INTERVIEWING STRATEGIES FOR HELPERS
Fundamental Skills and Cognitive Behavioral Interventions
Second Edition

INTERVIEWING STRATEGIES FOR HELPERS

FUNDAMENTAL SKILLS AND COGNITIVE BEHAVIORAL INTERVENTIONS
Second Edition

WILLIAM H. CORMIER
West Virginia University

L. SHERILYN CORMIER
West Virginia University

Brooks/Cole Publishing Company
Monterey, California

Brooks/Cole Publishing Company
A Division of Wadsworth, Inc.

Printed in the United States of America
10   9   8   7   6   5   4

Library of Congress Cataloging in Publication Data

Cormier, William H. (William Henry), [date].
  Interviewing strategies for helpers.

  Bibliography: p.
  Includes index.
  1. Counseling. 2. Helping behavior. 3. Interviewing.
4. Cognitive therapy. 5. Behavior therapy. I. Cormier,
L. Sherilyn (Louise Sherilyn), [date]. II. Title.
BF637.C6C584   1985   158′.3   84-19837
ISBN 0-534-04416-6

Sponsoring Editor: *Claire Verduin*
Editorial Assistant: *Pat Carnahan*
Production Editor: *Ellen Brownstein*
Manuscript Editor: *Rephah Berg*
Permissions Editor: *Carline Haga*
Interior and Cover Design: *Katherine Minerva*
Art Coordinator: *Michèle Judge*
Interior Illustration: *Precision Graphics*
Typesetting: *Progressive Typographers, Emigsville, Pennsylvania*
Printing and Binding: *R. R. Donnelly & Sons Co.*

To our parents,
Edith and Bill,
and Leona and Doc
with grateful appreciation
and affection

PREFACE

Counseling and therapy have been likened to a "craft" (Goldfried & Padawer, 1982). A skilled counselor is like a master craftsperson — someone who has acquired and mastered the basic "know-how" of his or her craft, coupled with individualized expression that gives the craft a unique form. Extremely skilled craftspersons have mastered the basic skills of their craft and also its more technical or complex features. *Interviewing Strategies for Helpers* is designed to help students and practitioners develop and refine the "craft" of counseling by acquiring and using various fundamental skills associated with helping and by acquiring and refining some of the more complex and comprehensive intervention strategies.

The skills and strategies selected for inclusion in this book are representative of those found in four major stages of the helping process: relationship, assessment and goal setting, strategy selection and implementation, and evaluation and termination. Chapters Two through Six describe relationship variables, nonverbal behavior, and verbal responses which are fundamental to any helping interaction, which are essential for developing an effective therapeutic relationship, and which seem to cut across varying theoretical orientations. In Chapters Seven through Twenty our focus shifts from rather basic skills considered important for a variety of theoretical orientations to a framework that is more cognitive-behavioral in orientation. Chapters Seven through Nine describe and model ways to help clients assess problems and define goals, or outcomes, in an interview setting. Chapter Ten describes a variety of ways in which helpers can, in rather practical ways, evaluate the effects of interventions and monitor client progress. Chapters Eleven through Twenty describe guidelines for selecting and implementing strategies, as well as a variety of intervention strategies, including ways to manage resistance, or "being stuck."

In part, the usefulness of this book may lie in its comprehensive coverage of skills and strategies associated with all the major phases of effective help-giving in counseling with individuals. It should be noted that although some of the material in this book is relevant to relationship, group, or systems interventions, the book focuses primarily on the "one to one" interaction.

Another feature of the book is its emphasis on practical application. The content of the book is designed to help developing counselors and therapists acquire and refine a repertoire of effective helpgiving behaviors. Coverage of theoretical concepts or research associated with the skills and strategies is limited because these areas are covered adequately in other texts.

The format of the book also emphasizes skill acquisition and application. Each chapter includes a brief introduction, chapter objectives, content material sprinkled with model examples, learning activities and feedback, a postevaluation, and a role-play interview assessment. The book can be completed by individuals on a self-instructional basis or within an organized course or in-service training. Identifying some ways to use this format may enhance the acquisition of the content. Chapter One describes the content and format of the book in greater detail. We urge you to read Chapter One before reading anything else in this book.

We have used the broad term *helping* in the title of the book to recognize that a variety of people —counselors, psychotherapists, social workers, nurses, and so on—engage in helping-oriented interactions with other persons. In this edition of the book, we have used the words *counselor* and *therapist* interchangeably. This is not meant to confuse anyone but simply to recognize the various kinds of practitioners and students who are covered under the broad term *helpers* and who are consumers of this book.

If you are familiar with the first edition, you might be interested in knowing about some of the changes reflected in this second edition. In addition to updated material on all skills and strategies, new or expanded coverage is given to—

- Relationship issues and the core facilitative conditions of empathy, genuineness, and positive regard.
- Selected skills associated with neurolinguistic programming (NLP).
- Environmental aspects of nonverbal behavior.
- Effective questions.
- Information giving.
- Ethical issues.
- Case conceptualization models.

- Diagnosis and *DSM-III*.
- History taking and intake interviews.
- Decision rules for strategy selection.
- Perceptual reframing.
- Clinically standardized meditation (CSM).
- Treatment contracts.

Two completely new chapters have been added. Chapter Three, on relationship enhancement variables (trustworthiness, interpersonal attractiveness, and competence), draws heavily from social influence models and concepts. The emphasis in this chapter is on how to demonstrate and convey these conditions in interviews with clients. The last chapter of the book, Chapter Twenty, on strategies to manage resistance, reflects the growing realization that therapeutic change is often a slow and difficult process and that occasionally clients resist giving up old and comfortable behavior patterns. Therapists, too, may resist doing therapy or, in severe burnout cases, resist even coming to work! This chapter reflects not only cognitive-behavioral strategies to deal with resistance but also family systems interventions.

We appreciate the helpful suggestions of all those persons who served as reviewers for the second edition: Gary L. Arthur, Georgia State University at Fort Benning; Gary Birchler, V.A. Medical Center, San Diego, California; John Elkhorn, Southern Mississippi University at Hattiesburg; Steven Fishman, Institute for Behavior Therapy, New York City; William Fremouw, West Virginia University at Morgantown; Pat Jaramillo, University of Texas at Odessa; Marva Larrabee, University of South Carolina at Columbia; Rosemery Nelson, University of North Carolina at Greensboro; Thomas A. Seay, Kutztown State College, Kutztown, Pennsylvania; Warren F. Shaffer, University of Minnesota at Minneapolis; and Karen K. Whitney, University of Houston at Clear Lake. We are also grateful to two of our colleagues, Robert Marinelli and David Srebalus of West Virginia University, who have used the first edition consistently in their sections of our Counseling Techniques course and have provided us with many "helpful hints" for the revision efforts. We also wish to acknowledge the help and contribution of Raymond Cooney, who developed some of the new learning activities and case examples for the first seven chapters.

We express heartfelt appreciation to our superb typist and good friend, Anne Drake. We are grateful for the instructive feedback provided by our own students. Their support, encouragement, and helpful criticism were vital to this second edition. Finally, wc want to acknowledge the support, expertise, and lack of intrusiveness demonstrated by our publisher and its employees and specifically by our project editor, Claire Verduin. She is indeed a master at her craft!

William Cormier
L. Sherilyn Cormier

CONTENTS

ONE ABOUT THIS BOOK 1
Purposes of the Book 2
An Overview of Helping 2
Format of the Book 4
One Final Thought 9

TWO INGREDIENTS OF AN EFFECTIVE
HELPING RELATIONSHIP 11
Objectives 11
Characteristics of Effective Helpers 11
Issues Affecting the Therapeutic
Relationship 16
Fundamental Helping Skills and Person-
Centered Therapy 21
Empathy, or Accurate Understanding 21
Genuineness 26
Positive Regard 31
Summary 36
Suggested Readings 41

THREE RELATIONSHIP ENHANCEMENT
VARIABLES AND INTERPERSONAL
INFLUENCE 43
Objectives 44
Strong's Model of Counseling as Interpersonal
Influence 44
The Interactional Nature of the Influence
Process 44
Counselor Characteristics or Relationship
Enhancers 46
Expertness 46
Attractiveness 52
Trustworthiness 55
Summary 60
Suggested Readings 63

FOUR NONVERBAL BEHAVIOR 65
Objectives 66
Client Nonverbal Behavior 66

How to Work with Client Nonverbal
  Behavior 79
Counselor Nonverbal Behavior 81
Summary 84
Suggested Readings 86

FIVE LISTENING RESPONSES 89
Objectives 90
Listening Is a Prerequisite 90
Listening and Sensory Modalities 90
Four Listening Responses 91
Summary 106
Suggested Readings 111

SIX ACTION RESPONSES 113
Objectives 113
Action Responses and Timing 114
Four Action Responses 114
Summary 136
Skill Integration 137
Suggested Readings 144

SEVEN CONCEPTUALIZING CLIENT
PROBLEMS 146
Objectives 146
What Is Assessment? 146
Methods of Conceptualizing Client
  Problems 147
Our Assumptions about Assessment and
  Cognitive Behavior Therapy 155
The ABC Model of Behavior 157
Diagnostic Classification of Client
  Problems 161
Summary 167
Suggested Readings 170

EIGHT DEFINING CLIENT PROBLEMS
WITH AN INTERVIEW ASSESSMENT 173
Objectives 174
Direct Assessment Interviewing 174
Intake Interviews and History 174
Mental-Status Examination 178
Eleven Categories for Assessing Client
  Problems 179

Limitations of Interview Leads in Problem
  Assessment 192
Model Dialogue for Problem Assessment: The
  Case of Joan 193
Forming Hypotheses about Problems 199
Notes and Record Keeping 202
Client Self-Monitoring Assessment 203
When Is "Enough" Assessment Enough? 207
Summary 207
Suggested Readings 216

NINE SELECTING AND DEFINING
OUTCOME GOALS 218
Objectives 219
Purposes of Goals 219
An Overview of Selecting and Defining
  Goals 220
Interview Leads for Selecting Goals 221
Model Dialogue: The Case of Joan 229
Interview Leads for Defining Goals 233
Model Dialogue: The Case of Joan 243
Summary 247
Suggested Readings 254

TEN EVALUATING PROCESSES AND
OUTCOMES IN HELPING 256
Objectives 257
Definition and Purpose of Helping
  Evaluation 257
Nontreatment Factors in Counseling 257
Conducting an Outcome Evaluation of
  Helping 259
What to Measure: Response Dimensions 260
How to Measure: Methods of
  Measurement 262
When to Measure: Time of Measurement 272
Conducting a Process Evaluation of
  Helping 286
Model Example: The Case of Joan 287
Summary 288
Suggested Readings 291

ELEVEN SELECTING HELPING
STRATEGIES 294
Objectives 295
Timing of Helping Strategies: Five
  Guidelines 295

Criteria for Selecting Strategies 296
Selecting Combinations of Strategies 303
Model Dialogue: The Case of Joan 303
Summary 306
Suggested Readings 307

TWELVE COMMON ELEMENTS OF
STRATEGY IMPLEMENTATION 309
Objectives 309
Rationale for Treatment Strategies 310
Modeling 310
Rehearsal, or Practice 312
Homework and Transfer of Learning 316
Model Dialogue: The Case of Joan 318
Model Treatment Contract: The Case of
Joan 322
Summary 323
Suggested Readings 325

THIRTEEN SYMBOLIC MODELING,
SELF-AS-A-MODEL, AND PARTICIPANT
MODELING 328
Objectives 329
Symbolic Modeling 329
Self-as-a-Model 331
Model Dialogue: Self-as-a-Model 333
Participant Modeling 335
Model Dialogue: Participant Modeling 340
Summary 344
Suggested Readings 348

FOURTEEN EMOTIVE IMAGERY AND
COVERT MODELING 351
Objectives 351
Assessment of Client Imagery 351
Emotive Imagery 352
Model Example: Emotive Imagery 355
Covert Modeling 356
Model Dialogue: Covert Modeling 363
Summary 368
Suggested Readings 375

FIFTEEN COGNITIVE MODELING AND
THOUGHT STOPPING 378
Objectives 378
Cognitive Modeling with Cognitive Self-
Instructional Training 379

Model Dialogue: Cognitive Modeling with
Cognitive Self-Instructional Training 382
Thought Stopping 385
Model Dialogue: Thought Stopping 390
Summary 392
Suggested Readings 401

SIXTEEN COGNITIVE RESTRUCTURING,
REFRAMING, AND STRESS
INOCULATION 403
Objectives 404
Cognitive Restructuring 404
Model Dialogue: Cognitive Restructuring 412
Reframing 417
Model Dialogue: Reframing 421
Stress Inoculation 423
Model Dialogue: Stress Inoculation 432
Summary 434
Suggested Readings 445

SEVENTEEN MEDITATION AND
MUSCLE RELAXATION 448
Objectives 449
Meditation 449
Steps for Relaxation Response and Zen
Meditation 450
Steps for Clinically Standardized
Meditation 454
Contraindications and Adverse Effects of
Meditation 455
Model Example: Meditation (CSM) 456
Muscle Relaxation 457
Model Dialogue: Muscle Relaxation 466
Summary 468
Suggested Readings 477

EIGHTEEN SYSTEMATIC
DESENSITIZATION 480
Objectives 481
Reported Uses of Desensitization 481
Comparison with Other Treatment
Approaches 482
Explanations of Desensitization 483
Components of Desensitization 484
Model Dialogue: Rationale 486

Model Dialogue: Identifying Emotion-
Provoking Situations 487
Model Dialogue: Hierarchy Construction 492
Model Dialogue: Selection of and Training in
Counterconditioning or Coping
Response 495
Model Dialogue: Imagery Assessment 497
Model Dialogue: Scene Presentation 503
Model Dialogue: Homework and Follow-
Up 505
Problems Encountered during
Desensitization 506
Variations of Systematic Desensitization 507
Summary 508
Suggested Readings 510

NINETEEN SELF-MANAGEMENT
STRATEGIES: SELF-MONITORING,
STIMULUS CONTROL, AND SELF-
REWARD 519
Objectives 520
Characteristics of an Effective Self-
Management Program 520
Steps in Developing a Client Self-Management
Program 522
Self-Monitoring 524
Steps in Self-Monitoring 526
Model Example: Self-Monitoring 533
Stimulus Control: Prearrangement of
Antecedents 534
Model Example: Stimulus Control 538
Self-Reward 539
Model Example: Self-Reward 544
Promoting Client Commitment to Use
Self-Management Strategies 545
Summary 546
Suggested Readings 547

TWENTY STRATEGIES FOR MANAGING
RESISTANCE 550
Objectives 550
Definition of Resistance 550
Resistance Due to Client Variables 552
Resistance Due to Environmental
Variables 555
Resistance Due to Therapist or Therapeutic
Variables 558
When All Else Fails: Last-Resort
Strategies 563
Paradoxical Interventions 567
Strategies for Involuntary Clients 575
A Final Note 576
Suggested Readings 579

APPENDIX A ETHICAL STANDARDS,
AMERICAN PERSONNEL AND
GUIDANCE ASSOCIATION 582

APPENDIX B ETHICAL PRINCIPLES OF
PSYCHOLOGISTS, AMERICAN
PSYCHOLOGICAL ASSOCIATION 589

APPENDIX C CODE OF ETHICS,
NATIONAL ASSOCIATION OF SOCIAL
WORKERS 597

APPENDIX D STANDARDS FOR THE
PRIVATE PRACTICE OF CLINICAL
SOCIAL WORK, NATIONAL
ASSOCIATION OF SOCIAL WORKERS 602

APPENDIX E MULTIMODAL LIFE
HISTORY QUESTIONNAIRE 606

APPENDIX F BEHAVIORAL ANALYSIS
HISTORY QUESTIONNAIRE (BAHQ) 615

References 623
Author Index 649
Subject Index 657

LEARNING ACTIVITIES AND FEEDBACKS

TWO

Learning Activity #1: Self-Image   15
  Feedback #1: Self-Image   19
Learning Activity #2: Personal Values   18
  Feedback #2: Personal Values   20
Learning Activities #3: Empathy   25
  Feedback #3: Empathy   28
Learning Activities #4: Self-Disclosure   30
  Feedback #4: Self-Disclosure   32
Learning Activities # 5: Immediacy   35
  Feedback #5: Immediacy   41
Postevaluation   36
  Feedback: Postevaluation   42

THREE

Learning Activities #6: Expertness   51
  Feedback # 6: Expertness   52
Learning Activities #7: Attractiveness   54
  Feedback #7: Attractiveness   56
Learning Activities #8: Trustworthiness   59
  Feedback #8: Trustworthiness   63
Postevaluation   61
  Feedback: Postevaluation   64

FOUR

Learning Activities #9: Client Nonverbal
  Communication   78
Learning Activities #10: Responding to Client
  Nonverbal Behavior   81
Learning Activity #11: Counselor Nonverbal
  Behavior   83
Learning Activity #12: Observation of
  Counselor and Client Nonverbal
  Behavior   84
Postevaluation   84
  Feedback: Postevaluation   86

FIVE
Learning Activity #13: Clarification   93
   Feedback #13: Clarification   96
Learning Activity #14: Paraphrase   97
   Feedback #14: Paraphrase   98
Learning Activity #15: Reflection of
   Feelings   101
   Feedback #15: Reflection of Feelings   104
Learning Activity #16: Summarization   105
   Feedback #16: Summarization   110
Postevaluation   107
   Feedback: Postevaluation   111

SIX
Learning Activity #17: Probes   117
   Feedback #17: Probes   121
Learning Activity #18: Mixed Messages   119
   Feedback #18: Mixed Messages   122
Learning Activity #19: Confrontation   123
   Feedback #19: Confrontation   126
Learning Activity #20: Interpretation   128
   Feedback #20: Interpretation   132
Learning Activity #21: Information Giving 135
   Feedback #21: Information Giving   142
Postevaluation   137
   Feedback: Postevaluation   144

SEVEN
Learning Activity #22: Methods of Case
   Conceptualization   154
Learning Activity #23: ABCs of Problem
   Assessment   166
   Feedback #23: ABCs of Problem
      Assessment   168
Postevaluation   168
   Feedback: Postevaluation   171

EIGHT
Learning Activity #24: Intake Interviews and
   History   178
Learning Activities #25: Interview
   Assessment   200
   Feedback #25: Interview Assessment   206
Postevaluation   208
   Feedback: Postevaluation   216

NINE
Learning Activity #26: Decision Point   228
Learning Activity #27: Defining Outcome
   Goals   237
Learning Activity #28: Identifying and
   Sequencing Subgoals   241
Postevaluation   248
   Feedback: Postevaluation   254

TEN
Learning Activity #29: Response
   Dimensions   262
   Feedback #29: Response Dimensions   264
Learning Activity #30: Methods of
   Measurement   272
   Feedback #30: Methods of
      Measurement   275
Learning Activity #31: Time of
   Measurement   282
   Feedback #31: Time of Measurement   284
Postevaluation   289
   Feedback: Postevaluation   292

ELEVEN
Learning Activities #32: Strategy
   Selection   305
Postevaluation   306
   Feedback: Postevaluation   308

TWELVE
Learning Activity #33: Strategy
   Implementation   321
   Feedback #33: Strategy
      Implementation   322
Postevaluation   324
   Feedback: Postevaluation   326

THIRTEEN
Learning Activity #34: Symbolic
   Modeling   331
   Feedback #34: Symbolic Modeling   332
Learning Activity #35: Self-as-a-Model   335
   Feedback #35: Self-as-a-Model   336

Learning Activity #36: Participant
  Modeling 343
Postevaluation 344
  Feedback: Postevaluation 349

FOURTEEN
Learning Activity #37: Emotive Imagery 356
Learning Activity #38: Covert Modeling 368
  Feedback #38: Covert Modeling 375
Postevaluation 368
  Feedback: Postevaluation 376

FIFTEEN
Learning Activity #39: Modeled Self-
  Guidance 381
  Feedback #39: Modeled Self-Guidance 382
Learning Activity #40: Cognitive Modeling
  with Cognitive Self-Instructional
  Training 385
  Feedback #40: Cognitive Modeling with
    Cognitive Self-Instructional Training 386
Learning Activities #41: Thought
  Stopping 392
  Feedback #41: Thought Stopping 400
Postevaluation 393
  Feedback: Postevaluation 401

SIXTEEN
Learning Activities #42: Cognitive
  Restructuring 416
  Feedback #42: Cognitive Restructuring 418
Learning Activity #43: Reframing 422
Learning Activities #44: Stress
  Inoculation 434
  Feedback #44: Stress Inoculation 444
Postevaluation 434
  Feedback: Postevaluation 445

SEVENTEEN
Learning Activities #45: Meditation
  (Relaxation Response and Zen Meditation or
  Clinically Standardized Meditation) 457

Learning Activity #46: Muscle
  Relaxation 467
Postevaluation 468
  Feedback: Postevaluation 478

EIGHTEEN
Learning Activity #47: Hierarchy
  Construction 493
Learning Activity #48: Scene
  Presentation 504
Postevaluation 508
  Feedback: Postevaluation 510

NINETEEN
Learning Activity #49: Self-Monitoring 534
Learning Activity #50: Stimulus Control 538
Learning Activity #51: Self-Reward 545
Postevaluation 546
  Feedback: Postevaluation 548

TWENTY
Learning Activity #52: Client Sources of
  Resistance 554
  Feedback #52: Client Sources of
    Resistance 556
Learning Activity #53: Environmental
  Sources of Resistance 558
  Feedback #53: Environmental Sources of
    Resistance 560
Learning Activity #54: Therapist Sources of
  Resistance 563
Learning Activities #55: Last-Resort
  Strategies 566
Learning Activities #56: Paradoxical
  Interventions 574
  Feedback #56: Paradoxical
    Interventions 576
Postevaluation 577
  Feedback: Postevaluation 580

INTERVIEWING STRATEGIES FOR HELPERS
Fundamental Skills and Cognitive Behavioral Interventions
Second Edition

ABOUT THIS BOOK

ONE

Imagine yourself as the helper in the following four situations. Try to see, hear, and sense what is happening to you.

A 14-year-old boy who is accused of setting fire to his family home walks in defiantly to see you. He has been "mandated" to see you by the judge. He sits down, crosses his arms and legs in front of him, and stares at the ceiling. He is silent after your initial greeting.

An 8-year-old girl walks in and can't hold back the tears and the sobs. After a while, she talks about how confused and upset she's been feeling. As she continues to talk almost without stopping, you discover that in the last year three of her very close relatives and friends have died and her parents have divorced. She can almost not get the words out fast enough.

An older, now retired gentleman appears at your door. He walks slowly with quite stooped shoulders. His face reflects resignation and discouragement and also a hint of pride. He speaks to you in a halting fashion and in a slow, soft voice. He seems to have difficulty concentrating and cannot always remember what you're saying to him.

A middle-aged woman comes in. She has been escorted to your facility by her husband. She is so afraid to go out of her house that she does not drive anymore. In talking with her, you discover that she has confined herself to her home almost exclusively for the last year because of incapacitating anxiety attacks. Her husband has recently turned down a lucrative job offer in order not to have to move her into a new environment.

Now try to process exactly what it is like for you to imagine helping or counseling each of these four clients. How were you feeling? What thoughts were running through your head? How did you see or hear yourself responding? What things about yourself were you aware of that helped you in the interaction; what things that hindered you? What skills did you utilize to deal with the client? What skills were you lacking? What did you observe about the client, and how did your observations affect your helpgiving? How did you know whether what you were doing was helpful?

Although it may be difficult for you to respond to these kinds of questions now, it will probably become easier as you go through the book and as you also acquire greater experience and more feedback. Specific purposes of the book are described in the following section.

□ PURPOSES OF THE BOOK

We hope that, in this book, you will find training experiences that facilitate personal growth, develop your counseling skills, and provide ways for you to evaluate your effectiveness. Personal growth is the most elusive and the most difficult to define of these three areas. Although it is beyond the scope of this book to focus primarily on self-development, you may engage in self-exploration as you go through certain parts of the book, particularly Chapters 2 and 3. We also encourage you to seek out additional experiences in which you can receive feedback from others about yourself, your strengths, and some behaviors that may interfere with counseling. These experiences might consist in individual or classroom activities and feedback, growth groups, and personal counseling. It is well documented that a counselor's warmth, empathy, and positive regard can contribute to client change. We feel that your demonstration of these relationship conditions will enhance the way you perform the skills and strategies presented in this book.

We created the book with three specific purposes. First, we think it will help you acquire a repertory of counseling interview skills and strategies. The book focuses on *interview* skills and strategies as used in a helping relationship. It is directed (but not restricted) to applying skills within a counselor/client dyadic relationship. Although some of the skills and strategies may be used appropriately in group counseling, organizational interventions, or marriage and family counseling, the major focus of this book is on the application of these skills with individuals.

In the first six chapters of this book, we present what we call "fundamental skills." These include relationship conditions, nonverbal behavior, and verbal responses that are useful for practitioners of varying theoretical orientations. In the remaining chapters, our selection of models and strategies reflects a cognitive-behavioral framework. The intervention strategies we have chosen to include have some supporting data base, although many of the existing research studies are analog ones (that is, conducted in simulated counseling settings) and the results may not always generalize to actual counseling situations.

In addition to the cognitive-behavioral "flavor" of the strategies, reference to skills and strategies based on other theoretical orientations is often mentioned throughout the book. This is because cognitive-behavioral therapies are increasingly broad-based in nature and focus (Goldfried, 1982) and also because of our own belief that skilled counselors are at least knowledgeable about, if not proficient in, more than one approach to working with client problems. For your benefit if you are not yet familiar with the concepts associated with various theoretical approaches to counseling and therapy, Table 1-1 presents a synopsis of ten major counseling theories.

Our second purpose is to assist you in identifying the potential applicability of many counseling strategies for different client problems. As Krumboltz and Thoresen (1976) point out, a variety of useful counseling methods are available for different problem areas. When you have finished the book, we hope you will be able to select and use appropriate counseling strategies when confronted with a depressed client, an anxious client, a nonassertive client, and so forth. We also hope you will be aware of cases in which approaches and strategies included in this book may not be very useful.

Thus, we hope to provide you with some ways to monitor and evaluate your behavior and the client's behavior during counseling. The recent emphasis on accountability requires each of us to explore the results of our helping activities more closely. Evaluation of counseling also assesses the extent to which the therapeutic goals are achieved.

Above all, we want to convey that the book is about *practical application* of selected skills and strategies. Our coverage of theoretical and research concepts is very limited because they are covered adequately in other texts.

□ AN OVERVIEW OF HELPING

A helping professional is someone who facilitates the exploration and resolution of issues and problems presented by a helpee or a client. Helping interactions have four recognized components: (1) someone seeking help, (2) someone willing to give

TABLE 1-1. Synopsis of theoretical approaches to counseling and psychotherapy

Theoretical system	General category	Personality theory base and founder or major contributors	Key philosophic, conceptual, process, and relationship identifiers
Psychoanalytic therapy	Psychodynamic approach	*Psychoanalysis Founder:* Sigmund Freud	Deterministic, topographic, dynamic, genetic, analytic, developmental, historical, insightful, unconscious, motivational
Adlerian theory	Social-psychological approach	*Individual psychology Founder:* Alfred Adler	Holistic, phenomenological, socially oriented, teleological, field-theoretical, functionalistic
Person-centered counseling	Humanistic, experiential, existential approaches	*Person-centered theory Founder:* Carl Rogers	Humanistic, experiential, existential, organismic, self-theoretical, phenomenological, person-centered, here-and-now-oriented
Gestalt therapy		*Gestalt therapy theory Founder:* Frederick Perls	Existential, experiential, humanistic, organismic, awareness-evocative, here-and-now-oriented, client-centered, confrontive
Transactional Analysis (TA)	Cognitive, behavioral, action-oriented approaches	*Transactional Analysis theory Founder:* Eric Berne	Cognitive, analytic, redecisional, contractual, interpretational, confrontational, action-oriented, awareness-evocative, social-interactive
Behavioral counseling, therapy, and modification	Cognitive, behavioral, action-oriented approaches (continued)	*Behavior theory and conditioning theory Major contributors:* B. F. Skinner J. Krumboltz A. Lazarus J. Wolpe D. Meichenbaum	Behavioristic, pragmatic, scientific, learning-theoretical, cognitive, action-oriented, experimental, goal-oriented, contractual
Rational-emotive therapy (RET)	Cognitive, behavioral, action-oriented approaches (continued)	*Rational-emotive theory Founder:* Albert Ellis	Rational, cognitive, scientific, philosophic, action-oriented, relativistic, didactic, here-and-now-oriented, decisional, contractual, humanistic
Reality therapy		*Reality theory Founder:* William Glasser	Reality-based, rational, antideterministic, cognitive, action-oriented, scientific, directive, didactic, contractual, supportive, nonpunitive, positivistic, here-and-now-oriented
Trait and factor counseling	Trait, factor, and decisional approach	*Trait-factor theory Contributors:* E. G. Williamson D. Paterson J. Darley D. Biggs	Scientific, empirical, decisional, informational, educational, vocational, evaluative, data-based, past/present/future-oriented, action-oriented, technological, person/environment interactive, problem-solving, objective, systematic, didactic, interpretative
Eclectic counseling and psycho-therapy	Integrative approach	*Eclecticism Contributors:* F. C. Thorne S. Garfield J. Palmer A. Ivey R. Carkhuff	Integrative, systematic, scientific, comprehensive, organismic/environmental, cognitive, past/present/future-oriented, behavioral, educational, developmental, humanistic, analytic, decisional

From Gilliland/James/Roberts/Bowman, *Theories and Strategies in Counseling and Psychotherapy,* © 1984, pp. 2–3. Reprinted by permission of Prentice-Hall, Inc., Englewood Cliffs, N.J.

help who is also (3) capable of or trained to help (4) in a setting that permits help to be given and received (Hackney & Cormier, 1979, p. 25).

Most helping or therapeutic interactions also involve certain stages or processes. In this book, we describe skills and strategies associated with four primary stages in helping:

1. Relationship
2. Assessment and goal setting
3. Strategy selection and implementation
4. Evaluation and termination

The first stage of the helping process involves *establishing an effective therapeutic relationship* with the client. This part of the process is based primarily on client- or person-centered therapy (Rogers, 1951) and more recently on social influence theory (Strong & Claiborn, 1982). The potential value of a sound relationship base cannot be overlooked, because the relationship is the specific part of the process that conveys the counselor's interest in and acceptance of the client as a unique and worthwhile person and builds sufficient trust for eventual self-disclosure and self-revelation to occur. For some clients, working with a counselor who stays primarily in this stage may be useful and sufficient. For example, as we mention in Chapter 11, for some clients who are troubled by generalized anxiety or low self-esteem, relationship-oriented therapy is often the first treatment of choice. For other clients, the relationship part of therapy is necessary but not sufficient to help them with the kinds of choices and changes they seek to make. These clients need additional kinds of action or intervention strategies.

The second phase of helping, assessment and goal setting, often begins concurrently with or shortly after relationship building. In both stages, the counselor is interested mainly in helping clients *explore* themselves and their concerns. Assessment is designed to help both the counselor and the client obtain a better picture, idea, or grasp of what is happening with the client and what prompted the client to seek the services of a helper at this time. The information gleaned during the assessment phase is extremely valuable in planning strategies and also can be used to manage resistance. After the problems and issues are identified and defined, the counselor and client together work through the process of developing outcome goals. Outcome goals refer to the specific results the client would like to occur as a result of

counseling. Outcome goals also provide useful information for planning action strategies.

In the third phase of helping, strategy selection and implementation, the counselor's task is to facilitate client *understanding and related action.* Insight can be useful, but insight alone is far less useful than insight accompanied by a supporting plan that helps the client translate new or different understandings into observable and specific actions or behaviors. Toward this end, the counselor and client select and sequence a plan of action or intervention strategies that are based on the assessment data and are designed to help the client achieve the designated goals. In developing action plans, it is important to select ones that relate to the identified problems and goals and also ones that are not in conflict with the client's primary beliefs and values.

The last major phase of helping, evaluation, involves *assessing the effectiveness* of your interventions and the progress the client has made toward the desired goals. This kind of evaluation assists you in knowing when to terminate or when your action plans need revamping. Additionally, observable and concrete signs of progress are often quite reinforcing to clients, who can easily get discouraged during the change process.

Table 1-2 presents an overview of the helping process as described in the remaining chapters of this book. In reviewing this table, you may note some flow and interrelationship among the four major stages of the helping process.

☐ FORMAT OF THE BOOK

We have used a learning format designed to help you to demonstrate and measure your use of the counseling competencies presented in this book. Each chapter includes a brief introduction, chapter objectives, content material interspersed with model examples, activities, and feedback, a post-evaluation, and a role-play interview assessment. People who have participated in field-testing this book have found that using these activities has helped them to get involved and to interact with the content material. You can complete the chapters by yourself or in a class. If you feel you need to go over an exercise several times, do so! If part of the material is familiar, jump ahead. Throughout each chapter, your performance on the learning activities and self-evaluations will be a clue to the pace at which you can work through the chapter.

TABLE 1-2. Four stages of helping and the chapters presenting related skills

Fundamental skills (relationship conditions, nonverbal behavior, verbal responses)	Assessment and goal-setting	Evaluation	Strategy selection and implementation
2—"Ingredients of an Effective Helping Relationship"	7—"Conceptualizing Client Problems"	10—"Evaluating Processes and Outcomes in Helping"	11—"Selecting Strategies"
3—"Relationship Enhancement Variables and Interpersonal Influence"	8—"Defining Client Problems with an Interview Assessment"		12—"Common Elements of Strategy Implementation"
4—"Nonverbal Behavior"	9—"Selecting and Defining Outcome Goals"		13—"Symbolic Modeling, Self-as-a-Model, and Participant Modeling"
5—"Listening Responses"			14—"Emotive Imagery and Covert Modeling"
6—"Action Responses"			15—"Cognitive Modeling and Thought Stopping"
			16—"Cognitive Restructuring, Reframing, and Stress Inoculation"
			17—"Meditation and Muscle Relaxation"
			18—"Systematic Desensitization"
			19—"Self-Management Strategies: Self-Monitoring, Stimulus Control, and Self-Reward"
			20—"Strategies for Managing Resistance"

To help you use the book's format to your advantage, we will explain each of its components briefly.

Objectives

As we developed each chapter, we had certain goals in mind for the chapter and for you. For each major topic, there are certain concepts and skills to be learned. We feel the best way to communicate this is to make our intentions explicit. After a short chapter introduction, you will find a section called "Objectives." The list of objectives describes the kinds of things that can be learned from the chapter. Using objectives for learning is similar to using goals in counseling. The objectives provide cues for your "end results" and serve as benchmarks for

you to assess your progress. As you will see in Chapter 9, an objective or goal contains three parts:

1. The behavior, or what is to be learned or performed.
2. The level of performance, or how much or how often to demonstrate the behavior.
3. The conditions of performance, or the circumstances or situations under which the behavior can be performed.

Part 1 of an objective refers to what you should learn or demonstrate. Parts 2 and 3 are concerned with evaluation of performance. The evaluative parts of an objective, such as the suggested level of performance, may seem a bit hard-nosed. However, there is evidence that setting objectives with a fairly high mastery level results in more-improved performance (Johnston & O'Neill, 1973; Semb, Hopkins, & Hursh, 1973). In this book, the objectives are stated at the beginning of each chapter so you know what to look for and how to assess your performance in the activities and self-evaluations. If you feel it would be helpful to see some objectives now, take a look at the beginning of Chapter 2.

Learning Activities

Learning activities that reflect the chapter objectives are interspersed throughout each chapter. These learning activities, which are intended to provide both practice and feedback, consist of model examples, exercises, and feedback. There are several ways you can use the learning activities. Many of the exercises suggest that you write your responses. Your written responses may help you or your instructor check the accuracy and specificity of your work. Take a piece of paper and actually write the responses down. Or you may prefer to work through an activity covertly and just think about your responses.

Some exercises instruct you to respond covertly by imagining yourself in a certain situation, doing certain things. We feel that this form of mental rehearsal can help you prepare for the kinds of counseling responses you might use in a particular situation. Covert responding does not require any written responses. However, if it would help you to jot down some notes after the activity is over, go ahead. You are the best person to determine how to use these exercises to your advantage.

Many of the exercises, particularly in the first six chapters, are based on cognitive self-instruction. The objective of this type of activity is to help you not only to acquire the skill in a "rote" manner but also to internalize it. Some research suggests that this may be an important addition to the more common elements of microtraining (modeling, rehearsal, feedback) found to be so helpful in skill acquisition (Richardson & Stone, 1981). The cognitive learning strategy is designed specifically to help you develop your own way to think about the skill or to "put it together" in a way that makes sense to you.

Another kind of learning activity involves a more direct rehearsal than the written or covert exercises. These "overt rehearsal" exercises are de-

signed to help you apply your skills in simulated counseling sessions with a role-play interview. The role-play activities involve three persons or roles: a counselor, a client, and an observer. Each group should trade roles so that each person can experience the role-play from these different perspectives. One person's task is to serve as the counselor and practice the skills specified in the instructions. The counselor role provides an opportunity to try out the skills in simulated counseling situations. A second person, the client, will be counseled during the role play.

We give one word of caution to whoever takes the client role. Assuming that "counselor" and "client" are classmates, or at least not close friends or relatives, each of you will benefit more when in the counselor's seat if the "client" shares a real concern. These concerns do not have to be issues of life or death. Often someone will say "I won't be a good client because I don't have a problem." It is hard to imagine a person who has no concerns. Maybe your role-play concern will be about a decision to be made, a relationship conflict, some uneasiness about a new situation, or feeling sorry for or angry with yourself or someone else. Taking the part of a client in these role-play exercises may require that you first get in touch with yourself.

The third person in the role-play exercise is the "observer." This is a very important role because it develops and sharpens observational skills that are an important part of effective counseling. The observer has three tasks to accomplish. First, this person should observe the process and identify what the client does and how the counselor responds. When the counselor is rehearsing a particular skill or strategy, the observer can also determine the strengths and limitations of the counselor's approach. Second, the observer can provide consultation at any point during the role play if it might facilitate the experience. Such consultation may occur if the counselor gets stuck or if the observer perceives that the counselor is practicing too many nonhelpful behaviors. In this capacity, we have often found it helpful for the observer to serve as a sort of "alter ego" for the counselor. The observer can then become involved in the role play to help give the counselor more options or better focus. It is important, however, not to take over for the counselor in such instances. The third and most important task of the observer is to provide feedback to the counselor about his or her performance following the role play. The person who role-played the client may also wish to provide feedback.

Giving helpful feedback is itself a skill that is used in some counseling strategies (see Chapter 12). The feedback that occurs following the role play should be considered just as important as the role play itself. Although everyone involved in the role play will receive feedback after serving as the counselor, it is still sometimes difficult to "hear" negative feedback. Sometimes receptiveness to feedback will depend on the way the observer presents it. We encourage you to make use of these opportunities to practice giving feedback to another person in a constructive, useful manner. Try to make your feedback specific and concise. Remember, the feedback is to help the counselor learn more about the role play; it should not be construed as the time to analyze the counselor's personality or lifestyle.

Another learning activity involves having people learn the strategies as partners or in small groups by teaching one another. We suggest that you trade off teaching a strategy to your partner or the group. Person A might teach covert modeling to Person B, and then Person B will teach Person A muscle relaxation. The "student" can be checked out in role play. Person B would check out on covert modeling (taught by A), and Person A would demonstrate the strategy learned from Person B. This method helps the teacher learn and teach at the same time. If the "student" does not master the skills, additional sessions with the "teacher" can be scheduled.

The role of feedback in learning activities. Most of the chapter learning activities are followed by some form of feedback. For example, if a learning activity involves identifying positive and negative examples of a counseling conversational style, the feedback will indicate which examples are positive and which are negative. We also have attempted in most of our feedback to give some rationale for the responses. In many of the feedback sections, several possible responses are included. Our purpose in including feedback is not for you to find out how many "right" and "wrong" answers you have given in a particular activity. The responses listed in the feedback sections should serve as a guideline for you to code and judge your own responses. With this in mind, we would like you to view the feedback sections as sources of information and alternatives. We hope you are not put off or dis-

couraged if your responses are different from the ones in the feedback. We don't expect you to come up with identical responses; some of your responses may be just as good as or better than the ones given in the feedback. Space does not permit us to list a plethora of possibly useful responses in the feedback for each learning activity.

Locating learning activities and feedback sections in the text. As we have indicated, each chapter contains a variety of learning activities and feedback. Usually a learning activity directly follows the related content section. We have placed learning activities in this way (rather than at the end of a chapter) to give you an immediate opportunity to work with and apply that content area before moving ahead to new material. Feedback for each learning activity is usually given on the *following* page. This is done in order to encourage you to work through the learning activity on your own without concurrently scanning the same page to see how we have responded. We believe this helps you work more independently and encourages you to develop and rely more on your own knowledge base and skills. A potential problem with this format is difficulty in finding a particular learning activity or its corresponding feedback section. To minimize this problem, we have done two things: (1) Each learning activity and its corresponding feedback section are numbered. For example, the first learning activity in the book is found on page 15; it is numbered #1. Its corresponding feedback section, found on page 19, is also labeled #1. (2) An index to all learning activities and feedback sections can be found in the front of the book.

Postevaluation

A postevaluation can be found at the end of each chapter. It consists of questions and activities related to the knowledge and skills to be acquired in the chapter. Because you respond to the questions after completing a chapter, this evaluation is called *post;* that is, it assesses your level of performance *after* receiving instruction. The evaluation questions and activities reflect the conditions specified in the objectives. When the conditions ask you to identify a response in a written statement or case, take some paper and write down your responses to these activities. However, if the objective calls for demonstrating a response in a role play, the evaluation will suggest how you can assess your performance level by setting up a role-play assessment. Other evaluation activities may suggest that you do something or experience something to heighten your awareness of or information about the idea or skill to be learned.

The primary purpose of the postevaluation is to help you assess your competencies after completing the chapter. One way to do this is to check your responses against those provided in the feedback at the end of each postevaluation. If there is a great discrepancy, the postevaluation can shed light on those areas still troublesome for you. You may wish to improve in these areas by reviewing parts of the chapter, redoing the learning activities, or asking for additional help from your instructor or a colleague.

Role-Play Evaluation

In actual counseling, you must demonstrate your skills orally—not write about them. To help you determine the extent to which you can apply and evaluate your skills, role-play evaluations are provided at the end of most chapters. Each role-play evaluation consists of a structured situation in which you are asked to demonstrate certain skills as a counselor with a role-play client. Your performance on the role-play interview can be assessed by using the role-play checklist at the end of the chapter. These checklists consist of steps and possible responses associated with a particular strategy. The checklist should be used only as a guideline. You should always adapt any helping strategy to the client and to the particular demands of the situation.

There are two ways to assess your role-play performance. You can ask your instructor, a colleague, or another person to observe your performance, using the checklist. Your instructor may even schedule you periodically to do a role-play "checkout" individually or in a small group. If you do not have anyone to observe you, assess yourself. Audiotape your interview and rate your performance on the checklist. Also ask your "client" for feedback. If you don't reach the criterion level of the objective on the first try, you may need some extra work. The following section explains the need for additional practice.

Additional Practice

You may find some skills more difficult to acquire the first time around than others. Often people are chagrined and disappointed when they do not demonstrate the strategy as well as they would like

on their first attempt. We ask these individuals whether they hold similar expectation levels for their clients! You cannot quickly and simply let go of behaviors you don't find useful in counseling and acquire others that are more helpful. It may be unrealistic to assume you will always demonstrate an adequate level of performance on *all* the evaluations on the first go-round. Much covert and overt rehearsal may be necessary before you feel comfortable with skill demonstration in the evaluations. On some occasions, it may be necessary for you to work through the learning activities and postevaluations more than once.

Some Cautions about Using This Format

Although we believe the format of this book will promote learning, we want you to consider several cautions about using it. As you will see, we have defined the skills and strategies in precise and systematic ways to make it easier for you to acquire and develop the skills. However, we do not intend that our definitions and guidelines be used like cookbook instructions. Perhaps our definitions and categories will give you some methodology and helping. But do not be restrained by this, particularly in applying your skills in the interview process. As you come to feel more comfortable with a strategy, we hope you will use the procedure creatively. Technical skills are not sufficient in counseling unless accompanied by inventiveness (Frey, 1975, p. 23), and "therapeutic guidelines cannot substitute for the clinical sensitivity and ingenuity of the therapist" (Goldfried & Goldfried, 1980, p. 125).

One of the most difficult parts of learning counseling skills seems to be trusting the skills to work and not being preoccupied with your own performance. We are reminded of a story in *Time* (November 29, 1976) about the conductor of the Berlin Philharmonic, Herbert Von Karajan. When asked why he didn't rely more on entry and cutoff cues in conducting a large orchestra, he replied "My hands do their job because they have learned what to do. In the performance I forget about them" (p. 82).

Preoccupation with yourself, your skills, or a particular procedure reduces your ability to relate to and be involved with another person. At first, it is natural to focus on the skill or strategy because it is new and feels a little awkward or cumbersome. But once you have learned a particular skill or strategy, the skills will be there when you need them. Gradually, as you acquire your repertory of skills and strategies, you should be able to change your focus from the procedure to the person.

Remember, also, that counseling is a complex process composed of many interrelated parts. Although different counseling stages, skills, and strategies are presented in this book in separate chapters, in practice there is a meshing of all these components. As an example, the relationship does not stop or diminish in importance when a counselor and client begin to assess problems, establish goals, or implement strategies. Nor is evaluation something that occurs only when counseling is terminated. Evaluation involves continual monitoring throughout the counseling interaction. Even obtaining a client's commitment to use strategies consistently and to monitor their effects may be aided or hindered by the quality of the relationship and the degree to which client problems and goals have been defined clearly. In the same vein, keep in mind that most client problems are complex and multifaceted. Successful counseling may involve changes in the client's feelings, observable behavior, beliefs, and cognitions. To model some of the skills and procedures you will learn, we have included cases and model dialogues in most chapters. These are intended to illustrate one example of a way in which a particular procedure can be used with a client. However, the cases and dialogues have been simplified for demonstration purposes, and the printed words may not communicate the sense of flow and direction that is normally present in counselor/client interchanges. Again, with actual clients, you will probably encounter more dimensions to the relationship and to the client's concerns than are reflected in the chapter examples.

Our third concern involves the way you approach the examples and practice opportunities in this book. Obviously, reading an example or doing a role-play interview is not as real as seeing an actual client or engaging in a live counseling interaction. However, some practice is necessary in any new learning program. Even if the exercises seem artificial, they probably will help you learn counseling skills. The structured practice opportunities in the book may require a great deal of discipline on your part, but the degree to which you can generalize your skills from practice to an actual counseling interview may depend on how much you invest in the practice opportunities.

One more word on such practice: Our Western culture regards practice as useful because "practice makes perfect." We prefer the Eastern concept—"practice makes different." Practice does not make perfect, because people are not intended to be perfect. However, practice may result in a change within ourselves, in our ideas, attitudes, beliefs, and actions. Practice can help all of us transform ourselves into more competent helpers.

Options for Using the Book

We have written this book in its particular format because each component seems to play a unique role in the learning process. But we are also committed to the idea that each person must determine the most suitable individual method of learning. With this in mind, we suggest a number of ways to use this book. First, you can go through the book and use the entire format in the way it is described in this chapter. If you do this, we suggest you familiarize yourself carefully with the format as described here. If you want to use this format but do not understand it, it is not likely to be helpful. Another way to use the book is to use only certain parts of the format in any combination you choose. You may want to experiment initially to determine which components seem especially useful. For example, you might use the postevaluation but not complete the chapter learning activities. Finally, if you prefer a "straight" textbook format, you can read only the content of the book and ignore the special format. Our intent is for you to use the book in whatever way is most suitable for your learning strategies.

☐ ONE FINAL THOUGHT

As you go through the book, you undoubtedly will get some feel for the particular ways to use each strategy. However, we caution you against using this book as a prescriptive device, like medicine handed over a counter automatically and without thought or imagination. We are discovering that no one method of learning is equally useful for all people (McKeachie, 1976; Snow, 1974). Similarly, one counseling strategy may not work well for all clients. As your counseling experience accumulates, you will find that one client does not use a strategy in the same way, at the same pace, or with similar results as another client. In selecting counseling strategies, it is helpful to be guided by the documentation concerning the ways in which the strategy has been used. But it is just as important to remember that each client may respond in an idiosyncratic manner to any particular approach. Mahoney and Mahoney (1976) emphasize that counseling is a "personalized science, in which each client's problems are given due recognition for their uniqueness and potential complexity" (p. 100). Finally, remember that almost anybody can learn and perform a skill in a rote and mechanistic manner. But not everyone shows the qualities of sensitivity and ingenuity to give the skills his or her own unique touch.

INGREDIENTS OF AN EFFECTIVE HELPING RELATIONSHIP

TWO

It is widely accepted today by persons of various theoretical orientations to counseling that the therapeutic relationship is an important part of the total helping process. According to Brammer and Shostrom (1982), the relationship is important not only because "it constitutes the principal medium for eliciting and handling significant feelings and ideas which are aimed at changing client behavior" but also because it often determines " whether counseling will continue at all" (p. 143). Without an effective therapeutic relationship, client change is unlikely to occur. An effective relationship provides the impetus and groundwork for more direct intervention strategies "to yield their intended effects" (Goldstein, 1980, p. 20).

☐ OBJECTIVES

After completing this chapter, you will be able to—

1. Identify attitudes and behaviors about yourself that might facilitate or interfere with establishing a positive helping relationship, given a written self-assessment checklist.
2. Identify issues related to values, ethics, and emotional objectivity that might affect the development of a therapeutic relationship, given six written case descriptions.
3. Communicate the three facilitative relationship conditions (empathy, genuineness, positive regard) to a client, given a role-play situation.

☐ CHARACTERISTICS OF EFFECTIVE HELPERS

The counselor's attitudes and skills are important determinants of the quality of the therapeutic relationship. (Client attitudes and behaviors also shape the relationship, since it is interactive and reciprocal.) The most effective helper is one who has successfully integrated the personal and scientific parts of himself or herself—in other words, who has achieved a balance of interpersonal and

11

technical competence. In this section we examine the qualities and behaviors present in very effective counselors and therapists.

Intellectual Competence

Counseling is an intellectually demanding process. In addition to being a "warm fuzzy," counseling and therapy require that one have a thorough and adequate knowledge base of many diverse areas. Counselors need to be knowledgeable and also to have a desire to learn, to be curious enough to want to check things out and know what is happening to clients. Intellectual competence also involves searching for data to make informed decisions about client treatment choice and progress (see also Chapter 10).

Energy

Counseling and therapy are emotionally demanding as well. Counselors who see several clients every day are likely to feel emotionally drained and physically fatigued at day's end—or sometimes even before! Passive, nonenergetic helpers are not likely to inspire much trust and confidence from their clients. Dynamism and intensity are more likely to produce client confidence and to encourage clients to work and to be active themselves during the session.

Flexibility

Effective therapists are also flexible—that is, they are not tied to a single ideology or methodology that they use for all clients. Flexible counselors adapt methods and technologies to clients rather than pushing clients and their problems to fit the use of a particular theoretical orientation or strategy. The flexible therapist's behavior is always mediated by the covert question posed by Kiesler (1966): Which technique will work best for this particular client with this set of problems?

Support

Effective therapists are supporting to clients. Support has a number of functions in the therapeutic relationship, including engendering hope, reducing client anxiety, and giving emotional security (Brammer & Shostrom, 1982). Giving support does not mean encouraging the client to lean on you, however, or taking responsibility away from the client. As Rogers (1951) notes, the counseling relationship "is experienced as basically supporting, but in no way supportive. The client does not

feel that someone is behind him, that someone approves of him. He does experience the fact that here is someone who respects him *as he is,* and is willing for him to take any direction which he chooses" (p. 209). (An exception would be in crisis intervention, where very direct supportive techniques are often the recommended treatment.) The counselor must maintain a careful balance between being supporting and being supportive in order to avoid promoting client dependence and to avoid "rescuing" the client, thus robbing clients of their own self-support system.

Good Will

Counselors who have good will work on behalf of their clients, not themselves. Their desire to help is not thwarted because of their own unmet needs. All of us who counsel get certain needs met through doing so. If we have "good will," however, we are not dependent on our counseling relationships as our *primary* source for meeting our own needs. Good will also implies that our motives and intentions are positive and constructive rather than negative and destructive. For example, we seek information about a client's sexual history because it is critical to the assessment of the particular problem, not because we are voyeuristic, curious, or in need of vicarious sexual reinforcement ourselves. Good will also suggests that we behave in ethical and responsible ways with clients (see also "Ethical Issues," later in this chapter).

Self-Awareness

The ability to be involved in an effective interpersonal interaction is influenced by our feelings and attitudes about ourselves. If we lack awareness about ourselves, we may be unable to establish the type of counseling relationship that is best for the client.

Our attitudes about ourselves can significantly influence the way we behave. People who have negative views of themselves will "put themselves down" and will either seek out or avoid types of interactions with others that confirm their negative self-image. This has serious implications for counselors. If we don't feel competent or valuable as people, we may communicate this attitude to the client. Or if we don't feel confident about our ability to counsel, we may inadvertently structure the counseling process to meet our own self-image problems or to confirm our negative self-pictures.

All our feelings and thoughts influence the way we handle certain things in the counseling relationship. Very strong feelings and attitudes about ourselves may significantly influence our behavior with clients. For instance a counselor who is very sensitive to rejection may be unduly careful not to offend a client or may avoid confronting a client when confrontation could be helpful. A counselor who has trouble dealing with negative feelings may structure the counseling interaction so that negative feelings are never "on the agenda."

In addition to skillful use of intervention strategies to produce client change, we need to be aware of our own strengths and limitations or "blind spots." In other words, it is just as important to keep track of our own personal growth as it is to keep track of which technique or change program we are using with a client. Otherwise, we run the risk of behaving incongruently in our relationships with clients. There are three areas that most counselors need to examine closely about themselves because they can have a significant impact on the quality of the relationship and the kind of service they give to clients: competence, power, and intimacy. These three areas and the possible feelings, attitudes, and behaviors associated with them are depicted in Table 2-1. We describe them in more detail in the next three sections.

TABLE 2-1. Effects of counselor's self-image on counseling interaction

Potential problem area and unresolved feelings and needs	Attitude about self	Possible counseling behaviors
Competence Incompetence Inadequacy Fear of failure Fear of success	1. Pollyanna; overly positive — fearful of failing	Structures counseling to maintain Pollyanna attitude, avoiding conflicts by— 1. discounting negative feedback 2. giving "fake" feedback 3. avoiding or smoothing over "heavy stuff"
	2. Negative; overly self-critical — fearful of succeeding	Structures counseling to maintain negative self-image by— 1. avoiding positive interactions 2. discounting positive feedback 3. giving self overly negative feedback 4. making goals and expectations too high 5. making self-deprecating or apologetic comments
	3. Not masculine enough or not feminine enough	Structures counseling to make self feel more secure as a male or female by— 1. overidentifying with or rejecting very masculine or very feminine clients 2. seducing clients of opposite sex 3. overreacting to or misinterpreting both positive and negative reactions from male and female clients
Power Impotence Control Passivity Dependence	1. Omnipotent — fearful of losing control	Structures counseling to get and stay in control by— 1. persuading clients to do whatever counselor wants 2. subtly informing client how good or right counselor is 3. dominating content and direction of interview 4. getting upset or irritated if client is resistant or reluctant

(continued)

TABLE 2-1. Effects of counselor's self-image on counseling interaction (continued)

Potential problem area and unresolved feelings and needs	Attitude about self	Possible counseling behaviors
Power		
Independence Counterdependence	2. Weak and unresourceful— fearful of control	Structures counseling to avoid taking control by— 1. being overly silent and nonparticipatory 2. allowing client too much direction, as in constant client rambling 3. frequently asking client for permission to do or say something 4. not expressing opinion; always referring back to client 5. avoiding any other risks
	3. Lifestyle converter	Structures counseling to convert client to counselor's beliefs or lifestyle by— 1. promoting ideology 2. getting in a power struggle 3. rejecting clients who are too different or who don't respond 4. "preaching"
Intimacy Affection Rejection	1. Needing warmth and acceptance—fearful of being rejected	Structures counseling to make self liked by— 1. eliciting positive feelings from client 2. avoiding use of confrontation 3. ignoring negative client cues 4. doing things for client—favors and so on
	2. Needing distance—fearful of closeness, affection	Structures counseling to maintain distance and avoid emotional intimacy by— 1. ignoring client's positive feelings 2. acting overly gruff or distant 3. maintaining professional role as "expert"

Competence. Your feelings of personal adequacy and professional competence can influence your covert and overt behavior in counseling interactions. Feelings of incompetence and inadequacy can be described as either fear of failure or fear of success. A counselor who is afraid of failure may approach counseling with an overly positive "Pollyanna" attitude. The fear of failure can be interfering if the counselor structures counseling to avoid conflicts. The counseling interaction may remain superficial because issues and negative topics are pushed under the table.

Other people may maintain a negative picture of themselves by being afraid of success and by avoiding successful situations and interactions. A counselor who fears success may structure counseling to maintain or confirm such a negative self-concept. This counselor tends to discount positive feedback and to have expectations that are out of reach.

Concerns about one's adequacy as a male or a female can also enter into the counseling relationship. Counselors who do not feel comfortable with themselves as men or women may behave in ways that add to their security in this area. For example, a counselor could promote his or her masculinity or femininity by overidentifying with or rejecting clients of the same sex, seducing clients of the opposite sex, and overreacting to or misinterpreting some client cues.

Power. Unresolved feelings about oneself in relation to power and control may include impotence, passivity, dependence. There are several ways that power can be misused in counseling. First, a counselor who fears being impotent or weak or who is afraid to give up control may try to be omnipotent. For this person, counseling is manageable only when it is controllable. Such a counselor may use a variety of maneuvers to stay in control, including persuading the client to do what the counselor wants, getting upset or defensive if a client is resistant or hesitant, and dominating the content and direction of the interview. The counselor who needs to control the interview may be more likely to engage in a power struggle with a client.

In contrast, a counselor may be afraid of power and control. This counselor may attempt to escape from as much responsibility and participation in counseling as possible. Such a counselor avoids taking control by allowing the client too much direction and by not expressing opinions. In other words, risks are avoided or ignored.

Another way that unresolved power needs can influence counseling is seen in the "lifestyle converter." This person has very strong feelings about the value of one particular lifestyle. Such a counselor may take unwarranted advantage of the influence processes in a helping relationship by using counseling to convert the client to that lifestyle or ideology. Counseling, in this case, turns into a forum for the counselor's views and pet peeves.

Intimacy. A counselor's unresolved intimacy needs can also significantly alter the direction and course of counseling. Generally, a counselor who has trouble with intimacy may fear rejection or be threatened by closeness and affection. A counselor who is afraid of rejection may behave in ways that meet the need to be accepted and liked by the client. For example, the counselor may avoid challenging or confronting the client for fear the client may be "turned off." Or the counselor may subtly seek positive client feedback as a reassurance of being valued and liked. Negative client cues also may be ignored because the counselor does not want to hear expressions of client dissatisfaction.

A counselor who is afraid of intimacy and affection may create excessive distance in the relationship. The counselor may avoid emotional intimacy in the relationship by ignoring expressions of positive feelings from the client or by behaving in a gruff, distant, or aloof manner and relating to the client through the "professional role."

LEARNING ACTIVITY #1: SELF-IMAGE

The following learning activity may help you explore some of your feelings and attitudes about yourself and possible effects on your counseling interactions. The activity consists of a Self-Rating Checklist divided into the three areas of competence, power, and intimacy. We suggest you work through each section separately. As you read the items listed for each section, think about the extent to which the item accurately describes your behavior *most* of the time (there are always exceptions to our consistent behaviors). If an item asks about you in relation to a client and you haven't had much counseling experience, try to project yourself into the counselor's role. Check the items that are most descriptive of you. Try to be as honest with yourself as possible. After completing the checklist, refer to the feedback that follows.

SELF-RATING CHECKLIST

Check the items that are most descriptive of you.

I. Competence Assessment

____ 1. Constructive negative feedback about myself doesn't make me feel incompetent or uncertain of myself.

____ 2. I tend to put myself down frequently.

____ 3. I feel fairly confident about myself as a helper.

____ 4. I am often preoccupied with thinking that I'm not going to be a competent counselor.

____ 5. When I am involved in a conflict, I don't go out of my way to ignore or avoid it.

____ 6. When I get positive feedback about myself, I often don't believe it's true.

____ 7. I set realistic goals for myself as a helper that are within reach.

____ 8. I believe that a confronting, hostile client could make me feel uneasy or incompetent.

____ 9. I often find myself apologizing for myself or my behavior.

____10. I'm fairly confident I can or will be a successful counselor.

____11. I find myself worrying a lot about "not making it" as a counselor.

____12. I'm likely to be a little scared by clients who would idealize me.

____13. A lot of times I will set standards or goals for myself that are too tough to attain.

____14. I tend to avoid negative feedback when I can.

(continued)

____15. Doing well or being successful does not make me feel uneasy.

II. Power Assessment

____ 1. If I'm really honest, I think my counseling methods are a little superior to other people's.

____ 2. A lot of times I try to get people to do what I want. I might get pretty defensive or upset if the client disagreed with what I wanted to do or did not follow my direction in the interview.

____ 3. I believe there is (or will be) a balance in the interviews between my participation and the client's.

____ 4. I could feel angry when working with a resistant or stubborn client.

____ 5. I can see that I might be tempted to get some of my own ideology across to the client.

____ 6. As a counselor, "preaching" is not likely to be a problem for me.

____ 7. Sometimes I feel impatient with clients who have a different way of looking at the world than I do.

____ 8. I know there are times when I would be reluctant to refer my client to someone else, especially if the other counselor's style differed from mine.

____ 9. Sometimes I feel rejecting or intolerant of clients whose values and lifestyles are very different from mine.

____10. It is hard for me to avoid getting into a power struggle with some clients.

III. Intimacy Assessment

____ 1. There are times when I act more gruff than I really feel.

____ 2. It's hard for me to express positive feelings to a client.

____ 3. There are some clients I would really like to be my friends more than my clients.

____ 4. It would upset me if a client didn't like me.

____ 5. If I sense a client has some negative feelings toward me, I try to talk about it rather than avoid it.

____ 6. Many times I go out of my way to avoid offending clients.

____ 7. I feel more comfortable maintaining a professional distance between myself and the client.

____ 8. Being close to people is something that does not make me feel uncomfortable.

____ 9. I am more comfortable when I am a little aloof.

____10. I am very sensitive to how clients feel about me, especially if it's negative.

____11. I can accept positive feedback from clients fairly easily.

____12. It is difficult for me to confront a client.

☐ ISSUES AFFECTING THE THERAPEUTIC RELATIONSHIP

Although each therapeutic relationship is always defined somewhat idiosyncratically by each therapeutic dyad, there are certain issues that will affect many of the therapeutic relationships you will encounter. These include (but are not limited to) values, ethics, and emotional objectivity.

Values

The word *value* denotes something we prize, regard highly, or prefer. Values are our feelings or attitudes about something and our preferred actions or behaviors. As an example, take a few minutes to think of (and perhaps list) five things you love to do. Now look over your list to determine how frequently and consistently you actually engage in each of these five actions. Your values are indicated by your frequent and consistent actions (Raths, Harmin, & Simon, 1966). If you say you value spending time with friends but you hardly ever do this, then other activities and actions probably have more value for you.

In interactions with clients, it is impossible to be "value-free." Values permeate every interaction. Counselors cannot be "scrupulously neutral" in their interactions with clients (Corey, Corey, & Callanan, 1984, p. 55). Okun (1982) asserts that "in recent years, we have recognized that in any interpersonal relationship, whether or not it is a helping relationship, values are transmitted either covertly or overtly between the participants" (p. 229). Interviewers may unintentionally influence a patient to embrace their values in subtle ways by what they pay attention to or by nonverbal cues of approval and disapproval (Corey et al., 1984, p. 81). If clients feel they need the counselor's approval, they may act in ways they think will please the counselor instead of making choices independently according to their own value system.

Obviously, not all of our values have an impact on the helping process. For example, the counselor who values sailing can probably work with a client who values being a landlubber without any problem. However, values that reflect our ideas about "the good life," morality, ethics, lifestyle, roles, interpersonal living, and so forth have a greater chance of entering into the helping process. The very fact that we have entered a helping profession suggests some of our values. As discussed in Chapter 9, there may be times when a referral is necessary because of an unresolved and interfering value conflict with a client. For example, a counselor who views rape as the most terrible and sexist act a person can perform might have difficulty counseling someone accused of rape. This counselor might tend to identify more with the rape victim than with the client. From an ethical viewpoint, if a counselor is unable to promote and respect the welfare of a client, a referral may be necessary (American Association for Counseling and Development, 1981; American Psychological Association, 1981).

There are other times in the counseling process when our values affect helping, not because they conflict with the client's values, but because they restrict or limit the client. In these instances, our values are getting in the way of helping the person reach her or his potential. Restricting or delimiting values are reflected in such areas as our expectations for different clients, our beliefs about change, and our values about an "ism" such as sexism, racism, culturism, or ageism. One of *our* values is the need for counselors to be aware of values that might prevent the client from developing his or her potential. We have acted on this value by including in Learning Activity #2 some ways to help you examine your values about a number of "isms" and about your expectations for client change.

Stereotypical values. There is a legitimate concern about the possible limiting effects of counselor stereotyping in the helping process. Maslin and Davis (1975, p. 87) define *stereotyping* as ascribing characteristics to a person on the basis of presumed knowledge about a group to which the person belongs. E. J. Smith (1977) asserts that stereotypes "are the conventions that people use for refusing to deal with one another on an individual basis" (p. 390). Stereotyping in counseling may occur when the counselor projects his or her biases on the client or applies cultural and sociological characteristics of a particular cultural group "indiscriminately to all members" of that group (p. 391).

The most damaging kinds of stereotyping have to do with sex roles and ethnicity. For example, there is some evidence that, during the helping process, many counselors communicate the stereotypical attitudes toward sex roles of our Western culture (Broverman, Broverman, Clarkson, Rosenkrantz, & Vogel, 1970). In other words, some counselors may try to influence male and female clients to behave according to stereotypical concepts of masculinity and femininity portrayed in our culture. Male clients may be reinforced for being strong, independent, and unemotional, whereas female clients are told it is more "healthy" to be less assertive and more passive, dependent, and "soft." Our sex-role values also may be used inappropriately in counseling even when our biases do not reflect the traditional male and female roles. Using nontraditional sex-role values to urge a nonworking mother to work is another example of limiting the client's choices. Okun (1982) suggests that sexist counseling occurs whenever the counselor employs her or his own sex-role ideology as a basis for helping.

Sexism is not the only area in which our values may dominate the helping process. Our biases can interfere when counseling people with handicaps and disabilities, people of limited abilities, and people of different cultures, races, and socioeconomic levels. E. J. Smith (1977) points out that stereotypical counseling treatment of Blacks occurs whenever the counselor applies assumptions and research findings about Black clients in a general, nonidiosyncratic manner. Smith adds that many of the proverbial conclusions about counseling Black clients — such as that Blacks have poor self-concepts, Black clients are nonverbal, or Black clients profit only from counseling that is highly structured and action-oriented — may be more myths than realities and may reflect White Anglo-Saxon interpretations and values. Okun (1982) observes that another common form of stereotypical counseling involves ageism, when we convey "our own beliefs and values about what a person can or should do at different ages" (p. 244). A counselor who becomes aware that his or her limiting expectations or stereotypical values are interfering with the helping process has the responsibility to modify the stereotypes or refer the client to another helper.

In some cases, a counselor may be unaware of tendencies toward "ism" counseling because of lack of opportunities to counsel different kinds of clients. For example, if you have never worked with an older person, a handicapped person, or a person of another culture, perhaps you have never confronted your values about such clients. Learning Activity #2 may give you a chance to simulate doing so.

LEARNING ACTIVITY #2: PERSONAL VALUES

This learning activity presents descriptions of six clients. If you work through this activity by yourself, we suggest that you imagine yourself counseling each of these clients. Try to generate a very vivid picture of yourself and the client in your mind. If you do this activity with a partner, you can role-play the counselor while your partner assumes the part of each client as described in the six examples. As you imagine or role-play the counselor, try to notice your feelings, attitudes, values, and behavior during the visualization or role-play process. After *each* example, stop to think about or discuss these questions:

1. What attitudes and beliefs did you have about the client?
2. Were your beliefs and attitudes based on actual or presumed information about the client?
3. How did you behave with the client?
4. What values are portrayed by your behavior?
5. Could you work with this person effectively?

There are no right or wrong answers. A reaction to this learning activity can be found after the client descriptions in the feedback section.

Client 1

This client is a young woman who is having financial problems. She is the sole supporter of three young children. She earns her living by prostitution and pushing drugs. She states that she is concerned about her financial problems but can't make enough money from welfare or from an unskilled job to support her kids.

Client 2

The client is an older man (age 60) who is approaching retirement. He has been working most of his life as a furniture salesperson. He has a high school diploma and has not been in school since he was 18 years old. Now he feels that he wants to go to college and earn a degree.

Client 3

You have been assigned a client who is charged with rape and sexual assault. The client, a man, tells you that he is not to blame for the incident because the victim, a woman, "asked for it."

Client 4

This client is concerned about general feelings of depression. Overweight and unkempt, the client is in poor physical condition and smokes constantly during the interview.

Client 5

The client is a middle-aged woman on welfare. She says she was raped and as a result gave birth to a child. She is torn between trying to keep this baby and giving it up.

Client 6

The client is a 12-year-old boy who recently lost a leg in an automobile accident. He was a strong swimmer before the accident; he wants to continue his swimming now so he can eventually make the high school swimming team. He wants to know your opinion about this decision.

Ethical Issues

The therapeutic relationship needs to be handled in such a way as to promote and protect the client's welfare. Indeed, as Brammer and Shostrom (1982, p. 149) observe, ethical handling of client relationships is a "distinctive mark" of the professional counselor/therapist. All professional groups of helpers have a code of ethics adopted by their profession, such as the ethical standards of the American Association for Counseling and Development (1981), the American Psychological Association (1981), and the National Association of Social Workers (1979) (see Appendixes A, B, C, and D). Marriage and family therapists, rehabilitation counselors, and health professionals also have their own sets of corresponding ethical standards.

FEEDBACK #1: SELF-IMAGE

1. For each of the three assessment areas you can look over your responses and determine the areas that seem to be OK and the areas that may be a problem for you or something to watch out for. You may find more problems in one area than another.
2. Do your "trouble spots" seem to occur with almost everyone or just with certain types of people? In all situations or some situations?
3. Compare yourself now with where you might have been four years ago or where you may be four years from now.
4. Identify any areas you feel you could use some help with, from a colleague, a supervisor, or a counselor.

The counselor's value system is an important factor in determining ethical behavior. Behaving unethically can have consequences such as loss of membership in professional organizations and malpractice lawsuits. Of most consequence is the detrimental effect that unethical behavior can have on clients and on the therapeutic relationship.

All student and practicing counselors and therapists should be familiar with the ethical codes of their profession. The following discussion highlights a few of the more critical issues and in no way is intended to be a substitute for careful scrutiny of existing ethical codes of behavior.

Client welfare. Counselors are obligated to protect the welfare of their clients. In most instances, this means putting the client's needs first. It also means ensuring that you are intellectually and emotionally ready to give the best that you can to each client — or to see that the client has a referral option if seeing you is not in the client's best interests.

Confidentiality. Closely related to protecting client well-being is the issue of confidentiality. Counselors who breach client confidences can do serious and often irreparable harm to the therapeutic relationship. Counselors are generally not free to reveal or disclose information about clients unless they have first received written permission from the client. An exception can be in instances in which the counselor believes the client poses a serious threat of harm to self or others and in states where the helping professional can be subpoenaed because of lack of a legal statute protecting counselor disclosure about the therapeutic relationship in a court of law (known as "privileged communication").

Dual relationships. A dual relationship is one in which the counselor is in a therapeutic relationship with the client and simultaneously also has another kind of relationship with that same person, such as an administrative, instructional, supervisory, social, or sexual relationship. Dual relationships are problematic because they reduce the counselor's objectivity, confuse the issue, and often put the client in a position of diminished consent. Counselors should avoid becoming involved in dual relationships. If such involvement is unavoidable, make use of the referral option so that two relationships are not carried on simultaneously.

Client rights. Establishing an effective therapeutic relationship entails being open with clients about their rights and options during the course of therapy. Nothing can be more damaging to trust and rapport than to have the client discover in midstream that the therapist is not qualified to help with a particular issue or that the financial costs of therapy are high or that therapy involves certain limitations or nonguarantees of outcomes. At the outset, the therapist should provide the client with enough information about therapy to help the client make informed choices (also called "informed consent"). Usually this means discussing four general aspects of counseling with clients: (1) confidentiality and its limitations, (2) the procedures and goals of therapy and any possible side effects of change (such as anxiety, pain, or disruption of the status quo), (3) the qualifications and practices of the therapist, and (4) other available resources and sources of help other than oneself and other than traditional therapy (for example, self-help groups) (Hare-Mustin, Maracek, Kaplan, & Liss-Levinson, 1979; see also "Structuring," in Chapter 3 and Informed Consent in Chapter 11).

Referral. It is important for counselors to handle referral effectively and responsibly. Referring a client to another therapist may be necessary when, for one reason or another, you are not able to provide the service or care that the client requires. Careful referral, however, involves more than just giving the client the name of another counselor. The client should be given a choice among therapists who are competent and are qualified to deal with the client's problems. The counselor must obtain written client permission before discussing the case with the new therapist. And to protect against abandonment, the counselor should follow up on the referral to determine whether the appropriate contact was made.

Emotional Objectivity

The therapeutic relationship has the capacity to invoke great emotional intensity, often experienced by both the counselor and the client. To some extent, counselors need to become emotionally involved in the relationship. If they are too aloof or distant, clients will feel that the counselor is cold, mechanical, and noncaring. However, if counselors are too involved, they may scare the client away or may lose all objectivity and cloud their judgment.

The degree of emotional objectivity and intensity felt by counselors can affect two relationship issues: transference and countertransference. *Transference* is the

> process whereby clients project onto their therapists past feelings or attitudes toward significant people in their lives. . . . In transference, a client's unfinished business produces a distortion in the way he or she perceives the therapist. The feelings that are experienced in transference may be positive or negative. . . . They are connected with the past but are now directed toward the therapist [Corey et al., 1984, pp. 42–43].

Transference can occur very easily with counselors of all theoretical orientations when the emotional intensity has become so great that the client loses his or her objectivity and starts to relate to the counselor as if he or she were some significant other person in the client's life.

Transference can have therapeutic value because

> it allows clients to express distorted feelings without getting the response they expect. . . . [For example], if a client is treating the therapist as a stern and rejecting parent, the therapist does not respond with the expected defensive and rejective feelings. Instead, the therapist accepts the client's feelings and helps the client understand them [Corey et al., 1984, p. 43].

Countertransference occurs when counselors lose their objectivity and develop a strong emotional reaction to the client. According to Corey et al. (1984, pp. 46–47), countertransference may be manifested in a number of ways, including—

1. The need for constant reinforcement and/or approval from your clients.
2. Seeing yourself and/or your problems or "unfinished business" in your clients.
3. Development of sexual or romantic feelings toward your clients.
4. Compulsive advice giving with clients.
5. A desire to develop a social relationship with clients.

To handle transference and countertransference effectively, the counselor needs, first of all, to be aware of when these dynamics occur. Clues to transference and countertransference include a sudden eruption of strong emotions (by either client or counselor) that seems inappropriate in timing or intensity, given the context in which the feelings arise (Reiser & Schroder, 1980, p. 150). The counselor who fails to recognize transference or countertransference may respond inappropriately to the client.

Second, counselors must be constantly aware of the various levels of impact that they have on clients and clients have on them (Brammer & Shostrom, 1982, p. 145). Either end of the continuum—too little impact or too intense an impact—can adversely affect the therapeutic relationship.

Finally, one must seek a level of emotional involvement that is sufficient to generate client involvement without clouding one's own objectivity about the client (Brammer & Shostrom, 1982).

☐ FUNDAMENTAL HELPING SKILLS AND PERSON-CENTERED THERAPY

In the remainder of this chapter, as well as in Chapters 3–6, we describe a number of fundamental, or *core,* skills of helping. Relationship, responding, and listening skills are parts of most current helping approaches. These skills have roots in a counseling theory developed by Rogers (1951), called "client-centered" or "person-centered" therapy. Because this theory is the basis of these fundamental skills, we will describe it briefly in this section.

The first stage of this theory (Rogers, 1942) was known as the *nondirective* period. The counselor essentially attended and listened to the client for the purpose of mirroring the client's communication. The second stage of this theory (Rogers, 1951) was known as the *client-centered* period. In this phase, the therapist not only mirrored the client's communication but also reflected underlying or implicit affect or feelings. (This is the basis of current concepts of the skill of empathy, discussed in the next section.)

In the most recent stage, known as *person-centered therapy* (Meador & Rogers, 1984), therapy is construed as an active partnership between two persons. In this current stage, emphasis is on client growth through *experiencing* of oneself and of the other person in the relationship.

Although client-centered therapy has evolved and changed, certain fundamental tenets have remained the same. One of these is that all people have an inherent tendency to strive toward growth, self-actualization, and self-direction. This tendency is realized when individuals have access to conditions (both within and outside therapy) that nurture growth. In the context of therapy, client growth is associated with high levels of three core, or facilitative, relationship conditions: *empathy* (accurate understanding), *respect* (positive regard), and *genuineness* (congruence) (Rogers, Gendlin, Kiesler, & Truax, 1967). If these conditions are absent from the therapeutic relationship, clients may not only fail to grow, they may deteriorate (Berenson & Mitchell, 1974; Carkhuff, 1969a, 1969b; Truax & Mitchell, 1971). Presumably, in order for these conditions to enhance the therapeutic relationship, they must be communicated by the counselor *and* perceived by the client (Rogers, 1951, 1957).

Gazda, Asbury, Balzer, Childers, and Walters (1984, p. 131) summarize a number of important purposes of facilitative conditions, including the following:

1. The use of facilitative conditions establishes a relationship of mutual trust and caring in which clients feel secure and able to express themselves in any way or form necessary.
2. The facilitative conditions help to define the counselor or therapist role; counselors utilize effective therapeutic behaviors and try to avoid ineffective skills and behaviors.
3. The use of facilitative conditions helps clients to obtain a more complete and concrete self-image, or self-picture, allowing them to see or understand things that formerly may have been hidden or only partly understood.
4. Facilitative responding is a concrete way to show clients they have your full attention without personal or environmental distractions.

Although Rogerian-based strategies for helping "are devoid of techniques that involve *doing* something to or for the client" (Gilliland, James, Roberts, & Bowman, 1984), in current writings Rogers (1977) asserts that these three core conditions represent a set of skills as well as an attitude on the part of the therapist. In recent years, a variety of persons have developed concrete skills associated with these three core conditions; much of this development is based on accumulating research evidence (Carkhuff, 1969a, 1969b; Egan, 1982; Gazda et al., 1984; Ivey, 1983). This delineation of the core conditions into teachable skills has made it possible for people to learn how to communicate these core conditions to clients. In the following three sections, we describe these three important relationship conditions and associated skills in more detail.

☐ EMPATHY, OR ACCURATE UNDERSTANDING

Empathy may be described as the ability to understand people from their frame of reference rather than your own. Responding to a client empathically may be "an attempt to think *with,* rather than *for* or *about* the client" (Brammer & Shostrom, 1982, p. 160). For example, if a client says "I've tried to get along with my father, but it doesn't work out. He's too hard on me," an empathic response would be something like "You feel discouraged about your unsuccessful attempts to get along with your father." In contrast, if you say something like "You ought to try harder," you are responding from your frame of reference, not the client's.

Empathy has received a great deal of attention from both researchers and practitioners over the years. Current concepts emphasize that empathy is far more than a single concept or skill. Empathy is believed to be a multistage process consisting of multiple elements (Barrett-Lennard, 1981; Gladstein, 1983).

Current research has abandoned the "uniformity myth" (Kiesler, 1966) with respect to empathy and seeks to determine when empathic understanding is most useful for particular clients and problems and at particular stages in the counseling process. As Gladstein (1983, p. 178) observes, "in counseling/psychotherapy, affective and cognitive empathy can be helpful in certain stages, with certain clients, and for certain goals. However, at other times, they can interfere with positive outcomes." Generally, empathy is useful in influencing the quality and effectiveness of the therapeutic relationship. Empathy helps to build rapport and elicit information from clients by showing understanding, demonstrating civility (Egan, 1982), conveying that both counselor and client are working "from the same side" (Krumboltz & Thoresen, 1976), and fostering client goals related to self-exploration (Gladstein, 1983) (see also Table 2-2).

Empathy is conveyed to clients by reflective and additive verbal messages (Carkhuff, 1969a; Carkhuff & Pierce, 1975; Egan, 1982), by nonverbal behavior (Maurer & Tindall, 1983; Smith-Hanen, 1977), and by the use of selected words or predicates that match clients' sensory systems (Lankton, 1980; Hammer, 1983).

Verbal Means of Conveying Empathy

Consider the following specific tools for conveying empathy:

- *Show desire to comprehend.* It is necessary not only to convey an accurate understanding from the client's perspective but also to convey your *desire* to comprehend from the client's frame of reference. This is evidenced by statements indicating your attempts to make sense of the client's world and by clarification and questions about the client's experiences and feelings.
- *Discuss what is important to the client.* Show by your questions and statements that you are aware of what is most important to the client. Respond in ways that relate to the client's basic problem or complaint. This should be a brief statement that captures the thoughts and feelings of the client and one that is directly related to the client's concerns.

TABLE 2-2. Components and purposes of facilitative, or core, relationship conditions (empathy, genuineness, positive regard)

Condition	Components	Purposes
Empathy (accurate understanding)	Desire to comprehend Reflection of implicit client messages Reference to client feelings Discussion of what is most important to client Pacing of client's experience	1. To build rapport 2. To elicit information by showing understanding 3. To foster client self-exploration
Genuineness (congruence)	Appropriate role behavior Congruence Spontaneity Openness and self-disclosure Supporting nonverbal behaviors	1. To reduce the emotional distance between client and counselor 2. To increase identification between client and counselor, thereby contributing to trust and rapport
Positive regard (respect)	Commitment Effort to understand Nonjudgmental behavior Warmth and immediacy	1. To communicate a willingness to work with the client 2. To show interest in the client as a person 3. To convey acceptance of the client

- Use verbal responses that *refer to client feelings.* One way to define empathy is through verbal statements that reflect the client's feelings (Uhlemann, Lea, & Stone, 1976). Use responses that convey your awareness of the client's feelings. Focus on the client's feelings by naming or labeling them. This is sometimes called "interchangeable" (Carkhuff, 1969a) or "primary" (Egan, 1982) empathy.
- Use verbal responses that bridge or *add on to implicit client messages.* Empathy also involves comprehension of the client's innermost thoughts and perspectives even when these are unspoken and implicit. According to Rogers (1977), "The therapist is so much inside the private world of the other that she can clarify not only the messages of which the client is aware but even those just below the level of awareness" (p. 11). The counselor bridges or adds on to client messages by conveying understanding of what the client implies or infers in order to add to the client's frame of reference or to draw out implications of the issue. This is sometimes called "additive empathy" (Carkhuff, 1969a) or "advanced empathy" (Egan, 1982).

Carkhuff and Pierce (1975) have developed a Discrimination Inventory that presents a scale for assessing both primary and additive empathy messages. On this scale, counselor responses are rated according to one of five levels; Level 3 is considered the *minimally* acceptable response. Level 3 responses on this scale correspond to Carkhuff and Pierce's concept of interchangeable empathy and Egan's (1975) concept of primary-level empathy; Level 4 corresponds to additive empathy (Carkhuff, 1969a) or advanced empathy (Egan); and Level 5 represents facilitating action. The scale can be used either to discriminate among levels of responses or to rate levels of counselor communication. Here is an example of a verbal empathic response at each level of Carkhuff and Pierce's Discrimination Inventory.

Client: I've tried to get along with my father, but it doesn't work out. He's too hard on me.
Counselor at Level 1: I'm sure it will all work out in time [reassurance and denial].
or
    You ought to try harder to see his point of view [advice].
or
    Why can't you two get along? [question].

Level 1 is a question, reassurance, denial, or advice.

Counselor at Level 2: You're having a hard time getting along with your father.

Level 2 is a response to only the *content,* or cognitive portion, of the message; feelings are ignored.

Counselor at Level 3: You feel discouraged because your attempts to get along with your father have not been very successful.

Level 3 has understanding but no direction; it is a reflection of feeling and meaning based on the client's explicit message. In other words, a Level 3 response reflects both the feeling and the situation. In this response, "You feel discouraged" is the reflection of the feeling, and "because of not getting along" is the reflection of the situation.

Counselor at Level 4: You feel discouraged because you can't seem to reach your father. You want him to let up on you.

Level 4 has understanding and some direction. A Level 4 response identifies not only the client's feelings but also the client's deficit that is implied. In a Level 4 response, the client's deficit is personalized, meaning the client owns or accepts responsibility for the deficit, as in "You can't reach" in this response.

Counselor at Level 5: You feel discouraged because you can't seem to reach your father. You want him to let up on you. One step could be to express your feelings about this to your father.

A Level 5 response contains all of a Level 4 response plus at least one action step the person can take to master the deficit and attain the goal. In this example, the action step is "One step could be to express your feelings about this to your father."

Nonverbal Means of Conveying Empathy
In addition to the use of selected verbal messages, empathy is conveyed by attentive nonverbal behaviors such as direct eye contact, a forward-leaning body position, facing the client (Haase & Tepper, 1972), and an open-arm position (Smith-Hanen, 1977). These nonverbal behaviors are particularly useful when they match (or pace) the client's nonverbal behavior. Pacing means simply moving as the client moves or matching the client's nonverbal behavior without mimicking the client or doing it so deliberately that the client becomes aware of it. For example, when the counselor's and client's body postures are similar, the client is likely to perceive the counselor as more empathic (Maurer & Tindall, 1983).

Matching the Client's Experience

People have different ways of mapping their experiences and of processing internal and external information. According to Lankton (1980, p. 17),

> We are constantly taking in information from the outside world through our sensory channels. Some of it we are conscious of and some of it not. What we sense externally . . . we translate into internal representations that, in turn, mediate our behavior. Consider the difference between seeing an appetizing dessert and hearing it described: both experiences involve different sensory channels yet either might trigger salivation.*

According to a communication theory called "neurolinguistic programming," or NLP (Bandler & Grinder, 1975; Grinder & Bandler, 1976), everyone has five sensory channels, or modalities (also called "representational systems," or "R systems"), for processing information: visual (what we see), auditory (what we hear), kinesthetic (what we feel, viscerally and tactically), olfactory (what we smell), and gustation (what we taste). For communication and therapy purposes, the visual, auditory, and kinesthetic channels are most important. Processing in the visual mode yields internal pictures or images; processing in the auditory mode yields words, sounds, tones, and internal dialogue; and processing in the kinesthetic mode results in felt bodily experiences such as proprioceptive information, tactile experiences, and affective and emotional sensations. For example, an individual who enjoys sailing may experience sailing simply by recalling a picture of a sailboat or constructing an image of a sailboat (visual channel), by hearing or constructing sounds associated with a sailing experience or by engaging in covert self-talk about sailing (auditory channel), or by experiencing "goose bumps" or similar felt sensations when recalling a memorable sailing experience (kinesthetic channel). According to NLP principles, each person also has a sensory modality that is most highly valued and utilized at any point in time—which NLP theorists refer to as the "primary representational system," or PRS (see also Birholtz, 1981).

Lankton (1980, p. 15) asserts that "clinical therapy tends to underemphasize the importance of the sensory data exchanged between people and

---

* Reprinted by permission of the author and publisher, S. R. Lankton, *Practical Magic,* 1980 by Meta Publications, P. O. Box 565, Cupertino, Calif., U.S.A.

between people and environments. . . . Therapy must, therefore, begin with the noticing of sensory input channels, especially sensory distinctions made within the kinesthetic, visual, and auditory channels." One of the most important reasons for noticing the client's sensory system is to be able to pace, or match, it. Research evidence suggests that counselors who match clients' sensory systems are perceived as more empathic (Brockman, 1980; Hammer, 1983) and trustworthy (Falzett, 1981). Empathy involves all three sensory channels: seeing with the client's eyes, hearing with the client's ears, and feeling with the client's experiences. Noticing and utilizing a client's sensory modalities also allows you to go beyond understanding the client's feelings and frame of reference to understand how clients construct or represent their experiences—their world—since sensory modalities are clues to the way in which people organize and process their experiences. Finally, pacing of clients' sensory systems emphasizes the importance of acknowledging aspects of their behavior and using their model of the world, not yours, to communicate.

In order to notice the client's sensory modalities, the therapist needs to be aware of certain aspects of the client's verbal and nonverbal behavior. NLP postulates that there are at least four major ways in which clients reveal which sensory system is used at any particular point in time: (1) verbal predicates, (2) eye movements, or accessing cues, (3) voice tone, and (4) self-report. Of these four ways to detect sensory systems, only #1, the tracking of verbal predicates, seems to be a reliable way to assess clients' preferred sensory systems (Sharpley, 1984). For this reason, it will be the only method we discuss.

The adjectives, adverbs, and verbs that clients select while talking reveal which sensory system they are using at that time (Lankton, 1980). For example, suppose you say something to your client and the client replies "I see what you mean." The client is making meaning of what you said by generating internal pictures or images. If another client responds with "I hear what you said," that client is probably processing your communication by generating internal sounds or dialogue. A third client may respond with "I can grasp it" or "I'm in touch with that, too." This client is processing your words with tactile, visceral, or internal sensations or feelings.

According to NLP, you can discover which system a client is attending to at any time by listening carefully to the predicates that the client chooses to describe her or his experience. Table 2-3 lists the most common predicates associated with the three commonly used sensory channels: visual, auditory, and kinesthetic.

Some research has found support for the notion that pacing, or matching, the client's sensory modality results in the counselor's empathy as perceived by the client, desire to see the counselor again, and perceived trustworthiness of the counselor (Brockman, 1980; Falzett, 1981; Hammer, 1983). However, as Hammer (1983) concludes, these results may or may not be explained strictly in terms of NLP principles. One might conclude either that matching of the client's sensory modality is useful or that simply classifying the client's words and responding with similar words is useful for activating empathy and trust. Regardless of the explanation, "the cueing effect of client verbalizations is valuable . . . to alert counselors to phrase their responses in such a way as to maximize empathy within the interview" (Sharpley, 1984, p. 247).

When you match the predicates of your clients, "you will literally be speaking the client's language" (Lankton, 1980, p. 19). Moreover, you will be on your way to expressing or communicating empathy by adopting a similar verbal style to the client's (Hammer, 1983). Matching predicates means that during a session you are able to track the client's ongoing use of predicates and select yours accordingly. It also means that you are aware of and can delete inappropriate (mis-

TABLE 2-3. Predicates associated with the visual, auditory, and kinesthetic modalities.

Visual	Auditory	Kinesthetic
see	listen	feel
clear	yell	touch, touchy
focus	tell, told	pressure
picture	talk	hurt
view	hear	pushy
perspective	ears	grasp
bright	discuss	relaxed
show	shout	sense
colorful	loud, noisy	experience
glimpse	call	firm
"now look"	"now listen"	"you know"

Adapted from Lankton (1980).

matched) predicates that may occur as a part of your habitual verbal style.

You can also match phrases the client uses repetitively from the same sensory system. For example, if a client says several times "Do you see what I mean?," you correspond by saying something like "From your point of view" or "Are you getting a clear picture?" In subsequent chapters on listening and action responses (see Chapters 5 and 6), we suggest ways for you to use responses that match the sensory-system predicates revealed by clients. Other examples of matching words and phrases are suggested in these chapters as well.

LEARNING ACTIVITIES #3: EMPATHY

Activity One: Empathy Discrimination Exercise

Using the description of Carkhuff and Pierce's (1975) Discrimination Inventory on page 23, decide whether each of the following counselor responses belongs in:

Level 1—No understanding, no direction. Counselor response is a question, a denial or reassurance, or advice.

Level 2—No understanding, some direction. Counselor response highlights only *content* of client's message; feelings are ignored.

Level 3—Understanding present; direction absent. Counselor responds to both *content* or meaning and *feelings*.

Level 4—Both understanding and direction present. Helper responds to client *feelings* and identifies *deficit*.

Level 5—Understanding, direction, and action present. Counselor response includes all of Level 4 plus one *action* step.

After rating each response, explain your choice. An example is provided at the beginning of the activity. Feedback can be found after the learning activities.

Example

Client: I've become burned out with teaching. I've thought about changing jobs, but you know it's hard to find a good job now.

Counselor response: Teaching is no longer too satisfying to you.
This response is: *Level 2.* Because: *Response is only to the content or the situation of teaching. Client's feelings are ignored.*

(continued)

LEARNING ACTIVITIES #3: EMPATHY (continued)

Practice Statements

1. *Client:* I've always wanted to be a doctor, but I've been discouraged from this.

   Counselor: Oh, I'm sure this is something you could do if you really wanted to.
   This response is:
   Because:

2. *Client:* I've had such a rough semester. I don't know what I got myself into. I'm not sure where to go from here.

   Counselor: You feel perturbed about the way your semester turned out and confused because of this.
   This response is:
   Because:

3. *Client:* My teacher always picks on me.

   Counselor: Why do you suppose she picks on you?
   This response is:
   Because:

4. *Client:* I'm bored with my job. It's getting to be the same old thing. But what else is there to do?

   Counselor: You feel dissatisfied with your job because of the routine. You can't find anything in it that really turns you on. You want to find some more appealing work. One step is to list the most important needs a job meets for you and to identify how those needs could be met by certain jobs.
   This response is:
   Because:

5. *Client:* I don't understand why this accident happened to me; I've always led a good life; now this.

   Counselor: You feel resentful because you can't explain why this sudden accident happened to you. You want to at least figure out some reason that might make it seem more fair.
   This response is:
   Because:

6. *Client:* My parents are getting a divorce. I wish they wouldn't.

   Counselor: You feel upset because your parents are divorcing.
   This response is:
   Because:

7. *Client:* It just seems like each year goes by without our being able to have children.

   Counselor: You feel discouraged because you can't seem to get pregnant. You want to have a child very much.
   This response is:
   Because:

8. *Client:* I'm caught in the middle. I'm not able to move into public housing unless my husband leaves for good. But I'd also want my husband to continue to come and live with me at least some of the time.

   Counselor: Moving into public housing might prevent you and your husband from living together.
   This response is:
   Because:

9. *Client:* It's been hard for me to adjust since I've retired. The days seem so empty.

   Counselor: You feel useless because of all the time on your hands now. You can't find a way to fill up your days. You want to find some meaningful things to do. One step is to think of some ways you can continue using your work interests even though you are no longer employed.
   This response is:
   Because:

Activity Two: Sensitivity to Sensory Modalities

To develop greater sensitivity to the sensory modalities of clients, list as many words and phrases as you can think of under each of the following categories: visual, auditory, kinesthetic. Carry a list around with you and add to it after conversations with friends or clients. Check your list with a colleague or instructor and see whether he or she has any additional input.

Activity Three: Identification of Sensory Modalities

Fifteen phrases are listed in this activity. Indicate in the blank provided which sensory modality is indicated by each phrase. Use *V* for visual, *A* for auditory, and *K* for kinesthetic. Feedback follows.

____ 1. Things are looking up
____ 2. Listening between the lines
____ 3. What a pain in the neck!
____ 4. My style is cramped
____ 5. Going blank
____ 6. Simply speechless
____ 7. Feel overloaded
____ 8. A brighter horizon
____ 9. How's that grab you?
____10. Rings a bell

(continued)

____11. Sick to my stomach
____12. Change your tune
____13. It bent my ear
____14. Seeing eye to eye
____15. A real eye opener

Activity Four: Tracking Speech Predicates and Phrases

To help you determine and track a client's use of various sensory modalities, engage in the following activities:

Using triads, identify one person as the client, another as the counselor, and the third as the observer. The activity will be done in three "rounds" — allow two to three minutes per round.

Round 1 — Both the client and the counselor are to talk using visual predicates and phrases. The observer keeps track by writing these words down and by interrupting if either person gets off track and switches to language of another sensory system.

Round 2 — Do as in Round 1, but switch roles and use auditory predicates and phrases.

Round 3 — Do as in Round 1, but switch roles again and use kinesthetic predicates and phrases.

After the third round, discuss the experience. Which role was hardest for you? Easiest? Which of the sensory systems was most comfortable to use? Least comfortable? What does this activity tell you about your own preferred sensory system?

☐ GENUINENESS

Genuineness means being oneself without being phony or playing a role. Although most counselors are trained to be "professionals," a counselor can convey genuineness by being human and by collaborating with the client. Genuineness contributes to an effective therapeutic relationship by reducing the emotional distance between the counselor and client and by helping the client to identify with the counselor, to perceive the counselor as another person similar to oneself. Genuineness has at least five components, summarized in Table 2-2: supporting nonverbal behaviors, role behavior, congruence, spontaneity, and openness (see also Egan, 1982).

Supporting Nonverbal Behaviors

Genuineness is communicated by the therapist's use of appropriate, or supporting, nonverbal behaviors. Nonverbal behaviors that convey genuineness include eye contact, smiling, and leaning toward the client while sitting (Seay & Altekruse, 1979). These two nonverbal behaviors, however, should be used discreetly and gracefully. For example, direct yet intermittent eye contact is perceived as more indicative of genuineness than is persistent gazing, which clients may interpret as staring. Similarly, continual smiling or leaning forward may be viewed as phony and artificial rather than genuine and sincere. As we mentioned during our discussion of empathy, when establishing rapport, the counselor should display nonverbal behaviors that parallel or match those of the client.

Role Behavior

Counselors who do not overemphasize their role, authority, or status are likely to be perceived as more genuine by clients. Too much emphasis on one's role and position can create excessive and unnecessary emotional distance in the relationship. Clients can feel intimidated or even resentful.

The genuine counselor also is someone who is comfortable with himself or herself and with a variety of persons and situations and does not need to "put on" new or different roles to feel or behave comfortably and effectively. As Egan (1982, p. 127) observes, genuine counselors "do not have to change when they are with different people — that is, they do not constantly have to adopt new roles in order to be acceptable to others."*

Congruence

Congruence means simply that the counselor's words, actions, and feelings match — they are consistent. For example, when a therapist becomes uncomfortable because of a client's constant verbal assault, she acknowledges this feeling of discomfort, at least to herself, and does not try to cover up or feign comfort when it does not exist. Counselors who are not aware of their feelings or of discrepancies between their feelings, words, and actions may send mixed, or incongruent, messages to clients — for example, saying "Sure, go ahead and tell me how you feel about me" while fidgeting

---

* This and all other quotations from this source are from *The Skilled Helper* by G. Egan (2nd ed.). Copyright © 1982 by Brooks/Cole. Reprinted by permission.

FEEDBACK #3: EMPATHY

Activity One

Counselor response 1 is at Level 1—no understanding and no direction. The response is a denial of client's concern and a form of advice.

Counselor response 2 is at Level 3—understanding is present; direction is absent. Responds to client's feelings (you feel perturbed) and to content or situation (about the semester).

Counselor response 3 is at Level 1—no understanding, no direction. Response is a question and ignores both the content and feelings of client's message.

Counselor response 4 is at Level 5—understanding, direction, and action are all present. Response tunes in to client's feelings, identifies client's deficit, and identifies one action step (to list the important needs a job meets).

Counselor response 5 is at Level 4—understanding and direction. Both client's feelings (you feel resentful) and client's deficit (you can't explain why) are included in counselor's response.

Counselor response 6 is at Level 3—understanding is there; no direction. Counselor responds to client's feelings (you feel upset) and to the content or situation (your parents are divorcing).

Counselor response 7 is at Level 4—understanding and direction. Response reflects client's feelings (you feel discouraged) and identifies her deficit (you can't seem to get pregnant).

Counselor response 8 is at Level 2—some direction but no understanding. Response is only to content of client's message; feelings are ignored.

Counselor response 9 is at Level 5—understanding, direction, and action are all there. Response picks up client's feelings and deficit and identifies one possible action step (to think of some ways).

Activity Three

1—V	6—A	11—K
2—A	7—K	12—A
3—K	8—V	13—A
4—K	9—K	14—V
5—V	10—A	15—V

or tapping feet or fingers. Such messages are likely to be very confusing and even irritating to clients.

Spontaneity

Spontaneity is the capacity to express oneself naturally without contrived or artificial behaviors. Spontaneity also means being tactful without deliberating about everything you say or do. Spontaneity, however, does not mean that counselors need to verbalize every passing thought or feeling to clients, particularly negative feelings. Rogers (1957) suggests that counselors express negative feelings to clients only if the feelings are constant and persistent or if they interfere with the counselor's ability to convey empathy and positive regard.

Openness and Self-Disclosure

Part of genuineness involves the ability to be open, to share yourself, to self-disclose. Because self-disclosure is a complex skill and should not be used indiscriminately, we will discuss it in some detail in this section.

Self-disclosure. Self-disclosure may be defined as any information counselors convey about themselves to their clients (Cozby, 1973). Typically, counselors may choose to reveal something about themselves through verbal sharing of such information. Self-disclosure is not confined to verbal behavior, of course. As Egan (1976, p. 55) points out, we always disclose information about ourselves through nonverbal channels and by our actions even when we don't intend to. This section, however, will focus on the purposeful use of verbal disclosure as a way to convey genuineness.

Although all self-disclosures reveal information about oneself, the type of information disclosed may vary. As shown in Figure 2-1, the content of a self-disclosure can be categorized as demographic or personal (Simonson, 1976) and as positive or negative (Hoffman-Graff, 1977).

In demographic disclosures, the counselor talks about nonintimate events. In personal disclosures, or self-involving statements (McCarthy & Betz, 1978), the counselor reveals more private, personal events and also refers directly to a feeling or feelings that the counselor believes will parallel the client's implicit feeling (McCarthy, 1982). Examples of demographic self-disclosure would be "I had some discouraging times during my schoolwork also" or "At first I had thought I didn't want children; then I changed my mind, so we had

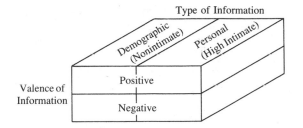

Figure 2-1. *Possible content of self-disclosive information*

them." A personal self-disclosure could mean saying something like "Well, I don't always feel loving toward my children. There are times when I feel pretty angry with them and just want some peace and quiet" or "I think it's pretty natural to have very warm feelings for your close friends. There are times when I've been a little scared of my deep feelings for my friends, too."

In addition, a counselor's self-disclosure may be positive or negative. Positive self-disclosure reveals personal strengths, successful experiences, and experiences similar to the client's. Negative self-disclosure provides information about personal limitations, unsuccessful or inappropriate behaviors and situations, and experiences dissimilar to the client's. Some examples of positive self-disclosure are—

> "I'm pretty honest with other people. If I have something to say, I usually try to tell them in a tactful way."
>
> "Sticking with my wife for 20 years has been a great experience. Sure, we've had our ups and downs, but overall we've had a really good relationship, and the stability makes me feel super."
>
> "I also had troubles in college, so I can relate to what you're experiencing now. I did a lot of partying, but in the long run I did settle down and finally made decent grades."

Examples of negative self-disclosure are—

> "I, too, have a really hard time making decisions on my own without the advice of others to depend on."
>
> "I, too, am divorced. My marriage was very rocky and just didn't work out."

There are several purposes for using self-disclosure with a client. Counselor self-disclosure may generate an open and facilitative counseling atmosphere. In some instances, a disclosive counselor may be perceived as more sensitive and warm than

a nondisclosive counselor (Nilsson, Strassberg, & Bannon, 1979). Counselor disclosure can reduce the role distance between a counselor and client (Egan, 1982). Counselor self-disclosure can also be used to increase the disclosure level of clients (Nilsson et al., 1979), to bring about changes in clients' perceptions of their behavior (Hoffman-Graff, 1977), and to increase client expression of feelings (McCarthy, 1982). Counselor self-disclosure may also help clients develop new perspectives needed for goal setting and action (Egan, 1982).

Ground rules. There are several ground rules that may help a counselor decide what, when, and how much to disclose. As Nilsson et al. (1979, p. 399) observe, "The issue is far more complex than whether a counselor should or should not disclose. . . . Content, timing, and client expectation, are critical mediating variables determining the influence of counselor disclosure." One ground rule relates to the "breadth," the cumulative amount of information disclosed (Cozby, 1973, p. 75). Most of the evidence indicates that a moderate amount of disclosure has more positive effects than a high or low level (Banikiotes, Kubinski, & Pursell, 1981). Some self-disclosure may indicate a desire for a close relationship and may increase the client's estimate of the helper's trustworthiness (Levin & Gergen, 1969). Counselors who disclose very little could add to the role distance between themselves and their clients. At the other extreme, too much disclosure may be counterproductive. The counselor who discloses too much may be perceived as lacking in discretion, being untrustworthy (Levin & Gergen), seeming self-preoccupied (Cozby), or needing assistance. A real danger in overdisclosing is the risk of being perceived as needing therapy as much as the client. This could undermine the client's confidence in the counselor's ability to be helpful.

Another ground rule concerns the duration of self-disclosure—the amount of time used to give information about yourself. Extended periods of counselor disclosure will consume time that could be spent in client disclosure. As one person reveals more, the other person will necessarily reveal less (Levin & Gergen, 1969). From this perspective, some conciseness in the length of self-disclosive statements seems warranted. Another consideration in duration of self-disclosure involves the capacity of the client to utilize and benefit from the information shared. As Egan (1982, p. 199) observes, counselors should avoid self-disclosing to the point of adding a burden to an already overwhelmed client.

A third ground rule to consider in using self-disclosure concerns the depth, or intimacy, of the information revealed (Cozby, 1973, p. 75). You should try to make your statements similar in content and mood to the client's messages. Ivey and Gluckstern (1976, p. 86) refer to this similarity as "parallelism," meaning that the counselor's self-disclosure is closely linked to the client's statements. For example:

Client: I just feel so down on myself. My husband is so critical of me, and often I think he's right. I really can't do much of anything well.

Counselor (parallel): There have been times when I've also felt down on myself, so I can sense how discouraged you are. Sometimes, too, criticism from a male has made me feel even worse, although I'm learning how to value myself regardless of critical comments from my husband or a male friend.

Counselor (nonparallel): I've felt bummed out, too. Sometimes the day just doesn't go well.

A counselor can alter the depth of a self-disclosure by adapting the content of the information revealed. For instance, if a client discloses about a nonintimate event, a demographic counselor disclosure may be more appropriate than a personal disclosure. Or if the client is discussing a negative experience, a negative counselor disclosure will be more similar than a positive disclosure. In fact, a positive counselor disclosure following client expression of negative feelings (or vice versa) can inhibit, rather than expand, the client's communication. Imagine how insensitive it would sound if a counselor said "I'm very happy today. Of course, I consider myself to be a very optimistic person" after a client had just revealed feelings of sadness or depression. Generally, the counselor can achieve the desired impact of self-disclosure as long as the depth or content of the information is not grossly discrepant from the client's messages and behavior.

The depth, or degree of intimacy, of your self-disclosure is also affected by the timing of the interaction. Demographic (nonintimate) disclosure may be very useful in initial phases because it informs the client that disclosure is part of the treatment process. Starting off with nonintimate disclosure is less threatening, and the client is not surprised later on by more intimate disclosures. Personal, or high-intimate, self-disclosures are more effective than demographic, or low-intimate, self-disclosures in eliciting client affect and in increasing client self-references and "present-tense talk" (McCarthy, 1982; McCarthy & Betz, 1978). Additionally, "high self-disclosure is 'additive' because it identifies previously unstated client feelings, thus adding to an understanding of the client's concern" (McCarthy, 1982, p. 130). Thus, personal, or highly intimate, disclosures may be more useful in subsequent sessions, after disclosure has already been made a part of the treatment contract in less threatening form.

In using self-disclosure, a counselor should be very aware of the effects it produces in the interview. There is always a danger of accelerating self-disclosure to the point where the counselor and client spend time swapping stories about themselves or playing "I've got one to top that." This effect does not reflect the intended purposes of self-disclosure.

In addition to being cognizant of the actual effects of self-disclosure, counselors should be aware of their motivation for using the response in the first place. Self-disclosure is appropriate only when you can explain how it may benefit the client. Counselors who are unaware of their own biases and vulnerabilities may self-disclose because they identify too much with a client or a topic area. Other helpers may self-disclose simply to reduce their anxiety level in the interview. As with all other counselor behavior, self-disclosure should be structured to meet the client's needs.

■
LEARNING ACTIVITIES #4: SELF-DISCLOSURE

I. Respond to the following three client situations with a self-disclosing response. Make sure you reveal something about yourself. It might help you to start your statements with "I." Also try to make your statements similar in content and depth to the client messages and situations. An example is given first, and feedback is provided on page 32.

Example

The client is having a hard time stating specific reasons for seeking counseling. Your self-disclosing statement: "I'm reluctant at times to share something that is personal about myself with someone I don't know; I know it takes time to get started."

(continued)

Now use your self-disclosure responses:

1. The client is feeling like a failure because "nothing seems to be going well."

Your self-disclosure:

2. The client is hinting that he or she has some concerns about sexual performance but does not seem to know how to introduce this concern in the session.

Your self-disclosure:

3. The client has started to become aware of feelings of anger for the first time and is questioning whether such feelings are legitimate or whether something is wrong with him or her.

Your self-disclosure:

II. In a conversation with a friend or in a group, use the skill of self-disclosure. You may wish to use the questions below as "starters." Consider the criteria listed in the feedback to assess your use of this response.

Preference Survey

1. What things or activities do you enjoy doing most?
2. What things or activities do you dislike?
3. What things or activities do you try to avoid?
4. When you're feeling down in the dumps, what do you do to get out of it?
5. What things or people do you think about most?
6. What things or people do you avoid thinking about?

□ POSITIVE REGARD

Positive regard, also called "respect," means the ability to prize or value the client as a person with worth and dignity (Rogers, 1957). Communication of positive regard has a number of important functions in establishing an effective therapeutic relationship, including the communication of willingness to work with the client, interest in the client as a person, and acceptance of the client. Raush and Bordin (1957) and Egan (1982) have identified four components of positive regard: having a sense of commitment to the client, making an effort to understand the client, suspending critical judgment, and expressing a reasonable amount of warmth (see also Table 2-2).

Commitment

Commitment means you are willing to work with the client and interested in doing so. It is translated into such actions as being on time for appointments, reserving time for the client's exclusive use, ensuring privacy during sessions, maintaining confidentiality, and applying skills to help the client. Lack of time and lack of concern are two major barriers to communicating a sense of commitment.

Understanding

Clients will feel respected to the degree that they *feel* the counselor is trying to understand them and to treat their problems with concern. Counselors can demonstrate their efforts to understand by being empathic, by asking questions designed to elicit information important to the client, and by indicating with comments or actions their interest in understanding the client (Raush & Bordin,

1957, p. 352). Counselors also convey understanding with the use of specific listening responses such as paraphrasing and reflecting client messages (see also Chapter 5).

Nonjudgmental Attitude

A nonjudgmental attitude is the counselor's capacity to suspend judgment of the client's actions or motives and to avoid condemning or condoning the client's thoughts, feelings, or actions. It may also be described as the counselor's acceptance of the client without conditions or reservations, although it does not mean that the counselor supports or agrees with all the client says or does. A counselor conveys a nonjudgmental attitude by warmly accepting the client's expressions and experiences without expressing disapproval or criticism. For example, suppose a client states "I can't help cheating on my wife. I love her, but I've got this need to be with other women." The counselor who responds with regard and respect might say something like "You feel pulled between your feelings for your wife and your need for other women." This response neither condones nor criticizes the client's feelings and behaviors. In contrast, a counselor who states "What a mess! You got married because you love your wife. Now you're fooling around with other women" conveys criticism and lack of respect for the client as a unique human being. The experience of having positive regard for clients can also be identified by the presence of certain (covert) thoughts and feelings such as "I feel good when I'm with this person" or "I don't feel bothered or uncomfortable with what this person is telling me."

A question that counselors frequently face is

FEEDBACK #4: SELF-DISCLOSURE

I. Here are some possible examples of counselor self-disclosure for these three client situations. See whether your responses are *similar;* your statements will probably reflect more of your own feelings and experiences. Are your statements fairly concise? Are they similar to the client messages in content and intensity?

1. "I, too, have felt down and out about myself at times."

   or

   "I can remember, especially when I was younger, feeling very depressed if things didn't turn out the way I wanted."

2. "For myself, I have sometimes questioned the adequacy of my sexual performance."

   or

   "I find it hard sometimes to start talking about really personal topics like sex."

3. "I can remember when I used to feel pretty afraid of admitting I felt angry. I always used to control it by telling myself I really wasn't angry."

   or

   "I know of times when some of my thoughts or feelings have seemed hard for me to accept."

II. Self-Disclosure Assessment

1. What was the amount of your self-disclosure in relation to the amount of the other person's — low, medium, or high?

2. What was the *total* amount of time you spent in self-disclosure?

3. Were your self-disclosure statements similar in content and depth to those expressed by the other person?

4. Did your self-disclosure detract from or overwhelm the other person?

---

clients "to move beyond behaviors, defenses, and facades that others (would) find offensive" (George & Cristiani, 1981, p. 152).

Warmth

According to Goldstein (1980), without the expression of warmth, particular strategies and helping interventions may be "technically correct but therapeutically impotent" (p. 39). Warmth reduces the impersonal nature or sterility of a given intervention or treatment procedure. In addition, warmth begets warmth. As Truax and Carkhuff (1967) observe, most clients respond to warmth with warmth. In interactions with hostile or reluctant clients, warmth and caring can disarm and diminish the intensity of the clients' angry feelings.

Nonverbal cues of warmth. A primary way in which warmth is communicated is with supporting nonverbal behaviors such as voice tone, eye contact, facial animation and expressions, gestures, and touch. Johnson (1981) describes some nonverbal cues that express warmth or coldness (see Table 2-4). Remember that these behaviors may be interpreted as warm or cold by clients from Western cultures. Clients from other cultures may perceive these nonverbal aspects of warmth and cold differently. Even clients from Western cul-

TABLE 2-4. Nonverbal cues of warmth and coldness

Nonverbal cue	Warmth	Coldness
Tone of voice	Soft, soothing	Callous, reserved, hard
Facial expression	Smiling, interested	Poker-faced, frowning, disinterested
Posture	Relaxed, leaning toward the other person	Tense, leaning away from the other person
Eye contact	Looking directly into the other person's eyes	Avoiding eye contact
Touching	Touching the other softly and discreetly	Avoiding all touch
Gestures	Open, welcoming	Closed, as if guarding oneself
Physical proximity	Close	Distant

From *Reaching Out: Interpersonal Effectiveness and Self-Actualization* (2nd ed.), by D. W. Johnson. Copyright © 1981 by Prentice-Hall. Reprinted by permission.

how they can overcome personal and cultural biases to deal effectively with an individual who is perceived as unlikable, worthless, or offensive by society at large—for example, a convicted rapist or a child abuser. George and Cristiani (1981) observe that the answer to this question lies partly in the fact that the nature of the relationship is a helping one. Counselors can create an atmosphere in which the client feels safe and behaves nondefensively and may be more responsive to the counselor than to people with whom he or she interacts in the course of ordinary life. In other words, the helping relationship can be the impetus for such

tures may vary in the amount of warmth they need or can handle.

An important aspect of the nonverbal dimension of warmth is touch (see also Chapter 4). In times of emotional stress, many clients welcome a well-intentioned touch. The difficulty with touch is that it may have a different meaning to the client than the meaning you intended to convey. In deciding whether to use touch, it is important to consider the level of trust between you and the client, whether or not the *client* may perceive the touch as sexual, and the client's past history associated with touch (occasionally a client will associate touch with punishment and will say "I can't stand to be touched"). To help you assess the probable impact of touch on the client, Gazda et al. (1984, p. 111) recommend asking yourself the following questions:

1. How does the other person perceive this? Is it seen as genuine or as a superficial technique?
2. Is the other person uncomfortable? (If the other person draws back from being touched, adjust your behavior accordingly.)
3. Am I interested in the person or in touching the person? Whom is it for — me, the other person, or to impress those who observe?

Verbal responses associated with warmth and immediacy. Warmth can also be expressed to clients through selected verbal responses. One way to express warmth is to use enhancing statements (Ivey & Simek-Downing, 1980) that portray some positive aspect or attribute about the client, such as "It's great to see how well you're handling this situation," "You're really expressing yourself well," or "You've done a super job on this action plan." Enhancing statements offer positive reinforcement to clients and must be sincere, deserved, and accurate in order to be effective.

Another verbal response used to express warmth is immediacy. Immediacy is a characteristic of a counselor verbal response describing something *as it occurs* within a session. Immediacy involves self-disclosure but is limited to self-disclosure of *current* feelings or what is occurring at the present time in the relationship or the session. When persons avoid being immediate with each other over the course of a developing relationship, distance sets in and coldness can quickly evaporate any warmth formerly established. Egan (1982, p. 202) describes the potential impact on a relationship when immediacy is absent:

People often fail to be immediate with one another in their interactions. For instance, a husband feels slighted by something his wife says. He says nothing and "swallows" his feelings. But he becomes a little bit distant from her the next couple of days, a bit more quiet. She notices this, wonders what is happening, but says nothing. Soon little things in their relationship that would ordinarily be ignored become irritating. Things become more and more tense, but still they do not engage in direct, mutual talk about what is happening. The whole thing ends as a game of "uproar" (see Berne, 1964) — that is, a huge argument over something quite small. Once they've vented their emotions, they feel both relieved because they've dealt with their emotions and guilty because they've done so in a somewhat childish way.

In using immediacy in counseling, the therapist reflects on a current aspect of (1) some thought, feeling, or behavior of the *counselor,* (2) some thought, feeling, or behavior of the *client,* or (3) some aspect of the *relationship.* Here are some examples of these three categories of immediacy.

1. *Counselor immediacy:* The counselor reveals his or her own thoughts or feelings in the counseling process as they occur "in the moment."
   "I'm glad to see you today."
   "I'm sorry, I am having difficulty focusing. Let's go over that again."
2. *Client immediacy:* The counselor provides feedback to the client about some client behavior or feeling as it occurs in the interview.
   "You're fidgeting and seem uncomfortable here right now."
   "You're really smiling now — you must be very pleased about it."
3. *Relationship immediacy:* The counselor reveals feelings or thoughts about how he or she experiences the relationship.
   "I'm glad that you're able to share that with me."
   "It makes me feel good that we're getting somewhere today."

Relationship immediacy may include references to specific "here and now" transactions or to the overall pattern or development of the relationship (Egan, 1982). For example, "I'm aware that right now as I'm talking again, you are looking away and tapping your feet and fingers. I'm wondering if you're feeling impatient with me or if I'm talking too much" (specific transaction). Consider another example in which immediacy is used to focus on the development and pattern of the relationship: "This session feels so good to me. I remember when we first started a few months ago and it seemed we were both being very careful and having trouble expressing what was on our minds. Today, I'm aware we're not measuring our words so carefully. It feels like there's more comfort between us."

Immediacy is not an end in and of itself but, rather, a means of helping the counselor and client work together better. If allowed to become a goal in and of itself, it can be distracting rather than helpful (Egan, 1982). Examples of instances in which immediacy might be useful include the following:

1. Hesitancy or "carefulness" in speech or behavior ("Mary, I'm aware that you [or I] seem to be choosing words very carefully right now—as if you [or I] might say something wrong").
2. Hostility, anger, resentment, irritation ("Joe, I'm feeling pretty irritated now because you're indicating you want me to keep this time slot open for you but you may not be able to make it next week. Since this has happened the last two weeks, I'm concerned about what might be happening in our relationship").
3. Attraction ("At first it seemed great that we liked each other so much. Now I'm wondering if we're so comfortable that we may be holding back a little and not sharing what's really on our minds").
4. Feeling of being "stuck"—lack of focus or direction ("Right now I feel like our session is sort of a broken record. We're just like a needle tracking in the same groove without really making any music or going anywhere").
5. Tension ("I'm aware there's some discomfort and tension we're both feeling now—about who we are as people and where this is going and what's going to happen").

Immediacy can also be used to deal with the issues of transference and countertransference described earlier in this chapter.

Immediacy has three purposes. One purpose is to bring out in the open something that you feel about yourself, the client, or the relationship that has not been expressed directly. Generally, it is assumed that covert, or unexpressed, feelings about the relationship may inhibit effective communication or may prevent further development of the relationship unless the counselor recognizes

and responds to these feelings. This may be especially important for negative feelings. As Eisenberg and Delaney (1977) note, "when stress occurs in the relationship between the client and counselor, it is generally more adaptive to deal openly with the stress than to avoid dealing with it" (p. 203). In this way, immediacy may reduce the distance that overshadows the relationship because of unacknowledged underlying issues.

A second purpose of immediacy is to generate discussion or to provide feedback about some aspects of the relationship or the interactions as they occur. This feedback may include verbal sharing of the counselor's feelings or of something the counselor sees going on in the interactive process. Immediacy is not used to describe every passing counselor feeling or observation to the client. But when something happens in the counseling process that influences the client's feelings toward counseling, then dealing openly with this issue has high priority. Usually it is up to the counselor to initiate discussion of unresolved feelings or issues (Eisenberg & Delaney, 1977, p. 202). Immediacy can be a way to begin such discussion and, if used properly, can strengthen the counselor/client relationship and help the counselor and client work together more effectively.

Finally, immediacy is useful to facilitate client self-exploration and to maintain the focus of the interaction on the client or the relationship rather than on the counselor (McCarthy, 1982; McCarthy & Betz, 1978).

Steps in immediacy. Immediacy is a complex set of skills. The first part of immediacy—and an important prerequisite of the actual verbal response—is awareness, or the ability to sense what is happening in the interaction (Egan, 1982; Turock, 1980). To do this, it is important to monitor the flow of the interaction in order to process what is happening to you, to the client, and to your developing relationship. Awareness also implies that you can read the clues without a great deal of decoding errors and without projecting your own biases and "blind spots" into the interaction. After awareness, the next step is to formulate a verbal response that somehow shares your sense or picture of the process with the client. The actual form of the response may vary and can include some of the listening or action responses we describe in Chapters 5 and 6. Regardless of the form, the critical feature of immediacy is its emphasis on the "here and now"—the present.

Turock (1980, p. 170) suggests some useful sentence stems for immediacy:

1. "Right now I'm feeling _____" (counselor immediacy).
2. "Even right now you're feeling _____ (feelings toward counselor) because _____" (client immediacy).
3. "When I see (hear, grasp) you _____ (client's behavior or feelings), I _____" (counselor's behavior or feelings).

Ground rules. There are several rules to consider in using immediacy effectively. First, the counselor should describe what she or he sees *as it happens.* If the counselor waits until later in the session or until the next interview to describe a feeling or experience, the impact is lost. In addition, feelings about the relationship that are discounted or ignored may build up and eventually be expressed in more intense or distorted ways. The counselor who puts off using immediacy to initiate a needed discussion runs the risk of having unresolved feelings or issues damage the relationship.

Second, to reflect the "here-and-nowness" of the experience, any immediacy statement should be in the present tense—"I'm feeling uncomfortable now," rather than "I just felt uncomfortable." This models expression of current rather than past feelings for the client.

Further, when referring to your feelings and perceptions, own them—take responsibility for them—by using the personal pronoun *I, me,* or *mine,* as in "I'm feeling concerned about you now" instead of "You're making me feel concerned." Expressing your current feelings with "I" language communicates that you are responsible for your feelings and observations, and this may increase the client's receptivity to your immediacy expressions.

Finally, as in using all other responses, the counselor should consider timing. Using a lot of immediacy in an early session may be overwhelming for some clients and can elicit anxiety in either counselor or client. As Gazda et al. (1984, p. 191) observe, "High level communication of immediacy of relationship involves talking about persons who are present and feelings that exist at that particular moment. Thus . . . it is desirable that a strong base relationship exist before using the dimension of immediacy." If a counselor uses immediacy and senses that this has threatened or scared the client, then the counselor should decide that the client is not yet ready to handle these feelings or issues. And not every feeling or observation a counselor has needs to be verbalized to a client. The session does not need to turn into a "heavy" discussion, nor should it resemble a confessional. Generally, immediacy is reserved for initiating exploration of the most significant or most influential feelings or issues. Of course, a counselor who never expresses immediacy may be avoiding issues that have a significant effect on the relationship.

There is some evidence that counselors tend to avoid immediacy issues even when raised directly by clients (Turock, 1980). Counselors who are not comfortable with their own self-image or who are struggling with intimacy issues in their own life (see "Characteristics of Effective Helpers," earlier in this chapter) are likely to have trouble with this skill or to try to avoid the use of it altogether. Unfortunately, this may result in the continuation of an unhealthy or somewhat stagnant therapeutic relationship (Turock, 1980).

LEARNING ACTIVITIES #5: IMMEDIACY

I. For each of the following client stimuli, write an example of a counselor immediacy response. An example has been completed below, and feedback can be found on p. 41.

Example

The client has come in late for the third time, and you have some concern about this.

Immediacy response: "I'm aware that you're having difficulty getting here on time, and I'm feeling uncomfortable about this."

Now use immediacy in the following five situations:

1. Tears begin to well up in the client's eyes as he or she describes the loss of a close friend.
   Your immediacy response:
2. The client stops talking whenever you bring up the subject of his or her academic performance.
   Your immediacy response:
3. The client has asked you several questions about your competence and qualifications.
   Your immediacy response:

(continued)

LEARNING ACTIVITIES #5: IMMEDIACY (continued)

4. You experience a great deal of tension and caution between yourself and the client; the two of you seem to be treating each other with "kid gloves." You notice physical sensations of tension in your body, and signs of tension are also apparent in looking at the client.
   Your immediacy response:

5. You and the client like each other a great deal and have a lot in common; lately you've been spending more time swapping life stories than focusing on or dealing with the client's presented concern of career indecision and dissatisfaction.
   Your immediacy response:

II. In a conversation with a close friend or in a group, use the sharing skill of immediacy. If possible, tape the conversation for feedback — or ask for feedback from the friend or the group. You should consider the criteria listed in the feedback in assessing your use of immediacy. You may wish to use the topics listed in the following Relationship Assessment Inventory as topics for discussion using immediacy.

Relationship Assessment Inventory
1. To what extent do we really know each other?

2. How do I feel in your presence?
3. How do you feel in my presence?
4. What areas do I have trouble sharing with you?
5. What is it about our relationship that makes it hard to share some things?
6. Do we both have a fairly equal role in maintaining our relationship, or is one of us dominant and the other passive?
7. How do we handle power and conflict in the relationship? Is one of us consistently "top dog" or "underdog"?
8. Do we express or avoid feelings of warmth and affection for each other?
9. How do our concepts of our sex roles affect the way we relate to each other?
10. How often do we give feedback to each other — and in what manner is it given?
11. How do we hurt each other?
12. How do we help each other?
13. Where do we want our relationship to go from here?

☐ SUMMARY

It is important to remember that the three core or facilitative conditions described in this chapter — empathy, genuineness, and positive regard — are mutually reinforcing and, in practice, work "hand in hand." The three core conditions are synergistic — the overall effect of all three is greater than the effect of any one alone.

The ability to communicate the core conditions to clients is a function not only of learned skills but also of your own biases and unresolved issues which could prevent you from adopting the client's frame of reference, could make you rely excessively on artificial or mechanistic roles and could interfere with your capacity to convey respect and warmth for your clients. Being in a relationship, thus, requires an awareness, scrutiny, and resolution of your own needs and behaviors before you can effectively relate to clients.

POSTEVALUATION

I. According to Chapter Objective One, you will be able to identify attitudes and behaviors about yourself that could facilitate or interfere with establishing a positive helping relationship. In this activity, we present a Checklist for Effective Helpers. This checklist refers to characteristics of effective helpers. Your task is to use the checklist to assess yourself *now* with respect to these attitudes and behaviors. If you haven't yet had any or much contact with actual clients, try to use this checklist to assess how you believe you would be in actual interactions. Identify any issues or areas you may need to work on in your development as a counselor. Discuss your assessment in small groups or with an instructor, colleague, or supervisor. There is no written feedback for this part of the postevaluation. (continued)

CHECKLIST FOR EFFECTIVE HELPERS

Instructions: Rate yourself on each item by circling the number and word that best describe you *now*. If an item represents a behavior or situation you have not yet encountered, rate yourself the way you *think* you would be or would handle the situation.

Intellectual Competence

1. I feel knowledgeable about counseling/psychotherapy theories and techniques and other counseling-related issues.

1	2	3	4	5
Not at all	A little	Somewhat	Quite a bit	Almost always

2. I feel curious about areas of knowledge related to counseling and try to seek information about areas in which I am uninformed.

1	2	3	4	5
Not at all	A little	Somewhat	Quite a bit	Almost always

3. It is important to me to monitor progress of clients throughout therapy in order to keep track of process and outcomes.

1	2	3	4	5
Not at all	A little	Somewhat	Quite a bit	Almost always

Energy

4. I have enough physical stamina to see several clients daily.

1	2	3	4	5
Not at all	A little	Somewhat	Quite a bit	Almost always

5. Even after seeing several clients in a row, I don't feel emotionally depleted.

1	2	3	4	5
Not at all	A little	Somewhat	Quite a bit	Almost always

6. I convey intensity and dynamism to my clients.

1	2	3	4	5
Not at all	A little	Somewhat	Quite a bit	Almost always

Flexibility

7. I adapt my counseling and therapy techniques to each client rather than having the client fit the technique or therapy.

1	2	3	4	5
Not at all	A little	Somewhat	Quite a bit	Almost always

8. I do not use a single methodology or theoretical orientation with all clients.

1	2	3	4	5
Not at all	A little	Somewhat	Quite a bit	Almost always

Support

9. I am supporting of a client's efforts to engage in self-directed choices and behaviors.

1	2	3	4	5
Not at all	A little	Somewhat	Quite a bit	Almost always

(continued)

POSTEVALUATION (continued)

10. I provide support to clients without rescuing them or taking more than my share of responsibility for therapy process and outcomes.

1	2	3	4	5
Not at all	A little	Somewhat	Quite a bit	Almost always

Good Will

11. I have other people and activities (outside my counseling relationship) where I get many of my own needs met.

1	2	3	4	5
Not at all	A little	Somewhat	Quite a bit	Almost always

12. I am clear about my motives for wanting to be a counselor.

1	2	3	4	5
Not at all	A little	Somewhat	Quite a bit	Almost always

13. I try to behave in ethical ways which meet the client's needs and which protect the client's welfare.

1	2	3	4	5
Not at all	A little	Somewhat	Quite a bit	Almost always

Self-Awareness

14. I am aware of my own unique strengths that I have to offer to clients.

1	2	3	4	5
Not at all	A little	Somewhat	Quite a bit	Almost always

15. I am aware of my limitations or self-defeating behaviors that may interfere with effective therapy.

1	2	3	4	5
Not at all	A little	Somewhat	Quite a bit	Almost always

16. I am aware of any unfinished or unresolved issues in my life right now.

1	2	3	4	5
Not at all	A little	Somewhat	Quite a bit	Almost always

II. According to Chapter Objective Two, you will be able to identify issues related to values, ethics, and emotional objectivity that could affect the development of a therapeutic relationship, given six written case descriptions. In this activity, read each case description carefully; then identify in writing the major kind of issue reflected in the case by matching the type of issue with the case descriptions listed below. Feedback follows the postevaluation (p. 42).

Type of Issue
A. Values conflict
B. Values stereotyping
C. Ethics—breach of confidentiality
D. Ethics—client welfare and rights
E. Ethics—referral
F. Transference
G. Countertransference

Case Description

____1. You are counseling a client who is almost flunking out of high school. The client states that he feels like a failure because all the other students are so smart. In an effort to make him feel better, you tell him about one of your former clients who also almost flunked out.

____2. A 58-year-old man who is having difficulty getting it together since his wife died comes to you for counseling. He has difficulty in discussing his concern or problem with you, and he is not clear about your role as a counselor and what counseling might do for him. He seems to feel that you can give him a tranquilizer. You tell him that you are not able to prescribe medication, and you suggest that he seek the services of a physician.

(continued)

_____3. You are leading a problem-solving group in a high school. The members are spending a lot of time talking about the flak they get from their parents. After a while, they start to "get the leader" and complain about all the flak they get from you.

_____4. A fourth-grade girl is referred to you by her teacher. The teacher states that the girl is doing poorly in class yet seems motivated to learn. After working with the girl for several weeks, including giving a battery of tests, you conclude that she has a severe learning disability. After obtaining her permission to talk to her teacher, you inform her teacher of this and state that the teacher might as well not spend too much more time working on what you believe is a "useless case."

_____5. You are counseling a person of the other sex who is the same age as yourself. After several weeks of seeing the client, you feel extremely disappointed and let down when the client postpones the next session.

_____6. You are counseling a couple who are considering a trial separation because of constant marital problems. You tell them you don't believe separation or divorce is the answer to their problems.

III. According to the third objective of this chapter, you will be able to communicate the three facilitative conditions to a client, given a role-play situation. Complete this activity in triads, one person assuming the role of the counselor, another the role of client, and the third acting as the observer. The counselor's task is to communicate the behavioral aspects of empathy, genuineness, and positive regard to the client. The client can share a concern with the counselor. The observer will monitor the interaction, using the accompanying Checklist for Facilitative Conditions as a guide, and provide feedback after completion of the session. Each role play can last about 10–15 minutes. Switch roles so each person has an opportunity to be in each of the three roles. If you do not have access to another person to serve as an observer, find someone with whom you can engage in a role-played helping interaction. Tape-record your interaction and use the accompanying checklist as a guide to reviewing your tape.

CHECKLIST FOR FACILITATIVE CONDITIONS

Counselor _____ Observer _____ Date _____ Instructions: Assess the counselor's communication of the three facilitative conditions by circling the number and word that best represent the counselor's overall behavior during this session.

Empathy

1. Did the counselor use verbal responses indicating a desire to comprehend the client?

1	2	3	4
A little	Somewhat	A great deal	Almost always

2. Did the counselor reflect _implicit,_ or hidden, client messages?

1	2	3	4
A little	Somewhat	A great deal	Almost always

3. Did the counselor refer to the client's feelings?

1	2	3	4
A little	Somewhat	A great deal	Almost always

4. Did the counselor discuss what appeared to be important to the client?

1	2	3	4
A little	Somewhat	A great deal	Almost always

5. Did the counselor pace (match) the client's nonverbal behavior?

1	2	3	4
A little	Somewhat	A great deal	Almost always

(continued)

POSTEVALUATION (continued)

6. Did the counselor match the client's predicates and phrases?

| 1 | 2 | 3 | 4 |
| A little | Somewhat | A great deal | Almost always |

Genuineness

7. Did the counselor avoid overemphasizing her or his role, position, and status?

| 1 | 2 | 3 | 4 |
| A little | Somewhat | A great deal | Almost always |

8. Did the counselor exhibit congruence, or consistency, among feelings, words, nonverbal behavior, and actions?

| 1 | 2 | 3 | 4 |
| A little | Somewhat | A great deal | Almost always |

9. Was the counselor appropriately spontaneous (for example, also tactful)?

| 1 | 2 | 3 | 4 |
| A little | Somewhat | A great deal | Almost always |

10. Did the counselor self-disclose, or share similar feelings and experiences?

| 1 | 2 | 3 | 4 |
| A little | Somewhat | A great deal | Almost always |

11. Did the counselor demonstrate supporting nonverbal behaviors such as eye contact, smiling, and leaning toward the client?

| 1 | 2 | 3 | 4 |
| A little | Somewhat | A great deal | Almost always |

Positive Regard

12. Did the counselor demonstrate behaviors related to commitment and willingness to see the client (for example, starting on time, responding with intensity)?

| 1 | 2 | 3 | 4 |
| A little | Somewhat | A great deal | Almost always |

13. Did the counselor respond verbally and nonverbally to the client without judging or evaluating the client?

| 1 | 2 | 3 | 4 |
| A little | Somewhat | A great deal | Almost always |

14. Did the counselor convey warmth to the client with supporting nonverbal behaviors (soft voice tone, smiling, eye contact, touch) and verbal responses (enhancing statements and/or immediacy)?

| 1 | 2 | 3 | 4 |
| A little | Somewhat | A great deal | Almost always |

Observer comments:_____

_____

_____

_____

FEEDBACK #5: IMMEDIACY

I. Here are some expressions of immediacy. See how these compare with yours.

1. "At this moment you seem to be experiencing this loss very intensely."
   or
   "I'm sensing now that it is very painful for you to talk about this."

2. "Every time I mention academic performance, like now, you seem to back off from this topic."
   or
   "I'm aware that, during this session, you stop talking when the topic of your grades comes up."

3. "You seem to be questioning now how qualified I am to help you."
   or
   "I'm wondering if it's difficult right now for you to trust me."

4. "I'm aware of how physically tight I feel now and how tense you look to me. I'm sensing that we're just not too comfortable with each other yet. We seem to be treating each other in a very fragile and cautious way right now."

5. "I'm aware of how well we get along and, because we have so much in common, how easy it is right now just to share stories and events instead of exploring your career concerns."

Are your immediacy responses in the present tense? Do you "own" your feelings and perceptions by using "I feel" rather than "You're making me feel"?

II. Immediacy Assessment

1. Did you express something personal about your feelings, the other person's feelings, or the relationship?

2. Were your immediacy statements in the present tense?

3. Did you use *I, me*, or *mine* when referring to *your* feelings and perceptions?

4. Did you express immediacy as your feelings occurred within the conversation?

☐ SUGGESTED READINGS

Barrett-Lennard, G. T. (1981). The empathy cycle: Refinement of a nuclear concept. *Journal of Counseling Psychology, 28,* 91–100.

Cavanaugh, M. E. (1982). *The counseling experience.* Monterey, CA: Brooks/Cole. Chapter 4, "The Person of the Counselor"; Chapter 11, "Problems That Counselors Face."

Corey, G., Corey, M., & Callanan, P. (1984). *Issues and ethics in the helping professions* (2nd ed.). Monterey, CA: Brooks/Cole. Chapter 2, "The Counselor as a Person and as a Professional"; Chapter 3, "Values and the Therapeutic Process"; Chapter 5, "Ethical Issues I: Therapist Responsibilities, Therapist Competence, and Confidentiality"; Chapter 6, "Ethical Issues II: The Client/Therapist Relationship."

D'Augelli, A., D'Augelli, J., & Danish, S. (1981). *Helping others.* Monterey, CA: Brooks/Cole. Chapter 2, "Helpers Are People Too."

Doster, J. A., & Nesbitt, J. G. (1979). Psychotherapy and self-disclosure. In G. J. Chelune (Ed.), *Self-disclosure: Origins, patterns, and implications of openness in interpersonal relationships.* San Francisco: Jossey-Bass.

Egan, G. (1982). *The skilled helper* (2nd ed.). Monterey, CA: Brooks/Cole. Chapter 4, "Stage 1: Problem Exploration and Clarification"; Part Two, "Helper Response and Client Self-Exploration"; Chapter 5, "Stage 1: Problem Exploration and Clarification"; Part Three, "The Foundations of Helping: Respect, Genuineness, and Social Influence."

Gazda, G. M., Asbury, F. S., Balzer, F. J., Childers, W. C., & Walters, R. P. (1984). *Human relations development: A manual for educators* (3rd ed.). Boston: Allyn & Bacon. Chapter 11, "Perceiving and Responding with Warmth."

Gladstein, G. (1983). Understanding empathy: Integrating counseling, developmental, and social psychology perspectives. *Journal of Counseling Psychology, 30,* 467–482.

Hammer, A. L. (1983). Matching perceptual predicates: Effect on perceived empathy in a counseling analogue. *Journal of Counseling Psychology, 30,* 172–179.

Johnson, D. W. (1981). *Reaching out: Interpersonal effectiveness and self-actualization* (2nd ed.). Englewood Cliffs, NJ: Prentice-Hall. Chapter 2, "Self-Disclosure."

Laborde, G. (1984). *Influencing with integrity.* Palo Alto: Science & Behavior Books.

Maurer, R. E., & Tindall, J. H. (1983). Effect of postural congruence on client's perception of counselor empathy. *Journal of Counseling Psychology, 30,* 158–163.

McCarthy, P. (1982). Differential effects of counselor self-referent responses and counselor status. *Journal of Counseling Psychology, 29,* 125–131.

Nilsson, D., Strassberg, D., & Bannon, J. (1979). Perceptions of counselor self-disclosure: An analogue study. *Journal of Counseling Psychology, 26,* 399–404.

Okun, B. F. (1982). *Effective helping.* (2nd ed.). Monterey, CA: Brooks/Cole. Chapter 9, "Issues Affecting Helping."

Schutz, B. (1982). *Legal liability in psychotherapy.* San Francisco: Jossey-Bass.

Seay, T. A., & Altekruse, M. K. (1979). Verbal and nonverbal behavior in judgments of facilitative conditions. *Journal of Counseling Psychology, 26,* 108–119.

Sharpley, C. F. (1984). Predicate matching in NLP: A review

of research on the preferred representational system. *Journal of Counseling Psychology, 31,* 238–248.

Turock, A. (1980). Immediacy in counseling: Recognizing clients' unspoken messages. *Personnel and Guidance Journal, 59,* 168–172.

Watkins, C. E., Jr. (1983). Transference phenomena in the counseling situation. *Personnel and Guidance Journal, 62,* 206–210.

FEEDBACK: POSTEVALUATION

1. C: Ethics—breach of confidentiality. The counselor broke the confidence of a former client by revealing his grade difficulties without his consent.

2. E: Ethics—referral. The counselor did not refer in an ethical or responsible way, because of failure to give the client names of at least several physicians or psychiatrists who might be competent to see the client.

3. F: Transference. The group members seem to be transferring their angry feelings toward their parents onto you.

4. B: Values stereotyping. The counselor is obviously stereotyping all kids with learning disabilities as useless and hopeless (the "label" is also not helpful or in the client's best interest).

5. G: Countertransference. You are having a more than usually intense emotional reaction to this client (disappointment), which suggests that you are developing some affectionate feelings for the client and countertransference is occurring.

6. A: Values conflict. Your values are showing: Although separation and divorce may not be your solution, be careful of persuading clients to pursue your views and answers to issues.

RELATIONSHIP ENHANCEMENT VARIABLES AND INTERPERSONAL INFLUENCE

THREE

In all human relationships, persons try to influence one another. The counseling relationship is no exception. The fact that counselors do influence clients is inescapable and, according to Senour (1982, p. 346), the desire to avoid influence is "patently absurd [since] there would be no point to counseling if we had no influence on those with whom we work." Moreover, the influence process that operates in counseling is a two-way street. Clients also seek to influence their counselors. As Dorn (1984b, p. 343) observes, "Although the client has sought counseling because of dissatisfaction with personal circumstances, this same client will attempt to influence the counselor's behavior."

Thus, the influence process in counseling and therapy is interpersonal—that is, between two persons—and reciprocal, or mutual. Some recent research (Heppner & Heesacker, 1982) provided a good illustration of the reciprocal and interpersonal influence exchanges. At the beginning of counseling, the highly motivated clients perceived their counselors to be attractive and likable. The counselors of these same clients also perceived their clients to be quite interpersonally attractive. These counselors also were the ones who believed they had the greatest impact or influence on their clients.

The interpersonal and reciprocal nature of this influence process makes for "very intricate dynamics" during counseling (Dorn, 1984b, p. 344). Dorn provides a useful example of how the influence process between the two parties occurs:

> Person A exhibits verbal and nonverbal behavior in an effort to have Person B respond in a specific manner. Person B responds, again with verbal and nonverbal behavior, and this behavior is immediate feedback to Person A about how successful his or her initial influence attempts were. Person A then assesses this feedback and compares it with his or her initial expectations. Person A then decides what behavior to exhibit next. Of course, Person B is simultaneously involved in the same process [p. 344].

□ OBJECTIVES

1. Given a role-play interaction, identify and challenge any deletions, distortions, and generalizations in the client's verbal messages in order to obtain specificity and concreteness.
2. Given written descriptions of six clients, match the client description with the corresponding client "test of trust."
3. Given a role-play interaction, conduct a 30-minute initial interview in which you demonstrate both descriptive and behavioral aspects of attractiveness.
4. Given a role-play interaction, conduct a 30-minute problem identification interview in which you demonstrate verbal and nonverbal behaviors of expertness and trustworthiness.

□ STRONG'S MODEL OF COUNSELING AS INTERPERSONAL INFLUENCE

In 1968 Strong published what is now regarded as a landmark paper on counseling as a social influence process. He hypothesized that counselors' attempts to change clients precipitate dissonance in clients because of the inconsistency, or discrepancy, between the counselor's and the client's attitudes. This dissonance feels uncomfortable to clients, and they try to reduce this discomfort in a variety of ways, including discrediting the counselor, rationalizing about the importance of their problem, seeking out information or opinions that contradict the counselor, attempting to change the counselor's opinion, or accepting the opinion of the counselor. Strong (1968) asserted that clients would be more likely to accept the counselor's opinions and less likely to discredit or refute the counselor if the clients perceive the counselor as expert, attractive, and trustworthy. These three helper characteristics (expertness, attractiveness, and trustworthiness) can also be called "relationship enhancers" (Goldstein, 1980) because they have been identified as ways of making the therapeutic relationship more positive.

Strong (1968) suggested a two-stage model of counseling:

1. The counselor establishes a power base, or influence base, with the client through the three relationship enhancers of expertness, attractiveness, and trustworthiness. This influence base enhances the quality of the relationship and also encourages client involvement in counseling. This stage of the model (drawing from social-psychology literature) assumes that counselors establish this influence base by drawing on power bases that can effect attitude change. Common power bases used by counselors include these:

- *Legitimate power:* power that occurs as a result of the counselor's role—a form that society at large views as acceptable and helpful.
- *Expert power:* power that results from descriptive and behavioral cues of expertness and competence.
- *Referent power:* power that results from descriptive and behavioral cues of interpersonal attractiveness, friendliness, and similarity between counselor and client (such as is found in "indigenous" helpers, for example).

2. The counselor actively uses this influence base to effect attitudinal and behavioral change in clients. In this second stage of the model, it is important that clients perceive the counselor as expert, attractive, and trustworthy, since it is the *client's* perception of these counselor characteristics that determines, at least in part, how much influence counselors will have with their clients.

During the last decade, an increasing number of research studies on Strong's social influence model have appeared, although much of the existing research consists of analogue (not "in the field") studies limited to one or two contacts between persons (Corrigan, Dell, Lewis, & Schmidt, 1980). The influence base that we describe above seems to have the most effect on clients during initial contacts, since that is when clients formulate their first impressions of counselors.

□ THE INTERACTIONAL NATURE OF THE INFLUENCE PROCESS

As we noted at the beginning of this chapter, counselor and client influence attempts are interdependent and interrelated. In considering counselor attributes and behaviors (expertness, attractiveness, and trustworthiness) that contribute to influence, it is also important to consider client variables that may enhance or mediate counselor influence effects.

Although most of this chapter will focus on the three counselor characteristics that contribute most to the influence process in counseling, remember that certain client characteristics may also enhance or mediate the counselor's influence attempts. In other words, some clients may be more susceptible or less susceptible to counselor influence, depending on such things as

- Gender, race, cultural background
- Attractiveness and social competence
- Conceptual level and cognitive style
- "Myths," beliefs, and expectations about counseling
- Motivation
- Satisfaction with outcomes of counseling
- Level of commitment required to change target behaviors

Additionally, since counseling is a *process* and involves distinctly different phases or stages, such as the ones mentioned in Chapter 1 (that is, relationship, assessment and goal setting, intervention and action, and evaluation and termination), it is also imperative to consider what kind of influence might be best suited for different phases of the process. For example, the descriptive aspects of expertness, such as role, reputation, education, and setting, are most useful and influential during the

first part of counseling, in which you are trying to encourage the client to continue counseling by demonstrating your credibility. Yet, as counseling ensues, these external trappings are *not* sufficient unless accompanied by behavioral demonstrations of expertness or competence that indicate the counselor is skilled enough to handle the client's concerns successfully. The relationship of various aspects of counselor expertness, attractiveness, and trustworthiness to stages of counseling is depicted in summary form in Table 3-1. *Descriptive* cues associated with these three relationship enhancers refer to nonbehavioral aspects of the counselor such as demeanor, attire, and appearance, to situational aspects such as the office setting, and to the counselor's reputation inferred from introductions, prior knowledge, and the display of diplomas and certificates. *Behavioral* aspects of these three variables refer to the counselor's verbal and nonverbal behaviors or specific things the counselor says and does. In the remainder of the chapter, we describe the behavioral components of these three variables and provide examples.

TABLE 3-1. Relationship of counselor expertness, attractiveness, and trustworthiness to stages of counseling

Stage of counseling	Purposes of influence efforts
Rapport and relationship (Stage 1)	
Descriptive aspects of *expertness:* education, role, reputation, setting	"Hook" client to continue counseling by communicating credibility
Physical demeanor and *attractiveness*	Create initial favorable impression
Interpersonal attractiveness conveyed by structuring	Reduce client anxiety, "check out" client expectations
Descriptive aspects of *trust* — role and reputation	Encourage client openness and self-expression
Assessment and goal setting (Stage 2)	
Behavioral aspects of *expertness:*	
Verbal and nonverbal attentiveness	Contribute to client understanding of self and of issues
Concreteness	Challenge client's language errors and omissions
Relevant and thought-provoking questions	Obtain specificity
Behavioral aspects of *attractiveness:*	
Responsive nonverbal behavior	Encourage relevant client self-disclosure and self-exploration
Self-disclosure	Convey likability and perceived similarity to client
Behavioral aspects of *trustworthiness:* nonverbal acceptance of client disclosures, maintaining of confidentiality, accurate paraphrasing, nondefensive reactions to client "tests of trust"	Convey yourself as trustworthy of client communications so client will feel comfortable "opening up" and self-disclosing

(continued)

TABLE 3-1. Relationship of counselor expertness, attractiveness, and trustworthiness to stages of counseling (continued)

Stage of counseling	Purposes of influence efforts
Intervention strategies and action steps (Stage 3)	
Behavioral aspects of *expertness:* directness, fluency, confidence in presentation, and delivery; interpretations	Use of selected skills and strategies and display of confidence to demonstrate ability to help client resolve problems and take necessary action
Behavioral aspects of *trustworthiness:* nonverbal dynamism, dependability and consistency of talk and actions, accurate and reliable information giving	Demonstrate dynamism, congruence, and reliability to encourage client to trust your suggestions and ideas for action; also to diffuse any resistance to action, especially if target behaviors require high level of commitment or change
Evaluation, termination, and follow-up (Stage 4)	
Behavioral areas of *expertness:*	
Relevant questions	Assess client progress and readiness for termination
Directness and confidence in presentation	Contribute to client confidence in maintenance of change through self-directed efforts
Interpersonal attractiveness: structuring	Reduce client anxiety about termination and dissolution of therapeutic relationship
Trustworthiness: reputation or demonstrated lack of ulterior motives or personal gain, honesty and openness	Increase client openness to dissolve relationship when appropriate and necessary

□ COUNSELOR CHARACTERISTICS OR RELATIONSHIP ENHANCERS

Earlier we described the importance of three counselor characteristics for establishing and using an influence base with clients: expertness, attractiveness, and trustworthiness. These three characteristics are also related and, in fact, intercorrelated (Zamostny, Corrigan, & Eggert, 1981) to the extent that counselors who are perceived by clients as competent are also likely to be viewed as interpersonally attractive and trustworthy. Additionally, of the three variables, expertness, or competence, seems to be the most important to client satisfaction (Zamostny et al., 1981) and client goal-related outcomes (LaCrosse, 1980). Expertness has also received the most attention in the research, followed by attractiveness. Very few studies have explored parameters of trustworthiness, despite its acknowledged importance to the developing therapeutic relationship.

□ EXPERTNESS

Expertness, also known as "competence" (Egan, 1982), is the client's perception that the counselor will be helpful in resolving the client's concerns. Clients develop this perception from such things as the counselor's apparent level of skill, relevant ed-

ucation, specialized training or experience, certificates or licenses, seniority, status, type of setting in which the counselor works, history of success in solving problems of others, and the counselor's ascribed role as a helper. Clients appear to formulate these perceptions from aspects of the counselor (language, attire, sex, and so on) and of the setting (display of diplomas, certificates, professional literature, title) that are *immediately* evident to a client — that is, in initial contacts. Thus, in the initial stage of counseling, in which the main goal is to establish an effective relationship and build rapport, descriptive cues such as those mentioned above (see also Table 3-2) associated with expertness play a predominant part in helping the counselor to establish an influence base with the client.

Initially, the *role* of counselor also contributes to client perceptions of counselor competence. In our society, a "helper" role is viewed as socially acceptable and valuable. Counselors convey legitimate power or influence simply by the role they hold. Thus, the "counselor role carries considerable initial influence regardless of its occupant" (Corrigan et al., 1980, p. 425). These authors believe that the legitimate power of our role is, in fact, so strong that demonstrated or behavioral cues of counselor expertness are masked in the initial stage of counseling because sufficient inher-

TABLE 3-2. Descriptive and behavioral cues of expertness, attractiveness, and trustworthiness

Expertness	Attractiveness	Trustworthiness
Descriptive cues		
Relevant education (diplomas)	Physical attractiveness	Role as helper (regarded as trustworthy by society)
Specialized training or experience		
Certificates or licenses		Reputation for honesty and "straightness," lack of ulterior motives
Seniority		
Status		
Type of setting		
Display of professional literature		
Attire		
Reputation (past history of success in resolving problems of others)		
Socially validated role of helper		
Behavioral cues		
Nonverbal behaviors	*Nonverbal behaviors (responsive)*	*Nonverbal behaviors*
Eye contact	Eye contact	Nonverbal congruence
Forward body lean	Direct body orientation facing client	Nonverbal acceptance of client disclosures
Fluent speech delivery	Forward body lean	
	Smiling	Nonverbal responsiveness/dynamism
	Head nodding	
Verbal behaviors	*Verbal behaviors*	*Verbal behaviors*
Relevant and thought-provoking questions	Structuring	Accurate and reliable information giving
Verbal attentiveness	Moderate level of self-disclosure	Accurate paraphrasing
Directness and confidence in presentation	Content of self-disclosure similar to client experiences and opinions	Dependability and consistency of talk and actions
Interpretations		Confidentiality
Concreteness		Openness, honesty
		Reflection of "tests of trust" nondefensively

ent power is ascribed to the role of a helper (Corrigan et al., 1980).

As shown in Table 3-1, in the initial stage of counseling, the counselor wants to create a favorable initial impression and also to encourage the client into counseling by communicating credibility. To some extent, such credibility will be conveyed for counselors by the inherent "power" of our roles as helpers. Additionally, counselors can seek to enhance evident and readily accessible descriptive cues associated with expertness by displaying diplomas, certificates, professional literature, titles, and so on. The helper's initial credibility is also enhanced when the counselor has acquired a positive reputation (based on past history of helping others to resolve their problems) and the client is aware of this reputation.

Role, reputation, and external or office "trappings," however, are insufficient to carry the counselor through anything but the initial phase of counseling. In subsequent phases, the counselor must show actual evidence of competence by his or her behavior. Behavioral expertise is measured by the extent to which the counselor actually helps clients achieve their goals (Egan, 1982). Behavioral demonstrations of expertness are particularly crucial in the second and third stages of counseling (assessment, goal setting, and intervention).

These stages require great skill or actual technical competence in order to make a thorough and accurate assessment of the client's problem, help the client set realistic and worthwhile goals, and help the client take suitable action to reach those goals. This is extremely important because having charisma or being a "good guy" or a "good gal" will not get you through successive interactions with clients. As Corrigan et al. note, "In longer term counseling . . . continued evidence of a lack of expertise might negate the power conferred on a counselor by virtue of his/her role" (1980, p. 425).

Perceived expertness does not seem to be equivalent to counselor experience—that is, experienced counselors are not automatically perceived as more competent or expert than less experienced or even paraprofessional helpers (Heppner & Heesacker, 1982). Instead, expertness is enhanced by the presence or absence of selected nonverbal *and* verbal counselor behaviors that, together, interact to convey behavioral manifestations of competence (Barak, Patkin, & Dell, 1982). *Nonverbal* behaviors associated with the communication of expertness include these:

1. Eye contact
2. Forward body lean
3. Fluent speech delivery (see also Chapter 4)

These nonverbal behaviors appear to contribute to perceived expertness by conveying counselor attentiveness and spontaneity and lack of hesitancy in speech and presentation (see also Table 3-2).

Certain *verbal* behaviors seem to contribute to perceived expertness by establishing the counselor as a source of knowledge and skill and by promoting counselor credibility. These include the following:

1. Use of relevant and thought-provoking questions (see Chapter 6)
2. Verbal indications of attentiveness, such as verbal following, lack of interruptions, listening responses (see Chapter 5)
3. Directness and confidence in presentation
4. Interpretations (see Chapter 6)
5. Concreteness

Concreteness

Because the skill of concreteness is not presented in any other part of the book, we will describe it in some detail in this section. What clients say to you is often an incomplete representation of their experience. Their words and language (sometimes called "surface structure") do not really represent their experience or the meaning of their communication (sometimes called "deep structure"). Not only is the language of clients an incomplete representation of their experience, it also is full of various sorts of "gaps"—three in particular:

Deletions—when things are left out, omitted.
Distortions—when things are not as they seem or are misconstrued.
Generalization—when a whole class of things or people is associated with one feeling or with the same meaning or when conclusions are reached without supporting data.

Because of these gaps, it is important for the counselor to use some linguistic tools to make meaning of the client's words and to fill in these gaps. The most efficient linguistic tool for achieving these two objectives is questions—not just any questions, but particular questions designed to extract exactness and concreteness from clients. These questions also help to ensure that you do not project your own sense of meaning onto the client, because your meaning may be irrelevant or inaccurate.

Consider the following example: A client says "I'm depressed." Therapist A responds by asking "About what, specifically?" Therapist B responds with "Depressed? Oh, yes, I know what that's like. How depressed?" The first therapist is likely to get a response from the client that leads to what depression is like for this client and eventually client responses that recover many missing pieces to the problem, since the client's initial statement is full of deletions, or omissions. The second therapist assumes that her sensory experience or meaning of the word *depressed* is the same as the client's and fails to determine how the client's model of reality (or depression) may differ from her own and even from those of other clients.

Concreteness is a way to ensure that general and common experiences and feelings such as depression, anxiety, anger, and so on are defined idiosyncratically for each client. Further, by requesting specific information from clients, you are relieved of having to search for your own equivalent meanings and interpretations. According to Lankton (1980, p. 52), "To translate a client's words into your own subjective experience, at best, results in valuable time and attention lost from the therapy session. At worst, the meaning you make of a client's experience may be wholly inaccurate."

Asking specific questions designed to elicit concreteness from clients is useful for assessing the client's current problems and also desired outcomes. Consequently, it is a facet of expertness that is particularly critical in the data-gathering and self-exploratory and understanding process characterized by the second stage of counseling—assessment and goal setting. Moreover, it helps you to identify client limitations and resources that could contribute to or militate against effective solutions to problems. Thus, it is also an important part of expertness in the third phase of counseling, in which action plans and intervention strategies are selected and applied.

As we mentioned earlier, client language contains linguistic errors known as deletions, distortions, and generalizations. Table 3-3 describes common categories of client incomplete linguistic communications and sample counselor responses designed to extract exactness and concreteness.

TABLE 3-3. Categories and examples of client linguistic errors and sample counselor responses designed to elicit concreteness

Category	Description	Examples	Sample therapist responses
Deletions			
Simple deletion	Some object, person, or event is left out	"I am going" "I'm scared"	"Going where?" "Of what?"
Comparative deletion	Basis for using a comparative or superlative is deleted	"She is the best" "My brother is better than me"	"Best compared with whom?" "Best when (or where)?" "Better when (or how or where)"?
Referential index, lack of	Object or person being referred to is left out or is unspecified	"They're always in my way" "It makes me sick"	"Who, specifically, is always in your way?" "What, specifically, makes you sick?"
Unspecified verb	Parts of the action are missing—for example, verb is introduced but not clarified	"He frustrates me" "I'm stymied"	"Specifically, how does he frustrate you?" "How, specifically, are you stymied?"
Modal operator of *necessity*	Assumption of no choice—"have to," "can't," "impossible," "necessary"	"I can't make sense of this list" "It's impossible to think straight"	"What stops you?" "What prevents you from thinking straight?"
Modal operator of *possibility*	Assumption of no choice—"should, "must not," "ought to"	"I should learn this list" "I must not neglect my studies"	"What would happen if you did not?" "What would happen if you did?"
Lost performative	Who is making a judgment or evaluation is omitted	"It is bad to neglect studying" "People should do better by each other"	"For whom it is bad?" "Bad in whose opinion?" "Who, specifically, should do better?" "Should do better in whose opinion?"
Distortions			
Nominalization	Action (verb) made into a thing (noun)—tends to delete person's responsibility for the action	"I do not have freedom" "I want security"	"How, specifically, do you not feel free? When, where, with whom?" "How do you want to be secure?"

(continued)

TABLE 3-3. Categories and examples of client linguistic errors and sample counselor responses designed to elicit concreteness (continued)

Category	Description	Examples	Sample therapist responses
Cause/effect	Assumption that one event *causes* another	"Your frowning makes me mad"	"Specifically, how does my frowning cause you to be mad?"
		"As long as my teacher is around, I feel happy"	"How, specifically, does the presence of your teacher cause you to be happy?"
Mind reading	Assumption of how the other person thinks or feels (inside) without specific evidence	"When you frown, I know you hate me"	"How, specifically, do you know that my frowning means I hate you?"
		"I know he doesn't love me"	"How, specifically, do you know this?"
Presuppositions	Some experience must be assumed for the statement to make sense	"You know I suffer" (Assumes that you know I suffer)	"How, specifically, do you suffer?"
		"My daughter is as stubborn as my husband" (Assumes husband is stubborn)	"How, specifically, does your husband seem stubborn to you?"
Generalizations			
Universal quantifiers	Generalization to whole class; "always," "never," "none," "all," "every"	"I always have trouble learning this kind of material"	"You *never* have learned any kind of material like this before, ever?"
		"I always lose arguments"	"Was there ever a time when you didn't lose an argument?"
Complex equivalence	Assuming that one experience means another (implied cause/effect)	"When he frowns, I know he hates me"	"Was there ever a time when he frowned and he loved you?" "Have you ever frowned at someone you love?"
		"My wife wants to work. She doesn't love me"	"Do you love your wife? And do you also work?"

Adapted from list compiled by R. Rittenhouse (personal communication, June 1982) and Bandler and Grinder (1975). The authors appreciate their contribution to this table.

Expertness Is Not "One Up"

It is extremely important to remember that expertness is not in any way the same as being dogmatic, authoritarian, or "one up." Expert helpers are those perceived as confident, attentive, and, because of background and behavior, capable of helping the client resolve problems and work toward goals. Helpers misuse this important variable when they come across as "the expert" or in a one-up position with clients. This may intimidate clients, who might then decide not to return for more counseling. In fact, particularly in initial sessions, helpers must do just the opposite: convey friendliness, equality, and likability. In later sessions, it is also important to deemphasize your influence efforts or make them inconspicuous in order to avoid engendering client resistance (see also Chapter 20). In the next section, we describe how helpers exercise likability and friendliness through the variable of attractiveness.

LEARNING ACTIVITIES #6: EXPERTNESS

I. Counselor Competence

A. With a partner or in small groups, describe the ideal counseling setting that would enhance most clients' initial impressions of counselor competence. Be very specific in your descriptions.

B. With your partner or in small groups, discuss any clients who might not view your ideal setting described above as indicative of counselor competence. Discuss the limitations of setting, role, and reputation as a means of enhancing the competence variable with these clients.

C. With your partner or in small groups, identify what you believe are the *three most important* things you can do behaviorally to enhance client perceptions of your competence. When you finish this part of the learning activity, you may want to share your descriptions of all three parts with another dyad or group, and vice versa.

II. Concreteness and Linguistic Errors

Twelve client statements are listed in this learning activity. Identify the category of the linguistic error contained in each statement (deletion, distortion, or generalization) and then write a sample counselor response that recovers the omission or challenges the distortion or generalization. An example is given. You may want to refer to Table 3-3 if you have difficulty. Feedback follows.

Example

1. a. Client statement: "I hate them."
   b. __✔__ Deletion   _____ Distortion
      _____ Generalization
   c. Counselor response: "Whom, specifically, do you hate?"

2. a. Client statement: "She upsets me."
   b. _____ Deletion   _____ Distortion
      _____ Generalization
   c. Counselor response:

3. a. Client statement: "I can't do this."
   b. _____ Deletion   _____ Distortion
      _____ Generalization
   c. Counselor response:

4. a. Client statement: "I know he thinks I'm dumb."
   b. _____ Deletion   _____ Distortion
      _____ Generalization
   c. Counselor response:

5. a. Client statement: "I always lose my cool in front of large groups."
   b. _____ Deletion   _____ Distortion
      _____ Generalization
   c. Counselor response:

6. a. Client statement: "The way you look makes me scared."
   b. _____ Deletion   _____ Distortion
      _____ Generalization
   c. Counselor response:

7. a. Client statement: "I'm sad."
   b. _____ Deletion   _____ Distortion
      _____ Generalization
   c. Counselor response:

8. a. Client statement: "I do not have independence."
   b. _____ Deletion   _____ Distortion
      _____ Generalization
   c. Counselor response:

9. a. Client statement: "My daughter wants to move out. I guess that means she doesn't like it here."
   b. _____ Deletion   _____ Distortion
      _____ Generalization
   c. Counselor response:

10. a. Client statement: "It is bad not to exercise."
    b. _____ Deletion   _____ Distortion
       _____ Generalization
    c. Counselor response:

11. a. Client statement: "It blows my top off."
    b. _____ Deletion   _____ Distortion
       _____ Generalization
    c. Counselor response:

12. a. Client statement: "I should do more work."
    b. _____ Deletion   _____ Distortion
       _____ Generalization
    c. Counselor response:

FEEDBACK #6: EXPERTNESS

II. Concreteness and Linguistic Errors

2. b. Deletion (unspecified verb)
   c. "Specifically, how does she upset you?"
3. b. Deletion (modal operator of necessity)
   c. "What is stopping you?"
4. b. Distortion (mind reading)
   c. "How, specifically, do you know this?"
5. b. Generalization (universal quantifier "always")
   c. "You *never* have kept it together in front of a large group?"
6. b. Distortion (cause/effect)
   c. "How, specifically, does the way I look cause you to feel afraid?"
7. b. Deletion (simple omission)
   c. "About what?"
8. b. Distortion (nominalization)
   c. "How, specifically, do you not act (or behave) independently?"
9. b. Generalization (complex equivalence)
   c. "Have you ever left a place or a person you liked or loved?"
10. b. Deletion (lost performative)
    c. "For whom is it bad?"
11. b. Deletion (lack of referential index)
    c. "What, specifically, blows your top off?"
12. b. Deletion (modal operator of possibility)
    c. "What would happen if you didn't do more work?"

☐ ATTRACTIVENESS

Attractiveness is inferred by clients from the counselor's apparent friendliness, likability, and similarity to the client. As we mentioned earlier, the counselor who is perceived as attractive by clients becomes an important source of referent power. The effects of attractiveness are apparently greatest when it is mutual—when the client likes the helper and the helper likes to work with the client (Heppner & Heesacker, 1982).

Attractiveness consists of both physical and interpersonal dimensions. Physical attractiveness is the primary descriptive cue associated with this relationship enhancer and, like the descriptive cues of expertness, appears to exert most influence in the *initial* stage of counseling—during relationship and rapport building, when impression formation by clients is based on relatively apparent and accessible cues (Cash & Salzbach, 1978). Dur-

ing later stages of counseling, the skills and competence, or behavioral manifestations, of expertness seem to outweigh the effects of physical attractiveness. In one study, clients did not want to return for counseling with counselors having poor skills even if the counselors were perceived as physically attractive (Vargas & Borkowski, 1982). Zlotlow and Allen (1981, p. 201) conclude that "although the physically attractive counselor may have a head start in developing rapport with clients as a result of widely held stereotypes about good-looking people, this advantage clearly is not an adequate substitute for technical skill or social competence."

In the initial stage of counseling, counselors can utilize the potential benefit from the attractiveness stereotype by trying to maximize their physical attractiveness, appearance, and demeanor. Although there is obviously little we can do to alter certain aspects of our appearance short of plastic surgery, other aspects of our appearance, such as attire, weight, personal hygiene, and grooming, are under our control and can be used to enhance, rather than detract from, initial impressions that clients formulate of us.

Selected nonverbal and verbal behaviors convey interpersonal attractiveness and also are quite important during the first two stages of counseling—relationship/rapport and assessment and goal setting. Interpersonal attractiveness helps clients to open up and self-disclose by reducing client anxiety (through structuring and self-disclosure) and by creating the belief that this counselor is someone with whom the client wants to work.

Nonverbal behaviors that contribute to attractiveness include eye contact, body orientation (facing client), forward body lean, smiling, and head nodding (Barak, Patkin, & Dell, 1982; see also Table 3-2). These and other aspects of counselor nonverbal behavior are discussed more extensively in Chapter 4.

Verbal behaviors that contribute to attractiveness include self-disclosure and structuring, discussed below. These behaviors appear to enhance the relationship by creating positive expectations, reducing unnecessary anxiety, and increasing the perceived similarity between client and counselor.

Self-Disclosure

With respect to attractiveness, three factors related to self-disclosure are worth reemphasizing:

1. Perceived attractiveness is related to a *mod-*

erate level of helper self-disclosure (Banikiotes, Kubinski, & Pursell, 1981). Too much or too little disclosure detracts from the client's perception of the helper as attractive.

2. The depth of intimacy reflected in self-disclosure statements needs to be adapted to the stage of counseling and the degree of the therapeutic relationship. In early sessions, self-disclosure of a factual, nonintimate nature is more useful; in later sessions, more personal or self-involving disclosures are more helpful (McCarthy, 1982).

3. Attractiveness is enhanced when helpers self-disclose problems and concerns previously experienced that are *similar* to the client's present problem. Similarity of self-disclosure may also promote the credibility and competence of the helper by suggesting that the counselor knows about and can understand the client's concern (Corrigan et al., 1980). Accordingly, "disclosure of any prior problem (now successfully resolved) may confer on the counselor some 'expertise in problem resolution' or credibility accorded to 'one who has also suffered'" (Corrigan et al., 1980, p. 425).

Structuring

Another way to maximize perceived similarity between counselor and client is by the use of direct structuring. *Structuring* refers to an interactional process between counselors and clients in which they arrive at similar perceptions of the role of the counselor, an understanding of what occurs in the counseling process, and an agreement on which outcome goals will be achieved (Brammer & Shostrom, 1982; Day & Sparacio, 1980). Structuring enhances perceived counselor/client similarity and interpersonal attractiveness (Goldstein, 1971) and also fulfills an ethical obligation that requires counselors to inform clients of such things as the purposes, goals, techniques, and limitations of counseling (American Association for Counseling and Development, 1981).

Direct structuring means that the counselor actively and directly provides structure to the clients concerning the elements mentioned above. Direct structuring contributes to attractiveness by enhancing helper/helpee agreement on basic information and issues, thereby establishing some security in the relationship. Insecurity results from excessive ambiguity and anxiety. Direct structuring is most important sometime in the first stage of counseling (relationship and rapport), in which ambiguity and anxiety and lack of information

about counseling are likely to be greatest and the need to promote helper/helpee similarity is critical. An example of the use of direct structuring with a new client in an initial interview follows:

Counselor: Mary, I understand this is the first time you have ever been to see a counselor. Is that accurate or not?

Client: Yes, it is. I've thought about seeing someone for a while, but I finally got the courage to actually do it just recently.

Counselor: I noticed you used the word *courage* as if perhaps you're feeling relieved you're here and also still somewhat uneasy about what happens in counseling.

Client: That's true. I'm glad I came, but I guess I'm also still a little unsure.

Counselor: One thing that might help with the uncertainty is to talk for a few minutes about what goes on in counseling, what my role and your role is, and the kinds of things you may want to talk about or work on. How does that sound?

Client: Great. I think that would help.

Counselor: OK. Many people come into counseling with something they need to get "off their chest" —at first sometimes they just need to talk and think about it. Later on it is usually important to also do something about the issue. My role is to help you identify, talk about, and understand issues of concern to you and then to help you take any action that seems important to resolve the issue or to take your life in a different direction. This process can take several months or longer. At first, it usually is a little hard to open up and share some personal things with someone you don't know, but one thing that might help you do this is to know that, short of feeling strongly like you are going to harm yourself or someone else, whatever you tell me is kept in this room between us. Now —what are your questions or reactions?

Direct structuring is also very useful during the last stage of counseling to ensure a smooth termination, to reduce client anxiety about dissolution of the therapeutic relationship, and to convey action expectations and information about what may happen after counseling terminates. Consider the following example as a counselor and client approach termination:

Counselor: Jim, we started seeing each other every week six months ago; the last two months you've been coming in every other week. Several times you've mentioned recently how good you feel and how your relationships with women are now starting to take off in a direction you want. It seems to me that after about one or two more contacts we will be ready to stop seeing each other because you are able to handle these issues on your own now. What is your reaction to this?

Client: That sounds about right. I do feel a lot more confident in the way my relationships are going. I guess it does seem a little strange to think of not coming in here.

Counselor: Yes. After you've been working together like we have, sometimes there's a little bit of strangeness or apprehension that accompanies the idea of finishing with counseling. However, I wouldn't suggest it at this time if I didn't feel very sure that you are ready to do this. It might help you to know that I'll be calling you several times after we finish to see how things are going, and of course, if anything comes up in the future you want to talk over, just give me a call.

According to Day and Sparacio (1980), structure is also helpful at major transition points in counseling, such as moving from one stage to another. This also reduces ambiguity, informs the client about any role and process changes in a different stage of therapy, and increases the likelihood that both counselor and client will approach the forthcoming stage with similar rather than highly discrepant perceptions.

To provide structure effectively with clients, consider the following ten guidelines for structuring suggested by Day and Sparacio (1980, pp. 248–249):

1. Structure should be negotiated or requested, not coerced. Clients should be given the opportunity to respond and react to structure as well as to be able to modify it.

2. Structure, particularly restrictions and limitations, should not be applied for punitive reasons or in a punitive manner (Bixler, 1949).

3. The counselor should be aware of his or her rationale for structuring and should explain the reasons at the time of structuring or be prepared to provide rationale in response to the client's request for explanation.

4. The counselor should be guided by the client's readiness for structure and by the context of the relationship and process.

5. Too much or a too-rigid structure can be constraining for both the client and the counselor (Pietrofesa, Hoffman, Splete, & Pinto, 1978).

6. Ill-timed, lengthy, or insensitive structuring can result in client frustration or resistance (Benjamin, 1974), and can interrupt the continuity of the therapeutic process (Pietrofesa et al., 1978).

7. Unnecessary and purposeless recitation of rules and guidelines can imply that the counselor is more concerned with procedure than with helpfulness. In fact, a compulsive approach to structuring can be indicative of low levels of counselor self-assurance (Hansen, Stevic, & Warner, 1977).

8. The counselor must relate structure to the client's emotional, cognitive, and behavioral predisposition. For example, the highly independent individual or the isolate may be expected to resist what she or he interprets as personal threats or infringements. In such cases, structuring must be accomplished by sensitivity, tentativeness, and flexibility.

9. Structuring can "imply that the relationship will continue with this particular client. It may turn out that the counselor will decide not to work with this client, or that the client may not be suitable for this counselor. Hence, the client or counselor may feel too committed to the relationship if it has been overstructured" (Brammer & Shostrom, 1982, p. 186).

10. Structure cannot replace or substitute for therapeutic competence. Structure is not a panacea. It is not the total solution to building a productive therapeutic relationship. Structure is complementary and supplementary to human relations, communications, diagnostic, and intervention skills.*

* From "Structuring the counseling process." by R. W. Day & R. T. Sparacio. *The Personnel and Guidance Journal,* (1981), *59,* 246–249. Copyright AACD. Reprinted with permission. No further reproduction authorized without permission from AACD.

LEARNING ACTIVITIES #7: ATTRACTIVENESS

I. Attributes of Attractive Persons

In a dyad or a small group, discuss the attributes of persons you know and consider to be "attractive" persons. Compile a written list of their attributes. Review your list to determine which attributes are descriptive ones, such as appearance and demeanor, and which attributes are behavioral — that is, things the person does. To what extent do the attributes of attractive people listed in your compilation generalize to effective helpers?

II. Structuring

In this activity, write an example of the use of direct structuring for each of the following four examples. Feedback follows.

(continued)

1. Write an example of structuring in an initial interview with a client who has never seen a counselor before.
2. Write an example of structuring in an initial interview with a client who is new to you but has seen three other counselors before.

3. Write an example of structuring prior to starting the termination phase with a client who has never been in counseling before.
4. Write an example of structuring prior to starting the termination phase with a client who has been in counseling several times before.

☐ TRUSTWORTHINESS

"Trust is the client's perception and belief that the counselor will not mislead or injure the client in any way"* (Fong & Cox, 1983, p. 163). According to the interpersonal influence model, trustworthiness is perceived by clients from such things as the counselor's role, reputation for honesty, demonstrated sincerity and openness, and lack of ulterior motives (Strong, 1968).

Establishing Trust

In the initial stage of counseling (relationship and rapport), clients are also dependent on readily accessible descriptive cues to judge the trustworthiness of counselors. For example, many clients are likely to find counselors trustworthy, at least initially, because of the status of their role in society. According to Egan (1975, p. 111), "In our society, people who have certain roles are usually considered trustworthy until the opposite is demonstrated. . . . When exceptions do occur (as when a dentist is convicted of molesting a patient), the scandal is greater because it is unexpected." Clients also are more likely to perceive a counselor as trustworthy if she or he has acquired a reputation for honesty and for ethical and professional behavior. Likewise, a negative reputation can erode initial trust in a helper. Thus, many clients may put their faith in the helper initially on the basis of role and reputation and, over the course of counseling, continue to trust the counselor unless the trust is in some way abused. This is particularly true for majority-group clients.

For clients who are members of minority groups, it may be the other way around. As La-Fromboise and Dixon (1981, p. 135) observe, "A member of the minority group frequently enters the relationship suspending trust until the person

proves that he/she is worthy of being trusted." For these and some other clients, counselors may have to earn initial trust. This is especially true as counseling progresses. Trust can be difficult to establish yet easily destroyed. Trust between counselor and client involves a series of "relationship interchanges" (Fong & Cox, 1983), takes time to develop fully, and is not a fixed phenomenon but changes constantly depending on the actions of both persons (Johnson, 1981). Initial trust based on external factors such as the counselor's role and reputation must be solidified with appropriate actions and behaviors of helpers that occur during successive interactions (see also Table 3-2).

During the second stage of counseling, assessment and goal setting, trust is essential in order for the client to be open and revealing of very personal problems and concerns. Clients' self-exploration of problems during this phase can be limited by the amount of trust that has developed in the relationship prior to this time. Trust is also critical during the third and fourth stages of counseling. In the third stage (action/intervention), the client often has to set in motion the difficult and vulnerable process of change. Trust can provide the impetus necessary for the client to do so. Trust is also critical to the fourth stage of counseling (evaluation and termination). Effective termination ensues when the client trusts the counselor's decision to terminate, trusts that it is not too early (leaving the client hanging) or too prolonged (creating excessive dependency for the client), and trusts that the counselor is reliable and concerned enough to check in with the client on a periodic basis as a follow-up to therapy.

The behaviors that contribute most importantly to trustworthiness include counselor congruence, or consistency, of verbal and nonverbal behavior, nonverbal acceptance of client disclosures, and nonverbal responsiveness and dynamism (see also Chapter 4). Incongruence, judgmental or evaluative reactions, and passivity quickly erode any initial trust.

Important verbal behaviors (see also Table 3-2) contributing to trust include accurate paraphras-

---

* This and all other quotations from this source are from "Trust as an underlying dynamic in the counseling process: How clients test trust." by M. L. Fong and B. G. Cox. *The Personnel and Guidance Journal, 62,* 163–166. Copyright AACD. Reprinted with permission. No further reproduction authorized without permission of AACD.

FEEDBACK #7: ATTRACTIVENESS

II. Structuring

1. "You're probably feeling uncertain about what to expect. It might help if we talked a little about what happens in counseling. You may have one or more things on your mind you want to talk about and work through. I'm here to help you do that and to do it in a safe and confidential place."

2. "You probably know what goes on in counseling generally. What I do might vary a little bit from the other counselors you've seen. I believe I'm here to listen to you, to help you understand some of your concerns, and to assist you in taking a course of action best for you to resolve these issues."

3. "I have the sense that you have really accomplished what you wanted to do. Let's take a few minutes to see . . . [reviews client's progress toward desired goals]. Since you also feel our work's about done, it seems like after two more sessions it will be time to close out our relationship for now. You may feel a little apprehensive about this, but I'll be calling you shortly after we finish to see how things are going. I imagine things will go quite smoothly for you. Once in a while, people find it's hard to start out on their own, but soon things start to fall into place. During these last three sessions, we'll also be working specifically on how you can take the things you've learned and done in our sessions out into your own world so things do fall into place for you out there."

4. "I believe after one or two more sessions, we're ready to finish. Since you've been through this before, do you have the same or a different opinion? [Time for client to respond.] One thing I want you to know about myself is that I'll call you once or twice after we stop to see how things are going, and of course, you can feel free to call me, too, if something comes up you need to discuss."

ing (see also Chapter 5), dependability and consistency between talk and actions, confidentiality, openness and honesty, accurate and reliable information giving (see also Chapter 6), and nondefensive reflections/interpretations of clients' "tests of trusts." This latter behavior is discussed in greater depth in the following section.

Client Tests of Counselor Trustworthiness

According to Johnson (1981), trust between counselors and clients does not always develop automatically. Clients need to be assured that counseling will be structured to meet their needs and that the counselor will not take advantage of their vulnerability (Johnson, 1981). Often clients do not ask about these issues directly. Instead, they engage in subtle maneuvers to obtain data about the counselor's trustworthiness. Fong and Cox (1983) call these maneuvers "tests of trust" and liken them to trial balloons sent up to "see how they fly" before the client decides whether to send up the big one or the real one.

Counselors may be insensitive to such "tests of trust" and fail to identify that trust is the real concern of the client. Instead of responding to the trust issue, counselors may respond just to the content, the surface level of the message. Or the counselor may view the client as "defensive, resistant, or hostile" and respond negatively (Fong & Cox, 1983, p. 163). If the trust issue is unresolved, the relationship may deteriorate or even terminate with the counselor unaware that "the real issue was lack of trust" (Fong & Cox, 1983, p. 163).

Fong and Cox observe that some client statements and behaviors are used repeatedly by many clients as "tests of trust." They state that "the specific content of clients' questions and statements is unique to individual clients, but the general form that tests of trust take — for example, requesting information or telling a secret — are relatively predictable" (p. 164). These authors have identified six common types of client "tests of trust," which we describe as follows.

Requesting information (or "Can you understand and help me?"). Counselors need to be alert to whether client questions are searches for factual information or for counselor opinions and beliefs. Clients who ask questions like "Do you have children?" or "How long have you been married?" are probably looking for something in addition to the factual response. Most often they are seeking verification from you that you will be able to understand, to accept, and to help them with their particular set of concerns. In responding to such client questions, it is important to convey your understanding and acceptance of the clients' concerns and of their need to feel understood. For example, a counselor might say "Yes, I do have two children. I'm also wondering whether you believe that the fact that I have children means I can better understand your concerns."

Telling a secret (or "Can I be vulnerable or take risks with you?"). Clients share secrets — very personal aspects of their lives — to test whether they can trust the counselor to accept them as they really are, to keep their communications confidential, and to avoid exploiting their vulnerability after they have disclosed very personal concerns. Usually, this secret is not even relevant to the client's presenting problem but, rather, is related to something the client does that has "embarrassment or shame attached to it" (Fong & Cox, 1983, p. 164). And "if the counselor becomes perceptively defensive in reaction to the client's revelation or makes some statement that seems to be judgmental, the client is almost certain to decide that it is unsafe to be vulnerable with this person. The level of trust drops. And further self-disclosure of any depth may not be forthcoming, at least for a very long time" (p. 164).

Counselors need to remember that clients who share secrets are really testing the waters to see how safe it is to self-disclose personal issues with you. Responding with nonverbal and verbal acceptance and listening assure clients that their private thoughts, feelings, and behaviors are safe with you. For example, suppose a client blurts out: "I had an affair several years ago. No one knows about this, not even my husband." The counselor must respond to the entire message, especially acknowledging the "risk" involved. "That is your way of saying to me that this is secret between you and me."

Asking a favor (or "Are you reliable?").   Clients may ask counselors to perform favors that may or may not be appropriate. According to Fong and Cox (1983, p. 165), "all requests of clients for a favor should be viewed, especially initially, as potential tests of trust." When clients ask you to lend them a book, see them at their home, or call their boss for them, whether you grant or deny the favor is not as important as how you handle the request and how reliably you follow through with your stated intentions. It is crucial to follow through on reasonable favors you have promised to do. For unreasonable favors, it is important to state tactfully but directly your reason for not granting the favor. Efforts to camouflage the real reason with an excuse or to grant an unreasonable favor grudgingly are just as damaging to trust as is failure to follow through on a favor (Fong & Cox, 1983, p. 165). For instance, if a client asks you to see her at her home in order to save her time and gas money, you might tactfully deny her favor by saying "Jane, I can certainly appreciate your need to save time and money. I would much prefer to continue

to see you in the office, however, because it is easier for me to concentrate and listen to you without any distractions I'm not used to." Asking favors is generally an indication that the client is testing your reliability, dependability, honesty, and directness. A good rule of thumb to follow is "Don't promise more than you can deliver, and be sure to deliver what you have promised as promised."

Putting oneself down (or "Can you accept me?").
Clients put themselves down to test the counselor's level of acceptance. This test of trust is designed to help clients determine whether the counselor will continue to be accepting even of parts of themselves that clients view as bad, negative, or dirty. Often this test of trust is conveyed by statements or behaviors designed to shock the counselor, followed by a careful scrutiny of the counselor's verbal and nonverbal reactions. Counselors need to respond neutrally to client self-putdowns rather than condoning or evaluating the client's statements and actions. As Fong and Cox note,

> In responding to the client's self-putdowns, the counselor reflects to the client what the counselor has heard and then responds with statements of interest and acceptance. If the counselor makes the mistake of reacting either positively or negatively to the client's descriptions of their "bad" behavior early in the relationship, trust is unlikely to be built. Clients will see the counselor as potentially judgmental or opinionated [1983, p. 165].

A client may say "Did you know I've had three abortions in the last three years? It's my own fault. I just get carried away and keep forgetting to use birth control." The counselor needs to respond with nonverbal acceptance and may say something like "You've found yourself with several unwanted pregnancies."

Inconveniencing the counselor (or "Do you have consistent limits?").   Clients often test trust by creating inconveniences to the counselor such as changing appointment times, canceling at the last minute, changing the location of sessions, or asking to make a phone call during the session. Counselors need to respond directly and openly to the inconvenience, especially if it occurs more than once or twice. When the counselor sets limits, clients may begin feeling secure and assured that the counselor is dependable and consistent. Setting limits often serves a reciprocal purpose: the clients realize they also can set limits in the relationship. As an example of this test of trust, consider the client who is repeatedly late to sessions. After three consecutive late starts, the counselor mentions "You know, Gary, I've realized that the last three weeks we've got off to quite a late start. This creates problems for me because if we have a full session, it throws the rest of my schedule off. Or if I stop at the designated time, you end up getting shortchanged of time. Can we start on time, or do we need to reschedule the appointment time?"

Questioning the counselor's motives (or "Is your caring real?"). As we mentioned earlier, one aspect of trustworthiness is sincerity. Clients test this aspect of trust by statements and questions designed to answer the question "Do you really care about me, or is it just your job?" Clients may ask about the number of other clients the counselor sees or how the counselor distinguishes and remembers all his clients or whether the counselor thinks about the client during the week (Fong & Cox, 1983). Fong and Cox observe that "unless counselors are alert to the fact that this is a form of testing trust, they may fail to respond adequately to the crucial issue; that is, the client's need to be seen as a worthwhile human being in the counselor's eyes and not just as a source of income for the counselor" (p. 166). For instance, suppose a client says to her counselor "I bet you get tired of listening to people like me all the time." The counselor may respond with something that affirms her interest in the client, such as "You're feeling unsure about your place here, wondering whether I really care about you when I see so many other persons. Suzanne, from you I've learned . . ." (follow through with a personal statement directly related to this client).

Table 3-4 presents a summary of these six tests of trust with sample client statements and helpful and nonhelpful counselor responses.

TABLE 3-4. Examples of client tests of trust and helpful and nonhelpful counselor responses

Test of trust	Client statement	Examples of nonhelpful responses	Example of helpful response
Requesting information (can you understand and help me?)	"Have you ever worked with anyone else who seems as mixed up as I am?"	"Yes, all the time" "No, not too often" "Once in a while" "Oh, you're not *that* mixed up"	"Many people I work with often come in feeling confused and over-whelmed. I'm also wondering whether you want to know that I have the experience to help you"
Telling a secret (can I be vulnerable with you?)	"I've never been able to tell anyone about this—not even my husband or my priest. But I did have an abortion several years ago. I just was not ready to be a good and loving mother"	"Oh, an abortion—really?" "You haven't even told your husband even though it might be his child too?"	"What you're sharing with me now is our secret, something between you and me"
Asking a favor (are you reliable?)	"Could you bring this information (or book) in for me next week?"	Promises to do it but forgets altogether or does not do it when specified	Promises to do it and does it when promised
Putting oneself down (can you accept me?)	"I just couldn't take all the pressure from the constant travel, the competition, the need to always win and be number one. When they offered me the uppers, it seemed like the easiest thing to cope with all this. Now I need more and more of the stuff"	"Don't you know you could hurt yourself if you keep going like this?" "You'll get hurt from this — is it really a smart thing to do?"	"The pressure has gotten so intense it's hard to find a way out from under it"

(continued)

TABLE 3-4. Examples of client tests of trust and helpful and nonhelpful counselor responses (continued)

Test of trust	Client statement	Examples of nonhelpful responses	Example of helpful response
Inconveniencing the counselor (do you have consistent limits?)	"Can I use your phone again before we get started?"	"Of course, go ahead—feel free any time" "Absolutely not"	"Marc, the last two times I've seen you, you have started the session by asking to use my phone. When this happens, you and I don't have the full time to use for counseling. Would it be possible for you to make these calls before our session starts, or do we need to change our appointment time?"
Questioning the counselor's motives (is your caring real?)	"I don't see how you have the energy to see me at the end of the day like this. You must be exhausted after seeing all the other people with problems, too"	"Oh, no, I'm really not" "Yes, I'm pretty tired"	"You're probably feeling unsure about how much energy I have left for you after seeing other people first. One thing about you that helps me keep my energy up is . . ."

LEARNING ACTIVITIES #8: TRUSTWORTHINESS

I. Identification of Trust-Related Issues
With a partner or in a small group, develop responses to the following questions:
A. For clients belonging to majority groups or from racial/cultural backgrounds similar to your own:
  1. How does trust develop during therapeutic interactions?
  2. How is trust during therapeutic interactions violated?
  3. How does it feel to have your trust in someone else violated?
  4. What are ten things a counselor can do (or ten behaviors to engage in) to build trust? Of the ten, select five that are most important and rank-order these from 1 (most critical, top priority to establish trust) to 5 (least critical or least priority to establish trust).
B. Complete the same four questions above for clients belonging to minority groups or from a racial/cultural background distinctly different from your own.

II. Client Tests of Trust
Listed below are six client descriptions. For each description, (a) identify the content and process reflected in the test of trust, and (b) write an example of a counselor response that could be used appropri-

ately with this type of trust test. You may wish to refer to Table 3-4. An example is completed. Feedback follows.

Example
1. The client asks whether you have seen other people before who have attempted suicide.
   a. Test of trust (content): request for information
                      (process): can you understand and help me?
   b. Example of counselor response: "Yes, I have worked with other persons before you who have thought life wasn't worth living. Perhaps this will help you know that I will try to understand what this experience is like for you and will help you try to resolve it in your own best way."
2. The client's phone has been disconnected, and the client wants to know whether he can come ten minutes early to use your phone.
   a. Test of trust (content): _____
   _____
      (process): _____
   _____
   b. Example of counselor response: _____
   _____

(continued)

LEARNING ACTIVITIES #8: TRUSTWORTHINESS (continued)

3. The client wonders aloud whether you make enough money as a counselor that you would choose this occupation if you had to do it over again.

   a. Test of trust (content): _____

   _____

   (process): _____

   _____

   b. Example of counselor response: _____

   _____

4. The client states that she must be kind of stupid because she now has to repeat third grade when all the other kids in her class are going on to fourth grade.

   a. Test of trust (content): _____

   _____

   (process): _____

   _____

   b. Example of counselor response: _____

5. The client has changed the appointment time at the last minute four times in the last several weeks.

   a. Test of trust (content): _____

   _____

   (process): _____

   b. Example of counselor response: _____

6. The client states that she is pregnant and doesn't know for sure whether the father is her husband or her husband's brother and doesn't know what to do and hasn't told anyone else about this.

   a. Test of trust (content): _____

   _____

   (process): _____

   b. Example of counselor response: _____

   _____

   _____

□ SUMMARY

In this chapter, we examined the social influence model of counseling. In this model, the counselor establishes an influence base with the client through the three relationship enhancers of expertness, attractiveness, and trustworthiness. The counselor then uses this influence base to effect client change.

Counselor characteristics contributing most to the influence process include expertness (or competence), attractiveness, and trustworthiness. Components of expertness include descriptive cues such as education and training, certificates and licenses, title and status, setting, reputation, and role. Behavioral cues associated with expertness include responsive nonverbal behaviors such as fluent speech delivery, nonverbal and verbal attentiveness, relevant and thought-provoking questions, interpretations, and concreteness.

Descriptive cues associated with attractiveness include physical attractiveness and demeanor. Behavioral cues of attractiveness are responsive nonverbal behavior, moderate level of counselor self-disclosure, similarity of the content of self-disclosure, and structuring.

Trustworthiness is based on one's role and reputation for honesty as well as nonverbal congruence, dynamism, and acceptance of client disclosures. Trustworthiness is also associated with accurate and reliable information giving, accurate paraphrasing, maintaining of confidentiality, openness and honesty, and nondefensive reactions to clients' "tests of trust."

Physical and interpersonal attractiveness and the role, reputation, and setting of the counselor contribute to early impressions of clients that the counselor is attractive, competent, and trustworthy. These aspects are most useful during the early sessions, in which the counselor strives to establish rapport and to motivate the client to continue with counseling. As therapy progresses, these aspects become less influential and must be substantiated by actual skills that demonstrate the counselor's competence and resourcefulness toward resolving client problems. Behavioral expressions of expertness and trustworthiness are particularly critical during all the remaining phases of counseling— assessment and goal setting, intervention and action, and evaluation and termination.

Clients also contribute to the influence process in counseling. Client variables that enhance or mediate the counselor's influence efforts include motivation; expectations; satisfaction and success of outcomes; conceptual level; sex, race, and gender; and degree of commitment required to make target behavior changes.

POSTEVALUATION

PART ONE

Complete this activity in triads, with one person assuming the role of client, another the counselor, and the third the observer. Engage in a ten-minute role-play interview *or* a ten-minute conversation. The client may present a problem *or* discuss a topic of interest to the client. The counselor's task is to listen for any deletions, distortions, and generalizations in the client's verbal messages. Once you identify these, challenge them. Challenge deletions to help the client recover or add the missing pieces; challenge distortions to help the client determine how the event is misconstrued; and challenge generalizations to help the client determine whether there are sufficient data to support his or her conclusion (Chapter Objective One). The observer should keep track of the interaction by jotting down instances of client deletions, distortions, and generalizations and by noting the subsequent counselor response. After the interaction is over, the observer can give feedback and you can trade roles so that each person has an opportunity to try out each of the three roles once.

PART TWO

Listed below are six written client descriptions. Your task is to match each description with the corresponding "test of trust" (Chapter Objective Two). Feedback for this part follows on p. 64.

Test of Trust

a. Information request
b. Telling a secret
c. Asking a favor
d. Putting oneself down
e. Inconveniencing the counselor
f. Questioning the counselor's motives

Client Situation

1. The client asks you whether you get "burned out" or fatigued talking to people with problems all day.
2. The client says she has been sexually abused by her stepfather.
3. The client asks to borrow a book she sees on your desk.
4. The client wants to know whether you have been married before.
5. The client wants you to see him on the weekend.
6. The client says some people consider her a whore because she sleeps around a lot.

PART THREE

This part of the postevaluation is to be completed in triads; the first person assumes the role of counselor, another takes the role of client, and the third assumes the role of observer. Trade roles so that each person has an opportunity to try out each of the three roles once. If triads are not available, an instructor can also observe you, or you can audiotape or videotape your interview for additional assessment.

Instructions to Counselors

Your task is to conduct a 30-minute *initial interview* with a client in which you demonstrate descriptive and behavioral aspects of attractiveness listed in the "Attractiveness Checklist" that follows (Chapter Objective Three). Remember, too, the purposes of trying to enhance your perceived attractiveness in initial interviews: to reduce client anxiety, to be perceived as likeable and friendly and similar to the client, and to increase the probability of client disclosure.

Instructions to Clients

Present a real or hypothetical concern to the counselor. Try to assume the role of a typical "new" client in an initial interview   somewhat apprehensive and a little reticent.

Instructions to Observers

Watch, listen, and assess the use of the counselor's physical and interpersonal cues associated with attractiveness. Use the Attractiveness Checklist that follows as a guide for your observation and feedback.

ATTRACTIVENESS CHECKLIST

I. Descriptive Cues

Instructions: Assess the counselor's degree of perceived attractiveness on these three items, using the following scale for rating: 1, not at all attractive, 2, minimally attractive; 3, somewhat attractive; 4, quite attractive; 5, very attractive.

1. Appearance

1	2	3	4	5

2. Demeanor

1	2	2	4	5

3. Grooming, hygiene

1	2	3	4	5

(continued)

POSTEVALUATION   (continued)

II. Behavioral Cues

Instructions: Check "Yes" if the counselor demonstrated the following skills and behaviors; "No" if they were not demonstrated.

4. Use of structure
   Yes   No
5. Moderate level of self-disclosure
   Yes   No
6. Content of self-disclosure similar to client's concerns and experiences
   Yes   No
7. Disclosure of factual, nonintimate material (since this is an initial session)
   Yes   No
8. Responsive nonverbal behaviors
   a. Eye contact
   Yes   No
   b. Direct body orientation facing client
   Yes   No
   c. Smiling (intermittent, not constant)
   Yes   No

Observer comments: _____
_____

PART FOUR

This part of the post evaluation will also be conducted in triads so that each person can assume the roles of counselor, client, and observer. For continuity, you may wish to stay in the same triads you used in Part Three of the postevaluation and trade roles in the same sequence.

Instructions to Counselors

You will be conducting a 30-minute *problem identification interview*—one in which you assess or explore the client's primary problems or concerns. During this interview, your task is to demonstrate behaviors associated with expertness and trustworthiness listed on the "Expertness and Trustworthiness Checklist" that follows (Chapter Objective Four). Remember, too, that the purposes of trying to enhance your perceived expertness and trustworthiness during this stage of counseling are to contribute to the client's exploration and understanding of self and of issues, to work toward specificity and concreteness, and to encourage the client to share personal and relevant information with you.

Instructions to Clients

Be sure to have a particular "presenting problem" in mind to discuss with the counselor during this role play. It will be helpful if the problem is something real for you, although it doesn't have to be "heavy." In addition to discussing your "presenting problem" try also to ask several questions related to at least one of the following "tests of trust"—requesting information, telling a secret, asking a favor, putting yourself down, inconveniencing the counselor, or questioning the counselor's motives.

Instructions to Observers

Watch, listen, and assess the use of the counselor's behaviors associated with competence and trustworthiness. Use the "Expertness and Trustworthiness Checklist" that follows as a guide for your observation and feedback.

EXPERTNESS AND TRUSTWORTHINESS CHECKLIST

I. Expertness

Instructions to observer: Check "Yes" if the counselor demonstrated the behavior; "No" if the counselor did not.

1. Did the counselor maintain eye contact with the client?
   Yes   No
2. Did the counselor lean toward the client during the interaction?
   Yes   No
3. Did the counselor talk fluently and without hesitation?
   Yes   No
4. Did the counselor use relevant and thought-provoking questions?
   Yes   No
5. Was the counselor attentive to the client?
   Yes   No
6. Was the counselor's presentation direct and confident?
   Yes   No
7. Did the counselor accurately interpret any implicit client messages?
   Yes   No
8. Did the counselor challenge any deletions, distortions, or generalizations apparent in the client's messages?
   Yes   No

(continued)

II. Trustworthiness

9. Did the counselor convey nonverbal and verbal acceptance of the client's disclosures?

   Yes   No

10. Was the counselor's nonverbal behavior responsive and dynamic?

    Yes   No

11. Did the counselor engage in accurate paraphrasing of the client's messages?

    Yes   No

12. Did the counselor appear to safeguard and respect confidentiality of the client's communication?

    Yes   No

13. Did the counselor seem open, honest, and direct with the client?

    Yes   No

14. Was the information the counselor gave "checked out" (or promised to be checked out) for accuracy and reliability?

    Yes   No

15. Were the counselor's verbal messages consistent with overt actions or behaviors?

    Yes   No

16. Did the counselor respond to any client "tests of trust" appropriately and nondefensively?

    Yes   No

Observer comments: _____

FEEDBACK #8: TRUSTWORTHINESS

II. Client Tests of Trust

2. a. Test of Trust (content): asking a favor
      (process): are you reliable and open with me?
   b. Example response: "I know how difficult it can be to manage without a telephone. Unfortunately, I see someone almost up until the minute you arrive for your session, and so my office is occupied. There's a pay phone in the outer lobby of the building if you find you need to make a call on a particular day or time."

3. a. Test of trust (content): questioning your motives
      (process): do you really care, or are you just going through the motions?
   b. Example response: "Perhaps, Bill, you're feeling unsure about whether I see people like yourself for the money or because I'm sincerely interested in you. One way in which I really enjoy [value] working with you is. . . ."

4. a. Test of trust (content): putting oneself down
      (process): can you accept me even though I'm not too accepting of myself right now?
   b. Example response: "You're feeling pretty upset right now that you're going to be back in the third grade again. I wonder if you're concerned, too, about losing friends or making new ones?"

5. a. Test of trust (content): inconveniencing you
      (process): do you have consistent limits?
   b. Example response: "Mary, I'm not really sure anymore when to expect you. I noticed you've changed your appointment time several times in the last few weeks at the last minute. I want to be sure I'm here or available when you do come in, so it would help if you could decide on one time that suits you and then just one back-up time in case the first time doesn't work out. If you can give some advance notice of a need to change times, then I won't have to post pone or cancel out on you because of my schedule conflicts."

6. a. Test of trust (content): telling you a secret
      (process): how much is it safe to disclose with you?
   b. Example response: "You're in a quandary right now about this pregnancy. It's probably hard enough just to tell me about it. You're also saying it's something you want to keep secret between the two of us."

□ SUGGESTED READINGS

Bandler, R., & Grinder, J. (1975). *The structure of magic: A book about language and therapy* (Vol. 1). Palo Alto, CA: Science & Behavior Books.

Barak, A., Patkin, J., & Dell, D. M. (1982). Effects of certain counselor behaviors on perceived expertness and attractiveness. *Journal of Counseling Psychology, 29,* 261–267.

Corrigan, J. D., Dell, D. M., Lewis, K. N., & Schmidt, L. D. (1980). Counseling as a social influence process: A review. *Journal of Counseling Psychology, 27,* 395–441.

Day, R. W., & Sparacio, R. T. (1980). Structuring the counseling process. *Personnel and Guidance Journal, 59,* 246–250.

Dorn, F. J. (1984). The social influence model: A social psychological approach to counseling. *Personnel and Guidance Journal, 62,* 342–345.

Dorn, F. J. (in press). *Counseling as applied social psychology: An introduction to the social influence model.* Springfield, IL: Charles C Thomas.

Fong, M. L., & Cox, B. G. (1983). Trust as an underlying dynamic in the counseling process: How clients test trust. *Personnel and Guidance Journal, 62,* 163–166.

Goldstein, A. P. (1980). Relationship-enhancement methods. In F. H. Kanfer & A. P. Goldstein (Eds.), *Helping people change* (2nd ed.). New York: Pergamon Press.

Goodyear, R., & Robyak, J. (1981). Counseling as an interpersonal influence process: A perspective for counseling practice. *Personnel and Guidance Journal, 60,* 654–657.

Heppner, P. P., & Heesacker, M. (1982). Interpersonal influence process in real-life counseling: Investigating client perceptions, counselor experience level, and counselor power over time. *Journal of Counseling Psychology, 29,* 215–223.

Heppner, P. P., & Heesacker, M. (1983). Perceived counselor attractiveness, client expectations, and client satisfaction with counseling. *Journal of Counseling Psychology, 30,* 31–39.

Johnson, D. W. (1981). *Reaching out: Interpersonal effectiveness and self-actualization.* Englewood Cliffs, NJ: Prentice-Hall. Chapter 3, "Developing and Maintaining Trust."

LaCrosse, M. B. (1980). Perceived counselor social influence and counseling outcomes: Validity of the Counselor Rating Form. *Journal of Counseling Psychology, 27,* 320–327.

LaFromboise, T. D., & Dixon, D. N. (1981). American Indian perception of trustworthiness in a counseling interview. *Journal of Counseling Psychology, 28,* 135–139.

Rothmeier, R. C., & Dixon, D. N. (1980). Trustworthiness and influence: A reexamination in an extended counseling analogue. *Journal of Counseling Psychology, 27,* 315–319.

Senour, M. (1982). How counselors influence clients. *Personnel and Guidance Journal, 60,* 345–350.

Siegel, J. C. (1980). Effects of objective evidence of expertness, nonverbal behavior, and subject sex on client-perceived expertness. *Journal of Counseling Psychology, 27,* 117–121.

Strong, S., & Claiborn, C. (1982). *Change through interaction: Social psychological processes of counseling and psychotherapy.* New York: Wiley-Interscience.

Vargas, A. M., & Borkowski, J. G. (1982). Physical attractiveness and counseling skills. *Journal of Counseling Psychology, 29,* 246–255.

FEEDBACK: POSTEVALUATION

PART TWO

1. f. Questioning your motives to see whether you really care

2. b. Telling you a secret, something she perhaps feels embarrassed about

3. c. Asking you a favor; in this case, it is probably a reasonable one

4. a. Requesting information overtly—but covertly wondering whether your personal life is together enough to help the client or whether you have enough significant life experiences similar to his own to help him

5. e. Trying to inconvenience you to see whether you have limits and how you set them and follow through on them

6. d. Putting herself down by revealing some part of herself she feels is "bad" and also something that will test your reaction to her

NONVERBAL BEHAVIOR

FOUR

Nonverbal behavior plays an important role in our communication and relationships with others. In communicating, we tend to emphasize the spoken word. Yet much of the meaning of a message, 65% or more, is conveyed by our nonverbal behavior (Birdwhistell, 1970). Knapp (1978, p. 38) defines nonverbal behavior as "all human communication events which transcend spoken or written words." Of course, many nonverbal behaviors are interpreted by verbal symbols. Nonverbal behavior is an important part of counseling because of the tremendous amount of information it communicates.

Counselors can learn much about a client by becoming sensitized to the client's nonverbal cues. Moreover, the counselor's nonverbal behavior has a great deal of impact on the client. One of the primary kinds of client verbal messages dealt with in counseling—the affective message—is highly dependent on nonverbal means of communication. Ekman and Friesen (1969a, p. 88) have noted that much of the information that can be gleaned from words of clients is derived from their nonverbal behavior. Schutz (1967), in his book *Joy: Expanding Human Awareness,* has stated that the "close connection between the emotional and the physical is evident in the verbal idioms that have developed in social interaction. Feelings and behavior are expressed in terms of all parts of the body, of body movement, and of bodily functions" (pp. 25–26). Schutz provided a list of some of these terms that associate the physical with the emotional: "lost your head, chin up, hair-raising, get it off your chest, no backbone, tight-fisted, hard-nosed, butterflies in the stomach, brokenhearted, stiff upper lip, eyebrow lifting, sweat of your brow, stand on your own feet, tight ass, choke up, and shrug it off"—to name a few (pp. 25–26).

Five dimensions of nonverbal behavior with significant effects on communication are *kinesics, paralinguistics, proxemics, environmental factors,* and *time.* Body motion, or kinesic behavior, includes gestures, body movements, facial expressions, eye behavior, and posture (Knapp, 1972,

p. 5). Associated with the work of Birdwhistell (1970), kinesics also involves physical characteristics that remain relatively unchanged during a conversation, such as body physique, height, weight, and general appearance. In addition to observing body motion, counseling involves identifying nonverbal vocal cues called paralanguage—the "how" of the message. Paralanguage includes voice qualities and vocalizations (Trager, 1958). Silent pauses and speech errors can also be considered part of paralanguage (Knapp, 1978, p. 19). Also of interest to counselors is the area of proxemics (Hall, 1966)—that is, one's use of social and personal space. As it affects the counseling relationship, proxemics involves the size of the room, seating arrangements, touch, and distance between counselor and client.

Perception of one's environment is another important part of nonverbal behavior because people react emotionally to their surroundings. Environments can produce effects on clients such as arousal or boredom and comfort or stress depending on the degree to which an individual tunes into or screens out relevant parts of the surroundings. A fifth aspect of nonverbal behavior involves perception and use of time. Time can be a significant factor in counseling. Time factors include promptness or delay in starting and ending sessions as well as the amount of time spent in communicating with a client about particular topics or events.

☐ OBJECTIVES

1. From a list of client descriptions and nonverbal client behaviors, describe one possible meaning associated with each nonverbal behavior.
2. In an interview situation, identify as many nonverbal behaviors of the person with whom you are communicating as possible. Describe the possible meanings associated with these behaviors. The nonverbal behaviors you identify may come from any one or all of the categories of kinesics, or body motion; paralinguistics, or voice qualities; proxemics, or room space and distance; and the person's general appearance.
3. Demonstrate effective use of counselor nonverbal behaviors in a role-play interview.
4. Identify at least four out of five occasions for responding to client nonverbal behavior in an interview.

☐ CLIENT NONVERBAL BEHAVIOR

An important part of a counselor's repertory is the capacity to discriminate various nonverbal behaviors of clients and their possible meanings. Recognizing and exploring client nonverbal cues is important in counseling for several reasons. First of all, clients' nonverbal behaviors are clues about their emotions. Even more generally, nonverbal behaviors are part of clients' expressions of themselves. As Perls states, "Everything the patient does, obvious or concealed, is an expression of the self" (1973, p. 75). Much of a client's nonverbal behavior may be obvious to you but hidden to the client. Passons (1975, p. 102) points out that most clients are more aware of their words than of their nonverbal behavior. Exploring nonverbal communication may give clients a more complete understanding of their behavior.

Nonverbal client cues may represent more "leakage" than client verbal messages do (Ekman & Friesen, 1969a). Leakage is the communication of messages that are valid yet are not sent intentionally. Passons (1975) suggests that, because of this leakage, client nonverbal behavior may portray the client more accurately than verbal messages (p. 102). He notes that "nonverbal behaviors are generally more spontaneous than verbal behaviors. Words can be selected and monitored prior to being emitted. . . . Nonverbal behaviors, on the other hand, are not as easily subject to control" (p. 102). A client may come in and *tell* you one story and in nonverbal language convey a completely different story (Erickson, Rossi, & Rossi, 1976).

Knapp (1978, p. 20) points out that nonverbal and verbal behavior are interrelated. It is helpful to recognize the ways nonverbal cues support verbal messages. Knapp identifies six such ways:

1. *Repetition:* The verbal message is to "come in and sit down"; the hand gesture pointing to the room and chair is a nonverbal repeater.
2. *Contradiction:* The verbal message is "I like you," communicated with a frown and an angry tone of voice. Some evidence suggests that when we receive contradictory verbal and nonverbal messages, we tend to believe the nonverbal one.
3. *Substitution:* Often a nonverbal message is used in lieu of a verbal one. For example, if you ask someone "How are you?" and you get

a smile, the smile substitutes for a "Very good today."

4. *Complementation:* A nonverbal message can complement a verbal message by modifying or elaborating the message. For example, if someone is talking about feeling uncomfortable and begins talking faster with more speech errors, these nonverbal messages add to the verbal one of discomfort.

5. *Accent:* Nonverbal messages can emphasize verbal ones and often heighten the impact of a verbal message. For example, if you are communicating verbal concern, your message may come through stronger with nonverbal cues such as furrow of the brows, frown, or tears. The kind of emotion one conveys is detected best by facial expressions. The body conveys a better description of the intensity of the emotion (Ekman, 1964; Ekman & Friesen, 1967).

6. *Regulation:* Nonverbal communication helps to regulate the flow of conversation. Have you ever noticed that when you nod your head at someone after he or she speaks, the person tends to keep talking? But if you look away and shift in body position, the person may stop talking, at least momentarily. Whether or not we realize it, we rely on certain nonverbal cues as feedback for starting or stopping a conversation and for indicating whether the other person is listening [pp. 21–24].*

Identifying the relation between the client's verbal and nonverbal communication may yield a more accurate picture of the client, the client's feelings, and the concerns that have led the client to seek help. In addition, the counselor can detect the extent to which the client's nonverbal behavior and verbal behavior match or are congruent. Frequent discrepancies between the client's expressions may indicate lack of integration or some conflict (Passons, 1975).

Nonverbal behavior has received a great deal of attention in recent years in newspapers, magazine articles, and popular books. These publications may have value in increasing awareness of nonverbal behaviors. However, the meanings that have been attached to a particular behavior may have become oversimplified. It is important to note that the meaning of nonverbal behavior will vary with people and situations (contexts). For example, water in the eyes may be a sign of happiness and glee for one person; for another, it may mean anger, frustration, or trouble with contact lenses. A person who has a lisp may be dependent; another may have a speech impediment. Twisting, rocking, or squirming in a seat might mean anxiety for one person and a stomach cramp for someone else. Further, nonverbal behaviors of one culture may have different or even opposite meanings in another culture. Watson (1970) reports significant differences among cultures in contact and noncontact nonverbal behaviors (distance, touch, eye contact, and so on). As an example, in some cultures, avoidance of eye contact is regarded as an indication of respect. We simply caution you to be careful not to assume that nonverbal behavior has the same meaning or effect for all. It is important to remember that much of what we know about client nonverbal behavior is extrapolated from research on "typical populations" or from analog studies, thus limiting the generalizability of the results.

Our Inventory of Nonverbal Behavior (Table 4-1) presents some possible categories of nonverbal behavior in kinesics, paralinguistics, proxemics, environment, and time and the *probable* or *possible* meanings associated with each nonverbal behavior. Remember, the effect or meaning of each nonverbal behavior we have presented is very tentative; these meanings will vary with people, context, and culture. We present some possible meanings only to help increase your awareness about different behaviors, not to make you an expert on client feelings by using an inventory to generalize meanings applicable to all clients. Any client nonverbal behavior must be interpreted with respect to both the antecedents of the behavior and the counselor's reaction that follows the behavior. To show you the importance of interpreting the meaning of nonverbal behavior within a given context, we present various counselor/client interaction descriptions to accompany the nonverbal cues and possible meanings in this inventory.

Kinesics

Kinesics involves eyes, face, head, gestures, body expressions, and movements.

* From *Nonverbal Communication in Human Interaction,* 2nd Ed., by Mark L. Knapp. Copyright © 1978 by Holt, Rinehart and Winston, Inc. Reprinted by permission of CBS College Publishing.

TABLE 4-1. Inventory of nonverbal behavior

Nonverbal dimension	Observed behavior	Example of counselor/client interaction (context)	Possible effect or meaning
I. *Kinesics*			

Eyes

_____	Direct eye contact	Client has just shared concern with counselor. Counselor responds; client maintains eye contact.	Readiness or willingness for interpersonal communication or exchange; attentiveness
_____	Lack of sustained eye contact	Each time counselor brings up the topic of client's family, client looks away.	Withdrawal or avoidance of interpersonal exchange; or respect or deference
		Client demonstrates intermittent breaks in eye contact while conversing with counselor.	Respect or deference
		Client mentions sexual concerns, then abruptly looks away. When counselor initiates this topic, client looks away again.	Withdrawal from topic of conversation; discomfort or embarrassment; or preoccupation
_____	Lowering eyes—looking down or away	Client talks at some length about alternatives to present job situation; pauses briefly and looks down; then resumes speaking and eye contact with counselor.	Preoccupation
_____	Staring or fixation on person or object	Counselor has just asked client to consider consequences of a certain decision. Client is silent and gazes at a picture on the wall.	Preoccupation; possibly rigidity or uptightness
_____	Darting eyes or blinking rapidly —rapid eye movements; twitching brow	Client indicates desire to discuss a topic yet is hesitant. As counselor probes, client's eyes move around the room rapidly.	Excitation or anxiety; or wearing contact lenses
_____	Squinting or furrow on brow	Client has just asked counselor for advice. Counselor explains role, and client squints and furrows appear in client's brow.	Thought or perplexity; or avoidance of person or topic
		Counselor suggests possible things for client to explore in difficulties with parents. Client doesn't respond verbally; furrow in brow appears.	Avoidance of person or topic
_____	Moisture or tears	Client has just reported recent death of father; tears well up in client's eyes.	Sadness; frustration; sensitive areas of concern
		Client reports real progress during past week in marital communication; eyes get moist.	Happiness
_____	Eye shifts	Counselor has just asked client to remember significant events in week; client pauses and looks away, then responds and looks back.	Processing or recalling material; or keen interest; satisfaction
_____	Pupil dilation	Client discusses spouse's sudden disinterest and pupils dilate.	Alarm; or keen interest
		Client leans forward while counselor talks and pupils dilate.	Keen interest; satisfaction

Mouth

_____	Smiles	Counselor has just asked client to report positive events of the week. Client smiles, then recounts some of these instances.	Positive thought, feeling, or action in content of conversation
		Client responds with a smile to counselor's verbal greeting at beginning of interview.	Greeting

(continued)

TABLE 4-1. Inventory of nonverbal behavior   (continued)

Nonverbal dimension	Observed behavior	Example of counselor/client interaction (context)	Possible effect or meaning
I. Kinesics (continued)			
Mouth			
	Tight lips (pursed together)	Client has just described efforts at sticking to a difficult living arrangement. Pauses and purses lips together.	Stress or determination; anger or hostility
		Client just expressed irritation at counselor's lateness. Client sits with lips pursed together while counselor explains the reasons.	Anger or hostility
	Lower lip quivers or biting lip	Client starts to describe her recent experience of being raped. As client continues to talk, her lower lip quivers; occasionally she bites her lip.	Anxiety or sadness
		Client discusses loss of parental support after a recent divorce. Client bites her lip after discussing this.	Sadness
	Open mouth without speaking	Counselor has just expressed feelings about a block in the relationship. Client's mouth drops open; client says he was not aware of it.	Surprise; or suppression of yawn — fatigue
		It has been a long session. As counselor talks, client's mouth parts slightly.	Suppression of yawn — fatigue
Facial Expressions			
	Eye contact with smiles	Client talks very easily and smoothly, occasionally smiling; maintains eye contact for most of session.	Happiness or comfortableness
	Eyes strained; furrow on brow; mouth tight	Client has just reported strained situation with a child. Then client sits with lips pursed together and a frown.	Anger; or concern; sadness
	Eyes rigid, mouth rigid (unanimated)	Client states she or he has nothing to say; there is no evident expression or alertness on client's face.	Preoccupation; anxiety; fear
	Face flushes, red blotches appear on neck	Client has started to discuss a sexual concern.	Anxiety, discomfort, embarrassment
Head			
	Nodding head up and down	Client just expressed concern over the status of her health; counselor reflects client's feelings. Client nods head and says "That's right."	Confirmation; agreement; or listening, attending
		Client nods head during counselor explanation.	Listening; attending
	Shaking head from left to right	Counselor has just suggested that client's continual lateness to sessions may be an issue that needs to be discussed. Client responds with "No" and shakes head from left to right.	Disagreement; or disapproval
	Hanging head down, jaw down toward chest	Counselor initiates topic of termination. Client lowers head toward chest, then says he is not ready to stop the counseling sessions.	Sadness; concern

(continued)

TABLE 4-1. Inventory of nonverbal behavior (continued)

Nonverbal dimension	Observed behavior	Example of counselor/client interaction (context)	Possible effect or meaning
I. Kinesics (continued)			
Shoulders			
	___ Shrugging	Client reports that spouse just walked out with no explanation. Client shrugs shoulders while describing this.	Uncertainty; or ambivalence
	___ Leaning forward	Client has been sitting back in the chair. Counselor discloses something about herself; client leans forward and asks counselor a question about the experience.	Eagerness; attentiveness, openness to communication
	___ Slouched, stooped, rounded, or turned away from person	Client reports feeling inadequate and defeated because of poor grades; slouches in chair after saying this.	Sadness or ambivalence; or lack of receptivity to interpersonal exchange
		Client reports difficulty in talking. As counselor pursues this, client slouches in chair and turns shoulders away from counselor.	Lack of receptivity to interpersonal exchange
Arms and hands			
	___ Arms folded across chest	Counselor has just initiated conversation. Client doesn't respond verbally; sits back in chair with arms crossed against chest.	Avoidance of interpersonal exchange or dislike
	___ Trembling and fidgety hands	Client expresses fear of suicide; hands tremble while talking about this.	Anxiety or anger
		In a loud voice, client expresses resentment; client's hands shake while talking.	Anger
	___ Fist clenching to objects or holding hands tightly	Client has just come in for initial interview. Says that he or she feels uncomfortable; hands are clasped together tightly.	Anxiety or anger
		Client expresses hostility toward boss; clenches fists while talking.	Anger
	___ Arms unfolded— arms and hands gesturing in conversation	Counselor has just asked a question; client replies and gestures during reply.	Accenting or emphasizing point in conversation; or openness to interpersonal exchange
		Counselor initiates new topic. Client readily responds; arms are unfolded at this time.	Openness to interpersonal exchange
	___ Rarely gesturing, hands and arms stiff	Client arrives for initial session. Responds to counselor's questions with short answers. Arms are kept down at side.	Tension or anger
		Client has been referred; sits with arms down at side while explaining reasons for referral and irritation at being here.	Anger
Legs and feet			
	___ Legs and feet appear comfortable and relaxed	Client's legs and feet are relaxed without excessive movement while client freely discusses personal concerns.	Openness to interpersonal exchange; relaxation
	___ Crossing and uncrossing legs repeatedly	Client is talking rapidly in spurts about problems; continually crosses and uncrosses legs while doing so.	Anxiety; depression

(continued)

TABLE 4-1. Inventory of nonverbal behavior (continued)

Nonverbal dimension	Observed behavior	Example of counselor/client interaction (context)	Possible effect or meaning
Legs and feet			
——	Foot tapping	Client is tapping feet during a lengthy counselor summary; client interrupts counselor to make a point.	Anxiety; impatience—wanting to make a point
——	Legs and feet appear stiff and controlled	Client is open and relaxed while talking about job. When counselor introduces topic of marriage, client's legs become more rigid.	Uptightness or anxiety; closed to extensive interpersonal exchange
Total body			
——	Facing other person squarely or leaning forward	Client shares a concern and faces counselor directly while talking; continues to face counselor while counselor responds.	Openness to interpersonal communication and exchange
——	Turning of body orientation at an angle, not directly facing person, or slouching in seat	Client indicates some difficulty in "getting into" interview. Counselor probes for reasons; client turns body away.	Less openness to interpersonal exchange
——	Rocking back and forth in chair or squirming in seat	Client indicates a lot of nervousness about an approaching conflict situation. Client rocks as this is discussed.	Concern; worry; anxiety
——	Stiff—sitting erect and rigidly on edge of chair	Client indicates some uncertainty about direction of interview; sits very stiff and erect at this time.	Tension; anxiety; concern
——	Repetitive twisting of hair, tapping of fingers	Client responds with short, minimal, non-self-revealing responses.	Feeling distracted, bored, or uncomfortable —or indication of some unexpressed emotion
——	Breathing becomes slower and deeper	Client begins to settle back in chair and relate a positive event that occurred during the week.	Client is feeling more comfortable and relaxed; breathing changes reflect the decreased arousal

II. *Paralinguistics*

Voice level and pitch			
——	Whispering or inaudibility	Client has been silent for a long time. Counselor probes; client responds, but in a barely audible voice.	Difficulty in disclosing
——	Pitch changes	Client is speaking at a moderate voice level while discussing job. Then client begins to talk about boss, and voice pitch rises considerably.	Topics of conversation have different emotional meanings
Fluency in speech			
——	Stuttering, hesitations, speech errors	Client is talking rapidly about feeling uptight in certain social situations; client stutters and makes some speech errors while doing so.	Sensitivity about topic in conversation; or anxiety and discomfort

(continued)

TABLE 4-1. Inventory of nonverbal behavior (continued)

Nonverbal dimension	Observed behavior	Example of counselor/client interaction (context)	Possible effect or meaning
II. *Paralinguistics (continued)*			
Fluency in speech			
	____ Whining or lisp	Client is complaining about having a hard time losing weight; voice goes up like a whine.	Dependency or emotional emphasis
	____ Rate of speech slow, rapid, or jerky	Client begins interview talking slowly about a bad weekend. As topic shifts to client's feelings about himself, client talks more rapidly.	Sensitivity to topics of conversation; or topics have different emotional meanings
	____ Silence	Client comes in and counselor invites client to talk; client remains silent.	Reluctance to talk; or preoccupation
		Counselor has just asked client a question. Client pauses and thinks over a response.	Preoccupation; or desire to continue speaking after making a point
III. *Proxemics*			
Distance			
	____ Moves away	Counselor has just confronted client; client moves back before responding verbally.	Signal that space has been invaded; increased arousal, discomfort
	____ Moves closer	Midway through session, client moves chair toward helper.	Seeking closer interaction, more intimacy
Position in room			
	____ Sits behind or next to an object in the room, such as table or desk	A new client comes in and sits in a chair that is distant from counselor.	Seeking protection or more space
	____ Sits near counselor without any intervening objects	Client who has been to see counselor before chooses chair closest to counselor.	Expression of adequate comfort level
Touch			
	____ Handshake accompanied by smile and verbal greeting	Client greets counselor and returns counselor's outstretched arm for handshake.	Desire to initiate interaction nonverbally
	____ Touch on client arm	Counselor touches client's arm when client is expressing concern over her extremely ill child.	Desire to convey support and comfort
IV. *Environment*			
	____ Counseling room is small, has subdued colors and soft lights	Client states he feels lethargic. Lack of self-disclosure is also evident.	So little arousal associated with counseling environment that client is too comfortable to "work"
V. *Time*			
	____ Client discusses many unrelated topics during session	Counselor starts to terminate session. Client then states she has a "big problem" to bring up.	Anxiety about bringing up problem or manipulation to get counselor to spend more time with her

TABLE 4-1. Inventory of nonverbal behavior (continued)

Nonverbal dimension	Observed behavior	Example of counselor/client interaction (context)	Possible effect or meaning
V. *Time (continued)*			
———	Repeated delays by client in responding to counselor	After counselor makes a statement or asks a question, client waits for a while before responding verbally.	Hesitation in responding to counselor or discomfort in relationship

Eyes. In our culture, we show a great deal of interest in one another's eyes. Western culture particularly emphasizes the importance of visual contact in interpersonal interactions. Therapists who are sensitive to the eye area of clients may detect various client emotions, such as the following:

Surprise: Eyebrows are raised so that they appear curved and high.
Fear: Brows are raised and drawn together.
Anger: Brows are lowered and drawn together. Vertical lines show up between the brows. The eyes may appear to have a "cold stare."
Sadness: Inner corners of the eyebrows are drawn up until the inner corners of the upper eyelids are raised.

Also significant to counselor/client interactions is eye contact (also called "direct mutual gaze"). Eye contact may indicate expressions of feeling, willingness for interpersonal exchange, or a desire to continue or stop talking. Lack of eye contact or looking away may signal withdrawal, embarrassment, or discomfort (Exline & Winters, 1965). Contrary to popular opinion, lack of eye contact does not seem to suggest deception or lack of truthfulness (Sitton & Griffin, 1981). People who generally avoid eye contact may nevertheless make eye contact when they seek feedback. Eye contact may also signal a desire to pause in the conversation or to say something (Knapp, 1978). The more shared glances there are between two persons, the higher the level of emotional involvement and comfort. An averted gaze may serve to hide shame over expressing a particular feeling that is seen as culturally or socially taboo (Exline & Winters, 1965). Any kind of reduced eye movement, such as staring or fixated eyes, may signal rigidity or preoccupation in thought (Singer, 1975). Darting or rapid eye movement may mean excitation, anger, or poorly fitting contact lenses. Excessive blinking (normal = 6 to 10 times per minute in adults) may be related to anxiety. During periods of attentiveness and concentration, blinking usually decreases in frequency. Moisture or tears in the eyes may have contrasting emotional meanings for different people. Eye shifts—away from the counselor to a wall, for example—may indicate that the client is processing or recalling material (Singer, 1975). Pupil dilation, which is an autonomic (involuntary) response, may indicate emotional arousal, attentiveness, and interest (Hess, 1975). Although pupil dilation seems to occur under conditions that represent positive interpersonal attitudes, little or no evidence supports the belief that the opposite (pupil constriction) is associated with negative attitudes toward people (Knapp, 1978).

In counseling, *more mutual gazing,* or eye contact, seems to occur when—

1. Greater physical distance exists between the counselor and client.
2. Comfortable, less personal topics are discussed.
3. Interpersonal involvement exists between the counselor and client.
4. You are listening rather than talking.
5. You are female.
6. You are from a culture that emphasizes visual contact in interaction.

Less gazing occurs when—

1. The counselor and client are physically close.
2. Difficult, intimate topics are being discussed.
3. Either the counselor or the client is not interested in the other's reactions.
4. You are talking rather than listening.
5. You are embarrassed, ashamed, or trying to hide something.
6. You are from a culture that has sanctions on visual contact during some kinds of interpersonal interactions.

Some behaviors of the eyes and their conjectured meanings are presented in Table 4-1; however, these meanings must be viewed idiosyncratically for each client, depending on the context and culture.

Mouth. Smiles are associated with the emotions of happiness and joy. Tight lips may mean stress, frustration, hostility, or anger. Lower-lip quivering or biting lips may connote anxiety or sadness. An open mouth without speaking may indicate surprise or difficulty in talking (see Table 4-1).

Facial expressions. The face of the other person may be the most important stimulus in an interaction, because it is the primary communicator of emotional information (Ekman, Friesen, & Ellsworth, 1972). Facial expressions are used to initiate or terminate conversation, provide feedback on the comments of others, underline or support verbal communication, and convey emotions. Most of the time, the face conveys multiple emotions (Ekman & Friesen, 1969b). For example, one emotion may be conveyed in one part of the face and another in a different area. It is rare for one's face to express only a single emotion at a time. More often than not, the face depicts a blend of varying emotions.

Different facial areas express different emotions. Happiness, surprise, and disgust may be conveyed through the lower face (mouth and jaw region) and the eye area, whereas sadness is conveyed with the eyes. The lower face and brows express anger; fear is usually indicated by the eyes (Ekman, Friesen, & Tomkins, 1971). Although it is hard to "read" someone by facial cues alone, these cues may support other nonverbal indexes of emotion within the context of an interview. The facial expressions listed in Table 4-1 are combinations of the mouth and eye regions.

Facial expressions conveying the basic emotions described above do *not* seem to vary much among cultures. According to Harper, Wiens, and Matarazzo (1978, p. 99), "There is considerable evidence that facial expressions of emotion themselves are 'universal' or not 'culture bound.'" In other words, primary or basic emotions such as anger, disgust, fear, sadness, and happiness do seem to be represented by the same facial expressions across cultures, although individual cultural norms may influence how and when such emotions are expressed.

Head. The movements of the head can be a rich source for interpreting a person's emotional or affective state. The head held erect, facing the other person in a relaxed way, indicates receptivity to interpersonal communication. Nodding the head up and down implies confirmation or agreement. Shaking the head from left to right may signal disapproval or disagreement. Shaking the head with accompanying leg movements may connote anger. Holding the head rigidly may mean anxiety or anger, and hanging the head down toward the chest may reflect disapproval or sadness. See Table 4-1 for an outline of these five behaviors and their associated meanings.

Shoulders. The orientation of the shoulders may give clues to a person's attitude about interpersonal exchanges. Shoulders leaning forward may indicate eagerness, attentiveness, or receptivity to interpersonal communication. Slouched, stooped, rounded, or turned-away shoulders may mean that the person is not receptive to interpersonal exchanges. This posture also may reflect sadness or ambivalence. Shrugging shoulders may mean uncertainty, puzzlement, ambivalence, or frustration.

Arms and hands. The arms and hands can be very expressive of an individual's emotional state. Arms folded across the chest may signal avoidance of interpersonal exchange or reluctance to disclose. Anxiety or anger may be reflected in trembling and fidgety hands or clenching fists. Arms and hands that rarely gesture and are stiffly positioned may mean tension, anxiety, or anger. Relaxed, unfolded arms and hands gesturing during conversation can signal openness to interpersonal involvement or accentuation of points in conversation. The autonomic response of perspiration of the palms may reflect anxiety or arousal.

Legs and feet. If the legs and feet appear comfortable and relaxed, the person may be signaling openness to interpersonal exchange. Shuffling feet or a tapping foot may mean that the person is experiencing some anxiety or impatience or wants to make a point. Repeatedly crossing and uncrossing legs may indicate anxiety, depression, or impatience. A person who appears to be very "controlled" or to have "stiff" legs and feet may be uptight, anxious, or closed to an extensive interpersonal exchange (see Table 4-1).

Total body and body movements. Most body movements do not have precise social meanings. Body movements are learned and culture-specific.

The body movements discussed in this section are derived from analyses of (and therefore most applicable to) White adults from middle and upper socioeconomic classes in the United States.

Body movements are not produced randomly. Instead, they appear to be linked to human speech. From birth, there seems to be an effort to synchronize body movements and speech sounds. In adults, lack of synchrony may be a sign of pathology. Lack of synchrony in body movements and speech between two persons may indicate an absence of listening behavior on the part of both (Condon & Ogston, 1966).

One of the most important functions of body movements is *regulation.* Various body movements regulate or maintain an interpersonal interaction. For example, important body movements that accompany the counselor's verbal greeting of a client include eye gaze, smiling, use of hand gestures, and a vertical or sideways motion of the head (Krivonos & Knapp, 1975). Body movements are also useful to terminate an interaction, as at the end of a counseling interview. Nonverbal exit or leave-taking behaviors accompanying a verbal summary statement include decreased eye gaze and positioning of your body near the exit. In terminating an interaction, particularly a therapeutic one, it is also important to display nonverbal behaviors that signify support, such as smiling, shaking the client's hand, touching the client on the arm or shoulder, and nodding your head. As Knapp (1978, p. 213) explains, "Supportiveness tends to offset any negativity which might arise from encounter termination signals while simultaneously setting a positive mood for the next encounter—that is, our conversation has terminated but our relationship hasn't."

Another way that body movements regulate an interaction involves *turn taking*—the exchange of speaker and listener roles within a conversation. Most of the time we take turns rather automatically. "Without much awareness for what we are doing, we use body movements, vocalizations, and some verbal behavior which often seems to accomplish this turn-taking with surprising efficiency" (Knapp, 1978, p. 213). Effective turn taking is important in a counseling interaction because it contributes to the perception that you and the client have a good relationship and that, as the counselor, you are a competent communicator. Conversely, ineffective turn taking may mean that a client perceives you as rude (too many inter-

ruptions) or as dominating (not enough talk time for the client).

Duncan (1972, 1974) has found a variety of nonverbal behaviors, called *turn signals,* that regulate the exchange of speaking and listening roles. These turn signals are described in this section. *Turn yielding* occurs when the therapist (as speaker) wants to stop talking and expects a response from the client (as listener). To engage in effective turn yielding, the counselor can ask a question and talk more slowly, slow down the rate of speech, drawl on the last syllable of the last word, utter a "trailer" such as "you know," or use silence. Terminating body movements and gazing at the client will also indicate that it is now the client's turn to talk. If, after a lengthy silence, the client does not respond, more explicit turn-yielding cues may be used, such as touching the client or raising and holding your eyebrows in expectation. Use of these more explicit nonverbal cues may be particularly important with a quiet, nontalkative client.

Turn maintaining occurs when the therapist (or client) wants to keep talking and not yield a turn to the other person, probably because an important idea is being expressed. Signals that indicate turn maintaining include talking louder and continuing or even increasing the gestures and other body movements accompanying your words. Counselors do not want to maintain their turns too often, or the client is likely to feel frustrated and unable to make a point. Conversely, overtalkative clients may try to take control of the interview by maintaining rather than yielding turns.

Turn requesting occurs when either the therapist or the client is listening and wants to talk. Turn requesting may be signified by an upraised index finger, often accompanied by an audible inspiration of breath and straightening or tightening of one's posture. The counselor can use turn-requesting signals more frequently with an overtalkative, rambling client who tends to hang on rather than give up his or her turn as speaker. In fact, to encourage a client to finish more quickly, the counselor can use rapid head nods accompanied by verbalizations of pseudoagreement such as "Yes," "Mm-hmm," and "I see" (Knapp, 1978).

Turn denying occurs when we get a turn-yielding cue from the speaker but don't want to talk. For example, if the client is nontalkative or if the counselor wants the client to take more responsibility for the interaction, the counselor may choose to deny or give up a turn in order to prompt the client to continue talking. Turn-denying signals include a relaxed body posture, silence, and eye gaze. The counselor will also want to exhibit behaviors that show continuing involvement in the ideas expressed by the client by smiling, nodding, or using minimal verbal prompts such as "Mm-hmm."

In addition to regulation, body movements also serve the function of *adaptors*. Adaptors may include such behaviors as picking, scratching, rubbing, and tapping. In counseling, it is important to note the frequency with which a client uses nonverbal adaptors, because these behaviors seem to be associated with emotional arousal and psychological discomfort (Dittmann, 1962; Ekman & Friesen, 1972). Body touching may reflect preoccupation with oneself and withdrawal from the interaction at hand (Freedman, 1972). A client who uses adaptors frequently may be uncomfortable with the counselor or with the topic of discussion. The counselor can use the frequency of client adaptors as an index of the client's overall comfort level during counseling.

Another important aspect of a client's total body is his or her breathing. Changes in breathing rate (slower, faster) or depth (shallower, deeper) provide clues about comfort level, feelings, and significant issues. As clients relax, for example, their breathing usually becomes slower and deeper. Faster, more shallow breathing is more often associated with arousal, distress, discomfort, and anxiety.

Paralinguistics

Paralinguistics includes such extralinguistic variables as voice level (volume), pitch (intonation), rate of speech, and fluency of speech. Pauses and silence also belong in this category. Paralinguistic cues are those pertaining to *how* a message is delivered, although occasionally these vocal cues represent what is said as well.

Vocal cues are important in counseling interactions for several reasons. First, they help to manage the interaction by playing an important role in the exchange of speaker and listener roles — that is, turn taking. As you may recall from the discussion of body movements, certain vocalizations are used to yield, maintain, request, or deny turns. For example, decreased pitch is associated with turn yielding, whereas increased volume and rate of speech are associated with turn maintaining. Second, vocal characteristics convey data about a client's emotional states. You can identify the presence of basic emotions from a client's vocal cues if you are able to make auditory discriminations. In recognizing emotions from vocal cues, it is also important to be knowledgeable about various vocal characteristics of basic emotions. For example, a client who speaks slowly and softly may be feeling sad or may be reluctant to discuss a sensitive topic. Increased volume and rate of speech are usually signs of anger or happiness (see also Table 4-1). Changes in voice level and pitch should be interpreted along with accompanying changes in topics of conversation and changes in other nonverbal behaviors.

Voice level may vary among cultures. Sue and Sue (1977) point out that some Americans have louder voice levels than people of other cultures. In counseling a client from a different cultural background, an American counselor should not automatically conclude that the client's lower voice volume indicates weakness or shyness (Sue & Sue, p. 427).

Vocal cues in the form of speech disturbances or aspects of *fluency* in speech also convey important information for therapists, since client anxiety or discomfort is often detected by identifying the type and frequency of client speech errors. Most speech errors become more frequent as anxiety and discomfort increase (Knapp, 1978).

Pauses and silence are another part of paralinguistics that can give the counselor clues about the level of arousal and anxiety experienced by the client. There are two types of pauses — filled and unfilled.

Filled pauses are those filled simply with some type of phonation such as "uh," or stutters, false starts, repetitions, and slips of the tongue (Knapp, 1978, p. 356). Filled pauses are associated with emotional arousal and anxiety (Knapp, 1978). A client may be more likely to make a false start or a slip of the tongue when anxious or uncomfortable.

Unfilled pauses are those in which no sound occurs. Unfilled pauses occur to give the person time to interpret a message and to make a decision about past, present, or future responses. Unfilled pauses, or periods of silence, serve various functions in a counseling interview. The purpose of an unfilled pause often depends on whether the pause is initiated by the counselor or client. Clients use silence to express emotions, to reflect about an issue, to recall an idea or feeling, to avoid a topic, or to catch up on the progress of the moment. Counselor-initiated silences are most effective when used with a particular purpose in mind, such as reducing the counselor's level of activity, slowing down the pace of the session, giving the *client* time to think, or transferring some responsibility to the client through turn yielding or turn denying. When therapists pause to meet their own needs, as, for example, because they are at a loss for words, the effects of silence may or may not be so therapeutic. As Hackney and Cormier (1979, p. 40) observe, in such instances, when the effect is therapeutic, the counselor is apt to feel lucky rather than competent.

Proxemics

Proxemics concerns the concept of environmental and personal space (Hall, 1966). As it applies to a counseling interaction, proxemics includes use of space relative to the counseling room, arrangement of the furniture, seating arrangements, and distance between counselor and client. Proxemics also includes a variable that seems to be very important to any human interaction — territoriality. Many people are possessive not only of their belongings but of the space around them. It is important for therapists to communicate nonverbal sensitivity to a client's need for space. A client who feels that his or her space or territory has been encroached on may behave in ways intended to restore the proper distance. Such behaviors may include looking away, changing the topic to a less personal one, or crossing one's arms to provide a "frontal barrier" (Knapp, 1978, p. 119).

In counseling, a distance of three to four feet between counselor and client seems to be the least anxiety-producing and most productive, at least for adult, middle-class Americans (Lecomte, Bernstein, & Dumont, 1981). For these Americans, closer distances may inhibit verbal productivity (Schulz & Barefoot, 1974), although females in Western cultures are generally more tolerant of less personal space than males, especially when interacting with other females (Harper et al., 1978). Disturbed clients also seem to require greater interaction distance (Harper et al., 1978). These spatial limits (three to four feet) may be inappropriate for clients of varying ages or cultures. The very young and very old seem to elicit interaction at closer distances. People from "contact" cultures (cultures where interactants face one another more directly, interact closer to one another, and use more touch and direct eye contact) may use different distances for interpersonal interactions than people from "noncontact" cultures (Watson,

1970). In short, unlike facial expressions, distance setting has no universals.

An important use of proxemics in counseling is to note proxemic *shifts* such as increasing or decreasing space or moving forward or backward. Some evidence suggests that proxemic shifts signal important segments or hiatus points of an interaction, such as the beginning or ending of a topic or a shift to a different subject (Erickson, 1975). Proxemic shifts can give counselors clues about when the client is initiating a new topic, is finishing with a topic, or is avoiding a topic by changing the subject.

Another aspect of proxemics involves seating and furniture arrangement. In Western cultures, most therapists prefer a seating arrangement with no intervening desk or objects, although many clients like to have the protective space or "body buffer" of a desk corner (Harper et al., 1978).

Seating and spatial arrangements are an important part of family therapy as well. Successful family therapists pay attention to family proxemics such as the following: How far apart do family members sit from each other? Who sits next to whom? Who stays closest to the therapist? Answers to these questions about family proxemics provide information about family rules, relationships, boundaries, alliances, roles, and so on.

A final aspect of proxemics has to do with touch. Although touch can be a powerful nonverbal stimulus, its effects in the counseling interaction have rarely been examined. A counselor-initiated touch may be perceived by the client as positive or negative, depending on the type of touch (expression of caring versus intimate gesture) and the context, or situation (supportive versus evaluative). In two recent studies, counseling touch consisting of handshakes and touches to the arm and back had a significant positive effect on the client's evaluation of counseling (Alagna, Whitcher, Fisher, & Wicas, 1979) and on the client's perceptions of the counselor's expertness (Hubble, Noble, & Robinson, 1981). According to Alagna et al. (1979, p. 471), these results

> point up the possibility of setting aside some of the reservations that practitioners experience when they think about physically contacting a client, since under no conditions did communication by touch lead to negative reactions. However, while the effect of touch in this experiment was consistently positive, it is obvious that under certain conditions (e.g. overtly sexual intent), touch in counseling could have negative effects.

Counselors should also be aware that ethical standards such as those adopted by the American Association for Counseling and Development (1981) and the American Psychological Association (1981) state that any form of sexual intimacy with clients, including sexuality in touch, is unethical.

Environment

Counseling and therapy take place in some surroundings, or environment—typically an office, although other indoor and outdoor environments can be used. The same surroundings can affect clients in different ways. Surroundings are perceived as arousing or nonarousing (Mehrabian, 1976). If a client reacts to an environment with low arousal and mild pleasure, the client will feel comfortable and relaxed. Environments need to be moderately arousing so that the client feels relaxed enough to explore her or his problems and to self-disclose. If the client feels so comfortable that the desire to work on a problem is inhibited, the therapist might consider increasing the arousal cues associated with the surroundings by moving the furniture around, using brighter colors, using more light, or even increasing vocal expressiveness. Therapists who talk louder and faster and use more expressive intonation patterns are greater sources of arousal for those around them (Mehrabian, 1976).

An important concept for considering the effects of environmental arousal on clients is *stimulus screening*—the extent to which a person characteristically screens out the less relevant parts of the environment and thereby effectively reduces the environmental load and the person's own arousal level (Mehrabian, 1976). This concept is useful for understanding different reactions of clients to the same room or office. Individuals who screen their environment well, or "screeners," select various parts of their surroundings to which they respond. As a result, they are more focused on key aspects of their surroundings because they screen out less relevant components. Nonscreeners, in contrast, are less selective in what they respond to in any environment. Consequently, nonscreeners experience places as more complex and loaded, which may result in too much arousal and even stress (Mehrabian, 1976). Overall, nonscreeners are more sensitive to the emotional reactions of others and to subtle changes in their environment and tend to react more strongly to such changes.

Time

Time has several dimensions that can affect a therapeutic interaction. One aspect has to do with the counselor's and client's perception of time and promptness or delays in initiating or terminating topics and sessions. Many clients will feel put off by delays or rescheduled appointments and, conversely, feel appreciated and valued when extra time is spent with them. Clients may communicate anxiety or resistance by being late or by waiting until the end of a session to bring up a significant topic. Perceptions of time also vary. Some persons have a highly structured view of time, so that being "on time" or ready to see the counselor (or client) is important. Others have a more casual view of time and do not feel offended or put off if the counselor is late for the appointment and do not expect the counselor to be upset when they arrive later than the designated time.

LEARNING ACTIVITIES #9: CLIENT NONVERBAL COMMUNICATION

I. The purpose of this activity is to have you sample some nonverbal behaviors associated with varying emotions for different regions of the body. You can do this in dyads or in a small group. Act out each of the five emotions listed below, using your face, body, arms, legs, and voice.

1. Sadness, depression
2. Pleasure, satisfaction
3. Anxiety, agitation
4. Anger
5. Confusion, uncertainty

As an example, if the emotion to be portrayed were "surprise," you would show how your eyes, mouth, face, arms, hands, legs and feet, and total body might behave in terms of movement or posture, and you would indicate what your voice level and pitch would be like and how fluent your speech might be. After someone portrays one emotion, other members of the group can share how their nonverbal behaviors associated with the same emotion might differ.

II. This activity will help you develop greater sensitivity to nonverbal behaviors of clients. It can be done

(continued)

in dyads or triads. Select one person to assume the role of the communicator and another to assume the role of the listener. A third person can act as observer. As the communicator, recall a recent time when you felt either (1) very happy, (2) very sad, and (3) very angry. Your task is to retrieve that experience *nonverbally*. Do *not say* anything to the listener, and do *not* tell the listener in advance which of the three emotions you are going to recall. Simply decide which of the three you will recall and tell the listener

when to begin. The listener's task is to *observe* the communicator, to *note* nonverbal behaviors and changes during the recall, and, from these, to *guess* which of the three emotional experiences the person was retrieving. After about three to four minutes, stop the interaction to process it. Observers can add behaviors and changes they noted at this time. After the communicator has retrieved one of the emotions, switch roles.

___

☐ HOW TO WORK WITH CLIENT NONVERBAL BEHAVIOR

Many theoretical approaches emphasize the importance of working with client nonverbal behavior. For example, behavioral counselors may recognize and point out particular nonverbal behaviors of a client that constitute effective or ineffective social skills (Eisler & Frederiksen, 1980). A client who consistently mumbles and avoids eye contact may find such behaviors detrimental to establishing effective interpersonal relationships. Use of effective nonverbal behaviors also forms a portion of assertion training programs (Otter & Guerra, 1976). In Transactional Analysis (TA), nonverbal behaviors are used to assess "ego states," or parts of one's personality used to communicate and relate to others. For example, the "critical" or controlling parent may be associated with a condescending and blaming voice tone, pointing fingers, frowning, hands on hips, and so forth (Woollams & Brown, 1979). TA therapists also note how a client's nonverbal behavior may keep communication going (complementary transactions) or break communication down (crossed transactions). Client-centered therapists use client nonverbal behaviors as indicators of client feelings and emotions. Gestalt therapists help clients recognize their nonverbal behaviors in order to increase awareness of themselves and of conflicts or discrepancies. For example, a client may say "Yes, I want to get my degree" and at the same time shake his head no and lower his voice tone and eyes. Body-oriented therapists actively use body language as a tool for understanding hidden and unresolved "business," conflicts, and personality. Adlerian counselors use nonverbal reactions of clients as an aid to discovering purposes (often hidden) of behavior and mistaken logic. Family therapists are concerned with a family's nonverbal (analogic) communication as well as verbal (digital) communication. A tool based on

family nonverbal communication is known as "family sculpture" (Duhl, Kantor, & Duhl, 1973). Family sculpture is a nonverbal arrangement of people placed in various physical positions in space to represent their relationship to one another. In an extension of this technique, family *choreography* (Papp, 1976), the sculptures or spatial arrangements are purposely moved to realign existing relationships and create new patterns.

Passons (1975) has described five ways of responding to client nonverbal behavior in an interview. His suggestions are useful because they represent ways of working with clients nonverbally that are consistent with various theoretical orientations. These five ways are the following:

1. Ascertain the congruence between the client's verbal and nonverbal behavior.
2. Note or respond to discrepancies, or mixed verbal and nonverbal messages.
3. Respond to or note nonverbal behaviors when the client is silent or not speaking.
4. Focus on nonverbal behaviors to change the content of the interview.
5. Note changes in client nonverbal behavior that have occurred in an interview or over a series of sessions.

Congruence between Behaviors

The counselor can determine whether the client's verbal message is congruent with his or her nonverbal behavior. An example of congruence is when the client expresses confusion about a situation accompanied by squinting of the eyes or furrowing of the brow. Another client may say "I'm really happy with the way things have been working since I've been coming to see you," which is correlated with eye contact, relaxed body posture, and a smile. The counselor can respond in one of two ways to congruence between the client's verbal and nonverbal behaviors. A counselor might make a *mental* note of the congruence in behaviors. Or the counselor could ask the client to explain the meaning of the nonverbal behaviors. For example, the counselor could ask: "While you were saying this is a difficult topic for you, your eyes were moist, your head was lowered, and your hands were fidgety. I wonder what that means?"

Mixed Messages

The counselor can observe the client and see whether what the client is saying and the client's nonverbal behavior are mixed messages. Contradictory verbal and nonverbal behavior would be apparent with a client who says "I feel really [pause] excited about the relationship. I've never [pause] experienced anything like this before" while looking down and leaning away. The counselor has at least three options for dealing with a verbal/nonverbal discrepancy. The first is to note mentally the discrepancies between what the client says and the nonverbal body and paralinguistic cues with which the client delivers the message. The second option is to describe the discrepancy to the client, as in this example: "You say you are excited about the relationship, but your head was hanging down while you were talking, and you spoke with a lot of hesitation." (Other examples of confronting the client with discrepancies can be found in Chapter 6.) The third option is to ask the client, "I noticed you looked away and paused as you said that. What does that mean?"

Nonverbal Behavior during Silence

The third way a counselor can respond to the nonverbal behavior of the client is during periods of silence in the interview. Silence does not mean that nothing is happening! Also remember that silence has different meanings from one culture to another. In some cultures, silence is a sign of respect, not an indication that the client does not wish to talk more (Sue & Sue, 1977). The counselor can focus on client nonverbal behavior during silence by noting the silence mentally, by describing the silence to the client, or by asking the client about the meaning of the silence.

Changing the Content of the Interview

It may be necessary with some clients to change the flow of the interview, because to continue on the same topic may be unproductive. Changing the flow may also be useful when the client is delivering a lot of information or is rambling. In such instances, the counselor can distract the client from the verbal content by redirecting the focus to the client's nonverbal behavior.

For "unproductive" content in the client's messages, the counselor might say "Our conversation so far has been dwelling on the death of your brother and your relationship with your parents. Right now, I would like you to focus on what we have been doing while we have been talking. Are you aware of what you have been doing with your hands?"

Such counselor distractions can be either productive or detrimental to the progress of therapy. Passons (1975) suggests that these distractions will be useful if they bring the client in touch with "present behavior." If they take the client away from the current flow of feelings, the distractions will be unproductive (p. 105). Passons also states that "experience, knowledge of the counselor, and intuition" all contribute to the counselor's decision to change the content of the interview by focusing on client nonverbal behavior.

Changes in Client Nonverbal Behavior

For some clients, nonverbal behaviors may be indexes of therapeutic change. For example, at the beginning of counseling, a client's arms may be folded across the chest. Later, the client may be more relaxed, with arms unfolded and hands gesturing during conversation. At the initial stages of counseling, the client may blush, perspire, and exhibit frequent body movement during the interview when certain topics are discussed. Later in counseling, these nonverbal behaviors may disappear and be replaced with a more comfortable and relaxed posture. Again, depending on the timing, the counselor can respond to nonverbal changes covertly or overtly.

This decision to respond to client nonverbal behavior covertly (with a mental note) or overtly depends not only on your purpose in focusing on nonverbal behavior but also on timing. Passons (1975) believes that counselors need to make overt responses such as immediacy (see Chapter 2) to client nonverbal behavior early in the therapeutic process. Otherwise, when you call attention to something the client is doing nonverbally after the tenth session or so, the client is likely to feel confused and bewildered by what is seen as a change in your approach. Another aspect of timing involves discriminating the likely effects of responding to the nonverbal behavior with immediacy. If the immediacy is likely to contribute to increased understanding and continuity of the session, it may be helpful. If, however, the timing of your response interrupts the client's flow of exploration, your response may be distracting and interfering.

When responding to client nonverbal behavior with immediacy, it is helpful to be descriptive rather than evaluative and to phrase your responses in a tentative way. For example, saying something like "Are you aware that as you're talking with Gene, your neck and face are getting red splotches of color?" is likely to be more useful than evaluative and dogmatic comments such as "Why is your face getting red?", "You sure do have a red face," or "You're getting so red — you must feel very embarrassed about this."

LEARNING ACTIVITIES #10: RESPONDING TO CLIENT NONVERBAL BEHAVIOR

I. The purpose of this activity is to practice verbal responses to client nonverbal behaviors. One person portrays a client (1) giving congruent messages between verbal and nonverbal behavior; (2) giving mixed messages, (3) being silent, (4) rambling and delivering a lot of information, and (5) portraying a rather obvious change from the beginning of the interview to the end of the interview in nonverbal behavior. The person playing the counselor responds verbally to each of these five portrayals. After going through all these portrayals with an opportunity for the role-play counselor to respond to each, switch roles. During these role plays, try to focus primarily on your responses to the other person's nonverbal behavior.

II. With yourself and several colleagues or members of your class to help you, use spatial arrangements to portray your role in your family and to depict your perceptions of your relationship to the other members of your family. Position yourself in a room and tell the other participants where to position themselves in relation to you and one another. (If you are short one or two participants, an object can fill a gap.) After the arrangement is complete, look around you. What can you learn about your own family from this aspect of nonverbal behavior? Do you like what you see and feel? If you could change your position in the family, where would you move? What effect would this have on you and on other family members?

III. In a role-play interaction or counseling session in which you function as the therapist, watch for some significant nonverbal behavior of the client, such as change in breathing, shifts in eye contact, voice tone, and proxemics. (Do not focus on a small nonverbal behavior out of context with the spoken words.) Focus on this behavior by asking the client whether she or he is aware of what is happening to her or his voice, body posture, eyes, or whatever. Do not interpret or assign meaning to the behavior for the client. Notice where your focus takes the client.

□ COUNSELOR NONVERBAL BEHAVIOR

As a counselor, it is important for you to pay attention to your nonverbal behavior for several reasons. First, some kinds of counselor nonverbal behavior seem to contribute to a facilitative relationship; other nonverbal behaviors may detract from the relationship. For example, "high," or facilitative, levels of such nonverbal behaviors as direct eye contact and body orientation and relaxed body posture can contribute to positive client ratings of counselor empathy even in the presence of a low-level, or detracting, verbal message (Fretz, Corn, Tuemmler, & Bellet, 1979). In addition, the degree to which clients perceive you as interpersonally attractive and as having some expertise is associated with effective nonverbal skills (Claiborn, 1979).

Because much of the research on counselor nonverbal behavior has been done with ratings of videotapes and photographs, it is difficult to specify precisely what counselor nonverbal behaviors are related to counseling effectiveness. Table 4-2 lists presumed effective and ineffective uses of counselor nonverbal behaviors. In assessing this list, it is also important to remember that the effects of various counselor nonverbal behaviors are related to contextual variables in counseling, such as type of client, verbal content, timing in session, and client's perceptual style (Hill, Siegelman, Gronsky, Sturniolo, & Fretz, 1981; Seay & Altekruse, 1979). Thus, clients who subjectively have a favorable impression of the therapist may not be adversely affected by an ineffective, or "low-level," nonverbal behavior such as tapping your finger or fiddling with your pen or hair (we still recommend you avoid such distracting mannerisms). Similarly, just engaging in effective use of

TABLE 4-2. Effective and ineffective counselor nonverbal behavior

Ineffective use	Nonverbal mode of communication	Effective use
Doing any of these things will probably close off or slow down the conversation		These behaviors encourage talk because they show acceptance and respect for the other person
Distant or very close	Space	Approximately arm's length
Away	Movement	Toward
Slouching; rigid; seated leaning away	Posture	Relaxed but attentive; seated leaning slightly toward
Absent; defiant; jittery	Eye contact	Regular
You continue with what you are doing before responding; in a hurry	Time	Respond at first opportunity; share time with the client
Used to keep distance between the persons	Feet and legs (in sitting)	Unobtrusive
Used as a barrier	Furniture	Used to draw persons together
Does not match feelings; scowl; blank look	Facial expression	Matches your own or other's feelings; smile
Compete for attention with your words	Gestures	Highlight your words; unobtrusive; smooth
Obvious; distracting	Mannerisms	None or unobtrusive
Very loud or very soft	Voice: volume	Clearly audible
Impatient or staccato; very slow or hesitant	Voice: rate	Average or a bit slower
Apathetic; sleepy; jumpy; pushy	Energy level	Alert; stays alert throughout a long conversation

From *Amity: Friendship in action, Part 1: Basic friendship skills.* Copyright © 1980 by Richard P. Walters, Boulder, Colo.: Christian Helpers, Inc. Reproduced by permission.

nonverbal behaviors such as those listed in Table 4-2 may not be sufficient to alter the negative impressions of a particular client about yourself.

In addition to the use of effective nonverbal behaviors such as those listed in Table 4-2, there are three other important aspects of a therapist's nonverbal demeanor: sensitivity, congruence, and synchrony.

Sensitivity

Presumably, skilled interviewers are better able to send effective nonverbal messages (encoding) and are more aware of client nonverbal messages (decoding) than ineffective interviewers. There is some evidence that females of various cultures are better decoders—that is, more sensitive to other persons' nonverbal cues—than males (Sweeney, Cottle, & Kobayashi, 1980). Male therapists may need to ensure that they are not overlooking important client cues. Nonverbal sensitivity is also related to representational systems. Since most of us may rely on one representational system (vi-

sual, auditory, kinesthetic) more than another, we can increase our nonverbal sensitivity by opening up all our sensory channels. For example, people who tend to process information through auditory channels can learn to pay closer attention to visual cues, and those who process visually can sensitize themselves to voice cues.

Congruence

Counselor nonverbal behaviors in conjunction with verbal messages also have some consequences in the relationship, particularly if these messages are mixed, or incongruent. Mixed messages can be confusing to the client. For example, suppose that a counselor says to a client "I am really interested in how you feel about your parents," while the counselor's body is turned away from the client with arms folded across the chest. The effect of this inconsistent message on the client could be quite potent. In fact, a *negative nonverbal* message mixed with a *positive verbal* one may have greater effects than the opposite (positive nonverbal and negative verbal). As Gazda et al. (1977, p. 93) point out, "When verbal and nonverbal messages are in contradiction, the helpee will usually believe the nonverbal message." Negative nonverbal messages are communicated by infrequent eye contact, body position rotated 45° away from the client, backward body lean (from waist up leaning back), legs crossed away from the client, and arms folded across the chest (Graves & Robinson, 1976; Smith-Hanen, 1977). The client may respond to inconsistent counselor messages by increasing interpersonal distance and may view such messages as indicators of counselor deception (Graves & Robinson, 1976). Further, mixed messages may reduce the extent to which the client feels psychologically close to the counselor and perceives the counselor as genuine.

In contrast, congruence between counselor verbal and nonverbal messages is related to both client and counselor ratings of counselor facilitativeness (Hill et al., 1981; Reade & Smouse, 1980). The importance of counselor congruence, or consistency, among various verbal, kinesic, and paralinguistic behaviors cannot be overemphasized. Congruence between verbal and nonverbal channels seems especially critical when confronting clients (see Chapter 6) or when discussing personal, sensitive, or stressful issues (Reade & Smouse, 1980). A useful aspect of counselor congruence involves learning to match the *intensity* of your nonverbal behaviors with those of the client. For example, if you are asking the client to recall a time when she or he felt strong, resourceful, or powerful, it is helpful to convey these feelings by your own nonverbal behaviors. Become more animated, speak louder, and emphasize key words such as "strong" and "powerful." Many of us overlook one of our most significant tools in achieving congruence—our voice. Changes in pitch, volume, rate of speech, and voice emphasis are particularly useful ways of matching our experience with the experience of clients.

Synchrony

Synchrony is the degree of harmony between the counselor's and client's nonverbal behavior. In helping interactions, especially initial ones, it is important to match, or pace, the client's nonverbal behaviors. Pacing of body posture and other client nonverbal behaviors contributes to rapport and builds empathy (Maurer & Tindall, 1983). Synchrony does not mean that the counselor mimics every move or sound the client makes. It does mean that the counselor's overall nonverbal demeanor is closely aligned with or very similar to the client's. For example, if the client is sitting back in a relaxed position with crossed legs, the counselor matches and displays similar body posture and leg movements. Dissynchrony, or lack of pacing, is evident when, for example, a client is leaning back, very relaxed, and the counselor is leaning foward, very intently, or when the client has a very sad look on her face and the counselor smiles, or when the client speaks in a low, soft voice and the counselor responds in a strong, powerful voice. The more nonverbal patterns you can pace, the more powerful the effect will be. However, when learning this skill, it is too overwhelming to try to match many aspects of a client's nonverbal behavior simultaneously. Find an aspect of the client's demeanor, such as voice, body posture, or gestures, that feels natural and comfortable for you to match, and concentrate on synchronizing this one aspect at a time.

LEARNING ACTIVITY #11: COUNSELOR NONVERBAL BEHAVIOR

The purpose of this activity is to have you experience the effects of different kinds of nonverbal behavior. You can do this in dyads or groups or outside a classroom setting.

1. Observe the response of a person you are talking with when—
   a. You look at the person or have relaxed eye contact.
   b. You don't look at the person consistently; you avert your eyes with only occasional glances.
   c. You stare at the person.
   Obtain a reaction from the other person about your behavior.
2. With other people, observe the effects of varying conversational distance. Talk with someone at a distance of (a) 3 feet (about 1 meter), (b) 6 feet (2 meters), and (c) 9 feet (3 meters).
   Observe the effect these distances have on the person.

(continued)

LEARNING ACTIVITY #11: COUNSELOR NONVERBAL BEHAVIOR (continued)

3. You can also do the same kind of experimenting with your body posture. For example, contrast the effects of two body positions in conversation: (a) slouching in seat, leaning back, and turning away from the person, compared with (b) facing the person, with a slight lean forward toward the person (from waist up) and with body relaxed.

LEARNING ACTIVITY #12: OBSERVATION OF COUNSELOR AND CLIENT NONVERBAL BEHAVIOR

The purpose of this activity is to apply the material presented in this chapter in an interview setting. Using the Nonverbal Behavior Checklist at the end of the chapter, observe a counselor and determine how many behaviors listed on the checklist she or he demonstrates. In addition, in the role play, see how much you can identify about the client's nonverbal behaviors. Finally, look for evidence of synchrony (pacing) or dissynchrony between the two persons and congruence or incongruence for each person.

□ SUMMARY

The focus of this chapter has been on counselor and client nonverbal behavior. The importance of nonverbal communication in counseling is illustrated by the trust that both counselor and client place in each other's nonverbal messages. Nonverbal behavior may be a more accurate portrayal of our real selves. Most nonverbal behaviors are very spontaneous and cannot easily be faked. Nonverbal behavior adds significantly to our interpretation of verbal messages.

Five significant dimensions of nonverbal behavior were discussed in this chapter: kinesics (face and body expressions), paralinguistics (vocal cues), proxemics (space and distance), environment, and time. Although much popular literature has speculated on the meanings of "body language," in counseling interactions it is important to remember that the meaning of nonverbal behavior varies with people, situations, and cultures and, further, cannot be easily interpreted without supporting verbal messages.

These categories of nonverbal behavior also apply to the counselor's use of effective nonverbal behavior in the interview. In addition to using nonverbal behaviors that communicate interest and attentiveness, counselors must ensure that their own verbal and nonverbal messages are congruent and that their nonverbal behavior is synchronized with, or matches, the client's nonverbal behavior. Congruence and synchrony are important ways of contributing to rapport and building empathy within the developing relationship.

POSTEVALUATION

PART ONE

Describe briefly one possible effect or meaning associated with each of the following ten client nonverbal behaviors (Chapter Objective One). Speculate on the meaning of the client nonverbal behavior from the client description and context presented. If you wish, write your answers on a piece of paper. Feedback follows the evaluation.

Observed Client Nonverbal Behavior	Client Description (Context)
1. Lowering eyes — looking down or away	Client has just described incestuous relationship with father. She looks away after recounting the episode.
2. Pupil dilation	Client has just been informed that she will be committed to the state hospital. Her pupils dilate as she sits back and listens.

(continued)

3. Lower lip quivers or biting lip

Client has just reported a recent abortion to the counselor. As she's finishing, her lip quivers and she bites it.

4. Nodding head up and down

Counselor has just described reasons for client to stop drinking. Client responds by nodding and saying "I know that."

5. Shrugging of shoulders

Counselor has just informed client that he is not eligible for services at that agency. Client shrugs shoulders while listening.

6. Fist clenching to objects or holding hands tightly.

Client is describing recent argument with spouse. Fists are clenched while relating incident.

7. Crossing and uncrossing legs repeatedly

Counselor has just asked client whether he has been taking his medicine as prescribed. Client crosses and uncrosses legs while responding.

8. Stuttering, hesitations, speech errors

Client hesitates when counselor inquires about marital fidelity. Starts to stutter and makes speech errors when describing extramarital affairs.

9. Moves closer

As counselor self-discloses an episode similar to client's, client moves chair toward helper.

10. Flushing of face and appearance of sweat beads

Counselor has just confronted client about provocative clothing and posture. Client's face turns red and sweat appears on the forehead.

PART TWO

Conduct a short interview as a helper and see how many client nonverbal behaviors of kinesics (body motion), paralinguistics (voice qualities), and proxemics (space) you can identify by debriefing with an observer after the session (Chapter Objective Two). Describe the possible effects or meanings associated with each behavior you identify. Confer with the observer about which nonverbal client behaviors you identified and which you missed.

PART THREE

In a role-play interview in which you are the counselor, demonstrate effective use of your face and body, your voice, and distance/space/touch (Objective Three). Be aware of the degree to which your nonverbal behavior matches your words. Also attempt to pace at least one aspect of the client's nonverbal behavior, such as body posture or breathing rate and depth. Use the Nonverbal Behavior Checklist at the end of the chapter to assess your performance from a videotape or have an observer rate you during your session.

PART FOUR

Recall that there are five occasions for responding to client nonverbal behavior:

a. Evidence of congruence between the client's verbal and nonverbal behavior
b. A client's "mixed" (discrepant) verbal and nonverbal message
c. Client's use of silence
d. Changes in client's nonverbal cues
e. Focusing on client's nonverbal behavior to change or redirect the interview

Identify four of the five occasions presented in the following client descriptions, according to Chapter Objective Four.

1. The client says that your feedback doesn't bother him; yet he frowns, looks away, and turns away.
2. The client has paused for a long time after your last question.
3. The client has flooded you with a great deal of information for the last five minutes.
4. The client says she feels angry about having to stay in the hospital. As she says this, her voice pitch gets louder, she clasps her hands together, and she frowns.
5. The client's face was very animated for the first part of the interview; now the client's face has a very serious look.

☐ SUGGESTED READINGS

Duhl, F. J., Kantor, D., & Duhl, B. S. (1973). Learning, space, and action in family therapy: A primer of sculpture. In D. A. Bloch (Ed.), *Techniques of family psychotherapy.* New York: Grune & Stratton.

Eisler, R. M., & Frederiksen, L. W. (1980). *Perfecting social skills.* New York: Plenum Press.

Ekman, P., & Friesen, W. V. (1975). *Unmasking the face.* Englewood Cliffs, NJ: Prentice-Hall.

Gazda, G. M., Asbury, F. S., Balzer, F. J., Childers, W. C., & Walters, R. P. (1984). *Human relations development* (3rd ed.). Boston: Allyn & Bacon. Chapter 6, "Awareness of Nonverbal Behaviors in Helping."

Harper, R. G., Wiens, A. N., & Matarazzo, J. D. (1978). *Nonverbal communication: The state of the art.* New York: Wiley.

Hess, E. H. (1975). *The tell-tale eye.* New York: Van Nostrand Reinhold.

Hill, C. E., Siegelman, L., Gronsky, B. R., Sturniolo, F., & Fretz, B. R. (1981). Nonverbal communication and counseling outcome. *Journal of Counseling Psychology, 28,* 203–212.

Hubble, M. A., Noble, F. C., & Robinson, S. E. (1981). The effect of counselor touch in an initial counseling session. *Journal of Counseling Psychology, 28,* 533–535.

King, M., Novik, L., & Citrenbaum, C. (1983). *Irresistible communication.* Philadelphia: Saunders.

Knapp, M. L. (1978). *Nonverbal communication in human interaction* (2nd ed.). New York: Holt, Rinehart and Winston.

Lecomte, C., Bernstein, B. L., & Dumont, F. (1981). Counseling interactions as a function of spatial-environmental conditions. *Journal of Counseling Psychology, 28,* 536–539.

Lee, D. Y., Hallberg, E. T., Kocsis, M., & Haase, R. F. (1980). Decoding skills in nonverbal communication and perceived interviewer effectiveness. *Journal of Counseling Psychology, 27,* 89–92.

Maurer, R. E., & Tindall, J. H. (1983). Effect of postural congruence on client's perception of counselor empathy. *Journal of Counseling Psychology, 30,* 158–163.

Mehrabian, A. (1976). *Public places and private spaces.* New York: Basic Books.

Otter, S. B., & Guerra, J. J. (1976). *Assertion training.* Champaign, IL: Resource Press.

Passons, W. R. (1975). *Gestalt approaches in counseling.* New York: Holt, Rinehart and Winston.

Reade, M. N., & Smouse, A. D. (1980). Effect of inconsistent verbal-nonverbal communication and counselor response mode on client estimate of counselor regard and effectiveness. *Journal of Counseling Psychology, 27,* 546–553.

Saha, G. B., Palchoudhury, S., & Mandal, M. K. (1982). A study on facial expression of emotion. *Psychologia, 25,* 255–259.

Sherer, M., & Rogers, R. (1980). Effects of therapist's nonverbal communication on rated skill and effectiveness. *Journal of Clinical Psychology, 26,* 696–700.

Sweeney, M. A., Cottle, W. C., & Kobayashi, M. J. (1980). Nonverbal communication: A cross-cultural comparison of American and Japanese counseling students. *Journal of Counseling Psychology, 27,* 150–156.

Young, D. W. (1980). Meanings of counselor nonverbal gestures: Fixed or interpretive? *Journal of Counseling Psychology, 27,* 447–452.

FEEDBACK: POSTEVALUATION

PART ONE

Some of the possible meanings of these client nonverbal behaviors are as follows:

1. This client's lowering of her eyes and looking away probably indicates her *embarrassment* and *discomfort* in discussing this particular problem.
2. Dilation of this client's pupils probably signifies *arousal* and *fear* of being committed.
3. In this example, the quivering of the client's lower lip and biting of the lip probably denote *ambivalence* and *sorrow* over her actions.
4. The client's head nodding indicates *agreement* with the counselor's rationale for remaining sober.
5. The client's shrugging of the shoulders may indicate *uncertainty* or *reconcilement.*
6. In this case, the client's fist clenching probably connotes *anger* with the spouse.
7. The client's crossing and uncrossing of his legs may signify *anxiety* or *discomfort.*
8. The client's hesitation in responding and subsequent stuttering and speech errors may indicate *sensitivity* to this topic, as well as *discomfort* in discussing it.
9. In this case, the client's moving closer to the counselor probably indicates *intrigue* and *identification* with what the counselor is revealing.
10. The client's sweating and blushing may be signs of *negative arousal*—that is, *anxiety* and/or *embarrassment* with the counselor's confrontation about suggestive dress and pose.

PART TWO

Have the observer debrief you for feedback or use the Nonverbal Behavior Checklist to recall which nonverbal behaviors you identified.

PART THREE

You or your observer can determine which desirable nonverbal behaviors you exhibited as a counselor, using the Nonverbal Behavior Checklist.

(continued)

PART FOUR

The five possible occasions for responding to client nonverbal cues as reflected in the postevaluation examples are these:

1. b. Responding to a client's mixed message; in this case the client's frown, break in eye contact, and shift in body position contradict the client's verbal message.
2. c. Responding to client silence; in this example the client's pause indicates silence.
3. e. Responding to client nonverbal behaviors to redirect the interview focus—in this example, to "break up" the flood of client information.
4. a. Responding to congruence in client verbal and nonverbal messages; in this case, the client's nonverbal behaviors "match" her verbal report of feeling angry.
5. d. Responding to changes in client nonverbal cues—in this example, responding to the change in the client's facial expression.

NONVERBAL BEHAVIOR CHECKLIST

Name of Counselor _____
Name of Observer _____
Instructions: Using a videotaped or live interview, use the categories below as guides for observing nonverbal behavior. The checklist can be used to observe the counselor, the client, or both. The left-hand column lists a number of behaviors to be observed. The right-hand column has spaces to record a √ when the behavior is observed and to fill in any descriptive comments about it—for example, "Blinking—*excessive*" or "Colors in room—*high arousal*."

I. Kinesics   (√)   *Comments*
1. *Eyes*
   Eyebrows raised, lowered, or drawn together   ___   _____
   Staring or "glazed" quality   ___   _____
   Blinking—excessive, moderate, or slight   ___   _____
   Moisture, tears   ___   _____
   Pupil dilation   ___   _____
2. *Face, mouth, head*
   Continuity or changes in facial expression   ___   _____
   Appropriate or inappropriate smiling   ___   _____
   Swelling, tightening, or quivering lips   ___   _____

(continued)

Changes in skin color   ___   _____
Flushing, rashes on upper neck, face   ___   _____
Appearance of sweat beads   ___   _____
Head nodding   ___   _____
3. *Body movements, posture, and gestures*
   Body posture—rigid or relaxed   ___   _____
   Continuity or shifts in body posture   ___   _____
   Frequency of body movements—excessive, moderate, or slight   ___   _____
   Gestures—open or closed   ___   _____
   Frequency of nonverbal adaptors (distracting mannerisms)—excessive, moderate, or slight   ___   _____
   Body orientation: direct (facing each other) or sideways   ___   _____
   Breathing—shallow or deep, fast or slow   ___   _____
   Continuity or changes in breathing depth and rate   ___   _____
   Crossed arms or legs   ___   _____

II. Paralinguistics
Continuity or changes in voice level, pitch, rate of speech   ___   _____
Verbal underlining—voice emphasis of particular words/phrases   ___   _____
Whispering, inaudibility   ___   _____
Directness or lack of directness in speech   ___   _____
Speech errors—excessive, moderate, or slight   ___   _____
Pauses initiated by counselor   ___   _____
Pauses initiated by client   ___   _____

III. Proxemics
Continuity or shifts in distance (closer, farther away)   ___   _____
Use of touch (handshake, shoulder pat, back pat, and so on)   ___   _____

(continued)

FEEDBACK: POSTEVALUATION (continued)

Position in room — behind
or next to object or person   ____ _____

IV. Environment

Arousal (high or low)
associated with:

Furniture arrangement   ____ _____
Colors   ____ _____
Light   ____ _____
Voice   ____ _____
Overall room   ____ _____

V. Time

Session started promptly or
late   ____ _____

Promptness or delay in
responding to other's
communication   ____ _____

Amount of time spent on
primary and secondary
problems — excessive,
moderate, or slight   ____ _____

Continuity or changes in
pace of session   ____ _____

Session terminated
promptly or late   ____ _____

VI. Synchrony and Pacing

Synchrony or dissynchrony
between nonverbal
behaviors and words   ____ _____

Pacing or lack of pacing
between counselor and
client nonverbal behavior   ____ _____

VII. Congruence

Congruence or
discrepancies:

Nonverbal — between
various parts of the
body   ____ _____

Nonverbal/verbal —
between nonverbal
behavior and words   ____ _____

VIII. Summary

Using your observations of nonverbal behavior and
the cultural/contextual variables of the interaction,
what conclusions can you make about the therapist?
The client? The counseling relationship? Consider
such things as emotions, comfort level, deception,
desire for more exchange, and liking/attraction.

LISTENING RESPONSES

FIVE

Communication is ever two-way. Listening is the other half of talking. Listening well is no less important than speaking well and it is probably more difficult. Could you listen to a 45-minute discourse without once allowing your thoughts to wander? Good listening is an art that demands the concentration of all your mental facilities. In general, people in the western world talk better than they listen [Potter, 1965, p. 6].

Listening is a prerequisite for all other counseling responses and strategies. Listening should precede whatever else is done in counseling. When a counselor fails to listen, the client may be discouraged from self-exploring, the wrong problem may be discussed, or a strategy may be proposed prematurely.

We define listening as involving three processes: receiving a message, processing a message, and sending a message. These three processes are illustrated in Figure 5-1.

Each client message (verbal or nonverbal) is a stimulus to be received and processed by the counselor. When a client sends a message, the counselor receives it. Reception of a message is a covert process; that is, we cannot see how or what the counselor receives. Failure to receive all of the message may occur when the counselor stops attending.

Once a message is received, it must be processed in some way. Processing, like reception, is covert, because it goes on within the counselor's mind and is not visible to the outside world — except, perhaps, from the counselor's nonverbal cues. Processing includes thinking about the message and pondering its meaning. Processing is important because a counselor's cognitions, self-talk, and mental (covert) preparation and visualization set the stage for overt responding (Richardson & Stone, 1981). Errors in processing a message accurately often occur when counselors' biases or blind spots prevent them from acknowledging parts of a message or from interpreting a message without distortion. Counselors may hear what they want to hear instead of the actual message sent.

The third process of listening involves the verbal and nonverbal messages sent by a counselor.

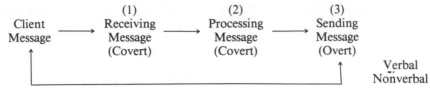

Figure 5-1. *Three processes of listening.*

Sometimes a counselor may receive and process a message accurately but have difficulty sending a message because of lack of skills. Fortunately, you can learn to use listening responses to send messages. Problems in sending messages can be more easily corrected than errors in the covert processes of receiving and processing messages. We hope that you are already able to receive and process a message without difficulty. Of course, this is a big assumption! If you think your own covert processes in listening are in need of further development, this may be an area you will need to work on by yourself or with someone else.

This chapter is designed to help you acquire four verbal listening responses that you can use to send messages to a client: clarification, paraphrase, reflection, and summarization.

□ OBJECTIVES

1. Using a written list of counselor responses, accurately identify at least nine of the twelve different types of counselor listening responses (clarification, paraphrase, reflection, summarization).
2. From a written list, match each of the four listening responses with its intended purposes.
3. From a list of three client statements, write an example of each of the four listening responses for each client statement.
4. In a 15-minute counseling interview in which you function as an observer, listen for and record five key aspects of client messages that form the basis of effective listening.
5. In a 15-minute role-play interview or a conversation in which you function as a listener, demonstrate at least two accurate examples of each of the four listening responses.

□ LISTENING IS A PREREQUISITE

We consider listening responses to be the foundation of the entire counseling process. If you conceptualize counseling and each interview as having a beginning, a middle, and an end, then attending and listening are the predominant counselor behaviors for the beginning part, or the first stage, of counseling. Listening also plays a major role in the beginning part of every interview.

One of the difficulties encountered in listening is to achieve a reasonable balance between too much and too little listening. If listening is the only tool used in counseling, the sessions will probably lack direction. However, if the counselor fails to listen, the sessions may be overly structured—at the client's expense. Egan (1982) points out that counselors who move into facilitating action too quickly are satisfying more of their own needs than those of the client.

□ LISTENING AND SENSORY MODALITIES

Effective listening involves all three major sensory modalities: sight (visual), sound (auditory), and experiencing/touch (kinesthetic). Recall from Chapter 2 that some clients use predominantly sensory words that are visual (such as *clear, look, appears, seems*), auditory *(hear, tell, sounds, listen)*, or kinesthetic *(feel, sense, grasp, touch)*. Others use a variety of words, or mixed modalities, in describing their experience, and occasionally a client may not use sensory-based words in a particular message.

Since listening responses are one way to communicate empathy and attentiveness, it is important to try to match the client's choice of sensory words in your listening response. If the client uses visually oriented words, you can select a sentence stem that matches these words—for example, "It looks as if . . ." or "I can see that. . . ." (The same matching can occur for auditory or kinesthetic words.) If the client selects words from mixed sensory modalities or does not include any words from sensory modalities, it is wise to use words in your response from two or three of the sensory channels rather than just one. Remember that clients will usually feel listened to and understood most when you let them know you have *seen* things from their frame of reference, *heard* what they have said, and *felt* or *grasped* their feelings and experiences.

□ FOUR LISTENING RESPONSES

This chapter will present four kinds of listening responses: clarification, paraphrase, reflection, and summarization. *Clarification* is a question, often used after an ambiguous client message. It starts with "Do you mean that . . ." or "Are you saying that . . ." along with a repetition or rephrasing of all or part of the client's previous message. Similar to a clarification is the *paraphrase,* defined as a rephrasing of the content part of the message, which describes a situation, event, person, or idea. In contrast, *reflection* is a rephrasing of the client's feelings, or the affect part of the message. Usually the affect part of the message reveals the client's feelings about the content; for example, a client may feel discouraged (affect) about not doing well in a class (content). *Summarization* is an extension of the paraphrase and reflection responses that involves tying together and rephrasing two or more different parts of a message or messages.

To illustrate these four responses, we present a client message with an example of each:

Client, a 35-year-old widow, mother of two young children: My whole life fell apart when my husband died. I keep feeling so unsure about my ability to make it on my own and to support my kids. My husband always made all the decisions for me. Now I haven't slept well for so long, and I'm drinking more heavily—I can't even think straight. Besides, I've put on 15 pounds. I look like a witch. Who would even want to think of hiring me the way I am now?

Counselor clarification: Are you saying that one of the hardest things facing you now is to have enough confidence in your ability to make the decisions alone?

Counselor paraphrase: Since your husband's death you have all the responsibilities and decisions on your shoulders.

Counselor reflection: You feel concerned about your ability to shoulder all the family responsibilities now.

Counselor summarization: Now that your husband has died, you're facing a few things that are very difficult for you right now . . . handling the family responsibilities, making the decisions, and trying to take better care of yourself.

Table 5-1 presents the definitions and the *intended* or hypothesized purposes of the four counselor listening responses of clarification, paraphrase, reflection, and summarization. The counselor responses may not have the same results

TABLE 5-1. Definitions and intended purposes of counselor listening responses

Response	Definition	Intended purpose
Clarification	A question beginning with, for example, "Do you mean that" or "Are you saying that" plus a rephrasing of the client's message	1. To encourage more client elaboration 2. To check out the accuracy of what you heard the client say 3. To clear up vague, confusing messages
Paraphrase (responding to content)	A rephrasing of the content of the client's message	1. To help the client focus on the content of his or her message 2. To highlight content when attention to feelings is premature or self-defeating
Reflection (responding to feelings)	A rephrasing of the affective part of the client's message	1. To encourage the client to express more of his or her feelings 2. To have the client experience feelings more intensely 3. To help the client become more aware of the feelings that dominate him or her 4. To help the client acknowledge and manage feelings 5. To help the client discriminate accurately among feelings
Summarization	Two or more paraphrases or reflections that condense the client's messages or the session	1. To tie together multiple elements of client messages 2. To identify a common theme or pattern 3. To interrupt excessive rambling 4. To review progress

for all clients. For example, a counselor may find that reflecting feelings prompts some clients to discuss feelings, whereas other clients may not even acknowledge the counselor's statements (Highlen & Baccus, 1977; Hill & Gormally, 1977). The point is that we are presenting some "modal" intentions for each counselor listening response; there are exceptions. The counselor responses will achieve their intended purposes most of the time. However, other dynamics within an interview may yield different client outcomes. Moreover, the effects of these verbal messages may vary depending on the nonverbal cues sent along with the message. It is helpful to have some rationale in mind for using a response. Keep in mind, however, that the influence a response has on the client may not be what you intended to achieve by selecting it. The guidelines in Table 5-1 should be used tentatively, *subject to modification by particular client reactions.*

The next three sections will describe the listening responses and will present model examples of each skill. Opportunities to practice each skill and receive feedback follow the examples.

Listening for Accuracy: The Clarification Response

Because most messages are expressed from the speaker's internal frame of reference, they may be vague or confusing. Messages that may be particularly confusing are those that include inclusive terms *(they* and *them),* ambiguous phrases *(you know),* and words with a double meaning *(stoned, trip)* (Hein, 1980, p. 35). When you aren't sure of the meaning of a message, it is helpful to clarify it.

According to Hein (1980, p. 56), a clarification asks the client to elaborate on "a vague, ambiguous, or implied statement." The request for clarification is usually expressed in the form of a question and may begin with phrases such as "Are you saying this . . ." or "Could you try to describe that . . ." or "Can you clarify that. . . ."

Purposes of clarification. A clarification may be used to make the client's previous message explicit and to confirm the accuracy of your perceptions about the message. A clarification is appropriate for any occasion when you aren't sure whether you understand the client's message and you need more elaboration. A second purpose of clarification is to check out what you heard of the client's message. Ivey and Gluckstern (1974, p. 26) point out that too often counselors "charge ahead without stopping to check out whether or not they have

really heard what the helpee has to say." In this case, the counselor often makes assumptions and draws conclusions about the client that are somewhat distorted or premature. Particularly in the beginning stages of counseling, it is important to verify client messages before jumping to quick conclusions. The following example may help you see the value of the clarification response.

Client: Sometimes I just want to get away from it all.
Counselor: It sounds like you have to split and be on your own.
Client: No, it's not that. I don't want to be alone. It's just that I wish I could get out from under all this work I have to do.

In this example, the counselor drew a quick conclusion about the initial client message that turned out to be inaccurate. The session might have gone more smoothly if the counselor had requested clarification before assuming something about the client, as in the next example:

Client: Sometimes I just want to get away from it all.
Counselor: Could you describe for me what you mean by getting away from it all?
Client: Well, I just have so much work to do—I'm always feeling behind and overloaded. I'd like to get out from under that miserable feeling.

In this case, the clarification helped both persons to establish exactly what was being said and felt. Neither the client nor the counselor had to rely on assumptions and inferences that were not explored and confirmed. The skilled counselor uses clarification responses to determine the accuracy of messages as they are received and processed. Otherwise, inaccurate information may not be corrected and distorted assumptions may remain untested.

Steps in clarifying. There are four steps in clarifying for accuracy. First, identify the content of the client's verbal and nonverbal messages—what has the client told you? Second, identify whether there are any vague or confusing parts to the message that you need to check out for accuracy or elaboration. Third, decide on an appropriate beginning, or sentence stem, for your clarification, such as "Could you describe," "Could you clarify," or "Are you saying." In addition, use your voice to deliver the clarification as a question rather than a statement. Finally, remember to assess the effectiveness of your clarification by listening and observing the client's response. If your clarification is useful, the client will elaborate on the ambiguous or confusing part of the message. If it is not useful, the client will clam up, ignore your request for clarification, and/or continue to make deletions or omissions. At this point, you can attempt a subsequent clarification or switch to an alternative response.

To help you formulate a clarification, decide when to use it, and assess its effectiveness, consider the following cognitive learning strategy:

1. What has this client told me?
2. Are there any vague parts or missing pictures to the message that I need to check out? If so, what? If not, decide on another, more suitable response.
3. How can I hear, see, or grasp a way to start this response?
4. How will I know whether my clarification is useful?

Notice how a counselor applies this cognitive learning strategy in clarifying the client's message given in the previous example:

Client: Sometimes I just want to get away from it all.
Counselor: 1. What has this client told me? That she wants to get away from something. [Asked and answered covertly]
2. Are there any vague parts or missing pictures in her message? If so, what? (If not, I'll decide on a more suitable response.)

Yes—I need to check out what she means by "getting away from it all."
3. Now, how can I begin a clarification response? I can see the start of it, hear the start of it, or grasp the start of it. Something like "Well, could you tell me, or could you describe. . . ."
4. Now, how will I know that the response will be helpful? I'll have to see, hear, and grasp whether she elaborates or not. Let's try it . . . .

Suppose that, at this juncture, the counselor's covert visualization or self-talk ends, and the following actual dialogue occurs:

Counselor clarification: Could you describe what you mean by "getting away from it all"?
Client response: Well, I just have so much work to do—I'm always feeling behind and overloaded. I'd like to get out from under that miserable feeling.

From the client's response, the counselor can determine that the clarification was effective because the client elaborated and added the missing parts or pictures from her previous message. The counselor can covertly congratulate himself or herself for not jumping ahead too quickly and for taking the time to check out the client's deletion and the resulting ambiguity.

The following learning activity gives you an opportunity to try out this cognitive learning strategy in order to develop the skill of clarification.

LEARNING ACTIVITY #13: CLARIFICATION

In this learning activity, you are presented with three client practice messages. For each client message, develop an example of a clarification response, using the cognitive learning strategy described earlier and outlined in the following example. In order to internalize this learning strategy, you may wish to talk through these self-questions overtly (aloud) and then covertly (silently to yourself). The end product will be a clarification response that you can say aloud or write down or both. An example precedes the practice messages. Feedback follows on page 96.

Example

Client, a 15-year-old high school student: My grades have really slipped. I don't know why; I just feel so down about everything:

Self-question 1: What has this client told me? That she feels down and rather discouraged.
Self-question 2: Are there any vague parts or missing pictures to the message that I need to check out—

if so, what? (If not, decide on a different response.) Yes, several—one is what she feels so down about. Another is what this feeling of being down is like for her.

Self-question 3: How can I hear, see, or grasp a way to start this response?
Well, "Are you saying there's something specific?" or "Can you describe this feeling . . . ?"
Self-question 4. Say aloud or write an actual clarification response:
"Are you saying there is something specific you feel down about?" or "Could you describe what this feeling of being down is like for you?"

Client Practice Messages

Client 1, a fourth-grader: I don't want to do this dumb homework anyway. I don't care about learning these math problems. Girls don't need to know this anyway.

Self-question 1: What has this client told me?

(continued)

LEARNING ACTIVITY #13: CLARIFICATION (continued)

Self-question 2: Are there any vague parts or missing pictures I need to check out — if so, what?

Self-question 3: How can I hear, see, or grasp a way to start my response?

Actual clarification response: _____

_____

Client 2, a middle-aged man: I'm really discouraged with this physical disability now. I feel like I can't do anything the way I used to. Not only has it affected me in my job, but at home. I just don't feel like I have anything good to offer anyone.

Self-question 1: What has this client told me?

Self-question 2: Are there any vague parts or missing pictures I need to check out — if so, what?

Self-question 3: How can I hear, see, or grasp a way to start my response?

Actual clarification response: _____

_____

Client 3, an older person: The company is going to make me retire even though I don't want to. What will I do with myself then? I find myself just thinking over the good times of the past, not wanting to face the future at all. Sometimes retirement makes me so nervous I can't sleep or eat. My family suggested I see someone about this.

Self-question 1: What has this client told me?

Self-question 2: Are there any vague parts or missing pictures I need to check out — if so, what?

Self-question 3: How can I hear, see, or grasp a way to start my response?

Actual clarification response: _____

_____

Listening for Content and Affect: Paraphrasing and Reflecting

In addition to clarifying the accuracy of client messages, the counselor needs to listen for information revealed in messages about significant situations and events in the client's life — and the client's feelings about these events. Each client message will express (directly or indirectly) some information about client situations or concerns and about client feelings. The portion of the message that expresses information or describes a situation or event is called the *content,* or the cognitive part, of the message. The cognitive part of a message includes references to a situation or event, people, objects, or ideas. Another portion of the message may reveal how the client feels about the content; expression of feelings or an emotional tone is called the *affective* part of the message (Hackney & Cormier, 1979). Generally, the affect part of the verbal message is distinguished by the client's use of an affect or feeling word, such as *happy, angry,* or *sad.* However, clients may also express their feelings in less obvious ways, particularly through various nonverbal behaviors.

The following illustrations may help you distinguish between the content and affective parts of a client's verbal message.

Client, a 6-year-old first-grader: I don't like school. It isn't much fun.

The first sentence ("I don't like school") is the affect part of the message. The client's feelings are suggested by the words "don't like." The second sentence ("It isn't much fun") is the content part of the message because it refers to a situation or an event in this child's life — not having fun at school. Here is another example:

Client, a 20-year-old woman: How can I tell my boyfriend I want to break off our relationship? He will be very upset. I guess I'm afraid to tell him.

In this example, the first two sentences are the content because they describe the situation of wanting to break off a relationship. The third sentence, the affect part, indicates the client's feelings about this situation — being *afraid* to tell the boyfriend of her intentions.

See whether you can discriminate between the content and affective parts of the following two client messages:

Client 1, a young man: I just can't satisfy my wife sexually. It's very frustrating for me.

In this example, the content part is "I can't satisfy my wife sexually." The affect part, or the client's feelings about the content, is "It's very *frustrating* for me."

Client 2, an institutionalized man: This place is a trap. It seems like I've been here forever. I'd feel much better if I weren't here.

In the second example, the statements referring to the institution as a trap and being there forever are the content parts of the message. The statement of "feeling better" is the affect part.

The skilled counselor tries to listen for both content and affect parts of client messages because it is important to deal with significant situations or relationships *and* with the client's feelings about the situations. Responding to cognitive or affective messages will direct the focus of the session in different ways. At some points, the counselor will respond to content by focusing on events, objects, people, or ideas. At other times, the counselor will respond to affect by focusing on the client's feelings and emotions. Generally, the counselor can respond to content by using a paraphrase and can respond to affect with a reflection.

Paraphrase. A paraphrase is a rephrasing of the client's primary words and thoughts. Paraphrasing involves selective attention given to the cognitive part of the message—with the client's key ideas translated into *your own words*. Thus, an effective paraphrase is more than just "parroting" the words of the client. The rephrasal should be carefully worded to lead to further discussion or increased understanding on the part of the client. It is helpful to stress the most important words and ideas expressed by the client. Consider the following example:

Client: I know it doesn't help my depression to sit around or stay in bed all day.
Counselor: You know you need to avoid staying in bed or sitting around all day to help your depression.

In this example, the counselor merely "parroted" the client's message. The likely outcome is that the client may respond with a minimal answer such as "I agree" or "That's right" and not elaborate further or that the client may feel ridiculed by what seems to be an obvious or mimicking response. A more effective paraphrase would be "You are aware that you need to get up and move around in order to minimize being depressed."

Purposes of paraphrasing. There are several purposes in using the paraphrase at selected times n client interactions. First, use of the paraphrase tells clients that you have understood their communication. If your understanding is complete, clients can expand or clarify their ideas. Second, paraphrasing can encourage client elaboration of a key idea or thought. Clients may talk about an important topic in greater depth. A third reason for use of paraphrases is to help the client focus on a particular situation or event, idea, or behavior.

Sometimes, by increasing focus, paraphrasing can help get a client "on track." For example, accurate paraphrasing can help stop a client from merely repeating a "story" (Ivey, 1983).

A fourth use of paraphrase is to help clients who need to make decisions. As Ivey and Simek-Downing (1980, p. 77) observe, "If the counselor feeds back the client's thinking in more succinct form, it frees the client to make clearer decisions." Finally, paraphrasing is useful when the therapist wants to emphasize content because attention to affect would be premature or counterproductive.

Steps in paraphrasing. There are five steps in paraphrasing content. First, attend to and recall the message by restating it to yourself covertly—what has the client told you? Second, identify the content part of the message by asking yourself "What situation, person, object, or idea is discussed in this message?" Third, select an appropriate beginning, or sentence stem, for your paraphrase. Paraphrases can begin with many possible sentence stems. Try to select one that is likely to match the client's choice of sensory words. Table 5-2 provides examples of typical sensory words that clients may use and corresponding counselor phrases. Next, using the sentence stem you se-

TABLE 5-2. Examples of client sensory words and corresponding counselor phrases

Client sensory words		Corresponding counselor phrases
Visual		
see	bright	It seems like
clear	show	It appears as though
focus	colorful	From my perspective
picture	glimpse	As I see it
view	"now look"	I see what you mean
perspective		It looks like
Auditory		
listen	discuss	Sounds like
yell	should	As I hear it
tell	loud	What you're saying is
told	noisy	I hear you saying
talk	call	Something tells you
hear	"now listen"	You're telling me that
ears		
Kinesthetic		
feel	relaxed	You feel
touch	sense	From my standpoint
pressure	experience	I sense that
hurt	firm	I have the feeling that
pushy	"you know"	
grasp		

Adapted from Lankton (1980).

FEEDBACK #13: CLARIFICATION

Client 1

1. What did the client say?
   That she doesn't want to do her math homework —that she thinks it's not important for girls.
2. Are there any vague parts or missing pictures?
   Yes—whether she really doesn't care about math or whether she's had a bad experience with it and is denying her concern.
3. Examples of clarification responses: "Are you saying that you really dislike math or that it's not going as well for you as you would like?"
   "Are you saying that math is not too important for you or that it is hard for you?"

Client 2

1. What did the client say?
   That he feels useless to himself and others.
2. Are there any vague parts or missing pictures?
   Yes—it's not clear exactly how things are different for him now and also whether it's the disability itself that's bothering him or its effects (inability to get around, reactions of others, and so on).
3. Examples of clarification responses: "Could you clarify exactly how things are different for you now than the way they used to be?"
   "Are you saying you feel discouraged about having the disability—or about the effects and constraints from it?"
   "Are you saying you feel differently about yourself now than the way you used to?"

Client 3

1. What did the client say?
   He is going to have to retire because of company policy. He doesn't want to retire now and feels upset about this. He's here at his family's suggestion.
2. Are there any vague parts or missing pictures?
   Yes—he says he feels nervous, although from his description of not eating and sleeping it may be sadness or depression. Also, is he here only because his family sent him or because he feels a need too? Finally, what specifically bothers him about retirement?
3. Examples of clarification responses: "Would you say you're feeling more nervous or more depressed about your upcoming retirement?"
   "Are you saying you're here just because of your family's feelings or because of your feelings too?"
   "Could you describe what it is about retiring that worries you?"

lected, translate the key content or constructs into your own words and verbalize this into a paraphrase. Remember to use your voice as you deliver the paraphrase so it sounds like a statement instead of a question. Finally, assess the effectiveness of your paraphrase by listening to and observing the client's response. If your paraphrase is accurate, the client will in some way—verbally and/or nonverbally—confirm its accuracy and usefulness. Consider the following example of the way a counselor uses the cognitive learning strategy to formulate a paraphrase:

Client, a 40-year-old woman: How can I tell my husband I want a divorce? He'll think I'm crazy. I guess I'm just afraid to tell him. [Said in a level, monotone voice]

1. What has this client told me?
   That she wants a divorce and she's afraid to tell her husband, as he will think she's crazy.
2. What is the content of this message—what person, object, idea, or situation is the client discussing?
   Wants divorce but hasn't told husband because husband will think she's crazy.
3. What is an appropriate sentence stem (one that matches the sensory words used by the client)?
   Client uses the verb *tell* two times and *think* once, so I'll go with a stem such as "You think," "I hear you saying," or "It sounds like."
4. How can I translate the client's key content into my own words?
   Want a divorce = break off, terminate the relationship, split.
5. How will I know whether my paraphrase is helpful?
   Listen and notice whether the client confirms its accuracy.

Suppose that at this point the counselor's self-talk stopped and the following dialogue ensued:

Counselor paraphrase: It sounds like you haven't found a way to tell your husband you want to end the relationship because of his possible reaction. Is that right?

Client: Yeah—I've decided—I've even been to see a lawyer. But I just don't know how to approach him with this. He thinks things are wonderful.

At this point, the counselor can congratulate herself or himself for having formulated a paraphrase that has encouraged client elaboration and focus on a main issue.

Learning Activity #14 gives you an opportunity to develop your own paraphrase responses.

LEARNING ACTIVITY #14: PARAPHRASE

In this learning activity, you are presented with three client practice messages. For each client message, develop an example of a paraphrase response, using the cognitive learning strategy outlined in the example below. In order to internalize this learning strategy, you may wish to talk through these self-questions overtly (aloud) and then covertly (silently to yourself). The end product will be a paraphrase response that you can say aloud or write down or both. Feedback is given on page 98.

Example

Client, a middle-aged graduate student: *It's just a rough time for me—trying to work, keeping up with graduate school, and spending time with my family. I keep telling myself it will slow down someday.* [Said in a level, monotone voice]

Self-question 1: What has this client told me?
That it's hard to keep up with everything he has to do.
Self-question 2: What is the content of this message —what person, object, idea, or situation is the client discussing?
Trying to keep up with work, school, and family.
Self-question 3: What is an appropriate sentence stem?
I'll try a stem like "It sounds like" or "There are."
Actual paraphrase response: It sounds like you're having a tough time balancing all your commitments *or* There are a lot of demands on your time right now.

Client Practice Statements

Client 1, a 30-year-old woman: *My husband and I argue all the time about how to manage our kids. He says I always interfere with his discipline—I* think he is too harsh with them. [Said in a level voice tone without much variation in pitch or tempo]

Self-question 1: What has this client told me?
Self-question 2: What is the content of this message —what person, object, idea, or situation is the client discussing?
Self-question 3: What is a useful sentence stem?
Actual paraphrase response: _____
_____

Client 2, a 6-year-old boy: *I wish I didn't have a little sister. I know my parents love her more than me.* [Said in slow, soft voice with downcast eyes]

Self-question 1: What has this client told me?
Self-question 2: What is the content of this message —what person, object, idea, or situation is this client discussing?
Self-question 3: What is a useful sentence stem?
Actual paraphrase response: _____
_____

Client 3, a college student: *I've said to my family before, I just can't compete with the other students who aren't blind. There's no way I can keep up with this kind of handicap. I've told them it's natural to be behind and do more poorly.* [Said in level, measured words with little pitch and inflection change]

Self-question 1: What has this client told me?
Self-question 2: What is the content of this message —what person, object, idea, or situation is the client discussing?
Self-question 3: What is a useful sentence stem?
Actual paraphrase response: _____
_____

Reflection of feeling. We have just seen that the paraphrase is used to restate the cognitive part of the message. Although the paraphrase and the reflection of feeling are not mutually exclusive responses, the reflection of feeling is used to rephrase the *affective* part of the message, the client's emotional tone. A reflection is similar to a paraphrase but different in that a reflection adds an emotional tone or component to the message that is lacking in a paraphrase. Here are two examples that may illustrate the difference between a paraphrase and a reflection of feeling.

Client: Everything is humdrum. There's nothing new going on, nothing exciting. All my friends are away. I wish I had some money to do something different.
Counselor paraphrase: With your friends gone and no money around, there is nothing for you to do right now.
Counselor reflection: You feel bored with the way things are for you right now.

Note the counselor's use of the affect word *bored* in the reflection response to turn into the feelings of the client created by the particular situation.

FEEDBACK #14: PARAPHRASE

Client 1

Question 1. What has the client said?

That she and her husband argue over child rearing.

Question 2. What is the content of her message?

As a couple, they have different ideas on who should discipline their kids and how.

Question 3. What is a useful sentence stem?

Try "It sounds like" or "Your ideas about discipline are."

Actual paraphrase response: Here are examples; see whether yours are similar.

It sounds like you and your husband disagree a great deal on which one of you should discipline your kids and how it should be done *or* Your ideas about discipline for your kids are really different from your husband's, and this creates disagreements between the two of you.

Client 2

Question 1. What has this client said?

He believes his little sister is loved more by his folks than he is, and he wishes she weren't around.

Question 2. What is the content of his message?

Client feels "dethroned"—wishes the new "queen" would go away.

Question 3. What is a useful sentence stem?

I'll try "It seems that" or "I sense that."

Actual paraphrase response: Here are examples. What are yours like?

It seems that you'd like to be "number one" again in your family *or* I sense you are not sure of your place in your family since your little sister arrived.

Client 3

Question 1. What has this client said?

He is behind in school and is not doing as well as his peers because he is blind—a point he has emphasized to his family.

Question 2. What is the content of his message?

Client wants to impress on his family that his blindness is a handicap that interferes with his doing as much or as well as other students.

Question 3. What is a useful sentence stem?

"It sounds like," "I hear you saying," or "You'd like."

Actual paraphrase response: Here are some examples.

It sounds like it's very important to you that your family realize how tough it is for you to do well in your studies here *or* You'd like your family to realize how difficult it is for you to keep up academically with people who don't have the added problem of being blind.

Purposes of reflection. Reflecting feelings has five intended purposes. First, this response, if used effectively and accurately, helps clients to feel understood. Clients tend to communicate more freely with persons whom they feel try to understand them. As Buggs (1975, p. 293) notes, "Understanding never makes feelings worse; it only gives them permission to be revealed."

Reflection is also used to encourage clients to express more of their feelings (both positive and negative) about a particular situation, person, or whatever. Some clients do not readily reveal feelings because they have never learned to do so, and other clients hold back feelings until the therapist gives permission to focus on them. Expression of feelings is not usually an end in itself; rather, it is a means of helping clients and counselors understand the scope of the problem or situation. Most if not all of the concerns presented by clients involve underlying emotional factors to be resolved (Ivey & Simek-Downing, 1980, p. 77). For example, in focusing on feelings, the client may become more aware of lingering feelings about an unfinished situation or of intense feelings that seem to dominate his or her reaction to a situation. Clients may also become aware of mixed, or conflicting, feelings. Ambivalence is a common way that clients express feelings initially about a problematic issue.

A third purpose of reflection is to help clients manage feelings. Learning to deal with feelings is especially important when a client experiences intense feelings such as fear, dependency, or anger. Strong emotions can interfere with a client's ability to make a rational response (cognitive or behavioral) to pressure.

A fourth use of reflection is with clients who express negative feelings about therapy or about the counselor. When a client becomes angry or upset with you or with the help you are offering, there is a tendency to take the client's remarks personally and become defensive. Using reflection in these instances "lessens the possibility of an emotional conflict, which often arises simply because two people are trying to make themselves heard and neither is trying to listen" (Long & Prophit, 1981, p. 89). The use of reflection in these situations lets clients know that the counselor understands their feelings in such a way that the intensity of the anger is usually diminished. As anger subsides, the client may become more receptive, and the counselor can again initiate action-oriented responses or intervention strategies.

Finally, reflection helps clients discriminate accurately among various feelings. Clients often use feeling words like *anxious* or *nervous* that, on occasion, mask deeper or more intense feelings (Ivey, 1983). Clients may also use an affect word that does not really portray their emotional state accurately. It is common, for instance, for a client to say "It's my nerves" or "I'm nervous" to depict other feelings, such as resentment and depression. Accurate reflections of feeling help clients to refine their understanding of various emotional moods.

Steps in reflecting feelings. Reflecting feelings can be a difficult skill to learn because often feelings are ignored or misunderstood (Long & Prophit, 1981). Reflection of feelings involves six steps that include identifying the emotional tone of the communication and verbally reflecting the client's feelings, using your own words.

The first step is to listen for the presence of feeling words, or affect words, in the client's messages. Positive, negative, and ambivalent feelings are expressed by one or more affect words falling into one of seven major categories: anger, fear, uncertainty, sadness, happiness, strength, and weakness. Table 5-3 presents a list of commonly used affect words. Becoming acquainted with such words may help you recognize them in client communications and expand your vocabulary for describing emotions.

A second way to identify the client's feelings is to watch the nonverbal behavior while the verbal message is being delivered. As you may remember

TABLE 5-3. Commonly used affect words

Level of Intensity	Category of feeling						
	Happiness	Sadness	Fear	Uncertainty	Anger	Strength, potency	Weakness, inadequacy
Strong	Excited	Despairing	Panicked	Bewildered	Outraged	Powerful	Ashamed
	Thrilled	Hopeless	Terrified	Disoriented	Hostile	Authoritative	Powerless
	Delighted	Depressed	Afraid	Mistrustful	Furious	Forceful	Vulnerable
	Overjoyed	Crushed	Frightened	Confused	Angry	Potent	Cowardly
	Ecstatic	Miserable	Scared		Harsh		Exhausted
	Elated	Abandoned	Overwhelmed		Hateful		Impotent
	Jubilant	Defeated			Mean		
		Desolate			Vindictive		
Moderate	"Up"	Dejected	Worried	Doubtful	Aggravated	Tough	Embarrassed
	Good	Dismayed	Shaky	Mixed up	Irritated	Important	Useless
	Happy	Disillusioned	Tense	Insecure	Offended	Confident	Demoralized
	Optimistic	Lonely	Anxious	Skeptical	Mad	Fearless	Helpless
	Cheerful	Bad	Threatened	Puzzled	Frustrated	Energetic	Worn out
	Enthusiastic	Unhappy	Agitated		Resentful	Brave	Inept
	Joyful	Pessimistic			"Sore"	Courageous	Incapable
	"Turned on"	Sad			Upset	Daring	Incompetent
		Hurt			Impatient	Assured	Inadequate
		Lost			Obstinate	Adequate	Shaken
						Self-confident	
						Skillful	
Weak	Pleased	"Down"	Jittery	Unsure	Perturbed	Determined	Frail
	Glad	Discouraged	Jumpy	Surprised	Annoyed	Firm	Meek
	Content	Disappointed	Nervous	Uncertain	Grouchy	Able	Unable
	Relaxed	"Blue"	Uncomfortable	Undecided	Hassled	Strong	Weak
	Satisfied	Alone	Uptight	Bothered	Bothered		
	Calm	Left out	Uneasy		Disagreeable		
			Defensive				
			Apprehensive				
			Hesitant				
			Edgy				

Adapted from *The Skills of Helping* by R. R. Carkhuff and W. A. Anthony. Copyright © 1979 by Human Resource Development Press, Inc., Amherst, Massachusetts. Reprinted by permission. All rights reserved.

from Chapter 4, nonverbal cues such as body posture, facial expression, and voice quality are important indicators of client emotion. In fact, nonverbal behavior is often a more reliable clue to client emotions because nonverbal behaviors are less easily controlled than words. Observing nonverbal behavior is particularly important when the client's feelings are implied or expressed very subtly.

After the feelings reflected by the client's words and nonverbal behavior have been identified, the next step involves verbally reflecting the feelings back to the client, using different words. The choice of words to reflect feelings is critical to the effectiveness of this skill. For example, if a client expresses feeling annoyed, interchangeable affect words would be *bothered, irritated,* and *hassled.* Words such as *angry, mad,* or *outraged,* however, probably go beyond the intensity expressed by the client. It is important to select affect words that accurately match not only the type of feeling but also its intensity—otherwise, the counselor makes an understatement, which can make a client feel ridiculed, or an overstatement, which can make a client feel put off or intimidated. Note the three major levels of intensity of affect words in Table 5-3—weak, moderate, and strong. You can also control the intensity of the expressed affect by the type of preceding adverb used—for example, *somewhat* (weak), *quite* (moderate), or *very* (strong) *upset.* Study Table 5-3 carefully so that you can develop an extensive affect-word vocabulary. Overuse of a few common affect words misses the varied nuances of the client's emotional experience.

The next step in reflecting is to start the reflection statement with an appropriate sentence stem—if possible, one that matches the client's choice of sensory words. These are some sample reflections to match the visual modality:

"It *appears* that you are *angry* now."
"It *looks* like you are *angry* now."
"It is *clear* to me that you are *angry* now."

Sample reflections to match the auditory modality:

"It *sounds* like you are *angry* now."
"I *hear* you saying you are *angry* now."
"My *ears tell* me that you are *angry* now."

Sample reflections to match kinesthetic words:

"I can *grasp* your *anger.*"

"You are *feeling angry* now."
"Let's get in *touch* with your *anger.*"

If you don't know how the client processes information, or if the client uses visual, auditory, and kinesthetic words interchangeably, you can do the same by varying the sentence stems you select (refer also to Table 5-2).

The next step in reflecting is to add on the context, or situation, around which the feelings occur. This takes the form of a brief paraphrase. Usually the context can be determined from the cognitive part of the client's message. For example, a client might say "I just can't take tests. I get so anxious I just never do well even though I study a lot." In this message, the affect is anxiety; the context is test taking. The counselor reflects the affect ("You feel uptight") *and* the context ("whenever you have to take a test").

The final step in reflecting feelings is to assess the effectiveness of your reflection after delivering it. Usually, if your reflection accurately identifies the client's feelings, the client will confirm your response by saying something like "Yes, that's right" or "Yes, that's exactly how I feel." If your response is off target, the client may reply with "Well, it's not quite like that" or "I don't feel exactly that way" or "No, I don't feel that way." When the client responds by denying feelings, it may mean your reflection was inaccurate or ill-timed. It is very important for counselors to decide when to respond to emotions. Reflection of feelings may be too powerful to be used *frequently* in the very early stage of counseling. At that time, overuse of this response may make the client feel uncomfortable, which can result in denial rather than acknowledgment of emotions. But do not ignore the potential impact or usefulness of reflection later on, when focusing on the client's feelings would promote the goals of the session. In the following example, notice the way a therapist uses a cognitive learning strategy (adapted from Richardson & Stone, 1981) to formulate a reflection of client feelings:

Client, a middle-aged man: You can't imagine what it was like when I found out my wife was cheating on me. I saw red! What should I do—get even—leave her—I'm not sure. [Said in loud, shrill, high-pitched voice, clenched fists]

1. What overt feeling words has this client used? None—except for the suggested affect phrase "saw red."

2. What feelings are implied in the client's voice and nonverbal behavior?
   Anger, outrage, hostility?
3. What is a good choice of affect words that accurately describe this client's feelings at a similar level of intensity?
   Furious, angry, vindictive, outraged.
4. What is an appropriate sentence stem that matches the sensory words used by the client?
   From the client's use of words like "imagine" and "saw red," I'll try visual sentence stems like "It seems," "It appears," "It looks like."
5. What is the context, or situation, surrounding his feelings that I'll paraphrase?
   Finding out wife was cheating on him.
6. How will I know whether my reflection is accurate and helpful?
   Watch and listen for the client's response — whether he confirms or denies the feeling of being angry and vindictive.

Actual examples of reflection:
   It looks like you're very angry now about your wife's going out on you.

It appears that you're furious with your wife's actions.
It seems like you're both angry and vindictive now that you've discovered your wife has been going out with other men.

Suppose that, following the reflection, the client said "Yes, I'm very angry, for sure — I don't know about vindictive, though I guess I'd like to make her feel as crappy as I do." The client has confirmed the counselor's reflection of the feelings of anger and vindictiveness but has also given a clue that the word *vindictive* was too strong for the client to accept *at this time.* The counselor can congratulate himself or herself for having picked up on the feelings, noting that the word *vindictive* might be used again later, after the client has sorted through his mixed feelings about his wife's behavior.
   Learning Activity #15 will give you an opportunity to try out the reflection-of-feeling response.

LEARNING ACTIVITY #15: REFLECTION OF FEELINGS

In this learning activity, you are presented with three client practice messages. For each message, develop an example of a reflection-of-feeling response, using the cognitive learning strategy (Richardson & Stone, 1981) described earlier and outlined below. To internalize this learning strategy, you may wish to talk through these self-questions overtly (aloud) and then covertly (silently to yourself). The end product will be a reflection-of-feeling response that you can say aloud or write down or both. An example precedes the practice messages. Feedback is given after the learning activity (on page 104).

Example

Client, a 50-year-old steelworker now laid off: Now look, what can I do? I've been laid off over a year now, I've got no money, no job, and a family to take care of. It's also clear to me that my mind and skills are just wasting away. [Said in a loud, critical voice, staring at the ceiling, brow furrowed, eyes squinting]

Self-question 1: What overt feeling words has the client used?
None.
Self-question 2: What feelings are implied in the client's nonverbal behavior?

Disgust, angry, upset, frustrated, resentful, disillusioned, discouraged.
Self-question 3: What is a good choice of affect words that accurately describes the client's feelings at a similar level of intensity?
Seem to be two feelings — anger and discouragement. Anger seems to be the stronger emotion of the two.
Self-question 4: What is an appropriate sentence stem that matches the sensory words used by the client?
Use stems like "I see you" or "It's clear to me that you" or "From where I'm looking, you" to match the client phrases "now look" and "it's clear."
Self-question 5: What is the context, or situation, surrounding his feelings that I'll paraphrase?
Loss of job, no resources, no job prospects in sight.
Reflection-of-feeling response: I can see you're angry about being out of work and discouraged about the future *or* It looks like you're very upset about having your job and stability taken away from you.

Client Practice Statements

Client 1, an 8-year-old girl: I'm telling you I don't like living at home anymore. I wish I could live with my friend and her parents. I told my mommy that one day I'm going to run away, but she doesn't listen

(continued)

LEARNING ACTIVITY #15: REFLECTION OF FEELINGS (continued)

to me. [Said in level, measured words, glancing from side to side, lips drawn tightly together, flushed face]

Self-question 1: What overt feeling words has the client used?

Self-question 2: What feelings are implied in the client's nonverbal behavior?

Self-question 3: What are accurate and similar interchangeable affect words?

Self-question 4: What is a useful sentence stem that matches the sensory words used by the client?

Self-question 5: What is the context, or situation, concerning her feelings that I'll paraphrase?

Actual reflection response: _____

_____

Client 2, a middle-aged man in marital therapy: As far as I'm concerned, our marriage turned sour last year when my wife went back to work. She's more in touch with her work than with me. [Said in soft voice tone with downcast eyes]

Self-question 1: What overt feeling words did the client use?

Self-question 2: What feelings are implied in the client's nonverbal behavior?

Self-question 3: What are accurate and similar interchangeable affect words?

Self-question 4: What is a useful sentence stem that matches the sensory words used by the client?

Self-question 5: What is the context, or situation, surrounding his feelings that I'll paraphrase?

Actual reflection response: _____

Client 3, an adolescent: Now look, we have too damn many rules around this school. I'm getting the hell out of here. As far as I can see, this place is a dump. [Said in loud, harsh voice]

Self-question 1: What overt feeling words has this client used?

Self-question 2: What feelings are implied in the client's nonverbal behavior?

Self-question 3: What are accurate and similar interchangeable affect words?

Self-question 4: What is a useful sentence stem that matches the sensory words used by the client?

Self-question 5: What is the context, or situation, surrounding his feelings that I'll paraphrase?

Actual reflection response: _____

_____

Listening for Themes: Summarization

Usually, after a client has expressed several messages or has talked for a while, her or his messages will suggest certain consistencies or patterns that we refer to as *themes*. Themes in client messages are expressed in topics that the client continually refers to or brings up in some way. The counselor can identify themes by listening to what the client repeats "over and over and with the most intensity" (Carkhuff, Pierce, & Cannon, 1977). The themes indicate what the client is trying to tell us and what the client needs to focus on in the counseling sessions. The counselor can respond to client themes by using a summarization response. For example, suppose you have been counseling a young man who, during the last three sessions, has made repeated references to homosexual relationships yet has not really identified this issue intentionally. You could use a summarization to identify the theme from these repeated references by saying something like "I'm aware that during our last few sessions you've spoken consistently about homosexual relationships. Perhaps this is an issue for you we might want to focus on."

As another example, suppose that in one session a client has given you several descriptions of different situations in which she feels concerned about how other people perceive her. You might discern that the one theme common to all these situations is the client's need for approval from others, or "other-directedness." You could use a summarization such as this to identify this theme: "One thing I see in all three of the situations you've described, Jane, is that you seem quite concerned about having the approval of the other people. Is this accurate?"

Purposes of summarization. One purpose of summarization is to tie together multiple elements of client messages. In this case, summarization can serve as a good feedback tool for the client by extracting meaning from vague and ambiguous messages. A second purpose of summarization is to identify a common theme or pattern that becomes apparent after several messages or sometimes after several sessions. Occasionally, a counselor may summarize to interrupt a client's incessant rambling or "storytelling." At such times, summarization is an important focusing tool that brings direction to the interview.

A fourth use of summarization is to moderate the pace of a session that is moving too quickly. In such instances, summaries provide psychological breathing space during the session. A final purpose of a summary is to review progress that has been made during one or more interviews.

A summarization can be defined as a collection of two or more paraphrases or reflections that condenses the client's messages or the session. In using a summarization, "a helper attends to the helpee's verbal and nonverbal statements over a period of time (e.g., three minutes to a complete session or even several sessions). The helper then selects out critical dimensions of the helpee's statements and behavior and restates them for the helpee as accurately as possible" (Ivey & Gluckstern, 1974, p. 48).

A summarization may represent collective rephrasings of either cognitive or affective data. Many summarization responses will include references to both cognitive and affective messages, as in the following four examples:

1. Example of summarization to *tie together multiple elements* of a client message:

Client, a college student: All my life I thought I wanted to be a teacher. Now I'm not sure. I always thought it was the ideal career for a woman. I don't know now if that's such a good reason. Maybe there's a career out there I'm more interested in.
Summarization: You are questioning whether being a teacher is what you really want or what you think as a woman you're supposed to be.

2. Example of summarization to *identify a theme:*

Client, a 35-year-old male: One of the reasons we divorced was because she always pushed me. I could never say no to her; I always gave in. I guess it's hard for me just to say no to requests people make.
Summarization: You're discovering that you tend to give in or not do what you want in many of your significant relationships, not just with your ex-wife.

3. Example of summarization *to regulate pace of session and to give focus:*

Client, a young woman: What a terrible week I had! The water heater broke, the dog got lost, someone stole my wallet, my car ran out of gas, and to top it all off, I gained five pounds. I can't stand myself. It seems like it shows all over me.

Summarization: Let's stop for just a minute before we go on. It seems like you've encountered an unending series of bad events this week.

4. Example of summarization *to review progress* (often used as termination strategy near end of session):

Client summary: Jane, we've got about five minutes left today. Could you summarize the key things we've been working on today?
Counselor summary: Jane, we've got about five minutes left today. It seems like most of the time we've been working on the ways you find to sabotage yourself from doing things you want to do but yet feel are out of your control. This week I'd like you to work on the following homework before our next session. . . .

Steps in summarizing.   Summarizing requires careful attention to and concentration on the client's verbal and nonverbal messages. Accurate use of this response involves good recall of client behavior, not only within a session but over time —across several sessions or even several months of therapy. Developing a summarization involves the following five steps:

1. Attend to and recall the message or series of messages by restating these to yourself covertly — what has the client been telling you, focusing on, working on? This is a key and difficult part of effective summaries because it requires you to be aware of many, varying verbal and nonverbal messages you have processed *over time.*

2. Identify any apparent patterns, themes, or multiple elements of these messages by asking yourself questions like "What has the client repeated over and over" or "What are the different parts of this puzzle?"

3. Select an appropriate beginning (sentence stem) for your summarization that uses the personal pronoun *you* or the client's name and matches one or more of the client's sensory words. (See Table 5-2.)

4. Next, using the sentence stem you've selected, select words to describe the theme or tie together multiple elements, and verbalize this as the summarization response. Remember to use your voice so that the summarization sounds like a statement instead of a question.

5. Assess the effectiveness of your summarization by listening for and observing whether the client confirms or denies the theme or whether the summary adds to or detracts from the focus of the session.

FEEDBACK #15: REFLECTION OF FEELINGS

Client 1

Question 1: What overt feeling words did the client use?
"Don't like."

Question 2: What feelings are implied in the client's nonverbal behavior?
Upset, irritation, resentment.

Question 3: What are interchangeable affect words?
Bothered, perturbed, irritated, upset.

Question 4: What sentence stem matches the client's sensory words?
"Seems like," "It sounds like," "I hear you saying that" match her words "tell" and "listen."

Question 5: What is the context, or situation, surrounding her feelings?
Living at home with her parents.

Actual examples of reflection: It sounds like you're upset about some things going on at your home now *or* I hear you saying you're bothered about your parents.

Client 2

Question 1: What overt feeling words did the client use?
No obvious ones except for phrases "turned sour" and "in touch with."

Question 2: What feelings are implied in the client's nonverbal behavior?
Sadness, loneliness, hurt.

Question 3: What are interchangeable affect words?
Hurt, lonely, left out, unhappy.

Question 4: What sentence stem matches the client's choice of sensory words?
"I sense," "You feel" match his phrases "turned sour" and "in touch with."

Question 5: What is the context, or situation, surrounding his feelings?
Wife's return to work.

Actual examples of reflection: You're feeling left out and lonely since your wife's gone back to work *or* I sense you're feeling hurt and unhappy because your wife seems so interested in her work.

Client 3

Question 1: What overt feeling words did the client use?
No obvious ones, but words like "damn," "hell," and "dump" suggest intensity of emotions.

Question 2: What feelings are implied in the client's nonverbal behavior?
Anger, frustration.

Question 3: What are interchangeable affect words?
Angry, offended, disgusted.

Question 4: What sentence stem matches the client's sensory words?
Stems such as "It seems," "It appears," "It looks like," "I can see" match his words "now look" and "I can see."

Question 5: What is the context surrounding the feelings?
School rules.

Actual examples of reflection: It looks like you're pretty disgusted now because you see these rules restricting you *or* It seems like you're very angry about having all these rules here at school.

To help you formulate a summarization, consider the following cognitive learning strategy:

1. What was this client telling me and working on today and over time? That is, what are the *key content* and *key affect?*
2. What has the client repeated over and over today and over time? That is, what is the *pattern* or *theme?*
3. What is a useful sentence stem that matches the client's sensory words?
4. How will I know whether my summarization is useful?

Notice how a counselor applies this cognitive learning strategy in developing a summarization in the following example:

Client, a middle-aged male fighting alcoholism who has told you for the last three sessions that his drinking is ruining his family life but he can't stop because it makes him feel better and helps him to handle job stress: I know drinking doesn't really help me in the long run. And it sure doesn't help my family. My wife keeps threatening to leave. I know all this. It's hard to stay away from the booze. Having a drink makes me feel relieved. [Said in low, soft voice, downcast eyes, stooped shoulders]

Self-question 1: What has this client been telling me today and over time?
Key content: results of drinking aren't good for him or his family.
Key affect: drinking makes him feel better, less anxious.

Self-question 2: What has this client repeated over and over today and over time—pattern or theme? That despite adverse effects and family deterioration, he continues to drink for stress reduction;

that is, stress reduction through alcohol seems worth losing his family.

Self-question 3: What sentence stem matches the client's sensory words?

I'll try "You're feeling," "My sense of it," and so on to match his words "know" and "feel."

Suppose that at this time the counselor delivered one of the following summarizations to the client:

> "Jerry, I sense that you feel it's worth having the hassle of family problems because of the good, calm feelings you get whenever you drink."

> "Jerry, you feel that your persistent drinking is creating a lot of difficulties for you in your

family, and I sense your reluctance to stop drinking in spite of these adverse effects."

> "Jerry, I sense that, despite everything, alcohol feels more satisfying (rewarding) to you than your own family."

If Jerry confirms the theme that alcohol is more important now than his family, the counselor can conclude that the summarization was useful. If Jerry denies the theme or issue summarized by the counselor, the counselor can ask Jerry to clarify how the summarization was inaccurate, remembering that the summary may indeed be inaccurate or that Jerry may not be ready to acknowledge the issue at this time.

LEARNING ACTIVITY #16: SUMMARIZATION

In this learning activity, you are presented with three client practice messages. For each message, develop a summarization response, using the cognitive learning strategy described earlier and outlined below. To internalize this learning strategy, you may wish to talk through these self-questions overtly (aloud) and then covertly—that is, silently to yourself. The end product will be a summarization response that you can say aloud or write down or both. An example precedes the practice messages. Feedback is given on pages 110–111.

Example

Client, a 10-year-old girl:

At beginning of the session: I don't understand why my parents can't live together anymore. I'm not blaming anybody, but it just feels very confusing to me. [Said in low, soft voice with lowered, moist eyes]

Near the middle of the same session: I wish they could keep it together. I guess I feel like they can't because they fight about me so much. Maybe I'm the reason they don't want to live together anymore.

Self-question 1: What has this client been telling me and looking at today in terms of key *content* and key *affect?*

Key content: wants parents to stay together.
Key affect: feels sad, upset, responsible.

Self-question 2: What has the client repeated over and over today or over time—that is, pattern or theme?

She's the one who's responsible for her parents' breakup.

Self-question 3: What is a useful sentence stem that matches the client's sensory words?

Try "I sense" or "You're feeling," to match her words such as "don't understand" and "feels."

Examples of summarization response: Joan, at the start of our talk today, you were feeling like no one person was responsible for your parents' separation. Now I sense you're saying that you feel responsible *or* Joan, earlier today you indicated you didn't feel like blaming anyone for what's happening to your folks. Now I'm sensing that you are feeling like you are responsible for their breakup.

Client Practice Messages

Client 1, a 30-year-old man who has been blaming himself for his wife's unhappiness: I really feel guilty about marrying her in the first place. It wasn't really for love. It was just a convenient thing to do. I feel like I've messed up her life really badly. I also feel obliged to her. [Said in low, soft voice tone with lowered eyes]

Self-question 1: What has this client been telling me and working on today?
Key content:
Key affect:

Self-question 2: What has this client repeated over and over today or over time in terms of patterns and themes?

Self-question 3: What is a sentence stem that matches the client's sensory words?
Summarization response: _____

_____

Client 2, a 35-year-old woman who focused on how her life has improved since having children: I never thought I would feel this great. I always thought being a parent would be boring and terri-
(continued)

LEARNING ACTIVITY #16: SUMMARIZATION (continued)

bly difficult. It's not, for me. It's fascinating and easy. It makes everything worthwhile. [Said with alertness and animation]

Self-question 1: What has this client been telling me and working on today?
Key content:
Key affect:
Self-question 2: What has this client repeated over and over today or over time in terms of patterns and themes?
Self-question 3: What is a sentence stem that uses the client's sensory words?
Summarization response: _____
_____

Client 3, a 27-year-old woman who has continually focused on her relationships with men and her needs for excitement and stability:
First session: I've been dating lots and lots of men for the last few years. Most of them have been married. That's great because there are no demands on me. [Bright eyes, facial animation, high-pitched voice]
Fourth session: It doesn't feel so good anymore. It's not so much fun. Now I guess I miss having some commitment and stability in my life. [Soft voice, lowered eyes]

Self-question 1: What has this client been telling me and working on today?
Key content:
Key affect:
Self-question 2: What has this client repeated over and over today or over time in terms of patterns and themes?
Self-question 3: What is a sentence stem that matches the client's sensory words?
Summarization response: _____
_____

□ SUMMARY

We often hear these questions: "What good does all this listening do? How does just rephrasing client messages really help?" In response, we will reiterate the rationale for using listening responses in counseling.

1. Listening to clients is a very powerful reinforcer and may strengthen clients' desire to talk about themselves and their concerns. Not listening may prevent clients from sharing relevant information (Morganstern & Tevlin, 1981, p. 85).

2. Listening to a client first may mean a greater chance of responding accurately to the client in later stages of counseling, such as problem solving (Carkhuff et al., 1977). By jumping to quick solutions without laying a foundation of listening, you may inadvertently ignore the primary problem or propose inadequate and ill-timed action steps.

3. Listening encourages the client to assume responsibility for selecting the topic and focus of an interview. Not listening may meet your needs to find information or to solve problems. In doing so, you may portray yourself as an expert rather than a collaborator. Simply asking a series of questions or proposing a series of action steps in the initial phase of helping can cause the client to perceive you as the expert and can hinder proper development of client self-responsibility in the interview.

4. Good listening and attending skills model socially appropriate behavior for clients (Gazda et al., 1984). Many clients have not yet learned to use the art of listening in their own relationship and social contacts. They are more likely to incorporate these skills to improve their interpersonal relationships when they experience them firsthand through their contact with a significant other, such as a therapist.

Some counselors can articulate a clear rationale for listening but nevertheless cannot listen in an interview because of blocks that inhibit effective listening. Some of the most common blocks to listening are these:

1. The tendency to judge and evaluate the client's messages.
2. The tendency to stop attending because of distractions such as noise, the time of day, or the topic.
3. The temptation to respond to missing pieces of information by asking questions.
4. The temptation or the pressure put on yourself to solve problems or find answers.
5. The preoccupation with yourself as you try to practice the skills. This preoccupation shifts the focus from the client to you and actually reduces, rather than increases, your potential for listening.

Effective use of listening responses requires you to

confront these blocks head-on. Too often a counselor will simply get discouraged and not listen because it is too difficult. Start slowly and work with each listening response until you feel comfortable with it. As you accumulate counseling experience and confidence, you can listen with greater ease and facility. As you go through the remainder of this book and add to your repertory of skills, we hope that you will treat listening responses as a permanent fixture.

POSTEVALUATION

PART ONE

This part is designed for you to assess your performance on Chapter Objective One. On a sheet of paper, classify each of the counselor listening responses in the following list as a clarification, paraphrase, reflection of feelings, or summarization. If you identify 9 out of 12 responses correctly, you have met this objective. You can check your answers against those provided in the feedback that follows on pages 111–112.

1. Client, an older, retired person: "How do they expect me to live on this little bit of Social Security? I've worked hard all my life. Now I have so little to show for it—I've got to choose between heat and food."

   C a. "Can you tell me who exactly expects you to be able to manage on this amount of money?"

   S b. "All your life you've worked hard, hoping to give yourself a secure future. Now it's very upsetting to have only a little bit of money that can't possibly cover your basic needs."

2. Client: "I don't like taking this medication. It makes me feel worse. I can't see how it can possibly help. I know I asked you to give me something to help calm me down, but I didn't imagine it would have these effects."

   C a. "Can you clarify exactly what effects these pills have seemed to have on you?"

   S b. "Originally you seemed to want very much to be given some medication to rely on to help calm your nerves. Now that you're taking it, it's hard for you to see whether it's been helping or hurting."

3. Client: "I feel so nervous when I have to give a speech in front of lots of people."

   R a. "You feel anxious when you have to talk to a group of people."

   P b. "You would rather not have to talk in front of large groups."

4. Client: "I always have a drink when I'm under pressure.

   C a. "Are you saying that you use alcohol to calm you down?"

   P b. "You think alcohol has a calming effect on you."

5. Client: "I don't know whether I've ever experienced orgasm. My husband thinks I have, though."

   C a. "Are you saying that you've been trying to have your husband believe you do experience orgasm?"

   R b. "You feel uncertain about whether you've ever really had an orgasm, even though your husband senses that you have."

6. Client: "I haven't left my house in years. I'm even afraid to hang out the clothes."

   R a. "You feel panicked and uneasy when you go outside the security of your house."

   P b. "Because of this fear, you've stayed inside your house for a long time."

PART TWO

Match the four listening responses listed in the right column with the intended purposes of these responses listed in the left column (Chapter Objective Two). Feedback follows the postevaluation.

Intended Purpose of Response	Listening Response
_C_ 1. To encourage greater expression of feeling	a. Clarification
_a_ 2. To confirm the accuracy of what you heard, saw, or grasped	b. Paraphrase
_b_ 3. To highlight the content part of a message	c. Reflection of feelings
_d_ 4. To interrupt rambling and provide focus to the session	d. Summarization
_a_ 5. To clear up vague or confusing client messages	
_c_ 6. To help the client discriminate accurately among feelings	

(continued)

POSTEVALUATION (continued)

7. To identify a common theme from client messages

8. To tie together multiple elements of a client message

PART THREE

Three client statements are presented. Objective Three asks you to verbalize or write an example of each of the four listening responses for each client statement.* In developing these responses, it may be helpful to use the cognitive learning strategy you practiced earlier for each response. Feedback follows the evaluation.

Client 1, a 28-year-old woman: My life is a shambles. I lost my job, my friends never come around anymore. It's been months now, but I still can't seem to cut down. I can't see clearly. It seems hopeless. [Said in high-pitched voice, with crossed legs, lots of nervous "twitching" in hands and face]
Clarification:
Paraphrase:
Reflection:
Summarization:

Client 2, a sophomore in high school: I can't seem to get along with my parents. They're always harassing me, telling me what to do. Sometimes I get so mad I feel like hitting them, but I don't, because it would only make the situation worse.
Clarification:
Paraphrase:
Reflection:
Summarization:

Client 3, a 54-year-old man: Ever since my wife died four months ago, I can't get interested in anything. I don't want to eat or sleep. I'm losing weight. Sometimes I just tell myself I'd be better off if I were dead, too.
Clarification:
Paraphrase:
Reflection:
Summarization:

PART FOUR

This part of the evaluation gives you an opportunity to develop your observation skills of key aspects of

client behavior that must be attended to in order to listen effectively:

1. Vague or confusing phrases and messages
2. Key content expressed
3. Use of affect words
4. Nonverbal behavior illustrative of feeling or mood states
5. Presence of themes or patterns

Objective Four asks you to observe these five aspects of a client's behavior during a 15-minute interview conducted by someone else. Record your observations on the Client Observation Checklist that follows. You can obtain feedback for this activity by having two or more persons observe and rate the same session—then compare your responses.

CLIENT OBSERVATION CHECKLIST

Name of counselor _____
Name of observer(s) _____
_____

Instructions: Given the five categories of client behavior to observe (left column), use the right column to record separate occurrences of behaviors within these categories as they occur during a short counseling interview.*

Observed category of behavior	*Selected key client words and nonverbal behavior*
1. Vague, confusing, ambiguous phrases, messages	1. _____ 2. _____ 3. _____ 4. _____ 5. _____
2. Key content (situation, event, idea, person)	1. _____ 2. _____ 3. _____ 4. _____ 5. _____
3. Affect words used	1. _____ 2. _____ 3. _____ 4. _____ 5. _____

(continued)

* These three client messages can be put on audiotape with pauses between statements. Instead of reading the message, you can listen to the message and write or verbalize your responses during the pause.

* If observers are not available, audiotape or videotape your sessions and complete the checklist while reviewing the tape.

4. Nonverbal behavior indicative of certain feelings

1. _____
2. _____
3. _____
4. _____
5. _____

5. Themes, patterns

1. _____
2. _____
3. _____
4. _____
5. _____

Observer impressions and comments _____
_____
_____

PART FIVE

This part of the evaluation gives you a chance to demonstrate the four listening responses. Objective Five asks you to conduct a 15-minute role-play interview in which you use at least two examples of each of the four listening responses. Someone can observe your performance, or you can assess yourself from an audiotape of the interview. You or the observer can classify your responses and judge their effectiveness using the Listening Checklist that follows. Try to select a listening response to use when you have a particular purpose in mind. Remember, in order to listen, it is helpful to—

1. refrain from making judgments
2. resist distractions
3. avoid asking questions
4. avoid giving advice
5. stay focused on the client

Obtain feedback for this activity by noting the categories of responses on the Listening Checklist and their judged effectiveness.

LISTENING CHECKLIST

Name of counselor _____
Name of observer _____

Instructions: In the far left column, "Counselor response," summarize a few key words of each counselor statement, followed by a brief notation of the client's verbal and nonverbal response in the next column, "Client response." Then classify the message as a clarification, paraphrase, reflection of feeling, summarization, or other under the corresponding column. Rate the *effectiveness* of each counselor response in the far right column, "Effectiveness of response," on the following 1–3 scale.

1 = not effective. Client ignored counselor message or gave indication that counselor message was inaccurate and "off target."
2 = somewhat effective. Client gave some verbal or nonverbal indication that counselor message was partly right, accurate, "on target."
3 = very effective. Client's verbal and nonverbal behavior confirmed that counselor response was very accurate, "on target," or "fit."

Remember to watch and listen for the *client's* reaction to the response for your effectiveness rating.

(continued)

POSTEVALUATION (continued)

Counselor response (key words)	Client Response (key words)	Type of counselor response					Effectiveness of response (determined by client response) Rate from 1 to 3 (3 = high)
		Clarification	Paraphrase	Reflection of feelings	Summarization	Other	
1.							
2.							
3.							
4.							
5.							
6.							
7.							
8.							
9.							
10.							
11.							
12.							
13.							
14.							
15.							
16.							
17.							
18.							
19.							
20.							

Observer comments and general observations _____

FEEDBACK #16: SUMMARIZATION

Client 1

Question 1: What has the client told me?

Key content: He married for convenience, not love.

Key affect: Now he feels both guilty and indebted.

Question 2: What has the client repeated over and over now and before in terms of patterns and themes?

Conflicting feelings—feels a strong desire to get out of the marriage yet feels a need to keep relationship going because he feels responsible for his wife's unhappiness.

Question 3: What is an appropriate sentence stem that matches the client's sensory words?

Use stems such as "You're feeling," "My grasp of it is," "I sense that" to match his constant use of the verb "feel."

Examples of summarization response: I sense you're feeling pulled in two different directions. For yourself, you want out of the relationship. For her sake, you feel you should stay in the relationship" *or* You're feeling like you've used her for your convenience and because of this you think you owe it to her to keep the relationship going *or* I can grasp how very much you want to pull yourself out of the marriage and also how responsible you feel for your wife's present unhappiness.

(continued)

Client 2

Question 1: What has the client told me?
  Key content: Children have made her life better, more worthwhile.
  Key affect: Surprise and pleasure.
Question 2: What has the client said over and over in terms of patterns and themes?
  Being a parent is uplifting and rewarding even though she didn't expect it to be. In addition, her children are very important to her. To some extent, they define her worth and value as a person.
Question 3: What is an appropriate sentence stem that matches the client's sensory words?
  There are no real clear-cut sensory words exhibited in this message, so I may want to emphasize several in my response—for example, "It *seems* like you're *feeling*" or "I *hear feelings* of."
Examples of summarization response: It seems like you're feeling surprise, satisfaction, and relief about finding parenting so much easier and more rewarding than you had expected it would be *or* I hear feelings of surprise and pleasure in your voice as you reveal how great it is to be a parent and how important your children are to you *or* You seem so happy about the way your life is going since you've had children—as if they make you and your life more worthwhile.

Client 3

Question 1: What has the client told me?
  Key content: She has been dating lots of men who have their own commitments.
  Key affect: It used to feel great; now she feels a sense of loss and emptiness.
Question 2: What has she repeated over and over in terms of patterns and themes?
  At first—feelings of pleasure, relief not to have demands in close relationships. Now, feelings are changing, feels less satisfied, wants more stability in close relationships.
Question 3: What is an appropriate sentence stem that matches the client's sensory words?
  There are no clear-cut sensory words except for "feel" in the fourth session, so I'll vary my own words in my response and also include the word "feel."
Examples of summarization response: Lee Ann, originally you said it was great to be going out with a lot of different men who didn't ask much of you. Now you're also feeling it's not so great—it's keeping you from finding some purpose and stability in your life *or* In our first session, you were feeling "up" about all those relationships with noncommittal men. Now you're feeling like this is

interfering with the stability you need and haven't yet found *or* At first it was great to have all this excitement and few demands. Now you're feeling some loss from lack of a more stable, involved relationship.

□ SUGGESTED READINGS

Brammer, L. M., & Shostrom, E. L. (1982). *Therapeutic psychology* (4th ed.). Englewood Cliffs, NJ: Prentice-Hall.

Carkhuff, R. R., & Anthony, W. A. (1979). *The skills of helping.* Amherst, MA: Human Resource Development Press.

Hackney, H., & Cormier, L. S. (1979). *Counseling strategies and objectives* (2nd ed.). Englewood Cliffs, NJ: Prentice-Hall.

Ivey, A. E. (1983). *Intentional interviewing and counseling.* Monterey, CA: Brooks/Cole.

Richardson, B., & Stone, G. L. (1981). Effects of a cognitive adjunct procedure within a microtraining situation. *Journal of Counseling Psychology, 28,* 168–175.

FEEDBACK: POSTEVALUATION

PART ONE
1. a. Clarification
   b. Summarization
2. a. Clarification
   b. Summarization
3. a. Reflection
   b. Paraphrase
4. a. Clarification
   b. Paraphrase
5. a. Clarification
   b. Reflection
6. a. Reflection
   b. Paraphrase

PART TWO
1. c. Reflection
2. a. Clarification
3. b. Paraphrase
4. d. Summarization
5. a. Clarification
6. c. Reflection
7. d. Summarization
8. d. Summarization

(continued)

FEEDBACK: POSTEVALUATION (continued)

PART THREE

Here are some examples of listening responses. See whether yours are similar:

Client statement 1

1. Clarification: "Can you describe what you mean by 'cutting down'?"
2. Paraphrase: "You seem to realize that your life is not going the way you want it to."
3. Reflection: "You appear frightened about the chaos in your life, and you seem uncertain of what you can do to straighten it out."
4. Summarization: "Your whole life seems to be falling apart. Your friends are avoiding you, and now you don't even have a job to go to. Even though you've tried to solve the problem, you can't seem to handle it alone. Coming here to talk is a useful first step in 'clearing up the water' for you."

Client statement 2

1. Clarification: "Can you describe what it's like when you don't get along with them?"
2. Paraphrase: "It appears that your relationship with your parents is deteriorating to the point where you feel you may lose control of yourself."
3. Reflection: "You feel frustrated and angry with your parents because they're always giving you orders."
4. Summarization: "It seems like the situation at home with your parents has become intolerable. You can't stand their badgering, and you feel afraid that you might do something you would later regret."

Client statement 3

1. Clarification: "Are you saying that since the death of your wife, life has become so miserable that you occasionally contemplate taking your own life?"
2. Paraphrase: "Your life has lost much of its meaning since your wife's recent death."
3. Reflection: "It sounds like you're very lonely and depressed since your wife died."
4. Summarization: "Since your wife died, you've lost interest in living. There's no fun or excitement anymore, and further, you're telling yourself that it's not going to get any better."

ACTION RESPONSES

SIX

Listening responses involve responding to client messages primarily from the client's point of view, or frame of reference. There are times in the counseling process when it is legitimate to move beyond the client's frame of reference and to use responses that include more counselor-generated data and perceptions. These responses, which we have labeled *action responses,* are active rather than passive and reflect a counselor-directed more than a client-centered style. Whereas listening responses influence the client indirectly, action responses exert a more direct influence on the client (Ivey, 1983). Action responses are based as much on the counselor's perceptions and hypotheses as on the client's messages and behavior. We have selected four such action responses: probes, confrontation, interpretation, and information giving. The general purpose of action responses, according to Egan (1982), is to help clients see the need for change and action through a more objective frame of reference.

☐ OBJECTIVES

1. Given a written list of counselor responses, be able to identify accurately at least six out of eight examples of the four counselor action responses.
2. Using a written list, match the four action responses with the intended purpose of each response.
3. With a written list of three client statements, write an example of each of the four action responses for each client statement.
4. In a 30-minute counseling interview in which you are an observer, listen for and record five key aspects of client behavior that form the basis for action responding.
5. Conduct at least one 20-minute counseling interview in which you integrate relationship variables (Chapters 2 and 3), nonverbal behavior (Chapter 4), listening responses (Chapter 5), and action responses (Chapter 6).

☐ ACTION RESPONSES AND TIMING

The most difficult part of using action responses is the timing, the point at which these responses are used in the interview. As you recall from Chapter 5, some helpers tend to jump into action responses before listening and establishing rapport with the client. Listening responses generally reflect clients' understanding of themselves. In contrast, action responses reflect the *counselor's* understanding of the client. Action responses can be used a great deal in the interview as long as the counselor is careful to lay the foundation with attending and listening. The listening base can heighten the client's receptivity to a counselor action message. If the counselor "lays on" his or her opinions and perceptions too quickly, the client may respond with denial, with defensiveness, or even with dropping out of counseling. When this happens, the counselor needs to "drop back" to a less obtrusive level of influence and do more listening, at least until a strong base of client trust and confidence has been developed.

☐ FOUR ACTION RESPONSES

We have selected four action responses to describe in this chapter: the probe, confrontation, interpretation, and information giving. A *probe* is an open or closed question or inquiry. A *confrontation* is a description of a client discrepancy. An *interpretation* is a possible explanation for the client's behavior. *Information giving* is the communication of data or facts about experiences, events, alternatives, or people.

Look at the way these four action responses differ in this illustration:

Client, a 35-year-old widow, mother of two young children: My whole life fell apart when my husband died. I keep feeling so unsure about my ability to make it on my own and to support my kids. My husband always made all the decisions for me. Now I haven't slept well for so long, and I'm drinking more heavily—I can't even think straight. Besides, I've put on 15 pounds. I look like a witch. Who would even want to think of hiring me the way I am now?

Counselor probe: What makes you think of yourself as not being able to make it on your own?
or
How do you think you could handle the situation?

Counselor confrontation: It seems that you're saying two things—first, that you aren't sure of your abil-

ity to work and support your family, but also that you're almost making it hard for someone else to see you as employable by some of the things you're doing, such as drinking and putting on weight.

Counselor interpretation: It's possible that your drinking heavily and not sleeping well are ways to continue to avoid accepting the responsibility of making decisions for yourself.

Counselor information giving: Perhaps you are still not over the grief process. It might help to acknowledge your feelings of loss and to take a look at where you are with respect to the different stages of grieving. For example, . . .

Table 6-1 describes the definitions and intended purposes of these four action responses. Remember, these intended purposes are presented only as tentative guidelines, not as "the truth." The remainder of the chapter will describe and present model examples of these four skills. You will have an opportunity to practice each skill and receive feedback about your responses.

Probes

Probes, or questions, are an indispensable part of the interview process. Their effectiveness depends on the type of question and the frequency of their use. Questions have the potential for establishing a desirable or undesirable pattern of interpersonal exchange, depending on the skill of the therapist (Long, Paradise, & Long, 1981). Beginning interviewers err by assuming that a helping interview is a series of questions and answers or by asking the wrong kind of question at a particular time. These practices are likely to make the client feel interrogated rather than understood. Research has shown that even more experienced counselors overuse this potentially valuable verbal response (Spooner & Stone, 1977). Unfortunately, asking a question is all too easy to do during silence or when you are at a loss for words. Questions should not be asked unless you have a particular purpose for the question in mind. For example, if you are using a question as an open invitation to talk, realize that you are in fact asking the client to initiate a dialogue and allow the client to respond in this way (Long et al., 1981).

Open and closed probes. Most effective questions are worded in an open-ended fashion, beginning with words such as *what, how, when, where,* or *who.* According to Ivey and Simek-Downing (1980, p. 75), "An open-ended question must be

TABLE 6-1. Definitions and intended purposes of counselor action responses

Response	Definition	Intended purpose
Probe	Open-ended or closed question or inquiry	*Open-ended questions* 1. To begin an interview 2. To encourage client elaboration or to obtain information 3. To elicit specific examples of client's behaviors, feelings or thoughts 4. To motivate client to communicate *Closed questions* 1. To narrow the topic of discussion 2. To obtain specific information 3. To identify parameters of a problem or issue 4. To interrupt an overtalkative client—for example, to give focus to the session
Confrontation	Description of client discrepancy	1. To identify client's mixed (incongruent) messages 2. To explore other ways of perceiving client's self or situation
Interpretation	Possible explanation of or association among various client behaviors	1. To identify the relation between client's implicit messages and behaviors 2. To examine client behavior from alternative view or with different explanation 3. To add to client's self-understanding as a basis for client action
Information giving	Verbal communication of data or facts	1. To identify alternatives 2. To evaluate alternatives 3. To dispel myths 4. To motivate clients to examine issues they may have been avoiding

answered with an explanation, requires discourse, and cannot easily be answered with a "yes" or "no." The particular word used to begin an open-ended question is important. Research has shown that "what" questions tend to solicit facts and information, "how" questions are associated with sequence and process or emotions, and "why" questions produce reasons and "intellectualizing" (Ivey & Simek-Downing, 1980). Similarly, "when" and "where" questions solicit information about time and place, and "who" questions are associated with information about people. The importance of using *different* words in formulating open-ended questions is critical. As Ivey and Simek-Downing note, "Frequently therapists develop a habit of asking only one type of open question, thus failing to see other dimensions of client experience" (1980, p. 75).

Open-ended probes have a number of purposes in different counseling situations (Hackney & Cormier, 1979; Ivey, 1983; Long et al., 1981).

1. Beginning an interview ("What would you like to discuss today?").

2. Encouraging the client to express more information ("What else can you tell me about this?").
3. Eliciting examples of particular behaviors, thoughts, or feelings so that the counselor can better understand the conditions contributing to the client's problem ("What are you doing in this situation? What are you thinking in this situation? How are you feeling about this?").
4. Developing client commitment to communicate by inviting the client to talk and guiding the client along a focused interaction.

In contrast to open-ended questions, closed, or focused, questions can be useful if the counselor needs a particular fact or seeks a particular bit of information. These questions begin with words such as *are, do, can, is, did* and can be answered with a yes, a no, or a very short response. As we will see in Chapter 8, questions are a major tool for obtaining information during the assessment process.

These are examples of closed questions:

1. "Of all the problems we discussed, which bothers you the most?"
2. "Is there a history of depression in your family?"
3. "Are you planning to look for a job in the next few months?"

The purposes of closed questions include the following:

1. Narrowing the area of discussion by asking the client for a specific response ("Is there a history of depression in your family?").
2. Gathering specific information ("Is your daughter still living at home?").
3. Identifying parameters of problems ("Have you noticed anything that makes the depression worse?").
4. Interrupting an overtalkative client who rambles or "storytells" ("Do you want to focus now on the family situation you mentioned earlier?").

Closed questions must be used sparingly within an interview. Too many closed questions may discourage discussion and may subtly give the client permission to avoid sensitive or important topics.

Guidelines in the use of probes.   Probes will be used more effectively and efficiently if you remember some important guidelines for their use. First, develop questions that center on the concerns of the client. Effective questions arise from what the client has already said, not from the counselor's curiosity or need for closure.

Second, after a question, use a pause to give the client sufficient time to respond. Remember that the client may not have a ready response. The feeling of having to supply a quick answer may be threatening and may encourage the client to give a response that pleases the therapist.

Third, ask only one question at a time. Some interviewers tend to ask multiple questions (two or more) before allowing the client time to respond. We call this "stacking questions." It confuses the client, who may respond only to the least important of your series of questions.

Fourth, avoid accusatory or antagonistic questions. These are questions that reflect antagonism either because of the counselor's voice tone or because of use of the word *why.* You can obtain the same information by asking "what" instead of "why." Accusatory questions can make a client feel defensive.

Finally, avoid relying on questions as a primary response mode during an interview (an exception would be when doing an intake, a history, or an assessment session). Remember that in some non-Western cultures questions may seem offensive and intrusive. In any culture, consistent overuse of questions can create a number of problems in the therapeutic relationship, including creating dependency, promoting yourself as an expert, reducing responsibility and involvement by the client, and creating resentment (Gazda et al., 1984). The feeling of being interrogated may be especially harmful with "reluctant" clients. Questions are most effective when they provoke new insights and yield new information. To determine whether it is really necessary to use a question at any particular time during a session, ask the question covertly to yourself and see whether you can answer it for the client. If you can, the question is probably unnecessary, and a different response would be more productive (D'Augelli, D'Augelli, & Danish, 1981).

Steps in the use of probes.   There are four steps in formulating effective probes. First, determine the purpose of your probe — is it legitimate and therapeutically useful? Often, before probing for information, it is therapeutically useful to demonstrate first that you have heard the client's message. Listening before probing is particularly important when clients reveal strong emotions. It also helps clients to feel understood rather than interrogated. For this reason, before each of our example probes, we use a paraphrase or reflection response. In actual practice, this "bridging" of listening and action responses is very important. Second, depending on the purpose, decide what type of question would be most helpful. Remember that open-ended probes foster client exploration, while closed or focused questions should be reserved for times when you want specific information or you need to narrow the area of discussion. Make sure your question centers on concerns of the client, not issues of interest only to you. Finally, remember to assess the effectiveness of your questioning by determining whether its purpose was achieved. A question is not useful simply because the client answered or responded to it. Additionally, examine how the client responded and the overall explanation, inquiry, and dialogue that ensued as a result of particular questions (Long et al., 1981).

These steps are summarized in the following cognitive learning strategy:

1. What is the purpose of my probe, and is it therapeutically useful?
2. Can I anticipate the client's answer?
3. Given the purpose, how can I start the wording of my probe to be most effective?
4. How will I know whether my probe is effective?

Notice how the counselor applies this cognitive learning strategy in the following example:

Client: I just don't know where to start. My marriage is falling apart. My mom recently died. And I've been having some difficulties at work.
Counselor:
  1. What is the purpose of my probe—and is it therapeutically useful?
    To get the client to focus more specifically on an issue of most concern to her.
  2. Can I anticipate the client's answer? No.
  3. Given the purpose, how can I start the wording of my probe to be most effective?
    "Which one of these?"
    "Do you want to discuss _____?"
  4. How will I know whether my probe is effective?

Examine the client's verbal and nonverbal response and resulting dialogue, as well as whether the purpose was achieved (whether client starts to focus on the specific concern).

Suppose that at this time the counselor's covert visualization or self-talk ends and the following dialogue ensues:

Counselor question: Things must feel overwhelming to you right now. [reflection] Of the three concerns you just mentioned, which one is of most concern to you now? [probe]
Client response: My marriage. I want to keep it together, but I don't think my husband does. [accompanied by direct eye contact; body posture, which had been tense, now starts to relax]

From the client's verbal and nonverbal response, the therapist can conclude the question was effective because the client focused on a specific concern and did not appear to be threatened by the question. The therapist can now covertly congratulate herself or himself for formulating an effective question with this client.

Learning Activity #17 gives you an opportunity to try out this cognitive learning strategy in order to develop effective probes.

LEARNING ACTIVITY #17: PROBES

In this learning activity, you are given three client practice statements. For each client message, develop an example of a probe, using the cognitive learning strategy described earlier and outlined below. To internalize this learning strategy, you may wish to talk through these self-questions overtly (aloud) and then covertly (silently to yourself). The end product will be a probe that you can say aloud or write down or both. An example precedes the practice messages. Feedback is at the end of the learning activity on page 121).

Example

Client 1, a middle-aged woman: I just get so nervous. I'm just a bunch of nerves.

Self-question 1: What is the purpose of my probe—and is it therapeutically useful?
  To ask for examples of times when she is nervous. This is therapeutically useful because it contributes to increased understanding of the problem.
Self-question 2: Can I anticipate the client's answer? No.
Self-question 3: Given the purpose, how can I start

the wording of my probe to be most effective? "When" or "what."
Actual probes: You say you're feeling pretty upset. [reflection] When do you feel this way? [probe] *or* What are some times when you get this feeling? [probe]

Client Practice Messages

The purpose of the probe is given to you for each message. Try to develop probes that relate to the stated purposes. Remember too, to precede your probe with a listening response such as paraphrase or reflection.

Client 1, a retired woman: To be frank about it, it's been pure hell around my house the last year.

Self-question 1: What is the purpose of my probe? To encourage client to elaborate on how and what has been hell for her.
Self-question 2: Can I anticipate the client's answer?
Self-question 3: Given the purpose, how can I start the wording of my probe to be most effective?
Actual probe(s): _____

(continued)

LEARNING ACTIVITY #17: PROBES (continued)

Client 2, a 40-year-old man: Sometimes I just feel kind of blue. It goes on for a while. Not every day but sometimes.

Self-question 1: What is the purpose of my probe? To find out whether client has noticed anything that makes the "blueness" better.
Self-question 2: Can I anticipate the client's answer?
Self-question 3: Given the purpose, how can I start the wording of my probe to be most effective?
Actual probe(s): _____
_____

Client 3, a 35-year-old woman: I just feel overwhelmed right now. Too many kids underfoot. Not enough time for me.

Self-question 1: What is the purpose of my probe? To find out how many kids are underfoot and in what capacity client is responsible for them.
Self-question 2: Can I anticipate the client's answer?
Self-question 3: Given the purpose, how can I start the wording of my probe to be most effective?
Actual probe(s): _____
_____

Confrontation

A confrontation is a verbal response in which the counselor describes discrepancies, conflicts, and mixed messages apparent in the client's feelings, thoughts, and actions. Patterson and Eisenberg (1983) believe that confrontation is a tool to focus "the client's attention on some aspect of his or her behavior that, if changed, would lead to more effective functioning" (p. 75). Confrontation has several purposes. One purpose is to help clients explore other ways of perceiving themselves or an issue, leading ultimately to different actions or behaviors. A second and major purpose of confrontation is to help the client become more aware of discrepancies or incongruities in thoughts, feelings, and actions. There are many instances within an interview in which a client says or does something that is inconsistent. For example, a client may say she doesn't want to talk to you because you are a male but then goes ahead and talks to you. In this case, the client's verbal message is inconsistent with her actual behavior. This is an example of an inconsistent, or mixed, message. The purpose of using a confrontation to deal with a mixed message is to describe the discrepancy or contradiction to the client. Often the client is unaware or only vaguely aware of the conflict before the counselor points it out. In describing the discrepancy, it is often most helpful to use a confrontation that presents or connects both parts of the discrepancy.

Six major types of mixed messages and accompanying descriptions of counselor confrontations are presented as examples (see also Egan, 1982; Ivey, 1983).

1. *Verbal and nonverbal behavior*
   a. The client says "I feel comfortable" (verbal message) and at the same time is fidgeting and twisting her hands (nonverbal message).
   Counselor confrontation: You say you feel comfortable, and you're also fidgeting and twisting your hands.
   b. Client says "I feel happy about the relationship being over—it's better this way" (verbal message) and is talking in a slow, low-pitched voice (nonverbal message).
   Counselor confrontation: You say you're happy it's over, and at the same time your voice suggests you have some other feelings, too.
2. *Verbal messages and action steps or behaviors*
   a. Client says "I'm going to call her" (verbal message) but reports the next week that he did not make the call (action step).
   Counselor confrontation: You said you would call her, and as of now you haven't done so.
   b. Client says "Counseling is very important to me" (verbal message) but calls off the next two sessions (behavior).
   Counselor confrontation: Several weeks ago you said how important counseling is to you; now I'm also aware that you called off our last two meetings.
3. *Two verbal messages* (stated inconsistencies)
   a. Client says "He's sleeping around with other people. I don't feel bothered [verbal message 1], but I think our relationship should mean more to him than it does" [verbal message 2].
   Counselor confrontation: First you say you feel OK about his behavior; now you're feeling upset that your relationship is not as important to him as it is to you.

b. Client says "I really do love little Georgie [verbal message 1], although he often bugs the hell out of me" [verbal message 2].
Counselor confrontation: You seem to be aware that much of the time you love him, and at other times you feel very irritated toward him, too.

4. *Two nonverbal messages* (apparent inconsistencies)
   a. Client is smiling (nonverbal message 1) and crying (nonverbal message 2) at the same time.
   Counselor confrontation: You're smiling and also crying at the same time.
   b. Client is looking directly at counselor (nonverbal message 1) and has just moved chair back from counselor (nonverbal message 2).
   Counselor confrontation: You're looking at me while you say this, and at the same time, you also just moved away.

5. *Two persons* (counselor/client, parent/child, teacher/student, spouse/spouse, and so on)
   a. Client's husband lost his job two years ago. Client wants to move; husband wants to stick around near his family.
   Counselor confrontation: Edie, you'd like to move. Marshall, you're feeling family ties and want to stick around.
   b. A woman presents anxiety, depression, and memory loss. You suggest a medical workup to rule out any organic dysfunction, and the client refuses.
   Counselor confrontation: Irene, I feel it's very important for us to have a medical workup so we know what to do that will be most helpful for you. You seem to feel very reluctant to have the workup done. How can we work this out?

6. *Verbal message and context or situation*
   a. A young child deplores her parents' divorce and states that she wants to help her parents get back together.
   Counselor confrontation: Juanita, you say you want to help your parents get back together. At the same time, you had no role in their breakup. How do you put these two things together?
   b. A young married couple have had severe conflicts for the past three years, and still they want to have a baby to improve their marriage.
   Counselor confrontation: The two of you have separated three times since I've been seeing you in therapy. Now you're saying you want to use a child to improve your relationship. Many couples indicate that having a child and being parents increases, rather than relieves, stress. How do you put this together?

LEARNING ACTIVITY #18: MIXED MESSAGES

An important part of developing effective confrontations is learning to identify accurately various client discrepancies and incongruities. In this learning activity, we present four client messages. For each message, use the list below to identify the type of mixed message you observe from the client's message, and identify concrete verbal/nonverbal cues that indicate the discrepancy. An example precedes the practice messages. Feedback is given after the learning activity (on page 122).

Types of mixed messages

1. Verbal and nonverbal behavior
2. Verbal messages and actions or behaviors
3. Two verbal messages
4. Two nonverbal messages
5. Two persons
6. Verbal messages and context

Example

Client: I'm very happy. [Said with lowered, moist eyes, stooped shoulders, impassive facial expression]

1. Identify the type of mixed message: #1 — verbal and nonverbal behavior.
2. Identify any cues that are indicative of the mixed message: Client *says* she's happy, but eyes, shoulders, and face suggest sadness.

Client Practice Messages

Client 1, a teenage girl with an obvious limp: I'd like to start ballet or gymnastics. I'd like to be a star gymnast or ballerina.

1. Identify the type of mixed message: _____

_____

(continued)

LEARNING ACTIVITY #18: MIXED MESSAGES (continued)

2. Identify any cues that are indicative of the mixed message: _____

_____

Client 2, a young man who has been talking very openly with you about some sexual concerns: A big part of the problem is that I can't talk to her about our sex life. I've just never been able to talk about sex.

1. Identify the type of mixed message: _____

_____

2. Identify any cues that are indicative of the mixed message: _____

_____

Client 3: My husband and I are thinking about having a baby. It would be a good way to fill this void we feel; to keep busy with someone who needs

you all the time. It will be great as long as it isn't too confining. I don't want to be too tied down.

1. Identify the type of mixed message: _____

_____

2. Identify any cues that are indicative of the mixed message: _____

_____

Client 4: My wife is always interested in sex. She could just wear me out. She wants it two or three times a night. I've told her I think that's a little much, especially for two persons who have been married as long as we have.

1. Identify the type of mixed message: _____

_____

2. Identify any cues that are indicative of the mixed message: _____

_____

Ground rules for confronting. Confrontation needs to be offered in a way that helps clients to examine the consequences of their behavior rather than defending their actions (Johnson, 1981). In other words, confrontation must be used carefully in order not to increase the very behavior or pattern that the therapist feels may need to be diminished or modified. The following ground rules may assist you in using this response to help rather than to harm. First, be aware of your own motives for confronting at any particular time. Although the word itself has a punitive or emotionally charged sound, confrontation in the helping process is not an attack on the client or an opportunity to badger the client (Patterson & Eisenberg, 1983). Confrontation is also not to be used as a way to ventilate or "dump" your frustration onto the client. It is a means of offering constructive, "growth-directed" feedback that is positive in context and intent, not disapproving or critical (Patterson & Eisenberg, 1983, p. 75). To avoid blame, focus on the incongruity as the problem, not on the person, and avoid "showing judgment through nonverbal displays of anger" (Ivey, 1983, p. 196). In describing the distortion or discrepancy, the confrontation should cite a *specific example* of the behavior rather than make a vague inference. A poor confrontation might be "You want people to like you, but your personality turns them off." In this case, the counselor is making a general inference about the client's personality and also is implying that the

client must undergo a major "overhaul" in order to get along with others. A more helpful confrontation would be "You want people to like you, and at the same time you make frequent remarks about yourself that seem to get in the way and turn people off."

Moreover, before a counselor tries to confront a client, rapport and trust should be established. Confrontation probably should not be used unless you, the counselor, are willing to maintain or increase your involvement in or commitment to the counseling relationship (Johnson, 1981). Some counselors, regardless of the status of the counseling relationship, sprinkle their counseling style with liberal doses of critical, negative messages. Egan (1975, p. 171) suggests that someone who specializes in confrontation may be a destructive person who isn't too adept at her or his chosen specialty. At the other extreme, some counselors may be so uncomfortable with anything other than positive communication, or "good news," that they totally avoid using confrontation even with long-term clients. The primary consideration is to judge what your level of involvement seems to be with each client and adapt accordingly. The stronger the relationship, the more receptive the client may be to a confrontation.

The *timing* of a confrontation is very important. Since the purpose is to help the person engage in self-examination, try to offer the confrontation at a time when the client is likely to use it. The per-

FEEDBACK #17: PROBES

Client 1

Sample probes based on defined purpose: It sounds like things have gotten out of hand. [paraphrase] What exactly has been going on that's been so bad for you? [probe] or How has it been like hell for you? [probe]

Client 2

Sample probes based on defined purpose: Now and then you feel kind of down. [reflection] What have you noticed that makes this feeling go away? [probe] or Have you noticed anything in particular that makes you feel better? [probe]

Client 3

Sample probes based on defined purpose: With everyone else to take care of, there's not much time left for you. [paraphrase] Exactly how many kids are underfoot? [probe] or How many kids are you responsible for? [probe]

ceived ability of the client to act on the confrontation should be a major guideline in deciding when to confront (Johnson, 1981). In other words, before you jump in and confront, determine the person's attention level, anxiety level, desire to change, and ability to listen.

Appropriate use of timing also means that the helper does not confront on a "hit and run" basis (Johnson, 1981, p. 230). Ample time should be given after the confrontation to allow the client to react to and discuss the effects of this response. For this reason, counselors should avoid confronting near the end of a therapy session.

It is also a good idea not to overload the client with confrontations that make heavy demands in a short time. The rule of "successive approximations" suggests that people learn small steps of behaviors gradually more easily than trying to make big changes overnight. Initially, you may want to confront the person with something that can be managed fairly easily and with some success. Carkhuff (1972) suggests that two successive confrontations may be too intense and should be avoided.

Finally, acknowledge the limits of confrontation. Confrontation usually brings about client awareness of a discrepancy or conflict. Awareness of discrepancies is an initial step in resolving conflicts. Confrontation, as a single response, may not

always bring about resolution of the discrepancy without additional discussion or intervention strategies such as role playing, role reversal, Gestalt dialoguing, and TA redecision work.

Client reactions. Sometimes counselors are afraid to confront because they are uncertain how to handle the client's reactions to the confrontation. Even clients who hear and acknowledge the confrontation may be anxious or upset about the implications. Generally, a counselor can expect four types of client reaction to a confrontation: denial, confusion, false acceptance, or genuine acceptance.

In a denial of the confrontation, the client does not want to acknowledge or agree to the counselor's message. A denial may indicate that the client is not ready or tolerant enough to face the discrepant or distorted behavior. Egan (1982, pp. 181–182) lists some specific ways the client might deny the confrontation:

1. Discredit the counselor (for example, "How do you know when you don't even have kids?").
2. Persuade the counselor that his or her views are wrong or misinterpreted ("I didn't mean it that way").
3. Devalue the importance of the topic ("This isn't worth all this time anyway").
4. Seek support elsewhere ("I told my friends about your comment last week and none of them had ever noticed that").

At other times, the client may indicate confusion or uncertainty about the meaning of the confrontation. In some cases, the client may be genuinely confused about what the counselor is saying. This may indicate that your confrontation was not concise and specific. At other times, the client may use a lack of understanding as a smokescreen — that is, as a way to avoid dealing with the impact of the confrontation.

Sometimes the client may seem to accept the confrontation. Acceptance is usually genuine if the client responds with a sincere desire to examine her or his behavior. Eventually such clients may be able to catch their own discrepancies and confront themselves. But Egan (1982) cautions that false acceptance also can occur, which is another client game. In this case, the client verbally agrees with the counselor. However, instead of pursuing the confrontation, the client agrees only to get the counselor to leave well enough alone.

FEEDBACK #18: MIXED MESSAGES

Client 1
1. #6—verbal messages and context.
2. Client says she wants to be a star in two sports that require considerable leg work and muscle dexterity; contraindicated by her obvious limp.

Client 2
1. #2—verbal message and behavior.
2. Client says he's never been able to talk about sex but has been talking about it openly with you.

Client 3
1. #3—two verbal messages.
2. Client says she wants to have a child to fill a void by keeping busy and also that she doesn't want to be too tied down or confined by a child.

Client 4
1. #5—two persons.
2. Client's wife wants frequent sex; client does not.

There is no set way of dealing with client reactions to confrontation. However, a general rule of thumb is to go back to the client-oriented listening responses of paraphrase and reflection and to continue to pace, or match, the client's primary representational system (predicates). A counselor can use these responses to lay the foundation before the confrontation and return to this foundation after the confrontation. The sequence might go something like this:

Counselor: You seem to feel concerned about your parents' divorce. [reflection]
Client: Actually, I feel pretty happy—I'm glad for their sake they got a divorce. [said with low, sad voice—mixed message]
Counselor: You say you're happy, and at the same time, from your voice I sense that you feel unhappy. [confrontation]
Client: I don't know what you're talking about, really. [denial]
Counselor: I feel that what I just said has upset you. [reflection]

Steps in confronting. There are four steps in developing effective confrontations. First, observe the client carefully to identify the type of discrep-

ancy, or mixed message, that the client presents. Note the specific verbal cues, nonverbal cues, and behaviors that support the type of discrepancy. Second, summarize the different elements of the discrepancy. In doing so, use a statement that *connects* the parts of the conflict rather than disputes any one part, since the overall aim of confrontation is to resolve conflicts and to achieve integration. A useful summary is "On the one hand, you _____, *and* on the other hand, _____." Note that the elements are connected with the word *and* rather than *but* or *yet*. Third, be sure to include words in your summary that reflect the client's choice of sensory words, or predicates, so that the confrontation paces the client's experience. Finally, remember to assess the effectiveness of your confrontation. A confrontation is effective whenever the client acknowledges the existence of the incongruity or conflict.

To help you formulate a confrontation, consider the following cognitive learning strategy:

1. What discrepancy, or mixed message, do I see, hear, or grasp in this client's communication?
2. How can I summarize the various elements of the discrepancy?
3. What words can I include in my response that match the client's sensory words?
4. How will I know whether my confrontation is effective?

Notice how a therapist uses this cognitive learning strategy for confrontation in the following example:

Client: It's hard for me to discipline my son. I know I'm too indulgent. I know he needs limits. But I just don't give him any. I let him do basically whatever he feels like doing. [Said in low, soft voice]
Counselor: 1. What discrepancy do I see, hear, or grasp in this client's communication?
   A discrepancy between two verbal messages and between verbal cues and behavior: client knows son needs limits but doesn't give him any.
   2. How can I summarize the various elements of the discrepancy?
   Client believes limits would help son; at the same time, client doesn't follow through.
   3. What words can I include in my response that match the client's sensory words?
   I'll use words in my response like "sense" and "feel" that match client's words "know" and "feel."

4. How will I know whether my confrontation is effective?
Observe the client's response and see whether he acknowledges the discrepancy.

Suppose that at this point the therapist's self-talk or covert visualization ends and the following dialogue occurs:

Counselor confrontation: William, on the one hand, you feel like having limits would really help your son, and at the same time, he can do whatever he pleases with you. How do you put this together?
Client response: Well, I guess that's right. I do feel

strongly he would benefit from having limits. He gets away with a lot. He's going to become very spoiled, I know. But I just can't seem to "put my foot down" or make him do something.

From the client's response, which confirmed the discrepancy, the counselor can conclude that the confrontation was initially useful (further discussion of the discrepancy seems necessary in order to help the client resolve the conflict between feelings and actions).

Learning Activity #19 gives you an opportunity to apply this cognitive learning strategy to develop the skill of confrontation.

LEARNING ACTIVITY #19: CONFRONTATION

We give you three client practice statements in this learning activity. For each message, develop an example of a confrontation, using the cognitive learning strategy described earlier and outlined below. To internalize this learning strategy, you may wish to talk through these self-questions overtly (aloud) and then covertly (silently to yourself). The end product will be a confrontation that you can say aloud or write down or both. An example precedes the practice messages. Feedback follows the learning activity (on page 126).

Example
Client, a college student: I'd like to get through nursing school with a flourish. I want to be at the top of my class and achieve a lot. All this partying is getting in my way and preventing me from doing my best work.

Counselor:
Self-question 1: What discrepancy do I see, hear, or grasp in this client's communication?
A discrepancy between verbal message and behavior; he says he wants to be at the top of his class and at the same time is doing a lot of partying.
Self-question 2: How can I summarize the various elements of the discrepancy?
He wants to be at the top of his class and at the same time is doing a lot of partying, which is interfering with his goal.
Self-question 3: What words can I include in my response that match the client's sensory words?
There are no clear-cut sensory words reflected in this example; so use words of varying modalities ("see," "hear," "feel").
Actual confrontation response: You're saying that

you feel like achieving a lot and being at the top of your class and also that you're doing a lot of partying, which appears to be interfering with this goal
or
Juan, you're saying that doing well in nursing school is very important to you. You have also indicated you are partying instead of studying. How important is being at the top for you?

Client Practice Messages
Client 1, a graduate student: My wife and child are very important to me. They make me feel it's all worth it. It's just that I know I have to work all the time if I want to make it in my field, and right now I can't be with them too much.

Self-question 1: What discrepancy do I see, hear, or grasp in this client's communication?
Self-question 2: How can I summarize the various elements of the discrepancy?
Self-question 3: What words can I include in my response that match the client's sensory words?
Actual confrontation response: _____
_____

Client 2, a 10-year-old girl: Sure, it would be nice to have mom at home when I get there after school. I don't feel lonely. It's just that it would feel so good to have someone close to me there and not to have to spend a couple of hours every day by myself.

Self question 1: What discrepancy do I see, hear, or grasp in this client's communication?

(continued)

LEARNING ACTIVITY #19: CONFRONTATION (continued)

Self-question 2: How can I summarize the various elements of the discrepancy?

Self-question 3: What words can I include in my response that match the client's sensory words?

Actual confrontation response: _____

_____

Client 3, a high school student: My dad thinks it's terribly important for me to get all As. He thinks I'm not working up to my potential if I get a B. I told him I'd much rather be well rounded and get a few Bs and also have time to talk to my friends and play basketball.

Self-question 1: What discrepancy do I see, hear, or grasp in this client's communication?

Self-question 2: How can I summarize the various elements of the discrepancy?

Self-question 3: What words can I include in my response that match the client's sensory words?

Actual confrontation response: _____

_____

Interpretation

Interpretation is a skill that involves understanding and communicating the meaning of a client's messages. In making interpretive statements, the counselor provides clients with a fresh look at themselves or with another explanation for their attitudes or behaviors (Ivey & Gluckstern, 1976). According to Brammer and Shostrom (1982, p. 251), interpretation involves "presenting the client with a *hypothesis* about *relationships* or *meanings* among his or her behaviors." Johnson (1981, p. 161) observes that interpretation is useful for clients because it leads to insight, and insight is a key to better psychological living and a precursor to effective behavior change.

Interpretive responses can be defined in a variety of ways (Brammer & Shostrom, 1982; Ivey & Gluckstern, 1976; Levy, 1963). An interpretation may vary to some degree according to your own perspective, your theoretical orientation, and what you decide is causing or contributing to the client's problems and behaviors (Johnson, 1981). We define an interpretation as a counselor statement that makes an association or a causal connection among various client behaviors, events, or ideas or presents a possible explanation of a client's behavior (including the client's feelings, thoughts, and observable actions). An interpretation differs from the listening responses (paraphrase, clarification, reflection, summarization) in that it deals with the *implicit* part of a message—the part the client does not talk about explicitly or directly. As Brammer and Shostrom (1982) note, when interpreting, a counselor will often verbalize issues that the client may have felt only vaguely. Our concept of interpretation is similar to what Egan (1982) calls "advanced accurate empathy," which is a tool to help the client "move from the less to the more" (p. 173). In other words, "If clients are not clear about some issue or if they speak guardedly, then the helper speaks directly, clearly, and openly."

There are many benefits and purposes for which interpretation can be used appropriately in a helping interview. First, effective interpretations can contribute to the development of a positive therapeutic relationship by reinforcing client self-disclosure, enhancing the credibility of the therapist, and communicating therapeutic attitudes to the client (Claiborn, 1982, p. 415). Another purpose of interpretation is to identify causal relations or patterns between clients' explicit and implicit messages and behaviors. A third purpose is to help clients examine their behavior from a different frame of reference or with a different explanation in order to achieve a better understanding of the problem. A final and most important reason for using interpretation is to motivate the client to replace self-defeating or ineffective behaviors with more functional ones.

The frame of reference selected for an interpretation should be consistent with one's preferred theoretical orientation(s) to counseling: a psychodynamic therapist might interpret unresolved anxiety or conflicts; an Adlerian therapist might highlight the client's mistaken logic; a Transactional Analysis interviewer may interpret client games and ego states; a cognitive therapist might emphasize irrational and rational thinking; and a behavioral counselor may emphasize self-defeating or maladaptive behavior patterns. *Traditional* (or "old guard") client-centered counselors often refrained from interpreting, but recent client-centered therapists do interpret and often emphasize such themes as self-image and intimacy in their interpretations (Egan, 1982). Gestalt therapists consider interpretation a "therapeutic mistake" because it takes responsibility away from the client.

Here is an example that may help you understand the nature of the interpretation response more clearly. Note how the frame of reference or content varies with the counselor's theoretical orientation.

Client 1, a young woman: Everything is humdrum. There's nothing new going on, nothing exciting. All my friends are away. I wish I had some money to do something different.

1. *Interpretation from Adlerian orientation:* It seems as if you believe you need friends, money, and lots of excitement in order to make your life worthwhile and to feel good about yourself.
2. *Interpretation from TA perspective:* It seems as if you function best only when you can play and have a lot of fun. Your "Child" seems in control of so much of your life.
3. *Interpretation from cognitive or rational-emotive perspective:* It sounds as if you're catastrophizing —because you have no friends around now and no money, things are going to be terrible. Yet where is the proof or data for this? I suspect your feelings of boredom would change if you could draw a different and more logical conclusion about not having friends and money right now.
4. *Interpretation from behavioral orientation:* You seem to be saying that you don't know how to get along or have fun without having other people around. Perhaps recognizing this will help you learn to behave in more self-reliant ways.

In all the above examples, the counselors use interpretation to point out that the client is more dependent on things or other people than on herself for making her life meaningful. In other words, the counselor is describing a possible association, or relationship, between the client's explicit feelings of being bored and her explicit behavior of depending on others to alleviate the boredom. The counselor hopes that this explanation will give the client an increased understanding of herself that she can use to create meaning and enjoyment in her life.

Content and wording of effective interpretations.
During the last several years, a variety of research studies have explored different parameters of interpretation (Beck & Strong, 1982; Claiborn, Ward, & Strong, 1981; Forsyth & Forsyth, 1982; Milne & Dowd, 1983; Strong, Wambach, Lopez, & Cooper, 1979). The results of these studies suggest three parameters that affect the content and wording of an effective interpretation: (1) depth, (2) focus, and (3) connotation. Depth is the degree

of discrepancy between the viewpoint expressed by the counselor and the client's beliefs. Presenting clients with a viewpoint discrepant from their own is believed to facilitate change by providing clients with a reconceptualization of the problem (Claiborn et al., 1981). An important question is to what extent the counselor's communicated conceptualization of the problem should differ from the client's beliefs. A study by Claiborn et al. (1981) addressed this question. The results supported the general assumption that highly discrepant (that is, very deep) interpretations are more likely to be rejected by the client, possibly because they are unacceptable, seem too preposterous, or evoke resistance. In contrast, interpretations that are either congruent with or only slightly discrepant from the client's viewpoint are most likely to facilitate change, possibly because these are "more immediately understandable and useful to the clients" (Claiborn et al., p. 108).

A second factor affecting the content and wording of interpretations has to do with the focus, or direction, of the interpretation. Research now suggests that interpretations that focus on control by highlighting causes the client can control are more effective than those that draw attention to causes the client cannot change (Strong et al., 1979). Focusing on controllable causes appears especially useful with clients who report a higher internal, as opposed to external, locus of control (Forsyth & Forsyth, 1982).

The third parameter that influences the content and wording of an interpretation is the connotation of the interpretation—that is, whether the counselor reframes or relabels the client's behavior and beliefs in a positive or a negative fashion. For example, an interpretation with a negative connotation would be "Harry, you seem to be saying it's too difficult for you to share your father with his new wife because you've been used to having him to yourself for the last ten years. I'm wondering if you're demanding that you be number one with him or else you won't 'play ball' [relate, cooperate]. It's almost as if you're coming across like a small child, begging for attention and then sulking if you don't get it." In contrast, an interpretation with a positive connotation goes like this: "Harry, you seem to be saying it's too difficult for you to share your father with his new wife because you've been used to having him to yourself for the past ten years. Perhaps the fact that you're recognizing that you feel shut out now will help you behave in ways that actually increase your chances of being included rather than excluded." Although both

FEEDBACK #19: CONFRONTATION

Client 1

Question 1: There is a discrepancy between the client's verbal message that his wife and child are very important and his behavior, which suggests he doesn't spend much time with them.

Question 2: He feels that his family is very valuable, while he also feels he must continually spend more time on his career than with his family.

Question 3: Use words like "sense" and "feel" to match the client's words "feel" and "know."

Examples of confrontation responses: Jerry, on the one hand, you feel your family is very important, and at the same time, you feel your work takes priority over them. How do you put this together? *or* Jerry, you're saying that your family makes things feel worthwhile for you. At the same time you're indicating you must make it in your field in order to feel worthwhile.

Client 2

Question 1: There is a discrepancy between two verbal messages—one denying she is lonely and the other indicating she doesn't want to be left alone.

Question 2: She doesn't feel lonely—and at the same time she wishes someone could be with her.

Question 3: Use "feel" to match client's repeated use of the word "feel."

Examples of confrontation responses: Shelley, you're saying that you don't feel lonely and also that you wish someone like your mom could be home with you. How do you put this together? *or* Shelley, it seems like you're trying to accept your mom's absence and at the same time still feeling like you'd rather have her home with you. I wonder if it does feel kind of lonely sometimes?

Client 3

Question 1: There is a discrepancy between two persons' views on this issue—the client and his father. A second discrepancy might be between the client's desire to please his father and to be well-rounded.

Question 2: The client feels getting all As is not as important as being well rounded, while his father values very high grades. Also, for discrep-

ancy #2, the client may want to please both his father and himself.

Question 3: Use words such as "saying," "believes," "tells," "hear" to match client words such as "told," "think," "talk."

Examples of confrontation responses: Gary, you're saying that doing a variety of things is more important than getting all As, while your father believes that all As should be your top priority.

or

Gary, you're saying you value variety and balance in your life; your father believes high grades come first.

or

Gary, you want to please your father and make good grades and, at the same time, you want to spend time according to your priorities and values.

(Note: Do not attempt to confront both discrepancies at once!)

types of interpretation may produce some immediate change, structuring interpretations to reflect a positive connotation seems to promote more enduring change (Beck & Strong, 1982).

To summarize, in constructing an interpretation, be sure that the viewpoint expressed in your statement is only slightly discrepant from the client's beliefs. Second, focus on causes that the client can control and modify, if desired. Finally, cast the new or different frame of reference into a positive, rather than negative, connotation.

Client reactions to interpretation. Client reactions to interpretation may range from expression of greater self-understanding and release of emotions to less verbal expression and more silence. Although research suggests that interpretations can contribute to self-exploration and behavior change (Auerswald, 1974; Beck & Strong, 1982; Claiborn et al., 1981; Elliott, Barker, Caskey, & Pistrang, 1982; Strong et al., 1979), clients can also react to interpretations with defensiveness and decreased disclosure. As Pope (1979) observes, interpretations often delve into material or experiences the client has resisted learning about because of the anxiety aroused by the particular situation.

If interpretation is met initially with defensiveness or hostility, it may be best to drop the issue temporarily and introduce it again later. Repetition is an important concept in the use of interpretations. As Brammer and Shostrom observe, "Since a useful and valid interpretation may be resisted, it may be necessary for the counselor to repeat the interpretation at appropriate times, in different forms, and with additional supporting evidence" (1982, p. 261). However, don't push an interpretation on a resistant client without first reexamining the accuracy of your response (Brammer & Shostrom, 1982). Another way to manage client resistance to a seemingly valid interpretation is to use a metaphor—that is, to tell the client a parable, story, or myth that serves as a mirror onto which the client can project his or her own life situation (Gordon, 1978; see also Chapter 20).

Ground rules for interpreting. Interpretation may be the one counselor activity that helps a client to face, rather than defend or avoid, a conflict or problem. However, the potential contribution of an interpretation depends somewhat on the counselor's ability to use this response effectively and at an advantageous time. There are several ground rules to consider in deciding to use interpretation. First, be careful about timing. The client should show some degree of readiness to explore or examine himself or herself before you use an interpretation. Generally, an interpretation response is reserved for later, rather than initial, sessions, because some data must be gathered as a basis for an interpretive response and because the typical client requires several sessions to become accustomed to the type of material discussed in counseling. The client may be more receptive to your interpretation if she or he is comfortable with the topics being explored and shows some readiness to accept the interpretive response. As Brammer and Shostrom (1982, p. 257) note, a counselor usually does not interpret until the time when the client can almost formulate the interpretation for herself or himself.

Timing of an interpretation within a session is also important. Generally, an interpretation is more helpful in the initial or middle phase of an interview, so that the counselor and client have sufficient time to work through the client's reaction. If the counselor suspects that the interpretation may produce anxiety or resistance or break the client's "emotional dam," it may be a good idea to postpone it until the beginning of the next session (Brammer & Shostrom, 1982).

A second ground rule is to make sure your interpretation is based on the client's actual message rather than your own biases and values projected onto the client. This requires that you be aware of your own blind spots. As an example, if you have had a bad experience with marriage and are biased against people's getting or staying married, be aware of how this could affect the way you interpret client statements about marriage. If you aren't careful with your values, you could easily advise all marital-counseling clients away from marriage, which might not be in the best interests of some of them. As Ivey and Gluckstern (1976, p. 135) state, "psychological imperialism" must be avoided—especially in the use of an interpretation. Try to be aware of whether you are interpreting to present helpful data to the client or only to show off your expertise. Make sure your interpretation is based on sufficient data, and offer the interpretation in a collaborative spirit, making the client an active participant.

A third ground rule in using interpretation effectively concerns the way the counselor phrases the statement and offers it to the client. Although preliminary research suggests there is no difference between interpretations offered with absolute and with tentative phrasing (Milne & Dowd, 1983), we believe that in most cases the interpretation should be phrased tentatively, using phrases such as "perhaps," "I wonder whether," "it's possible that," or "it appears as though." Using tentative rather than absolute phrasing helps to avoid putting the counselor in a one-up position and engendering client resistance or defensiveness to the interpretation. After an interpretation, check out the accuracy of your interpretive response by asking the client whether your message fits. Returning to a clarification is always a useful way to determine whether you have interpreted the message accurately.

Steps in interpreting. There are five steps in formulating effective interpretations. First, listen for and identify the *implicit* meaning of the client's communication—what the client conveys subtly and indirectly. Second, formulate an interpretation that provides the client with a *slightly* different way to view the problem or issue. This alternative frame of reference should be consistent with your theoretical orientation and not too discrepant from the client's beliefs. Third, make sure your view of the issue, your frame of reference, emphasizes positive factors rather than negative factors or things the client can't change or modify. Next, select words in the interpretation that match the client's sensory words, or predicates. Finally, examine the effectiveness of your interpretation by assessing the client's reaction to it. Look for non-verbal "recognition" signs such as a smile or contemplative look as well as verbal and behavioral cues that indicate the client is considering the issue from a different frame of reference.

To help you formulate an effective interpretation and assess its usefulness, consider the following cognitive learning strategy:

1. What is the implicit part of the client's message?
2. What is a slightly different way to view this problem or issue that is consistent with the theoretical orientation I am using with this client?
3. What are positive aspects of the problem that are under the client's control?
4. What words can I use that will match the client's sensory words, or predicates?
5. How will I know whether my interpretation is useful?

Notice how a therapist applies this cognitive learning strategy in the following example:

Client: I really don't understand it myself. I can always have good sex whenever we're not at home —even in the car. But at home it's never too good.
Counselor: 1. What is the implicit part of the client's message? That sex is not good or fulfilling unless it occurs in special, out-of-the-ordinary circumstances or places.
  2. What is a slightly different way to view this problem or issue consistent with the theoretical orientation I am using with this client?
  Behavioral—Adaptive response learned in special places, hasn't generalized to home setting, perhaps because of different "setting events" there (for example, fatigue, lack of novelty).
  Cognitive—Client is catastrophizing about "no good" sex when it occurs at home; continued reindoctrination prevents spontaneity, increases preoccupation with himself.
  Psychodynamic—Problem with sex at home is indicative of unresolved anxiety or possible unresolved oedipal issue.
  Transactional Analysis—Sex is good in places

that are novel and exciting, where the "Child" ego state can be predominant; not as good at home, where Child ego state is probably excluded.
  Adlerian—Client has developed a lifestyle and accompanying mistaken logic that emphasizes novelty, excitement, out-of-the-ordinary events in order for things (like sex) to be good or great.
3. What are positive aspects of the problem that are under the client's control?
  That client does experience sex as good some of the time; has potential for good sex more of the time.
4. What words can I use that will match the client's primary representational system?
  There are no clear-cut sensory words in this example, so vary the words used in the actual interpretation that reflect all three major sensory modalities.

Suppose that at this point the counselor's covert visualization or self-talk ends and the following dialogue ensues:

Counselor interpretation: Shawn, I might be wrong about this—it seems that you get psyched up for sex only when it occurs in out-of-the-ordinary places where you feel there's a lot of novelty and excitement. Is that possible? [Note: This is an interpretation that could be consistent with a behavioral, Adlerian, or eclectic orientation.]
Client: [Lips part, slight smile, eyes widen] Well, I never thought about it quite that way. I guess I do need to feel like there's some thrills around when I do have sex—maybe it's that I find unusual places like the elevator a challenge.

At this point, the counselor can conclude that the interpretation was effective because of the client's nonverbal "recognition" behavior and because of the client's verbal response suggesting the interpretation was "on target." The therapist might continue to help the client explore whether he needs thrills and challenge to function satisfactorily in other areas of his life as well.

Learning activity #20 gives you an opportunity to try out the interpretation response.

LEARNING ACTIVITY #20: INTERPRETATION

Three client practice statements are given in this learning activity. For each message, develop an example of an interpretation, using the cognitive learning strategy described earlier and outlined below. To

internalize this learning strategy, you may want to talk through these self-questions overtly (aloud) and then covertly (silently to yourself). The end product
(continued)

will be an interpretation that you can say aloud or write down or both. An example precedes the practice messages. Feedback follows the learning activity (on page 132).

Example

Client, a young woman: I don't know what to do. I guess I just never thought I'd ever be asked to be a supervisor. I feel so content just being an assistant. But my husband says I'd be foolish to pass up this opportunity.

Self-question 1: What is the implicit part of the client's message?
That the client feels afraid to achieve more than she's presently doing.

Self-question 2: What is a slightly different way to view this problem or issue consistent with the theoretical orientation I am using with this client?
Behavioral—Client has acquired anxiety about job success, possibly because of lack of exposure to other successful female models and also because of lack of reinforcement from significant others for job achievement. It is also possible that she has been punished for being successful or achieving in the past, which is maintaining her present avoidance behavior on this issue.
Cognitive—Client is indoctrinating herself with irrational or self-defeating thoughts of possible failure or loss of friends if she moves up the job ladder.
Psychodynamic—Client has anxiety about a job situation; suggests possible unresolved conflict and also identity issue.
Transactional Analysis—Client is confronted with a decision that her Adapted Child ego state is afraid to make, possibly because in the role of supervisor she would have to function in more of her Parent ego state, which is probably excluded from her personality to some degree.
Alderian—Client's lifestyle and family background haven't accommodated personal achievement; possibly client has relied on others, such as husband, to take care of her rather than putting herself in roles where she is responsible for others.

Self-question 3: What are positive aspects of the problem that are under the client's control?
She has a job she feels satisfied with; further, that she was given an opportunity for a promotion suggests she is doing good work.

Self-question 4: What words can I use that will match the client's sensory words?
Use words like "feel," "sense" to match client words "don't know," "guess," "feel."

Actual interpretation responses: Despite your husband's encouragement and your obvious success at your present position, you seem to feel like holding back. I wonder whether you're afraid to move up for fear that someone close to you will be upset with you or won't like you if you're more successful? [This interpretation is consistent with the behavioral and cognitive frameworks.] or I wonder whether a big part of you feels more comfortable in situations where others can take care of you? So it feels scary to think of being in a situation where you are in charge and responsible for other people. [This interpretation is consistent with the TA and Adlerian frameworks.]

Client Practice Statements

Client 1, a 35-year-old male factory worker: I know I don't get along very well with my buddies [co-workers], but they tease me all the time because I'm very religious, especially compared with them.

Self-question 1: What is the implicit part of the client's message?
Self-question 2: What is a slightly different way to view this problem or issue consistent with my theoretical orientation?*
Self-question 3: What are positive aspects of the problem that are under the client's control?
Self-question 4: What words can I use that will match the client's sensory words?
Actual interpretation response: _____

_____

Client 2, a 50-year-old man: Sure, I seemed upset when I got laid off several years ago. After all, I'd been an industrial engineer for almost 23 years. At least I didn't have to put myself on welfare. I have a clear conscience about that, and I can support my family with my job supervising these custodial workers. So I should be very thankful. Then why do I seem so depressed?

Self-question 1: What is the implicit part of this message?
Self-question 2: What is a slightly different way to view this problem or issue consistent with my theoretical orientation?*
Self-question 3: What are positive aspects of the problem that are under the client's control?
Self-question 4: What words can I use that will match the client's sensory words?
Actual interpretation response: _____

_____

(continued)

* If you have not yet had much exposure to counseling theories, you may find it useful just to reframe the client statement in a slightly different manner without trying to conceptualize it according to a counseling theory.

LEARNING ACTIVITY #20: INTERPRETATION (continued)

Client 3: I have a great time with Susie [his girl-friend], but I've told her I don't want to settle down. She's always so bossy and tries to tell me what to do. She always decides what we're going to do and when and where and so on. I get real upset at her.

Self-question 1: What is the implicit part of the client's message?

Self-question 2: What is a slightly different way to view this problem or issue consistent with my theoretical orientation?*

Self-question 3: What are positive aspects of the problem that are under the client's control?

Self-question 4: What words can I use that will match the client's sensory words?

Actual interpretation response: _____
_____

* If you have not yet had much exposure to counseling theories, you may find it useful just to reframe the client statement in a slightly different manner without trying to conceptualize it according to a counseling theory.

Information Giving

There are many times in the counseling interview when a client may have a legitimate need for information. For instance, a client who reports being abused by her husband may need information about her legal rights and alternatives. A client who has recently become physically disabled may need some information about employment and about lifestyle adaptations such as carrying out domestic chores or engaging in sexual relationships. According to Selby and Calhoun (1980, p. 236), "Conveying information about the psychological and social changes accompanying a particular problem situation (. . . such as divorce) may be a highly effective addition to any therapeutic strategy." Selby and Calhoun assert that information giving has been neglected as an explicit and important part of treatment "in spite of evidence indicating the therapeutic value of information about the client's problem situation" (p. 236).

We define information giving as the verbal communication of data or facts about experiences, events, alternatives, or people. As summarized in Table 6-1, there are four intended purposes of information giving in counseling. First, information is necessary when the client does not know her or his options. Giving information is a way to help the client identify possible alternatives. As Gelatt, Varenhorst, Carey, and Miller (1973, p. 6) suggest, a "person's choices are increased if he can create new alternatives based on information." For example, you may be counseling a pregnant client who says she is going to get an abortion because it is her only choice. Although she may eventually decide to pursue this choice, she should be aware of other options before making a final decision. Information giving is also helpful when a client is not aware of the possible outcomes of a particular choice or plan of action. Giving information can help the client evaluate different choices and actions. For example, if the client is a minor and is not aware that she may need her parents' consent for an abortion, this information may influence her choice. In the preceding kinds of situations, information is given to counteract ignorance. According to Egan (1982, p. 164), this is especially critical "when ignorance is either one of the principal causes of a problem situation or it is making an existing problem worse." Information giving can also be useful to correct invalid or unreliable data or to dispel a myth. In other words, information giving may be necessary when the client is misinformed about something. For example, a pregnant client may decide to have an abortion on the erroneous assumption that an abortion is also a means of subsequent birth control.

A final purpose of information giving is to help clients examine issues or problems they have been successfully avoiding (Egan, 1982). For example, a client who hasn't felt physically well for a year may be prompted to explore this problem when confronted with information about possible effects of neglected treatment for various illnesses.

Differences between information giving and advice. It is important to note that information giving differs from advice. In giving advice, a person usually recommends or prescribes a particular solution or course of action for the listener to follow. In contrast, information giving consists in presenting relevant information about the issue or problem, and the decision concerning the final course of action—if any—is made by the client. Consider the differences between the following two responses:

Client, a young mother: I just find it so difficult to refuse requests made by my child—to say no to her—even when I know they are unreasonable requests or could even be dangerous to her.

Counselor (advice giving): Why don't you start by saying no to her just on one request a day for now —anything that you feel comfortable with refusing—and then see what happens?

Counselor (information giving): I think there are two things we could discuss that may be affecting the way you are handling this situation. First, we could talk about what you feel might happen if you say no. We also need to examine how your requests were handled in your own family when you were a child. Very often as parents we repeat with our children the way we were parented—in such an automatic way we don't even realize it's happening.

In the first example, the counselor has recommended action that may or may not be successful. If it works, the client may feel elated and expect the counselor to have other magical solutions. If it fails, the client may feel even more discouraged and question whether counseling can really help her resolve this problem. Appropriate and effective information giving is presented as what the client *could* ponder or do, not what the client *should* do, and what the client *might* consider, not *must* consider (D'Augelli et al., 1981, p. 80).

Several dangers are associated with advice giving that make it a potential trap for counselors. First, the client may reject not only this piece of advice but any other ideas presented by the therapist in an effort to establish independence and thwart any conspicuous efforts by the counselor to influence or coerce. Second, if the client accepts the advice and the advice leads to an unsatisfactory action, the client is likely to blame the counselor and may terminate therapy prematurely. Third, if the client follows the advice and is pleased with the action, the client may become overly dependent on the counselor and expect, if not demand, more "advice" in subsequent sessions. Finally, there is always the possibility that an occasional client may misinterpret the advice and may cause injury to self or others in trying to comply with it.

Ground rules for giving information. Lewis (1970) observes that information should be a tool for counseling, not an end in itself. Information giving is generally considered appropriate when the need for information is directly related to the client's concerns and goals and when the presentation and discussion of information are used to help the client achieve these goals (p. 135).

To use information giving appropriately, a counselor should consider three major guidelines. These cover when to give information, what information is needed, and how the information should be delivered. Table 6-2 summarizes the "when,"

TABLE 6-2. The "when," "what," and "how" of information giving in helping

When—recognizing client's need for information	*What—identifying type of information*	*How—delivery of information in interview*
1. Identify information presently available to client.	1. Identify kind of information useful to client.	1. Avoid jargon.
2. Evaluate client's present information—is it valid? data-based? sufficient?	2. Identify reliable sources of information to validate accuracy of information.	2. Present all the relevant facts; don't protect client from negative information.
3. Wait for client cues of readiness to avoid giving information prematurely.	3. Identify any sequencing of information (option A before option B).	3. Limit amount of information given at one time; don't overload.
		4. Ask for and discuss client's feelings and biases about information.
		5. Know when to stop giving information so action isn't avoided.
		6. Use paper and pencil to highlight key ideas or facts.

FEEDBACK #20: INTERPRETATION

Client 1

Question 1: The implicit part of the client's message is "I'm better than they [buddies] are."

Question 2: Different ways to view this issue, depending on your theoretical orientation, include the following:

Behavioral—Client and buddies have set up a relationship based on negative and reciprocal contingencies; each punishes rather than reinforces the other.

Cognitive—Client is "awfulizing" about how terrible it is not to be liked by his buddies and also is imposing his religious "shoulds" on them.

Psychodynamic—Client has unresolved sexual identity issue that surfaces when in competition with other males.

Transactional Analysis—Communication between client and co-workers has broken down because of crossed transactions in which they are communicating with each other from different and noncomplementary ego states. Additionally, they seem to be playing games with each other. Client may be playing games such as "They'll be glad they knew me" or "I'm only trying to help."

Adlerian—Client has not learned much "social interest"; lifestyle is based on acting superior to others while actually feeling inferior.

Question 3: Client's values or religion can be reframed to help him get along rather than compete or fight with his buddies.

Question 4: No one sensory modality seems predominant in this example, so use words in interpretation that emphasize all modalities.

Examples of interpretations:

1. Could there be something you are doing or saying that makes your buddies feel threatened or irritated—perhaps you seem better or more religious or perhaps because they feel you are telling them how they should live? [This is consistent with the Adlerian and cognitive frameworks.]

2. Could you be using your religiousness to avoid having to get along with them and work things out? [Eclectic framework.]

3. It seems that you and your buddies have got off on the wrong track and good communication is sort of stymied. Perhaps you sort of tear each other down instead of building each other up, so no one feels like a winner. [Behavioral and TA frameworks.]

Client 2

Question 1: Implicit part of this client's message is that he's sort of an independent, self-made man whose independence, masculinity, and pride have been damaged by being laid off and by doing "menial" work.

Question 2: Alternative ways to view this issue, depending on your theoretical orientation, include the following:

Behavioral: Depression was precipitated and is maintained by loss of powerful positive, or reinforcing, contingencies (job loss, lack of satisfying current employment).

Cognitive: Depression is maintained by client's negative and irrational thoughts or self-statements about his lack of human worth due to job loss and subsequent type of employment.

Psychodynamic: Depression is the result of his loss of masculinity.

Transactional Analysis: Depressed feelings are the result of the adapted child ego state, which probably became a greater part of his personality after the job loss, while other ego states formerly functional, such as nurturing parent, are being somewhat excluded now from his personality.

Adlerian: Client has developed lifestyle and image of self in which he is independent, intelligent, strong, and masculine. Self-image is now challenged by job loss and menial work, resulting in depression.

Question 3: Positive aspects of the problem include the fact that he has a job that is economically sufficient. In this way, he continues to be independent, self-reliant, and resourceful.

Question 4: Use words like "seems," "appears," "looks like" to match client's visual words "should," "seem," "clear."

Examples of interpretations:

1. It seems like when you lost your job as an engineer, you let your masculinity and strength go out the window, too. [Consistent with psychodynamic and Adlerian frameworks.]

2. Probably at some level you keep picturing yourself as worthless and weak because of the type of work you're doing. The more of these pictures you keep flashing in your head, the worse you feel. [Consistent with cognitive framework, but "pictures" is used instead of "ideas" or "self-statements" to match the visual sensory modality.]

3. The depression is probably the result of having to give up a big part of your life—a part of yourself

(continued)

— that was very important and rewarding to you. What you're doing instead hasn't seemed to fill the void for you even though you appear to be behaving in an independent, self-reliant, and re-sourceful manner. [Consistent with behavioral framework.]

Client 3

Question 1: Implicit part of this message is that client doesn't want to settle down with a controlling woman; he's also upset with himself for giving her so much control.

Question 2: Different ways to view this issue, de-pending on your theoretical orientation:

Behavioral: Client uses a relationship with a con-trolling female to maintain avoidance behavior against settling down.

Cognitive: Client allows himself to get upset with Susie because of all the negative things he tells himself about her and her need to control his life.

Psychodynamic: Client's need to be controlled by a domineering female suggests unresolved oedipal issue.

Transactional Analysis: Client is both attracted to and repelled by Susie; he is hooked because he relates to her out of his Child ego state, which hooks or maintains her Parent ego state. At the same time, he dislikes feeling so "trapped" or con-trolled by her. He needs to find ways of relating to her from other ego states.

Adlerian: Client has developed lifestyle in which he feels adequate by giving up control to others. He may also have been parented by a controlling mother who made all his decisions for him.

Question 3: Client enjoys being with Susie; her boss-iness can be reframed as her need to take care of him and his letting her do so.

Question 4: Use words like "feel," "say," "hear" to match client words "tell,""say," "hear."

Examples of interpretations:

1. You say you have great times with Susie although you told her you don't want to settle down. I may be wrong—I'm wondering whether you've got yourself hooked up with a controlling woman as a way to avoid settling down. [Consistent with be-havioral framework.]

2. You seem to be both attracted to and turned off to Susie. I wonder what your relationship with your mother was like and whether you see any similar-ities between that relationship and the present one? [Consistent with psychodynamic and Adler-ian frameworks.]

3. You seem to be blaming Susie for being so control-ling and nurturing. Perhaps you haven't thought about how what you say to her might encourage her to be this way. Could it be that you relate to her as a child might relate to a parent? [Consistent with Transactional Analysis framework.]

"what," and "how" guidelines for information giving in counseling. The first guideline, the "when," involves recognizing the client's need for information. If the client does not have all the data or has invalid data, a need exists.

To be effective, information must also be well timed. The client should indicate receptivity to the information before it is delivered. As Lewis (1970, p. 135) observes, a client may ignore information if it is introduced too early in the interaction.

The counselor also needs to determine what in-formation is useful and relevant to the client. Gen-erally, information is useful if it is something the client is not likely to find on her or his own and if the client has the resources to act on the informa-tion. The counselor also needs to determine whether the information must be presented se-quentially in order to make most sense to the client. Since clients may remember initial infor-mation best, presenting the most significant infor-mation *first* may be a good rule of thumb in se-quencing information. Finally, in selecting information to give, be careful not to impose in-formation on the client, who is ultimately respon-sible for deciding what information to use and act on (Lewis, 1970). In other words, information giv-ing should not be used as a forum for the counselor to subtly push his or her own values on the client (Egan, 1982).

In the interview itself, the actual delivery of in-formation, the "how" of information giving, is crucial. The information should be discussed in a way that makes it "usable" to the client and en-courages the client to "hear and apply" the infor-mation (Gazda et al., 1984). Moreover, informa-tion should be presented objectively. Don't leave out facts simply because they aren't pleasant. Watch out, too, for information overload. Most people are not "bionic" and cannot assimilate a great deal of information in "one shot." Limit the amount of information presented at any one time. Usually, the more information you give the clients, the less they remember. Clients recall information best when you give no more than several pieces of information at one time (Ley, 1976). Be aware that information differs in depth and may have an emotional impact on clients. Clients may not react emotionally to relatively simple or factual information such as information about a counseling procedure or an occupation or a résumé. However, clients may react with anger, anxiety, or relief to information that has more depth or far-reaching consequences, such as the results of a test. Ask about and discuss the client's reactions to the information you give. In addition, make an effort to promote client understanding of the information. Avoid jargon in offering explanations. Use paper and pencil as you're giving information to draw a picture or diagram highlighting the most important points, or give clients paper and pencil so they can get down key ideas. Remember to ask clients to verify their impression of your information either by summarizing it or by repeating it back to you. Try to determine, too, when it's time to stop dealing with information. Continued information giving may reinforce a client's tendency to avoid taking action (Gelatt et al., 1973).

Steps in information giving. There are six steps in formulating the what, when, and how of presenting information to clients. First, assess what information the client lacks about the issue or problem. Second, determine the most important parts to include in your presentation. Third, decide how the information can be sequenced in a way that facilitates client comprehension and retention. Fourth, consider how you can deliver the information in such a way that the client is likely to comprehend it. Fifth, assess the emotional impact the information is likely to have on the client. Finally, determine whether your information giving was effective. Note client reactions to it and follow up on client use of the information in a subsequent session. Remember, too, that some clients may "store" information and act on it at a much later date — often even after therapy has terminated.

To facilitate your use of information giving, we have put these six steps in the form of questions that you can use as a cognitive learning strategy:

1. What information does this client lack about the problem or issue?
2. What are the most important parts of this information to include in my presentation?
3. How can I best sequence this information?
4. How can I deliver this information so that the client is likely to comprehend it?
5. What emotional impact is this information likely to have on this client?
6. How will I know whether my information giving has been effective?

Consider the way a therapist uses this cognitive learning strategy in the following example. The therapist is counseling with a woman who has been advised by three physicians to have a mastectomy because of a breast carcinoma (cancer). Although the client admits she realizes that her decision not to have surgery could have negative health consequences, she expresses reluctance to undergo surgery because of possible public reactions to her "deformity" after the operation.

1. What information does this client lack about this problem or issue?
   The client seems to lack information about a prosthesis and about special clothing designed to make her look as "typical" as she did prior to surgery. (Note — in this particular situation, because of this type of problem, it would be important to check out whether she has all the necessary medical and health-related information as well.)
2. What are the most important parts of this information to include in my presentation?
   a. That if this is the only concern she has about surgery, it is potentially remedied with a prosthesis and good choices of clothing.
   b. That other women in a Reach for Recovery group who have dealt with this concern after similar surgery are available to share their insights with her.
3. How can I best sequence this information?
   Mention the prosthesis first, since it may be most important to her, and how it is fitted especially for her, followed by information about clothing and then about the Reach for Recovery group.
4. How can I deliver this information so that the client is likely to comprehend it?
   Make sure she knows what I mean by the term *prosthesis;* show her one or pictures of one so she can see how it really looks and feels.
5. What emotional impact is this information likely to have on the client?
   May be relieved to know these options exist or anxious because the options remove her reason

for avoiding the operation.

6. How will I know whether my information giving has been effective?

Watch and listen to her reactions to it; follow up in subsequent session to determine what she did with the information—whether she acted on it and, if so, in what ways.

Suppose that at this point the counselor responds to the client with the following information:

Sheila, I'm aware of your reluctance to have this operation. One of the major reasons for your reluctance seems to be your concern about how you will look to yourself and to others after the surgery is over. I'd like to share some information with you that you may not be aware of. I'm not giving this information to persuade you to have the surgery. That's a decision only you can make. This infor-

mation is something you can use to decide the best possible course of action for you under the circumstances. Now you mentioned the word *deformity*. Did you know you can get a prosthesis that is made especially for you and your body? I have one here [or can get one] to show you. When this is properly fitted, your body will look just as it does now. In fact, you can even wear any type of bathing suit that you choose and feel comfortable with. It also might be helpful for you to talk with some of the women in the "Reach for Recovery" group. These women have all had some type of mastectomy and would be happy to talk with you about your feelings concerning your body image. After you've thought about this, maybe you could share your reactions to this information with me.

Learning Activity #21 gives you an opportunity to try out the skill of information giving.

LEARNING ACTIVITY #21: INFORMATION GIVING

In this learning activity, three client situations are presented. For each situation, determine what information the client lacks and develop a suitable information-giving response, using the cognitive learning strategy described earlier and outlined below. To internalize this learning strategy, you may want to talk through these self questions overtly (aloud) and then covertly (silently to yourself). The end product will be an information-giving response that you can say aloud or write down or both. An example precedes the practice situations. Feedback follows the learning activity (on pages 142–143).

Example

The clients are a married couple in their thirties who disagree about the way to handle their 4-year-old son. The father believes he is a "spoiled brat" and states that he thinks the best way to keep him in line is to give him a spanking. The mother believes that her son is just a "typical boy" and the best way to handle him is to be understanding and loving. The couple admit that there is little consistency in the way the two of them deal with their son. The typical pattern is for the father to reprimand him and swat him while the mother stands, watches, comforts him, and often intercedes on the child's behalf.

Self-question 1: What information do these clients lack about this problem or issue?
Information about effective parenting and child-rearing skills.

Self-question 2: What are the most important parts

of this information to include in my presentation?

a. All children need discipline.
b. Discipline involves setting and enforcing limits, not spanking, getting revenge, or giving in to a child.
c. All disciplining should occur in a manner that enhances rather than destroys a child's self-esteem.
d. There is a hierarchy in parent/child relationships: parents are there to be in charge and to take care of children, not the other way around.
e. Kids behave better and feel better and more secure when their parents work together rather than argue on how to handle and respond to them.

All five of these things are too much to emphasize at one time, so for today, I'll concentrate on a, b, and c only.

Self-question 3: How can I best sequence this information?
Discuss children's need for discipline first, followed by what discipline is and then how it should help rather than hurt a child's self-esteem.

Self-question 4: How can I deliver this information so that the clients are likely to comprehend it?
Define what I mean by *discipline* and define it in such a way that it appeals to the values of both parents. The mother values understanding, support, and nurturing, while the father values authority, respect, and control.

Self-question 5: What emotional impact is this information likely to have on these clients?

(continued)

LEARNING ACTIVITY #21: INFORMATION GIVING (continued)

If I frame the information positively, it will appeal to both parents. I have to be careful not to take sides or cause one parent to feel relieved while the other feels anxious, guilty, or put down.

Self-question 6: How will I know whether my information giving has been effective?

I'll watch and listen to their nonverbal and verbal reactions to it to see whether they support the idea and also follow up on their use of the information in a later session.

Example of information-giving response: You know, Mary and Gus, I sense that you are in agreement on the fact that you love your child and want what is best for him. So what I'm going to say next is based on this idea that you are both trying to find a way to do what is best for Timmy. In discussing how you feel about Timmy and his behavior, I think it is important to remember that all children need discipline or limits. Kids ask for limits in all kinds of ways and don't get along very well without them. So when I talk about discipline for Timmy, I mean the idea of setting some limits the two of you agree on and sticking to them. I don't mean spanking or getting revenge, or giving in to him and letting him have his own way. But discipline does involve taking charge, being in control —and doing so in a nurturing way that can help Timmy feel good rather than bad about himself.

Client Practice Situations

Client 1 is a young adolescent, sexually active female. She has already been pregnant three times and has had three abortions. She says she is not too worried about getting pregnant again because either she and her partners abstain on certain days or her partner withdraws "before anything happens." She also indicates that if she did happen to get pregnant again, she would just get another abortion, because it's an easy solution with no physical or emotional aftereffects.

Self-question 1: What information does this client lack about this problem or issue?

Self-question 2: What are the most important parts of this information to include in my presentation?

Self-question 3: How can I best sequence this information?

Self-question 4: How can I deliver this information so that the client is likely to comprehend it?

Self-question 5: What emotional impact is this information likely to have on this client?

Client 2 is a high school girl who is expressing her desire to be a nurse because it's an "easy curriculum, and in a field where lots of jobs are available." The client has very good grades in English and history and very poor grades in math and science.

Self-question 1: What information does this client lack about this problem or issue?

Self-question 2: What are the most important parts of this information to include in my presentation?

Self-question 3: How can I best sequence this information?

Self-question 4: How can I deliver this information so that the client is likely to comprehend it?

Self-question 5: What emotional impact is this information likely to have on this client?

Client 3 is a 35-year-old woman with two teenage daughters. She is employed as an executive secretary in a large engineering firm. Her husband is a department store manager. She and her husband have had a stormy relationship for several years. She wants to get a divorce but is hesitant to do so for fear that she will be labeled a troublemaker and will lose her job. She is also afraid that she will not be able to support her daughters financially on her limited income. However, she indicates that she believes getting a divorce will make her happy and will essentially solve all her own internal conflicts.

Self-question 1: What information does this client lack about this problem or issue?

Self-question 2: What are the most important parts of this information to include in my presentation?

Self-question 3: How can I best sequence this information?

Self-question 4: How can I deliver this information so that the client is likely to comprehend it?

Self-question 5: What emotional impact is this information likely to have on this client?

□ SUMMARY

Listening responses reflect clients' perceptions of their world. Action responses provide alternative ways for clients to view themselves and their world. A change in the client's way of viewing and explaining things may be one indication of positive movement in counseling. According to Egan (1975, p. 132), counselor statements that move beyond the client's frame of reference are a "bridge" between listening responses and concrete change programs. To be used effectively, action responses require a great deal of counselor concern and judgment. Effective use of action responses presupposes high levels of relationship conditions and enhancers such as those described in Chapters 2 and 3. In an actual interview, these responses must be used flexibly, sensitively, and in the context of a client's nonverbal cues as well as verbal messages.

□ SKILL INTEGRATION

In Chapters 2 and 3 you learned about important relationship conditions and variables such as empathy, genuineness, positive regard, competence, trustworthiness, and interpersonal attractiveness. In Chapter 4 you discovered valuable reasons for atending to and working with client nonverbal behavior as well as important aspects of your own nonverbal behavior, including kinesics, paralinguistics, proxemics, environment, and time variables. Synchrony, or matching, between counselor and client nonverbal behavior and congruence be-

tween your verbal and nonverbal messages were also emphasized. In Chapters 5 and 6 you acquired a base of various verbal responses to use in counseling interactions to facilitate client exploration, understanding, and action. These responses included clarification, paraphrase, reflection, summarization, probes, confrontation, interpretation, and information giving. You have also had various types of practice in which you have demonstrated each set of skills in role-play interactions. In actual counseling, these skills are blended together and used in complementary fashion. In Part Five of the postevaluation, we structure a practice opportunity designed to simulate an actual initial helping interview with a client. The purpose of this activity is to help you "put the skills together"—that is, integrate them for yourself in some meaningful, coherent fashion. It is analogous to learning anything else that requires a set of skills for successful performance. To swim, for example, you have to learn first to put your face in the water, then to float, then to kick, then to move your arms in strokes, and finally to do it all at once. Initial attempts feel awkward, but out of such first steps evolve championship swimmers.

POSTEVALUATION

PART ONE

This part is designed for you to assess your performance on Objective One. Using the written list of client statements and counselor responses below, take a sheet of paper and identify the type of action response—probe, confrontation, interpretation, or information giving—reflected in each counselor message. If you can accurately identify six out of eight responses, you have met this objective. You can check your answers against those provided in the feedback that follows the postevaluation.

1. *Client:* "The pressure from my job is starting to get to me. I'm always in a constant rush, trying to hurry and get several things done at the same time. There's never enough time."

P a. "What is it about your job that is causing you to feel so stressed?"

I b. "It's important you are aware of this. Continued anxiety and stress like this can lead to health problems if they go unchecked."

2. *Client:* "I'm tired of sitting home alone, but I feel so uptight when I ask a girl for a date."

C a. "You seem to be saying that you feel lonely

and also that you're not willing to risk asking a girl to go out with you."

P b. "What makes you so anxious when you speak with girls?"

3. *Client:* "I don't know why I tolerate his abuse. I really don't love him."

C a. "On the one hand, you say that you don't love him, and on the other hand, you remain in the house and allow him to beat you. How do you put these two things together?"

I b. "You may be caught up in a vicious cycle about whether your feelings for him, even though they're not love, outweigh your regard for yourself. It might be helpful for you to know the process other women in your shoes go through before they finally get enough courage to leave for good."

4. *Client:* "I don't know why we ever got married in the first place."

P a. "What qualities attracted you to each other originally?"

I b. "You're having a difficult time right now,

(continued)

POSTEVALUATION (continued)

which has led you to question the entire marriage. I wonder whether you would react this way if this present problem weren't causing such distress."

PART TWO

Match the four action responses, listed below, with the appropriate intended purposes of these responses (Chapter Objective Two). Feedback follows the postevaluation.

Action Response
(a) Probe
(b) Confrontation
(c) Interpretation
(d) Information giving

Intended purpose of response
_b_1. To identify mixed (incongruent) messages and behavior
_A_2. To begin an interview
_C_3. To examine client behavior or issues from an alternative frame of reference
_D_4. To identify alternatives/options available to clients
_A_5. To obtain information
_A_6. To broaden or narrow the topic of discussion
_C_7. To identify implicit messages
_D_8. To dispel myths

PART THREE

For each of the following three client statements, Objective Three asks you to verbalize or write an example of each of the four action responses. In developing these responses, it may be helpful to use the cognitive learning strategy you practiced earlier for each response. Example responses are given in the Postevaluation Feedback.

Client 1, a frustrated parent: My house looks like a mess. I can't seem to get anything done with these kids always under my feet. I'm afraid that I may lose my temper and hit them one of these days.
Probe:
Confrontation:
Interpretation:
Information giving:

Client 2, a graduate student: I feel so overwhelmed. I've got books to read, papers to write. My money is running low and I don't even have a job. Plus my roommate is thinking of moving out.

Probe:
Confrontation:
Interpretation:
Information giving:

Client 3, a nurse: These doctors drive me crazy. They tell me whenever I make a mistake but never say a word when I do a good job. I'm getting tired of hearing them order me around the way they do. At my salary, who needs the aggravation?
Probe:
Confrontation:
Interpretation:
Information giving:

PART FOUR

This part of the evaluation gives you an opportunity to develop your observation skills of key aspects of client behavior that must be attended to in order to develop effective and accurate action responses:

1. Issues and messages that need more elaboration, information, or examples
2. Discrepancies and incongruities
3. Implicit messages and themes
4. Distorted perceptions and ideas
5. Myths and inaccurate information

Objective Four asks you to observe these five aspects of client behavior during a 30-minute interview. Record your observations on the Client Observation Checklist that follows. You can obtain feedback for this activity by having two or more persons observe and rate the same session—then compare your responses.

CLIENT OBSERVATION CHECKLIST
Name of counselor _____
Name of observer(s) _____
_____

Instructions: Given the five categories of client behavior (left column), use the right column to record separate occurrences of behaviors within these categories as they occur during a 30-minute counseling interview.*

* If observers are not available, audiotape or videotape your session and complete the checklist while reviewing the tape.

(continued)

Observed category	Selected key client words and behavior
1. Issues and messages that need more elaboration, information, or examples	1. _____ 2. _____ 3. _____ 4. _____
2. Discrepancies and incongruities	1. _____ 2. _____ 3. _____ 4. _____
3. Implicit messages and themes	1. _____ 2. _____ 3. _____ 4. _____
4. Distorted perceptions and ideas	1. _____ 2. _____ 3. _____ 4. _____
5. Myths or inaccurate information	1. _____ 2. _____ 3. _____ 4. _____

Observer impressions and comments _____

PART FIVE

In order to have an opportunity to integrate your skills (Chapter Objective Five), conduct at least one role-play interview that is approximately 20 minutes long. You may want to consider this an initial helping interview. Your objective is to use as many of the verbal responses (listening, action) and the nonverbal behaviors as seem appropriate within this time span. Also give some attention to the quality of your relationship with the client. Try to regard this interview as an opportunity to get involved with the person in front of you, not as just another practice. If you feel some discomfort in using your verbal and nonverbal skills, you may wish to do several more interviews with different clients with this goal in mind. To assess your interview, use the Interview Inventory that follows. You may wish to copy the inventory or superimpose a piece of paper over it for your ratings. After all the ratings are completed, look at your ratings in the light of these questions:

1. Which relationship variables were easiest for you to demonstrate? Hardest?
2. Examine the total number of the verbal responses

you used in each category. Did you use responses from each category with the same frequency? Did most of your responses come from one category? Did you seem to avoid using responses from one category? If so, for what reason?
3. Was it easier to integrate the verbal responses or the nonverbal skills?
4. Which nonverbal skills were easiest for you to demonstrate? Which ones did you find most difficult to use in the interview?
5. What do you see that you have learned about your counseling interview behavior so far? What do you think you need to improve?

INTERVIEW INVENTORY

Interview No. _____ Counselor _____
Client _____ Rater _____ Date _____

Instructions for rating: This rating form has three parts. Part One (Relationship Variables) measures aspects of establishing and enhancing a therapeutic relationship. Part Two (Verbal Behavior) assesses listening and action responses. Part Three (Nonverbal Behavior) evaluates your use of various nonverbal behaviors. To use the Interview Inventory for rating, follow the instructions found on each part of the inventory.

PART ONE: RELATIONSHIP VARIABLES

Instructions: Using the 5-point scale, indicate which number on the scale best represents the counselor's behavior during the observed interaction. Circle the appropriate number on the chart on p. 140.

PART TWO: VERBAL BEHAVIOR

Instructions: Check (✔) the *type* of verbal response represented by each counselor statement in the corresponding category on the rating form. At the end of the observation period, tally the total number of checks associated with each verbal response on the chart on p. 141.

PART THREE: NONVERBAL BEHAVIOR

Instructions: This part of the inventory lists a number of significant dimensions of nonverbal behavior. Check (✔) any that you observe and provide a brief description of the key aspects and appropriateness of the behavior. An example is given on the chart on p. 142.

(continued)

POSTEVALUATION (continued)

PART ONE: RELATIONSHIP VARIABLES

1. Conveyed accurate understanding of the client.

1	2	3	4	5
Not at all	Minimally	Somewhat	A great deal	Almost always

2. Conveyed support and warmth without approving or disapproving of the client.

1	2	3	4	5
Not at all	Minimally	Somewhat	A great deal	Almost always

3. Focused on the person rather than on the procedure or on counselor's "professional role."

1	2	3	4	5
Not at all	Minimally	Somewhat	A great deal	Almost always

4. Conveyed spontaneity, was not "mechanical" when responding to client.

1	2	3	4	5
Not at all	Minimally	Somewhat	A great deal	Almost always

5. Responded to feelings and issues as they occurred within the session (that is, "here and now").

1	2	3	4	5
Not at all	Minimally	Somewhat	A great deal	Almost always

6. Displayed comfort and confidence in working with the client.

1	2	3	4	5
Not at all	Minimally	Somewhat	A great deal	Almost always

7. Responded with dynamism and frequency; was not "passive."

1	2	3	4	5
Not at all	Minimally	Somewhat	A great deal	Almost always

8. Displayed sincerity in intentions and responses.

1	2	3	4	5
Not at all	Minimally	Somewhat	A great deal	Almost always

9. Conveyed friendliness and "good will" in interacting with client.

1	2	3	4	5
Not at all	Minimally	Somewhat	A great deal	Almost always

10. Informed client about expectations and what would or would not happen in session (that is, structuring).

1	2	3	4	5
Not at all	Minimally	Somewhat	A great deal	Almost always

11. Shared similar attitudes, opinions, and experiences about oneself with client when appropriate (that is, when such sharing added to, not detracted from, client focus).

1	2	3	4	5
Not at all	Minimally	Somewhat	A great deal	Almost always

12. Other significant relationship aspects _____

_____

_____

_____

PART TWO: VERBAL BEHAVIOR

	Listening responses				Action responses					
	Clarification	Paraphrase	Reflecting feeling	Summarization	Open question	Closed question	Focused question	Confrontation	Interpretation	Information giving
1										
2										
3										
.										
.										
.										
.										
.										
.										
20										
Total										

POSTEVALUATION (continued)

PART THREE: NONVERBAL BEHAVIOR

Behavior	Check (✓) if observed	Key aspects of behavior	Behavior	Check (✓) if observed	Key aspects of behavior
Example Body posture	✓	Tense, rigid until last part of session, then relaxed	*Example* Body posture	✓	Tense, rigid until last part of session, then relaxed
1. Eye contact			19. Time in responding to messages		
2. Facial expression			20. Time in ending session		
3. Head nodding			21. Autonomic response (for example, breathing, sweat, skin flush, rash)		
4. Body posture					
5. Body movements					
6. Body orientation					
7. Gestures					
8. Nonverbal adaptors			22. Congruence/ incongruence between counselor verbal and nonverbal behavior		
9. Voice level and pitch					
10. Rate of speech					
11. Verbal underlining (voice emphasis)			23. Synchrony/ dissynchrony between counselor/client nonverbal behavior		
12. Speech errors					
13. Pauses, silence					
14. Distance					
15. Touch					
16. Position in room					
17. Environmental arousal			24. Other		
18. Time in starting session					

FEEDBACK #21: INFORMATION GIVING

Client 1

Question 1: The client seems to lack information about effective birth control and about possible effects of multiple abortions.

Question 2: a. Rhythm is not a foolproof pregnancy prevention method.

b. Withdrawal also may not prevent pregnancy, particularly if semen is around the vaginal opening.

c. Multiple abortions can have physical and/or emotional complications, depending on the individual.

Question 3: Present the problems of withdrawal and rhythm first, since this could result in another pregnancy; followed by information about effects of multiple abortions.

Question 4: Be very specific, accurate, and factual. Avoid making any value judgments. May want to use paper and pencil to draw how withdrawal could result in pregnancy.

Question 5: Probably a lot, as she is using lack of information to avoid the issue. She may initially be upset or angry.

Examples of information-giving response: Marie, since you've said you're not worried about getting pregnant again because you and your partner practice rhythm and withdrawal, let me share some information about these methods with you.

(continued)

I'm not telling you these things to say "Do this"—or "Don't do this"—but more to give you some facts that you can use to decide what might be best for you with this issue. First, withdrawal can and often does result in pregnancy, because in withdrawing, sometimes some semen is left around this vaginal opening [draws a diagram]. What can happen then is that the semen can travel up the opening and reach these tubes [continues drawing] and can fertilize an egg and result in pregnancy, just as if you had had a complete act of intercourse. Rhythm is also something that doesn't have a very high rate of preventing pregnancy—about half the time it works, half it doesn't. That's because it can get awfully difficult and tedious to know for sure when to have sex and when not to and also because women can ovulate at any time in their menstrual cycle. I mention this because depending on the person, having several abortions can result in physical or emotional complications. Since you seem to be interested in preventing another pregnancy at this time, you may want to consider other, more foolproof methods.

Client 2

Question 1: The client seems to lack information about the type of curriculum found in a nursing program, about the present job market for nurses, and about her own academic abilities and achievements as well as limitations.

Question 2: a. The nursing curriculum may or may not be easy, depending on a person's strengths. It requires ability and facility with science and math.

b. In some areas of the country, nursing jobs are now very scarce.

c. Since your record of achievement has been consistently good in English and history and consistently poor in math and science, you may find nursing to be a hard curriculum.

Question 3: Perhaps begin with the fact that jobs are not always readily available, since this is so important to her, followed by information about the amount of math and science required in a nursing curriculum and how this fits with her past record of achievement.

Question 4: Be specific and objective—dig out some statistics of the nursing job market for her in different areas of the country. Perhaps have her look through catalogues of nursing programs and assess her interest and ability in each individual course.

Question 5: Depending on her motivation to be a

nurse, she may feel relieved or upset and frustrated by the information.

Example of information-giving response: Renee, you mentioned you are interested in getting into nursing because it is an easy curriculum and because there are so many nursing jobs always available. I'd like to share some facts and figures with you about the nursing field you may not be aware of. I'm not trying to say "Pursue nursing" or "Don't pursue it"—just look at the information and then at yourself in making this important decision. First, it was true at one time that nurses were always in short supply. During the last few years, however, this has changed. In some parts of the country, there are many more nurses than there are jobs. If you take a look at these figures for these five geographical areas, you'll see what I mean. So, depending on where you live, it could be easy or very difficult to get the kind of job you want in the nursing field. Second, whether nursing is easy or hard as a curriculum depends on you and your interests and abilities. I've pulled out several catalogues listing courses in typical nursing programs. Nursing involves a lot of math and science course work, which, as you know, has not seemed to be as easy for you as English and history. It may be helpful for you to look at these courses individually and see whether you think you have the interest and inclination to achieve in them.

Client 3

Question 1: Client seems to lack certain legal information about possible management and consequences of divorce. Also seems to lack information about possible psychological effects of divorce.

Question 2: a. Getting a divorce rarely results in loss of job.

b. In most situations, the husband would be legally required to give financial support for the children.

c. Although divorce may make a person feel happy and relieved, it can also be unsettling, can result in temporary feelings of loss and depression, and is not an antidote for all other life issues.

Question 3: Present the need for legal information about her job status and child support, followed by other possible effects of divorce.

Question 4: Be factual and concrete. Possibly ask her to list pros and cons of divorce on paper.

Question 5: Her feelings could range from relief about the legal issues to disappointment that divorce is not a panacea.

FEEDBACK #21: (continued)

Example of information-giving response: Leslie, in discussing your situation with you, there are a couple of things I want to mention. First, it might be useful for you to consider seeing a competent lawyer who specializes in divorce mediation. This person could give you detailed information about the legal effects and processes of a divorce. Usually, however, a person does not lose a job because of a divorce. Besides, in most instances, the husband is required to make support payments as long as the children are of minor age. I would encourage you to express these same concerns to the lawyer. The other thing I'd like to spend some time discussing is your belief that you will feel very happy after the divorce. That might be very true. It is also important to remember, though, that just the process of ending a relationship — even a bad relationship — can be very unsettling and can bring not only relief but often some temporary feelings of loss and maybe sadness.

☐ SUGGESTED READINGS

Beck, J. T., & Strong, S. R. (1982). Stimulating therapeutic change with interpretations: A comparison of positive and negative connotation. *Journal of Counseling Psychology, 29,* 551–559.

Borck, L. E., & Fawcett, S. B. (1982). *Learning counseling and problem-solving skills.* New York: Haworth Press. Chapter 7, "How to Ask a Client Questions."

Brammer, L. M., & Shostrom, E. L. (1982). *Therapeutic psychology: Fundamentals of counseling and psychotherapy.* Englewood Cliffs, N.J.: Prentice-Hall. Chapter 9, "Interpretation and Body Awareness Strategies."

Claiborn, C. D. (1982). Interpretation and change in counseling. *Journal of Counseling Psychology, 29,* 439–453.

Claiborn, C. D., Ward, S. R., & Strong, S. R. (1981). Effects of congruence between counselor interpretations and client beliefs. *Journal of Counseling Psychology, 28,* 101–109.

Elliott, R., Barker, C. B., Caskey, N., & Pistrang, N. (1982). Differential helpfulness of counselor verbal response modes. *Journal of Counseling Psychology, 29,* 354–361.

Gazda, G. M., Asbury, F. S., Balzer, F. J., Childers, W. C., & Walters, R. P. (1984). *Human relations development: A manual for educators.* Boston: Allyn & Bacon. Chapter 18, "Perceiving and Responding with Confrontation."

Hudson, J., & Danish, S. (1980). The acquisition of information: An important life skill. *Personnel and Guidance Journal, 59,* 164–167.

Ivey, A. E. (1983). *International interviewing and counseling.* Monterey, CA: Brooks/Cole. Chapter 3, "Questions: Opening Communication."

Johnson, D. W. (1981). *Reaching out: Interpersonal effectiveness and self-actualization.* Englewood Cliffs, NJ: Prentice-Hall. Chapter 11, "Confrontation and Negotiation."

Leaman, D. R. (1978). Confrontation in counseling. *Personnel and Guidance Journal, 56,* 630–633.

Long, L., Paradise, L., & Long, T. (1981). *Questioning: Skills for the helping process.* Monterey, CA: Brooks/Cole.

Milne, C. R., & Dowd, E. T. (1983). Effect of interpretation style on counselor social influence. *Journal of Counseling Psychology, 30,* 603–606.

Selby, J. W., & Calhoun, L. G. (1980). Psychodidactics: An undervalued and underdeveloped treatment tool for psychological intervention. *Professional Psychology, 11,* 236–241.

Strong, S. R., Wambach, C. A., Lopez, F. G., & Cooper, R. K. (1979). Motivational and equipping functions of interpretation in counseling. *Journal of Counseling Psychology, 26,* 98–107.

FEEDBACK: POSTEVALUATION

PART ONE
1. a. Probe
   b. Information giving
2. a. Confrontation
   b. Probe
3. a. Confrontation
   b. Information giving
4. a. Probe
   b. Interpretation

PART TWO
1. b. Confrontation
2. a. Probe
3. c. Interpretation
4. d. Information giving
5. a. Probe
6. a. Probe
7. c. Interpretation
8. d. Information giving

PART THREE
Here are some examples of action responses. Are yours similar?

(continued)

2. To identify the controlling or contributing variables associated with the problem.

3. To determine the client's goals/expectations for counseling outcomes.

4. To gather baseline data that will be compared with subsequent data to assess and evaluate client progress and the effects of treatment strategies. This evaluation helps the practitioner decide whether to continue or modify the treatment plan or intervention strategy.

5. To educate and motivate the client by sharing your views of the problem with the client, increasing the client's receptivity to treatment, and contributing to therapeutic change through reactivity (that is, when behavior changes as a consequence of the assessment interview or procedure rather than as a result of a particular action or change strategy).

6. To use the information obtained from the client to plan effective treatment interventions and strategies. The information obtained during the assessment process should help to answer this well-thought-out question: "*What* treatment, by *whom*, is most effective for *this* individual with *that* specific problem and under *which* set of circumstances?" (Paul, 1967, p. 111).

This chapter focuses primarily on the first two purposes of assessment mentioned above: defining the problem and identifying the controlling variables associated with the problem. The next section presents several ways to conceptualize client problems.

□ METHODS OF CONCEPTUALIZING CLIENT PROBLEMS

Interviewing the client and having the client engage in other assessment procedures are only part of the overall assessment process in counseling and therapy. Equally important is the therapist's own mental, or covert, activity that goes on during the process. The therapist typically gathers a great amount of information from clients during this stage of counseling. Unless the therapist can integrate and synthesize the data, they are of little value and use. The *counselor's* tasks during the assessment process include knowing what information to obtain and how to obtain it, putting it together in some meaningful way, and using it to generate clinical hunches, or hypotheses, about client problems, hunches that lead to tentative ideas for treatment planning. This mental activity

of the counselor's is called "conceptualization"—which simply means the way the counselor thinks about the client's problem configuration.

The assessment methods we describe later in this chapter and in Chapter 8, and our interview assessment model particularly, are based on a model of conceptualization we have used over the years in our teaching and in clinical practice. The origins of this model were first described by Kanfer and Saslow (1969). Before describing our model in detail, we would first like to describe three other current models of client or case conceptualization proposed by Swensen (1968), Seay (1978), and Lazarus (1976, 1981) that have influenced the development of our own clinical model of problem conceptualization.

The four models of problem conceptualization we present in this chapter have some distinct differences but are also similar in several respects. First, they represent a framework the therapist can use to develop hunches (educated guesses) about the client's presenting problem. Second, they recognize that problem behavior is usually multifaceted and affects how people think and feel as well as behave. Finally, they provide information about the problem that the therapist can use in selecting and planning relevant treatments. Although the major focus of the chapter is on the model we use for case conceptualization, we present three others because they are important historically in the development of case conceptualization models and because they enable the reader to look at client problems from more than one perspective.

Swensen's Model of Problem Conceptualization:

Drawing on the works of Lewin (1951) and Pascal (1959), Swensen has developed a model of case conceptualization based on the following formula:

Deviant behavior (symptomatology; undesired result or outcome)	=	function of the degree of stress, maladaptive behaviors, habits, and defenses
		versus
		supports, strengths, and adaptive habits and defenses

Deviant behavior. Deviant behavior is any behavior that is different from what is typical or ordinary and would be expected of a person in a similar role and may include symptomatology such as feeling anxious or depressed or more unusual (in the negative sense) behavior such as overeating and vomiting or hearing voices.

Stress. Stress includes situations that are pressure-packed or tense or uncomfortable for the client, usually resulting in noticeable physiological sensations such as rapid heartbeat, dizziness, sweating, or stomach upset.

Maladaptive behaviors, habits, and defenses. Maladaptive behaviors, habits, and defenses are habitual behaviors and defenses that are negative or destructive in the sense that they prevent clients from achieving their goal of a satisfying life. In other words, maladaptive habits and defenses are things that contribute to deviant behavior. For example, an adolescent is removed from a normal classroom and placed in a behavior-disorders classroom because of continued and repetitive behavioral problems, including starting fights with other kids, stealing their personal property, and swearing at teachers. In discussion with his parents, you find that this 15-year-old boy has almost never received any parental-enforced consequences for irresponsible behavior. The parents also indicate that their son's behavior has resulted in a constant strain on their own marital relationship. They say as well that this boy's behavior is especially hard for them to tolerate because of the excellent behavior of their older son, who is a "model child." They don't understand why the younger son can't act more responsibly, as his brother does. Interviews with the boy suggest that he feels very inferior to his older brother and many of his peers. The client also states that, if his parents didn't have him to fight about, they would "split" because they argue about him constantly. In this case, the undesirable result, or deviant behavior, is represented by the boy's learned and inappropriate behaviors that get him into trouble at school, such as fighting, stealing, and swearing. Maladaptive defenses/behavioral habits would be his lack of responsibility at home and his possible belief that his "problem" provides a good reason for his parents to stay together.

Supports and strengths. Supports include resources that currently exist for the client—namely, persons or situations in the client's environment who are supportive or helpful. Strengths include accomplishments or positive performance of the client in some area. Strengths are indicators of the client's "basic abilities or talents" and "sug-

gest areas in which the psychotherapist may work with some prospect of success. . . . [However], strengths are impossible to assess without successful performance of some kind. Strength is evidenced by prior success at some endeavor" (Swensen, 1968, p. 57).

Adaptive behaviors, habits, and defenses. Adaptive behaviors, habits, and defenses include constructive defenses or habitual behaviors which help clients achieve their goals and which contribute to a satisfying life. Adaptive behaviors are those that are learned, are appropriate given the context, and ultimately result in success or reinforcement for the client. For example, in the case of the adolescent mentioned earlier, the client also is a member of the school's swim team. Successful performance in swimming is a strength for the client. Behaviors that contribute to this accomplishment, such as attending practices daily, being on time, and following instructions from the coach, are adaptive behavior habits or patterns that ultimately contribute to success or reinforcement for this client in this one area.

Swensen's case conceptualization model can be used by practitioners in several ways. First, it is a tool to help counselors see, hear, or grasp what is going on with a client in order to develop some hypotheses or hunches about the client's concerns. For example, consider the case analysis depicted in Figure 7-1 of the adolescent boy described earlier. In studying the figure, we get a picture of a boy who exhibits a lot of school-related "behavioral problems" and who feels a lot of pressure on him from his older brother and his parents as well as pressure to help keep together his parents' disintegrating marital relationship. This same boy has learned to respond to these stresses or pressures with maladaptive defenses and behavioral patterns, including constant unfavorable comparisons with his older brother, lack of responsibility at home, and anxiety in unstructured situations, especially at school. He does, however, have two persons in school willing to work with him—the counselor and the swim coach. He also has several other positive things in his favor, including good health, intelligence, and membership on the school swim team. And he has demonstrated adaptive defenses and behavioral patterns in certain situations, such as swim meet competitions and test-taking situations. We can use this information to generate some hunches about the client's presenting behavioral symptomatology—including (but not limited to) the following:

Deviant Behaviors	Stresses	Maladaptive Defenses and Behavioral Habits
Starts fights with other kids Steals personal property from other kids Swears at teachers Has received low grades (Cs and Ds) in four out of five classes	Older brother who is smart, well behaved, well liked at school and elsewhere Parents' relationship—constant tension Unstructured classes in school	Compares self unfavorably with older brother Lack of responsibility/tasks at home Feels anxious in unstructured situations, especially school-related

Supports	Strengths	Adaptive Habits and Defenses
School counselor is willing to work with him and with family Swim coach wants to help so he can remain on swim team	Member of swim club—performs well in competitions Good health—good appetite and sleep patterns Received high scores on intelligence tests	Attends daily practice promptly for swim club practices Follows instructions of swim club coach Applies himself to a test-taking (intelligence) situation; follows instructions on the test Generally feels comfortable and handles himself well in structured and competitive situations

Figure 7-1. *Case analysis using Swensen's case conceptualization model*

1. There is a lot of competition between himself and his older brother for his parents' attention. Most of the time, the client feels his older brother wins this one.
2. The client has never really had to be responsible for himself or his behavior.
3. The client may feel his problems provide a reason for his parents to stay together.
4. The client feels uncomfortable in unstructured situations and shows evidence of adaptive responses in situations that are structured and somewhat competitive. In fact, the client seems to thrive on competition so that he can demonstrate that he is capable of winning.

Second, this model provides ways for therapists to decide which treatment approach (or combination of strategies) they will use to help a particular client. Often this decision will be made according to theoretical models, biases, and related strengths. For example, a client-centered therapist might focus on the lack of awareness, congruence, and self-actualization of this client, who doesn't seem to have generated his own ideas about how to live his life. The reality therapist might focus on the client's prevalent irresponsible behavior and how he could learn to take responsibility for his actions. The Adlerian therapist would want to deal more with the competition between the client and his brother as well as with helping the client acquire social interest or a better sense of belonging at home and at school. The TA therapist would view the client as relating to others out of his "adapted child" ego state and might focus on how he could use other ego states to produce different results. The Gestalt therapist would focus on the splits, or incongruence, displayed in some of the client's feelings and actions and also on ideas the client has introjected and/or projected. The cognitive or RET therapist would look at the cognitions, or internal thoughts or self-statements, behind some of the client's maladaptive behavior habits and help him learn to dispute them. The family therapist would focus on the roles and boundaries of the client's family and on the marital relationship between his parents. The behavioral therapist would focus on changing the contributing causes (maladaptive behavioral habits) and on strengthening the client's adaptive behavioral habits in order to produce change in the presenting symptoms. Ideally, the decision about which approaches to use should be based on a number of factors, not just on the therapist's particular allegiance to or preference for a particular counseling theory (see also Chapter 11). It is particularly important to select intervention approaches that are related to the identified problems and goals and have the best chance of helping the client resolve those problems.

A third, more general way in which Swensen's case conceptualization model can be used is to examine the ratio of factors in the numerator of the formula to factors present in the denominator. According to Swensen (1968, p. 31), "Any *decrease* in the factors listed in the numerator of the formula (stress, maladaptive habits, and defenses) should reduce psychological deficit, as will any *increase* in the factors listed in the denominator (supports, adaptive habits and defenses, strengths)."

Seay's Model of Problem Conceptualization

Seay's model of case conceptualization (1978) integrates thematic content and therapy techniques. It is based on major life themes (and lifestyles) drawn from the three primary modalities for human functioning: cognition, affect, and behavior (CAB).

Seay (1978) proposes the following categories to describe the client problems:

1. Major environmental contingencies—includes environmental setting events, consequences, history.
2. Cognitive themes—consists of both misconceptions and irrationalities held by the client.
3. Affective themes—consists of barriers or emotional conflicts and felt or expressed emotions that are barriers or are interfering and counterproductive.
4. Behavioral patterns—consists of overt, observable behaviors. May include verbal and nonverbal behaviors exhibited during counseling, such as rapid speech and frequent gestures, as well as behavioral patterns exhibited outside counseling and often in problem-related situations, such as overeating, periodic drug and alcohol use, or poor study skills.

As an example of Seay's conceptualization model, consider a client who reports having limited options because she is afraid to drive; she also reports depression caused by constant criticism from her husband of some 20 years. She is having difficulty sleeping (wakes up and can't go back to sleep) and also has lost weight recently. History reveals that she grew up in a home with an abusive father. The client is also approaching 40 years of age and is unsure whether she wants to spend her next 20 years as she has spent the last 20 years. The client states that she has been moderately successful in getting some people to drive her here and there but is unable to leave town on her own or do things at her convenience. She also states that, as a child, she tolerated the abuse from her father. With her husband, she listens to his criticism and then withdraws either by leaving the room or by saying nothing. Even though she reports feeling "fed up" and "upset" with her husband's constant badgering, she also reports believing that she is a failure and not capable of making good decisions independently, despite the facts that test data reveal she is of superior intelligence and that she has had a very responsible position in a business company for the last 15 years. During the initial interview, she cries often and speaks slowly and softly in a very halting style. Figure 7-2 shows an analysis of this case according to Seay's case conceptualization model.

Information revealed from Seay's case conceptualization model can also be used to generate hypotheses, or educated guesses, about the client and to plan a comprehensive treatment program. For example, in the case given, one of the major themes is cognitive and involves the client's negative perceptions about herself, especially in relationship to men. This theme probably originated with her father's abuse and is maintained by her husband's constant criticism. One could speculate that she may have sought out a particular type of male for a spouse who reinforces her negative image of herself. Although constant verbal abuse may seem punitive to her, it may also serve a purpose in confirming her self-perceptions as dependent and as a failure and help her to avoid anxiety-producing situations such as driving alone. The affective barriers of anxiety and depression represent anger/dissatisfaction turned inward. These emotions, like the cognitive theme, underscore her lack of confidence or the way she deprecates herself. These emotions are produced both by environmental contingencies and by her cognitive misperceptions. Observed behaviors such as crying, speech patterns, sleep difficulties, and weight loss corroborate her self-report of depression. Both the cognitive misperceptions and the affective barriers are contributing conditions to her withdrawal from her husband's criticism and her not driving by herself.

For treatment planning, initial focus areas might deal with the environmental contingencies and cognitive misconceptions that produce the maladaptive emotional and behavioral patterns. For example, the client might benefit from such things as Gestalt and TA strategies and/or assertion training to explore her feelings related to being abused and to help her change her reactions to her husband's criticism. Both rational-emotive and cognitive-behavioral techniques might be useful as treatment interventions for the cognitive

Environmental Contingencies	Cognitive Misconceptions	Affective Barriers	Behavioral Patterns
E_1 Abuse from father	C_1 Thoughts of failure	A_1 Anxiety/emotional dependence	B_1 Docs not drive by herself
E_2 Constant criticism from husband	C_2 Negative or self-deprecating talk and perception	A_2 Depression	B_2 Withdraws from husband's criticism
E_3 Approaching 40: midlife assessment period	C_3 Lack of trust in her decisions	A_3 Anger — directed toward self and husband	B_3 Periodic crying during session
E_4 Successful and responsible job with stable work pattern	C_4 Superior intelligence		B_4 Slow, halting soft speech pattern
			B_5 Interrupted sleep pattern
			B_6 Appetite and weight loss

Figure 7-2. *Case analysis using Seay's case conceptualization model*

misperceptions. It would also be important to deal with some of the problematic behavioral patterns she exhibits, such as not driving by herself. Taking driving lessons and engaging in various driving tasks with the therapist (see also participant modeling, Chapter 13) are two ways to deal with this particular behavior pattern.

Seay's model is similar to other recent case conceptualizations proposed by Hutchins (1979 — the TFA, or "thought, feelings, action," model) and by L'Abate (1981 — the ERA, or "emotionality, rationality, activity," model). Both these models also stress the interrelatedness of thoughts, feelings, and actions (overt behaviors) and the importance of choosing interventions designed to focus on one or more of these elements that will maximize the probability of desired outcomes for the client and will "increase the likelihood of an optimum match between the behavior and the method used to improve that behavior" (L'Abate, 1981, p. 263).

Lazarus' Model of Problem Conceptualization: The BASIC ID

According to Arnold Lazarus, who is associated with broad-spectrum behavior therapy and with "technical eclecticism" (1971), people "are beings who move, feel, sense, imagine, think, and relate" (1976, p. 4).* Whenever stress or psychological disturbance exists, these functions are affected. According to Lazarus (1976, 1981), there are seven modalities to explore in assessment and intervention. To refer to these seven areas of assessment and treatment in abbreviated fashion, Lazarus uses the acronym "BASIC ID." A brief discussion

of each component of the BASIC ID follows. In using this model of conceptualization, it is important to remember that each modality described by Lazarus interacts with the other modalities and should not be treated in isolation.

B: Behavior. Behavior includes simple and more complex psychomotor skills and activities such as smiling, talking, writing, eating, smoking, and having sex. In most clinical interviewing, the therapist has to infer what the client does or does not do on the basis of client self-report, although occasionally other measures of behavior can corroborate client verbal report. Lazarus (1976) notes that it is especially important to be alert to behavioral excesses and deficits — things the client does too much or too little.

A: Affect. Affect includes felt or reported feelings and emotions. According to Lazarus, it is perhaps classically the most "overworked" area in psychotherapy and also one of the least understood (p. 33). Included in this category would be presence or absence of particular feelings as well as hidden or distorted feelings.

S: Sensation. Sensation includes the five major senses mentioned in Chapter 2 with respect to sensory processing of information: visual (sight), kinesthetic (touch), auditory (hearing), olfactory (smell), and gustation (taste). Focus on sensory elements of experience is important in order to develop personal fulfillment. Sometimes, too, presenting complaints are presented by way of felt body sensations such as stomach distress or dizziness (Lazarus, 1976). Therapists need to be alert to pleasant and unpleasant reported sensations as well as sensations of which clients seem unaware.

* From Arnold A. Lazarus, *Multimodal Behavior Therapy*, pp. 4, 33, 34. Copyright © 1976 by Arnold A. Lazarus. Published by Springer Publishing Company, Inc., New York. Used by permission of the publisher.

I: Imagery. According to Lazarus, imagery comprises various "mental pictures" that exert influence on a client's life (1976, p. 37). For example, a husband who was nagged by what he called repetitive ideas about his wife having an affair (apparently with no realistic basis) actually was troubled because he generated constant pictures or images of his wife in bed with another man. Lazarus (1976) believes that this modality is especially useful with clients who tend to overuse the cognitive modality and intellectualize their feelings.

C: Cognition. Cognitions are thoughts and beliefs, and Lazarus is most interested in exploring the client's mistaken beliefs—the illogical or irrational ones. He usually looks for three faulty assumptions that he believes are common and also potentially more damaging than others:

1. The tyranny of the SHOULD (Horney, 1950). Often this belief can be inferred from the client's actions and behaviors as well as from self-report.
2. Perfectionism—understanding ways in which clients expect perfectionism or infallibility, often not only of themselves but of others as well.
3. External attributions—the myths that clients verbalize when they feel they are the victims of outside persons or circumstances and have no control over or responsibility for what is happening to them.

I: Interpersonal relationships. Many therapists (including Sullivan, Horney, and Fromm) have stressed the importance of interpersonal relationships, or "social interest" (Adler, 1964). Lazarus (1976) notes that problems in the way clients relate to others can be detected not only through self-report and role playing but also by observation of the therapist/client relationship. Assessment of this modality includes observing the way clients express and accept feelings communicated to them by others as well as the way they behave and react to others.

D: Drugs. Lazarus asserts that this is an important nonpsychological modality to assess (and potentially treat), because neurological and biochemical factors can affect behavior, affective responses, cognitions, sensations, and so on. In addition to specific inquiries about psychotropic medications, assessment of this modality includes the following:

1. Overall appearance—attire, skin or speech disturbances, tics, psychomotor disorders.
2. Physiological complaints or diagnosed illnesses.
3. General health and well-being—physical fitness, exercise, diet and nutrition, avocational interests and hobbies, and leisure time pursuits.

This modality may often require consultation with or examination by a physician or other type of health professional.

Lazarus (1976) asserts that most therapists, including eclectic ones, fail to assess and treat these seven basic modalities. Instead, they deal with only one or two modalities, depending on their personal preferences and theoretical orientation, even though "durable results are in direct proportion to the number of specific modalities deliberately invoked by any therapeutic system" (p. 13).

The BASIC ID model of case conceptualization is applied to the following case and summarized in the modality profile (Lazarus, 1976, 1981) shown in Figure 7-3.

The client is a 35-year-old female who looks about 50–75 pounds overweight, though well groomed, well dressed, and articulate. The client states that she is in generally good health, does little exercise, and works either on the job or at home and has little free time. Free time is spent mainly in sedentary activities such as reading or watching TV. The client is divorced and has two school-age daughters. She does report occasional stomach distress—often as much as once or twice weekly. The client's presenting problem is overall "dissatisfaction with myself and my life." The client notes that she lives in a small town and has been unable to meet many available partners. She would like to have a good relationship with a male. She was divorced four years ago and states that her husband became interested in another woman and "took off." She says that she also has poor relationships with her two daughters, whom she describes as "irresponsible and lazy." On inquiry, it appears that the client is easily exploited and rather submissive in most of her relationships with significant others. In her job, she agrees to take work home with her even though she receives no overtime pay. She describes herself as feeling alone, lonely, and sometimes unloved or unlovable. She

Modality	Observations
B: Behavior	Passive responding; some withdrawal from conversation
	Slow rate of speech
	Frequent shrugging of shoulders
	Overeating
A: Affect	Alone — loneliness
	Unloved
	Denies concern or upset over weight
S: Sensation	Muscular tension — upper torso particularly
I: Imagery	Frequent fantasies of a move and different lifestyle
	Persistent dreams of being rescued
C: Cognition	Negative self-verbalizations and perceptions
	Self-perfectionistic standards
	Attributes problems to forces outside herself
I: Interpersonal relationships	Is exploited by ex-husband, daughters, boss
	Submissive in interactions with others
D: Drugs	Well groomed
	Well dressed
	50 – 75 pounds overweight
	Articulate
	Stomach distress — weekly
	Good health — mostly sedentary activity
	Little leisure time

Figure 7-3. *Modality profile of client case using BASIC ID (Lazarus, 1976, 1981)*

also reports that she often has thoughts that her life has been a failure and that she is not the kind of person she could be, although she portrays herself as a victim of circumstances (divorce, job, small town) beyond her control. However, she also reports rather frequent fantasies of moving and living in a different town and having a different job. She also describes repetitive dreams in which she can recall vividly the image of being rescued. She behaves very passively in the session — talks slowly, shrugs her shoulders, and occasionally withdraws from the conversation. Some muscular tension is apparent during the interview, particularly in her upper body. She states that overeating is a major problem, one that she attributes to not having her life go the way she wants it to and being unable to do much about it. At the same time, she appears to deny any concern about her weight, stating that if she's not worried about it, then it shouldn't matter to anyone else either.

In treatment planning, the first areas of focus would be the two modalities about which the client is most concerned — affective and interpersonal. If the interpersonal modality is selected as the initial area of change, it is likely that changes in this modality will lead to changes in the affective one also,

since the client's feelings of loneliness are a direct result of lack of effective interpersonal relationships. Skill training programs (see Chapter 12) such as assertion training and social skills training are likely to be most effective in helping the client establish new relationships and avoid further exploitation in her present ones. Such skill training could also be directed toward some of her overt behaviors that may interfere with establishing new relationships, such as her speech rate and her style of responding in conversations. Although the client denies any concern about her weight, she may also allow her weight to prevent her from engaging in the very kind of social interactions and relationships she finds absent from her life. Strategies such as Gestalt dialoguing, TA redecision work, and NLP reframing may help her to examine her conflicting feelings about being overweight. If and when she decides to make weight reduction a goal, cognitive strategies (such as cognitive restructuring, Chapter 16) aimed at modifying any problem-related cognitive misperceptions would be useful, as would behavioral strategies (such as self-management, Chapter 16) targeted toward helping her modify her overeating behavior and supporting environmental contingencies.

LEARNING ACTIVITY #22: METHODS OF CASE CONCEPTUALIZATION

Using the case of Mrs. X, described later in this Learning Activity, conceptualize the case according to the three models previously described: Swensen's, Seay's, and Lazarus'. We provide specific questions below to consider for each model. You can do this exercise by yourself, although it may be a better learning experience if you work with it in small groups. You can then share your ideas with your group or your instructor or supervisor. For additional work with these three models, you may also wish to apply the questions below to actual cases of your own or to the cases presented in the postevaluation at the end of this chapter.

1. Swensen's model
   a. Identify the client's deviant behavior or presenting symptomatology.
   b. Identify the client's stressors.
   c. Identify the client's maladaptive behaviors, habits, and defenses.
   d. Identify the client's supports and strengths.
   e. Identify the client's adaptive behaviors, habits, and defenses.
   f. Speculate on which of the above would need to be targets of change in order to resolve the presenting symptoms.
2. Seay's model
   a. Identify environmental contingencies present in the client's situation.
   b. Identify cognitive misperceptions held by the client.
   c. Identify emotions or affective barriers.
   d. Identify behavioral patterns exhibited by the client.
   e. Speculate on which of the above would be appropriate targets of change in order to resolve the major issues.
3. Lazarus' model
   a. Identify the behavior exhibited by the client, particularly excesses and deficits.
   b. Identify the primary affect (feelings and emotions) reported by the client.
   c. Identify any major sensations or sensory experiences/processing reported by the client. Speculate on the client's primary sensory system.
   d. Identify the imagery or mental pictures that exert influence on the client.
   e. Identify the apparent cognitions (thoughts, beliefs) reported by the client.

f. Assess the nature of the client's interpersonal relationships.
g. Identify any physiological factors/complaints apparent in the problem.
h. Speculate on which of these seven areas would be *primary* targets of change and which might be *secondary* targets in order to resolve the problems and issues this client presents.

The Case of Mrs. X

Mrs. X is a 28-year-old married woman who reports that an excessive fear of having her husband die has led her to seek therapy. She further states that because this is her second marriage, it is important for her to work out her problem so that it doesn't ultimately interfere with her relationship with her husband. However, her husband is a sales representative and occasionally has to attend out-of-town meetings. According to Mrs. X, whenever he has gone away on a trip during the two years of their marriage, she "goes to pieces" and feels "utterly devastated" because of recurring thoughts that he will die and not return. She states that this is a very intense fear and occurs even when he is gone on short trips, such as a half day or a day. She is not aware of any coping thoughts or behaviors she uses at these times. She indicates that she feels great as soon as her husband does get home. She states that this was also a problem for her in her first marriage, which ended in divorce five years ago. She believes this happens because her father died unexpectedly when she was 11 years old. She states that whenever her husband tells her he has to leave, or actually does leave, she reexperiences the pain of being told her father has died. She feels plagued with thoughts that her husband will not return and then feels intense anxiety. She states that she is constantly thinking about never seeing her husband again during these anxiety episodes. According to Mrs. X, her husband has been very supportive and patient and has spent a considerable amount of time trying to reassure her and to convince her, through reasoning, that he will return from a trip. She states that this has not helped her to stop worrying excessively that he will die and not return. She also states that in the past few months her husband has canceled several business trips just to avoid putting her through all this pain.

Mrs. X also reports that this anxiety has resulted in some insomnia during the past two years. She states

(continued)

that as soon as her husband informs her that he must leave town, she has difficulty going to sleep that evening. When he has to be gone on an overnight trip, she reports, she doesn't sleep at all. She simply lies in bed and worries about her husband dying and also feels very frustrated that it is getting later and later and that she is still awake. She reports sleeping fairly well as long as her husband is home and a trip is not impending.

Mrs. X reports that she feels very satisfied with her present marriage except for some occasional times when she finds herself thinking that her husband does not fulfill all her expectations. She is not sure exactly what her expectations are, but she is aware of feeling anger toward him after this happens. When she gets angry, she just "explodes" and feels as though she lashes out at her husband for no apparent reason. She reports that she doesn't like to explode at her husband like this but feels relieved after it happens. She indicates that her husband continues to

be very supportive and protective in spite of her occasional outbursts. She suspects the anger may be her way of getting back at him for going away on a trip and leaving her alone. She also expresses feelings of hurt and anger since her father's death in being unable to find a "father substitute." She also reports feeling intense anger toward her ex-husband after the divorce — anger she still sometimes experiences.

Mrs. X has no children. She is employed in a responsible position as an executive secretary and makes $18,500 a year. She reports that she enjoys her work, although she constantly worries that her boss might not be pleased with her and that she could lose her job, even though her work evaluations have been satisfactory. She reports that another event she has been worried about is the health of her brother, who was injured in a car accident this past year. She further reports that she has an excellent relationship with her brother and strong ties to her church.

☐ OUR ASSUMPTIONS ABOUT ASSESSMENT AND COGNITIVE BEHAVIOR THERAPY

Like the previously described case conceptualization models, our model of assessment in counseling and therapy is based on several assumptions about clients, problems, and behavior. These assumptions are drawn from the cognitive-behavioral approach to counseling. Cognitive behavior therapy includes a variety of techniques and strategies that are based on principles of learning and designed to produce constructive change in human behaviors. This approach was first developed in the 1950s under the term *behavior therapy* by, among others, Skinner, Wolpe, Lazarus, and Krumboltz. Early behavior therapists focused on the importance of changing clients' observable behavior. Since the 1950s, there have been significant developments in behavior therapy. Among the most important is the emergence of cognitive behavior therapy, which arose in the 1970s as a result of the work of such persons as Meichenbaum and Beck. Cognitive behavior therapy emphasizes the effects of private events such as cognitions, beliefs, and internal dialogue on resulting feelings and performance. This orientation to counseling now recognizes that both overt responding (observed behavior) and covert respond-

ing (feelings and thoughts) are important targets of change as long as they can be clearly specified (Rimm & Masters, 1979, p. 1).

Most Problem Behavior Is Learned

Problem (maladaptive) behavior is developed, maintained, and subject to alteration or modification in the same manner as normal (adaptive) behavior. Both prosocial and maladaptive, or self-defeating, behaviors are assumed to be developed and maintained either by external situational events or cues, by external reinforcers, or by internal processes such as cognition, mediation, and problem solving. For the most part, maladaptive behavior is not thought to be a function of physical disease or of underlying intrapsychic conflict. This fundamental assumption means that we do not spend a great deal of time sorting out or focusing on possible unresolved early conflicts or underlying pathological states. It does not mean, however, that we rule out or overlook possible organic and physiological causes of problem behavior. For example, clients who complain of "anxiety" and report primarily somatic (body-related) symptoms such as heart palpitations, stomach upset, chest pains, and breathlessness may be chronic hyperventilators (Lum, 1976), although this can be considered only after the client has had a physical examination to rule out cardiopathy. Physical examinations also may reveal the presence of mitral valve heart dysfunction for some individuals who complain of "panic attacks." Other somatic symptoms suggesting anxiety, such as sweating, tachycardia, lightheadedness, and dizziness, could also result from organic disorders such as hypoglycemia, hyperthyroidism or other endocrine disorders, or a low-grade infection.

Physiological variables should always be explored, particularly when the results of the assessment do not suggest the presence of other specific stimuli eliciting the problem behavior. It is also important to recognize the need for occasional physiological management of psychological problems—for example, in the kinds of disorders mentioned above. Medications may be necessary in addition to psychological intervention. Antidepressants are typically recommended for some forms of depression, particularly the endogenous type as distinct from the more reactive (situational) type. They have been found helpful as a supplement to psychological treatment for some instances of agoraphobia, a disorder typified by a marked fear of being alone or in public places. Anxiety or panic attacks often are also managed with antidepressants but additionally with beta blockers and/or other antianxiety agents. Furthermore, a biological element, such as biochemical imbalance, seems to be present in many of the psychoses, such as schizophrenia, and these conditions usually require antipsychotic drugs to improve the client's overall level of functioning.

Causes of Problems and Therefore Treatments/Interventions Are Multidimensional

Rarely is a problem caused by only one factor, and rarely does a single, unidimensional treatment program work in actual practice. For example, with a client who reports depression, we may find evidence of organic contributing factors such as Addison's disease (dysfunction of the adrenal gland), of environmental contributing conditions such as being left by his wife after moving to a new town, and of internal contributing factors such as self-deprecatory thoughts and images. Causes and contributing conditions of most client problems are multiple and include overt behavior, environmental events and relationships with others, covert behavior such as beliefs, images, and cognitions, feelings and bodily sensations, and possibly physiological/organic conditions. Intervention is usually more effective when directed toward all these multiple factors. For the client described

above, his endocrine balance must be restored and maintained, he must be helped to deal with his feelings of rejection and anger about his wife's departure, he needs to develop alternative resources and supports, including self-support, and he needs help in learning how to modify his self-deprecating thoughts and images. Additionally, he may benefit from problem-solving skills in order to decide the direction he wants his life to take. The more complete and comprehensive the treatment, the more successful the therapy tends to be, and also the less chance of relapse. According to Lazarus (1976, pp. 13–14),

> Comprehensive treatment at the very least calls for the correction of irrational beliefs, deviant behaviors, unpleasant feelings, intrusive images, stressful relationships, negative sensations, and possible biochemical imbalance. To the extent that problem identification (diagnosis) systematically explores each of these modalities, whereupon therapeutic intervention remedies whatever deficits and maladaptive patterns emerge, treatment outcomes will be positive and long-lasting. To ignore any of these modalities is to practice a brand of therapy that is incomplete.

Problems Are to Be Viewed Operationally

We suggest a way to view client problems that defines the client's present problem behaviors and some contributing problem conditions. This approach is called defining the problem "operationally," or "concretely." An operational problem definition functions like a measure, a barometer, or a "behavioral anchor." Operational definitions indicate some very specific problem behaviors; they do not infer vague traits or labels from the client's problem statement. Mischel (1968, p. 10) has contrasted these two approaches to problem conceptualization: "The emphasis is on what a person *does* in situations rather than on inferences about what attributes he *has* more globally."

Consider the following example of a way to view a client's problem operationally. In working with the "depressed" client, we would try to define precisely what the client means by "depressed" in order to avoid any misinterpretation of this self-report feeling statement. Instead of viewing the client's problem as "depression," we would try to specify some problem thoughts, feelings, actions, situations, and persons that are associated with the client's depression. We would find out whether the client experiences certain physiological changes during depression, what the client is thinking about while depressed, and what activities and behaviors occur during the depressed periods.

In other words, the therapist, in conjunction with the client, identifies a series of referents that are indicative of the state of being depressed, anxious, withdrawn, lonely, and so on. The advantage of viewing the problem this way is that vague phenomena are translated into specific and observable experiences. When this occurs, we not only have a better idea of what is happening with the client, we also have made the problem potentially measurable, allowing us to assess therapy progress and outcome (see also Chapter 10).

Most Problems Occur in a Social Context and Are Functionally Related to Internal and External Antecedents and Consequences

Problems do not usually occur in a vacuum but are related to observable events (verbal, nonverbal, and motoric responses) and to less visible covert or indirect events (thoughts, images, moods and feelings, body sensations) that precipitate and maintain the problem. These internal and external events are called "antecedents" or "consequences." They are functionally related to the problem in that they exert control over it, so that a change in one of these variables often brings about a change in related variables. For example, a child's inability to behave assertively with his teacher may be a function of learned fears, lack of social skills, and the fact that he has moved, is in a new school, and also has his first male teacher. Changing one part of this overall problem—for example, helping him reduce and manage his fears—will exert an effect on all other variables in the situation.

As we discuss in Chapter 9, on goals, the therapist must be alert not only to the way different parts of the problem are related but also to the impact that change in one variable may have on the others. Occasionally a symptom may perform a very useful function for the client, and removing it could make things worse. For example, in the above illustration, add to the case the fact that the child had on one occasion been sexually abused by a male house intruder. The symptom of fear may be serving the function of protection in his relationships with unknown males. Removal of the fear without consideration of the other parts of the problem could make the presenting problem worse or could bring about the onset of other issues. We describe the functional relationship between behavior and antecedents and consequences in greater detail in the next section.

☐ THE ABC MODEL OF BEHAVIOR

One way to identify the relationship between problem behavior and environmental events is by the ABC model (Goldiamond, 1965; Goodwin, 1969; Kanfer & Saslow, 1969; Mahoney & Thoresen, 1974; Thoresen & Mahoney, 1974). The ABC model of behavior suggests that the behavior (B) is influenced by events that precede it, called "antecedents" (A), and by some types of events that follow behavior, called "consequences" (C). An antecedent (A) event is a cue or signal that can tell a person how to behave in a situation. A consequence (C) is defined as an event that strengthens or weakens a behavior. Note that these definitions of antecedents and consequences suggest that an individual's behavior is directly related to or influenced by certain events. For example, a behavior that appears to be caused by antecedent events such as anger may also be maintained or strengthened by consequences such as reactions from other people. Assessment interviews focus on identifying the particular antecedent and consequent events that influence or are functionally related to the client's defined problem behavior.

As a very simple example of the ABC model, consider a behavior (B) that most of us engage in frequently—talking. Our talking behavior is usually occasioned by certain cues, such as starting a conversation with another person, being asked a question, or the presence of a friend. Antecedents that might decrease the likelihood that we will talk may include worry about getting approval for what we say or how we answer the question or being in a hurry to get somewhere. Our talking behavior may be maintained by the verbal and nonverbal attention we receive from another person, which is a very powerful consequence, or reinforcer. Other positive consequences that might maintain our talking behavior may be feeling good or happy and engaging in positive self-statements or evaluations about the usefulness or relevance of what we are saying. We may talk less when the person's eye contact wanders or when he or she tells us more explicitly that we've talked enough. These are negative consequences (C) that decrease our talking behavior. Other negative consequences that may decrease our talking behavior could include bodily sensations of fatigue or vocal hoarseness that occur after talking for a while or thoughts and images that what we are saying is of little value to attract the interest of others. As you will see in the next three sections, not only do the components of problem behavior often vary among clients, but what functions as an antecedent or consequence for one person is often very different for someone else.

Behavior

Behavior includes things a client does as well as things a client thinks about. *Overt* behavior is behavior that is visible or could be detected by an observer, such as verbal behavior (talking), nonverbal behavior (for example, gesturing or smiling), or motoric behavior (engaging in some action such as betting, walking, or drinking). *Covert* behavior includes events that are usually internal—inside the client—and are not so readily visible to an observer, who must rely on client self-report and nonverbal behavior to detect such events. Examples of covert behavior include thoughts, beliefs, images, feelings, moods, and body sensations.

As we indicated earlier, problem behavior that clients report rarely occurs in isolated fashion. Most reported problems typically are part of a larger chain or set of behaviors. Moreover, each problem behavior mentioned usually has more than one component. For example, a client who complains of "anxiety" or "depression" is most likely using the label to refer to an experience consisting of an *affective* component (feelings, mood states), a *somatic* component (physiological and body-related sensation), a *behavioral* component (what the client does or doesn't do), and a *cognitive* component (thoughts, beliefs, images, or internal dialogue). Additionally, the experience of anxiety or depression may vary for the client, depending on *contextual* factors (time, place, concurrent events) and on *relational* factors such as presence or absence of other people. All these components may or may not be related to a particular reported problem. For example, suppose that our client who reports "anxiety" is afraid to venture out in public places except for home and work because of heightened anxiety and/or "panic attacks." Her reported concern of anxiety seems to be part of a chain that starts with a cognitive component in which she thinks worried thoughts and produces images in which she sees herself alone and unable to cope or to get the assistance of others if necessary. The cognitive component leads to somatic discomfort and tension and to feelings of apprehension and dread. These three components work together to influence her overt behavior—for the last few years, she has successfully avoided almost

all public places and functions like the grocery store, theater, or church, and she functions well only at home or at work. She consequently depends on the support of family and friends to help her function adequately in the home and at work and particularly on the few occasions when she attends public functions or uses public transportation.

It is important to determine the relative importance of each component of the reported problem behavior in order to select appropriate intervention strategies (see also Chapter 11). In Chapter 8 we describe ways to obtain descriptions of these various components of problem behavior with an interview assessment method. It is often valuable to list, in writing, the various components identified for any given problem behavior.

Antecedents

According to Mischel (1968), behavior is situationally determined. This means that given behaviors tend to occur only in certain situations. For example, most of us brush our teeth in a public or private bathroom rather than during a concert or a church service. Antecedents may elicit emotional and physiological reactions such as anger, fear, joy, headaches, or elevated blood pressure. Antecedents influence behavior by either increasing or decreasing its likelihood of occurrence. For example, a child in a first-grade class may behave differently at school than at home or differently with a substitute than with the regular teacher.

Antecedent events that occur immediately before a problem behavior exert influence on it. Events that are not in temporal proximity to the problem behavior can similarly increase or decrease the probability that the behavior will occur. Antecedents that occur in immediate temporal proximity to the problem behavior are technically called *stimulus events* (Bijou & Baer, 1961) and include any external or internal event or condition that either cues the behavior or makes it more or less likely to occur under that condition. Antecedents that are temporally distant from the problem are called *setting events* (Kantor, 1970) and include behavioral circumstances that the person has recently or previously passed through. Setting events may end well before the problem and yet, like stimulus events, still facilitate or inhibit its occurrence. Examples of setting events to consider in assessing client problems are age, developmental stage, physiological state of the client, characteristics of the client's work, home, or school setting, and behaviors that emerge to affect subsequent behaviors (Wahler & Fox, 1981). Both stimulus and setting antecedent conditions must be identified and defined individually for each client.

Antecedents also usually involve more than one source or type of event. Sources of antecedents may be *affective* (feelings, mood states), *somatic* (physiological and body-related sensations), *behavioral* (verbal, nonverbal, and motoric responses), *cognitive* (thoughts, beliefs, images, internal dialogue), *contextual* (time, place, concurrent events), and *relational* (presence or absence of other people). For example, with our client who reported "anxiety," there may be a variety of antecedent sources that cue or occasion each aspect of the problem behavior, such as fear of losing control (cognitive/affective), negative self-statements and misperceptions of self and others (cognitive), awareness of apprehension-related body sensations, fatigue, and hypoglycemic tendencies (somatic), staying up late and skipping meals (behavioral), presence of public places or need to attend public functions (contextual), and absence of significant others such as friends and family (relational).

There are also a variety of antecedent sources that make components of the client's anxiety problem less likely to occur. These include feeling relaxed (affective), being rested (somatic), eating regularly (behavioral), decreasing the client's dependent behavior on her husband (behavioral), decreased fear of separation from spouse (affective), positive appraisal of self and others (cognitive), expectation of being able to handle situations (cognitive), absence of need to go to public places or functions (contextual), and being accompanied to a public place by a significant other (relational).

The influence that antecedents have on our behavior may vary with each of us, depending on our learning history. It is also important to keep in mind that antecedents are overt or covert events that in some way influence the problem behavior either by cuing it or by increasing or decreasing the likelihood that it will occur under certain conditions. In other words, not everything that precedes a behavior is automatically considered an antecedent—only those things that influence a behavioral response in some manner. Problem behavior may, however, also be affected by other situational factors (props) that are usually present in the problem situation but do not directly influ-

ence the behavior. This is especially true if any of these situational factors changes dramatically (Goldiamond & Dyrud, 1967). For instance, a child's behavior in school may be at least temporarily affected if the child's only sibling is hospitalized for injuries received in an automobile accident or if the child's father, who has been a household spouse for ten years, starts to work full-time outside the home.

During the assessment phase of counseling, it is important to identify those antecedent sources that facilitate desirable behaviors and those that are related to inappropriate responses. The reason is that, during the intervention (treatment) phase, it is important to select strategies that not only facilitate the occurrence of desirable behavior but also decrease the presence of cues for unwanted behavior. In Chapter 8 we describe and model ways to elicit information about antecedent sources and their effects on problem behavior with an interview assessment approach.

Consequences

The consequences of a behavior are events that follow a behavior and exert some influence on the behavior or are functionally related to the behavior. In other words, not everything that follows a behavior is automatically considered a consequence. For example, suppose you are counseling an overweight woman who tends occasionally to go on eating binges. She reports that, after a binge, she feels guilty, regards herself as even more unattractive, and tends to suffer from insomnia. Although these events are *results* of her eating-binge behavior, they are not consequences unless in some way they directly influence her binges, either by maintaining or by decreasing them. In this case, other events that follow the eating binges may be the real consequences. For instance, perhaps the client's binges are maintained by the enjoyment she gets from eating; perhaps they are temporarily decreased when someone else, such as her husband, notices her behavior and reprimands her for it or refuses to go out with her on their regular weekend splurge.

Consequences are categorized as positive or negative. Positive consequences can be referred to technically as *rewards* or *reinforcers;* negative ones can be labeled *punishers.* Like antecedents, the things that function as consequences will always vary with clients. By definition, positive consequences (rewarding events) will maintain or increase the behavior. Positive consequences often maintain or strengthen behavior by positive reinforcement, which involves the presentation of an overt or covert event following the behavior which increases the likelihood that the behavior will occur again in the future. People tend to repeat behaviors that result in pleasurable effects.

People also tend to engage in behaviors that have some "payoffs," or value, even if the behavior is very dysfunctional (such payoffs are called *secondary gains*). For example, a client may abuse alcohol and continue to do so even after she loses her job or her family because she likes the feelings she gets after drinking and because the drinking helps her to avoid responsibility. Another client may continue to verbally abuse his wife despite the strain it causes in their relationship because the abusive behavior gives him a feeling of power and control. In these two examples, the problem behavior is often hard to change, because the immediate consequences make the person feel better in some way. As a result, the problem behavior is reinforced, even if its delayed or long-term effects are unpleasant. In other words, in these examples, the client "values" the behavior that he or she is trying to eliminate. Often the secondary gain, the payoff derived from a manifest problem, is a cover for more severe problems that are not always readily presented by the client. According to Fishman and Lubetkin (1983), it is important for therapists to be alert to this fact in order to focus on the core problem that, when ameliorated, will generalize to other problem areas as well. For example, consider a client who is overweight and wants to "lose weight" as her goal for therapy. Yet assessment of this presenting problem reveals that the client's obesity allows her to avoid social interaction with others, particularly men. Successful therapy would need to be targeted not only to the manifest problem (weight and overeating) but also to the core, or underlying, problem that the weight masks — namely, avoidance of social interactions, particularly with the other sex. Otherwise, attempts to maintain weight reduction programs are likely to be unsuccessful. Similarly, the client described above who uses alcohol to avoid responsibility will need a treatment program targeted not only toward eliminating alcohol abuse but also toward changing her pattern of avoiding responsibility. As Fishman and Lubetkin note, many cognitive behavior therapists "are too wedded to the 'prima facie' problems that clients bring to therapy. We have observed from our own clinical experience that 'under material' may often be responsible for maintaining the manifest behavior" (1983, p. 27). Clients may not always know the reasons they engage in problem behavior. Part of therapy involves making reasons or secondary gains more explicit.

Positive consequences can also maintain behavior by negative reinforcement — removal of an unpleasant event following the behavior, increasing the likelihood that the behavior will occur again. People tend to repeat behaviors that get rid of annoying or painful events or effects. They also use negative reinforcement to establish *avoidance* and *escape* behavior. Avoidance behavior is maintained when an *expected* unpleasant event is removed. For example, staying at home stops agoraphobia fears. Avoidance of public places is maintained by removal of these expected fears. Escape behavior is maintained when a negative (unpleasant) event *already occurring* is removed or terminated. For example, abusive behavior toward a child temporarily stops the child's annoying or aversive behaviors. Termination of the unpleasant child behaviors maintains the parental escape behavior.

Negative consequences weaken or eliminate the behavior. A behavior is typically decreased or weakened (at least temporarily) if it is followed by an unpleasant stimulus or event (punishment), if a positive, or reinforcing, event is removed or terminated (response cost), or if the behavior is no longer followed by reinforcing events (operant extinction). As an example, the overweight woman may maintain her eating binges because of the feelings of pleasure she receives from eating (a positive reinforcing consequence). Or her binges could be maintained because they allow her to escape from a boring work situation (negative reinforcing consequence). In contrast, her husband's reprimands or sarcasm or refusal to go out with her may, at least temporarily, reduce her binges (punishing consequence). Although using negative contingencies to modify behavior has many disadvantages, in real-life settings such as home, work, and school, punishment is widely used to influence the behavior of others. Therapists must be alert to the presence of negative consequences in a client's life and its effects on the client. Therapists must also be careful to avoid the use of any verbal or nonverbal behavior that may seem punitive to a client, because such behavior may contribute to unnecessary problems in the therapeutic relationship and subsequent client termination of (escape from) therapy.

Consequences also usually involve more than one source or type of event. Like antecedents, sources of consequences may be *affective, somatic, behavioral, cognitive, contextual,* and/or *relational.* For example, with our client who reports "anxiety," her avoidance of public places and functions is maintained because it results in a reduction of anxious feelings (affective), body tension (somatic), and worry (cognitive). Additional consequences that may help to maintain the problem may include avoidance of routine chores (behavioral) and increased attention from family and friends (relational).

It would be inaccurate to simply ask about whatever follows the problem behavior and automatically classify it as a consequence without determining its particular effect on the behavior. As Cullen (1983, p. 137) notes, "If variables are supposed to be functionally related to behavior when, in fact, they are not, then manipulation of those variables by the client or therapist will, at best, have no effect on the presenting difficulties or, at worst, create even more difficulties."

Occasionally students seem to confuse consequences as we present the concept in this chapter with the kind of consequences that are often the results of problem behavior—for example, Julie frequently procrastinates on studying and, as a consequence, receives poor grades. Although poor grades are the result of frequent procrastination, they are not a consequence in the way we are defining it unless the poor grades in some way increase, decrease, or maintain the procrastination behavior. Otherwise, poor grades are simply the result of studying too little. One way to distinguish consequences from mere effects of problem behavior is to remember a rule of thumb termed "gradient of reinforcement." This term refers to the belief that consequences that occur soon after the behavior are likely to have a stronger impact than consequences that occur after a long time has elapsed (Hull, 1952). Poor grades are so far removed in time from daily studying (or lack of it) that they are unlikely to exert much influence on the student's daily study behavior.

During the assessment phase of counseling, it is important to identify those consequences that maintain, increase, or decrease both desirable and undesirable behaviors related to the client's problem. In the intervention (treatment) phase, this information will help you to select strategies and approaches that will maintain and increase desirable behaviors and will weaken and decrease undesirable behaviors such as behavioral excesses and deficits. Information about consequences is also useful in planning treatment approaches that rely directly on the use of consequences to facilitate behavior change, such as self-reward (see also Chapter 19). In Chapter 8 we describe and model ways to elicit information about consequences and their effects on problem behavior with an interview assessment approach.

It is important to reiterate that antecedents, consequences, and components of the problem must be assessed and identified for each particular client. Two clients might complain of anxiety or "nerves," and the assessments might reveal very different components of the problem behavior and different antecedents and consequences. It is also important to keep in mind that there is often some overlap among antecedents, components of problem behavior, and consequences. For example, negative self-statements or irrational beliefs might function in some instances as both antecedents and consequences for a given component of the identified problem. Consider a college student who reports depression after situations with less than desired outcomes, such as asking a girl out and being turned down, getting a test back with a B or C on it, and interviewing for a job and not receiving a subsequent offer of employment. Irrational beliefs in the form of perfectionistic standards may function as an antecedent by cuing, or setting off, the resulting feelings of depression—for example, "Here is a solution that didn't turn out the way I wanted; it's awful; now I feel lousy." Irrational beliefs in the form of self-deprecatory thoughts may function as a consequence by maintaining the feelings of depression for some time even after the situation itself is over—for example, "When things don't turn out the way they should, I'm a failure."

☐ DIAGNOSTIC CLASSIFICATION OF CLIENT PROBLEMS

Our emphasis throughout this chapter is on the need to conduct a thorough and precise assessment with each client in order to be able to define client problems in very concrete ways. In addition, counselors need to be aware that client problems can be organized in some form of diagnostic taxonomy (classification).

The official classification system used currently is found in the American Psychiatric Association's *Diagnostic and Statistical Manual of Mental Dis-*

orders, third edition *(DSM-III)* (1980). The reader is urged to consult this original source as well as the *DSM-III Casebook* (Spitzer, Skodol, Gibbon, & Williams, 1981) for additional information. Our interest is simply to summarize the basic diagnostic codes and categories found in *DSM-III* so that the reader will not be caught off guard if a colleague or supervisor begins talking about "Axis I, II," and so on.

DSM-III consists largely of descriptions of various mental and psychological disorders broken down into 16 major diagnostic classes, with additional subcategories within these major categories. Specific diagnostic criteria are provided for each category. These criteria are supposed to provide the practitioner with a way to evaluate and classify the client's problems. The particular evaluation system used by *DSM-III* is called "multiaxial" because it consists of an assessment on five codes, or "axes":

Axis I, clinical syndromes and conditions not attributable to a mental disorder that are a focus of attention or treatment.
Axis II, personality disorders (adult) and specific developmental disorders (child).
Axis III, physical disorders or conditions.
Axis IV, severity of psychosocial stressors.
Axis V, highest level of adaptive functioning during past year.

Axes I and II comprise the clinical disorders and conditions not attributable to a mental disorder that are a focus of attention or treatment. On Axis III the practitioner indicates any current physical disorder or condition of the client. Axis IV provides a 7-point rating scale for assessing the overall severity of stress that is judged to have been a significant contributor to the development or exacerbation of the current disorder. Each scale level is anchored with examples for children, adolescents, and adults. The information on this axis is important because the person's prognosis may be better when a disorder develops as a consequence of marked stress than when it develops after minimal or no stress. This information may also be important in developing a treatment plan to reduce the severity and frequency of "stressors" in the client's life. Axis V permits the interviewer to indicate his or her judgment of the person's highest level of adaptive functioning, for at least a few months, during the past year. A 7-point scale is provided. It is also anchored with examples for children, ado-

lescents, and adults. Adaptive functioning is defined as a composite of three areas: social relations, occupational functioning, and use of leisure time. Examples of this multiaxial evaluation system can be found following the analyses of the client cases in this chapter. Table 7-1 describes the 16 major diagnostic categories of *DSM-III* that are classified on Axis I and Axis II.

Taylor (1983) observes that, in spite of apparent conceptual and practical limitations of diagnosis, the process can aid therapists in assessing problem behaviors and in selecting appropriate interventions for treatment. For instance, knowledge about selected features of various types of clinical pathology, such as the usual age of the onset of some disorder or whether the disorder is more common in men or in women, can aid in assessment. In one case study reported by Evans (1970), the therapist was working with an "exhibitionist." The exhibitionistic behavior started at age 30, a time of life when such behavior usually diminishes rather than begins. The alert and sensitive therapist recognized this discrepancy, and a very careful assessment ensued. The assessment revealed an organic condition of hypoglycemia (abnormal decrease of sugar in the blood), leading to periods of confusion, at which times the client exhibited himself. In this case, the target of treatment became relief of hypoglycemia, although it was not immediately apparent to the clinician.

Nelson and Barlow (1981) note that selected features of *DSM-III* are useful for suggesting additional information about the problem behaviors and the controlling variables. For example, the operational criteria found in *DSM-III* often indicate further target behaviors associated with a particular disorder that should be assessed, and the associated features of a disorder often suggest controlling or contributing variables to be assessed. For instance, if a client describes behaviors related to depression, the therapist can use the operational criteria for major depressive episodes to ask about other target behaviors related to depression that the client may not mention. Therapists can also be guided by the associated features of this disorder to question the client about possible controlling variables typically associated with the disorder (for example, for depression, events such as life changes, loss of reinforcers, and family history of depression).

Nelson and Barlow (1981) also observe that diagnoses may be useful in suggesting treatments

TABLE 7-1. The 16 major diagnostic classes of *DSM-III*

Disorders usually first evident in infancy, childhood, or adolescence—behavioral, intellectual, emotional, physical, and developmental disturbances that usually are first observed during infancy, childhood, or adolescence

Organic mental disorders—behavioral or psychological disturbances related to temporary or permanent brain dysfunction

Substance use disorders—disorders of abuse and/or dependence caused by taking substances such as alcohol, drugs, and tobacco that affect the central nervous system

Schizophrenic disorders—five subtypes of schizophrenia; all emphasize the presence of one of the following: delusions, hallucinations, or certain thought disturbances

Paranoid disorders—three types of disorders, features of which are persistent persecutory delusions and delusions of jealousy not attributable to some other psychotic disorder

Psychotic disorders not elsewhere classified—includes three other categories that do not fit into any of the other categories

Affective disorders—includes two classes of disorders in which there is a disturbance of mood accompanied by related symptoms

Anxiety disorders—includes four categories in which the predominant symptom is some form of anxiety

Somatoform disorders—disorders in which physical symptoms are involved but with no evidence of organic disease

Disassociative disorders—includes a variety of disorders in which there is a sudden and usually temporary alteration in the person's identity and/or consciousness

Psychosexual disorders—disorders involving some disturbance or disruption of psychosexual identity and/or function

Factitious disorders—disorders in which physical or psychological symptoms are present that are produced by the client and under the client's voluntary control

Disorders of impulse control not elsewhere classified—disorders that do not fit elsewhere and are characterized by failure to resist an impulse to perform an act potentially harmful to oneself and/or others

Adjustment disorders—eight disorders characterized by a maladaptive reaction to an identifiable psychosocial stressor, occurring within three months of the onset of the stressor and resulting in other impairment in social or occupational functioning or symptoms that are in excess of a normal reaction to such a stressor.

Psychological factors affecting physical condition—although physical conditions are noted on Axis III, this category is available to describe psychological factors that have some temporal proximity to the physical condition and appear to precipitate or exacerbate it

Personality disorders—includes three classes of personality disorders; all reflect features of maladaptive patterns of perception and relationships that are severe enough to create either subjectively felt distress or impairment in overall level of functioning

V codes—conditions that are included in treatment/intervention but not attributable to any of the previously described disorders can be noted here; this code often includes problems not involving a mental disorder or other problems (in addition to a specific disorder) that warrant attention

that have been found effective with similar problems. For example, clients with phobias typically benefit from modeling (see Chapters 13 and 14) or from fear-reduction approaches such as systematic desensitization (see Chapter 18) and may also require antianxiety medication (see also Chapter 11).

Diagnostic classification presents certain limitations, and these are most apparent when a client is given a diagnostic classification without the benefit of a thorough and complete assessment. The most common criticisms of diagnosis are that it places labels on clients, often meaningless ones, and that the labels themselves are not well defined and do not describe what the clients do or don't do that makes them "histrionic" or "a conduct disorder" and so on. Despite the apparent disadvantages of diagnosis, many counselors and therapists find themselves in field placement and work settings in which they are required to make a diagnostic classification of the client's problems. Often even clients request this in order to receive reimbursement from their health insurance carrier for payment made for therapeutic services. We feel comfortable with the *DSM-III* system of classification as long as it is applied within the context of a complete assessment approach and is not used as a substitute for more idiographic assessment of the specified problem events and behaviors. This latter kind of assessment is illustrated in the following example case.

An ABC Model Case

To assist you in conceptualizing client problems from an ABC model, we provide a case illustration followed by two practice cases for you to complete. The conceptual understanding you should acquire from this chapter will help you actually define client problems and contributing variables with an interview assessment, described in Chapter 8. The following hypothetical case will assist you in identifying the overt and covert ABCs of a client problem. Extensions of this case will be used as illustrations in remaining chapters of the book.

The Case of Joan

Joan is a 15-year-old student completing her sophomore year of high school and presently taking a college preparatory curriculum. Her initial statement in the first counseling session is that she is "unhappy" and feels "dissatisfied" with this school experience but feels unable to do anything about it. On further clarification, Joan reveals that she is unhappy because she doesn't think she is measuring up to her classmates and that she dislikes being with these "top" kids in some of her classes, which are very competitive. She reports particular concern in one math class, which she says is composed largely of "guys" who are much smarter than she is. She states that she thinks about the fact that "girls are so dumb in math" rather frequently during the class. She reports that as soon as she is in this class, she gets anxious and "withdraws." She states that she sometimes gets anxious just thinking about the class, and when this happens, she gets "butterflies" in her stomach, her palms get sweaty and cold, and her heart beats faster. When asked what she means by "withdrawing," she says she sits by herself, doesn't talk to her classmates, and doesn't volunteer answers or go to the board. Often, when called on, she says nothing. As a result, she reports, her grades are dropping. She also states that her math teacher has spoken to her several times about her behavior and has tried to help her do better. However, Joan's nervousness in the class has resulted in her cutting the class whenever she can find any reason, and she has almost used up her number of excused absences

from school. She states that her fear of competitive academic situations has been a problem since junior high, when her parents started to compare her with other students and put "pressure" on her to do well in school so she could go to college. When asked how they "pressure" her, she says they constantly talk to her about getting good grades, and whenever she doesn't, they lash out at her and withdraw privileges, like her allowance. She reports that, during this year, since the classes are tougher and more competitive, school is more of a problem to her and she feels increasingly anxious in certain classes, especially math. Joan also states that sometimes she thinks she is almost failing on purpose to get back at her parents for their pressure. Joan reports that all this has made her dissatisfied with school and she has questioned whether she wants to stay in a college prep curriculum. She states that she has considered switching to a work-study curriculum so she can learn some skills and get a job after high school. However, she says she is a very indecisive person and does not know what she should do. In addition, she is afraid to decide this because if she changed curriculums, her parents' response would be very negative. Joan states that she cannot recall ever having made a decision without her parents' assistance. She feels they have often made decisions for her. She says her parents have never encouraged her to make decisions on her own, because they say she might not make the right decision without their help. Joan is an only child. She indicates that she is constantly afraid of making a bad or wrong choice.

Analysis of Case

Problem situations.   First of all, there are two related but distinct problem situations for Joan. Her "presenting" problem is that she feels anxious in certain competitive classes in school. She identifies math class as the primary problem class. Second, she is having difficulty making a decision about the type of curriculum she should pursue. More generally, another problem is that she considers herself indecisive in most situations. The analysis of this case will explore Joan's problem behaviors and the antecedents and consequences for each of these two problem areas.

Analysis of School Problem

1. *Problem Behaviors*
   Joan's problem behaviors at school include

a. Self-defeating labeling of her math class as "competitive" and of herself as "not as smart as the guys."

b. Sitting alone, not volunteering answers in math class, not answering the teacher's questions or going to the board, and cutting class.

Her self-defeating labels are a covert behavior; her sitting alone, not volunteering answers, and cutting class are overt behaviors.

2. *Antecedent Conditions*
Joan's problem behaviors at school are elicited by anxiety about certain "competitive" classes, particularly math. Previous antecedent conditions would include verbal comparisons about Joan and her peers made by her parents and verbal pressure for good grades and withholding of privileges for bad grades by her parents. Note that these antecedent conditions do not occur at the same time. The antecedent of the anxiety in the "competitive" class occurs in close proximity to Joan's problem behaviors and is a "stimulus event." However, the verbal comparisons and parental pressure began several years ago and probably function as a "setting event."

3. *Consequences*
Joan's problem behaviors at school are maintained by

a. An increased level of attention to her problems by her math teacher.

b. Feeling relieved of anxiety through avoidance of the situation that elicits anxiety. By not participating in class and by cutting class, she can avoid puting herself in an anxiety-provoking situation.

c. Her poorer grades, possibly because of two "payoffs," or secondary gains. (1) If her grades get too low, she may not qualify to continue in the college prep curriculum. This would be the "ultimate" way to avoid putting herself in competitive academic situations that elicit anxiety. (2) The lowered grades could also be maintaining her problem behaviors because she labels the poor grades as a way to "get back at" her parents for their pressure.

Analysis of Decision-Making Problem

1. *Problem Behaviors*
Joan's problem behavior can be described as not making a decision for herself—in this case, about a curriculum change. Depending on the client, problems in making decisions can be either a covert or an overt problem. In people who have the skills to make a decision but are blocking themselves because of their "labels" or "internal dialogue" about the decision, the problem behavior would be designated as covert. In Joan's case, her indecisive behavior seems based on her past learning history of having many decisions either made for her or made with parental assistance. The lack of opportunities she has had to make choices suggests she has not acquired the skills involved in decision making. This would be classified as an overt problem.

2. *Antecedent Conditions*
Joan's previous decision-making history is the primary antecedent condition. This consists of (1) having decisions made for her and (2) a lack of opportunities to acquire and use the skills of decision making.

3. *Consequences*
The consequences that seem to be maintaining her problem behavior of not deciding include:

a. Getting help with her decisions, thereby avoiding the responsibility of making a choice.

b. Anticipation of parental negative reactions (punishment) to her decisions through her "self-talk."

c. Absence of positive consequences or lack of encouragement for any efforts at decision making in the past.

d. In the specific decision of a curriculum change, her low grades, which, if they get too bad, may help her avoid making a curriculum decision by automatically disqualifying her from the college prep curriculum.

DSM-III Diagnosis

Axis I: V62.89, phase-of-life problem.
Axis II: none.
Axis III: none.
Axis IV: 4, *moderate* severity of psychosocial stressors (school, parents).
Axis V: 4, *fair* level of adaptive functioning during past year (poorer grades, skipping school, deteriorating relationship with parents).

LEARNING ACTIVITY #23: ABCs OF PROBLEM ASSESSMENT

To help you in conceptualizing a client's problem from the ABC model, the following two cases are provided. We suggest that you work through the first case completely before going on to the second one. After reading each case, by yourself or with a partner, respond to the questions following the case. Then check your reponses with the feedback.

The Case of Ms. Weare and Freddie

Ms. Weare and her 10-year-old son, Freddie, have come to counseling at the referral of Family Services. Their initial complaint is that they don't get along with each other. Ms. Weare complains that Freddie doesn't dress by himself in the morning and this makes her mad. Freddie complains that his mother yells and screams at him frequently. Ms. Weare agrees she does, especially when it is time for Freddie to leave for school and he isn't dressed yet. Freddie agrees that he doesn't dress himself and points out that he does this just to "get mom mad." Ms. Weare says this has been going on as long as she can remember. She states that Freddie gets up and usually comes down to breakfast not dressed. After breakfast, Ms. Weare always reminds him to dress and threatens him that she'll yell or hit him if he doesn't. Freddie usually goes back to his room, where, he reports, he just sits around until his mother comes up. Ms. Weare waits until five minutes before the bus comes and then calls Freddie. After he doesn't come down, she goes upstairs and sees that he's not dressed. She reports that she gets very mad and yells "You're dumb. Why do you just sit there? Why can't you dress yourself? You're going to be late for school. Your teacher will blame me, since I'm your mother." She also helps Freddie dress. So far, he has not been late, but Ms. Weare says she "knows" he will be if she doesn't "nag" him and help him dress. On further questioning, Ms. Weare says this does not occur on weekends, only on school days. She states that, as a result of this situation, she feels very nervous and edgy after Freddie leaves for school, often not doing some necessary work because of this. Asked what she means by "nervous" and "edgy," she reports that her body feels tense and jittery all over. She reports that since Freddie's father is not living at home, all the child rearing is on her shoulders. Ms. Weare also states that she doesn't spend much time with Freddie at night after school.

DSM-III Diagnosis for Ms. Weare

Axis I: V61.20, parent/child problem.

Axis II: none.

Axis III: none.

Axis IV: 3, *mild* severity of psychosocial stressors (age of child, single-parent status of mother).

Axis V: 3, *good* level of adaptive functioning during past year. (Slight improvement in her work and her relationship with her son; much of this is a result of single parent status.)

Respond to these questions. Feedback follows the Learning Activity.

1. What problem behavior(s) does Freddie demonstrate in this situation?
2. Is each problem behavior you have listed overt or covert?
3. What problem behavior(s) does Ms. Weare exhibit in this situation?
4. Is each problem behavior you have listed overt or covert?
5. List one or more antecedent conditions that seem to bring about each of Freddie's problem behavior(s).
6. List one or more antecedent conditions that seem to bring about each of Ms. Weare's problem behavior(s).
7. List one or more consequences (including any secondary gains) that influence each of Freddie's problem behavior(s). After each consequence listed, identify how the consequence seems to influence his behavior.
8. List one or more cosequences that seem to influence each of Ms. Weare's behaviors. After each consequence listed, identify how the consequence seems to influence her behavior.

The Case of Mrs. Turner

Mrs. Turner is a 34-year-old mother of two sons: Jason, age 5, and Andrew, age 2. She was brought to the emergency room by the police after her bizarre behavior in a local supermarket. According to the police report, Mrs. Turner became very aggressive toward another shopper, accusing the man of "following me around and spying on me." When confronted by employees of the store about her charges, she stated "God speaks to me. I can hear His voice guiding me in my mission." On mental-status exami-

(continued)

nation, the counselor initially notes Mrs. Turner's unkempt appearance. She appears unclean. Her clothing is somewhat disheveled. She seems underweight and looks older than her stated age. Her tense posture seems indicative of her anxious state, and she smiles inappropriately throughout the interview. Her speech is loud and fast, and she constantly glances suspiciously around the room. Her affect is labile, fluctuating from anger to euphoria. On occasion, she looks at the ceiling and spontaneously starts talking. When the counselor asks to whom she was speaking, she replies, "Can't you hear Him? He's come to save me!" Mrs. Turner is alert and appears to be of average general intelligence. Her attention span is short. She reports no suicidal ideation and denies any past attempts. She does, however, express some homicidal feelings for those who "continue to secretly follow me around." When the family members arrive, the counselor is able to ascertain that Mrs. Turner has been in psychiatric treatment on and off for the last ten years. She has been hospitalized several times in the past ten years during similar episodes of unusual behavior. In addition, she has been treated with several antipsychotic medicines for her problem. There is no evidence of organic pathology or any indication of alcohol or drug abuse. Her husband indicates that she recently stopped taking her medicine

after the death of her sister and up until then had been functioning adequately during the past year with not much impairment.

DSM-III Diagnosis

Axis I: 295.3x, paranoid schizophrenia, chronic with acute exacerbation.

Axis II: none.

Axis III: none.

Axis IV: 6, *extreme* severity of psychosocial stressors (death of sister).

Axis V: 4, *fair* level of adaptive functioning during past year. (Moderate problems with other persons, lifestyles, carrying out of daily responsibilities.)

Respond to these questions. Feedback follows.

1. List several of the problem behaviors that Mrs. Turner demonstrates.
2. Is each problem behavior you have listed overt or covert?
3. List one or more antecedents that seem to elicit Mrs. Turner's problem behaviors.
4. List one or more consequences that appear to influence the problem behavior(s), including any secondary gains. Describe how each consequence seems to influence the behavior.

☐ SUMMARY

Assessment is the basis for development of the entire counseling program. Assessment has important informational, educational, and motivational functions in therapy. Although the major part of assessment occurs early in the counseling process, to some extent assessment, or identification of client concerns, goes on constantly during therapy.

An important part of assessment is the counselor's ability to conceptualize client problems. In this chapter we described the models of case or problem conceptualizations proposed by Swensen (1968), Seay (1978), and Lazarus (1976, 1981). Conceptualization models help the counselor think clearly about the complexity of client problems.

The ABC model of assessment described in this chapter is based on several assumptions, including these:

1. Most problem behavior is learned, although this does not rule out organic (biological) causes of psychological problems.
2. Causes of problems are multidimensional.
3. Problems need to be viewed operationally, or concretely.
4. Problems occur in a social context and are affected by internal and external antecedents that are functionally related to or exert influence on the problem in various ways.
5. Components of the problem as well as sources of antecedents and consequences can be affective, somatic, behavioral, cognitive, contextual, and relational.

In addition to the need to identify components of the problem behavior and sources of antecedents and consequences, another part of assessment may involve a multiaxial diagnosis of the client. Current diagnosis is based on the *Diagnostic and Statistical Manual*, third edition, and involves classifying the problems and assessing the severity of psychosocial stressors and the client's highest level of adaptive functioning during the past year. Diagnosis can be a useful part of assessment. For example, knowledge about selected features of various types of clinical syndromes can add to understanding of the client's concern. Diagnosis, however, is not an adequate *substitute* for other assessment approaches and is not an effective basis for specifying goals and selecting intervention strategies unless it is part of a comprehensive treatment approach in which components of the problem are identified in a concrete, or operational, manner.

FEEDBACK #23: ABCs OF PROBLEM ASSESSMENT

The Case of Ms. Weare and Freddie

1. Freddie's problem behavior is sitting in his room and not dressing for school.
2. This is an overt behavior, since it is visible to someone else.
3. Ms. Weare's problem behaviors are (a) feeling mad and (b) yelling at Freddie.
4. (a) Feeling mad is a covert behavior, since feelings can only be inferred. (b) Yelling is an overt behavior that is visible to someone else.
5. Receiving a verbal reminder and threat from his mother at breakfast elicits Freddie's behavior.
6. Ms. Weare's behavior seems to be cued by a five-minute period before the bus arrives on school days.
7. Two consequences seem to influence Freddie's problem behavior of not dressing for school. (a) He gets help in dressing himself; this influences his behavior by providing special benefits. (b) He gets some satisfaction from seeing that his mother is upset and is attending to him. This seems to maintain his behavior because of the attention he gets from her in these instances. A possible secondary gain is the control he exerts over his mother at these times. According to the case description, he doesn't seem to get much attention at other times from his mother.
8. The major consequence that influences Ms. Weare's behavior is that she gets Freddie ready on time and he is not late. This appears to influence her behavior by helping her avoid being considered a poor mother by herself or someone else.

The Case of Mrs. Turner

1. There are various problem behaviors for Mrs. Turner: (a) disheveled appearance, (b) inappropriate affect, (c) delusional beliefs, (d) auditory hallucinations, (e) homicidal ideation, (f) noncompliance with treatment (medicine).
2. Disheveled appearance, inappropriate affect, and noncompliance with treatment are overt behaviors—they are observable by others. Delusions, hallucinations, and homicidal ideation are covert behaviors as long as they are not expressed by the client and therefore not visible to someone else. However, when expressed or demonstrated by the client, they become overt behaviors as well.
3. In this case, Mrs. Turner's problem behaviors appear to be elicited by the cessation of her medicine, which is the major antecedent. Apparently, when she stops taking her medication, an acute psychotic episode results.
4. This periodic discontinuation of her medicine and subsequent psychotic reaction may be influenced by the attention she receives from the mental health profession, her family, and even strangers when she behaves in a psychotic, helpless fashion. Additional possible secondary gains include avoidance of responsiblity and of being in control.

POSTEVALUATION

Read the case descriptions of Mr. Brown and of John that follow and then answer the following questions:

1. What are the client's problem behaviors?
2. Are the problem behaviors overt or covert?
3. What are the antecedent conditions of the client's concern?
4. What are the consequences of the problem behaviors? Secondary gains?
5. In what way do the consequences influence the problem behaviors?

Answers to these questions are provided in the Feedback section that follows the Postevaluation.

The Case of Mr. Brown

A 69-year-old man, Mr. Brown, came to counseling because he felt his performance on his job was ''slip-
(continued)

ping." Mr. Brown had a job in a large automobile company. He was responsible for producing new car designs. Mr. Brown revealed that he noticed he had started having trouble about six months before, when the personnel director came in to ask him to fill out retirement papers. Mr. Brown, at the time he sought counseling, was due to retire in nine months. (The company's policy made it mandatory to retire at age 70.) Until this incident with the personnel director and the completion of the papers, Mr. Brown reported, everything seemed to be "OK." He also reported that nothing seemed to be changed in his relationship with his family. However, on some days at work, he reported having a great deal of trouble completing any work on his car designs. When asked what he did instead of working on designs, he said "Worrying." The "worrying" turned out to mean that he was engaging in constant repetitive thoughts about his approaching retirement, such as "I won't be here when this car comes out" and "What will I be without having this job?" Mr. Brown stated that there were times when he spent almost an entire morning or afternoon "dwelling" on these things and that this seemed to occur mostly when he was alone in his office actually working on a car design. As a result, he was not turning in his designs by the specified deadlines. Not meeting his deadlines made him feel more worried. He was especially concerned that he would "blow" his previously established reputation in the eyes of his colleagues and superiors, who, he felt, always could have counted on him "to get the job done." He was afraid that his present behavior would jeopardize the opinion others had of him, although he didn't report any other possible "costs" to him. In fact, Mr. Brown said that it was his immediate boss who had suggested, after several talks and after-work drinks, that he see a counselor. The boss also indicated the company would pay for Mr. Brown's counseling. Mr. Brown said that his boss had not had any noticeable reactions to his missing deadlines, other than reminding him and being solicitous, as evidenced in the talks and after-work drinks. Mr. Brown reported that he enjoyed this interaction with his boss and often wished he could ask his boss to go out to lunch with him. However, he stated that these meetings had all been at his boss's request. Mr. Brown felt somewhat hesitant about making the request himself. In the last six months, Mr. Brown had never received any sort of reprimand for missing deadlines on his drawings. Still, he was concerned with maintaining his own sense of pride about his work, which he felt might be jeopardized since he's been having this trouble.

DSM-III Diagnosis

> Axis I: 309.23, adjustment disorder with work inhibition.
>
> Axis II: none.
>
> Axis III: none.
>
> Axis IV: 5, *severe* psychosocial stressors (impending retirement).
>
> Axis V: 3, *good* level of adaptive functioning during past year (work performance good before onset of work-related problems six months ago; has affected some social interactions with his boss, but family interactions remain good).

The Case of John

This is a complicated case with three presenting problems: (1) work, (2) sexual, and (3) alcohol. We suggest that you complete the analysis of ABCs (Questions 1–5 listed at the beginning of this post-evaluation) *separately* for each of these three problems.

John, a 30-year-old business manager, has been employed by the same large corporation for two years, since his completion of graduate school. During the first counseling session, he reports a chronic feeling of "depression" with his present job. In addition, he mentions a recent loss of interest and pleasure in sexual activity, which he describes as "frustrating." He also relates a dramatic increase in his use of alcohol as a remedy for the current difficulties he is experiencing.

John has never before been in counseling and admits to feeling "slightly anxious" about this new endeavor. He appears to be having trouble concentrating when asked a question. He traces the beginning of his problems to the completion of his master's degree a little over two years ago. At that time, he states, "everything was fine." He was working part-time during the day for a local firm and attending college during the evenings. He had been dating the same woman for a year and a half and reports a great deal of satisfaction in their relationship. Drinking occurred infrequently, usually only during social occasions or a quiet evening alone. On completion of his degree, John relates, "things changed. I guess maybe I expected too much too soon." He quit his job in the expectation of finding employment with a larger company. At first there were few offers, and he was beginning to wonder whether he had made a mistake. After several interviews, he was finally offered a job with a business firm that specialized in computer technology, an area in which John was intensely

(continued)

POSTEVALUATION (continued)

interested. He accepted and was immediately placed in a managerial position. Initially, John was comfortable and felt confident in his new occupation; however, as the weeks and months passed, the competitive nature of the job began to wear him down. He relates that he began to doubt his abilities as a supervisor and began to tell himself that he wasn't as good as the other executives. He began to notice that he was given fewer responsibilities than the other bosses, as well as fewer employees to oversee. He slowly withdrew socially from his colleagues, refusing all social invitations. He states that he began staying awake at night obsessing about what he might be doing wrong. Of course, this lack of sleep decreased his energy level even further and produced a chronic tiredness and lessening of effectiveness and productivity at work. At the same time, his relationship with his girlfriend began to deteriorate slowly. He relates that "she didn't understand what I was going through." Her insistence that his sexual performance was not satisfying her made him even more apprehensive and lowered his self-esteem even further. After a time, his inhibition of sexual desire resulted in inconsistency in maintaining an erection throughout the sexual act. This resulted in an even greater strain on their relationship, so that she threatened to "call it quits" if he did not seek treatment for his problem. He reports that it was at this time that he began to drink more heavily. At first it was just a few beers at home alone after a day at the office. Gradually, he began to drink during lunch, even though, he states, "I could

have stopped if I had wanted to." However, his repeated efforts to reduce his excessive drinking by "going on the wagon" met with little success. He began to need a drink every day in order to function adequately. He was losing days at work, was becoming more argumentative with his friends, and had been involved in several minor traffic accidents. He states, "I think I'm becoming an alcoholic." John points out that he has never felt this low before in his life. He reports feeling very pessimistic about his future and doesn't see any way out of his current difficulties. He's fearful that he might make the wrong decisions, and that's why he's come to see a counselor at this time in his life.

DSM-III Diagnosis

Axis I: 300.40, dysthymic disorder (depressive neurosis).
305.01, alcohol abuse, continuous.
302.72, inhibited sexual excitement.
Axis II: none.
Axis III: none.
Axis IV: 5, *severe* psychosocial stressors (new type of job position; deterioration in relationship with girlfriend).
Axis V: 5, *poor* level of adaptive functioning during past year. (Marked and steady deterioration of relationship with colleagues, supervisor, and girlfriend, as well as marked impairment of work and increasing use of alcohol during leisure time.)

□ SUGGESTED READINGS

Barlow, D. H. (Ed.). (1981). *Behavioral assessment of adult disorders.* New York: Guilford Press.

Barlow, D. H., Hayes, S. C., & Nelson, R. O. (1984). *The scientist practitioner.* New York: Pergamon Press.

Celotta, B., & Telasi-Golubscow, H. (1982). A problem taxonomy for classifying clients' problems. *Personnel and Guidance Journal, 61,* 73–76.

Fishman, S. T., & Lubetkin, B. S. (1983). Office practice of behavior therapy. In M. Hersen (Ed.), *Outpatient behavior therapy: A clinical guide.* New York: Grune & Stratton.

Hutchins, D. E. (1979). Systematic counseling: The T-F-A model for counselor intervention. *Personnel and Guidance Journal, 57,* 529–531.

Kendall, P. C., & Hollon, S. D. (Eds.). (1981). *Assessment strategies for cognitive-behavioral interventions.* New York: Academic Press.

L'Abate, L. (1981). Toward a systematic classification of counseling and therapy theorists, methods, processes, and goals: The E-R-A model. *Personnel and Guidance Journal, 59,* 263–266.

Lazarus, A. A. (1981). *The practice of multimodal therapy.* New York: McGraw-Hill.

Meyer, V., & Turkat, I. (1979). Behavioral analysis of clinical cases. *Journal of Behavioral Assessment, 1,* 259–270.

Nelson, R. O. (1983). Behavioral assessment: Past, present, and future. *Behavioral Assessment, 5,* 195–206.

Owens, R. G., & Ashcroft, J. B. (1982). Functional analysis in applied psychology. *British Journal of Clinical Psychology, 21,* 181–189.

Seay, T. A. (1978). *Systematic electic therapy.* Jonesboro, TN: Pilgrimage Press.

Slade, P. (1982). Towards a functional analysis of anorexia nervosa and bulimia nervosa. *British Journal of Clinical Psychology, 21,* 167–179.

Spitzer, R. L., Skodol, A. E., Gibbon, M., & Williams, J.

(1981). *DSM-III Case-Book.* Washington, DC: American Psychiatric Association.

Swensen, C. H., Jr. (1968). *An approach to case conceptualization.* Boston: Houghton Mifflin.

Taylor, C. B. (1983). DSM-III and behavioral assessment. *Behavioral Assessment, 5,* 5–14.

Wahler, R. G., & Fox, J. J. (1981). Setting events in applied behavior analysis: Toward a conceptual and methodological expansion. *Journal of Applied Behavior Analysis, 14,* 327–338.

Webb, L. J., DiClemente, C. C., Johnstone, E. E., Sanders, J. L., & Perley, R. A. (1981). *DSM-III training guide.* New York: Brunner/Mazel.

■
FEEDBACK: POSTEVALUATION

The Case of Mr. Brown

1. Mr. Brown's self-reported problem behaviors include worry about retirement and not doing work on his automobile designs.

2. Worrying about retirement is a covert behavior. Not doing work on designs is an overt behavior.

3. One antecedent condition occurred six months ago, when the personnel director conferred with Mr. Brown about retirement and papers were filled out. This is an overt antecedent in the form of a setting event. The personnel director's visit seemed to elicit Mr. Brown's worry about retirement and his not doing his designs. A covert antecedent is Mr. Brown's repetitive thoughts about retirement, getting older, and so on. This is a stimulus event.

4. The consequences include Mr. Brown's being excused from meeting his deadlines and receiving extra attention from his boss.

5. Mr. Brown's problem behaviors appear to be maintained by the consequence of being excused from not meeting his deadlines, with only a "reminder." He is receiving some extra attention and concern from his boss, whom he values highly. He may also be missing deadlines and therefore not completing required car designs as a way to avoid or postpone retirement; that is, he may expect that if his designs aren't done, he'll be asked to stay longer until they are completed.

The Case of John
Analysis of Work Problem

1. John's problem behaviors at work include (a) over-emphasis on the rivalry that he assumes exists with his fellow administrators and resulting self-doubts about his competence compared with his peers and (b) missing days at work because of his feelings of depression as well as his alcohol abuse.

2. His discrediting of his skills is a covert behavior, as is much of his current dejection. Avoiding his job is an overt behavior.

3. The antecedent conditions of John's difficulties at work are his apparent misperceptions surrounding the competitiveness with his co-workers. These misperceptions constitute a stimulus event. This apprehension has led him to feel inadequate and fosters his depressive symptomatology. It should be recognized that John's occupational difficulties arose only after he obtained his present job, one that requires more responsibility than any of his previous positions. Acquisition of this job and its accompanying managerial position is a setting event.

4. The consequences that maintain John's difficulties at work are (a) failing to show up for work each day and (b) alcohol abuse.

5. Failing to show up for work each day amounts to a variable-interval schedule of reinforcement, which is quite powerful in maintaining John's evasion of the workplace. A possible secondary gain of his absenteeism is the resulting decrease in his feelings of incompetence and depression. His abuse of alcohol provides him with a ready-made excuse to miss work whenever necessary or whenever he feels too depressed to go. It should be noted that alcohol as a drug is a central nervous system depressant as well. Alcohol abuse is also a common complication of depressive episodes.

Analysis of Sexual Problem

1. John's problem behavior is an apparent loss of interest in or desire for sexual activity, which is a significant change from his previous behavior. His feelings of excitement have been inhibited so that he is unable to attain or maintain an erection throughout the sexual act.

2. The inability to achieve and/or sustain an erection is an overt problem. We may also assume that whatever John is telling himself is somehow influencing his observable behavior. His self-talk is a covert problem.

3. There are apparently no organic factors contributing to the disturbance. Therefore, it appears likely that the antecedent conditions of John's current
(continued)

FEEDBACK: POSTEVALUATION (continued)

sexual problem are the anxiety and depression associated with the work situation.

4. The consequences maintaining John's sexual problem appear to be (a) the lack of reassurance from his girlfriend and (b) his current alcohol abuse. The girlfriend's ultimatum that he begin to regain his normal sexual functioning is creating psychological stress that will continue to prevent adequate sexual response. Although alcohol may serve as a relaxant, it also acts to physiologically depress the usual sexual response.

Analysis of Alcohol Problem

1. Problem behavior is frequent consumption of alcoholic beverages during the day as well as at night.

2. Although alcohol abuse is certainly an overt problem behavior, we might also assume that John is engaging in some self-defeating covert behaviors to sustain his alcohol abuse.

3. It is quite apparent that John's maladaptive use of alcohol occurred only after his difficulties with his job became overwhelming. It also appears to be linked to the onset of his sexual disorder. There is no history of previous abuse of alcohol or other drugs.

4. Consequences include the payoffs of avoidance of tension, responsibility, and depression related to his job as well as possible increased attention from others.

5. By abusing alcohol, John has been missing days at work and thus avoids the tension he feels with his job. Alcohol abuse is serving as a negative reinforcer. Moreover, his use of alcohol, which is a depressant, allows him to maintain his self-pitying behavior, which, owing to the attention he derives from this, may also be maintaining the alcohol abuse. Finally, alcohol may also provide a ready-made excuse for his poor sexual functioning with his girlfriend.

DEFINING CLIENT PROBLEMS WITH AN INTERVIEW ASSESSMENT

EIGHT

In Chapter 7 we described a number of important functions of the assessment process in therapy and noted that assessment is a way of identifying and defining a client's problems in order to make decisions about therapeutic treatment. A variety of tools or methods are available to the therapist that can help identify and define the range and parameters of client problems. These methods include standardized tests, such as interest and personality inventories; psychophysiological assessment, such as monitoring of muscle tension for chronic headaches with an electromyograph (EMG) machine; self-report checklists, such as assertiveness scales or anxiety inventories; observation by others, including observation by the therapist or by a significant person in the client's environment; self-observation, in which the client observes and records some aspect of the problem; imagery, in which the client uses fantasy and directed imagery to vicariously experience some aspect of the problem; role playing, in which the client may demonstrate some part of the problem in an *in vivo* yet simulated enactment; and direct interviewing, in which the client and counselor identify the problem through verbal and nonverbal exchanges. All these methods are also used to evaluate client progress during therapy, in addition to their use in assessment for the purpose of collecting information about client problems. Specific uses, advantages, and limitations of each of these methods as an evaluation tool are described in greater detail in Chapter 10. In this chapter we concentrate on direct interviewing, not only because it is the focus of the book but also because it is the one method readily available to all therapists without additional cost in time or money. We also, however, will mention ancillary use of some of the other methods of assessment named above. In actual practice, it is very important not to rely solely on the interview for assessment data but to use several methods of obtaining information about client problems.

□ OBJECTIVES

1. Given a written description of a selected client problem, outline in writing at least two questions for each of the 11 problem assessment categories that you would ask during an assessment interview with this person.
2. In a 30-minute role-play interview, demonstrate leads and responses associated with 9 out of 11 categories for assessing the problem. An observer can rate you, or you can rate your performance from a tape, using the Problem Assessment Interview Checklist at the end of the chapter. After the interview, identify orally or in writing some hypotheses about antecedent sources that cue the problem, consequences that maintain it, secondary gains, or "payoffs," and client resources, skills, and assets that might be used during intervention.
3. Given a written client case description, construct in writing a self-monitoring assessment plan for the client and an example of a log to use for self-recording the data.
4. Conduct a role-play interview in which you explain at least three parts of a self-monitoring assessment plan to a client (rationale, instructions, follow-up).

□ DIRECT ASSESSMENT INTERVIEWING

According to cognitive-behavioral literature, the interview is the most common behavioral assessment instrument (Haynes & Jensen, 1979; Nelson, 1983). A recent article noted that "while elaborate behavioral and psychophysiological assessment procedures have been developed and evaluated, the assessment instrument most frequently employed in the clinical setting remains the behavioral interview" (Keane, Black, Collins, & Venson, 1982, p. 53). Nelson (1983) observes that the interview is the one assessment strategy used more consistently than any other procedure —perhaps because of its practicality in applied settings and its potential efficiency. Despite the overwhelming evidence confirming the popularity of the interview as an assessment tool, some persons believe it is the most difficult assessment approach for the therapist to enact. Successful assessment interviews require specific guidelines and training in order to obtain accurate and valid information from clients that will make a difference in treatment planning (Duley, Cancelli, Kratochwill, Bergan, & Meredith, 1983).

In this chapter we describe a structure and some guidelines to apply in assessment interviews in order to identify and define client problems. This chapter and other chapters in this book describe interview leads that, in applied settings, are likely to elicit certain kinds of client information. However, as Morganstern and Tevlin (1981) observe, little research on the effects of interview procedures has been conducted. The leads suggested in this chapter are supported more by practical considerations than by empirical data. As a result, you will need to be very attentive to the effects of using these questions with each client.

□ INTAKE INTERVIEWS AND HISTORY

Part of assessment involves eliciting information about the client's background, especially as it may relate to *current* problems or complaints. Past, or historical, information is not sought as an end in itself or because the therapist is necessarily interested in exploring or focusing on the client's "past" during treatment. Rather, it is used as a part of the overall assessment process that helps the therapist fit the pieces of the puzzle together concerning the client's presenting problems and current life difficulties. Often a client's current problems are precipitated and maintained by events found in the client's history. For example, with one middle-aged client who felt conflicted between the demands of her job and the demands of her family, it became apparent that she carried around with her an ever-present image of the way her now-deceased mother had functioned in her own family when the client was growing up— totally nurturing, self-sacrificing, expecting her daughter to do the same, and reinforcing her for doing so. Although the client hadn't lived in her family of origin for over 25 years, this image and all the beliefs and feelings associated with it were having a very strong influence on her present complaint. The complaint was exacerbated by the client's age and stage in the life cycle: she was feeling a strong need to ascend the job ladder, to be productive, and to establish herself as an individual in her own right. At the same time, the learnings from her family of origin, particularly her mother, were holding her back and were also interfering with successful completion of an important developmental life task. In cases such as this one, history may serve as a retrospective baseline measure for the client and may help to identify cognitive or historical antecedent conditions that still exert influence on the problem behavior and might otherwise be overlooked.

The process of gathering this type of information is called "history taking." In many agency settings, history taking occurs during an initial interview called an "intake interview." An intake interview is viewed as informational rather than therapeutic and, to underscore this point, is often conducted by someone other than the therapist assigned to see the client. In these situations, someone else, such as an intake worker, sees the client for an hour interview (shorter for children and adolescents), summarizes the information in writing, and passes the information along to the therapist. In other places, the therapists conduct their own intakes. For therapists who work either in private practice or in a school or agency in which intakes are not required, it is still a good idea to do some history taking with the client.

Various kinds of information can be solicited during history taking, but the most important areas are the following:

1. Identifying information about the client
2. General appearance and demeanor
3. History related to the presenting problem(s)
4. Past psychiatric and/or counseling history
5. Educational and job history
6. Health (medical) history
7. Social/developmental history (including religious and cultural background and affiliations, predominant values, description of past problems, chronological/developmental events, military background, social/leisure activities, present social situation)
8. Family, marital, sexual history
9. Assessment of client communication patterns
10. Results of mental status; diagnostic summary

Table 8-1 presents specific questions or content areas to cover for each of these ten areas.

TABLE 8-1. History-taking interview content

I. *Identifying information*
Client's name, address, home and work telephone numbers
Age
Sex
Ethnic/cultural affiliation
Marital status
Occupation

II. *General appearance*
Approximate height
Approximate weight
Brief description of client's dress, grooming, overall demeanor

III. *Presenting problems* (do for *each* problem or complaint that client presents)
Note the presenting complaint (quote client directly):
When did it start? What other events were occurring at that time?
How often does it occur?
What are thoughts, feelings, and observable behaviors associated with it?
Where and when does it occur most? least?
Are there any events or persons that precipitate it? make it better? make it worse?
How much does it interfere with the client's daily functioning?
What previous solutions/plans have been tried for the problem and with what result?
What made the client decide to seek help at this time (or, if referred, what influenced the referring party to refer the client at this time)?

IV. *Past psychiatric/counseling history*
Previous counseling and/or psychological/psychiatric treatment:
Type of treatment
Length of treatment
Treatment place or person
Presenting complaint
Outcome of treatment and reason for termination
Previous hospitalization and/or prescription drugs for emotional/psychological problems

(continued)

TABLE 8-1. History-taking interview content (continued)

    V. *Educational/job history*
        Trace academic progress (strengths and weaknesses) from grade school through last level of education completed
        Relationships with teachers and peers
        Types of jobs held by client
        Length of jobs
        Reason for termination or change
        Relationships with co-workers
        Training/education received for jobs
        Aspects of work that are most stressful or anxiety-producing
        Aspects of work that are least stressful or most enjoyable
        Overall degree of current job satisfaction

    VI. *Health/medical history*
        Childhood diseases, prior significant illnesses, previous surgery
        Current health-related complaints or illnesses (for example, headache, hypertension)
        Treatment received for current complaints: what type and by whom
        Date of last physical examination and results
        Significant health problems in client's family of origin (parents, grandparents, siblings)
        Client's sleep patterns
        Client's appetite level
        Current medications (including such things as aspirin, vitamins, birth control pills, recreational drug use)
        Drug and nondrug allergies
        Client's typical daily diet, including caffeine-containing beverages/food; alcoholic beverages
        Exercise patterns

    VII. *Social/developmental history*
        Current life situation (typical day/week, living arrangements, occupation and economic situation, contact
            with other people)
        Social/leisure time activities, hobbies
        Religious affiliation
        Military background/history
        Predominant values, priorities, and beliefs expressed by client
        Significant chronological/developmental events noted by client:
            Earliest recollections
         Significant events reported for the following developmental periods:
            Preschool (0–6 years)
            Middle childhood (6–13 years)
            Adolescence (13–21 years)
            Young adulthood (21–30 years)
            Middle adulthood (30–65 years)
            Late adulthood (65 years and over)

    VIII. *Family, marital, sexual history*
        Identifying data for client's mother and father
        Ways in which mother rewarded and punished client
        Ways in which father rewarded and punished client
        Significant "parent tapes"
        Activities client typically did with mother
        How well client got along with mother
        Activities client typically did with father
        How well client got along with father
        How well parents got along with each other
        Identifying information for client's siblings (including those older and younger and client's birth order, or
            position in family)
        Which sibling was most like client? least like client?

TABLE 8-1. History-taking interview content (continued)

Which sibling was most favored by mother? father? least favored by mother? father?
Which sibling did client get along with best? worst?
History of previous psychiatric illness/hospitalization among members of client's family of origin
Dating history
Engagement/marital history—reason for termination of relationship
Current relationship with spouse (how well they get along, problems, stresses, enjoyment, satisfaction, and so on)
Number and ages of client's children
Other people living with or visiting family frequently
Description of previous sexual experience, including first one
(note whether heterosexual, homosexual, or bisexual experiences are reported)
Present sexual activity—masturbation, intercourse, and so on; note frequency
Any present concerns or complaints about sexual attitudes or behaviors
For female clients: obtain menstrual history (onset of first period, regularity of current ones, degree of stress
    and comfort before and during period)

IX. *Assessment of client's communication patterns*
(Typically completed by interviewer after the intake or initial interview)
Client's predominant representational (sensory) system
Nonverbal behavior during session:
    Kinesics (eye contact, body movements, gestures)
    Paralinguistics (voice level, pitch, fluency, vocal errors)
    Proxemics (personal space, territoriality)

X. *Diagnostic summary* (if applicable)
Axis I. Clinical syndromes   *DSM-III* Code

_____
_____
_____

Axis II. Personality and specific developmental disorders

_____
_____
_____

Axis III. Physical disorders

_____
_____
_____

Avis IV. Psychological stressors (include relevant occupational, educational, legal, recreational, financial, and
    social problems):
    A. Ranked list:
        1._____
        2._____
        3._____
        4._____
    B. Overall stressor severity:

1	2	3	4	5	6	7	0
None	Minimal	Mild	Moderate	Severe	Extreme	Catastrophic	Unspecified

Axis V. Adaptive Functioning:
    A. Highest level during the past year:

1	2	3	4	5	6	7	0
Superior	Very good	Good	Fair	Poor	Very poor	Grossly impaired	Unspecified

    B. Current functioning:

Work/school:	___satisfactory	___marginal	___unsatisfactory
Family:	___satisfactory	___marginal	___unsatisfactory
Other individuals and groups	___satisfactory	___marginal	___unsatisfactory

The sequence of obtaining this information in a history or intake interview is important. Generally, the interviewer begins with the least threatening topics and saves more sensitive topics (such as #6, #7, and #8) until near the end of the session, when a greater degree of rapport has been established and the client feels more at ease about revealing personal information to a total stranger.

In addition to or even in lieu of asking the client to give the history *during* the session, the therapist may give the client a written history questionnaire or form to complete as homework before another scheduled session. Two very useful forms developed for this purpose are the Life History Questionnaire (Lazarus, 1976) and the History Questionnaire (Cautela, 1976). These appear in Appendixes E and F.

☐ MENTAL-STATUS EXAMINATION

If, after conducting an initial interview, you are in doubt about the client's psychiatric status or suspicious about the possibility of an organic brain disorder, you may wish to conduct (or refer the client for) a mental-status examination. According to Kaplan and Sadock (1981), the mental-status exam is one that classifies and describes the areas and components of mental functioning involved in making diagnostic impressions and classifications. The major categories covered in a mental-status exam are general description and appearance of the client, mood and affect, perception, thought processes, level of consciousness, orientation to time, place, and people, memory, and impulse control. Additionally, the examiner may note the degree to which the client appeared to report the information accurately and reliably. Of these categories, disturbances in consciousness (which involves ability to perform mental tasks, degree of effort, degree of fluency/hesitation in task performance) and orientation (whether or not clients know when, where, and who they are and who other people are) are usually indicative of organic brain impairment or disorders and require neurological assessment and follow-up as well. It is important for counselors and therapists to know enough about the functions and content of a mental-status exam in order to refer an occasional client who might benefit from this additional assessment procedure. For additional information about mental-status examinations and neurophysiological assessment, see Kaplan and Sadock (1981) and Meyer (1983). A standardized extension of the mental-status exam, called the "Present State Exam," has been developed by Wing, Cooper, and Sartorius (1974). This published version also includes reliability data and sample questions.

History taking (and mental-status exams, if applicable) usually occur near the very beginning of counseling. After obtaining this sort of preliminary information about the client as well as an idea of the range of presenting complaints, you are ready to do some direct assessment interviewing with the client in order to define the parameters of problems and concerns more specifically. We present guidelines for assessment interviews in the next section, after Learning Activity #24.

LEARNING ACTIVITY #24: INTAKE INTERVIEWS AND HISTORY

To give you a sense of the process involved in doing an intake or history interview (if you don't already do lots of these on your job), we suggest you pair up with someone else in your class and complete intake/history interviews with each other. Conduct a 30–45 minute session with one person serving as the counselor and the other taking the client's role; then switch roles. As the counselor, you can use the format in Table 8-1 as a guide. You may wish to jot down some notes. After the session, it might be helpful to write a brief summary of the session, also using the major categories listed in Table 8-1 as a way to organize your report. As the client, in this particular activity, rather than "playing a role," it will be more helpful to be yourself so that you can respond easily and openly to the counselor's questions and also so that both of you can more readily identify the way in which your particular history has influenced the current issues in your life.

☐ ELEVEN CATEGORIES FOR ASSESSING CLIENT PROBLEMS

To help you acquire the skills associated with problem assessment interviews, we will describe 11 categories of information you need to seek from each client. Most of this information is based on the case conceptualization models presented in Chapter 7. These 11 categories are illustrated and defined in the following list and subsections. They are also summarized in the Interview Checklist at the end of the chapter.

1. Explanation of *purpose* of assessment—presenting rationale for assessment interview to the client.
2. Identification of *range* of problems—using leads to help the client identify all the relevant primary and secondary issues in order to get the "big picture."
3. *Prioritization* and *selection* of issues and problems—using leads to help the client prioritize problems and select the initial area of focus.
4. Identification of *present problem behaviors*—using leads to help the client identify the six components of problem behavior(s): affective, somatic, behavioral, cognitive, contextual, and relational.
5. Identification of *antecedents*—using leads to help the client identify sources of antecedents and their effect on the problem behavior.
6. Identification of *consequences*—using leads to help the client identify sources of consequences and their influence on the problem behavior.
7. Identification of *secondary gains*—using leads to help the client identify underlying controlling variables that serve as "payoffs" to maintain the problem behavior.
8. Identification of *previous solutions*—using leads to help the client identify previous solutions or attempts to solve the problem and their subsequent effect on the problem.
9. Identification of *client coping skills*—using leads to help client identify past and present coping or adaptive behavior and how such skills might be used in working with the present issue.
10. Identification of the *client's perceptions* of the problem—using leads to help the client describe her or his understanding of the problem.
11. Identification of *problem intensity*—using leads and/or client self-monitoring to identify impact of problem on client's life, including (a) degree of problem severity and (b) frequency or duration of problem behaviors.

The first three categories—explanation of the purpose of assessment, identification of the range of problems, and prioritization and selection of problem concerns—are a logical starting place. First, it is helpful to give the client a rationale, a reason for conducting an assessment interview, before gathering information. Next, some time must be spent in helping the client explore all the relevant issues and prioritize problems to work on in order of importance, annoyance, and so on.

The other eight categories follow problem prioritization and selection. After the counselor and client have identified and selected the problem(s) to work on, these eight categories of counselor leads are used to define and analyze parameters of the problem. The counselor will find that the order of the problem assessment leads varies among clients. A natural sequence will evolve in each interview, and the counselor will want to use the leads associated with these content categories in a pattern that fits the flow of the interview and follows the lead of the client. It is very important in assessment interviews not to impose your structure at the expense of the client. The amount of time and number of sessions required to obtain this information will vary with problems and with clients. It is possible to complete the assessment in one session, but with some clients, three or four assessment interviews may be necessary. A complete analysis of the problem may go beyond "first appearances" in counseling (Morganstern & Tevlin, 1981, p. 73). Although the counselor may devote several interviews to assessment, the information gathering and hypothesis testing that go on do not automatically stop after these few sessions. Some degree of problem assessment continues throughout the entire therapy process (Linehan, 1977).

Explaining the Purpose of Assessment

In explaining the purpose of problem assessment, the counselor gives the client a rationale for doing an assessment interview. The intent of this first category of problem assessment is to give the client a "set," or an expectation, of what will occur during the interview and why assessment is important to both client and counselor. We also usually tell clients that we may be asking more questions during this session than we have before or will in the future so that clients are not caught off guard if our interviewing style changes. One way the counselor can communicate the purpose of the assessment interview is "Today I'd like to focus on some concerns that are bothering you most. In order to find out exactly what you're concerned about, I'll be asking you for some specific kinds of information. This information will help both of us identify what you'd like to work on in counseling. How does this sound [or appear] to you?" After presenting the rationale, the counselor looks for some confirmation or indication that the client understands the importance of assessing problems. If client confirmation or understanding is not forthcoming, the counselor may need to provide more explanation before proceeding to other areas. It is also important in initial interviews with clients to create expectations that inspire hope (Lazarus, 1981). Most clients are so focused on their pain that they are unable to see, hear, or grasp much beyond it. So you need to be in touch not only with their pain but also with their potential, their possibilities, and their future.

Identifying the Range of Problems

In this category, the counselor uses open-ended leads to help clients identify all the major issues and concerns in their life now. Often clients will initially describe only one problem, and on further inquiry and discussion, the counselor discovers a host of other problems, some of which may be more severe or stressful or have greater significance than the one the client originally described. If the counselor does not try to get the "big picture," the client may reveal additional concerns either much later in the therapy process or not at all.

These are examples of range-of-problem leads:

"What are your concerns in your life now?"
"Could you describe some of the things that seem to be bothering you?"
"What are some present stresses in your life?"
"What situations are not going well for you?"
"Is there anything else that concerns you now?"

After using range-of-problem leads, the counselor should look for the client's indication of some general areas of concern or things that are troublesome for the client or difficult to manage. An occasional client may not respond affirmatively to these leads. Krumboltz and Thoresen

(1976, p. 29) point out that sometimes a client may have a "vested interest" in not identifying a problem or may come in with a "hidden agenda" that is not readily disclosed. Other clients may be uncertain about what information to share with the counselor. In such cases, the counselor may need to use a different approach from verbal questioning to elicit problem statements. For example, Lazarus (1981, p. 55) has recommended the use of an "Inner Circle" strategy to help a client disclose problem areas.* The client is given a picture like this:

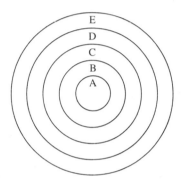

The counselor points out that topics in circle A are very personal, whereas topics in circle E are more or less public information. The counselor can provide examples of types of topics likely to be in the A circle, such as sexual concerns, feelings of hostility, marriage problems, and dishonesty. These examples may encourage the client to disclose personal concerns more readily. The counselor also emphasizes that good therapy takes place in the A and B circles and may say things like "I feel we are staying in Circle C" or "Do you think you've let me into Circle A or B yet?" (Lazarus, 1981, p. 56). Sometimes the counselor may be able to obtain more specific problem descriptions from a client by having the client role-play a typical problem situation. Another client might provide more information by describing a fantasy or visualization about the problem. This last method has been used by Meichenbaum (1976), who asks the client "to run a movie through your head" in order to recall various aspects of the problem (p. 151).

Exploring the range of problems is also a way to

* This and all other quotations from this source are from *The Practice of Multimodal Therapy* by A. A. Lazarus. Copyright © 1981 by McGraw-Hill. Reprinted by permission.

establish who is the appropriate client. A client may attribute the problem or the undesired behavior to an event or to another person. For instance, a student may say "That teacher always picks on me. I can never do anything right in her class." Since most clients seem to have trouble initially "owning" their role in their problem or tend to describe it in a way that minimizes their own contribution (Watzwalick, Beavin, & Jackson, 1967), the counselor will need to determine who is most invested in having the problem resolved and who is the real person requesting assistance. Often it is helpful to ask clients who it is that feels it is most important for the problem to be resolved— themselves or someone else. It is important for therapists not to assume that the person who arrives at their office is always the client. As Fay (1980) observes, the client is the person who wants a change and who seeks assistance for it. In the example above, if the student had desired a change and had requested assistance, the student would be the client; if it were the teacher who wanted a change and requested assistance, the teacher would be the client. (Sometimes, however, the therapist gets "stuck" in a situation in which a family or a client wants a change and the person whose behavior is to be changed is "sent" to counseling as the client. In Chapter 20 we discuss strategies for handling these "involuntary" clients.)

The question of who is the appropriate client is also tricky when the problem involves two or more persons, such as a relationship, marital, or family problem. Many family therapists view family problems as devices for maintaining the status quo of the family and recommend that either the couple or the entire family be involved in counseling, rather than one individual. Although this is a great concept in theory, in practice it is sometimes difficult to implement. Further, as Lazarus notes, "It should not be a question of *whether* to treat the individual or the family but *when* to concentrate on one or both" (1981, p. 41).

Prioritizing and Selecting Problems

Rarely do clients or the results of assessment suggest only one area or problem that needs modification or resolution. Typically, a presenting problem turns out to be one of several unresolved issues in the client's life. For example, the assessment of a client who reports depression may also reveal that the client is troubled by her relationship with her teenage daughter and her obesity. After the client describes all of her or his concerns, the counselor and client will need to select the problems that best represent the client's purpose for seeking counseling. The primary question to be answered by these leads is "What is the specific problem situation the client chooses to start working on?"

Prioritizing problems is an important part of assessment and goal setting. If clients try to tackle too many issues simultaneously, they are likely to soon feel overwhelmed and anxious and may not experience enough success to stay in therapy. Karoly (1975) points out that the selected target for change is sometimes difficult for a client to identify. Generally, a selected problem area represents something that is "harmful" to the person's safety, "disruptive" of the person's emotions, or "damaging" to the person's effectiveness (p. 205). Selection of the problem is the client's responsibility, although the counselor may help with the client's choice. If the client selects a problem that severely conflicts with the counselor's values, a referral to another counselor may be necessary. Otherwise, the counselor may inadvertently or purposely block the discussion of certain client problem areas by listening selectively to only those problems that the counselor can or wants to work with (Kanfer & Grimm, 1977).

The following guidelines form a framework to help clients select and prioritize problems to work on:

1. Start with the presenting problem, the one that best represents the reason the client sought help. Fensterheim (1983, p. 63) observes that relief of the presenting problem often improves the client's level of functioning and may then make other, related problems more accessible to treatment. Leads to use to help determine the initial or presenting problem include "Which issue best represents the reason you are here?" and "Out of all these problems you've mentioned, identify the one that best reflects your need for assistance."

2. Start with the problem that is primary or most important to the client to resolve. Often this is the one that causes the client the most pain or discomfort or annoyance or is most interfering to the client. Modifying the more important issues seems to lead to lasting change in that area, which may then generalize to other areas (Fensterheim, 1983). Responses to determine the client's most important priority include "How much happiness or relief would you experience if this issue were resolved?," "Of these concerns, which is the most stressful or painful for you?," "Rank-order these

concerns, starting with the one that is most important for you to resolve to the one least important," and "How much sorrow or loss would you experience if you were unable to resolve this issue?"

3. Start with the problem or behavior that has the best chance of being resolved successfully and with the least effort. Some problems/behaviors are more resistant to change than others and require more time and energy to modify. Initially, it is important for the client to get reinforced for seeking help. One significant way to do this is to help the client resolve something that makes a difference without much cost to the client.

Responses to determine what problems might be resolved most successfully include "Do you believe there would be any unhappiness or discomfort if you were successful at resolving this concern?," "How likely do you think we are to succeed in resolving this issue or that one?," and "Tell me which of these problems you believe you could learn to manage most easily with the greatest success."

4. Start with the problem that needs resolution before other problems can be resolved or mastered. Sometimes the presence of one problem sets off a chain of other ones; when this problem is resolved or eliminated, the other issues either improve or at least move into a position to be explored and modified. Often this problem is one that, in the range of elicited problems, is central or prominent.

Questions to ask to help determine the most central problem include "Out of all the problems we've discussed, which is the most predominant one?" and "Out of all the problems we've discussed, describe the one that, when resolved, would have the greatest impact on the rest of the issues."

If, after this process, the counselor and client still have difficulty prioritizing problems and selecting the initial area of focus, try the procedure recommended by Goldfried (1976a). The client asks the following question about each identified problem: "What are the consequences of my *not* doing anything therapeutically to handle this particular problem?" As Goldfried notes, "Depending on the severity of the consequences associated with ignoring—at least temporarily—each of the different presenting problems, one can obtain a clearer picture as to what is most important" (p. 319).

Understanding the Problem Behaviors

After selecting the initial area of focus, it is important to determine the components of the problem behavior. For example, if the identified problem is "not getting along very well with people at work," with an expected outcome of "improving my relationships with people at work," we would want to identify the client's *feelings* (affect), *body sensations* (somatic phenomena), *actions* (overt behavior), and *thoughts and beliefs* (cognitions) that occur during the problem situations at work. We would also explore whether these problematic feelings, sensations, actions, and thoughts occurred with all *people* at work or only some *people* (relationships) and whether they occurred only at work or in other *situations,* at what *times,* and under what *conditions* or *concurrent events* (context). Without this sort of exploration, it is impossible to define the problem operationally (concretely). Furthermore, it is difficult to know whether the client's work problems result from the client's actions or observable behaviors, from covert responses such as feelings of anger or jealousy, from cognitions and irrational beliefs such as "When I make a mistake at work, it's terrible" from the client's transactions with significant others that suggest an "I'm not OK—they're OK" position, or from particular events that occur in certain times or situations during work, as during a team meeting or when working under a supervisor.

Without this kind of information about when and how the problem behavior is manifested, it would be very difficult and even presumptuous to select intervention strategies or approaches. The end result of this kind of specificity is that the problem is defined or stated in terms such that two or more persons can agree on when it exists (Brown & Brown, 1977, p. 7). In the following sections, we describe specific things to explore for each of these six components and suggest some leads and responses to facilitate this exploration with clients.

Affect and mood states. Affective components of problem behavior include self-reported feelings or mood states, such as "depression," "anxiety," and "happiness." Feelings are generally the result of complex interactions among behavioral, physiological, and cognitive systems rather than unitary experiential processes (Woolfolk, 1976, p. 49). Clients often seek therapy because of this component of the problem—that is, they feel bad, uptight, sad, angry, confused, and so on and want to get rid of such unpleasant feelings. Hence, the affective component is often "overworked" in therapy. As Lazarus observes, "It is within the domain of 'emotional disturbance' that we labor, and we consider our therapeutic interventions successful or worthwhile to the extent that we are able to alleviate suffering while also promoting new adaptive responses" (1976, p. 33).

One category of things to ask the client about to get a handle on feelings or mood states is feelings about the problem behavior. After eliciting them, note the content (pleasant/unpleasant) and level of intensity. Example leads for this are the following:

"How do you feel about this?"
"What kinds of feelings do you have when you do this or when this happens?"

A second category is concealed or distorted feelings—that is, feelings that the client seems to be hiding from, such as anger, or a feeling like anger that has been distorted into hurt. Example responses for this:

"You seem to get headaches every time your husband criticizes you. What feelings are these headaches masking?"
"When you talk about your son, you raise your voice and get a very serious look on your face. What feelings do you have—deep down—about him?"
"You've said you feel hurt and you cry whenever you think about your family. What other feelings do you have besides hurt?"
"You've indicated you feel a little guilty whenever your friends ask you to do something and you don't agree to do it. Try on resentment instead of guilt. Try to get in touch with those feelings now."

The practitioner can always be on the lookout for concealed anger, which is the one emotion that tends to get "shoved under the rug" more easily than most. Lazarus observes that "it is often easy to deny, displace, conceal, and suppress anger. It is less easy to conceal anxiety or misery, especially from oneself" (1976, p. 34). Distorted feelings that are common include reporting the feeling of hurt or anxiety for anger, guilt for resentment, and sometimes anxiety for depression, or vice versa. It is also important to be aware that exploration of the affective component may be very productive

initially for clients who process information easily in a kinesthetic manner. For clients who do not, however, asking "How do you feel?" can draw a blank, uncomprehending look accompanied by an "I don't know what you mean" statement. Like any other response, "How do you feel?" is not equally productive with all clients and tends to be a tremendously overused lead in counseling sessions.

Somatic sensations. Closely tied to feelings are body sensations. Some clients are very aware of these "internal experiencings"; others are not. Some persons are so "tuned into" each and every body sensation that they become hypochondriacal, while others seem to be switched off "below the head" (Lazarus, 1976, p. 35). Neither extreme is desirable. Somatic reactions are quite evident in problems such as sexual dysfunction, depression, and anxiety. Some persons may describe complaints in terms of body sensations rather than as feelings or thoughts—that is, as headaches, dizzy spells, back pain, and so on. Problem behavior can also be affected by other physiological processes, such as nutrition and diet, exercise and lifestyle, substance use, hormone levels, and physical illness. Usually, when this is the case, some form of physiological treatment is warranted as well as psychological intervention. The therapist will want to elicit information about physiological complaints, about lifestyle and nutrition, exercise, substance use, and so on and about other body sensations relating to the problem. Some of this information is gathered routinely during the health history portion of the intake interview.

Useful leads to elicit this component of the problem behavior include these:

"What goes on inside you when you do this or when this happens?"
"What are you aware of when this occurs?"
"What sensations do you experience in your body when this happens?"
"When this happens, are you aware of anything that feels bad or uncomfortable inside you—aches, pains, dizziness, and so on?"

Overt behaviors or motoric responses. Clients often describe a problem "behavior" in very nonbehavioral terms. In other words, they describe a situation or a process without describing their actions or specific behaviors within that event or process. For example, clients may say "I'm not getting along with my wife" or "I feel lousy" or "I have a hard time relating to authority figures" without specifying what they do to get along or not get along or to relate or not relate. In this part of the assessment interview, you are interested in finding out precisely what the client does and doesn't do related to the problem. Examples of overt behaviors might be compulsive handwashing, crying, excessive eating, stealing, and making deprecatory or critical comments about self or others.

When inquiring about the behavioral domain, the therapist will want to elicit descriptions of both the presence and absence of concrete overt behaviors connected to the problem — that is, what the client does and doesn't do. The therapist also needs to be alert to the presence of behavioral *excesses* and *deficits*. Excesses are things that the person does too much or too often or that are too extreme, such as binge eating, excessive crying, or assaultive behavior. Deficits are responses that occur too infrequently or are not in the client's repertoire or do not occur in the expected context or conditions, such as failure to initiate requests on one's behalf, inability to talk to one's partner about sexual concerns and desires, or lack of physical exercise and body conditioning programs. The therapist may also wish to inquire about "behavioral opposites" (Lazarus, 1976) by asking about times when the person does *not* behave that way.

These are examples of leads to elicit information about overt behaviors and actions:

"Describe what happens in this situation."
"What do you mean when you say you're 'having trouble at work'?"
"What are you doing when this occurs?"
"What do you do when this happens?"
"What effect does this situation have on your behavior?"
"Describe what you did the last few times this occurred."
"If I were photographing this scene, what actions and dialogue would the camera pick up?"

Occasionally the counselor may want to supplement the information gleaned about behavior from the client's oral self-report with more objective assessment approaches, such as using role plays that approximate the problem or accompanying clients into their environments. These additional assessment devices will help therapists improve their knowledge of how the client does and doesn't act in the problematic situation. Additionally, when such observations are coupled with the interview data, the therapist can develop more reliable hunches about how the problem manifests itself and how the problem and the client may respond to treatment.

Cognitions, beliefs, and internal dialogue. In the last few years, therapists of almost all orientations have emphasized the relative importance of cognitions or symbolic processes (Bandura, 1969; Ellis, 1984) in contributing to, exacerbating, or improving problematic situations that clients bring to therapy. Irrational expectations of oneself and of others are often related to presenting problems, as are disturbing images, self-labeling and self-statements, and cognitive distortions. Gambrill (1977, pp. 112–113) elucidates various ways in which cognitions and symbolic processes influence problems:

Fear of elevators may be associated with vivid images of the elevator plunging to the ground. Anger may be fueled by the vivid reliving of perceived slights. Self-labeling may be involved in problematic reactions. A client may experience an unusual feeling state and consider it indicative of mental illness. He may become unduly attentive to the possible occurrence of such states, and may label ones that are only similar as also being indicators that he is "going crazy." A depressed client may engage in very few positive self-evaluative statements and a great number of punishing self-statements. Cognitive distortions may include arbitrary inference, in which conclusions are drawn in the absence of supporting evidence or in direct contradiction to such evidence; magnification, in which the meaning of an event is exaggerated; overgeneralization, in which a single incident is considered indicative of total incompetence; and dichotomous reasoning, in which polar differences are emphasized (Beck, 1970) . . . . [In addition], it is assumed that there is a close relationship between the nature of self-statements and overt behavior, in that someone who copes well in a given situation has an internal dialog that is different from that of someone who does not cope well. Clients who complain of anxiety and depression often have an internal dialog consisting of anticipated bad consequences.*

* This and all other quotations from this source are from *Behavior Modification: Handbook of Assessment, Intervention, and Evaluation* by E. Gambrill. Copyright © 1977 by Jossey-Bass. Reprinted by permission.

When the cognitive component is a very strong element of the problem, part of the resulting treatment is usually directed toward this component and involves altering irrational ideas and beliefs and cognitive distortions and misconceptions.

Not all clients process cognitions or symbolic processes in the same way. Therefore, the therapist has to be sensitive to how this component may manifest itself with each client and respond accordingly. For example, some clients can easily relate to the term *irrational ideas;* others, particularly adolescents, seem to be offended by such terminology and prefer phrases like "clean up your thinking" (Baker, 1981). Clients who process information kinesthetically may have a great deal of difficulty exploring the cognitive component because they typically don't "think" this way. In contrast, people who process visually may report cognitions as images or pictures. For example, if you ask "What do you *think* about when this happens?," the client may say "I *see* my wife getting into bed with someone else." Imagery may be a very useful supplemental assessment device with such clients. Clients who process in an auditory modality may report cognitions as "talking to myself" or "telling myself" and can probably verbalize aloud for you a chain of internal dialogue connected to the problem.

Assessment of the cognitive component is accordingly directed toward exploring the presence of both irrational and rational beliefs and images related to the identified problem. Irrational beliefs will later need to be altered. Rational beliefs are also useful during intervention. Although irrational beliefs take many forms, the most damaging ones seem to be related to "shoulds" about oneself, others, relationships, work, and so on, "awfulizing" or "catastrophizing" about things that don't turn out as we expect, "perfectionistic standards" about ourselves and often projected onto others, and "externalization," the tendency to think that outside events are responsible for our feelings and problems. The therapist will also want to be alert for the presence of cognitive distortions and misperceptions, such as overgeneralization, exaggeration, and drawing conclusions without supporting data. Finally, it is important to note what clients do and do not "say" or "think" to themselves and how that relates to the identified problem.

Leads to use to assess these aspects of the cognitive component of the identified problem include the following:

"What beliefs [or images] do you hold that contribute to this problem? make it worse? make it better?

"Complete the following sentences for me—
I should . . .
People should . . .
My husband [or mother, and so on] should . . .
Work [or school] should . . .
Sex should . . .""

"When something doesn't turn out the way you want or expect, how do you usually feel?"

"What data do you have to support these beliefs or assumptions?"

"What are you thinking about or dwelling on when this [problem] happens?"

"Can you describe what kinds of thoughts or images go through your mind when this occurs?"

"What do you say to yourself when this happens?"

"What do you say to yourself when it doesn't happen [or when you feel better, and so on]?"

"Let's set up a scene. You imagine that you're starting to feel a little upset with yourself. Now run through the scene and relate the images or pictures that come through your mind. Tell me how the scene changes [or relate the thoughts or dialogue—what you say to yourself as the scene ensues]."

Context: Time, place, and concurrent events. Problem behaviors occur in a social context, not in a vacuum. Indeed, what often makes a behavior a "problem" is the context surrounding it or the way it is linked to various situations, places, and events. For example, it is not a problem to undress in your home, but the same behavior on a public street in Western culture would be called "exhibitionism." In some other cultures, this same behavior might be more commonplace and would not be considered abnormal or maladaptive. Lazarus asserts that "if a therapist is genuinely interested in promoting constructive changes in a client . . . it is essential that he or she first obtain a comprehensive understanding of the total context in which the behaviors occur" (1976, p. 25). Looking at the context surrounding the problem has implications not only for assessment but also for intervention, because a client's cultural background, lifestyle, and values can affect how the client views the problem and also the treatment approach to resolve it. As Gambrill observes, "The norms present in given racial and cultural subgroups may expand or limit the possibilities for change" (1977, p. 118).

Assessing the context surrounding the problem is also important because most problems are "situation-specific"—that is, they are linked to certain events and situations, and they occur at certain times and places. For example, clients who say "I'm uptight" or "I'm not assertive" usually do not mean they are *always* uptight or nonassertive but, rather, in particular situations or at particular times. It is important that the therapist not reinforce the notion or belief in the client that the feeling, cognition, or behavior is pervasive. Otherwise, clients are even more likely to adopt the identity of the problem and begin to regard themselves as possessing a particular trait such as "nervousness," "social anxiety," or "nonassertiveness." They are also more likely to incorporate the problem into their lifestyle and daily functioning.

In assessing contextual factors associated with the problem, you are interested in discovering—

1. Any *cultural, ethnic, and racial affiliations,* any particular *values* associated with these affiliations, and how these values affect the client's perception of the problem and of change.
2. *Situations* or *places* in which the problem usually occurs and situations in which it does not occur (*where* the problem occurs and where it does not).
3. *Times* during which the problem usually occurs and times during which it does not occur (*when* the problem occurs and when it does not).
4. *Concurrent events*—events that typically occur at or near the same time as the problem. This information is important because sometimes it suggests a pattern or a significant chain of events related to the problem that clients might not be aware of or may not report on their own.

These are example responses to elicit information about contextual components of the problem:

"Do you have [or feel] an affiliation with any particular culture or ethnic group? [In addition to the more apparent ones, don't overlook ones such as Italian American, French Canadian, Polish American, and so on.] If so, how do the values of this group affect the way you [think about, grasp] the problem? How

do these values affect what you want to do about this problem?"

"Describe some recent situations in which this problem occurred. What are the similarities in these situations? In what situations does this usually occur? Where does this usually occur?"

"Describe some situations when this problem does not occur."

"In what situations does this not occur?"

"When does this usually occur? not occur?"

"Can you identify certain times of the day [week, month, year] when this is more likely to happen? less likely?"

"Does the same thing happen at other times or in other places?"

"What else is going on when this problem occurs?"

"Describe a typical day for me when you feel 'uptight.' "

"Are you aware of any other events that normally occur at the same time as this problem?"

In addition to the information obtained from the client's oral self-report during the assessment interviews, often both counselor and client can obtain a better idea of the context of the problem by having the client self-monitor such things as when and where the problem occurs and concurrent events.

Relationships and significant others. Just as problems are often linked to particular times, places, and events, they are also often connected to the presence or absence of other people. People around the client can bring about or exacerbate a problem. Someone temporarily or permanently absent from the client's life can have the same effect. Assessing the client's relationships with others is a significant part of many theoretical orientations to counseling, including dynamic theories, Adlerian theory, family systems theory, and behavioral theory.

Interpersonal problems may occur because of a lack of significant others in the client's life or because of the way the client relates to others or because of the way significant others respond to the client. Gambrill (1977, p. 109) observes that "social reinforcement from significant others may become an important maintaining factor [in a problem], even though it was not involved in the initial occurrence of a problematic reaction." Negative reactions from others or lack of social reinforcement can also discourage a client from seeking help or from trying to change.

Other persons involved in the problem often tend to discount their role in it. It is helpful if the therapist can get a handle on what other persons are involved in the problem, how they perceive the problem, and what they might have to gain or lose from a change in the problem or the client. As Gambrill (1977) observes, such persons may anticipate negative effects of improvement in a problem and covertly try to sabotage the client's best efforts. For example, a husband may preach "equal pay and opportunity" yet secretly sabotage his wife's efforts to move up the career ladder for fear that she will make more money than he does or that she will find her new job opportunities more interesting and rewarding than her relationship with him. Other people can also influence a client's behavior by serving as role models (Bandura, 1969). People whom clients view as significant to them can often have a great motivational effect on clients in this respect.

Example leads to use to assess the relational component of the problem include the following:

"How many significant close relationships or friendships do you have in your life now?"

"What effects does this problem have on your relationships with significant others in your life?"

"What effects do these significant others have on this problem?"

"Who else is involved in this problem besides yourself? How are these persons involved? What would their reaction be if you resolved this issue?"

"From whom do you think you learned to act or think this way?"

"What persons *present* in your life now have the greatest positive impact on you? negative impact?"

"What persons *absent* from your life have the greatest positive impact on you? negative impact?"

"Whom do you know and respect who handles this issue in a way that you like?"

Identifying Antecedents

You may recall from Chapter 7 that there are usually certain things that happen before or after a problem that contribute to it. In other words, people are not born feeling depressed or thinking of themselves as inadequate. Other events may contribute to the problem by maintaining, strengthening, or weakening the problem behaviors, thoughts, or feelings. Much of the assessment process consists in exploring contributing variables that precede and cue the problem (antecedents) and things that happen after the problem (consequences) that, in some way, influence or maintain it.

To review our previous discussion of the ABC model, remember that, like problem behaviors, the sources of antecedents and consequences are varied and may be affective, somatic, behavioral, cognitive, contextual, or relational. Further, antecedents and consequences are likely to differ for each client. Antecedents are external or internal events that occasion or cue the problem behaviors and make them more or less likely to occur. Some antecedents occur immediately before the problem; other antecedents (setting events) may have taken place a long time ago.

In helping clients explore antecedents of the problem, you are particularly interested in discovering (1) what *current* conditions (covert and overt) exist *before* the problem that make it *more likely* to occur, (2) what *current* conditions (covert and overt) exist that occur *before* the problem that make it *less likely* to occur, and (3) what *previous* conditions, or setting events, exist that *still* influence the problem.

Example leads to identify antecedents follow and are categorized according to the six possible sources of antecedents, described in Chapter 7:

Affective
"What are you usually feeling before this happens?"

"When do you recall the first time you felt this way?"

"What are the feelings that occur before the problem and make it stronger or more constant?"

"What are the feelings that occur before the problem that make it weaker or less intense?"

"Are there any holdover feelings or unfinished feelings from past events in your life that still affect this problem?"

Somatic
"What goes on inside you just before this happens?"

"Are you aware of any particular sensations in your body before this happens?"

"Are there any body sensations that occur right before this problem that make it weaker or less intense?"

"Is there anything going on with you physically —an illness or physical condition—or anything about the way you eat, smoke, exercise, and so on that affects or leads to this problem?"

Behavioral

"If I were photographing this, what actions and dialogue would I pick up before this happens?"

"Can you identify any particular behavior patterns that occur right before this happens?"

"What do you typically do before this happens?"

"Can you think of anything you do that makes this problem more likely to occur? less likely to occur?"

Cognitive

"What kinds of pictures or images do you have before this happens?"

"What are your thoughts before this happens?"

"What are you telling yourself before this happens?"

"Can you identify any particular beliefs that seem to set the problem off?"

"What do you think about [see or tell yourself] before the problem occurs that makes it stronger or more likely to occur? weaker or less likely to occur?"

Contextual

"Has this ever occurred at any other time in your life? If so, describe that."

"How long ago did this happen?"

"Where and when did this occur the first time?"

"How do you see those events related to your problem?"

"What things happened that seemed to lead up to this?"

"When did the problem start—what else was going on in your life at that time?"

"What were the circumstances under which the problem first occurred?"

"What was happening in your life when you first noticed this?"

"Are there any ways in which your cultural affiliation and values set off this problem? make it more likely to occur? less likely?"

"Are you aware of any events that occurred before this problem that in some way still influence it or set it off?"

Relational

"Can you identify any particular people that seem to bring on this problem?"

"Are you usually with certain people right before or when this occurs?"

"Whom are you usually with right before this problem occurs?"

"Can you think of any person—or of any particular reaction from a person—that makes this problem more likely to occur? less likely?"

"Are there any people or relationships from the past that still influence or set off or lead to this problem in some way?"

Identifying Consequences

Recall from Chapter 7 that consequences are external or internal events that influence the problem behavior by maintaining it, strengthening or increasing it, or weakening or decreasing it. Consequences occur after the problem behavior and are distinguished from results or effects of the problem behavior by the fact that they have direct influence on the problem by either maintaining or decreasing the problem in some way.

In helping clients explore consequences, you are interested in discovering both internal and external events that maintain and strengthen the problem behavior and also events that weaken or decrease it.

Example leads to identify consequences follow and are categorized according to the six sources of consequences described in Chapter 7.

Affective

"How do you feel after _____?"

"How does this feeling affect the problem (for example, keep it going, stop it)?"

"Are you aware of any particular feelings or emotions that you have after the problem that strengthen or weaken it?"

Somatic

"What are you aware of inside you just after this happens? How does this affect the problem?"

"Are there any body sensations that seem to occur after the problem that strengthen or weaken it?"

"Is there anything you can think of about your- self physically—illness, diet, exercise, and so on—that seems to occur after this problem? How does this affect the problem?"

Behavioral

"What do you do after this happens, and how does this make the problem worse? better?"

"How do you usually react after this is over? In what ways does your reaction keep the prob- lem going? weaken it or stop it?"

"Can you identify any particular behavior pat- terns that occur after this? How do these pat- terns keep the problem going? stop the prob- lem?"

Cognitive

"What do you usually think about afterward? How does this affect the problem?"

"What do you picture after this happens?"

"What do you tell yourself after this occurs?"

"Can you identify any particular thoughts [or beliefs or self-talk] during or after the prob- lem that make the problem better? worse?"

"Are there certain thoughts or images you have afterward that either strengthen or weaken the problem?"

Contextual

"What happened after this?"

"When does the problem usually stop or go away? get worse? get better?"

"Where are you when the problem stops? gets worse? gets better?"

"Can you identify any particular times, places, or events that seem to keep the problem going? make it worse or better?"

"Are there any ways in which your cultural affil- iation and values seem to keep this problem going? stop it or weaken it?"

Relational

"Are you usually with certain people during and after the problem? when the problem gets worse? better?"

"Can you identify any particular people who can make the problem worse? better? stop it? keep it going?"

"Can you identify any particular reactions from other people that occur after the problem? In what ways do these reactions affect the issue?"

Identifying Secondary Gains: A Special Case of Consequences

As we mentioned in Chapter 7, occasionally clients have a "vested interest" in maintaining the status quo of the problem because of the "payoffs" that the problem produces. For example, a client who is overweight may find it difficult to lose weight, not because of unalterable eating and exer- cise habits, but because the extra weight has al- lowed her to avoid or escape such things as new social situations or sexual relationships and has produced a safe and secure lifestyle that she is re- luctant to give up (Fishman & Lubetkin, 1983). A child who is constantly disrupting his school classroom may be similarly reluctant to give up such disruptive behavior even though it results in loss of privileges, because it has given him the status of "class clown," resulting in a great deal of peer attention and support.

It is always extremely important to explore with clients the "payoffs," or secondary gains, they may be getting from having the problem, because often during the intervention phase such clients seem "resistant." In these cases, the resistance is a sign the payoffs are being threatened (see also Chapter 20). The most common payoffs include money, attention from significant others, immediate grati- fication of needs, avoidance of responsibility, se- curity, and control.

Questions you can use to help clients identify possible secondary gains include these:

"The good thing about _____ is . . . ."

"What happened afterward that was pleasant?"

"What was unpleasant about what happened?"

"Has your concern or problem ever produced any special advantages or considerations for you?"

"As a consequence of your concern, have you got out of or avoided things or events?"

"What are the reactions of others when you do this?"

"How does this problem help you?"

"What do you get out of this situation that you don't get out of other situations?"

"Do you notice anything that happens after- ward that you try to prolong or to produce?"

"Do you notice anything that occurs afterward that you try to stop or avoid?"

"Are there certain feelings or thoughts that go on afterwards that you try to prolong?"

"Are there certain feelings or thoughts that go on afterwards that you try to stop or avoid?"

Exploring Previous Solutions

Another important part of the assessment interview is to explore what things the client has already tried to resolve the problem and with what effect. This information is important for two reasons. First, it helps you to avoid recommendations for problem resolution that amount to "more of the same." Second, in many instances, solutions attempted by the client either create new problems or make the existing one worse (see also Chapter 20).

Fisch, Weakland, and Segal (1982, pp. 13–14) explain how clients' attempted solutions are often responsible for the origin or persistence of problems:

Problems begin from some ordinary life difficulty, of which there is never any shortage. This difficulty may stem from an unusual or fortuitous event. More often, though, the beginning is likely to be a common difficulty associated with one of the transitions regularly experienced in the course of life — marriage, the birth of a child, going to school, and so on. . . . Most people handle most such difficulties reasonably adequately—perfect handling is neither usual nor necessary—and thus we do not see them in our offices. But for a difficulty to turn into a problem, only two conditions need to be fulfilled: (1) the difficulty is mishandled, and (2) when the difficulty is not resolved, more of the same "solution" is applied. Then the original difficulty will be escalated, by a vicious-circle process, into a problem—whose eventual size and nature may have little apparent similarity to the original difficulty.*

Leads to help the client identify previous "solutions" include the following:

"How have you dealt with this or other problems before? What was the effect? What made it work or not work?"

"How have you tried to resolve this problem?"

"What kinds of things have you done to improve this situation?"

* From *The Tactics of Change* by R. Fisch, J. H. Weakland, and L. Segal. Copyright © 1982 by Jossey-Bass. Reprinted by permission.

"What have you done that has made the problem better? worse? kept it the same?"

"What have others done to help you with this?"

Identifying the Client's Coping Skills, Strengths, and Resources

When clients come to therapists, they usually are in touch with their pain and often only with their pain. Consequently, they are shortsighted and find it hard to believe that they have any internal or external resources that can help them deal with the pain more effectively. In the assessment interview, it is useful to focus not solely on the problems and pains but also on the person's positive assets and resources (which the pain may mask). This achieves several purposes. First, it helps to convey to clients that, in spite of the psychological pain, they do have at least internal resources available that they can muster to produce a different outcome. Second, it emphasizes wholeness—the client is *more* than just his or her "problem." Third, it gives you information on potential problems that may crop up during an intervention. Finally, information about the client's past "success stories" may be applicable to current problems. Such information is extremely useful in planning intervention strategies that are geared to using the kind of problem-solving and coping skills already available in the client's repertoire.

Information to be obtained in this area includes the following:

1. Behavioral assets and problem-solving skills— at what times does the client display adaptive behavior instead of problematic behavior? Often this information can be obtained by inquiring about "opposites"—for example, "When don't you act that way?" (Lazarus, 1981).

2. Cognitive coping skills—such as rational appraisal of a situation, ability to discriminate between rational and irrational thinking, selective attention and feedback from distractions, and the presence of coping or calming "self-talk" (Meichenbaum & Cameron, 1983).

3. Self-control and self-management skills— including the client's overall ability to withstand frustration, to assume responsibility for self, to be self-directed, to control problematic behavior by either self-reinforcing or self-punishing consequences, and to perceive the self as being in control rather than being a victim of

external circumstances (Gambrill, 1977; Lazarus, 1981).

The following leads are useful in identifying these kinds of client resources and assets:

"What skills or things do you have going for you that might help you with this concern?"

"Describe a situation when this concern or problem is not interfering."

"What strengths or assets can you use to help resolve this problem?"

"When don't you act this way?"

"What kinds of thoughts or self-talk help you handle this better?"

"When don't you think in self-defeating ways?"

"What do you say to yourself to cope with a difficult situation?"

"Identify the steps you take in a situation you handle well. What do you think about and what do you do? How could these steps be applied to the present issue?"

"In what situations is it fairly easy for you to manage or control this reaction or behavior?"

"Describe any times you have been able to avoid situations in which these problems have occurred."

"To what extent can you do something for yourself in a self-directed way without relying on someone else to prod you to do it?"

"How often do you get things done by rewarding yourself in some way?"

"How often do you get things done by punishing yourself in some way?"

Exploring the Client's Perception of the Problem

Most clients have their own perception of and explanation for their problem. It is important to elicit this information during an assessment session for several reasons. First, it adds to your understanding of the problem. The therapist can note which aspects of the problem are stressed and which are ignored during the client's assessment of the issue. Second, this process gives you valuable information about "patient position," a concept we describe in greater detail in Chapter 20. Briefly stated, *patient position* refers to the client's strongly held beliefs and values—in this case, about the nature of the issue or problem (Fisch et al., 1982). Usually clients allude to such "positions" in the course of presenting their perception of the problem. Ignoring the client's position may cause the therapist to "blunder into a strategy that

will be met with resistance" (Fisch et al., 1982, p. 92). You can get clients to describe their view of the problem very concisely simply by asking them to give the problem a one-line title as if it were a movie, play, or book. Another way to elicit the client's perception of the problem that Lazarus (1981) recommends is to describe the problem in only one word and then to use the selected word in a sentence. For example, a client may say "guilt" and then "I have a lot of guilt about having an affair." The same client might title the problem "Caught between Two Lovers." This technique also works extremely well with children, who typically are quick to think of titles and words without a lot of deliberation.

Leads to use to help clients identify and describe their view of the problem include these:

"What is your understanding of this issue?"

"How do you explain this problem to yourself?"

"What does the problem mean to you?"

"What is your interpretation [analysis] of this problem?"

"What else is important to you about the problem that we haven't mentioned?"

"Give the problem a title."

"Describe the issue with just one word."

Ascertaining the Frequency, Duration, and Severity of the Problem

It is also useful to determine the intensity of the problem. In other words, you want to check out how much the problem is affecting the client and the client's daily functioning. If, for example, a client says "I feel anxious," does the client mean a little anxious or very anxious? Is this person anxious all the time or only some of the time? And does this anxiety affect any of the person's daily activities, such as eating, sleeping, or working? There are two kinds of intensity to assess: the degree of problem intensity or severity and the frequency (how often) or duration (how long) of the problem.

Degree of problem intensity.   Often it is useful to obtain a client's subjective rating of the degree of discomfort, stress, or intensity of the problem. The counselor can use this information to determine how much the problem affects the client and whether the client seems to be incapacitated or immobilized by it. As you may recall from Chapter 7, assessing the severity of the stressors in the client's life is also part of the multiaxial system of diagnostic classification of problems. To assess the degree of problem intensity, the counselor can use leads similar to these:

"You say you feel anxious. On a scale from 1 to 10, with 1 being very calm and 10 being extremely anxious, where would you be now?"
"How strong is your feeling when this happens?"
"How has this interfered with your daily activities?"
"How would your life be affected if this issue were not resolved in a year?"

In assessing degree of intensity, you are looking for a client response that indicates how strong, interfering, or pervasive the problem seems to be.

Frequency or duration of problem behaviors. In asking about frequency and duration, your purpose is to have the client identify how long (duration) or how often (frequency) the problem behaviors occur. Data about how long or how often the problem occurs *before* a counseling strategy is applied are called "baseline data." Baseline data provide information about the *present* extent of the problem. They can also be used later to compare the extent of the problem before and after a counseling strategy has been used (also see our discussion of evaluation in Chapter 10).

Leads to assess the frequency and duration of the problem behavior include the following:

"How often does this happen?"
"How many times does this occur?"
"How long does this feeling usually stay with you?"
"How much does this go on, say, in an average day?"

Some clients can discuss the severity, frequency, or duration of the problem behavior during the interview rather easily. However, many clients may be unaware of the number of times the problem occurs, how much time it occupies, or how intense it is. Most clients can give the counselor more accurate information about frequency and duration by engaging in self-monitoring of the problem behaviors with a written log. Use of logs to supplement the interview data is discussed later in this chapter.

Table 8-2 provides a review of the 11 categories of problem assessment. This table may help you

TABLE 8-2. Review of 11 problem assessment categories

I.	*Purpose* of assessment
II.	*Range* of problems
III.	*Prioritization* of problems
IV, V, VI, VII.	Identification of:

Antecedents	Problem behaviors	Consequences and secondary gains (payoffs)
Affective	Affective	Affective
Somatic	Somatic	Somatic
Behavioral	Behavioral	Behavioral
Cognitive	Cognitive	Cognitive
Contextual	Contextual	Contextual
Relational	Relational	Relational

VIII.	*Previous solutions*
IX.	*Coping skills*
X.	*Client perceptions* of problem
XI.	*Frequency, duration, severity* of problem

conceptualize and summarize the types of data you will seek during assessment interviews.

☐ LIMITATIONS OF INTERVIEW LEADS IN PROBLEM ASSESSMENT

According to Lazarus (1973, p. 407), "Faulty problem identification . . . is probably the greatest impediment to successful therapy." As we mentioned earlier in this chapter, the ABC model for viewing client problems is reflected in the problem assessment leads presented in this chapter. The leads are simply tools that the counselor can use to elicit certain kinds of client information. They are designed to be used as a "road map" to provide some direction for assessment interviews. However, the leads alone are an insufficient basis for problem assessment, because they represent only about half of the process at most—the counselor responses. The other part of the process is reflected by the responses these leads generate from the client. A complete problem assessment includes not only asking the right questions but also synthesizing and integrating the client responses.

A useful way to synthesize client responses during assessment interviews is to continue to build on and use all the fundamental helping skills presented earlier in this book. Think of it this way: In an assessment interview, you are simply *supplementing* your basic skills with some specific leads designed to obtain certain kinds of information. Many of your leads will consist of open-ended questions or probes. However, even assessment interviews should not disintegrate into a question-and-answer or interrogation session. You can obtain information and give the information some meaning through other verbal responses, such as summarization, clarification, confrontation, and reflection. It is extremely important to clarify and reflect the information the client gives you before jumping ahead to another question. The model dialogue that follows will illustrate this process.

☐ MODEL DIALOGUE FOR PROBLEM ASSESSMENT: THE CASE OF JOAN

To help you identify how these problem assessment leads are used in an interview, a dialogue of the case of Joan (from Chapter 7) is given. An explanation of the counselor's response and the counselor's rationale for using it appear in italics before the responses.

Counselor response 1 is a **rationale** *to explain to the client the* **purpose** *of the assessment interview.*

1. *Counselor:* Joan, last week you dropped by to schedule today's appointment, and you mentioned you were feeling unhappy and dissatisfied with school. It might be helpful today to take some time just to explore exactly what is going on with you and school and anything else that concerns you. I'm sure there are ways we can work with this dissatisfaction, but first I think it would be helpful to both of us to get a better idea of what all the issues are for you now. Does this fit with where you want to start today?
   Client: Yeah. I guess school is the main problem. It's really bugging me.

Counselor response 2 is a lead to help Joan identify the **range** *of her concerns.*

2. *Counselor:* OK, you just said school is the *main* problem. From the way you said that and the way you look right now, I have the feeling school isn't the *only* thing you're concerned about in your life.
   Client: Well, you're right about that. I'm also kind of not getting along too well with my folks. But that's kind of related to this school thing, too.

In the next response, the counselor will simply **listen** *to Joan and synthesize what she's saying by using a* **paraphrase** *response.*

3. *Counselor:* So from your point of view, the school thing and the issue with your parents are connected.
   Client: Yeah, because I'm having trouble in

some of my classes. There's too much competition. I feel the other kids are better than I am. I've thought about changing from this college prep program to the work-study program, but I don't know what to do. I don't like to make decisions anyway. At the same time, my folks put a lot of pressure on me to perform well, to make top grades. They have a lot of influence with me. I used to want to do well, but now I'm kind of tired of it all.

In the next response, the counselor continues to listen to Joan and **reflect her feelings.**

4. *Counselor:* It seems like you're feeling pretty overwhelmed and discouraged right now.
   Client: Yeah, I am. [Lowers head, eyes, and voice tone]

Counselor senses Joan has strong feelings about these issues and doesn't want to cut them off initially. **Instructs** *Joan to continue focusing on the feelings.*

5. *Counselor:* [Pause] Let's stay with these feelings for a few minutes and see where they take you.
   Client: [Pause; eyes fill with tears] I guess I just feel like all this stuff is coming down on me at once. I'd like to work something out, but I don't know how—or where, even—to start.

Counselor continues to **attend,** *to* **listen,** *and to* **reflect** *the client's current experience:*

6. *Counselor:* It seems like you feel you're carrying a big load on your shoulders—
   Client: Yeah.

In response 7, the counselor **summarizes** *Joan's concerns, followed by a lead to determine whether Joan has* **prioritized** *her problems.*

7. *Counselor:* I think before we're finished I'd like to come back to these feelings, which seem pretty strong for you now. Before we do, it might help you to think about not having to tackle everything all at once. You know you mentioned three different things that are bothering you—your competitive classes, having trouble making decisions, and not getting along with your parents. Which of these problems bothers you most?
   Client: I'm not really sure. I'm concerned right now about having trouble in my classes. But sometimes I think if I were in another type of curriculum, I wouldn't be so tense about these classes. But I'm sort of worried about deciding to do this.

Counselor response 8 is a **clarification.** *The counselor wants to see whether the client's interest in work-study is real or is a way to avoid the present problem.*

8. *Counselor:* Do you see getting in the work-study

program as a way to get out of your present problem classes, or is it a program that really interests you?

Client: It's a program that interests me. I think sometimes I'd like to get a job after high school instead of going to college. *But* I've been thinking about this for a year and I can't decide what to do. I'm not very good at making decisions on my own.

Counselor response 9 is a **summarization** *and* **instruction.** *The counselor goes back to the three problem areas mentioned in "Identifying the Range of Problems." Note that the counselor does not draw explicit attention to the client's last self-deprecating statement.*

9. *Counselor:* Well, your concerns of your present class problems and of making this and other decisions are somewhat related. Your parents tie into this, too. Maybe you could explore all concerns and then decide later about what you want to work on first.
Client: That's fine with me.

Counselor response 10 is a lead to **identify some present problem behaviors** *related to Joan's concern about competitive classes. Asking the client for examples can elicit specificity about what does or does not occur during the problem situation.*

10. *Counselor:* OK, what is an example of some trouble you've been having in your most competitive class?
Client: Well, I withdraw in these classes. I've been cutting my math classes. It's the worst. My grades are dropping, especially in math class.

Counselor response 11 is a **problem behavior** *lead regarding the* **context** *of the problem to see whether the client's concern occurs at other* **times** *or other* **places.**

11. Counselor: Where else do you have trouble — in any other classes, or at other times or places outside school?
Client: No, not outside school. And, to some degree, I always feel anxious in any class because of the pressures my parents put on me to get good grades. But my math class is really the worst.

Counselor response 12 is a lead to help the client identify **overt problem behaviors** *in math class (* **behavioral** *component of problem).*

12. *Counselor:* Describe what happens in your math class that makes it troublesome for you. [could also use imagery assessment at this point]
Client: Well, to start with, it's a harder class for me. I have to work harder to do OK. In this class I get nervous whenever I go in it. So I withdraw.

Client's statement "I withdraw" is vague. So counselor response 12 is another **overt problem behavior** *lead to help the client specify what she means by "withdrawing." Note that since the counselor did not get a complete answer to this after response 8, the same type of lead is used again.*

13. *Counselor:* What do you do when you withdraw? [This is also an ideal place for a role-play assessment.]
Client: Well, I sit by myself, I don't talk or volunteer answers. Sometimes I don't go to the board or answer when the teacher calls on me.

Now that the client has identified certain overt behaviors associated with the problem, the counselor will use a **covert problem behavior** *lead to find out whether there are any predominant* **thoughts** *the client has during the math class (* **cognitive** *component of problem).*

14. *Counselor:* What are you generally thinking about in this class?
Client: What do you mean — am I thinking about math?

The client's response indicated some confusion. The counselor will have to use a more specific **covert problem behavior** *lead to assess cognition, along with some* **self-disclosure,** *to help the client respond more specifically.*

15. *Counselor:* Well, sometimes when I'm in a situation like a class, there are times when my mind is in the class and other times I'm thinking about myself or about something else I'm going to do. So I'm wondering whether you've noticed anything you're thinking about during the class?
Client: Well, some of the time I'm thinking about the math problems. Other times I'm thinking about the fact that I'd rather not be in the class and that I'm not as good as the other kids.

The client has started to be more specific, and the counselor thinks perhaps there are still other thoughts going on. To explore this possibility, the counselor uses another **covert problem behavior** *lead in response 16 to assess* **cognition.**

16. *Counselor:* What else do you recall that you tell yourself when you're thinking you're not as good as other people?
Client: Well, I think that I don't get grades that are as good as some other students'. My parents have been pointing this out to me since junior high. And in the math class I'm one of four girls. The guys in there are really smart. I just keep thinking how can a girl ever be as smart as a guy in math class? No way. It just doesn't happen.

The client identifies more specific problem-related

thoughts and also suggests two possible antecedents — parental comparison of her grades and cultural stereotyping (girls shouldn't be as good in math as boys). The counselor's records show that the client's test scores and previous grades indicate that she is definitely not "dumb" in math. The counselor will **summarize** *this and then, in the next few responses, will focus on these and on other possible* **antecedents,** *such as the nervousness the client mentioned earlier.*

17. *Counselor:* So what you're telling me is that you believe most of what you've heard from others about yourself and about the fact that girls automatically are not supposed to do too well in math.
    Client: Yeah, I guess so, now that you put it like that. I've never given it much thought.

18. *Counselor:* Yes. It doesn't sound like you've ever thought about whether *you, Joan,* really feel this way or whether these feelings are just adopted from things you've heard others tell you.
    Client: No, I never have.

19. *Counselor:* That's something we'll also probably want to come back to later.
    Client: OK.

20. *Counselor:* You know, Joan, earlier you mentioned that you get nervous about this class. When do you notice that you feel this way — before the class, during the class, or at other times?
    Client: Well, right before the class is the worst. About ten minutes before my English class ends — it's right before math — I start thinking about the math class. Then I get nervous and feel like I wish I didn't have to go. Recently, I've tried to find ways to cut math class.

The counselor still needs more information about how and when the nervousness affects the client, so 21 is another **antecedent** *lead.*

21. *Counselor:* Could you tell me more about when you feel most nervous and when you don't feel nervous about this class?
    Client: Well, I feel worst when I'm actually walking to the class and the class is starting. Once the class starts, I feel better. I don't feel nervous about it when I cut it or at other times. However, once in a while, if someone talks about it or I think about it, I feel a little nervous.

The client has indicated that the nervousness seems to be more of an antecedent than a problem behavior. She has also suggested that cutting class is a consequence that maintains the problem, because she uses this to avoid the math class that brings on the nervousness. The counselor realizes at this point that the word **nervous** *has not been defined and goes back in the*

next response to a **covert problem behavior** *lead to find out what Joan means by* **nervous** *(affective component).*

22. *Counselor:* Tell me what you mean by the word *nervous* — what goes on with you when you're nervous?
    Client: Well, I get sort of a sick feeling in my stomach, and my hands get all sweaty. My heart starts to pound.

In the next response, the counselor continues to **listen** *and* **paraphrase** *to clarify whether the nervousness is experienced somatically.*

23. *Counselor:* So your nervousness really consists of things you feel going on inside you.
    Client: Yeah.

Next the counselor will use an **intensity** *lead to determine the* **severity** *of nervousness.*

24. *Counselor:* How strong is this feeling — a little or very?
    Client: Before class, very strong — at other times, just a little.

The client has established that the nervousness seems mainly to be exhibited in somatic forms and is more intense before class. The counselor will pursue the relationship between the client's nervousness and overt and covert problem behaviors described earlier to verify that the nervousness is an **antecedent.** *Another* **antecedent** *lead is used next.*

25. *Counselor:* Which seems to come first — feeling nervous, not speaking up in class, or thinking about other people being smarter than you?
    Client: Well, the nervousness. Because that starts before I get in the class.

The counselor will **summarize** *this pattern and confirm it with the client in the next response.*

26. *Counselor:* Let's see. So you feel nervous — like in your stomach and hands — before class and when math class starts. Then during class, on days you go, you start thinking about not being as smart in math as the guys and you don't volunteer answers or don't respond sometimes when called on. But after the class is over, you don't notice the nervousness so much. Is that right?
    Client: That's pretty much what happens.

The counselor has a clue from the client's previous comments that there are other antecedents in addition to nervousness that have to do with the client's problem behavior — such as the role of her parents. The counselor will pursue this in the next response, using an **antecedent** *lead.*

27. *Counselor:* Joan, you mentioned earlier that you have been thinking about not being as smart

as some of your friends ever since junior high. When do you recall you really started to dwell on this?

Client: Well, probably in seventh grade.

The counselor didn't get sufficient information about what happened to the client in the seventh grade, so another **antecedent** *lead will be used to identify this possible* **setting event.**

28. *Counselor:* Well, what things seemed to happen then when you began to compare yourself with others?

Client: Well, my parents said when you start junior high, your grades become really important in order to go to college. So for the last three or four years they have been telling me some of my grades aren't as good as other students'. Also, if I get a B, they will withhold a privilege, like my allowance.

The counselor has no evidence of actual parental reaction but will work with the client's report at this time, since this is how the client perceives parental input. If possible, a parent conference could be arranged later with the client's permission. The parents **seem** *to be using negative rather than positive consequences with Joan to influence her behavior. The counselor wants to pursue the relationship between the parents' input and the client's present behavior to determine whether parental reaction is eliciting part of Joan's present concerns and will use a lead to identify this as a possible* **antecedent.**

29. *Counselor:* How do you think this reaction of your parents' relates to your present problems in your math class?

Client: Well, since I started high school, they have talked more about needing to get better grades for college. And I have to work harder in math class to do this. I guess I feel a lot of pressure to perform—which makes me withdraw and just want to hang it up. Now, of course, my grades are getting worse, not better.

The counselor, in the next lead, will **paraphrase** *Joan's previous comment.*

30. *Counselor:* So the expectations you feel from your parents seem to draw out pressure in you.

Client: Yes, that happens.

In response 31, the counselor will explore another possible **antecedent** *that Joan mentioned before— thinking that girls aren't as good as boys in math.*

31. *Counselor:* Joan, I'd like to ask you about something else you mentioned earlier that I said we would come back to. You said one thing that you think about in your math class is that you're only

one of four girls and that, as a girl, you're not as smart in math as a boy. Do you know what makes you think this way?

Client: I'm not sure. Everyone knows or says that girls have more trouble in math than boys. Even my teacher. He's gone out of his way to try to help me because he knows it's tough for me.

The client has identified a possible consequence of her problem behavior as teacher attention. The counselor will return to this later. First, the counselor is going to respond to the client's response that "everyone" has told her this thought. Counselors have a responsibility to point out things that clients have learned from stereotypes or irrational beliefs rather than actual data, as is evident in this case from Joan's academic record. Counselor will use **confrontation** *in the next response.*

32. *Counselor:* We can deal more with this later, but it's evident to me from your records that you have a lot of potential for math. Yet you've learned to think of yourself as less capable, especially less capable than guys. This is a popular idea that people throw around in our culture. But in your case I don't see any evidence for it.

Client: You mean I really could do as well in math as the guys?

Counselor response 33 is an **interpretation** *to help the client see the relation between overt and covert behaviors.*

33. *Counselor:* I don't see why not. But lots of times the way someone acts or performs in a situation is affected by how the person thinks about the situation. I think some of the reason you're having more trouble in your math class is that your performance is hindered a little by your nervousness and by the way you put yourself down.

In the next response, the counselor **checks out** *and* **clarifies** *the client's reaction to the previous interpretation.*

34. *Counselor:* I'm wondering now from the way you're looking at me whether this makes any sense or whether what I just said "muddies the waters" more for you?

Client: No, I guess I was just thinking about things. You mentioned the word *expectations.* But I guess it's not just that my parents expect too much of me. I guess in a way I expect too little of myself. I've never really thought of that before.

35. *Counselor:* That's a great observation. In a way the two sets of expectations are probably connected. These are some of the kinds of issues we may want to work on in counseling if this track we're on seems to fit for you.

Client: Yeah. OK, it's a problem.

The counselor is going to go back now to pursue possible consequences that are influencing the client's problem behavior. The next response is a lead to identify **consequences.**

36. *Counselor:* Joan, I'd like to go back to some things you mentioned earlier. For one thing, you said your teacher has gone out of his way to help you. Would you say that your behavior in his class has got you any extra attention or special consideration from him?

    Client: Well, certainly extra attention. He's talked to me more frequently. And he doesn't get upset when I don't go to the board.

Counselor response 37 will continue to explore the teacher's behavior as a possible **consequence.**

37. *Counselor:* Do you mean he may excuse you from board work?

    Client: For sure, and I think he, too, almost expects me *not* to come up with the answer. Just like I don't expect myself to.

The teacher's behavior may be maintaining the client's overt problem behaviors in class by giving extra attention to her for her problems and by excusing her from some kinds of work. A teacher conference may be necessary at some later point. The counselor, in the next two responses, will continue to use other leads to identify possible **consequences.**

38. *Counselor:* What do you see you're doing right now that helps you get out of putting yourself through the stress of going to math class?

    Client: Do you mean something like cutting class?

39. *Counselor:* I think that's perhaps one thing you do to get out of the class. What else?

    Client: Nothing I can think of.

The client has identified cutting class as one way to avoid the math class. The counselor, in the next response, will suggest another **consequence** *that the client mentioned earlier, though not as a way to get out of the stress associated with the class. The counselor will suggest that this consequence functions as a* **secondary gain,** *or* **payoff,** *in a tentative* **interpretation** *that is "checked out" with the client in the next three responses:*

40. *Counselor:* Well, Joan, you told me earlier that your grades were dropping in math class. Is it possible that if these grades—and others—drop too much, you'll automatically be dropped from these college prep classes?

    Client: That's right.

41. *Counselor:* I'm wondering whether one possible reason for letting your grades slide is that it is almost an automatic way for you to get out of

these competitive classes.

    Client: How so?

42. *Counselor:* Well, if you became ineligible for these classes because of your grades, you'd automatically be out of this class and others that you consider competitive and feel nervous about. What do you think about that?

    Client: I guess that's true. And then my dilemma is whether I want to stay in this or switch to the work-study program.

In the next response, the counselor uses **summarization** *and ties together the effects of "dropping grades" to math class and to the earlier-expressed concern of a curriculum-change decision.*

43. *Counselor:* Right. And letting your grades get too bad will automatically mean that decision is made for you, so you can take yourself off the hook for making that choice. In other words, it's sort of a way that part of you has rather creatively come up with to get yourself out of the hassle of having to decide something you don't really want to be responsible for deciding about.

    Client: Wow! Gosh, I guess that might be happening.

44. *Counselor:* That's something you can think about. We didn't really spend that much time today exploring the issue of having to make decisions for yourself, so that will probably be something to discuss the next time we get together. I know you have a class coming up in about ten minutes, so there's just a couple more things we might look at.

    Client: OK—what next?

In the next few responses (45–52), the counselor continues to demonstrate **listening responses** *and to help Joan explore* **solutions** *she's tried already to resolve the problem. They look together at the* **effects** *of the use of the solutions Joan identifies.*

45. *Counselor:* OK, starting with the nervousness and pressure you feel in math class—is there anything you've attempted to do to get a handle on this problem?

    Client: Not really—other than talking to you about it and, of course, cutting class.

46. *Counselor:* So cutting class is the only solution you've tried.

    Client: Yeah.

47. *Counselor:* How do you think this solution has helped?

    Client: Well, like I said before—it helps mainly because on the days I don't go, I don't feel uptight.

48. *Counselor:* So you see it as a way to get rid of these feelings you don't like.
   Client: Yeah, I guess that's it.

49. *Counselor:* Can you think of any ways in which this solution has not helped?
   Client: Gee, I don't know. Maybe I'm not sure what you're asking.

50. *Counselor:* OK, good point! Sometimes when I try to do something to resolve a problem, it can make the issue better or worse. So I guess what I'm really asking is whether you've noticed that your "solution" of cutting class has in any way made the problem worse or in any way has even contributed to the whole issue?
   Client: [Pause] I suppose maybe in a way. [Pause] In that, by cutting class, I miss out on the work, and then I don't have all the input I need for tests and homework, and that doesn't help my poor grades.

51. *Counselor:* OK. That's an interesting idea. You're saying that when you look deeper, your solution also has had some negative effects on one of the problems you're trying to deal with and eliminate.
   Client: Yeah. But I guess I'm not sure what else I could do.

52. *Counselor:* At this point, you probably are feeling a little bit stuck, like you don't know which other direction or road to take.
   Client: Yeah, kind of like a broken record.

At this point, the counselor shifts the focus a little to exploration of Joan's **assets, strengths, and resources.**

53. *Counselor:* Well, one thing I sense is that your feelings of being so overwhelmed are sort of covering up the resources and assets you have within you to handle the issue and work it out. For example, can you identify any particular skills or things you have going for you that might help you deal with this issue?
   Client: [Pause] Well, are you asking me to brag about myself?

Clients often talk about their pain or limitations freely but feel reluctant to reveal their strengths, so in the next response, the counselor gives Joan a specific **directive** *and* **permission** *to talk about her* **assets.**

54. *Counselor:* Sure. Give yourself permission. That's certainly fine in here.
   Client: Well, I am pretty responsible. I'm usually fairly loyal and dependable. It's hard to make decisions for myself, but when I say I'm going to do something, I usually do it.

55. *Counselor:* OK, great. So what you're telling me is you're good on follow-through once you decide something is important to you.

Client: Yeah. Mm-hmm. Also, although I'm usually uptight in my math class, I don't have the same feeling in my English class. I'm really doing well in there.

In response 56, the counselor will pick up on these "pluses" and use another **coping skills** *lead to have the client identify particular ways in which she handles positive situations, especially her English class. If she can demonstrate the steps to succeed in one class, this is useful information that can be applied in a different and problematic area. This topic is continued in response 57.*

56. *Counselor:* So there are some things about school that are going OK for you. You say you're doing well in your English class. What can you think of that you do or don't do to help you perform well in this class?
   Client: Well, I go to class, of course, regularly. And I guess I feel like I do well in reading and writing. I don't have the hangup in there about being one of the few girls.

57. *Counselor:* So maybe you can see some of the differences between your English and math classes—and how you handle these. This information is useful because if you can start to identify the things you do and think about in English that make it go so well for you, then you potentially can apply the same process or steps to a more difficult situation, like math class.
   Client: That sounds hopeful!

In the next few responses, the counselor tries to elicit **Joan's perception and assessment of the main issue.**

58. *Counselor:* Right. It is. I feel hopeful, too. Just a couple more things. Changing the focus a little now, could you think about the issues that you came in with today—and describe the main issue in one word?
   Client: Ooh—that's a hard question!

59. *Counselor:* I guess it could be. Take your time. You don't have to rush.
   Client: [Pause] Well, how about "can't?"

60. *Counselor:* OK, now, to help me get an idea of what that word means to you, use it in a sentence.
   Client: Any sentence?

61. *Counselor:* Yeah. Make one up. Maybe the first thing that comes in your head.
   Client: Well, "I can't do a lot of things I think I want to or should be able to do."

In response 62, the counselor uses a **confrontation** *to depict the incongruity revealed in the sentence Joan made up about her problem. This theme is continued in response 63.*

62. *Counselor:* OK, that's interesting too, because

on the one hand, you're saying there are some things you *want* to do that aren't happening, and on the other hand, you're also saying there are some things that aren't happening that you think you *should* be doing. Now, these are two pretty different things mixed together in the same sentence.

Client: Yeah. [Clarifies] I think the wanting stuff to happen is from me and the should things are from my folks and my teachers.

63. *Counselor:* OK, so you're identifying part of the whole issue as wanting to please yourself and others at the same time.

Client: M-m-hmm.

*In response 64, the counselor identifies this issue as an extension of the **secondary gain** mentioned earlier—avoiding deliberate decisions.*

64. *Counselor:* I can see how after a while that would start to feel like so much trouble that it would be easier to try to let situations or decisions get made for you rather than making a conscious or deliberate choice.

*In the next two responses, the counselor explores the **context** related to these issues and sets up some **self-monitoring** homework to obtain additional information. Note that this is a task likely to appeal to the client's dependability, which she revealed during exploration of **coping skills**.*

65. *Counselor:* That's something else we'll be coming back to, I'm sure. One last thing before you have to go. Earlier we talked about some specific times and places connected to some of these issues—like where and when you get in the rut of putting yourself down and thinking you're not as smart as other people. What I'd like to do is give you sort of a diary to write in this week to collect some more information about these kinds of problems. Sometimes writing these kinds of things down can help you start making changes and sorting out the issues. You've said that you're pretty dependable. Would doing this appeal to your dependability?

Client: Sure. That's something that wouldn't be too hard for me to do.

66. *Counselor:* OK, let me tell you specifically what to keep track of, and then I'll see you next week—bring this back with you. [Goes over instructions for Joan's log sheet—see Figure 8-2, p. 205].

At this time, the counselor also has the option of giving Joan a history questionnaire to complete and/or a brief self-report inventory to complete, such as an anxiety inventory or checklist.

☐ FORMING HYPOTHESES ABOUT PROBLEMS

During and after the assessment process, the therapist is constantly developing hunches, guesses, or hypotheses about what is going on with the client and about the client's problem. Hypotheses about functional relationships among the problem, antecedents, and consequences and about "patient position" and coping skills are also generated, since these "educated guesses" provide important clues for making valid treatment decisions. The counselor relies on all the assessment information available, including that obtained from interviews, history, self-monitoring, inventories, and so on. This is also a time when the therapist's intuition is useful to help put the pieces together. To provide you with an illustration of this process, we might generate the following ideas about "the case of Joan," based on the case description given in Chapter 7 and on the interview dialogue and self-monitoring log presented in this chapter on page 205.

Joan's presenting problem of having trouble in competitive classes such as math is cued by nervousness, by pressure she has felt from her parents to perform, by being female and by the cultural stereotyping she has bought into, and by her general tendency to put herself down. The problem is maintained by the attention she receives from her math teacher, who also excuses her from doing required work, and by her low expectations and irrational beliefs and misconceptions about herself. A secondary gain at stake is that by continuing to perform poorly in her college prep classes, she will automatically be disqualified from this curriculum, thereby effectively eliminating her need to make a deliberate choice about her curriculum, which is another presenting problem. This second problem (difficulty in making independent decisions) is also cued by her low expectations for herself and by her lack of confidence in her decision-making ability. It is maintained by a desire to please her parents, a lack of opportunities to make decisions, and perhaps by negative parental reactions when she made independent decisions in the past. Another secondary gain may be that this problem keeps her from taking too many risks and from becoming self-reliant and allows her to continue to be rather dependent on others for security and protection. (A way to look at this from an alternative treatment orientation would be that having the problem allows her to stay in her Child ego state, which is also heavily reinforced by her parents, who transact with her from Parental rather than Adult ego states. Another alternative interpretation is that she has never learned or has never been challenged to assume *self* rather than environmental support until recently, which is creating a push/pull conflict for her.) Information gleaned from the interview suggests that she views the problem as an extension of the decision-making issue — as something she can't do rather than something she chooses not to do. At the same time, she seems to be somewhat dependable and has demonstrated the steps and processes required to handle one class successfully. This information can be helpful for selecting strategies that appeal to

her dependability and also capitalize on the behavioral and cognitive coping skills she has been able to use in successful situations. Her tenacity and coping skills will be assets during intervention. A major difficulty will be devising and implementing strategies that challenge her to rely on herself and assume more responsibility and self-direction without unduly threatening her present "payoffs" for dependence and support from others.

In the chapter Postevaluation you will have an opportunity to develop hunches about the client based on information obtained in an assessment interview.

LEARNING ACTIVITIES #25: INTERVIEW ASSESSMENT

I. The following activity is designed to assist you in identifying problem assessment leads in an interview. You are given a counselor/client dialogue of the case of Ms. Weare and Freddie (Chapter 7). This dialogue consists of an interview with the mother, Ms. Weare. For each counselor response, your task is to identify and write down the type of problem assessment lead used by the counselor. You may find it helpful to use the Interview Checklist at the end of the chapter as a guide for this learning activity. There may be more than one example of any given lead in the dialogue. Also, responses from previous chapters (listening and action) may be used. Other basic verbal interview responses are also included. Feedback follows the Learning Activities (on page 206).

Dialogue with Ms. Weare and Counselor

1. *Counselor:* Hello, Ms. Weare. Could you tell me about some things going on now that are concerning you?
   Client: Not too much. Family Services sent me here.
2. *Counselor:* So you're here just because they sent you — or is there something bothering you?
   Client: Well, they don't think my kid and I get along too well. My kid is Freddie.
3. *Counselor:* What do you think about the way you and Freddie get along?
   Client: Well, I yell at him a lot. I don't like to do that but sometimes he gets me so mad. I don't like to, but he needs to learn.
4. *Counselor:* So there are times when you get real mad at Freddie and then you yell at him. You don't like to do this, but you see it as a way to help him learn right and wrong.
   Client: That's it. I don't like to, but there are

times when he needs to know something. Like yesterday, I bought him new pants and he came home from school with a big hole in them. Now I just don't have money to keep buying him new pants.
5. *Counselor:* You just mentioned the incident with Freddie's pants. What are some other times that you get mad at Freddie?
   Client: Every morning. Freddie's in fifth grade now. But he still doesn't dress himself in the morning. I want to be a good mother and get him to school on time, and he tries to be late. He waits around not getting dressed.
6. *Counselor:* Any other times you can remember getting mad?
   Client: Well, not too long ago he was playing outside and broke a window. I got mad then. But that doesn't happen every day like his not getting dressed does.
7. *Counselor:* So one thing that really bothers you is what goes on in the mornings. Could you tell me exactly what does happen each morning at your house?
   Client: Well, I call Freddie to get up and tell him to dress before he comes down for breakfast. He comes down all right — in his pajamas. I warn him after breakfast to get ready. Usually about five minutes before the bus comes, I'll go up. He'll just be sitting in his room! He's still not dressed. I'll yell at him and then dress him so he's not late.
8. *Counselor:* And your main feeling at this point is that you're mad. Anything else you feel?
   Client: No, just very mad.
9. *Counselor:* And what exactly do you do when you go upstairs and he's not dressed?
   Client: I yell at him. Then I help dress him.
   (continued)

10. *Counselor:* What kinds of things do you usually say to him?

    Client: I tell him he's dumb and he's going to be late for school, and that I have to make sure he won't be.

11. *Counselor:* You mentioned this happens in the morning. Does this situation go on every morning or only some mornings?

    Client: Just about every morning except weekends.

12. *Counselor:* When did these incidents seem to begin?

    Client: Ever since Freddie started going to school.

13. *Counselor:* So it appears that this has been going on for about five or six years, then?

    Client: Yes, I guess so.

14. *Counselor:* OK, now let's go back over this situation. You told me you remind Freddie every morning to get dressed. He never dresses by breakfast. You remind him again. Then, about five minutes before the bus comes, you go upstairs to check on him. When do you notice that you start to feel mad?

    Client: I think about it as soon as I realize it's almost time for the bus to come and Freddie isn't down yet. Then I feel mad.

15. *Counselor:* And what exactly do you think about right then?

    Client: Well, that he's probably not dressed and that if I don't go up and help him, he'll be late. Then I'll look like a bad mother if I can't get my son to school on time.

16. *Counselor:* So in a sense you actually go help him out so he won't be late. How many times has Freddie ever been late?

    Client: Never.

17. *Counselor:* You believe that helping Freddie may prevent him from being late. However, your help also excuses Freddie from having to help himself. What do you think would happen if you stopped going upstairs to check on Freddie in the morning?

    Client: Well, I don't know, but I'm his only parent. Freddie's father isn't around. It's up to me, all by myself, to keep Freddie in line. If I didn't go up and if Freddie was late all the time, his teachers might blame me. I wouldn't be a good mother.

18. *Counselor:* Of course, we don't *really* know what would happen if you didn't go up and yell at him or help him dress. It might be so different for Freddie after the first day or two he would dress himself. It could be that he thinks it's easier to wait and get your help than to dress himself.

He might think that by sitting up there and waiting for you to help, he's getting a special advantage or attention from you.

    Client: You mean like he's getting a favor from me?

19. *Counselor:* Sure. And when we find a way to get a favor from someone, we usually do as much as we can to keep getting the favor. Ms. Weare, I'd like to ask you about something else. Do you think maybe that you see helping Freddie out as a way to avoid having Freddie be late and then not having someone blame you for this?

    Client: Sure. I'd rather help him than get myself in hot water.

20. *Counselor:* OK, so you're concerned about what you think might happen to you if he's late. You see getting him ready on time as a way to prevent you from getting the heat for him.

    Client: Yes.

21. *Counselor:* How do you usually feel after these incidents in the morning are over?

    Client: Well, it upsets me.

22. *Counselor:* OK, you feel upset. Do these feelings seem to make you want to continue or to stop helping Freddie?

    Client: Probably to stop. I get worn out. Also, sometimes I don't get my work done then.

23. *Counselor:* So helping Freddie so he won't be late and you won't be blamed sort of makes you want to keep on helping him. Yet when you feel upset and worn out afterward, you're tempted to stop helping. Is this right?

    Client: I guess that could be true.

24. *Counselor:* Gee, I imagine that all the responsibility for a 10-year-old boy would start to feel like a pretty heavy burden after a while. Would it be right to say that it seems like you feel very responsible for Freddie and his behavior?

    Client: Yeah. I guess a lot of the time I do.

25. *Counselor:* Those may be feelings we'll want to talk about more. I'm also wondering whether there are any other things in your life causing you any difficulty now?

    Client: No, this is about it.

26. *Counselor:* Ms. Weare, we've been talking a lot about some problem situations you've had with Freddie. Could you tell me about some times when the two of you get along OK?

    Client: Well, on weekends we do. Freddie dresses himself whenever he gets up. I sleep later.

27. *Counselor:* What happens on weekends when the two of you get along better?

    Client: Sometimes I'll take him to a movie or a

(continued)

LEARNING ACTIVITIES #25: INTERVIEW ASSESSMENT (continued)

game. And we eat all our meals together. Usually weekends are pleasant. He can be a good boy and I don't scream all the time at him.

28. *Counselor:* So you realize it is possible for the two of you to get along. How do you feel about my talking with Freddie and then with both of you together?
Client: That's OK.

II. To incorporate the interview leads into your verbal repertory. We suggest that you try a role-play interview of the case of Ms. Weare (Chapter 7) or the case of Mr. Brown (Chapter 7) with a triad. One person can take the role of the client (Ms. Weare or Mr. Brown), another can be the counselor. Your task is to assess the client's concerns using the interview leads described in this chapter. The third person can be the observer, providing feedback to the counselor during

or following the role-play, using the Interview Checklist at the end of the chapter as a guide.

III. A 40-year-old married woman with two young children complains of listlessness, fatigue, and depression. You also discover that she has become dependent on sleeping pills in order to go to sleep at night. She says that if she does not take the pills, she lies awake at night and so many thoughts and worries run through her head that she cannot go to sleep for several hours. Outline in writing the kinds of information you would seek from her during an assessment interview. An example is given to start with.

Example

Range of problems: Are there any other problems not reported, such as problems with her children, marital stress, or boredom?

□ NOTES AND RECORD KEEPING

Generally, some form of written record is started from the time the client requests an appointment. Identifying data about the client are recorded initially, as well as appointment times, cancellations, and so on. The intake or initial history-taking session is recorded next. In writing up an intake or history, it is important to avoid labels, jargon, and inferences. If records were subpoenaed, such statements could appear inflammatory or slanderous. Be as specific as possible. Don't make evaluative statements or clinical judgments without supporting documentation. For example, instead of writing "This client is homicidal," you might write "This client reports engaging in frequent (at least twice daily) fantasies of killing an unidentified or anonymous victim," or instead of "The client is disoriented," consider "The client could not remember where he was, why he was here, what day it was, and how old he was."

It is also important to keep notes of subsequent treatment sessions and of client progress. These can be recorded on a standardized form such as the Individualized Client Treatment Plan (Table 8.3) or in narrative form. Generally, treatment notes are brief and highlight only the major activities of each session and client progress and improvement (or lack of it). These notes are usually started during intakes, with additional information added from the assessment interview(s). As therapy progresses, notations about goals, intervention strategies, and client progress are also included. Again,

TABLE 8-3. Individualized client treatment plan

Client's name _____

Date _____

DSM-III diagnosis
    Axis I _____
    Axis II _____
    Axis III _____
    Axis IV _____
    Axis V _____

Identified problems
    1. _____
    2. _____
    3. _____
    4. _____
    5. _____

Problem antecedents
    P1[a] _____
    P2 _____
    P3 _____
    P4 _____
    P5 _____

Problem consequences
    P1 _____
    P2 _____
    P3 _____
    P4 _____
    P5 _____

Treatment goals
    P1 _____
    P2 _____
    P3 _____
    P4 _____
    P5 _____

TABLE 8-3. (continued)

Intervention strategies and treatment modalities
P1 _____
P2 _____
P3 _____
P4 _____
P5 _____

Evaluation
  A. Expected length of treatment _____
  B. Method of assessing treatment process _____
  C. Method of assessing goals or treatment outcomes
_____
_____
_____

---

[a] *P* stands for problem; *P1* refers to #1 under "Identified problems," *P2* to #2, and so on.
Adapted from a form developed by Albert Scott and Karen Scott. Reprinted by permission of authors.

labels and inferences should always be avoided in written notes and records.

It is also important to document in detail anything that has ethical or legal implications, particularly facts about case management. For example, with a client who reports depression and suicidal fantasies, it would be important to note that you conducted a suicide assessment and what its results were, that you consulted with your supervisor, and whether you did anything else to manage the case differently, such as seeing the client more frequently or setting up a contract with the client.

☐ CLIENT SELF-MONITORING ASSESSMENT

The data given by the client in the interview can be supplemented by client self-monitoring outside the interview. Self-monitoring can be defined as the process of observing specific things about oneself and one's interaction with others and the environment. In using self-monitoring as a problem assessment tool, the client is asked to record her or his observations in writing. These written recordings can be entered on a log (Schwartz & Goldiamond, 1975) or a daily record sheet.

One purpose of client self-monitoring is to help the counselor and client gain information about what actually occurs with respect to the problem in real-life settings. Another purpose is to validate the accuracy of the client's oral reports during the interviews. As Linehan (1977, p. 45) points out, sometimes the client's interview description is not a complete report of the events that occur, or the way the client describes the events differs from the way the client actually experiences them. Client self-monitoring of problem situations and behaviors outside the interview should add more accuracy and specificity to the information discussed in the interview. As a result, client self-monitoring may accelerate treatment and enhance the client's expectations for change (Shelton & Ackerman, 1974, p. 7). Self-monitoring is also a useful way to test out hunches about the problem and to identify relations between classes of events such as thoughts, feelings, and behaviors (Hollon & Kendall, 1981).

As we mentioned earlier, a client can record observations on some type of written record, or log. Two types of logs can be used for different observations a client might make during problem definition. A *descriptive log* can be used to record data about identification and selection of problem concerns. A *behavior log* can be used to record information about the problem behaviors and their antecedents and consequences or the relation between these classes of events related to the problem.

Descriptive Logs

In an initial session with a client, a simple descriptive or exploratory log can be introduced to find out what is going on with the client, where, and when (Schwartz & Goldiamond, 1975). Such a descriptive log could be set up as shown in Figure 8-1. The descriptive log is extremely useful when the client has difficulty identifying problem concerns or pinpointing problem situations. However, once the problem concerns have been identified and selected, a counselor and client may find that a behavior log is helpful as an interview adjunct for defining the ABCs of the problem.

Behavior Logs

The ABCs of a problem situation and the intensity of the problem can be clarified with client self-monitoring of the problem behaviors, the contributing conditions, and the frequency or duration of the problem behavior. All this information can be recorded in a behavior log, which is simply an extension of the descriptive log. Figure 8-2 is an example of a behavior log for our client Joan.

The client is also asked to observe and record how long (duration) or how often (frequency) the problem behaviors occur. Determining the level of the present problem serves as a baseline — that is, the rate or level of the problem *before* any counsel-

DAILY RECORD SHEET

Date	Time	Place	Activity	People	Observed behavior

Figure 8-1. *A descriptive log*

ing interventions have been started. The baseline is useful initially in helping establish the direction and level of change desired by the client. This information, as you will see in Chapter 9, is essential in establishing client goals. And as counseling progresses, these baseline data may help the client compare progress during and near the end of counseling with progress at the beginning of counseling (see Chapter 10).

In a behavior log, the defined problem behaviors are listed at the left. The client records the date, time, and place when these behaviors occur. To record contributing conditions, the client is asked to write down the behaviors and events that occur before and after the problem behaviors. This information helps to establish a pattern among the problem behaviors, things that cue or elicit the problem behaviors, and activities that maintain, strengthen, or weaken those behaviors.

Uses of Logs

The success of written logs may depend on the client's motivation to keep a log as well as on the instructions and training given to the client about the log. Five guidelines may increase the client's motivation to engage in self-monitoring:

1. Establish a rationale for the log, such as "We need a written record in order to find out what is going on. This will help us make some decisions about the best way to handle your problem." A client is more likely to keep a log if he or she is aware of a purpose for doing so.

2. Provide specific, detailed instructions regarding how to keep the log. The client should be told *what, how, when,* and for *how long* to record. The client should be given an example of a model log to see how it may look. Providing adequate instructions may increase the likelihood that the client will record data consistently and accurately.

3. Adapt the type of log to the client's ability to do self-monitoring. At first, you may need to start

with a very simple log that does not require a great deal of recording. Gradually, you can increase the amount of information the client observes and records. If a client has trouble keeping a written log, a substitute can be used, such as a tape recorder, golf wrist counter, or, for children, gold stars or pictures. Schwartz and Goldiamond (1975, p. 106) point out that even clients who seem "out of contact" with themselves are able to keep a log if they are not overwhelmed with entries and if attention to their entries is given promptly.

4. Adapt the log and the instructions to the client's problem and degree and type of pathology, if present. Recent evidence suggests that clients exhibiting certain types of problems appear to experience predictable types of problems in implementing self-monitoring, particularly of covert, or cognitive, events (Bemis, 1980). Hollon and Kendall (1981, pp. 350–351) summarize some of these reactions:

Depressed clients either frequently report being overwhelmed by what seems to be an unmanageable task and/or fail to initiate or maintain monitoring because they do not anticipate that it can provide any help. Anxious clients (e.g., Beck & Emery, 1979) frequently avoid attending to cognitions because doing so seems to increase distress. Anorexic clients rarely report effects, per se. Rather, they list strings of inferential descriptions when asked to record how they feel. If asked to evaluate the validity of their beliefs, they are likely to respond with moralistic prescriptions, reminiscent of "New Year's resolutions" (Bemis, 1980). Obsessive clients, as might be expected, rarely get beyond listing their thoughts—frequently working long and hard to get it just "right."*

* From "*In vivo* assessment techniques for cognitive-behavioral processes" by S. D. Hollon and P. C. Kendall. In *Assessment Strategies for Cognitive-Behavioral Interventions* by P. C. Kendall and S. D. Hollon (Eds.). Copyright © 1981 by Academic Press. Reprinted by permission.

For Joan _____

Week of Nov. 6–13 _____

(Problem behaviors) Behavior observing	Date	Time	Place	(Frequency/ duration) Number or amount	(Antecedents) What precedes behavior	(Consequences) What follows behavior
1. Thinking of self as not as smart as other students	Mon., Nov. 6	10:00 A.M.	Math class	IIII	Going into class, know have to take test in class	Leaving class, being with friends
	Tues., Nov. 7	10:15 A.M.	Math class	IIII IIII	Got test back with a B	Teacher consoled me
	Tues., Nov. 7	5:30 P.M.	Home	IIII II	Parents asked about test. Told me to stay home this weekend	Went to bed
	Thurs., Nov. 9	9:30 A.M.	English class	II	Thought about having to go to math class	Got to math class. Had substitute teacher
	Sun., Nov. 12	8:30 P.M.	Home	III	Thought about school tomorrow	Went to bed
2. a. Not volunteering answers	Tues., Nov. 7	10:05 A.M. 10:20	Math class	II	Felt dumb	Nothing
b. Not answering teacher questions	Thurs., Nov. 9	10.10 A.M. 10:20 10:40	Math class	III	Felt dumb	Nothing
c. Not going to board	Thurs., Nov. 9	10:30 A.M.	Math class	I	Teacher called on me	Nothing
	Fri., Nov. 10	10:10 A.M. 10:35 A.M.	Math class	II	Teacher called on me	Nothing
	Thurs., Nov. 9	10:45 A.M.	Math class	I	Didn't have a substitute teacher	Nothing
	Fri., Nov. 10	10:15 A.M.	Math class	I	Teacher asked girls to go up to board	Teacher talked to me after class
3. Cutting class	Wed., Nov. 8	9:55 A.M.	School	1 hour	Didn't want to hassle class or think about test	Cut class. Played sick. Went to nurse's office for an hour

Figure 8-2. Example of behavior log

FEEDBACK #25: INTERVIEW ASSESSMENT

I. Identifications of the responses in the dialogue between Ms. Weare and the counselor are as follows:

1. Open-ended question (probe)
2. Clarification response
3. Open-ended question (probe)
4. Summarization response
5. Paraphrase response and problem behavior lead: exploration of context
6. Problem behavior lead: exploration of context
7. Paraphrase response and problem behavior lead: exploration of overt behavior
8. Reflection-of-feeling response and problem behavior lead: exploration of affect
9. Problem behavior lead: exploration of overt behavior
10. Problem behavior lead: exploration of overt behavior
11. Paraphrase and problem behavior lead: exploration of context
12. Antecedent lead: context
13. Clarification response
14. Summarization response and antecedent lead: affect
15. Problem behavior lead: exploration of cognitions
16. Paraphrase and probe responses
17. Consequences: overt behavior
18. Consequences: secondary gains for Freddie
19. Consequences: secondary gains for Ms. Weare
20. Summarization response and exploration of secondary gains for Ms. Weare
21. Consequences: affect
22. Consequences: affect
23. Summarization (of consequences)
24. Reflection-of-feeling and interpretation responses
25. Range-of-problems lead
26. Coping skills
27. Coping skills
28. Paraphrase and open-ended question

III. In addition to range and prioritization of problems, pertinent information to seek includes the following:

1. *Description of problem behaviors*—listlessness, fatigue, depression, insomnia:
   a. *Feelings* associated with each
   b. *Body sensations* and/or *physiological responses,* illness, and so on associated with each
   c. *Behavioral reactions/patterns* associated with each
   d. *Cognitions*—thoughts, self-talk, belief systems associated with each
   e. *Times and places* when these problems occur
   f. *People* connected with these problems
2. *Antecedent sources* that set off the listlessness, fatigue, depression, insomnia—including feelings, body sensations, and physiological responses, behavioral reactions and patterns, cognitions, self-talk, times and places, and people.
3. *Consequences* that influence the listlessness, fatigue, depression, and insomnia—and ways in which they influence these behaviors. Potential sources of consequences to "check out" include feelings, body sensations and physiological responses, behavioral reactions/patterns, thoughts, beliefs, self-talk, times, situations, and reactions from other people.
4. *Secondary gains* that client may be receiving from reported symptoms, such as undivided attention from spouse and avoidance of child care or household duties.
5. *Previous solutions*—explore what, if anything, client has done to solve these concerns and the effects the solutions have had on the symptoms.
6. *Coping skills*—times when the client does not feel fatigued and depressed and what is different at these times. In addition, behavioral and cognitive assets and coping skills of client that might be applied to problems—that is, things client does or thinks about that are effective rather than self-defeating. Also explore degree to which client typically engages in self-reliant and self-directed behavior.
7. *Client's perceptions of problems*—find out how client explains these symptoms to herself; ask her to summarize her main issue in one word.
8. *Intensity of problem*—frequency, duration, severity; explore how often these symptoms occur, how long they last, and how severe they are. Determine to what degree they affect the client's level of daily functioning.

5. Involve the client in discussing and analyzing the log within the interview. At first, the counselor can begin by putting together "hunches" about

patterns of problem behavior and contributing conditions. As counseling progresses, the client can take a more active role in analyzing the log. Increasing the client's involvement in analyzing the log should serve as an incentive to the client to continue the time and effort required to collect the data.

The counselor should remember that the process of client self-monitoring can be reactive. In other words, the very act of observing oneself can influence that which is being observed. This reactivity may affect the data reflected in the log. Reactivity can be helpful in the overall counseling program when it changes the behavior in the desired direction. There are times when self-monitoring is used deliberately as a change strategy to increase or decrease a particular behavior (see Chapter 19).

Occasionally, when self-monitoring is used as an assessment tool, reactivity may cause an aspect of the problem behavior to get worse. This seems especially true when the client is monitoring negative affect, such as anxiety, anger, or depression (Hollon & Kendall, 1981). In such instances, sometimes the self-monitoring becomes a signal for the mood state, causing it to increase in frequency or intensity. If this happens, the use of self-monitoring as an *assessment* device should be discontinued, although using it as a change strategy and changing what and how the client self-records may create reactivity in the desired direction (see also Chapter 19).

The data obtained from client self-monitoring are used not only during the assessment process but also in establishing client goals. During assessment sessions, the self-monitoring data will help the client and counselor to determine the ABCs of the problem. The baseline data will be the starting place for the discussion of desired counseling outcomes (see Chapter 9).

for clients in crisis or for practitioners in high-demand, high-caseload work settings. Regardless of the type of clients with whom you work or your work setting, we encourage you to view the assessment phase of counseling with healthy respect. Skipping or glossing over assessment can actually result in longer treatment and end up costing more of your time and of the client's money. Epstein and Bishop (1981) observe that a thorough assessment usually results in a more active and shorter course of treatment by eliminating a lot of guesswork. Epstein and Bishop (1981) also observe that thorough assessment seems to prevent client dropout from therapy.

Occasionally, even after a thorough assessment period, you may still feel that there are chunks of missing information or pieces to the puzzle. It is difficult to know whether additional assessment strategies are warranted in terms of time and cost and, most important, whether they will contribute to the effectiveness of treatment for this client. At this point, the counselor must make a deliberate therapeutic decision—to conduct additional assessments or to begin intervention strategies and work on what is known about the client. Fensterheim (1983) suggests three key questions to consider before making this decision:

1. Is enough information present to make a start on treatment?
2. How urgent is the need for immediate relief?
3. How pessimistic and despondent is the patient?

We would like to conclude this chapter with one caution: above all, remember that assessment is not an end in itself! The time, structure, and tools you use for assessment are of little value unless assessment has sufficient "treatment validity" (Nelson, 1983) or contributes to greater effectiveness of therapy treatment and outcome for clients.

□ WHEN IS "ENOUGH" ASSESSMENT ENOUGH?

Occasionally people will wonder whether assessment goes on forever—or when it stops! As we mentioned earlier, assessment is something of a continuous process during therapy, in that clients are people and can't—or shouldn't—be pigeonholed, and occasionally problems are shifted and redefined.

Shorter assessment periods are often necessary

□ SUMMARY

This chapter focused on the use of direct interviewing to assess client concerns. In many settings, initial assessment interviews often begin with an intake interview to gather information about the client's presenting problems and primary symptoms as well as information about such areas as previous counseling, social/developmental history, educational/vocational history, health history, and family, marital, and sexual history. This interview often yields information that the counselor can use to develop hypotheses about the nature of the client's problems. History interviews also serve as a retrospective baseline of how the client was functioning before and what events contributed to the present difficulties and coping styles. For occasional clients, intakes or history interviews may be followed by a mental-status exam, which aids the therapist in assessing the client's psychiatric status.

The model presented in this chapter for direct assessment interviewing is based on the ABC model described in Chapter 7. Specifically, counselors are interested in defining six components of problem behavior—affective, somatic, behavioral, cognitive, contextual, and relational. They also seek to identify antecedent events that occur before the problem and cue it and consequent events that follow the problem and in some way influence it or maintain it. Consequences may include "payoffs," or secondary gains, which give value to the dysfunctional behavior and thus keep the problem going. Antecedent and consequent sources may also be affective, somatic, behavioral, cognitive, contextual, and relational. Other important components of direct assessment interviewing include identifying previous solutions the client has tried for resolving the problem, exploring client coping skills and assets, exploring the client's perceptions of the issue, and identifying the frequency, duration, or severity of the problem.

In addition to direct assessment interviewing, other assessment tools include role playing, imagery, self-report measures, and self-monitoring. All these techniques can be useful for obtaining more specific information about the identified problems.

POSTEVALUATION

PART ONE

A client is referred to you with a presenting problem of "free-floating," or generalized (pervasive), anxiety. Outline the questions you would ask during an assessment interview with this client that pertain directly to her presenting component. Your objective (Objective One) is to identify at least 2 questions for each of the 11 problem assessment categories described in this chapter and summarized in Table 8-2. Feedback follows the postevaluation.

PART TWO

Using the description of the above client, conduct a 30-minute role-play assessment interview in which your objective is to demonstrate leads and responses associated with at least 9 out of the 11 categories described for problem assessment (Chapter Objective Two). You can do this activity in triads in which one person assumes the role of counselor, another the "anxious" client, and the third person the role of observer; trade roles two times. If groups are not available, audiotape or videotape your interview. Use the Interview Checklist at the end of the chapter as a guide to assess your performance and to obtain feedback.

After completing your interview, develop some hypotheses, or hunches, about the client. In particular, try to develop "guesses" about—

1. Antecedent sources that cue or set off the anxiety, making its occurrence more likely.

2. Consequences that maintain the anxiety, keep it going, or make it worse.
3. Consequences that diminish or weaken the anxiety.
4. Secondary gains, or "payoffs," attached to the anxiety.
5. Ways in which the client's "previous solutions" may contribute to the anxiety or make it worse.
6. Particular strengths, resources, and coping skills of the client and how these might be best used during treatment/intervention.

You may wish to continue this part of the activity in triads or to do it alone, jotting down ideas as you proceed. At some point, it may be helpful to share your ideas with your group or your instructor.

PART THREE

Devise a self-monitoring assessment procedure you could give to this client for homework, to obtain information about the time, place, frequency, duration, and severity of her anxious feelings. Write an example of a log you could give to her to obtain this information (Chapter Objective Three).

PART FOUR

Conduct a role-play interview with this client in which you assign the self-monitoring plan you devised as homework (Chapter Objective Four).

(continued)

1. Provide a *rationale* to the client about the usefulness of the assignment.
2. Provide the client with detailed *instructions* about *what, how, when,* and for *how long* to monitor.
3. Follow-up—clarify and check out the client's understanding of your assignment.

If possible, continue with this activity in your triads and obtain feedback from the observer on the specificity and clarity of your instructions. If an observer is not available, tape your interview for self-assessment of its playback.

INTERVIEW CHECKLIST FOR ASSESSING CLIENT PROBLEMS

Scoring		Category of information	Examples of counselor leads or responses	Client response
Yes	No			
____	____	1. Explain purpose of assessment interview	"I am going to be asking you more questions than usual so that we can get an idea of what is going on. Getting an accurate picture about your concern (or problem) will help us to decide what we can do about it. Your input is important."	____(check if client confirmed understanding of purpose)
____	____	2. Identify range of concerns and/or problems (if you don't have this information from history)	"What would you like to talk about today?" "How would you describe the things that are really bothering you now?" "What are some things that bug you?" "What specifically led you to come to see someone now?" "What things are not going well for you?" "Are there any other issues you haven't mentioned?"	____(check if client described additional concerns)
____	____	3. Prioritize and select primary or most immediate problem to work on	"What issue best represents the reason you are here?" "Of all these concerns, which one is most stressful (or painful) for you?" "Rank-order these concerns, starting with the one that is most important for you to resolve to the one least important." "Tell me which of these problems you believe you could learn to deal with most easily and with the most success." "Which one of the things we discussed do you see as having the best chance of being solved?" "Out of all the problems we've discussed, describe the one that, when resolved, would have the greatest impact on the rest of the issues."	____(check if client selected problem to focus on)
____	____	4.0. Present problem-behavior		____(check if client identified the following components of problem)
		4.1. Affective aspects of problem: feelings, emotions, mood states	"What are you feeling when this happens?" "How does this make you feel when this occurs?" "What other feelings do you have when this occurs?" "What feelings is this problem hiding or covering up?"	____(check if client identified feelings)
				(continued)

POSTEVALUATION (continued)

Scoring	Category of information	Examples of counselor leads or responses	Client response
—— ——	4.2. *Somatic* aspects of problem: body sensations, physiological responses, organic dysfunction and illness, medications	"What goes on inside you then?" "What do you notice in your body when this happens?" "What are you aware of when this happens?" "When this happens, are you aware of anything that goes on in your body that feels bad or uncomfortable — aches, pains, and so on?"	——(check if client identified body sensations)
—— ——	4.3. *Behavioral* aspects of problem: overt behaviors/actions (excesses and deficits)	"In photographing this scene, what actions and dialogue would the camera pick up?" "What are you doing when this occurs?" "What do you mean by 'not communicating'?" "Describe what you did the last few times this occurred."	——(check if client identified overt behavior)
—— ——	4.4. *Cognitive* aspects of problem: automatic, helpful, unhelpful, rational, irrational thoughts and beliefs; internal dialogue; perceptions and misperceptions	"What do you say to yourself when this happens?" "What are you usually thinking about during this problem?" "What was going through your mind then?" "What kinds of thoughts can make you feel _____ ?" "What beliefs [or images] do you hold that affect this issue?" Sentence completions: I should _____, people should _____, it would be awful if _____, _____ makes me feel bad.	——(check if client identified thoughts, beliefs)
—— ——	4.5. *Contextual* aspects of problem: time, place, or setting events	"Describe some recent situations in which the problem occurred. Where were you? When was it?" "When does this usually occur?" "Where does this usually occur?" "Does this go on all the time or only sometimes?" "Does the same thing happen at other times or places?" "At what time does this *not* occur? places? situations?" "Do you have any affiliation with a cultural or ethnic group, and if so, how do the values of this group affect this issue?"	——(check if client identified time, places, other events)
—— ——	4.6. *Relational* aspects of problem: other people	"What effects does this problem have on significant others in your life?" "What effects do significant others have on this problem?" "Who else is involved in the problem? How?"	——(check if client identified people)

(continued)

Scoring	Category of information	Examples of counselor leads or responses	Client response
		"From whom do you think you learned to act or react this way?" "How many significant close relationships do you have in your life now?" "Whom do you know and respect who handles the issue the way you would like to?" "What persons *present* in your life now have the greatest positive impact on this problem? negative impact?" "What about persons *absent* from your life?"	
____ ____	5.0. Antecedents— past or current conditions that cue, or set off, the problem		____ (check if client identified following antecedent sources)
____ ____	5.1. *Affective* antecedents	"What are you usually feeling before this?" "When do you recall the first time you felt this way?" "What are the feelings that occur before the problem and make it more likely to happen? less likely?" "Are there any holdover or unfinished feelings from past events in your life that still affect this problem? How?"	____ (feelings, mood states)
____ ____	5.2. *Somatic* antecedents	"What goes on inside you just before this happens?" "Are you aware of any particular sensations or discomfort just before the problem occurs or gets worse?" "Are there any body sensations that seem to occur before the problem or when it starts that make it more likely to occur? less likely?" "Is there anything going on with you physically—like illness or a physical condition or in the way you eat or drink—that leads up to this problem?"	____ (body sensations, physiological responses)
____ ____	5.3. *Behavioral* antecedents	"If I were photographing this, what actions and dialogue would I pick up before this happens?" "Can you identify any particular behavior patterns that occur right before this happens?" "What do you typically do before this happens?"	____ (overt behavior)
____ ____	5.4. *Cognitive* antecedents	"What kinds of pictures do you have before this happens?" "What are your thoughts before this happens?"	____ (thoughts, beliefs, internal dialogue)

(continued)

POSTEVALUATION (continued)

Scoring	Category of information	Examples of counselor leads or responses	Client response
		"What are you telling yourself before this happens?" "Can you identify any particular beliefs that seem to set the problem off?" "What do you think about [or tell yourself] before the problem occurs that makes it more likely to happen? less likely?"	
___ ___	5.5. *Contextual* antecedents	"How long ago did this happen?" "Has this ever occurred at any other time in your life? If so, describe that." "Where and when did this occur the first time?" "How do you see those events as related to your problem?" "What things happened that seemed to lead up to this?" "What was happening in your life when you first noticed the problem?" "Are there any ways in which your cultural values and affiliations set off this problem? make it more likely to occur? less likely?" "How were things different before you had this concern?" "What do you mean, this started 'recently'?"	___(time, places, other events)
___ ___	5.6. *Relational* antecedents	"Are there any people or relationships from past events in your life that still affect this problem? How?" "Can you identify any particular people that seem to bring on this problem?" "Are you usually with certain people right before or when this problem starts?" "Are there any people or relationships from the past that trigger this issue in some way? Who? How?"	___(other people)
___ ___	6.0. Identify consequences — conditions that maintain and strengthen problem or weaken or diminish it		___(check if client identified following sources of consequences)
___ ___	6.1. *Affective* consequences	"How do you feel after this happens?" "How does this affect the problem?" "When did you stop feeling this way?" "Are you aware of any particular feelings or reactions you have after the problem that strengthen it? weaken it?"	___(feelings, mood states)

(continued)

Scoring	Category of information	Examples of counselor leads or responses	Client response
____ ____	6.2. *Somatic* consequences	"What are you aware of inside you—sensations in your body—just after this happens?" "How does this affect the problem?" "Are there any sensations inside you that seem to occur after the problem that strengthen or weaken it?" "Is there any physical condition, illness, and so on about yourself that seems to occur after this problem? If so, how does it affect the problem?"	____(body or internal sensations)
____ ____	6.3. *Behavioral* consequences	"What do you do after this happens, and how does this make the problem better? worse?" "How do you usually react after this is over?" "In what ways does your reaction keep the problem going? weaken it or stop it?" "Can you identify any particular behavior patterns that occur after this?" "How do these patterns keep the problem going? stop it?"	____(overt responses)
____ ____	6.4. *Cognitive* consequences	"What do you usually think about afterward?" "How does this affect the problem?" "What do you picture after this happens?" "What do you tell yourself after this occurs?" "Can you identify any particular thoughts [beliefs, self-talk] that make the problem better? worse?" "Are there certain thoughts or images you have afterward that either strengthen or weaken the problem?"	____(thoughts, beliefs, internal dialogue)
____ ____	6.5. *Contextual* consequences	"When does this problem usually stop or go away? get worse? get better?" "Where are you when the problem stops? gets worse? gets better?" "Can you identify any particular times, places, or events that seem to keep the problem going? make it worse or better?" "Are there any ways in which your cultural affiliation and values seem to keep this problem going? stop it or weaken it?"	____(time, places, other events)
____ ____	6.6. *Relational* consequences	"Can you identify any particular reactions from other people that occur following the problem?" "In what ways do their reactions affect the problem?" "Are you usually with certain people when the problem gets worse? better?"	____(other people)

(continued)

POSTEVALUATION (continued)

Scoring	Category of information	Examples of counselor leads or responses	Client response
		"Can you identify any particular people who can make the problem worse? better? stop it? keep it going?"	
____ ____	7. Identify possible secondary gains from problem	"What happened afterward that was pleasant?" "What was unpleasant about what happened?" "Has your concern or problem ever produced any special advantages or con- siderations for you?" "As a consequence of your concern, have you got out of or avoided things or events?" "How does this problem help you?" "What do you get out of this situation that you don't get out of other situa- tions?" "Do you notice anything that happens afterward that you try to prolong or to produce?" "Do you notice anything that occurs after the problem that you try to stop or avoid?" "Are there certain feelings or thoughts that go on after the problem that you try to prolong?" "Are there certain feelings or thoughts that go on after the problem that you try to stop or avoid?" "The good thing about _____ [problem] is . . . ."	____(check if client identified payoffs)
____ ____	8. Identify solutions already tried to solve the problem	"How have you dealt with this or other problems before? What was the effect? What made it work or not work?" "How have you tried to resolve this problem?" "What kinds of things have you done to improve this situation?" "What have you done that has made the problem better? worse? kept it the same?" "What have others done to help you with this?"	____(check if client identified prior solutions)
____ ____	9. Identify client coping skills, strengths, resources	"What skills or things do you have going for you that might help you with this concern?" "Describe a situation when this concern or problem is not interfering." "What strengths or assets can you use to help resolve this problem?" "When don't you act this way?" "What kinds of thoughts or self-talk help you handle this better?"	____(check if client identified assets, coping skills)

(continued)

Scoring	Category of information	Examples of counselor leads or responses	Client response
		"When don't you think in self-defeating ways?" "What do you say to yourself to cope with a difficult situation?" "Identify the steps you take in a situation you handle well — what do you think about and what do you do? How could these steps be applied to the present problem?" "To what extent can you do something for yourself without relying on someone else to push you or prod you to do it?" "How often do you get things done by rewarding yourself in some way? by punishing yourself?"	
____ ____	10. Identify client's description/assessment of the problem (note which aspects of problem are stressed and which are ignored)	"What is your understanding of this issue?" "How do you explain this problem to yourself?" "What does the problem mean to you?" "What is your interpretation [analysis] of the problem?" "What else is important to you about the problem that we haven't mentioned?" "Sum up the problem in just one word." "Give the problem a title."	____(check if client explained problem)
____ ____	11. Estimate frequency, duration, or severity of problem behavior/symptoms (assign monitoring homework, if useful)	"How often [how much] does this occur during a day — a week?" "How long does this feeling stay with you?" "How many times do you _____ a day? a week?" "To what extent has this problem interfered with your life? How?" "You say sometimes you feel very anxious. On a scale from 1 to 10, with 1 being very calm and 10 being very anxious, where would you put your feelings?" "How has this interfered with other areas of your life?" "What would happen if the problem were not resolved in a year?"	____(check if client estimated amount or severity of problem)

Yes	No		Other skills
____	____	12.	The counselor listened attentively and recalled accurately the information given by the client.
____	____	13.	The counselor used basic listening responses to clarify and synthesize the information shared by the client.
____	____	14.	The counselor followed the client's lead in determining the sequence or order of the information obtained.

Observer comments _____

☐ SUGGESTED READINGS

Cautela, J. R. (1977). *Behavior analysis forms for clinical intervention.* Champaign, IL: Research Press.

Cautela, J. R. (1981). *Behavior analysis forms for clinical intervention* (Vol. 2). Champaign, IL: Research Press.

Duley, S. M., Cancelli, A. A., Kratochwill, T. R., Bergan, J. R., & Meredith, K. E. (1983). Training and generalization of motivational analysis interview assessment skills. *Behavioral Assessment, 5,* 281–293.

Epstein, N. B., & Bishop, D. S. (1981). Problem-centered systems therapy of the family. *Journal of Marital and Family Therapy, 7,* 23–31.

Goldfried, M. R. (1982). Behavioral assessment: An overview. In A. S. Bellack, M. Hersen, & A. E. Kazdin (Eds.), *International handbook of behavior modification and therapy.* New York: Plenum.

Haynes, S. N., Jensen, B. J., Wise, E., & Sherman, D. (1981). The marital intake interview: A multimethod criterion validity assessment. *Journal of Consulting and Clinical Psychology, 49,* 379–387.

Haynes, S. N., & Wilson, C. C. (1979). *Behavioral assessment.* San Francisco: Jossey-Bass.

Hersen, M., & Bellack, A. S. (Eds.). (1981). *Behavioral assessment: A practical handbook* (2nd ed.). New York: Pergamon Press.

Keane, T. M., Black, J. L., Collins, F. L., Jr., & Vensen, M. C. (1982). A skills training program for teaching the behavioral interview. *Behavioral Assessment, 4,* 53–62.

Lazarus, A. A. (1978). Multimodal behavior therapy (Part 3). In E. Shostrom (Ed.), *Three approaches to psychotherapy II* [16-mm film or ¾″ videocassette]. Orange, CA: Psychological Films.

Nay, W. R. (1979). *Multimethod clinical assessment.* New York: Gardner Press.

Nelson, R. O., & Barlow, D. H. (1981). Behavioral assessment: Basic strategies and initial procedures. In D. H. Barlow (Ed.), *Behavioral assessment of adult disorders.* New York: Guilford Press.

■
FEEDBACK: POSTEVALUATION

PART ONE

See whether the questions you generated are similar to the following ones:

Is this the only issue you're concerned about now in your life, or are there other issues you haven't mentioned yet? (Range of problems)

When you say you feel anxious, what exactly do you mean? (Problem behavior — affective component)

When you feel anxious, what do you experience inside your body? (problem behavior — somatic component)

When you feel anxious, what exactly are you usually doing? (problem behavior — behavioral component)

When you feel anxious, what are you typically thinking about [or saying to yourself]? (Problem behavior — cognitive component)

Try to pinpoint exactly what times the anxiety occurs or when it is worse. (Problem behavior — contextual component)

Describe where you are or in what situations you find yourself when you get anxious. (Problem behavior — contextual component)

Describe what other things are usually going on when you have these feelings. (Problem behavior — contextual component)

Can you tell me what persons are usually around when you feel this way? (Problem behavior — relational component)

Are there any feelings that lead up to this? (Antecedent source — affective)

What about body sensations that might occur right before these feelings? (Antecedent source — somatic)

Have you noticed any particular behavioral reactions or patterns that seem to occur right before these feelings? (Antecedent source — behavioral)

Are there any kinds of thoughts — things you're dwelling on — that seem to lead up to these feelings? (Antecedent source — cognitive)

When was the first time you noticed these feelings? where were you? (Antecedent source — contextual)

Can you recall any other events or times that seem to be related to these feelings? (Antecedent source — contextual)

Does the presence of any particular people in any way set these feelings off? (Antecedent source — relational)

Are you aware of any particular other feelings that make the anxiety better or worse? (Consequence source — affective)

Are you aware of any body sensations or physiological responses that make these feelings better or worse? (Consequence source — somatic)

Is there anything you can do specifically to make these feelings stronger or weaker? (Consequence source — behavioral)

Can you identify anything you can think about or

focus on that seems to make these feelings better or worse? (Consequence source — cognitive)

At what times do these feelings diminish or go away? get worse? in what places? in what situations? (Consequence source — contextual)

Do certain people you know seem to react in ways that keep these feelings going or make them less intense? If so, how? (Consequence source — relational)

As a result of this anxiety, have you ever gotten out of or avoided things you dislike? (Consequence — secondary gain)

Has this problem with your nerves ever resulted in any special advantages or considerations for you? (Consequence — secondary gain)

What have you tried to do to resolve this issue? How have your attempted solutions worked out? (Previous solutions)

Describe some times and situations when you don't have these feelings or you feel calm and relaxed. What goes on that is different in these instances? (Coping skills)

How have you typically coped with other difficult situations or feelings in your life before? (Coping skills)

If you could give this problem a title — as if it were a movie or a book — what would that title be? (Client perceptions of problem)

How do you explain these feelings to yourself? (Client perceptions of problem)

How many times do these feelings crop up during a given day? (Frequency of problem)

How long do these feelings stay with you? (Duration of problem)

On a scale from 1 to 10, with 1 being not intense and 10 being very intense, how strong would you say these feelings usually are? (Severity of problem)

PART THREE

To start with, you may want to obtain information directly related to time and place of anxiety occurrence. The log might look something like this:

Date   Time   Place   Activity

The client would be asked to record anxious feelings daily. Later, you may wish to add recording of information about direction and severity. You could add these two columns to the log:

How long   Intensity (1 to 10)

Although it might be valuable to ask the client to also observe and record cognitions (thoughts, beliefs), there is some evidence that many anxious clients fail to complete this part of self-monitoring because attending to cognitions is reactive and may cue, or increase, rather than decrease, the anxiety (Hollon & Kendall, 1981).

SELECTING AND DEFINING
OUTCOME GOALS

NINE

Pause for a few minutes to answer the following questions to yourself or with someone else.

1. What is one thing you would like to change about yourself?
2. Suppose you succeeded in accomplishing this change. How would things be different for you?
3. Does this outcome represent a change in yourself or for someone else?
4. How feasible is this change?
5. What are some of the risks — to you or others — of this change?
6. What would be your payoffs for making this change?
7. What would you be doing, thinking, or feeling as a result of this change you would like to make for yourself?
8. In what situations do you want to be able to do this?
9. How much or how often would you like to be able to do this?
10. Looking at where you are now and where you'd like to be, are there some steps along the way to get from here to there? If so, rank them in an ordered list from "easiest to do now" to "hardest to do."
11. Identify any obstacles (people, feelings, ideas, situations) that might interfere with attainment of your goal.
12. Identify any resources (skills, people, knowledge) that you need to use or acquire to attain your goal.
13. How could you monitor and review progress toward this outcome?

These steps reflect the process of selecting and defining goals for counseling. Goals represent desired results or outcomes and function as milestones of client progress. In this chapter we describe and model concrete guidelines you can use to help clients select and define outcome goals for counseling.

☐ OBJECTIVES

1. Identify a situation about you or your life that you would like to change. Select and define one desired outcome for this issue, using the Goal-Setting Worksheet in the postevaluation as a guide.
2. Given a list of ten hypothetical client outcome goals, discriminate, with an 80% accuracy rate, those goals that are statements of changes owned by the client, are based on realistic ideas, and are behaviorally defined from those that are not.
3. Given a written client case description, describe the steps you would use with this client to explore, select, and define desired outcome goals, with at least 11 of the 15 categories for selecting and defining goals represented in your description.
4. Demonstrate at least 11 of the 15 categories associated with selecting and defining outcome goals, given a role-play interview.

☐ PURPOSES OF GOALS

Goals have six important purposes in counseling. First, they provide some directions for counseling. Clearly defined goals reflect the areas of client concern that need most immediate attention (Hill, 1975). Establishing goals can also clarify the client's initial expectations of counseling (Smith, 1976). Goals may help both counselor and client anticipate more precisely what can and cannot be accomplished through counseling (Krumboltz, 1966).

Although each theoretical orientation has its own direction for counseling (Frey & Raming, 1979), specifying goals individually for each client helps to ensure that counseling is structured specifically to meet the needs of *that* client. Clients are much more likely to support and commit themselves to changes that they create than changes imposed by someone else. Without goals, counseling may be "directionless" or may be based more on the theoretical biases and personal preferences of the counselor (Bandura, 1969, p. 70). Some clients may go through counseling without realizing that the sessions are devoid of direction or are more consistent with the counselor's preferences than the client's needs and aims. In other aspects of our lives, however, most of us would be quite aware of

analogous situations. If we boarded an airplane destined for a place of our choice, and the airplane went around in circles or the pilots announced a change of destination that they desired, we would be upset and indignant.

Second, goals permit counselors to determine whether or not they have the skills, competencies, and interest for working with a particular client toward a particular outcome. Depending on the client's choice of goals and the counselor's values and level of expertise, the counselor decides whether to continue working with the client or to refer the client to someone else who may be in a better position to give services.

Another often overlooked purpose of goals is their role in human cognition and problem solving. Goals facilitate successful performance and problem resolution because they are usually rehearsed in our working memory and because they direct our attention to the resources and components in our environment that are most likely to facilitate the solution of a problem (Dixon & Glover, 1984, pp. 128–129). This purpose of goals is quite evident in the performance of successful athletes who set goals for themselves and then use the goals not only as motivating devices but also as standards against which they rehearse their performance over and over, often cognitively or with imagery. Running backs, for example, constantly "see themselves" getting the ball and running downfield, over and past the goal line. Champion skiers are often seen closing their eyes and bobbing their heads in the direction of the course before the race.

A fourth purpose of goals is to have some basis for selecting and using particular counseling strategies and interventions. The changes the client desires will, to some degree, determine the kinds of action plans and treatment strategies that can be used with some likelihood of success. Without an explicit identification of what the client wants from counseling, it is almost impossible to explain and defend one's choice to move in a certain direction or to use one or more counseling strategies. Without goals, the counselor may use a particular approach without any "rational basis" (Bandura, 1969, p. 70). Whether the approach will be helpful is left to chance rather than choice.

A fifth and most important purpose of goals is their role in an outcome evaluation of counseling. Goals can indicate the difference between what and how much the client is able to do now and what and how much the client would like to do in the future. With the ultimate goal in mind, the counselor and client can monitor progress toward the goal and compare progress before and after a counseling intervention. These data provide continuous feedback to both counselor and client (Smith, 1976). The feedback can be used to assess the feasibility of the goal and the effectiveness of the intervention. Bandura (1969, p. 74) has summarized very aptly the role of well-defined outcomes in evaluation of counseling:

> When desired outcomes are designated in observable and measurable terms, it becomes readily apparent when the methods have succeeded, when they have failed, and when they need further development to increase their potency. This self-corrective feature is a safeguard against perpetuation of ineffective approaches, which are difficult to retire if the changes they are supposed to produce remain ambiguous.

Finally, goal-planning systems are useful because, like assessment procedures, they are often reactive; that is, clients make progress in change as a result of the goal-planning process itself. Lloyd (1983, p. 60) explains how reactivity in goal setting seems to work:

> It seems likely that therapists who help their clients set objectives may find a clearer focus for case planning and treatment and that therapists who are aware of their own goal attainment statistics may be more motivated to have their clients do well. It is also possible that clients who are aware of their own specific objectives may do better in therapy than those who are not. The more involved both therapists and clients are in the details of goal attainment procedures, the more likely is the system to be reactive.*

☐ AN OVERVIEW OF SELECTING AND DEFINING GOALS

The sequence of selecting and defining goals is shown in Figure 9-1, which represents the following steps in this process.

---

* This and all other quotations from this source are from "Selecting systems to measure client outcome in human service agencies" by M. E. Lloyd. *Behavioral Assessment, 5,* 55–70. Copyright © 1983 by Association for Advancement of Behavior Therapy. Reprinted by permission.

Selecting Goals

1. Explain the *purpose* of goals.
2. Ask the client to specify *positive change(s)* desired as a result of counseling.
3. Determine whether the goal selected represents changes *owned by the client.*
4. Explore whether the goal is *realistic.*
5. Identify possible *advantages* of goal attainment.
6. Identify possible *disadvantages* of goal attainment.
7. Make a *decision.* Using the information obtained about client-stated goals, select one of the following alternatives: to adopt these goals as the direction for counseling, to reconsider the client's goals, or to seek a referral.

The process of selecting goals may also involve values clarification between the client and the counselor.

Defining Goals

As illustrated in Figure 9-1, defining goals occurs after the goals have been selected and *agreed to* by both counselor and client. Defining goals includes eight steps.

1. Define the overt and covert *behaviors* associated with the goal.
2. Determine the circumstances or *conditions* of change.
3. Establish the *level* of the goal behavior or the extent to which it is to occur.
4. Identify *subgoals* or intermediate action steps.
5. *Sequence* the action steps by immediacy and degree of difficulty.
6. Identify *obstacles* that prevent goal attainment.
7. Identify necessary *resources.*
8. Review *progress.*

The counselor can facilitate the development of counseling goals by using leads in the interview that are directed toward selection and definition of goals. In this chapter we offer examples of leads for selecting and defining goals, and more can be found in the Interview Checklist at the end of the chapter. These leads are merely suggested examples. You can provide examples that are equally good or better for each category.

The areas illustrated in Figure 9-1 reflect the process of selecting and defining goals in counseling. In one of the first articles to describe counseling goals, Krumboltz (1966) suggested two basic guidelines for the goal-setting process. First, the goal should be stated for each client individually. Second, the goal should be stated in terms of visible outcomes. These two guidelines help to ensure that the process of developing counseling goals is highly individualized and that the goals will be observable.

Selecting and defining goals is a highly interactive process between the counselor and the client. The client usually determines the outcome of goals of counseling. However, the counselor's input is essential in helping the client identify the desired results of counseling in clearly defined, visible goal statements. The following section describes interview leads you can use to help clients identify and select desired outcomes for counseling.

□ INTERVIEW LEADS FOR SELECTING GOALS

Purpose of Goals

The first step in selecting goals is to give the client a *rationale* about goals. This statement should describe goals, the purpose of having them, and the client's participation in the goal-setting process. The counselor's intent is to convey the importance of having goals, as well as the importance of the client's participation in developing them. An example of what the counselor might say about the purpose of goals is "We've been talking about these two areas that bother you. It might be helpful now to discuss how you would like things to be different. We can develop some goals to work

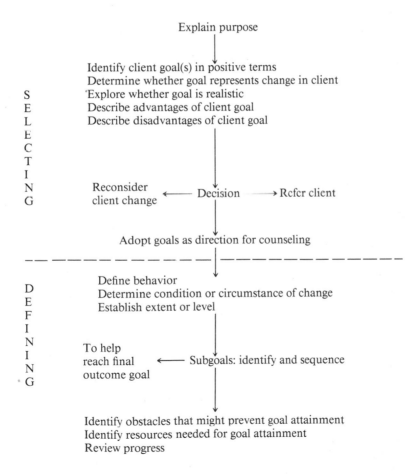

Figure 9-1. Selecting and defining goals

toward during our sessions. These goals will tell us what you want as a result of counseling. So today, let's talk about some things *you* would like to work on."

The counselor might also emphasize the role that goals play in resolving problems through attention and rehearsal. "Dean, you've been saying how stuck you feel in your marriage and yet how hopeful you feel, too. If we can identify specifically the ways that you want to relate differently, this can help you attend to the things you do that cause difficulty as well as the things you know you want to handle differently." Occasionally, offering examples of how other persons, such as athletes or dancers, use goal setting to facilitate performance may be useful to clients.

After this explanation, the counselor will look for a client response that indicates understanding. If the client seems confused, the counselor will need to explain further the purposes of goals and their benefits to the client or to clarify and explore the client's confusion.

Identifying Client Goals

What does an outcome goal represent? At the simplest level, an outcome goal represents what the client wants to happen as a result of the counseling process. Stated another way, outcome goals are an extension of the type of problem(s) the client experiences. Outcome goals represent two major classifications of problems: *choice* and *change* (Dixon & Glover, 1984). In choice problems, the client has the requisite skills and resources for problem resolution but is caught between two or more choices, often conflicting ones. In these instances, the outcome goal represents a choice or a decision the client needs to make, such as "to decide between College A and College B" or "to choose either giving up my job and having lots of free time or keeping my job and having money and stability."

In change issues, the outcome goal is a change the client wants to make. In such instances the client does not have the requisite skills and resources to solve the problem. Additionally, clients faced with change issues enter counseling with what Gottman & Leiblum (1974) call a "performance discrepancy"; in some way or in some situation, the client is performing in a manner that needs to be changed. The performance discrepancy is represented by the difference between the client's perception of current functioning and the

client's expectations of alternative ways of functioning (p. 25). The desired changes may be in overt behaviors or situations, covert behaviors, or combinations of the two. These outcome goals may be directed at eliminating something, increasing something, developing something, or restructuring something, but in all cases the change is expected to be an improvement over what currently exists (Srebalus, 1975, p. 415). Client goals based on a performance discrepancy reflect a typical definition of change cited by Srebalus as movement from one state of being to another (p. 416). This concept of change indicates a discrepancy between what the client is doing now and what the client wants to accomplish. These changes may result from developmental changes, counseling interventions, or both.

Occasionally, in addition to choice or change goals, clients want to maintain certain aspects of their life or certain behaviors at the same rate or in the same way. For example, a client may want to continue his sexual relationship with his wife (maintaining a behavior) the way it is even though he may wish to change other aspects of the relationship.

Interview leads to identify client goals. These are examples of leads the counselor can use to elicit goal statements from the client:

> "Suppose some distant relative you haven't seen for a while sees you after counseling. What would be different then from the way things are now?"
> "Assuming we are successful, what would you be doing or how would these situations change?"
> "What do you expect to accomplish as a result of counseling? Is this a choice or a change?"
> "How would you like counseling to benefit you?"
> "What do you *want* to be doing, thinking, or feeling?"

The counselor's purpose in using these sorts of leads is to have the client identify some desired outcomes of counseling. The counselor is looking for some verbal indication of the results the client expects. If the client does not know of desired changes or cannot specify a purpose for engaging in counseling, some time should be spent in exploring this area before moving on. The counselor can assist the client in selecting goals in several ways: by assigning homework ("Make a list of what you can do now and what you want to do one year from now"), by using imagery ("Imagine being someone you admire. Who would you be? What would you be doing? How would you be different?"), by additional questioning ("If you could wave a magic wand and have three wishes, what would they be?"), or by self-report questionnaires or inventories such as the Behavioral Self-Rating Checklist (BSRC) developed by Cautela and Upper (1975). This checklist asks the client which of 73 adaptive overt and covert behaviors the client needs to learn in order to function more effectively (Cautela & Upper, 1976, p. 91).

Stating the goal in positive terms. An effective outcome goal is stated in *positive* rather than negative terms — as what the client *does* want to do, not what the client does not want to do. This is very important because of the role that goal setting plays in human cognition and performance, as mentioned earlier. When the goal is stated positively, clients are more likely to encode and rehearse the things they want to be able to *do* rather than the things they want to avoid or stop. For example, it is fairly easy to generate an image of yourself sitting down and watching TV. However, picturing yourself *not* watching TV is difficult. Instead of forming an image of not watching TV, you are likely to form images (or sounds) related to performing other activities instead, such as reading a book, talking to someone, or being in the TV room and doing something else. Maultsby (1984) explains the implications for goal setting and change as follows:

> Resolutions not to keep doing something are behavioral resolutions. To keep such behavioral resolutions, people must get rid of the undesirable habit of doing the act they have resolved not to do anymore. But in psychological science as in physical science nature seems to abhor a vacuum. Therefore, people can *not* just get rid of a habit; people have to replace every old habit with a new habit.
>
> Now, what do people have to do to form a new habit? They have to have the same mental image of themselves acting out the same new behavior, in the same way, every time they normally would act out the old, undesirable, but habitual behavior. . . . To learn a new behavioral habit, people must have the same specific, mental images, or behavioral picture-maps of themselves acting out the new behavior in the same way, every time. In addition, the people must be willing to act in the new

way every time they have a cue for the old behavior. [p. 45]*

The counselor will have to help clients "turn around" their initial goal statements, which are usually stated as something the person doesn't want to do, can't do, or wants to stop doing. Such statements reveal the "dead man's error" (Lindsley, 1968), in that these objectives are ones that could be realized by a dead person. Stating goals positively represents a self-affirming position. If the client responds to the counselor's initial leads with a negative answer, the counselor can help turn this around by saying something like "That is what you *don't* want to do. Describe what you *do* want to do [think, feel]" or "What will you do instead, and can you see [hear, feel] yourself doing it every time?"

Who Owns the Goal?

As we mentioned in Chapter 8, clients often describe problems in a way that minimizes their own contribution. The likely result is that the client projects the blame or responsibility for the problem onto someone else — for example, "I didn't do this," "It's all her fault," "If it weren't for them." Similarly, in stating goals, some clients display the same tendency and initially want to select goals that call for someone else to change rather than themselves — a teenager who says "I want my mom to stop yelling at me," a teacher who says "I want this kid to shut up so I can get some teaching done," or a husband who says "I want my wife to stop bitching." The tendency to project the desired change onto someone else is particularly evident in change problems that involve relationships with two or more persons.

Without discounting the client's feelings, the counselor needs to help get this tendency turned around. The client is the identified person seeking help and services and is the only person who can make a change. When two or more clients are involved simultaneously in counseling, such as a couple or a family, all identified clients need to contribute to the desired choice or change, not just one party or one "identified patient." More specifically, any persons directly affected by a choice or change need some involvement in selection and implementation of the desired outcomes (Gam-

* From *Rational behavior therapy* by M. C. Maultsby, Jr. Copyright © 1984 by Prentice-Hall. Reprinted by permission.

brill, 1977). The counselor may have a special responsibility to protect the rights of clients in "low power" positions, such as children and the elderly, to ensure that this happens, because their rights are so often easily overlooked (Gambrill, 1977).

Who owns the change is usually directly related to the degree of *control* or *responsibility* that the client has in the situation and over the choice or change. For example, suppose you are counseling an 8-year-old girl whose parents are getting a divorce. The child says she wants you to help her persuade her parents to stay married. This goal would be very difficult for the child to attain, since she has no responsibility for her parents' relationship.

The counselor will need to use leads to help clients determine whether they or someone else owns the change and whether anyone else needs to be involved in the goal selection process. If the client steers toward a goal that requires a change by someone else, the counselor will need to point this out and help the client identify his or her role in the change process.

Interview leads to determine who owns the change. To help the client explore who owns the change, the counselor can use leads similar to the following ones:

> "How much control do you have over making this happen?"
> "What changes will this goal require of you?"
> "What changes will this goal require someone else to make?"
> "Can this goal be achieved without the help of anyone else?"
> "To whom is this goal most important?"
> "Who, specifically, is responsible for making this happen?"

The intent of these leads is to have the client identify a goal that represents choice or change for the client, not for others unless they are directly affected. If the client persists in selecting a goal that represents change for others rather than oneself, the counselor and client will have to decide whether to pursue this goal, to negotiate a reconsidered goal, or to refer the client to another helper, as we shall discuss shortly.

Is the Goal Realistic?

Realistic goals are ones that are *feasible* and within the client's control and capabilities to achieve. Realistic goals also represent outcomes that are based on realistic expectations rather than unrealistic, irrational, or perfectionistic ideas, standards, or self-demands.

When clients select goals, the counselor needs to be on the lookout for goals that are unrealistic either because they are too high to be reached or because they are too low and either inconsequential or likely to be attained anyway during the natural course of events. Clients who set goals that are too high usually operate from perfectionistic standards and self-demands. Dixon and Glover (1984) note that often these clients also fear failure, and the selection of unrealistically high goals removes the possibility of failure in their eyes because they do not feel anyone would blame them for not reaching such a lofty objective. For example, a client who states "I want to get all As during my four years of college" knows that no one will hold her to this goal because it is so "ideal" and difficult to reach. Setting high goals is also a way to avoid trying or taking any risk, thus preventing the possibility of failing at one risk or attempt.

Clients who set goals that are inconsequential or too low also usually fear failure and select such goals because they know they can be attained. Unfortunately, the result is usually as inconsequential as the goal itself and often feels like a "hollow victory" with no sense of accomplishment (Dixon & Glover, 1984, p. 133). A client who states "I just want to maintain a C average in college" is likely to do so successfully but may feel little or no pride when the goal has been reached or even surpassed. Challenging goals are more likely to lead to higher performance than "easy" goals (Locke, Shaw, Saari, & Latham, 1981).

The counselor can help clients explore the degree to which the identified goals are realistic and are based on potential for change and on rational standards, as well as any anxiety that may be reflected by the client's choice of unrealistic goals. Counselors can also help clients examine any inappropriate attributions or notions about who is responsible for success or failure to attain the goals. Inappropriate attributions would be those in which the client attributes success or failure to factors outside the client's control (Dixon & Glover, 1984). In selecting goals that are realistic, both the counselor and the client should be careful not to overestimate or underestimate the client's potential.

Interview leads to explore feasibility. To help the client determine the realism of the identified goal(s), the counselor can use any of the following example leads:

"How feasible is it for you to do _____?"

"Is it reasonable to effect a change in _____?"

"How are you likely to feel after you have reached this goal?"

"To what extent are you leaning toward this goal because you know it's something you can achieve with little effort and/or little risk?"

"To what extent are you leaning toward this goal because it's out of your reach and may excuse you from blame if you don't try or don't make it?"

"To what extent do you want to achieve this goal?"

"To what extent do you feel you should achieve this goal?"

"To what degree is this goal based on realistic expectations?"

"To what degree does this goal represent wishful thinking?"

"Does this goal alleviate in any way a possible fear of failure on your part?"

"When you reach this goal, how will you explain your success [or if you don't reach it, how will you explain failure to reach it]?"

The intent of these leads is to have the *client* assess the degree to which a goal can be attained in a realistic way and within a practical amount of time. The counselor is looking for a response that indicates the client has some evidence that the goal is realistic and can be attained in a reasonable time and manner. If the client selects a goal and considers it feasible but the counselor does not agree, renegotiation and/or referral are options.

Advantages and Disadvantages of the Goal

It is important to explore the *cost/benefit* effect of all identified goals — that is, what is being given up (cost) versus what is being gained (benefit) from goal attainment (Dixon & Glover, 1984). We think of this step as exploration of *advantages,* or positive effects, and *disadvantages,* or negative effects, of goal attainment. Clients are unlikely to commit themselves to a goal or are likely to give up working toward a goal when the stakes become too high and the payoffs too low. Exploration of advantages and disadvantages helps the client anticipate what price will be paid to achieve the goal and then decide whether the change is worth the cost to oneself or to significant others. Many clients tend

to jump into change without considering that attainment of a desired goal may also involve a cost. Costs are usually less obvious than the benefits of change. If the counselor and client fail to explore possible costs, the client may reach the goal and solve the original problem but create new problems in the process (Dixon & Glover, 1984). Sometimes removal of or change in a symptom creates adverse effects or new problems that the client did not bargain for and the counselor did not anticipate. For example, a client may choose to give up his job to get more free time and, after doing so, become despondent because of lack of money and security and loss of an important social network and feeling of "community." Advantages and disadvantages of particular goals may be emotional and cognitive as well as behavioral (Gambrill, 1977): goal attainment may result in desirable or undesirable feelings and mood states; self-enhancing or self-defeating thoughts, images, and internal dialogue; and appropriate or inappropriate reactions and motoric responses.

Generally, the goals selected by clients should lead to benefits rather than losses. Gambrill (1977, p. 169) notes that making such a selection "calls for careful identification of the situations in which new behaviors will be displayed and anticipation of the possible consequences that might occur." Advantages and disadvantages may be both short-term and long-term. The counselor helps the client identify various kinds of short- and long-term advantages and disadvantages associated with goal attainment and offers options to expand the client's range of possibilities (Gambrill, 1977). Sometimes it is helpful to write these down in the form of a list, which can be expanded or modified at any time, such as the one found in Figure 9-2 (see also Goldfried & Goldfried, 1980).

Interview leads for advantages.   Most clients can readily identify some positive consequences associated with their desired changes. Nevertheless, it is still a good idea with all clients to explore positive consequences of the change, for at least four reasons: to determine whether the advantages the client perceives are indicative of actual benefits; to point out other possible advantages for the client or for others that have been overlooked; to strengthen the client's incentive to change; and to determine to what degree the identified goal is relevant and worthwhile, given the client's overall functioning. These are examples of leads to explore advantages of client change:

Goal	Immediate Advantages	Long-Term Advantages	Immediate Disadvantages	Long-Term Disadvantages
Goal #1				
Goal #2				
Goal #3				

Figure 9-2. *List for recording advantages and disadvantages of identified goals*

"In what ways is it worthwhile to pursue this goal?"
"What do you see as the benefits of this change?"
"Who would benefit from this change and how?"
"What are some positive consequences that may result from this change?"
"What are some advantages of attaining this goal?"
"Will attainment of this goal lead to solution of the issue?"

In using these leads, the counselor is looking for some indication that the client is selecting a goal on the basis of the positive consequences the goal may produce. If the client overlooks some advantages, the counselor can describe them to add to the client's incentive to change.

If the client is unable to identify any benefits of change for herself or himself, this may be viewed as a signal for caution. Failure to identify advantages of change for oneself may indicate that the client is attempting to change at someone else's request or that the identified goal is not very relevant, given the "total picture." For instance, if a client wants to find a new job while she is also fighting off a life-threatening illness, the acquisition of a new job at this time may not be in the best interests of her desire to regain her health. Further exploration may indicate that another person is a more appropriate client or that other goals should be selected.

Interview leads for disadvantages. The counselor can also use leads to have the client consider some risks or side effects that might accompany the desired change. Some examples of leads the counselor might use to explore the risks or disadvantages of change are the following:

"Will pursuing this goal affect your life in any adverse ways?"
"What might be some possible risks of doing this?"
"How would your life be changed if this happened?"
"What are some possible disadvantages of going in this direction? How willing are you to pay this price?"

"What are some negative consequences this change might have for you—or for others?"
"How will this change limit or constrain you?"
"What new problems in living might pursuing this goal create for you?"

The counselor is looking for some indication that the client has considered the possible costs associated with the goal. If the client discounts the risks or cannot identify any, the counselor can use immediacy or confrontation to point out some disadvantages. However, the counselor should be careful not to persuade or coerce the client to pursue another alternative simply because the counselor believes it is better. As Eisenberg and Delaney (1977) note, "It is one thing to help a person be aware of the consequences of the choice he or she has made and another thing to persuade the client to prefer another alternative" (p. 202).

Decision Point

The process of developing goals to this point has involved the client as the primary agent in choosing goals. The counselor's role has been secondary, confined mainly to helping the client explore the feasibility, risks, and disadvantages of change. At this point in the process, the primary issue for the counselor is whether she or he can help the client attain the selected goals. Most people agree that this is one of the biggest ethical and, to some extent, legal questions the counselor faces during the helping process (Bandura, 1969; Gottman & Leiblum, 1974; Krumboltz, 1966; Morganstern & Tevlin, 1981).

According to Gambrill (1977, p. 1035),

There *is* an obligation to help the client obtain desired goals, within the limits of the counselor's personal value system and theoretical orientation and the likely short- and long-term effects on the client and society. However, both the counselor's personal value system and his theoretical orientation may place unethical restrictions on the help that he or she can offer the client. In such instances, the counselor has an ethical obligation to refer the client to someone else who can view the client's desired outcomes more objectively.

The counselor and client will need to choose whether to continue with counseling and pursue the selected goals, to continue with counseling but reevaluate the client's initial goals, or to seek the services of another counselor. The particular decision is always made on an individual basis and is based on two factors: *willingness* and *competence* to help the client pursue the selected goals (Brown & Brown, 1977). Willingness involves your interest in working with the client toward identified goals and issues, your values, and your acceptance of the goals as worthwhile and important, given the overall functioning of the client. Competence involves your skills and "know-how" and whether you are familiar with alternative intervention strategies and multiple ways to work with particular problems.

We offer the following ideas as food for thought in this area. First of all, as much as possible, be responsive to the *client's* requests for change (Gottman & Leiblum, 1974, p. 64) even if these goals do not reflect your theoretical biases or personal preferences. This sort of responsiveness has been described by Gottman and Leiblum (1974, p. 64): "If [the client] wants help in accepting his homosexuality, do not set up a treatment program designed to help him find rewards in heterosexuality. Respect for your client implies respect for his diagnosis of his needs and wishes."

Too often, either knowingly or unwittingly, counselors may lead a client toward a goal they are personally comfortable with or feel more competent to treat. As Gambrill observes, "Personal values and theoretical assumptions with no empirical basis have caused profound distress to many clients over the years" (1977, p. 1035).

Second, if you have a *major* reservation about pursuing selected goals, a referral might be more helpful to the client (Gottman & Leiblum, p. 43).

Major reservations of a counselor.   A counselor might have several reservations or limitations that would affect this decision point. One possible major reservation for you, the counselor, is any previous difficulty you have had in working with similar clients. Your own unresolved conflicts in the area the client wants to pursue may block successful counseling. Other reservations may surface when your values are not compatible with those reflected in the client's choice of goals. When goals

pose harm to the client or others, you may decide it would be ethically irresponsible to help the client pursue them. Some clients may select "self-defeating" goals. Self-defeating goals may constrict freedom of activity, may be impractical to achieve, or may be chosen because of political pressure or demands from others (Gambrill, 1977). Brown and Brown (1977, p. 100) observe that "sanctioning such goals reinforces a client's avoidance of the problem or reinforces the selection of inappropriate means of handling a problem situation." You also might have some reservations if the client insists that you use a technique that data suggest is ineffective or harmful or if the client insists on a treatment approach that is beyond your skill level or the realm of counseling. Finally, you may feel counseling would not help when the contributing problem conditions are outside the client's control or when the client is unwilling to change these factors.

Making the decision.   If the client selects goals and neither you nor the client has any major reservations, you will probably decide to continue with counseling to help the client attain her or his goal. You might summarize this to the client as in the following example: "You stated that you want to do _____ as a result of counseling. You seem to be willing and able to change the factors that are part of this problem. The benefits of this change for you seem to outweigh the disadvantages." After this point, assuming the client confirms this statement, the counselor and client will move on to defining the goal.

In other cases, you may decide to continue with the client on the basis of some reevaluation of the client's selected goals. Morganstern and Tevlin (1981) observe that there may be times when it would be difficult to accept the client's goals without offering "reeducation." For example, if the client wants to have a child and cannot identify any risks or disadvantages posed by this choice, the counselor may point out some constraints. Or if a client chooses as his goal "I want to be just exactly like my best friend," the counselor might point out the difficulty in achieving this goal. In reconsidering the client's goal, the counselor might say something like "I can't help you be just like your best friend, because each of us is a little different from everyone else. Our differences are what make us unique. If there is something about yourself you'd like to work on, I can help with that."

Reevaluation of the client's goals is a very sticky

issue. Bandura (1969) observes that a redefinition of the client's goal by the counselor, especially "unilateral redefinition," is a prevailing but "largely ignored ethical issue" (p. 103). Bandura recommends that, when initiating reevaluation or redefinition of the client's goals, the counselor should make this path explicit to the client. Moreover, the counselor should inform the client that such comments are based on information *and* on the counselor's own belief system (p. 103). Reevaluation of client goals should be pursued only "with the understanding and consent of the client," who is "free to exert 'counter-control'—that is, to challenge, refute, or refuse to comply with the therapist's suggestions" (Gottman & Leiblum, 1974, p. 68). The counselor's influence in reconsideration should be explicit, not implicit, open rather than disguised.

Referral may be appropriate in any of the following cases: if the client wants to pursue a goal that is incompatible with your value system; if you are unable to be objective about the client's concern; if you are unfamiliar with or unable to use a treatment requested by the client; if you would be exceeding your level of competence in working with the client; or if more than one person is involved and, because of your emotions or biases, you favor one person instead of another. Referral may be a better choice than continuing to work with the client in the midst of serious limitations or reservation. Referral is a way to provide an alternative counseling experience and, we hope, one that will leave the client with a positive impression of counseling.

In deciding to refer a client, the counselor does have certain responsibilities. From the initial counseling contacts, the counselor and client have entered into at least an unwritten contract. Once the counselor agrees to counsel a client, he or she "assumes a degree of loyalty and responsibility for the outcomes of therapy" (Van Hoose & Kottler, 1977, p. 82). In deciding to terminate this "contract" by a referral, the referring counselor can be considered legally liable if the referral is not handled with due care (Dawidoff, 1973). Due care implies that

> when referral is undertaken the referring therapist has the responsibility for ascertaining the appropriateness of the referral, including the skill of the receiving therapist. Furthermore, he should provide the receiving therapist with information sufficient to enable him to give proper help to the client. It is also important that the therapist attempt to follow up on the status of his client's well-being. [Van Hoose & Kottler, p. 83]

Therapists are also responsible for giving clients choices of referral therapists (when available) and for ensuring that referred therapists are considered competent and do not have a reputation for poor service or unethical practices (M. Boston, personal communication, December 1980).

LEARNING ACTIVITY #26: DECISION POINT

For practice in thinking through the kinds of decisions you may face in the goal-setting process, you may want to use this learning activity. The exercise consists of three hypothetical situations. In each case, assume that you are the counselor. Read through the case. Then sit back, close your eyes, and try to imagine being in the room with the client and being faced with this dilemma. How would you feel? What would you say? What would you decide to do and why?

There are no "right" or "wrong" answers to these cases. You may wish to discuss your responses with another classmate, a co-worker, or your instructor.

Case 1

You are counseling a family with two teenage daughters. The parents and the younger daughter seem closely aligned; the elder daughter is on the periphery of the family. The parents and the younger daughter report that the older daughter's recent behavior is upsetting and embarrassing to them because she has been caught cheating in school and is hanging out with a "fast crowd." They state that they want you to help them get this girl "back in line" with the rest of the family and get her to adopt their values and socially acceptable behavior. What do you do?

Case 2

You are counseling a fourth-grader. You are the only counselor in this school. One day you notice that this boy seems to be all bruised. You inquire about this. After much hesitation, the child blurts out that he is often singled out on his way home by two big sixth-grade "bullies" who pick a fight, beat him up for a while, and then leave him alone until another time.

(continued)

Your client asks you to forget this information. He begs you not to say or do anything for fear of reprisal from these two bullies. He states he doesn't want to deal with this in counseling, since he has come to see you about something else. What do you do?

Case 3

You are working with an elderly man whose relatives are dead. After his wife died six months ago, he moved from their family home to a retirement home. Although the client is relatively young (70) and is in good health and alert, the staff has requested your help because he seems to have become increasingly morbid and discouraged. In talking with you, he indicates that he has sort of given up on everything, including himself, because he doesn't feel he has anything to live for. Consequently, he has stopped going to activities, isolates himself in his room, and has even stopped engaging in self-care activities such as personal hygiene and grooming, leaving such things up to the staff. He indicates that he doesn't care to talk with you if these are the kinds of things you are going to want to talk about. What do you do?

☐ MODEL DIALOGUE: THE CASE OF JOAN

To help you see how the leads for selecting goals are used with a client, the case of Joan, introduced in Chapter 7, is continued here as a dialogue in a counseling session directed toward goal selection. Counselor responses are prefaced by an explanation (in italics).

In response 1, the counselor starts out with a **review** *of the last session.*

1. *Counselor:* Joan, last week we talked about some of the things that are going on with you right now that you're concerned about. What do you remember that we talked about?

   Client: Well, we talked a lot about my problems in school—like my trouble in my math class. Also about the fact that I can't decide whether or not to switch over to a vocational curriculum—and if I did my parents would be upset.

2. *Counselor:* Yes, that's a good summary. We did talk about a lot of things—such as the pressure and anxiety you feel in competitive situations like your math class and your difficulty in making decisions. I believe we mentioned also that you tend to go out of your way to please others, like your parents, or to avoid making a decision they might not like.

   Client: Mm-hmm. I tend to not want to create a hassle. I also just have never made many decisions by myself.

In response 3, the counselor will move from problem definition to goal selection. Response 3 will consist of an **explanation** *about goals and their* **purpose.**

3. *Counselor:* Yes, I remember you said that last week. I've been thinking that since we've kind of got a handle on the main issues you're concerned about, today it might be helpful to talk about things you might want to happen—or how you'd like things to be different. This way we know

exactly what we can be talking about and working on that will be most helpful to you. How does that sound?

   Client: That's OK with me. I mean, do you really think there are some things I can do about these problems?

The client has indicated some uncertainty about possible change. The counselor will pursue this in response 4 and indicate more about the **purpose** *of goals and possible effects of counseling for this person.*

4. *Counselor:* You seem a little uncertain about how much things can be different. To the extent that you have some control over a situation, it is possible to make some changes. Depending on what kind of changes you want to make, there are some ways we can work together on this. It will take some work on your part, too. How do you feel about this?

   Client: OK. I'd like to get out of the rut I'm in.

In response 5, the counselor will explore the ways in which the client would like to change. The counselor will use a lead to **identify client goals.**

5. *Counselor:* So you're saying that you don't want to continue to feel stuck. Exactly how would you like things to be different—say, in three months from now—from the way things are now?

   Client: Well, I'd like to feel less pressured in school, especially in my math class.

The client has identified one possible goal, although it is stated in negative terms. In response 6, the counselor will help the client identify the goal in **positive terms.**

6. *Counselor:* OK, that's something you *don't* want to do. Can you think of another way to say it that would describe what you *do* want to do?

   Client: Well, I guess I'd like to feel confident about my ability to handle tough situations like math class.

In the next response, the counselor paraphrases Joan's goal and "checks" it out to see whether she has restated it accurately.

7. *Counselor:* So you're saying you'd like to feel more positively about yourself in different situations — is that it?

    Client: Yeah, I don't know if that is possible, but that's what I would like to have happen.

In responses 8–14, the counselor continues to help Joan explore and identify desired outcomes.

8. *Counselor:* Well, in a little while we'll take some time to explore just how feasible that might be. Before we do that, let's make sure we don't overlook anything else you'd like to work on — in what other areas is it important to you to make a change or to turn things around for yourself?

    Client: Well, I'd like to start making some decisions for myself for a change, but I don't know exactly how to start.

9. *Counselor:* OK, that's part of what we'll do together — we'll look at how you can get started on some of these things. So far, then, you've mentioned two things you'd like to work toward — increasing your confidence in your ability to handle tough situations like math and starting to make some decisions by yourself without relying on help from someone else. Is that about it, or can you think of any other things you'd like to work on?

    Client: Well, I guess it's related to making my own decisions, but I'd like to decide whether to stay in this curriculum or switch to the vocational one.

10. *Counselor:* So you're concerned also about making a special type of decision about school that affects you now.

    Client: That's right. But I'm sort of afraid to, because I know if I decided to switch, my parents would have a terrible reaction when they found out about it.

11. *Counselor:* It seems that you're mentioning another situation that we might need to try to get a different handle on. As you mentioned last week, in certain situations, like math class or with your parents, you tend to back off and kind of let other people take over for you.

    Client: That's true, and I guess this curriculum thing is an example of it. It's like a lot of things I do know what I want to do or say, but I just don't follow through. Like not telling my folks about my opinion about this college prep curriculum. Or not telling them how their harping at me about grades makes me feel. Or even in math class, just sitting there and sort of letting the teacher do a lot of the work for me when I really

do probably know the answer or could go to the board.

12. *Counselor:* So what you're saying is that in certain situations with your folks or in math class, you may have an idea or an opinion or a feeling, yet you usually don't express it.

    Client: Mm-hmm. Usually I don't because sometimes I'm afraid it might be wrong or I'm afraid my folks would get upset.

13. *Counselor:* So the anticipation that you might make a mistake or that your folks might not like it keeps you from expressing yourself in these situations?

    Client: Yup, I believe so.

14. *Counselor:* Then is this another thing that you would like to work on?

    Client: Yes, because I realize I can't go on withdrawing forever.

Since Joan has again stated the outcome in negative terms, in the next four responses (15, 16, 17, 18), the counselor helps Joan restate the goal in positive terms.

15. *Counselor:* OK, now again you're sort of suggesting a way that you don't want to handle the situation. You don't want to withdraw. Can you describe something you *do* want to do in these situations in a way that you could see, hear, or grasp yourself doing it each time the situation occurs?

    Client: I'm not exactly sure what you mean.

16. *Counselor:* Well, for instance, suppose I want to lose weight. I could say "I don't want to eat so much, and I don't want to be fat." But that just describes not doing what I've been doing. So it would be more helpful to describe something I'm going to do instead, like "Instead of eating between meals, I'm going to go out for a walk, or talk on the phone, or create a picture of myself in my head as a thinner person."

    Client: Oh, yeah, I do see what you mean. So I guess instead of withdrawing, I — well, what is the opposite of that? I guess I think it would be more helpful if I volunteered the answers or gave my ideas or opinions — things like that.

17. *Counselor:* OK, so you're saying that you want to express yourself instead of holding back. Things like expressing opinions, feelings, things like that.

    Client: Yeah.

18. *Counselor:* OK, now we've mentioned three things you want to work on — anything else?

    Client: No, I can't think of anything.

In the next response, the counselor asks Joan to select one of the goals to work on initially. Tackling all three outcomes simultaneously could be overwhelming to a client.

19. *Counselor:* OK, as time goes on and we start working on some of these things, you may think of something else — or something we've talked about today may change. What might be helpful now is to decide which of these three things you'd like to work on first.
Client: Gee, that's a hard decision.

In the previous response, Joan demonstrated in vivo *one of her problems — difficulty in making decisions. In the next response, the counselor* **provides guidelines** *to help Joan make a choice but is careful not to make the decision for her.*

20. *Counselor:* Well, it's one decision I don't want to make for you. I'd encourage you to start with the area you think is most important to you now — and also maybe one that you feel you could work with successfully.
Client: [Long pause] Can this change, too?

21. *Counselor:* Sure — we'll start with one thing, and if later on it doesn't feel right, we'll move on.
Client: OK, well, I guess it would be the last thing we talked about — starting to express myself in situations where I usually don't.

In the next response, the counselor will discuss the degree to which Joan believes the **change represents something she will do** *rather than someone else.*

22. *Counselor:* OK, sticking with this one area, it seems like these are things that you could make happen without the help of anyone else or without requiring anyone else to change too. Can you think about that for a minute and see whether that's the way it feels to you?
Client: [Pause] I guess so. You're saying that I don't need to depend on someone else; it's something I can start doing.

In the next three responses (23, 24, 25), this counselor helps Joan explore the **feasibility and realistic nature of the goal.**

23. *Counselor:* Yes, it's a case where you are in the driver's seat. You know, too, earlier you mentioned this was something you wanted to do if it was possible, and I said we'd come back to this. Do you feel this change is realistic?
Client: I think so. In what way?

24. *Counselor:* Well, assuming you have some help from me, how feasible do you think it will be to start expressing yourself in these difficult situations?
Client: Well, I think it's feasible in the long run. I guess at first it will be hard because it's something I'm not used to doing and also because I get pretty uptight in some of these situations.

25. *Counselor:* So it feels possible for you to pursue this. At the same time, you realize your lack of skills and your nervousness are roadblocks that may make it difficult. Once we remove the roadblocks, I imagine your journey will be lot faster and a lot smoother. What do you think?
Client: Yeah. If I can just get past these initial hurdles.

In the next response, the counselor shifts to exploring **possible advantages** *of goal achievement. Note that the counselor asks the client first to express her opinion about advantages; the counselor is giving her in* vivo *practice of one of the skills related to her goal.*

26. *Counselor:* We're going to remember these hurdles and come back to them later. Then we can develop a plan to cope with and master them, so they don't get the best of you. One thing I'm wondering about — and this will probably sound silly because in a way it's obvious — but exactly how will making this change help you or benefit you?
Client: Mm — [Pause] — I'm thinking — well, what do you think?

In the previous response, the client shifted responsibility to the counselor and "withdrew," as she does in other anxiety-producing situations, such as math class and interactions with her parents. In the next response, the counselor **confronts** *this behavior pattern.*

27. *Counselor:* You know, it's interesting, I just asked you for your opinion about something, and instead of sharing it, you asked me to sort of handle it instead. Are you aware of this?
Client: Now that you mention it, I am. But I guess that's what I do so often it's sort of automatic.

In the next three responses (28, 29, 30), the counselor does some in vivo *assessment of Joan's problems, which results in information that can be used later for* **planning of subgoals and action steps.**

28. *Counselor:* Can you run through exactly what you were thinking and feeling just then?
Client: Well, just that I had a couple of ideas, but then I didn't think they were important enough to mention.

29. *Counselor:* I'm wondering if you also may have felt a little concerned about what I would think of your ideas.
Client: [Face flushes] Well, yeah. I guess it's silly, but yeah.

30. *Counselor:* So is this sort of the same thing that happens to you in math class or around your parents?
Client: Yeah — only in those two situations, I feel much more uptight than I do here.

In the next four responses, the counselor continues to explore **potential advantages** *for Joan of attaining this goal.*

31. *Counselor:* OK, that's real helpful because that information gives us some clues on what we'll need to do first in order to help you reach this result. Before we explore that, let's go back and see whether you can think of any ways in which making this change will help you.
    Client: Well, I think sometimes I'm like a doormat. I just sit there and let people impose on me. Sometimes I get taken advantage of.

32. *Counselor:* So you're saying that at times you feel used as a result?
    Client: Yeah. That's a good way to put it.

33. *Counselor:* OK, other advantages or benefits to you?
    Client: Well, I'd become less dependent and more self-reliant. If I do decide to go to college, that's only two years away, and I will need to be a whole lot more independent then.

34. *Counselor:* OK, that's a good thought. Any other ways that this change would be worthwhile for you, Joan?
    Client: Mm—I can't think of any. That's honest. But if I do, I'll mention them.

In the next responses (35–38), the counselor initiates exploration of **possible disadvantages** *of this goal.*

35. *Counselor:* OK, great! And the ones you've mentioned I think are really important ones. Now, I'd like you to flip the coin, so to speak, and see whether you can think of any disadvantages that could result from moving in this direction?
    Client: Well, I can't think of any in math. Well, no, in a way I can. I guess it's sort of the thing to do there to act like a dumb broad. If I start expressing myself more, people might wonder what is going on.

36. *Counselor:* So you're concerned about the reaction from some of the other students?
    Client: Yeah, in a way. Although there are a couple of girls in there who are pretty popular and also made the honor roll. So I don't think it's like I'd be a social outcast.

37. *Counselor:* It sounds, then, like you believe that is one disadvantage you could live with. Any other ways in which doing this could affect your life in a negative way—or could create another problem for you?
    Client: Well, I think a real issue there is how my parents would react if I started to do some of these things. I don't know. Maybe they would welcome it. But I sort of think they would consider it a revolt or something on my part and would want to squelch it right away.

38. *Counselor:* You seem to be saying you believe your parents have a stake in keeping you somewhat dependent on them.
    Client: Yeah, I do.

This is a difficult issue. Without observing her family, it would be impossible to say whether this is Joan's perception (and a distorted one) or whether the parents do play a role in this problem—and, indeed, from a diagnostic standpoint, family members are often significantly involved when one family member has a dependent personality. The counselor will thus **reflect both possibilities** *in the next response.*

39. *Counselor:* That may or may not be true. It could be that you see the situation that way and an outsider like myself might not see it the same way. On the other hand, it is possible your parents might subtly wish to keep you from growing up too quickly. This might be a potentially serious enough disadvantage for us to consider whether it would be useful for all four of us to sit down and talk together.
    Client: Do you think that would help?

In the next two responses, the counselor and Joan continue to discuss potential **negative effects or disadvantages** *related to this goal. Note that in the next response, instead of answering the client's previous question directly, the counselor shifts the responsibility to Joan and solicits her opinion, again giving her in vivo opportunities to demonstrate one skill related to the goal.*

40. *Counselor:* What do you think?
    Client: I'm not sure. They are sometimes hard to talk to.

41. *Counselor:* How would you feel about having a joint session—assuming they were agreeable?
    Client: Right now it seems OK. How could it help exactly?

In the following response, the counselor changes from an **individual to a systemic focus,** *since the parents may have an investment in keeping Joan dependent on them or may have given Joan an injunction "Don't grow up." The systemic focus avoids blaming any one person.*

42. *Counselor:* I think you mentioned it earlier. Sometimes when one person in a family changes the way she or he reacts to the rest of the family, it has a boomerang effect, causing ripples throughout the rest of the family. If that's going to happen in your case, it might be helpful to sit down and talk about it and anticipate the effects, rather than letting you get in the middle of a situation that starts to feel too hard to handle. It could be

helpful to your parents, too, to explore their role in this whole issue.

Client: I see. Well, where do we go from here?

43. *Counselor:* Our time is about up today. Let's get together in a week and map out a plan of action. (*Note:* The same process of goal selection would also be carried out in subsequent sessions for the other two outcome goals Joan identified earlier in this session.)

□ INTERVIEW LEADS FOR DEFINING GOALS

Most clients will select more than one goal. Ultimately, it may be more realistic for the client to work toward "attainment of a variety of specific objectives rather than a single, omnibus outcome" (Bandura, 1969, p. 104). For example, in our model case, Joan has selected three terminal outcome goals: acquiring and demonstrating at least four initiating skills, increasing positive self-talk about her ability to function adequately in competitive situations, and acquiring and using five decision-making skills (see Joan's goal chart on pp. 246–247). These three outcomes reflect the three core problems revealed by the assessment interview (Chapter 8). Selection of one goal may also imply the existence of other goals. For example, if a client states "I want to get involved in a relationship with a man that is emotionally and sexually satisfying," the client may also need to work on meeting men and her approach behaviors, developing communications skills designed to foster intimacy, and learning about what responses might be sexually satisfying for her.

At first, it is useful to have the client specify one or more desired goals for each separate problem. However, to tackle several outcome goals at one time would be unrealistic. The counselor should ask the client to choose one of the outcome goals to pursue first. After selecting an initial outcome goal to work toward, the counselor and client can define the three parts of the goal and identify subgoals. The next section of this chapter will introduce some counselor leads used to help the client define the outcome goals of counseling and will present some probable responses that indicate client responsiveness to the leads.

Defining Behaviors Related to Goals

Carkhuff and Anthony (1979, pp. 136–137) assert that "to achieve any goal, a helper must *act.* And to ensure that the goal to be achieved is both functional and real, the helper must begin his or her

sequence of activity by defining this goal. . . . This is a step that all too many people overlook entirely."* Defining goals involves specifying in operational or behavioral terms what the client (whether an individual, group member, or organization) is to *do* as a result of counseling. This part of an outcome goal defines the particular behavior the client is to perform and answers the question "*What* will the client do, think, or feel differently?" Examples of behavior outcome goals include exercising more frequently, asking for help from a teacher, verbal sharing of positive feelings about oneself, and thinking about oneself in positive ways. As you can see, both overt and covert behaviors, including thoughts and feelings, can be included in this part of the outcome goal as long as the behavior is defined by what it means for each client. Defining goals behaviorally makes the goal-setting process specific, and specifically defined goals are more likely to create incentives and guide performance than vaguely stated intentions (Bandura & Simon, 1977, p. 178). When goals are behaviorally or operationally defined, it is easier to evaluate the effects of counseling (see also Chapter 10). Further, "clearly stated goals tend to make problems seem more manageable and solutions more attainable" (Dixon & Glover, 1984, p. 133).

Interview leads for defining goal behavior. The following are some leads a counselor can use to identify the behavior part of a goal:

"When you say you want to _____, what do you see yourself doing?"

"What could I see you doing, thinking, or feeling as a result of this change?"

"You say you want to be more self-confident. What things would you be thinking and doing as a self-confident person?"

"Describe a good (and a poor) example of this goal."

It is important for the counselor to continue to pursue these leads until the client can define the overt and covert behaviors associated with the goal. This is not an easy task, for most clients talk about changes in vague or abstract terms. If the client has trouble specifying behaviors, the counselor can help with further instructions, informa-

---

* This and all other quotations from this source are from *The Skills of Helping* by R. R. Carkhuff and W. A. Anthony. Copyright © 1979 by Human Resource Development Press. Reprinted by permission.

tion giving, or self-disclosing a personal goal. The counselor can also facilitate behavioral definitions of the goal by encouraging the client to use action verbs to describe what will be happening when the goal is attained (Dixon & Glover, 1984). As we mentioned earlier, it is important to get clients to specify what they *want* to do, not what they don't want or what they want to stop. The goal is usually defined sufficiently when the counselor can accurately repeat and paraphrase the client's definition.

Another way to obtain behavioral goal descriptions, suggested by Hill (1975), is to use the Counseling Outcome Inventory (COI). In using the COI, the client is asked to list some characteristics, qualities, or descriptions that are important to the client to acquire or to demonstrate. Then, for each of these descriptors, the client is asked to list one or more actual behaviors of this quality, which Hill calls "behavioral anchors" (p. 573). For instance, the vague descriptor "self-confidence" might be translated into a behavioral anchor of "making fewer negative self-statements"; the descriptor "be more attractive" might be translated into the behavioral anchors of "lose 10 pounds" and "smile more often." The COI procedure helps to make the outcome goals observable and also helps to develop goals that are stated meaningfully for different clients.

Defining the Conditions of an Outcome Goal

The second part of an outcome goal specifies the conditions — that is, the *context* or *circumstances* — where the behavior will occur. This is an important element of an outcome goal for both the client and the counselor. The conditions suggest a particular *person* with whom the client may perform the desired behaviors or a particular *setting* and answers the question "*Where, when,* and *with whom* is the behavior to occur?" Specifying the conditions of a behavior sets boundaries and helps to ensure that the behavior will occur only in desired settings or with desired people and will not generalize to undesired settings. This idea can be illustrated vividly. For example, a woman may wish to increase the number of positive verbal and nonverbal responses she makes toward her husband. In this case, time spent with her husband would be the condition or circumstances in which the behavior occurs. However, if this behavior generalized to include all men, it might have negative effects on the very relationship she is trying to improve.

Interview leads for the conditions of a goal. Leads used to determine the conditions of the outcome goal include these:

"Where would you like to do this?"
"In what situations do you want to be able to do this?"
"When do you want to do this?"
"Whom would you be with when you do this?"
"In what situations is what you're doing now not meeting your expectations?"

The counselor is looking for a response that indicates where or with whom the client will make the change or perform the desired behavior. If the client gives a noncommittal response, the counselor may suggest client self-monitoring to obtain these data. The counselor can also use self-disclosure and personal examples to demonstrate that a desired behavior may not be appropriate in all situations or with all people.

Defining a Level of Change

The third element of an outcome goal specifies the level or *amount* of the behavioral change. In other words, this part answers "*How much* is the client to do or to complete in order to reach the desired goal?" The level of an outcome goal serves as a barometer that measures the extent to which the client will be able to perform the desired behavior. For example, a man may state that he wishes to decrease cigarette smoking. The following week, he may report that he did a better job of cutting down on cigarettes. However, unless he can specify how much he actually decreased smoking, both he and the counselor will have difficulty determining how much the client really completed toward the goal. In this case, the client's level of performance is ambiguous. In contrast, if he had reported that he reduced cigarette smoking by two cigarettes per day in one week, his level of performance could be determined easily. If his goal were to decrease cigarette smoking by eight cigarettes per day, this information would help to determine progress toward the goal.

Like the behavior and condition parts of an outcome goal, the level of change should always be established individually for each client. The amount of satisfaction derived from goal attainment often depends on the level of performance established (Bandura & Simon, 1977, p. 178). A suitable level of change will depend on such factors as the present level of the problem behavior, the present level of the desired behavior, the resources available for change, the client's readiness to change, and the degree to which other conditions or people are maintaining the present level of problem behavior. Hosford and de Visser (1974) point out that such factors often make the level of a goal the most difficult part to define.

As an example, suppose a client wants to increase the number of assertive opinions she expresses orally with her husband. If she now withholds all her opinions, her level of change might be stated at a lower level than that defined for another client who already expresses some opinions. And if the client's husband is accustomed to her refraining from giving opinions, this might affect the degree of change made, at least initially. The counselor's and client's primary concern is to establish a level that is manageable, that the client can attain with some success. Occasionally the counselor may encounter a client who always wants to achieve more change than is desirable or even possible. As Krumboltz and Thoresen (1976) note, progressively raising levels of change has a limit (p. 105). These authors suggest that, in such cases, the counselor must avoid reinforcing the client's perfectionistic goal statements (p. 104). In addition, if the level is set too high, the desired behavior may not occur, thus ruling out chances for success and subsequent progress and rewards. Brown and Brown (1977) recommend that, as a general rule of thumb, it is better to err by moving too slowly and thus set the level too low rather than too high.

One way to avoid setting the level of a goal too high or making it too restrictive is to use a scale that identifies a series of *increasingly desired* outcomes for each given problem area. This concept, introduced by Kiresuk and Sherman (1968), is called "goal-attainment scaling" (GAS) and has been used increasingly in agencies that must demonstrate certain levels of client goal achievement in order to receive or maintain funding. In goal-attainment scaling, the counselor and client devise five outcomes for a given problem and arrange these by level or extent of change on a scale in the following order (each outcome is assigned a numerical value): most unfavorable outcome (−2), less than likely expected outcome (−1), most likely or expected outcome (0), more than likely expected outcome (+1), most favorable outcome (+2). Table 9-1 shows an example of the use of GAS for a client with ulcerative colitis.

A review of this GAS model and four similar models is presented by Lloyd (1983).

TABLE 9-1. Goal-attainment scale for client with ulcerative colitis

Date: 10/24/73	Frequency of colitis attacks	Cognitive hypothesis testing
Most unfavorable outcome thought likely	One per day	Every stress transaction per week seen as attack on self
Less than expected success with treatment	One every other day	One out of four times per week considers that a stress transaction might not be attack on self
Expected level of treatment success	One per week	Completes Treatment Steps 4 and 5 *after* every stress transaction
More than expected success with treatment	One every two weeks	Completes Treatment Steps 4 and 5 *during* stress transactions some of the time
Best expected success with treatment	None per month	Completes Treatment Steps 4 and 5 *during* stress transactions all the time

Adapted From "Behavioral treatment of mucous colitis" by K. J. Youell & J. P. McCullough. *Journal of Consulting and Clinical Psychology, 43,* 740–745. Copyright © 1975 by American Psychological Association. Reprinted by permission.

Leads to identify the level of change. Here are some leads you can use to help identify the client's desired extent or level of change:

"How much would you like to be able to do this, compared with how much you're doing it now?"

"How often do you want to do this?"

"From the information you obtained during self-monitoring, you seem to be studying only about an hour a week now. What is a reasonable amount for you to increase this without getting bogged down?"

"You say you'd like to lose 40 pounds. Let's talk about a reasonable amount of time this might take and, to start with, what amount would be easy for you to lose just in the next 3 weeks."

"What amount of change is realistic, considering where you are right now?"

The counselor is looking for some indication of the present and future levels of the desired behavior. This level can be expressed by either the number of times or the amount the client wants to be able to do something. In some cases, an appropriate level may be only one, as when a client's outcome goal is to make one decision about a job change. The counselor can help the client establish an appropriate level of change by referring to the self-monitoring data collected during problem assessment. If the client has not engaged in monitoring, this is another point where it is almost imperative to have the client observe and record the present amounts of the problem behavior and the goal behavior. This information will give some idea of the present level of behavior, referred to as the "base-rate" or "baseline" level. This information is important because in setting the desired level, it should be contrasted with the present level of the overt or covert behavior(s). As you may recall from Chapter 8, a client's data gathering is very useful for defining problems and goals and for monitoring progress toward the goals.

Level as an indicator of type of problem and goal. The level reflected in an outcome goal reflects both the type of problem and the type of goal. From our earlier discussion about what outcome goals represent, recall that problems can be classified as either choice or change. In a choice problem, the level of the goal reflects a conflict to be resolved or a choice or decision to be made—for example, the client needs to decide on one of three options or decide between two different directions. In a change problem, the level reflected in the goal specifies both the direction and the type of change desired. In the example of the client who wants to be more assertive, if the client's present level of a specified assertive response is zero, then the goal would be to acquire the assertive skill. When the base rate of a behavior is zero, or when the client does not seem to have certain skills in her or his repertoire, the goal is stated as acquiring a behavior. If, however, the client wants to improve or increase something that she or he can already do (but at a low level), the goal is stated as increasing a behavior. Increas-

ing or acquiring overt and/or covert behaviors is a goal when the client's problem is a *response deficit,* meaning that the desired response occurs with insufficient intensity or frequency or in inappropriate form (Gambrill, 1977). Sometimes a client has an overt behavioral response in his or her repertoire, but it is masked or inhibited by the presence of certain feelings—in which case the goal would be directed toward the feelings rather than the overt behavior. In this instance, the problem stems from *response inhibition,* and the resulting goal is a disinhibition of the response, usually by the working through of the emotional reactions standing in the way.

In contrast, if the client is doing too much of something and wants to lower the present level, the goal is stated as decreasing a behavior and possibly, later on, eliminating it from the client's repertoire. Decreasing or eliminating overt and/or covert behaviors is a goal when the client's problem is a *response excess,* meaning that a response occurs so often, so long, with such excessive intensity, or in socially inappropriate contexts that it is often annoying to the client and to others (Gambrill, 1977). In problems of response excesses, it is usually the frequency or amount of the response, rather than its form, that is problematic. It is almost always easier to work on developing or increasing a behavior (response increment or acquisition) than on stopping or decreasing a response (response decrement or elimination). This is another reason to encourage clients to state their goals in positive terms, working toward doing something or doing it more, rather than stopping something or doing it less.

Sometimes, when the client wants to eliminate something, she or he wishes to replace whatever is eliminated with a more appropriate or self-enhancing behavior. For instance, a client trying to lose weight may desire to replace junk-food snacks with low-calorie snacks. This client's goal is stated in terms of "restructuring" something about her or his environment—in this case, the type of snack eaten. Although this is an example of restructuring an overt behavior, restructuring can be cognitive as well. For example, a client may want to eliminate negative, self-defeating thoughts about difficulty in taking tests and replace these with positive, self-enhancing thoughts about the capacity to perform adequately in test-taking situations. Restructuring also often takes place during family counseling when boundaries and alliances between and among family members are shifted so that, for instance, a member on the periphery is pulled into the family, or triangles are broken up, or overinvolved alliances between two persons are rearranged. Restructuring overt or covert behaviors is a goal when the problem is *inadequate, inappropriate, or defective stimulus control,* meaning that the necessary supporting environmental conditions either are missing or are arranged in such a way as to make it impossible or difficult for the desired behavior to occur.

In some instances, the level of a goal reflects maintenance of a particular overt or covert response at the current rate or frequency or under existing conditions. As you recall from our earlier discussion of client change in this chapter, not all goals will reflect a discrepancy between the client's present and future behavior. Some goals may be directed toward maintaining a desired or satisfying situation or response. Such goals may be stated as, for example, "to maintain my present amount (three hours daily) of studying," "to maintain the present balance in my life between work on weekdays and play on weekends," "to maintain the positive communication I have with my spouse in our daily talks," or "to maintain my present level (two a day) of engaging in relaxation sessions." A maintenance goal suggests that the client's present level of behavior is satisfying and sufficient, at least at this particular time. A maintenance goal may

help to put things in perspective by acknowledging the areas of the client's life that are going well. Maintenance goals are also useful and necessary when one of the change goals has been achieved. For example, if a client wanted to lose weight and has done so successfully, then the counselor and client need to be concerned about how the client can maintain the weight loss. Often maintenance goals and programs are harder to achieve and take greater effort and planning than initial change attempts.

To summarize, the level stated by the outcome goal will usually reflect one of the categories of problems and goals summarized in Table 9-2. Since most clients have more than one outcome goal, a client's objectives may reflect more than one of these directions of change. Knowledge of the direction and level of change defined in the client's goals is important in selecting counseling strategies. For example, self-monitoring (see Chapter 19) is used differently depending on whether it is applied to increase or to decrease a response. One counseling strategy might be used appropriately to help a client acquire responses; yet another strategy may be needed to help a client restructure some responses. It is very important for the counselor and client to spend sufficient time on specifying the level of the goal, even if this process seems elusive and difficult.

LEARNING ACTIVITY #27: DEFINING OUTCOME GOALS

We have found that the most difficult part of developing goals with a client is specifying the three parts of the outcome goal. We believe the reason is that the concept is foreign to most of us and difficult to internalize. This is probably because, in our own lives, we think about small, very mundane goals. With more complex goals, we still don't assess the individual overt and covert behaviors to be changed, where and with whom change will occur, and the extent of the change. This learning activity is intended to help you create some *personal* meaning from these three parts of an outcome goal. If you feel comfortable with this, you are more likely to help a client define her or his goals.

1. During the next week, keep a log of any concerns, issues, or problems you're experiencing.
2. At the end of the week, go over your log and label each problem according to type: choice or change. If change, describe the problem as re-

sponse deficit, response inhibition, response excess, or inadequate/inappropriate stimulus control (refer also to Table 9-2).
3. Select one problem you are interested in resolving and specify the corresponding type of goal (as listed in Table 9-2): decision or resolution of conflict, response increment, response acquisition, disinhibition or working through a response, response decrement, response elimination, or response restructuring.
4. Define the goal by identifying—
   a. What you'll be doing (overt behavior) and thinking and feeling (covert behavior) as a result of this goal—make sure you state this in positive terms.
   b. Where, when, and with whom you want to do this (conditions).
   c. How much or how often you want to do this (level).

(continued)

LEARNING ACTIVITY #27: DEFINING OUTCOME GOALS (continued)

Your goal is probably defined sufficiently if an objective observer can paraphrase it accurately, stating exactly what, when, where, with whom, and how much you will be doing.

5. In addition to your definition above, create a goal-attainment scale for your outcome, using the example given in Table 9-1. Your scale should specify the following five levels of possible outcomes: most unfavorable outcome (−2), less than likely expected outcome (−1), most likely or expected outcome (0), more than likely expected outcome (+1), and most favorable outcome (+2).

6. Review your responses to this activity with a colleague, instructor, supervisor, or partner.

TABLE 9-2. Categories of types of client problems and related goals

Type of problem	Type of goal
1. Choice	Decision between two or more alternatives
	Resolution of at least two conflicting issues
2. Change	
A. Response deficit	Response increment
	Response acquisition
B. Response inhibition	Disinhibition of response
	Working through of emotional reactions
C. Response excess	Response decrement
	Response elimination
D. Inadequate or inappropriate stimulus control	Response restructuring
3. Maintenance	Response maintenance at current frequency or amount or in current context

Identifying and Sequencing Subgoals or Action Steps

All of us can probably recall times when we were expected to learn something so fast that the learning experience was overwhelming and produced feelings of frustration, irritation, and discouragement. The change represented by counseling goals can be achieved best if the process is gradual. Any change program should be organized into an "orderly learning sequence" that guides the client through small steps toward the ultimate desired behaviors (Bandura, 1969, p. 74). In defining goals, this gradual learning sequence is achieved by breaking down the ultimate goal into a series of smaller goals called *subgoals* or *action steps.* Subgoals help clients move toward the solution of problems in a "planful way" (Dixon & Glover, 1984, p. 136). The subgoals are usually arranged in a hierarchy, so that the client completes subgoals at the bottom of the ranked list before the ones near the top. Although an overall outcome goal can provide a "general directive" for change, the specific subgoals may determine a person's immediate activities and degree of effort in making changes (Bandura & Simon, 1977, p. 178). As these authors note, "By focusing on the distant future, it is easy to put off efforts at change in the present. . . . Exercising control over behaviors in the present increases the likelihood that desired futures will be realized" (p. 170). In a study reported by Seidner and Kirschenbaum (1980), commitment to identified goals was enhanced more when individuals agreed to participate fully in key aspects of a change program than when they agreed to pursue distant, long-range goals.

Bandura (1969) suggests that sequencing goals into smaller subgoals is more likely to produce the desired results for two reasons. First, completion of subgoals may keep failure experiences to a minimum. Completing subgoals successfully will encourage the client and will help maintain the client's motivation to change (p. 75). Jeffery (1977) found that progressively increasing subgoals sustained a high level of client motivation even when the overall outcomes were difficult to attain. Second, arranging the ultimate goal into subgoals indicates that immediate, daily subgoals may be more potent than distant, weekly subgoals.

Subgoals identified may represent covert as well as overt behavior, since a comprehensive change program usually involves changes in the client's thoughts and feelings as well as in overt behaviors and environmental situations. Subgoals may arise out of treatment approaches or recommended ways to resolve a particular problem or, when formal procedures are not available, from more informal and common-sense ideas. In any event, they are always actions that move the client in the direction of the desired outcome goal (Carkhuff & Anthony, 1979).

After subgoals are identified and selected, they

are rank-ordered in a series of tasks—a hierarchy —according to *complexity and degree of difficulty and immediacy.* Since some clients are put off by the word *hierarchy,* we use the term *goal pyramid* instead and pull out an 8½" × 11" sheet of paper that has a drawing of a blank pyramid on it, such as the one in Figure 9-3 (p. 240). A series of subgoal tasks may represent either increasing requirements of the same (overt or covert) behavior or demonstrations of different behaviors, with simpler and easier responses sequenced before more complex and difficult ones (Gambrill, 1977). The second criterion for ranking is immediacy. For this criterion, subgoals are ranked according to prerequisite tasks—that is, what tasks must be done before others can be achieved.

The sequencing of subgoals in order of complexity is based on learning principles called *shaping* and *successive approximations.* Shaping helps someone learn a small amount at a time, with reinforcement or encouragement for each task completed successfully. Gradually, the person learns the entire amount or achieves the overall result through these day-to-day learning experiences that successively approximate the overall outcome.

Steps in identifying and sequencing subgoals. Identification and arrangement of subgoals are critical to the client's success with the outcome goal. The following steps are involved in this process.

First, the client identifies the *first* step he or she must take—that is, the first things that need to be done to move in the desired direction. The first step will be some action that is both comfortable and achievable (Gambrill, 1977). As Carkhuff and Anthony (1979) note, "The great majority of people who abandon [change] programs do so because they find they are unable to complete the first step successfully. . . . Conversely, successful completion of the first step invariably reinforces a helpee's determination to go on by promoting self-confidence" (pp. 185–186). If the client identifies an action as the initial step but cannot answer affirmatively the following two questions suggested by Carkhuff and Anthony, then selecting that action as the initial step is not a good idea, and the choice needs further exploration and consideration. The two questions are "Will [the client] be able to take this first step successfully?" and "Does this first step lead directly toward the goal?" (Carkhuff & Anthony, 1979, p. 185).

Second, if the client progresses satisfactorily on

the first step, additional intermediate steps that bridge the gap between the first step and the terminal goal are identified and ranked. (If the client does not progress on the first step, discuss this issue and consider revising the initial step.) Effective intermediate steps are ones that build on existing client assets and resources, do not conflict with the client's value system, are decided on and owned by the client, and represent immediate, daily, or short-term actions rather than weekly, distant, long-term actions (see also Bandura & Simon, 1977; Carkhuff & Anthony, 1979; Gambrill, 1977).

There is no hard and fast rule concerning the number of intermediate steps identified, other than ensuring that the gap between adjacent steps is not too great. Each successive step gradually begins where the last step left off. Clients can consider two questions in ranking successive intermediate steps: "Where will I be when I have completed this step?" and "What should my next major step be?" (Carkhuff & Anthony, 1979, p. 184). The counselor also needs to make sure that each intermediate step requires only one basic action or activity by the client; if two or more activities are involved, it is usually better to make this two separate steps (Carkhuff & Anthony, 1979).

As we mentioned earlier, intermediate steps are ranked on two aspects:

1. Degree of difficulty and complexity—"Which is easier; which is harder?" Less complex and demanding tasks are ranked ahead of others.
2. Immediacy—"What do I need to do before I can do this?" Prerequisite tasks are ranked before others.

Ranked steps are then filled in on the goal pyramid—usually in pencil, because in the process of moving through the hierarchy, the subgoals may need to be modified or rearranged. As Dixon and Glover observe, "Subgoals represent an early representation of the problem and may well be revised by the client and counselor as strategies are tested" (1984, p. 136).

Third, after all the steps have been identified and sequenced, the client starts to carry out the actions represented by the subgoals, beginning with the initial step and moving on. Usually, it is wise not to attempt a new subgoal until the client has successfully completed the previous one on the pyramid. Progress made on initial and subsequent steps provides useful information about whether the gaps between steps are too large or just right and whether the sequencing of steps is appropriate. As the subgoals are met, they become part of the client's current repertoire that can be used in additional change efforts toward the terminal goals (Schwartz & Goldiamond, 1975, p. 117).

An example may clarify the process of identifying and sequencing subgoals for a client. Suppose you are working with a person who wishes to lose 40 pounds. Losing 40 pounds is not a goal that anyone can accomplish overnight or without small requisite changes along the way. First of all, the person will need to determine a reasonable weekly level of weight loss, such as 1 to 2 pounds. Next, you and the client will have to determine the tasks the client will need to complete in order to lose weight. These tasks can be stated as subgoals that the client can strive to carry out each day, starting with the initial subgoal, the one that feels most comfortable and easy to achieve, and working the way up the pyramid as each previous step is successfully completed and maintained in the client's repertoire.

Although weight loss generally may include action steps such as alteration of eating levels, increase in physical activity, restructuring of cognitions and belief systems, and development of additional social skills, the exact tasks chosen by two or more clients who want to lose weight may be quite different. The therapist should be sensitive to such differences and not impose his or her method for solving the problem (such as weight loss) on the client. Similarly, each client will have a different idea of how subgoals will be best sequenced. In Figure 9-3 we illustrate how one particular client sequenced her identified subgoals on the goal pyramid. This client's rationale was that if she increased exercise and relaxation *first,* it would be easier to alter eating habits. For her, more difficult and also less immediate goals included restructuring her thoughts about herself and her body image and developing social skills necessary to initiate new relationships. This last subgoal she viewed as the most difficult one because her weight served partly to protect her from social distress situations. After all six subgoals are achieved, the

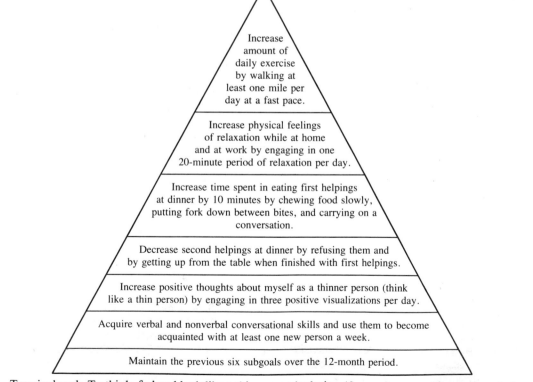

Terminal goal: To think, feel and look like a thin person by losing 40 pounds over a 12-month period

Weekly goal: To think, feel, and look like a thin person by losing 1 pound per week

Figure 9-3. Goal pyramid subgoals for example client

final subgoal is simply to keep these actions going for at least a 12-month period. At the bottom of the pyramid, it would be important to discuss with her ways in which she can maintain the subgoals over an extended period of time. Note, too, in this example that her terminal goal is stated in positive terms—not "I don't want to be fat" but "I do want to feel, think, and look like a thin person." The subgoals represent actions she will take to support this desired outcome. Also note that all the subgoals are stated in the same way as the terminal outcome goal—with the definition of the behaviors to be changed, the level of change, and the conditions or circumstances of change so that the client knows what to do, where, when, with whom, and how much or how often.

Interview leads for identifying subgoals. In identifying subgoals, the counselor uses leads similar to the following to help the client determine appropriate subgoals or action steps:

"How will you go about doing [or thinking, feeling] this?"

"What exactly do you need to do to make this happen?"

"Let's brainstorm some actions you'll need to take to make your goal work for you."

"What have you done in the past to work toward this goal? How did it help?"

"Let's think of the steps you need to take to get from where you are now to where you want to be."

The counselor is always trying to encourage and support client participation and responsibility in goal setting, remembering that clients are more likely to carry out changes that they originate. Occasionally, however, after using leads like the ones above, some clients are unable to specify any desirable or necessary action steps or subgoals. The counselor may then have to prompt the client either by asking the client to think of other people who have similar problems and to identify their strategies for action or by providing a statement illustrating an example or model of an action step or subgoal (Dixon & Glover, 1984). Counselors do not prompt in these instances to give clients the answer but to "demonstrate that there are always alternatives" (Dixon & Glover, p. 97).

Interview leads for sequencing subgoals. General leads to use to sequence and rank subgoals include the following:

"What is your first step?"

"What would you be able to do most easily?"

"What would be most difficult?"

"What is most important for you to do now? least important?"

"How could we order these steps to maximize your success in reaching your goal?"

"Let's think of steps you need to take to get from where you are now to where you want to be—and arrange them in an order from what seems easiest to you to the ones that seem hardest for you."

"Can you think of some things you need to do before some other things as you make progress toward your goal?"

LEARNING ACTIVITY #28: IDENTIFYING AND SEQUENCING SUBGOALS

This learning activity is an extension of Learning Activity #27. Continue to work with the same goal you selected and defined in that activity. In this activity, we suggest the following steps:

1. First, identify the initial step you need to take to move toward your goal. Ask yourself:
   a. Does this step move directly toward the goal?
   b. Will I be able to take this step comfortably and successfully?
   Unless the answer to both questions is yes, redefine your initial step. Your initial step then becomes your first subgoal.
2. Generate a list of intermediate steps that bridge the gap between this initial step and your desired outcome. Consider where you will be after completing each step and what comes next. These intermediate steps become remaining subgoals. For each step in your list, consider:
   a. Does the step represent only one major activity?
   b. Is the step based on my existing assets and resources?
   c. Does the step support most of my major values and beliefs?
   d. Is the step something I want for myself?
   e. Does the step represent immediate, short-term activities rather than distant, long-term ones?
   If the answer to any of these questions for any particular step is no, rework that step.

(continued)

3. Write each step on a 3 × 5 index card. Then assign a numerical rating to each card for degree of difficulty, using a 0 to 100 scale: 0 = least complex, least difficult; 100 = most complex, most difficult.

4. Rank-order your steps or subgoals by arranging your cards in order, starting with the one closest to zero and ending with the one closest to 100. This represents the sequence in which you will complete your subgoals.

Identifying Obstacles

To ensure that the client can complete each subgoal step successfully, it is helpful to identify any *obstacles* that could interfere. Obstacles may include overt and/or covert behavior. *Potential* obstacles to "check out" with the client include the presence or absence of certain feelings or mood states, thoughts, beliefs and perceptions, other people, and situations or events. Another obstacle could be lack of knowledge or skill. As Gambrill (1977) points out, identification of lack of knowledge or skill is important because the client probably needs information or training before the subgoal action can be attempted.

Interview leads to identify obstacles. Clients are often not very aware of any factors that might interfere with completing a subgoal and may need prompts from the counselor, such as the following ones, to identify obstacles:

> "What are some obstacles you may encounter in trying to take this action?"
> "What people [feelings, ideas, situations] might get in the way of getting this done?"
> "What or who might prevent you from working on this activity?"
> "In what ways might you have difficulty completing this task successfully?"
> "What information or skills do you need in order to complete this action effectively?"

Occasionally the counselor may need to point out apparent obstacles that the client overlooks. If significant obstacles are identified, a plan to deal with or counteract the effects of these factors needs to be developed. Often this is similar to an "antisabotage plan" (see Chapter 20), in which the counselor and client try to predict ways in which the client might not do the desired activity and then work around the possible barriers. For example, suppose you explore obstacles with the client we described in the earlier section who wants to lose weight and become thin. Perhaps in exploring

the first subgoal, walking at least one mile a day, she identifies two things that might keep her from doing this: rain and being alone. Ways to prevent these two factors from interfering with her walking might be using an indoor facility and walking with an exercise partner.

Identifying Resources

The next step is to identify *resources* — factors that will help the client complete the subgoal task effectively. Like obstacles, resources include overt and covert behaviors. *Potential* resources to explore include feelings, thoughts and belief systems, people, situations, information, and skills. In this step, the counselor tries to help clients identify already present or developed resources that, if used, can make completion of the subgoal task(s) more likely and more successful.

Interview leads for identifying resources. Possible leads include the following:

> "Which resources do you have available to help you as you go through this activity [or action]?"
> "What specific feelings [or thoughts] are you aware of that might make it easier for you to _____?"
> "What kind of support system do you have from others that you can use to make it easier to _____?"
> "What skills [or information] do you possess that will help you do _____ more successfully?"

For example, the weight-loss client might identify a friend or other social support as a resource she could use for daily exercise, as well as her belief that exercise promotes wellness and good feelings.

Review of Progress

As any one subgoal is completed, it is helpful for the counselor and the client to review it together to assess *progress* and to determine whether the next-ranked subgoal is still relevant to the appropriate place on the goal pyramid. In any case where a subgoal is not met, the counselor and client should discuss what went wrong and what can be done more successfully in the future. According to Gambrill (1977), the most common reason for failure to carry out a subgoal is that the gaps between steps are too big. In this instance, the "failure" is a useful indication, letting the counselor know that smaller approximations are needed. Other areas to explore when subgoals are not met include whether the subgoal was really selected and owned by the client to begin with, whether it was carried out as specified, and whether the client had the resources to achieve it. If this exploration turns up nothing, then consider what the maladaptive behavior is trying to preserve and protect. Perhaps additional secondary gains yet to be identified are operating.

Counselors need to support, encourage, and reinforce the client for completion of subgoal tasks in order to help maintain client enthusiasm and commitment. It is also important to realize that goal setting has broader implications for clients than simply reaching a target objective. It is helpful to explore with clients what they are learning from this process and how this can be applied to other areas of their life as well. As Carkhuff and Anthony observe, clients "should gain more from the helping process itself than the limited ability to reach a single, isolated goal" (1979, p. 231).

Interviewing leads for reviewing progress. Leads to use during the review process include the following:

"Can you describe how you carried out the plan [action] we worked out last week?"

"What problems, if any, did you encounter in taking this action?"

"What have you learned from doing this? Is it sufficient to move on now or do we need to work on this some more?"

☐ MODEL DIALOGUE: THE CASE OF JOAN

The dialogue for the case of Joan is continued to help you see how the leads for defining goals are used with a client. The session for selecting goals was presented earlier in this chapter. We pick up with the next session. As in the previous dialogue, each counselor response is prefaced by an explanation of what the counselor is doing.

The counselor will start by **summarizing** *the previous session and by checking out whether Joan's goals have changed in any way. Goal setting is a flexible process, subject to revisions along the way.*

1. *Counselor:* OK, Joan, last week when we talked, just to recap, you mentioned three areas you'd like to work on. Is this still accurate, or have you added anything or modified your thinking in any way about these since we last met?

   Client: No, that's still where I want to go right now. And I still want to start with this whole issue of expressing myself and not worrying so much about what other people think. I've been doing a lot of thinking about that this week, and I think I'm really starting to see how much I let other people use me as a doormat and also control my reactions in a lot of ways.

2. *Counselor:* Yes, you mentioned some of those things last week. They seem to be giving you some incentive to work on this.

   Client: Yeah. I guess I'm finally waking up and starting to feel a little fed up about it.

In the next response, the counselor explains the **purpose** *of the session and solicits Joan's opinion, again giving her another opportunity to express her opinions.*

3. *Counselor:* Last week I mentioned it might be helpful to map out a plan of action. How does that sound to you? If it isn't where you want to start, let me know.

   Client: No, I do. I've been kind of gearing up for this all week.

In the next two responses, the counselor helps Joan define the **behaviors** *associated with the goal — what she will be doing, thinking, or feeling.*

4. *Counselor:* OK, last week when we talked about this area of change, you described it as wanting to express yourself more without worrying so much about the reactions of other people. Could you tell me what you mean by expressing yourself — to make sure we're on the same wavelength?

   Client: Well, like in math class, I need to volunteer the answers when I know them, and volunteer to go to the board. Also, I hesitate to ask questions. I need to be able to ask a question without worrying if it sounds foolish.

5. *Counselor:* OK, you've mentioned three specific ways in math class you want to express yourself. [makes a note] I'm going to jot these down on this paper in case we want to refer to these later. Anything else you can think of in math class?

   Client: No, not really. The other situation I have trouble with is with my folks.

"Trouble" is not very specific. Again, a **behavioral definition** *of the goal is sought in the next two responses.*

6. *Counselor:* OK, "trouble." Again, can you describe exactly how you'd like to express yourself when interacting with them?

    Client: Well, kind of the same stuff. Sometimes I would like to ask them a question. Or ask for help or something. But I don't. I almost never express my ideas or opinions to them, especially if I don't agree with their ideas. I just keep things to myself.

7. *Counselor:* So you'd like to be able to make a request, ask a question, talk about your ideas with them, and express disagreement.

    Client: Yeah. Wow—sounds hard.

In the following response, the counselor prepares Joan for the idea of working in **small steps** *and also explores* **conditions (situations, people)** *associated with the goal.*

8. *Counselor:* It will take some time, and we won't try to do everything at once. Just one step at a time. Now, you've mentioned two different situations where these things are important to you— math class and with your parents. I noticed last week there was one time when you were reluctant to express your opinion with me. Is this something you want to do in any other situations or with any other people?

    Client: Well, sure—in that it does crop up occasionally at different times or with different people, even friends. But it's worse in math and at home. I think if I could do it there, I could do it anywhere.

In the next response, the counselor starts to explore the **level** *or* **desired extent of change.** *The counselor is attempting to establish a* **current base rate** *in order to know how much the client is doing now.*

9. *Counselor:* OK, I'm making a note of this, too. Now could you estimate how often you express yourself in the ways you've described above *right now,* either in math class or with your folks, during the course of an average week?

    Client: You mean how many times do I do these things during the week?

10. *Counselor:* Yes.

    Client: Probably almost never—at least not in math class or at home. Maybe once or twice at the most.

The counselor continues to help Joan identify a **practical** *and* **realistic level of change.**

11. *Counselor:* OK, if you express yourself in one of these ways once or twice a week now, how often would you like to be doing this? Think of something that is also practical or realistic.

    Client: Mm. Well, I don't really know. Offhand, I'd guess about four or five times—that's about once a day, and that would take a lot of energy for me to be able to do that in these situations.

At this point, the **behavior, conditions, and level of change** *for this terminal goal are defined. The counselor asks Joan whether this definition is the way she wants it.*

12. *Counselor:* OK, I'll make a note of this. Check what I have written down—does it seem accurate? [Joan reads what is listed as the first terminal goal on her goal chart at the end of this dialogue.]

    Client: Yeah. Boy, that sort of makes it official, doesn't it?

This is the second time Joan has expressed a little hesitation. So the counselor will check out **her feelings** *about the process in the next response.*

13. *Counselor:* Yes. What kinds of feelings are you having about what we're doing now?

    Client: Kind of good and a little scared too. Like do I really have what it takes to do this?

In the next response, the counselor responds to Joan's concern. Joan has already selected this goal, yet if she has difficulty later on moving toward it, they will need to explore **what her present behavior is trying to protect.**

14. *Counselor:* One thing I am sure of is that you do have the resources inside you to move in this direction as long as this is a direction that is important to you and one that is not necessary to protect any parts of you. If we move along and you feel stuck, we'll come back to this and see how you keep getting stuck at this point.

    Client: OK.

In the next response, the counselor introduces the idea of **subgoals** *that represent small action steps toward the terminal goal and asks Joan to identify the* **initial step.**

15. *Counselor:* Another thing that I think might help with your apprehension is to map out a plan of action. What we've just done is to identify exactly where you want to get to—maybe over the course of the next few months. Instead of trying to get there all at once, let's look at different steps you could take to get there, with the idea of taking just one step at a time, just like climbing a staircase. For instance, what do you think would be your first step—the first thing you would need to do to get started in a direction that moves directly to this end result?

Client: Well, the first thing that comes to my mind is needing to be less uptight. I worry about what other people's reactions will be when I do say something.

In the next two responses, the counselor helps Joan define the **behavior and conditions associated with this initial subgoal,** *just as she did previously for the terminal goal.*

16. *Counselor:* OK, so you want to be less uptight and worry less about what other people might think. When you say other people, do you have any particular persons in mind?
    Client: Well, my folks, of course, and to some degree almost anyone that I don't know too well or anyone like my math teacher, who is in a position to evaluate me.
17. *Counselor:* So you're talking mainly about lessening these feelings when you're around your folks, your math teacher, or other people who you think are evaluating you.
    Client: Yes, I think that's it.

In response 18, the counselor is trying to establish the **current level of intensity** *associated with Joan's feelings of being uptight. She does this by using an* **imagery assessment.** *If Joan had trouble engaging in imagery,* **role-play assessment** *could be used.* **Self-reported ratings of intensity** *are used in conjunction with the imagery.*

18. *Counselor:* OK, now I'm going to ask you to close your eyes and imagine a couple of situations that I'll describe to you. Try to really get involved in the situation — put yourself there. If you feel any nervousness, signal by raising this finger. [Counselor shows Joan the index finger of her right hand and describes three situations — one related to parents, one related to math class, and one related to a job interview with a prospective employer. In all three situations, Joan raises her finger. After each situation, the counselor stops and asks Joan to rate the intensity of her anxiety on a 100-point scale, 0 being complete calm and relaxation and 100 being total panic.]

After the imagery assessment for base rate, the counselor asks Joan to **specify a desired level of change for this subgoal.**

19. *Counselor:* OK. Now, just taking a look at what happened here in terms of the intensity of your feelings, you rated the situation with your folks about 75, the one in math class 70, and the one with the employer 65. Where would you like to see this drop down to during the next couple of weeks?
    Client: Oh, I guess about a 10.

It is understandable that someone with fairly intense anxiety wants to get rid of it, and it is possible to achieve that within the next few months. However, such goals are more effective when they are **immediate rather than distant.** *In the next two responses, the counselor asks Joan to* **specify a realistic level of change** *for the immediate future.*

20. *Counselor:* OK, that may be a number to shoot for in the next few months, but I'm thinking that in the next three or four weeks the jump from, say, 70 to 10 is pretty big. Does that gap feel realistic or feasible?
    Client: Mm. I guess I was getting ahead of myself.
21. *Counselor:* Well, it's important to think about where you want to be in the long run. I'm suggesting three or four weeks mainly so you can start to see some progress and lessening of intensity of these feelings in a fairly short time. What number seems reasonable to you to shoot for in the short run?
    Client: Well, maybe a 45 or 50.

At this point, the counselor and Joan continue to **identify other subgoals or intermediate steps** *between the initial goal and the terminal outcome.*

22. *Counselor:* OK, that seems real workable. Now, we've sort of mapped out the first step. Let's think of other steps between this first one and this end result we've written down here. [Counselor and client continue to generate possible action steps. Eventually they select and define the remaining three shown on Joan's goal chart.]

Assuming the remaining subgoals are selected and defined, the next step is to **rank-order** *or* **sequence** *the subgoals and* **list them in order on the goal pyramid.**

23. *Counselor:* OK, we've got the first step, and now we've mapped out three more. Consider where you will be after this first step is completed — which one of these remaining steps comes next? Let's discuss it, and then we'll fill it in, along with this first step, on this goal pyramid, which you can keep so you know exactly what part of the pyramid you're on and when. [Counselor and Joan continue to rank-order subgoals, and Joan lists them in sequenced order on a goal pyramid.]

In response 24, the counselor points out that **subgoals may change in type or sequence.** *The counselor then shifts the focus to exploration of potential* **obstacles for the initial subgoal.**

24. *Counselor:* OK, now we've got our overall plan mapped out. This can change, too. You might find later on you may want to add a step or reorder the steps. Now, let's go back to your first

step—decreasing these feelings of nervousness and worrying less about the reactions of other people. Since this is what you want to start working on this week, can you think of anything or anybody that might get in your way or would make it difficult to work on this?

Client: Not really, because it is mostly something inside me. In this instance, I guess I am my own worst enemy.

25. *Counselor:* So you're saying there don't seem to be any people or situations outside yourself that may be obstacles. If anyone sets up an obstacle course, it will be you.

Client: Yeah. Mostly because I feel I have so little control of those feelings.

The client has identified herself and her perceived lack of control over her feelings as **obstacles.** *Later on, the counselor will need to help Joan select and work with one or two* **intervention strategies.**

26. *Counselor:* So one thing we need to do is to look at ways you can develop skills and know-how to manage these feelings so they don't get the best of you.

Client: Yup. I think that would help.

In the next response, the counselor explores **existing resources and support systems** *that Joan might use to help her work effectively with the subgoal.*

27. *Counselor:* OK, that's where I'd like to start in just a minute. Before we do, can you identify any people who could help you with these feelings—

or anything else you could think of that might help instead of hinder you?

Client: Well, coming to see you. It helps to know I can count on that. And I have a real good friend who is sort of the opposite of me, and she's real encouraging.

"Social allies" *are an important principle in effecting change, and the counselor uses this word in response 28 to underscore this point.*

28. *Counselor:* OK, so you've got at least two allies.

Client: Yeah.

In response 29, the counselor helps Joan develop a way to continue the **self-ratings of the intensity** *of her nervous feelings. This gives both of them a* **benchmark to use in assessing progress and reviewing** *the adequacy of the first subgoal selected.*

29. *Counselor:* The other thing I'd like to mention is a way for you to keep track of any progress you're making. You know how you related these situations I described today? You could continue to do this by keeping track of situations in which you feel uptight and worry about the reactions of others—jot down a brief note about what happened and then a number on this 0 to 100 scale that best represents how intense your feelings are at that time. As you do this and bring it back, it will help both of us see exactly what's happening for you on this first step. Does that sound like something you would find agreeable?

Client: Yeah—do I need to do it during the situation or after?

Joan's goal chart

Terminal goal	Related subgoals
Goal 1 (B) to acquire and demonstrate a minimum of four different initiating skills (asking a question or making a reasonable request, expressing differences of opinion, expressing positive feelings, expressing negative feelings, volunteering answers or opinions, going to the board in class) (C) in her math class and with her parents (L) in at least 4 situations a week	1. (B) to decrease anxiety associated with anticipation of failure (C) in math class or rejection by parents (L) from a self-rated intensity of 70 to 50 on a 100-point scale during the next 2 weeks 2. (B) to restructure thoughts or self-talk by replacing thoughts that "girls are dumb" with "girls are capable" (C) in math class and in other threatening or competitive situations (L) from 0–2 per day to 4–5 per day 3. (B) to increase attendance (C) at math class (L) from 2–3 times per week to 4–5 times per week 4. (B) to increase verbal participation skills (asking and answering questions, volunteering answers or offering opinions) (C) in math class and with her parents (L) from 0–1 times per day to 3–4 times per day

(continued)

Terminal goal	Related subgoals

Goal 2
(B) to increase positive perceptions about herself and her ability to function effectively
(C) in competitive situations such as math class
(L) by 50% over the next 3 months
	1. (B) to eliminate conversations
	    (C) with others in which she discusses her lack of ability
	    (L) from 2–3 per week to 0 per week
	2. (B) to increase self-visualizations in which she sees herself as competent and adequate to function independently
	    (C) in competitive situations or with persons in authority
	    (L) from 0 per day to 1–2 per day
	3. (B) to identify negative thoughts and increase positive thoughts
	    (C) about herself
	    (L) by 25% in the next 2 weeks

Goal 3
(B) to acquire and use five different decision-making skills (identifying an issue, generating alternatives, evaluating alternatives, selecting the best alternative, and implementing action)
(C) at least one of which represents a situation in which significant others have given her their opinion or advice on how to handle it
(L) in at least two different situations during a month
	1. (B) to decrease thoughts and worry about making a bad choice or poor decision
	    (C) in any decision-making situation
	    (L) by 25% in the next 2 weeks
	2. (B) to choose a course of action and implement it
	    (C) in any decision-making situation
	    (L) at least once during the next 2 weeks

Key: B = behavior; C = condition; L = level.

Clients are more likely to do **self-ratings or self-monitoring if it falls into their daily routine,** *so this is explored in the next response.*

30. *Counselor:* What would be most practical for you?

    Client: Probably after, because it's hard to write in the middle of it.

The counselor encourages Joan to make her notes soon after the situation is over. **The longer the gap, the less accurate or reliable** *the data might be.*

31. *Counselor:* That's fine; try to write it down as soon as it ends or shortly thereafter, because the longer you wait, the harder it will be to remember.

Before the session ends, they have to work on the **obstacle** *Joan identified earlier — that she is her own worst enemy because her feelings are in control of her. At this point, some of the real nuts and bolts of counseling begin. The counselor will need to select an intervention strategy or theoretical approach to use with Joan in this instance. (Two such options, thought stopping and cognitive restructuring, are described and modeled in Chapters 15 and 16.)*

32. *Counselor:* Now, let's go back to that obstacle you mentioned earlier — that your feelings are in control of you. . . .

☐ SUMMARY

The primary purpose of selecting goals is to convey to the client the responsibility and participation she or he has in contributing to the results of counseling. Without active client participation, counseling may be doomed to failure, resembling little more than a benevolent dictatorship. The selection of goals should reflect client choices. The counselor's role is mainly to use leads that facilitate the client's goal selection. Together, the counselor and client explore whether the goal is owned by the client, whether it is realistic, and what advantages and disadvantages are associated with it. However, some value judgments by both counselor and client may be inevitable during this process. If the client selects goals that severely conflict with the counselor's values or exceed the counselor's level of competence, the counselor may decide to refer the client or to renegotiate this goal. If counselor and client agree to pursue the selected goals, these goals must be defined clearly and specifically.

Well-defined goals make it easier to note and assess progress and also aid in guiding the client toward the desired goal(s). Goals are defined when you are able to specify the overt and covert behaviors associated with the goal, the conditions or context in which the goal is to be carried out or achieved, and the level of change. After the outcome goal(s) is defined, the counselor and client work jointly to identify and sequence subgoals that represent intermediate action steps and lead directly to the goal. Obstacles that might hinder goal attainment and resources that may facilitate goal attainment are also explored.

As you go through the process of helping clients develop goals, remember that goal setting is a dynamic and flexible process. "Decisions about objectives are not irrevocable" (Bandura, 1969, p. 103). Goals may change or may be redefined substantially as counseling progresses (Thompson & Wise, 1976). Once the person begins to change in a certain direction, the actual consequences of the change may lead to modification of the initial goals. Changes that the client originally perceived as feasible may turn out to be unrealistic. Moreover, as Bandura points out, at different points during the counseling process, some "previously ignored areas of behavioral functioning may become more important" (p. 104).

For these reasons, the outcome goals should always be viewed as temporary and subject to change. Client "resistance" at later stages in counseling may be the client's way of saying that the original goals need to be modified or redefined. The counselor who is committed to counseling to meet the client's needs will remember that, at any stage, the client always has the prerogative of changing or modifying directions. If the counselor is "highly sensitive to feedback from resultant changes," any or all parts of the original goal may be reevaluated and modified (Bandura, 1969, p. 104).

The flexibility required in modifying outcome goals should also be a part of the interview process for defining goals. Do not get so bogged down in checking off the interview categories that you lose touch with the client. As you become more comfortable in defining outcome goals, we hope you will not become encapsulated by the procedure. Remember, there is much more to counseling than carrying out a procedure in an assembly-line fashion.

POSTEVALUATION

PART ONE

Objective one asks you to identify a problem for which you select and define an outcome goal. Use the Goal-Setting Worksheet below for this process. You can obtain feedback by sharing your worksheet with a colleague, supervisor, or instructor.

Goal-Setting Worksheet

1. Identify a concern or problem.
2. State the desired outcome of the problem.
3. Assess the desired outcome (#2 above):
   a. Does it specify what you want to do? (If not, reword it so that you state what you want to do instead of what you don't want to do.)
   b. Is this something you can see (hear, grasp) yourself doing every time?
4. In what ways is achievement of this goal important to you? to others?
5. What will achieving this goal require of you? of others?
6. To what extent is this goal something you want to do? something you feel you should do or are expected to do?
7. Is this goal based on:
   ____ rational, logical ideas?

   ____ realistic expectations, ideas?
   ____ irrational ideas and beliefs?
   ____ logical thinking?
   ____ perfectionistic standards (for self or others)?
8. How will achieving this goal help *you?* help significant others in your life?
9. What problems could achieving this goal create for you? for others?
10. If the goal requires someone else to change, is not realistic or feasible, is not worthwhile, or poses more disadvantages than advantages, rework the goal. Then move on to #11.
11. Specify exactly *what* you will be
    a. doing _____
    b. thinking _____
    c. feeling _____
    as a result of goal achievement. Be specific.
12. Specify your goal definition in #11 by indicating:
    a. *where* this will occur: _____
    b. *when* this will occur: _____
    c. *with whom* this will occur: _____
    d. *how much or how often* this will occur: ___
13. Develop a plan that specifies *how* you will attain your goal by identifying action steps included in the plan.

(continued)

a. _____

b. _____

c. _____

d. _____

e. _____

f. _____

g. _____

h. _____

i. _____

j. _____

k. _____

l. _____

14. *Check* your list of action steps:

   a. Are the gaps between steps small? If not, add a step or two.

   b. Does each step represent only one major activity? If not, separate this one step into two or more steps.

   c. Does each step specify what, where, when, with whom, and how much or how often? If not, go back and define your action steps more concretely.

15. Use the goal pyramid below to sequence your list of action steps, starting with the easiest, most immediate step on the top and proceeding to the bottom of the pyramid by degree of difficulty and immediacy or proximity to the goal.

16. For each action step (starting with the first), brainstorm what could make it difficult to carry out or could interfere with doing it successfully. Consider feelings, thoughts, places, people, and lack of knowledge or skills. Write down the obstacles in the space provided on page 250.

17. For each action step (starting with the first), identify existing resources such as feelings, thoughts, situations, people and support systems, information, and skills that would make it more likely for you to carry out the action or complete it more successfully. Write down the resources in the space provided on page 250.

18. Identify a way to monitor and reinforce yourself for completion of each action step.

19. Develop a plan to help yourself maintain the action steps once you have attained them.

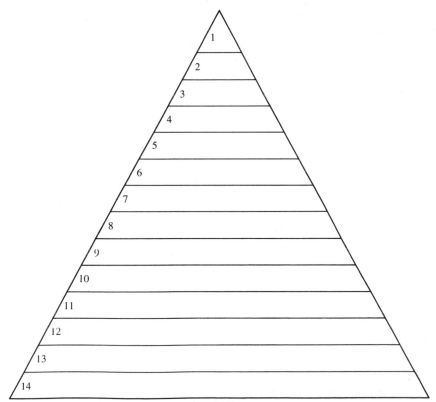

GOAL PYRAMID

(continued)

POSTEVALUATION (continued)

Obstacles		Action Steps	Resources
_____	1. _____		_____
_____	2. _____		_____
_____	3. _____		_____
_____	4. _____		_____
_____	5. _____		_____
_____	6. _____		_____
_____	7. _____		_____
_____	8. _____		_____
_____	9. _____		_____
_____	10. _____		_____
_____	11. _____		_____
_____	12. _____		_____

PART TWO

In this section of the postevaluation, you are to identify, from among 10 examples of client outcome goals, those that represent changes owned by the client, are based on realistic ideas, and are behaviorally defined, with an 80% accuracy rate (Chapter Objective Two). Examine carefully the following list of goals, and note in writing whether each goal is OK or not OK. If you decide a goal is not OK, identify which of the following are apparent problems with the goal (there may be more than one):

a. Change not owned by client
b. Goal based on irrational or magical thinking
c. Goal not behaviorally defined

Check your responses against those given in the feedback following the postevaluation.

1. I'd feel content if I could have a good sexual experience with my husband where I experience orgasm at least once a week.
2. I want him to like me.
3. I want to be more loving toward my child.
4. I wish she would see it my way.
5. I just want my dad to stop yelling at me for at least once a day.
6. I'd like to be able to get up at least in front of people I know and be able to role-play or talk without having this terrible knot in my stomach.
7. I don't ever want to get in trouble at school.
8. I'd like to get 100s on all my homework.
9. I wish my girlfriend would agree to have sex with me at least four or five times every day.
10. I want to be able to say no to any request my family makes of me that I feel is unreasonable.

PART THREE

In this part of the postevaluation, we describe a client case, the case of Jerry. Assuming that Jerry is your client, describe the steps you would go through to help him explore, select, and define desired actions, given his stated problem (Chapter Objective Three). Try to include at least 11 of the 15 steps or categories we described in this chapter for selecting and defining outcome goals. You can do this orally with a partner, in small groups, or by yourself. If you do it by yourself, you may want to jot down your ideas in writing for someone else to look at. Feedback follows the postevaluation.

The Case of Jerry

Jerry Bolwin is a 52-year-old manager of an advertising firm. He has been with the firm for 17 years and has another 12–15 years to go before drawing a rather lucrative retirement package. Over the last three years, however, Jerry has become increasingly dissatisfied with his job specifically and with the work world in general. He says he feels as if he would want nothing better than to quit and go hop on a steamer and sail off to China. Jerry is divorced and no longer has any financial obligations to his ex-wife and his only son. He does state, however, that he'd like to build up a "nest egg" for his son's two young children, as his grandchildren are very important to him. He realizes that if he left the firm now, he would lose many of his retirement benefits. Jerry defines his problem as feeling burned out with the "nine to five" job routine.

PART FOUR

According to Objective Four, you will be able to demonstrate, in an interview setting, at least 11 of the 15
(continued)

categories identified for selecting and defining client outcome goals. We suggest you complete this part of the postevaluation in triads. One person assumes the role of the counselor and demonstrates helping the client with the goal-setting process in a 20- or 30-minute interview. The second person takes the role of the client. You may wish to portray the role and problem described for Jerry Bolwin in Part Three. (If you choose to present something unfamiliar to the counselor, be sure to inform the counselor of your identi-fied problem or concern before you begin.) The third person assumes the role of the observer. The observer may act as the counselor's alter ego and cue the counselor during the role play if necessary. The observer also provides feedback to the counselor after the interview, using the Interview Checklist for Selecting and Defining Goals that follows below as a guide. If you do not have access to an observer, tape-record your interview so you can assess it yourself.

INTERVIEW CHECKLIST FOR SETTING AND DEFINING GOALS

Instructions: Determine which of the following leads or questions the counselor demonstrated. Check each counselor question or lead demonstrated. Also check whether the client answered the content of the counselor's question. Example counselor leads and questions are provided next to each item of the checklist. These are only suggestions—be alert to other responses used by the counselor.

Scoring	Category of information	Examples of counselor leads or questions	Client response
___Yes___No	1. Explain the purpose and importance of having goals or positive outcomes to the client.	"Let's talk about some areas you would like to work on during counseling. This will help us to do things that are related to what you want to accomplish."	___indicates understand-ing
___Yes___No	2. Determine *positive* changes desired by client ("I would like" versus "I can't").	"What would you like to be doing [thinking, feeling] differently?" "Suppose some distant relative you haven't seen for a while comes here in several months. What would be different then from the way things are now?" "Assuming we are successful, what do you want to be doing, or how would this change for you?" "In what ways do you want to benefit from counseling?"	___identifies goal in positive terms
___Yes___No	3. Determine whether the goal selected represents changes owned by the client rather than someone else ("I want to talk to my mom without yelling at her," rather than "I want my mom to stop yelling at me").	"How much control do you have to make this happen?" "What changes will this goal require of you?" "What changes will this goal require someone else to make?" "Can this goal be achieved without the help of anyone else?" "To whom is this goal most important?"	___identifies who owns the goal
___Yes___No	4. Determine whether the goal is based on realistic expectations rather than unrealistic or irra-tional ideas or self-de-mands ("I want to have more friends," rather than "I want to be liked by everyone").	"To what extent do you want to achieve this goal?" "To what extent do you feel you should achieve this goal?" "To what degree is this goal based on realistic expectations?" "To what degree does this goal represent wishful thinking?" "How feasible is it for you to _____?"	___identifies underlying expectations

(continued)

POSTEVALUATION (continued)

Scoring	Category of information	Examples of counselor leads or questions	Client response
		"Is it reasonable to expect to effect a change in this area?" "To what extent are you leaning toward this goal because you know it's something you can achieve with little effort or little risk?" "To what extent are you leaning toward this goal because it's out of your reach and you'll be excused if you don't make it?"	
____Yes____No	5. Identify advantages (positive consequences) to client and others of goal achievement.	"In what ways is it worthwhile to you and others to achieve this goal?" "How will achieving this goal help you?" "What problems will continue for you if you don't pursue this goal?" "What are the advantages of achieving this goal—for you? others?" "Who will benefit from this change—and how?"	—identifies advantages
____Yes____No	6. Identify disadvantages (negative consequences) of goal achievement to client and others.	"What new problems in living might achieving this goal pose for you?" "Are there any disadvantages to going in this direction?" "How will achieving this goal affect your life in adverse ways?" "How might this change limit or constrain you?"	—identifies disadvantages
____Yes____No	7. Identify whether, as the helper, you are willing and competent to help the client with the stated goals (decision point).	"These are things I am able to help you work with." "I feel uncomfortable working with you on this issue because of my own personal values [or lack of knowledge]. I'd like to give you the names of several other counselors . . . ." "This would be hard for me to help you with because it seems as if you're choosing something that will restrict you and not give you any options. Let's talk more about this."	—responds to counselor's decision
____Yes____No	8. Identify what the client will be doing, thinking, or feeling in a concrete, observable way as a result of goal achievement ("I want to be able to talk to my mom without yelling at her," rather than "I want to get along with my mom").	"What do you want to be able to do [think, feel] differently?" "What would I see you doing [thinking, feeling] after this change?" "Describe a good and a poor example of this goal."	—specifies overt and covert behaviors
____Yes____No	9. Specify under what conditions and what situations goals will be achieved: when, where, and with whom ("I want to be able to	"When do you want to accomplish this goal?" "Where do you want to do this?" "With whom?" "In what situations?"	—specifies people and places

(continued)

Scoring	Category of information	Examples of counselor leads or questions	Client response
	talk to my mom at home during the next month without yelling at her'').		
____Yes____No	10. Specify how often or how much client will do something to achieve goal (''I want to be able to talk to my mom at home during the next month without yelling at her at least once a day'').	''How much [or how often] are you doing this [or feeling this way] now?'' ''What is a realistic increase or decrease?'' ''How much [or how often] do you want to be doing this to be successful at your goal?'' ''What amount of change is realistic, considering where you are right now?''	____specifies amount
____Yes____No	11. Identify and list small action steps the client will need to take to reach the goal (that is, break the big goal down into little subgoals). *List of Action Steps* 1. 2. 3. 4. 5. 6. 7. 8. 9. 10.	''How will you go about doing [thinking, feeling] this?'' ''What exactly do you need to do to make this happen?'' ''Let's brainstorm some actions you'll need to take to make your goal work for you.'' ''What have you done in the past to work toward this goal?'' ''How did it help?'' ''Let's think of the steps you need to take to get from where you are now to where you want to be.''	____lists possible action steps
____Yes____No	12. Sequence the action steps on the goal pyramid (a hierarchy) in terms of a. degree of difficulty (least to most) b. immediacy (most to least immediate)	''What is your first step?'' ''What would you be able to do most easily?'' ''What would be most difficult?'' ''What is your foremost priority?'' ''What is most important for you to do soon? least important?'' ''How could we order these steps to maximize your success in reaching your goal?'' ''Let's think of the steps you need to take to get from where you are now to where you want to be and arrange them in an order from what seems easiest to you to the ones that seem hardest.'' ''Can you think of some things you need to do before some other things as you make progress toward this outcome?''	____assists in rank-ordering

Least difficult, most immediate
1
2
3
4
5
6
7
8
9
10
Most difficult, least immediate

(continued)

POSTEVALUATION (continued)

Scoring	Category of information	Examples of counselor leads or questions	Client response
___Yes___No	13. Identify any people, feelings, or situations that could prevent the client from taking action to reach the goal.	"What are some obstacles you may encounter in trying to take this action?" "What people [feelings, ideas, situations] might get in the way of getting this done?" "In what ways could you have difficulty completing this task successfully?" "What do you need to know to take this action?" or "What skills do you need to have?"	___identifies possible obstacles
___Yes___No	14. Identify any resources (skill, knowledge, support) that client needs to take action to meet the goal.	"What resources do you have available to help you as you complete this activity?" "What particular thoughts or feelings are you aware of that might make it easier for you to ___?" "What kind of support system do you have from others that you can use to make it easier to ___?" "What skills [or information] do you possess that will help you do this more successfully?"	___identifies existing resources and supports
___Yes___No	15. Develop a plan to monitor and review progress toward the goal.	"Would it be practical for you to rate these feelings [count the times you do this] during the next two weeks? This information will help us determine the progress you are making." "Let's discuss a way you can keep track of how easy or hard it is for you to take these steps this week."	___agrees to monitor in some fashion

Observer Comments: _____

_____

_____ ∎

☐ SUGGESTED READINGS

Carkhuff, R. R., & Anthony, W. A. (1979). *The skills of helping.* Amherst, MA: Human Resource Development Press. Chapter 5, "Helping People Define Goals and Select Courses of Action"; Chapter 6, "Helping People Develop Programs to Reach Goals"; Chapter 7, "Helping People Take Steps to Reach Their Goals."

Dixon, D. N., & Glover, J. A. (1984). *Counseling: A problem-solving approach.* New York: Wiley. Chapter 8, "Goal Selection."

Frey, D. H., & Raming, H. E. (1979). A taxonomy of counseling goals and methods. *Personnel and Guidance Journal, 58,* 26–33.

Lloyd, M. E. (1983). Selecting systems to measure client outcome in human service agencies. *Behavioral Assessment, 5,* 55–70.

Locke, E. A., Shaw, K. N., Saari, L. M., & Latham, G. P. (1981). Goal-setting and task performance; 1969–1980. *Psychological Bulletin, 90,* 125–152.

Rosen, A., & Proctor, E. (1981). Distinctions between treatment outcomes and their implications for treatment evaluation. *Journal of Consulting and Clinical Psychology, 49,* 418–425.

Seidner, M. L., & Kirschenbaum, D. S. (1980). Behavioral contracts: Effects of pretreatment information and intervention statements. *Behavior Therapy, 11,* 689–698.

FEEDBACK: POSTEVALUATION

PART TWO
1. Goal OK.
2. Goal not OK:
    a. Change is not owned by this client.
    b. Goal may represent wishful and magical thinking.
    c. Goal is not behaviorally defined.

3. Goal not OK.
   c. Goal is not behaviorally defined.
4. Goal not OK.
   a. Change is not owned by this client.
   b. Goal represents wishful and irrational thinking.
   c. Goal is not behaviorally defined.
5. Goal not OK.
   a. Change is not owned by this client.
6. Goal OK.
7. Goal not OK.
   b. Goal is based on negative and irrational thinking.
   c. Goal is not behaviorally defined.
8. Goal not OK.
   d. Goal is based on wishful thinking.
9. Goal not OK.
   a. Change is not owned by this client.
   b. Goal is *probably* not realistic or is based on wishful thinking, given the stated frequency —at least neither person would get much else done!
10. Goal OK.

PART THREE

1. First, explain to Jerry the *purpose and importance* of developing goals.
2. Help Jerry state the goal or desired change in *positive terms*.
3. Help Jerry determine whether the goal he is moving toward represents *changes owned by him* and whether such factors are under his control. Probably, deciding to give up his job and/or take a leave of absence would be changes under his control.
4. Determine whether Jerry's ideas about change are *realistic*. There seems to be a little bit of an element of wishful thinking (sail off to China). However, the degree to which his goal reflects *realistic expectations* would need to be explored with him.
5. Help Jerry identify *advantages* or *benefits* to be realized by achieving his goal. He seems to be thinking about increased leisure time as a major benefit—are there others?
6. Help Jerry identify *disadvantages* or *possible costs* of making the desired change. He has mentioned loss of retirement benefits as one cost. Are there others? Do the perceived benefits outweigh the costs?
7. If Jerry's goal is not realistic or if it looks as if it will have too many costs, explore other options with him, leaving the final decision about goals up to him. At this point, you will need to *decide whether you are able to help* him pursue his goal.
8. Assuming you will continue to work with Jerry, help him *define his goal behaviorally* by specifying exactly *what* he will be doing, thinking, and feeling as a result of goal achievement.
9. Further specification of the goal includes *where*, *when*, and *with whom* this will occur and
10. *how much* or *how often* it will occur. An option that might be useful for Jerry is to develop and scale five possible outcomes, ranging from the most unfavorable one to the most expected one to the best possible one.
11. Help Jerry explore and *identify action steps or subgoals* that represent small approximations toward the overall goal. Help him choose action steps that are practical, are based on his resources, and support his values.
12. Help Jerry *sequence the action steps* according to *immediacy and difficulty* so he knows what step he will take first and what step will be his last one.
13. Explore any *obstacles* that could impede progress toward the goal, such as the presence or absence of certain feelings, ideas, thoughts, situations, responses, people, and knowledge and skills.
14. Explore existing *resources* that could help Jerry complete the action steps more successfully. Like obstacles, exploration of resources also includes the presence or absence of certain feelings, ideas, thoughts, situations, responses, people, and knowledge and skills.
15. Help Jerry develop a *plan to review completion of the action steps* and *progress toward the goal*, including a way to monitor and reward himself for progress and a plan to help him maintain changes.

EVALUATING PROCESSES AND OUTCOMES IN HELPING

TEN

A primary part of helping involves monitoring and evaluating the effects of the helping process. We view evaluation as a major component of helping that is just as vital to the conduct of therapy as all the other components. An evaluation of helping provides encouragement to both counselor and client and also indicates the extent to which counseling goals have been achieved. As Egan points out,

> Tangible results form the backbone of the reinforcement process in counseling. If the client is to be encouraged to move forward, he must see results. Therefore, both counselor and client should be able to judge whether the action program is or is not being implemented, and to what degree, and the results of this implementation [1975, p. 225].

The remaining chapters contain many references to analogue and clinical research studies that have demonstrated "effective" outcomes resulting from a particular therapeutic strategy applied to certain clinical problems. These studies are examples of experimental research. The experimental designs used in research studies have been described in a variety of sources (Barlow, Hayes, & Nelson, 1984; Hersen & Barlow, 1976; Huck, Cormier, & Bounds, 1974; Kazdin, 1973b, 1976d, 1980a, 1981). It is not the purpose of this chapter to describe the potential use and relevance of experimental designs. Our objective is to present some practical techniques that a counselor can use to evaluate the process and outcomes of therapy.

Although some of the methodology and schemes for evaluation presented in this chapter are the same as some research designs, the purpose of counseling evaluation is often different from the objectives of experimental research. Empirical research can be considered a quest for causality or "truth." In contrast, a counseling evaluation is more of a hypothesis-testing process (Shapiro, 1966). The data collected in a helping evaluation are used to make decisions about selection of treatment strategies and about the extent to which a client's stated goals were achieved. Mahoney has summarized the use of data collection in making decisions about helping processes and outcomes:

The most efficient therapist is sensitively tuned to the personal data of the client. He is not collecting data for the sake of scientific appearances or because that is what is considered proper. . . . The effective therapist uses data to guide his or her own efforts at having an impact, and—regardless of theoretical bias or procedural preference—he adjusts therapeutic strategies in tune with that feedback [1977b, p. 241].

□ OBJECTIVES

1. Given a client case description and a description of data-collection and evaluation procedures, identify:
   a. Response dimensions used with this client.
   b. Methods of measurement used with this client.
   c. Times of measurement.
2. Given examples of client self-monitoring data during baseline, treatment, and posttreatment assessment periods, graph these data and identify trends reflected in the graphs.
3. With yourself, another person, or a client, conduct an outcome evaluation of one real or hypothetical outcome goal, specifying the response dimensions, methods, and times of measurement.

□ DEFINITION AND PURPOSE OF HELPING EVALUATION

In evaluation of helping, the counselor and client monitor and assess change. There are two purposes for conducting an evaluation of helping. The primary purpose is to assess therapeutic outcomes. The evaluation helps the counselor and client to determine the type, direction, and amount of change in behavior (overt or covert) shown by the client during and after therapy. Stated another way:

Individual measures of change fall within three categories. First, most measures are simply designed to find out whether a client changed during the course of treatment, e.g. pre-post global ratings of the client's overall level of functioning or pre-post multiple ratings of client symptoms. Second, and much less frequently, measures are designed to find out whether a client changed as a *result* of treatment as in single subject designs. Third, measures have been designed to find out if a client changed *enough* during treatment to produce an improvement in his or her everyday functioning [Lloyd, 1983, p. 56].

A second purpose is to evaluate the helping process. Specifically, the data collected during counseling can be used to monitor whether a strategy is helping a client in the designated way and whether a client is using the strategy accurately and systematically. Hosford and de Visser (1974) define the evaluation process in helping this way:

Observations of the client's behavior near the termination point of counseling can easily be compared with the base rate data if the counselor records the same target behavior, in the same way, and for the same period of time as was done during the initial observations. This provides the counselor with an objective measure of the success of his learning interventions. If the data indicate that little or no behavioral change occurred, the learning strategies should be reevaluated and perhaps changed [p. 81].

Although an evaluation of helping can yield valuable information about the process and outcome of therapy, it is naturally not so rigorous as an evaluation conducted under carefully controlled experimental conditions. In other words, a counseling evaluation cannot establish that the client's change resulted *solely* from this or that strategy. The results of counseling may be influenced by factors other than the particular counseling intervention used. These factors, often called "nonspecific" or "nontreatment" conditions, may contribute to the client's change. In the final analysis, it is difficult to rule out the possible effects of other sources of influence in counseling. Some of the primary nontreatment sources of influence are described in the next section.

□ NONTREATMENT FACTORS IN COUNSELING

A variety of factors occur in counseling, either independently of or in conjunction with the application of a helping strategy, that may affect counseling outcomes. Important nontreatment factors include the influence of the counselor and the counseling relationship, demand characteristics, instructions and expectancy set, and the potential reactivity of measurement.

Influence of the Counselor and the Relationship

The chemistry of the client/counselor relationship is reciprocal: client and counselor are mutual sources of influence. Client changes in counseling can result from "nonspecific aspects of attention, suggestion and faith (in the therapist or his techniques) that are common to most interpersonal situations" (Paul, 1966, p. 5). As Mahoney (1977a) observes, a counselor engages in a great deal of persuasive communication to encourage the client to behave, think, or feel differently. To the extent that the client regards the counselor with trust, respect, and regard, the counselor's "power of suggestion" is greatly enhanced. In other words, the reinforcing value of the counselor is increased. As we discussed in Chapters 2 and 3, certain relationship conditions and social influence variables initiated and displayed by the counselor can motivate the client to change or to behave in certain ways.

Demand Characteristics

According to Orne (1969), demand characteristics include any cues that influence a person's perception of his or her role in a particular setting. In counseling, these cues not only may influence a client's perception of his or her role but also may affect the client's behavior during and between sessions. For example, perceiving that it is very important to complete therapy assignments systematically will probably motivate the client to complete assignments regularly and conscientiously. In this example, the demand characteristic prompts the client to use therapy in a certain way —which may affect the degree and direction of change. Another demand characteristic that may influence counseling outcomes is the client's desire to please the therapist. This may affect the client's behavior in a number of ways, ranging from the degree of improvement the client reports to the investment and "work" she or he conducts during the counseling process. Other factors that can influence counseling outcomes by communicating certain "demands" include instructions and expectancies.

Instructions and Expectancy Set

A client's motivation to change and to work at the change process is also influenced by instructions and belief factors. Clients who receive specific and detailed instructions about counseling or about a treatment strategy may be more likely to use the strategy accurately and to offer unbiased self-reports (Bootzin, 1972; Nicassio & Bootzin, 1974). In addition, clients who are given high-demand instructions emphasizing the critical importance of a task or behavior may respond to counseling differently than people who receive low-demand instructions (Jacobson, 1981). Martinez and Edel-

stein (1977) indicate that clients' behavior may fluctuate, depending on the instructions they receive and on the context or situation in which they are seen or evaluated.

Clients who receive suggestions of therapeutic improvement without "formal" treatment may demonstrate a great deal of clinical progress (Kazdin, 1973b). Client expectations about the helpfulness of therapy can significantly affect both the course and the outcomes of counseling (see Kazdin & Krouse, 1983). As Frank (1961, pp. 70–71) has indicated, "Part of the success of all forms of psychotherapy may be attributed to the therapist's ability to mobilize the patient's expectation of help." If the client views the counselor and the treatment as highly credible, the client's change efforts may be enhanced. Some research has indicated that therapy outcomes are improved after a positive expectancy set has been established for the client (Woy & Efran, 1972).

Reactivity of Measurement

Some of the procedures used to measure client change in counseling may be reactive; that is, the process of collecting data may itself contribute to client change. Reactivity can be defined as the changes in behavior that occur as a consequence of observing and recording the behavior despite, or in addition to, treatment intervention.

A great deal of reactivity is associated with client self-monitoring measurement techniques (Barlow et al., 1984; Nelson, Lipinski, & Black, 1976b). For example, a client may be instructed to observe and record instances of smoking cigarettes or of self-defeating thoughts for two weeks at the beginning of counseling, before any treatment strategy is used. At the end of the two weeks, decreases in the client's smoking or self-defeating thoughts may be apparent even though the counselor has not yet implemented any strategies to help the client reduce these behaviors. Other types of measures of client change, such as standardized tests, questionnaires, and simulated laboratory or role-play measures, may also have reactive qualities (Hughes & Haynes, 1978; Lick & Unger, 1977). In assessing change, the counselor should be aware of possible reactive properties of the measures used to monitor change.

Practically speaking, the influence of the counselor, the demand characteristics associated with counseling, the client's expectancy set, and the reactivity of certain types of measures can be assets for maximizing desired therapeutic changes. However, from an empirical perspective, these factors are potentially confounding sources of influence when one wishes to infer that the selected counseling strategy was the only cause of therapeutic change. In evaluating the effects of counseling, it is important to recognize the potential impact of some of the nontreatment sources of influence we have just described.

☐ CONDUCTING AN OUTCOME EVALUATION OF HELPING

The client's problem must be clearly defined and the goal behaviors specified before the therapist can conduct an outcome evaluation. There may be occasions when the client's problem is redefined and the goals changed. In such cases, the method of assessment, the target behavior, and the response dimensions may have to be altered to reflect the redefined problem. If the method of assessment of outcome is not altered when the problem has been redefined, the reliability and validity of the assessment methods may be limited. Reliability is the consistency or generalizability of the target behavior. For example, counselors want to know whether a particular assessment method will produce consistent client reponses if no intervention occurs and if the natural environment remains stable (R. O. Nelson, 1981). They also want to know, for example, whether the data recorded by the client in the natural environment will be comparable with observational data recorded at the same time by a significant other (R. O. Nelson, 1981, p. 178).

The essential question of validity for assessment methods is how well a method does the job it is employed to do (Cureton, 1951). There are four types of validity: content, concurrent, predictive, and construct. Content validity answers the question whether the method of assessment being used describes a person's present behavior (Livingston, 1977, p. 323) or adequately assesses the response of interest to the therapist and client (R. O. Nelson, 1981, p. 178). Predictive validity answers the question whether the current assessment method predicts the client's future behavior. Concurrent validity refers to whether client responses on assessment measures in the clinic are the same as those responses recorded in the natural environment. Construct validity refers to the client's status on some unobservable variable or construct such as intelligence, shyness, or introversion. Multitrait (two or more categories of behavior) assessment and multiple methods of assessment can enhance reliability and validity for evaluating client outcomes.

Figure 10-1 summarizes the major components of an evaluation procedure for monitoring and evaluating the outcomes of therapy. These components comprise five response dimensions for the target behaviors, seven methods of measurement, and four time periods for measuring the response

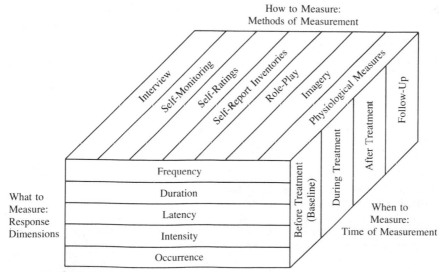

Figure 10-1. A model of monitoring and evaluating therapy outcomes

dimensions. The therapist is responsible for arranging the evaluation procedures and explaining them to the client, who is an active participant in the data-collection process. The model pictured in Figure 10-1 is not intended to connote that evaluation of therapy is easy or simple. Evaluation can be a very complex process; however, we do not believe its complexity should discourage our attempts as therapists to assess therapeutic change.

□ WHAT TO MEASURE: RESPONSE DIMENSIONS

The therapist and client are interested in assessing the degree to which the defined outcome goal or goal behavior has been achieved (R. O. Nelson, 1981). Because the client typically monitors the covert and overt goal behaviors, evaluation of therapy outcomes depends on a clear specification of the behavior, level, and conditions of the client's goals of therapy (see Chapter 9). A therapist and client may assess one or several goals or target behaviors, depending on the number of changes they have agreed to during the goal definition process. Multiple measures of the goal behaviors are desirable for each client. The same goal behaviors should be assessed repeatedly before, during, and after treatment. Further, measures of goal behavior should be made under similar stimulus conditions (R. O. Nelson, 1981). For example, if a client records the degree of intensity of muscle tension three times a day, the intensity should be rated at about the same time each day so that comparisons can be made daily for each of the three time periods.

The goal behaviors are evaluated by having the client assess the amount or level of the defined behaviors. Five dimensions commonly used to measure the direction and level of change in goal behaviors are frequency, duration, latency, magnitude (intensity), and occurrence. A client may use one or a combination of these response dimensions, depending on the nature of the goal, the method of assessment, and the feasibility of obtaining particular data. R. O. Nelson (1981) recommends that behaviors that are inconvenient to record be assessed less frequently. For example, sexual arousal to diverse stimuli could be assessed only at each treatment session (Nelson, p. 169). The response dimensions should be individualized, particularly because they vary in the time and effort they cost the client.

Frequency

Frequency reflects the number (how many, how often) of overt or covert behaviors and is determined by obtaining measures of each occurrence of the goal behavior. Frequency counts are typically used when the goal behavior is discrete and of short duration. Panic episodes and headaches are examples of behaviors that can be monitored with frequency counts. Frequency data can also be obtained from comments written in a diary or daily journal. For example, the number of positive (or negative) self-statements before and after each snack or binging episode, reported in a daily diary, can be tabulated.

Sometimes frequency counts should be obtained as percentage data. For example, knowing the number of times a behavior occurred may not be meaningful unless data are also available on the number of *possible* occurrences of the behavior. Ciminero, Nelson, and Lipinski (1977) recommend that percentage measures be obtained when it is important to determine the number of opportunities to perform the target behavior as well as the number of times the behavior actually occurs. For example, data about the number of times an overweight client consumes snacks might be more informative if expressed as a percentage. In this example, the denominator would reflect the number of opportunities the person had to eat snacks; the numerator would indicate the number of times the person actually did snack. The advantage of percentage scores is that they indicate whether the change is a function of an actual increase or decrease in the number of times the response occurs or merely a function of an increase or decrease in the number of opportunities to perform the behavior. Thus, a percentage score may give more accurate and more complete information than a simple frequency count. However, when it is hard to detect the available opportunities, or when it is difficult for the client to collect data, percentage scores may not be useful.

Duration

Duration reflects the length of time a particular response or collection of responses occurs. Ciminero et al. indicate that duration measurement is appropriate whenever the goal behavior is not discrete and lasts for varying periods (p. 198). Thinking about one's strengths for a certain period of time, the amount of time spent on a task or with another person, the period of time for depressive thoughts, and the amount of time that anxious feelings lasted are examples of behaviors that can be measured with duration counts.

Latency

Another type of duration measure involves observing the latency of a particular response. Latency refers to the amount of time that elapses before a response or behavior occurs. The number of minutes before falling asleep is an example of a latency response. Another is the amount of time that elapsed before self-disclosing to another person or in a group. Duration and latency measures can be used in combination. For example, a client can record both the latency of self-disclosing responses and the duration of those responses in a group situation. Observing the latency of a response provides useful information about the target behavior even though the data may not always be precise. For example, clients often overestimate sleep latency. If the client can obtain information about response latency using a timer or a clock, the data are likely to be more accurate.

Frequency counts, percentage scores, duration, and latencies can be obtained in one of two ways: continuous recording or time sampling. If the client can obtain data *each time* he or she engages in the goal behavior, then the client is collecting data continuously. Sometimes continuous recording is impossible, particularly when the goal behavior occurs very often or when its onset and termination are hard to detect. In such cases, a time-sampling procedure may be more practical. In time sampling, a day is divided into equal time intervals—90 minutes, 2 hours, or 3 hours, for example. The client keeps track of the frequency or duration of the goal behavior only during randomly selected intervals. In using time sampling, data should be collected during at least three time intervals each day and during *different* time intervals each day, so that representative and unbiased data are recorded. One variation of time sampling is to divide time into intervals and indicate the presence or absence of the target behavior for each interval in an "all or none" manner (Mahoney & Thoresen, 1974, p. 31). If the behavior occurred during the interval, a *yes* would be recorded; if it did not occur, a *no* would be noted. Time sampling is less precise than continuous recordings of frequency or duration of a behavior. Yet it does provide an estimate of the behavior and may be a useful substitute in monitoring high-frequency or nondiscrete target responses (Mahoney & Thoresen).

Intensity

The intensity or degree of the goal behavior can be assessed with a rating scale. For example, intensity of anxious feelings can be measured with ratings of 1 (not anxious) to 5 (panic). Cronbach (1984) suggests three ways of decreasing sources of error frequently associated with rating scales. First, the therapist should be certain that what is to be rated is well defined and specified in the client's language. For example, if a client is to rate depressed thoughts, the counselor and client specify, with examples, what constitutes depressed thoughts (such as "Nothing is going right for me," "I can't do anything right"). These definitions should be tailored to each client, on the basis of an analysis of the client's problem behavior and contributing conditions. Second, rating scales should be designed that include a description for each point on the scale. For example, episodes of anxious feelings in a particular setting can be rated on a 5-point scale, with 1 representing little or no anxiety, 2 equal to some anxiety, 3 being moderately anxious, 4 representing strong anxious feelings, and 5 indicating very intense anxiety. Third, rating scales should be unidirectional, starting with 0 or 1. Negative points (points below 0) should not be included. In addition, the therapist should consider the range of points in constructing the scale. There should be at least 4 points and no more than 7. A scale of less than 4 points may limit a person's ability to discriminate, whereas a scale that includes more than 7 points may not produce reliable ratings by the client because too many discriminations are required.

Occurrence

Occurrence refers to presence or absence of target behaviors. Checklists can be used to rate the occurrence of behaviors. They are similar to rating scales. The basic difference is the type of judgment one makes. On a rating scale, a person can indicate the degree to which a behavior is present; a checklist simply measures the presence or absence of a behavior. Checklists describe a cluster or collection of behaviors that a client may demonstrate. A checklist assesses the client's *capability* "to emit a particular behavior to a given standard under a given condition" (Walls, Werner, Bacon, & Zane, 1977, pp. 79–80). For example, suppose a counselor is using either covert or participant modeling as a treatment strategy for teaching a person job-interview skills. The nonverbal and verbal behaviors associated with demonstrating appropriate job-interview skills can be listed on a checklist. If the client demonstrates a particular behavior in a naturalistic or simulated situation, he or she will receive a check on a list for that behavior. A checklist can also be used in conjunction with frequency and duration counts and rating scales.

As evaluative tools, checklists may be very useful, particularly when the reference points on the list are clearly defined and are representative of the particular performance domain being assessed. In the example just given, a checklist of observable job-interview skills could be a useful tool. Walls et al. (1977, pp. 90–146) provide a list and review of 166 behavior checklists.

Any or all of these five response dimensions can be used to assess the magnitude and direction of change reflected in the goal behaviors. The next section explores how the therapist and client can go about actually collecting data to be used in evaluating helping outcomes.

LEARNING ACTIVITY #29: RESPONSE DIMENSIONS

Read the following client case description and decide which response dimensions of the target behavior would be most appropriate for the client to monitor. As a review, there are five response dimensions:

1. Frequency: (a) how often the behavior occurs or (b) how often the behavior occurs in proportion to the number of opportunities available (percentage score).
2. Duration: how long the behavior lasts.
3. Latency: amount of time elapsed before the behavior occurs.
4. Intensity: ratings of intensity, severity, or degree of the behavior.
5. Occurrence: presence or absence of the behavior.

Case Description

The client is a 38-year-old single female who referred herself for counseling because of recurring fears about having cancer. Although the client is in excellent health, over the last two years she has had re-peated ruminations about the possibility that she will contract cancer. She reports that this concern began after a close friend died suddenly from an undiagnosed cancer. The client reports that she has several anxiety attacks a day about this. These occur both at work and at home. She also reports that some of the attacks are mild, but others are more severe and result in headaches and nausea. Her attacks are centered on thoughts of "worrying that I have or will get cancer and it will be too late to do anything about it." Her goal is to reduce these anxiety-producing ruminations and the concurrent feelings of anxiety and panic.

Assume that the client is going to evaluate her anxiety attacks as the outcome measure. If you were her counselor, what response dimensions would you have her use to collect data about these attacks? List your choices on a sheet of paper and briefly describe a rationale for each type you suggest. Feedback follows.

☐ HOW TO MEASURE: METHODS OF MEASUREMENT

There are at least seven methods a therapist and client can use to measure progress toward desired outcomes: interviews, self-monitoring, self-ratings, self-report inventories, role playing, imagery, and physiological measures. Any one of these methods or a combination can be used to provide indications of whether the desired goal behaviors are being achieved.

Interviews

As we have described in previous chapters, the interview is very useful for gathering data about the client's problems and for defining client goals. The interview can also be used to evaluate informally the degree to which the goal behaviors are achieved. There are at least two ways a therapist can use the interview as a measurement method. First, the helper can use open-ended verbal leads to elicit client self-report data about progress toward the desired goals. Specifically, the helper can draw on some of the leads we suggested for problem and goal definition later in counseling to find out whether progress has been made. The interview leads for determining the intensity of the problem (Chapter 8) and for specifying desired changes (Chapter 9) are particularly appropriate for eliciting client verbal descriptions of therapeutic progress. Presumably, if changes are occurring, the client will indicate that the extent and severity of the problem have decreased as helping strategies are introduced and implemented.

A second way the interview can be used in data collection is to audiotape randomly selected interview sessions at the beginning, middle, and end points of the helping process. Segments of these tapes or entire sessions can be rated independently by the therapist or by other raters on dimensions of client verbal responses that may be representative of the counseling goals. For example, if the client's goal is to reduce depressed thoughts, defined as thoughts such as "Life is rotten," "I'm no good," or "Nothing is going well for me," these operationally defined client verbalizations can be scored and rated across taped interviews. Positive statements such as "I'm getting more out of life now," "I'm realizing I'm a worthwhile person," or "Good things are starting to happen for me now" can also be scored. As counseling continues, if the client is making progress toward the goal, there should be a decrease across the interview sessions in the negative statements and an increase in the positive statements.

Advantages.   The interview is perhaps the easiest and most convenient method of data collection available (Haynes & Jensen, 1979). It is a relatively "low cost" measurement method, requiring very little extra time and effort from either counselor or client. It is also a good way to elicit the client's perceptions about the value of the helping process. These perceptions may be especially important in cases where the client believes that therapy is helping (or hurting) but these beliefs are not supported by quantified data. Interviews can also provide greater flexibility and more information than self-report inventories or questionnaires. The interview can facilitate obtaining accurate and complete information from illiterate and less educated clients (Jayaratne & Levy, 1979).

Limitations.   The interview is the least systematic and standardized way to collect data, however, and the resulting information is often not very precise or specific. For example, the client may be able to report the duration of change (increase or decrease, positive or negative) but not the exact level of change (increase or decrease by two per day, three hours per week, and so on). Another disadvantage involves the reliability of client verbalizations, since the information obtained in the interview is based on recall and is retrospective (Kendall & Hollon, 1981). If the interview is the only measurement method used, the helper must rely totally on the client's reports of progress. There is always a danger that some clients will report that they feel good or are making desired changes simply to please the counselor (Okun, 1982).

Haynes and Jensen (1979) enumerate several possible sources of error and bias in interviews. These sources are likely to be of more consequence in *unstructured* interviews and include such variables as differences in race, sex, or social class between interviewer and client, interviewer knowledge about or classification of the client, type of information being requested, and the nature of the interviewee (age, population group, and so on).

Guidelines for use.   The interview method may be more effective as an evaluation tool when used in the following ways:

1. The helper should determine in advance some *structured,* open-ended leads to elicit client descriptions of progress. These leads should include client indications of the present extent of the problem, the present severity of the problem, and how things are different than they were at the beginning of counseling.
2. These interview leads should be used at several points during the helping process; the helper should use the same leads at each of these "sampling points."
3. Where feasible, the helper should supplement the use of interview leads with ratings of various audiotaped interview segments on dimensions of client goal-related verbal behavior.

Self-Monitoring

Self-monitoring is a process of observing and recording aspects of one's own covert or overt behavior (Kazdin, 1974f). Self-monitoring can be used in the helping process in three ways: to define client problems (see Chapter 8), to increase or decrease desired target behaviors (see Chapter 19), and to evaluate the effects of helping. The discussion of self-monitoring in this chapter is limited to its role as an evaluation method. For the purpose of evaluating goal behaviors, a client uses self-monitoring to collect data about the amount (frequency, latency, duration, or intensity) of the goal

FEEDBACK #29: RESPONSE DIMENSIONS

At least three types of responses could be used very appropriately with this client to collect data about dimensions of the goal behavior:

1. Frequency of attacks. The counselor and client need to know how many times these attacks occur and, ultimately, whether counseling is helping the client reduce their number.
2. Duration of attacks. If each attack lasted as long as 30 minutes, this could impede the client's overall functioning.
3. Intensity or severity of attacks. Using, perhaps, a 5- or 7-point scale, the client could rate each attack according to its severity. This information would be a clue to the overall intensity of the attacks. These data also might suggest whether more severe attacks were linked to any particular antecedent conditions.

behaviors. The monitoring involves not only noticing occurrences of the goal behavior but also recording them with paper and pencil, mechanical counters, timers, or electronic devices (Ciminero et al., 1977).

Advantages. This method has a number of advantages as a way to collect data about client progress toward goal behaviors. Self-monitoring, or an ongoing account of what happens in a person's daily environment, can have more concurrent validity than some other data-collection procedures (Lick & Unger, 1977). In other words, self-monitoring may produce data that more closely approximate the goals of counseling than such measures as inventories or standardized instruments. Moreover, the predictive validity of self-monitoring may be superior to that of other measurement methods, with the exception of direct observation (Mischel, 1968). As McFall (1977b) explains, "The best way to predict an individual's future behavior in a particular situation is to observe his past behavior in that same situation, but the next best way is to simply ask the person how he typically behaves in that situation" (p. 199).* Self-monitoring can also provide a thorough and repre-

---

* This and all other quotations from this source are from "Parameters of Self-Monitoring," by R. McFall. In R. B. Stuart (Ed.), *Behavioral self-management: Strategies, techniques and outcomes.* Copyright 1977 by Brunner/Mazel, Inc. Reprinted by permission.

sentative sample of the ongoing behaviors in the client's environment. And self-monitoring is relatively objective. McFall notes that it is more objective than informal or verbal self-reports, mainly because "it prompts subjects to use a formal structure for their self-observation and reporting" (p. 199). Finally, self-monitoring is flexible. It can be used to collect data on covert and physiological indexes of change as well as more observable behaviors (Lick & Katkin, 1976, p. 183).

Limitations. Self-monitoring should not be used by clients who cannot engage in observation because of the intensity or diagnostic nature of their problems or because of medication. Kazdin (1974f) points out that some clients may not monitor as accurately as others. In addition, not all clients will agree to engage in self-monitoring (Ciminero et al., 1977). Some clients may resist continual or quantifiable data collection. Self-monitoring can be a "high cost" method for the client because of the time and effort required to make such frequent records of the goal behavior. Finally, as an evaluation tool, self-monitoring data are subject to two potential problems: reactivity and reliability.

As we suggested earlier in this chapter, the major problem associated with any self-report measure is its potential reactivity. Simply observing oneself and one's behavior may produce a change in the behavior. However, one can argue that other methods of data collection, such as standardized tests, questionnaires, and role-play assessments, are subject to as much reactivity and invalidity as self-report procedures (Lick & Unger, 1977). And as Mahoney (1977b, p. 243) notes, the reactive effects of self-monitoring are often "variable" and "short-lived."

Another problem associated with self-monitoring is its reliability, the consistency and accuracy with which the client collects and reports the data. Some have argued that individuals do not collect and report data about themselves in a reliable manner, particularly when they know that no one else will check on their observations (Barlow et al., 1984; Lipinski & Nelson, 1974). The reliability of self-report data seems to be a problem mainly when the target behaviors are subtle or not easily discriminable.

Both reactivity and reliability can affect the use of self-monitoring as a measurement method. As Nelson (1977) notes, the potential reactivity of self-monitoring should be maximized for therapeutic change yet minimized for evaluation. In using self-monitoring solely as a helping strategy (Chapter 19), the need for reliability is not as critical as when self-monitoring is as a measurement method or for assessment and evaluation. However, for use as a measurement method, accurate reporting of self-monitored data is essential. The next section describes some guidelines that may enhance the accuracy of client self-monitoring as a data-collection method.

Guidelines for use. There are eight guidelines a counselor and client can use to increase the accuracy of self-monitoring as a data-collection procedure. Many of these have been reviewed by McFall (1977b).

1. The behaviors to be observed should be defined clearly so that there is no ambiguity about what is to be observed and reported. Reliability of self-monitoring can be increased if the behaviors to be observed are well defined and easy to discriminate (Lick & Unger, 1977; Simkins, 1971). Hawkins and Dobes (1977) suggest three criteria for an adequate response definition: objectivity, clarity, and completeness. For example, a client should be instructed to observe particular responses associated with aggressiveness instead of just recording "aggressive behavior." In this case, the client might observe and record instances of raising one's voice above a conversational tone, hitting another person, or using verbal expressions of hostility. Usually any definition of the target behavior should be accompanied by examples so the client can discriminate instances of the observed behavior from instances of other behaviors.

2. Obtaining from the client an oral and written commitment to engage in self-monitoring activity may increase compliance with the self-monitoring task (Levy, 1977).

3. The accuracy of a client's report may be increased by having the client record the target behaviors immediately rather than after a delay (Frederiksen, Epstein, & Kosevsky, 1975).

4. Bootzin (1972) and Nicassio and Bootzin (1974) suggest that increasing the specificity of self-monitoring may offset any potential client biases arising from self-report. The counselor should spell out clearly the procedures for *what, where, when, how,* and *how long* to report the behaviors. McFall (1977b, p. 200) points out that "the more systematic the [self-monitoring] method used, the more reliable and accurate it is likely to be."

5. Reliability of recording can be increased when clients are trained to make *accurate* recordings (Nelson, Lipinski, & Boykin, 1978). Mahoney (1977b, p. 252) recalls that, following his instructions to a client to record her intake of sweets, the client asked: "But what if I get three pieces of candy in my mouth at once, is that one or three responses?" Mahoney accordingly recommends that clients practice self-monitoring before leaving the session. He advocates the following training sequence:

1. Give explicit definitions and examples of the behavior(s).
2. Give explicit self-monitoring instructions.
3. Illustrate data collection with a sample (model) form — possibly one of your own.
4. Ask the client to repeat the definitions and instructions.
5. Have the client practice or monitor several trial instances you describe [p. 252].

6. Self-monitoring should not be too much of a chore for the client. Sometimes a reluctant client can be encouraged to self-monitor if the demands are minimal (Mahoney, 1977b). A client may be discouraged from self-monitoring or may record inaccurately if required to record many behaviors. The client should self-monitor at least one response dimension associated with the major goal behavior; other response dimensions can be added at the counselor's discretion. If possible, clients should be instructed to self-monitor *in vivo* when the behavior occurs, rather than self-recording at the end of the day, when the client is dependent on retrospective recall.

7. Accuracy of the data from self-monitoring increases if the client is aware that accuracy of the data could be substantiated with his or her permission. For example, a parent or spouse can monitor aspects of the target behavior to be evaluated against the concurrent self-monitored data collected by the client (R. O. Nelson, 1981).

8. The counselor may need to "sell" the client on the importance of the self-recording process and its accuracy, for the client must be motivated to use it. The counselor can point out that accurate self-recording may provide the counselor and client with an awareness of varying parameters of the problem, the possible strategies for treatment, and the extent to which the therapeutic goals are reached. Accuracy of reporting may also be increased if the counselor positively reinforces the client for producing accurate self-monitored data

(McFall, 1977b; R. O. Nelson, 1981) and if the counselor stresses the personal honesty and integrity of the client in reporting these data (Bornstein, Hamilton, Carmody, Rychtarik, & Veraldi, 1977).

Self-Ratings

Self-ratings are used to assess the magnitude, or intensity, of the client's subjective state. The rating scales may use a variety of gradations (for example, 1–5, 0–100). Self-ratings have been used to measure client mood on a 5-point scale before and after eating (Fremouw & Heyneman, 1983), severity of headaches on a 6-point scale (Blanchard, Theobald, Williamson, Silver, & Brown, 1978), and general mood states on a 0–100 scale (Kendall & Hollon, 1981). Sherman and Cormier (1972) have used the Subjective Units of Irritation (SUI) scale, with points from 0 to 100, for self-ratings of interpersonal interactions with teachers, students, and family members. Self-ratings may be used in therapy sessions or in the natural environment. Ratings may be made with particular persons or at particular times or at random intervals during the day or during a 24-hour period.

Table 10-1 illustrates two examples of self-ratings. The self-rating of headache severity (Blanchard et al., 1978) can be used to rate headaches each time they occur during the day. Orlinsky and Howard's (1965) ratings of the therapy session include the client's ratings about progress made in the session and about what the client felt he or she got from the session.

Advantages. Self-ratings are useful in at least three ways: (1) they collect data about a client's subjective mood, feelings, tension, or behavior, (2) they are individualized for the particular client problem, and (3) they are easy to administer and interpret and can help the therapist and client to focus on the specific client concern.

Limitations. Some problems with self-rating scales are that responses from self-ratings are susceptible to selectivity, demand or expectancy, and social desirability. Additionally, self-ratings are unstandardized and have undetermined norms, reliability, and validity.

Guidelines for use. Three guidelines should be considered if a therapist wishes to use self-ratings to collect data about goal behaviors.

1. The therapist and client should define and specify in the client's language what is to be rated. Ratings of feelings, thoughts, tension, or behavior should be based on the target behavior for each client.
2. Each point on the rating scale should be described so that there is no ambiguity about any point to be rated.
3. Use the individualized self-rating consistently at each point in the evaluation process. Specify where and when the client is to use the self-ratings.

Self-Report Inventories

Self-report inventories can focus on the client's reports of particular overt behaviors, on fear, on anxiety, or on perceptions of the environment (Goldfried, 1976a). Inventories range from a global focus, such as those of the Minnesota Multiphasic Personality Inventory (Hathaway & McKinley, 1951) and the Symptom Checklist (SCL-90) (Derogatis, Rickels, & Rock, 1976), to a more specific focus, such as those of the Rathus Assertiveness Scale (Rathus, 1973), the College Self-Expression Scale (Galassi, Delo, Galassi, & Bastien, 1974), and the Assertion Inventory (Gambrill & Richey, 1975). Another example of an inventory with a specific focus is the Fear Survey Schedule (Wolpe & Lang, 1964). Watson and Friend (1969) have developed two anxiety inventories—the Social Avoidance and Distress Scale and the Fear of Negative Evaluation Scale. Locke and Wallace (1957) have developed the Marital Adjustment Test for couples in counseling, LoPiccolo and Steger (1974) have created the Sexual Interaction Inventory to assess sexual dysfunction between couples, and the Beck Depression Inventory (Beck, Ward, Mendelson, Mock, & Erbaugh, 1961) was developed to assess depressed clients. Moos (1972) has devised inventories assessing a person's social environment. Cautela (1977, 1981) has developed inventories and surveys for a variety of client problems. These self-report inventories are used to measure reports of covert and overt behaviors and global traits (Cautela, 1977, 1981). Descriptive lists and summarizations of self-report instruments in these and related areas are reported by Bellack and Hersen (1977), Cautela and Upper (1976), Haynes (1978), Haynes and Wilson (1979), Nelson and Hayes (1979), and Tasto (1977). Self-report inventories can be used to assess the client's progress (outcome) before, during, and after therapy.

TABLE 10-1. Examples of self-ratings: headache severity and therapy session

*Headache severity**

0 = No headache
1 = Aware of headache only when attention is devoted to it
2 = Mild headache, could be ignored at times
3 = Headache is painful but person can do his or her job
4 = Very severe headache, difficult to concentrate, can do only undemanding task
5 = Intense, incapacitating headache

*Therapy session***

How much progress do you feel you made in dealing with your problems this session? (Circle one.)
1. A great deal of progress
2. Considerable progress
3. Moderate progress
4. Some progress
5. Didn't get anywhere this session
6. In some ways my problems seem to have gotten worse this session

What do you feel that you got out of this session? (For each item, circle the answer that best applies.)

	No	A little	Some	A lot
I feel that I got:				
Help in talking about what was really troubling me	0	1	2	3
Relief from tension or unpleasant feelings	0	1	2	3
More understanding of the reasons behind my behavior and feelings	0	1	2	3
Reassurance and encouragement about how I'm doing	0	1	2	3
Confidence to try to do things differently	0	1	2	3
More ability to feel my feelings to know what I really want	0	1	2	3
Ideas for better ways of dealing with people and problems	0	1	2	3

* Blanchard, Theobald, Williamson, Silver, & Brown, 1978
** From Orlinsky, D. E. & Howard, K. I. (1965). *Therapy session report.* Chicago: Institute for Juvenile Research.

Advantages.   Bellack and Hersen (1977, p. 55) note that self-report inventories are useful in at least two ways: to collect data about a client's overt and covert behaviors and to obtain data about the person's subjective evaluation of these behaviors. As Lick and Katkin (1976, p. 179) note, inventories are relatively easy to administer, take little time to complete, and can help the therapist and client identify important clinical material. Self-report inventories generally have norms, have determined reliability and validity, and are easy to interpret.

Limitations.   One problem of self-report inventories is that they may not measure *particular* client behaviors. For example, the items in an inventory may not represent the behaviors of interest in relation to fear, assertion, depression, or anxiety. Another drawback is that the wording of items may be subject to a variety of interpretations (Cronbach, 1984). Inventory responses may be biased because of the practice effect, reactivity, demand characteristics, and client faking (R. O. Nelson, 1981). The psychometric properties of self-report inventories, such as reliability, content validity and concurrent validity, and norms may not be established for all client groups or problems (Jayaratne & Levy, 1979; Nelson, 1981; Nelson & Hayes, 1979). Finally, the readability of some self-report inventories may be too difficult for clients having a limited educational background (Dentch, O'Farrell, & Cutter, 1980).

Guidelines for use.   In selecting self-report inventories, the therapist might be aided by the following guidelines.

1. Select instruments that have been used and validated with more than one population. As Bellack and Hersen note, "Although data derived from studies with the college volunteer subjects are of academic interest, they frequently are of limited value when the assessor is confronted with the clinical situation in an applied setting" (1977, p. 75). However, self-report inventories used in evaluating goal behaviors may not have to be validated beyond the agreement between what a client says he or she does and what actually occurs. For example, selected individual items from the Beck Depression Scale (Beck, 1972), administered daily, provide continuous data about how the individual responds to items related to depression. One does not have to "interpret" or "score" the answers on the scale for comparison with norms.

2. Select inventories in which the wording of the items or questions is objective and is related specifically to the client's concerns. An inventory may have more meaning when the terms reflected in the items are defined explicitly (Bellack & Hersen, 1977, p. 58).

3. Select inventories in which the response choices are, in some way, quantifiable and unambiguous. Words such as *always, seldom,* or *hardly* or points along a continuum such as "1 to 7" should be clearly defined (Cronbach, 1984).

Role Play

Role play can be a valuable tool to assess the client's behavior. The procedure consists of scenarios designed by the therapist to prompt the occurrence of behaviors and to evaluate the client's performance of the goal behaviors. Role play can easily be video- or audiotape-recorded in interview situations. It can occur in the therapist's office or in the client's natural environment with the presence of other stimuli or persons. For example, role play with stimuli or "contrived situations" (Barlow et al., 1984) can be used with clients who are phobic or fearful about some particular situation or object, such as dental chairs, physicians' exam-

ining tables, automobiles, water, elevators, spiders, and darkness. Role-play scenes can also be created to evaluate interpersonal behaviors, such as those between parent and child, distressed couples, employer and potential employee, or colleagues.

Self-ratings and checklists can be used to assess the client's behavior during the role play. The particular self-ratings and checklists used should specify the major response dimensions of each outcome goal or target behavior. For example, clients could rate their degree of felt apprehension during the role plays on a 1-to-10 scale. Concurrently, the therapist may be evaluating the presence or absence of particular verbal and nonverbal behaviors associated with anxiety (or lack of it). The therapist can have the client take part in role plays before, during, and after a therapeutic intervention. Role-play evaluations of the goal behavior may be especially useful as an adjunct to self-monitoring, imagery, or self-report inventories.

Advantages.   Role-play assessments have some advantages. First, direct observation of clients' verbal and nonverbal behaviors requires little inference (Barlow et al., 1984). Second, role-play assessments of target behaviors are easily conducted in the therapist's presence either in a clinic setting or in the client's natural and often stressful situation. Thus, as Lick and Unger (1977) note, role-play assessment is an "ideal context" for making "precise, multichannel assessments" of client responses to problem stimuli and provides a rich record of client responses (p. 301).

Limitations.   Role play as an assessment procedure has several drawbacks. The role–play scenes must be carefully designed in order to have external validity—that is, to provide accurate data about how the client actually functions in his or her natural environment. Role–play assessments may impose "artificial constraints" on a client (McFall, 1977a, p. 162). The therapist must be aware that a client's performance, even in a well-constructed role–play test with a variety of scenarios or stimulus situations, may not correspond to how the client might behave in the actual environment. Kazdin, Matson, and Esveldt-Dawson (1984) found that role play of social skills among children did not have concurrent validity. Further, the client's performance on a role–play test may be affected by the presence of the therapist (or someone else) and by the client's knowledge that he or she is being observed (Lick & Katkin, 1976;

Lick & Unger, 1977). Small variations in the role-play scenes, the demand characteristics, the instructions, and the rationale given to the client have implications for the validity of the responses obtained (Galassi & Galassi, 1976; Higgins, Frisch, & Smith, 1983; Hopkins, Krawitz, & Bellack, 1981; Kern, 1982; Kern, Miller, & Eggers, 1983; Lick & Unger, 1977; Mahaney & Kern, 1983; Martinez & Edelstein, 1977; Orne, 1969).

Guidelines for use.   Three guidelines should be considered if a therapist wishes to use role play to collect data about goal behaviors.

1. A variety of role–play scenes should be developed as vividly as possible in order to approximate a number of situations in the client's actual environment. The scenes should approximate the real-life situations to which the goal behavior is directed. This is important because, in reality, clients have to deal with a variety of stimulus situations requiring responses across different dimensions.

2. The scenes used for the role play should be developed on the basis of an individual analysis of problematic situations encountered by each client. Lick and Unger (1977, p. 302) recommend that the counselor have the client identify a series of problem situations that have "maximum relevance" for the client's everyday life. The role–play assessments can replicate some of these scenes. Basing the role-play test on an individual analysis helps to ensure that this assessment does not misrepresent or underrepresent the most important dimensions to which the client will respond in the "real world" (Lick & Unger, 1977).

3. There should be some standardization of instructions on how to role-play and of the role-play scenarios used across time. For example, suppose a counselor has developed a variety of scenes to assess a client's assertive behavior of making refusals. The nature of the scene and the responses of the other person in the scene should be standardized—that is, consistent across repeated role-play measures. This ensures that evaluation of the client's behavior is not based on changes in the nature of the scene or in the behavior of the other person in the scene.

A client's performance in role-play scenarios can be assessed with frequency counts, duration counts, rating scales, or checklists. For example, a therapist may record the number of times the client expresses opinions during the role play or the amount of time the client spends in verbal expression of opinions. The client's behavior in role plays could also be rated on a scale according to the degree of effectiveness or competence. Finally, the presence or absence of a collection of responses can be checked using a behavior checklist.

Imagery

Imagery can be used to assess the client's perception of problem situations before, during, and after treatment. Clients are instructed to relax, to close their eyes, to imagine the problem situation or problem event with detailed instructions, and to focus on as many of the sensations associated with the particular problem situation as possible (for example, sounds, visual features and colors, temperature, and smell). The purpose of focusing on the sensations is to heighten the client's awareness or vividness of recalling specific details associated with the problems.

There are three ways a therapist can use imagery as an outcome measure or a measure of progress toward the goal behaviors. First, the therapist can do a *content analysis* of the client's description of the problem after the client has imagined the problem situation. The therapist performs the content analysis by tape-recording the client's imagined description of the problem or by writing down what and how the client describes the problem. Ratings of the content can reflect changes in the way the client describes the problem situation. For example, the adjectives connoting anxiety in the client's description may decrease in frequency.

The second technique is to have the client *rate the intensity or severity* of the imagined problem situation. The client can rate descriptions of imagined problem scenes on a 0-to-4 or 0-to-100 scale, where the highest number represents the greatest degree of intensity. Another variation of rating the intensity of the imagined problem situation is the *card-sort* procedure (Barlow et al., 1984; R. O. Nelson, 1981). The card-sort procedure can be used when there are several (five to ten) variations of the problem situation, such as phobic or social situations. A scene is developed for each problem situation. A brief description of each scene is typed on an index card. After the client imagines the scene described on one card, it is placed in one of five envelopes or piles. The five envelopes or piles represent the degree of intensity or aversiveness for the particular scene: 0 equals not aversive, 1 equals a little, 2 a fair amount, 3 very aversive, and 4 extremely aversive.

A third technique is to develop a *hierarchy of imagery scenes* individualized for the client's problem. The range of intensity for the hierarchy of scenes is from neutral (0) to extremely aversive (100). The therapist helps the client to develop five to ten scenes. One or two scenes associated with the problem situation are neutral and are rated 0. The rest of the scenes reflect varying degrees of aversiveness up to extremely aversive (100). The client imagines each scene and places the scene in the hierarchy or assigns a value to the scene from 0 to 100. Presumably, therapeutic intervention is successful when the client gives lower point values to aversive scenes.

Advantages. There are several advantages associated with imagery assessments. They are easy to administer within the interview setting, they take little time to complete, and they can be individualized for the client. Imagery assessments also can be used to reflect the degree of change in the client's perception of the problem over time.

Limitations. Imagery assessment should not be used by clients who cannot relax because of the intensity of the problem or who are on medications that might distort imagery. Additionally, because the imagery process is retrospective, reliability and validity about the client's perception of the problem are undetermined. The demand characteristics or expectations created by instructions to engage in imagery may influence what the client imagines or may distort the vividness of the recalled problem.

Guidelines for use. There are several guidelines to consider in using imagery evaluation methods with clients.

1. Assess the client's potential to construct believable scenes in her or his imagination.
2. Individualize the scenes to be used for each client so that they reflect the major response dimensions of the target behavior.
3. Standardize the selected scenes for each client; that is, be sure to use the same scenes at each point in the overall measurement process.
4. Select one of the three methods described earlier for imagery evaluation to use with each client. Use this method consistently at each point in the measurement process.

Physiological Measures

Another method for assessing outcome is to measure directly the client's psychophysiological responses. Barlow et al. (1984) indicate that psycho-

physiological measures have been most frequently used to assess outcome of three types of disorders: (1) anxiety or phobic behavior (heart rate, pulse rate, and skin conductance), (2) psychophysiological disorders (blood pressure, headaches), and (3) sexual disorders (male or female genital arousal). A variety of instruments are used to obtain physiological measures. For example, to measure heart rate, a portable electrocardiogram machine can be used. A common device for measuring blood pressure includes a sphygmomanometer and a stethoscope. A popular technique for recording muscular activity is the electromyogram (EMG). The EMG has been used to assess tension in the frontalis muscle for clients who suffer from tension headaches. A thermistor is used to measure digital skin temperature. Instruments are also available in treatment of sexual disorders to measure male genital arousal (penile circumference and volume) and female genital arousal (vaginal photoplethysmograph).

Advantages. Psychophysiological measures are easy to administer in an interview setting. Some devices, such as the sphygmomanometer to measure blood pressure and the manual recording of pulse rate to measure heart rate, are not so expensive and require less expertise to apply (R. O. Nelson, 1981). Furthermore, direct measurement of the client's physiological responses can minimize therapist-introduced bias about problem behavior (Jayaratne & Levy, 1979).

Limitations. Possible disadvantages of some psychophysiological measures are the expense and expertise required for suitable instrumentation (R. O. Nelson, 1981). These disadvantages may limit the availability of such instrumentation in some clinical settings. The complex instrumentation may also exert demand characteristics and reactive effects on the person being assessed (Ray & Raczynski, 1981).

Guidelines for use. Three guidelines are applicable to the use of physiological measures:

1. Make every effort to obtain the most reliable equipment possible.
2. Make sure you are trained to use the equipment selected. Obtain supervision for your initial attempts.
3. Establish a fairly lengthy baseline to minimize any reactive effects of the procedure.

In the previous sections, we discussed use of the evaluation methods by the therapist (or a staff member) and/or the client to collect outcome data. Some of these methods for assessing outcomes can be used in the clinic or the natural environment. Data collected from these procedures can be verified with direct observations made by others about the client in his or her environment. For example, a spouse or parent can observe the behavior of the other spouse or child in the home environment (Margolin, 1981; Prinz, Foster, Kent, & O'Leary, 1979). Observation by others may be especially helpful when clients have altered "negative" behaviors but are still mislabeled by others in their environment. As Kazdin (1977) indicates,

> The evaluation of behavior by others is important independently of the behaviors that the clients perform after treatment. The problem with many deviant populations is not merely their behavior but how they are perceived by others and perceive themselves. . . . Thus, it is possible that changing behavior of clients will not necessarily alter the evaluation of individuals with whom the target clients have interacted [pp. 446–447].

Outside observation does, however, pose ethical problems. Before contacting any other person, the counselor must obtain the client's permission, and in contacting observers or significant others, problems of confidentiality may arise. Another major drawback of using observers or of contacting other people is the possibility of communicating mistrust of the client. This could damage the counseling relationship and interventions. An alternative might be to have the client bring in representative tape-recorded samples of his or her behavior in the environment. These samples would have to be drawn from situations in which the client could use a tape recorder unobtrusively and without violating the rights of others. The client might be unable to tape-record all the clinically important situations encountered in the environment. Still, this method provides data about the client's functioning in the environment and does not pose a threat to the confidentiality and trust necessary for an effective therapeutic relationship. Another alternative is to have the therapist accompany the client into various environmental situations. Although this is very time-consuming, it does lend objectivity and reliability to client self-report data.

Selecting Methods of Evaluation

Four guidelines should be considered when selecting methods of evaluation to assess the client's progress toward the target behavior.

1. The client's problems must be clearly defined and the goal behaviors of therapy specified. If a problem is redefined, the goal behaviors and methods of outcome measurement may have to change to reflect the redefined problem. Once the problems have been defined for the client, appropriate evaluation methods can be selected and developed.

2. Methods of evaluation and outcome measures should be developed idiographically for the client. Standardized self-report inventories can be used as global measures. Interview, self-ratings, self-monitoring, role plays, and/or imagery should be developed to reflect the client's unique concerns or problems. Not all seven methods of assessment have to be used for each client. Therapists should select a global method (for example, self-report inventories) to be used at baseline, at treatment, after treatment, and as a follow-up several months or a year later. More specific methods can be used weekly (for example, interview, role play, imagery, or physiological measures) or can be recorded daily (for example, self-monitoring or self-ratings). The specific method should be designed to measure the particular client problem.

3. The therapist should provide a rationale to the client for evaluating client outcomes, stressing the importance of sufficient feedback about the degree of success of the treatment. The therapist should also explain that if the treatment is not successful, the therapist can make whatever adjustments are needed to increase its effectiveness. Otherwise, the helping process is incomplete or unfinished (Egan, 1982).

4. Once the treatment strategy or intervention has started, the therapist should monitor its application. Monitoring involves recording four aspects of treatment: (a) What treatment or variation was used? (b) When and how often was the treatment applied? (c) Where was the treatment applied? (d) Who applied the treatment?

Regardless of which of these methods is used to collect outcome data, it is important to remember that none of the methods is perfect—and all may suffer from what we refer to as "the validity of external validity." In other words, any outcome measure is effective only to the degree that it is tied directly to the clinical criterion or goal behaviors. This point was well stated by Lick and Katkin (1976, p. 182):

> Clients do not, in our estimation, seek therapy to change responses on questionnaires, physiological and behavioral reactions to imagined animals, or unassertive responses to videotaped unreasonable requests. Regardless of the reliability of such measures or the thoroughness with which they assess behavioral, cognitive, and physiological reactions,

they have little *clinical value* as outcome measures unless they correlate highly with a client's reactions to problematic stimuli encountered in the natural environment.

Generally, these procedures can be used to collect data on the goal behavior at four times — before counseling (baseline), during counseling, after counseling, and at follow-up. The next section explores the ways data are collected at these four times.

LEARNING ACTIVITY #30: METHODS OF MEASUREMENT

Read the client case description in Learning Activity #29 again. Assuming you are the therapist for this client:

1. On a sheet of paper write the measurement method you believe to be most appropriate for

this case.
2. Provide a brief rationale for your choice.
3. Write sample instructions you would give to this client about how to use this method. Feedback follows.

☐ WHEN TO MEASURE: TIME OF MEASUREMENT

There are several times during which a counselor and client can log progress toward the goal behaviors. Generally, it is important to assess the client's performance before counseling (baseline), during counseling or during application of a counseling strategy, immediately after counseling, and some time after counseling at a follow-up. Repeated measurements of client change may provide more precise data than only two measurement times, such as before and after counseling (Barlow et al., 1984; Hersen & Barlow, 1976; Jayaratne & Levy, 1979; Kazdin, 1980b, 1981). Limited measurements often reflect "random fluctuation," whereas "frequent and repeated" measurements indicate stability of client change (Chassan, 1962, p. 615).

Baseline (Pretreatment) Assessment

Baseline assessment measures the goal behaviors before treatment. The baseline period is a reference point against which therapeutic change in the client's goal behavior can be compared during and after treatment. The length of the baseline period can be three days, a week, two weeks, or longer. One criterion for the length of the baseline period is that it should be long enough or contain enough data points to serve as a *representative sample* of the client's behavior. Usually a minimum of three

data points for the baseline are necessary — for example, three interviews, three role plays, three instances of self-ratings or self-monitoring. The length should also be sufficient to establish estimates of level, trend, and stability (Barlow et al., 1984). *Level* refers to the number of a particular behavior, such as number of self-critical thoughts. *Trend* refers to whether the behavior is increasing, decreasing, or remaining constant over a period of time. *Stability* is the variability or fluctuation of the behavior. Regularity or stability in behavior can be quite variable; that is, if variability in the data reflects a representative sample of the client's behavior, then these data may be considered stable.

Collecting interview, self-monitoring, and self-ratings data during baseline. Typically, during the baseline period, the client is asked to self-monitor instances of the problem and goal behaviors. All the guidelines for using self-monitoring described earlier should be followed at this time. The behaviors to be observed should be defined clearly, and the client should rehearse the process of self-observing and recording. The client will self-monitor the frequency or duration of a behavior and, in some cases, both. For example, suppose a client wants to decrease the number of self-critical thoughts. During the baseline period, the client would be instructed to observe and record (with some device) each time she or he noticed the onset of a self-critical thought. The client would be counting the number, or frequency, of self-critical thoughts.

Typically, the frequency or duration of the observed behavior during baseline can be seen more clearly if it is displayed visually. This pictorial display can be accomplished with a graph. Usually, the counselor will be responsible for taking the client's data and displaying them graphically; however, the graph should be shared with the client because of its informational value. To make a graph for our example of self-critical thoughts, a counselor would plot the number of self-critical thoughts (one to ten) along the vertical axis (the ordinate) as a function of the number of days the behavior was observed. The number of days (1 to 14) would be plotted along the horizontal axis (the abscissa). Generally, in graphing baseline data, the observed behavior is plotted along the vertical line, and the time (or days) is plotted along the horizontal line.

Graphic display of self-monitored data is very important in evaluation. The client can continue to self-monitor instances of the goal behavior during and after the application of counseling strategies. The baseline graph can be compared with the graphs of data collected at these later points to see whether there is evidence of change in the observed behavior. Graphic display of data is also of informational value to the counselor and client, particularly the graph of the baseline data. Self-monitored baseline data can give clues about the nature and intensity of problem and goal behaviors and contributing problem conditions.

A graph can also provide information about the *relative* stability or instability of the observed behavior. The observed behavior may be stable or unstable over time. If the observed behavior occurs consistently over time — even with increasing or decreasing trends or fluctuations in frequency or duration — it is usually considered stable. Unstable baseline data present more of a problem in evaluation because the irregular fluctuations in the data make comparisons more difficult. However, instability can be an important source of information for problem assessment (Chapters 7 and 8) and definition of goal behaviors (Chapter 9). For example, unstable baseline data may be a clue that different contexts (perhaps times, places, or situations) in which the behavior occurs may have been overlooked during assessment (Gambrill, 1977). The instability of baseline

data may add new dimensions to the defined problem or may help to refine the goal behaviors.

To demonstrate some of the ways self-monitored baseline data may look pictorially, Figure 10-2 presents five hypothetical baseline graphs for the client who observed the daily number of self-critical thoughts. Graph A illustrates relatively unvarying data. The level is about six per day, the thoughts are relatively stable, and there is no increasing or decreasing trend. Graph B illustrates an increase in the behavior over the baseline period: the level of the thoughts increases from three on the first day to nine on day 14. The increase might have been caused by the reactivity of the self-recording of self-critical thoughts. Another possibility is that greater job or home demands were imposed on the client, causing more self-critical thoughts. The counselor and client should discuss the increasing trend in these thoughts to discover possible contributing factors. Graph C depicts a decreasing trend, from nine thoughts on day 1 to three on day 14. As in Graph B, reactivity or situational demands could have contributed to the decreasing trend. Again, the counselor would query the client about what might have contributed to decreases in these thoughts. It is also possible for baseline data to reflect a combination of an increasing trend or a decreasing and increasing trend. Graph D reveals such variable data. An explanation for these fluctuations in self-critical thoughts might be that more of these thoughts occurred during days on which the client had unsuccessful experiences in his or her environment or context. A counselor might also discover that, on days in which relatively low numbers of self-critical thoughts occurred (days, 1, 2, 4, 7, and 11), the client was at home, faced fewer demands, or reported more "successful" activities.

Graphs A through D could all be considered stable if the data reflected a consistent pattern in each case. In other words, stability of data and trends in data are not mutually exclusive. In contrast, Graph E can be described as unstable because there is no indication of consistent variability, level, or trend in the goal behavior. As with the previous graph patterns, the counselor could use the hypothetical data in Graph E to determine contributing factors that might account for the varying number of self-critical thoughts. Such discussion can help define the antecedents and consequences of the problem behavior. In some cases, irregular fluctuations in the baseline data may

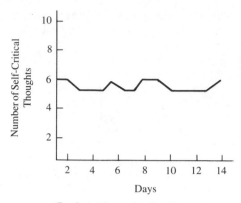

Graph A. Unvarying Baseline

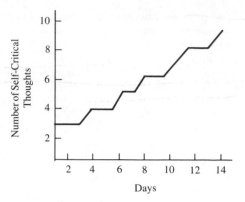

Graph B. Increasing Baseline Trend

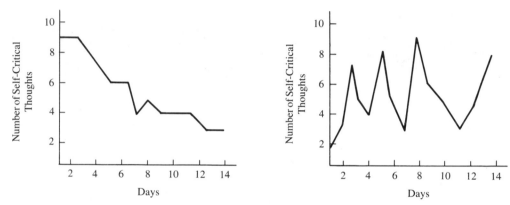

Graph C. Decreasing Baseline Trend

Graph D. Variable Baseline

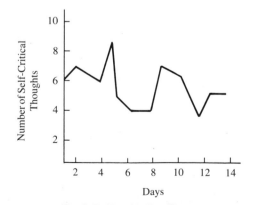

Graph E. Unstable Baseline

Figure 10-2. *Graphs of unvarying, increasing, decreasing, variable, and unstable baselines*

mean that the client is not self-monitoring accurately or regularly—or that another, more important goal behavior has been overlooked. In addition to context, it is also important to note that stability in goal behavior can be affected by the *unit of time* in which data are collected and

FEEDBACK #30: METHODS OF MEASUREMENT

The method of measurement that would be most useful for this client is self-monitoring. Note that the way the therapist instructs the client to self-monitor (see below) also includes *self-ratings* of intensity of feelings. The behavior to be assessed is primarily covert, and self-monitoring lends itself to assessment of covert behavior more readily than role plays or therapist observation. In addition, because this client is concerned about a very specific anxiety-provoking situation, most of the self-report inventories typically used for fear assessment are too general to be helpful.

The client would be instructed to self-monitor the frequency and intensity of the anxiety attacks. Your instructions for this method might go something like this:

"I would like you to get some very specific information this week about these anxiety attacks. I am going to ask you to carry this note card and pencil with you during the week. Whenever you have an anxiety attack—that is, whenever you are thinking about or feeling anxious about the idea of getting cancer—I want you to mark this down with a check mark on the note card, like this:

Mon	Tues	Wed	Thurs	Fri	Sat	Sun
✓						

"Be sure you note even the slightest bit of anxiety. Sometimes the thoughts will lead up to an attack. Also, as you do this, write down the intensity or severity of your attacks, using a 5-point scale: 1 would be complete calm and 5 would be complete panic. If, for example, you feel just a little anxious, your number would be 2. If you feel very, very anxious, you would select a higher number, such as 4 or 5. See—after the check mark, indicate your rating of the intensity of the attack with a number, like this:

Mon	Tues	Wed	Thurs	Fri	Sat	Sun
✓ - 4						
✓ - 2						
✓ - 3						
✓ - 4						

"Now, to make sure we're clear on this, could you tell me what you're going to do on this note card this week? . . . OK, let's practice this. Assume you're having an anxiety attack now. You're thinking about having cancer and not knowing it until it's too late. Use the card now to mark these things down." The self-monitoring data collected by the client during *in vivo* situations can also be supplemented by the therapist's ratings of the client's self-reported anxiety in the interviews, either in response to structured leads or during imagery assessments.

graphed. If the unit of time is expanded, instability in the data will decrease.

Graphs can also be used to display client self-ratings of problem intensity during the baseline period. Remember that, in addition to self-monitoring the frequency or duration of a behavior, the client can record self-ratings of the intensity of the behavior. For example, a client might rate the level of anxiety on a 5-point scale in addition to noting the number of times anxious feelings occur. When self-rating intensity, one should try to provide anchor points that are not directly related to the problem. If anxious about public speaking, for example, one can use anxiety experienced while climbing stairs or approaching a busy intersection as an anchor point. The rationale for providing neutral anchor points is that the client's ratings can be confounded by overall reductions in anxiety, thus altering the rating scale. The self-ratings of the anxiety level can be displayed pictorially in the same way that frequency or duration counts are displayed. The time (days) would be plotted along the horizontal line and the client's ratings plotted along the vertical line (see Figure 10-3).

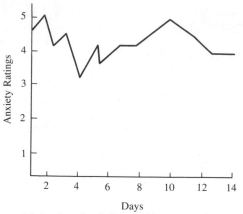

Figure 10-3. *Graph of client self-ratings of anxiety level during baseline period*

Graphs can also be used to display data obtained from the interview. For example, suppose you wanted to use the interview as a method of obtaining baseline data on the number of self-deprecatory comments a client makes. You would need to use at least three interviews as data points; you could audiotape the interviews and then, in listening to the tapes, count the self-critical comments during each session. These numbers would be plotted on the vertical axis of the graph, with the interview sessions plotted on the horizontal axis (see Figure 10-4 for an example).

Collecting role-play, imagery, and physiological data during baseline. The counselor may wish to obtain corroborative measures of the client's progress in therapy in addition to data collected from interviews, self-monitoring, or self-ratings. Moreover, self-monitoring or self-ratings may not always be feasible. In such cases, other procedures must be used. For example, consider a male client who lacks social confidence, defined as feelings of anxiety and lack of verbal skills in being able to approach and ask females for dates. It may not be possible to have this client self-report or self-rate feelings, thoughts, or behaviors in actual situations, because his reported anxiety is so high that he cannot focus on his own behavior.

In this case, the counselor might create several situations in which the client would role-play asking someone for a date. Several (at least three) role-play scenarios could be used during the baseline period. A checklist used during the role plays could indicate whether the client demonstrated a particular collection of behaviors associated with asking for a date. This topography, or collection, of behaviors is defined in the interview session in which the goals for counseling are established. As you may remember from our discussion of the role-play evaluation method, the behaviors and scenarios that make up the role play should be defined on the basis of a situational problem analysis for each client. A checklist or a rating list can be used for each role-play session during the baseline period, and the collection of behaviors the client demonstrates during role play can be scored. For example, 0 = demonstrated none of the desired

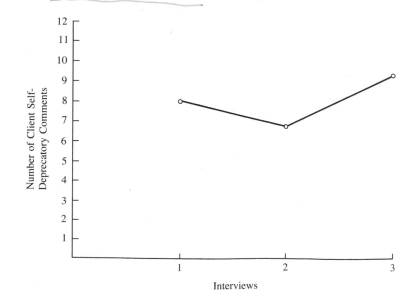

Figure 10-4. *Graph of interview baseline data*

behaviors associated with asking a female for a date, 10 (or more) = exhibited all the goal behaviors. If the client consistently demonstrates the same behaviors across all the role plays, these behaviors may reflect skills already in the client's repertory. Then the focus of counseling should be the skills that were *not* exhibited during the role plays.

The data could be plotted on a graph. Assuming that the range for the role-play checklist is 0 to 10, Figure 10-5 illustrates how data from three hypothetical role-play sessions might be graphed. The observed behaviors are plotted on the vertical axis; the three role-play occasions are plotted on the horizontal axis. Note from the graph that the client demonstrated two of the desired behaviors in the first role play and three in the second and third ones.

Data collected from imagery methods of evaluation and physiological measures can also be graphically displayed. For example, frequency of words connoting anxiety while describing an imagery scene, ratings of intensity for different scenes (card sorts), and placing of imagined scenes on a hierarchy can all be plotted on the ordinate (vertical axis) of a graph. Physiological measures taken during baseline such as heart rate, blood pressure, and digital temperature can be depicted graphically as well.

Collecting self-report inventory data during baseline. The counselor can also administer a self-report schedule or an inventory to a client during the baseline period. For example, with our male client, the Fear of Negative Evaluation (FNE) Scale or the Social Avoidance and Distress (SAD) Scale (Watson & Friend, 1969) could be used. The scores obtained on each scale each time it was adminis-

tered during the baseline period can be recorded and graphed. Figure 10-6 shows hypothetical graphs in which this client's scores on the questionnaires are plotted on the vertical axes and the two scale administrations are plotted on the horizontal axes.

It is not always necessary to plot all the baseline data graphically. The counselor can simply keep a record of the client's self-monitored data, role-play checklists, and scores on self-report schedules or inventories. However, the graphic display of data has more practical use to the client and also may make progress toward the goal behavior more observable.

A baseline measurement may not be possible with all clients. The client's problem concern may be too urgent or intense to take time to gather baseline data. For example, if a client reports "exam panic" and is faced with an immediate and very important test, the counselor and client will need to start working on reducing the test anxiety at once. In such cases, the treatment or counseling strategy must be applied immediately. Baseline measurement is also often omitted in crisis counseling.

Assessment during Treatment Strategies

According to Cronbach (1975, p. 126), any evaluator is engaged in monitoring an ongoing operation. In therapy, the therapist and client monitor the effects of a designated treatment on the goal behaviors after collecting baseline data and selecting a counseling treatment strategy. The monitoring during the treatment phase of counseling is conducted by continuing to collect data about the client's performance of the goal behavior. The same types of data collected during the baseline period are collected during treatment. For example, if the client self-monitored the frequency and duration of self-critical thoughts during the baseline period, this self-monitoring would continue during the application of a helping strategy. Or if inventories and role-play assessments of the client's social skills were used during the baseline period, these same methods would be used to collect data during treatment. Data collection during treatment is a feedback loop that gives both the counselor and the client important information about the usefulness of the selected treatment strategy and the client's demonstration of the goal behavior. Monitoring the goal behavior during treatment is analogous to what Cronbach (1975) calls "short-run empiricism," the idea of taking

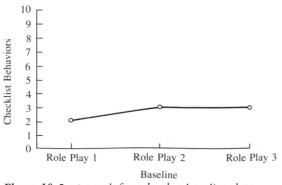

Figure 10-5. *A graph for role-play baseline data*

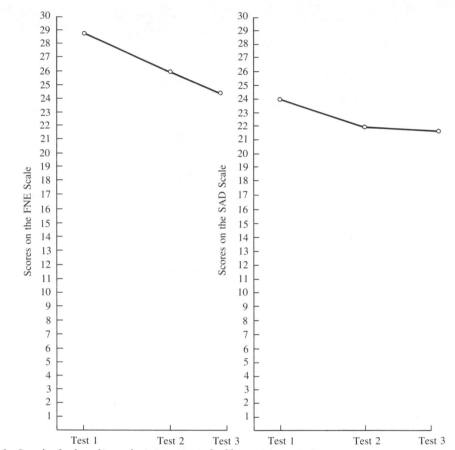

Figure 10-6. *Graphs for baseline administration of self-report inventories*

depth soundings as one moves into unknown waters (p. 126). The data collected during treatment can indicate the need for adjustments in the client's goals or in the treatment plan.

As an example, consider the client who was instructed to self-monitor instances of self-critical thoughts during a baseline period. Before working with any treatment strategies, this client and the therapist would have spent several sessions assessing the problem and establishing and defining desired outcome goals. During portions of this time, the client would have been self-monitoring instances of self-critical thoughts; data from the interviews, role plays, and self-report inventories might also have been obtained. After defining the problem and goal behaviors and collecting baseline data, the therapist and client would select and use one or several counseling (treatment) strategies to help the client achieve the designated goal behaviors. For instance, with the client who wanted to decrease self-critical thoughts, the counselor and client might decide to use a thought-stopping

procedure (Chapter 15). During the first treatment session, suppose the therapist helped this client learn how to stop instances of these thoughts. Following this session, the client would monitor application of this part of thought stopping by continuing to observe and record instances of self-critical thoughts. If role-play assessments and self-report inventories had been used during the baseline period, these sources of data would also be used at one or several points during application of the thought-stopping procedure.

Effects of treatment measures. Measures of the effects of treatment on the goal behavior can have the same degree of stability or instability as baseline measures (see Figure 10-2). For example, suppose our client continued to monitor instances of self-critical thoughts during and after thought stopping. Graphs of the effects of the treatment on this behavior might show decreasing, increasing, or variable trends, as depicted in Figure 10-7.

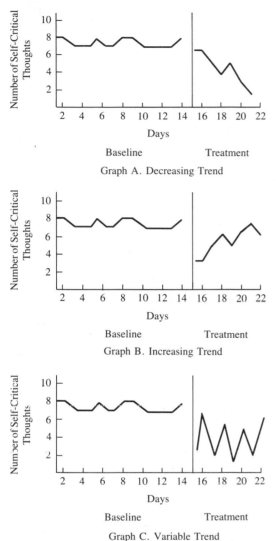

Figure 10-7. Graphs of decreasing, increasing, and variable trends in behavior during treatment application

In Graph A, the client's self-observed instances of self-critical thoughts decreased after thought stopping was applied. Note the decreasing trend in the self-reported thoughts from the end of the baseline, or beginning of treatment (day 15), to the last day of treatment (day 22). In this example, the client's goal behavior is changing in the desired direction (a decrease in self-critical thoughts). Such a graph indicates that treatment is having the desired effect. It is likely that the treatment is contributing to the desired change, although nontreatment factors such as the relationship, reactivity, and demand characteristics may also be at work.

The counselor and client can discuss the client's reaction to the treatment strategies used (in this case, thought stopping) and to additional factors contributing to the desired change.

In an occasional case, the opposite of the desired effect seems to occur when treatment is applied. In Graph B of Figure 10-7, for example, the client's number of self-critical thoughts increases from the beginning of treatment (day 15) to the last day data were collected (day 22). In this example, the increasing trend does not reflect the desired direction of change in the goal behavior.

When treatment has an unintended effect, several factors may be involved, and the counselor and client should discuss these to determine what might be going on. First of all, the reactivity of the measurement may be creating change in an unintended direction. For example, self-monitoring these thoughts may increase the client's attention to them. Occasionally, a heightened awareness or attention to an undesired behavior may result in an increase (although usually a temporary one) in the behavior. Another possible explanation for a behavior change in an undesired direction concerns the way the data are being collected. Perhaps the client is recording inaccurately or is monitoring the wrong behavior. An undesired effect of treatment may also be a function of time. In this case, the client's self-critical thoughts increased during the first week of treatment. A longer time period may achieve a different effect—perhaps these thoughts may increase initially and then decrease two to three weeks later. It is also possible that the nature of the client's problem behavior is contributing to a temporary setback or movement away from the desired goals. For instance, it is not uncommon for clients trying to decrease addictive behaviors to reduce their level of addiction initially—but later during treatment to increase it. Another reason for undesired effects of treatment or variability of goal behaviors may be the inappropriate application of treatment. For example, perhaps, in using the thought-stopping strategy outside therapy, the client does not regularly use a signal such as a covert or overt "Stop!" to terminate the thoughts or does not replace the thoughts with more adaptive alternatives, or the client may be practicing the strategy at home infrequently. As mentioned earlier under "Selecting Methods of Evaluation," the therapist should monitor the what, when, where, and who of the application of treatment to ensure its proper application and to make whatever adjustments to the treatment strategy are needed.

Obtaining an unintended effect of treatment may require that some adjustments be made in the way the client monitors or what the client monitors. Or the counselor may decide to extend the time period during which the treatment is applied. If such adjustments are made and the trend still continues in the undesired direction, the counselor may conclude that the selected treatment strategy is inappropriate for this client or for the target behavior. Changes in the particular counseling strategy being applied may be warranted. However, the counselor should be careful not to jump to quick conclusions about the ineffectiveness of a strategy and to terminate its use before exploring possible contributing factors.

Sometimes the effects of treatment are not so clear-cut as those depicted in Graphs A and B. Graph C in Figure 10-7 depicts variability in the goal behavior during treatment application (days 15–22). Such variability may indicate that the client is not using the treatment regularly or accurately or that more time is required for the treatment to have an effect. In some cases, a second procedure or strategy may be needed to contribute to changes in the desired level of the goal behavior. Variability in the goal behavior during treatment may also indicate a need to reexamine and possibly revise the client's goals.

Treatment without a baseline. Some client problems are so intense that treatment or a counseling strategy must be applied immediately, without obtaining baseline measures of the goal behavior. In such cases, the client can be instructed to self-monitor during treatment, and inventories or role-play assessments of the goal behavior can be made. For instance, a depressed client might be instructed to report the number of depressed thoughts per day while the counselor is applying treatment and the client is practicing the procedure. Figure 10-8 is a graph of how this client's self-monitored data of depressed thoughts would appear when treatment is applied without a baseline. Note that the average number of depressed thoughts for this client remained constant during the first five weeks of treatment and then decreased during weeks 6 through 10. The counselor and client might have used something like a cognitive restructuring counseling strategy (Chapter 16) that required some time before the client's depressed thoughts were reduced.

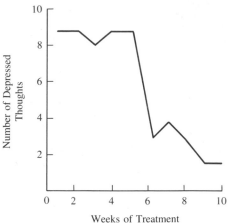

Figure 10-8. *Graph of self-monitoring data during treatment without a baseline*

Posttreatment: Assessment after Counseling

At the conclusion of a counseling treatment strategy or at the conclusion of counseling, the counselor and client should conduct a posttreatment assessment to indicate in what ways and how much counseling has helped the client achieve the desired results. Specifically, the data collected during a posttreatment assessment are used to compare the client's demonstration and level of the goal behavior after treatment with the data collected during the baseline period (before counseling) and during treatment.

The posttreatment assessment may occur at the conclusion of a counseling strategy or at the point when counseling is terminated—or both. For instance, if a counselor is using cognitive restructuring (Chapter 16) to help a client reduce depressed thoughts, the counselor and client could collect data on the client's level of depressed thoughts after they have finished working with the thought-stopping strategy. This assessment may or may not coincide with counseling termination. If the counselor plans to use a second treatment strategy, then data would be collected at the conclusion of the cognitive restructuring strategy and prior to the use of another strategy. This example is depicted in Figure 10-9. Note that the client continued to self-monitor the number of depressed thoughts for two weeks between cognitive restructuring and stimulus control and for four weeks after stimulus control, when counseling was terminated. In some cases, the final data point of treatment can serve as the posttreatment assessment.

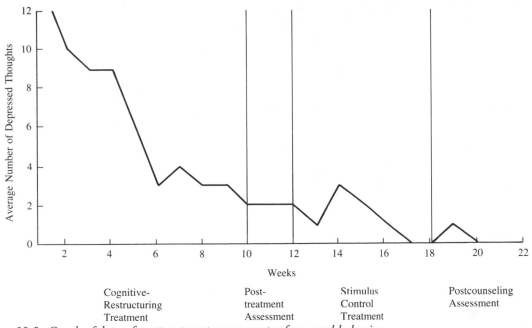

Figure 10-9. Graph of data of posttreatment assessments of one goal behavior

Ideally, the same types of measures used to collect data before and during counseling should be employed in the posttreatment assessment. For instance, if the client self-monitored depressed thoughts before and during treatment, then, as Figure 10-9 illustrates, self-monitoring data would also be collected during posttreatment assessment. If the counselor had also employed questionnaires or structured role-play assessments during the baseline period and treatment, these measures would be used during posttreatment data collection as well.

Follow-up Assessment

After the counseling relationship has terminated, some type of follow-up assessment should be conducted. A counselor can conduct both a short-term and a long-term follow-up. A short-term follow-up can occur three to six months after therapy. A long-term follow-up would occur six months to a year (or more) after counseling has been terminated. Generally the counselor should allow sufficient time to elapse before conducting a follow-up in order to determine to what extent the client is maintaining desired changes without the counselor's assistance.

There are several reasons for conducting follow-up assessments. First, a follow-up can indicate the counselor's continued interest in the client's welfare. As Okun observes, follow-up "is a form of recognition that both parties can appreciate in that it can communicate genuine caring and interest" (1982, p. 195). Second, a follow-up provides information that can be used to compare the client's performance of the goal behavior before and after counseling. Another important reason for conducting a follow-up is to determine to what extent the client is able to perform the goal behaviors in his or her environment without relying on the support and assistance of counseling. In other words, a follow-up can give some clues about the degree to which the counseling treatment has been effective or has generalized to the client's actual environment. This reflects one of the most important evaluative questions to be asked: Has counseling helped the client to maintain desired behaviors and to prevent the occurrence of undesired ones in some self-directed fashion?

Many practitioners are legitimately concerned about the long-term effects of therapy. Although a short-term follow-up may reflect significant gains, all too often, 6, 9, or 12 months after counseling, the client is back where he or she started. As Bandura (1976a) asserts, the value of a counseling approach must be judged not only in terms of successful "initial elimination" of a problem behavior but also in terms of the client's "vulnerability to defensive" or maladaptive "re-learning" after counseling is over (p. 261).

Both short-term and long-term follow-ups can take several forms. The kind of follow-up a counselor conducts often depends on the client's availability to participate in a follow-up and the time demands of each situation. Here are some ways a follow-up can be conducted:

1. Invite the client in for a follow-up interview. The purpose of the interview is to evaluate how the client is coping with respect to his or her "former" concern or problem. The interview may also involve client demonstrations of the goal behavior in simulated role plays.
2. Mail an inventory or questionnaire to the client, seeking information about her or his current status in relation to the original problem or concern. Be sure to include a stamped, self-addressed envelope.
3. Send a letter to the client asking about the current status of the problem.

4. Telephone the client for an oral report.

These examples represent one-shot follow-up procedures that take the form of a single interview, letter, or telephone call. A more extensive (and sometimes more difficult to obtain) kind of follow-up involves the client's engaging in self-monitoring or self-rating of the goal behavior for a designated time period, such as two or three weeks. Figure 10-10 shows the level of depressed thoughts

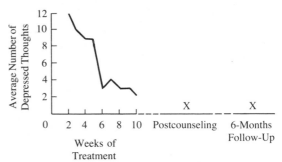

Figure 10-10. *Graph of self-monitored follow-up data*

LEARNING ACTIVITY #31: TIME OF MEASUREMENT

Continue with the client case description found in Learning Activity #29 and work through the following questions and instructions. Feedback is provided after the learning activity.

1. Assume that you asked the client to rate and self-monitor the frequency and severity of the anxiety attacks for a two-week (14-day) baseline period. Here are the client's self-recorded baseline data:

Day	Frequency	Average severity rating
1	3	1
2	2	5
3	4	2
4	3	3
5	3	5
6	4	1
7	3	2
8	4	5
9	3	1
10	3	4
11	4	3
12	3	2
13	3	4
14	3	2

On paper, plot these data on two graphs. Both should have days as the horizontal axis. The first graph should show the number of attacks on the vertical axis; the second, the average daily ratings of the severity of attacks.

a. Does the baseline for the number of attacks reflect unvarying, variable, decreasing, or increasing trends? Do the data seem to reflect a regular (stable) or irregular (unstable) pattern?
b. Does the baseline for the severity of attacks indicate unvarying, variable, decreasing, or increasing trends? Are consistent or irregular patterns reflected?
c. What hunches or clues do the baseline data give you about the client or about things to explore with the client?

2. Assume that, after two weeks of baseline data collection and four sessions of problem and goal definition, you teach the client, in session 5, the thought-stopping strategy. You work on thought stopping during sessions 5 through 8. During this time (days 15–42), you ask the client to continue to self-observe and record the frequency and severity of the anxiety attacks. Here are the client's data collected during treatment (thought stopping):

(continued)

Day	Frequency	Average severity rating
15	3	1
16	4	5
17	3	4
18	4	3
19	5	1
20	4	4
21	3	3
22	2	1
23	2	2
24	1	4
25	2	5
26	1	1
27	1	2
28	1	4
29	2	3
30	2	2
31	3	4
32	1	1
33	1	5
34	0	1
35	0	1
36	1	2
37	0	1
38	1	5
39	0	1
40	0	1
41	0	1
42	0	1

Plot these data on the same sorts of graphs you used in question 1.

a. What do the data for the number of attacks suggest about the effects of the thought-stopping strategy? Is this an intended or unintended effect?

b. What do the data for the severity of attacks indicate about the effects of the thought-stopping strategy? Is this an intended or unintended effect?

c. As the counselor, what hunches might you draw from these data? What directions would you pursue with this client in counseling?

3. Imagine that, after four weeks of thought stopping, you terminate this strategy and ask the client to continue to self-monitor the frequency and severity of attacks for two more weeks (days 43–56). Here are the client's data for this postassessment period:

Day	Frequency	Average severity rating
43	0	1
44	0	1
45	1	5
46	0	1
47	0	1
48	1	4
49	0	1
50	1	5
51	0	1
52	0	1
53	1	3
54	2	1
55	0	1
56	0	1

Plot these data on the same sorts of graphs you used in questions 1 and 2.

a. Compare these data with the data shown on your baseline graphs. To what extent have the client's counseling goals been achieved?

b. On the basis of these data, would you, at this point, suggest continuing or terminating counseling? If you continue, what direction or plan would you pursue?

c. What factors in your counseling might have contributed to the positive effects of counseling other than your treatment strategy?

d. What kind of one-shot follow-up assessment might you use with this client? When would you initiate follow-up?

a client self-monitored in a follow-up six months after counseling. Note in this graph that the client's level of depressed thoughts six months after counseling had remained at the same low level indicated by the posttreatment assessment. These data suggest that the client had been able to control his or her level of depressed thoughts while functioning in the environment without the counselor's assistance. If the number of depressed thoughts had risen substantially from the postcounseling assessment to the follow-up assessment, this might indicate a need for some additional counseling or a booster treatment. It also could be an indication that, at the end of counseling, the counselor had

FEEDBACK #31: TIME OF MEASUREMENT

1. Here are graphs for the client's baseline data:

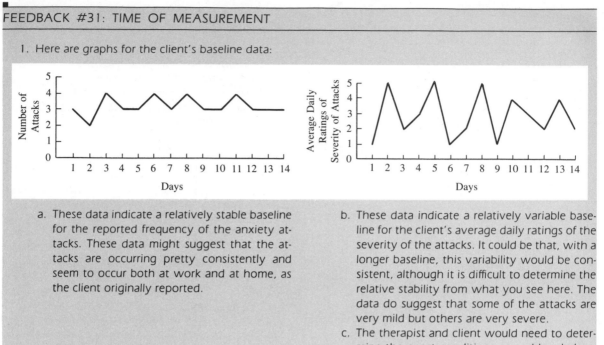

a. These data indicate a relatively stable baseline for the reported frequency of the anxiety attacks. These data might suggest that the attacks are occurring pretty consistently and seem to occur both at work and at home, as the client originally reported.

b. These data indicate a relatively variable baseline for the client's average daily ratings of the severity of the attacks. It could be that, with a longer baseline, this variability would be consistent, although it is difficult to determine the relative stability from what you see here. The data do suggest that some of the attacks are very mild but others are very severe.

c. The therapist and client would need to determine the exact conditions or problem behaviors reflected in the more intense attacks. The counselor may also need to determine whether the client understands the 5-point rating scale and is using it accurately.

2. Here are the graphs of the client's data collected during treatment:

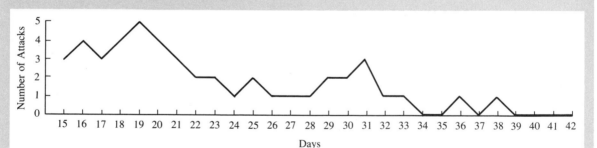

a. These data indicate that, during application of the thought-stopping strategy, the client's number of anxiety attacks did decrease, particularly after the first week of treatment (days 22–42). Clearly, the intended effect was obtained, suggesting that this approach was useful in decreasing and possibly eliminating the anxiety attacks.

(continued)

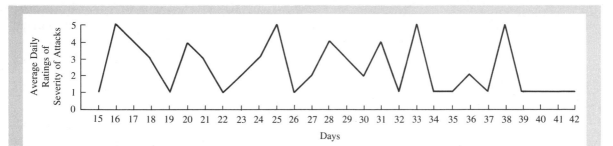

b. These data are variable, indicating that the client's ratings of severity of attacks still range from very mild to very intense. It does not appear that the thought stopping is reducing the severity of the attacks—at least during this time period. Even though the number of attacks is being reduced, the client still rates an attack occurring at the end of this period as pretty severe.

c. This may suggest that another strategy, directed more at the client's felt or experienced distress, is necessary. It also may indicate that there are times in the natural setting when the client does not stop the anxiety-producing thoughts but continues to ruminate about them. It may also be a cue that some other, unidentified thoughts are occurring that are very distressful to the client.

3. Here are the graphs for the client's post-strategy-assessment data:

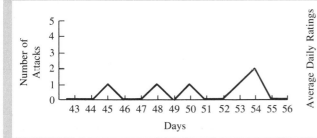

a. These data indicate that the client's goal of decreasing anxiety attacks has been achieved, although when an attack occurs, it is still rated as moderately severe or severe.

b. Because the severity of the attacks is still moderate, therapy might be continued to explore this variable. The counselor and client might focus directly on reducing the client's physiological or cognitive index of severity or stress. Or they might determine whether certain factors that could be resolved or eliminated are contributing to the severity.

c. In addition to the usefulness of thought stopping, it is possible that nontreatment variables might have contributed to the reduction of the anxiety attacks. The nature of the relationship and such therapist-initiated relationship conditions as empathy and positive regard might have helped to extinguish some of the client's anxiety, particularly in the therapy sessions. If the counselor had provided a positive expectancy set about the thought-stopping strategy, this could have enhanced the client's belief in the possibility of change. Finally, the client's self-monitoring of the anxiety attacks could have had some reactive properties that contributed to the decrease in the attacks.

d. A one-shot follow-up would occur about three months after counseling had been terminated. The follow-up could take the form of an interview, telephone call, or letter asking the client to report the general incidence and severity of anxiety attacks during this three-month period.

failed to incorporate some treatment or strategy to help the client apply coping skills to manage depressed thoughts in a self-directed manner.

A follow-up in the form of client self-monitoring has some advantages over an interview or telephone call because the data collected are more specific. However, some clients may not be willing or able to collect such data at this point. In lieu of client self-monitoring or self-ratings, an interview, letter, or telephone call is better than no follow-up at all. In addition, if possible, the counselor can incorporate structured role plays and self-report inventories into the follow-up if these measures were used during the previous assessments. Now go back to page 282 and complete Learning Activity 31.

☐ CONDUCTING A PROCESS EVALUATION OF HELPING

The data collected from evaluation of helping outcomes should be of practical value to both counselor and client. The evaluation data serve as a feedback loop to help confirm or redefine the selected problem area and the established goals. They also aid the counselor in selecting and using strategies that are likely to help the client. The primary benefit to be realized from an outcome evaluation is the information about the extent to which the client's goals are being achieved.

In addition to the ongoing data collection about outcomes, an evaluation of helping involves some ongoing monitoring of processes. Such a *process evaluation* provides information about the means used to achieve the results—that is, about the particular counseling treatments and any nontreatment factors that may contribute to the outcomes. Both outcome and process evaluation involve continual data collection during the helping process. The primary difference between these two types of evaluation is in what is monitored. An outcome evaluation assesses the goals, or the dependent variables; a process evaluation monitors the treatment and action strategies, or the independent variables.

A process evaluation helps a counselor answer the question "What happened, or what did I do, that helped the client achieve the desired outcomes?" Answers to this question—though speculative and tentative—can help the counselor plan future cases and determine what important factors might be reproduced in future helping sessions and how. As Rinn and Vernon (1975) note,

"Outcome measures generally are not useful for further planning *unless* the intervention technique is quantifiable and its consistent application insured. Thus, the inclusion of process evaluation is mandatory for interpretation of outcome data" (p. 11).

Table 10-2 presents one example of a process measure. The example provides questions that the client answers about the therapy session. The client rates any change that occurred during the session. Questions A and B describe the positive changes that occurred, and Question C specifies particular things that happened in the session that contributed to these changes.

TABLE 10-2. An example of a process instrument

Therapy Session Report*

Significantly Helpful Events: (to be completed by the client)

A. Now take a minute to think back over the session. Do you feel that anything really *significantly positive* happened? In other words, did anything about you or your concern really *change* or *shift positively* for you during the session? (Circle one).

No	*Maybe*	*Probably*	*Definitely*
0	1	2	3

B. Describe briefly the positive change(s) that occurred.

C. What specific thing(s) happened in the session that helped to bring about the positive change(s) (for example, thing(s) your therapist or you said or did, including particular therapist responses)?

---

* Adapted from Elliott, R. (1980). *Therapy session report: Short-forms for client and therapist,* unpublished instrument, University of Toledo, Client form, p. 6. Reprinted by permission of author.

Sometimes process evaluations of therapy are at variance with outcome measures (Dixon & Glover, 1984). For example, clients may give very positive ratings about therapy although, at the same time, the outcome measures do not suggest much progress is being made. There may be at least three reasons for this difference. First, the outcome measures may be insensitive to the actual progress that is occurring. Second, the intervention strategy may require more time before its effects are reflected in the outcome measure(s). Finally, the client may be reporting high process evaluations of the session in order to please the therapist or to justify being in therapy. For whatever reasons the process evaluation differs from the outcome measures, the therapist should examine the monitored treatment data, assess the validity and sensitivity of the outcome measures, or discuss the disparity with the client.

These forms of process evaluation or others can be used to collect data on each session or at different times during baseline, during treatment, and after treatment. Descriptions of treatment strategies used can also be recorded and monitored on standardized forms such as the one shown in Chapter 8 (Table 8-3).

☐ MODEL EXAMPLE: THE CASE OF JOAN

Throughout this book, we provide model illustrations of processes and strategies with our hypothetical client, Joan. We now provide sample illustrations of how a counselor could use the process and outcome evaluation procedures described in this chapter with Joan.

Description of Problem and Goal Definition Sessions
In Chapters 8 and 9, three sessions with Joan were illustrated: session 1 (Chapter 8) was used to assess the problem; session 2 (Chapter 9) was devoted to selecting goals; and session 3 (Chapter 9) was used to define Joan's outcome goals for counseling. After each of these sessions, the counselor recorded the description of the session and the defined problems and goals on the Individualized Client Treatment Plan (reproduced in Chapter 8).

Selection of Treatment Strategies
In session 4, Joan and the counselor decide to work on Joan's goals in the order reflected on Joan's goal chart (from p. 246, Chapter 9) and selected corresponding treatment strategies (see Chapter 11).

Baseline Data Collection for Goal 1
Joan's first outcome goal has been defined as "to acquire and demonstrate a minimum of four initiating skills, including four of the following: (1) asking questions and making reasonable requests, (2) expressing differences of opinion, (3) expressing positive feelings, (4) expressing negative feelings, and (5) volunteering answers or opinions in at least four situations a week with her parents and in math class" (see Chapter 9). Four subgoals are associated with the first goal:

1. To decrease anxiety associated with anticipation of failure in math class and rejection by parents from self-ratings of intensity of 70 to 50 on a 100-point scale during the next two weeks of treatment.
2. To increase positive self-talk and thoughts that "girls are capable" in math class and other competitive situations from zero or two times a week to four or five times a week over the next two weeks during treatment.
3. To increase attendance in math class from two or three times a week to four or five times a week during treatment.
4. To increase verbal participation and initiation in math class and with her parents from none or once a week to three or four times a week over the next two weeks during treatment. Verbal participation is defined as asking and answering questions with teacher or parents, volunteering answers or offering opinions, or going to the chalkboard.

The therapist and Joan need to establish the method of evaluating progress on each of the four subgoals and to determine the response dimension for each subgoal. We would recommend that a global self-report assessment inventory of anxiety (Lehrer & Woolfolk, 1982) be used to measure reductions in anxiety (subgoal 1). For subgoal 1, Joan could also use self-ratings of intensity of anxiety associated with anticipated failure in math class and rejection from parents, on a scale ranging from 0 to 100. For subgoal 2, we recommend that Joan self-monitor her self-talk during math class and other competitive situations. She could be instructed to write (in vivo) her self-talk on note cards during baseline and treatment. Subgoal 3 is to increase her attendance in math class. Joan could keep a record of the days she attended class, and these data could be verified from the teacher's attendance records, with Joan's permission. For subgoal 4, verbal participation and initiation in math class and with her parents could be self-monitored (in vivo) by recording each time Joan performed these verbal responses. (Additionally, these data could be corroborated by imagery and role-play assessments within the interviews.)

Let's assume that Joan collected two weeks of baseline data on the behavior associated with the first subgoal (anxiety). Global measures of cognitive, somatic, and behavioral anxiety from the self-report inventory indicated that, at three administrations, the somatic anxiety was higher than the cognitive or behavioral anxiety, but all three anxieties were relatively high for each of the three baseline measures. In addition, Joan's daily self-ratings of the intensity of her anxiety averaged about 70, with a range of 60 to 80 during the two-week baseline. The self-rating data are shown in Figure 10-11.

Treatment Strategies and Data Collection for Goal 1

We illustrate several treatment strategies used as possible ways to help Joan with each of her four subgoals. To help Joan with her anxiety of anticipation of failure in math class and rejection by her parents (subgoal 1), muscle relaxation (Chapter 17) and stress inoculation (Chapter 16) could be used. Joan would continue to self-rate her anxiety during the application of treatment. Joan is taught muscle relaxation during the therapy session on day 15. She is instructed to practice the relaxation exercise twice a day with the help of audiotape-recorded instructions given to her by the therapist. Verification of Joan's home practice session can be obtained (see Chapter 17). Figure 10-11 reflects a decrease in Joan's ratings of anxiety between days 15 and 24; the range of self-ratings is 40 to 60, with an average of about 50. In the therapy session on day 25, a stress inoculation strategy is applied (see Chapter 16). The graph in Figure 10-11 shows a decline in the self-ratings of the intensity of anxiety to 20 on days 25 through 28.

For subgoal 2, thought stopping (Chapter 15) and cognitive restructuring (Chapter 16) could be used conjointly to help Joan increase positive self-talk. These strategies would be applied only after Joan had made sufficient progress toward subgoal 1. The treatments to help Joan with her attendance (subgoal 3) could be self-monitoring and self-reward (Chapter 19). These strategies would not be used until the treatments for subgoal 2 were concluded. Again, we would assume that the application of self-monitoring and self-reward would increase her attendance but only after Joan's anxiety had decreased and her positive self-talk increased.

Perhaps the most difficult subgoal is the fourth. The therapist could apply two modeling strategies: participant modeling (Chapter 13) and cognitive modeling (Chapter 15). It might not be necessary to terminate self-monitoring and self-reward in subgoal 3 before applying the strategies for subgoal 4. Self-monitoring and self-reward would probably not interfere with the application of the modeling strategies used for subgoal 4. After applying the modeling strategies, we would expect the frequency of participation to increase. Again, all four measures of the subgoals could be graphed during and after treatments and the graphed data kept in Joan's file. The therapist could compare data for all measures for the subgoals with baseline during and after treatment applied to each subgoal. These comparisons would help the therapist and client determine the effectiveness of treatment and/or adjustments needed in the treatment strategies.

Follow-up Data Collection

About three to six months after this (or earlier, if school will be over for the year), the counselor would initiate a follow-up with Joan to discuss her maintenance of change for this goal. The counselor could ask Joan to report orally or to self-monitor frequency of absences from math class. Follow-up could be conducted with any of the methods described on page 282.

☐ SUMMARY

Evaluation of therapy is designed to assess the degree to which treatment has helped the client achieve the desired goals. There are a variety of

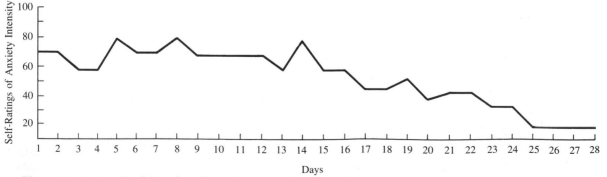

Figure 10-11. *Graph of data for subgoal 1 — intensity of anxiety*

methods for measuring outcome goals: client responses in the interview, self-monitoring, self-ratings, self-report inventories, role play, imagery, and physiological measures. The particular method for measuring outcomes should reflect the response dimension associated with the client's goal—frequency, duration, latency, intensity, or occurrence. Outcome data can be verified with direct observations made by the therapist and others in the client's natural environment. It is important that outcome data be collected at four time periods: before treatment (baseline), during treatment, after treatment, and at follow-up 3 to 12 months after therapy.

There are some sources of influence in therapy in addition to the treatment: the influence of the therapist, demand characteristics, instructions and expectancy set, and reactivity of measurement. Process evaluation of sessions provides information about the means used to achieve outcome goals, including nontreatment factors and particular intervention strategies that contribute to success of outcomes.

We believe that most therapists feel committed to making the necessary efforts to provide the best possible service they can for each of their clients. To do so, we believe, each therapist must feel personally dependent on the collection and availability of data during her or his therapy efforts. As an integral part of the entire therapy process, evaluation should occur for one primary reason—to promote the welfare of the client.

POSTEVALUATION

PART ONE

Objective One asks you to use a client case description to identify appropriate response dimensions, methods of measurement, and times of measurement.

Recall that *response dimensions* include (1) frequency, (2) duration, (3) latency, (4) intensity, and (5) occurrence. *Methods of measurement* include (1) interview, (2) self-monitoring, (3) self-ratings, (4) self-report inventories, (5) role play, (6) imagery, and (7) physiological measures. *Times* include (1) before treatment, (2) during treatment, (3) immediately after treatment, and (4) follow-up, three months to a year after treatment. Now read over the following client case description and respond in writing or covertly to the questions after the case. Feedback follows the Postevaluation.

The Case of Joe

Joe is 36 years old, is married, and has two children. Joe is a production manager for a large steel-fabrication plant in a large city and is active in several community and church organizations. He comes to a counselor concerned about his "uptightness" in crowds. After several initial sessions of problem assessment and goal definition, Joe and the counselor define the problem and goals in the following way:

Problem:

Setting—Small groups or crowds of people such as meetings at work, church services, waiting in line for a movie or restaurant, or sporting events such as swim meets or baseball games.

Thoughts—Thoughts are generally negative when in these settings. For example, "Wish I didn't have to stand in line—there are too many people," "I have to present this stuff in front of this group—boy, I'll screw up if I'm not careful," "These people are making too much noise."

Feelings—General feelings of tension in these settings—hands sweat, butterflies in stomach, heart beating faster.

Behaviors—Performance before groups generally OK, although at times his speech may be faulty (stuttering), but generally no real or obvious anxious behaviors in crowds or small groups other than stuttering occasionally.

Goals:

1. To reduce feelings of tension and discomfort and increase feelings of relaxation in group and crowd situations.

2. To reduce self-defeating thoughts and to increase positive or coping thoughts in group and crowd situations.

3. To speak without any evident stuttering when speaking in front of groups of more than two persons.

After the problem and goal definition sessions, Joe was instructed to self-monitor his level of tension on a 7-point scale (what), each time (when) he is in a crowd or in a small group, (where) on a note card he can carry in his pocket, and to self-record this tension level for the next two weeks (baseline). Joe was also instructed to make a note or count of each time he

(continued)

POSTEVALUATION   (continued)

was aware of a negative or self-defeating thought and of a positive or coping thought about his ability to speak in front of groups. He was instructed to make these tallies also on the note card during the next two weeks.

Before deciding on any treatment strategies, the counselor was interested in obtaining a general index of Joe's anxiety over receiving negative evaluations. For this purpose, Joe completed the Fear of Negative Evaluation Scale (FNE), developed by Watson and Friend (1969). The counselor also structured several role plays in which Joe was asked to talk informally to six persons. These role plays were audiotaped so that any evidence of Joe's stuttering could be rated.

During role playing, a thermistor was used to measure Joe's skin conductance. These digital temperature measures were to assess Joe's level of anxiety (for example, highly anxious, low temperature; low anxiety, normal temperature).

The therapist used imagery (the card-sort procedure) to have Joe rate on a 0-to-5 scale six situations that provoked stuttering. The six situations were typed on index cards, and Joe was instructed to imagine each situation (scene). After imagining one scene, Joe rated the intensity of tension and discomfort for that scene. The total of all six ratings was also used as a measure.

After these data were collected for two weeks, in consultation with Joe, the counselor used stress inoculation for six weeks. During these six weeks and for two weeks following, Joe continued to collect data on ratings of his tension level and frequency of self-defeating and coping thoughts in group or crowd situations. After three weeks of using stress inoculation and again following the use of this strategy, the counselor readministered the FNE Scale and the structured role-play assessments with the thermistor and the imagery card-sort procedure. According to the data collected, Joe's tension level and number of self-defeating thoughts had decreased substantially, and his coping thoughts had increased. However, Joe's level of stuttering exhibited in the role plays and imagery scenes remained at about the same level. Therefore, the counselor introduced the self-as-a-model strategy to help Joe speak in public-speaking situations without any evidence of stuttering. This strategy was used for four weeks. After two weeks and at the end of these four weeks, additional role-play assessments were made. At the end of four weeks in these role-play assessments and the imagery scenes, Joe was able to speak without any evi-

dence of stuttering in more than 50% of these assessments.

Six months after counseling, the counselor contacted Joe by telephone to see how things were going — specifically, to see how Joe felt now in talking in front of groups. The counselor also asked Joe to complete the FNE Scale again and sent it to him in the mail with a stamped, self-addressed envelope.

Now respond to these questions.

1. What response dimensions were used?
2. What methods of data collection were used?
3. At what specific times were data collected?

PART TWO

Objective Two asks you to graph examples of Joe's self-monitored data and to explain the trends reflected in the graphs. Make a graph of the data that appears in the table on p. 291 and explain what the trends for the baseline period, for the treatment period, and for the posttreatment period might mean. Feedback follows the Postevaluation. The tension rating runs from 1 (no tension) to 7 (maximum tension).

PART THREE

Objective Three asks you to conduct an outcome evaluation with yourself, another person, or a client, specifying response dimensions, methods, and times of measurement. You may wish to do so using the following guidelines.

1. Define and give examples of a desired goal behavior.
2. Specify what type of data you or the other person will collect (for example, verbal reports, frequency, duration, ratings, or occurrence of the behavior).
3. a. Identify the methods to be used to collect these data (such as interview, self-monitoring, inventories, self-ratings, role plays, or imagery).
   b. For *each* method to be used, describe very specifically the instructions you or the client would need to use this method.
4. Collect baseline data on the goal behavior for one to four weeks; graph these data.
5. Following baseline data collection, implement some treatment strategy for a designated time period. Continue to have data collected during treatment; graph these data.

(continued)

6. Collect data for one to four weeks after treatment; graph these data.

7. Compare the three graphs and note what changes have occurred in the goal behavior.

Baseline data		Data collected during four weeks of stress inoculation treatment		Data collected for two weeks after stress inoculation treatment	
Day	Tension rating	Day	Tension rating	Day	Tension rating	Day	Tension rating
1	7	15	4	29	3	43	2
2	2	16	5	30	2	44	1
3	4	17	6	31	3	45	2
4	5	18	7	32	2	46	1
5	6	19	5	33	2	47	1
6	6	20	4	34	1	48	2
7	7	21	3	35	1	49	1
8	4	22	4	36	2	50	2
9	7	23	3	37	1	51	1
10	7	24	3	38	1	52	1
11	3	25	4	39	2	53	1
12	5	26	5	40	2	54	1
13	3	27	4	41	2	55	2
14	6	28	3	42	1	56	1

☐ SUGGESTED READINGS

Barlow, D. H., Hayes, S. C., & Nelson, R. O. (1984). *The scientist practitioner.* New York: Pergamon Press.

Beck, A. T., Ward, C. H., Mendelson, M., Mock, J., & Erbaugh, J. (1961). An inventory for measuring depression. *Archives of General Psychiatry, 4,* 561–571.

Blanchard, E. B., Theobald, D. E., Williamson, D. A., Silver, B. V., & Brown, D. A. (1978). Temperature biofeedback in the treatment of migraine headaches. *Archives of General Psychiatry, 35,* 581–588.

Cautela, J. R. (1977). *Behavior analysis forms for clinical intervention* (Vol. 1). Champaign, IL: Research Press.

Cautela, J. R. (1981). *Behavior analysis forms for clinical intervention* (Vol. 2). Champaign, IL: Research Press.

Ciminero, A. R., Nelson, R., & Lipinski, D. (1977). Self-monitoring procedures. In A. R. Ciminero, K. S. Calhoun, & H. E. Adams (Eds.), *Handbook of behavioral assessment.* New York: Wiley.

Cureton, E. E. (1951). Validity. In E. F. Lindquist (Ed.), *Educational measurement.* Washington, DC: American Council on Education.

Dentch, G. E., O'Farrell, T. J., & Cutter, H. S. G. (1980). Readability of mental assessment measures used by behavioral marriage therapists. *Journal of Consulting and Clinical Psychology, 48,* 790–792.

Derogatis, L. R., Rickels, K., & Rock, A. F. (1976). The SCL-90 and the MMPI: A step in the validation of a new self-report scale. *British Journal of Psychiatry, 128,* 280–289.

Jayarantne, S., & Levy, R. L. (1979). *Empirical clinical practice.* New York: Columbia University Press.

Hay, W. M., Hay, L. R., Angle, H. V., & Nelson, R. O. (1979). The reliability of problem identification in the behavioral interview. *Behavioral Assessment, 1,* 107–118.

Haynes, S. N. (1978). *Principles of behavioral assessment.* New York: Gardner Press.

Haynes, S. N., & Jensen, B. J. (1979). The interview as a behavioral assessment instrument. *Behavioral Assessment, 1,* 97–106.

Haynes, S. N., & Wilson, C. C. (1979). *Behavioral assessment.* San Francisco: Jossey-Bass.

Hersen, M., & Barlow, D. (1976). *Single case experimental designs: Strategies for studying behavioral change.* New York: Pergamon Press.

Higgins, R. L., Frisch, M. B., & Smith, D. (1983). A comparison of role-played and natural responses to identical circumstances. *Behavior Therapy, 14,* 148–169.

Hopkins, J., Krawitz, G., & Bellack, A. S. (1981). The effects of situational variations in role-play scenes on assertive behavior. *Journal of Behavioral Assessment, 3,* 271–280.

Kazdin, A. E. (1980). *Research design in clinical psychology.* New York: Harper & Row.

Kazdin, A. E. (1981). Drawing valid inferences from case studies. *Journal of Consulting and Clinical Psychology, 49,* 183–192.

Kazdin, A. E., Matson, J. L., & Esveldt-Dawson, K. (1984). The relationship of role-play assessment of children's social skills to multiple measures of social competence. *Behaviour Research and Therapy, 22,* 129–139.

Kern, J. M. (1982). The comparative external and concurrent validity of three role-plays for assessing heterosocial performance. *Behavior Therapy, 13,* 666–680.

Kern, J. M., Miller, C., & Eggers, J. (1983). Enhancing the validity of role-play tests: A comparison of three role-play methodologies. *Behavior Therapy, 14,* 482–492.

Lehrer, P. M., & Woolfolk, R. L. (1982). Self-report assessment of anxiety: Somatic, cognitive, and behavioral modalities. *Behavioral Assessment, 4,* 167–177.

Levy, R. L. (1977). Relationship of an overt commitment to task compliance in behavior therapy. *Journal of Behavior Therapy and Experimental Psychiatry, 8,* 25–29.

Livingston, S. A. (1977). Psychometric techniques for criterion-referenced testing and behavioral assessment. In J. D. Cone & R. P. Hawkins (Eds.), *Behavioral assessment: New directions in clinical psychology.* New York: Brunner/Mazel.

Locke, H. J., & Wallace, K. N. (1957). Short marital adjustment and prediction tests: Their reliability and validity. *Marriage and Family Living, 21,* 251–255.

LoPiccolo, J., & Steger, J. C. (1974). The Sexual Interaction Inventory: A new instrument for assessment of sexual dysfunction. *Archives of Sexual Behavior, 6,* 585–595.

Margolin, G. (1981). Behavior exchange in happy and unhappy marriages: A family cycle perspective. *Behavior Therapy, 12,* 329–343.

Nelson, R. O. (1981). Realistic dependent measures for clinical use. *Journal of Consulting and Clinical Psychology, 49,* 168–182.

Nelson, R. O., & Hayes, S. C. (1979). Some current dimensions of behavioral assessment. *Behavioral Assessment, 1,* 1–16.

Nietzel, M. T., & Bernstein, D. A. (1981). Assessment of anxiety and fear. In M. Hersen & A. S. Bellack (Eds.), *Behavioral assessment: A practical handbook* (2nd ed.). New York: Pergamon Press.

Orne, M. T. (1969). Demand characteristics and the concept of quasi-controls. In R. Rosenthal & R. Rosnow (Eds.), *Artifact in behavioral research.* New York: Academic Press.

Prinz, R. J., Foster, S., Kent, R. N., & O'Leary, K. D. (1979). Multivariate assessment of conflict in distressed and nondistressed mother-adolescent dyads. *Journal of Applied Behavior Analysis, 12,* 691–700.

Ray, W. J., & Raczynski, J. M. (1981). Psychophysiological assessment. In M. Hersen & A. S. Bellack (Eds.), *Behavioral assessment: A practical handbook* (2nd ed.). New York: Pergamon Press.

Stiles, W. B. (1980). Measurement of the impact of psychotherapy sessions. *Journal of Consulting and Clinical Psychology, 48,* 176–185.

Walls, R. T., Werner, T. J., Bacon, A., & Zane, T. (1977). Behavior checklists. In J. D. Cone & R. P. Hawkins (Eds.), *Behavioral assessment: New directions in clinical psychology.* New York: Brunner/Mazel.

Wolf, M. M. (1978). Social validity: The case for subjective measurement, or how applied behavior analysis is finding its heart. *Journal of Applied Behavior Analysis, 11,* 203–214.

FEEDBACK: POSTEVALUATION

PART ONE

1. For the case of Joe, the following response dimensions were collected:
   a. Intensity ratings of Joe's level of tension
   b. Frequency counts of self-defeating and coping thoughts about Joe's speaking ability
   c. Occurrence of Joe's fear of negative evaluation
   d. Checklist of presence or absence of Joe's stuttering behavior in public-speaking situations (occurrence)
   e. Intensity of skin conductance and temperature
   f. Intensity ratings of anxiety on imagery scenes
2. The methods used to collect these data were:
   a. Self-monitoring for tension ratings (a above) and for thoughts (b above)
   b. Completion of a self-report inventory (Fear of Negative Evaluation Scale) (c above)
   c. Structured role-play assessments simulating public-speaking situations (d above)
   d. Digital temperature with a thermistor (or physiological measure; e above)
   e. Imagery ratings of six imagined scenes (f above)
3. These data were collected at the following times:
   a. Two-week baseline (before treatment)
   b. During stress inoculation treatment
   c. After stress inoculation treatment
   d. During self-as-a-model treatment
   e. After self-as-a-model treatment
   f. At a six-month follow-up

PART TWO

Figure 10-12 shows Joe's baseline, treatment, and posttreatment self-recorded data of tension levels. According to these data, Joe's tension level before treatment is variable. During the first two weeks of

(continued)

treatment (days 15–28), some variability persists; however, during the last two weeks of treatment (days 29–42), there is a decreasing trend in his re-ported tension level. This trend is maintained in the posttreatment data, which also reflect less variability than the baseline data.

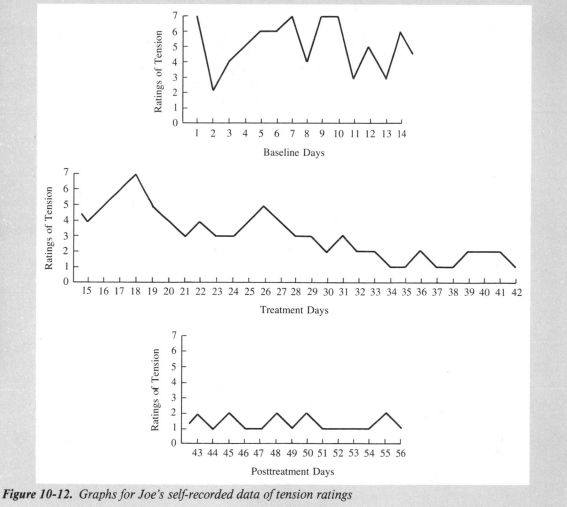

Figure 10-12. *Graphs for Joe's self-recorded data of tension ratings*

SELECTING HELPING STRATEGIES

ELEVEN

Helping strategies are "modi operandi," or plans of action, tailored to meet the particular goals of each client (Hackney & Cormier, 1979, p. 102). Strategies, along with an effective counseling relationship, "can expedite the helpee's emotional, cognitive, or behavioral changes" (Okun, 1982, p. 190). In a nutshell, helping strategies represent the procedural plan to help the client get from point A to point B. And, as in traveling from one place to another, no single means of transportation is suitable for all travelers. Hosford and de Visser (1974, p. 97) explain the emphasis on the variety of counseling strategies this way: "Just as there is no one perfect way to understand the client's problem, so there is no single perfect counseling strategy that fits all situations. Different techniques work differently for different individuals, for different problems, and for different goals."

Tailoring the treatment plan to the client is a move away from the "all-purpose single-method" therapies (Bandura, 1969, p. 89) or the "uniformity myth" (Kiesler, 1966). Goldstein and Stein (1976) charge that, all too often, helpers counsel according to the "one true light" assumption; that is, they assume that their preferred approach is "equally and widely applicable" to most or all clients (p. 3). As a result, these helpers fail to develop treatment plans on the basis of assessment and fail to orient the plan to the desired outcomes (Bandura, 1969; Goldstein & Stein, 1976). Instead, such helpers manage to mold their clients' problems to fit their "brand" of therapy and encourage clients to behave in ways that meet the assumptions of this brand (Lazarus, 1981).

In contrast to the all-purpose counseling approach, we advocate the judicious selection of treatment strategies tailored to the individual client. We believe that counselors need to ask themselves constantly "Which treatment strategy, or combination of strategies, will be most effective for this client with these desired outcomes?" (Paul,

We are extremely appreciative of the invaluable assistance of Warren Shaffer in developing the revision of this chapter.

1967, p. 111). We realize that this concept is easy to discuss but difficult to practice. Our purpose in this chapter is twofold: to propose some criteria a counselor can use to select treatment strategies and to describe an interview process in which both counselor and client can be involved in strategy selection.

OBJECTIVES

1. For at least four out of six written client situations, identify the corresponding guideline(s) for the timing of helping strategies.
2. For at least two out of three written client descriptions, identify accurately which of the seven criteria for strategy selection would be used.

TIMING OF HELPING STRATEGIES: FIVE GUIDELINES

Many counselors wonder when a helping strategy should be introduced. There is no easy answer, and the answer varies with clients. As Goldfried (1983) observes,

> Quite often, the rules for selecting the technique that is "appropriate" are poorly spelled out. In order to make such difficult clinical decisions, one needs to depend on the sensitivity of the therapist to pick upon subtle cues within the clinical interaction, the understanding of how various behavior patterns and life styles interrelate, and a keen appreciation of the environmental forces and contingencies that direct people's lives. Much of this knowledge and the rules that follow from it are not readily found in the literature, but instead come from clinicians' earlier social learning experiences, their personal experiences as human beings, and the accumulation of actual clinical experience [p. 45].

Sometimes beginning helpers tend to use intervention strategies too quickly and offer premature recommendations or action steps because of their own need to be "helpful." It is impossible (and, in our judgment, inappropriate) to state that "the time" for a strategy is the third, fifth, or eighth session. Nor do we wish to convey the erroneous idea that a treatment procedure will *always* be used with every client. We do believe that a counselor should always try to have a plan or a rationale for whatever route is taken. The transition from building a strong relationship and from problem and goal definition to selecting and implementing a counseling procedure is crucial. Eisenberg and Delaney (1977) point out that the timing of this transition is vital to the successful use of a strategy. These authors note that premature use of a procedure may have a "disastrous impact" (p. 145). Although it is hard to define what "premature use" might be in every case, we think there are a few guidelines to help you make this transition more effectively. The five guidelines you can use to help yourself judge the timing for a strategy involve the quality of the relationship, the assessment of the problem, the development of desired counseling goals, client cues of readiness and commitment, and collection of baseline measures.

Quality of the Relationship

Hackney and Cormier (1979) and Okun (1982) indicate that a counseling strategy may not be effective unless it is used with a strong counseling relationship. When the client begins working with a plan or a procedure, the counselor's support remains vital. A strong therapeutic relationship helps the client make the transition from environmental, or external, support to self-support.

How do you know when the relationship is strong enough to provide the support the client will need? Again, this may vary with clients, but here are a few indicators of "quality" in the relationship:

1. The client has given you verbal feedback that you are understanding his or her feelings or concerns accurately.
2. The client has demonstrated a willing (as opposed to reluctant) involvement in counseling through such behaviors as being on time, coming to sessions, completing homework, self-disclosing personal concerns, and sharing feelings with you.
3. The client and the counselor have discussed anything that might impede open communication.
4. You, the counselor, feel comfortable in confronting, disclosing, and using immediacy with this person.

If you sense these conditions in your relationship, it is probably sufficiently well developed to introduce a helping strategy.

Assessment of the Problem

It is always premature to suggest a plan of action unless the client's problem has been assessed adequately. Otherwise, inappropriate or irrelevant strategies may be selected. As soon as you find yourself wanting to suggest some steps the client should take, ask yourself mentally some of these questions:

1. Do I know why the client is here?
2. Is the client's presenting concern all or only part of the entire problem?
3. Do I know the problem behaviors and situations for this person?
4. Can I describe the conditions contributing to the client's problem?
5. Am I aware of the present severity and intensity of the problem?

If you can answer these questions affirmatively, then follow through on your plan. If not, maybe you should check your impulse to move into an action plan until a more thorough assessment has been completed. In some instances, the client should also be given an opportunity to respond to these questions in order to have a role in deciding the appropriate time for introducing action strategies.

Development of Counseling Goals

If you introduce a strategy before establishing counseling goals, you may be barking up the wrong tree. Because a strategy is a way to promote the goals, clearly specified outcomes are a prerequisite for strategy selection. Be sure that you and the client can describe the desired behavioral outcomes of counseling before you suggest a way to reach them. This information helps you determine whether the selected intervention(s) point toward the targeted results.

Client Readiness and Commitment

The client's readiness for and commitment to action is the fourth guideline you can use to judge the timing of strategy selection. It is always easier to move slowly and then speed up the process than to move into action plans too quickly and possibly scare clients or discourage them from taking further steps. Egan (1975) cautions counselors to "take the client where he is. Never put demands on a client for which he is not sufficiently prepared" (p. 194). For example, clients who are seeking some advice, a panacea, or a quick way to solve their problems probably are not ready for the slow and sometimes painful growth that may be involved in working toward their goals. Clients who have a history of avoidance behaviors may need

extra time before being ready to put aside their typical escape or denial patterns. Clients' motivation and incentive to change affect their use of a procedure. A client might indicate readiness to "work" by giving verbal permission, by demonstrating awareness of the positive consequences of change, and by doing at least some covert work or hard thinking between sessions. Sometimes a client's readiness to pursue the outcomes is indicated by a shift in one part of his or her behavior. For example, the client may become more disclosive or may do more initiating in the interview. Another client may demonstrate readiness for action by starting to assert his or her right to begin the session on time.

Collection of Baseline Measures

As we mentioned in the previous chapter, problem and goal definition are usually accompanied by some baseline data collection, unless the client's concerns are so urgent that immediate intervention is required. Baseline measures can provide valuable information about the nature of the client's concerns and desired goals. Collecting baseline data before implementing strategies is essential in order to determine to what extent the strategies are helping the client.

To summarize, there are no hard and fast rules about moving into the strategy phase of helping. Introduction of a strategy will depend on the quality of the helping relationship, accurate assessment of the client's problem, establishment of observable counseling goals, client behaviors that indicate readiness for action, and collection of baseline measures.

☐ CRITERIA FOR SELECTING STRATEGIES

Once you believe that the prerequisites for appropriate timing of a strategy have been met, you may be ready to move into the strategy phase of counseling. In our own counseling endeavors, in consultation with our clients, we use some criteria for selecting strategies. Our description of these criteria reflects our own preferences; however, we have been aided by the thoughtful work of Gambrill (1977), Goldfried and Davison (1976), Okun (1982), and Shaffer (1976). Seven important criteria to consider in selecting helping strategies involve counselor characteristics and preferences, the documentation for strategies, environmental factors, the nature of the client's problem behavior, type of desired outcomes, client characteristics and preferences, and diagnostic cues and patterns.

In selecting strategies, all seven of these criteria should be considered, although perhaps the most important ones are the nature of the client's problems and diagnostic cues and patterns. Counseling strategies should be used that have the best chance of helping clients resolve their particular concerns most effectively. To a lesser degree, the other five parameters will affect the choice of strategies made by the counselor and client.

Generally speaking, effective intervention strategies meet the following twelve criteria:

Are easy to carry out

Match the unique characteristics and preferences of the client

Match the characteristics of the problem and related factors

Are positive rather than punitive

Encourage the development of self-management skills

Strengthen the client's expectations of personal effectiveness or self-efficacy

Are supported by the literature

Are feasible and practical to implement

Do not create additional problems for the client or significant others

Do not burden the client or significant others with too many things to do

Do not require more of the counselor than the counselor is able to give or responsible for giving

Do not repeat or build on previous unsuccessful solutions

Counselor Characteristics and Preferences

"The best helper is the one who has the widest repertory of helping skills and who can readily call upon any of these skills to meet the different needs of any client" (Egan, 1975, p. 187). We value the counselor who keeps abreast of new procedures and is adept at using a variety of procedures in the counseling process. We question whether a counselor will be able to function adequately with many clients with only a limited range of skills. To paraphrase Maslow (1966, pp. 15–16), if your only tool is a hammer, you will probably treat everything as if it were a nail. However, our enthusiasm for a multiplicity of treatment strategies does not mean that a helper should abandon principles of human behavior just to offer "the latest thing." Nor do we believe that you should propose a strat-

egy that you know little or nothing about. As Okun (1982, p. 189) points out, "Pretending to be an expert when you're not can backfire and even if it doesn't, it is ethically questionable." Misrepresenting yourself and your qualifications to a client may also have serious legal consequences (Van Hoose & Kottler, 1977).

We are suggesting that you use *your* skills, comfort level, and values as criteria for judging which strategy may be most appropriate. Your previous use of a procedure and your attitude about it are major factors affecting your preferences. At the same time, don't restrict yourself to your old stand-bys. Be open to using different techniques —but be aware of when you need supervision or consultation to accompany your testing out a new approach. Don't hesitate to share your preferences with a client. In addition, your preferences for strategies may reflect your particular orientation to therapy; this, too, should be shared with the client at the beginning of therapy.

Documentation about Strategies

Varying amounts of data exist for different counseling procedures. These data can help you determine the ways in which the strategy has been used successfully and with what types of client problems. All the strategies presented in the remainder of this book have some empirical support. Whether a strategy has been documented should be one, but not the only, criterion to consider in deciding whether to use it. As Gambrill (1977) observes, the best strategy is not always the one the literature suggests, particularly if it poses operational problems or if the client favors another one instead. However, don't restrict yourself to past use. Participant modeling (Chapter 13), for example, has been documented most extensively for reduction of fears. We have used it also in helping clients acquire new skills. When using strategies based on documentation in the literature, it is often useful to point out to the client that procedure X and Y both have been documented to some extent and have worked for clients who had similar concerns or shared characteristics related to the problem.

Environmental Factors

Factors within the counseling environment or the client's environment may affect whether a strategy is practical or impractical. These include time, cost, equipment, role of significant others, and availability of reinforcing consequences in the natural environment (Gambrill, 1977). The amount of time you can spend with a client for each session and for the totality of counseling affects the strategies you propose. In time-limited counseling, specific, concrete procedures that are easy to work with are more practical. Your counseling setting may also limit the choice of procedures. For example, it would be difficult to train a client in deep relaxation (Chapter 17) without a comfortable chair.

The client's environment is also important. Egan (1975, pp. 221–222) points out that an action plan that may occur in an unbending environment or may meet with a lot of resistance is not a practical strategy. The availability of role models and reinforcers in the client's environment may also bear on what strategies are possible (Goldfried & Davison, 1976). It is not helpful to depend on a procedure that requires a great deal of encouragement from significant others if the client has very few close relationships.

Nature of Client Problem and Response Systems Involved

The counselor must assume some responsibility for generating suggestions of strategies that are based on the previous assessment of the client's problem. The strategies should reflect the nature of the problem behaviors. Of course, this requires a thorough problem assessment and definition, as well as knowledge about the purpose of particular procedures. As an example, if a client wanted to improve test grades and the assessment revealed the student didn't study, the counselor would have a basis for suggesting some type of study skills training. But if the assessment revealed that the client studied frequently but panicked on tests, the counselor would have a basis for suggesting an approach for managing test anxiety, such as systematic desensitization (Chapter 18), cognitive restructuring (Chapter 16), or both.

Furthermore, the counselor will need to know the nature of the response systems, or components, associated with the problem—thoughts, feelings, somatic expressions, overt behavior, and so on—in order to match the treatment strategies accordingly. For example, a client such as the one described above with test anxiety or some other kind of focal anxiety may experience anxiety in at least three response systems: *cognitive, somatic* (physiological), and *behavioral* (avoidance behavior) (Lehrer & Woolfolk, 1982). One client may report that anxiety is manifested in all three of these response systems during the problem situa-

tion; another may react behaviorally with no physiological arousal or vice versa; and still another may report only the cognitive component of anxiety. Depending on which response systems are involved, the counselor would present different treatment options (Lehrer & Woolfolk, 1984). Cognitive reactors would benefit most from cognitive-therapeutic strategies, such as thought stopping, cognitive restructuring, and rational-emotive approaches, and from coping skills desensitization. Somatic reactors would benefit more from anxiety-lessening techniques, such as muscle relaxation training, systematic desensitization, biofeedback, and some of the body approaches that work with chronic muscle tension. Behavioral reactors seem to benefit more from skills training, participant modeling (graduated exposure), and contact desensitization. Persons reacting in both cognitive and somatic ways may benefit from meditation, while those who are troubled by all three of these response systems may do better with a multiform treatment package such as stress inoculation training.

In contrast to these cognitive-behavioral approaches for focal anxiety and phobias (highly situation-specific forms of anxiety), client-centered therapy is often the initial treatment of choice for persons with generalized or free-floating anxiety (Mitchell, Bozarth, & Krauft, 1977; Shaffer, 1976). As Meyer (1983) observes, "The focus on empathy and warmth, combined with the initial low demand for specific discussion material, proves helpful here" (p. 120). It is also presumed that consistently high levels of the three facilitative conditions associated with this approach (empathy, positive regard, respect) gradually extinguish some of the generalized anxiety.

Data in which response components of various problems are matched to corresponding treatments are just beginning to appear. Preliminary evidence does suggest that best results are achieved when clients are treated with methods that fit their particular response pattern (Lehrer & Woolfolk, 1984; Öst, Jerremalm, & Johannson, 1981). In the absence of additional available data, the therapist will need to assess carefully the components, or response systems, associated with the client's problem(s) (as we illustrated in Chapters 7 and 8) and scrutinize the relevant parameters of possible treatment approaches in order to determine a good fit or a good match. As Lazarus notes, "This is the point at which clinical experience and a degree of artistry" are both terribly important (1981, p. 55).

Nature of Outcome Goals

The choice of strategies also depends on the nature of the identified goal and what the goal represents. As we mentioned in Chapter 9, outcome goals may reflect choice or change issues (Dixon & Glover, 1984). This is an important distinction because each kind of issue requires different intervention strategies. Choice issues are usually best served by such strategies or approaches as educational and vocational counseling, decision making and conflict resolution, role playing and role reversal, Gestalt dialoguing, and TA redecision work.

Recall that, for change issues, the outcome goal will be a response acquisition, response increment, response decrement, or response restructuring (*response* includes both overt and covert behaviors). For goals that reflect response acquisition, the skill training components described in Chapter 12 and the modeling approaches described in Chapters 13, 14, and 15 are often most helpful. Usually, the greater the deficit, the more modeling, practice, and feedback are required. For goals that reflect response increments, modeling approaches, imagery, stress inoculation, meditation, muscle relaxation, self-monitoring, self-reward, and paradoxical intention may all be applied idiosyncratically to work toward increasing desired behaviors. For goals that reflect response decrements, imagery, thought stopping, stress inoculation, meditation, muscle relaxation, systematic desensitization, self-monitoring, self-reward, and paradoxical intention may be used to work toward decreasing undesired responses. For goals that reflect response restructuring, thought stopping with covert assertion, cognitive restructuring, stress inoculation, coping skills or self-control desensitization, stimulus control, and reframing or relabeling may be particularly useful.

Client Characteristics and Preferences

In our opinion, the choice of appropriate counseling strategies is a joint decision in which both counselor and client are actively involved. We believe it is a misuse of the inherent influence of the helping process for the counselor to select a strategy or to implement a treatment plan independent of the client's input. We believe, as Frey (1975) does, that the client should be a coproducer of the therapy process.

The client's preference for a treatment plan is important, and most clients do have definite preferences of therapist style and therapy orientation (Manthei, 1983). Attempts to meet client expectations and preferences often yield more positive therapy results (Devine & Fernald, 1973). Exceptions to this general rule might include working with highly manipulative clients or with "emotional saboteurs," in which cases it is difficult to take their often self-serving interests at face value without further exploration and clarification (Lazarus, 1981, pp. 159–160).

During the last decade, we have also witnessed an increasing consumerism movement in counseling and therapy. This movement has at least four implications (Sue, 1977):

1. The client needs to be an active, rather than passive, participant in therapy.
2. The client's rights need to be made explicit.
3. The counseling process needs to be demystified. This demystification can occur by having the counselor explain what will take place during counseling and/or when a particular treatment approach is used.
4. The client must consent to treatment.

These implications are important for all clients, regardless of the setting in which they are helped. Counselors also must usually take special precautions with clients of "low power," such as minors and institutionalized persons, to ensure that their rights are not violated and that treatment programs are not implemented without their participation and consent. Occasionally, some therapists argue that they are withholding information about treatment in order to base a therapeutic strategy on "confusion." Limited data, however, as well as ethical and legal principles, suggest that each client has the right to choose services and strategies appropriate to his or her needs. Unfortunately, this choice means little "unless accurate, prior information about available alternatives is readily accessible" (Manthei, 1983, p. 339).

We believe the counselor is acting in good faith to protect clients' rights and welfare by providing the following kinds of information to clients about strategies:

1. A description of *all* relevant and potentially useful treatment approaches for this particular client with this particular problem.
2. A rationale for each procedure.
3. A description of the therapist's role in each procedure.
4. A description of the client's role in each procedure.
5. Discomforts or risks that may occur as a result of the procedure.

6. Benefits expected to result from the procedure.
7. The estimated time and cost of each procedure.

The therapist also needs to state that he or she will try to answer any questions the client has now or later about the procedure and that the client is always free to discontinue participation in the procedure at any time. If the client is a minor, consent must be obtained from a parent or legal guardian, just as consent must be obtained from a guardian or legal representative if the client has been declared mentally incompetent to give consent.

For the therapist's protection, it is a good idea to have some record of the session(s) in which informed consent is given, in either written or taped form. For example, the treatment contract we describe in Chapter 12 contains a paragraph summarizing the main elements of informed consent. This contract is signed and dated by both therapist and client. As we mentioned before, informed consent is extremely important with minors and institutionalized clients and also when the therapist wants to use experimental "nonstandard" procedures.

In addition to explaining and considering client preferences for treatment strategies, it is helpful to consider any client characteristics that might affect the use of a strategy. Goldfried and Davison (1976, p. 27) point out that, in some techniques, a client's ability to report specific examples is very important. In other procedures, such as covert modeling (Chapter 14) and systematic desensitization (Chapter 18), the client's ability to generate and sustain mental images is crucial. The counselor will need to determine whether the client can generate clear and vivid images before using such strategies.

Other client characteristics to consider include the client's social and self-control skills that may facilitate the use of a particular strategy. A physical condition or strongly held attitudes may preclude the use of a particular strategy (Gambrill, 1977). In Chapter 20, for instance, we describe the notion of "patient position"—the strongly held values and beliefs that are likely to support or reject the use of a particular approach. If the therapist is insensitive to the client's beliefs and values and forges ahead with a strategy that runs counter to them, the client is likely either to resist the procedure or to fail to really invest herself or himself in working with it. Occasionally, a client will reject a proposed strategy quite openly: "That sounds pretty silly to me!", "How in the world would that help?", or "I didn't even try it." Other clients convey their disapproval far more subtly, requiring the counselor from the very beginning to be alert to the client's cues, often nonverbal, for "yes" and "no." For instance, some clients' lack of acceptance of a proposed procedure may be communicated by a change in face color, eye or mouth movements, or breathing patterns.

Proposed strategies also need to take into account prior successes and failures of the client (Dixon & Glover, 1984). As we indicated in Chapter 8, the assessment interview includes identifying any previous solutions the client has used to resolve the problem and with what effect. This information is particularly useful at the strategy solution juncture in counseling. According to Watzlawick (1978), by identifying clients' previous unsuccessful attempts to resolve problems, the counselor can avoid using strategies that build on or duplicate those prior attempts, thus avoiding "problem-engendering pseudo-solutions" (Lazarus, 1981, p. 147). We discuss this concept in greater detail in Chapter 20.

Diagnostic Cues and Patterns

According to Shaffer (1976), an important category to use in selecting and ordering particular treatment interventions involves diagnostic cues and patterns that are readily observable and exhibited by the client during interviews. These diagnostic cues and patterns (or "templates") are the basis of what Shaffer (1976) calls "decision rules" —ways to select and sequence the kind of interventions most useful for a given client with a given problem and related goal. A decision rule is a series of mental questions or heuristics that the counselor constantly asks himself or herself during interviews in order to match techniques to clients and their identified concerns. In Shaffer's model, the first guideline, or heuristic, is the client-centered, or relationship, approach. According to Shaffer, it is useful to start with the Rogerian modality because listening and reflecting elicit a vast amount of client information without interrogation and because it is easier to exit from this modality than to reenter it. In subsequent sessions, the therapist's task is to observe and process certain diagnostic cues and patterns and, on the basis of these patterns, to decide to stay in the client-centered modality or to move out of it and use a different approach that is likely to be more effective. *Which* approach is selected again depends on the particular pattern of diagnostic cues exhibited by the client.

Table 11.1 describes eight major diagnostic criteria and corresponding treatment approaches delineated by Shaffer (1976). These eight diagnostic categories as well as the corresponding treatments are derived from existing empirical literature. Shaffer (1984) has also developed lists of corresponding measures to assess the effects of these treatment approaches.

It is important to note that the strategies we present in the remainder of this book reflect primarily a cognitive-behavioral approach and are most useful when the following conditions exist:

1. The client's defined problem and goal represent *change* rather than choice. As we mentioned earlier, choice issues are better served by other approaches, such as educational and vocational information and counseling, decision making, TA redecision work, and Gestalt dialoguing.
2. The client is generally intact (is not so disoriented that he or she cannot respond to treatment), is not suffering from organic impairment or dysfunction, and wants to work on a limited number of overt and/or covert behaviors.
3. The client or the client's behavior rather than the system is responsible for the problem. If not, system interventions (marriage, family, or organizational development) are warranted.
4. The client is not terribly rigid and has not found successive attempts to change behavior, either alone or with a therapist, unsuccessful. Otherwise, the client may benefit more from group rather than individual treatment modalities.
5. The counselor has the expertise, resources, and interest for working with the client. If not, a referral option is warranted.

Additionally, in Table 11-2 we present examples of some particular kinds of client problems and associated treatment strategies. This list is not exhaustive, but it does represent the general kinds of problems presented by individual clients for which the strategies in this book are used frequently as primary intervention strategies. The table also includes references to other useful treatment approaches not covered in this book in order to give you some idea of the various alternative

TABLE 11-1. Eight categories of diagnostic and corresponding treatment modalities

Diagnostic cues	Corresponding treatment
1. Low self-esteem High generalized anxiety No acting out	Rogerian/relationship approach
2. Focal anxiety Intact client Gradient of anxiety	Desensitization, other counterconditioning and anxiety reduction approaches
3. Client needs to increase or decrease three or fewer specific behaviors	Operant treatment and traditional noncognitive behavioral techniques
4. Role discrepancy Lack of information about self in relation to educational or vocational environments	Educational/vocational counseling, decision making and problem solving, other "choice" strategies such as Gestalt dialogue, NLP reframing, TA redecision work
5. Client cannot introduce change System rather than client is causing the problem Therapist can get entry into the system	Organizational or systems interventions
6. "Rigidity" More than three behaviors to change Prior attempts to change behavior have failed Nonpsychotic client	"Group work"
7. Lack of cognitive sophistication Errors in cognitive conceptualizations or appraisals High degree of cognitive involvement	Interpretive and cognitive therapies
8. Therapist's belief that someone else can handle the case better owing to training, skills, values, time, cost, or convenience or availability	Referral

Adapted from *Heuristics for the initial diagnostic interview* by Warren F. Shaffer, 1976. Reprinted by permission of the author.

TABLE 11-2. Examples of client problems and corresponding treatment approaches and strategies

DEPRESSION	ANXIETY DISORDERS

(neurotic or reactive rather than major or endogenous; also adjustment disorder with depressed mood)
  Cognitive therapy (cognitive restructuring and reframing, rational-emotive therapy, personal construct therapy)
  Self-monitoring
  Imagery
  Thought stopping
  Stimulus control
  Supportive measures
  (Anti-depressants may or may not be required)
	Phobias and focal anxiety disorders
	  Systematic desensitization
	  Participant modeling (graduated exposure)
	  Stress inoculation
	  Neurolinguistic programming "phobia fix"
	  Self-help groups
	  (Antianxiety medication—or antidepressants in the case of agoraphobias—may or may not be required)
	Anxiety disorders with panic attacks
	  Muscle relaxation
	  Meditation
	  Participant modeling and graduated exposure
	  (Antianxiety medication will probably be required initially)

ANGER CONTROL AND MANAGEMENT
Cognitive restructuring
Reframing
Relaxation training
Meditation
Stress inoculation
Skills training
	Generalized (free-floating, or nonspecific) anxiety
	  Client-centered therapy
	  Biofeedback
	  Meditation
	  Muscle relaxation
	  (Mild tranquilizers may or may not be required)
	Obessive-compulsive disorders
	  Thought stopping
	  Paradoxical intention
	  Participant modeling
	  Cognitive modeling with self-instructional training
	  Systematic desensitization—if there is an anxiety component
	  Gestalt approaches
	  Group work

SKILL DEFICITS
(for example, social skills, assertive skills, job-interview skills)
  Skills training
  Modeling approaches
	PERSONALITY DISORDERS
	Avoidant personality disorders
	  Skills training (assertiveness)
	  Cognitive restructuring and rational-emotive approaches
	  Paradoxical intention
	  Adlerian therapy
	  Existential approaches
	  Gestalt approaches

BEHAVIORAL EXCESSES
(for example, weight, procrastination, smoking)
  Self-management techniques
  Paradoxical intention
  Imagery
	Dependent personality disorders
	  Assertive (skill) training
	  Covert modeling
	  Group work
	  Marriage and family counseling

treatment options for a given problem area. Problems for which these strategies are often used as secondary components, such as sexual dysfunction and alcohol abuse, are not included. The table is intended to be used as a resource, not as a cookbook. From our earlier discussion of criteria for selecting strategies, remember that it is extremely important to match the strategies used to the response components of the defined problem. For additional information on treatment considerations, see Meyer (1983), Reid (1983), and Lehrer and Woolfolk (1984).

☐ SELECTING COMBINATIONS OF STRATEGIES

Helping strategies are rarely used in isolation. Although the counseling strategies in the remainder of this book are presented one at a time for instructional purposes, in the "real world" these strategies are often used in combination. Further, there can be a great deal of overlap among strategies in the actual implementation.

It is necessary to select and sequence a variety of strategies in order to treat the complexity and range of problems presented by a single client. It is uncommon to encounter a client with only one very straightforward concern (such as fear of flying in airplanes) that can be treated successfully with only one strategy (such as systematic desensitization). As M. J. Mahoney (1974, p. 273) asserts, "Unidimensional presenting problems appear to be a myth propagated by research conventions. The average client is not simply snake phobic — he often expresses desires to improve personal adjustment along a wide range of foci."

Because most client problems are multidimensional and are controlled by diverse variables, the targets of change and corresponding treatment strategies usually need to be multiple. Furthermore, increasing evidence indicates a strong correlation between performance changes and cognitive changes. Performance accomplishments in the form of personal mastery experiences can strengthen clients' expectations of personal effectiveness or self-efficacy (Bandura & Adams, 1977; Bandura, Adams, & Beyer, 1977). A well-integrated helping program will employ all the necessary strategies to work with a client's performance skills, cognitive skills, emotional responses, body processes, and environmental factors.

☐ MODEL DIALOGUE: THE CASE OF JOAN

In this dialogue, the counselor will explore with Joan some of the strategies they could use to work with the first subgoal on Joan's goal chart (Chapter 9) for Terminal Outcome Goal #1. This dialogue is a continuation of the ones described in Chapters 8 and 9. In this session Joan and the counselor will explore strategies that could help Joan decrease her nervousness about math class and anticipation of rejection from her parents. Note that all three strategies suggested are based on Joan's diagnostic pattern of specific, or focal, anxiety, as opposed to generalized anxiety.

In the initial part of the interview, the counselor will summarize the previous session and will introduce Joan to the idea of **exploring** *strategies.*

1. *Counselor:* Last week, Joan, we talked about some of the things you would like to see happen as a result of counseling. One of the things you indicated was pretty important to you was being able to be more initiating. You had mentioned things like wanting to be able to ask questions or make responses, express your opinions, and express your feelings. We had identified the fact that one thing that keeps you from doing these things more often is the apprehension you feel in certain situations with your parents or in math class. There are several ways we might deal with your apprehension. I thought today we might explore some of the procedures that may help. These procedures are things we can do together to help you get where you want to be. How does that sound?
Client: It's OK. So we'll find a way, maybe, that I could be less nervous and more comfortable at these times.

In the second response, the counselor tries to explain to Joan what strategy selection involves and the importance of **Joan's input.**

2. *Counselor:* Yes. One thing to keep in mind is that there are no easy answers and there is not necessarily one right way. What we can do today is explore some ways that are typically used to help people be less nervous in specific situations and try to come up with a way that *you* think is most workable for you. I'll be giving you some information about these procedures for your input in this decision.
Client: OK.

In responses 3 and 4, the counselor suggests possible strategies for Joan to consider. The counselor also explains how one strategy, relaxation, **is related to Joan's concerns and can help her achieve her goal.**

3. *Counselor:* From my experience, I believe that there are a couple of things that might help you manage your nervousness to the point where you don't feel as if you have to avoid the situation. First of all, when you're nervous, you're tense. Sometimes when you're tense, you feel bad or sick or just out of control. One thing we could do is to teach you some relaxation methods [Chapter 17]. The relaxation can help you learn to identify when you're starting to feel nervous, and it can help you manage this before it gets so strong you just skip class or refuse to speak up. Does this make sense?

Client: Yes, because when I really let myself get nervous, I don't want to say anything. Sometimes I force myself to, but I'm still nervous and I don't feel like it.

4. *Counselor:* That's a good point. You don't have the energy or desire to do something you're apprehensive about. Sometimes, for some people, just learning to relax and control your nervousness might be enough. If you want to try this first and it helps you be less nervous to the point where you can be more initiating, then that's fine. However, there are some other things we might do also, so I'd like you to know about these action plans, too.

Client: Like what?

*The counselor proposes an additional strategy in response 5 and indicates how this procedure can help Joan decrease her nervousness by **describing how it is also related to Joan's problem and goal.***

5. *Counselor:* Well, one procedure has a very interesting name—it's called "stress inoculation" [Chapter 16]. You know when you get a shot like a polio inoculation, the shot helps to prevent you from getting polio. Well, this procedure helps you to prevent yourself from getting so overwhelmed in a stressful situation, such as your math class or with your folks, that you want to avoid the situation or don't want to say anything.

Client: Is it painful like a shot?

*The counselor provides more information about what stress inoculation would involve from Joan in terms of the **time, advantages, and risks of the procedure;** this information should help Joan assess her preferences.*

6. *Counselor:* No, not like that, although it would involve some work on your part. In addition to learning the relaxation training I mentioned earlier, you would learn how to cope with stressful situations—through relaxing your body and thinking some thoughts that would help you handle these difficult or competitive situations. When you are able to do this successfully with me, you would start to do it in your math class and with your folks. Once you learned the relaxation, it would take several sessions to learn the other parts. The advantage of stress inoculation is that it helps you learn how to cope with rather than avoid a stressful situation. Of course, it does require you to practice the relaxation and the coping thoughts on your own, and this takes some time each day. Without this sort of daily practice, this procedure may not be that helpful.

Client: It does sound interesting. Have you used it a lot?

*The counselor indicates some **information and advantages** about the strategy based on the **counselor's experience** and use of it with others.*

7. *Counselor:* I believe I tend to use it, or portions of it, whenever I think people could benefit from learning to manage nervousness and not let stressful situations control them. I know other counselors have used it and found that people with different stresses can benefit from it. It has a lot of potential if you're in a situation where your nervousness is getting the best of you and where you can learn to cope with the stress. Another advantage of this procedure is that it is pretty comprehensive. By that I mean it deals with different parts of a nervous reaction—like the part of you that gets sweaty palms and butterflies in your stomach, the part of you that thinks girls are dumb in math or girls don't have much to say, and then the part of you that goes out of your way to avoid these sticky situations. It's kind of like going shopping and getting a whole outfit—skirt, blouse, and shoes—rather than just the shoes or just the skirt.

Client: Well, it sounds OK to me. I also like the idea of the relaxation that you mentioned earlier.

*The counselor moves on in response 8 to describe another possible strategy, explains what this involves and how it might help Joan manage her nervousness, and **relates the use of the procedure to her problem and goal.***

8. *Counselor:* There's also another procedure called "desensitization" that is a pretty standard one to help a person decrease anxiety about situations [Chapter 18]. It is a way to help you desensitize yourself to the stress of your math class.

Client: Well, how exactly does that work—to desensitize yourself to something?

*The counselor explains how this strategy helps Joan decrease her nervousness and **explains elements, advantages, and risks of this strategy.***

9. *Counselor:* It works on the principle that you can't be relaxed and nervous at the same time. So, after teaching you how to relax, then you imagine situations involving your math class—or with your folks. However, you imagine a situation only when you're relaxed. You practice this way to the point where you can speak up in class or with your folks without feeling all the nervousness you do now. In other words, you become desensitized. Most of this process is something we would do together in these sessions and is an advantage over something requiring a lot of outside work on your part.

Client: Does that take a long time?

The counselor gives Joan some information about the **time** *involved in the desensitization procedure.*

10. *Counselor:* This may take a little longer than the other two procedures. This procedure has helped a great many people decrease their nervousness about specific situations—like taking a test or flying. Of course, keep in mind that any change plan takes some time.

    Client: It sounds helpful.

The counselor points out some of the **environmental factors** *involved in these procedures.*

11. *Counselor:* Another thing I should point out is that all these procedures will require you to practice on your own once or twice a day in a quiet place. Is that possible?

    Client: Sure, as long as it's something I can do at home. I don't know—what do you think will help me most?

In response 12, the counselor indicates **his or her preferences** *and provides information about* **documentation.**

12. *Counselor:* I'd like us to make the decision together. I feel comfortable with all of these things I've mentioned. Also, all three of these procedures have been found to be pretty effective in dealing with the different fears of many people who are concerned about working on their nervousness in situations so it isn't a handicap.

    Client: I'm wondering exactly how to decide where to go from here.

In responses 13 and 14, the counselor elicits information about **client preferences.**

13. *Counselor:* Well, perhaps if we reviewed the action plans I've mentioned and go over them, you can see which one you feel might work best for

you, at least now. We can always change at a later point. How does that sound?

    Client: Good. There's a lot of information and I don't know if I remember everything you mentioned.

14. *Counselor:* OK. Well, we talked first about relaxation as something you could learn here and then do on your own to help you control the feelings and physical sensations of nervousness. Then we discussed stress inoculation, which involves giving you a lot of different skills to use to cope with the stressful situations in your math class. The third plan, desensitization, involves using relaxation first but also involves having you imagine the scenes related to your math class and to interactions with your parents. This procedure is something we would work on together, although the relaxation requires daily practice from you. What do you think would be most helpful to you at this point?

    Client: I think maybe the relaxation might help, since I can practice with it on my own. It also sounds like the simplest to do, not so much in time but just in what is involved.

In the last response, the counselor pursues the option that Joan has been leaning toward during the session, thus building on **client preferences.**

15. *Counselor:* That's a good point. Of the three procedures I mentioned, relaxation training is probably the easiest and simplest to learn to use. You have also mentioned once or twice before in our session that you were intrigued with this idea, so it looks as if you've been mulling it over for a little while and it still sounds appealing and workable to you. If so, we can start working with it today.

LEARNING ACTIVITIES #32: STRATEGY SELECTION

I. Using the case of Mr. Brown, presented in Chapter 7 (p. 168), select and define an outcome goal for the client, based on the assessed problem described in that chapter. In small groups, brainstorm to generate as many action plans or strategies as possible that might be most workable for this client, given the identified problem and goal. List these strategies on paper. After the brainstorming, assess the usefulness and potential efficacy of each strategy by applying the 12 criteria for effective strategies listed earlier in this chapter on page 297.

II. This activity provides practice in eliciting informed consent from a client. If possible, use role-play triads

in which one person assumes the role of the client, another the counselor, and the third the observer. This activity will work best if you continue to use the case of Mr. Brown. The counselor's task is to select two or three strategies that your group judged effective and to describe them to the client. Be sure to include information about the activities involved, the rationale for the strategy, the client's role or expected participation, your role, possible discomforts or risks, and expected benefits. The observer can use the Checklist for Informed Consent that follows as a guide for observation and feedback.

(continued)

CHECKLIST FOR INFORMED CONSENT

Instructions: Determine whether the counselor did or did not convey the following elements of information to the client about proposed procedures.

Yes	No	Item
___	___	1. Description of each strategy, including activities involved
___	___	2. Rationale for or purpose of the strategy
___	___	3. Description of the therapist's role
___	___	4. Description of the client's role
___	___	5. Description of possible risks or discomforts

Yes	No	Item
___	___	6. Description of expected benefits
___	___	7. Estimated time and cost of each strategy
___	___	8. Offer made to answer client's questions about strategy
___	___	9. Client advised of the right to discontinue strategy at any time
___	___	10. Explanations given in clear and nontechnical language
___	___	11. Summary and/or clarifications used to explore and understand client reactions

☐ SUMMARY

Most clients will present complex problems with a diverse set of counseling goals. This will require a set of interventions and combinations of strategies designed to work with all the major target areas of a person's functioning. Both counselor and client should be active participants in choosing counseling treatment strategies that are appropriate for the client's problem and desired outcomes. The strategies reflected by the overall treatment plan should be sufficient to deal with all the important target areas of change and matched, as well as possible, to the response components of the defined problem. After the strategies have been selected, the counselor and client will continue to work together to implement the procedures. Some common elements of strategy implementation are considered in the next chapter.

POSTEVALUATION

PART ONE

Instructions: Listed below in the left column are six client situations. Listed in the right column are the five guidelines for appropriate timing of strategy introduction and selection. Decide which of these five guidelines is represented in each of the six client situations (Chapter Objective One). There may be more than one guideline that "fits" for any given situation. Feedback follows the postevaluation.

Situations

___1. The client has been late the last few weeks and on one occasion "forgot" the appointment.

___2. You asked the client to complete a self-report inventory during the week. The client started it but says he needs another week to finish it.

___3. The client shifts the focus during the third session from not being able to decide on a major to the concern that she is "going crazy."

___4. The clients keep changing their minds about how they want their relationship to be different.

___5. The client repeatedly asks you to solve issues for him.

___6. The client has left the session early the last two times.

Guidelines

a. Quality of the relationship
b. Assessment of the problem
c. Development of counseling goals
d. Client readiness and commitment
e. Collection of baseline measures

(continued)

PART TWO

In this part of the postevaluation, we present three descriptions of client cases. Read each case carefully and then determine and list in writing which among the seven criteria for strategy selection (listed below) would be the predominant or primary criteria for selecting strategies *for this particular client case* (Chapter Objective Two). Provide a rationale for your choice. You may also want to speculate on a choice of suitable intervention strategies, given the primary criteria you have identified. Feedback is provided after the postevaluation.

Criteria for Strategy Selection

1. Counselor characteristics and preferences
2. Documentation about strategies
3. Environmental factors
4. Nature of client problem and response systems
5. Nature of outcome goals
6. Client characteristics and preferences
7. Diagnostic cues and patterns

Case 1

The client, a college student, reports failing grades because of what he calls "procrastination." He says he puts off everything related to classes until the last possible moment. As a result, his work is often sloppy and/or late, and he has insufficient time to prepare adequately for tests. He says he has tried to deal with this in two ways: (1) by depriving himself of things he enjoys doing until the work is completed and (2) by forcing himself to sit at his desk for a certain amount of time. He reports that neither solution has helped at all. He also reports that he has sought therapy for this problem before and that it was unsuccessful. He states that it is difficult to study in his room because of

noise but that he is too lazy to get up and walk to the library all the time. He describes himself as a slow starter, as someone who needs a lot of pushing and prodding to get things done.

Case 2

The client, in her midtwenties, has just returned from two years of travel in Europe, which she completed after earning a college degree in art. Her funds have run out, and her traveling companion has come back to school. She would like to return to Europe to live but needs first to find work and build up her funds. Despite this realization, she says she is reluctant to "buckle down" and work, preferring the more creative life of a roving artist. She states that she read in a national newsmagazine about an approach called "CP"—creative processing—which she would like you to try with her to see whether she can start to work full-time without losing touch with the creative part of herself that she discovered during her recent travels.

Case 3

The client, a middle-aged married woman, has become increasingly anxious over a variety of things during the past year. Her anxiety began when she was shopping. Now she also can no longer drive without having panic attacks. During the last two months, she has confined herself to her house because of increasing anxiety over being out of the house. She indicates that her anxiety mainly takes the form of a terrible feeling in her stomach, rapid heart rate, shortness of breath, dizziness, and thoughts that she is going crazy or is going to die. She wants help in getting control of these feelings and not being such a bundle of nerves.

☐ SUGGESTED READINGS

Dixon, D., & Glover, J. (1984). *Counseling: A problem-solving approach.* New York: Wiley. Chapter 9, "Selecting an Intervention Strategy."

Lazarus, A. A. (1981). *The practice of multimodal therapy.* New York: McGraw-Hill. Chapter 8, "The Selection of Techniques."

Lehrer, P. M., & Woolfolk, R. L. (1984). Are stress-reduction techniques interchangeable, or do they have specific effects? A review of the comparative empirical literature. In R. L. Woolfolk & P. N. Lehrer (Eds.), *Principles and practice of stress management.* New York: Guilford Press.

Lidz, C. W., Meisel, A., Zerbavel, G. E., Carter, M., Sestak, R., & Roth, L. (1984). *Informed consent.* New York: Guilford Press.

Manthei, R. J. (1983). Client choice of therapist in therapy. *Personnel and Guidance Journal, 61,* 339–340.

Meyer, R. G. (1983). *The clinician's handbook.* Boston: Allyn & Bacon.

Öst, L. G., Jerremalm, A., & Johannson, J. (1981). Individual response patterns and the effects of different behavioral methods in the treatment of social phobia. *Behaviour Research and Therapy, 19,* 1–16.

Reid, W. H. (1983). *Treatment of the DSM-III psychiatric disorders.* New York: Brunner/Mazel.

Shaffer, W. F. (1976). *Heuristics for the initial diagnostic interview.* Paper presented at the annual meeting of the American Psychological Association, Washington, DC.

Widiger, T. A., & Rorer, L. G. (1984). The responsible psychotherapist. *American Psychologist, 39,* 503–515.

Yeaton, W. H., & Sechrest, L. (1981). Critical dimensions in the choice and maintenance of successful treatments: Strength, integrity, and effectiveness. *Journal of Consulting and Clinical Psychology, 49,* 156–167.

FEEDBACK: POSTEVALUATION

PART ONE

1. a, d
2. a, d, e
3. b
4. c
5. d
6. a, d

PART TWO

Case 1

Nature of client problem—procrastination, avoidance behavior.

Client characteristics—a slow starter; uses punitive means to manage his own behavior, and these have perhaps made problem worse.

Environmental factors—difficulty in finding quiet place to study.

Diagnostic cues—previous attempts by self and another therapist to change the pattern have been unsuccessful.

Possible treatment strategies—paradoxical intervention; group counseling/therapy.

Case 2

Counselor characteristics—counselor may not feel comfortable using the "CP" approach requested by the client.

Documentation—there is a hint that the "CP procedure" is a novel and somewhat experimental one, without much supporting demonstration of its clinical effectiveness.

Diagnostic cues—client seems to lack realistic information about herself and her environment.

Possible treatment strategies—ones related to choice issues such as vocational counseling; Gestalt dialoguing; TA redecision work.

Case 3

Nature of client problem and response systems—phobia (agoraphobia) with panic attacks; anxiety involves both somatic and cognitive components.

Nature of goal—client wants to learn to manage anxiety and control panic attacks.

Diagnostic cues—anxiety is focal rather than generalized.

Possible treatment strategies—specific anxiety management procedures such as desensitization; presence of panic attacks may indicate initial need for medication.

COMMON ELEMENTS OF
STRATEGY IMPLEMENTATION

TWELVE

Many helping strategies share four elements when used with clients: the rationale for the strategy, modeling of goal behaviors, rehearsal of goal behaviors, and *in vivo* homework and transfer of learning. Each strategy is described to the client with a treatment rationale in which the counselor explains the purpose of the procedure and provides an overview of it. Some strategies also involve some form of modeling, in which the goal behaviors are demonstrated, live or symbolically. And typically the modeling is followed by some form of rehearsal within the interview, often accompanied by coaching and feedback from the helper. Finally, most strategies include a transfer-of-learning element in which the client engages in homework or self-directed practice in the environment. These four elements of strategy implementation, when used in combination, comprise a variety of skill training programs, such as assertive behavior (Galassi & Galassi, 1977), social skills (Eisler & Frederiksen, 1980), and job-interview skills (Azrin & Besalel, 1980), and for some self-help therapy programs (Glasgow & Rosen, 1979). This chapter will describe the major ways in which these elements are used in implementing helping strategies. We also describe components of written treatment contracts.

☐ OBJECTIVES

1. Given a simulated client case, describe how you would apply the four elements of strategy implementation with this client.
2. With a partner, demonstrate the four elements of strategy implementation in a skill-building program.
3. Given a written client case, design a written treatment contract including the five components of such contracts.

☐ RATIONALE FOR TREATMENT STRATEGIES

Before implementing any strategy, the therapist should give the client a rationale about the treatment. Wilson and Evans (1977, p. 555) suggest what a rationale should be in order to foster realistic expectations about a particular treatment:

> Essentially the strategy is . . . to provide clients with information which will produce a cognitive structure whereby they can organize their experience in therapy. Structuring would include an explanation of the development, maintenance, and modification of the client's problems, a persuasive rationale for the specific treatment methods to be employed, a description of the procedural steps involved and the client's own responsibilities in actively participating in the treatment.

An adequate rationale about treatment consists of a *reason* for the procedure and a brief *overview* of its components (Kazdin & Krouse, 1983). After providing the rationale, you should seek the client's willingness to try out the strategy. As with any part of the counseling process, clients should never be forced or coerced to use something without their express commitment.

In the remaining chapters, examples of a rationale that might be used to explain each particular strategy to a client are modeled. Here is an example of a counselor providing a rationale about using modeling and role play as part of a skill-building program for a young girl who would like to talk more honestly with her best friend.

Counselor: Kathy, you've said you'd like to be able to learn to tell your friend Tammy when she has hurt your feelings, but you aren't sure how to do this. I think I can show you a way to talk to Tammy, and then you can pretend that I am Tammy and talk to me about how I have hurt your feelings. [overview] I believe if you can pretend I'm your friend and talk to me about this, then later on you will be able to talk to Tammy the way you want to. [rationale] How does this sound to you? [client's willingness]

Client: OK. We pretend in my class sometimes.

Counselor: So would you like for us to go ahead and try this out?

Client: Sure. It's fine with me.

To summarize, there are two things a counselor can explain in giving the client an adequate rationale about any counseling strategy: a reason, or purpose, for the strategy and an overview of the strategy.

☐ MODELING

Modeling is a procedure by which a person can learn through observing the behavior of another person. In some instances, modeling alone is used as a therapy strategy to help a client acquire responses or extinguish fears (see Chapter 13). In other cases, modeling is a component of a strategy in which the counselor provides demonstrations of the goal behaviors. Models can be live or symbolic. Live models are people: the therapist, a teacher, a friend, or a peer. As Nye (1973) points out, a counselor can be a live model "by demonstrating a desired behavior and arranging optimal conditions for the client to do the same" (p. 381). Symbolic models can be provided through written materials such as manuals or handbooks, films, audio- or videotapes, slide tapes, or photographs. Modeling can also take place by having the client imagine someone performing the target behaviors, as is done in covert modeling (see Chapter 14).

Processes Involved in Modeling

Bandura and Jeffery (1973) claim that there are four processes involved in modeling: attention, retention, reproduction, and motivation. *Attention* refers to the activity of the observer in focusing on what is modeled. For example, it might be very difficult for a client to attend to a model when feeling anxious. In such cases, the counselor may have to introduce relaxation procedures (Chapter 17) before modeling can be used. One way the counselor can facilitate client attention is to cue or instruct the client about what to look for before the model is presented.

Retention refers to symbolic or linguistic coding, cognitive organization, or covert rehearsal of what has been modeled or demonstrated. A counselor can enhance the retention processes by sequencing the presentation of the model in a series of brief modeled scenarios. After the model has been presented, a summarization of what has been demonstrated by the counselor or client may also aid retention.

The third process involved in modeling is *reproduction,* which refers to the ability of the observer to reproduce, rehearse, or practice the modeled behavior.

The last process common to all modeling procedures is *motivation*. A counselor can encourage motivation by giving the client a rationale for using modeling. For example, a counselor might explain how the procedure is applied and the benefits the client might derive from its use. Motivation can also be increased if the client successfully performs the modeled behavior. This can be arranged by practice of small, successful steps. These four processes of attention, retention, reproduction, and motivation overlap. For example, client motivation can be enhanced by successful reproduction of the modeled behavior. These processes may be enhanced by the characteristics of the model and by the presentation of the modeling procedure.

Characteristics of the Model

The characteristics of the model can be important factors contributing to the success of modeling. The model characteristics described in this section represent the ideal. However, it may not be practical or feasible for the counselor to apply all the ideal characteristics, particularly when the counselor has to be the model or when other live models are used. It is perhaps easier to incorporate these model characteristics into symbolic models (see Chapter 13).

Research indicates that the effects of modeling may be enhanced when there is a great deal of similarity between the model and the client (Bandura, 1971a; Rosenthal & Bandura, 1978). The model selected should be like the client in age and sex. The prestige of the model and similarity in cultural and ethnic background and racial origin may also have important effects for some clients (Cormier & Cormier, 1975).

A coping model is perhaps better than a mastery model (Kazdin, 1973a, 1974a, 1974b; Meichenbaum, 1971). That is, a model who shows some fear or anxiety, makes errors in performance, and shows some degree of struggle or coping while performing the behavior or activity may be less threatening than a model who comes across as flawless. A client may be able to identify more easily with a coping model or with what Marlatt and Perry (1975) call a "slider" model, who displays gradual improvement during a complex series of modeled behaviors. For example, a phobic client may improve more quickly if timid models gradually attain calmness than if they perform fearlessly at once. Model displays should be tuned to the perspective of the clients and not be beyond their reach. In addition, models who have concerns similar to those of the client may contribute a great deal to the success of a modeling procedure. Models who share yet overcome handicaps are therapeutically beneficial when seen by clients as having similar concerns and similar histories (Rosenthal, 1976).

Repeated demonstrations of the same response are often necessary. As Bandura (1976a, p. 250) indicates, multiple modeling demonstrations show the client how something can be performed best and also that any feared consequences do not occur. Multiple demonstrations can be arranged by having a single model repeat the demonstration or by having several models demonstrate the same response. For example, one model could demonstrate several times how our client Kathy could talk to her friend, or several models could demonstrate this same activity. The multiple models would be portrayed as possessing characteristics and concerns similar to those of the client (Perry & Furukawa, 1980). The use of multiple models may also increase the generalizability and efficacy of modeling. Multiple models may give more cues to the client and can have greater impact than a single model, because clients can draw on the strengths of each model.

Remember that, in some cases, a therapist may not be able to use multiple models in an interview setting. The selection of particular model characteristics will be dictated by the parameters of the client's problem and goals and the individual characteristics of the client. Sometimes the client is the best model (see "Self-as-a-Model," Chapter 13).

Presentation of Live Modeling

When using live modeling in the interview, the model first engages in role reversal; that is, the model plays the part of the client while the client plays the part of a significant other person in the client's environment. It is important to instruct the client to portray this person as realistically as possible. This provides an opportunity for the behaviors to be modeled under conditions that closely resemble the client's extratherapeutic environment. At the same time, it enables the model to identify the kind of person who should be portrayed later in the client's practice sequences. When using live modeling, try to remember that the modeling is a suggestion — not a decision for the client. Encourage the client to adapt the modeling to his or her own style.

Here is an example of a live modeling sequence with the counselor modeling the goal behavior for Kathy:

Counselor: We're going to pretend for a bit. I'd like you to pretend to be Tammy. Just be the way she is and tell me what she says about your clothes. I'm going to pretend to be you. Only instead of biting my lip and being quiet like you tell me you are, I'm going to tell her my feelings are hurt. OK. Now you start as Tammy.

Client (as Tammy, in a jeering voice): You know, Kathy, that dress looks funny on you today. Are those clothes yours or are they hand-me-downs from your sister?

Counselor (as Kathy, silent for a moment, starts to bite lip, then stops herself): No, they're mine. Hey, Tammy, what's the big deal about clothes? We only have so much money. . . . I have hurt feelings when you say something about my clothes like that.

Client (as Tammy): Oh, let's forget it. I'm sorry. Can you come over after school today?

After the demonstration, the client can summarize the main points of the modeled presentation. At this time, general principles that the client should remember during later practice attempts can be reviewed. These guidelines may help the client code the modeled input in a way that facilitates recall. If the client has trouble summarizing or reviewing, additional modeling may be required before practice attempts are initiated. The client should be encouraged to select for practice only those parts of the modeled demonstration that he or she finds comfortable. For example:

Counselor: OK, Kathy, let's talk about our pretending. Did you feel like you acted the way Tammy does?

Client: Yes. I believe she did feel sorry, too. I don't think she wants to be mean.

Counselor: That's probably right. But as long as you don't say anything, she doesn't know how you feel. What did you see me do?

Client: Well, you started to bite your lip. But it looked like you got brave then and told her your feelings were hurt.

Counselor: Do you think you could say something like I did to Tammy?

Client: Sure, I think so.

Counselor: Well, we can try another pretend, only this time I'll be Tammy and you be yourself. If you see that you forget to say something and start to bite your lip, just stop, take your time, and then tell me in your own words that your feelings are hurt.

To summarize, the counselor should implement modeling with the following guidelines in mind:

1. Instruct the client in what to look for before the modeled demonstration.
2. Select a model who is similar to the client and who can demonstrate the goal behaviors in a coping manner.
3. Present the modeled demonstration in a sequence of scenarios that minimize stress for the client.
4. Ask the client to summarize or review what he or she saw after the demonstration.

Typically, modeling of goal behaviors will be followed by practice or rehearsal of these responses. Modeling is used as a necessary precondition for rehearsal when the client's behavioral repertory is deficient or defective and when the goal of rehearsal is *response acquisition.* The rationale for this is very simple: if a person wants to do something but doesn't know how, without a modeled demonstration it would be very difficult to practice the desired behavior. Modeling provides the client with some response choices he or she can use during practices of the goal behaviors.

☐ REHEARSAL, OR PRACTICE

Most strategies involve some form of response practice in which the client rehearses the goal behaviors. Usually these rehearsal attempts follow the sequence in which the goal behaviors have been arranged. The actual practice of each response should be very similar to the situations that occur in the client's environment. As Mischel (1971) asserts, "Generalization is enhanced to the degree that the stimulus conditions sampled in treatment are similar to those in the life situation in which the new behaviors will be used" (p. 468). To simulate these situations realistically, the practice attempts should include any necessary props and should portray any other people involved with the client as accurately as possible. This portrayal should include acting out the probable responses of these other persons to the client's goal behavior.

Overt and Covert Rehearsal

The actual rehearsal attempts may be covert or overt. A client can rehearse covertly by imagining and reflecting about the desired response. In overt rehearsal, the client can verbalize and act out the desired behaviors in a role-play scene. Both overt and covert rehearsal have some empirical support (McFall & Twentyman, 1973). The combined effects of overt and covert rehearsal may be better than the effects of either alone (Kazdin, 1982; Kazdin & Mascitelli, 1982b). When the target response consists in sexual behaviors or acquisition or discrimination of covert responses, covert rehearsal may be more appropriate. For clients who have difficulty generating and maintaining real-life images, overt rehearsal may be more helpful. With many clients, both covert and overt practice can be used. Initially, it may be useful to have the client engage in covert rehearsal, because it is less visible and may decrease the client's concern about being observed by the counselor. Gradually, the client can approximate overt rehearsals, first by verbalizing while practicing covertly and then by acting out the situation in a role play.

Coaching and Induction Aids

Immediately before a goal behavior is rehearsed, it may help to have the client review covertly or aloud what he or she is going to do and say during the practice. In addition, the client's fear of "fouling up" may be decreased if the counselor stops to prompt, or coach, when the client gets stuck. Coaching consists in giving the client instructions about the general principles for performing the desired behavior effectively. Coaching can provide the cues for the person to make discriminations about the appropriate use of the target responses. The counselor can coach by giving verbal suggestions or by flashing cue cards to the client during practice. If a client has repeated difficulty in rehearsing one particular response, it may be necessary to go back to the previous response. In some cases, additional modeling and coaching may be required, or the order of the rehearsed responses may need rearrangement.

Sometimes a client has difficulty practicing the desired responses unless the practice attempts are supplemented with *induction aids,* performance or supportive aids arranged by the counselor to assist a client in performing a feared or difficult response. Induction aids are safeguards that are introduced temporarily during initial practice attempts to help clients do what they are too frightened to think about or too hesitant to initiate on their own (Bandura, 1976a, p. 250). Bandura describes the use of induction aids as follows: "During the early phases of treatment, therapists use whatever supplementary aids are necessary to initiate behavioral changes. As treatment progresses,

however, the supportive aids and practice controls are gradually removed until clients function effectively without assistance" (p. 251).

These are examples of induction aids, adapted from Bandura (pp. 250–251), to be used with practice attempts:

1. Practice with the counselor's (or model's) assistance.
2. Verbal or physical guidance, support, or coaching by the counselor.
3. Repeated practice of only one activity or response.
4. Use of graduated time intervals for practice, such as a shorter to a longer duration.
5. Graduated levels of severity, risk, or threat in a practice situation (low risk to high risk).
6. Any arrangement of protective practice conditions to reduce the likelihood of feared or undesired consequences.

Induction aids are useful to help clients who cannot perform an activity or behavior by themselves or to assist a client through difficult performances. A client should never be coerced to perform a behavior or engage in a particular activity. However, a client's refusal to practice might indicate a need for help in the form of induction aids, not necessarily a desire to stop trying (R. W. Jeffery, 1976, p. 304). If the counselor has difficulty thinking of suitable induction aids, she or he should ask the client to recommend induction aids that would help the client to practice or engage in the desired activity or behavior in either the interview or the natural setting. The counselor and client can use any induction aids that are necessary to initiate behavioral change and to ensure successful performance. The more aids the counselor can use, the greater the probability of success for treatment. The importance of a wide array of induction aids was demonstrated with phobic, incapacitated clients (Bandura, Jeffery, & Wright, 1974). Bandura (1976a) suggests that the number of supportive aids should be a function of the severity of the client's disabilities or deficits.

Client Self-Directed Practice

As the client becomes able to master the activity or behavior with aids, support, and guidance from the counselor, the coaching or induction aids should be *gradually* withdrawn so that the client performs the activities or behaviors unassisted. Dispense with aids and coaching when clients can perform the desired activities. But remember, encourage the client to practice only what is clearly within the client's *immediate capabilities* and what the client is *willing* to do. The counselor can decide when and how to decrease the amount of coaching and induction aids by relying on such indicators as client performance and verbal feedback. Gradually, clients should be able to rehearse a response, directing themselves with self-cuing.

Criteria for Effective Practice

One response in the sequence should be covered adequately before moving on to the next task. The therapist can use three criteria proposed by Lazarus (1966, p. 210) to determine when a practice attempt has been rehearsed satisfactorily:

1. The client is able to enact the response without feeling anxious.
2. The client's general demeanor supports his or her words.
3. The client's words and actions would seem fair and reasonable to an objective onlooker.

In addition, as Goldfried and Davison (1976, p. 147) suggest, the client should take an active role in deciding when a scene has been rehearsed sufficiently.

In the following dialogue, Kathy and the counselor are starting the practice attempts of the first response on their ordered list:

Counselor: Kathy, let's try another pretending. This time you just be yourself and I'll pretend to be Tammy. Let's just be walking home from school together. Nothing touchy has come up. Now can you tell me what you think you could say if I said something to hurt your feelings—like about your clothes? [review of target response]

Client: Well, I'd think I could just say "Tammy, I don't think my clothes should matter. But when you say they do, my feelings are hurt."

Counselor: That's great. I think it would help if you could just go over that for a few minutes, using your imagination. Just pretend Tammy makes a remark about your clothes and imagine telling her your feelings are hurt. Then imagine what she would say to you. [covert rehearsal]

[Pause]

Counselor: OK, tell me what happened in your imagination.

Client? Well, it was after school. She brought up the Girl Scout banquet and told me she thought I should borrow her dress, since our troop decided not to wear our uniforms. I told her I had a dress I

wanted to wear and it bothered me when she said something like that. [Pauses]

Counselor: And then what happened?

Client: Tammy was surprised. She said she was sorry.

Counselor: OK, let's try this out again. This time I'll be Tammy and you be yourself. [overt rehearsal]

Counselor (as Tammy): You know, Kathy, I've been noticing that your clothes look like, well, I mean don't you think you should get a new dress for the banquet—or borrow one of mine?

Client: Tammy, we don't have a lot of money right now for clothes. Besides, I'd rather spend my allowance on my bike. [somewhat defensively]

Counselor: Let's stop there. Did you say to Tammy what you really wanted to tell her? [counselor coaching]

Client: No, not really. I left out the part about my hurt feelings, didn't I?

Counselor: Yes. You got off to a good start, but you did leave it out. Sometimes you can remember that part by the words *I feel,* like "I feel hurt or upset when you talk about my clothes." Let's go over it again. [counselor coaching and repeated practice of same response]

After several successful practices, the counselor would encourage Kathy to practice the scene without any assistance from the counselor. Then practice with the next response would begin. The rehearsal attempts would continue until each response in the sequence had been completed satisfactorily. At this point, Kathy should be able to demonstrate the desired behaviors in appropriate ways, and any anxiety that was present should be decreased. However, the rehearsal efforts might be of limited value unless accompanied by some form of feedback or analysis of performance.

Feedback

Feedback is a way to observe and evaluate oneself and one's behavior and, under the right circumstances, to initiate corrective action (Melnick, 1973). Feedback that follows rehearsal provides a basis for recognizing successful performance and for recognizing and correcting any problems encountered during practice (Geis & Chapman, 1971, p. 40). Feedback should be designed to help the client improve performance and to recognize desirable and undesirable aspects of her or his rehearsal. For feedback to have a positive effect, it must be used cautiously and with some guidelines. Too much feedback, particularly if it comes from an external source, can be threatening or punishing. Thomas (1977, p. 95) summarizes the role of feedback in a behavior-change program as follows: "The problem with feedback . . . is that while it generally informs the recipient and sometimes changes his behavior favorably, its behavioral function is uncertain."

According to McKeachie (1976, p. 824), feedback is most likely to be facilitative if three conditions are met:

1. The person receiving the feedback is motivated to improve.
2. The feedback provides an adequate, but not an excessive, dose of information.
3. The feedback helps the person to identify or implement other response alternatives.

The extent to which these conditions of effective feedback are met will depend on the type, timing, and amount of feedback used in conjunction with a client's practice sessions.

The following three guidelines can be used to apply feedback in conjunction with a practice effort.

1. Give the client the first opportunity to assess his or her own performance. As Rose (1973) points out, if the client is responsible for a great deal of the feedback, this sensitizes the client to his or her behavior and helps the client to monitor performance between sessions.

2. Verbal assessment (by either the counselor or the client) should be supplemented with a periodic objective assessment, such as a playback of a video- or audiotape. Initially a taped playback may seem threatening to a client. But as a client becomes accustomed to being on tape, the playback will not be viewed with apprehension. At first, the counselor and client can go over the playback together. Eventually, the client should be able to take the tape home and evaluate progress alone. The advantage of the taped feedback is that it allows the client to see or hear objective evidence of successive rehearsals with greater refinement of the desired skills. Moreover, the knowledge of being taped may itself bring about change by activating the client's self monitoring system (Melnick & Stocker, 1977). If it is impossible to tape-record any rehearsal sessions, a substitute playback using role reversal can be used. In this method, the counselor takes the part of the client and tries to mirror exactly the way in which the client completed the previous rehearsal attempt.

This may be more accurate than verbal analysis, which is subject to more distortions and biases.

3. Verbal assessment by the counselor should contain encouragement for some part of the client's practice attempt and some suggestions for how the client might improve or do something differently. Krumboltz and Thoresen (1976) suggest the use of Homme's "sandwiching" technique for counselor feedback. In this technique, the first part (a slice of bread) is a positive stroke, followed by a suggestion or a criticism (the filling), followed by another positive stroke (the other slice of bread). It is important to give some positive feedback for *each* rehearsal attempt. Don't wait for a perfect performance before giving encouragement. Each successive attempt should be reinforced by the counselor. Gradually, the counselor can reduce the amount of praise given and help clients learn to reinforce themselves for successes. This will help clients learn how to praise themselves after a rehearsal effort. Clients are usually able to do this after a sufficient amount of modeling or coaching has provided a basis for discriminating improved performance.

Here is an example of the counselor and Kathy using feedback after a practice attempt.

Counselor: OK, Kathy, let's stop for a minute. What do you think just happened in our practice?
Client: Well, I did tell Tammy my feelings were hurt. It wasn't as hard as I thought. Uh, well, it's harder to talk to her than to you.
Counselor: So maybe you think a little more practice might be needed. Would you like to listen to the way we sound on this tape?
Client (giggles): Sure.
[Tape is turned on and replayed. Immediately after Kathy has responded with the desired behavior, counselor adds feedback.]
Counselor: Right there, Kathy. I can play this part back again. Notice how you just told Tammy your feelings were hurt—you didn't hem and haw around. [stroke] You may want to speak up a little the next time—hear how soft your voice is. [suggestion] That was a good effort [stroke].
Client: Yeah, I didn't realize I talked softly.
Counselor: You don't seem to usually. Perhaps it was because you're learning something new. What did you hear on the tape that you liked about the way you handled the situation? [cuing Kathy for self-reinforcement]
Client: Well, I liked saying "Tammy, I have hurt feelings." As my older brother says, "Tell it like it is."

Counselor: Yes, you were being honest, and yet you were doing it in a way that was not putting down your friend, either.

To summarize, rehearsal of the goal behaviors involves the following steps:

1. A review of the target responses to practice.
2. Covert and/or overt rehearsal attempts of sequenced responses.
3. Therapist coaching and induction aids during initial practice attempts.
4. Reduction of coaching and induction aids.
5. Client self-directed practice of response.
6. Adequate practice of one response before moving on to another.
7. Therapist and client feedback, oral and taped.

After the client is able to demonstrate the goal behaviors during practice attempts in the interview, *in vivo* practice opportunities can be arranged. Typically these take the form of homework tasks that make up a transfer-of-training program.

☐ HOMEWORK AND TRANSFER OF LEARNING

Facilitating the transfer of behavior from the counseling or training session to the "natural" environment should be an integral part of the helping process. Generalization of desired changes can be achieved by homework assignments that are part of a transfer-of-training program. Martin and Worthington (1982) indicate that homework can increase the client's self-awareness about the problem and can improve the acquisition of new behavior or the elimination of old responses because the homework is to be completed between therapy sessions. Shelton and Levy (1981, pp. 12–14) suggest that homework can result in a number of benefits, including the following:

1. Provides access to private behaviors.
2. Allows treatment to continue after therapy sessions.
3. Increases the efficiency of treatment.
4. Increases client's perceptions of self-control.
5. Facilitates transfer of learning.

Homework experiences are arranged by tailoring a transfer-of-training program for each client. In an adequate program, the client's new skills are used first in low-risk situations in the client's natural environment or in any situation in which the client will probably experience success or favorable outcomes. Gradually, the client extends the application of the skills to natural situations that are more unpredictable and involve a greater threat. The particular homework developed and assigned will vary with each client and with the client's desired goal. If the client is learning to express feelings, then the homework would be structured to assist the client in that goal. For a very thorough description of various homework activities, see Shelton and Levy's *Behavioral Assignments and Treatment Compliance* (1981).

Components of Effective Homework

Whatever the homework assignment is, it should be something clients can instigate by themselves that is likely to meet with some success. Initially, the homework should involve a fairly simple task; gradually, more complex situations can be added. Kazdin and Mascitelli (1982a) found that homework is necessary to maintain desired behavior change after the treatment intervention has ended.

Homework assignments should start with a *rationale* for the homework. Jacobson and Margolin (1979, p. 127) give couples the following rationale for homework tasks for marital counseling:

"Now I'm going to assign a task which may be the most important task which you will do from now until the end of therapy. As part of our evaluation procedure, you will begin to record some of the events that take place between the two of you every day. This will give us some information that we can't get in any other way, namely, the patterns of interactions and exchanges that go on at home. You will be doing this from now until the end of therapy, if we should decide to pursue that. So, later we will be using this information to begin working on some of the problems. We'll look at it every week and see how we're doing. So, we'll be making a lot of use of this information, and I find that it functions like a seeing eye dog for me. I am blind without it. So, it is necessary that you do the work every day and do it carefully."*

In addition to the rationale, homework assignments should contain six other components: *what* the client is to do, *when* the behavior should occur,

* From *Marital Therapy: Strategies Based on Social Learning and Behavior Exchange Principles* by N. S. Jacobson and G. Margolin. Copyright © 1979 Brunner/Mazel. Reprinted by permission.

where the behavior is to be performed, *how much* or *how often* the behavior is to occur, *how* the behavior is to be recorded, and a *reminder* to bring the homework log to the next therapy session (Shelton & Levy, 1981).

To increase the probability that the client will carry out the assignment accurately, Rose (1973) suggests that self-directed prompts in the form of cue cards be made up for the client. The client can go over the cue cards just before carrying out the assignment. Both the type of homework assignment and the prompts on the cue cards should be developed in conjunction with the client. A client who has had a major role in selecting and developing the assignment is more likely to complete the homework. In lieu of using cue cards, sometimes the counselor or another person can accompany the client on a homework assignment. Ascher and Phillips (1975) suggest that a trained aide who functions in this capacity can model for the client and also can reinforce the client's progress in the *in vivo* setting.

Self-Monitoring of Homework

The client should be encouraged to self-monitor certain aspects of the completed homework. Specifically, the client should record both the use or application of the strategy and some measure of the goal behaviors. Goldfried and Davison (1976, p. 150) suggest that giving the client a daily log sheet to monitor homework completion has certain demand characteristics that may facilitate the client's written observations. Log sheets can be developed that enable the client to gather data germane to each therapy strategy. For example, a log sheet used to record homework associated with muscle relaxation is presented in Chapter 17, and one used for cognitive restructuring can be found in Chapter 16. The data the client collects during homework completion may be used as part of evaluating the overall effects of the counseling strategy, as described in Chapter 10. The counselor should also arrange for an interview or a telephone follow-up after the client has completed some part of the homework.

Here is an example of a homework assignment the counselor developed with Kathy.

Purpose: to help Kathy think about expressing her feelings to Tammy outside the counselor's office (task 1, a simple situation that Kathy can initiate).

Instructions:

Rationale:
1. "Kathy, I'm going to assign a task for you to do during the week outside our weekly sessions. The homework assignment is really important because it will help you later express your feelings to Tammy. You will keep a 'Daily Log' and check it each time you feel OK *thinking* about telling Tammy about your hurt feelings. At the next session, bring the log so that we can look it over and discuss it. How does that sound?"

"What" to do:
2. "Read over the card that says 'Feelings' on it [cue card; see Figure 12-1]. Then sit back, close your eyes, and think about telling Tammy about your hurt feelings."

"When" to do the behavior:
3. "*Each day,* (1) before school, (2) after school, and (3) before bed, take out the cue card."

Kathy's Cue Card

FEELINGS
"Tammy, I feel hurt when . . . "

Kathy's Homework Log

DAILY LOG					
Time	Mon	Tue	Wed	Thur	Fri
Before school					
During school					
After school					

Figure 12-1. Homework cue card and log

"How often" to do the behavior:
4. "Three times a day for one week."

"Where" the behavior is performed (context):
5. "At home."

"How" the behavior is to be recorded:
6. "Each time you are able to do this and feel OK with it, check this on this 'Daily Log'" (see Figure 12-1).

"Follow-up":
7. "At the end of the week, bring the log in to discuss and to review with me."

In vivo homework in the form of client self-directed practice or independent mastery results in more generalization of behavioral changes, more evidence of coping skills, and enhancement of self-competence levels (Bandura, Jeffery, & Gajdos, 1975). Self-competence, or confidence, is enhanced more by independent practice, because a client is more likely to attribute the stress to his or her own capabilities than to external aids or supports (Bandura et al., p. 142).

☐ MODEL DIALOGUE: THE CASE OF JOAN

Recall from Chapter 9 that one of Joan's three outcome goals was to acquire and utilize various decision-making skills in situations in which she typically relies on the advice of others. In this dialogue we illustrate how these four components of various helping strategies can be used in combination as a decision-making skill training program for you.

First, the counselor gives Joan a **rationale** *about the strategies being used.*
1. *Counselor:* I believe today we can start working on some of the skills involved in making a decision. I think there is a way we could go about doing this that you might find helpful. It involves talking about the skills and practicing the skills in some role plays. It gives you a chance to practice making decisions without having to worry about what happens. As you feel more skillful about making decisions in this way, it will be easier for you to do so on your own. How does this sound to you?
Client: Pretty good. It sounds like it might be fun. We act out things in my English class.

The counselor gives an **overview** *of how they will proceed.*

2. *Counselor:* Well, what we'll do is go over one situation at a time. We'll work on the first one until you feel comfortable with it and then move on.
Client: OK.

The counselor introduces both **symbolic and live modeling** *of the first target response and situation and gives* **instructions** *about what to look for.*
3. *Counselor:* Since there are a couple of skills to work on, let's work on one at a time, and then we can practice putting all the skills together later on. I believe that it might be a good idea if you read over this book, *Deciding,** before our next session. It will give you a good overview of the decision-making skills. Or, if you prefer, you can come in and watch a filmstrip. We'll be starting with how you learn to find all the alternatives in a situation, so perhaps you can pay close attention to that area in the book or the filmstrip. Also, we could go over this today. Let's take a decision about how you spend your time. This time why don't you be your friend, Barbara, and I'll be you? As we do this, notice how many options I can find in this decision. I'll start out. (as Joan) Say, Barbara, what are you planning to do after school today?
Client (as Barbara): Oh, I've got to go to the store for Mom. Want to come along?
4. *Counselor* (as Joan): Well, that's a possibility. Actually, I don't have anything I really have to do today after school. I've been thinking all day about what I'm going to do.
Client (as Barbara): Well, what else do you need to do?
Counselor (as Joan): Well, I guess I should go home and work on my English theme. If I don't, I'll have to do it all tomorrow night. But it's so nice outside, I'd rather either go out with you or just go shopping.
Client (as Barbara): Well, make up your mind.
Counselor (as Joan): Well, I've got three choices—go with you, go shopping alone, or go home and do my English theme. Of course, those are all things I usually do. I also could go play tennis, go down and watch my little brother's baseball game, stay after school and work on the newspaper, or go see that movie the French Club is showing.
Client (as Barbara): You never usually do those things.

---

* Gelatt, H., Varenhorst, B., & Carey, R. *Deciding.* Princeton, N. J.: College Entrance Examination Board, 1972.

Counselor (as Joan): I know, but I'm trying to think of all my possible options.

Client (as Barbara): Well, why stay after school anyway? If you're going to do that, you might as well go home and work on your English theme — that's the safest thing to do.

Counselor (as Joan): Yeah, but I'm not concerned right now about whether my choices are good or bad. I'm just trying to think of all my possible choices.

The counselor stops live modeling and **coaches** *Joan on a way to generate different alternatives in a situation.*

5. *Counselor:* OK, Joan, let's stop here. What I was trying to do was to come up with all the ways I could spend my free time that day, if I were you. The idea of generating options is like brainstorming — the more ideas, the better. And you're only trying to *find* options right now, not evaluate them.

The counselor asks Joan **to review** *what she saw during the modeled demonstration.*

6. *Counselor:* What did you notice about what went on in this role play?

Client: Well, at first you sounded just like me — doing what is easy or necessary. I usually would either just let Barbara talk me into going with her, or I would probably study. When you started listing all those other ideas, it made me realize how automatic my decisions really are.

The counselor asks Joan **to review** *what she is going to try to do during* **her practice** *of this situation.*

7. *Counselor:* OK, let's switch roles now. This time let's give you a chance to practice this for yourself. You be yourself and I'll be Barbara. Could you briefly review what it is you're going to try to do during the practice?

Client: Well, I'm not going to make a snap decision. I'm going to hold out and try to come up with as many options as possible. Also, I'm not going to worry whether the ideas sound good or bad.

The counselor asks Joan **to practice the scene covertly** *at first.*

8. *Counselor:* OK, that's great. Sounds like you've got this well in mind. You know, I think before we practice this in a role play, it might be helpful if you went over this situation first in your imagination. Just put yourself in the situation and rehearse thinking about all your options. Do you understand?

Client: Yeah. How long should I do this?

9. *Counselor:* Spend as much time as you like.
Client: OK. [Closes eyes, pauses for several minutes]

The counselor **cues Joan to report** *what went on during* **covert rehearsal.**

10. *Counselor:* Now, tell me what happened.
Client: Well, I didn't tell Barbara right away I'd go with her. I could feel myself holding out longer. But it was still hard to think of some things I don't usually do after school. I did think of going to the library and reading some magazines.

The counselor **initiates overt practice** *with audiotape recording.*

11. *Counselor:* Well, let's try this in a role-play practice. If it's OK with you, I'll audiotape this and then we can both listen to a playback.
Client: That's fine. I've never heard myself on tape before, so it will be a surprise.

12. *Counselor:* OK, let's begin. I'll be Barbara and you be yourself now. (as Barbara) Hey, Joan, want to go to the store with me after school?
Client: Well, I'm not sure. I was thinking I should go home and study.
Counselor (as Barbara): Do you have a big test?
Client: No, I just didn't want to get behind. You know, though, Barbara, have you ever felt like doing something different?
Counselor (as Barbara): What do you mean?
Client: Well, I was thinking I usually just make snap judgments like this. I usually either go with you or go study. I was trying to think of something different to do.

[Note the counselor's use of the friend's **possible response** *next.]*
Counselor (as Barbara): Don't you like to go places with me?
Client: Sure, I do. But I was only trying to think of some things we could do together that we don't usually do.
Counselor (as Barbara): Like what?
Client: I'm not sure. Can you think of anything?

Joan has just gotten "stuck" in trying to get her friend to think of options. Counselor **stops and asks Joan to report** *what happened.*

13. *Counselor:* What did you just do there?
Client: I guess I sort of tried to get you to come up with the ideas.

The counselor **coaches Joan and** **initiates overt practice** *again.*

14. *Counselor:* Right. And I remember you said earlier that you haven't always been happy with

having Barbara make the decisions. Let's pick up there again. (as Barbara) Well, Joan, what kinds of things could we do together?

Client: Well, we could go to the library and read magazines. Or maybe go play some video games.

Counselor (as Barbara): That's sort of neat.

Client: Or we could go down to the record shop and look at records and tapes.

Counselor (as Barbara): You know, that sounds like fun. I guess we just usually do the same things. Maybe it would be fun to try something different.

The counselor asks Joan **to give herself feedback.**

15. *Counselor:* OK, let's stop here, Joan. What do you think about what just happened?

Client: Well, it seemed to go better than when I tried to imagine it. I realize I did sort of do my same old trick when you stopped me. After I realized it was up to me, it didn't seem too hard to think of some ideas.

The counselor gives **verbal feedback.** *Note* **use of "sandwiching"** — *positive feedback, followed by suggestion, followed by positive feedback. Then the counselor initiates playback feedback.*

16. *Counselor:* You know, you were able to come up with three good ideas of things that you and Barbara don't usually do together. At first you did want to shift the decision to her. That's something to work on. But after that it seemed like you were able to think of some alternatives pretty easily. How about listening to the playback?

Counselor plays back the tape and asks Joan **to assess herself** *from the playback.*

17. *Counselor:* What did you notice from the playback that you liked about this practice?

Client: Well, I seemed pretty persistent. I wasn't too put off by your comments, and I didn't make a snap judgment.

Note that the counselor **reinforces Joan's own positive assessment.**

18. *Counselor:* That's right. Even by the end of our practice you had successfully managed not to make an automatic decision.

The counselor assesses the extent to which the scene has been **practiced sufficiently.**

19. *Counselor:* What kinds of feelings did you have during this role play?

Client: I felt pretty comfortable. It wasn't as hard as I thought.

The counselor points out a way in which the target response might need more work and **initiates another practice** *of the same scene.*

20. *Counselor:* You seem pretty comfortable. I think the main area where you got bogged down was just getting started. Once you got past that point, you really got going. How would you feel about practicing a similar situation again?

Client: I think that would be good.

During the second practice, the counselor instructs Joan **to direct herself** *during practice* **(withdraws coaching).**

21. *Counselor:* OK, let's go over it again. This time try to direct yourself. If you feel like you're getting stuck, stop and talk yourself through the problem. I'll keep a low profile now.

After the second practice, the counselor **encourages** *Joan to direct herself and* **initiates playback feedback.**

22. *Counselor:* OK, let's stop. I think it would be a good idea for you to hear the playback. That practice really went smoothly and you didn't need much help from me.

Client: You know, this is sort of fun. Let's hear the tape.

The counselor plays the tape and **points out the way Joan was able to get herself out of being "stuck."**

23. *Counselor:* Did you notice the way you stopped and got yourself back on the track?

Client: Yeah. I was also able to come up with more ideas that time.

The counselor initiates possible in vivo **homework.**

24. *Counselor:* Right I'm wondering if this situation is something that you could initiate with Barbara this week?

Client: Sure. We do a lot of things together after school at least a couple of days a week.

The counselor provides a **rationale for the homework.**

25. *Counselor:* OK, I'd like to give you a homework assignment. It will be very similar to what we did today, only you'll be carrying it out with Barbara. You'll initiate a conversation with Barbara where you discuss different ways you could spend your time. You can record these on a daily log sheet and write down the number of ideas you've found during the discussion. Next, we'll discuss your log sheet for each day. The homework assignment will help you become more skillful in making decisions. How does this sound to you?

Client: OK. What exactly will I do?

In responses 26 and 27, the counselor gives **instructions** *about homework and specifies* **what** *and* **how much** *Joan is to do.*

26. *Counselor:* Well, I'd like you to initiate a situation with Barbara where you try to discuss different ways you could spend your time. Don't worry about actually deciding what to do. Your main goal is to come up with as many alternatives as possible—let's say at least three options. Does that sound reasonable to you?
Client: Sure. We did that today.

27. *Counselor:* Right. I'll write this down for you on this card—"To initiate a conversation with Barbara in which I identify at least three different ways we could spend our after-school time together."

*Counselor and client work out **cue cards** to help Joan carry out the homework successfully.*

28. *Counselor:* Now, maybe we could list some guidelines for you that we discussed today to help you carry out the homework. We'll call them cue cards—just like they use in the movies to help them remember. What cues would help you carry this out?
Client: Well, the one thing would be for me to come up with some ideas rather than asking Barbara.

29. *Counselor:* OK, I'll put down here—"I'll find ideas." What else?
Client: Mm [thinking]

30. *Counselor:* What about coming up with as many ideas as possible without evaluating them for now.
Client: Yes. You mean, don't worry if the idea is good or bad.

31. *Counselor:* Right. So your second cue can be "Think of many ideas. Don't evaluate now."

*The counselor instructs Joan in **how to record use of the homework** during the week, using log sheets.*

32. *Counselor:* OK, Joan. On these daily record sheets here, take a blank sheet for each day of the week. Every time you complete this assignment, make a check. Also, write the number of ideas *you* found during the discussion. Does that seem clear?
Client: Yes. Do I bring it back?

*The counselor initiates **a follow-up.***

33. *Counselor:* Yes. Bring it with you next week at this time and we can see how your assignment worked out. Also, feel free to call me and report on your progress, all right? Next week, we'll go over the next situation on our list that we put together.
Client: OK, I'll probably call or stop in later on this week.

LEARNING ACTIVITY #33: STRATEGY IMPLEMENTATION

This activity consists of examples of counselor responses associated with the four components of strategy implementation for the case of John (from Chapter 7). Identify in writing which of the four components of strategy implementation (rationale, modeling, rehearsal, homework) is represented by each response. Feedback follows.

1. "John, your thinking gets in the way of what you're doing at work. It's possible to learn to control such thinking and to make it less interfering. You can control your thinking by first becoming aware of when you are producing negative self-statements and by identifying the negative self-talk. You can replace your negative self-talk with coping statements."

2. "I'm going to show you some coping statements you can use to replace your negative statements. Then, I'll show you how I replace the negative statements with positive coping statements."

3. "Now I'd like you to imagine that you are experiencing negative self-talk. Then imagine that you are replacing this talk with positive coping statements."

4. "Replacing your negative self-talk with positive coping statements can influence your attitude and how you feel about your job responsibilities. Positive coping statements can create positive attitudes and feelings about your work."

5. "Think of the negative self-talk or statements and then try to replace it with the three positive coping statements we developed."

6. "During this week I'd like you to replace your negative self-talk with positive coping statements every time you start thinking these thoughts throughout the day."

7. "At the end of the first day, call me and we can see how you are working with this procedure."

□ WRITTEN TREATMENT CONTRACTS

The four elements of strategy implementation described in the previous sections of this chapter imply a contract between the therapist and the client. The therapist may wish to use an explicit or written treatment contract with some clients. The written contract can facilitate the therapeutic process and decrease ambiguity about the therapeutic relationship. A written treatment contract is an agreement between the therapist and the client. Contracts can be made with an individual client, a couple, or an entire family. Treatment contracts can have two forms: (1) contingency contract or (2) informational contract. A contingency contract is usually *quid pro quo,* in which bonuses are given for performing behaviors agreed to in the contract or sanctions are imposed on an individual for failure to perform behaviors as specified in the contract (Framer & Sanders, 1980; Stuart, 1971; Taylor, Pfenninger, & Candelaria, 1980; Wysocki, Hall, Iwata, & Riordan, 1979). The form of contract we present in this section is the informational treatment contract.

The informational contract has five elements: (1) information about the treatment strategies, (2) statements about goal (outcome) expectations, (3) client intention statements stipulating agreement to participate fully in a key aspect of the treatment, (4) duration (weeks or sessions) of the contract, and (5) an informed consent statement (Seidner & Kirschenbaum, 1980). A treatment contract has several advantages (Goodyear & Bradley, 1980, pp. 513–514). The contract reduces game playing because client and therapist are working toward clearly stated goal(s). The contract provides a standard for evaluating progress toward the outcome goal. It protects the client and therapist by specifying parameters of the treatment relationship. Finally, the contracting process provides a facilitative means for client self-exploration.

□ MODEL TREATMENT CONTRACT: THE CASE OF JOAN

We illustrate a treatment contract for Joan. Recall the defined goals and the proposed treatments for Joan. In Chapter 9, we described Joan's overall goals for therapy. Four subgoals were specified for the first terminal outcome goal. Suppose we design a treatment contract for subgoal 1 of the first goal. This subgoal was to decrease Joan's anxiety associated with anticipation of failure in math class and rejection by parents. The level for the goal was to reduce the self-ratings of intensity from about 70 to 50 on a 100-point scale during the next two weeks. In Chapter 9, deep muscle relaxation (Chapter 17) and stress inoculation (Chapter 16) were mentioned as the two treatment strategies used to help Joan reduce her anxiety (subgoal 1).

Elements of a Treatment Contract for Joan

We model the five elements of the contract with the case of Joan. Figure 12-2 illustrates the five elements of a treatment contract. The first element is to provide information about the two treatment strategies used with Joan: muscle relaxation and stress inoculation.

Information about treatment strategies. Two strategies are listed in the contract (Figure 12-2). The counselor would describe *muscle relaxation* to Joan in the interview, somewhat as follows:

"This process, if you practice it regularly, can help you become relaxed. The relaxation benefits can help you recognize better when you feel tension in your body because of stress or anxiety. This procedure involves learning to tense and relax 16 different muscle groups in your body. By doing this, you can contrast the difference between tenseness and relaxation. This will help you to recognize tension so you can instruct yourself to relax. Muscle relaxation is a skill, and the learning process will be gradual and will require regular practice."

Stress inoculation might be explained like this:

"You find yourself confronted with situations in which your stress gets out of hand. It is difficult to manage your anxiety when you are confronted with these stressful situations. Stress inoculation can help you learn to cope with these situations and can help inoculate you when you are in these situations so the anxiety does not overwhelm you. I will help you understand the nature of your anxious feelings. Next, you will learn some ways to manage

TREATMENT CONTRACT

Treatment strategies: Muscle relaxation and stress inoculation

Goal: My self-ratings of anxiety intensity on a 0-to-100-point scale will decrease from 70 to 50 points in math class and in situations with my parents.

Intention statements: Muscle relaxation — I will practice tensing and relaxing all 16 muscle groups at home once after getting up in the morning and once after school or before dinner each day.

  Stress inoculation — I will use the coping statements developed by the counselor and me for my math class and when confronted with situations with my parents. I will also use relaxation techniques and coping statements every time I am confronted with a stressful situation.

Duration of treatment: Treatment procedures will be used at least six weeks but no longer than ten weeks.

Informed consent: I agree that the counselor has explained the nature and purpose of muscle relaxation and stress inoculation and other alternative treatment options available to me. I understand the reasonable benefits and the potential disadvantages involved as well as the estimated length of these procedures. I understand that I am free to discontinue participation in these procedures at any time.

_____   _____

Signature of client   Signature of counselor

_____

Date   Date

Figure 12-2. Sample treatment contract

your anxious feelings and to cope with these two stressful situations."

Goal statement. The counselor might say to Joan:

"Your self-ratings of anxiety intensity on a 0-to-100 point scale will decrease from about 70 to 50 in math class and in situations with your parents."

Client intention statements. The next portion of the contract consists of client intention statements indicating agreement to participate fully in a key aspect of the treatment. The contract in Figure 12-2 shows intention statements for the two treatment strategies (muscle relaxation and stress inoculation).

Information about duration. The next section of the contract specifies the duration of the terms of the contract:

You understand that the duration of the contract will be at least six weeks and not to exceed ten weeks. During the first two weeks, we will work on muscle relaxation treatment. Stress inoculation will be used during the next four weeks. It is important for you to continue to practice muscle relaxation exercises at home twice daily while using stress inoculation.

Informed consent statement. One final element of the contract is an informed consent paragraph and

a place for the date and the client's and counselor's signatures, as shown in Figure 12-2.

☐ SUMMARY

Most counseling strategies or action plans involve similar components. The use of any strategy should be prefaced by a rationale about the procedure. Modeling, rehearsal, feedback, and homework tasks are important ingredients in any therapeutic change program. In addition, the four elements described in this chapter are the components used in all skill-building programs. For example, assertion training consists of modeling assertive skills, practicing assertive skills in simulated conditions with feedback, and practicing these responses in the actual environment. Written treatment contracts can also facilitate client change and reduce ambiguity about the action phase of counseling. In the following chapters, which present various treatment strategies, you will discover the importance of these components for strategy implementation.

  As Lazarus (1981) cautions, however, the effectiveness of a particular intervention strategy depends not only on the components of the strategy but also on the skill of the therapist. Lazarus states:

I have been impressed by the fact that skillful therapists, especially great psychotherapeutic artists, share certain features regardless of their backgrounds, school affiliations, or professional identifications. They are responsible and flexible individuals with a high degree of respect for people. They are essentially nonjudgmental and firmly committed to the view that infringement on the rights and satisfactions of others is to be strongly discouraged. They will not compromise human interests, values, and dignity. . . . They bring warmth, wit, and wisdom to the therapeutic situation, and, when appropriate, they introduce humor and fun. They seem to have an endless store of relevant anecdotes and narratives. They are good role models (they practice what they preach) and are authentic, congruent, and willing to self-disclose. . . . The final orchestration of successful therapy depends on what techniques are selected, how they are implemented, and by whom they are delivered. As surgeons are apt to point out, it is the person behind the scalpel who can wield it as an instrument of destruction or of healing. In psychotherapy, it is even more difficult to separate the specific technique from the person who administers it [pp. 155–156].

■

POSTEVALUATION

PART ONE

Objective One asks you to take a simulated client case and describe how you would apply the four common elements of strategy implementation (rationale, modeling, rehearsal, homework) with this client.

As you may recall with our client Mr. Brown (from Chapter 7), one of his desired counseling goals was to be able to initiate social contacts with his boss. Although Mr. Brown had acquired some reasonably useful social skills, he was hesitant to initiate requests with his boss. In other words, his social skills were inhibited in his boss's presence. Mr. Brown stated that he felt awkward about initiating a social contact with his boss, although he did initiate such contacts with other people apparently quite successfully and without any discomfort. On the basis of Mr. Brown's desired goal, as well as this description, describe how you would use the four components of strategy implementation to help Mr. Brown demonstrate social skills with his boss. Feedback follows the Postevaluation.

PART TWO

Objective Two asks you to demonstrate the four components of strategy implementation in a skill-building program. Here's how you might do this:

1. Ask a partner to select a skill or skills he or she would like to learn. The person might wish to learn to give compliments to others, to initiate a conversation with strangers, or to give constructive feedback, for example.
2. Use modeling, rehearsal, and homework to teach the person the skill. Provide a rationale to the person about this process.
3. Tape your teaching and rate it using the Checklist for Strategy Implementation, or have an observer sit in and observe you. This checklist can be found at the end of the chapter.

PART THREE

For the third objective of this chapter, you are to design a written contract, given a hypothetical client case. Again use the case of Mr. Brown (from Chapter 7). Using the description in Part One of the postevaluation and the description of a skills training program to use with him in Part One of the feedback, design a treatment contract that you could use in conjunction with this skills training program. (Assume that you will be working with him for six to ten weeks.) Make sure your contract includes a description of the five components:

1. Treatment strategies
2. Goal
3. Intention statement
4. Duration of the skills training program
5. Informed consent statement

Feedback follows the Postevaluation.

CHECKLIST FOR STRATEGY IMPLEMENTATION

Check to see which of the following steps the counselor used.

I. Rationale for treatment

_____ 1. Did the counselor provide a rationale to the client about the strategy?

_____ 2. Did the counselor provide an overview of the strategy?

_____ 3. Did the counselor obtain the client's willingness to try the strategy?

II. Modeling of goal behaviors

_____ 4. Were instructions about what to look for in the modeled demonstration given to the client?

(continued)

_____ 5. Did the model demonstrate the goal behaviors in a coping manner?

_____ 6. Was the modeled demonstration presented in a series of sequential scenarios?

_____ 7. Did the client review or summarize the goal behaviors after the modeled demonstration?

III. Rehearsal of goal behaviors

_____ 8. Did the counselor ask the client to review the target responses before the practice attempts?

_____ 9. Did the client engage in:
_____ Covert rehearsal
_____ Overt rehearsal
_____ Both

_____ 10. During initial rehearsal attempts, did the counselor provide:
_____ Coaching
_____ Induction aids
_____ Both

_____ 11. Were the amount of coaching and the number of induction aids decreased with successive practice attempts?

_____ 12. Did the client engage in self-directed practice of each goal behavior?

_____ 13. Was each practice attempt covered satisfactorily before moving on to another goal behavior? (Check which criteria were used in this decision.)
_____ The decision to move on was a joint one (counselor and client)
_____ The client was able to enact the scene without feeling anxious
_____ The client was able to demonstrate the target responses, as evidenced by demeanor and words
_____ The client's words and actions during the scene would seem realistic to an objective onlooker

_____ 14. Did the counselor and client go over or arrange for a taped playback of the rehearsal?

_____ 15. Did the counselor provide feedback to the client about the rehearsal? (Check if the counselor's feedback included these elements.)
_____ Counselor's feedback contained a positive reinforcer statement, a suggestion for improvement, and another positive reinforcer
_____ Counselor encouraged each successive rehearsal attempt

IV. Homework and transfer of training

_____ 16. After successful practices in the interview, did the counselor assign rehearsal homework in the client's environment?

_____ 17. Did the homework assignment include (check any that apply):
_____ Situations the client could easily initiate
_____ Graduated tasks in which the client could gradually demonstrate the target response
_____ A rationale for the task
_____ Specification of what the client was to do
_____ Specification of when the task would be performed
_____ Specification of where the task would be performed
_____ Specification of how much or how often the client would perform or engage in the task

_____ 18. Was the client given self- or other-directed assistance in carrying out the homework through:
_____ Written cue cards
_____ A trained counselor's aide

_____ 19. Did the counselor instruct the client to make written self-recordings (how to record) of both the strategy (homework) and the goal behaviors?

_____ 20. Did the counselor arrange for a face to face or telephone follow-up after the client's completion of some of the homework?

☐ SUGGESTED READINGS

Bandura, A., & Jeffery, R. W. (1973). Roles of symbolic coding and rehearsal processes in observational learning. *Journal of Personality and Social Psychology, 26,* 122–130.

Bourque, P., & Ladouceur, R. (1980). An investigation of various performance-based treatments with acrophobics.

Behaviour Research and Therapy, 18, 161–170.

Coe, W. C. (1980). Expectation, hypnosis, and suggestion methods. In F. H. Kanfer & A. P. Goldstein (Eds.), *Helping people change* (2nd ed.). New York: Pergamon Press.

Flowers, J. V., & Booraem, C. D. (1980). Simulation and role-playing methods. In F. A. Kanfer & A. P. Goldstein

(Eds.), *Helping people change (2nd ed.)*. New York: Pergamon Press.

Goldfried, M. R., & Davison, G. C. (1976). *Clinical behavior therapy*. New York: Holt, Rinehart and Winston. Chapter 7, "Behavior Rehearsal."

Goodyear, R. K., & Bradley, F. O. (1980). The helping process as contractual. *Personnel and Guidance Journal, 58,* 512–515.

Kazdin, A. E. (1982). The separate and combined effects of covert and overt rehearsal in developing assertive behavior. *Behaviour Research and Therapy, 20,* 17–25.

Kazdin, A. E., & Krouse, R. (1983). The impact of variations in treatment rationales on expectations for therapeutic change. *Behavior Therapy, 14,* 657–671.

Kazdin, A. E., & Mascitelli, S. (1982a). Behavioral rehearsal, self-instructions, and homework practice in developing assertiveness. *Behavior Therapy, 13,* 346–360.

Kazdin, A. E., & Mascitelli, S. (1982b). Covert and overt rehearsal and homework practice in developing assertiveness. *Journal of Consulting and Clinical Psychology, 50,* 250–258.

Martin, G. A., & Worthington, E. L. (1982). Behavioral homework. In M. Hersen, R. M. Eisler, & P. M. Miller (Eds.), *Progress in behavior modification* (Vol. 13). New York: Academic Press.

Perry, M. A., & Furukawa, M. J. (1980). Modeling methods. In F. H. Kanfer & A. P. Goldstein (Eds.), *Helping people change (2nd ed.)*. New York: Pergamon Press.

Sarason, I. G., & Sarason, B. R. (1981). Teaching cognitive and social skills to high school students. *Journal of Consulting and Clinical Psychology, 49,* 908–918.

Shelton, J. L., & Levy, R. L. (1981). *Behavioral assignments and treatment compliance*. Champaign, IL: Research Press.

Stuart, R. B. (1971). Behavioral contracting within the families of delinquents. *Journal of Behavior Therapy and Experimental Psychiatry, 2,* 1–11.

FEEDBACK: POSTEVALUATION

PART ONE

1. *Rationale for treatment*

   You might explain to Mr. Brown that this strategy will help him practice the skills he needs in approaching his boss in low-threat situations. You can tell him this involves seeing someone else (like yourself) demonstrate these skills and then having him practice them—first in the interview and then actually with the boss. You might emphasize that this method can help him gain confidence in the skills he needs to approach his boss.

2. *Modeling*

   Beginning with the easiest goal behavior (social skill), you or someone else could model this for Mr.

Brown, taking his part while he assumes the role of his boss. You would instruct him about what to look for before the demonstration—which would be portrayed in a coping manner. After the modeled presentation, you would ask Mr. Brown to summarize what he saw.

3. *Rehearsal*

   Beginning with the easiest goal behavior, you would use a role play to help Mr. Brown practice this. The enactment of this scene should be as similar to Mr. Brown's actual environment as possible, in order to help Mr. Brown see how his behavior might affect others and to give him practice under conditions that will approximate those he will find outside counseling. You might ask Mr. Brown to practice the response covertly (in his head) at first, especially if he seems nervous about going over it with you. The reason is to reduce some of his concern about having you observe this initial performance. Gradually, though, you would ask Mr. Brown to shift into an overt rehearsal or an actual enactment of the response. If Mr. Brown tends to get stuck during the scene, you can prompt him or use cue cards; or you can go back to the previous scene. Consistent trouble in Mr. Brown's rehearsals may call for more coaching or for some introduction of induction aids, such as joint practice. You would make sure that each response was rehearsed satisfactorily before going on to another one. The decision to move on should be made jointly. Mr. Brown should be able to practice the response without feeling anxious and also be able to demonstrate the target response adequately before moving on. After each practice attempt, you should provide feedback that will help Mr. Brown assess his prior performance. First, you may want to give Mr. Brown an opportunity to assess his own practice. Periodically, a taped playback of the practice would be helpful to provide objective feedback. As the counselor, you want to be sure to encourage Mr. Brown for small indications of improvement as well as to give suggestions for the next practice. Gradually, you should encourage Mr. Brown to direct his own practice attempts and to assess and reinforce himself for a successful rehearsal.

4. *Homework*

   Finally, you should assign homework to Mr. Brown that will help him practice the target re-

(continued)

sponse outside the sessions. The homework, at first, may consist simply of mental rehearsal. Gradually, Mr. Brown might be assigned tasks in which he initiates a simple social contact with his boss, such as going on a coffee break. The nature of the tasks can be changed as Mr. Brown successfully and comfortably completes requisite tasks. Cue cards might be given to Mr. Brown to help him remember any guidelines for carrying out the homework. Mr. Brown should be instructed to observe his performance while carrying out the homework and to monitor his completion of the homework on log sheets. You should follow up the homework assignments with a face-to-face or telephone check-in.

PART TWO

Use the Checklist for Strategy Implementation on pages 324–325 as a guide to assess your teaching of a skill to a partner.

PART THREE

Here is a sample treatment contract for Mr. Brown:

Treatment strategy: Skills training (social skills)

Goal: To initiate social contacts with my boss (at least one a week).

Intention statements: I understand that I will be practicing situations involving social contacts with my boss with the counselor initially and later on by myself.

Duration of treatment: The skills training program will last between six and ten weeks.

Informed consent: I agree that the counselor has explained to me the nature and purpose of the skills training program we will be using as well as alternative treatment options available. I understand the reasonable benefits and potential disadvantages associated with this program and its expected length. I also understand that I am free to discontinue participation at any time.

_____   _____
Signature of client   Signature of counselor

_____   _____
Date   Date

SYMBOLIC MODELING, SELF-AS-A-MODEL, AND PARTICIPANT MODELING

THIRTEEN

Picture the following series of events. A young girl is asked what she wants to be when she grows up. Her reply: "A doctor, just like my mom." Think of a child who points a toy gun and says "Bang, bang, you're dead" after watching a police program on television. Think of people flocking to stores to buy clothes that reflect the "outdoor" or "leisure look," or "warm-up suit look," which has been described and featured in some magazines. All these events are examples of a process called imitation, copying, mimicry, vicarious learning, identification, observational learning, or modeling. Perry and Furukawa (1980, p. 131) define modeling as "the process of observational learning in which the behavior of an individual or a group, the model, acts as a stimulus for the thoughts, attitudes, or behaviors on the part of another individual who observes the model's performance."

There are several ways people can learn through modeling. A person can acquire new behaviors from live or symbolic modeling. Modeling can help a person perform an already acquired behavior in more appropriate ways or at more desirable times. Modeling can also extinguish client fears. Modeling procedures have been used to help clients acquire social skills, modify verbal behavior, acquire emotional responses, modify study behaviors, modify phobic responses, and treat drug addiction (Perry & Furukawa, 1980). According to Rachman (1972, p. 393), the clinical significance of modeling lies in the strength of the procedure to eliminate fearful and undesired behavior and to promote acquisition of desired responses.

In this chapter, we present three modeling procedures: symbolic modeling, self-as-a-model, and participant modeling. The steps we present for each procedure should be viewed only as guidelines for application. The creative variation of or departure from a particular procedure is a decision based on the counselor, the client, the nature of the assessed concern or problem, the goals for counseling, and the setting in which the problem behavior occurs.

☐ OBJECTIVES

1. Develop and try out a script for one symbolic model with a client or a group of clients of your choice. After completing the script, evaluate it on the Checklist for Developing Symbolic Models at the end of the chapter.
2. Given a case description of a client and a counseling goal, describe how the five components of the self-as-a-model strategy could be used with this client.
3. Demonstrate at least 13 out of 16 steps of the self-as-a-model strategy in a role-play interview with a client.
4. Describe how you would apply the four components of participant modeling in a simulated client case.
5. Demonstrate at least 14 out of 17 steps associated with participant modeling with a role-play client.

☐ SYMBOLIC MODELING

In symbolic modeling, the model is presented through written materials, audio- or videotapes, films, or slide tapes. Symbolic models can be developed for an individual client or can be standardized for a group of clients. For example, M. L. Russell (1974) used cartoon characters as models to teach decision-making skills to children. These characters were presented in a self-contained set of written materials and a cassette audiotape. Counselors may find that developing a standardized model is more cost-effective because it can reach a greater number of clients. For instance, a school counselor who sees many students with deficits in information-seeking skills could develop one tape that could be used by many of these students.

In this section, we present some suggestions for developing self-instructional symbolic modeling procedures. A self-instructional model contains demonstrations of the target behavior, opportunities for client practice, and feedback. In developing a self-instructional symbolic modeling procedure, the counselor will have to consider the following elements: the characteristics of the consumers who will use the model; the goal behaviors to be modeled or demonstrated; the media to be used; the content of the script; and the field testing of the model. These five steps are summarized in the Checklist for Developing Symbolic Models at the end of the chapter.

Characteristics of Consumers

The first consideration in developing a symbolic model is to determine the characteristics of the people for whom the model is designed. For example, the age, sex, cultural practices, racial characteristics, and problems of the people who will use the procedure should be assessed. For example, to determine problem situations, Sarason and Sarason (1981) conducted extensive interviews to assess what social skills are needed for low-achieving high school students. The authors interviewed teachers, counselors, students attending the school, former students who had dropped out, and employers who typically hired the students (Sarason & Sarason, 1981, p. 910).

The characteristics of the symbolic model should be similar to those of the people for whom the procedure is designed, as described in Chapter 12. The counselor should also consider the degree of variation that may exist in these characteristics among the users of the symbolic model. Including several persons as models (using multiple models) can make a symbolic model more useful for a variety of clients. For example, Sarason and Sarason's models were high school students who "represented several racial/ethnic groups—Western European, Mexican-American, Filipino, and black" (1981, p. 911). Gilbert, Johnson, Spillar, McCallum, Silverstein, & Rosenbloom (1982) used as peer models two children aged 6 and 8—a Black male and White female—who were trained for self-injection of insulin. One model may be satisfactory in some situations. Peterson and Shigetomi (1981) presented a film, *Ethan Has an Operation* (produced by Melamed & Siegel, 1975), that showed a 7-year-old White male as a model. Also, an 8-year-old Caucasian boy was used as a coping and a mastery model with children who were pedodontic patients (Klorman, Hilpert, Michael, LaGana, & Sveen, 1980).

In some instances, former clients may serve as appropriate symbolic models on audio- and videotapes. Reeder and Kunce (1976) used ex-addict paraprofessional staff members and "advanced" residents of a drug-abuse treatment program as the models for their six video-model scenarios. The models in each scenario displayed a coping attitude while performing the various skills required for achieving the goal behaviors associated with one of six problem areas. For example:

The model was initially shown as being pessimistic and ineffective in the given problem area. The model would then reflect upon his problem and discuss it with a peer or staff member. Following reflection and discussion, the model would try out new problem-solving behaviors. As the scenarios progressed, the model would progressively display more independence in solving problems, becoming less dependent upon the advice of the others [p. 561].

Goal Behaviors to Be Modeled

The goal behavior, or what is to be modeled, should be specified. A counselor can develop a series of symbolic models to focus on different behaviors, or a complicated pattern of behavior can be divided into less complex skills. For instance, Reeder and Kunce (1976) developed scenarios for their video models for six problem areas: accepting help from others, capitalizing on street skills, job interviewing, employer relations, free-time management, and new lifestyle adjustment. Craigie and Ross (1980) employed actors who modeled appropriate and inappropriate target behaviors for pretherapy training programs to encourage alcohol detoxification patients to seek treatment. Webster-Stratton (1981a, 1981b) used videotaped vignettes of parent models who displayed appropriate parent behaviors (nurturant, playful) and inappropriate behaviors (rigid and controlling) to train mothers. Gilbert et al. (1982) used videotaped models who gave information about self-injection of insulin, described feelings about the procedure, modeled appropriate coping statements, and used self-instructions and self-praise statements (p. 189). Gresham and Nagle (1980) had female and male 9- and 10-year-olds model on videotape such social skills as participation, cooperation, communication, friendship making, and initiating and receiving positive and negative peer interaction. Finally, Sarason and Sarason (1981) used models who displayed social and cognitive skills for the following situations: "job interview, resisting peer pressure, asking for help in school, asking questions in class, getting along with the boss, dealing with frustration on the job, cutting class, asking for help at work, and getting along with parents" (p. 911).

Whether one model or a series of models is developed, the counselor should structure the model around three questions: What behaviors are to be acquired? Should these behaviors or activities be divided into a sequence of less complex skills? How should the sequence of skills be arranged?

Media

In an attempt to help you acquire counseling skills, we have presented written symbolic models throughout the book in the form of modeled examples, practice exercises, and feedback. Any of these modeled examples could be filmed, audio- or videotaped, or presented on slide tape. The choice of the medium will depend on where, with whom, and how symbolic modeling will be used. Written, filmed, audiotaped, and videotaped symbolic models can be checked out for the client and used independently in a school, in an agency, or at home. We have found that audiotaped models (cassettes) are economical and extremely versatile. However, in some instances, audiotapes may not be as effective because they are not visual. Written models can serve as a bibliotherapeutic procedure (reading) by portraying a person or situation similar to the client and the desired goal (Nye, 1973). However, a self-instructional written symbolic model differs from traditional bibliotherapy procedures by including additional components of self-directed practice and feedback. In other words, self-instructional symbolic models can be administered by the client without therapist contact (Glasgow & Rosen, 1978, 1979).

Content of the Presentation

Regardless of the medium used to portray the modeled presentation, the counselor should develop a script to reflect the content of the modeling presentations. The script should include five parts: instructions, modeling, practice, feedback, and a summarization.

Instructions. Instructions should be included for each behavior or sequence of behaviors to be demonstrated. Brief but explicit and detailed instructions presented before the model will help the client identify the necessary components of the modeled display (McGuire, Thelen, & Amolsch, 1975). Instructions provide a rationale for the modeling and cues to facilitate attention to the model. The instructions can also describe the type of model portrayed, such as "The person you are going to see or hear is similar to yourself."

Modeling. The next part of the script should include a description of the behavior or activity to be modeled and possible dialogues of the model engaging in the goal behavior or activity. This part of the script should present complex patterns of behavior in planned sequences of skills.

Practice. The effects of modeling are likely to be greater when presentation of the modeled behavior is followed by opportunities to practice. In symbolic modeling, there should be opportunities for clients to practice what they have just read, heard, or seen the model do.

Feedback. After the client has been instructed to practice and sufficient time is allowed, feedback in the form of a description of the behavior or activity should be included. The client should be instructed to repeat the modeling and practice portions again if the feedback indicates some trouble spots.

Summarization. At the conclusion of a particular scenario or series, the script should include a summary of what has been modeled and the importance for the client of acquiring these behaviors.

Field Testing of the Model

It is a good idea to check out the script before you actually construct the symbolic model from it. You can field-test the script with some colleagues or some people from the target or client group. The language, the sequencing, the model, practice time, and feedback should be examined by the potential consumer before the final symbolic model is designated as ready for use. If at all possible, a pilot program should be designed for the initial use of the symbolic model. For example, M. L. Russell and C. E. Thoresen (1976) validated a written symbolic model on decision-making skills for children by comparing the performance of children who completed the workbook (the model) with children who did not (controls). The resulting data enabled the authors to validate the effectiveness of their written model for teaching decision-making skills to children. As another example, Sarason and Sarason (1981) conducted a series of pilot studies after identifying social skills in a variety of situations. For example, students critiqued the role-play scripts, and the language was changed or the situation was altered to enhance credibility of the scene and script. Data from the field testing can be used to make any necessary revisions before the finished product is used with a client.

☐ SELF-AS-A-MODEL

The self-as-a-model procedure uses the client as the model. The procedure as we present it in this chapter has been developed primarily by Hosford. Hosford and de Visser (1974) have described self-modeling as a procedure in which the client sees himself or herself as the model—performing the goal behavior in the desired manner. The client also practices with a tape. Successful practices are rewarded and errors are corrected. Note that this procedure involves not only modeling but also practice and feedback.

Why have the client serve as the model? As we mentioned in Chapter 12, the literature indicates that such model characteristics as prestige, status, age, sex, and ethnic identification have differential influence on clients (Bandura, 1969, 1971a). For some people, observing another person—even one with similar characteristics—may produce negative reactions (McDonald, 1973). Some people may attend and listen better when they see or hear themselves on a tape or in a movie (Hosford, Moss, & Morrell, 1976). For example, when we perform in front of a video camera or a tape recorder, we have to admit there is a little exhibitionism and "ham" in each of us.

LEARNING ACTIVITY #34: SYMBOLIC MODELING

You are working with a Caucasian client in her late twenties who is employed as a salesperson in a local department store. The client's goal at this point is to lose 20 pounds. The client has previously tried unsuccessfully to lose weight and is now seeking your assistance. One approach you believe might help the client is to portray someone like herself who models some weight reduction procedures. You decide to select an appropriate person as the model and use this person in an audiotaped symbolic model of weight reduction procedures.

1. Describe the type of model you would select, including age, sex, race, a coping or mastery model, and concerns presented by the model.
2. Develop an outline for a script you would use for the audiotaped model. Include in the script instructions to the client; a description of the model; a brief example of one modeled scenario, perhaps about one weight reduction procedure; an example of a practice opportunity; feedback about the practice; and a summarization of the script. Feedback follows.

FEEDBACK #34: SYMBOLIC MODELING

1. You would probably select a female, Caucasian model in her late twenties. Since your client has tried unsuccessfully to lose weight before, a mastery model may be too discouraging, and a coping model would be preferable. The concern presented by the model would be similar to that of your client—weight reduction. If possible, a model who has overcome a weight problem would be best.

2. After you have developed your script, check it with guideline 4 on the Checklist for Developing Symbolic Models on page 345.

Several studies have explored the effects of self-as-a-model with different populations. Miklich, Chida, and Danker-Brown (1977) used the procedure to promote bedmaking for hospitalized children. Hosford (1980) found self-as-a-model a good instructional procedure for training counselors. Davis (1979) used the strategy to decrease problem behavior of three children in an elementary school setting. Finally, Dowrick and Dove (1980) used self-modeling to improve the swimming performance of children with spina bifida.

We have adopted five steps associated with the self-as-a-model procedure from Hosford and de Visser (1974). These five components, which are illustrated in the Interview Checklist for Self-as-a-Model at the end of the chapter, are the following:

1. Rationale about the strategy
2. Recording the desired behavior on tape
3. Editing the tape
4. Demonstrating with the edited tape
5. Homework: client self-observation and practice

Treatment Rationale

After the client and counselor have reviewed the problem behaviors and the goal behaviors for counseling, the counselor presents a treatment rationale for the self-as-a-model procedure to the client. The counselor might say something like this:

"The procedure we are going to use is based on the idea that people learn new habits or skills by observing other people in various situations. [reason] The way this is done is that people watch other people doing things or they observe a film or tape of people doing things. What we are going to do is vary this procedure a little by having you observe yourself rather than someone else. The way we can do this is to videotape [or audiotape] your desired behavior, and then you can see [hear] yourself on the tape performing the behavior. After that, you will practice the behavior that you saw [heard] on the tape, and I will give you feedback about your practice performance. I think that seeing yourself perform and practice these behaviors will help you acquire these skills. [overview] How does this sound to you?" [client's willingness]

Of course, this is only one version of the rationale for the self-as-a-model procedure a counselor might use. A counselor could add "Seeing yourself perform these behaviors will give you confidence in acquiring these skills." This statement emphasizes the cognitive component of the self-as-a-model strategy: by using oneself as the model, one sees oneself coping with a formerly anxiety-arousing or difficult situation.

Recording the Desired Behaviors

The desired goal behaviors are recorded on audio- or videotape first. For example, one particular client may need to acquire several assertion skills, such as expression of personal opinions using a firm and strong voice tone, delivery of opinions without errors in speech, and delivery of the assertive message without response latency (within five seconds after the other person's message). For this example, the counselor and client might start with voice tone and record the client expressing opinions to another person in a firm, strong voice. The counselor might have to coach the client so that at least some portion of the taped message reflects this desired response. The tape should be long enough that the client will later be able to hear himself or herself expressing opinions in a firm voice throughout several verbal exchanges with the other person. The counselor might have to spend a great deal of time staging the recording sessions in order to obtain tapes of the client's goal behavior. A dry run might be helpful before the actual tape is made.

Sometimes the counselor can instruct clients to obtain recordings of their behavior *in vivo*. For example, clients who stutter could be asked to audiotape their interactions with others during designated times of the week. We have also suggested such recordings to people who felt incompetent in talking with those of the other sex. The advantage of *in vivo* recordings is that examples of the client's actual behavior in real-life situations are obtained. However, it is not always possible or desirable to do this, particularly if the client's baseline level of performing the desired skill is very low. Whether tapes are made *in vivo* or in the session, the recording is usually repeated until a sample of the desired behavior is obtained.

Editing the Tape

Next, the counselor will edit the audio- or videotape recordings so that the client will see or hear *only* the appropriate (goal) behavior. Hosford et al. (1976) recommend that the "inappropriate" behaviors be deleted from the tape, leaving a tape of only the desired responses. The purpose in editing out the inappropriate behaviors is to provide the client with a positive, or self-enhancing, model. It is analogous to weeding out the dandelions in a garden and leaving the daffodils. In our example, we would edit out portions of the tape when the client did not express opinions in a strong voice and leave in all the times when the client did use a firm voice tone. For the stutterer, the stuttering portions of the tape would be deleted so that the edited tape included only portions of conversations in which stuttering did not occur.

Demonstrating with the Edited Tape

After the tape has been edited, the counselor plays it for the client. First, the client is told what to observe on the tape. For our examples of stuttering and assertion training, the counselor might say "Listen to the tape and notice that, in these conversations you have had, you are able to talk without stuttering," or "Note that you are maintaining eye contact when you are delivering a message to the other person."

After these instructions, the counselor and client play back the tape. If the tape is long, it can be stopped at various points to obtain the client's reaction. At these points, or after the tape playback, it is important for the counselor to give encouragement or positive feedback to the client for demonstrating the desired behavior.

After the tape playback, the client should practice behaviors that were demonstrated on the tape. The counselor can facilitate successful practice by coaching, rewarding successes, and correcting errors. This component of self-as-a-model relies heavily on practice and feedback.

Homework: Client Self-Observation and Practice

The client may benefit more from the self-as-a-model strategy when the edited tape is used in conjunction with practice outside the interview. The counselor can instruct the client to use a self-model audiotape as a homework aid by listening to it daily. (For homework purposes, the use of a videotape may not be practical.) After each daily use of the taped playback, the client should practice the target behavior covertly or overtly. The client could also be instructed to practice the behavior without the tape. Gradually, the client should be instructed to use the desired responses in actual instances outside the interview setting. In addition, the client should record the number of practice sessions and the measurement of the goal behaviors on a log sheet. And, as with any homework assignment, the counselor should arrange for a follow-up after the client completes some portion of the homework.

☐ MODEL DIALOGUE: SELF-AS-A-MODEL

To assist you in identifying the steps of a self-as-a-model strategy, the following dialogue is presented with our client Joan. In this dialogue, the strategy is used to help Joan achieve one of her counseling goals described in Chapter 9, increasing her initiating skills in her math class.

Session 1

*In response 1, the counselor provides Joan with a **rationale** for the self-as-a-model strategy. One initiating skill, that of volunteering answers to questions, will be worked with using this strategy. Note that the counselor presents a **rationale** and also confirms the **client's willingness** to try the strategy.*

1. *Counselor:* One of the things we discussed that is a problem for you now in your math class is that you rarely volunteer answers or make comments during class. As we talked about before, you feel awkward doing this and unsure about how to do it in a way that makes you feel confident. One thing we might try that will help you build up your skills for doing this is called "self-as-a-model." It's sort of a fun thing because it involves not only you but also this tape recorder. It's a way for you to actually hear how you come across when volunteering answers. It can help you do this the way you want to and also can build up your confidence about this. What do you think about trying this?

   Client: Well, I've never heard myself on tape too much before. Other than that, it sounds OK.

In response 2, the counselor **responds to Joan's concern** *about the tape recorder and initiates a period of using it so it doesn't interfere with the strategy.*

2. *Counselor:* Sometimes the tape recorder does take a little time to get used to, so we'll work with it first so you are accustomed to hearing your voice on it. We might spend some time doing that now. [Joan and the counselor spend about 15 minutes recording and playing back their conversation.]

In response 3, the counselor gives Joan an **overview** *of what is involved in the self-as-a-model strategy.*

3. *Counselor:* You seem to feel more comfortable with the recorder now. Let me tell you what this involves so you'll have an idea of what to expect. After we work out the way you want to volunteer answers, you'll practice this and we'll tape several practice sessions. Then I'll give you feedback, and we'll use the tape as feedback. We'll take the one practice that really sounds good to you, and you can take that and the recorder home so you can listen to it each day. Does that seem pretty clear?
Client: I think so. I guess the tape is a way for me to find out how I really sound.

In response 4, the counselor emphasizes the cognitive or **coping part** *of self-as-a-model.*

4. *Counselor:* That's right. The tape often indicates you can do something better than you think, which is the reason it does help.
Client: I can see that. Just hearing myself a little while ago helped. My voice doesn't sound as squeaky as I thought.

In this case, the client's verbal participation has already been defined by three behaviors. One behavior, volunteering answers, will be worked with at this point. The other two can be added later. In response 5, the counselor will **coach** *Joan on ways to perform this skill.*

5. *Counselor:* OK, Joan, let's talk about what you might do to volunteer answers in a way that you would feel good about. What comes to your mind about this?
Client: Well, I just hardly ever volunteer in the class now. I just wait until Mr. _____ calls on me. It's not that I don't know the answer, because lots of times I do. I guess I just need to raise my hand and give out the answer. See, usually he'll say, "OK, who has the answer to this problem?" So all I need to do is raise my hand and give the answer, like 25 or 40 or whatever. I don't know why I don't do it. I guess I'm afraid I will sound silly or maybe my voice will sound funny.

In the next response, the counselor uses a **clarification** *to determine Joan's particular concern about this skill.*

6. *Counselor:* So are you more concerned with the way you sound than with what you have to say?
Client: I think so.

In response 7, the counselor continues to **coach** *Joan about ways to perform the desired skill, volunteering answers, and also initiates a* **trial practice.**

7. *Counselor:* Well, let's try this. Why don't I pretend to be Mr. _____ and then you raise your hand and give me an answer? Just try to speak in a firm voice that I can easily hear. Maybe even take a deep breath at first. OK? [Counselor turns on tape recorder.] (as Mr. _____) Who has the answer to this problem?
[Joan raises her hand.]
Counselor (as Mr. _____, looks around room, pauses): Joan?
Client (in a pretty audible voice): 25.

After the dry run, the counselor, in responses 8, 9, and 10, gives **feedback** *(using tape playback) about Joan's performance of the target behavior.*

8. *Counselor:* OK, let's stop. What did you think about that?
Client: Well, it wasn't really that hard. I took a deep breath.
9. *Counselor:* Your voice came across pretty clear. Maybe it could be just a little stronger. OK. Let's hear this on tape. [Playback of tape]
10. *Counselor:* How do you feel about what you just heard?
Client: Well, I sound fine. I mean my voice didn't squeak.

In response 11, the counselor initiates **tape recordings** *of Joan's demonstration of the skill (volunteering answers). This tape will be edited and used as a modeling tape.*

11. *Counselor:* No, it was pretty strong. Let's do this several times now. Just take a deep breath and speak firmly. [Practice ensues and is recorded.]

In response 12, the counselor explains the **tape-editing process;** *the tape is edited before their next session.*

12. *Counselor:* OK, I'm going to need to go over this tape before we use it for feedback. So maybe that's enough for today. We can get together next week, and I'll have this tape ready by then. Basically, I'm just going to edit it so you can hear the practice examples in which your voice sounded clear and firm. [Before the next session, the counselor erases any portions of the tape in which Joan's answers were inaudible or high-pitched, leaving only audible, firm, level-pitched answers.]

Session 2

After a brief warm-up period in this session, the counselor **instructs** *Joan about what to listen for in the* **demonstration with the edited tape playback.**

1. *Counselor:* Well, Joan, I've got your tape ready. I'd like to play back the tape. When I do, I'd like you to note how clearly and firmly you are able to give the answers. [Tape is played.]

2. *Counselor:* What did you think?
   Client: You're right. I guess I don't sound silly, at least not on that tape.

In response 3, the counselor gives **positive feedback** *to Joan about demonstrating the skill.*

3. *Counselor:* You really sounded like you felt very confident about the answers. It was very easy to hear you.
   Client: But will I be able to sound like that in class?

In response 4, the counselor instructs Joan on how to use the tape as **daily homework** *in conjunction with practice. Note that the homework assignment specifies* **what** *and* **how much** *Joan will do.*

4. *Counselor:* Yes, and we'll be working on that as our next step. In the meantime, I'd like you to work with this tape during the week. Could you set aside a certain time each day when you could listen to the tape, just like we did today? Then after you listen to the tape, practice again. Imagine Mr. _____ is asking for the answer. Just raise your hand, take a deep breath, and speak firmly. Do you understand how to use this now?

Client: Yes, just listen to it once a day and then do another round of practice.

In response 5, the counselor asks Joan to **record her use of homework on log sheets.**

5. *Counselor:* As you do this, I'd like you to use these log sheets and mark down each time you do this homework. Also, rate on this 5-point scale how comfortable you feel in doing this before and each time you practice.
   Client: That doesn't sound too difficult, I guess.

In response 6, the counselor encourages Joan to **reinforce herself** *for progress and* **arranges for follow-up** *on homework at their next session.*

6. *Counselor:* Well, this recording on your log sheet will help you see your progress. You've made a lot of progress, so give yourself a pat on the back after you hear the tape this week. Next week we can talk about how this worked out and then we'll see whether we can do the same type of thing in your classes.

The next step would be to obtain some tape-recorded samples of Joan's volunteering in a class situation. A nonthreatening class in which Joan presently does volunteer might be used first, followed by her trying this out in math class. The biggest problem in this step is to arrange for tape-recorded samples in a way that is not embarrassing to Joan in the presence of her classmates.

LEARNING ACTIVITY #35: SELF-AS-A-MODEL

You may recall from the case of Ms. Weare and Freddie that Ms. Weare wanted to eliminate the assistance she gave Freddie in getting ready for school in the morning. One of Ms. Weare's concerns is to find a way to instruct Freddie about the new ground rules —mainly that she will not help him get dressed and will not remind him when the bus is five minutes away. Ms. Weare is afraid that after she delivers her instructions, Freddie will either pout or talk back to her. She is concerned that she will not be able to follow through with her plan or else will not be firm in the way she delivers the ground rules to him.

Describe how you could use the five components of the self-as-a-model strategy to help Ms. Weare accomplish these four things:

1. Deliver clear instructions to Freddie.
2. Talk in a firm voice.
3. Maintain eye contact while talking.
4. Avoid talking down, giving in, or changing her original instructions.

Feedback follows.

☐ PARTICIPANT MODELING

Participant modeling consists of modeled demonstration, guided practice, and successful experiences (Bandura, 1976a). Participant modeling assumes that a person's successful performance is an effective means of producing change. Bandura, Jeffery, and Gajdos (1975) indicate that participant modeling is an effective way to provide "rapid reality testing, which provides the correc-

FEEDBACK #35: SELF-AS-A-MODEL

1. *Rationale for strategy*

   First, you would explain to Ms. Weare how the self-as-a-model procedure could help her (rationale) and what is involved in the procedure (overview). Then, ask Ms. Weare how she feels about trying this procedure (client's willingness).

2. *Recording the desired behavior*

   According to the case description, there are four things Ms. Weare wants to learn to do in delivering her instructions to Freddie. It would be useful to work on one thing at a time, starting with the one subskill that may be easiest for her, such as maintaining eye contact when she talks to Freddie. After each subskill is worked with separately, she can work on doing all four skills in combination.

   The counselor will probably need to coach Ms. Weare on a successful way to perform the skill before recording her demonstration of it, and a dry run may be necessary.

   When the counselor believes Ms. Weare can demonstrate the skill at least sometimes, a video or audio recording will be made. (For eye contact, a videotape would be necessary.) Since Ms. Weare presently is not engaging in these behaviors with Freddie, an in-session tape would be more useful than an *in vivo* tape at this point. The counselor can role play the part of Freddie during the taping. The taping should continue until an adequate sample of each of the four skills is obtained.

3. *Editing the tape*

   After the tape has been recorded, the counselor will edit it. Only inappropriate examples of the skill would be deleted. For example, instances when Ms. Weare looks away would be erased from the tape. The edited tape would consist only of times when she maintains eye contact. A final tape in which she uses all four skills would consist only of times when she was using the desired skills.

4. *Demonstrating with the edited tape*

   After the edited tape is ready, it would be used for demonstration and practice with Ms. Weare. The counselor would instruct Ms. Weare about what to look for and then play back the tape. The counselor would give positive feedback to Ms. Weare for instances of demonstrating eye contact and the other three skills. After the playback, Ms. Weare would practice the skill and receive feedback from the counselor about the practice performance.

5. *Homework: Client self-observation and practice*

   After Ms. Weare was able to practice the skills with the counselor, she would use the self-modeling tape as homework. Specifically, the counselor would instruct her to listen to or view the tape on her own if possible. She could also practice the skills—first covertly and later overtly—with Freddie. This practice could occur with or without the tape. A follow-up should be arranged to check on her progress.

tive experiences for change" (p. 141). By successfully performing a formerly difficult or fearful response, a person can achieve potentially enduring changes in behavior. For example, Etringer, Cash, and Rimm (1982) found that participant modeling quickly achieved very high levels of change on behavioral, attitudinal, and perceived self-efficacy measures in dealing with a feared stimulus; Ladouceur (1983) found that participant modeling and self-verbalizations (thinking aloud) reduced cat and dog phobias for adults. Participant modeling has been used to reduce avoidance behavior and the person's associated feelings about fearful activities or situations (Bandura, Blanchard, & Ritter, 1969; Bandura, Jeffery, & Gajdos, 1975; Bandura, Jeffery, & Wright, 1974; Smith & Coleman, 1977). For example, imagine an outside house painter who develops acrophobia. Participant modeling could be used to help the painter gradually climb "scary" heights by dealing directly with the anxiety associated with being in high places. In participant modeling with phobic clients, successful performance in fearful activities or situations helps the person learn to cope with the feared situation. There is probably nothing more persuasive than successful performance in feared situations (Bandura, 1969).

Another application of participant modeling is with people who have behavioral deficits or who lack such skills as social communication, assertiveness, child management, or physical fitness. Some of these skills might be taught as preventive measures in schools or community agencies. For example, parents can be taught child-management skills by modeling and practicing effective ways of dealing with and communicating with their children.

There are four major components of participant modeling: rationale, modeling, guided participation, and successful experiences (homework). These components are essentially the same whether participant modeling is used to reduce fearful avoidance behavior or to increase some behavior or skill. As you can see from the Interview Checklist for Participant Modeling at the end of the chapter, each component includes several parts. We present a description for each component, followed by a hypothetical counselor/client dialogue illustrating the implementation and use of the participant modeling strategy. We are indebted to the work of Bandura (1969, 1976a) in our description of this strategy.

Treatment Rationale

Here is an example of a rationale the counselor might give for participant modeling:

"This procedure has been used to help other people overcome fears or acquire new behaviors. [rationale] There are three primary things we will do. First, you will see some people demonstrating _____. Next, you will practice this with my assistance in the interview. Then we'll arrange for you to do this outside the interview in situations likely to be successful for you. This type of practice will help you perform what is now difficult for you to do [overview] Are you willing to try this now?" [client's willingness]

Modeling

The modeling component of participant modeling consists of five parts:

1. The goal behaviors, if complex, are divided into a series of subtasks or subskills.
2. The series of subskills is arranged in a hierarchy.
3. Models are selected.
4. Instructions are given to the client before the modeled demonstration.
5. The model demonstrates each successive subtask with as many repetitions as necessary.

Dividing the goal behaviors. Before the counselor (or someone else) models the behavior to be acquired by the client, it should be determined whether the behavior should be divided. Complex patterns of behavior should be divided into subskills or tasks and arranged by small steps or by a graduated series of tasks in a hierarchy. Dividing patterns of behavior and arranging them in order

of difficulty may ensure that the client can perform initial behaviors or tasks. This is a very important step in the participant modeling strategy, because you want the client to experience success in performing what is modeled. Start with a response or a behavior the client can perform.

One example of dividing behaviors involved in competence training into subskills is assertion behaviors. A counselor and client might decide to divide assertive behavior into three categories: (1) eye contact with the person who is receiving the assertive message, (2) delivery of the assertive message without errors in speech, and (3) delivery of the assertive message without latency (time between the end of the other person's message and the beginning of the client's assertive response).

For our acrophobic house painter, the target behavior might be engaging in house painting at a height of 30 feet off the ground. This response could be divided into subtasks of painting at varying heights. Each task might be elevated by several feet at a time.

Arranging the subskills or tasks in a hierarchy. The counselor and client then arrange the subskills or subtasks in a hierarchy. The first situation in the hierarchy is the least difficult or threatening; other skills or situations of greater complexity or threat follow. Usually, the first behavior or response in the hierarchy is worked with first. After each of the subtasks has been successfully practiced one at a time, the client can practice all the subskills or tasks. With a nonassertive client, the counselor and client may decide it would be most helpful to work on eye contact first, then speech errors, then response latency, and finally all these behaviors at once.

In phobic cases, the content and arrangement of each session can be a hierarchical list of feared activities or objects. According to Bandura (1976a), you would first work with the situation that poses the least threat or provokes the least fear for the client. For our acrophobic house painter, we would begin with a situation involving little height and gradually progress to painting at greater heights.

Selecting a model. Before implementing the modeling component, an appropriate model should be selected. At times, it may be most efficient to use the therapist as the model. However, as you may recall from Chapter 13, therapeutic gains may be greater when multiple models are used who are somewhat similar to the client. For example, phobia clinics have successfully employed participant modeling to extinguish phobias by using several formerly phobic clients as the multiple models.

Prior instructions to the client. Immediately before the modeled demonstration, to draw the client's attention to the model, the counselor should instruct the client about what will be modeled. The client should be told to note that the model will be engaging in certain responses without experiencing any adverse consequences. With our nonassertive client, the counselor might say something like "Notice the way this person looks at you directly when refusing to type your paper." With the house painter, the counselor might say "Look to see how the model moves about the scaffolding easily at a height of five feet."

Modeled demonstrations. In participant modeling, a live model demonstrates one subskill at a time. Often, repeated demonstrations of the same response are necessary. As Bandura (1976a) indicates, multiple modeling demonstrations show the client how something can be performed best and also that any feared consequences do not occur (p. 250). Multiple demonstrations can be arranged by having a single model repeat the demonstration or by having several models demonstrate the same activity or response. For example, one model could show moving about on the scaffolding without falling several times, or several models could demonstrate this same activity. When it is feasible to use several models, you should do so. Multiple models lend variety to the way the activity is performed and believability to the idea that adverse consequences will not occur.

Guided Participation

After the demonstration of the behavior or activity, the client is given opportunities and necessary guidance to perform the modeled behaviors. Guided participation or performance is one of the most important components of learning to cope, to reduce avoidance of fearful situations, and to acquire new behaviors. People must experience success in using what has been modeled. The client's participation in the counseling session should be structured in a nonthreatening manner aimed at "fostering new competencies and confidence, rather than at exposing deficiencies" (Bandura, 1976a, p. 262).

Guided participation consists of the following five steps:

1. Client practice of the response or activity with counselor assistance.
2. Counselor feedback.
3. Use of various induction aids for initial practice attempts.
4. Fading of induction aids.
5. Client self-directed practice.

Each of these steps will be described and illustrated.

Client practice. After the model has demonstrated the activity or behavior, the client is asked to do what has been modeled. The counselor has the client perform each activity or behavior in the hierarchy. The client performs each activity or behavior, starting with the first one in the hierarchy, until he or she can do this skillfully and confidently. It is quite possible that, for an occasional client, there does not need to be a breakdown of the behaviors or activities. For these clients, guided practice of the entire ultimate goal behavior may be sufficient without a series of graduated tasks.

Our nonassertive client would first practice delivering an assertive message using direct eye contact. When the client was able to do this easily, she or he would practice delivering a message using eye contact while concentrating on making as few speech errors as possible. When the client was able to do this successfully, the next practices would focus on decreasing response latency. Finally, the client would practice delivering assertive messages and simultaneously using direct eye contact, limiting speech errors, and shortening the amount of time between others' responses and his or her replies.

Our house painter would practice moving about on a ladder or scaffolding at a low height. Practices would continue at this height until the painter could move about easily and comfortably; then practices at the next height would ensue.

Counselor feedback. After each client practice attempt, the counselor provides verbal feedback to the client about his or her performance. There are two parts to the feedback: (1) praise or encouragement for successful practice and (2) suggestions for correcting or modifying errors. For example, after the nonassertive client delivered a message while attempting to use direct eye contact, the counselor might say "That time you were able to look at me while you were talking. You looked away after you finished talking, which did reduce the impact of your message. Your eye contact is definitely improving; let's try it again." Or, with the painter, the counselor might say "You seem comfortable at this height. You were able to go up and down the ladder very easily. Even looking down didn't seem to bother you. That's really terrific."

Use of induction aids.   As you may recall from Chapter 12, induction aids are supportive aids arranged by the counselor to assist a client in performing a feared or difficult response. Many people consider successful performance a good way to reduce anxiety. However, most people are just not going to participate in something they dread simply because they are told to do so. For instance, can you think of something you really fear, such as holding a snake, riding in an airplane or a boat, climbing a high mountain, or getting in a car after a severe accident? If so, you probably realize you would be very reluctant to engage in this activity just because at this moment you read the words *do it*. However, suppose we were to be there and hold the snake first, and hold the snake while you touch it, and then hold its head and tail while you hold the middle, then hold its head while you hold the tail, and so on. You might be more willing to do this or something else you fear under conditions that incorporate some supportive aids. (However, as Bourque and Ladouceur [1980, p. 167] indicate, induction aids such as physical contact or therapist proximity may have a greater impact for people with animal phobias than for clients with territorial phobias.)

With our nonassertive client, the counselor might assist the client in initial practice attempts with verbal cues about the desired performance. Repeated practice of one type of assertive behavior could also be used. Graduated time intervals might be another feasible aid: the counselor could arrange for the client to practice short intervals of direct eye contact, followed by longer durations.

To help our acrophobic painter reduce fear of heights, an initial induction aid might be joint practice. If actual practice with a ladder or scaffold is possible, nothing may be more supportive than having the counselor up on the scaffold with the painter or standing directly behind or in front of the painter on a ladder. This also functions as a type of protective aid. Of course, this assumes that the counselor is not afraid of heights. In our own experience, the one of us who is the nonacrophobic induces the other (no names mentioned) to climb lighthouses, landmarks, hills, and other such "scenic views" by going first and extending a hand. This type of induction aid enables both of us to enjoy the experience together. As a result, the fears of one person have never interfered with the pleasures of the other, because continued practice efforts with some support have reduced the fear level substantially.

Induction aids can be used in the counseling session, but they should also be applied in settings that closely approximate the natural setting. If at all possible, the counselor or a model should accompany the client into the "field," where the client can witness further demonstrations and can participate in the desired settings. For example, teaching assertive behavior to a client in the interview must be supplemented with modeling and guided participation in the natural setting in which the final goal behavior is to occur. It is doubtful that a counselor would be equipped with scaffolds so that our acrophobic house painter could practice the modeled activities at different heights. The counselor could use covert rehearsal instead of overt practice. Our point is that the counselor who uses live participant modeling procedures must be prepared to provide aids and supports that help the client practice as closely as possible the desired goal behavior. If this is not possible, the next best alternative is to simulate those activities as closely as possible in the client's real situation.

Fading of induction aids.   Induction aids can be withdrawn gradually. With our nonassertive client, the use of four induction aids initially might be gradually reduced to three, two, and one. Or, with the painter, a very supportive aid, such as joint practice, could be replaced by a less supportive aid, such as verbal coaching. The gradual withdrawal of induction aids bridges the gap between counselor-assisted and client-directed practice.

Client self-directed practice.   At some point, the client should be able to perform the desired activities or responses without any induction aids or assistance. A period of client self-directed practice may reinforce changes in the client's beliefs and self-evaluation and may lead to improved behavioral functioning. Therefore, the counselor should arrange for the client to engage in successful performance of the desired responses independently unassisted. Ideally, client self-directed practice would occur both within the interview and in the client's natural setting. Our nonassertive client would practice the three desired assertion responses unassisted. The house painter would practice moving on the ladder or scaffold alone. Client self-directed practice is likely to be superior to therapist-directed practice (Smith & Coleman, 1977).

In addition to application of the participant modeling procedures in the counseling sessions, facilitating the transfer of behavior from the training session to the natural environment should be an integral part of counseling. Generalization of desired changes can be achieved by success or by reinforcing experiences that occur as part of a transfer-of-training program.

Success, or Reinforcing, Experiences

The last component of the participant modeling procedure is success (reinforcing) experiences. Clients must experience success in using what they are learning. Further, as Bandura points out, psychological changes "are unlikely to endure unless they prove effective when put into practice in everyday life" (1976a, p. 248). Success experiences are arranged by tailoring a transfer-of-training program for each client. In an adequate transfer-of-training program, the client's new skills are used first in low-risk situations in the client's natural environment or in any situation in which the client will probably experience success or favorable outcomes. Gradually, the client extends the application of the skills to natural situations that are more unpredictable and involve a greater threat.

Bandura (1976a) describes a possible transfer-of-training program for nonassertive clients:

After the clients have perfected their social skills and overcome their timidity, they accompany the therapist on excursions into the field where they witness further demonstrations of how to handle situations calling for assertive action. The therapist then reduces the level of participation to background support and guidance as the clients try their skills in situations likely to produce favorable results. By means of careful selection of encounters of increasing difficulty, the assertion requirements can be adjusted to the clients' momentary capabilities to bolster their sense of confidence. As a final step in the program, the clients are assigned a series of assertive performance tasks to carry out on their own [pp. 262–263].

To summarize, success experiences are ar-

ranged through a program that transfers skill acquisition from the interview to the natural setting. This transfer-of-training program involves the following steps:

1. The counselor and client identify situations in the client's environment in which the client desires to perform the target responses.
2. These situations are arranged in a hierarchy, starting with easy, safe situations in which the client is likely to be successful and ending with more unpredictable and risky situations.
3. The counselor accompanies the client into the environment and works with each situation on the list by modeling and guided participation. Gradually the counselor's level of participation is decreased.
4. The client is given a series of tasks to perform in a self-directed manner.

Bandura (1976a) concludes that participant modeling achieves results, given adequate demonstration, guided practice, and positive experiences. One advantage of participant modeling is that "a broad range of resource persons," such as peers or former clients, can serve as therapeutic models (p. 249). Bandura also points out that participant modeling helps clients to learn new responses under "lifelike conditions." As a result, the problems of transfer of learning from the interview to the client's real-life environment are minimized.

☐ MODEL DIALOGUE: PARTICIPANT MODELING

Here is an example of the use of participant modeling with our client Joan. The participant modeling will be used to help Joan perform the four behaviors in math class that she typically avoids. The rationale for the counselor responses is set off by the italicized comments that precede the responses.

Session 1

In the first response, the counselor will provide a **rationale** *about the strategy and a brief* **overview** *of the procedure.*

1. *Counselor:* This procedure has been of help to other people who have trouble in classroom participation. We'll take each of the ways you would like to participate, and either I myself or maybe one of your classmates will show you a way to do this, then help you practice it. At first we'll just practice

here. Then gradually you'll try this out in your other classes and, of course, finally in your math class. What do you think about this?

Client: It's OK with me. It's just something I know I can do but I don't because I'm a little nervous.

The counselor will pick up on Joan's previous response and use it to provide an **additional rationale** *for the participant modeling strategy.*

2. *Counselor:* And nervousness can keep you from doing something you want. This procedure helps you to learn to do something in small steps. As you accomplish each step, your confidence in yourself will increase and your nervousness will decrease.

Client: I think that will definitely help. Sometimes I just don't believe in myself.

In response 3, the counselor ignores Joan's previous self-effacing comment. The counselor instead begins with the **modeling component** *by reviewing the ways Joan wanted to increase selected initiating skills in math class.*

3. *Counselor:* You know, last week I believe we found some ways that you would like to increase your participation in math class. And I think we arranged these in an order, starting with the one that you thought was easiest for you now, to the one that was hardest for you. Can you recall these things and this order?

Client: Yes, I believe it was like this: answering questions, going to the board, volunteering answers, and then volunteering opinions or ideas.

The counselor asks the client **whether additional activities** *need to be added or* **whether the hierarchy order** *needs to be rearranged.*

4. *Counselor:* OK, after thinking about it for a week, have you thought of any other ways you'd like to participate—or do you think this order needs to be rearranged at all?

Client: Well, one more thing—I would like to be able to work the problems on my own after I ask Mr. _____ for help. That's where I want to begin. He usually takes over and works the problems for me.

In response 5, the counselor will explore **a potential model** *for Joan and obtain Joan's input about this decision.*

5. *Counselor:* OK, one thing we need to do now is to consider who might model and help you with these activities. I can do it, although if you can think of a classmate in math who participates the way you want to, this person could assist you when you try this out in your class. What do you think?

Client: Is it necessary to have someone in the class

with me? If so, I think it would be less obvious if it were someone already in the class.

The counselor picks up on Joan's discomfort about the counselor's presence in her class and **suggests another classmate as the model.**

6. *Counselor:* Well, there are ways to get around it, but it would be more helpful if someone could be there in your class, at least initially. I think you would feel more comfortable if this person were another classmate rather than me. If there is someone you could pick who already does a good job of participating, I'd like to talk to this person and have him or her help during our next sessions. So try to think of someone you like and respect and feel comfortable around.

Client: Well, there's Debbie. She's a friend of mine, and she hardly ever gets bothered by answering Mr. _____'s questions or going to the board. I could ask her. She'd probably like to do something like this. She works independently, too, on her math problems.

The counselor provides **a rationale** *for how Joan's friend will be used as the model so that Joan understands how her friend will be involved. Note that Joan's reaction to this is solicited. If Joan were uncomfortable with this, another option would be explored.*

7. *Counselor:* OK, if you could ask her and she agrees, ask her to drop by my office. If that doesn't work out, stop back and we'll think of something else. If Debbie wants to do this, I'll train her to help demonstrate the ways you'd like to participate. At our session next week, she can start modeling these things for you. How does that sound?

Client: OK. It might be kind of fun. I've helped her with her English themes before, so now maybe she can help with this.

The counselor encourages the idea of these two friends' providing **mutual help** *in the next response.*

8. *Counselor:* That's a good idea. Good friends help each other. Let me know what happens after you talk to Debbie.

After session 1, Joan stopped in to verify that Debbie would be glad to work with them. The counselor then arranged a meeting with Debbie to explain her role in the participant modeling strategy. Specifically, Debbie practiced modeling the other four participation goals Joan had identified. The counselor gave Debbie instructions and feedback so that each behavior was modeled clearly and in a coping manner. The counselor also trained Debbie in ways to assist Joan during the guided-participation phase. Debbie practiced this, with the counselor taking the role of Joan. In these practice attempts, Debbie also practiced using various induction aids that she might use with Joan, such as joint practice, verbal coaching, and graduated time intervals and difficulty of task. Debbie also practiced having the counselor (as Joan) engage in self-directed practice. Classroom simulations of success experiences were also rehearsed so Debbie could learn her role in arranging for actual success experiences with Joan. When Debbie felt comfortable with her part in the strategy, the next session with Joan was scheduled.

Session 2

In response 1, the counselor gives **instructions to Joan about what to look for** *during the modeled demonstration. Note that the counselor also points out the* **lack of adverse consequences** *in the modeling situation.*

1. *Counselor:* It's good to see you today, Joan. I have been working with Debbie, and she is here today to do some modeling for you. What we'll do first is to work with one thing you mentioned last week, telling Mr. _____ you want to work the problems yourself after you ask him for an explanation. Debbie will demonstrate this first. So I'll play the part of Mr. _____ and Debbie will come up to me and ask me for help. Note that she tells me what she needs explained, then firmly tells Mr. _____ she wants to try to finish it herself. Notice that this works out well for Debbie — Mr. _____ doesn't jump at her or anything like that. Do you have any questions?
   Client: No, I'm ready to begin. [Modeling ensues.]
   Debbie (as model): Mr. _____, I would like some explanation about this problem. I need you to explain it again so I can work it out all right.
   Counselor (as Mr. _____): OK, well, here is the answer . . .
   Debbie (as model, interrupts): Well, I'd like to find the answer myself, but I'd like you to explain this formula again.
   Counselor (as Mr. _____): OK, well, here's how you do this formula . . .
   Debbie (as model): That really helps. Thanks a lot I can take it from here. [Goes back to seat.]

After the modeling, the counselor **asks Joan to react** *to what she saw.*

2. *Counselor:* What reactions did you have to that, Joan?
   Client: Well, it looked fairly easy. I guess when I do ask him for help, I have a tendency just to let him take over. I am not really firm about telling him to let me finish the problem myself.

The counselor picks up on Joan's concern and **initiates a second modeled demonstration.**

3. *Counselor:* That's an important part of it — first being able to ask for an additional explanation and then being able to let him know you want to apply the information and go back to your seat and try that out. It might be a good idea to have Debbie do this again — see how she initiates finishing the problem so Mr. _____ doesn't take over.
   Client: OK.
   [Second modeled demonstration ensues.]

In response 4, the counselor asks Joan for her opinion about **engaging in a practice.**

4. *Counselor:* How ready do you feel now to try this out yourself in a practice here?
   Client: I believe I could.

Before the first practice attempt, the counselor will introduce **one induction aid, verbal coaching,** *from Debbie.*

5. *Counselor:* OK. Now I believe one thing that might help you is to have Debbie sort of coach you. For instance, if you get stuck or start to back down, Debbie can step in and give you a cue or a reminder about something you can do. How does that sound?
   Client: Fine. That makes it a little easier.

The first practice attempt begins.

6. *Counselor:* OK, let's begin. Now I'll be Mr. _____ and you get up out of your seat with the problem.
   Client: Mr. _____, I don't quite understand this problem.
   Counselor (as Mr. _____): Well, let me just give you the answer; you'll have one less problem to do then.
   Client: Well, uh, I'm not sure the answer is what I need.
   Counselor (as Mr. _____): Well, what do you mean?
   Debbie (intervenes to prompt): Joan, you might want to indicate you would prefer to work out the answer yourself, but you do need another explanation of the formula.
   Client: Well, I'd like to find the answer myself. I do need another explanation of the formula.
   Counselor (as Mr. _____): OK. Well, it goes like this . . .
   Client: OK, thanks.
   Debbie: Now be sure you end the conversation there and go back to your seat.

The counselor will **assess Joan's reactions** *to the practice.*

7. *Counselor:* OK, what did you think about that, Joan?
   Client: It went pretty well. It *was* a help to have Debbie here. That is a good idea.

In the next response, the counselor **provides positive feedback** *to Debbie and to Joan.* **Another practice is initiated;** *this also serves as an* **induction aid.**

8. *Counselor:* I think she helps, too. You seemed to be able to start the conversation very well. You did need a little help in explaining to him what you wanted and didn't want. Once Debbie cued you, you were able to use her cue very effectively. Perhaps it would be a good idea to try this again. Debbie will only prompt this time if she really needs to.
   [Second practice ensues; Debbie's amount of prompting is decreased.]

The counselor explores the idea of **a self-directed practice.**

9. *Counselor:* That seemed to go very smoothly. I think you are ready to do this again without any assistance. How does that sound?
   Client: I think so, too.

After obtaining an affirmative response from Joan, the counselor asks Debbie to leave the room. Just Debbie's physical presence could be a protective condition for Joan, which is another induction aid, so Debbie leaves to make sure the **self-directed practice occurs.**

10. *Counselor:* I'm going to ask Debbie to leave the room so you'll be completely on your own this time.
    [Self-directed practice ensues.]

Next the counselor cues Joan to provide herself with **feedback** *about her self-directed practice.*

11. *Counselor:* How did you feel about that practice, Joan?
    Client: Well, I realized I was relying a little on Debbie. So I think it was good to do it by myself.

The counselor notes the link between self-directed performance and confidence and starts to work on **success experiences** *outside counseling.*

12. *Counselor:* Right. At first it does help to have someone there. Then it builds your confidence to do it by yourself. At this point, I think we're ready to discuss ways you might actually use this in your class. How does that sound?
    Client: Fine. A little scary, but fine.

The counselor introduces the idea of **Debbie's assistance as an initial aid in Joan's practice outside the session.**

13. *Counselor:* It's natural to feel a little apprehensive at first, but one thing we will do to help you get started on the right foot is to use Debbie again at first.
    Client: Oh, good. How will that work?

In response 14, the counselor **identifies a hierarchy of situations** *in Joan's math class. Joan's first attempts will be assisted by Debbie to ensure success at each step.*

14. *Counselor:* Well, apparently math is the only class where you have difficulty doing this, so we want to work on your using this in math class successfully. Since Debbie is in the class with you, instead of going up to Mr. _____ initially by yourself, first you can go with her. In fact, she could initiate the request for help the first time. The next time you could both go up and you could initiate it. She could prompt you or fill in. Gradually, you would get to the point where you would go up by yourself. But we will take one step at a time.
    Client: That really does help. I know the first time it would turn out better if she was there, too.

15. *Counselor:* Right. Usually in doing anything new, it helps to start slowly and feel good each step of the way. So maybe Debbie can come in now and we can plan the first step.

Debbie will model and guide Joan in using these responses in their math class. Next, the entire procedure will be repeated to work with the other initiating skills Joan wants to work on.

LEARNING ACTIVITY #36: PARTICIPANT MODELING

This activity is designed to be completed for a behavior of yours that you wish to change. You will need a partner to complete this activity.

1. Select a skill that you wish to acquire, such as a social or assertive skill or a particular counseling skill.

2. Define the skill by describing what you would be doing, thinking, and/or feeling differently. Decide whether the skill is so broad that it needs to be divided into a series of subskills. If so, identify

(continued)

LEARNING ACTIVITY #36: PARTICIPANT MODELING (continued)

these and arrange them on a hierarchy in order of difficulty.

3. Ask your partner to model or demonstrate the skill for you. (You can also arrange to observe other people you know and respect who might be likely to use similar skills in naturally occurring circumstances.)

4. With the help of your partner, prepare for your own initial practice of the skill or of the first subskill on the hierarchy. Your partner should facilitate your initial practice attempts with at least one or two induction aids, such as joint practice or verbal coaching. With successive practice attempts,

these induction aids will gradually be removed. Your partner also needs to provide feedback after each practice.

5. With your partner, identify actual situations in which you want to apply your newly acquired skill. Rehearse such attempts and identify any induction aids that may be necessary in your initial efforts at skill application in these situations.

6. Call or see your partner to report on how you handled rehearsal efforts in step 5. Identify whether you need additional modeling, practice, or induction aids.

☐ SUMMARY

The three modeling strategies presented in this chapter can be used to help clients acquire new responses or extinguish fears. These modeling strategies promote learning by providing a model to demonstrate the goal behaviors for the client. The way the model is presented differs slightly among the modeling procedures. Symbolic modeling and self-modeling use media for modeled presentations; participant modeling usually employs a live modeling demonstration. Modeling can also be carried out by means of the client's imagination. Two therapeutic strategies based on imagery, emotive imagery and covert modeling, are described in the next chapter.

POSTEVALUATION

PART ONE

Objective One asks you to develop a script for a symbolic model. Your script should contain—

1. Examples of the modeled dialogue
2. Opportunities for practice
3. Feedback
4. Summarization

Use the Checklist for Symbolic Models (p. 345) as a guide.

PART TWO

Objective Two asks you to describe how you would use the five components of the self-as-a-model procedure with a client case. Recall from the case of Mr. Brown (Chapter 7) that one of his concerns was not being able to initiate social contacts with his boss. Describe how you would use the five components of the self-as-a-model procedure to help Mr. Brown initiate social contacts with his boss (Objective Two). The five components are: (1) rationale, (2) recording the desired behavior, (3) editing the tape, (4) demonstrating with the edited tape, and (5) homework: client self-observation and practice.

PART THREE

Objective Three asks you to demonstrate at least 13 out of 16 steps associated with the self-as-a-model strategy with a role-play interview. Assess yourself or have someone else assess you, using the Interview Checklist for Self-as-a-Model on pages 345–346.

PART FOUR

Objective Four asks you to describe how you would apply the four components of participant modeling with a hypothetical client case. Using the case of Mr. Brown, describe how you would use the four components of participant modeling (rationale, modeling, guided practice, and success experiences) to help Mr. Brown acquire verbal and nonverbal skills necessary to initiate social contacts with his boss.

PART FIVE

Objective Five asks you to demonstrate 14 out of 17 steps of participant modeling with a role-play client. The client might take the role of someone who is

(continued)

afraid to perform certain responses or activities in certain situations. You can assess yourself, using the Interview Checklist for Participant Modeling on pages 347–348. Feedback for the postevaluation follows on page 349.

CHECKLIST FOR DEVELOPING SYMBOLIC MODELS

Instructions: Determine whether the following guidelines have been incorporated into the construction of your symbolic model.

Check if completed:

_____1. Determine what consumers will use the symbolic modeling procedure and identify their characteristics.
_____Age
_____Sex

_____Ethnic origin, cultural practices, and/or race
_____Coping or mastery model portrayed
_____Possesses similar concern or problem to that of client group or population
_____2. Goal behaviors to be modeled by client have been enumerated.
_____3. Medium is selected (for example, written script, audiotape, videotape, film, slide tape).
_____4. Script includes the following ingredients:
_____Instructions
_____Modeled dialogue
_____Practice
_____Written feedback
_____Written summarization of what has been modeled, with its importance for client
_____5. Written script has been field-tested.

INTERVIEW CHECKLIST FOR SELF-AS-A-MODEL

Instructions: Indicate with a check which of the following leads were used by the counselor in the interview. Some examples of possible leads are provided in the right column; however, these are only suggestions.

Item	Examples of counselor leads
I. Rationale about Strategy	
1. Counselor provides rationale about strategy.	"This procedure can help you improve your communication with each other, using yourselves. We'll use your own examples of good interactions to help you learn these skills."
_____ 2. Counselor provides overview of strategy.	"We'll have you practice communicating with each other and we'll tape-record your interactions. Then I'll edit the tape. You'll have a tape that consists of only positive examples of communication. You'll use the tape for homework and practice."
_____ 3. Counselor checks client's willingness to try strategy.	"How willing would you be to try this process to help you learn these communication skills?"
II. Recording the Desired Behavior	
_____ 4. Counselor and client break down desired behaviors into subskills.	"There are several things we can work on to improve your communication with each other. One thing we might start with is to help you learn to express your feelings to each other about the other person and his or her behavior."
_____ 5. For each subskill, counselor coaches client about ways to perform skill successfully.	"The basic idea here is to use an 'I' message, coupled with a word that describes how you feel, such as 'I feel angry' or 'I feel happy,' instead of 'You made me angry.'"
_____ 6. Client performs a dry run of skill, using counselor or tape for feedback.	"Let's try this out in a short role play. Just try to express a feeling you have right now to your spouse, using an 'I' message."

(continued)

POSTEVALUATION (continued)

_____ 7. Client demonstrates skill while being recorded on video- or audiotape.

_____a. Recording took place in the interview.

"This time while you're practicing this with each other, I'm going to tape it."

_____b. Recording took place in _in vivo_ situations outside the session.

"In addition to the tape we made today, I'd like you to tape some of your interactions you have at home with each other."

_____c. Recording is repeated until sample of desired behavior is obtained.

"Remember, start with 'I feel.' Let's try this again."

III. Editing the Tape

_____ 8. Counselor edits tape so that a clear picture of client's desired behavior is evident and instances of undesired behavior are deleted.

"I'm going to take the tape we made in our session and the one you made at home and edit them before our next session. Basically, I'm going to edit the tape so only your best interactions are left. This gives you a chance to hear yourselves communicating with each other the way you'd like to."

IV. Demonstrating with the Edited Tape

_____ 9. Counselor instructs client about what to look or listen for during tape playback.

"While we play this tape, listen to all the times you were able to say 'I feel _____' to each other."

_____10. Counselor initiates playback of edited tape for client observation.

"OK, we'll spend some time now listening to these tapes."

_____11. Counselor provides positive feedback to client for demonstration of desired behavior on tape.

"The tapes show clearly that you are both able to express your feelings to each other in this constructive way."

_____12. Counselor initiates client practice of taped behaviors; successes are rewarded and errors corrected.

"Now that you've heard yourselves do this on the tape, let's work on it here."

V. Homework: Client Self-Observation and Practice

_____13. Using model tape, counselor assigns homework:

_____a. By asking client to observe or listen to model tape and to practice goal responses overtly or covertly.

_____b. Daily for a designated period of time.

"I'd like you to take these tapes home and set aside a period of time each day when you can go over and listen to them. After you listen to the tapes, I'd like you to practice this with each other."

_____14. Counselor provides some sort of self-directed prompts, such as cue cards.

"To help you remember this, I'll give you this card. The card tells you to start each expression of feeling with 'I feel,' then to stop and listen for the other person's response."

_____15. Counselor asks client to record number of practice sessions and to rate performance of goal behaviors on a homework log sheet.

"I'd like you to use these log sheets and mark down each time you practice these skills — with or without the tape. Also, try to rate how well you think you demonstrated these skills at each practice on a 1-to-5 scale, 1 being very poor and 5 being excellent."

_____16. Counselor initiates a face-to-face or telephone follow-up to assess client's use of homework and to provide encouragement.

"Why don't you give me a call in three or four days and check in?"

Observer Comments: _____

INTERVIEW CHECKLIST FOR PARTICIPANT MODELING

Instructions: Determine which of the following leads the counselor used in the interview. Check the leads used.

Item	Examples of counselor leads

I. Rationale about Strategy

_____ 1. Counselor provides rationale about participant modeling strategy.

"This procedure has been used with other people who have concerns similar to yours. It is a way to help you overcome your fear of _____ or to help you acquire these skills."

_____ 2. Counselor provides brief description of components of participant modeling.

"It involves three things. I'll model what you want to do, you'll practice this with my assistance, and then you'll try this out in situations that at first will be pretty easy for you so you can be successful."

_____ 3. Counselor asks for client's willingness to use strategy.

"Would you be willing to try this now?"

II. Modeling

_____ 4. Counselor and client decide whether to divide goal behaviors into a series of subtasks or skills.

"Well, let's see . . . Right now you hardly ever go out of the house. You say it bothers you even to go out in the yard. Let's see whether we can identify different activities in which you would gradually increase the distance away from the house, like going to the front door, going out on the porch, out in the yard, out to the sidewalk, to the neighbor's house, and so on."

_____ 5. If goal behaviors were divided (step 4), these subskills are arranged by counselor and client in a hierarchy according to order of difficulty.

"Perhaps we can take our list and arrange it in an order. Start with the activity that is easiest for you now, such as going to the door. Arrange each activity in order of increasing difficulty."

_____ 6. Counselor and client determine and select appropriate model.

"I could help you learn to do this, or we could pick someone whom you know or someone similar to yourself to guide you through this. What are your preferences?"

_____ 7. Counselor provides instructions to client before demonstration about what to look for.

"Notice that when the doorbell rings, I will go to the door calmly and quickly and open it without hesitation. Also notice that after I go to the door, I'm still calm; nothing has happened to me."

_____ 8. Model demonstrates target response at least once; more demonstrations are repeated if necessary.

"OK, let me show this to you again."

_____ If hierarchy is used, first skill is modeled, followed successively by all others, concluding with demonstration combining all subskills.

"Now that I've done the first scene, next I'll show you stepping out on the porch. Then we'll combine these two scenes."

III. Guided Participation

_____ 9. Client is asked to perform target response. If a hierarchy is used, first skill in hierarchy is practiced first, successfully followed by second, third, and so on.

"This time you try going to the door when the doorbell rings. I will assist you as you need help."

_____10. After each practice, model or counselor provides feedback consisting of positive feedback and error corrections.

"That was quite smooth. You were able to go to the door quickly. You still hesitated a little once you got there. Try to open the door as soon as you see who is there."

(continued)

POSTEVALUATION (continued)

Item	Examples of counselor leads
___11. Initial practice attempts of each skill by client include a number of induction aids, such as —	"I'm going to assist you in your first few practices."
___a. Joint practice with model or counselor.	"Let's do it together. I will walk with you to the door."
___b. Verbal and/or physical coaching or guiding by model or counselor.	"Let me give you a suggestion here. When you open the door, greet the person there. Find out what the person wants."
___c. Repeated practice of one subtask until client is ready to move on to another.	"Let's work on this a few more times until you feel really comfortable."
___d. Graduated time intervals for practice (short to long duration).	"This time we'll increase the distance you have to walk to the door. Let's start back in the kitchen."
___e. Arrangement of protective conditions for practice to reduce likelihood of feared or undesired consequences.	"We'll make sure someone else is in the house with you."
___f. Graduated levels of severity of threat or complexity of situation.	"OK, now we've worked with opening the door when a good friend is there. This time let's pretend it's someone you are used to seeing but don't know as a friend, like the person who delivers your mail."
___12. In later practice attempts, number of induction aids is gradually reduced.	"I believe now that you can do this without my giving you so many prompts."
___13. Before moving on, client is able to engage in self-directed practice of all desired responses.	"This time I'm going to leave. I want you to do this by yourself."
IV. Success Experiences (Homework)	
___14. Counselor and client identify situations in client's environment in which client desires to perform target responses.	"Let's list all the actual times and places where you want to do this."
___15. Situations are arranged in hierarchy from easy with least risk to difficult with greater risk.	"We can arrange these in an order. Put the easiest one first, and follow it by ones that are successively harder or more threatening for you."
___16. Starting with easiest and least risky situation, counselor (or model) and client use live or symbolic modeling and guided practice in client's real-life environment. Steps 4 – 11 are repeated outside session until gradually counselor (or model) reduces level of assistance.	"Starting with the first situation, we're going to work with this when it actually occurs. At first I'll assist you until you can do it on your own."
___17. Client is assigned a series of related tasks to carry out in a self-directed manner.	"Now you're ready to tackle this situation without my help. You have shown both of us you are ready to do this on your own."

□ SUGGESTED READINGS

Bandura, A. (1976). Effecting change through participant modeling. In J. D. Krumboltz & C. E. Thoresen (Eds.), *Counseling methods.* New York: Holt, Rinehart and Winston.

Bandura, A., Jeffery, R. W., & Gajdos, E. (1975). Generalizing change through participant modeling with self-directed mastery. *Behaviour Research and Therapy, 13,* 141–152.

Bandura, A., Jeffery, R. W., & Wright, C. (1974). Efficacy of participant modeling as a function of response induction aids. *Journal of Abnormal Psychology, 83,* 56–64.

Bourque, P., & Ladouceur, R. (1980). An investigation of various performance-based treatments with acrophobics. *Behaviour Research and Therapy, 18,* 161–170.

Craigie, F. C., Jr., & Ross, S. M. (1980). The case of a videotape pretherapy training program to encourage treatment-seeking among alcohol detoxification patients. *Behavior Therapy, 11,* 141–147.

Davis, A., Rosenthal, T. L., & Kelley, J. E. (1981). Actual fear cues, prompt therapy, and rationale enhance participant modeling with adolescents. *Behavior Therapy, 12,* 536–542.

Davis, R. (1979). The impact of self-modeling on problem behaviors in school-age children. *School Psychology Digest, 8,* 128–132.

Dowrick, P. W., & Dove, C. (1980). The use of self-modeling to improve the swimming performance of spina bifida children. *Journal of Applied Behavior Analysis, 13,* 51–56.

Edelstein, B., & Eisler, R. (1976). Effects of modeling and modeling with instructions and feedback on the behavioral components of social skills. *Behavior Therapy, 7,* 382–389.

Etringer, B. D., Cash, T. F., & Rimm, D. C. (1982). Behavioral, affective, and cognitive effects of participant modeling and an equally credible placebo. *Behavior Therapy, 13,* 476–485.

Gilbert, B. O., Johnson, S. B., Spillar, R., McCallum, M., Silverstein, J. H., & Rosenbloom, A. (1982). The effects of a peer-modeling film on children learning to self-inject insulin. *Behavior Therapy, 13,* 186–193.

Glasgow, R. E., & Rosen, G. M. (1979). Self-help behavior therapy manuals: Recent developments and clinical usage. *Clinical Behavior Therapy Review, 1,* 1–20.

Gresham, F. M., & Nagle, R. J. (1980). Social skills training with children: Responsiveness to modeling and coaching as a function of peer orientation. *Journal of Consulting and Clinical Psychology, 48,* 718–729.

Hosford, R. (1974). *Counseling techniques: Self-as-a-model film.* Washington, DC: American Personnel and Guidance Press.

Ladouceur, R. (1983). Participant modeling with or without cognitive treatment for phobias. *Journal of Consulting and Clinical Psychology, 51,* 930–932.

Miklich, D., Chida, T., & Danker-Brown, P. (1977). Behavior modification by self-modeling without subject awareness. *Journal of Behavior Therapy and Experimental Psychiatry, 8,* 125–130.

Perry, M. A., & Furukawa, M. J. (1980). Modeling methods. In F. A. Kanfer & A. P. Goldstein (Eds.), *Helping people change.* New York: Pergamon Press.

Peterson, L., & Shigetomi, C. (1981). The use of coping techniques to minimize anxiety in hospitalized children. *Behavior Therapy, 12,* 1–14.

Sarason, I. G., & Sarason, B. R. (1981). Teaching cognitive and social skills to high school students. *Journal of Consulting and Clinical Psychology, 49,* 908–918.

Webster-Stratton, C. (1981a). Modification of mothers' behaviors and attitudes through a videotape modeling group discussion program. *Behavior Therapy, 12,* 634–642.

Webster-Stratton, C. (1981b). Videotape modeling: A method of parent education. *Journal of Clinical Child Psychology, 10,* 93–98.

FEEDBACK: POSTEVALUATION

PART ONE
Check the contents of your script outline with item 4 on the Checklist for Developing Symbolic Models on page 345.

PART TWO
1. *Rationale*
   First, you explain to Mr. Brown what the self-as-a-model procedure consists of and how it could help him practice and gain confidence in his skills of initiating social contacts with his boss.

2. *Recording of behavior*
   After a practice attempt and some coaching of the behaviors required in initiating a contact, have Mr. Brown practice initiating a social contact with you role-playing the part of his boss. Record these practices until you have obtained an adequate sample of his behavior.

3. *Editing the tape*
   After the practice tape has been made, you would edit the tape so that any inappropriate behaviors are deleted; only appropriate behaviors are left on the tape.

4. *Demonstrating with the tape*
   The edited tape would be used as the model for Mr. Brown, who would hear it replayed. After the playback, you might suggest additional practice.

5. *Homework*
   Mr. Brown would arrange to listen to or view the tape daily, followed by role play or covert (mental) practice of the behaviors involved in initiating social contacts with his boss.

PART THREE
Rate your taped interview or have someone else rate you, using the Interview Checklist for Self-as-a-Model.

PART FOUR
Here is a brief description of how you might use participant modeling to help Mr. Brown.

Rationale
First, you would explain to Mr. Brown that the procedure can help him acquire the kinds of skills he will need to initiate social contacts with his boss. You

(continued)

FEEDBACK: POSTEVALUATION (continued)

would also tell him that the procedure involves modeling, guided practice, and success experiences. You might emphasize that the procedure is based on the idea that change can occur when the desired activities are learned in small steps with successful performance emphasized at each step. This successful performance will help Mr. Brown do what he wants to do but presently avoids.

Modeling
You and Mr. Brown would explore the verbal and nonverbal responses that might be involved in Mr. Brown's approaching his boss and asking him out to lunch, for a drink, and so on. For example, these skills might be divided into direct eye contact, making a verbal request, speaking without hesitation or errors, and speaking in a firm, strong voice. After specifying all the components of the desired response, you and Mr. Brown would arrange them in a hierarchy according to order of difficulty for him. If there are any other situations in which he has trouble making a request, these could also be included.

You and Mr. Brown would select the appropriate model—yourself, an aide, or possibly one of Mr. Brown's colleagues. The model selected would demonstrate the first response in the hierarchy (followed by all the others) to Mr. Brown. Repeated demonstrations of any response might be necessary.

Guided participation
After the modeled demonstration of a response, you would ask Mr. Brown to perform it. His first attempts would be assisted with induction aids administered by you or the model. For example, you might verbally coach him or start with a short message and gradually increase it. After each practice, you would give Mr. Brown feedback, being sure to encourage his positive performance and make suggestions for improvement. Generally, Mr. Brown would practice each response several times, and the number of induction aids would be reduced gradually. Before moving on to practice a *different* response, Mr. Brown should be able to perform the response in a self-directed manner without your presence or support.

Success experiences
You and Mr. Brown would identify situations in his environment in which he would like to use the skills he has learned. In his case, most of the situations would center on social situations with his boss. For example, the situations for Mr. Brown might include

visiting his boss in his boss's office, going over to speak to his boss during a break or at lunch, asking his boss to accompany him on a coffee break, asking his boss out for lunch, and inviting his boss to his home for dinner or drinks. As you may note, some of these situations involve more risk than others. The situations should be arranged in order, from the least to the most risky. Mr. Brown would work on the least risky situation until he was able to do that easily and successfully before going on. Ideally, it would help to have the counselor or model go along with Mr. Brown to model and guide. If the model was one of his colleagues, this would be possible. If this was not possible, Mr. Brown could telephone the counselor just before his "contact" to rehearse and to receive coaching and encouragement.

PART FIVE
Use the Interview Checklist for Participant Modeling to assess your performance or to have someone else rate you.

EMOTIVE IMAGERY
AND COVERT MODELING

FOURTEEN

With some client problems, a counselor may find that it is impossible or unrealistic to provide live or symbolic models or to have the client engage in overt practice of the goal behaviors. In these cases, it may be more practical to employ strategies that use the client's imagination for the modeling or rehearsal. This chapter describes two therapeutic procedures that rely heavily on client imagery: emotive imagery and covert modeling. In both these strategies, scenes are developed that the client visualizes or rehearses by imagination. It has been assumed that the client must be able to generate strong, vivid images to use these procedures, but we do not know at present to what extent the intensity of the client's imagery correlates with therapeutic outcomes (M. J. Mahoney, 1974).

☐ OBJECTIVES

1. Given seven examples of counselor leads, identify which of the five steps of the emotive imagery procedure are presented in each counselor lead. You should be able to identify accurately at least six out of seven examples.
2. Demonstrate 10 out of 13 steps of emotive imagery with a role-play client, using the Interview Checklist for Emotive Imagery at the end of the chapter to assess your performance.
3. Describe how you would apply the five components of covert modeling, given a simulated client case.
4. Demonstrate at least 22 out of 28 steps associated with covert modeling with a role-play client, using the Interview Checklist for Covert Modeling at the end of the chapter to assess your use of this strategy.

☐ ASSESSMENT OF CLIENT IMAGERY

In both emotive imagery and covert modeling, it is essential to assess the client's potential for engaging in imagery or fantasy. To some extent, the success of these two strategies may depend on the client's capacity to generate vivid images. As Kazdin points out, "Presumably, the effect of treatment is influenced by the extent to which the client is imagining the material presented by the therapist" (1976b, p. 480). Some clients may be "turned off" by imagery; others may find it difficult to picture vivid scenes in their minds.

There are several ways the counselor can assess the intensity and clarity of client images. First, the client's level of imagery could be assessed before using emotive imagery or covert modeling with a self-report questionnaire such as the Visual and Auditory Imagery parts of the Imaginal Processes Inventory (Singer & Antrobus, 1972), the Betts QMI (Sheehan, 1967), the Imagery Survey Schedule (Cautela, 1977), or other such measures as reviewed by White, Sheehan, and Ashton (1977). The counselor and client can also develop practice scenes that the client can use to generate images. For example, the counselor might instruct the client to "visualize a scene or event that makes you feel relaxed and pleasant. Select a scenario that you really enjoy and feel good about—try to be aware of all your sensations while in the scene." Kazdin (1976b) suggests that the client can narrate aloud the events in the practice scene as they are imagined. Or, after 30 seconds to a minute of imagery, the counselor can ask the client to describe the scene in detail. After the client's description, the counselor might probe about the colors, sounds, movement, temperature, or smell reflected in the scene. The idea is to ascertain how vividly the client imagined the scene. (Additionally, the counselor might ask how the client was feeling during the imagined scene. This question helps the counselor get an impression of how much the client can "get into," or become involved in, the scene.)

If a client has some difficulty imagining specific details, the counselor can train the client to engage in more detailed imagery (Lazarus, 1982; Phillips, 1971). If this seems too time-consuming or if the client is reluctant to use or uninterested in using imagery, a strategy that does not involve imagery may be more appropriate. If a client has good feelings about imagery and can "get into" the practice scene, then the counselor and client may decide to continue with either emotive imagery or covert modeling, depending on the client's problem and goal behavior.

☐ EMOTIVE IMAGERY

In using the emotive imagery procedure, a person focuses on positive thoughts or images while imagining a discomforting or anxiety-arousing activity or situation. By focusing on positive and pleasant images, the person is able to "block" the painful, fearful, or anxiety-provoking situation. One can think of blocking in emotive imagery as a process that takes advantage of the difficulty of focusing on pleasant thoughts and on anxiety, pain, or tension at the same time. This is difficult because these emotions are incompatible.

Imagery is very frequently used as an induction procedure for hypnosis (Clarke & Jackson, 1983), and several studies have reported the use of emotive imagery as a therapeutic strategy. Lazarus and Abramovitz (1962) were among the first to report such a study. Children with phobias were instructed to engage in enjoyable fantasies while experiencing phobic stimuli. For example, a child's school phobia was eliminated by introducing imagery scenes about school centered on a fictional character, Noddy. As these authors point out, "The essence of this procedure was to create imagined situations where Noddy played the role of a truant and responded fearfully to the school setting. The patient (child) would then protect him, either by active reassurance or by 'setting a good example'" (pp. 191–195). Lazarus (1968) has used relaxing images to enhance muscle relaxation. The client selects any imagined scene that she or he finds relaxing and focuses on the scene while engaging in deep muscle relaxation. Lazarus claims that he can obtain deeper and more satisfying levels of relaxation with the use of relaxing images. Horan (1973) has used emotive imagery with pregnant women to reduce the discomfort and anxiety associated with childbirth. Stone, Demchik-Stone, and Horan (1977) found that emotive imagery was as effective as the Lamaze method of prophylactic childbirth in controlling pain-tolerance levels of pregnant women. In an analogue study, Horan and Dellinger (1974) found that people who listened to tape-recorded relaxation-producing images were able to hold their hands immersed in ice water more than twice as long as people who did not use relaxing images. Horan, Layng, and Pursell (1976) reported that heart rates of women who experienced discomfort while having their teeth cleaned declined, on the average, from 77 beats per minute to 65 beats after five minutes of tape-recorded relaxation-producing emotive images. Worthington and Shumate (1981) and Varni (1981) found that imagery was an effective method of pain control. Progressive muscle-relaxation training plus emotive imagery was used effectively to reduce the aversiveness of chemotherapy for cancer patients (Lyles, Burish, Krozely, & Oldham, 1982). Pickett and Cloum (1982) found that patients who had had gall-bladder surgery were able to reduce postsurgical anxiety by imagining a pleasant situation. Three types of imagery scenes—neutral (going to the library), positive (jogging on a beautiful, clear, sunny day), and self-generated scenes—were found to be equally effective in reducing depression (Jarvinen & Gold, 1981). A novel use of imagery has been applied to cancer patients (Simonton & Simonton, 1975). These researchers found that some terminal cancer patients instructed to imagine their disease and their body's own immune mechanisms (white blood cells) attacking the diseased and weakened cancer cells extended their lives past the predicted life expectancy.

Emotive imagery can be applied to a variety of client concerns and problems. Situations in which positive images can be used concurrently to reduce discomfort include "receiving injections, minor surgery and chronic recurring pain" (Horan, 1976, p. 318). Emotive imagery is also applicable to situations in which people experience boredom or tension created by daily routine. This use of the procedure can be viewed as a cognitive "time-out" or a "rest-and-recuperation" (R-and-R) strategy. In vivo emotive imagery can be applied as a single strategy or used with other procedures to increase relaxation and to reduce discomfort or tension. Lazarus (1982) has developed a series of audiotapes instructing the listener to use imagery to help cope with fears, phobias, and daily problems, to overcome sadness, to maintain achievement goals, and to achieve habit control.

Emotive imagery involves five steps: a rationale, assessment of the client's imagery potential, development of imagery scenes, practice of scenes, and homework. See the Interview Checklist for Emotive Imagery at the end of the chapter for some examples of counselor leads associated with these steps.

Treatment Rationale
The following illustration of the purpose and overview of emotive imagery has been given to pregnant women about the procedure for reducing childbirth anxiety and for relieving discomfort during labor (Horan, 1976):

Here is how in vivo emotive imagery works: In this culture women often learn to expect excruciat-

ing pain in childbirth. Even intelligent sophisticated women have a hard time shaking this belief. Consequently, the prospect of childbirth is often fraught with considerable anxiety. In the labor room, early contractions are seen as signals for unbearable pain to follow. The result is that even more anxiety occurs.

Now, since anxiety has a magnifying effect on childbirth discomfort, the more anxious you become the more actual pain you will probably experience. This "vicious circle" happens all too frequently.

The process of in vivo emotive imagery involves having you focus on scenes or events which please you or make you feel relaxed, while the contractions are occurring. You simply cannot feel calm, happy, secure—or whatever other emotion the scenes engender—and anxious at the same time. These opposing emotions are incompatible with each other.

So, in vivo emotive imagery blocks the anxiety which leads to increased childbirth discomfort. There is also some evidence which suggests that the holding of certain images can raise your pain threshold. Thus, in vivo emotive imagery not only eliminates anxiety-related discomfort, but it also has a dulling effect on what might be called real pain! [pp. 317–318]*

The rationale ends with a request for the client's willingness to try the strategy.

Assessment of Client's Imagery Potential
Because the success of the emotive imagery procedure may depend on the amount of positive feelings and calmness a client can derive from visualizing a particular scene, it is important for the counselor to get a feeling for the client's potential for engaging in imagery. The counselor can assess the client's imagery potential by the methods discussed at the beginning of this chapter: a self-report questionnaire, a practice scene with client narration, or counselor "probes" for details.

Development of Imagery Scenes
If the decision is made to continue with the emotive imagery procedure, the client and counselor will then develop imagery scenes. They should develop at least two, although one scene might be

* From Counseling Methods by John D. Krumboltz and Carl E. Thoresen. Copyright © 1976 by Holt, Rinehart and Winston, Inc. Reprinted by permission of CBS College Publishing.

satisfactory for some clients. The exact number and type of scenes developed will depend on the nature of the concern and the individual client.

Two basic ingredients should be included in the selection and development of the scene. First, the scenario should promote calmness, tranquility, or enjoyment for the client. Examples of such client scenes might include skiing on a beautiful slope, hiking on a trail in a large forest, sailing on a sunny lake, walking on a secluded beach, listening to and watching a symphony orchestra perform a favorite composition, or watching an athletic event. The scenes can involve the client as an active participant or as a participant observer or spectator. For some clients, the more active they are in the scene, the greater the degree of their involvement.

The second ingredient of the scene should be as much sensory detail as possible, such as sounds, colors, temperature, smell, touch, and motion. There may be a high positive correlation between the degree and number of sensations a scene elicits for the client and the amount or intensity of pleasant and enjoyable sensations the client experiences in a particular imagery scene. The counselor and client should decide on the particular senses that will be incorporated into the imagery scenes.

As an example, the following imagery scene was used by Horan (1976) for people who experience discomfort having their teeth cleaned. Note the sensations described in the scene instructions:

Now close your eyes, sit back, and relax. Eyes closed, sitting back in the chair, relaxing. Now visualize yourself standing by the shore of a large lake, looking out across an expanse of blue water and beyond to the far shore. Immediately in front of you stretches a small beach, and behind you a grassy meadow. The sun is bright and warm. The air is fresh and clean. It's a gorgeous summer day. The sky is pale blue with great billowy clouds drifting by. The wind is blowing gently, just enough to make the trees sway and make gentle ripples in the grass. It's a perfect day. And you have it entirely to yourself, with nothing to do, nowhere to go. You take from your car a blanket, towel, and swim-suit, and walk off through the meadow. You find a spot, spread the blanket, and lie down on it. It's so warm and quiet. It's such a treat to have the day to yourself to just relax and take it easy. Keep your eyes closed, thinking about the warm, beautiful day. You're in your suit now, walking toward the water, feeling the soft, lush grass under your feet. You reach the beach and start across it. Now you can feel the warm sand underfoot. Very warm and very nice. Now visualize yourself walking out into the

water up to your ankles; out farther, up to your knees. The water's so warm it's almost like a bath. Now you're moving faster out into the lake, up to your waist, up to your chest. The water's so warm, so comfortable. You take a deep breath and glide a few feet forward down into the water. You surface and feel the water run down your back. You look around; you're still all alone. You still have this lovely spot to yourself. Far across the lake you can see a sailboat, tiny in the distance. It's so far away you can just make out the white sail jutting up from the blue water. You take another breath and kick off this time toward the shore swimming with long easy strokes. Kicking with your feet, pulling through with your arms and hands. You swim so far that when you stop and stand the water's only up to your waist, and you begin walking toward the beach, across the warm sand to the grass. Now you're feeling again the grass beneath your feet. Deep, soft, lush. You reach your blanket and pick up the towel, and begin to dry yourself. You dry your hair, your face, your neck. You stretch the towel across your shoulders, dry your back, your legs. You can feel the warm sun on your skin. It must be ninety degrees, but it's clear and dry. The heat isn't oppressive; it's just nice and warm and comfortable. You lie down on the blanket and feel the deep, soft grass under your head. You're looking up at the sky, seeing those great billowy clouds floating by, far, far, above [p. 319].*

Practice of Imagery Scenes

After the imagery scenes have been developed, the client is instructed to practice using them. There are two types of practice. In the first type, the client is instructed to focus on one of the scenes for about 30 seconds and to picture as much detail as was developed for that scene and feel all the sensations associated with it. The counselor cues the client after the time has elapsed. After the client uses the scene, the counselor obtains an impression of the imagery experience — the client's feelings and sensory details of the scene. If other scenes are developed, the client can be instructed to practice imagining them. Variations on this type of practice might be to have the client use or hold a scene for varying lengths of time.

The second type of practice is to have the client use the scenes in simulated anxious, tense, fearful, or painful situations. The counselor and client

* From *Counseling Methods* by John D. Krumboltz and Carl E. Thoresen. Copyright © 1976 by Holt, Rinehart and Winston, Inc. Reprinted by permission of CBS College Publishing.

should simulate the problem situations while using the imagery scenes. Practice under simulated conditions permits the counselor and client to assess the effectiveness of the scenes for blocking out the discomfort or for reducing the anxiety or phobic reaction. Simulated situations can be created by describing vividly the details of an anxiety-provoking situation while the client uses a scene. For example, the counselor can describe the pleasant scene while interweaving a description of the discomforting situation (Lazarus & Abramovitz, 1962). The counselor can simulate painful situations by squeezing the client's arm while the client focuses on one of the scenes. Or, to simulate labor contractions, the labor coach squeezes the woman's thigh while she focuses on a pleasant image. Another simulation technique is to have clients hold their hands in ice water for a certain length of time. Simulated practice may facilitate generalization of the scene application to the actual problem situation. After the simulated practices, the counselor should assess the client's reactions to using the scene in conjunction with the simulated discomfort or anxiety.

Homework and Follow-up

The client is instructed to apply the emotive imagery *in vivo*—that is, to use the scenes in the fearful, painful, tense, or anxious situation. The client can use a homework log to record the day, time, and situation in which emotive imagery was used. The client can also note reactions before and after using emotive imagery with a 5-point scale, 1 representing minimum discomfort and 5 indicating maximum discomfort. The client should be told to bring the homework log to the next session or to a follow-up session.

☐ MODEL EXAMPLE: EMOTIVE IMAGERY

In this model example, we are going to deviate from our usual illustrations of hypothetical cases and present a narrative account of how the two of us used emotive imagery before and during labor for the birth of our two children.

1. *Rationale*
   First, we discussed a rationale for using emotive imagery during labor in conjunction with the breathing and relaxation techniques (see Chapter 17) we had learned in our prepared-childbirth class. We decided before labor started that we would try emotive imagery at a point during

labor when the breathing needed to be supplemented with something else. We also worked out a finger-signaling system to use during contractions so Sherry could inform Bill whether to continue or stop with the imagery scenes, depending on their effectiveness.

2. *Assessment of imagery potential*
   We also discussed whether Sherry was able to use fantasy effectively enough to concentrate during a labor contraction. We tested this out by having Bill describe imagery stimuli and having Sherry imagine these and try to increase use of all sensations to make the imagery scenes as vivid as possible.

3. *Development of imagery scenes*
   Together we selected two scenes to practice with before labor and to use during labor. One scene involved being on a sailboat on a sunny, warm day and sailing quite fast with a good breeze. We felt this scene would be effective because it produced enjoyment and also because it seemed to evoke a lot of sensory experience. The second scene involved being anchored at night on the boat with a full moon, a soft breeze, and some wine. Since both these scenes represented actual experiences, we felt they might work better than sheer fantasy.

4. *Practice of imagery scenes*
   We knew that much of the success of using emotive imagery during labor would depend on the degree to which we worked with it before labor. We practiced with our imagery scenes in two ways. First, Sherry imagined these scenes on her own, sometimes in conjunction with her self-directed practice in breathing and relaxation, and sometimes just as something to do —for instance, in a boring situation. Second, Sherry evoked the scenes deliberately while Bill simulated a contraction by tightly squeezing her upper arm.

5. *Homework: In vivo*
   We had a chance to apply emotive imagery during labor itself. We started to use it during the active phase of labor—about midway through the time of labor, when the contractions were coming about every 2 minutes. In looking back, we felt it was a useful supplement to the breathing and relaxation typically taught in the Lamaze childbirth method. Sherry felt that a lot of the effectiveness had to do with the soothing effect of hearing Bill's vocal descriptions of the scenes—in addition to the images she produced during the scene descriptions.

LEARNING ACTIVITY #37: EMOTIVE IMAGERY

This learning activity is designed to help you learn the process of emotive imagery. It will be easier to do this with a partner, although you can do it alone if a partner is not available. You may wish to try it with a partner first and then by yourself.

Instructions for Dyadic Activity

1. In dyads, one of you can take the helper role; the other takes the part of the helpee. Switch roles after the first practice with the strategy.
2. The helper should give an explanation about the emotive imagery procedure.
3. The helper should determine the helpee's potential for imagination: ask the helpee to imagine several pleasant scenes and then probe for details.
4. The helper and helpee together should develop two imagery scenes the helpee can vividly imagine. Imagination of these scenes should produce pleasant, positive feelings.
5. The helpee should practice imagining these scenes — as vividly and as intensely as possible.
6. The helpee should practice imagining a scene while the helper simulates a problem situation. For

example, the helper can simulate an anxiety-provoking situation by describing it while the helpee engages in imagery, or the helper can stimulate pain by squeezing the helpee's arm during the imagination.

Instructions for Self-Activity

1. Think of two scenes you can imagine very vividly. These scenes should produce positive or pleasant feelings for you. Supply as many details to these scenes as you can.
2. Practice imagining these scenes as intensely as you can.
3. Next, practice imagining one of these scenes while simulating a problem (discomforting) situation such as holding a piece of ice in your hands or running your hands under cold water. Concentrate very hard on the imagery as you do so.
4. Practice this twice daily for the next three days. See how much you can increase your tolerance for the cold temperature with daily practice of the imagery scene.

☐ COVERT MODELING

Covert modeling is a procedure developed by Cautela (1971) in which the client imagines a model performing behaviors by means of instructions. The covert modeling procedure assumes that a live or symbolic performance by a model is not necessary. Instead, the client is directed to imagine someone demonstrating the desired behavior. Flannery (1972) used covert modeling as part of a treatment strategy with a college dropout. Cautela, Flannery, and Hanley (1974) compared covert and overt (live) modeling in reducing avoidance behaviors of college students; both procedures were effective. In the last decade, most of the supportive data for the covert modeling procedure have resulted from studies conducted by Kazdin (1973a, 1974a, 1974b, 1974c, 1974d, 1975, 1976a, 1976b, 1976c, 1979a, 1979b, 1980a, 1982). Rosenthal and Reese (1976) explored the effectiveness of covert modeling in developing assertive behaviors. The procedure has also been used to treat alcoholism and obsessive-compulsive behaviors (Hay, Hay, & Nelson, 1977) and to decrease smoking (Nesse & Nelson, 1977). L. Watson (1976)

found that covert modeling was effective in helping prison inmates acquire job-interview skills. Covert modeling has also been used to decrease test anxiety (Gallagher & Arkowitz, 1978) and has been used with hypnosis in the treatment of obesity (Bornstein & Devine, 1980).

Covert modeling has several advantages: the procedure does not require elaborate therapeutic or induction aids; scenes can be developed to deal with a variety of problems; the scenes can be individualized to fit the unique concerns of the client; the client can practice the imagery scenes alone; the client can use the imagery scenes as a self-control procedure in problem situations; and covert modeling may be a good alternative when live or filmed models cannot be used or when it is difficult to use overt rehearsal in the interview.

Some questions about certain aspects of covert modeling remain unanswered, such as the importance of the identity of the model, the role of reinforcing consequences, and the type and duration of imagery scenes best used in the procedure. We have tried to point out the possible alternatives in our description of the components of the covert modeling strategy. Our description is based not only on our own experience with it but also on the pioneering efforts of Cautela (1971) and Kazdin (1976b). The five major components of covert modeling are rationale about the strategy, practice scenes, developing treatment scenes, applying treatment scenes, and homework. Within each of these five components are several substeps. If you would like an overview of the procedure, see the Interview Checklist for Covert Modeling at the end of the chapter.

Treatment Rationale

After the counselor and client have reviewed the problem behaviors and the goal behaviors for counseling, the counselor presents the rationale for covert modeling. Here is Kazdin's (1976b) explanation of a treatment rationale for using covert modeling in assertiveness training:

In developing behavior such as assertive skills, it is essential to rehearse or practice elements of the skills. Specifically, it is important to rehearse the situations in which assertiveness is the appropriate response. Numerous situations in life require an assertive response of some sort. Learning what these situations are and being able to discriminate appropriate responses are important. People can rehearse situations in their imagination. Imagining certain selected situations can alter one's behavior in those actual situations. For example, to get rid of one's fear, one can imagine carefully selected scenes related to fear and remove the fear. So imagination can strongly influence behavior [p. 477].

The rationale should also provide a brief description of the process of covert modeling. Cautela (1976) provides an illustration of the way he describes the covert modeling process to a client:

In a minute, I'll ask you to close your eyes and try to imagine, as clearly as possible, that you are observing a certain situation. Try to use all the senses needed for the particular situation, e.g., try to actually hear a voice or see a person very clearly. After I describe the scene, I will ask you some questions concerning your feelings about the scene and how clearly you imagined it [p. 324].

Practice Scenes

After providing a rationale to the client, the counselor may decide to try out the imagery process with several practice scenes. For most clients, imagining a scene may be a new experience and may seem foreign. Kazdin (1976b, p. 478) suggests that practice scenes may help to familiarize clients

with the procedure and sensitize them to focus on specific details of the imagery. Use of practice scenes also helps the counselor to assess the client's potential for carrying out instructions in the imagination.

The practice scenes usually consist of simple, straightforward situations that are unrelated to the goal behaviors. For example, if you are using covert modeling to help a client acquire job-interview skills, the practice scenes would be unrelated to job-seeking responses. You might use some of the following as practice scenes:

1. Imagine a person in a library checking out a book.
2. Imagine someone lying on the beach in the hot sun.
3. Imagine someone eating a gourmet meal at an elegant restaurant.
4. Imagine someone being entertained at a night spot.

In using practice scenes with a client, the counselor usually follows six steps.

1. The counselor instructs the client to close his or her eyes and to sit back and relax. The client is instructed to tell the counselor when he or she feels relaxed. If the client does not feel relaxed, the counselor may need to decide whether relaxation procedures (Chapter 17) should be introduced. The effect of relaxation on the quality of imagery in covert modeling has not been evaluated. However, research on live and symbolic modeling suggests that modeling may be facilitated when the client is relaxed (Bandura, Blanchard, & Ritter, 1969).

2. The counselor describes a practice scene and instructs the client to imagine the scene and to raise an index finger when the scene has been imagined vividly. The practice scenes are similar to the four previous examples. The counselor reads the scene or instructs the client about what to imagine.

3. The counselor asks the client to open his or her eyes after the scene is vividly imagined (signal of index finger) and to describe the scene or to narrate the imagined events.

4. The counselor probes for greater details about the scene — the clothes or physical features of a person in the imagery, the physical setting of the situation, the amount of light, colors of the furniture, decorative features, noises, or smells. This probing may encourage the client to focus on details of the imagery scene.

5. The counselor may suggest additional details for the client to imagine during a subsequent practice. Working with practice scenes first can facilitate the development of the details in the actual treatment scenes.

6. Usually each practice scene is presented several times. The number of practice scenes used before moving on to developing and applying treatment scenes will depend on several factors. If the client feels comfortable with the novelty of the imagined scenes after several presentations, the counselor might consider this a cue to stop using the practice scenes. Additionally, if the client can provide a fairly detailed description of the imagery after several practice scenes, this may be a good time to start developing treatment scenes. If a client reports difficulty in relaxing, the counselor may need to introduce relaxation training before continuing. For a client who cannot generate images during the practice scenes, another modeling strategy may be needed in lieu of covert modeling.

Developing Treatment Scenes

The treatment scenes used in covert modeling are developed in conjunction with the client and grow out of the desired client outcomes or goals. The scenes consist of a variety of situations in which the client wants to perform the target response in the real-life environment. If the client wants to develop assertion skills, the treatment scenes represent different situations requiring assertive responses. If a client wants to acquire effective job-interview skills, the treatment scenes are developed around job-interview situations.

Five things should be considered in the development of treatment scenes: the model characteristics, whether to use individualized or standardized scenes, whether to use vague or specific scenes, the ingredients of the scenes, and the number of scenes. It is important for the client to help in the development of treatment scenes because client participation can provide many specifics about situations in which the goal behavior is to be performed.

Model characteristics. As you may recall from Chapter 12, research about model characteristics in live and symbolic modeling indicates that similarity between the model and the client contributes to client change (Bandura, 1971a). Kazdin (1974b) found that, in covert modeling, a same-

sex and similar-age model produced greater avoidance reduction with college students than an older model or a model of the other sex. Further, clients who imagined several models showed more change than clients who imagined only one model (Kazdin, 1974a, 1976c). Coping models also seemed to be generally more effective in covert modeling than mastery models (Bornstein & Devine, 1980; Kazdin, 1973a; Meichenbaum, 1971). A coping model who self-verbalizes his or her anxiety and uses covert self-talk for dealing with fear may enhance and facilitate the behaviors to be acquired (Tearnan, Lahey, Thompson, & Hammer, 1982, p. 180).

One of the most interesting questions about the covert model is the identity of the model. Kazdin (1974a) found no differences between college-age subjects who imagined *themselves* as the model and subjects who imagined *another person* as the model. Using a somewhat different population, incarcerated youth offenders, Watson (1976) found that covert self-modeling (imagining oneself) was superior to covert modeling (imagining someone else) on some measures. As Krumboltz and Thoresen (1976, p. 484) point out, no one is more similar to the client than the client! At present there are not sufficient data to indicate who the model should be in the covert modeling procedure. We suspect that the answer varies with clients and suggest that you give clients the option of deciding whether to imagine themselves or another person as the model. One key factor may involve the particular identity the client can imagine most easily and comfortably. For clients who feel some stress at first in imagining themselves as models, imagining someone else might be introduced first and later replaced with self-modeling.

Individualized versus standardized scenes. The treatment scenes used in covert modeling can be either standardized or individualized. Standardized scenes cover different situations in everyday life and are presented to a group of clients or to all clients with the same target responses. For example, Kazdin (1976b) used a series of standardized scenes describing situations requiring assertive responses for nonassertive clients. Individualized scenes represent situations specifically tailored to suit an individual client. For example, one nonassertive client may need scenes developed around situations with strangers; another may need scenes that involve close friends. Generally, treatment scenes should be individualized for those who have unique concerns and who are counseled individually, since some standardized scenes may not be relevant for a particular client.

Kazdin (1979b, 1980a) found that clients who were instructed to individualize (elaborate) scenes increased their assertive behavior. In these two studies, clients were permitted to change (elaborate or improvise) the "scene in any way as long as the model engaged in an assertive response" (1979b, p. 727). (See also "Verbal Summary Codes and Personalization" a few pages ahead.)

Degree of specificity of scenes.   Another consideration in developing treatment scenes is the degree of specificity of instruction that should be included. Some clients may benefit from very explicit instructions about the details of what to imagine. Other clients may derive more gains from covert modeling if the treatment scenes are more general, allowing the client to supply the specific features. A risk of not having detailed instructions is that some clients will introduce scene material that is irrelevant or detracts from the desired outcomes. Kazdin (1976b) has explored clients' imagery during the treatment scenes and found that clients do make some changes. However, he indicates that such changes appear to be infrequent and that there do not seem to be any particular features of a scene introduced by a client that are consistently related to treatment outcome (p. 481). At this point, the data on the necessary degree of specificity of a treatment scene are limited. Again, we suggest this decision should consider the client's preferences.

Here is an example of a fairly general treatment scene for a prison inmate about to be released on parole who is seeking employment:

"Picture yourself (or someone else like you) in a job interview. The employer asks why you didn't complete high school. You tell the employer you got in some trouble, and the employer asks what kind of trouble. You feel a little uptight but tell her you have a prison record. The employer asks why you were in prison and for how long. The employer then asks what makes you think you can stay out of trouble and what you have been doing while on parole. Imagine yourself saying that you have been looking for work while on parole and have been thinking about your life and what you want to do with it."

The generality of the treatment scene in this example assumes that the client knows what type of response to make and what details to supply in the scene.

A more detailed treatment scene would specify more of the actual responses. For example:

"Picture yourself (or someone else) in a job interview and imagine the following dialogue. The employer says, 'I see that you have only finished three years of high school. You don't intend to graduate?' Picture yourself saying (showing some anxiety): 'Well, no, I want to go to vocational school while I'm working.' The employer asks: 'What happened? How did you get so far behind in school?' Imagine yourself (or someone else) replying: 'I've been out of school for awhile because I've been in some trouble.' Now imagine the employer is showing some alarm and asks: 'What kind of trouble?' You decide to be up front as you imagine yourself saying: 'I want you to know that I have a prison record.' As the employer asks: 'Why were you in prison?' imagine yourself feeling a little nervous but staying calm and saying something like: 'I guess I was pretty immature. Some friends and I got involved with drugs. I'm on parole now. I'm staying away from drugs and I'm looking hard for a job. I really want to work'" [L. Watson, 1976].

Remember, the degree of specificity of each scene will depend largely on the client, the problem or concern, and the goals for counseling.

Ingredients for the scene.   Three ingredients are required for a treatment scene in the covert modeling procedure: a description of the situation or context in which the behavior is to occur, a description of the model demonstrating the behavior to be acquired, and a depiction of some favorable outcome of the goal behavior. Kazdin (1976b) gives an example of a covert modeling scene for assertive behavior in which the situation and the goal behavior are illustrated:

Situation: Imagine the person (model) is staying at a hotel. After one night there, he (she) notices that the bed springs must be broken. The bed sags miserably and was very uncomfortable during the night.

Model demonstrating the behavior: In the morning, the person goes to the clerk at the desk and says: "The bed in my room is quite uncomfortable. I believe it is broken. I wish you would replace the bed or change my room" [p. 485].

Hay et al. (1977) developed covert modeling scenes that included a favorable outcome for an adult male alcoholic. This is an example of one of the scenes for their client:

> Imagine yourself walking in town and running into a group of your old drinking buddies. They have already been drinking heavily and ask you to join them. They are drinking white lightning. They look happy and you are alone. In the past you would have taken a drink and probably have become drunk. Now cope with the situation. Imagine yourself feeling the "urge" to drink, but refusing and slowly turning and walking down the street [p. 71].

Here the model (the client) is depicted as coping with a situation and then refusing to drink and walking away, which is a favorable outcome.

Inclusion of a favorable consequence as a scene ingredient is based on research indicating that if a client sees a model rewarded for the behavior, the client is more likely to perform the response (Bandura, 1976b). Moreover, specifying a possible favorable outcome to imagine may prevent a client from inadvertently imagining an unfavorable one. Kazdin (1974c, 1976c) found that clients who received covert modeling treatment scenes that were resolved favorably were more assertive than clients who imagined scenes without any positive consequences.

We believe that the favorable outcome in the scene should take the form of some action initiated by the client or of covert self-reinforcement or praise. For example, the favorable outcome illustrated in the scene for the alcoholic client was the client's self-initiated action of walking away from the alcohol (Hay et al., 1977). We prefer that the action be initiated by the client or model instead of someone else in the scene because, in a real situation, it may be too risky to have the client rely on someone else to deliver a favorable outcome in the form of a certain response. We cannot guarantee that clients will always receive favorable responses from someone else in the actual situation.

In some previous reports of covert modeling, nonassertive clients experienced a favorable response by another person through the person's compliance. But as Nietzel, Martorano, and Melnick (1977) point out, using compliance of someone else as a favorable outcome might reinforce inaccurate client expectations and also could fail to help a client learn how to respond to noncompliance. These authors compared the effectiveness of covert modeling with and without "reply training." In other words, some clients were trained to visualize (1) an initial assertive response by the model, (2) another person's noncomplying response, and (3) a second assertive counterreply by the model. The clients who received the extra "reply training" were more assertive and more persevering in their assertions than the clients who were trained only to make an initial assertive response that was followed by compliance from the other person. Reply training to noncompliance may be more realistic and provide more response alternatives than training someone to receive automatic compliance as a positive consequence.

Another way to incorporate a favorable outcome into a treatment scene is to include an example of client (or model) self-reinforcement or praise. For instance, models might congratulate themselves by saying "That is terrific. I am proud of myself for what I said to the hotel clerk." A favorable consequence in the form of model or client self-praise is self-administered. Again, in a real-life situation, it may be better for clients to learn to reward themselves than to expect external encouragement that might not be forthcoming.

The person who experiences the favorable outcomes will be the same person the client imagines as the model. If the client imagines someone else as the model, then the client would also imagine that person initiating a favorable outcome or reinforcing himself or herself. Clients who imagine themselves as the models would imagine themselves receiving the positive consequences. There is very little actual evidence on the role of reinforcement in covert modeling. Some of the effectiveness of adding favorable consequences to the treatment scene may depend on the identity of the covert model and the particular value of the consequences for the client (Watson, 1976).

Number of scenes. The counselor and client can develop different scenes that portray the situation in which the client experiences difficulty or wants to use the newly acquired behavior. Multiple scenes can depict different situations in which assertive behavior is generally appropriate. In a series of studies, Kazdin (1979a, 1979b, 1982) and Kazdin and Mascitelli (1982b) presented 5 scenes during the first session and 10 in each of the next three sessions, for a total of 35 scenes. Thirty-five is perhaps too many for use in therapy. The number of scenes the therapist and client develop will depend on the client and his or her problem. Although there is no set number of scenes that should be developed, certainly several scenes provide more variety than only one or two.

Applying Treatment Scenes

After all the scenes have been developed, the counselor can apply the treatment scenes by having the client imagine each scene. The basic steps in applying the treatment scenes are these:

1. Arranging the scenes in a hierarchy.
2. Instructing the client before scene presentation.
3. Presenting one scene at a time from the hierarchy.
4. Presenting a scene for a specified duration.
5. Obtaining the client's reactions to the imagined scene.
6. Instructing the client to develop verbal summary codes and/or to personalize each treatment scene.
7. Presenting each scene at least twice with the aid of the counselor or tape recorder.
8. Having the client imagine each scene at least twice while directing himself or herself.
9. Selecting and presenting scenes from the hierarchy in a random order.

Hierarchy.   The scenes developed by the counselor and client should be arranged in a hierarchy for scene presentation (Rosenthal & Reese, 1976). The hierarchy is an order of scenes beginning with one that is relatively easy for the client to imagine with little stress. More difficult or stressful scenes would be ranked by the client.

Instructions.   It may be necessary to repeat instructions about imagery to the client if a great amount of time has elapsed since using the practice scenes. The counselor might say:

> In a minute I will ask you to close your eyes and to sit back and relax. I want you to try to imagine as vividly and clearly as possible that you are observing a certain scene. Try to use *all* the senses needed for the particular situation—for example, try to actually hear the voice(s), see the colors, and picture features of a person (or people). After I describe the scene. I will ask you some questions concerning your feelings about the scene and how clearly you imagined it [Cautela et al., 1974].

If a person other than the client is the model, the client is instructed to picture someone his or her own age and sex whom he or she knows. The client

is told that the person who is pictured as the model will be used in all the treatment scenes. The counselor also instructs the client to signal by raising an index finger as soon as the scene is pictured clearly and to hold the scene in imagery until the counselor signals to stop.

Sequence of scene presentation.   Initially, the first scene in the hierarchy is presented to the client. Each scene is presented alone. When one scene has been covered sufficiently, the next scene in the hierarchy is presented. This process continues until all scenes in the hierarchy have been covered.

Duration of scenes.   There are no general ground rules for the amount of time to hold the scene in imagery once the client signals. In Kazdin's (1976c) research, the client held the imagery for 15 seconds after signaling; in two other studies the scene duration was 30 seconds (Bornstein & Devine, 1980; Nesse & Nelson, 1977). More recently, Kazdin (1979b, 1980b) and Kazdin and Mascitelli (1982b) have instructed clients to hold the scene for 40 seconds. We do not know whether this duration is optimal. For some clients, a longer duration may be more beneficial; for others, a shorter duration may be. We feel that the choice will depend on the counselor's personal preference and experience with the covert modeling procedure, the nature of the client's problem, the goal behavior for counseling, and—perhaps most important—the client's input about the scene duration. After one or two scenes have been presented, the counselor can query the client about the suitability of the scene duration. Generally, a scene should be held long enough for the client to imagine the three scene ingredients vividly without rushing.

Client reactions to the scene.   After the client has imagined a particular scene, the counselor queries the client about how clearly it was imagined. The client is asked to describe feelings during particular parts of the scene. The counselor should also ask whether the scene was described too rapidly or the duration of the scene was adequate for the client to imagine the scene ingredients clearly. These questions enable the counselor and client to modify aspects of a scene before it is presented the second time. Client input about possible scene revision can be very helpful. If particular episodes of the scene elicit intense feelings of anxiety, the content of the scene or the manner of presentation can be revised. Perhaps the order of the scenes in the hierarchy needs rearrangement.

Another way to deal with the client's unpleasant feelings or discomfort with a scene is to talk it over. If the client feels stressful when the model (or the self) is engaging in the behavior or activity in the scene, examine with the client what episode in the scene is producing the discomfort. In addition, if the client is the model and has difficulty performing the behavior or activity, discuss and examine the block. Focus on the adaptive behavior or the coping with the situational ingredient of the scene, rather than on the anxiety or discomfort.

After each scene presentation, the counselor should assess the rate of delivery for the scene description, the clarity of the imagery, and the degree of unpleasantness of the scene for the client. Perhaps if the client has a great deal of input in developing the scenes, the level of discomfort produced will be minimized. In addition, the intensity of the imagined scene can be enhanced by using verbal summary codes or by personalizing the scene.

Verbal summary codes and personalization. Kazdin (1979a, 1979b, 1980a) found that clients who were instructed to use verbal summary codes and/or to elaborate, or personalize, each treatment scene showed higher levels of assertiveness than clients who received only covert modeling. You may wish to use either or both of these techniques with covert modeling.

Verbal summary codes are brief descriptions about the behavior to be acquired and the context in which the behavior is to occur *in the client's own words* (Kazdin, 1979a). Verbal coding of the modeling cues can facilitate acquisition and retention of the behaviors to be modeled and may maintain client performance during and after treatment by helping clients encode desired responses in their working memory. The verbalizations (or verbal summary codes) of the scene provide an alternative representational process to imagery or covert modeling (Kazdin, 1979a). The therapist instructs the client to use his or her descriptions of the behavior and the situation. Kazdin (1979a) recommends that clients rehearse using verbal summary codes with *practice* scenes and receive feedback from the therapist about the descriptions of the practice scenes. The practice should occur before presentation of the *treatment* scenes. Then the treatment scenes are presented and the client is instructed to develop his or her own verbal summary codes (descriptions of behavior and situa-

tion) for the scene. Have the client "try out" the treatment scene on the first presentation *without* the use of the summary code. On the second presentation of the scene, instruct the client to use the summary code and to say aloud exactly what it is.

Personalization of treatment scenes is another technique that can enhance covert modeling. Kazdin (1979b) calls this procedure "imagery elaboration." After the scene has been presented once as developed, then the client is instructed *to change the treatment scene in any way as long as the model responses to be acquired are represented in the scene* (Kazdin, 1979b, p. 727). As with verbal summary codes, the client is asked to rehearse personalizing (individualizing) or elaborating a scene using a practice scene and receives feedback about the elaboration. The counselor should encourage the client to use variations within the context of the situation presented by the scene. Variations include more details about the model responses and the situation in which the responses are to occur. The client is asked to elaborate the scene the second time the treatment scene is presented. Elaboration may lead to more client involvement because the scenes are individualized.

Remember to have the client experience imagining a scene first without instructions to use verbal summary codes or to personalize the scene. Then, on the second presentation of the treatment scene, the client is instructed to use one of these techniques. To verify that the client is complying with the instructions, the therapist can instruct the client to say aloud the verbal summary code or elaboration being used.

Counselor-directed scene repetition. In the analogue studies of Kazdin (1976b, 1976c), each scene is presented twice by the counselor or on a tape recording. However, Cautela (1976) recommends that after presenting the first scene and making any necessary revisions, the counselor repeat the scene four times. The number of scene repetitions may be dictated by the degree of comfort the client experiences while imagining the scene and the complexity of the activities or behaviors the client is to acquire. A complex series of motor skills, for example, may require more repetitions; and engaging in some situations may require more repetition until the client feels reasonably comfortable. Again, make the decision about the number of scene repetitions on the basis of client input: ask the client. If you use the verbal summary codes or personalization of the scene, remember to instruct the client to use the technique during later repetitions of each scene.

Client-directed scene repetition.   In addition to counselor-directed scene practice, the client should engage in self-directed scene practice. Again, the number of client practices is somewhat arbitrary, although perhaps two is a minimum. Generally, the client can repeat imagining the scenes alone until he or she feels comfortable in doing so. The client can either use the verbal summary codes without saying the codes aloud or can personalize the scenes. Overt rehearsal of the scene can facilitate acquisition and retention of the imagined behaviors. The client should be instructed to overtly enact (rehearse) the scene with the therapist after the second or third time each scene is presented (Kazdin, 1980a, 1982; Kazdin & Mascitelli, 1982b).

Random presentation of scenes.   After all the scenes in the hierarchy have been presented adequately, the counselor can check out the client's readiness for self-directed homework practice by presenting some of the scenes in random order. This random presentation guards against any "ordering" effect that the hierarchy arrangement may have had in the scene presentation.

Homework and Follow-up

Self-directed practice in the form of homework is perhaps the most important therapeutic ingredient for generalization. If a person can apply or practice the procedure outside the counseling session, the probability of using the "new" behavior or of coping in the actual situation is greatly enhanced. Kazdin and Mascitelli (1982a, 1982b) found that homework enhanced performance, possibly because clients were instructed to use the newly acquired behaviors *in vivo* between therapy sessions. Homework can consist in having clients identify several situations in their everyday lives in which they could use the desired responses (Kazdin & Mascitelli, 1982b, p. 252). Cautela (1976) recommends that the counselor instruct the client to practice each scene at home *at least* ten times a day. Nesse and Nelson (1977) also recommend to their clients that they rehearse the scenes ten times daily. They found that most clients did rehearse scenes about eight times a day.

Some clients may find it difficult to practice the scenes at home this frequently. The counselor might encourage more frequent and more reliable home practice by providing the client with a "phone-mate" on a clinic phone. With a phone-mate, clients can call and verbalize their practice imagery over the phone. This procedure not only creates a demand characteristic to facilitate client practice but also enables the helper to assess the quality of the client's use of the homework. A client could also rehearse the treatment scenes at home with the aid of a tape recorder (Hay et al., 1977). In arranging the homework tasks, the counselor and client should specify how often, how long, what times during the day, and where practice should occur. The counselor should also instruct the client to record the daily use of the modeling scenes on log sheets. The counselor should verify whether the client understands the homework and should arrange for a follow-up after some portion of the homework is completed.

☐ MODEL DIALOGUE: COVERT MODELING

Here is an example of a covert modeling dialogue with our client Joan to help her increase initiating skills in her math class.

In response 1, the counselor briefly describes the **rationale** *and gives an* **overview** *of the strategy.*

1. *Counselor:* Joan, one way we can help you work on your initiating skills in math class is to help you learn the skills you want through practice. In this procedure, you will practice using your imagination. I will describe situations to you and ask you to imagine yourself or someone else participating in the way described in a situation. How does that sound?
Client: OK. You mean I imagine things like daydreaming?

Further **instructions** *about the strategy are provided in counselor response 2.*

2. *Counselor:* It has some similarities. Only instead of just letting your mind wander, you will imagine some of the skills you want to use to improve your participation in your math class.
Client: Well, I'm a pretty good daydreamer, so if this is similar, I will probably learn from it.

In response 3, the counselor initiates the idea of using **practice scenes** *to determine Joan's level and style of imagery.*

3. *Counselor:* Well, let's see. I think it might help to see how easy or hard it is for you to actually imagine a specific situation as I describe it to you. So maybe we could do this on a try-out basis to see what it feels like for you.
Client: OK, what happens?

In response 4, the counselor instructs Joan to **sit back and relax before imagining the practice scene.**

4. *Counselor:* First of all, just sit back, close your eyes, and relax. [Gives Joan a few minutes to do this.] You look pretty comfortable. How do you feel?

   Client: Fine. It's never too hard for me to relax.

In response 5, the counselor instructs Joan **to imagine the scene vividly and to indicate this by raising her finger.**

5. *Counselor:* OK, now, Joan, I'm going to describe a scene to you. As I do so, I want you to imagine the scene as vividly as possible. When you feel you have a very strong picture, then raise your index finger. Does that seem clear?

   Client: Yes.

The counselor will offer a practice scene next. Note that the **practice scene** *is simple and relatively mundane. It asks Joan only to imagine another person.*

6. *Counselor:* OK, imagine that someone is about to offer you a summer job. Just picture a person who might offer you a job like this. [Gives Joan time until Joan raises her index finger.]

In response 7, the counselor asks Joan **to describe what she imagined.**

7. *Counselor:* OK, Joan, now open your eyes. Can you tell me what you just imagined?

   Client: Well, I pictured myself with a middle-aged man who asked me if I wanted to lifeguard this summer. Naturally I told him yes.

Joan's imagery report was specific in terms of the actions and dialogue, but she didn't describe much about the man, so the counselor **will probe for more details.**

8. *Counselor:* OK, fine. What else did you imagine about the man? You mentioned his age. What was he wearing? Any physical characteristics you can recall?

   Client: Well, he was about 35 [a 16-year-old's impression of "middle age" is different from a 30-, 40-, or 50-year-old person's definition], he was wearing shorts and a golf shirt — you see, we were by the pool. That's about it.

Joan was able to describe the setting and the man's dress but no other physical characteristics, so the counselor **will suggest that Joan add this to the next practice attempt.**

9. *Counselor:* OK, so you were able to see what he was wearing and also the setting where he was talking to you. I'd like to try another practice

with this same scene. Just imagine everything you did before, only this time try to imagine even more details about how this man actually looks. [Counselor presents the same scene, which goes on until Joan raises her finger.]

In response 10, the counselor will **again query Joan about the details of her imagery.**

10. *Counselor:* OK, let's stop. What else did you imagine this time about this person or the situation?

    Client: Well, he was wearing white shorts and a blue shirt. He was a tall man and very tanned. He had dark hair, blue eyes, and had sunglasses on. He was also barefoot. We were standing on the pool edge. The water was blue and the sun was out and it felt hot.

In response 11, the counselor will **try to determine how comfortable Joan is with imagery** *and whether more practice scenes are necessary.*

11. *Counselor:* OK, that's great. Looks like you were able to imagine colors and temperature — like the sun feeling hot. How comfortable do you feel now with this process?

    Client: Oh, I like it. It was easier the second time you described the scene. I put more into it. I like to imagine this anyway.

In response 12, the counselor decides Joan can move ahead and **initiates development of treatment scenes.**

12. *Counselor:* Well, I believe we can go on now. Our next step is to come up with some scenes that describe the situations you find yourself in now with respect to participation in math class.

    Client: And then I'll imagine them in the same way?

The counselor sets the stage to **obtain all the necessary information to develop treatment scenes.** *Note the emphasis in response 13 on Joan's* **participation** *in this process.*

13. *Counselor:* That's right. Once we work out the details of these scenes, you'll imagine each scene as you just did. Now we have sort of a series of things we need to discuss in setting up the scenes in a way that makes it easiest for you to imagine, so I'll be asking you some questions. Your input is very valuable here to both of us.

    Client: OK, shoot.

In response 14, the counselor **asks Joan whether she would rather imagine herself or someone else** *as the model.*

14. *Counselor:* Well, first of all, in that practice

scene I asked you to imagine someone else. Now, you did that, but you were also able to picture yourself from the report you gave me. In using your class scenes, which do you feel would be easiest and least stressful for you to imagine—yourself going through the scene or someone else, maybe someone similar to you, but another person? [Gives Joan time to think.]

Client (pauses): Well, that's hard to say. I think it would be easier for me to imagine myself, but it might be a little less stressful to imagine someone else . . . . [Pauses again.] I think I'd like to try using myself.

In the next response, the counselor **reinforces Joan's choice and also points out the flexibility of implementing the procedure.**

15. *Counselor:* That's fine. And besides, as you know, nothing is that fixed. If we get into this and that doesn't feel right and you want to imagine someone else, we'll change.

Client: Okey-dokey.

In response 16, the counselor **introduces the idea of a coping model.**

16. *Counselor:* Also, sometimes it's hard to imagine yourself doing something perfectly to start with, so when we get into this, I might describe a situation where you might have a little trouble but not much. That may seem more realistic to you. What do you think?

Client: That seems reasonable. I know what you mean. It's like learning to drive a car. In Driver's Ed, we take one step at a time.

In response 17, the counselor **will pose the option of individualizing the scenes** *or using* **standardized scenes.**

17. *Counselor:* You've got the idea. Now we have another choice also in the scenes we use. We can work out scenes just for you that are tailored to your situation, or we can use scenes on a cassette tape I have that have been standardized for many students who want to improve their class-participation skills. Which sounds like the best option to you?

Client: I really don't know. Does it really make a difference?

It is not that uncommon for a client not to know which route to pursue. In the next response, the counselor will **indicate a preference** *and check it out with Joan.*

18. *Counselor:* Probably not, Joan. If you don't have a choice at this point, you might later. My preference would be to tailor-make the scenes we use here in the session. Then, if you like, you could use the taped scenes to practice with at home later on. How does that sound to you?

Client: It sounds good, like maybe we could use both.

In responses 19 and 20, the counselor asks Joan to **identify situations in which Joan desires to increase these skills.** *This is somewhat a review of goal behavior described in Chapter 9.*

19. *Counselor:* Yes, I think we can. Now let's concentrate on getting some of the details we need to make up the scenes we'll use in our sessions. First of all, let's go over the situations in math class in which you want to work on these skills.

Client: Well, it's some of those things we talked about earlier, like being called on, going to the board, and so on.

Next the counselor **explores whether Joan prefers a very general decription or a very specific one.** *Sometimes this makes a difference in how the person imagines.*

20. *Counselor:* OK, Joan, how much detail would you like me to give you when I describe a scene —a little detail, to let you fill in the rest, or do you want me to describe pretty completely what you should imagine?

Client: Maybe somewhere in between. I can fill in a lot, but I need to know what to fill in.

In response 21, the counselor **is asking about the specific situations** *in which Joan has trouble participating in her math class.*

21. *Counselor:* OK, let's fill out our description a little more. We're talking about situations you confront in your math class. I remember four situations in which you wanted to increase these skills—you want to answer more when Mr. _____ calls on you, volunteer more answers, go to the board, and tell Mr. _____ you want to work the problems yourself after you ask for an explanation. Any others, Joan?

Client: I can't think of any offhand.

In responses 22 through 27; the counselor asks Joan to **identify the desired behaviors for these situations.** *Again, much of this is a review of identifying outcome goals (Chapter 9).*

22. *Counselor:* OK, so we've got about four different situations. Let's take each of these separately. For each situation, can we think of what you would like to do in the situation—like when Mr. _____ calls on you, for instance?

Client: Well, I'd like to give him the answer instead of saying nothing or saying "I don't know."

23. *Counselor:* OK, good. And if you did give him

the answer—especially when you do know it—how would you feel?

Client: Good, probably relieved.

24. *Counselor:* OK. Now what about volunteering answers?

Client: Well, Mr. _____ usually asks who has the answer to this; then he calls on people who raise their hand. I usually never raise my hand even when I do know the answer, so I need to just raise my hand and, when he calls on me, give the answer. I need to speak clearly, too. I think sometimes my voice is too soft to hear.

25. *Counselor:* OK, now, how could you tell Mr. _____ to let you work out the problems yourself?

Client: Well, just go up to him when we have a work period and tell him the part I'm having trouble with and ask him to explain it.

26. *Counselor:* So you need to ask him for just an explanation and let him know you want to do the work.

Client: Yup.

27. *Counselor:* OK, now, what about going to the board?

Client: Well, I do go up. But I always feel like a fool. I get distracted by the rest of the class so I hardly ever finish the problem. Then he lets me go back to my seat even though I didn't finish it. I need to concentrate more so I can get through the entire problem on the board.

Now that the content of the scenes has been developed, the counselor asks Joan to **arrange the four scenes in a hierarchy.**

28. *Counselor:* OK, so we've got four different situations in your math class where you want to improve your participation in some way. Let's take these four situations and arrange them in an order. Could you select the situation that right now is easiest for you and least stressful to you and rank the rest in terms of difficulty and degree of stress?

Client: Sure, let me think. . . . Well, the easiest thing to do out of all of these would be to tell Mr. _____ I want to work out the problems myself. Then I guess it would be answering when he calls on me and then going to the board. I have a lot of trouble with volunteering answers, so that would be hardest for me.

The counselor emphasizes the **flexibility of the hierarchy** *and provides* **general instructions to Joan about how they will work with these scenes.**

29. *Counselor:* OK. Now, this order can change. At any point if you feel it isn't right, we can reorder these situations. What we will do is to take one situation at a time, starting with the easiest one,

and I'll describe it to you in terms of the way you want to handle it and ask you to imagine it. So the first scene will involve you telling Mr. _____ what you need explained in order to work the problems yourself.

Client: So we do this just like we did at the beginning?

The counselor will **precede the scene presentation with very specific instructions** *to Joan.*

30. *Counselor:* Right. Just sit back, close your eyes, and relax . . . . [Gives Joan a few minutes to do so.] Now remember, as I describe the scene, you are going to imagine yourself in the situation. Try to use all your senses in your imagination—in other words, get into it. When you have a very vivid picture, raise your index finger. Keep imagining the scene until I give a signal to stop. OK?

Client: Yeah.

The counselor **presents the first scene in Joan's hierarchy slowly** *and with ample pauses to give Joan time to generate the images.*

31. *Counselor:* OK, Joan, picture yourself in math class . . . . [Pause] Mr. _____ has just finished explaining how to solve for x and y. . . . Now he has assigned problems to you and has given you a work period. . . . You are starting to do the problems and you realize there is some part of the equation you can't figure out. You take your worksheet and get up out of your seat and go to Mr. _____'s desk. You are telling Mr. _____ what part of the equation you're having trouble with. You explain to him you don't want him to solve the problem, just to explain the missing part. Now you're feeling good that you were able to go up and ask him for an explanation. [The counselor waits for about 10 seconds after Joan signals with her finger.]

The counselor **signals Joan to stop** *and in responses 32 through 35* **solicits Joan's reactions** *about the imagery.*

32. *Counselor:* OK, Joan, open your eyes now. What did you imagine?

Client: Well, it was pretty easy. I just imagined myself going up to Mr. _____ and telling him I needed more explanation but that I wanted to find the answers myself.

33. *Counselor:* OK, so you were able to get a pretty vivid picture?

Client: Yes, very much so.

34. *Counselor:* What were your feelings during this—particularly as you imagined yourself?

Client: I felt pretty calm. It didn't really bother me.

35. *Counselor:* OK, so imagining yourself wasn't too stressful. Did I give you enough time before I signaled to stop?
Client: Well, probably. Although I think I could have gone on a little longer.

On the basis of Joan's response about the length of the first scene, the counselor will modify the length during the next presentation.

36. *Counselor:* OK, I'll give you a little more time the next time.

Before the counselor presents the treatment scenes the second time, the counselor explores whether the client would like to use verbal summary codes or to personalize the treatment scenes.

37. *Counselor:* Joan, there are two techniques that you can use to enhance your imagery scene of Mr. _____'s math class. One technique is to describe briefly the behavior you want to do and the situation in Mr. _____'s class when you will perform the behavior. All that you are doing is just describing the scene in your own words. This process can help you remember what to do. With the other technique, you can change the scene or elaborate on the scene in any way as long as you still imagine engaging in the behaviors you want to do. Do you have any questions about these two techniques?
Client: You think these techniques might help me imagine the scene better?

38. *Counselor:* That's right. Is there one technique you think might be more helpful to you?
Client: Yes, I think that for me to describe the scene in my own words might work better for me. It might help me to remember better what to do.

39. *Counselor:* OK, for the first scene, what verbal summary or description would you use?
Client: Well—after Mr. _____ explains how to solve for *x* and *y* and assigns problems, I might find something I can't figure out. I get out of my seat and go up to Mr. _____ and tell him I need more explanation but I want to find the answer myself.

40. *Counselor:* That's great, Joan!

The counselor presents the same scene again. Usually each scene is presented a minimum of two times by the counselor or on a tape recorder. If the client has chosen one or both treatment-scene enhancement techniques, instruct the client on the technique with each scene.

41. *Counselor:* Let's try it again. I'll present the same scene, and I'll give you more time after you signal to me you have a strong picture. [Presents the same scene again and checks out Joan's reactions after the second presentation.]

After the counselor-presented scenes, the counselor asks Joan to self-direct her own practice. This also occurs a minimum of two times on each scene.

42. *Counselor:* You seem pretty comfortable now in carrying out this situation the way you want to. This time instead of my describing the scene orally to you, I'd like you just to go through the scene on your own—sort of a mental practice without my assistance.
Client: OK. [Pauses to do this for several minutes.]

43. *Counselor:* OK, how did that feel?
Client: It was pretty easy even without your instructions, and I think I can see where I can actually do this now with Mr. _____.

The other scenes in the hierarchy are worked through in the same manner.

44. *Counselor:* Good. Now we will work through the other three scenes in the same manner, sticking with each one until you can perform your desired behaviors in your imagination pretty easily. [The other three situations in the hierarchy are worked through.]

45. *Counselor:* Well, how do you feel now that we've gone over every scene?
Client: Pretty good. I never thought that my imagination would help me in math class!

After the hierarchy has been completed, the counselor picks scenes to practice at random. This is a way to see how easily the client can perform the scene when it is not presented in the order of the hierarchy.

46. *Counselor:* Well, sometimes imagining yourself doing something helps you learn how to do it in the actual situation. Now I'd like to just pick a scene here at random and present it to you and have you imagine it again. [Selects a scene from the hierarchy at random and describes it.]
Client: That was pretty easy, too.

The counselor initiates homework practice for Joan.

47. *Counselor:* OK, I just wanted to give you a chance to imagine a scene when I took something out of the order we worked with today. I believe you are ready to carry out this imagination practice on your own during the week.
Client: Is this where I use the tapes?

The purpose of homework is explained to Joan.

48. *Counselor:* Sure. This tape has a series of scenes dealing with verbal class participation. So instead of needing me to describe a scene, the tape can do this. I'd like you to practice with this daily, because daily practice will help you learn to participate more quickly and easily.
Client: So I just go over a scene the way we did today?

The counselor instructs Joan on **how to complete the homework practice.**

49. *Counselor:* Go over the scenes one at a time— maybe about four times for each scene. Make your imagination as vivid as possible. Also, each time you go over a scene, make a check on your log sheets. Indicate the time of day and place where you use this—also, the length of each practice. And after each practice session, rate the vividness of your imagery on this scale: 1 is not vivid and 5 is very vivid. How about summarizing what you will do for your homework?

Client: Yes. I just do what we did today and check the number of times I practice each scene and assign a number to the practice according to how strongly I imagined the scene.

At the termination of the session, the counselor **indicates that a follow-up on the homework** *will occur at their next meeting.*

50. *Counselor:* Right. And bring your log sheets in at our next meeting and we'll go over this homework then. OK? We had a really good session today. You worked hard. I'll see you next Tuesday.

LEARNING ACTIVITY #38: COVERT MODELING

As you may recall from reading the goals and subgoals of Ms. Weare (Chapter 9), one of her subgoals was to arrange a school conference with Freddie's teacher. Ms. Weare was going to use the conference to explain her new strategy in dealing with Freddie and request help and cooperation from the school. Specifically, Ms. Weare might point out that one of the initial consequences of her strategy might be an increase in Freddie's tardiness at school. Assume that Ms. Weare is hesitant to initiate the conference because she is unsure about what to say during the meeting. Describe how you could use covert modeling to help Ms. Weare achieve this subgoal. Describe specifically how you would use (1) a rationale, (2) practice scenes, (3) development of treatment scenes, (4) application of treatment scenes, and (5) homework to help Ms. Weare in this objective. Feedback is provided; see whether some of your ideas are similar.

Feedback follows on page 375.

☐ SUMMARY

Emotive imagery and covert modeling are procedures that may be useful when media modeling and live modeling are not feasible. These two strategies can be used without elaborate therapeutic aids or expensive equipment. Both strategies involve imagery, which makes the procedures quite easy for a client to practice in a self-directed manner. The capacity of clients to generate vivid images may be important for the overall effectiveness of emotive imagery and covert modeling. Assessment of client potential to engage in imagery is a necessary prerequisite before using either of these procedures. Assuming that clients can produce clear images, counselors may use emotive imagery to deal with fears or discomfort or covert modeling to promote desired responses.

POSTEVALUATION

PART ONE

According to Objective One, you should be able to identify accurately six of the seven steps of emotive imagery represented in written examples of counselor leads. For each of the following seven counselor leads, write down which part of emotive imagery the counselor is implementing. More than one counselor lead may be associated with any part of the procedure, and the leads given here are not in any particular order. The five major parts of emotive imagery are as follows:

1. Rationale
2. Determining the client's potential to use imagery
3. Developing imagery scenes
4. Imagery-scene practice training
5. Homework and follow-up

Feedback follows the Postevaluation on page 376.

(continued)

1. "Can you think of several scenes you could imagine that give you calm and positive feelings? Supply as many details as you can. You can use these scenes later to focus on instead of the anxiety."
2. "It's important that you practice with this. Try to imagine these scenes at least several times each day."
3. "This procedure can help you control your anxiety. By imagining very pleasurable scenes, you can block out some of the fear."
4. "Let's see whether you feel that it's easy to imagine something. Close your eyes, sit back, and visualize anything that makes you feel relaxed."
5. "Now, select one of these scenes you've practiced. Imagine this very intensely. I'm going to apply pressure to your arm, but just focus on your imaginary scene."
6. "What we will do, if you feel that imagination is easy for you, is to develop some scenes that are easy for you to visualize and that make you feel relaxed. Then we'll practice having you focus on these scenes while also trying to block out fear."
7. "Now I'd like you just to practice these scenes we've developed. Take one scene at a time, sit back, and relax. Practice imagining this scene for about 30 seconds. I will tell you when the time is up."

PART TWO

Objective Two asks you to demonstrate 10 out of 13 steps of emotive imagery with a role-play client. You or an observer can rate your performance, assisted by the Interview Checklist for Emotive Imagery following this Postevaluation.

PART THREE

Objective Three asks you to describe how you would use the five components of covert modeling with a simulated client case. Use the case of Mr. Brown (Chapter 7) and his stated goal of wanting to decrease his worrying about retirement and increase his positive thoughts about retiring, particularly in his work setting. Describe how you would use a rationale, practice scenes, developing treatment scenes, applying treatment scenes, and homework to help Mr. Brown do this. Feedback follows the Postevaluation.

PART FOUR

Objective Four asks you to demonstrate at least 22 out of 28 steps associated with covert modeling with a role-play client. The client might take the part of someone who wants to acquire certain skills or to perform certain activities. Use the Interview Checklist for Covert Modeling on page 371 to help you assess your interview.

INTERVIEW CHECKLIST FOR EMOTIVE IMAGERY

Instructions: In a role-play counselor/client interview, determine which of the following counselor leads or questions were demonstrated. Indicate by a check the leads used by the counselor. A few examples of counselor leads are presented in the right column.

Item	Examples of counselor leads
I. Rationale	
_____ 1. Counselor describes purpose of emotive imagery.	"The procedure is called emotive imagery because you can emote pleasant thoughts or images in situations that evoke fear, pain, tension, anxiety, or routine boredom. The procedure helps you block your discomfort or reduce the anxiety that you experience in the problem situation. The technique involves focusing on imaginary scenes that please you and make you feel relaxed while in the uncomfortable situation. This procedure works because it is extremely difficult for you to feel pleasant, calm, happy, secure, or whatever other emotion is involved in the scene and anxious (tense, fearful, stressed) at the same time. These emotions are incompatible."
_____ 2. Counselor gives an overview of procedure.	"What we will do is, first, see how you feel about engaging in imagery and look at the details of the scene you used. Then, we will decide whether emotive imagery is a procedure we want to use. If we decide to use it,

(continued)

POSTEVALUATION (continued)

Item	Examples of counselor leads
	we will develop scenes that make you feel calm and good and generate positive feelings for you. We will practice using the scenes we have developed and try to rehearse using those scenes in a simulated fashion. Later, you will apply and practice using the scene in the real situation. Do you have any questions about my explanation?''
_____ 3. Counselor assesses client's willingness to try strategy.	''Would you like to go ahead and give this a try now?''

II. Assessment of Client's Imagery Potential

_____ 4. Counselor instructs client to engage in imagery that elicits good feelings and calmness.	''Close your eyes, sit back, and relax. Visualize a scene or event that makes you feel relaxed and pleasant. Select something you really enjoy and feel good about. Try to be aware of all your sensations in the scene.''
_____ 5. After 30 seconds to a minute, the counselor probes to ascertain the sensory vividness of the client's imagined scene (colors, sounds, movement, temperature, smell). Counselor asks client's feelings about imagery and about ''getting into'' the scene (feeling good with imaginal process).	''Describe the scene to me.'' ''What sensations did you experience while picturing the scene?'' ''What temperature, colors, sounds, smells, and motions did you experience in the scene?'' ''How do you feel about the imagery?'' ''How involved could you get with the scene?''
_____ 6. Counselor discusses with client the decision to continue or discontinue emotive imagery. Decision is based on client's attitude (feelings about imagery) and imaginal vividness.	''You seem to feel good with the imagery and are able to picture a scene vividly. We can go ahead now and develop some scenes just for you.'' ''Perhaps another strategy that would reduce tension without imagery would be better, since it is hard for you to 'get into' a scene.''

III. Development of Imagery Scenes

_____ 7. Counselor and client develop at least two scenes that promote positive feelings for client and involve many sensations (sound, color, temperature, motion, and smell).	''What I would like to do now is to develop an inventory of scenes or situations that promote calmness, tranquility, and enjoyment for you. We want to have scenes that will have as much sensory detail as possible for you, so that you can experience color, smell, temperature, touch, sound, and motion. Later, we will use the scenes to focus on instead of anxiety. What sort of scenes can you really get into?''

IV. Practice of Imagery Scene

_____ 8. Counselor instructs client to practice focusing on the scene for about 30 seconds.	''Take one of the scenes, close your eyes, sit back, and relax. Practice or hold this scene for about 30 seconds, picturing as much sensory detail as possible. I will cue you when the time is up.''
_____ 9. Counselor instructs client to practice focusing on scene with simulated discomfort or anxiety.	''Let us attempt to simulate or create the problem situation and to use the scenes. While I squeeze your arm to have you feel pain, focus on one of the imagery scenes we have developed.'' ''While I describe the feared situation or scene to you, focus on the scene.''
_____ 10. Counselor assesses client's reaction after simulated practice.	''How did that feel?'' ''What effects did my describing the discomforting situ- (continued)

Item	Examples of counselor leads
	ation [my application of pain] have on your relaxation?" "Rate your ability to focus on the scene with the discomfort." "How comfortable did you feel when you imagined this fearful situation then?"

V. Homework and Follow-up

Item	Examples of counselor leads
____11. Counselor instructs client to apply emotive imagery *in vivo*.	"For homework, apply the emotive imagery scenes to the discomforting situation. Focus on the scene as vividly as possible while you are experiencing the activity or situation."
____12. Counselor instructs client to record use of emotive imagery and to record level of discomfort or anxiety on log sheets.	"After each time you use emotive imagery, record the situation, the day, the time, and your general reaction on this log. For each occasion that you use imagery, record also your level of discomfort or anxiety, using a 5-point scale, with 5 equal to maximum discomfort and 1 equal to minimum discomfort."
____13. Counselor arranges a follow-up session.	"Let's get together again in two weeks to see how your practice is going and to go over your homework log."

Observer comments: _____

INTERVIEW CHECKLIST FOR COVERT MODELING

Instructions: Determine which of the following leads the counselor used in the interview. Check the leads used.

Item	Examples of counselor leads
I. Rationale	
____ 1. Counselor describes purpose of strategy.	"This strategy can help you learn how to discuss your prison record in a job interview. I will coach you on some things you could say. As we go over this, gradually you will feel as if you can handle this situation when it comes up in an actual interview."
____ 2. Counselor provides overview of strategy.	"We will be relying on your imagination a lot in this process. I'll be describing certain scenes and asking you to close your eyes and imagine that you are observing the situation I describe to you as vividly as you can."
____ 3. Counselor confirms client's willingness to use strategy.	"Would you like to give this a try now?"
II. Practice Scenes	
____ 4. Counselor instructs client to sit back, close eyes, and relax in preparation for imagining practice scenes.	"Just sit back, relax, and close your eyes."
____ 5. Counselor describes a practice scene unrelated to goal and instructs client to imagine scene as counselor describes it and to raise index finger when scene is vividly imagined.	"As I describe this scene, try to imagine it very intensely. Imagine the situation as vividly as possible. When you feel you have a vivid picture, raise your index finger."
____ 6. After client indicates vivid imagery, counselor instructs client to open eyes and describe what was imagined during scene.	"OK, now let's stop — you can open your eyes. Tell me as much as you can about what you just imagined."

(continued)

POSTEVALUATION (continued)

Item	Examples of counselor leads
_____ 7. Counselor probes for additional details about scene to obtain a very specific description from client.	"Did you imagine the color of the room? What did the people look like? Were there any noticeable odors around you? How were you feeling?"
_____ 8. Counselor suggests ways for client to attend to additional details during subsequent practice.	"Let's do another scene. This time try to imagine not only what you see but what you hear, smell, feel, and touch."
_____ 9. Counselor initiates additional practices of one scene or introduces practice of new scene until client is comfortable with the novelty and is able to provide a detailed description of imagery.	"Let go over another scene. We'll do this for a while until you feel pretty comfortable with this."
_____10. After practice scenes, counselor:	
_____a. Decides to move on to developing treatment scenes.	"OK, this seems to be going pretty easily for you, so we will go on now."
_____b. Decides that relaxation or additional imagery training is necessary.	"I believe before we go on it might be useful to try to help you relax a little more. We can use muscle relaxation for this purpose."
_____c. Decides to terminate covert modeling because of inadequate client imagery.	"Judging from this practice, I believe another approach would be more helpful where you can actually see someone do this."

III. Developing Treatment Scenes

Item	Examples of counselor leads
_____11. Counselor and client decide on appropriate characteristics of model to be used in treatment scenes, including:	
_____a. Identity of model (client or someone else).	"As you imagine this scene, you can imagine either yourself or someone else in this situation. Which would be easier for you to imagine?"
_____b. Coping or mastery model.	"Sometimes it's easier to imagine someone who doesn't do this perfectly. What do you think?"
_____c. Single or multiple models.	"We can have you imagine just one other person—someone like yourself—or several other people."
_____d. Specific characteristics of model to maximize client/model similarity.	"Let's talk over the specific type of person you will imagine."
_____12. Counselor and client specify:	"We have two options in developing the scenes you will imagine. We can discuss different situations and develop the scenes just to fit you, or else we can use some standardized scenes that might apply to anyone going through a job interview with a prison record. What is your preference?"
_____a. Individualized scenes.	
_____b. Standardized scenes.	
_____13. Counselor and client decide to use either:	"On the basis of these situations you've just described, I can present them to you in one of two ways. One way is to give you a general description and leave it up to you to fill in the details. Or I can be very detailed and tell you specifically what to imagine. Which approach do you think would be best for you?"
_____a. General descriptions of scenes.	
_____b. Specific, detailed descriptions of scenes.	
_____14. Counselor and client develop specific ingredients to be used in scenes. Ingredients include:	"Let's decide the kinds of things that will go in each scene."
_____a. Situations or context in which behaviors should occur.	"In the scene in which you are interviewing for a job, go over the type of job you might seek and the kind of employer who would be hard to talk to."
_____b. Behaviors and coping methods to be demonstrated by model.	"Now, what you want to do in this situation is to discuss your record calmly, explaining what happened and

(continued)

Item	Examples of counselor leads

| | emphasizing that your record won't interfere with your job performance." |

____c. Favorable outcome of scene, such as:

____1. Favorable client self-initiated action.

"At the end of the scene you might want to imagine you have discussed your record calmly without getting defensive."

____2. Client self-reinforcement.

"At the end of the scene, congratulate yourself or encourage yourself for being able to discuss your record."

____15. Counselor and client generate descriptions of multiple scenes.

"OK, now, the job interview is one scene. Let's develop other scenes where you feel it's important to be able to discuss your record—for example, in establishing a closer relationship with a friend."

IV. Applying Treatment Scenes

____16. Counselor and client arrange multiple scenes in a hierarchy for scene presentation according to:

____a. Client degree of discomfort in situation.

____b. Degree of difficulty or complexity of situation.

"Now I'd like you to take these six scenes we've developed and arrange them in an order. Start with the situation that you feel most comfortable with and that is easiest for you to discuss your record in now. End with the situation that is most difficult and gives you the most discomfort or tension."

____17. Counselor precedes scene presentation with instructions to client, including:

____a. Instructions to sit back, relax, close eyes.

____b. Instructions on whom to imagine.

"I'm going to tell you now what to do when the scene is presented."

"First, just sit back, close your eyes, and relax."

"Now come up with an image of the person you're going to imagine."

____c. Instructions to imagine intensely, using as many senses as possible.

"As I describe the scene, imagine it as vividly as possible. Use all your senses . sight, smell, touch, and so on."

____d. Instructions to raise index finger when vivid imagery occurs.

____e. Instructions to hold imagery until counselor signals to stop.

"When you start to imagine very vividly, raise your finger."

"And hold that vivid image until I tell you when to stop."

____18. Counselor presents one scene at a time, by describing the scene orally to client or with a tape recorder.

"Here is the first scene. . . . Imagine the employer is now asking you why you got so far behind in school. Imagine that you are explaining what happened in a calm voice."

____19. Duration of each scene is determined individually for client and is held until client imagines model performing desired behavior as completely as possible (perhaps 20–30 seconds).

"You should be able to imagine yourself saying all you want to about your record before I stop you."

____20. After first scene presentation, counselor solicits client reactions about:

____a. Rate of delivery and duration of scene.

____b. Clearness and vividness of client imagery.

"How did the length of the scene seem to you?"

"How intense were your images? What did you imagine?"

____c. Degree of discomfort or pleasantness of scene.

"How did you feel while doing this?"

____21. On basis of client reactions to first scene presentation:

____a. Scene is presented again as is.

____b. Scene or manner of presentation is revised before second presentation.

"I'm going to present this same scene again."

"Based on what you've said. let's change the type of employer. Also, I'll give you more time to imagine this the next time."

(continued)

POSTEVALUATION (continued)

Item	Examples of counselor leads
____c. Scene order in hierarchy is changed and another scene is presented next.	"Perhaps we need to switch the order of this scene and use this other one first."
____d. Relaxation or discussion of client discomfort precedes another presentation of scene.	"Let's talk about your discomfort."
____22. Imagery enhancement techniques explained to client:	
____a. Verbal summary codes.	"You can briefly describe the scene in your own words, which can help you remember the behaviors to perform in the situation."
____b. Personalization or elaboration of treatment scene.	"You can change or elaborate on the scene in any way as long as you still imagine the behavior you want to do."
____23. Each scene is presented a minimum of two times by counselor or on tape recorder.	"Ok, now I'm going to present the same scene one or two more times."
____24. Following counselor presentations of scene, client repeats scene at least twice in a self-directed manner.	"This time I'd like you to present the scene to yourself while imagining it, without relying on me to describe it."
____25. After each scene in hierarchy is presented and imagined satisfactorily, counselor presents some scenes to client in a random order, following steps 18–20.	"Now I'm just going to pick a scene at random and describe it while you imagine it."

V. Homework

____26. Counselor instructs client to practice scenes daily outside session and explains purpose of daily practice.	"During the week, I'd like you to take these cards where we've made a written description of these scenes and practice the scenes on your own. This will help you acquire this behavior more easily and quickly."
____27. Instructions for homework include:	
____a. What to do.	"Just go over one scene at a time — make your imagination as vivid as possible."
____b. How often to do it.	"Go over this five times daily."
____c. When and where to do it.	"Go over this two times at home and three times at school."
____d. A method for self-observation of homework completion.	"Each time you go over the scene, make a tally on your log sheet. Also, after each practice session, rate the intensity of your imagery on this scale."
____28. Counselor arranges for a follow-up after completion of some amount of homework.	"Bring these sheets next week so we can discuss your practices and see what we need to do as the next step."

Observer comments: _____

FEEDBACK #38: COVERT MODELING

1. *Rationale*

   First, you would explain that covert modeling could help Ms. Weare find ways to express herself and could help her practice expressing herself before initiating the actual conference. Second, you would briefly describe the strategy, emphasizing that she will be practicing her role and responses in the school conference, using her imagination.

2. *Practice Scenes*

   You would explain that it is helpful to see how she feels about practicing through her imagination. You would select several unrelated scenes, such as imagining someone coming to her home, imagining an old friend calling her, or imagining a new television show about a policewoman. You would present one practice scene and instruct Ms. Weare first to close her eyes, imagine the scene intensely, and signal to you with her finger when she has a strong picture in her mind. After this point, you could tell her to open her eyes and to describe the details of what she imagined. You might suggest additional details and present the same scene again or present a different scene. If Ms. Weare is able to use imagery easily and comfortably, you could move on to developing the actual treatment scenes.

3. *Developing Treatment Scenes*

   At this point, you would seek Ms. Weare's input about certain aspects of the scenes to be used as treatment scenes. Specifically, you would decide who would be used as the model, whether individualized or standardized scenes would be used, and whether Ms. Weare felt she could benefit from general or specific scenes. Our preference would be to use pretty specific, individualized scenes in which Ms. Weare imagines herself as the model, since she will ultimately be carrying out the action. Next, you should spec

ify the three ingredients of the scenes: (1) the situation in which the behaviors should occur, (2) the behaviors to be demonstrated, and (3) a favorable outcome. For example, the scenes could include Ms. Weare calling the teacher to set up the conference, beginning the conference, explaining her strategy in the conference, and ending the conference. Specific examples of things she could say would be included in each scene. Favorable outcomes might take the form of covert self-praise or of relief from stressful, anxious feelings.

4. *Applying Treatment Scenes*

   After all the treatment scenes have been developed, Ms. Weare would arrange them in a hierarchy from least to most difficult. Starting with the first scene in the hierarchy, you would again instruct Ms. Weare about how to imagine. After the first scene presentation, you would obtain Ms. Weare's reactions to the clearness of her imagery, the duration of the scene, and so on. Any needed revisions could be incorporated before a second presentation of the same scene. You would also encourage Ms. Weare to develop a verbal summary code for each scene after the initial presentation of that scene. You would present each scene to Ms. Weare several times; then have her self-direct her own scene-imagining several times. After all the scenes in the hierarchy had been covered adequately, Ms. Weare would be ready for homework.

5. *Homework*

   You would instruct Ms. Weare to continue to practice the scenes in her imagination outside the session. A follow-up should be arranged. You should be sure that Ms. Weare understands how many times to practice and how such practice can benefit her. Ms. Weare might record her practice sessions on log sheets. She could also call in and verbalize the scenes, using a phone-mate.

☐ SUGGESTED READINGS

Bornstein, P. H., & Devine, D. A. (1980). Covert modeling-hypnosis in the treatment of obesity. *Psychotherapy: Theory, Research and Practice, 17,* 272–275.

Bry, A., & Bair, M. (1979). *Visualization: Directing the movies of your mind.* New York: Barnes & Noble.

Cautela, J. R. (1976). The present status of covert modeling. *Journal of Behavior Therapy and Experimental Psychiatry, 6,* 323–326.

Cautela, J. R. (1977). *Behavior analysis forms for clinical intervention.* Champaign, IL: Research Press.

Clarke, J. C., & Jackson, J. A. (1983). *Hypnosis and behavior therapy.* New York: Springer.

Horan, J. J. (1976). Coping with inescapable discomfort through in vivo emotive imagery. In J. D. Krumboltz & C. E. Thoresen (Eds.), *Counseling methods.* New York: Holt, Rinehart and Winston.

Jarvinen, P. J., & Gold, S. R. (1981). Imagery as an aid in reducing depression. *Journal of Clinical Psychology, 37,* 523–529.

Kazdin, A. E. (1979a). Effects of covert modeling and coding of modeled stimuli on assertive behavior. *Behaviour Research and Therapy, 17,* 53–61.

Kazdin, A. E. (1979b). Imagery elaboration and self-efficacy in covert modeling treatment of unassertive behavior. *Journal of Consulting and Clinical Psychology, 47,* 725–733.

Kazdin, A. E. (1980). Covert and overt rehearsal and elaboration during treatment in development of assertive behavior. *Behaviour Research and Therapy, 18,* 191–201.

Kazdin, A. E., & Mascitelli, S. (1982b). Covert and overt rehearsal and homework practice in developing assertiveness. *Journal of Consulting and Clinical Psychology, 50,* 250–258.

Lazarus, A. A. (1982). *Personal enrichment through imagery,* Workbook [Audiotape]. New York: BMA Audio Cassettes.

Lyles, J. N., Burish, T. G., Krozely, M. G., & Oldham, R. K. (1982). Efficacy of relaxation training and guided imagery in reducing the aversiveness of cancer chemotherapy. *Journal of Consulting and Clinical Psychology, 50,* 509–524.

Pickett, C., & Cl-oum, G. A. (1982). Comparative treatment strategies and their interaction with locus of control in the reduction of post surgical pain and anxiety. *Journal of Consulting and Clinical Psychology, 50,* 439–441.

Sheikh, A. A. (Ed.). (1983). *Imagery: Current theory, research and application.* New York: Wiley.

Shorr, J. E., Sobel-Whittington, G., Robin, P., & Connella, J. A. (Eds.). (1984). *Imagery.* Vol. 3: *Theoretical and clinical applications.* New York: Plenum.

Tearnan, B. H., Lahey, B. B., Thompson, J. R., & Hammer, D. (1982). The role of coping self-instructions combined with covert modeling in specific fear reduction. *Cognitive Therapy & Research, 6,* 185–190.

Varni, J. W. (1981). Self-regulation techniques in the management of chronic arthritic pain in hemophilia. *Behavior Therapy, 12,* 185–194.

FEEDBACK: POSTEVALUATION

PART ONE

1. Instructing the client to *develop imagery scenes.* These are used as the scenes to focus on to block the unpleasant sensation.
2. Part of *homework*—*in vivo* application of imagery.
3. *Rationale*—giving the client a reason for emotive imagery.
4. The counselor is determining *the client's potential to use imagery.*
5. *Imagery-scene practice*—with a pain-provoking situation.
6. *Rationale*—the counselor is giving an overview of the procedure.
7. *Imagery-scene practice*—the client is trained to imagine the scenes very vividly before using them in simulation of anxiety-provoking situations.

PART TWO

Rate your performance with the Interview Checklist for Emotive Imagery found after the Postevaluation.

PART THREE

Rationale

First you would give Mr. Brown an explanation of covert modeling. You would briefly describe the process to him and explain how using his imagination to "see" someone doing something could help him perform his desired responses.

(continued)

Practice Scenes

Next you would present a couple of unrelated practice scenes. You would instruct Mr. Brown to close his eyes, relax, and imagine the scene as you describe it. When Mr. Brown signals he is imagining the scene, you would stop and query him about what he imagined. You might suggest additional details for him to imagine during another practice scene. Assuming Mr. Brown feels relaxed and can generate vivid images, you would go on to develop treatment scenes.

Developing Treatment Scenes

You and Mr. Brown would specify certain components to be included in the treatment scenes, including the identity of the model (Mr. Brown or someone else), type of model (coping or mastery), single or multiple models, and specific characteristics of the model to maximize client/model similarity. Next you would decide whether to use individualized or standardized scenes; perhaps in Mr. Brown's case, his own scenes might work best. You would also need to decide how detailed the scene should be. In Mr. Brown's case, a scene might include some examples of positive thoughts and allow room for him to add his own. You and Mr. Brown would generate a list of scenes to be used, specifying:

1. The situation (which, for him, would be at work when the negative thoughts crop up).
2. The behavior and coping methods he would acquire (stopping interfering thoughts, generating positive thoughts about retirement, and getting back to his project at work).
3. Favorable outcomes (for Mr. Brown, this might be being able to get his work done on time).

Applying Treatment Scenes

You and Mr. Brown would arrange the scenes in order—starting with a work situation in which his thoughts are not as interfering and proceeding to situations in which they are most interfering. Starting with the first scene, you would give Mr. Brown specific instructions on imagining. Then you would present the scene to him and have him hold the scene in imagination for a few seconds after he signaled a strong image. After the scene presentation, you would get Mr. Brown's reactions to the scene and make any necessary revisions in duration, scene content, order in the hierarchy, and so on. At this time Mr. Brown could either develop a verbal summary code or personalize the scene by changing or elaborating on it in some way. The same scene would be presented to Mr. Brown at least one more time, followed by several practices in which he goes through the scene without your assistance. After you had worked through all scenes in the hierarchy, you would present scenes to him in a random order.

Homework

After each scene presentation in the session, you would instruct Mr. Brown to practice the scenes daily outside the session. A follow-up on this homework should be arranged.

PART FOUR

Assess your interview or have someone else assess it, using the Interview Checklist for Covert Modeling on pages 371–374.

COGNITIVE MODELING
AND THOUGHT STOPPING

FIFTEEN

Most systems of therapy recognize the importance of overt behavior change *and* cognitive and affective, or covert, behavior change. In recent years, more attention and effort have been directed toward developing and evaluating procedures aimed at modifying thoughts, attitudes, and beliefs. These procedures come under the broad umbrella of cognitive therapy (Beck, 1970) or cognitive behavior modification (M. J. Mahoney, 1974; Meichenbaum, 1977). Several assumptions are made about cognitive-change procedures. One of the basic assumptions is that a person's thoughts and beliefs can contribute to maladaptive behavior. Another is that maladaptive behaviors can be altered by dealing directly with the person's beliefs, attitudes, or thoughts (Beck, 1970). Krumboltz and Thoresen (1976) point out that, in many instances, a client's unreasonable self-standards and negative self-thoughts can diminish the power of a treatment program. Attention to the client's beliefs and expectations may be necessary in order for other therapeutic strategies to be successful.

Four cognitive-change procedures are presented in this chapter and in Chapter 16. This chapter describes cognitive modeling and thought stopping, and Chapter 16 describes cognitive restructuring and stress inoculation. All four of these procedures are efforts to eliminate "cognitive pollution."

□ OBJECTIVES

1. Using a simulated client case, describe how you would apply the seven components of cognitive modeling and self-instructional training.
2. Demonstrate 16 out of 21 steps of cognitive self-instructional modeling with a role-play client, using the Interview Checklist for Cognitive Modeling at the end of the chapter to rate your performance.
3. Using a counselor/client dialogue, identify the six steps of the thought-stopping strategy reflected in at least 20 out of 25 counselor responses.

4. Demonstrate 21 out of 26 steps of thought stopping in a role-play interview, using the Interview Checklist for Thought Stopping at the end of the chapter to assess your performance.

☐ COGNITIVE MODELING WITH COGNITIVE SELF-INSTRUCTIONAL TRAINING

Cognitive modeling is a procedure in which counselors show people what to say to themselves while performing a task. Sarason (1973), who used cognitive modeling to decrease test anxiety in college students, views the procedure as "efforts by the model to make explicit for observers the process by which he arrives at the overt responses he makes" (p. 58). Sarason points out that the uniqueness of cognitive modeling is that "the implicit or covert responses related to performance" are modeled (p. 58). These implicit factors may be just as important as the overt responses of a modeled display.

Meichenbaum and Goodman (1971) used cognitive modeling to develop self-control in young, impulsive children. The children saw a person model a set of verbalizations and behaviors that characterized a strategy they could use in performing a task. For example, the model verbalized:

> I have to remember to go slowly to get it right. Look carefully at this one (the standard), now look at these carefully (the variants). Is this one different? Yes, it has an extra leaf. Good, I can eliminate this one. Now, let's look at this one (another variant). I think it's this one, but let me first check the others. Good. I'm going slow and carefully. Okay, I think it's this one [p. 121].

The performance of the children exposed to this cognitive model was compared with that of a group in which the children received cognitive modeling plus self-instructional training (Meichenbaum & Goodman, 1971). In the latter group, in addition to viewing the model, the children were trained to produce the self-instructions the model emitted while performing the task. The children performed the task while instructing themselves as the model had done. Over the course of the practice trials, the children's self-verbalizations were faded from an overt to a covert level (p. 122). This group not only decreased decision time but also significantly reduced performance errors.

Kendall and Braswell (1982) found that problem children aged 8–12 years who received cognitive modeling with cognitive self-instructional training improved on teachers' ratings of self-control. Copeland (1981) recommends that client variables should be examined when designing self-instructional programs for impulsive children. For example, indexes of cognitive maturity such as age, IQ, cognitive style, and internal versus external attributions should be considered.

Cognitive self-instruction used in combination with rehearsal and homework practice was effective in developing assertive skills (Kazdin & Mascitelli, 1982a). Written symbolic models of self-instructional statements were designed to "help the person adopt a set to facilitate the assertive response, to identify the situation as one requiring action, and to prompt a specific response (e.g., 'This person always says things to me and I must answer them now to put an end to this,' or 'This is unfair, and I have to speak up for my rights')" (Kazdin & Mascitelli, 1982a, p. 350).

Cognitive modeling plus self-instructional training was also used effectively to train hospitalized schizophrenics to alter their thinking, attention, and language behaviors (self-talk) while performing tasks (Meichenbaum & Cameron, 1973b). According to these authors, cognitive modeling with a self-instructional training strategy consists of five steps:

1. The counselor serves as the model (or a symbolic model can be used) and first performs the task while talking aloud to himself or herself.
2. The client performs the same task (as modeled by the counselor) while the counselor instructs the client aloud.
3. The client is instructed to perform the same task again while instructing himself or herself aloud.
4. The client whispers the instructions while performing the task.
5. Finally, the client performs the task while instructing himself or herself covertly.

Note that cognitive modeling is reflected in step 1, whereas steps 2 through 5 consist of client practice of self-verbalizations while performing a task or behavior. The client's verbalizations are faded from an overt to a covert level.

We propose that cognitive modeling and self-instructional training should be implemented with seven steps as guidelines:

1. A rationale about the procedure
2. Cognitive modeling of the task and of the self-verbalizations

Client practice in the form of:

3. Overt external guidance
4. Overt self-guidance
5. Faded overt self-guidance
6. Covert self-guidance
7. Homework and follow-up

Each of these steps will be explained in the following section. Illustrations are also provided in the Interview Checklist for Cognitive Modeling at the end of the chapter.

Treatment Rationale

Here is an example of a rationale for cognitive modeling:

> "It has been found that some people have difficulty in performing certain kinds of tasks. Often the difficulty is not because they don't have the ability to do it but because of what they say or think to themselves while doing it. In other words, a person's 'self-talk' can get in the way or interfere with performance. For instance, if you get up to give a speech and you're thinking 'What a flop I'll be,' this sort of thought may affect how you deliver your talk. This procedure can help you perform something the way you want to by examining and coming up with some helpful planning or self-talk to use while performing [rationale]. I'll show what I am saying to myself while performing the task. Then I'll ask you to do the task while I guide or direct you through it. Next, you will do the task again and guide yourself aloud while doing it. The end result should be your performing the task while thinking and planning about the task to yourself [overview]. How does this sound to you? [client willingness]"

After the rationale has been presented and any questions have been clarified, the counselor begins by presenting the cognitive model.

Model of Task and Self-Guidance

First, the counselor instructs the client to listen to what the counselor says to herself or himself while performing the task. Next, the counselor models performing a task while talking aloud. Meichenbaum and Goodman (1971, p. 8) describe an example of the modeled self-instructions that were given to train impulsive children to copy line patterns:

Questions
1. What has to be done?

2. Answers question in form of planning what to do.
3. Self-guidance and focused attention.
4. Self-reinforcement.
5. Coping self-evaluative statements with error correction options.

Dialogue
1. "Okay, what is it I have to do?"
2. "You want me to copy the picture with different lines."
3. "I have to go slow and be careful. Okay, draw the line down, down, good; then to the right, that's it; now down some more and to the left."
4. "Good. Even if I make an error I can go on slowly and carefully. Okay, I have to go down now."
   "Finished. I did it."
5. "Now back up again. No, I was supposed to go down. That's okay. Just erase the line carefully."

As this example indicates, the counselor's modeled self-guidance should include five parts. The first part of the verbalization asks a question about the nature and demands of the task to be performed. The purposes of the question are to compensate for a possible deficiency in comprehending what to do, to provide a general orientation, and to create a cognitive set. The second part of the modeled verbalization answers the question about what to do. The answer is designed to model cognitive rehearsal and planning in order to focus the client's attention on relevant task requirements. Self-instruction in the form of self-guidance while performing the task is the third part of the modeled verbalization. The purpose of self-guidance is to facilitate attention to the task and to inhibit any possible overt or covert distractions or task irrelevancies. In the example, modeled self-reinforcement is the fourth part and is designed to maintain task perseverance and to reinforce success. The last part in the modeled verbalization contains coping self-statements to handle errors and frustration, with an option for correcting errors. The example of the modeled verbalization used by Meichenbaum and Goodman depicts a coping model. In other words, the model does make an error in performance but corrects it and does not give up at that point. See whether you can identify these five parts of modeled self-guidance in Learning Activity #39.

LEARNING ACTIVITY #39: MODELED SELF-GUIDANCE

The following counselor verbalization is a cognitive model for a rehabilitation client who is learning how to use a wheelchair. Identify the five parts of the message: (1) questions of what to do, (2) answers to the question in the form of planning, (3) self-guidance and focused attention, (4) coping self-evaluative statements, and (5) self-reinforcement. Feedback for this activity follows.

"What is it that I have to do to get from the parking lot over the curb onto the sidewalk and then to the building? I have to wheel my chair from the car to the curb, get over the curb and onto the sidewalk, and then wheel over to the building entrance. Okay, wheeling the chair over to the curb is no problem. I have to be careful now that I am at the curb. Okay, now I've just got to get my front wheels up first. They're up now. So now I'll pull up hard to get my back wheels up. Whoops, didn't quite make it. No big deal—I'll just pull up very hard again. Good. That's better, I've got my chair on the sidewalk now. I did it! I've got it made now."

Overt External Guidance

After the counselor models the verbalizations, the client is instructed to perform the task (as modeled by the counselor) while the counselor instructs or coaches. The counselor coaches the client through the task or activity, substituting the personal pronoun *you* for *I* (for example, "What is it that *you* . . . , *you* have to wheel your chair . . . , *you* have to be careful"). The counselor should make sure that the coaching contains the same five parts of self-guidance that were previously modeled: question, planning, focused attention, coping self-evaluation, and self-reinforcement. Sometimes in the client's real-life situation, other people may be watching when the client performs the task—as could be the case whenever the wheelchair client appears in public. If the presence of other people appears to interfere with the client's performance, the counselor might say "Those people may be distracting you. Just pay attention to what you are doing." This type of coping statement can be included in the counselor's verbalizations when using overt external guidance in order to make this part of the procedure resemble what the client will actually encounter.

Overt Self-Guidance

The counselor next instructs the client to perform the task while instructing or guiding himself or herself aloud. The purpose of this step is to have the client practice the kind of self-talk that will strengthen attention to the demands of the task and will minimize outside distractions. The counselor should attend carefully to the content of the client's self-verbalizations. Again, as in the two preceding steps, these verbalizations should include the five component parts, and the client should be encouraged to use his or her own words. If the client's self-guidance is incomplete or if the client gets stuck, the counselor can intervene and coach. If necessary, the counselor can return to the previous steps—either modeling again or coaching the client while the client performs the task (overt external guidance). After the client completes this step, the counselor should provide feedback about parts of the practice the client completed adequately and about any errors or omissions. Another practice might be necessary before moving on to the next step, faded overt self-guidance.

Faded Overt Self-Guidance

The client next performs the task while whispering (lip movements). This part of cognitive modeling serves as an intermediate step between having the client verbalize aloud, as in overt self-guidance, and having the client verbalize silently, as in the next step, covert self-guidance. In other words, whispering the self-guidance is a way for the client to approximate successively the end result of the procedure: thinking to oneself while performing. In our own experience with this step, we have found that it is necessary to explain this to an occasional client who seems hesitant or concerned about whispering. If a client finds the whispering too foreign or aversive, it might be more beneficial to repeat overt self-guidance several times and finally move directly to covert self-guidance. If the client has difficulty in performing this step or leaves out any of the five parts, an additional practice may be required before moving on.

FEEDBACK #39: MODELED SELF-GUIDANCE

Question: "What is it that I have to do to get from the parking lot over the curb onto the sidewalk and then to the building?"

Answers with planning: "I have to wheel my chair from the car to the curb, get onto the curb and onto the sidewalk, and then wheel over to the building entrance."

Self-guidance and focused attention: "Okay, wheeling the chair over to the curb is no problem. I have to be careful now that I am at the curb. Okay, now I've just got to get my front wheels up first. They're up now. So now I'll pull up hard to get my back wheels up."

Coping self-evaluation and error-correction option: "Whoops, didn't quite make it. No big deal—I'll just pull up very hard again."

Self-reinforcement: "Good. That's better, I've got my chair on the sidewalk now. I did it! I've got it made now."

Covert Self-Guidance

Finally, the client performs the task while guiding or instructing covertly, or "in one's head." It is very important for clients to instruct themselves covertly after practicing the self-instructions overtly. After the client does this, the counselor might ask for a description of the covert self-instructions. If distracting or inhibiting self-talk has occurred, the counselor can offer suggestions for more appropriate verbalizations or self-talk and can initiate additional practice. Otherwise, the client is ready to use the procedure outside the session.

Homework and Follow-up

Assigning the client homework is essential for generalization to occur from the interview to the client's environment. The therapist should instruct the client to use the covert verbalizations while performing the desired behaviors alone, outside the counseling session. The homework assignment should specify what the client will do, how much or how often, and when and where the homework is to be done. The counselor should also provide a way for the client to monitor and reward himself or herself for completion of homework. A follow-up on the homework task should also be scheduled.

These seven components of cognitive modeling are modeled for you in the following dialogue with

our client Joan. Again, this strategy is used as one way to help Joan achieve her goal of increasing her verbal participation in math class.

□ MODEL DIALOGUE: COGNITIVE MODELING WITH COGNITIVE SELF-INSTRUCTIONAL TRAINING

*In response 1, the counselor introduces the possible use of cognitive modeling to help Joan achieve the goal of increasing initiating skills in her math class. The counselor is giving a **rationale** about the strategy.*

1. *Counselor:* One of the goals we developed was to help you increase your participation level in your math class. One of the ways we might help you do that is to use a procedure in which I demonstrate the kinds of things you want to do—and also I will demonstrate a way to think or talk to yourself about these tasks. So this procedure will help you develop a plan for carrying out these tasks, as well as showing you a way to participate. How does that sound?
   Client: OK. Is it hard to do?

*In response 2, the counselor provides an **overview** of the procedure, which is also a part of the rationale.*

2. *Counselor:* No, not really, because I'll go through it before you do. And I'll sort of guide you along. The procedure involves my showing you a participation method and, while I'm doing that, I'm going to talk out loud to myself to sort of guide myself. Then you'll do that. Gradually, we'll go over the same participation method until you do it on you own and can think to yourself how to do it. We'll take one step at a time. Does that seem clear to you?
   Client: Well, pretty much. I've never done anything like this, though.

*In response 3, the counselor determines **Joan's willingness** to try out the procedure.*

3. *Counselor:* Would you like to give it a try?
   Client: Sure—I'm willing.

*In responses 4 and 5, the counselor sets the stage for **modeling of the task** and accompanying **self-guidance** and **instructs the client in what will be done and what to look for in this step.***

4. *Counselor:* We mentioned there were at least four things you could do to increase your initiating skills—asking Mr. _____ for an explanation only, answering more of Mr. _____'s questions, going to the board to do problems, and volunteering answers. Let's just pick one of these to start with. Which one would you like to work with first?

Client: Going to the board to work algebra problems. If I make a mistake there, it's visible to all the class.

5. *Counselor:* Probably you're a little nervous when you do go to the board. This procedure will help you concentrate more on the task than on yourself. Now, in the first step, I'm going to pretend I'm going to the board. As I move out of my chair and up to the board, I'm going to tell you what I'm thinking that might help me do the problems. Just listen carefully to what I say, because I'm going to ask you to do the same type of things afterwards. Any questions?

Client: No, I'm just waiting to see how you handle this. I'll look like Mr. _____. His glasses are always down on his nose and he stares right at you. It's unnerving.

In responses 6 and 7, the counselor **initiates and demonstrates** *the task with accompanying* **self-guidance.** *Note, in the modeled part of response 7, the* **five components of the self-guidance process.** *Also note that a simple problem has been chosen for illustration.*

6. *Counselor:* OK, you do that. That will help set the scene. Why don't you start by calling on me to go to the board?

Client (as teacher): Joan, go to the board now and work this problem.

7. *Counselor* (gets out of seat, moves to imaginary board on the wall, picks up the chalk, verbalizing aloud): What is it I need to do? He wants me to find *y*. OK, I need to just go slowly, be careful, and take my time. OK, the problem here reads $4x + y = 10$, and *x* is 2.8. OK, I can use *x* to find *y*. [Counselor asks *question* about task.] OK, I'm doing fine so far. Just remember to go slowly. OK, *y* has to be $10 - 4x$. If *x* is 2.8, then *y* will be $10 - 4$ multiplied by 2.8. [Counselor focuses *attention* and uses *self-guidance.*] Let's see, 4×2.8 is 10.2. Oops, is this right? I hear someone laughing. Just keep on going. Let me refigure it. No, it's 11.2. Just erase 10.2 and put in $y = 10 - 11.2$. OK, good. If I keep on going slowly, I can catch any error and redo it. [Counselor uses *coping self-evaluation* and makes *error correction.*] Now it's simple. $10 - 11.2$ is -1.2 and *y* is -1.2. Good, I did it, I'm done now and I can go back to my seat. [Counselor *reinforces self.*]

In responses 8 and 9, the counselor initiates **overt external guidance:** *the client performs the task while the counselor continues to verbalize aloud the self-guidance, substituting* **you** *for* **I** *as used in the previous sequence.*

8. *Counselor:* OK, that's it. Now let's reverse roles. This time I'd like you to get up out of your seat, go to the board, and work through the problem. I will coach you about what to plan during the process. OK?

Client: Do I say anything?

9. *Counselor:* Not this time. You just concentrate on carrying out the task and thinking about the planning I give you. In other words, I'm just going to talk you through this the first time.

Client: OK, I see.

In response 10, the counselor **verbalizes self-guidance while the client performs** *the problem.*

10. *Counselor:* OK, I'll be Mr. _____. I'll ask you to go to the board, and then you go and I'll start coaching you. (as teacher): Joan, I want you to go to the board now and work out this problem: If $2x + y = 8$ and $x = 2$, what does *y* equal? [Joan gets up from chair, walks to imaginary board, and picks up chalk.] (as counselor): OK, first you write the problem on the board. $2x + y = 8$ and $x = 2$. Now ask yourself "What is it I have to do with this problem?" OK, now answer yourself [question].

You need to find the value of *y* [answer to question]. OK, just go slowly, be careful, and concentrate on what you're doing. You know $x = 2$, so you can use *x* to find *y*. Your first step is to subtract $8 - 2x$. You've got that up there. OK, you're doing fine—just keep going slowly [focuses attention and uses self-guidance].

$8 - 2$ multiplied by 2, you know is $8 - 4$. Someone is laughing at you. But you're doing fine, just keep thinking about what you're doing. $8 - 4$ is 4, so $y = 4$ [coping self-evaluation].

Now you've got *y*. That's great. You did it. Now you can go back to your seat [self-reinforcement].

In response 11, the counselor **assesses the client's reaction** *before moving on to the next step.*

11. *Counselor:* OK, let's stop. How did you feel about that?

Client: Well, it's such a new thing for me. I can see how it can help. See, usually when I go up to the board I don't think about the problem. I'm usually thinking about feeling nervous or about Mr. _____ or the other kids watching me.

In response 12, the counselor reiterates the **rationale** *for the cognitive modeling procedure.*

12. *Counselor:* Yes, well, those kinds of thoughts distract you from concentrating on your math problems. That's why this kind of practice may help. It gives you a chance to work on concentrating on what you want to do.

Client: I can see that.

*In responses 13 and 14, the counselor instructs the client to perform the task while verbalizing to herself (**overt self-guidance**).*

13. *Counselor:* This time I'd like you to go through what we just did—only on your own. In other words, you should get up, go to the board, work out the math problem, and as you're doing that, plan what you're going to do and how you're going to do it. Tell yourself to take your time, concentrate on seeing what you're doing, and give yourself a pat on the back when you're done. How does that sound?

    Client: OK, I'm just going to say something similar to what you said the last time—is that it?

14. *Counselor:* That's it. You don't have to use the same words. Just try to plan what you're doing. If you get stuck, I'll step in and give you a cue. Remember, you start by asking yourself what you're going to do in this situation and then answering yourself. This time let's take the problem $5x + y = 10$; with $x = 2.5$, solve for y.

    Client (gets out of seat, goes to board, writes problem): What do I need to do? I need to solve for y. I know $x = 2.5$. Just think about this problem. My first step is to subtract $10 - 5x$. 5 multiplied by 2.5 is 12.5. So I'll subtract $10 - 12.5$. [Counselor laughs; Joan turns around.] Is that wrong?

    Counselor: Check yourself but stay focused on the problem, not on my laughter.

    Client: Well, $10 - 12.5$ is -2.5. $y = -2.5$. Let's see if that's right. $5 \times 2.5 = 12.5 - 2.5 = 10$. I've got it. Yeah.

*In response 15, the counselor **gives feedback** to Joan about her practice. Note the use of "sandwich" feedback, discussed in Chapter 12—a positive comment, followed by a suggestion or criticism, followed by a positive comment.*

15. *Counselor:* That was really great. You only stumbled one time—when I laughed. I did that to see whether you would still concentrate. But after that, you went right back to your work and finished the problem. It seemed pretty easy for you to do this. How did you feel?

    Client: It really was easier than I thought. I was surprised when you laughed. But then, like you said, I just tried to keep going.

*In responses 16, 17, and 18, the counselor instructs Joan on how to **perform the problem while whispering instructions** to herself (**faded overt self-guidance**).*

16. *Counselor:* This time we'll do another practice. It will be just like you did the last time, with one change. Instead of talking out your plan aloud, I

just want you to whisper it. Now you probably aren't used to whispering to yourself, so it might be a little awkward at first.

Client (laughs): Whispering to myself? That seems sort of funny.

17. *Counselor:* I can see how it does. But it is just another step in helping you practice this to the point where it becomes a part of you—something you can do naturally and easily.

    Client: Well, OK. I guess I can see that.

18. *Counselor:* Well, let's try it. This time let's take a problem with more decimals, since you get those, too. If it seems harder, just take more time to think and go slowly. Let's take $10.5x + y = 25$, with $x = 5.5$.

    Client (gets out of seat, goes to board, writes on board, whispers): OK, what do I need to do with this problem? I need to find y. This has more decimals, so I'm just going to go slowly. Let's see, $25 - 10.5x$ is what I do first. I need to multiply 10.5 by 5.5. I think it's 52.75. [Counselor laughs.] Let's see, just think about what I'm doing. I'll redo it. No, it's 57.75. Is that right? I'd better check it again. Yes, it's OK. Keep going. $25 - 57.75$ is equal to -32.75, so $y = -32.75$. I can check it—yes, 10.5×5.5 is $57.75 - 32.75 = 25$. I got it!

*Counselor **gives feedback** in response 19.*

19. *Counselor:* That was great, Joan—very smooth. When I laughed, you just redid your arithmetic rather than turning around or letting your thoughts wander off the problem.

    Client: It seems like it gets a little easier each time. Actually, this is a good way to practice math, too.

*In responses 20 and 21, the counselor gives Joan instructions on how to **perform the problem while instructing herself covertly (covert self-guidance).***

20. *Counselor:* That's right. Not only for what we do in here, but even when you do your math homework. Now, let's just go through one more practice today. You're really doing this very well. This time I'd like you to do the same thing as before—only this time I'd like you to just think about the problem. In other words, instead of talking out these instructions, just go over them mentally. Is that clear?

    Client: You just want me to think to myself what I've been saying?

21. *Counselor:* Yes—just instruct yourself in your head. Let's take the problem $12x - y = 36$, with $x = 4$. Solve for y. [Joan gets up, goes to the board, and takes several minutes to work through this.]

In response 22, the counselor **asks the client to describe what happened during covert self-guidance** *practice.*

22. *Counselor:* Can you tell me what you thought about while you did that?

    Client: Well, I thought about what I had to do, then what my first step in solving the problem would be. Then I just went through each step of the problem, and then after I checked it, I thought I was right.

In response 23, the counselor **checks to see whether another practice is needed** *or whether they can move on to homework.*

23. *Counselor:* So it seemed pretty easy. That is what we want you to be able to do in class—to instruct youself mentally like this while you're working at the board. Would you like to go through this type of practice one more time, or would you rather do this on your own during the week?

    Client: I think on my own would help right now.

In response 24, the counselor sets up Joan's **homework assignment** *for the following week.*

24. *Counselor:* OK. I think it would be helpful if you could do this type of practice on your own this week—where you instruct yourself as you work through math problems.

    Client: You mean my math homework?

In response 25, the counselor **instructs Joan on how to do homework,** *including what to do, where, and how much to do.*

25. *Counselor:* Well, that would be a good way to start. Perhaps you could take seven problems a day. As you work through each problem, go through these self-instructions mentally. (Do this at home.) Does that seem clear?

    Client: Yes, I'll just work out seven problems a day the way we did here for the last practice.

In response 26, the counselor instructs Joan **to observe her homework completion on log sheets** *and* **arranges for a follow-up** *of homework at their next session.*

26. *Counselor:* Right. One more thing. On these blank log sheets, keep a tally of the number of times you actually do this type of practice on math problems during the day. This will help you keep track of your practice. And then next week bring your log sheets with you and we can go over your homework.

LEARNING ACTIVITY #40: COGNITIVE MODELING WITH COGNITIVE SELF-INSTRUCTIONAL TRAINING

You may recall from the case of Ms. Weare and Freddie (Chapter 7) that Ms. Weare wanted to eliminate the assistance she gave Freddie in getting ready for school in the morning. One of Ms. Weare's concerns is to find a successful way to instruct Freddie about the new ground rules—mainly that she will not help him get dressed and will not remind him when the bus is five minutes away. Ms. Weare is afraid that after she delivers her instructions, Freddie will either pout or talk back to her. She is concerned that she will not be able to follow through with her plan or else will not be firm in the way she delivers the ground rules to him. (a) Describe how you would use the seven major components of cognitive modeling and self-instructional training to help Ms. Weare to do this, and (b) write out an example of a cognitive modeling dialogue that Ms. Weare could use to accomplish this task. Make sure this dialogue contains the five necessary parts of the self-guidance process: question, answer, focused attention, self-evaluation, and self-reinforcement. Feedback follows.

☐ THOUGHT STOPPING

Thought control was introduced as early as 1928 by Bain. The thought-control procedure of thought stopping was developed by Taylor (1963) and described by both Wolpe (1982) and Lazarus (1971). Rimm and Masters (1979) have described an elaboration of the procedure, which includes the addition of covert assertion.

Thought stopping is used to help a client control unproductive or self-defeating thoughts and images by suppressing or eliminating these negative cognitions. Often the use of a thought-stopping survey (Cautela, 1977) can help clients identify potential maladaptive thoughts. Thought stopping is particularly appropriate with a client who ruminates about a past event that cannot be changed ("crying over spilled milk"), with a client who ruminates about an event that is unlikely to

FEEDBACK #40: COGNITIVE MODELING WITH COGNITIVE SELF-INSTRUCTIONAL TRAINING

a. Description of the seven components:
1. *Rationale.* First, you would explain to Ms. Weare how cognitive modeling could help her in instructing Freddie and what the procedure would involve. You might emphasize that the procedure would be helpful to her in both prior planning and practice.
2. *Model of task and self-guidance.* In this step, you would model a way Ms. Weare could talk to Freddie. Your modeling would include both the task (what Ms. Weare could say to Freddie) and the five parts of the self-guidance process.
3. *Overt external guidance.* Ms. Weare would practice giving her instructions to Freddie while you coach her on the self-guidance process.
4. *Overt self-guidance.* Ms. Weare would perform the instructions while verbalizing aloud the five parts of the self-guidance process. If she gets stuck or if she leaves out any of the five parts, you can cue her. This step also may need to be repeated before moving on.
5. *Faded overt self-guidance.* Assuming Ms. Weare is willing to complete this step, she would perform the instructions to give Freddie while whispering the self-guidance to herself.
6. *Covert self-guidance.* Ms. Weare would practice giving the instructions to Freddie while covertly guiding herself. When she is able to do this comfortably, you would assign homework.
7. *Homework.* You would assign homework by asking Ms. Weare to practice the covert self-guidance daily and arranging for a follow-up after some portion had been completed.

b. Example of a model dialogue:
"OK, what is it I want to do in this situation [question]? I want to tell Freddie that he is to get up and dress himself without my help, that I will no longer come up and help him even when it's time for the bus to come [answer]. OK, just remember to take a deep breath and talk firmly and slowly. Look at Freddie. Say "Freddie, I am not going to help you in the morning. I've got my own work to do. If you want to get to school on time, you'll need to decide to get yourself ready" [focused attention and self-guidance]. Now, if he gives me flak, just stay calm and firm. I won't back down [coping self-evaluation]. That should be fine. I can handle it [self-reinforcement].

occur (what Lazarus [1971, p. 230] calls a "low-probability catastrophe"), or with a client who engages in repetitive, unproductive, negative thinking or repetitive anxiety-producing or self-defeating images. The bothersome cognitions may take the form of thoughts or visual images. For example, a person who is always bothered by the idea of his or her spouse's having an affair may engage in repetitive thoughts such as "What if this happens to me?" or "It would be my luck to have _____ cheat on me." Another client, concerned over the same event, might report repetitive images such as visualizing the spouse with another person.

Olin (1976) suggests that thought stopping may not be appropriate for clients who have such intense troubling thoughts that they cannot control them. In our own counseling experience, we have found that thought stopping works better with clients who are troubled by intermittent, rather than continuous, self-defeating thoughts. Of course, thought stopping should be used only with clients whose thoughts are clearly counterproductive. Wolpe (1971) distinguishes between problem-solving thoughts that lead to action — desirable thoughts — and those that lead to a dead end — negative thoughts.

Thought stopping has been used in a number of clinical cases. It has been used to reduce hallucinatory images (Bucher & Fabricatore, 1970; Samaan, 1975), to reduce fantasies of dressing in clothes of the other sex (Gershman, 1970), to reduce obsessive thoughts (Martin, 1982; Tryon & Pallandino, 1979), self-critical thoughts (Mahoney, 1971), to eliminate repetitive images of colors (Yamagami, 1971), to reduce anxiety attacks about epileptic seizures (Anthony & Edelstein, 1975), and to eliminate a husband's constant thoughts and images of his wife's past extramarital affair (Rosen & Schnapp, 1974). Thought stopping was also effective in reducing smoking (Wisocki & Rooney, 1974) and helpful in reducing obsessive thinking among ten outpatients (Hackmann & McLean, 1975). There is not a great deal of evidence from controlled studies to support empirically the validity of the procedure (Tryon, 1979). However, one empirical study did compare the efficacy of thought stopping and covert assertion, thought stopping alone, covert assertion alone, and no treatment (Arrick, Voss, & Rimm, 1981). All three groups receiving experimental treatments showed more fear reduction than the control group.

Despite the limited amount of empirical evidence for the validity of the procedure, thought stopping continues to be used frequently, often in conjunction with other strategies. As Wisocki and Rooney point out, thought stopping has several advantages: it is administered easily, it is usually understood by a client, and it is readily employed by the client in a self-regulatory manner (1974, p. 192).

The thought-stopping strategy has six major components: treatment rationale, counselor-directed thought stopping (overt interruption), client-directed thought stopping (overt interruption), client-directed thought stopping (covert interruption), a shift to assertive, positive, or neutral thoughts, and homework and follow-up. Some of these steps have been described in a study and case examples (Arrick et al., 1981; Hackmann & McLean, 1975; Rimm, 1973; Rimm & Masters, 1979; Yamagami, 1971). The steps associated with each component can be found in the Interview Checklist for Thought Stopping at the end of the chapter.

Treatment Rationale

First, the counselor will explain the rationale for thought stopping. Before using the strategy, clients should be aware of the nature of their self-defeating thoughts or images. Wolpe (1982) suggests that the counselor should point out how the client's thoughts are futile and in what ways the client would be better off without being plagued by such thoughts or images. Here is an example of a way the counselor might explain the purpose of thought stopping:

"You say you are bothered by constant thoughts that you might die in some horrible way. These thoughts take up a lot of energy and really are unnecessary. You would feel better if you weren't contantly thinking about this or having images of a horrible death scene flash through your mind. This procedure can help you learn to break this habit of thinking. How does this sound to you?"

If the client agrees to try to work with thought stopping, the counselor should describe the procedure without displaying too graphically the way in which the thoughts are stopped, because the initial surprise is very effective. The counselor might say:

"I will ask you to sit back and just let thoughts come into my mind. When you tell me you have a thought or an image related to this horrible death scene, I will interrupt you. Then I will teach you how to break this chain of thoughts yourself so you can do this whenever these thoughts crop up."

Counselor-Directed Thought Stopping: Overt Interruption

In this first phase of thought stopping, the counselor assumes the responsibility for interrupting the thoughts. The interruption is overt, consisting of a loud *Stop!* that can be accompanied by a noise such as a hand clap, a ruler hitting a desk, or a whistle. In the first counselor-directed sequence, the client is instructed to verbalize all thoughts and images aloud. The verbalization enables the counselor to determine the precise point when the client shifts from positive thinking to negative thinking. The sequence goes like this:

1. The counselor instructs the client to sit back and let any thoughts come to mind: "Sit back, relax, and just let thoughts and images flow into your mind."
2. The counselor instructs the client to verbalize aloud these thoughts or images as they occur: "Whenever you start to think about anything or you see an image, just share with me verbally what you're thinking or seeing."
3. At the point where the client verbalizes a self-defeating thought or image, the counselor interrupts with a loud *Stop!* Sometimes, in addition, a loud noise stimulus such as a hand clap, a whistle, or a ruler hitting the desk is used.
4. The counselor points out whether the unexpected interruption was effective in terminating the client's negative thoughts or images: "Perhaps you realize that as soon as I said *Stop!* and interrupted you, your self-defeating thought stopped and didn't go on as often happens." At this time it is often very effective for the counselor to point out how the client *can* learn to control his or her thoughts.

After this sequence, the counselor directs another thought-stopping sequence in which the client does not verbalize thoughts aloud but uses a hand signal to inform the counselor of the onset of a self-defeating thought or image. This sequence is similar to the first one with the exception of the hand signal:

1. The counselor asks the client to sit back and let thoughts come naturally to mind.
2. The counselor instructs the client to signal with a raised hand or finger when the client notices thinking about the self-defeating or negative ideas.
3. When the client signals, the counselor interrupts with *Stop!*

These three steps are repeated within the session as often as necessary—generally until a pattern of inhibiting the client's self-defeating thoughts by the counselor's command is established.

Client-Directed Thought Stopping: Overt Interruption

After the client has learned to control negative thoughts in response to the counselor's interruption, the client assumes responsibility for the interrupting. At first the client directs himself or herself in the thought-stopping sequence with the same overt interruption used by the counselor—a loud *Stop!* Here is the way this step might proceed:

1. The client deliberately evokes thinking about something and lets all kinds of thoughts come to mind.
2. The counselor instructs the client to say aloud *Stop!* whenever the client notices a self-defeating thought or image: "This time you can direct yourself in thought stopping. When you first notice you're thinking about a horrible way of dying, interrupt yourself with a loud *Stop!*"

These two steps are repeated until the client is able to suppress self-defeating thoughts by overt self-interruption. Sometimes a client may report that even the word *Stop* or a clap is not a strong enough stimulus to help actually terminate the undesired thought. In these cases, a snap of a rubber band worn on the wrist at least for a short time may add to the potential of these stimuli to stop the negative thoughts (Mahoney, 1971; Tryon & Pallandino, 1979).

Client-Directed Thought Stopping: Covert Interruption

In many cases, it would be impractical and unwise for clients to interrupt themselves overtly. Imagine what might happen if a client were riding on an airplane, bus, or subway and suddenly yelled *Stop!* Because of this, in the next sequence of thought stopping, the client substitutes a covert interruption for the overt one. The same two-step sequence occurs:

1. The client lets any thoughts or images come to mind.
2. When the client becomes aware of a self-defeating thought, the client stops by covertly saying *Stop!*

These two steps are repeated until the client is able to terminate the self-defeating thoughts with only the covert interruption.

Shift to Assertive, Positive, or Neutral Thoughts

In some instances, a client's negative thoughts may contribute to a greater level of anxiety. In other cases, the client's thought patterns may be cued by some preceding anxiety or tension. In both cases, some degree of anxiety or arousal may be present in addition to the ruminative thinking patterns. In order to reduce any residual anxiety, Rimm and Masters (1979) suggest that the client learn to think assertive thoughts after the self-defeating thoughts are interrupted. Since assertive behavior inhibits anxiety, it is assumed that assertive thoughts will also inhibit any anxiety or arousal that may occur even after the client has learned to suppress the undesired thoughts (Arrick et al., 1981). Essentially, the client is taught to shift thoughts to assertive responses after the interruption. These responses may either contradict the content of the negative thoughts or be unrelated. For example, in working with a client who was constantly worrying about having a nervous breakdown, Rimm and Masters helped the client learn to think "Screw it. I'm OK. I'm normal." This assertive thought clearly contradicts the nature of the client's self-defeating thoughts. An example of an unrelated, yet still assertive, thought this same client could use might be "Some of the new things I'm going to start in my job this week are . . ." or "I've got some important ideas to express the next time I . . . ."

Rimm and Masters (1979) point out that the assertive thoughts should be realistic and geared toward any actual danger in a situation. For example, if a client is in police work and is constantly thinking about the hazards of the job, it would be unrealistic for this client to use an assertive response that denies real hazards, such as "Being a police officer is a very safe job." However, the client could think about skills and past successes in coping with apparent hazards, such as "When something comes up, I know how to handle it." Although Rimm and Masters refer to these kinds of thoughts as "assertive," there is a great deal of similarity between these thoughts and the coping thoughts the client is taught in cognitive restructuring (see Chapter 16).

Not all counselors who use thought stopping have the client shift from self-defeating thoughts to assertive ones. In lieu of using assertive thoughts, the client can be asked to focus on a pleasurable or reinforcing scene (Anthony & Edelstein, 1975; Gershman, 1970; Yamagami, 1971) or a neutral scene, such as an object in the environment (Wolpe, 1971). In an interesting report of thought stopping, clients who were constantly engaging in self-degrading thoughts were taught to stop the chain of thoughts and replace them with a variety of self-reinforcing thoughts (Hays & Waddell, 1976). For example, someone who catches herself thinking "I'll never be a superstar. What do I have to offer anyway?" stops these thoughts and shifts to thoughts such as "I'm a really good piano player" or "In my own quiet way I can contribute." In our opinion, it is important to have the client learn to shift to other kinds of thoughts after the self-defeating ones are stopped. However, the particular kinds of thoughts that are substituted should be adapted for the client and the nature of the self-defeating thoughts.

Here are the steps involved in teaching the client to shift from self-defeating to assertive, positive, or neutral thoughts:

1. The counselor explains the purpose of substituting different thoughts for the negative or unproductive ones: "In addition to stopping yourself from ruminating over all the horrible ways you might die, it's helpful to substitute different kinds of thoughts that are unrelated to death. This part of the procedure will help you learn to shift to different thoughts after you stop yourself from the self-defeating thinking."

2. The counselor models the type of thoughts the client could substitute after terminating the self-defeating ones and gives some examples. The client is asked to identify others and to practice using these aloud: "After you signal Stop! to yourself, shift your thoughts to something positive, like a beautiful sunset, something fun you did during the day, or an interesting object in the room, like a picture on the wall. See whether you can think of several things like this you could think about from time to time. Then just practice saying these things aloud."

3. Next, the client is asked to practice this shift after another sequence of self-directed thought stopping with overt interruption. As soon as the client says Stop!, the shift to another kind of thought should be made. The client should verbalize aloud the particular thought used: "This time, repeat the thought stopping where you stop your negative thoughts by saying Stop! aloud. Then practice substituting one of these thoughts you've picked, like thinking about what a good movie you saw last night. Share these positive thoughts aloud."

4. After this practice, the client engages in another practice, which is done covertly. The client stops covertly and substitutes different thoughts without verbalizing them aloud: "Now we'll do the same type of thing — only all in your head. When you notice any thoughts related to a horrible death popping into your mind, think Stop! and then think about lying on the beach on a warm day."

5. The client should be encouraged to practice substituting assertive, positive, or neutral thoughts several times. Each time, the client should use a different thought so that satiation from constant repetition of only one thought does not occur (Rimm & Masters, 1979).

If a client has difficulty making the shift from the negative thoughts to other ones, a cuing device might help. For example, the client can write positive or assertive responses on small note cards and carry these around. Or the client can wear a wrist golf counter and click it as a cue for making the shift in thoughts.

Homework and Follow-up

Once the client learns the thought-stopping procedure, it is time to use it outside the interview. At first, the client should be instructed to practice the thought-stopping sequence several times each day. This homework practice strengthens the client's control over stopping a chain of self-defeating thoughts as they occur. Samaan (1975) had a client use a tape recording of his Stop! messages in the initial phase of homework practice to strengthen thought control. Gradually, the client's use of the tape-recorded messages with daily practice was eliminated.

In addition to daily practice, clients can initiate thought stopping whenever they notice that they are engaging in negative or self-defeating thinking. The client should be cautioned about the amount of time that is often necessary to break a well-learned habit of thinking a certain way. The client can keep track of the daily practice and the number of times thought stopping was used in vivo on a log sheet. And, as with the application of any counseling strategy, a later follow-up session should be arranged.

☐ MODEL DIALOGUE: THOUGHT STOPPING

As you may recall, one of Joan's goals was to increase positive thoughts about her ability to do well in math. One of her subgoals was to stop negative or self-degrading thoughts about her potential and to replace these with more realistic, positive thoughts. Her dialogue with the counselor illustrates a combination of thought stopping and cognitive restructuring. As you will see from the explanations that precede the counselor's responses, thought stopping is used to help Joan stop her negative thoughts, while cognitive restructuring is used to help her learn to replace the self-defeating thoughts with coping thoughts. Thought stopping is illustrated in session 1. The cognitive restructuring dialogue is presented in Chapter 16.

Session 1

In this session, the counselor will give Joan a rationale and an overview of both strategies and teach Joan how to use thought stopping to control her negative thoughts about math.

In responses 1 and 2, the counselor **reviews the things Joan wants to change** *and emphasizes that cognitive change requires practice in addition to willpower. Note the use of* **a prop** *(tape recorder) to illustrate this concept.*

1. *Counselor:* Joan, we've talked about how you constantly put yourself down about your ability to do well in math — even though you know you have the ability. You know that thinking you can't do math doesn't really reflect your ability, but you find yourself thinking this way anyway. These kinds of thoughts also probably add to the nervousness you feel before and during math class.
   Client: I know what you're saying, and I agree. I just can't seem to make myself think I can do it.
2. *Counselor:* Right. Well, thinking about a situation in a certain way is something you learn like a habit, and it takes time to change it. It's not changed easily by just willpower — but by systematic practice of new, more productive ways of thinking. It's like this tape recorder I have here (holds up a cassette tape player). There's a tape in here of your negative thoughts about math. You've been playing it over and over inside your head for a long time. Now it's time to eject it and

put in a new tape. You'll need to start listening to the new tape just as frequently as you did to this one we're getting rid of.
   Client: And you think that if I could think about my ability positively, this would help?

Joan, like many clients, is questioning how changing her thoughts can help. The counselor will respond to her concern **by pointing out the difference between self-defeating and self-enhancing thoughts** *and how these different ways of thinking can affect performance.*

3. *Counselor:* Well, let's look at it this way. Whenever you think "I'm a girl, I can't do math" or "This problem is too hard for me, I'll give up," that is just one way to think about math — and it's negative. If you think something like "Girls can do well in math if they want to" or "I know I have the ability, so I'm going to work at it," these thoughts are more positive. The negative thoughts can interfere with your doing OK in math, because you start to convince yourself it's useless. Also, when you think you can't do it, you get nervous and want to give up or get out of the situation. But the positive thoughts give you a way to cope with the situation and help you feel more relaxed. Both these things can help you improve your performance in math class.
   Client: That makes some sense.

In response 4, the counselor describes the **rationale** *for the procedure.*

4. *Counselor:* OK. Well, let me explain a little about what we will do so you can see exactly how this can help. First, I'll ask you to tell me the specific kinds of things you're usually thinking about yourself and your capacity in math. For any of these thoughts that are negative or self-defeating, I'll teach you a way to stop these kinds of thoughts so they don't just continue [thought stopping]. Then after you feel you have some control in stopping these thoughts, we'll learn some more positive thoughts. We call these "coping thoughts" because they help you cope with the situation. We'll practice these so you get used to using coping thoughts instead of the negative thoughts [cognitive restructuring]. How does this sound?
   Client: Well, I think it gives me an idea. It sounds like it will take a while.

Joan is continuing to express some concern about the idea, so in response 5 the counselor will respond to this before going ahead with the strategies.

5. *Counselor:* It will take some time. We'll need to spend some time learning these things, and then it will be important for you to practice what you

learn on your own. I'm wondering if you're concerned about the time it might take or about what we might do?

Client: No, not really. Actually it sounds like it has to help. I guess I'm still just getting used to the idea that you can change the way you think.

The counselor realizes that, especially for young people, the idea of thought control may seem foreign. The counselor will attempt to make this more understandable to Joan **by pointing out some situations and books using thought control** *that a client of Joan's age can relate to.*

6. *Counselor:* I realize that often the idea does sound a little unfamiliar. Have you heard of any of the popular books out like _____ or _____ that teach mind control? These books work with the idea that you can have control over the way you think and that your thinking can influence you. For example, the way athletes or musicians perform in the Olympics or a concert depends to some extent on the way they think about themselves and their ability.

Client: That's true. I hadn't made a connection between that and myself, but I can see where it's the same idea.

Up to this point, the counselor has been giving information about how Joan's thoughts affect her performance. This information given is common to thought stopping and cognitive restructuring, since both strategies emphasize the effects of self-defeating thinking on one's feelings and behaviors. In the next sequence, the counselor will work on helping Joan **identify and stop the kinds of self-defeating thoughts** *she has about math. This part of the strategy is primarily the "nuts and bolts" of thought stopping, although it is also part of cognitive restructuring. In response 7, the counselor asks Joan to describe aloud her typical thoughts about math; as soon as she describes a chain of negative thoughts, the counselor interrupts her with a loud* **Stop!** *in response 8.*

7. *Counselor:* Why don't you sit back now and just think about math class? Then tell me what you're thinking.

Client: Well, I'm thinking how hard math is for me. I'm dumb in it and I'm a girl and that doesn't help and . . .

8. *Counselor: Stop!*
Client (startled): Wow, you surprised me!

In responses 9 and 10, the counselor **points out how the unexpected interruption stopped Joan's negative thoughts,** *emphasizing the* **potential control** *Joan has over her thoughts.*

9. *Counselor:* I can see I did. Joan, what happened when I did that?

Client: Well, I was startled. I stopped thinking about how dumb I am in math.

10. *Counselor:* Right. You were starting to tell me some very negative thoughts about math and your ability—so I interrupted you. Then you shut those thoughts off. The interruption like that is startling, but it shows you that you don't *have* to let these kinds of thoughts go on.

Client: I can see what you mean, but can I do the same thing?

Next the counselor shows Joan how she controls her thoughts by having Joan **interrupt herself with a loud Stop!**

11. *Counselor:* Yes, with lots of practice. That's where the new tape comes in. And that's what I'll show you now—how to interrupt yourself. This time, think about math class again. Whenever you start to think these things like "You can't do it" or "You're dumb," shout *Stop!*
Client (thinks, then): *Stop!*

12. *Counselor:* OK—what happened?
Client: Well, I stopped. Of course, it seems a little strange.

13. *Counselor:* It will at first, and gradually we'll get to the point where you can stop yourself by *thinking* the word *stop.* But for now let's do this several times until you get used to it. [Client-directed overt interruption is repeated as necessary.]

Next, the counselor introduces **covert interruption;** *Joan practices interrupting her negative thoughts with a* **subvocal Stop!**

14. *Counselor:* OK, I'd like you to try the same thing. Only this time when you notice the self-defeating thoughts, stop these just by saying *Stop!* to yourself so no one can hear you. [Joan does this and practices repeatedly until she feels she has control over stopping these thoughts.]

15. *Counselor:* That's really good. It seems like you're able to cut off the thoughts pretty well.
Client: I can. But will I forget how to do this?

The counselor responds to Joan's concern by emphasizing the importance of practice. A **daily homework assignment** *is given. In addition, to get an idea of how often Joan needs to use thought stopping, the counselor asks her to record other instances of usage in her log.*

16. *Counselor:* Not if you practice at it. Keep inserting the new tape and ejecting the old one. What I'd like you to do before our next meeting is to practice these at least three times each day just like you've done today. Then, as you need to, if these thoughts crop up at other times, you can use the thought stopping then, too. Could you keep track of your daily practices and the num-

ber of other times you do this on these log sheets and bring these next week?

Client: Sure. Just write down each practice and each other time I do this—right?

17. *Counselor:* Right. Remember to put down how often, where, and how long you work with this. Have a good week.

LEARNING ACTIVITIES #41: THOUGHT STOPPING

I. Listed below are four client descriptions. Read each and, on the basis of the description, determine whether thought stopping would be an appropriate strategy to use with the client. Write down why or why not. You may wish to distinguish between problem-solving thoughts and "dead end" thoughts in your analysis. Feedback follows on page 400.

1. The client is unhappy with his present job and reports spending a great deal of time thinking about various job alternatives.
2. The clients, a retired couple, are unsure whether their health and age permit them to stay in their large house. They are spending a lot of time trying to decide whether they should move and, if so, what options are available.
3. The client is a young woman whose first baby died several years ago soon after birth. The client reports spending a great deal of time thinking about what she did or didn't do that may have contributed to the baby's death.
4. The client is afraid to go out of her house because she is worried that something bad will happen to her.

II. This learning activity is designed for you to use thought stopping with yourself as a kind of self-management procedure.

1. Identify some pervasive "dead end" thoughts you have about a situation. Make sure the thoughts are self-defeating or unproductive. Perhaps you are even faced with ruminating over some "what if's" about being a helper, such as "What if I don't say the right thing" or "What if I don't help the client" or "What if the client doesn't come back."
2. Sit back and think about the situation—let any thoughts flow into your mind. As soon as you notice a self-defeating thought, say *Stop!* very loudly. Repeat this step about five times.
3. This time, think about the situation, and when you become aware of a self-defeating thought, say *Stop!* subvocally so no one can hear you. Repeat this step about five times.
4. Identify some assertive or positive thoughts you could substitute for the self-defeating ones. If, for example, you wish to eliminate self-defeating thoughts about not being a good helper, some assertive thoughts might be "I will do my best," "There will always be times when I don't say the best thing," "My attitude toward clients is one of caring."
5. Now think again about the situation. Stop any self-defeating thoughts subvocally. Then concentrate on an assertive or positive thought. Repeat this about five times, using a different assertive or positive thought each time.
6. Practice this every day for a week or two. Also use this whenever the self-defeating thoughts you are trying to eliminate appear spontaneously.

☐ SUMMARY

Cognitive modeling is a procedure designed to help people learn how to use self-talk to enhance performance. In this strategy, implicit or covert responses as well as overt responses are modeled. Thought stopping is used to help clients control unproductive or obsessive thinking. In this strategy, unproductive thoughts are inhibited or terminated, first with the counselor's assistance and then in a self-directed fashion. Both cognitive modeling and thought stopping can be used to help clients deal with distracting ruminations.

In the next chapter we will see how clients can be taught to stop self-defeating thoughts and to replace these with incompatible coping thoughts and skills. Both the strategies of cognitive restructuring and stress inoculation, presented in Chapter 16, are directed toward *replacement,* not merely elimination, of self-defeating cognitions.

POSTEVALUATION

PART ONE

Describe how you would use the seven components of cognitive modeling and self-instructional training to help Mr. Brown (from Chapter 7) initiate social contacts with his boss (Objective One). These are the seven components:

1. Rationale
2. Model of task and self-guidance
3. Overt external guidance
4. Overt self-guidance
5. Faded overt self-guidance
6. Covert self-guidance
7. Homework and follow-up

Feedback follows the evaluation.

PART TWO

Objective Two asks you to demonstrate at least 16 out of 21 steps of the cognitive self-instructional modeling procedure with a role-play client. You can audiotape your interview or have an observer assess your performance, using the Interview Checklist for Cognitive Modeling that follows the Postevaluation.

PART THREE

Objective Three asks you to identify at least 20 of 25 leads associated with the steps of thought stopping used by the counselor in a counselor/client dialogue. As you may recall from the case of Mr. Brown (Chapter 7), Mr. Brown wanted to decrease his negative, self-defeating thoughts about retirement and increase his positive thoughts about retirement. In the following dialogue, the counselor uses thought stopping to help Mr. Brown achieve these two goals. Your task is to identify each counselor lead by writing down which particular component of thought stopping it illustrates. The six major components of the thought-stopping strategy are as follows:

1. Rationale about strategy.
2. Counselor-directed thought stopping: overt interruption
3. Client-directed thought stopping: overt interruption
4. Client-directed thought stopping: covert interruption
5. Shift from self-defeating to assertive, positive, or neutral thoughts
6. Homework and follow-up

Remember, there may be more than one counselor lead associated with each of these parts of the strategy throughout the dialogue. Feedback is provided on page 401.

1. *Counselor:* I'm glad to see you today, Mr. Brown. Last week we talked about some of the ways we might work together to reach your counseling goals. You indicated an interest in learning a procedure we call thought stopping. I'm wondering whether you have thought of any questions about this or whether you'd like me to review how this might help you.
Client: No, I really don't have any questions, but it might help if you could just tell me again exactly what we would be doing.

2. *Counselor:* Sure. First, we talked before about how your negative thoughts about retirement interfere with your work. You'd like to be able to stop these, but you haven't been able to do so just by willpower. Thought stopping is a way to hand over the responsibility to you for gaining control of these thoughts, so they don't remain in control of you.
Client: Is it sort of like telling yourself to stop these thoughts?

3. *Counselor:* Well, it helps you learn to stop your thoughts by using the word *stop* to interrupt your thoughts. However, it is a matter of not only telling yourself but practicing   to the point where, on your own command, you can break this habit of continually ruminating at work about the terrible aspects of retirement. Anything else that doesn't seem clear?
Client: No. I think I'd like to give it a try.

4. *Counselor:* OK. Now, first I am going to show you how your negative thoughts can be interrupted. Then I'll show you how to interrupt your thoughts in a way that you can use at work, when you need to. Are you ready?
Client: Yes.

5. *Counselor:* OK, Mr. Brown. Can you imagine you're at your desk now, working on one of your car projects? As you notice any thoughts that you think of, just share these with me aloud.
Client: Well, I'm thinking that I need to get busy on this design. It's a neat design. What a car! But hell, I won't even be around when it comes out, why can't I . . .

6. *Counselor* (loudly): *Stop!*
Client: Wow! I stopped. I wasn't expecting that.

(continued)

POSTEVALUATION   (continued)

7. *Counselor:* The surprise element sometimes helps, even though I realize it is startling. Do you see how you stopped thinking about not being around to see that car when I interrupted you that way?

   Client: Yes, I do. It was quite effective.

8. *Counselor:* What does this suggest to you?

   Client: Well, that I don't have to let my thoughts like this go on and on.

9. *Counselor:* Right. With enough practice, you can learn to stop your thoughts in this sort of way. Now I'd like you to try something similar. Imagine again that you are at your desk. This time, as you become aware of any thoughts, just keep them to yourself. But as soon as you notice that you are starting to get into those negative thoughts, signal this to me by raising your hand. OK?

   Client: Yes. [Closes his eyes, pauses, then signals.]

10. *Counselor* (loudly): *Stop!*

    Client: I stopped. I sure did.

11. *Counselor:* You seem to be working really well with this. I think it would help if we went over this several more times now. [Additional practice ensues.]

12. *Counselor:* Do you feel that you're at the point where you now automatically stop when you hear this word, or do you think more practice like this is needed before you learn to do this yourself?

    Client: I think I'm ready to go on.

13. *Counselor:* OK. This time I'd like you to interrupt yourself the way I just did. Sit back and imagine you're at your desk working on this car design. When you notice a self-defeating thought, say *Stop!* loudly.

    Client (pauses): *Stop!*

14. *Counselor:* Well, what happened?

    Client: Well, it felt strange to say that, but I did stop.

15. *Counselor:* It does seem strange at first. But if it works, that's what counts. As you practice this, it won't seem as strange as it does now. I'd like you to practice this more. [Additional practice.]

16. *Counselor:* How do you feel about this now?

    Client: Pretty good. It's not as strange. Of course it does seem a little like talking to yourself.

17. *Counselor:* True, and in a sense you are. Of course, it wouldn't always be possible for you to actually yell *Stop!* like this, especially if you weren't alone. So what we'll do is practice the same sort of thing again. Only this time you will keep the signal to yourself. Just imagine again that you're at your desk with this project. Let any thoughts come into your mind. This time when you notice a self-defeating thought, just say *Stop!* to yourself subvocally like this [mouths the word]—so no one else hears. [Client pauses, mouths *Stop!*]

18. *Counselor:* OK. Now this is the way you will use thought stopping when you need to in your office. Let's work with this until you feel there's a pattern established when you mouth or think the word *stop*. [More practice.]

    Client: I feel pretty comfortable with this now. I believe I've got this under control.

19. *Counselor:* OK, good. Now so far we've practiced helping you decrease or stop your negative thoughts about retirement. In this next part of thought stopping, you can learn to shift to some positive thoughts about retirement after you stop the negative ones. This helps you replace the interfering thoughts with other ones that are realistic yet positive. Does this seem clear?

    Client: Yes, I think so.

20. *Counselor:* The first thing we need to do is to find some things about retirement that you feel are positive that you can start thinking about. For example, retirement brings some advantages, such as having time to spend with your family or having time to travel somewhere. Perhaps becoming active in an organization or a group you enjoy is an advantage. Maybe entertaining more or engaging in your woodworking hobby is another advantage. What other positive things about retirement could you think of?

    Client: Well, some of the things you mentioned. I've never had enough time to do things I enjoy or to spend time with my family. I guess having more free time is one positive aspect of retirement. Actually, I believe retirement will have some pluses for my marriage. It will be good for my wife to see more of me. I've never been home as much as I'd like or she'd like.

21. *Counselor:* OK, so those are at least two positive things—having free time and enhancing your marriage. Maybe during the week you can think of a few more. What might be helpful now is for you to practice with these positive thoughts. Imagine you're at your desk and think the word *stop* if you start those self-defeating thoughts. This time, right after you stop these thoughts, start thinking about one of the positive things about retirement, like having more

(continued)

time. Share with me aloud what your positive thought is.

Client: OK. [Pause and reflects.] Well, I'm thinking about all the things I will do with some free time.

22. *Counselor:* OK. Now let's try this again. This time, after you signal *Stop!* to yourself, substitute a different positive thought, like the pluses this will have for your marriage. And this time you don't need to share these thoughts with me — just spend time concentrating on them to yourself.

Client (pauses and reflects): OK.

23. *Counselor:* Now that is how you can use thought stopping at work. You'll stop a self-defeating thought and substitute some of these positive thoughts. How about doing this a little more? [Repeated practice.]

24. *Counselor:* You've really done a good job with

learning this. As you know, it will take some time and practice, so during the next week I'd like you to practice what you just did about three times each day. OK?

Client: Yes, I think practice will help me remember this.

25. *Counselor:* It will also help you use it when you need to. Keep track of each of your practices on your log and we'll go over this again next week.

PART FOUR

Objective Four asks you to demonstrate 21 out of 26 steps associated with the thought-stopping strategy in a role-play interview. You can audiotape your interview or have an observer rate it, using the Interview Checklist for Thought Stopping at the end of the chapter.

INTERVIEW CHECKLIST FOR COGNITIVE MODELING

Instructions: Determine which of the following leads the counselor used in the interview. Check each of the leads used. Some examples of counselor leads are provided in the right column; however, these are only suggestions.

Item	Examples of counselor leads
I. Rationale about Strategy	
___ 1. Counselor provides a rationale for the strategy.	"This strategy is a way to help you do this task and also plan how to do it. The planning will help you perform better and more easily."
___ 2. Counselor provides overview of strategy.	"We will take it step by step. First, I'll show you how to do it and I'll talk to myself aloud while I'm doing it so you can hear my planning. Then you'll do that. Gradually, you'll be able to perform the task while thinking through the planning to yourself at the same time."
___ 3. Counselor checks client's willingness to use strategy.	"Would you like to go ahead with this now?"
II. Model of Task and Self-Guidance	
___ 4. Counselor instructs client in what to listen and look for during modeling.	"While I do this, I'm going to tell you orally my plans for doing it. Just listen closely to what I say as I go through this."
___ 5. Counselor engages in modeling of task, verbalizing self-guidance aloud.	"OK, I'm walking in for the interview. [Counselor walks in.] I'm getting ready to greet the interviewer and then wait for his cue to sit down [sits down]."
___ 6. Self-guidance demonstrated by counselor includes five components:	
___a. *Question* about demands of task.	"Now what is it I should be doing in this situation?"
___b. *Answers* question by planning what to do.	"I just need to greet the person, sit down on cue, and answer the questions. I need to be sure to point out why they should take me."

(continued)

POSTEVALUATION (continued)

Item	Examples of counselor leads
____c. *Focused attention* to task and *self-guidance* during task.	"OK, just remember to take a deep breath, relax, and concentrate on the interview. Just remember to discuss my particular qualifications and experiences and try to answer questions completely and directly."
____d. *Coping self-evaluation* and, if necessary, *error correction.*	"OK, now, if I get a little nervous, just take a deep breath. Stay focused on the interview. If I don't respond too well to one question, I can always come back to it."
____e. *Self-reinforcement* for completion of task.	"OK, doing fine. Things are going pretty smoothly."

III. Overt External Guidance

____ 7. Counselor instructs client to perform task while counselor coaches.	"This time you go through the interview yourself. I'll be coaching you on what to do and on your planning."
____ 8. Client performs task while counselor coaches by verbalizing self-guidance, changing *I* to *you.* Counselor's verbalization includes the five components of self-guidance:	"Now just remember you're going to walk in for the interview. When the interview begins, I'll coach you through it."
____a. Question about task.	"OK, you're walking into the interview room. Now ask yourself what it is you're going to do."
____b. Answer to question.	"OK, you're going to greet the interviewer. [Client does so.] Now he's cuing you to sit down. [Client sits.]"
____c. Focused attention to task and self-guidance during task.	"Just concentrate on how you want to handle this situation. He's asking you about your background. You're going to respond directly and completely."
____d. Coping self-evaluation and error correction.	"If you feel a little nervous while you're being questioned, just take a deep breath. If you don't respond to a question completely, you can initiate a second response. Try that now."
____e. Self-reinforcement.	"That's good. Now remember you want to convey why you should be chosen. Take your time to do that. [Client does so.] Great. Very thorough job."

IV. Overt Self-Guidance

____ 9. Counselor instructs client to perform task and instruct self aloud.	"This time I'd like you to do both things. Talk to yourself as you go through the interview in the same way we have done before. Remember, there are five parts to your planning. If you get stuck, I'll help you."
____10. Client performs task while simultaneously verbalizing aloud self-guidance process. Client's verbalization includes five components of self-guidance:	
____a. Question about task.	"Now what is it I need to do?"
____b. Answer to question.	"I'm going to greet the interviewer, wait for the cue to sit down, then answer the questions directly and as completely as possible."
____c. Focused attention and self-guidance.	"Just concentrate on how I'm going to handle this situation. I'm going to describe why I should be chosen."

(continued)

Item	Examples of counselor leads
____d. Coping self-evaluation and error correction.	"If I get a little nervous, just take a deep breath. If I have trouble with one question, I can always come back to it."
____e. Self-reinforcement.	"OK, things are going smoothly. I'm doing fine."
____11. If client's self-guidance is incomplete or if client gets stuck, counselor either—	
____a. Intervenes and cues client or	"Let's stop here for a minute. You seem to be having trouble. Let's start again and try to. . . ."
____b. Recycles client back through step 10.	"That seemed pretty hard, so let's try it again. This time you go through the interview and I'll coach you through it."
____12. Counselor gives feedback to client about overt practice.	"That seemed pretty easy for you. You were able to go through the interview and coach yourself. The one place you seemed a little stuck was in the middle, when you had trouble describing yourself. But overall, it was something you handled well. What do you think?"

V. Faded Overt Self-Guidance

Item	Examples of counselor leads
____13. Counselor instructs client on how to perform task while whispering.	"This time I'd like you to go through the interview and whisper the instructions to yourself as you go along. The whispering may be a new thing for you, but I believe it will help you learn to do this."
____14. Client performs task and whispers simultaneously.	"I'm going into the room now, waiting for the interviewer to greet me and to sit down. I'm going to answer the questions as completely as possible. Now I'm going to talk about my background."
____15. Counselor checks to determine how well client performed.	
____a. If client stumbled or left out some of the five parts, client engages in faded overt practice again.	"You had some difficulty with ____. Let's try this type of practice again."
____b. If client performed practice smoothly, counselor moves on to next step.	"You seemed to do this easily and comfortably. The next thing is . . . ."

VI. Covert Self-Guidance

Item	Examples of counselor leads
____16. Counselor instructs client to perform task while covertly (thinking only) instructing self.	"This time while you practice, simply *think* about these instructions. In other words, instruct yourself mentally or in your head as you go along."
____17. Client performs task while covertly instructing.	Only client's actions are visible at this point.
____18. After practice (step 17), counselor asks client to describe covert instructions.	"Can you tell me what you thought about as you were doing this?"
____19. On basis of client report (step 18):	
____a. Counselor asks client to repeat covert self-guidance.	"It's hard sometimes to begin rehearsing instructions mentally. Let's try it again so you feel more comfortable with it."
____b. Counselor moves on to homework.	"OK, you seemed to do this very easily. I believe it would help if you could apply this to some things that you do on your own this week. For instance. . . ."

(continued)

POSTEVALUATION (continued)

Item	Examples of counselor leads
VII. Homework	
____20. Counselor instructs client on how to carry out homework. Instructions include:	"What I'd like you to do this week is to go through this type of mental practice on your own."
____a. What to do.	"Specifically, go through a simulated interview where you mentally plan your responses as we've done today."
____b. How much or how often to do the task.	"I believe it would help if you could do this two times each day."
____c. When and where to do it.	"I believe it would be helpful to practice at home first, then practice at school [or work]."
____d. A method for self-monitoring during completion of homework.	"Each time you do this, make a check on this log sheet. Also, write down the five parts of the self-instructions you used."
____21. Counselor arranges for a face-to-face or telephone follow-up after completion of homework assignment.	"Bring in your log sheets next week or give me a call at the end of the week and we'll go over your homework then."

Observer Comments: _____

INTERVIEW CHECKLIST FOR THOUGHT STOPPING

Instructions: Determine whether the counselor demonstrated each of the following leads in applying the thought-stopping strategy. Check each lead demonstrated by the counselor.

Item	Examples of counselor leads
I. Rationale about Strategy	
____ 1. Counselor explains purpose of thought stopping to client.	"We've agreed that you are bothered by constant thoughts when you're left alone that are upsetting and self-defeating and cannot be supported by evidence. This procedure is a way for you to learn to inhibit these kinds of thoughts."
____ 2. Counselor gives brief description of strategy.	"First I will ask you to imagine being alone in your hospital room and to tell me what you usually think about then. As soon as you mention a self-defeating thought, I will interrupt you. Then I will teach you how to interrupt yourself and shift your thoughts to something else."
____ 3. Counselor asks client to try strategy.	"Would you like to try it now?"
II. Counselor-Directed Thought Stopping: Overt Interruption	
____ 4. Counselor instructs client to imagine specific problem situation in which chronic self-defeating thoughts occur or just to sit back and let any thoughts come to mind.	"Just close your eyes and imagine now that you are all alone in your room. No one is around. It is very quiet. Just let any thoughts you have come into your mind."
____ 5. Counselor asks client to verbalize aloud typical thoughts (both positive and negative) while imagining situation.	"Now, as you start to think about anything, share with me whatever you are thinking about."
____ 6. When client verbalizes a self-defeating thought, counselor loudly says *Stop!* (may be accompanied by	"OK, *Stop!*" (with a hand clap or noise)

(continued)

Item	_Examples of counselor leads_

a hand clap or some other noise, such as a ruler hitting a desk or a whistle).

_____ 7. After counselor's overt interruption, counselor points out that the unexpected interruption terminated client's self-defeating chain of thoughts.

"Did you notice that as soon as I said _Stop!_, you didn't think about being alone anymore?"

_____ 8. Counselor instructs client to imagine the situation and to concentrate covertly on any thoughts client has.

"This time just imagine again being alone in your room, and notice but don't verbalize any thoughts you have while you're imagining this."

_____ 9. Counselor instructs client to signal with a raised hand or finger whenever client first notices a self-defeating thought.

"When you first start to notice that you're thinking about hearing all these noises, signal to me by raising your hand."

_____10. As soon as client signals, counselor says "_Stop!_"

Client raises hand. "_Stop!_"

_____11. Steps 8 through 10 are repeated until a pattern of inhibiting self-defeating thoughts at counselor's command is established.

"Let's try this again. The idea is to get a pattern established so that on hearing _Stop!_ you discontinue these negative thoughts."

III. Client-Directed Thought Stopping: Overt Interruption

_____12. Counselor instructs client to sit back and notice any thoughts that come to mind.

"Just imagine you're all alone in your room now; imagine what you would be thinking in this situation."

_____13. Counselor instructs client to say aloud _Stop!_ whenever client first notices a self-defeating thought while imagining the situation.

"When you notice a self-defeating thought, say _Stop!_ aloud. This time you'll interrupt yourself by saying _Stop!_ This gives you control over interrupting this chain of thought."

_____14. Steps 12 and 13 are repeated until client feels comfortable interrupting overtly.

"Why don't you try this another time or two until you feel very comfortable interrupting yourself like this?"

IV. Client-Directed Thought Stopping: Covert Interruption

_____15. Counselor instructs client to imagine situation and to notice covertly any thoughts during this time.

"Just imagine the same situation and what your thoughts are."

_____16. Counselor instructs client to _subvocally_ say _Stop!_ when a self-defeating thought occurs.

"This time, when you are aware of a negative thought, just say _Stop!_ to yourself. Say it silently so no one can hear you."

_____17. Counselor instructs client to repeat steps 15 and 16 until client feels comfortable using covert interruption.

"Let's do this again until you feel this is very natural."

V. Shift from Self-Defeating to Assertive, Positive, or Neutral Thoughts

_____18. Counselor explains purpose of shifting from self-defeating to assertive, positive, or neutral thoughts.

"So far we've practiced helping you keep these negative thoughts from getting out of hand by interrupting yourself. Now we're going to learn something that should help you even more. In addition to stopping a thought, you can learn to shift to a very different kind of thought. This helps you manage your feelings of anxiety and gives you a more constructive thing to think about."

_____19. Counselor models assertive, positive, or neutral thoughts. Client is asked to identify others and to verbalize aloud at least three thoughts client could think about after stopping a negative thought.

"An assertive thought is something you might do or think about in the situation that is realistic and focuses on a rational part of the situation, like 'I've been alone before and I've been able to handle whatever has come up.' Or you could think about something positive, like something you enjoy doing, or you could

(continued)

POSTEVALUATION   (continued)

Item	Examples of counselor leads
	just concentrate on an object in the room. I'd like you to think of thoughts similar to these and just to get a feel for them. Practice saying these aloud.''
——20. Counselor asks client to engage in steps 12 and 13 (client-directed overt interruption) again and to follow overt interruption by verbalizing aloud a different thought.	''This time I'd like you to imagine the situation again and tell yourself to stop when you notice a self-defeating thought. In addition, after you say *Stop!,* verbalize aloud one of the thoughts you just selected to substitute for the negative thoughts.''
——21. Step 20 is repeated, with client using a different assertive, positive, or neutral thought with each practice.	''Let's do this a couple of times. Each time after you say *Stop!,* use a different assertive or positive thought. This gives you more options and prevents you from getting tired of just one idea.''
——22. Counselor instructs client to repeat steps 15 and 16 (client-directed covert interruption) and to follow covert interruption with *covert* use of an assertive, positive, or neutral thought.	''Now we're going to do the same type of thing— this time all covertly. You'll say *Stop!* only to yourself —then shift by thinking to yourself a different thought.''
——23. Counselor instructs client to repeat step 22 several times, using a different assertive or positive thought after each covert interruption.	''Let's do this another time so you can try out substituting a different thought than you used the last time.''

VI. Homework and Follow-up

Item	Examples of counselor leads
——24. Counselor instructs client to practice using thought stopping several times daily and any time self-defeating thoughts occur outside the session.	''You've done a really great job teaching this to yourself here. Now you are ready to use it when you need it outside our session. You should practice this three times each day. You'll also be able to use this procedure whenever a self-defeating thought comes up. It will take time, because you're breaking an old habit, so don't get discouraged or expect too much too fast.''
——25. Counselor instructs client to record on a log daily practices and number of times thought stopping is used *in vivo.*	''Record each practice session on your log sheet. Each time you use thought stopping for these negative thoughts as they crop up, write it down on your log. You'll write down the situation you used it for, the time and place, and the specific assertive or positive thought you used after you stopped the negative thought.''
——26. Counselor arranges for follow-up session.	''I'd like to see you in two weeks to see how this has helped. We can go over your log data then.''

Observer Comments: ————————————————————————————————

——

——

FEEDBACK #41: THOUGHT STOPPING

1. We would not select thought stopping for this client because the thoughts are related to a realistic present problem of job dissatisfaction. This is a situation the client may be able to change. In order to do so, he would need to spend some time thinking about different employment alternatives.

2. We would not use thought stopping with this couple. They also are faced with a realistic decision and must think about their options before making a final decision.

3. Although some ruminating over the death of a loved one is natural and realistic, this client is continuing to do so several years after the baby's death. And the client's thoughts center mainly on trying to reconstruct what she did or didn't do — something that, in actuality, she cannot change. Thought stopping could be used with her.

4. This is a good example of a client whose behavior is influenced by thoughts that reflect a "low-probability catastrophe." Although there are reasonable precautions she could take, such as not going out alone at night, her thoughts about something happening to her at other times are unrealistic and interfering. Thought stopping could be used with her.

☐ SUGGESTED READINGS

Arrick, M., Voss, J. R., & Rimm, D. C. (1981). The relative efficacy of thought-stopping and covert assertion. *Behaviour Research and Therapy, 19*, 17–24.

Beck, A. T. (1976). *Cognitive therapy and the emotional disorders.* New York: International Universities Press.

Copeland, A. P. (1981). The relevance of subject variables in cognitive self-instructional programs for impulsive children. *Behavior Therapy, 12*, 520–529.

Kazdin, A. E., & Mascitelli, S. (1982). Behavioral rehearsal, self-instructions, and homework practice in developing assertiveness. *Behavior Therapy, 13*, 346–360.

Kendall, P. C., & Braswell, L. (1982). Cognitive-behavioral self-control therapy for children: A component analysis. *Journal of Consulting and Clinical Psychology, 50*, 672–689.

Mahoney, M. J. (1974). *Cognition and behavior modification.* Cambridge, MA: Ballinger.

Martin, G. L. (1982). Thought-stopping and stimulus control to decrease resistant disturbing thoughts. *Journal of Behavior Therapy and Experimental Psychiatry, 13*, 215–220.

Meichenbaum, D. (1977). *Cognitive behavior modification: An integrative approach.* New York: Plenum.

Meichenbaum, D., & Cameron, R. (1973). Training schizophrenics to talk to themselves: A means of developing attentional controls. *Behavior Therapy, 4*, 515–534.

Meichenbaum, D., & Goodman, J. (1971). Training impulsive children to talk to themselves: A means of developing self-control. *Journal of Abnormal Psychology, 77*, 115–126.

Rimm, D. C., & Masters, J. C. (1979). *Behavior therapy: Techniques and empirical findings* (2nd ed.). New York: Academic Press.

Sarason, I. G. (1973). Test anxiety and cognitive modeling. *Journal of Personality and Social Psychology, 28*, 58–61.

Tryon, G. S. (1979). A review and critique of thought stopping research. *Journal of Behavior Therapy and Experimental Psychiatry, 10*, 189–192.

Tryon, G. S., & Pallandino, J. J. (1979). Thought stopping: A case study and observation. *Journal of Behavior Therapy and Experimental Psychiatry, 10*, 151–154.

■ FEEDBACK: POSTEVALUATION

PART ONE

1. *Rationale*

   First, you would explain the steps of cognitive modeling and self-instructional training to Mr. Brown. Then you would explain how this procedure could help him practice and plan the way he might approach his boss.

2. *Model of task and self-guidance*

   You would model for Mr. Brown a way he could approach his boss to request a social contact. You would model the five parts of the self-guidance process: (1) the question about what he wants to do, (2) the answer to the question in the form of planning, (3) focused attention on the task and guiding himself through it, (4) evaluating himself and correcting errors or making adjustments in his behavior in a coping manner, and (5) reinforcing himself for adequate performance.

3. *Overt external guidance*

   Mr. Brown would practice making an approach or contact while you coach him through the five parts of self-guidance as just described.

4. *Overt self-guidance*

   Mr. Brown would practice making a social contact while verbalizing aloud the five parts of the self-guidance process. If he got stuck, you could prompt him, or else you could have him repeat this step or recycle step 3.

5. *Faded overt self-guidance*

   Mr. Brown would engage in another practice attempt, only this time he would whisper the five parts of the self-guidance process.

6. *Covert self-guidance*

   Mr. Brown would make another practice attempt while using the five parts of the self-guidance process covertly. You would ask him afterward to describe what happened. Additional practice with covert self-guidance or recycling to step 4 or 5 might be necessary.

7. *Homework*

   You would instruct Mr. Brown to practice the self-
   (continued)

FEEDBACK: POSTEVALUATION   (continued)

guidance process daily before actually making a social contact with his boss.

PART TWO

Rate an audiotape of your interview or have an observer rate you, using the Interview Checklist for Cognitive Modeling on pages 395–398.

PART THREE

1. Rationale. The counselor reviews the strategy and clarifies Mr. Brown's questions about it.
2. Rationale. The counselor explains the purpose of thought stopping.
3. Rationale. The counselor explains what thought stopping is and how it works.
4. Rationale. The counselor gives a brief overview of what will happen.
5. Counselor-directed thought stopping: overt interruption. The counselor asks Mr. Brown to imagine the problem situation and report any thoughts.
6. Counselor-directed overt interruption. The loud *Stop!* is the overt interruption. In this first sequence, it is administered by the counselor as a demonstration of how thoughts can be interrupted or terminated.
7. Counselor-directed overt interruption. The counselor points out how the interruption terminates the self-defeating thoughts.
8. Counselor-directed overt interruption. The counselor gets the client to acknowledge potential control over terminating the self-defeating thoughts.
9. Counselor-directed overt interruption. The counselor asks the client to signal a self-defeating thought that the counselor then interrupts overtly.
10. Overt interruption directed by the counselor.
11. Counselor-directed overt interruption. The counselor initiates repetitive practice until the word *stop* exerts control over the client's self-defeating thoughts.
12. Counselor-directed overt interruption. The counselor checks out Mr. Brown's use of this part of thought stopping before going on.
13. Client-directed overt interruption. Mr. Brown is instructed to terminate his self-defeating thoughts by interrupting them with the word *stop.*

14. Client-directed overt interruption. The counselor queries Mr. Brown about his reaction to this practice attempt.
15. Client-directed overt interruption. The counselor initiates additional practices in which Mr. Brown interrupts his self-defeating thoughts overtly.
16. Client-directed overt interruption. The counselor assesses Mr. Brown's reactions to these practices.
17. Client-directed covert interruption. This time Mr. Brown will interrupt his self-defeating thoughts covertly with a subvocal *Stop!*
18. Client-directed covert interruption. The counselor initiates additional practices in which Mr. Brown interrupts his negative thoughts covertly.
19. Shift from self-defeating to positive thoughts. The counselor explains the purpose of this part of the strategy to Mr. Brown.
20. Shift from self-defeating to positive thoughts. The counselor gives some examples of positive thoughts and asks Mr. Brown to identify some he can use.
21. Shift from self-defeating to positive thoughts. The counselor asks Mr. Brown to practice covert interruption of self-defeating thoughts, followed by substituting a positive thought. This first time, Mr. Brown verbalizes the positive thought aloud.
22. Shift from self-defeating to positive thoughts. The counselor instructs Mr. Brown to practice this covertly, this time using a different positive response. A variety of positive responses should be used by the client to prevent satiation.
23. Shift from self-defeating to positive thoughts. The counselor instructs Mr. Brown to engage in additional practice of the shift.
24. Homework and follow-up. The counselor assigns daily homework practice of the procedure.
25. Homework and follow-up.

PART FOUR

Rate an audiotape of your interview or have someone else rate it, using the Interview Checklist for Thought Stopping on pages 398–400.

COGNITIVE RESTRUCTURING, REFRAMING, AND STRESS INOCULATION

SIXTEEN

Risley and Hart (1968, p. 267) suggest that "much of psychotherapy . . . is based on the assumption that reorganizing and restructuring a patient's verbal statements about himself and his world will result in a corresponding reorganization of the patient's behavior with respect to that world." Cognitive restructuring, reframing, and stress inoculation assume that maladaptive emotions and overt responses are influenced or mediated by one's beliefs, attitudes, and perceptions —one's "cognitions." These procedures help clients to determine the relation between their perceptions and cognitions and the resulting emotions and behaviors, to identify faulty or self-defeating cognitions, or perceptions, and to replace these cognitions with self-enhancing perceptions. In all strategies, clients learn how to cope; indirect benefits may include an increase in feelings of resourcefulness, greater ability to handle a problem, and enhancement of self-concept.

Although the procedures described in this chapter reflect a behavioral perspective, no description of these strategies would be complete without some discussion of a major historical antecedent —rational-emotive therapy, or RET. RET, which was developed by Ellis (1975), assumes that most problems are the result of "magical" thinking or irrational beliefs. According to Morris and Kanitz (1975), some of the irrational ideas discussed by Ellis lead to self-condemnation or anger, and others lead to a low tolerance for frustration. The RET therapist helps clients identify which of the irrational ideas are evidenced by their belief systems and emotional reactions.

Ten major irrational ideas cited by Ellis are the following:

1. The idea that it is a dire necessity for an adult to be loved or approved by virtually every significant person in his or her community.
2. The idea that one should be thoroughly competent, adequate, and achieving in all possible respects if one is to consider oneself worthwhile.

3. The idea that human unhappiness is externally caused and that people have little or no ability to control their sorrows and disturbances.

4. The idea that one's past history is an all-important determinant of one's present behavior and that because something once strongly affected one's life, it should indefinitely have a similar effect.

5. The idea that there is invariably a right, precise, and perfect solution to human problems and that it is catastrophic if this perfect solution is not found.

6. The idea that if something is or may be dangerous or fearsome, one should be terribly concerned about it and should keep dwelling on the possibility of its occurring.

7. The idea that certain people are bad, wicked, or villainous and that they should be severely blamed and punished for their villainy.

8. The idea that it is awful and catastrophic when things are not the way one would very much like them to be.

9. The idea that it is easier to avoid than to face certain life difficulties and self-responsibilities.

10. The idea that one should become quite upset over other people's problems and disturbances [Ellis, 1974, pp. 152–153].*

According to RET, it is possible to resolve a client's problems by "cognitive control of illogical emotional responses" (Morris & Kanitz, 1975, p. 8). In RET, such control is achieved primarily by reeducating the client through the use of what Ellis (1975) calls the "ABCDE model." This model involves showing the client how irrational beliefs (B) about an activity or action (A) result in irrational or inappropriate consequences (C). The client is then taught to dispute (D) the irrational beliefs (B), which are not facts and have no supporting evidence, and then to recognize the effects (E). Usually, the effects (E) are either cognitive effects (cE) or behavioral effects (bE).

As you may realize, one of the major assumptions that RET and these three cognitive change strategies share is that a person's beliefs, thoughts, and perceptions can create emotional distress and maladaptive responding. Another shared assumption is that a person's cognitive system can be changed directly and that such change results in different, and presumably more appropriate, consequences. Ullmann and Krasner (1969) note that any cognitive change approach involves punishing a client's emotional labels and reinforcing more appropriate evaluations of a situation.

As you will note in this chapter's discussion of cognitive restructuring, reframing, and stress inoculation, there are some differences between RET and cognitive behavior modification procedures. One difference is that cognitive-behavior procedures do not assume that certain irrational ideas are generally held by all. In cognitive restructuring and stress inoculation, each client's *particular* irrational thoughts or perceptions are identified and are assumed to be idiosyncratic, although some elements may be shared by others as well. A second difference involves the method of change. In RET the therapist tries to help the client alter irrational beliefs by verbal persuasion and teaching. Emphasis is placed on helping the client discriminate between irrational beliefs, which have no evidence, and rational beliefs, which can be supported by data. In cognitive restructuring, reframing, and stress inoculation, in addition to these kinds of discriminations, the client is taught the skill of using alternative cognitions or perceptions in stressful or distressing situations.

□ OBJECTIVES

1. Identify and describe the six components of cognitive restructuring from a written case description.

2. Teach the six major components of cognitive restructuring to another person, or demonstrate these components in a role-play interview.

3. Demonstrate 8 out of 11 steps of reframing in a role-play interview.

4. Using a simulated client case, describe how the five components of stress inoculation would be used with a client.

5. Demonstrate 17 out of 21 steps of stress inoculation in a role-play interview.

□ COGNITIVE RESTRUCTURING

Although cognitive restructuring was described earlier by Lazarus (1971) and has its roots in ratio-

---

* From *Humanistic psychotherapy,* by A. Ellis. Copyright 1974 by McGraw-Hill, Inc. Reprinted by permission of the publisher, McGraw-Hill Book Company, and the author.

nal-emotive therapy (Ellis, 1975), it has been developed by Meichenbaum (1972) under the name *cognitive behavior modification* and by Goldfried, Decenteceo, and Weinberg (1974) under the name *systematic rational restructuring.* Cognitive restructuring focuses on identifying and altering clients' irrational beliefs and negative self-statements or thoughts. Much of the supporting evidence for cognitive restructuring has come from a series of studies conducted by Fremouw and associates (Fremouw & Harmatz, 1975; Fremouw & Zitter, 1978; Glogower, Fremouw, & McCroskey, 1978). Cognitive restructuring has been used to help clients with test anxiety (Cooley & Spiegler, 1980; McCordick, Kaplan, Smith, & Finn, 1981), social anxiety (Elder, Edelstein, & Fremouw, 1981; Gormally, Varvil-Weld, Raphael, & Sipps, 1981), assertive behaviors (Jacobs & Cochran, 1982; Kaplan, 1982; Safran, Alden, & Davidson, 1980; Valerio & Stone, 1982), and musical performance anxiety (Sweeney & Horan, 1982). Baker (1981) and associates (Baker & Butler, in press; Baker, Thomas, & Munson, 1983); have developed a primary prevention unit entitled "Cleaning Up Our Thinking" for junior and senior high students. Hamilton and Fremouw (in press) implemented a cognitive restructuring procedure to improve the foul-shooting performance of male Division II college basketball players. Forman (1980) used cognitive restructuring to modify aggressive behavior of elementary school children. Dush, Hirt, and Schroeder (1983) performed a meta-analysis of controlled studies incorporating direct modification of covert self-statements. They found that self-statement modification made considerable gains beyond no-treatment controls. Finally, in a review of 48 studies, Miller and Berman (1983) found that sex, age, or experience of therapist, duration of treatment, and group or individual presentation of treatment did not affect the efficacy of cognitive behavior therapies.

Several factors can limit or enhance the value of cognitive restructuring. Elder et al. (1981) found cognitive restructuring to be more effective for highly socially anxious clients and found negligible effects for clients reporting relatively low levels of social anxiety. In contrast, Safran et al. (1980) found that cognitive restructuring used to train nonassertive clients was not as effective as skill training for clients with high levels of anxiety. Highly anxious clients may be focusing on the "negative" features or details of the problem situation (Greenberg & Safran, 1981). Bruch, Juster, and Heisler (1982) suggest that individuals with a high degree of conceptual complexity may report more internal attributions and fewer negative task statements. For these types of clients, emphasis should be placed on internal rather than external causal factors when designing coping statements (Bruch et al., 1982). Another factor that can inhibit the use of cognitive restructuring may be the complexity of the treatment (Baker & Butler, in press; Woodward & Jones, 1980); however, the issue of complexity may be related to how well clients understand the presentation of the procedure. For this reason, it is important that counselors carefully explain the rationale for cognitive restructuring to clients.

Our presentation of cognitive restructuring reflects these sources and our own adaptations of it based on clinical usage. We present cognitive restructuring in six major parts:

1. Rationale: purpose and overview of the procedure.
2. Identification of client thoughts during problem situations.
3. Introduction and practice of coping thoughts.
4. Shifting from self-defeating to coping thoughts.
5. Introduction and practice of positive or reinforcing self-statements.
6. Homework and follow-up.

Each of these parts will be described in this section. A detailed description of these six components can be found in the Interview Checklist for Cognitive Restructuring at the end of the chapter.

Treatment Rationale

The rationale used in cognitive restructuring attempts to strengthen the client's belief that "self-talk" can influence performance and particularly that self-defeating thoughts or negative self-statements can cause emotional distress and can interfere with performance.

Rationale. Meichenbaum (1974) has provided a *rationale* he used in training test-anxious and speech-anxious college students to use cognitive restructuring. His example of the purpose for treatment follows; the language can be adapted.

One goal of treatment is for each member to become aware of the factors which are maintaining his test (speech) anxiety. Once we can determine what these factors are, then we can change or combat them. One of the surprising things is that the factors contributing to anxiety are not something secretive, but seem to be the thinking processes you go through in evaluative situations. Simply, there seems to be a correlation between how anxious and tense people feel and the kinds of thoughts they are experiencing. For example, the anxiety you experienced in the test (speech) situation may be tied to the kinds of thoughts you had, what you chose to think about, or how you chose to focus your attention. Somehow your thinking gets all tied up with how you are feeling [pp. 9–10].

Overview.   Here is an example of an overview of the procedure:

We will learn how to control our thinking processes and attention. The control of our thinking, or what we say to ourselves, comes about by first becoming aware of when we are producing negative self-statements, catastrophizing, being task-irrelevant, etc. (Once again, give examples of the clients' thinking styles.) The recognition that we are in fact doing this will be a step forward in changing. This recognition will also act as a reminder, a cue, a bell-ringer for us to produce different thoughts and self-instructions, to challenge our thinking styles and to produce incompatible, task-relevant self-instructions and incompatible behaviors. We will learn how to control our thinking processes in our group discussion, by some specific techniques which I will describe a bit later on. (Pause.) I'm wondering about your reactions to what I have described. Do you have any questions? [pp. 11–12].*

Contrast of self-defeating and self-enhancing thoughts.   In addition to providing a standard rationale such as the one just illustrated, the cognitive restructuring procedure should be prefaced by some contrast between self-enhancing, or rational, thoughts and self-defeating, or irrational, thoughts. This explanation may help clients discriminate between their own self-enhancing and self-defeating thoughts during treatment. Many clients who could benefit from cognitive restructuring are all too aware of their self-defeating thoughts and are unaware of or unable to generate self-enhancing thoughts. Providing a contrast may help them see that more realistic thinking styles can be developed.

Although some therapists describe beliefs as ei-

ther rational or irrational (Ellis, 1975; Goldfried et al., 1974), we prefer to label them positive, self-enhancing thoughts or negative, self-defeating ones. In our opinion, this description is less likely to confuse clients who have trouble distinguishing between their *thoughts* as irrational and *themselves* as irrational or "crazy." Besides, as Thorpe (1973) points out, the aim of cognitive restructuring is to show clients how negative thoughts are unproductive, how they defeat purposes or goals, rather than that clients' ideas are irrational and wrong.

One way to contrast these two types of thinking is to model some examples of both positive, enhancing self-talk and negative, defeating self-talk. These examples can come out of your personal experiences or can relate to the client's problem situations. The examples might occur *before, during,* or *after* a problem situation (Fremouw, 1977). For example, you might say to the client that in a situation that makes you a little uptight, such as meeting a person for the first time, you could get caught up in very negative thoughts:

Before meeting:
"What if I don't come across very well?"
"What if this person doesn't like me?"
"I'll just blow this chance to establish a good relationship."

During meeting:
"I'm not making a good impression on this person."
"This person is probably wishing our meeting were over."
"I'd just like to leave and get this over with."
"I'm sure this person won't want to see me after this."

After meeting:
"Well, that's a lost cause."
"I can never talk intelligently with a stranger."
"I might as well never bother to set up this kind of meeting again."
"How stupid I must have sounded!"

In contrast, you might demonstrate some examples of positive, self-enhancing thoughts about the same situation:

Before meeting:
"I'm just going to try to get to know this person."
"I'm just going to be myself when I meet this person."
"I'll find something to talk about that I enjoy."
"This is only an initial meeting. We'll have to get together more to see how the relationship develops."

---

* From *Therapist manual for cognitive behavior modification,* by D. Meichenbaum. Unpublished manuscript, 1974. Reprinted by permission of the author.

During meeting:

"I'm going to try to get something out of this conversation."

"This is a subject I know something about."

"This meeting is giving me a chance to talk about _____."

"It will take some time for me to get to know this person, and vice versa."

After meeting:

"That went OK; it certainly wasn't a flop."

"I can remember how easy it was for me to discuss topics of interest to me."

"Each meeting with a new person gives me a chance to see someone else and explore new interests."

"I was able just to be myself then."

Influence of self-defeating thoughts on performance. The last part of the rationale for cognitive restructuring should be an *explicit* attempt to point out how self-defeating thoughts or negative self-statements are unproductive and can influence emotions and behavior. You are trying to convey to the client that, whatever we tell ourselves, we are likely to believe it and to act on that belief. However, it is also useful to point out that, in some situations, people don't *literally* tell themselves something. In many situations, our thoughts are so well learned that they are automatic (Goldfried et al., 1974, p. 250). For this reason, you might indicate that you will often ask the client to monitor or log what happens during actual situations between counseling sessions.

Thorpe (1973) has provided an example of a description for nonassertive clients about how unproductive thinking can influence emotions and behavior:

Many difficulties in social situations are simply based on the way in which we think about them. In other words, it is not that a certain situation is really, in itself, difficult, anxiety-provoking, or uncomfortable, but that we simply look on it that way. What usually happens is that we spend so much time telling ourselves negative things, that we are bound to fail, that we are no good, etc., that we cannot possibly handle the situation well. What we will be doing in therapy is to examine some of the unproductive trains of thought that we have when in a demanding situation. Research has shown that if we can only learn to get rid of such unproductive, self-defeating thoughts, and replace them with realistic, sensible ones, then difficult situations become much easier, simply by looking on them in a more positive way [p. 3].

The importance of providing an adequate rationale for cognitive restructuring cannot be overemphasized. If one begins implementing the procedure too quickly, or without the client's agreement, the process can backfire. Some research indicates that people may be more resistant to changing beliefs if they are pushed or coerced to abandon them and adopt someone else's (Brehm, 1966; Watts, Powell, & Austin, 1973). As Goldfried and associates (1974) point out, the procedure should be implemented slowly "by having clients gradually agree to the underlying rationale" (p. 249). The counselor should not move ahead until the client's commitment to work with the strategy is obtained.

Identification of Client Thoughts in Problem Situations

Assuming that the client accepts the rationale provided about cognitive restructuring, the next step involves an analysis of the client's thoughts in anxiety-provoking or distressing situations. Both the range of situations and the content of the client's thoughts in these situations should be explored (Meichenbaum, 1974).

Description of thoughts in problem situations. Within the interview, the counselor should query the client about the particular distressing situations encountered and the things the client thinks about before, during, and after these situations. The counselor might say something like "Sit back and think about the situations that are really upsetting to you. What are they?" and then "Can you identify exactly what you are thinking about or telling yourself before you go to _____? What are you thinking during the situation? And afterward?"

In identifying negative or self-defeating thoughts, the client might be aided by a description of possible cues that compose a self-defeating thought. The counselor can point out that a negative thought may have a "worry quality" such as "I'm afraid . . . ," or a "self-oriented quality" such as "I won't do well" (Meichenbaum, 1974, p. 16). Negative thoughts may also include elements of catastrophizing ("If I fail, it will be awful") or exaggerating ("I *never* do well" or "I *always* blow it"). Goldfried (1976b) suggests that clients can identify the extent to which unrealistic thinking contributes to situational anxiety by answering three questions about each anxiety-provoking situation:

Do I make unreasonable demands of myself?
Do I feel that others are approving or disapproving of my actions?
Do I often forget that this situation is only one part of my life?

Modeling of links between events and emotions. If the client has trouble identifying negative thoughts, Meichenbaum (1974) suggests asking the client to recall the situation as if running a movie through his or her head. The counselor may need to point out that the thoughts are the link between the situation and the resulting emotion and ask the client to notice explicitly what this link seems to be. If the client is still unable to identify thoughts, the counselor can model this link, using either the client's situations or situations from the counselor's life. For example, the counselor might say

"Here is one example that happened to me. I was a music major in college, and several times a year I had to present piano recitals that were graded by several faculty members and attended by faculty, friends, and strangers. Each approaching recital got worse—I got more nervous and more preoccupied with failure. Although I didn't realize it at the time, the link between the event of the recital and my resulting feelings of nervousness was things I was thinking that I can remember now—like "What if I get out there and blank out?" or "What if my arms get so stiff I can't perform the piece?" or "What if my shaking knees are visible?" Now can you try to recall the specific thoughts you had when you felt so upset about _____?"

Client modeling of thoughts. The counselor can also have the client identify situations and thoughts by monitoring and recording events and thoughts outside the interview in the form of homework. For example, Fremouw (1977, p. 3) suggests that an initial homework assignment might be to have the client observe and record at least three negative self-statements a day in the stressful situation for a week. For each day of the week, the client could record on a daily log the negative self-statements and the situations in which these statements were noted (see Figure 16-1).

Using the client's data, the counselor and client can determine which of the thoughts were self-enhancing and productive and which were self-defeating and unproductive. The counselor should try to have the *client* discriminate between the two types of statements and identify why the negative

ones are unproductive. The identification serves several purposes. First, it is a way to determine whether the client's present repertory consists of both positive and negative self-statements or whether the client is generating or recalling only negative thoughts. These data may also provide information about the degree of distress in a particular situation. If some self-enhancing thoughts are identified, the client becomes aware that alternatives are already present in his or her thinking style. If no self-enhancing thoughts are reported, this is a cue that some specific attention may be needed in this area. The counselor can demonstrate how the client's unproductive thoughts can be changed by showing how self-defeating thoughts can be restated more constructively (Fremouw, 1977, p. 3).

Introduction and Practice of Coping Thoughts

At this point in the procedure, there is a shift in focus from the client's self-defeating thoughts to other kinds of thoughts that are incompatible with the self-defeating ones. These incompatible thoughts may be called coping thoughts, coping statements, or coping self-instructions. They are developed for each client. There is no attempt to have all clients accept a common core of rational beliefs, as is often done in rational-emotive therapy (Meichenbaum, 1974).

Introduction and practice of coping statements is, as far as we know, crucial to the overall success of the cognitive restructuring procedure. As Meichenbaum observes, "It appears that the awareness of one's self-statements is a necessary but *not* sufficient condition to cause behavior change. One needs to produce incompatible self-instructions and incompatible behaviors" (1974, p. 51). A well-controlled investigation of the components of cognitive restructuring conducted by Glogower et al. (1978) seems to support Meichenbaum's contention. These authors found that, with communication-anxious college students, simply identifying negative self-statements was no more effective than extinction (repeated exposure to anxious feelings). The crucial component appeared to be the learning and rehearsal of coping statements, which, by itself, was almost as effective as the combination of identifying negative statements and replacing these with incompatible coping thoughts.

Explanation and examples of coping thoughts. The purpose of coping thoughts should be explained clearly. The client should understand that

Name: _____   Week: _____
Date: _____

      Negative Self-Statements: *Situations:*

1. _____   1. _____
2. _____   2. _____
3. _____   3. _____

Figure 16-1. *Example of daily log. From* A Client Manual for Integrated Behavior Treatment of Speech Anxiety, *by W. Fremouw. Copyright © 1977 by the Division of Psychotherapy, American Psychological Association. Reprinted by permission.*

it is difficult to think of failing at an experience (a self-defeating thought) while concentrating on just doing one's best, regardless of the outcome (a coping thought). The counselor could explain the purpose and use of coping thoughts like this:

> "So far we've worked at identifying some of the self-defeating things you think during _____. As long as you're thinking about those kinds of things, they can make you feel anxious. But as soon as you replace these with coping thoughts, then the coping thoughts take over, because it is almost impossible to concentrate on both failing at something and coping with the situation at the same time. The coping thoughts help you to manage the situation and to cope if you start to feel overwhelmed."

The counselor should also model some examples of coping thoughts so that the client can clearly differentiate between a self-defeating and a coping thought. Some examples of coping thoughts to use *before* a situation might be—

> "I've done this before, and it is never as bad as I think."
> "Stay calm in anticipating this."
> "Do the best I can. I'm not going to worry how people will react."
> "This is a situation that can be a challenge."
> "It won't be bad—only a few people will be there."

Examples of coping thoughts to use *during* a situation include—

> "Focus on the task."
> "Just think about what I want to do or say."
> "What is it I want to accomplish now?"
> "Relax so I can focus on the situation."
> "Step back a minute, take a deep breath."
> "Take one step at a time."
> "Slow down, take my time, don't rush."
> "OK, don't get out of control. It's a signal to cope."

If you go back and read over these lists of coping examples, you may note some subtle differences among them. Some of them refer to the nature of the situation itself, such as "It won't be too bad," "It can be a challenge," or "Only a few people will be watching me." Fremouw (1977) refers to these as *context-* or *situation-oriented coping statements.* These coping statements help the client reduce the potential level of threat or severity of the anticipated situation. Other coping statements refer more to the plans, steps, or behaviors the person will need to demonstrate during the stressful situation, such as "Concentrate on what I want to say or do," "Think about the task," or "What do I want to accomplish?" These may be called *task-oriented coping statements* (Fremouw, 1977). Another set of coping thoughts can be used to help the client stay calm and relaxed at tense moments. Meichenbaum (1974) refers to these as *coping with being overwhelmed.* These statements include such self-instructions as "Keep cool," "Stay calm," or "Relax, take a deep breath." A fourth type of coping statement, which we call *positive self-statements,* is used to have clients reinforce or encourage themselves for having coped. These include such self-instructions as "Great, I did it," or "I managed to get through that alright." Positive self-statements can be used during a stressful situation and especially after the situation. The use of positive self-statements in cognitive restructuring is described in more detail later in this chapter.

In explaining about and modeling potential coping thoughts, the counselor may want to note the difference between *coping* and *mastery* thoughts. Coping thoughts are ones that help a client deal with or manage a situation, event, or person adequately. Mastery thoughts are ones that are directed toward helping a person "conquer" or master a situation in almost a flawless manner. For some clients, mastery self-instructions may function as perfectionistic standards that are, in reality, too difficult to attain. For these clients, use of mastery thoughts can make them feel more pressured rather than more relieved. For these reasons we recommend that counselors avoid modeling the use of mastery self-statements and also remain alert to clients who may spontaneously use mastery self-instructions in subsequent practice sessions during the cognitive restructuring procedure.

Client examples of coping thoughts. After providing some examples, the counselor should ask the client to think of additional coping statements. The client may come up with self-enhancing or positive statements she or he has used in other situations. The client should be encouraged to select coping statements that feel most natural. Goldfried (1976b) recommends that clients identify coping thoughts by discovering convincing counterarguments for their unrealistic thoughts.

Client practice. Using these client-selected coping statements, the counselor should ask the client to practice verbalizing coping statements aloud. This is very important, because most clients are not accustomed to using coping statements. Such practice may reduce some of the client's initial discomfort and can strengthen confidence in being able to produce different "self-talk." In addition, clients who are "formally" trained to practice coping statements systematically may use a greater variety of coping thoughts, may use more specific coping thoughts, and may report more consistent use of coping thoughts *in vivo* (Glogower et al., 1978).

At first, the client can practice verbalizing the individual coping statements she or he selected to use before and during the situation. Gradually, as the client gets accustomed to coping statements, the coping thoughts should be practiced in the natural sequence in which they will be used. First, the client would anticipate the situation and practice coping statements before the situation to prepare for it, followed by practice of coping thoughts during the situation — focusing on the task and coping with feeling overwhelmed.

It is important for the client to become actively involved in these practice sessions. The counselor should try to ensure that the client does not simply rehearse the coping statements by rote. Instead, the client should use these practices to try to internalize the meaning of the coping statements (Meichenbaum, 1977, p. 89). One way to encourage more client involvement and self-assertion in

these practice attempts is to suggest that the client pretend that he or she is talking to an audience or a group of persons and needs to talk in a persuasive, convincing manner in order to get his or her point across.

Shifting from Self-Defeating to Coping Thoughts

After the client has identified negative thoughts and has practiced alternative coping thoughts, the counselor introduces rehearsal of shift from self-defeating to coping thoughts during stressful situations. Practice of this shift helps the client use a self-defeating thought as a cue for an immediate switch to coping thoughts.

Counselor demonstration of shift. The counselor should model this process before asking the client to try it. This gives the client an accurate idea of how to practice this shift. Here is an example of a counselor modeling for a high school student who constantly "freezes up" in competitive situations.

"OK, I'm sitting here waiting for my turn to try out for cheerleader. Ooh, I can feel myself getting very nervous. [anxious feeling] Now, wait, what am I so nervous about? I'm afraid I'm going to make a fool of myself. [self-defeating thought] Hey, that doesn't help. [cue to cope] It will take only a few minutes, and it will be over with before I know it. Besides, only the faculty sponsors are watching. It's not like the whole school. [situation-oriented coping thoughts]

Well, the person before me is just about finished. Oh, they're calling my name. Boy, do I feel tense. [anxious feelings] What if I don't execute my jumps? [self-defeating thought] OK, don't think about what I'm not going to do. OK, start out, it's my turn. Just think about my routine — the way I want it to go." [task-oriented coping thoughts]

Client practice of the shift. After the counselor demonstration, the client should practice identifying and stopping self-defeating thoughts and replacing them with coping thoughts. The counselor can monitor the client's progress and coach if necessary. Rehearsal of this shift involves four steps:

1. The client imagines the stressful situation or carries out his or her part in the situation by means of a role play.
2. The client is instructed to recognize the onset of any self-defeating thoughts and to signal this by raising a hand or finger.
3. Next, the client is told to stop these thoughts. If

the client cannot stop the thoughts covertly, a hand clap by the counselor after the signal may work (see "Thought Stopping," in Chapter 15).

4. After the self-defeating thought is stopped, the client immediately replaces it with the coping thoughts. The client should be given some time to concentrate on the coping thoughts. Initially, it may be helpful for the client to verbalize coping thoughts; later, this can occur covertly.

As the client seems able to identify, stop, and replace the self-defeating thoughts, the counselor can gradually decrease the amount of assistance. Before homework is assigned, the client should be able to practice and carry out this shift in the interview setting in a completely self-directed manner.

Introduction and Practice of Reinforcing Self-Statements

The last part of cognitive restructuring involves teaching clients how to reinforce themselves for having coped. This is accomplished by counselor modeling and client practice of positive, or reinforcing, self-statements. Many clients who could benefit from cognitive restructuring report not only frequent self-defeating thoughts but also few or no positive or rewarding self-evaluations. Some clients may learn to replace self-defeating thoughts with task-oriented coping ones and feel better but not satisfied with their progress (Mahoney & Mahoney, 1976). The purpose of including positive self-statements in cognitive restructuring is to help clients learn to praise or congratulate themselves for signs of progress. Although the counselor can provide social reinforcement in the interview, the client cannot always be dependent on encouragement from someone else when confronted with a stressful situation.

Purpose and examples of positive self-statements. The counselor should explain the purpose of reinforcing self-statements to the client and provide some examples. An explanation might sound like this:

"You know, Joan, you've really done very well in handling these situations and learning to stop those self-defeating ideas and to use some coping thoughts. Now it's time to give yourself credit for your progress. I will help you learn to encourage yourself by using rewarding thoughts, so that each time you're in this situation and you cope, you also give yourself a pat on the back for handling the situation and not getting overwhelmed by it. This

kind of self-encouragement helps you to note your progress and prevents you from getting discouraged."

Then the counselor can give some examples of reinforcing self-statements:

"Gee, I did it."
"Hey, I handled that OK."
"I didn't let my emotions get the best of me."
"I made some progress, and that feels good."
"See, it went pretty well after all."

Client selection of positive self-statements. After providing examples, the counselor should ask the client for additional positive statements. The client should select those statements that feel suitable. This is particularly important in using reinforcing statements, because the reinforcing value of a statement may be very idiosyncratic.

Counselor demonstration of positive self-statements. The counselor should demonstrate how the client can use a positive self-statement after coping with a situation. Here is an example of a counselor modeling the use of positive self-statements during and after a stressful situation. In this case, the client was an institutionalized adolescent who was confronting her parents in a face-to-face meeting.

"OK, I can feel them putting pressure on me. They want me to talk. I don't want to talk. I just want to get the hell out of here. [self-defeating thought] Slow down, wait a minute. Don't pressure yourself. Stay cool. [coping with being overwhelmed] Good. That's better. [positive self-statement]
    Well, it's over. It wasn't too bad. I stuck it out. That's progress." [positive self-statement]

Client practice of positive self-statements. The client should be instructed to practice using positive self-statements during and after the stressful situation. The practice occurs first within the interview and gradually outside the interview with *in vivo* assignments. Mahoney and Mahoney (1976) reported an ingenious type of daily self-directed practice to help increase the frequency of a client's positive self-evaluations. The client was taught to cue positive self-statements, to practice these by calling a telephone-answering device, and to verbalize self-praise for her efforts to modify and cope with negative thoughts. These recordings were reviewed by both the client and her counselor. This review served as another way to strengthen the client's positive self-evaluative thoughts (p. 104).

Homework and Follow-up

Although homework is an integral part of every step of the cognitive restructuring procedure, the client ultimately should be able to use cognitive restructuring whenever it is needed in actual distressing situations. The client should be instructed to use cognitive restructuring *in vivo* but cautioned not to expect instant success (Goldfried & Davison, 1976). As with thought stopping, clients can be reminded of the time they have spent playing the old tape over and over in their heads and of the need to make frequent and lengthy substitutions with the new tape. The client can monitor and record the instances in which cognitive restructuring was used over several weeks.

The counselor can facilitate the written recording by providing a homework log sheet that might look something like Figure 16-2. The client's log data can be reviewed at a follow-up session to determine the number of times the client is using cognitive restructuring and the amount of progress that has occurred. The counselor can also use the follow-up session to encourage the client to apply the procedure to stressful situations that could arise in the future. This may encourage the client to generalize the use of cognitive restructuring to situations other than those that are presently considered problematic.

Occasionally, a client's level of distress may not diminish even after repeated practice of restructuring self-defeating thoughts. In some cases, negative self-statements do not precede or contribute to the person's strong feelings. Some emotions may be classically conditioned and therefore treated more appropriately by a counterconditioning procedure, such as systematic desensitization (see Chapter 18). However, even in classically conditioned fears, cognitive processes may also play some role in maintaining or reducing the fear (Davison & Wilson, 1973).

When cognitive restructuring does not reduce a client's level of distress, depression, or anxiety, the counselor and client may need to redefine the problem and goals. As Goldfried and Davison (1976, p. 174) observe, the therapist should "consider the possibility that his assessment has been inaccurate, and that there are, in fact, no internal sentences which are functionally tied to this particular client's problem." Remember that assessment of initial problems may not always turn out to be valid or accurate.

Assuming that the original problem assessment is accurate, perhaps a change in parts of the cognitive restructuring procedure is necessary. Here are some possible revisions:

1. The amount of time the client uses to shift from self-defeating to coping thoughts and to imagine coping thoughts can be increased.
2. The particular coping statements selected by the client may not be very helpful; a change in the type of coping statements may be beneficial.
3. Cognitive restructuring may need to be supplemented either with additional coping skills, such as deep breathing or relaxation, or with skill training [Goldfried & Davison, 1976, p. 174].

Another reason for failure of cognitive restructuring may be that the client's problem behaviors result from errors in encoding rather than errors in reasoning. We describe a strategy designed to alter encoding or perceptual errors in the next section, after the dialogue and learning activity.

☐ MODEL DIALOGUE: COGNITIVE RESTRUCTURING

Session 2

In session 2, the counselor will follow up and review the thought stopping Joan learned the previous week (see Chapter 15). The rest of the interview will be directed toward helping Joan replace self-defeating thoughts with coping thoughts. This is the "nuts and bolts" of cognitive restructuring; it is similar to the substitution of assertive or positive thoughts in thought stopping and is also a major part of stress inoculation, described later in this chapter.

1. *Counselor:* Good to see you again, Joan. How did your week go?
   Client: Pretty good. I did a lot of practice. I also tried to do this in math class. It helped some, but I still felt nervous. Here are my logs.

In response 2, the counselor **reinforces Joan for completing her logs** *and her daily practice. Joan is usually good at completing these; nevertheless, such work on the client's part should not go unnoticed.*

2. *Counselor:* OK, these look good. Let's go over

Daily record of dysfunctional thoughts

Date	Situation	Emotion(s)	Automatic thought(s)	Rational response	Outcome
	Describe: 1. Actual event leading to unpleasant emotion or 2. Steam of thoughts, daydream, or recollection leading to unpleasant emotion.	1. Specify sad-anxious. etc. 2. Rate degree of emotion, 1–100%.	1. Write automatic thought(s) that preceded emotion(s). 2. Rate belief in automatic thought(s), 0–100%.	1. Write rational response to automatic thought(s). 2. Rate belief in rational response, 0–100%.	1. Rerate belief in automatic thought(s), 0–100%. 2. Specify and rate subsequent emotions, 0–100%.
EXAMPLE 2/5	Not getting filing and lots of other stuff done.	Anxious-sad-angry 85%	A failure again, I can never get my work done, I'm no good. 85%	I have got filing and other work done in the past, but usually in smaller bites, not all at once. 80%	1. 45% 2. Anxious-sad 50%

Explanation of rating categories: When you experience an unpleasant emotion, note the situation that seemed to stimulate the emotion. (If the emotion occurred while you were thinking, daydreaming, etc., please note this.) Then note the automatic thought associated with the emotion. Record the degree to which you believe this thought: 0% = not at all; 100% = completely. In rating degree of emotion: 1 = a trace; 100 = the most intense possible.

"*In vivo assessment techniques for cognitive-behavioral processes" by S. D. Hollon & P. C. Kendall. In *Assessment strategies for cognitive-behavioral interventions* by P. C. Kendall and S. D. Hollon (Eds.). Copyright © 1981 by Academic Press. Reprinted by permission.

Figure 16-2. *Example of homework log sheet**

them. Looks like you did a lot of daily practice. This is terrific. Now, according to your log, you needed to use the thought stopping before your class and several times during the class.

Client: Right. Especially when we had a test or I had to go to the board. You know how that makes me feel—nervous.

The counselor uses this opportunity **to reiterate how Joan's negative thoughts can, to some extent, contribute to her nervous feelings** *and explains that the physical sensations of nervousness will be dealt with later and cautions Joan not to expect too much change all at once.*

3. *Counselor:* Yes, and some of the nervousness is created by the negative thoughts. However, you've indicated you feel nervous physically, so we'll work with this in another way later on. So it's understandable if you still feel nervous this week. It won't be an overnight change—just one step at a time. (Shows Joan a cassette tape recorder.) Remember this tape recorder. You've been playing the old tape in your head for a long time and it will take some practice to eject it and put a new one in.

Client: Yes. Well, I could definitely tell that I cut off these thoughts sooner than I used to.

In response 4, the counselor gives a **rationale** *for cognitive restructuring,* **explains the purpose of "coping" thoughts to Joan,** *and gives an* **overview** *of the strategy.*

4. *Counselor:* That's great. And I bet your daily practice helped you do that when you needed to. Today we're going to go one step further. In addition to having you stop the negative thoughts, we're going to work on having you learn to use some more constructive thoughts. I call these *"coping thoughts."* You can replace the negative thoughts with coping thoughts that will help you when you're anticipating your class, in your class itself, and when things happen in your class that are especially hard for you—like taking a test or going to the board. What questions do you have about this?

Client: I don't think any—although I don't know if I know exactly what you mean by a coping thought.

The counselor, in response 5, will **explain and give some examples of coping thoughts** *and particular times or phases when Joan might need to use them.*

5. *Counselor:* OK, let me explain about these and give you some examples. Then perhaps you can think of your own examples. The first thing is

that there are probably different times when you could use coping thoughts—like before math class when you're anticipating it. Only, instead of worrying about it, you can use this time to prepare to handle it. For example, some coping thoughts you might use before math class are "No need to get nervous. Just think about doing OK" or "You can manage this situation" or "Don't worry so much—you've got the ability to do OK." Then, during math class, you can use coping thoughts to get through the class and to concentrate on what you're doing, such as "Just psych yourself up to get through this" or "Look at this class as a challenge, not a threat" or "Keep your cool, you can control your nervousness." Then, if there are certain times during math class that are especially hard for you, like taking a test or going to the board, there are coping thoughts you can use to help you deal with really hard things, like "Think about staying very calm now" or "Relax, take a deep breath" or "Stay as relaxed as possible. This will be over shortly." After math class, or after you cope with a hard situation, then you can learn to encourage yourself for having coped by thinking things like "You did it" or "You were able to control your negative thoughts" or "You're making progress." Do you get the idea?

Client: Yes, I think so.

Next, in responses 6 through 9, the counselor will instruct Joan **to select and practice coping thoughts at each critical phase,** *starting with* **preparing for class.**

6. *Counselor:* Joan, let's take one thing at a time. Let's work just with what you might think before your math class. Can you come up with some coping thoughts you could use when you're anticipating your class?

Client: Well. [Pauses] I could think about just working on my problems and not worrying about myself. I could think that when I work at it, I usually get it even if I'm slow.

7. *Counselor:* OK, good. Now just to get the feel for these, practice using them. Perhaps you could imagine you are anticipating your class—just say these thoughts aloud as you do.

Client: Well, I'm thinking that I could look at my class as a challenge. I can think about just doing my work. When I concentrate on my work, I usually do get the answers.

8. *Counselor:* OK—good! How did that feel?

Client: Well, OK. I can see how this might help. Of course, I don't usually think these kinds of things.

9. *Counselor:* I realize that, and later on today we will practice actually having you use these

thoughts after you use the thought stopping that you learned last week. You'll get to the point where you can use your nervousness as a signal to cope. You can stop the self-defeating thoughts and use these coping thoughts instead. Let's practice this some more. [Additional practice ensues.]

In responses 10, 11, and 12, the counselor asks Joan **to select and practice verbalizing coping thoughts** *she can use* **during class.**

10. *Counselor:* OK, Joan, now you seem to have several kinds of coping thoughts that might help you when you're anticipating math class. What about some coping thoughts you could use during the class? Perhaps some of these could help you concentrate on your work instead of your tenseness.

    Client: Well, I could tell myself to think about what I need to do — like to get the problems. Or I could think — just take one situation at a time. Just psych myself up 'cause I know I really can do well in math if I believe that.

11. *Counselor:* OK, it sounds like you've already thought of several coping things to use during class. This time, why don't you pretend you're sitting in your class? Try out some of these coping thoughts. Just say them aloud.

    Client: OK. Well, I'm sitting at my desk, my work is in front of me. What steps do I need to take now? Well, I could just think about one problem at a time, not worry about all of them. If I take it slowly, I can do OK.

12. *Counselor:* OK, that seemed pretty easy for you. Let's do some more practice like this just so these thoughts don't seem unfamiliar to you. As you practice, try hard to think about the meaning of what you're saying to yourself. [More practice occurs.]

Next, Joan **selects and practices coping thoughts** *to help her deal with especially* **stressful or critical situations** *that come up in math class (responses 13, 14, and 15).*

13. *Counselor:* This time, let's think of some particular coping statements that might help you if you come up against some touchy situations in your math class — things that are really hard for you to deal with, like taking a test, going to the board, or being called on. What might you think at these times that would keep the lid on your nervousness?

    Client: Well, I could think about just doing what is required of me — maybe, as you said earlier taking a deep breath and just thinking about

staying calm, not letting my anxiety get the best of me.

14. *Counselor:* OK, great. Let's see — can you practice some of these aloud as if you were taking a test or had just been asked a question or were at the board in front of the class?

    Client: OK. Well, I'm at the board, I'm just going to think about doing this problem. If I start to get really nervous, I'm going to take a deep breath and just concentrate on being calm as I do this.

15. *Counselor:* OK, let's practice this several times. Maybe this time you might use another tense moment, like being called on by your teacher. [Further practice goes on.]

Next, the counselor **points out how Joan may discourage or punish herself after class** *(responses 16 and 17). Joan selects and* **practices encouraging or self-rewarding thoughts** *(responses 18, 19, and 20).*

16. *Counselor:* OK, Joan, there's one more thing I'd like you to practice. After math class, what do you usually think?

    Client: I feel relieved. I think about how glad I am it's over. Sometimes I think about the fact that I didn't do well.

17. *Counselor:* Well, those thoughts are sort of discouraging, too. What I believe might help is if you could learn to encourage yourself as you start to use these coping thoughts. In other words, instead of thinking about not doing well, focus on your progress in coping. You can do this during class or after class is over. Can you find some more positive things you could think about to encourage yourself — like giving yourself a pat on the back?

    Client: You mean like I didn't do as bad as I thought?

18. *Counselor:* Yes, anything like that.

    Client: Well, it's over, it didn't go too badly. Actually I handled things OK. I can do this if I believe it. I can see progress.

19. *Counselor:* OK, now, let's assume you've just been at the board. You're back at your seat. Practice saying what you might think in that situation that would be encouraging to you.

    Client: Well, I've just sat down. I might think that it went fast and I did concentrate on the problem, so that was good.

20. *Counselor:* OK. Now let's assume class is over. What would you say would be positive, self-encouraging thoughts after class?

    Client: Well, I've just gotten out. Class wasn't that bad. I got something out of it. If I put my mind to it, I can do it. [More practice of positive self-statements occurs.]

In response 21, the counselor instructs Joan **to practice the entire sequence** *of stopping a self-defeating thought and using a coping thought before, during, and after class. Usually the client practices this by* **imagining the situation.**

21. *Counselor:* So far we've been practicing these coping thoughts at the different times you might use them so you can get used to these. Now let's practice this in the sequence that it might actually occur—like before your class, during the class, coping with a tough situation, and encouraging yourself after class. We can also practice this with your thought stopping. If you imagine the situation and start to notice any self-defeating thoughts, you can practice stopping these. Then switch immediately to the types of coping thoughts that you believe will help you most at that time. Concentrate on the coping thoughts. How does this sound?

    Client: OK, I think I know what you mean. [Looks a little confused.]

Sometimes long instructions are confusing. Modeling may be better. In responses 22 and 23, the counselor **demonstrates how Joan can apply thought stopping and coping thoughts in practice.**

22. *Counselor:* Well, I just said a lot, and it might make more sense if I showed this to you. First, I'm going to imagine I'm in English class. It's almost time for the bell, then it's math class. Wish I could get out of it. It's embarrassing. *Stop!* That's a signal to use my coping thoughts. I need to think about math class as a challenge. Something I can do OK if I work at it. [Pauses.] Joan, do you get the idea?

    Client: Yes, now I do.

23. *Counselor:* OK, I'll go on and imagine now I'm actually in the class. He's given us a worksheet to do in 30 minutes. Whew! How will dumb me ever do that! *Stop!* I know I can do it, but I need to go slowly and concentrate on the work, not on me. Just take one problem at a time.

    Well, now he wants us to read our answers. What if he calls on me? I can feel my heart pounding. *Stop!* If I get called on, just take a deep breath and answer. If it turns out to be wrong, it's not the end of the world.

    Well, the bell rang. I am walking out. I'm glad it's over. Now, wait a minute—it didn't go that badly. Actually I handled it pretty well.

    Client: I'm seeing now how this fits together with thought stopping. After you stop a negative thought, you go to a coping thought.

Next, the counselor encourages Joan **to try this out in practice attempts.**

24. *Counselor:* That's it. The idea is to stop the negative thoughts and use more constructive ones. Now, why don't you try this? [Joan practices the sequence of thought stopping and shifting to coping thoughts several times, first with the counselor's assistance, gradually in a completely self-directed manner.]

Before terminating the session, the counselor **assigns daily homework practice.**

25. *Counselor:* This week I'd like you to practice this several times each day—just like you did now. Keep track of your practices on your log. And you can use this whenever you feel it would be helpful—such as before, during, or after math class. Jot these times down too, and we'll go over this next week.

LEARNING ACTIVITIES #42: COGNITIVE RESTRUCTURING

I. Listed below are eight statements. Read each statement carefully and decide whether it is a self-defeating or a self-enhancing statement. Remember, a self-defeating thought is a negative, unproductive way to view a situation; a self-enhancing thought is a realistic, productive interpretation of a situation or of oneself. Write down your answers. Feedback is given after the learning activities on page 418.

1. "I'll never be able to pass this test."
2. "How can I ever give a good speech when I don't know what I want to say?"
3. "What I can do is to take one thing at a time."
4. "I know I'm going to blow it with all those people looking at me."

5. "What I need to think about is what I *want* to say, not what I think I *should* say."
6. "What if I'm imposing? Maybe I'm just wasting their time."
7. "Why bother? She probably wouldn't want to go out with me anyway."
8. "I may not win, but I'll do my best."

II. This learning activity is designed to help you personalize cognitive restructuring in some way by using it yourself.

1. Identify a problem situation for yourself—a situation in which you don't do what you want to, not

(continued)

because you don't have the skills, but because of your negative, self-defeating thoughts. Some examples:

   a. You need to approach your boss about a raise, promotion, or change in duties. You know what to say, but you are keeping yourself from doing it because you aren't sure it would have any effect and you aren't sure how the person might respond.

   b. You have the skills to be an effective helper, yet you constantly think that you aren't.

   c. You continue to get positive feedback about the way you handle a certain situation, yet you are constantly thinking you don't do this very well.

2. For about a week, every time this situation comes up, monitor all the thoughts you have *before, during,* and *after* the situation. Write these thoughts in a log. At the end of the week:

   a. Identify which of the thoughts are self-defeating.

   b. Identify which of the thoughts are self-enhancing.

   c. Determine whether the greatest number of self-defeating thoughts occur before, during, or after the situation.

3. In contrast to the self-defeating thoughts you have, identify some possible coping or self-enhancing thoughts you could use. On paper, list some you could use before, during, and after the situation, with particular attention to the time period when you tend to use almost all self-defeating thoughts. Make sure that you include in your list some positive or self-rewarding thoughts, too—for coping.

4. Imagine the situation—before, during, and after it. As you do this, stop any self-defeating thoughts and replace them with coping and self-rewarding thoughts. You can even practice this in role play. This step should be practiced until you can feel your coping and self-rewarding thoughts taking hold.

5. Construct a homework assignment for yourself that encourages you to apply this as needed when the self-defeating thoughts occur.

☐ REFRAMING

Recall that the focus of cognitive restructuring is on faulty reasoning and illogical or irrational inferences and beliefs. The goal is to alter irrational beliefs or negative self-statements. Some clients, however, may exhibit maladaptive response patterns because of errors in encoding and/or encoding bias. For example:

> A parent who explodes in anger at [a] child's demands for help does so because s/he focuses on cues related to his/her dependence and inability to do anything for herself/himself. S/he might selectively attend to his/her statement "I can't do it" and to the pleading look in his/her eyes or tone in his/her voice and automatically thinks "I can't stand this child. I wish I were free of her/him." S/he feels overwhelmed by his/her demands and inadequate as a parent. However, a focus on the child's tired eyes and partial achievement of the task in which the child is asking for help results in a different encoding, one of an overtired child who attempts to do things independently. This encoding would produce a different response to the child and no subsequent thoughts of personal inadequacy for the parent [Greenberg & Safran, 1981, p. 165].*

As this example illustrates, typical dysfunctional encoding activity consists of a series of discrete peripheral responses that are "linked together in a cyclical and self-perpetuating fashion" (Greenberg & Safran, 1981, p. 165). For clients who are making mistakes in encoding, identifying and modifying their perceptions—what they attend to—may be useful. This is the goal of a strategy we call "reframing." This strategy is based on the work of Greenberg and Safran (1981), Safran et al. (1980), Safran and Greenberg (1982), Bandler and Grinder (1982) and Watzlawick, Weakland, and Fisch (1974). Occasionally, *both* cognitive restructuring and reframing are useful for a client.

Reframing (sometimes also called relabeling) is an approach that modifies or restructures a client's perceptions or views of a problem or a behavior. Reframing is used frequently in family therapy as a way to redefine presenting problems in order to

* This and other quotations from this source and from "Encoding and cognitive therapy: Changing what clients attend to" by L. S. Greenberg and J. D. Safran. *Psychotherapy: Theory, Research and Practice, 18,* 163–169. Copyright © 1981 by the American Psychological Association. Reprinted by permission.

FEEDBACK #42: COGNITIVE RESTRUCTURING

I. 1. Self-defeating: the word *never* indicates the person is not giving himself or herself any chance for passing.
   2. Self-defeating: the person is doubting both the ability to give a good speech and knowledge of the subject.
   3. Self-enhancing: the person is realistically focusing on one step at a time.
   4. Self-defeating: the person is saying with certainty, as evidenced by the word *know*, that there is no chance to do well; this is said without supporting data or evidence.
   5. Self-enhancing: the client is realistically focusing on his or her own opinion, not on the assessment of others.
   6. Self-defeating: the person is viewing the situation only from a negative perspective, as if rejection were expected and deserved.
   7. Self-defeating: the person predicts a negative reaction without any supporting evidence.
   8. Self-enhancing: the person recognizes a win may not occur yet still concentrates on doing the best job.

---

shift the focus off of an "identified patient" or "scapegoat" and onto the family as a whole, as a system in which each member is an interdependent part (Watzlawick et al., 1974). When used in this way, reframing changes the way a family encodes an issue or a conflict.

With individual clients, reframing has a number of uses as well. By changing or restructuring what clients encode and perceive, reframing can reduce defensiveness and mobilize the client's resources and forces for change. Secondly, it can shift the focus from overly simplistic trait attributions of behavior that clients are inclined to make ("I am lazy." or "I am not assertive.") to analyses of important contextual and situational cues associated with the behavior (Alexander & Parsons, 1982). Finally, reframing can be a useful strategy for dealing with client "resistance" (see also positive connotation in Chapter 20).

Meaning Reframes

Counselors reframe whenever they ask or encourage clients to see an issue from a different perspective. In this chapter, we propose a more systematic way for counselors to help clients reframe a prob-

lem behavior. The most common method of reframing—and the one that we illustrate in this chapter—is to reframe the *meaning* of a problem situation or behavior. When you reframe meaning, you are challenging the meaning that the client (or someone else) has assigned to a given problem behavior. Usually, the longer a particular meaning (or label) is attached to a client's behavior, the more necessary the behavior itself becomes in maintaining predictability and equilibrium in the client's functioning. Also, when meanings are attached to client behavior over a long period of time, clients are more likely to develop "functional fixity"—that is, seeing things in only one way or from one perspective or being fixated on the idea that this particular situation or attribute is *the* issue. Reframing helps clients by providing alternative ways to view a problem behavior without directly challenging the behavior itself and by loosening a client's perceptual frame, thus setting the stage for other kinds of therapeutic work. Once the *meaning* of a behavior or a situation changes, the person's response to the situation or the person's typical behavior usually also changes, providing the reframe is valid and acceptable to the client. The essence of a meaning reframe is to give a situation or a behavior a new label or a new name that has a different meaning. This new meaning always has a different connotation, and usually it is a positive one. For example, client "stubbornness" might be reframed as "independence" or "greediness" might be reframed as "ambitiousness." Meaning reframes are based on two assumptions: (1) that it is possible to reframe whatever a person does (or doesn't do) as a success (Erickson, in Watzlawick et al., 1974); and (2) that persons will be cooperative if positive aspects of their behavior are stressed.

Reframing involves six steps:

1. Rationale: purpose and overview of the procedure.
2. Identification of client perceptions and feelings in problem situations.
3. Deliberate enactment of selected perceptual features.
4. Identification of alternative perceptions.
5. Modification of perceptions in problem situations.
6. Homework and follow-up.

A detailed description of the steps associated with these components can be found in the Interview Checklist for Reframing at the end of this chapter.

Treatment Rationale

The rationale used to present reframing attempts to strengthen the client's belief that perceptions or attributions about the problem situation can cause emotional distress. Here is a rationale that can be used to introduce reframing:

"When we think about or when we are in a problem situation, we automatically attend to selected features of the situation. As time goes on, we tend to get fixated on these same features of the situation and ignore other aspects of it. This can lead to some uncomfortable emotions, such as the ones you're feeling now. In this procedure, I will help you identify what you are usually aware of during these problem situations. Then we'll work on increasing your awareness of other aspects of the situation that you usually don't notice. As this happens, you will notice that your feelings about and responses to this problem will start to change. Do you have any questions?"

Identification of Client Perceptions and Feelings

Assuming that the client accepts the rationale the counselor provides, the next step is to help clients become aware of what they automatically attend to in problem situations. Clients are often unaware of what features or details they attend to in a problem situation and what information about these situations they encode. For example, one person may attend to a long hospital corridor and encode it as cold and impersonal, while someone else may attend to the people on the corridor and encode the feature as healthy, caring, and clean (Greenberg & Safran, 1981). Or clients who have a fear of water may attend to how deep the water is because they cannot see the bottom and encode the perception that they might drown. Clients who experience test anxiety might attend to the large size of the room or how quickly the other people seem to be working. These features are encoded and lead to feeling overwhelmed, anxious, and lacking in confidence. In turn, these feelings can lead to impaired performance in or avoidance of the situation.

Within the interview, the therapist helps clients discover what they typically attend to in problem situations. The therapist can use imagery or role play to help clients reenact the situation(s) in order to become aware of what they notice and encode. While engaging in role play or in imagining the problem situation, the therapist can help the client become more aware of typical encoding patterns by asking questions like these:

"What are you attending to now?"
"What are you aware of now?"

"What are you noticing about the situation?"

In order to link feelings to individual perceptions, these questions can be followed with further inquiries like

"What are you feeling at this moment?" or
"What do you experience?" (Greenberg & Safran, 1981).

The counselor may have to help clients engage in role play or imagery several times so that they can reconstruct the situation and become more aware of salient encoded features. The therapist may also suggest what the client might have felt and what the experience appears to mean to the client in order to bring these automatic perceptions into awareness (Greenberg & Safran, 1981). The therapist also helps clients notice "marginal impressions"—fleeting images, sounds, feelings, and sensations that were passively rather than deliberately processed by the client yet affect the client's reaction to the situation (Greenberg & Safran, 1981).

Deliberate Enactment of Selected Perceptual Features

After clients become aware of their rather automatic attending, they are asked to reenact the situation and intentionally attend to the selected features that they have been processing automatically. For example, the water-phobic client reenacts (through role play or imagery) approach situations with the water and deliberately attends to the salient features such as the depth of the water and inability to see the bottom of the pool. By deliberately attending to these encoded features, clients are able to bring these habitual attentional processes fully into awareness and under direct control (Greenberg & Safran, 1981, p. 165). This sort of "dramatization" seems to sharpen the client's awareness of existing perceptions. When these perceptions are uncovered and made more visible through this deliberate re-enactment, it is harder for the client to maintain old illusions (Andolfi, 1979). This step may need to be repeated several times during the session or assigned as a homework task.

Identification of Alternative Perceptions

The counselor can help the client change his or her attentional focus by selecting other features of the problem situation to attend to rather than ignore. For example, the water-phobic client who focuses on the depth of the water might be instructed to focus on how clear, clean, and wet the water appears. For the test-anxious client who attends to the size of the room, the counselor can redirect the client's attention to how roomy the testing place is or how comfortable the seats are. Both clients and counselors can suggest other features of the problem situation or person to utilize that have a positive or at least a neutral connotation. The following kinds of questions may help both counselor and client identify new meanings: "Is there a larger or different frame in which this behavior would have a positive value?" "What else could this behavior mean?" "How else could this same situation be described?" "What other aspect of this same situation that isn't apparent to the client could provide a different meaning frame?" (Bandler & Grinder, 1982, p. 15).

For reframing to be effective, the alternative perceptions you identify must be acceptable to the client. The best reframes are the ones that are accurate and are "*as* valid a way of looking at the world as the way the person sees things now. Reframes don't necessarily need to be more valid, but they really can't be less valid" (Bandler & Grinder, 1982, p. 42). Thus, all reframes or alternative perceptions have to be tailored to the clients' values, style, sociocultural context, and have to fit the clients' experience and model of their world. The alternative perceptions or reframes you suggest obviously also need to match the external reality of the situation enough to be plausible. If, for example, a husband is feeling very angry with his wife because of her extramarital affair, reframing his anger as "loving concern" is probably not representative enough of the external situation to be plausible to the client. A more plausible reframe might be something like "frustration over not being able to control your wife's behavior" or "frustration from not being able to protect the (marital) relationship."

The delivery of a reframe is also important. When suggesting alternative perceptions to clients, it is essential that the counselor's nonverbal behavior be congruent with the tone and content of the reframe. It is also important to use your voice effectively in delivering the reframe by emphasizing key words or phrases.

Modification of Perceptions in Problem Situations

Modifying what clients attend to can be facilitated with role play or imagery. The therapist instructs the client to attend to other features of the problem situations during the role play or imagery enact-

ment. This step may need to be repeated several times. According to Greenberg and Safran (1981, p. 166), these attempts to create new perceptual responses "are explicitly designed to break old encoding patterns and lay the blueprint for new, more effective patterns."

Homework and Follow-up

The therapist can suggest that the client follow during *in vivo* situations the same format used in therapy. The client is instructed to become more aware of salient encoded features of a stressful or arousing situation, to link these to uncomfortable feelings, to engage in deliberate enactments or practice activities, and to try to make "perceptual shifts" during these situations to other features of the situation previously ignored.

As the client becomes more adept at this process, the therapist will need to be alert to slight perceptual shifts and point these out to clients. Typically, clients are unskilled at detecting these shifts in encoding (Greenberg & Safran, 1981). Helping the client discriminate between old and new encodings of a problem situation can be very useful in promoting the overall goal of the reframing strategy — to alleviate and modify encoding or perceptual errors and bias.

Context Reframes

Although the steps we propose for reframing involve reframing of meaning, another way you can also reframe is to reframe the *context* of a problem behavior. Reframing the context helps a client to explore and decide *when, where,* and *with whom* a given problem behavior is *useful* or appropriate. Context reframing helps clients answer the question "In what place in your life is behavior X useful and appropriate?" (Bandler & Grinder, 1982). Context reframing is based on the assumption that every behavior is useful in *some* but not all contexts or conditions. Thus, when a client states "I'm too lazy," a context reframe would be "In what situations (or with what people) is it useful or even helpful to be lazy?" The client may respond by noting that it is useful to be lazy whenever she wants to play with the children. At this point the counselor can help the client sort out and contextualize a given problem behavior so that clients can see where and when they do and do not want the behavior to occur. Context reframes are most useful when dealing with client generalizations — for example "I'm *never* assertive," "I'm *always* late," and so on.

☐ MODEL DIALOGUE: REFRAMING

Session 3

In this session, the counselor continues to help Joan work on the anxiety she feels in math class. In the previous session, they focused on her negative self-statements. In this session, they will work with reframing the meaning associated with Joan's math class.

1. *Counselor:* Good to see you again, Joan. How did things go for you this week?
   Client: Not too bad. I did cut math class once. I still have some nervousness there, although it seems to be getting a little bit more under control.

In response 2, the counselor introduces the idea of **how perceptions can create distressing feelings.**

2. *Counselor:* Great. As we talked about last week, some of the nervousness is created by those negative thoughts. Some of it is also created by how you see math class, which is what I'd like to focus on today if that's OK.
   Client: All right.

In response 3, the counselor gives a **rationale** *for reframing.*

3. *Counselor:* OK, today we're going to go one step further. In addition to having you stop the negative thoughts, we're going to work on having you look at how you perceive the math class. Right now, if I asked you to think about math class, you would probably think about negative features of the class. By attending only to these negative features, you exclude positive or neutral aspects of math class. Just seeing the negative features of the class contributes to your nervous feelings about the class. Today, I'll help you identify what things you notice in math class. Once we become aware of this, we will modify what you attend to by focusing on the ignored positive or neutral attributes of the math class. What questions do you have about this?
   Client: I don't have any—but I'm not sure what you mean by my "perception" and "features."

The counselor, in response 4, will help Joan **identify what she attends to** *when she thinks of math class.*

4. *Counselor:* Yes, those terms are confusing! Let's work with math class and see whether this becomes more clear to you. Let's try to see what it is you are attending to in math class. For example, when you think of math class, try to identify what comes into your mind.
   Client: Well, some of the time I think about math problems and how difficult they are. And I

don't get grades that are as good as some others in the class. I get nervous and I wish I didn't have to go.

The client has identified some of her thoughts and reactions related to math class. However, the counselor wants to identify some specific features the client attends to **initially when she thinks of math class.** *In response 5, the counselor instructs the client to* **engage in imagery** *to help Joan* **increase her awareness of what she initially thinks about** *when she starts to think of math class.*

5. *Counselor:* OK, that's a good start. Now, what I want us to focus on is specific things you first think about when you start to think about math class. What are the specific features that come to your mind when I say "math class?" To help you identify these initial features, I want you to close your eyes, and I'll instruct you to imagine being in math class and being aware of all the reactions you experience. After you imagine being in class for a while, I'll ask you to identify what specific things about your math class you're focusing on. Ok, now close your eyes and imagine you are in math class. Experience all the sensations you have. After a few minutes, I'll tell you to open your eyes. [Twenty seconds elapse.] Now open your eyes and tell me what you saw in this situation.
   Client: Well, I think that math is really not important for women. I think that math won't help me and girls shouldn't be as good in math as boys.

Joan is now describing an irrational belief. The counselor provides an **example** *to show Joan what kinds of things to attend to during the imagery.*

6. *Counselor:* OK, that's an example of something you *think* about. I'm interested now in what you *notice* about the situation when you're there. For instance, right now I'm noticing that it is hot in this room, that you have a perplexed look on your face, that I have a gurgling sensation in my stomach. Let's try it again, and this time I'll ask you some questions as you imagine this. [Instructs Joan to engage in another imagery scene of math.]

In response 7, the counselor queries Joan about **present awareness of selected features.**

7. *Counselor:* OK, now, Joan, what are you aware of as you do this? Just describe whatever comes into your mind.
   Client: Well—the teacher. He is there with a smirk on his face, like he thinks I'm stupid. And all the other guys in the room. They are all look-

ing at me, especially when I get called on or have to go to the board—like I'm dumb.

This time, Joan did identify significant perceptual features she encodes in math class. The counselor **clarifies** *this in response 8.*

8. *Counselor:* OK, great. So you attend mostly to the teacher, to the guys, and to their faces. Is that accurate?

    Client: Well, I never really gave it much thought, but yes, I guess I do.

In response 9 the counselor suggests **how these perceptual features are linked to Joan's anxious feelings.**

9. *Counselor:* So you feel nervous whenever you see these guys looking at you and when you see your teacher with this smirk on his face.

    Client: Well, I guess I do because they are all guys and they all seem so smart in math.

In the next responses, the counselor instructs Joan to reenact the situation in imagery by **deliberately attending to or focusing on these identified features.**

10. *Counselor:* Well, again that is one of your beliefs that isn't necessarily true. What I was thinking was that by noticing just *them,* you might fail to notice other things that might create different feelings for you, like the other female students or other facial expressions of these people. Now this may seem a little strange, but I'd like you to imagine this situation again and this time deliberately pay attention to the teacher and to the guys. Even exaggerate the smirk and frowns and stares on their faces. [Gives instructions for imagery.]

11. *Counselor:* OK, what was that like?

    Client: Well, OK. Actually, it almost made me laugh. Like I was silly to see them like that. Because they don't look *that* bad!

In response 12, the counselor starts to help Joan **identify alternative perceptions about math class by reframing the meaning.**

12. *Counselor:* OK, that's a good point. Actually, what you see as a smirk on the teacher's face may just be what the teacher thinks is an encouraging smile. Now, along these lines, what else could you pay attention to about math class that you usually overlook or don't notice? Try to think of

things that are more positive or at least neutral.

    Client: [Pauses] Well, there are times when the teacher and the guys do offer to help, and they look encouraging or sincere. Plus the fact, as you mentioned, I'm not the only girl there. There are three others, and I don't usually notice them.

The counselor **suggests another alternative feature or a new reframe** *to focus on in the next response.*

13. *Counselor:* Great. Another thing I might add is being aware of times when other people in the class also have trouble with the answers or working at the board.

    Client: That's true. I tend to only see myself like that. But sometimes even some of the guys have difficulty.

In responses 14 through 16, the counselor helps Joan **modify the original perceptions** *by setting up a practice opportunity in imagery.*

14. *Counselor:* OK, now I'm going to ask you to imagine this situation in math class again. This time, I want you to deliberately focus on these other things—the other girls, the times when the teacher offers help, the times when other guys can't get the answer. Is that clear?

    Client: You mean try to notice these things instead of their smirks?

15. Counselor: Exactly. [Gives instructions for imagery.]

16. *Counselor:* OK, what happened?

    Client: Well, it was interesting. I could do it, but I kept shifting back to the smirks at times.

In response 17, the counselor provides information about **successive practice attempts,** *in the session and as* **homework.**

17. *Counselor:* Well, it takes practice! Again remember the tape recorder. You've been playing the tape that has the teacher smirking and the guys laughing at you for a long time. Now it is time to insert a tape with new pictures and sounds on it. We'll keep working on it today, and then I'll show you a way to use it in math class during the week.

    Client: OK, I think I can see how it might prove to be helpful if I can do it.

LEARNING ACTIVITY #43: REFRAMING

This activity is designed to help you use the reframing procedure with yourself.

1. Identify a situation that typically produces uncomfortable or distressing feelings for you. Examples:

a. You are about to initiate a new relationship with someone of the other sex.

b. You are presenting a speech in front of a large audience.

(continued)

2. Try to become aware of what you rather automatically attend to or focus on during this situation. Role-play it with another person or pretend you're sitting in a movie theater and project the situation onto the screen in front of you. As you do so, ask yourself:

"What am I aware of now?"

"What am I focusing on now?"

Be sure to notice fleeting sounds, feelings, images, and sensations.

3. Establish a link between these encoded features of the situation and your resulting feelings. As you reenact the situation, ask yourself: "What am I feeling at this moment?" "What am I experiencing now?"

4. After you have become aware of the most salient features of this situation, reenact it either in role play or in imagination. This time, deliberately attend to these selected features during the reenactment. Repeat this process until you feel that you have awareness and control of the perceptual process you engage in during this situation.

5. Next, select other features of the session (previously ignored) that you focus could on or attend to during this situation which would allow you to view and handle the situation differently. Consider images, sounds, and feelings as well as people and objects. Ask yourself questions like: "What other aspects of this same situation aren't readily apparent to me that would provide me with a different way to view the situation?" You may wish to query another person for ideas. After you have identified alternative features, again reenact the situation in role play or imagination— several times if necessary—in order to break old encoding patterns.

6. Construct a homework assignment for yourself that encourages you to apply this process as needed for use during actual situations.

□ STRESS INOCULATION

Stress inoculation is an approach to teaching both physical and cognitive coping skills. The procedure was developed by Meichenbaum and Cameron (1973a), who use it to help clients with severe phobic reactions to manage anxiety in stressful situations. Meichenbaum and Turk (1976) describe stress inoculation as a type of psychological protection that functions in the same way as a medical inoculation that provides protection from disease. According to these authors, stress inoculation gives the person "a prospective defense or set of skills to deal with future stressful situations. As in medical inoculations, a person's resistance is enhanced by exposure to a stimulus strong enough to arouse defenses without being so powerful that it overcomes them" (p. 3). Although the procedure has been used as remediation, as the name implies, it can also be used for prevention.

Stress inoculation has three major components: educating the client about the nature of stressful reactions, having the client rehearse various physical and cognitive coping skills, and helping the client apply these skills during exposure to stressful situations. Of these three components, the second, which provides training in coping skills, seems to be the most important (Horan, Hackett, Buchanan, Stone, & Demchik-Stone, 1977). Stress inoculation has been used to help manage anxiety reactions (Altmaier, Ross, Leary, & Thornbrough, 1982; Meichenbaum & Cameron, 1973a), to help people with chronic headaches, bronchial asthma, and essential hypertension (Holroyd, Appel, & Andrasik, 1983), to help patients undergoing cardiac catheterization (Kendall, 1983), to help people learn how to tolerate and cope with physiological pain (Hackett & Horan, 1980; Klepac, Hauge, Dowling, & McDonald, 1981; Turk & Genest, 1979; Wernick, 1983), to help people deal with dental anxiety (Nelson, 1981), to help juvenile delinquents control anger (Feindler & Fremouw, 1983; Schlichter & Horan, 1981), to help nurses on an acute care unit deal with occupational stress (West, Horan, & Games, 1984), with Type A people (Roskies, 1983), with dating anxiety (Jaremko, 1983), and with rape victims (Veronen & Kilpatrick, 1983). Meichenbaum and Cameron (1973a) found that stress inoculation was superior to systematic desensitization and two other anxiety-relief treatments in reducing avoidance behavior and in promoting treatment generalization of multiphobic clients. Novaco (1975) found that, for anger control, the entire stress inoculation procedure was more effective than the use of only coping thoughts or physical relaxation. One of the advantages of stress inoculation, compared with either cognitive restructuring or relaxation (Chapter 17), is that both relaxation and cognitive coping skills are learned and applied as part of the stress inoculation procedure.

We wish to acknowledge the work of Meichenbaum and Cameron (1973a), Novaco (1975), and Meichenbaum and Turk (1976) in our presentation of stress inoculation. The process of modification of perceptions described under "Reframing" can also be used in conjunction with stress inoculation (Leventhal & Nerenz, 1983). We describe the procedure in seven major components:

1. Rationale.
2. Information giving.
3. Acquisition and practice of direct-action coping skills.
4. Acquisition and practice of cognitive coping skills.
5. Application of all coping skills to problem-related situations.
6. Application of all coping skills to potential problem situations.
7. Homework and follow-up.

A detailed description of each step associated with these seven parts can be found in the Interview Checklist for Stress Inoculation at the end of this chapter.

Treatment Rationale

Here is an example of a rationale that a counselor might use for stress inoculation.

Purpose. The counselor might explain as follows the purpose of stress inoculation for a client having trouble with anger control:

"You find yourself confronted with situations in which your temper gets out of hand. You have trouble managing your anger, especially when you feel provoked. This procedure can help you learn to cope with provoking situations and can help you manage the intensity of your anger when you're in these situations so it doesn't control you."

Overview. Then the counselor can give the client a brief overview of the procedure:

"First, we will try to help you understand the nature of your feelings and how certain situations may provoke your feelings. Next you will learn some ways to manage your anger and to cope with situations in which you feel angry. After you learn these coping skills, we will set up situations where you can practice using these skills to help you control your anger. How does this sound to you?"

Information Giving

In this procedure, before learning and applying various coping strategies, it is important that the client be given some information about the nature of a stress reaction and the possible coping strategies that might be used. Most clients view a stress reaction as something that is automatic and difficult to overcome. It is helpful for the client to understand the nature of a stress reaction and how various coping strategies can help manage the stress. It appears that this education phase of stress inoculation is "necessary but insufficient for improvement" (Horan et al., 1977, p. 219). As these authors indicate, "The other components of stress inoculation are built on the education framework and cannot be logically examined or clinically administered in isolation" (p. 219).

Three things should be explained to the client: a framework for the client's emotional reaction, information about the phases of reacting to stress, and examples of types of coping skills and strategies.

Framework for client's reaction. First, the counselor should explain the nature of the client's reaction to a stressful situation. Although understanding one's reaction may not be sufficient for changing it, the conceptual framework lays some groundwork for beginning the change process. Usually an explanation of some kind of stress (anxiety, anger, pain) involves describing the stress as having two components: physiological arousal and covert self-statements or thoughts that provoke anxiety, anger, or pain. This explanation may help the client realize that coping strategies must be directed toward the arousal behaviors *and* the cognitive processes. For example, to describe this framework to a client who has trouble controlling anger, the counselor could say something like

"Perhaps you could think about what happens when you get very angry. You might notice that certain things happen to you physically—perhaps your body feels tight, your face may feel warm, you may experience more rapid breathing, or your heart may pound. This is the physical part of your anger. However, there is another thing that probably goes on while you're very angry—that is, what you're thinking. You might be thinking such things as 'He had no right to attack me; I'll get back at him; Boy, I'll show him who's boss; I'll teach her to keep her mouth shut,' and so on. These kinds of thoughts only intensify your anger. So the way you interpret and think about an anger-provoking situation also contributes to arousing hostile feelings."

Phases of stress reactions. After explaining a framework for emotional arousal, it is helpful to describe the kinds of times or phases when the client's arousal level may be heightened. Meichenbaum and Turk (1976, p. 4) point out that anxious or phobic clients tend to view their anxiety as one "massive panic reaction." Similarly, clients who are angry, depressed, or in pain may interpret their feelings as one large, continuous reaction that has a certain beginning and end. Clients who interpret their reactions this way may perceive the reaction as too difficult to change because it is so massive and overwhelming.

One way to help the client see the potential for coping with feelings is to describe the feelings by individual stages or phases of reacting to a situation. Meichenbaum and Cameron (1973a), Novaco (1975), and Turk (1975) all used four similar stages to help the client conceptualize the various critical points of a reaction: (1) preparing for a stressful, painful, or provoking situation, (2) confronting and handling the situation or the provocation, (3) coping with critical moments or with feelings of being overwhelmed or agitated during the situation, and (4) rewarding oneself after the stress for using coping skills in the first three phases. Explanation of these stages in the preliminary part of stress inoculation helps the client understand the sequence of coping strategies to be learned. To explain the client's reaction as a series of phases, the counselor might say

"When you think of being angry, you probably just think of being angry for a continuous period of time. However, you might find that your anger is probably not just one big reaction but comes and goes at different points during a provoking situation. The first critical point is when you anticipate the situation and start to get angry. At this point you can learn to prepare yourself for handling the situation in a manageable way. The next point may come when you're in the middle of the situation and you're very angry. Here you can learn how to confront a provoking situation in a constructive way. There might also be times when your anger really gets intense and you can feel it starting to control you—and perhaps feel yourself losing control. At this time, you can learn how to cope with intense feelings of agitation. Then, after the situation is over, instead of getting angry with yourself for the way you handled it, you can learn to encourage yourself for trying to cope with it. In this procedure, we'll practice using the coping skills at these especially stressful or arousing times."

Information about coping skills and strategies. Finally, the counselor should provide some information about the kinds of coping skills and strategies that can be used at these critical points. The counselor should emphasize that there are a *variety* of useful coping skills; clients' input in selecting and tailoring these for themselves is *most* important. Some research has indicated that coping strategies are more effective when clients choose those that reflect their own preferences (Chaves & Barber, 1974). In using stress inoculation, both "direct action" and "cognitive" coping skills are taught (Meichenbaum & Turk, 1976). *Direct-action* coping strategies are designed to help the client use coping behaviors to handle the stress; *cognitive* coping skills are used to give the client coping thoughts (self-statements) to handle the stress. The client should understand that *both* kinds of coping skills are important and that the two serve different functions. To provide the client with information about the usefulness of these coping skills, the counselor might explain

"In the next phase of this procedure, you'll be learning a lot of different ways to prepare for and handle a provoking situation. Some of these coping skills will help you learn to cope with provoking situations by your actions and behaviors; others will help you handle these situations by the way you interpret and think about the situation. Not all the strategies you learn may be useful or necessary for you, so your input in selecting the ones you prefer to use is important."

Acquisition and Practice of Direct-Action Coping Skills

In this phase of stress inoculation, the client acquires and practices some direct-action coping skills. Horan et al. (1977) found that coping skills training was highly effective in helping people deal with the type of pain they were trained to cope with. The counselor first discusses and models possible action strategies; the client selects some to use and practices them with the counselor's encouragement and assistance. As you may recall, direct-action coping skills are designed to help the client acquire and apply coping behaviors in stressful situations. The most commonly used direct-action coping strategies are—

1. Collecting objective or factual information about the stressful situation.
2. Identifying short-circuit or escape routes or ways to decrease the stress.

3. Palliative coping strategies.
4. Mental relaxation methods.
5. Physical relaxation methods.

Information collection. Collecting objective or factual information about a stressful situation may help the client evaluate the situation more realistically. Moreover, information about a situation may reduce the ambiguity for the client and indirectly reduce the level of threat. For example, for a client who may be confronted with physical pain, information about the source and expected timing of pain can reduce stress. This coping method is widely used in childbirth classes. The women and their "labor coaches" are taught and shown that the experienced pain is actually a uterine contraction. They are given information about the timing and stages of labor and the timing and intensity of contractions so that when labor occurs, their anxiety will not be increased by misunderstanding or lack of information about what is happening in their bodies.

Collecting information about an anxiety- or anger-engendering situation serves the same purpose. For example, in using stress inoculation to help clients control anger, collecting information about the people who typically provoke them may help. Clients can collect information that can help them view provocation as a *task* or a problem to be solved, rather than as a *threat* or a personal attack (Novaco, 1975).

Identification of escape routes. Identifying escape routes is a way to help the client cope with stress before it gets out of hand. The idea of an escape route is to short-circuit the explosive or stressful situation or to deescalate the stress before the client behaves in a way that may "blow it." This coping strategy may help abusive clients learn to identify cues that elicit their physical or verbal abuse and to take some preventive action before "striking out." This is similar to the stimulus-control self-management strategy discussed in Chapter 19. These escape or prevention routes can be very simple things that the client can *do* to prevent losing control or losing face in the situation. An abusive client could perhaps avoid striking out by counting to 60, leaving the room, or talking about something humorous.

Palliative coping strategies. Meichenbaum and Cameron (1983, pp. 135–138) describe three pal-liative coping strategies that may be particularly useful for aversive or stressful situations that cannot be substantially altered or avoided, such as chronic or life-threatening illnesses:

1. Perspective taking — thinking about or examining positive, alternative, or useful features in the stressful situation. (This is similar to the perceptual restructuring strategy.)
2. Creation of a social support network.
3. Appropriate expression of affect, such as "ventilation of feelings" or "getting things off one's chest."

Mental relaxation. Mental relaxation can also help clients cope with stress. This technique may involve attention-diversion tactics: angry clients can control their anger by concentrating on a problem to solve, counting floor tiles in the room, thinking about a funny or erotic joke, or thinking about something positive about themselves. Attention-diversion tactics are commonly used to help people control pain. Instead of focusing on the pain, the person may concentrate very hard on an object in the room or on the repetition of a word (a mantra) or a number. Again, in the Lamaze method of childbirth, the women are taught to concentrate on a "focal point" such as an object in the room or, as the authors used, a picture of a sailboat. In this way, the woman's attention is directed to an object instead of to the tightening sensations in her lower abdomen.

Some people find that mental relaxation is more successful when they use imagery or fantasy. People who enjoy daydreaming or who report a vivid imagination may find imagery a particularly useful way to promote mental relaxation. Generally, imagery as a coping method helps the client go on a fantasy trip instead of focusing on the stress, the provocation, or the pain. For example, instead of thinking about how anxious or angry he feels, the client might learn to fantasize about lying on a warm beach, being on a sailboat, making love, or eating a favorite food (see "Emotive Imagery" in Chapter 14). For pain control, the person can imagine different things about the pain. A woman in labor can picture the uterus contracting like a wave instead of thinking about pain. Or a person who experiences pain from a routine source, such as extraction of a wisdom tooth, can use imagery to change the circumstances producing the pain. Instead of thinking about how terrible and painful it is to have a tooth pulled, the person can imagine that the pain is only the aftermath of intense training for a marathon race or is from being the underdog who was hit in the jaw during a fight with the world champion (Knox, 1972).

Physical relaxation. Physical relaxation methods are particularly useful for clients who report physiological components of anxiety and anger, such as sweaty palms, rapid breathing or heartbeat, or nausea. Physical relaxation is also a very helpful coping strategy for pain control, because body tension will heighten the sensation of pain. Physical relaxation may consist of muscle relaxation or breathing techniques. Chapter 17 describes these procedures in more detail.

Each direct-action strategy should first be explained to the client with discussion of its purpose and procedure. Several sessions may be required to discuss and model all the possible direct-action coping methods. After the strategies have been described and modeled, the clients should select the particular methods to be used. The number of direct-action strategies used by a client will depend on the intensity of the reaction, the nature of the stress, and the client's preferences. With the counselor's assistance, the client should practice using each skill in order to be able to apply it in simulated and *in vivo* situations.

Acquisition and Practice of Cognitive Coping Skills

This part of stress inoculation is very similar to the cognitive restructuring strategy described earlier in this chapter. The counselor models some examples of coping thoughts the client can use during stressful phases of problem situations, and then the client selects and practices substituting coping thoughts for negative or self-defeating thoughts.

Description of four phases of cognitive coping. As you remember from our discussion of information giving, the counselor helps the client understand the nature of an emotional reaction by conceptualizing the reaction by phases. In helping the client acquire cognitive coping skills, the counselor may first wish to review the importance of learning to cope at crucial times. The counselor can point out that the client can learn a set of cognitive coping skills for each important phase: preparing for the situation, confronting and handling the situation, coping with critical moments in the situation, and

stroking oneself after the situation. Note that the first phase concerns coping skills *before* the situation; the second and third phases, coping *during* the situation; and the fourth phase, coping *after* the situation. The counselor can describe these four phases to the client with an explanation similar to this:

> "Earlier we talked about how your anger is not just one giant reaction but something that peaks at certain stressful points when you feel provoked or attacked. Now you will learn a method of cognitive control that will help you control any negative thoughts that may make you more angry and also help you use coping thoughts at stressful points. There are four times that are important in your learning to use coping thoughts, and we'll work on each of these four phases. First is how you interpret the situation initially, and how you think about responding or preparing to respond. Second is actually dealing with the situation. Third is coping with anything that happens during the situation that *really* provokes you. After the situation, you learn to encourage yourself for keeping your anger in control."

Modeling coping thoughts. After explaining the four phases of using cognitive coping skills to the client, the counselor would model examples of coping statements that are especially useful for each of the four phases.

Meichenbaum and Turk (1976) have provided an excellent summary of the coping statements used by Meichenbaum and Cameron (1973a) for anxiety control, by Novaco (1975) for anger control, and by Turk (1975) for pain control. These statements, presented in Table 16-1, are summarized for each of the four coping phases: preparing for the situation, confronting the situation, coping with critical moments, and reinforcing oneself for coping. The counselor would present examples of coping statements for each of the four phases of a stress reaction.

Client selection of coping thoughts. After the counselor models some possible coping thoughts for each phase, the client should add some or select those that fit. The counselor should encourage the client to "try on" and adapt the thoughts in whatever way feels most natural. The client might look for coping statements he or she has used in other stress-related situations. At this point in the procedure, the counselor should be helping to tailor a coping program *specifically* for this client. If the

TABLE 16-1. Examples of coping thoughts used in stress inoculation

Anxiety	Anger	Pain
I. *Preparing for a stressor* (Meichenbaum & Cameron, 1973a) What is it you have to do? You can develop a plan to deal with it. Just think about what you can do about it. That's better than getting anxious. No negative self-statements; just think rationally. Don't worry; worry won't help anything. Maybe what you think is anxiety is eagerness to confront it.	*Preparing for a provocation* (Novaco, 1975) What is it that you have to do? You can work out a plan to handle it. You can manage this situation. You know how to regulate your anger. If you find yourself getting upset, you'll know what to do. There won't be any need for an argument. Time for a few deep breaths of relaxation. Feel comfortable, relaxed and at ease. This could be a testy situation, but you believe in yourself.	*Preparing for the painful stressor* (Turk, 1975) What is it you have to do? You can develop a plan to deal with it. Just think about what you have to do. Just think about what you can do about it. Don't worry; worrying won't help anything. You have lots of different strategies you can call upon.
II. *Confronting and handling a stressor* (Meichenbaum & Cameron, 1973a) Just "psych" yourself up — you can meet this challenge. One step at a time; you can handle the situation. Don't think about fear; just think about what you have to do. Stay relevant. This anxiety is what the doctor said you would feel. It's a reminder to use your coping exercises. This tenseness can be an ally, a cue to cope. Relax; you're in control. Take a slow deep breath. Ah, good.	*Confronting the provocation* (Novaco, 1975) Stay calm. Just continue to relax. As long as you keep your cool, you're in control here. Don't take it personally. Don't get all bent out of shape; just think of what to do here. You don't need to prove yourself. There is no point in getting mad. You're not going to let him get to you. Don't assume the worst or jump to conclusions. Look for the positives. It's really a shame that this person is acting the way she is. For a person to be that irritable, he must be awfully unhappy. If you start to get mad, you'll just be banging your head against the wall. So you might as well just relax. There's no need to doubt yourself. What he says doesn't matter.	*Confronting and handling the pain* (Turk, 1975) You can meet the challenge. One step at a time; you can handle the situation. Just relax, breathe deeply and use one of the strategies. Don't think about the pain, just what you have to do. This tenseness can be an ally, a cue to cope. Relax. You're in control; take a slow deep breath. Ah. Good. This anxiety is what the trainer said you might feel. That's right; it's the reminder to use your coping skills.

(continued)

client's self-statements are too general, they may lead only to "rote repetition" and not function as effective self-instructions (Meichenbaum, 1977, p. 160). The counselor might explain this to the client in this way:

"You know, your input in finding coping thoughts that work for you is very important. I've given you some examples. Some of these you might feel comfortable with, and there may be others you can think of too. What we want to do now is to come up with some specific coping thoughts you can and will use during these four times that fit for *you,* not me or someone else."

TABLE 16-1. Examples of coping thoughts used in stress inoculation (continued)

Anxiety	Anger	Pain
III. *Coping with the feeling of being overwhelmed* (Meichenbaum & Cameron, 1973a) When fear comes, just pause. Keep the focus on the present; what is it you have to do? Label your fear from 0 to 10 and watch it change. You should expect your fear to rise. Don't try to eliminate fear totally; just keep it manageable. You can convince yourself to do it. You can reason your fear away. It will be over shortly. It's not the worst thing that can happen. Just think about something else. Do something that will prevent you from thinking about fear. Describe what is around you. That way you won't think about worrying.	*Coping with arousal and agitation* (Novaco, 1975) Your muscles are starting to feel tight. Time to relax and slow things down. Getting upset won't help. It's just not worth it to get so angry. You'll let him make a fool of himself. It's reasonable to get annoyed, but let's keep the lid on. Time to take a deep breath. Your anger is a signal of what you need to do. Time to talk to yourself. You're not going to get pushed around, but you're not going haywire either. Try a cooperative approach. Maybe you are both right. He'd probably like you to get really angry. Well, you're going to disappoint him. You can't expect people to act the way you want them to.	*Coping with feelings at critical moments* (Turk, 1975) When pain comes just pause; keep focusing on what you have to do. What is it you have to do? Don't try to eliminate the pain totally; just keep it manageable. You were supposed to expect the pain to rise; just keep it under control. Just remember, there are different strategies; they'll help you stay in control. When the pain mounts you can switch to a different strategy; you're in control.
IV. *Reinforcing self-statements* (Meichenbaum & Cameron, 1973a) It worked; you did it. Wait until you tell your therapist about this. It wasn't as bad as you expected. You made more out of the fear than it was worth. Your damn ideas—that's the problem. When you control them, you control your fear. It's getting better each time you use the procedures. You can be pleased with the progress you're making. You did it!	*Self-reward* (Novaco, 1975) It worked! That wasn't as hard as you thought. You could have gotten more upset than it was worth. Your ego can sure get you in trouble, but when you watch that ego stuff you're better off. You're doing better at this all the time. You actually got through that without getting angry. Guess you've been getting upset for too long when it wasn't even necessary.	*Reinforcing self-statements* (Turk, 1975) Good, you did it. You handled it pretty well. You knew you could do it! Wait until you tell the trainer about which procedures worked best.

From "The Cognitive-Behavioral Management of Anxiety, Anger, and Pain," by D. Meichenbaum and D. Turk. In P. O. Davidson (Ed.), *The behavioral management of anxiety, depression and pain*. Copyright 1976 by Brunner/Mazel, Inc. Reprinted by permission.

Client practice of coping thoughts. After the client selects coping thoughts to use for each phase, the counselor will instruct the client to practice these self-statements by saying them aloud. This verbal practice is designed to help the client become familiar with the coping thoughts and accustomed to the words. After this practice, the client should also practice the selected coping thoughts in the sequence of the four phases. This practice helps the client learn the timing of the coping thoughts in the application phase of stress inoculation.

The counselor can say something like

"First I'd like you to practice using these coping thoughts just by saying them aloud to me. This will help you get used to the words and ideas of coping. Next, let's practice these coping thoughts in the sequence in which you would use them when applying them to a real situation. Here, I'll show you. OK, first I'm anticipating the situation, so I'm going to use coping statements that help me prepare for the situation, like 'I know this type of situation usually upsets me, but I have a plan now to handle it' or 'I'm going to be able to control my anger even if this situation is rough.' Next, I'll pretend I'm actually into the situation. I'm going to cope so I can handle it. I might say something to myself like 'Just stay calm. Remember who I'm dealing with. This is her style. Don't take it personally' or 'Don't overreact. Just relax.'

OK, now the person's harassment is continuing. I am going to cope with feeling more angry. I might think 'I can feel myself getting more upset. Just keep relaxed. Concentrate on this' or 'This is a challenging situation. How can *I* handle myself in a way I don't have to apologize for?' OK, now afterwards I realize I haven't got abusive or revengeful. So I'll think something to encourage myself, like 'I did it' or 'Gee, I really kept my cool.'

Now you try it. Just verbalize your coping thoughts in the sequence of preparing for the situation, handling it, coping with getting really agitated, and then encouraging yourself."

Application of All Coping Skills to Problem-Related Situations

The next part of stress inoculation involves having the client apply both the direct-action and the cognitive coping skills in the face of stressful, provoking, or painful situations. Before the client is instructed to apply the coping skills *in vivo,* she or he practices applying coping skills under simulated conditions with the counselor's assistance. The application phase of stress inoculation apears to be important for the overall efficacy of the procedure. As Meichenbaum and Cameron (1973a) point out, simply having a client rehearse coping skills *without* opportunities to apply them in stressful situations seems to result in an improved but limited ability to cope.

The application phase involves modeling and rehearsal to provide the client with exposure to simulations of problem-related situations. For example, the client who wanted to control anger would have opportunities to practice coping in a variety of anger-provoking situations. During this application practice, it is important that the client be faced with a stressful situation and also that the client practice the skills in a coping manner. In other words, the application should be arranged and conducted as realistically as possible. The angry client can be encouraged to practice feeling very agitated and to rehearse even starting to lose control—but then applying the coping skills to gain control (Novaco, 1975). This type of application practice is viewed as the client's providing a self-model of how to behave in a stressful situation. By imagining faltering or losing control, experiencing anxiety, and then coping with this, the person practices the thoughts and feelings as they are likely to occur in a real-life situation (Meichenbaum, 1977, p. 178). In the application phase of stress inoculation, the client's anxiety, anger, or distressful emotions is used as a cue or reminder to cope.

Modeling of application of coping skills. The counselor should first model how the client can apply the newly acquired skills in a coping manner when faced with a stressful situation. Here is an example of a counselor demonstration of this process with a client who is working toward anger control (in this case, with his family):

"I'm going to imagine that the police have just called and told me that my 16-year-old son was just picked up again for breaking and entering. I can feel myself start to get really hot. Whoops, wait a minute. That's a signal [arousal cue for coping]. I'd better start thinking about using my relaxation methods to stay calm and using my coping thoughts to prepare myself for handling this situation constructively.

OK, first of all, sit down and relax. Let those muscles loosen up. Count to ten. Breathe deeply [direct-action coping methods]. OK, now I'll be seeing my son shortly. What is it I have to do? I know it won't help to lash out or to hit him. That won't solve anything. So I'll work out another plan. Let him do most of the talking. Give him the chance to make amends or find a solution [cognitive coping: preparing for the situation]. OK, now I can see him walking in the door. I feel sort of choked up. I can feel my fists getting tight. He's starting to explain. I want to interrupt and let him have it. But wait [arousal cue for coping]. Concentrate on counting and on breathing slowly [direct-action coping]. Now just tell myself—keep cool.

Let him talk. It won't help now to blow up [cognitive coping: confronting situation]. Now I can imagine myself thinking back to the last time he got arrested. Why in the hell doesn't he learn? No son of mine is going to be a troublemaker [arousal]. Whew! I'm pretty damn angry. I've got to stay in control, especially now [cue for coping]. Just relax, muscles! Stay loose [direct-action coping]. I can't expect him to live up to my expectations. I can tell him I'm disappointed, but I'm not going to blow up and shout and hit [cognitive coping: feelings of greater agitation]. OK, I'm doing a good job of keeping my lid on [cognitive coping: self-reinforcement]."

Client application of coping skills in imaginary and role-play practice. After the counselor modeling, the client should practice a similar sequence of both direct-action and cognitive coping skills. The practice can occur in two ways: imagination and role play. We find it is often useful to have the client first practice the coping skills while imagining problem-related situations. This practice can be repeated until the client feels very comfortable in applying the coping strategies to imagined situations. Then the client can practice the coping skills with the counselor's aid in a role play of a problem situation. The role-play practice should be similar to the *in vivo* situations the client encounters. For instance, our angry client could identify particular situations and people with whom he or she is most likely to blow up or lose control. The client can imagine each situation (starting with the most manageable one) and imagine using the coping skills. Then, with the counselor taking the part of someone else such as a provoker, the client can practice the coping skills in role play.

Application of All Coping Skills to Potential Problem Situations

Any therapeutic procedure should be designed not only to help clients deal with current problems but also to help them anticipate constructive handling of potential problems. In other words, an adequate therapeutic strategy should prevent future problems as well as resolve current ones. The prevention aspect of stress inoculation is achieved by having clients apply the newly learned coping strategies to situations that are not problematic now but could be in the future. If this phase of stress inoculation is ignored, the effects of the inoculation may be very short-lived. In other words, if clients do not have an opportunity to apply the

coping skills to situations other than the current problem-related ones, their coping skills may not generalize beyond the present problem situations.

Application of coping skills to other potentially stressful situations is accomplished in the same way as application to the present problem areas. First, after explaining the usefulness of coping skills in other areas of the client's life, the counselor demonstrates the application of coping strategies to a potential, hypothetical stressor. The counselor might select a situation the client has not yet encountered, one that would require active coping of anyone who might encounter it, such as not receiving a desired job promotion or raise, facing a family crisis, moving to a new place, anticipating retirement, or being very ill. After the counselor has modeled application of coping skills to these sorts of situations, the client would practice applying the skills in these situations or in similar ones that she or he identifies. The practice can occur in imagination or in role-play enactments. Turk (1975) used a novel method of role play to give clients opportunities to apply coping skills. The counselor or trainee role-played a novice, while the client took the part of a trainer or helper. The client's task in the role play was to train the novice in how to cope with stress — in this case, the stress of experiencing pain. Although Turk did not specifically assess the effects of this particular type of application practice, Fremouw and Harmatz (1975) found that speech-anxious students who acted as helpers and taught anxiety-reduction procedures to other speech-anxious students showed more improvement than other speech-anxious students who learned how to help but were not given an opportunity to do so (latent helpers). Putting the client in the role of a helper or a trainer may provide another kind of application opportunity that may also have benefits for the client's acquisition of coping strategies.

Homework and Follow-up

When the client has learned and used stress inoculation within the interviews, she or he is ready to use coping skills *in vivo.* The counselor and client should discuss the potential application of coping strategies to actual situations. The counselor might caution the client not to expect to cope beautifully with every problematic situation initially. The client should be encouraged to use a daily log to record the particular situations and the number of times the coping strategies are used.

The log data can be used in a later follow-up as one way to determine the client's progress.

In our opinion, stress inoculation training is one of the most comprehensive therapeutic treatments presently in use. Teaching clients both direct-action and cognitive coping skills that can be used in current and potential problematic situations provides skills that are under the clients' own control and are applicable to future as well as current situations. Stress inoculation deserves much more empirical investigation than it has yet received, but the results of the limited previous investigations point to its clinical potential.

☐ MODEL DIALOGUE: STRESS INOCULATION

Session 1

In this session, the counselor will teach Joan some direct-action coping skills for mental and physical relaxation to help her cope with her physical sensations of nervousness about her math class. Imagery manipulations and slow, deep breathing will be used.

1. *Counselor:* Hi, Joan. How was your week?
   Client: Pretty good. You know, this, well, whatever you call it, it's starting to help. I took a test this week and got an 85—I usually get a 70 or 75.

The counselor introduces the **idea of other coping skills to deal with Joan's nervousness.**
2. *Counselor:* That really is encouraging. And that's where the effects of this count—on how you do in class. Since what we did last week went well for you, I believe today we might work with some other coping skills that might help you decrease your nervous feelings.
   Client: What would this be?

In responses 3 and 4, the counselor explains and **models possible direct-action coping skills.**
3. *Counselor:* Well, one thing we might do is to help you learn how to imagine something that gives you very calm feelings, and while you're doing this to take some slow, deep breaths—like this [counselor models closing eyes, breathing slowly and deeply]. When I was doing that, I thought about curling up in a chair with my favorite book—but there are many different things you could think of. For instance, to use this in your math class, you might imagine that you are doing work for which you will receive some prize or award. Or you might imagine that you are learning problems so you'll be in a

position to be a helper for someone else. Do you get the idea?
   Client: I think so. I guess it's like trying to imagine or think about math in a pretend kind of way.
4. *Counselor:* Yes—and in a way that reduces rather than increases the stress of it for you.
   Client: I think I get the idea. It's sort of like when I imagine that I'm doing housework for some famous person instead of just at my house—it makes it more tolerable.

In response 5, the counselor asks Joan to **find some helpful imagery manipulations to promote calm feelings.**
5. *Counselor:* That's a good example. You imagine that situation to prevent yourself from getting too bored. Here, you find a scene or scenes to think about to prevent yourself from getting too nervous. Can you take a few minutes to think about one or two things you could imagine—perhaps about math—that would help you to feel calm instead of nervous?
   Client: (Pauses) Well, maybe I could pretend that the math class is part of some training I need in order to do something exciting, like being one of the females in the space program.

In responses 6 and 7, the counselor instructs Joan to **practice these direct-action coping skills.**
6. *Counselor:* OK, good. We can work with that, and if it doesn't help, we can come up with something else. Why don't you try first to practice imagining this while you also breathe slowly and deeply, as I did a few minutes ago? [Joan practices.]
7. *Counselor:* OK. How did that feel?
   Client: OK—it was sort of fun.

In response 8, the counselor gives **homework**—*asks Joan to engage in* **self-directed practice** *of these coping skills before the next session.*
8. *Counselor:* Good. Now this week I'd like you to practice this in a quiet place two or three times each day. Keep track of your practice sessions in your log and also rate your tension level before and after you practice. Next week we will go over this log and then work on a way you can apply what we did today—and the thought stopping and coping thoughts we learned in our two previous sessions. So I'll see you next week.

Session 2

In this session, the counselor helps Joan integrate the strategies of some previous sessions (thought stopping, coping thoughts, and imagery and breathing coping skills). Specifically, Joan learns to apply all these coping skills in imagery and role-play practices of some stressful situations related to math class. Application of coping skills to problem-related situations is a part of stress inoculation and helps the client to generalize the newly acquired coping skills to *in vivo* situations as they occur.

In responses 1 and 2, the counselor will **review Joan's use of the direct-action skills homework.**

1. *Counselor:* How are things going, Joan?
   Client: OK. I've had a hard week—one test and two pop quizzes in math. But I got 80s. I also did my imagination and breathing practice. You know, that takes a while to learn.
2. *Counselor:* That's natural. It does take a lot of practice before you really get the feel of it. So it would be a good idea if you continued the daily practice again this week. How did it feel when you practiced?
   Client: OK—I think I felt less nervous than before.

The counselor introduces the idea of **applying all the coping skills in practice situations** *and* **presents a rationale for this application phase.**

3. *Counselor:* That's good. As time goes on, you will notice more effects from it. Up to this point, we've worked on some things to help you in your math class—stopping self-defeating thoughts and using imagination and slow breathing to help you cope and control your nervousness. What I think might help now is to give you a chance to use all these skills in practices of some of the stressful situations related to your math class. This will help you use the skills when you need to during the class or related situations. Then we will soon be at a point where we can go through some of these same procedures for the other situations in which you want to express yourself differently and more frequently, such as with your folks. Does this sound OK?
   Client: Yes.

Next, the counselor **demonstrates (models) how Joan can practice her skills in an imaginary practice.**

4. *Counselor:* What I'd like you to do is to imagine some of the situations related to your math class and try to use your coping thoughts *and* the imagination scene and deep breathing to control your nervousness. Let me show you how you might do this. OK, I'm imagining that it's almost time for math class. I'm going to concentrate on thinking about how this class will help me train for the space program. If I catch myself thinking I wish I didn't have to go, I'm going to use some coping thoughts. Let's see—class will go pretty fast. I've been doing better. It can be a challenge. Now, as I'm in class,

I'm going to stop thinking about not being able to do the work. I'm going to just take one problem at a time. One step at a time. Oops! Mr. _____ just called on me. Boy, I can feel myself getting nervous. Just take a deep breath. . . . Do the best I can. It's only one moment anyway. Well, it went pretty well. I can feel myself starting to cope when I need to. OK, Joan, why don't you try this several times now? [Joan practices applying coping thoughts and direct action with different practice situations in imagination.]

In response 5, the counselor **checks Joan's reaction** *to applying the skills in practice through imagination.*

5. *Counselor:* Are you able to really get into the situation as you practice this way?
   Client: Yes, although I believe I have to work harder to use this when it really happens.

Sometimes **role play makes the practice more real.** *The counselor introduces this next. Note that the counselor will add a stress element by calling on Joan at unannounced times.*

6. *Counselor:* That's right. This kind of practice doesn't always have the same amount of stress as the "real thing." Maybe it would help if we did some role-play practice. I'll be your teacher this time. Just pretend to be in class. I'll be talking, but at an unannounced time, I'm going to call on you to answer a question. Just use your coping thoughts and your slow breathing as you need to when this happens. [Role-play practice of this and related scenarios occurs.]

The counselor **assesses Joan's reaction** *to role-play practice and* **asks Joan to rate her level of nervousness** *during the practice.*

7. *Counselor:* How comfortable do you feel with these practices? Could you rate the nervousness you feel as you do this on a 1-to-5 scale, with 1 being not nervous and 5 being very nervous?
   Client: Well, about a 2.

The counselor encourages Joan to **apply coping statements in the math-related problem situations** *as they occur, assigns* **homework,** *and schedules a* **follow-up.**

8. *Counselor:* Well, I think you are ready to use this as you need to during the week. Remember, any self-defeating thought or body tenseness is a cue to cope, using your coping thoughts and imagination and breathing skills. I'd like you to keep track of the number of times you use this on your log sheets. Also rate your level of nervousness before, during, and after math class on the log sheet. How about coming back in two weeks to see how things are going?
   Client: Fine.

LEARNING ACTIVITIES #44: STRESS INOCULATION

I. Listed below are 12 examples of various direct-action coping skills. Using the coding system that precedes the examples, identify on paper the *type* of direct-action coping skill displayed in each example. Feedback follows on page 444.

Code
Information (I)
Escape route (ER)
Social support network (SSN)
Ventilation (V)
Perspective taking (PT)
Attention diversion (AD)
Imagery manipulations (IM)
Muscle relaxation (MR)
Breathing techniques (B)

Examples

1. "Learn to take slow, deep breaths when you feel especially tense."
2. "Instead of thinking just about the pain, try to concentrate very hard on one spot on the wall."
3. "Imagine that it's a very warm day and the warmth makes you feel relaxed."
4. "If it really gets to be too much, just do the first part only—leave the rest for a while."
5. "You can expect some pain, but it is really only the result of the stitches. It doesn't mean that something is wrong."
6. "Just tighten your left fist. Hold it and notice the tension. Now relax it—feel the difference."
7. "Try to imagine a strong, normal cell attacking the weak, confused cancer cells when you feel the discomfort of your treatment."
8. "When it gets very strong, distract yourself—listen hard to the music or study the picture on the wall."
9. "If you talk about it and express your feelings about the pain, you might feel better."
10. "Your initial or intuitive reaction might cause you to see only selected features of the situation. There are also some positive aspects we need to focus on."
11. "It would be helpful to have your family and neighbors involved to provide you feedback and another perspective."
12. "Social skills are important for you to learn in order to develop the support you need from other people. Others can lessen the effects of the aversive situation."

II. Listed below are eight examples of cognitive coping skills used at four phases: preparing for a situation, confronting or handling the situation, dealing with critical moments in the situation, and self-encouragement for coping. On paper, identify which phase is represented by each example. Feedback follows.

1. "By golly, I did it."
2. "What will I need to do?"
3. "Don't lose your cool even though it's tough now. Take a deep breath."
4. "Think about what you want to say—not how people are reacting to you now."
5. "Relax, it will be over shortly. Just concentrate on getting through this rough moment now."
6. "Can you feel this—the coping worked!"
7. "When you get in there, just think about the situation, not your anxiety."
8. "That's a signal to cope now. Just keep your mind on what you're doing."

☐ SUMMARY

The five cognitive change procedures of cognitive modeling, thought stopping, cognitive restructuring, reframing, and stress inoculation are being used more frequently in counseling and therapy—even to the point of achieving acceptance, notoriety, and "best seller" status (Dyer, 1976). Yet thorough investigative efforts into the components and effects of these strategies have only just begun. We wholeheartedly agree with the plea of Mahoney and Mahoney (1976, p. 105): "As clinical scientists, our research has only recently begun to examine the functional role of cognitive processes in maladjustment and therapeutic behavior change. Our understanding of the 'inside story' needs rigorous cultivation."

POSTEVALUATION

PART ONE

Objective One asks you to identify and describe the six major components of cognitive restructuring in a client case. Using the case described here, explain briefly how you would use the steps and compo-

(continued)

nents of cognitive restructuring with *this* client. You can use the six questions following the client case to describe your use of this procedure. Feedback follows on pages 445–447.

Description of client: The client is a junior in college, majoring in education and getting very good grades. She reports that she has an active social life and has some good close friendships with both males and females. Despite obvious "plusses," the client reports constant feelings of being worthless and inadequate. Her standards for herself seem to be unrealistically high: although she has almost a straight-A average, she still chides herself that she does not have all As. Although she is attractive and has an active social life, she thinks that she should be more attractive and more talented.

1. How would you explain the rationale for cognitive restructuring to this client?
2. Give an example you might use with this client to point out the difference between a self-defeating and a self-enhancing thought. Try to base your example on the client's description.
3. How would you have the client identify her thoughts about herself — her grades, appearance, social life, and so on?
4. What are some coping thoughts this client might use?
5. Explain how, in the session, you would help the client practice shifting from self-defeating to coping thoughts.
6. What kind of homework assignment would you use to help the client increase her use of coping thoughts about herself?

PART TWO

Objective Two asks you to teach the six components of cognitive restructuring to someone else or to demonstrate these components with a role-play client. Use the Interview Checklist for Cognitive Restructuring on pages 436–439 as a teaching and evaluation guide.

PART THREE

Objective Three asks you to demonstrate at least 8 out of 11 steps of the reframing procedure with a role-play client. Assess this activity using the Interview Checklist for Reframing on pages 439–441.

PART FOUR

Objective Four asks you to describe how you would apply the five major components of stress inoculation with a client case. Using the client description below, respond to the five questions following the case description as if you were using stress inoculation with this client. Feedback follows.

Description of client: The client has been referred to you by Family Services. He is unemployed, is receiving welfare support, and has three children. He is married to his second wife; the oldest child is hers by another marriage. He has been referred because of school complaints that the oldest child, a seventh-grader, has arrived at school several times with obvious facial bruises and cuts. The child has implicated the stepfather in this matter. After a long period of talking, the client reports that he has little patience with this boy and sometimes does strike him in the face as his way of disciplining the child. He realizes that maybe, on occasion, he has gone too far. Still, he gets fed up with the boy's "irresponsibility" and "lack of initiative" for his age. At these times, he reports, his impatience and anger get the best of him.

1. Explain the purpose of stress inoculation as you would to this client.
2. Briefly give an overview of the stress inoculation procedure.
3. Describe and explain one example of each of the following kinds of direct-action coping skills that might be useful to this client.
   a. Information about the situation
   b. An escape route
   c. An attention-diversion tactic
   d. An imagery manipulation
   e. Physical relaxation
   f. A palliative coping strategy (perspective taking, social support, or ventilation)
4. Explain, as you might to this client, the four phases of an emotional reaction and of times for coping. For each of the four phases, give two examples of cognitive coping skills (thoughts) that you would give to this client. The four phases are preparing for a disagreement or argument with the boy; confronting the situation; dealing with critical, very provoking times; and encouraging himself for coping.
5. Describe how you would set up practice opportunities in the interview with this client to help him practice applying the direct-action and cognitive coping skills in simulated practices of the provoking situations.

PART FIVE

Objective Five asks you to demonstrate 17 out of 21 steps of the stress inoculation procedure with a role-play client. Assess this activity using the Interview Checklist for Stress Inoculation on pages 441–444.

(continued)

POSTEVALUATION (continued)

INTERVIEW CHECKLIST FOR COGNITIVE RESTRUCTURING

Instructions to observer: Determine whether the counselor demonstrated the lead listed in the checklist. Check which leads the counselor used.

Item	*Examples of counselor leads*
I. Rationale and Overview	
_____ 1. Counselor explains purpose and rationale of cognitive restructuring.	"You've reported that you find yourself getting anxious and depressed during and after these conversations with the people who have to evaluate your work. This procedure can help you identify some things you might be thinking in this situation that are just beliefs, not facts, and are unproductive. You can learn more realistic ways to think about this situation that will help you cope with it in a way that you want to."
_____ 2. Counselor provides brief overview of procedure.	"There are three things we'll do in using this procedure. *First,* this will help you identify the kinds of things you're thinking before, during, and after these situations that are self-defeating. *Second,* this will teach you how to stop a self-defeating thought and replace it with a coping thought. *Third,* this will help you learn how to give yourself credit for changing these self-defeating thoughts."
_____ 3. Counselor explains difference between rational, or self-enhancing, thoughts (facts) and irrational, or self-defeating, thoughts (beliefs) and provides examples of each.	"A self-defeating thought is one way to interpret the situation, but it is usually negative and unproductive, like thinking that the other person doesn't value you or what you say. In contrast, a self-enhancing thought is a more constructive and realistic way to interpret the situation—like thinking that what you are talking about has value to you."
_____ 4. Counselor explains influence of irrational and self-defeating thoughts on emotions and performance.	"When you're constantly preoccupied with yourself and worried about how the situation will turn out, this can affect your feelings and your behavior. Worrying about the situation can make you feel anxious and upset. Concentrating on the situation and not worrying about its outcome can help you feel more relaxed, which helps you handle the situation more easily."
_____ 5. Counselor confirms client's willingness to use strategy.	"Are you ready to try this now?"
II. Identifying Client Thoughts in Problem Situations	
_____ 6. Counselor asks client to describe problem situations and identify examples of rational, self-enhancing thoughts and of irrational, self-defeating thoughts client typically experiences in these situations.	"Think of the last time you were in this situation. Describe for me what you think before you have a conversation with your evaluator. . . . What are you usually thinking during the conversation? . . . What thoughts go through your mind after the conversation is over? Now, let's see which of those thoughts are actual facts about the situation or are constructive ways to interpret the situation. Which ones are your beliefs about the situation that are unproductive or self-defeating?"
_____ 7. If client is unable to complete step 6, counselor models examples of thoughts or "links" between event and client's emotional response.	"OK, think of the thoughts that you have while you're in this conversation as a link between this event and your feelings afterward of being upset and depressed. What is the middle part? For instance, it might be something like 'I'll never have a good evaluation, and I'll lose this position' or 'I always blow this conversation and never make a good impression.' Can you recall thinking anything like this?"
_____ 8. Counselor instructs client to monitor and record content of thoughts *before, during,*	"One way to help you identify this link or your thoughts is to keep track of what you're thinking in these situations as they happen. This week I'd like you to use this log each day. Try to identify and write down at least three specific (continued)"

Item	Examples of counselor leads
and *after* stressful or upsetting situations before next session.	thoughts you have in these situations each day and bring this in with you next week."
____ 9. Using client's monitoring, counselor and client identify client's self-defeating thoughts.	"Let's look at your log and go over the kinds of negative thoughts that seem to be predominant in these situations. We can explore how these thoughts affect your feelings and performance in this situation — and whether you feel there is any evidence or rational basis for these."

III. Introduction and Practice of Coping Thoughts

____10. Counselor explains purpose and potential use of "coping thoughts" and gives some examples of coping thoughts to be used: ____a. Before the situation —preparing for it ____b. During the situation ____1. Focusing on task ____2. Dealing with feeling overwhelmed	"Up to this point, we've talked about the negative or unproductive thoughts you have in these situations and how they contribute to your feeling uncomfortable, upset, and depressed. Now we're going to look at some alternative, more constructive ways to think about the situation — using coping thoughts. These thoughts can help you prepare for the situation, handle the situation, and deal with feeling upset or overwhelmed in the situation. As long as you're using some coping thoughts, you avoid giving up control and letting the old self-defeating thoughts take over. Here are some examples of coping thoughts."
____11. Counselor instructs client to think of additional coping thoughts client could use or has used before.	"Try to think of your own coping thoughts — perhaps ones you can remember using successfully in other situations, ones that seem to fit for you."
____12. Counselor instructs client to practice verbalizing selected coping statements. ____a. Counselor instructs client first to practice coping statements individually. Coping statements to use before a situation are practiced, then coping statements to use during a situation.	"At first you will feel a little awkward using coping statements. It's like learning to drive a stick shift after you've been used to driving an automatic. So one way to help you get used to this is for you to practice these statements aloud." "First just practice each coping statement separately. After you feel comfortable with saying these aloud, practice the ones you could use before this conversation. OK, now practice the ones you could use during this conversation with your evaluator."
____b. Counselor instructs client to practice sequence of coping statements as they would be used in actual situation.	"Now let's put it all together. Imagine it's an hour before your meeting. Practice the coping statements you could use then. We'll role-play the meeting. As you feel aroused or overwhelmed, stop and practice coping thoughts during the situation."
____c. Counselor instructs client to become actively involved and to internalize meaning of coping statements during practice.	"Try to really put yourself into this practice. As you say these new things to yourself, try to think of what these thoughts really mean."

(continued)

POSTEVALUATION (continued)

Item	Examples of counselor leads

IV. Shifting from Self-Defeating to Coping Thoughts

____13. Counselor models shift from recognizing a self-defeating thought and stopping it to replacing it with a coping thought.

"Let me show you what we will practice today. First, I'm in this conversation. Everything is going OK. All of a sudden I can feel myself starting to tense up. I realize I'm starting to get overwhelmed about this whole evaluation process. I'm thinking that I'm going to blow it. No, I stop that thought at once. Now, I'm just going to concentrate on calming down, taking a deep breath, and thinking only about what I have to say."

____14. Counselor helps client practice shift from self-defeating to coping thoughts. Practice consists of four steps:

"Now let's practice this. You will imagine the situation. As soon as you start to recognize the onset of a self-defeating thought, stop it. Verbalize the thought aloud, and tell yourself to stop. Then verbalize a coping thought in place of it and imagine carrying on with the situation."

____a. Having client imagine situation or carry it out in a role play (behavior rehearsal).

____b. Recognizing self-defeating thought (which could be signaled by a hand or finger).

____c. Stopping self-defeating thought (which could be supplemented with a hand clap).

____d. Replacing thought with coping thought (possibly supplemented with deep breathing).

____15. Counselor helps client practice using shift for each problem situation until anxiety or stress felt by client while practicing situation is decreased to a reasonable or negligible level and client can carry out practice and use coping thoughts in self-directed manner.

"Let's keep working with this situation until you feel pretty comfortable with it and can shift from self-defeating to coping thoughts without my help."

V. Introduction and Practice of Positive, or Reinforcing, Self-Statements

____16. Counselor explains purpose and use of positive self-statements and gives some examples of these to client.

"You have really made a lot of progress in learning to use coping statements before and during these situations. Now it's time to learn to reward or encourage yourself. After you've coped with a situation, you can pat yourself on the back for having done so by thinking a positive or rewarding thought like 'I did it' or 'I really managed that pretty well.' "

____17. Counselor instructs client to think of additional positive

"Can you think of some things like this that you think of when you feel good about something or when you feel like you've accomplished something? Try

(continued)

Item	Examples of counselor leads
self-statements and to select some to try out.	to come up with some of these thoughts that seem to fit for you."
____18. Counselor models application of positive self-statements as self-reinforcement for shift from self-defeating to coping thoughts.	"OK, here is the way you reward yourself for having coped. You recognize the self-defeating thought. Now you're in the situation using coping thoughts, and you're thinking things like 'Take a deep breath' or 'Just concentrate on this task.' Now the conversation is finished. You know you were able to use coping thoughts, and you reward yourself by thinking 'Yes, I did it' or 'I really was able to manage that.'"
____19. Counselor instructs client to practice use of positive self-statements in interview following practice of shift from self-defeating to coping thoughts. This should be practiced in sequence (coping *before* and *during* situation and reinforcing oneself *after* situation).	"OK, let's try this out. As you imagine the conversation, you're using the coping thoughts you will verbalize. . . . Now, imagine the situation is over, and verbalize several reinforcing thoughts for having coped."

VI. Homework and Follow-Up

____20. Counselor instructs client to use cognitive restructuring procedure (identifying self-defeating thought, stopping it, shifting to coping thought, reinforcing with positive self-statement) in situations outside the interview.	"OK, now you're ready to use the entire procedure whenever you have these conversations in which you're being evaluated—or any *other* situation in which you recognize your negative interpretation of the event is affecting you. In these cases, you recognize and stop any self-defeating thoughts, use the coping thoughts before the situation to prepare for it, and use the coping thoughts during the sitution to help focus on the task and deal with being overwhelmed. After the situation is over, use the positive self-thoughts to reward your efforts."
____21. Counselor instructs client to monitor and record on log sheet number of times client uses cognitive restructuring outside the interview.	"I'd like you to use this log to keep track of the number of times you use this procedure and to jot down the situation in which you're using it. Also rate your tension level on a 1-to-5 scale before and after each time you use this."
____22. Counselor arranges for follow-up.	"Do this recording for the next two weeks. Then let's get together for a follow-up session."

Observer comments: _____

_____

INTERVIEW CHECKLIST FOR REFRAMING

Instructions to observer: Determine whether the counselor demonstrated the lead listed in the checklist. Check which leads were used.

Item	Examples of counselor leads
I. Rationale for Reframing	
____ 1. Counselor explains purpose of reframing.	"Often when we think about a problem situation, our initial or intuitive reaction can lead to emotional distress. For example, we focus only on the nega-

(continued)

POSTEVALUATION (continued)

Item	Examples of counselor leads
	tive features of the situation and overlook other details. By focusing only on the selected negative features of a situation, we can become nervous or anxious about the situation."
____ 2. Counselor provides overview of reframing.	"What we'll do is to identify what features you attend to when you think of the problem situation. Once you become aware of these features, we will look for other neutral or positive aspects of the situation that you may ignore or overlook. Then we will work on incorporating these other things into your perceptions of the problem situation."
____ 3. Counselor confirms client's willingness to use the strategy.	"How does this all sound? Are you ready to try this?"

II. Identification of Client Perceptions and Feelings in Problem Situations

____ 4. Counselor has client identify features typically attended to during problem situation. (May have to use imagery with some clients.)	"When you think of the problem situation or one like it, what features do you notice or attend to? What is the first thing that pops into your head?"
____ 5. Counselor has client identify typical feelings during problem situation.	"How do you usually feel?" "What do you experience [or are you experiencing] during this situation?"

III. Deliberate Enactment of Selected Perceptual Features

____ 6. Counselor asks client to reenact situation (by role play or imagery) and to deliberately attend to selected features. (This step may need to be repeated several times.)	"Let's set up a role play [or imagery] in which we act out this situation. This time I want you to deliberately focus on these aspects of the situation we just identified. Notice how you attend to _____."

IV. Identification of Alternative Perceptions

____ 7. Counselor instructs client to identify positive or neutral features of problem situation. The new reframes are plausible and acceptable to the client and fit the client's values and experiences.	"Now, I want us to identify other features of the problem situation that are neutral or positive. These are things you have forgotten about or ignored. Think of other features." "What other aspects of this situation that aren't readily apparent to you could provide a different way to view the situation?"

V. Modification of Perceptions in Problem Situations

____ 8. Counselor instructs client to modify perceptions of problem situation by focusing on or attending to the neutral or positive features. (Use of role play or imagery can facilitate this process for some clients.) (This step may need to be repeated several times.)	"When we act out the problem situation, I want you to change what you attend to in the situation by thinking of the neutral or positive features we just identified. Just focus on these features."

(continued)

Item	Examples of counselor leads

VI. Homework and Follow-Up

_____ 9. Counselor encourages client to practice modifying perceptions during *in vivo* situations.

"Practice is very important for modifying your perceptions. Every time you think about or encounter the problem situation, focus on the neutral or positive features of the situation."

_____ 10. Counselor instructs client to monitor aspects of the strategy on homework log sheet.

"I'd like you to use this log to keep track of the number of times you practice or use this. Also record your initial and resulting feelings before and after these kinds of situations."

_____ 11. Counselor arranges for a follow-up. (During follow-up, counselor comments on client's log and points out small perceptual shifts.)

"Let's get together in two weeks. Bring your log sheet with you. Then we can see how this is working for you."

Observer comments: _____

_____

_____

INTERVIEW CHECKLIST FOR STRESS INOCULATION

Instructions to observer: Determine which of the following steps the counselor demonstrated in using stress inoculation with a client or in teaching stress inoculation to another person. Check any step the counselor demonstrated in the application of the procedure.

Item	Examples of counselor leads

I. Rationale

_____ 1. Counselor explains purpose of stress inoculation.

"Stress inoculation is a way to help you cope with feeling anxious so that you can manage your reactions when you're confronted with these situations."

_____ 2. Counselor provides brief overview of stress inoculation procedure.

"First we'll try to understand how your anxious feelings affect you now. Then you'll learn some coping skills that will help you relax physically — and help you use coping thoughts instead of self-defeating thoughts. Then you'll have a chance to test out your coping skills in stressful situations we'll set up."

_____ 3. Counselor checks to see whether client is willing to use strategy.

"How do you feel now about working with this procedure?"

II. Information Giving

_____ 4. Counselor explains nature of client's emotional reaction to a stressful situation.

"Probably you realize that when you feel anxious, you are physically tense. Also, you may be thinking in a worried way — worrying about the situation and how to handle it. Both the physical tenseness and the negative or worry thoughts create stress for you."

_____ 5. Counselor explains possible *phases* of reacting to a stressful situation.

"When you feel anxious, you probably tend to think of it as one giant reaction. Actually, you're probably anxious at certain times or phases. For example, you might feel very uptight just anticipating the situation. Then you might feel uptight during the situation, especially if it starts to overwhelm you. After the situation is over, you may feel relieved — but down on yourself, too."

_____ 6. Counselor explains specific kinds of coping skills to be learned in stress inoculation

"We'll be learning some action kinds of coping strategies — like physical or muscle relaxation, mental relaxation, and just common-sense ways to minimize the stress of the situation. Then also you'll learn some different ways to

(continued)

POSTEVALUATION (continued)

Item	Examples of counselor leads
and importance of client's input in tailoring coping strategies.	view and think about the situation. Not all of these coping strategies may seem best for you, so your input in selecting the ones you feel are best for you is important."

III. Acquisition and Practice of Direct-Action Coping Skills

Item	Examples of counselor leads
____ 7. Counselor discusses and models direct-action coping strategies (or uses a symbolic model):	"First, I'll explain and we can talk about each coping method. Then I'll demonstrate how you can apply it when you're provoked."
____a. Collecting objective or factual information about stressful situation	"Sometimes it helps to get any information you can about things that provoke and anger you. Let's find out the types of situations and people that can do this to you. Then we can see whether there are other ways to view the provocation. For example, what if you looked at it as a situation to challenge your problem-solving ability rather than as a personal attack?"
____b. Identifying short-circuit or escape routes — alternative ways to deescalate stress of situation	"Suppose you're caught in a situation. You feel it's going to get out of hand. What are some ways to get out of it or to deescalate it *before* you strike out? For example, little things like counting to 60, leaving the room, using humor, or something like that."
Mental relaxation:	
____c. Attention diversion	"OK, one way to control your anger is to distract yourself — take your attention away from the person you feel angry with. If you have to stay in the same room, concentrate very hard on an object in the room. Think of all the questions about this object you can."
____d. Imagery manipulations	"OK, another way you can prevent yourself from striking out is to use your imagination. Think of something very calming and very pleasurable, like your favorite record or like being on the beach with the hot sun."
Physical relaxation:	
____e. Muscle relaxation	"Muscle relaxation can help you cope whenever you start to feel aroused and feel your face getting flushed or your body tightening up. It can help you learn to relax your body, which can, in turn, help you control your anger."
____ f. Breathing techniques	"Breathing is also important in learning to relax physically. Sometimes, in a tight spot, taking slow, deep breaths can give you time to get yourself together before saying or doing something you don't want to."
Palliative coping strategies:	
____g. Perspective taking	"Let's try to look at this situation from a different perspective — what else about the situation might you be overlooking?"
____h. Social support network	"Let's put together some people and resources you could use as a support system."
____ i. Ventilation of feelings	"Perhaps it would be helpful just to spend some time getting your feelings out in the open." [You could use Gestalt dialoging as one ventilation tool in addition to discussion.]
____ 8. Client selects most useful coping strategies and practices each under counselor's direction.	"We've gone over a lot of possible methods to help you control your anger so it doesn't result in abusive behavior. I'm sure that you have some preferences. Why don't you pick the methods that you think will work best for you, and we'll practice with these so you can get a feel for them?"

IV. Acquisition and Practice of Cognitive Coping Skills

Item	Examples of counselor leads
____ 9. Counselor describes four phases of using cognitive	"As you may remember from our earlier discussion, we talked about learning to use coping procedures at important points during a stressful or provoking

(continued)

Item	Examples of counselor leads
coping skills to deal with a stressful situation.	situation. Now we will work on helping you learn to use coping thoughts during these four important times — preparing for the situation, handling the situation, dealing with critical moments during the situation, and encouraging yourself after the situation."
____10. For each phase, counselor models examples of coping statements.	"I'd like to give you some ideas of some possible coping thoughts you could use during each of these four important times. For instance, when I'm trying to psych myself up for a stressful situation, here are some things I think about."
____11. For each phase, client selects most natural coping statements.	"The examples I gave may not feel natural for you. What I'd like you to do is to pick or add ones that you could use comfortably, that wouldn't seem foreign to you."
____12. Counselor instructs client to practice using these coping statements for each phase.	"Sometimes, because you aren't used to concentrating on coping thoughts at these important times, it feels a little awkward at first. So I'd like you to get a feel for these just by practicing aloud the ones you selected. Let's work first on the ones for preparing for a provoking situation."
____13. Counselor models and instructs client to practice sequence of all four phases and verbalize accompanying coping statements.	"OK, next I'd like you to practice verbalizing the coping thoughts aloud in the sequence that you'll be using when you're in provoking situations. For example, [counselor models]. Now you try it."

V. Application of All Coping Skills to Problem-Related Situations

____14. Using coping strategies and skills selected by client, counselor models how to apply these in a coping manner while imagining a stressful (problem-related) situation.	"Now you can practice using all these coping strategies when confronted with a problem situation. For example, suppose I'm you and my boss comes up to me and gives me criticism based on misinformation. Here is how I might use my coping skills in that situation."
____15. Client practices coping strategies while imagining problem-related stressful situations. (This step is repeated as necessary.)	"OK, this time why don't you try it? Just imagine this situation — and imagine that each time you start to lose control, that is a signal to use some of your coping skills."
____16. Client practices coping strategies in role play of problem-related situation. (This step is repeated as necessary.)	"We could practice this in role play. I could take the part of your boss and initiate a meeting with you. Just be yourself and use your coping skills to prepare for the meeting. Then, during our meeting, practice your skills whenever you get tense or start to blow up."

VI. Application of All Coping Skills to Potential Problem Situations (Generalization)

____17. Counselor models application of client-selected coping strategies to non-problem-related or other potentially stressful situations.	"Let's work on some situations now that aren't problems for you but could arise in the future. This will give you a chance to see how you can apply these coping skills to other situations you encounter in the future. For instance, suppose I just found out I didn't get a promotion that I believe I really deserved. Here is how I might cope with this."
____18. Client practices, as often as needed, applying coping	"OK, you try this now."

(continued)

POSTEVALUATION (continued)

Item	Examples of counselor leads
strategies to potentially stressful situations by:	
——a. Imagining a potentially stressful situation.	"Why don't you imagine you've just found out you're being transferred to a new place? You are surprised by this. Imagine how you would cope."
——b. Taking part in a role-play practice.	"This time let's role-play a situation. I'll be your husband and tell you I've just found out I am very ill. You practice your coping skills as we talk."
——c. Taking part of a teacher in a role play and teaching a novice how to use coping strategies for stressful situations.	"This time I'm going to pretend that I have chronic arthritis and am in constant pain. It's really getting to me. I'd like you to be my trainer or helper and teach me how I could learn to use some coping skills to deal with this chronic discomfort."

VII. Homework and Follow-Up

——19. Counselor and client discuss application of coping strategies to *in vivo* situations.	"I believe now you could apply these coping skills to problem situations you encounter during a typical day or week. You may not find that these work as quickly as you'd like, but you should find yourself coping more and not losing control as much."
——20. Counselor instructs client how to use log to record uses of stress inoculation for *in vivo* situations.	"Each time you use the coping skills, mark it down on the log and briefly describe the situation in which you used them."
——21. Counselor arranges for a follow-up.	"We could get together next week and go over your logs and see how you're doing."

Observer comments: _____

_____

_____

_____

_____

_____

_____

_____

_____

_____

_____

_____

FEEDBACK #44: STRESS INOCULATION

I.
1. B
2. AD
3. IM
4. ER
5. I
6. MR
7. IM
8. AD
9. V
10. PT
11. SSN
12. SSN

If this was difficult for you, you might review the information presented in the text on direct-action coping skills.

II.
1. Encouraging phase
2. Preparing for the situation
3. Dealing with a critical moment
4. Confronting the situation

(continued)

5. Dealing with a critical moment
6. Encouragement for coping
7. Preparing for the situation
8. Confronting the situation

If you had trouble identifying the four phases of cognitive coping skills, you may want to review Table 16-1.

□ SUGGESTED READINGS

Baker, S. B., & Butler, J. N. (in press). Effects of preventive cognitive self-instruction training on adolescent attitudes, experiences and state anxiety. *Journal of Prevention.*

Bandler, R., & Grinder, J. (1982). *Reframing.* Moab, Utah: Real People Press.

Bruch, M. A., Juster, H. R., & Heisler, B. D. (1982). Conceptual complexity as a mediator of thought content and negative affect: Implications for cognitive restructuring interventions. *Journal of Counseling Psychology, 29,* 343–353.

Dush, D. M., Hirt, M. L., & Schroeder, H. (1983). Self-statement modification with adults: A meta-analysis. *Psychological Bulletin, 94,* 408–422.

Elder, J. P., Edelstein, B. A., & Fremouw, W. J. (1981). Client by treatment interactions in response acquisition and cognitive restructuring approaches. *Cognitive Therapy and Research, 5,* 203–210.

Feindler, E. L., & Fremouw, W. J. (1983). Stress inoculation training for adolescent anger problems. In D. H. Meichenbaum & M. E. Jaremko (Eds.), *Stress reduction and prevention.* New York: Plenum.

Greenberg, L. S., & Safran, J. D. (1981). Encoding and cognitive therapy: Changing what clients attend to. *Psychotherapy: Theory, Research and Practice, 18,* 163–169.

Hamilton, S. A., & Fremouw, W. J. (in press). Cognitive-behavioral training for college basketball foul-shooting performance. *Cognitive Therapy and Research.*

Janis, I. L. (1983). Stress inoculation in health care: Theory and research. In D. H. Meichenbaum & M. E. Jaremko (Eds.), *Stress reduction and prevention.* New York: Plenum.

Kendall, P. C. (1983). Stressful medical procedures: Cognitive-behavioral strategies for stress management and prevention. In D. H. Meichenbaum & M. E. Jaremko (Eds.), *Stress reduction and prevention.* New York: Plenum.

Klepac, R. K., Hauge, G., Dowling, J., & McDonald, M. (1981). Direct and generalized effects of three components of stress inoculation for increased pain tolerance. *Behavior Therapy, 12,* 417–424.

Leventhal, H., & Nerenz, D. R. (1983). A model for stress research with some implications for the control of stress disorders. In D. H. Meichenbaum & M. E. Jaremko (Eds.), *Stress reduction and prevention.* New York: Plenum.

McCordick, S. M., Kaplan, R. M., Smith, S., & Finn, M. E. (1981). Variations in cognitive behavior modification for test anxiety. *Psychotherapy: Theory, Research and Practice, 18,* 170–178.

Meichenbaum, D. (1985). *Stress-inoculation training.* Elmsford, New York: Pergamon Press.

Meichenbaum, D., & Cameron, R. (1983). Stress inoculation training: Toward a general paradigm for training coping skills. In D. H. Meichenbaum & M. E. Jaremko (Eds.), *Stress reduction and prevention.* New York: Plenum.

Miller, R. C., & Berman, J. S. (1983). The efficacy of cognitive behavior therapies: A quantitative review of the research evidence. *Psychological Bulletin, 94,* 39–53.

Novaco, R. W. (1975). *Anger control: The development and evaluation of an experimental treatment.* Lexington, MA: Heath.

Roskies, E. (1983). Stress management for Type A individuals. In D. H. Meichenbaum & M. E. Jaremko (Eds.), *Stress reduction and prevention.* New York: Plenum.

Safran, J. D., Alden, L. E., & Davidson, P. O. (1980). Client anxiety level as a moderator variable in assertion training. *Cognitive Therapy and Research, 4,* 189–200.

Safran, J. D., & Greenberg, L. S. (1982). Cognitive appraisal and reappraisal: Implications for clinical practice. *Cognitive Therapy and Research, 6,* 251–258.

Sweeney, G. A., & Horan, J. J. (1982). Separate and combined effects of cue-controlled relaxation and cognitive restructuring in the treatment of musical performance anxiety. *Journal of Counseling Psychology, 29,* 486–497.

Turk, D., & Genest, M. (1979). Regulation of pain: The application of cognitive and behavioral techniques for prevention and remediation. In P. Kendall & S. Hollon (Eds.), *Cognitive-behavioral intervention: Theory, research, and procedures.* New York: Academic Press.

Veronen, L. J., & Kilpatrick, D. G. (1983). Stress management for rape victims. In D. H. Meichenbaum & M. E. Jaremko (Eds.), *Stress reduction and prevention.* New York: Plenum.

Wernick, R. L. (1983). Stress inoculation in the management of clinical pain: Application to burn pain. In D. H. Meichenbaum & M. E. Jaremko (Eds.), *Stress reduction and prevention.* New York: Plenum.

West, D. J., Jr., Horan, J. J., & Games, P. A. (1984). Component analysis of occupational stress inoculation applied to registered nurses in an acute care hospital setting. *Journal of Counseling Psychology, 31,* 209–218.

FEEDBACK: POSTEVALUATION

PART ONE

1. You might emphasize that the client thinks of herself as inadequate although there are, in actuality, many indications of adequacy. You can explain
(continued)

FEEDBACK #44: (continued)

that CR would help her identify some of her thoughts about herself that are beliefs, not facts, and are unrealistic thoughts, leading to feelings of depression and worthlessness. In addition, CR would help her learn to think about herself in more realistic, self-enhancing ways. See the Interview Checklist for Cognitive Restructuring on pages 436–439 for another example of the CR rationale.

2. Self-enhancing or realistic thoughts for this client would be thinking that an almost straight-A average is good. A self-defeating thought is that this average is not good enough. In this case, almost any self-degrading thought is self-defeating because, for this client, these thoughts are only beliefs. Thinking that she is not good enough is self-defeating. Self-enhancing or positive thoughts about herself are more realistic interpretations of her experiences — good grades, close friends, active social life, and so on. Recognition that she is intelligent and attractive is a self-enhancing thought.

3. You could ask the client to describe different situations and the thoughts she has about herself in them. She could also observe this during the week. You could model some possible thoughts she might be having. See leads 6, 7, 8, and 9 in the Interview Checklist for Cognitive Restructuring.

4. There are many possible coping thoughts she could use. Here are some examples: "Hey, I'm doing pretty well as it is." "Don't be so hard on myself. I don't have to be perfect." "That worthless feeling is a sign to cope — recognize my assets." "What's more attractive anyway? I am attractive." "Don't let that one B get me down. It's not the end of the world."

5. See leads 13 through 16 on the Interview Checklist for Cognitive Restructuring.

6. Many possible homework assignments might help. Here are a few examples:
   a. Every time the client uses a coping thought, she could record it on her log.
   b. She could cue herself to use a coping thought by writing these down on note cards and reading a note before doing something else, like getting a drink or making a phone call, or by using a phone-answering device to report and verbalize coping thoughts.
   c. She could enlist the aid of a close friend or roommate. If the roommate notices that the client starts to "put herself down," she could interrupt her. The client could then verbalize a coping statement.

PART TWO

Use the Interview Checklist for Cognitive Restructuring on pages 436–439 to assess your teaching or counseling demonstration of this procedure.

PART THREE

Use the Interview Checklist for Reframing to assess your interview.

PART FOUR

1. Your rationale to this client might sound something like this:

   "You realize that there are times when your anger and impatience do get the best of you. This procedure can help you learn to control your feelings at especially hard times — when you're very upset with this child — so that you don't do something you will regret later."

2. Here is a brief overview of stress inoculation:

   "First, we'll look at the things the child can do that really upset you. When you realize you're in this type of situation, you can learn to control how upset you are — through keeping yourself calm. This procedure will help you learn different ways to keep calm and not let these situations get out of hand."

3. Information — See lead 7, part a, on the Interview Checklist for Stress Inoculation for some examples.
   Escape route — See lead 7, part b.
   Attention diversion — See lead 7, part c.
   Imagery manipulations — See lead 7, part d.
   Physical relaxation — See lead 7, parts e and f.
   Palliative coping — See lead 7, parts g, h, and i.

4. Here are some examples of a possible explanation of the four coping phases and of cognitive coping skills you might present to this client.

Phase	Explanation	Cognitive coping
Preparing for a provoking	Before you have a	"What do I want to say to (continued)

situation	disagreement or discussion, you can plan how you want to handle it.	him that gets my point across?" "I can tell him how I feel without shouting."
Confronting a provoking situation	When you're talking to him, you can think about how to stay in control.	"Just keep talking in a normal voice, no yelling." "Let him talk, too. Don't yell a lot; it doesn't help."
Dealing with a very provoking moment	If you feel very angry, you really need to think of some things to keep you from blowing your cool.	"Wait a minute. Slow down. Don't let the lid off." "Keep those hands down. Stay calm now."
Encouraging self for coping	Recognize when you do keep your cool. It's important to do this, to give yourself a pat on the back for this.	"I kept my cool that time!" "I could feel myself getting angry, but I kept in control then."

5. Practice opportunities can be carried out by the client in imagination or by you and the client in role play. In a role-play practice, you could take the part of the child. See leads 14, 15, and 16 on the Interview Checklist for Stress Inoculation for some examples of this type of practice.

PART FIVE

Use the Interview Checklist for Stress Inoculation to assess your role-play interview.

MEDITATION AND MUSCLE RELAXATION

SEVENTEEN

Feeling uptight? stressful? anxious?

Does your blood pressure zoom up at certain times or in certain situations?

Having trouble sleeping?

Does your head pound and ache at the end of the day?

A great number of people would respond affirmatively to one or more of these four questions. Anxiety is one of the most common problems reported by clients; stress is related to physiological discomfort such as headaches and indigestion. Stress is also correlated with heart disease, cancer, and other serious diseases. Perhaps as a consequence of the "stress syndrome," the last few years have produced an explosion in procedures for stress or anxiety management, originally introduced in 1929 as "progressive relaxation" (Jacobson, 1929). Related books have appeared on nonfiction best-seller lists (Benson, 1976; Bloomfield, Cain, Jaffe, & Kory, 1975; Denniston & McWilliams, 1975), and a flurry of research endeavors has explored the relative strengths and weaknesses of stress-management approaches (Nicassio & Bootzin, 1974; Lehrer & Woolfolk, 1984; Shoemaker & Tasto, 1975; Smith, 1975).

This chapter presents three stress-management or relaxation strategies. Two meditation procedures are described — Benson's (1974, 1976) relaxation response and Carrington's (1978a, 1978b) clinically standardized meditation — as well as muscle-relaxation training. These three strategies are typically used to treat both cognitive and physiological indexes of stress, including anxiety, anger, pain, and hypertension. The strategies differ somewhat in that both meditation strategies are primarily cognitive relaxation procedures, whereas muscle relaxation focuses on physical, or somatic, sensations (Marlatt & Marques, 1977, p. 131). The benefits of both procedures may not be realized unless they are used to prevent, as well as to remediate, stress-related symptoms. Lehrer, Woolfolk, Rooney, McCann, and Carrington (1983) suggest that meditation might be preferable if client motivation is a problem; the clients may enjoy practice more because cognitive absorption of attention may be greater. In contrast, clients who experience skeletal-muscle tension or tension headaches might benefit more from progressive muscle relaxation (Lehrer et al., 1983). A combination of one form of meditation and muscle relaxation may be better than one strategy alone.

□ OBJECTIVES

1. Identify which step of the relaxation response is reflected by each of ten counselor responses, accurately identifying at least eight of the ten examples.
2. Identify which step of the clinically standardized meditation procedure is reflected by at least six of eight counselor responses.
3. Select either the relaxation response or clinically standardized meditation and teach the procedure to another person. Audiotape your teaching and assess your steps with the Interview Checklist for Muscle Relaxation or the Interview Checklist for Clinically Standardized Meditation, or have an observer evaluate your teaching, using the checklist.
4. Describe how you would apply the seven major components of the muscle-relaxation procedure, given a simulated client case.
5. Demonstrate 13 out of 15 steps of muscle relaxation with a role-play client, using the Interview Checklist for Muscle Relaxation to assess your performance.

□ MEDITATION

"Meditation refers to a family of techniques which have in common a conscious attempt to focus attention in a nonanalytical way and an attempt not to dwell on discursive ruminating thought" (Shapiro, 1982, p. 268). The word *meditation* is associated with the mystical traditions of the East. For example, Zen (Zazen) breath meditation was developed many centuries ago as a technique for attaining religious insight (Shapiro & Zifferblatt, 1976). Transcendental Meditation (TM) is another procedure used to turn one's attention inward toward more subtle levels of thought. In a review of meditation as psychotherapy, Smith (1975, p. 558) states that "such exercises vary widely and can involve sitting still and counting breaths, attending to a repeated thought, or focusing on virtually any simple external or internal stimulus." Carrington (1978a) defines *clinically*

standardized meditation (CSM) as a Western version of the Indian practice called "mantra meditation." CSM uses a soothing sound that the client repeats mentally without conscious effort or concentration. Benson (1974, 1976) refers to meditation as the *relaxation response.*

Several studies have reported on the effectiveness of meditation as a therapeutic strategy. Smith's (1975) review of research about meditation as a therapeutic procedure yielded three general findings. First, experienced meditators who volunteer without pay for meditation research appear "healthier" than nonmeditators. Second, people who are beginners and who practice meditation for four to ten weeks show more "improvement" on a variety of tests than nonmeditators measured for the same period of time. Third, four to ten weeks of regular practice of meditation is associated with greater decrements in "psychopathology" than those experienced by control nonmeditators. However, Smith points out that none of the studies reviewed had controlled for the expectation of relief ("I want to and will get better") or the regular practice of sitting quietly.

In other studies, Boudreau (1972) found that TM relieved symptoms associated with claustrophobia in one case and excessive perspiration in another. Girodo (1974) found that people with a short history of anxiety neurosis effectively reduced their anxiety symptoms with meditation. Zen breath meditation and self-management techniques were applied to reduce methadone dosage of two drug addicts (Shapiro & Zifferblatt, 1976), to treat anxiety (Lehrer et al., 1983), and to reduce nonattending behaviors of children (Redfering & Bowman, 1981). Attention-focusing techniques derived from meditation procedures were as effective as progressive relaxation in treating 24 insomniacs to reduce latency of sleep onset (Woolfolk, Carr-Kaffashan, McNulty, & Lehrer, 1976). Breath meditation was effective in reducing systolic and diastolic blood pressure of a 71-year-old hypertensive from 170/105 before treatment to 135/90 several months after treatment (Rappaport & Cammer, 1977). Both the relaxation response and muscle relaxation significantly decreased alcohol consumption of many clients (Marlatt & Marques, 1977) and decreased daily manifestations of cognitive and somatic stress (Woolfolk, Lehrer, McCann, & Rooney, 1982).

Shapiro and Zifferblatt (1976, p. 522) have described the process of Zen meditation in five overlapping steps:

1. There is a reactive effect when a person begins to focus on breathing. For example, breathing may be faster.
2. Later, the person's attention wanders from the breathing and he or she becomes habituated in the exercise.
3. The person is taught to catch himself or herself whenever attention wanders and return to breathing. Either this process may cause another reactive effect or, with practice, one may learn to breathe effortlessly.
4. The person is able to continue to focus on breathing and at the same time passively observe new thoughts as they come into awareness.
5. The last process (step 4) may have two functions: (a) the person becomes desensitized to distracting thoughts, and (b) the person eventually removes thoughts by focusing on breathing.

Barber (1980) and Clarke and Jackson (1983) indicate that there is a great deal of commonality between meditation and hypnosis, particularly with respect to the central role of attentional focusing in both procedures. Barber noted the similarity of the two procedures:

> The overlap between self-hypnosis and meditation is tremendous. In fact it seems to me that the variability within self-hypnosis and meditation is almost as large as the variability between these procedures. There seems to me to be so many parallels so that it appears possible to at least conceptualize self-hypnosis as one type of meditation, or vice versa, meditation as one type of self-hypnosis [quoted in Shapiro, 1980, p. 57].

Benson (1974, 1976) has described meditation, or the relaxation response, as a counterbalancing technique for alleviating the environmental effects of stress. Often, when people feel stress, "fight or flight" is the coping response used. Regular practice of the relaxation response can stimulate the area of the hypothalamus in the brain that can decrease systolic and diastolic blood pressure, heart rate, respiratory rate, and oxygen consumption. The fight-or-flight response to stress can raise these physiological rates (Benson, 1976). According to Benson (1974, 1976), four basic elements are needed to elicit the relaxation response: a quiet environment, a mental device, a passive attitude, and a comfortable position. The components of clinically standardized meditation are similar: a mantra, or sound, a quiet environment free of distractions, a passive attitude in which the client flows with the process, and a comfortable and relaxed sitting position.

Shapiro (1980, p. 33) has described several characteristics of people who are successful at meditation. Some of the characteristics are high level of internal locus of control ("I'm in control of my behavior"), a great deal of enthusiasm, high interest in subjective experiences (Lehrer et al., 1983), and good ability to maintain attentional focus.

Meditation can be used alone or in conjunction with other procedures (see D. H. Shapiro & S. M. Zifferblatt, 1976). The elements listed by Benson (1976) for eliciting the relaxation response and the processes described by Shapiro and Zifferblatt have been interwoven into the following description of the steps for the relaxation response (RR) and Zen meditation (ZM).

☐ STEPS FOR RELAXATION RESPONSE AND ZEN MEDITATION

We describe the relaxation response (RR) and Zen meditation (ZM) combined in one eight-step procedure (see Table 17-1).

1. The counselor gives the client a rationale for the procedure.
2. The counselor and client select a mental device.
3. The counselor instructs the client about body comfort.
4. The counselor instructs the client about breathing and use of a mental device.
5. The counselor instructs the client about a passive attitude.
6. The client tries to meditate for 10 to 20 minutes.
7. The counselor probes the client about the meditative experience.
8. Finally, the client is assigned homework and is instructed to keep a daily log of meditative experiences.

The Interview Checklist for Relaxation Response and Zen Meditation at the end of the chapter summarizes these steps.

Treatment Rationale
Here is an example of a *rationale* for meditation used by Shapiro (1978b):

> . . . Meditation is nothing magical. It takes patience and practice; you have to work at it; and, just

TABLE 17-1. Steps for relaxation response (RR) and Zen meditation (ZM) combined and clinically standardized meditation (CSM)

RR and ZM combined	*Clinically standardized meditation (CSM)*

1. Rationale
  a. Describe purpose of procedure.
  b. Give overview of procedure.
	1. Rationale
	  a. Describe purpose of procedure.
	  b. Give overview of procedure.

2. Selection of a mental device
  a. Provide rationale for mental device.
  b. Provide examples of mental device.
	2. Selection of mantra or sound
	  a. Instruct client to select a mantra.
	  b. Choose or make up a meaningless sound or word that has few associations and is not emotionally charged.

3. Instructions to patient
  a. Get in quiet environment.
  b. Relax all muscles in body and keep them relaxed.
  c. Close eyes and assume comfortable body position.
	3. Preparation for meditation
	  a. Select a quiet environment free from distractions (such as the telephone).
	  b. Should not be interrupted while meditating.
	  c. Should not take any alcoholic beverages or nonprescription drugs at least 24 hours before meditation.
	  d. Should not drink any beverages containing caffeine one hour before meditation.
	  e. Should not eat for one hour before meditation. No smoking for half an hour before. No chewing gum while meditating.
	  f. Select a comfortable straight-backed chair in a room free of clutter. Face away from direct light in dimly lit room.
	  g. Loosen tight clothing and shoes.

4. Instructions about breathing and use of mental device: Breathe through your nose and focus on your breathing. Let the air come to you. As you do this, say the mental device for each inhalation and exhalation: "Breathe in . . . out 'one,' in . . . out, 'one.'" Breathe in and out while saying your mental device silently to yourself. Try to achieve effortless breathing.	4. Instructions to meditate
	  a. Sit quietly for about a half minute before you say your mantra or sound. Be relaxed and quiet.
	  b. First, close your eyes and say your mantra or sound aloud, say it softly, whisper, think the sound to yourself without moving your lips or tongue. After the first session, hear or think your sound.
	  c. CSM is not an exercise in discipline—it is a quiet, peaceful time with yourself. It requires no effort.
	  d. Allow distracting thoughts to flow. Flow with the process—allow memories, images, thoughts to occur. Don't try to influence these. Your mantra will return to you.
	  e. Meditate for five to ten minutes. You can open your eyes to look at watch periodically.
	  f. Come out of meditation slowly. Sit with your eyes closed for two minutes—take time to absorb what is happening. Get up slowly and open eyes slowly.

5. Instructions about passive attitude: When distracting thoughts occur, let them pass. Keep your mind open and return to your mental device.	
6. Meditate for 10 to 20 minutes. Instruct the client to meditate 10 minutes at first. Later, the time can be extended.	

7. Probe about meditation experience
  a. How does it feel?
  b. How did you handle distracting thoughts?
	5. Discuss client's reaction to first meditation.

8. Instruct client to meditate daily
  a. Don't meditate within one hour after eating.
  b. Meditate in quiet environment.
  c. Meditate several hours before bedtime.
  d. Meditate twice daily.
	6. Homework
	  a. Meditate for three weeks, twice a day.
	  b. Meditate first thing in the morning after arising and during the afternoon or early evening.

Reprinted with permission from Deane H. Shapiro, Jr., *Meditation: Self-regulation strategy and altered state of consciousness* (New York: Aldine Publishing Company). Copyright © 1980 by Deane H. Shapiro.

by meditating, all life's problems will not be solved. On the other hand, meditation is potentially a very powerful tool, and it is equally important to suggest what you might be able to expect from meditation the first month you practice it. Studies have shown that Zen meditation can have a strong effect within the first two to four weeks. Some of these effects can be measured physiologically—e.g., brain wave states, slower breathing, slower heart rate. These all contribute to a state of relaxation and inner calm. Meditation may help you become more aware, both of what is going on outside you, and what is happening within you—your thoughts, feelings, hopes, fears. Thus, although meditation won't solve all your problems, it can give you the calmness, the awareness, and the self-control to actively work on solving those problems (p. 71).*

Here is an illustration of an *overview* of the strategy:

"What we will do first is select a focusing or mental device. You will then get in a relaxed and comfortable position. Afterward, I will instruct you about focusing on your breathing and using your mental device. We will talk about a passive attitude while meditating. You will meditate about 10 to 20 minutes. Then we will talk about the experience."

Selection of a Mental Device

Most forms of meditation can be classified as "concentrative" meditation, in which one tries to clear one's mind of intruding thoughts by focusing for a time on a single stimulus (Ornstein, 1972). Often this stimulus takes the form of a mental device. A mental device, or "mantra," is usually a single-syllable sound or word such as *in, out, one,* or *zum,* although concentration on a mental riddle is also possible. The client repeats the syllable or word silently or in a low tone while meditating. The rationale for the repetition of the syllable or word is to free the client from focusing on logical and externally oriented thought. Instead, the client focuses on a constant stimulus—the word, sound, syllable, or phrase. Repetition of the word assists in breaking the stream of distracting thoughts (Ben-

son, 1976). The mental device is used to help the client focus on breathing. The counselor should describe the rationale for the mental device to the client and give examples of possible options for a mental device. Benson (1974) suggests use of the word *one* "because of its simplicity and neutrality" (p. 54). The client then selects his or her own mental device to use while meditating.

Instructions about Body Comfort

The first prerequisite for body comfort is a quiet environment in which to meditate. The counselor should create a quiet, calm environment that is as free of distractions as possible. Benson (1976) claims that some background noise may prevent the relaxation response. A quiet environment is less distracting and may facilitate elimination of intrusive thoughts. The counselor tells the client that there are several ways to meditate or to elicit the relaxation response and says that he or she will show the client one way. Then the counselor instructs the client to get into a comfortable position. This may be sitting in a comfortable chair with the head and arms supported, or the person might wish to sit on the floor, assuming a semilotus position (this is particularly good for "private" practice sessions). As in muscle relaxation, the client should wear comfortable clothing. Getting into a comfortable position minimizes muscular effort. When in a comfortable position, the client is instructed to close her or his eyes and to relax all muscles deeply. The counselor might name a few muscle groups—"Relax your face, your neck, your head, shoulders, chest, your lower torso, your thighs, going to your calves, and to your feet." The muscle groups described in Table 17-2, later in this chapter, can be used at this point. After the client is relaxed, the counselor gives instructions about breathing and using the mental device.

Instructions about Breathing and Use of the Mental Device

The counselor instructs the client to breathe through the nose and to focus on or become aware of breathing. It is believed that the focused-breathing component of meditation helps a person learn to relax and to manage tension (Shapiro, 1978a). At first, it may be difficult for some people to be natural when focusing on breathing. The counselor should encourage the client to breathe easily and naturally with a suggestion to "allow the air to

---

* This and all other quotations from this source are from "Instructions for a Training Package Combining Formal and Informal Zen Meditation with Behavioral Self-Control Strategies," by D. H. Shapiro. From *Psychologia.* Copyright 1978 by Kyoto University. Reprinted by permission of the publisher.

come to you" on each inhalation. For each exhalation, the client is instructed to exhale slowly, letting all the air out of the lungs. While focusing on breathing, the client uses the mental device by saying it silently. Clients are instructed to repeat the mental device silently for each inhalation and each exhalation and are encouraged to keep their attention on the breathing and the mental device.

Instructions about a Passive Attitude

The counselor instructs the client to maintain a passive attitude and to allow relaxation to occur at its own pace. In addition, the client is instructed, if attention wanders and distracting images or thoughts occur, not to dwell on them and to return to repeating the mental device or word. The client should allow the distracting thoughts to pass through the mind and just be passive. If distracting thoughts occur for several minutes, instruct the client not to be evaluative and to return to repeating the mental device. As Benson states, "The purpose of the response is to help one rest and relax, and this requires a completely passive attitude. One should not scrutinize his performance or try to force the response, because this may well prevent the response from occurring. When distracting thoughts enter the mind, they should simply be disregarded" (1974, p. 54). The relaxation response is not an occasion for thinking things over or for problem solving. Shapiro (1978a) hypothesizes that this emphasis in meditation on the "ongoing present" may alert people to notice when they become distracted from tasks and also may represent a way to return to the present, or the "here and now."

Meditation for 10 to 20 Minutes

The client is instructed to meditate for about 10 to 20 minutes. The counselor tells the client to open her or his eyes to check the time if desired. A clock or watch that the client can see easily should be provided. The counselor also instructs the client in what to do after the meditative session. For example, some clients may wish to keep their eyes closed for a couple of minutes after meditating — or just to sit quietly for several minutes.

Probe about the Meditative Experience

The counselor asks the client about the experience with meditation. For example, the counselor should ask how the client felt, how the mental device was used, what happened to any distracting thoughts, and whether the client was able to maintain a passive attitude.

Homework and Follow-up

As homework, the counselor asks the client to practice the relaxation response once or twice a day at home or at work. Each practice session may last 10 to 15 minutes. Practice should not occur within two hours after any meal, because the digestive processes appear to interfere with relaxation. Practice should occur in a quiet environment free from distractions or interruptions. For some people, practice several hours before bedtime can interfere with going to sleep. The client should be instructed to keep a daily log of each time the relaxation response is used. The log might include the time of day meditation was used, the setting, the period of time spent in practice, and the client's reaction to the experience or the level of relaxation as rated on a 5-point scale. Individualize the homework for the client. Some clients may feel that they cannot practice twice daily. In such cases, encourage the client to practice several times weekly.

Another homework assignment proposed by Shapiro and Zifferblatt (1976) is *informal meditation.* This requires that a person be conscious and aware and observe or attend very closely to ordinary daily activities (pp. 521–522). A client could be instructed simply to observe all events and behaviors that occur throughout the day. This type of informal meditation is similar to what Ornstein (1972) describes as "opening up" — meditative exercises in which the person simply focuses on whatever is happening as it occurs, in the "here and now." Informal meditation may be used more frequently as homework than formal meditation because it is somewhat easier, is less structured, and takes less time.

Another way to use informal meditation as homework is to ask the client to observe some selected problem or stress-related environmental event in a detached, nonevaluative fashion. For such events that might produce tension, anxiety, anger, fear, or pain, the client could be instructed to focus on breathing and to initiate calmness and relaxation. Here is an example of this type of assignment developed by Shapiro (1980, pp. 128–130), which he refers to as "contingent informal meditation":

Awareness: List below current problems, difficulties, or concerns which you are having or have had that cause you to become tense and anxious:

a. _____

b. _____

c. _____

Let's pick a situation *a*, now, and see if you can make it as specific as possible. Who is present; where are you; what kinds of things are you doing, saying, thinking. Now close your eyes and imagine yourself in that situation, and allow yourself to experience the tension that you normally feel.

Interruption of sequence and competing response. Once you have observed these thoughts and actions, say to yourself "Stop!" as you clench your fist and your jaw. Then relax your fingers and your jaw and imagine yourself beginning informal breath meditation: you are closing your eyes and beginning to focus on your breathing. Now, actually take two deep breaths through your nose, and as you exhale let your "center" sink into your stomach. Say to yourself:

1. Your name: "I am _____."
2. "I am breath" (and take another deep breath).
3. "I am calm and relaxed and am in control" (and take two more deep breaths, letting your "center" sink to your stomach as you exhale).

Now imagine yourself becoming more and more relaxed; imagine yourself meditating, feeling calm, and in control. At the count of ten you may open your eyes, and you will feel calm, relaxed, and wide awake. [Repeat this process for situations *b* and *c*.]*

In addition to the formal practice of the relaxation response, informal meditation can be assigned as an *in vivo* application of the procedure. The client can also be instructed to keep a log of informal meditation applied *in vivo* to stressful situations. After the client has used the meditation homework for about a month, a follow-up session should be scheduled. This session can use the client's log data to check on the frequency of use of the homework, the client's reactions to the homework, and the client's recorded stress level.

* Reprinted with permission from Deane H. Shapiro, Jr., *Meditation: Self-regulation strategy and altered state of consciousness* (New York: Aldine Publishing Company). Copyright © 1980 by Deane H. Shapiro.

☐ STEPS FOR CLINICALLY STANDARDIZED MEDITATION

We divide the clinically standardized meditation (CSM) procedure, based on Carrington's (1978a) descriptions, into six steps:

1. Rationale.
2. Selection of a mantra, or sound.
3. Preparation for meditation.
4. Instructions to meditate.
5. Discussion of client's reaction to first meditation.
6. Homework and follow-up.

Table 17-1 summarizes these steps, and the Interview Checklist for Clinically Standardized Meditation at the end of the chapter models the steps.

Treatment Rationale

Here is one version of a rationale and overview (adapted from Carrington, 1978b) that a counselor might give:

"The procedure called 'clinically standardized meditation' is a simple relaxation exercise. A variety of positive effects can come from meditating. For example, meditation has benefited people by reducing tension, stress, headaches, anxiety, and the time it takes to fall asleep. It has also been reported to increase athletic performance and energy. People who meditate report that they are more alert, are closer to their feelings, and have clearer thinking. Meditation may be an alternative to tranquilizers and other drugs. If you choose to try meditation as a relaxation technique, you will be asked to select a sound, or mantra, that you will use while you are relaxed and comfortable in a quiet environment. You can allow images and thoughts to flow freely. You will not have to concentrate, and meditation will require no effort. Let your thoughts or feelings come and go. Your mantra will come back to you. We will meditate for five or ten minutes at first. Then we will talk about your reaction to this quiet and peaceful experience" [after Cormier & Cormier, & Weisser, 1984, p. 270].

Selection of a Mantra

Carrington's course workbook (*Learning to Meditate,* 1978b) contains a list of 16 Sanskrit words from which a client may choose (p. 10). Alternatively, we have found that clients can create a meaningless sound or word that has few associations and is not emotionally charged. *Grik, shalom,* and *rava* are examples of sounds or words.

Whatever sound is chosen, it should be soothing to the client.

Preparation for Meditation

Carrington (1978b) provides extensive instructions on preparing to meditate (see Table 17-1). First, clients should be instructed to select a quiet, uncluttered environment, free from interruptions and distractions such as ringing telephones or people talking. The idea is for people not to be interrupted or externally distracted while meditating. Clients should not consume any alcoholic beverages or nonprescription drugs for at least 24 hours before meditation. They should not meditate within one hour after consuming solid food or beverages containing caffeine. Smoking is discouraged for at least a half hour before meditation.

Clients should be instructed to loosen tight-fitting clothing or shoes and select a comfortable straight-backed chair away from direct light. These instructions are provided to enhance the quality of the meditation. The instructions can also serve as stimulus controls, or cues to increase the probability of meditating (see "Stimulus Control," in Chapter 19).

Instructions to Meditate

It is important that clients know to relax their muscles before beginning to meditate (see the next section of this chapter). Carrington (1978b) recommends sitting quietly for about half a minute before saying the mantra, or sound. After this brief period of quiet relaxation, clients are to close their eyes and focus on the mantra. At first, they pronounce the mantra aloud. Gradually, they begin to say it more softly, then to whisper it, and finally to think or hear the sound without moving their lips or tongue. It is important that clients be reminded that meditation is not an exercise in discipline but a quiet, peaceful time alone, requiring no effort or concentration. Clients should allow distracting thoughts or feelings to flow, as if they were clouds floating by. They should not actively try to influence distracting thoughts or feelings but should merely allow their mantra to return to them. Clients should be instructed to meditate for five to ten minutes, opening their eyes occasionally to peek at a watch or clock. Finally, they should end each meditative session slowly. Carrington (1978b) advises that clients sit with closed eyes for about two minutes and take time to absorb what is happening at that moment.

Client's Reaction to First Meditation

Discuss or probe the client's reaction to meditation. People experience a variety of reactions to meditation; no two meditative experiences are alike. Clients may feel unsure of themselves when meditating, possibly because *there are no rules* for the process.

Homework and Follow-up

The therapist should tell the client when and how often to meditate. Novices should practice twice daily for at least the initial three-week period. Carrington (1978b) recommends that people regularly meditate in the morning after arising and in the late afternoon or early evening.

☐ CONTRAINDICATIONS AND ADVERSE EFFECTS OF MEDITATION

Carrington (1978a) and Shapiro (1980, 1982) have recommended that meditation not be used with some patients unless *closely* supervised by the therapist. Meditation for some clients may not be a useful therapeutic procedure, and some clients may experience adverse effects.

Carrington (1978a) has indicated that severely disturbed or psychotic patients should not meditate unless supervised by a therapist competent in the use of meditation. Shapiro (1980) suggests that meditation may not be useful for chronically depressed clients or for people with somatic anxiety but low cognitive anxiety, for those with high external locus of control, or for those with chronic headaches or Raynaud's disease. Patients suffering from physical or emotional symptoms should be informed that meditation is not a substitute for treatment by a competent health professional (Carrington, 1978a, p. 11). Carrington advises that patients under medical treatment, particularly those who are receiving medication for endocrine or metabolic control, for pain, or for psychiatric symptoms, should have their meditation experience supervised by a therapist familiar with the effects of profound relaxation on medical conditions and on drug therapy (1978a, p. 11). Persons using insulin, thyroxin, or antihypertensive drugs *may* need to have their dosages decreased while they are regularly practicing meditation; at the very least, dosages of drugs such as these need to be monitored.

Particular types of clients may experience adverse effects from meditation. For example, Shapiro (1980) indicates that some clients may be attracted to meditation for inappropriate reasons, such as to use meditation as a strong cognitive avoidance strategy or to use it as a technique to block out most of the unpleasant events in their lives. In addition, Shapiro (1980, 1982) suggests that self-critical, perfectionistic, goal-oriented Type A people may bring this same orientation to meditation. Finally, people who meditate too long may have such adverse effects as increased anxiety, boredom, confusion, depression, restlessness, and impaired reality testing (Shapiro, 1980, p. 47).

Carrington (1978a) recommends that, to decrease the probability of adverse effects, the therapist should have the client meditate initially with and under the supervision of the therapist. As we suggested in Chapter 10, the therapist should monitor the instruction, training, and use of meditation. Monitoring the meditative process may reveal that clients need to decrease the length of time they meditate, decrease the frequency of daily sessions of meditation, or select another treatment strategy.

☐ MODEL EXAMPLE: MEDITATION (CSM)

In this model example, we present a narrative account of how meditation (CSM) might be used with a 42-year-old male client. Nick, an air traffic controller, has reported that he would like to decrease the stress he experiences in his job. He believes that decreasing this stress will help his ulcer and help him cope better with his job. In addition to the physical signs of stress (hypertension), Nick also reports that he worries constantly about making mistakes in his job.

1. *Rationale*

First, we explain to Nick that CSM has been used to help people cope with job-related stress. We tell Nick that the procedure has also been used to help people with high blood pressure, anxiety, and those who want to feel more alert. We provide Nick with an overview of CSM, telling him that the procedure is a technique in which a sound is selected and said while in a quiet place, with eyes closed, while allowing thoughts to flow freely, for a period of about five to ten minutes. Finally, we confirm Nick's willingness to use meditation and answer any questions he may have about the procedure.

2. *Selection of a Mantra*

We explain to Nick that he needs to select a mantra—a word or sound that has few associations and is not emotionally charged. We discuss the purpose of the sound as a device that helps him avoid becoming distracted by other thoughts. We give examples of sounds, such as *gome, rance,* and *shalom.* We help Nick think of a sound that is neutral and soothing. Nick selects his own sound.

3. *Instructions about Preparation for Meditation*

We inform Nick about how to prepare for meditation—for example, arranging a quiet environment free of distraction and interruption. We instruct him not to meditate within 24 hours of taking alcoholic beverages or nonprescription drugs or right after eating or after drinking beverages containing caffeine and not to chew gum while meditating. We discuss how all these might interfere with meditation. We also inform Nick that it is important to wear comfortable clothing and sit in a comfortable chair while meditating.

4. *Instructions to Meditate*

We instruct Nick to sit quietly and get relaxed for about a minute. Then he is to close his eyes and say his sound aloud, to say it softly, then to whisper the sound several times, and finally to think the sound without moving his lips or tongue. We tell Nick that meditation is not an exercise or discipline and requires no effort—don't force it. We mention that if distracting thoughts occur, he should allow them to come and not try to influence these thoughts—the sound will return. We tell Nick that he will meditate for about five to ten minutes. We will keep time. When Nick meditates alone, he can open his eyes to check the time. When the time is up, we ask Nick to come out of meditation slowly by sitting there with his eyes closed for about two minutes. We instruct Nick to try to absorb what he is experiencing and then to open his eyes slowly.

5. *Discussion of Nick's Reaction to Meditation*

We ask Nick a series of questions about his experience with meditation: "How did your sound work for you? How did you feel about the CSM experience? What thoughts or images occurred? How did your sound return to you?"

6. *Homework and Follow-up*

We instruct Nick to meditate twice a day, once after getting up in the morning and later in the late afternoon or early evening. We remind him of the things to do to prepare—quiet environment, no alcoholic beverages or nonprescription drugs at least 24 hours before meditating, wait for an hour after taking solid foods or caffeine, do not smoke half an hour before meditating, select a comfortable place, and do meditation at the same time and place each day.

Nick is instructed to keep a weekly log of each meditative experience: where he used it, time of day used, and each use rated on a 5-point scale: 5 = great, 4 = good, 3 = fair, 2 = not smooth, 1 = poor. We instruct Nick about the use of informal meditation at work and schedule an appointment the following week to talk about the meditative experiences and discuss his log.

LEARNING ACTIVITIES #45: MEDITATION (RELAXATION RESPONSE AND ZEN MEDITATION OR CLINICALLY STANDARDIZED MEDITATION)

I. Teaching relaxation response/Zen meditation or clinically standardized meditation to a client is an informational process. The counselor provides the instructions, and the client engages in meditation in a self-directed manner. To practice giving instructions to someone about meditation, select a partner or a role-play client and give instructions as described in the Interview Checklist for Relaxation Response and Zen Meditation or the Interview Checklist for Clinically Standardized Meditation at the end of the chapter. Then assess how well your partner was able to implement your instructions. If you wish, reverse roles so that you can experience being instructed by another person.

II. This learning activity provides an opportunity to try out formal meditation. Do this in a quiet, restful place when you will not be interrupted for 20 minutes. Do *not* do this within two hours *after* a meal or within two hours of going to sleep.
1. Get in a comfortable sitting position and close your eyes.
2. Relax your entire body. Think about all the tension draining out of your body.

3. Meditate for about 15 to 20 minutes.
   a. Breathe easily and naturally through your nose.
   b. Focus on your breathing with the thought of a number (one) or a word. Say (think) your word silently each time you inhale and exhale.
   c. If other thoughts or images appear, don't dwell on them but don't force them away. Just relax and focus on your word or breathing.
4. Try to assess your reactions to your meditative experience:
   How do you feel about it?
   How do you feel afterward?
   What sorts of thoughts or images come into your mind?
   How much difficulty did you have with distractions?
5. Practice the relaxation response systematically — twice daily for a week, if possible.

III. To experience "informal meditation," we suggest you follow the homework assignment developed by Shapiro described on pp. 453–454. Try to do this daily for at least a week.

☐ MUSCLE RELAXATION

In muscle relaxation, a person is taught to relax by becoming aware of the sensations of tensing and relaxing major muscle groups. Take a few moments to feel and to become aware of some of these sensations. Make a fist with your preferred (dominant) hand. Clench your fist of that hand. Clench it tightly and study the tension in your hand and forearm. Become aware and feel those sensations of tension. Now let the tension go in your fist, hand, and forearm. Relax your hand and rest it. Note the difference between the tension and the relaxation. Do the exercise once more, only this time close your eyes. Clench your fist tightly; become aware of the tension in your hand and fore-arm; then relax your hand and let the tension flow out. Note the different sensations of relaxing and tensing your fist. Try it.

If you did this exercise, you may have noticed that your hand and forearm *cannot* be tense and relaxed at the same time. In other words, relaxation is incompatible with tension. You may also have noted that you instructed your hand to tense up and then to relax. You sent messages from your head to your hand to impose tension and then to create relaxation. You can cue a muscle group (the hand and forearm, in this case) to perform or respond in a particular manner (tense up and relax). This exercise was perhaps too brief for you to notice changes in other bodily functions. For example, tension and relaxation can affect one's blood pressure, heart rate, and respiration rate and can also influence covert processes and the way one performs or responds overtly. The long-range goal of muscle relaxation is "for the body to monitor instantaneously all of its numerous control signals, and automatically to relieve tensions that are not desired" (McGuigan, 1984, p. 15).

Relaxation training is not new, but it has recently become a popular technique to deal with a variety of client concerns. Jacobson (1929, 1964) developed an extensive procedure called "progressive relaxation." Later, Wolpe (1958) described muscle relaxation as an anxiety-inhibiting procedure with his systematic desensitization strategy (see Chapter 18). Bernstein and Borkovec (1973) wrote a thorough relaxation manual entitled *Progressive Relaxation Training.* Goldfried and Davison (1976) have described relaxation training in their book about behavior therapy.

In a procedural analysis and review of 80 relaxation training studies, Hillenberg and Collins (1982) found that relaxation training has been used with clients who have sleep disturbance, headache, hypertension, test anxiety, speech anxiety, general anxiety, asthma, excessive drinking, hyperactivity, and problems with anger control (p. 252). The Lamaze (1958) method of childbirth uses relaxation training to facilitate a more relaxed and less painful labor and delivery. Cautela and Groden (1978) have developed a relaxation training manual for children.

Studies have also compared the effectiveness of relaxation training instructions administered in person (live) and by a tape recording. Hillenberg and Collins (1982) and Lehrer (1982) indicate that live presentation of relaxation instructions is probably better than taped instructions. Our preference is to have a counselor administer relaxation training within the interview. Tape-recorded instructions can be used for homework or outside practice sessions.

The effects of muscle relaxation, like those of any other strategy, are related to satisfactory problem assessment, client characteristics, and the therapist's ability to apply the procedure competently and confidently. There are also precautions therapists should heed — one should not apply relaxation training indiscriminately.

Some Cautions in Using Muscle Relaxation

There are two areas the counselor should assess before applying muscle relaxation (Bernstein & Borkovec, 1973). First, make sure the client is medically cleared to engage in muscle relaxation (p. 12). For example, a person who suffers headaches or lower-back pain may have an organic basis for these complaints, or a person may be taking a drug that is incompatible with the purposes of muscle relaxation. For some clients, tensing certain muscle groups may have detrimental effects. The counselor should obtain a medical clearance from the client's physician or encourage the client to have a physical examination if there is a complaint that might be organically caused. Relaxation exercises may have to be adjusted for handicapped clients or for clients who cannot perform exercises for particular muscle groups.

The next caution is to discover the causes of the client's reported tension (Bernstein & Borkovec, 1973, p. 12). The counselor would probably have achieved this during problem assessment (see Chapters 7 and 8). For example, is muscle relaxation a reasonable strategy for alleviating the client's problem? If the client is experiencing tension in a job situation, the counselor and client may prefer to deal first with the client's external situation (the job). Bernstein and Borkovec point out that there is a difference between dealing with the tension of daily problems and handling the tension of someone who is on the verge of financial disaster. In the latter case, combinations of therapeutic strategies may be necessary. As Goldfried (1977, p. 84) notes, relaxation training may be more effective on a short-term basis and when supplemented with other therapeutic strategies, and the clinical potential of relaxation may be enhanced when the procedure is presented to clients as a coping skill.

Steps of Muscle Relaxation

Muscle relaxation consists of the following seven steps:

1. Rationale.
2. Instructions about dress.
3. Creation of a comfortable environment.
4. Counselor modeling of the relaxation exercises.
5. Instructions for muscle relaxation.
6. Posttraining assessment.
7. Homework and follow-up.

These steps are described in detail in the Interview Checklist for Muscle Relaxation at the end of the chapter.

Treatment rationale. Here is an example of one way a counselor might explain the *purpose* of relaxation: "This process, if you practice it regularly, can help you become relaxed. The relaxation benefits you derived can help you sleep better at night." An *overview* of the procedure might be "This procedure involves learning to tense and relax different muscle groups in your body. By doing this, you can contrast the difference between tenseness and relaxation. This will help you to recognize tension so you can instruct yourself to relax."

In addition, the counselor should explain that muscle relaxation is a *skill*. The process of learning will be gradual and will require regular practice. Finally, the counselor might explain that some discomfort may occur during the relaxation process. If so, the client can just move his or her body to a more comfortable position. Finally, the client may experience some floating, warming, or heavy sensations typical for some people learning muscle relaxation. The counselor should inform the client about these possible sensations. The rationale for muscle relaxation should be concluded by asking the client about willingness to try the procedure.

Instructions about dress.   Before the actual training session, the client should be instructed about appropriate clothing. The client should wear comfortable clothes such as slacks, a loose-fitting blouse or shirt, or any apparel that will not be distracting during the exercises. Clients who wear contact lenses should be told to wear their regular glasses for the training. They can take off the glasses while going through the exercises. It is uncomfortable to wear contact lenses when your eyes are closed.

Creation of a comfortable environment.   A comfortable environment is necessary for effective muscle-relaxation training. The training environment should be quiet and free of distracting noises such as telephone rings, workers outside breaking up the street, and airplane sounds. A padded recliner chair should be used if possible. If the counseling facility cannot afford one, an aluminum lawn chair or recliner covered with a foam pad may be satisfactory. If relaxation training is to be applied to groups, pads or blankets can be placed on the floor, with pillows used to support the head (Gershman & Clouser, 1974). The clients can lie on the floor on their backs, with their legs stretched out and their arms along their sides with palms down.

Counselor modeling of the relaxation exercises. Just before the relaxation training begins, the counselor should model briefly at least a few of the muscle exercises that will be used in training. The counselor can start with either the right or the left hand (make a fist, then relax the hand, opening the fingers; tense and relax the other hand; bend the wrists of both arms and relax them; shrug the shoulders and relax them) and continue demonstrating some of the rest of the exercises. The counselor should tell the client that the demonstration is going much faster than the speed at which the client will perform the exercises. The counselor should also punctuate the demonstration with comments like "When I clench my biceps like this, I feel the tension in my biceps muscles, and now, when I relax and drop my arms to my side, I notice the difference between the tension that was in my biceps and the relative relaxation I feel now." These comments are used to model discriminating the contrast between tension and relaxation.

Instructions for muscle relaxation.   Muscle-relaxation training can start after the counselor has given the client the rationale for the procedure, answered any questions about relaxation training, instructed the client about what to wear, created a comfortable environment for the training, and modeled some of the various muscle-group exercises. In delivering (or reading) the instructions for the relaxation training exercises, the counselor's voice should be conversational, not dramatic. Goldfried and Davison (1976) recommend that the counselor practice along with the client during the beginning exercises. Practicing initial relaxation exercises with the client can give the counselor a sense of timing for delivering the verbalizations of relaxing and tension and may decrease any awkwardness the client feels about doing "body type" exercises.

In instructing the client to tense and relax muscles, remember that you do *not* want to instruct the client to tense up as hard as possible. You do not want the client to strain a muscle. Be careful of your vocabulary when giving instructions. Do not use phrases like "as hard as you can," "sagging or drooping muscles," or "tense the muscles until they feel like they could snap." Sometimes you can supplement instructions to tense and relax with comments about the client's breathing or the experiencing of warm or heavy sensations. These comments may help the client to relax.

The various muscle groups used for client training can be categorized into 17 groups, 7 groups, or 4 groups. These sets of muscle groups, adapted from Bernstein and Borkovec (1973), are listed in Table 17-2. Generally, in initial training sessions, the counselor instructs the client to go through all 17 muscle groups. When the client can alternately tense and relax any of the 17 muscle groups on command, you can abbreviate this somewhat long procedure and train the client in relaxation using 7 muscle groups. After this process, the client can practice relaxation using only four major muscle groups. Start with either 17 or 7 muscle groups. This may help the client to discriminate sensations of tension and relaxation in different parts of the body. Then the number of muscle groups involved in the relaxation can be reduced gradually. When the client gets to the point of using the relaxation *in vivo,* 4 muscle groups are much less unwieldy than 17!

The following section illustrates how the counselor can instruct the client in relaxation using all 17 muscle groups. First, the counselor instructs the client to settle back as comfortably as possible — either in the recliner chair or on the floor with the head on a pillow. The arms can be alongside the body, resting on the arms of the chair or on the floor with the palms of the hands down. The counselor then instructs the client to close her or his eyes. In some instances, a client may not wish to do this; at other times, the counselor and the client may decide that it might be more therapeutic to keep the eyes open during the training. In such cases, the client can focus on some object in the room or on the ceiling. Tell the client to *listen* and to *focus* on your instructions. When presenting instructions for each muscle group, direct the client's attention to the tension, which is held for five to seven seconds, and then to the feelings of relaxation that follow when the client is instructed to relax. Allow about ten seconds for the client to enjoy the relaxation associated with each muscle group before delivering another instruction. Intermittently throughout the instructions, make muscle-group comparisons — for example, "Is your forehead as relaxed as your biceps?" While delivering the instructions, gradually lower your voice and slow the pace of delivery. Usually in initial training sessions, each muscle group is presented twice.

Here is a way the counselor might proceed with initial training in muscle relaxation, using the list of 17 muscle groups in Table 17-2 (adapted from a relaxation tape recording by Lazarus, 1970):

1. *Fist of dominant hand.* "First think about your right arm, your right hand in particular. Clench your right fist. Clench it tightly and study the tension in the hand and in the forearm. Study those sensations of tension. [Pause.] Now let go. Just relax the right hand and let it rest on the arm of the chair [or floor]. [Pause.] And note the difference between the tension and the relaxation." [Ten-second pause.]

2. *Fist of nondominant hand.* "Now we'll do the same with your left hand. Clench your left fist. Notice the tension [five-second pause] and now relax. Enjoy the difference between the tension and the relaxation." [Ten-second pause.]

3. *Wrist of one or both arms.* The counselor can instruct the client to bend the wrists of both arms at the same time or to bend each separately. You might start with the dominant arm if you instruct the client to bend the wrists one at a time. "Now bend both hands back at the wrists so that you tense the muscles in the back of the hand and in the forearm. Point your fingers toward the ceiling. Study the tension, and now relax. [Pause.] Study the difference between tension and relaxation." [Ten-second pause.]

4. *Biceps.* The counselor can instruct the client to work with both biceps or just one at a time. If you train the client to do one at a time, start with the dominant biceps. The instructions for this exercise are "Now clench both your hands into fists and bring them toward your shoulders. As you do this, tighten your biceps muscles, the ones in the upper part of your arm. Feel the tension in these muscles. [Pause.] Now relax. Let your arms drop down to your sides. See the difference between the tension and the relaxation." [Ten-second pause.]

5. *Shoulders.* Usually the client is instructed to shrug both shoulders. However, the client could be instructed to shrug one shoulder at a time. "Now we'll move to the shoulder area. Shrug your shoulders. Bring them up to your ears. Feel and hold the tension in your shoulders. [Pause.] Now, let both shoulders relax. Note the contrast between the tension

TABLE 17-2. Relaxation exercises for 17, 7, and 4 muscle groups (from *Progressive relaxation training,* by D. Bernstein and T. Borkovec. Copyright 1973 by Research Press. Used by permission.)

17 muscle groups	*7 muscle groups*	*4 muscle groups*
1. Clenching *fist* of dominant *hand.* 2. Clenching *fist* of nondominant *hand.* 3. Bending *wrist* of one or both arms. 4. Clenching *biceps* (one at a time or together). 5. Shrugging *shoulders* (one at a time or together). 6. Wrinkling *forehead.* 7. Closing *eyes* tightly. 8. Pressing *tongue* or clenching *jaws.* 9. Pressing *lips* together. 10. Pressing *head* back (on chair or pillow). 11. Pushing *chin* into chest. 12. Arching *back.* 13. Inhaling and holding *chest muscles.* 14. Tightening *stomach* muscles. 15. Contracting *buttocks.*[a] 16. Stretching *legs.* 17. Pointing *toes* toward head.	1. Hold *dominant arm* in front with elbow bent at about 45-degree angle while making a *fist* (hand, lower arm, and biceps muscles). 2. Same exercise with *nondominant arm.* 3. Facial muscle groups. Wrinkle *forehead* (or frown), squint *eyes* wrinkle up *nose,* clench *jaws* or press *tongue* on roof of mouth, press *lips* or pull corners of mouth back. 4. Press or bury *chin* in chest (neck and throat). 5. *Chest, shoulders, upper back,* and *abdomen.* Take deep breath, hold it, pull shoulder blades back and together, while making stomach hard (pulling in). 6. *Dominant thigh, calf,* and *foot.* Lift foot off chair or floor slightly while pointing toes and turning foot inward. 7. Same as 6, with *nondominant thigh, calf,* and *foot.*	1. Right and left *arms, hands,* and *biceps* (same as 1 and 2 in 7-muscle group). 2. *Face* and *neck* muscles. Tense all *face* muscles (same as 3 and 4 in 7-muscle group) 3. *Chest, shoulders, back* and *stomach* muscles (same as 5 in 7-muscle group). 4. Both left and right upper *leg, calf,* and *foot* (combines 6 and 7 in 7-muscle group).

[a] This muscle group can be eliminated; its use is optional.

and the relaxation that's now in your shoulders." [Ten-second pause.]

6. *Forehead.* This and the next three exercises are for the facial muscles. The instructions for the forehead are "Now we'll work on relaxing the various muscles of the face. First, wrinkle up your forehead and brow. Do this until you feel your brow furrow. [Pause.] Now relax. Smooth out the forehead. Let it loosen up." [Ten-second pause.]

7. *Eyes.* The purpose of this exercise is for the client to contrast the difference between tension and relaxation for the muscles that control the movements of the eyes. "Now close your eyes tightly. Can you feel tension all around your eyes? [Five-second pause.] Now relax those muscles, noting the difference between the tension and the relaxation." [Ten-second pause.]

8. *Tongue or jaws.* You can instruct some clients to clench their jaws: "Now clench your jaws by biting your teeth together. Pull the corners of your mouth back. Study the tension in the jaws. [Five-second pause.] Relax your jaws now. Can you tell the difference between tension and relaxation in your jaw area?" [Ten-second pause.] This exercise may be difficult for some clients who wear dentures. An alternative exercise is to instruct them: "Press your tongue into the roof of your mouth. Note the tension within your mouth. [Five-second pause.] Relax your mouth and tongue now. Just concentrate on the relaxation." [Ten-second pause.]

9. *Pressing the lips together.* The last facial exercise involves the mouth and chin muscles. "Now press your lips together tightly. As you do this, notice the tension all around the mouth. [Pause.] Now relax those muscles around the mouth. Enjoy this relaxation in your mouth area and your entire face. [Pause.] Is your face as relaxed as your biceps [inter-muscle-group comparison]?"

10. *The head.* "Now we'll move to the neck muscles. Press your head back against your chair. Can you feel the tension in the back of your

neck and in your upper back? Hold the tension. [Pause.] Now let your head rest comfortably. Notice the difference. Keep on relaxing." [Pause.]

11. *Chin in chest.* This exercise focuses on the muscles in the neck, particularly the front of the neck. "Now continue to concentrate on the neck area. Bring your head forward. See whether you can bury your chin into your chest. Note the tension in the front of your neck. Now relax and let go." [Ten-second pause.]

12. *The back.* Be careful here—you don't want the client to get a sore back. "Now direct your attention to your upper back area. Arch your back as if you were sticking out your chest and stomach. Can you feel tension in your back? Study that tension. [Pause.] Now relax. Note the difference between the tension and the relaxation." [Ten-second pause.]

13. *Chest muscles.* Inhaling (filling the lungs) and holding the breath focuses the client's attention on the muscles in the chest and down into the stomach area. "Now take a deep breath, filling your lungs, and hold it. Feel the tension all through your chest and into your stomach area. Hold that tension. [Pause.] Now relax and let go. Let your breath out naturally. Enjoy the pleasant sensations." [Ten-second pause.]

14. *Stomach muscles.* "Now think about your stomach. Tighten up the muscles in your abdomen. Hold this. Make the stomach like a knot. Now relax. Loosen those muscles now. [Ten-second pause.] Is your stomach as relaxed as your back and chest [muscle-group comparison]?" An alternative instruction is to tell the client to "pull in your stomach" or "suck in your stomach."

15. *The buttocks.* Moving down to other areas of the body, the counselor instructs or coaches the client to tighten the buttocks. This muscle group is optional; with some clients, the counselor may delete it and move on to the legs. The model instructions are "Now tighten [tense or contract] your buttocks by pulling them together and pushing them into the floor [or chair]. Note the tension. And now relax. Let go and relax." [Ten-second pause.]

16. *Legs.* "I'd like you now to focus on your legs. Stretch both legs. Feel tension in the thighs. [Five-second pause.] Now relax. Study the difference again between tension in the thighs

and the relaxation you feel now." [Ten-second pause.]

17. *Toes.* "Now concentrate on your lower legs and feet. Tighten both calf muscles by pointing your toes toward your head. Pretend a string is pulling your toes up. Can you feel the pulling and the tension? Note that tension. [Pause.] Now relax. Let your legs relax deeply. Enjoy the difference between tension and relaxation." [Ten-second pause.]

After each muscle group has been tensed and relaxed twice, the counselor usually concludes relaxation training with a summary and review. The counselor goes through the review by listing each muscle group and asking the client to dispel any tension that is noted as the counselor names the muscle area. Here is an example:

"Now, I'm going to go over once more the muscle groups that we've covered. As I name each group, try to notice whether there is any tension in those muscles. If there is any, try to concentrate on those muscles and tell them to relax. Think of draining the tension completely out of your body as we do this. Now relax the muscles in your feet, ankles, and calves. [Pause.] Get rid of tension in your knees and thighs. [Five-second pause.] Loosen your hips. [Pause.] Let the muscles of your lower body go. [Pause.] Relax your abdomen, waist, lower back. [Pause.] Drain the tension from your upper back, chest, and shoulders. [Pause.] Relax your upper arms, forearms, and hands. Loosen the muscles of your throat and neck. [Pause.] Relax your face. [Pause.] Let all the tension drain out of your body. [Pause.] Now just sit quietly with your eyes closed."

The therapist can conclude the training session by evaluating the client's level of relaxation on a scale from 0 to 5 or by counting aloud to the client to instruct him or her to become successively more alert. For example:

"Now I'd like you to think of a scale from 0 to 5, where 0 is complete relaxation and 5 is extreme tension. Tell me where you would place yourself on that scale now."
"I'm going to count from 5 to 1. When I reach the count of 1, open your eyes. 5 . . . 4 . . . 3 . . . 2 . . . 1. Open your eyes now."

Posttraining assessment. After the session of relaxation training has been completed, the counselor asks the client about the experience. The counselor can ask "What is your reaction to the procedure?", "How do you feel?", "What reaction did you have when you focused on the tension?", "What about relaxation?", or "How did the contrast between the tension and relaxation feel?" The counselor should be encouraging about the client's performance, praise the client, and build a positive expectancy set about the training and practice.

People experiencing relaxation training may have several problems (Bernstein & Borkovec, 1973). Some of these potential problem areas are cramps, excessive laughter or talking, spasms or tics, intrusive thoughts, falling asleep, inability to relax individual muscle groups, and unfamiliar sensations. If the client experiences muscle cramps, possibly too much tension is being created in the particular muscle group. In this case, the counselor can instruct the client to decrease the amount of tension. If spasms and tics occur in certain muscle groups, the counselor can mention that these occur commonly, as in one's sleep, and possibly the reason the client is aware of them now is that he or she is awake. Excessive laughter or talking would most likely occur in group-administered relaxation training. Possibly the best solution is to ignore it or to discuss how such behavior can be distracting.

The most common problem is for the client to fall asleep during relaxation training. The client should be informed that continually falling asleep can impede learning the skills associated with muscle relaxation. By watching the client throughout training, the counselor can confirm whether the client is awake.

If the client has difficulty or is unable to relax a particular muscle group, the counselor and client might work out an alternative exercise for that muscle group. If intrusive client thoughts become too distracting, the counselor might suggest changing the focus of the thought to something less distracting or to more positive or pleasant thoughts. It might be better for some clients to gaze at a picture of their choosing placed on the wall or ceiling throughout the training. Another strategy for dealing with interfering or distracting thoughts is to help the client use task-oriented coping statements or thoughts (see Chapter 16), which would facilitate focusing on the relaxation training.

The last potential problem is the occurrence of unfamiliar sensations, such as floating, warmth, and headiness. The counselor should point out that these sensations are common and that the client should not fear them. Bernstein and Borkovec (1973) provide a more detailed discussion of these potential problems and their possible solutions. The counselor need not focus on these problems unless they are reported by the client or noted by the counselor during a training session.

Homework and follow-up. The last step in muscle relaxation is assigning homework. Four or five therapist training sessions with two daily home practice sessions between therapy sessions are probably sufficient. Some therapists found that a minimal therapist contract with the client (2½ hours) and home-based relaxation training using manuals and audiotapes with telephone consultation (two times, ten minutes each) were just as effective in reducing tension headaches as six hours of therapist training (Teders et al., 1984). Regardless of the amount of time or number of therapist training sessions with the client, the therapist should inform the client that relaxation training, like learning any skill, requires a great deal of practice.

The more the client practices the procedure, the more proficient he or she will become in gaining control over tension, anxiety, or stress. The client should be instructed to select a quiet place for practice, free from distracting noise. The client should be encouraged to practice the muscle-relaxation exercises about 15 to 20 minutes twice a day. The exercises should be done when there is no time pressure. Some clients may not be willing to practice twice a day. The therapist can encourage these clients to practice several times or as often as they can during the week. The exercises can be done in a recliner chair or on the floor with a pillow supporting the head.

The client should be encouraged to complete a homework log after each practice. Figure 17-1 is an example of a homework log. Clients can rate their reactions on a scale from 1 (little or no tension) to 5 (extremely tense) before and after each practice. They can practice the relaxation exercises using a tape recording of the relaxation instructions or from memory. After client homework practices, a follow-up session should be scheduled.

There are several techniques a therapist can use to promote client compliance with relaxation homework assignments. One technique is to ask the client to demonstrate during the therapy session how the exercises for the muscles in the neck or the calf, for example, were done during last week's home practice. The counselor can select randomly from four or five muscle groups for the client to demonstrate. If the exercises are demon-

HOMEWORK LOG SHEET

DATE	TAPE NUMBER	ALL MUSCLE GROUPS EXERCISED. TONE PRESENT FOR WHICH MUSCLE GROUP	PRACTICE SESSION NUMBER	LOCATION OF SESSION	LEVEL OF TENSION (1–5)	
					BEFORE SESSION	AFTER SESSION

Note: 1 = slightly or not tense; 2 = somewhat tense; 3 = moderately tense; 4 = very tense; 5 = extremely tense.

Figure 17-1. *Example of homework log sheet for relaxation training*

strated accurately, the client probably practiced. The "cue-tone compliance procedure" (Martin, Collins, Hillenberg, Zabin, & Katell, 1981) is an objective measure of client compliance. The technique involves recording cue tones on some audiotaped relaxation exercises and not on other tapes. The cue tones can be recorded for randomly selected exercises on the tape and not for others. The tapes are numbered, and the client is instructed to listen to different tapes for the two daily practice sessions. The client is instructed to listen to a different tape during each practice session and to record on the homework log sheet whether she or he heard the tone and for which exercises. The cue-tone compliance technique does not appear to interfere with relaxation (Collins, Martin, & Hillenberg, 1982). After client homework practices, a follow-up session should be scheduled. Agras, Schneider, and Taylor (1984) found that routine booster sessions may be more effective than retraining when a client relapse occurs after initial relaxation training.

Variations of the Muscle-Relaxation Procedure

There are several variations of the muscle-relaxation training procedure as we've described it. These variations, which include recall, counting, and differential relaxation, are arranged and designed in successive approximations from the counselor assisting the client to acquire the skills to the client applying the relaxation skills in real-life situations. The four-muscle-group exercises listed in Table 17-2 can be used in combination with the recall and counting procedures described by Bernstein and Borkovec (1973).

Recall. Recall proceeds according to the relaxation exercises for the four muscle groups (Table 17-2) without muscular tension. The counselor first instructs the client about the rationale for using this variation of relaxation training: "to increase your relaxation skills without the need to tense up the muscles." The client is asked to focus on each muscle group. Then the counselor instructs the client to focus on one of the four muscle groups (arms; face and neck; chest, shoulders, back, and stomach; legs and feet) and to relax and just recall what it was like when the client released the tension (in the previous session) for that particular muscle group. The counselor might suggest that if there is tension in a particular muscle group, the client should just relax or send a message for the muscle to relax and should allow what tension there is to "flow out." The counselor gives similar instructions for all four muscle groups. Again, the client is to recall what the relaxation felt like for each muscle group. Recall can generally be used after first using the tension/relaxation-contrast procedure for the four muscle groups. Gradually, the client can use recall to induce relaxation in self-directed practices. Recall can also be used in combination with counting.

An example of a recall procedure follows. This procedure can also be used as an induction aid in hypnosis.

"I'm going to help you relax even more deeply now. Just go along with the things I suggest . . . and you will experience a much deeper sense of relaxation . . . you will enjoy the experience . . . just listen to what I say . . . and let things happen. Now feel this relaxation coming into the small muscles around the eyes . . . they are feeling so relaxed that presently . . . the eyelids will feel heavy . . . very heavy . . . like lead shutters . . . almost too heavy to move . . . feeling as though they are glued together . . . and you feel this relaxation spreading outward . . . just as ripples spread out on a still pool when the water is disturbed . . . spreading out into the muscles of the face . . . so that your jaw feels relaxed and your lips part a little . . . into the forehead and scalp . . . the neck . . . notice how your head feels so heavy and relaxed . . . so comfortable against the back of the chair . . . the shoulders feel quite limp and relaxed . . . the arms are relaxing . . . heavy . . . loose and floppy by your side . . . from your shoulders right through to the tips of your fingers. Your back, too, is becoming more and more relaxed . . . sinking deeply into the chair . . . especially the small of your back . . . your muscles in your stomach and your chest are relaxing more and more . . . notice that each time you breathe out . . . you go deeper and deeper into this pleasant relaxed state . . . notice this, just let yourself be aware of this . . . don't try to do anything . . . and now your legs are gradually letting go of all the tension as well . . . all through your hips . . . your thighs . . . your knees . . . calf muscles . . . even the ankles and feet are relaxing. You feel as though all the tension within you . . . is flowing out through your toes . . . and being replaced by this very pleasant feeling of relaxation. As this grows you'll also become more aware of how fleeting and unimportant all of your thoughts are . . . aware of the quiet deep within you . . . the quiet" [Clarke & Jackson, 1983, pp. 83–84].*

* From J. Christopher Clarke and J. Arthur Jackson, *Hypnosis and behavior therapy: The treatment of anxiety and phobias*, pp. 83–84. Copyright © 1983 by Springer Publishing Company, Inc., New York. Used by permission.

Counting.   The rationale for counting is that it helps the client become very deeply relaxed. Again, the counselor explains the rationale for using counting. The counselor says that she or he will count from one to ten and that this will help the client to become more relaxed after each number. The counselor might say slowly:

"One—you are becoming more relaxed; two—notice that your arms and hands are becoming more and more relaxed; three—feel your face and neck becoming more relaxed; four, five—more and more relaxed are your chest and shoulders; six—further and further relaxed; seven—back and stomach feel deeply relaxed; eight—further and further relaxed; nine—your legs and feet are more and more relaxed; ten—just continue to relax as you are—relax more and more."

The counselor can use this counting procedure with recall. The client can also be instructed to use counting in real situations that provoke tension. For a more detailed presentation of counting, see Bernstein and Borkovec (1973) and Goldfried and Davison (1976). As you may remember from Chapter 16, counting is one type of direct-action coping skill used in stress inoculation. Counting can increase relaxation and decrease tension, and the client should be encouraged to practice it outside the session.

Differential relaxation.   This variation may contribute to generalization of the relaxation training from the treatment session to the client's world. The purpose of differential relaxation is to help the client recognize what muscles are needed in various situations, body positions, and activities in order to differentiate which muscle groups are used and which are not. Table 17-3 illustrates some possible levels for the differential-relaxation procedure.

As an example of differential relaxation, the counselor might have the client sit in a regular chair (not a recliner) and ask the client to identify which muscles are used and which are not when

TABLE 17-3. Levels of differential-relaxation procedure

Situation	Body position	Activity level
Quiet	Sitting	Low—inactive
Noisy	Standing	High—routine movements

sitting. If tension is felt in muscles that are not used (face, legs, and stomach), the client is instructed to induce and to maintain relaxation in the muscles not required for what the client is doing (sitting). The counselor can instruct the client to engage in different levels of the differential-relaxation procedure—for example, sitting down in a quiet place while inactive, or standing up. After several practice sessions, the client can be assigned homework to engage in various levels of these activities. Examples might be sitting in a quiet cafeteria, sitting in a noisy cafeteria while eating, standing in line for a ticket to some event, or walking in a busy shopping center. In practicing differential relaxation, the client tries to recognize whether any tension exists in the nonessential muscle groups. If there is tension in the nonengaged muscles, the client concentrates on dispelling it.

☐ MODEL DIALOGUE: MUSCLE RELAXATION

In this dialogue, the counselor demonstrates relaxation training to help Joan deal with her physical sensations of nervousness.

First, the counselor gives Joan a **rationale** *for relaxation. The counselor explains the* **purpose** *of muscle relaxation and gives Joan a brief* **overview** *of the procedure.*

1. *Counselor:* Basically, we all learn to carry around some body tension. Some is OK. But in a tense spot, usually your body is even more tense, although you may not realize this. If you can learn to recognize muscle tension and relax your muscles, this state of relaxation can help to decrease your nervousness or anxiety. What we'll do is to help you recognize when your body is relaxed and when it is tense, by deliberately tensing and relaxing different muscle groups in your body. We should get to the point where, later on, you can recognize the sensations that mean tension and use these as a signal to yourself to relax. Does this make sense?
   Client: I think so. You'll sort of tell me how to do this?

Next, the counselor will **"set up" the relaxation by attending to details about the room** *and the client's comfort.*

2. *Counselor:* Yes. At first I'll show you so you can get the idea of it. One thing we need to do before we start is for you to get as comfortable as possible. So that you won't be distracted by light, I'm going to turn off the light. If you are wearing your contact lenses, take them out if they're uncomfortable, because you may feel more comfortable if you go through this with your eyes closed. Also, I use a special chair for this. You know the straight-backed chair you're sitting on can seem like a rock after a time. That might distract, too. So I have a padded chaise you can use for this. [Gets lounge chair out.]
   Client (sits in chaise): Umm. This really is comfortable.

Next the counselor begins **to model the muscle relaxation** *for Joan. This shows Joan how to do it and may alleviate any embarrassment on her part.*

3. *Counselor:* Good. That really helps. Now I'm going to show you how you can tense and then relax your muscles. I'll start first with my right arm. [Clenches right fist, pauses and notes tension, relaxes fist, pauses and notes relaxation; models several other muscle groups.] Does this give you an idea?
   Client: Yes. You don't do your whole body?

The counselor provides **further information about muscle relaxation, describes sensations** *Joan might feel, and checks to see whether Joan is completely clear on the procedure before going ahead.*

4. *Counselor:* Yes, you do. But we'll take each muscle group separately. By the time you tense and relax each muscle group, your whole body will feel relaxed. You will feel like you are "letting go," which is very important when you tense up—to let go rather than to tense even more. Now, you might not notice a lot of difference right away—but you might. You might even feel like you're floating. This really depends on the person. The most important thing is to remain as comfortable as possible while I'm instructing you. Do you have any questions before we begin, anything you don't quite understand?
   Client: I don't think so. I think that this is maybe a little like yoga.

The counselor proceeds with **instructions to alternately tense and relax** *each of 17 muscle groups.*

5. *Counselor:* Right. It's based on the same idea—learning to soothe away body tension. OK, get very comfortable in your chair and we'll begin. [Gives Joan several minutes to get comfortable, then uses the relaxation instructions. Most of the session is spent in instructing Joan in muscle relaxation as illustrated on pp. 459–462.]

After the relaxation, the counselor **queries Joan** *about her feelings during and after the relaxation. It is important to find out how the relaxation affected the client.*

6. *Counselor:* OK, Joan, how do you feel now?
   Client: Pretty relaxed.
7. *Counselor:* How did the contrast between the tensed and relaxed muscles feel?
   Client: It was pretty easy to tell. I guess sometimes my body is pretty tense and I don't think about it.

The counselor assigns **relaxation practice** *to Joan as* **daily homework.**

8. *Counselor:* As I mentioned before, this takes regular practice in order for you to use it when you need it— and to really notice the effects. I have put these instructions on this audiotape, and I'd like you to practice with this tape two times each day during the next week. Do the practice in a quiet place at a time when you don't feel pressured, and use a comfortable place when you do practice. Do you have any questions about the practice?
   Client: No, I think I understand.

Counselor **explains the use of the log.**

9. *Counselor:* Also, I'd like you to use a log sheet with your practice. Mark down where you practice, how long you practice, what muscle groups you use, and your tension level before and after each practice on this 5-point scale. Remember, 0 is complete relaxation and 5 is complete or extreme tension. Let's go over an example of how you use the log. . . . Now, any questions?
   Client: No. I can see this will take some practice.

Finally, the counselor arranges a **follow-up.**

10. *Counselor:* Right, it really is like learning any other skill—it doesn't just come automatically. Why don't you try this on your own for two weeks and then come back, OK?

LEARNING ACTIVITY #46: MUSCLE RELAXATION

Because muscle relaxation involves the alternate tensing and relaxing of a variety of muscle groups, it is sometimes hard to learn the procedure well enough to use it with a client. We have found that the easiest way to learn this is to do muscle relaxation yourself. Using it not only helps you learn what is involved but also may have some indirect benefits for you—increased relaxation!

This learning activity is designed for you to apply the muscle-relaxation procedure you've just read about to yourself. You can do this by yourself or with a partner. You may wish to try it out alone and then with someone else.

By Yourself

1. Get in a comfortable position, wear loose clothing, and remove your glasses or contact lenses
2. Use the written instructions in this chapter to practice muscle relaxation. This can be done by putting the instructions on tape or by reading the instructions to yourself. Go through the procedure quickly to get a feel for the process; then do it again slowly without trying to rely too much on having to read the instructions. As you go through the relaxation, study the differences between tension and relaxation.
3. Try to assess your reactions after the relaxation.

On a scale from 0 to 5 (0 being very relaxed and 5 being very tense), how relaxed do you feel? Were there any particular muscle groups that were hard for you to contract or relax?

4. One or two times through muscle relaxation is not enough to learn it or to notice any effects. Try to practice this procedure on yourself once or twice daily over the next several weeks.

With a Partner

One of you can take the role of a helper; the other can be the person learning relaxation. Switch roles so you can practice helping someone else through the procedure and trying it out on yourself.

1. The helper should begin by giving an explanation and a rationale for muscle relaxation and any instructions about it before you begin.
2. The helper can read the instructions on muscle relaxation to you. The helper should give you ample time to tense and relax each muscle group and should encourage you to note the different sensations associated with tension and relaxation.
3. After going through the process, the helper should query you about your relaxation level and your reactions to the process.

□ SUMMARY

In this chapter we described two meditation strategies and a procedure for muscle relaxation. A combination of the relaxation response and the Zen meditation strategies or the clinically standardized meditation strategy presented in this chapter can be used as an informal meditation procedure applied in one's natural environment. There are contraindications and adverse effects of meditation for some clients. The muscle-relaxation strategy can be used with 17, 7, or 4 muscle groups. Three variations of muscle relaxation were presented: recall, counting, and differential relaxation. All these strategies are often used as a single treatment to prevent stress and to deal with stress-related situations. In addition, these strategies may be used to countercondition anxiety as part of another therapeutic procedure called "systematic desensitization," which is presented in the next chapter.

POSTEVALUATION

PART ONE

For Objective One, you will be able to identify accurately the steps of the relaxation response/Zen meditation procedure represented by at least eight out of ten examples of counselor instructive responses. On paper, for each of the following counselor responses, identify which part of the meditation procedure is being implemented. There may be more than one counselor response associated with a part. These examples are not in any particular order. The eight major parts of meditation are as follows:

1. Rationale.
2. Selection of a mental device.
3. Instructions for body comfort.
4. Breathing and word instruction.
5. Instruction about passive attitude.
6. Meditating for 10 to 20 minutes.
7. Probing about the meditative experience.
8. Homework and practice.

Feedback for the Postevaluation follows on pages 478–479.

1. "It is very important that you practice this at home regularly. Usually there are no effects without regular practice — about twice daily."
2. "One position you may want to use is to sit on the floor Indian-style — crossing your legs and keeping your back straight. If this feels uncomfortable, then just assume any sitting position that is comfortable for you."
3. "This procedure has been used to help people with high blood pressure and people who have trouble sleeping and just as a general stress-reduction process."
4. "Breathe through your nose and focus on your breathing. If you can concentrate on one word as you do this, it may be easier."
5. "Be sure to practice at a quiet time when you don't think you'll be interrupted. And do not practice within two hours after a meal or within two hours before going to bed."
6. "Just continue now to meditate like this for 10 or 15 minutes. Sit quietly then for several minutes after you're finished."
7. "The procedure involves learning to focus on your breathing while sitting in a quiet place. Sometimes concentrating on just one word may help you do this. You continue to do this for about 15 minutes each time."
8. "How easy or hard was this for you to do?"
9. "There may be times when other images or thoughts come into your mind. Try to just maintain a passive attitude. If you're bothered by other thoughts, don't dwell on them, but don't force them away. Just focus on your breathing and your word."
10. "Pick a word like *one* or *zum* that you can focus on — something neutral to you."

PART TWO

Objective Two asks you to identify accurately the steps for the clinically standardized meditation procedure represented by at least six out of eight counselor instructive responses. Do this on paper. There may be more than one response for a given step. The counselor examples are not in order. The six major steps of CSM are as follows:

1. Rationale.
2. Selection of a mantra or sound.
3. Preparation for meditation.
4. Instructions to meditate.
5. Discussion of client's reaction to first meditation.
6. Homework and practice.

Feedback follows.

(continued)

1. "Meditation has benefited people by reducing tension, anxiety, stress, and headaches."
2. "Meditate for three weeks and at the same times twice a day."
3. "Allow distracting thoughts to flow. Allow memories, images, and thoughts to occur. Don't try to influence them."
4. "Do not take any alcoholic beverages or nonprescription drugs for at least 24 hours before meditating."
5. "Think of a meaningless sound or word that has few associations and is not emotionally charged."
6. "Come out of meditation slowly. Sit with your eyes closed for two minutes — take time to absorb what is happening. Slowly open your eyes."
7. "First, close your eyes and say your mantra aloud, say it softly, then whisper it, and then think the sound to yourself without moving your lips."
8. "Do not chew gum while meditating. Face away from direct light in a dimly lit room."

PART THREE

Objective Three asks you to teach the process of meditation to another person. Select either relaxation response/Zen meditation or clinically standardized meditation to teach. You can have an observer evaluate you, or you can audiotape your teaching session and rate yourself. You can use the Interview Checklist for Relaxation Response and Zen Meditation or the Interview Checklist for Clinically Standardized Meditation that follows as a teaching guide and evaluation tool.

PART FOUR

Objective Four asks you to describe how you would apply the seven major parts of the muscle-relaxation procedure. Using this client description and the seven questions following it, describe how you would use certain parts of the procedure with this person. You can check your responses with the feedback that follows.

Description of client: The client is a middle-aged man who is concerned about his inability to sleep at night. He has tried sleeping pills but does not want to rely on medication.

1. Give an example of a rationale you could use about the procedure. Include the purpose and an overview of the strategy.
2. Give a brief example of instructions you might give this client about appropriate dress for relaxation training.
3. List any special environmental factors that may affect the client's use of muscle relaxation.
4. Describe how you might model some of the relaxation exercises for the client.
5. Describe some of the important muscle groups that you would instruct the client to tense and relax alternately.
6. Give two examples of probes you might use with the client after relaxation to assess his use of and reactions to the process.
7. What instructions about a homework assignment (practice of relaxation) would you give to this client?

PART FIVE

Objective Five asks you to demonstrate 13 out of 15 steps of muscle relaxation with a role-play client. An observer or the client can assess your performance, or you can assess yourself, using the Interview Checklist for Muscle Relaxation on pages 473–477.

INTERVIEW CHECKLIST FOR RELAXATION RESPONSE AND ZEN MEDITATION

Instructions: Determine which of the following counselor leads or questions were demonstrated in the interview. Check each of the leads used by the counselor. Some examples of counselor leads are provided in the right column.

Item	Examples of counselor leads
I. Rationale	
_____ 1. Counselor describes purpose of procedure.	"I would like to teach you a mental exercise called the relaxation response, or meditation. The relaxation response has been used to relieve fatigue caused by anxiety, to decrease stress that can lead to high blood pressure, and to help people who have difficulty getting to sleep at night. It can be used to have you become more relaxed. The procedure helps you become more relaxed and deal more effectively with your tension and stress. It may give you a new awareness."

(continued)

POSTEVALUATION (continued)

Item	Examples of counselor leads
_____ 2. Counselor gives client an overview.	"What we will do first is select a focusing device, or mental device. You will then get into a relaxed and comfortable position. Afterward, I will instruct you about focusing on your breathing and using your mental device. We will talk about a passive attitude while meditating. You will meditate about 10 to 20 minutes. Then, we will talk about the experience."
_____ 3. Counselor confirms client's willingness to use strategy.	"How do you feel now about working with meditation?"

II. Selecting a Mental Device

_____ 4. Counselor provides rationale for mental device.	"First, we want to select a mental device. It is a word, syllable, or phrase that helps you focus on breathing, and by repeating it you can become free of distracting thoughts or images."
_____ 5. Counselor gives examples of mental devices.	"Examples of a mental device are *one, zum, in, Rama*. Think of something you can say to yourself that is easy and will be fairly neutral to you."

III. Instructions about Body Comfort

_____ 6. Counselor conducts meditation training in quiet environment.	"We want to meditate in a quiet environment, free of distractions and interruption."
_____ 7. Counselor tells client to close eyes and get into comfortable position.	"There are several ways to meditate. I'll show you one. I want you to get into a comfortable position while you are sitting there. Now, close your eyes."
_____ 8. Counselor instructs client to relax major muscle groups.	"Relax all the muscles in your body — relax [said slowly] your head, face, neck, shoulders, chest, your torso, thighs, calves, and your feet. Keep all your muscles relaxed."

IV. Instructions about Breathing and Use of Mental Device

_____ 9. Counselor instructs client to focus on breathing and to use mental device with each inhalation and exhalation.	"Breathe through your nose and focus on [or become aware of] your breathing. It is sometimes difficult to be natural when you are doing this. Just let the air come to you. Breathe easily and naturally. As you do this, say your mental device for each inhalation and exhalation. Say your mental device silently to yourself each time you breathe in and out."

V. Instructions about Passive Attitude

_____10. Counselor instructs client to maintain passive attitude and to allow relaxation to occur at its own pace. Client is also instructed, if attention wanders and unrelated images and thoughts occur that take away from breathing, not to dwell on them but return to repeating mental device.	"Be calm and passive. If distracting thoughts or images occur, attempt to be passive about them by not dwelling on them. Return to repeating the mental device. Try to achieve effortless breathing. After more practice, you will be able to examine these thoughts or images with greater detachment." "After a while, you may become aware that you were busy with distracting thoughts or images and you have not said your mental device for a couple of minutes. When this happens, just return to saying your word. Do not attempt to keep the thoughts out of your mind; just let them pass through. Keep your mind open — don't try to solve problems or think things over. Allow the thoughts to flow smoothly into your mind and then drift out. Say your mental device and relax. Don't get upset with distracting thoughts. Just return to your mental device."

(continued)

Item	Examples of counselor leads

VI. Instructions to Meditate for 10 to 20 Minutes

_____11. Counselor is instructed to meditate for 10 to 20 minutes. Counselor instructs client on what to do after meditative session.

"Continue to meditate for about 10 [15 or 20] minutes. You can open your eyes to check on the time. After you have finished, sit quietly for several minutes. You may wish to keep your eyes closed for a couple of minutes and later open them. You may not want to stand up for a few minutes."

VII. Probe about the Meditative Experience

_____12. Counselor asks client about experience with meditation.

"How do you feel about the experience?"
"What sort of thoughts or images flowed through your mind?"
"What did you do when the distracting thoughts drifted in?"
"How did you feel about your mental device?"

VIII. Homework and Follow-up

_____13. Formal meditation: Counselor instructs client to practice formal meditation (relaxation response) once or twice a day at home or at work. Counselor cautions client not to meditate within two hours after a meal or within a couple of hours before bedtime.

"Practice meditation [relaxation response] two times a day. Like anything else we are trying to learn, you will become better with practice. You can do it at work or at home. Get comfortable in your meditative [relaxation-response] position. Practice in a quiet place away from noise and interruptions. Do not use meditation [relaxation response] as a substitute for sleep. Usually, meditation before sleep might make you feel very awake. Also, do not meditate within two hours after a meal or within a couple of hours before bedtime. Keep a log for each meditative experience, including where it was used and time of day used, and rate each use on a 5-point scale."

_____14. Informal meditation: Counselor instructs client to apply informal meditation _in vivo_.

"Also, I think it would be helpful for you to apply an informal meditation in problem or stressful situations that may occur daily. The way you can do this is, when in the situation, be detached and passive. Observe yourself and focus on being calm and on your breathing. Be relaxed in the situations that evoke stress. How does that sound?"

_____15. Counselor schedules follow-up session.

"After you have practiced the homework daily for the next two weeks, bring in your logs and we'll see what has happened."

Observer comments: _____

INTERVIEW CHECKLIST FOR CLINICALLY STANDARDIZED MEDITATION (CSM)

Instructions: Indicate by a check mark each counselor lead demonstrated in the interview. Example leads are provided in the right column.

Item	Examples of counselor leads

I. Rationale

_____ 1. Counselor describes purpose of procedure.

"I would like to teach you a simple relaxation exercise. People who have used this procedure have reduced tension and stress, headaches, anxiety, and the time it takes to fall asleep. Meditation has been reported to increase athletic performance

(continued)

POSTEVALUATION (continued)

Item	Examples of counselor leads
	and energy. People have also reported that they are more alert and closer to their feelings and have clearer thinking when they use meditation."
_____ 2. Counselor gives client an overview of procedure.	"If you want to use meditation as a relaxation method, you will select a soothing sound (mantra) that you will use. You will close your eyes, say the sound, and be in a quiet environment, and you will allow your images and thoughts to flow freely. You will meditate for about five to ten minutes. Then we will talk about the experience."
_____ 3. Counselor confirms client's willingness to use strategy.	"How do you feel about using this strategy?"

II. Selection of a Mantra, or Sound

Item	Examples of counselor leads
_____ 4. Counselor helps client select a sound and gives the reason for using the sound.	"Before we begin, we want to select a sound. The type of sound or word we want is one that has few associations and is not emotionally charged for you. The sound should be soothing to you. The mantra, or sound, helps you not to become distracted by other thoughts."
_____ 5. Counselor gives examples of sounds.	"Some examples of a sound are *shaham, rama,* and *gome.* Think of a sound you can say to yourself that is neutral and soothing."

III. Instructions about Preparation for Meditation

Item	Examples of counselor leads
_____ 6. Counselor conducts meditation training in quiet environment free from distractions and interruptions.	"We want to meditate in a quiet environment free of distractions and interruptions. If you decide to use meditation, you want to select a quiet place at home."
_____ 7. Counselor instructs client about alcoholic beverages, nonprescription drugs, beverages with caffeine, eating, smoking, and chewing gum.	"When you meditate, you don't want to do things that might interfere with meditation. For example, you should not take any alcoholic beverages or nonprescription drugs at least 24 hours before meditation. And you should not meditate right after you consume solid food or beverages containing caffeine. If you do these things, wait an hour before you meditate. Finally, do not chew gum while meditating."
_____ 8. Counselor instructs client about sitting, focusing away from light, and loosening tight shoes.	"Before we meditate, get comfortable in the chair, and if your shoes feel tight, loosen them. If you decide to meditate at home, you will want to wear comfortable clothing."

IV. Instructions to Meditate

Item	Examples of counselor leads
_____ 9. Counselor instructs client about sitting quietly and relaxed for a minute.	"Sit quietly for a while — just relax — don't say your sound yet."
_____10. Counselor instructs client to close eyes, to say aloud the sound, to say it softly, to whisper, and then to think the sound without moving lips or tongue.	"Close your eyes and say your sound aloud. Then say it softly. Now whisper your sound. [Allow the client to say aloud, say softly, and whisper several times for each.] Think your sound without moving your lips or tongue."
_____11. Counselor tells client that CSM is not a discipline and to allow distracting thoughts to flow.	"Remember that meditation is not an exercise in discipline — it is a quiet, peaceful time with yourself. It does not require effort. Don't force it. If distracting thoughts, memories, or images occur, allow them to come. Don't try to influence them. Your sound will return to you."
_____12. Counselor tells client that she or he will meditate for about five to ten minutes.	"I will keep time and have you meditate for about five to ten minutes. I will tell you when to stop. When you meditate alone, you can open your eyes to check the time periodically."

(continued)

Item	Examples of counselor leads
___13. Counselor instructs client to come out of meditation slowly.	"Our time is about up. I want you to come out of meditation slowly. Sit with your eyes closed for two minutes — take time to experience and absorb what is happening. Open your eyes slowly."

V. Discussion of Client's Reaction to Meditation

___14. Counselor asks client about experience with meditation.	"How did you feel about your sound?" "How did you feel about CSM?" "What thoughts, images, or memories flowed through your mind?" "How did your sound return to you?"

VI. Homework and Follow-up

___15. Counselor instructs client to meditate at home two times a day, once after getting up in the morning and once during late afternoon or early evening. Reminds client about preparations for meditation.	"Practice meditation two times a day, once after getting up in the morning and later in late afternoon or early evening. Remember the things to do to prepare for meditation. Select a quiet environment without distractions. Do not take any alcoholic beverages or nonprescription drugs at least 24 hours before meditating. Wait for an hour before meditating after eating solid foods or drinking beverages containing caffeine. Do not smoke half an hour before meditating. Select a comfortable chair away from direct light. Meditate in the same place and the same time each day. Keep a log of each meditative experience — where you used it, time of day, and rating on a 5-point scale."
___16. Informal meditation: counselor instructs client about informal meditation in stressful situations.	"You can meditate informally when you are in stressful situations that may occur daily. Just relax and say the sound to yourself, and you'll find how peaceful the situation will become."
___17. Counselor schedules follow-up session.	"After you have practiced a couple of times a day at home for a week, bring your log in and we'll discuss your home meditative experiences."

Observer comments: _____

_____

_____

INTERVIEW CHECKLIST FOR MUSCLE RELAXATION

Instructions: Indicate with a check mark each counselor lead demonstrated in the interview. Some example leads are provided in the right column.

Item	Examples of counselor leads
I. Rationale	
___ 1. Counselor explains purpose of muscle relaxation.	"The name of the strategy that I believe will be helpful is *muscle relaxation*. Muscle relaxation has been used very effectively to benefit people who have a variety of concerns like insomnia, high blood pressure, anxiety, or stress or for people who are bothered by everyday tension. Muscle relaxation will be helpful in decreasing your tension. It will benefit you because you will be able to control and to dispel tension that interferes with your daily activities."

(continued)

POSTEVALUATION (continued)

Item	Examples of counselor leads
_____ 2. Counselor gives overview of how muscle relaxation works.	"What we will do is that I will ask you to tense up and relax various muscle groups. All of us have some tensions in our bodies—otherwise we could not stand, sit, or move around. Sometimes we have too much tension. By tensing and relaxing, you will become aware of and contrast the feelings of tension and relaxation. Later we will train you to send a message to a particular muscle group to relax when nonessential tension creeps in. You will learn to control your tension and relax when you feel tension."
_____ 3. Counselor describes muscle relaxation as a skill.	"Muscle relaxation is a skill. And, as in learning any skill, it will take a lot of practice to learn it well—a lot of repetition and training are needed to acquire the muscle-relaxation skill."
_____ 4. Counselor instructs client about moving around if uncomfortable and informs client of sensations that may feel unusual.	"At times during the training and muscle exercises, you may want to move while you are on your back on the floor [or on the recliner]. Just feel free to do this so that you can get more comfortable. You may also feel heady sensations as we go through the exercise. These sensations are not unusual. Do you have any questions concerning what I just talked about? If not, do you want to try this now?"

II. Client Dress

_____ 5. Counselor instructs client about what to wear for training session.	"For the next session, wear comfortable clothing." "Wear regular glasses instead of your contact lenses."

III. Comfortable Environment

_____ 6. Counselor uses quiet environment, padded recliner chair, or floor with a pillow under client's head.	"During training, I'd like you to sit in this recliner chair. It will be more comfortable and less distracting than this wooden chair."

IV. Modeling the Exercises

_____ 7. Counselor models some exercises for muscle groups.	"I would like to show you [some of] the exercises we will use in muscle relaxation. First, I make a fist to create tension in my right hand and forearm and then relax it. . . . ."

V. Instructions for Muscle Relaxation

_____ 8. Counselor reads or recites instructions from memory in conversational tone and practices along with client.	
_____ 9. Counselor instructs client to get comfortable, close eyes, and listen to instructions.	"Now, get as comfortable as you can, close your eyes, and listen to what I'm going to be telling you. I'm going to make you aware of certain sensations in your body and then show you how you can reduce these sensations to increase feelings of relaxation."
_____10. Counselor instructs client to tense and relax alternately each of the 17 muscle groups (*two* times for each muscle group in initial training). Also occasionally makes muscle-group comparisons.	

(continued)

Item	Examples of counselor leads
____a. Fist of dominant hand	"First study your right arm, your right hand in particular. Clench your right fist. Clench it tightly and study the tension in the hand and in the forearm. Study those sensations of tension. [Pause.] And now let go. Just relax the right hand and let it rest on the arm of the chair. [Pause.] And note the difference between the tension and the relaxation." [Ten-second pause.]
____b. Fist of nondominant hand	"Now we'll do the same with your left hand. Clench your left fist. Notice the tension [five-second pause] and now relax. Enjoy the difference between the tension and the relaxation." [Ten-second pause.]
____c. One or both wrists	"Now bend both hands back at the wrists so that you tense the muscles in the back of the hand and in the forearm. Point your fingers toward the ceiling. Study the tension, and now relax. [Pause.] Study the difference between tension and relaxation." [Ten-second pause.]
____d. Biceps of one or both arms	"Now, clench both your hands into fists and bring them toward your shoulders. As you do this, tighten your bicep muscles, the ones in the upper part of your arm. Feel the tension in these muscles. [Pause.] Now relax. Let your arms drop down again to your sides. See the difference between the tension and the relaxation." [Ten-second pause.]
____e. Shoulders	"Now we'll move to the shoulder area. Shrug your shoulders. Bring them up to your ears. Feel and hold the tension in your shoulders. Now, let both shoulders relax. Note the contrast between the tension and the relaxation that's now in your shoulders. [Ten-second pause.] Are your shoulders as relaxed as your arms?"
____f. Forehead	"Now we'll work on relaxing the various muscles of the face. First, wrinkle up your forehead and brow. Do this until you feel your brow furrow. [Pause.] Now relax. Smooth out the forehead. Let it loosen up." [Ten-second pause.]
____g. Eyes	"Now close your eyes tightly. Can you feel tension all around your eyes? [Five-second pause.] Now relax those muscles, noting the difference between the tension and the relaxation." [Ten-second pause.]
____h. Tongue or jaw	"Now clench your jaw by biting your teeth together. Pull the corners of your mouth back. Study the tension in the jaws. [Five-second pause.] Relax your jaws now. Can you tell the difference between tension and relaxation in your jaw area?" [Ten-second pause.]
____i. Lips	"Now, press your lips together tightly. As you do this, notice the tension all around the mouth. [Pause.] Now relax those muscles around the mouth. Just enjoy the relaxation in your mouth area and your entire face." [Pause.]
____j. Head backward	"Now we'll move to the neck muscles. Press your head back against your chair. Can you feel the tension in the back of your neck and in the upper back? Hold the tension. Now let your head rest comfortably. Notice the difference. Keep on relaxing." [Pause.]

(continued)

POSTEVALUATION (continued)

Item	Examples of counselor leads
____k. Chin in chest	"Now continue to concentrate on the neck area. See whether you can bury your chin into your chest. Note the tension in the front of your neck. Now relax and let go." [Ten-second pause.]
____l. Back	"Now direct your attention to your upper back area. Arch your back as if you were sticking out your chest and stomach. Can you feel tension in your back? Study that tension. [Pause.] Now relax. Note the difference between the tension and the relaxation."
____m. Chest muscles	"Now take a deep breath, filling your lungs, and hold it. See the tension all through your chest and into your stomach area. Hold that tension. [Pause.] Now relax and let go. Let your breath out naturally. Enjoy the pleasant sensations. Is your chest as relaxed as your back and shoulders?" [Ten-second pause.]
____n. Stomach muscles	"Now think about your stomach. Tighten the abdomen muscles. Hold this tension. Make your stomach like a knot. Now relax. Loosen these muscles now." [Ten-second pause.]
____o. Buttocks	"Focus now on your buttocks. Tense your buttocks by pulling them in or contracting them. Note the tension that is there. Now relax — let go." [Ten-second pause.]
____p. Legs	"I'd like you now to focus on your legs. Stretch both legs. Feel tension in the thighs. [Five-second pause.] Now relax. Study the difference again between the tension in the thighs and the relaxation you feel now." [Ten-second pause.]
____q. Toes	"Now concentrate on your lower legs and feet. Tighten both calf muscles by pointing your toes toward your head. Pretend a string is pulling your toes up. Can you feel the pulling and the tension? Note that tension. [Pause.] Now relax. Let your legs relax deeply. Enjoy the difference between tension and relaxation." [Ten-second pause.]
____11. Counselor instructs client to review and relax all muscle groups.	"Now, I'm going to go over again the different muscle groups that we've covered. As I name each group, try to notice whether there is any tension in those muscles. If there is any, try to concentrate on those muscles and tell them to relax. Think of draining any residual tension out of your body. Relax the muscles in your feet, ankles, and calves. [Pause.] Let go of your knee and thigh muscles. [Pause.] Loosen your hips. [Pause.] Loosen the muscles of your lower body. [Pause.] Relax all the muscles of your stomach, waist, lower back. [Pause.] Drain any tension from your upper back, chest, and shoulders. [Pause.] Relax your upper arms, forearms, and hands. [Pause.] Let go of the muscles in your throat and neck. [Pause.] Relax your face. [Pause.] Let all the muscles of your body become loose. Drain all the tension from your body. [Pause.] Now sit quietly with your eyes closed."

(continued)

Item	Examples of counselor leads
____12. Counselor asks client to rate relaxation level following training session.	"Now I'd like you to think of a scale from 0 to 5, where 0 is complete relaxation and 5 extreme tension. Tell me where you would place yourself on that scale now."

VI. Posttraining Assessment

____13. Counselor asks client about first session of relaxation training, discusses problems with training if client has any.	"How do you feel?" "What is your overall reaction to the procedure?" "Think back about what we did—did you have problems with any muscle group?" "What reaction did you have when you focused on the tension? What about relaxation?" "How did the contrast between the tension and relaxation feel?"

VII. Homework and Follow-up

____14. Counselor assigns homework and requests that client complete homework log for practice sessions.	"Relaxation training, like any skill, takes a lot of practice. I would like you to practice what we've done today. Do the exercises twice a day for about 15 to 20 minutes each time. Do them in a quiet place in a reclining chair, on the floor with a pillow, or on your bed with a head pillow. Also, try to do the relaxation at a time when there is no time pressure—like arising, after school or work, or before dinner. Try to avoid any interruptions, like telephone calls and people wanting to see you. Complete the homework log I have given you. Make sure you fill it in for each practice session. Do you have any questions?"
____15. Counselor arranges for follow-up session.	"Why don't you practice with this over the next two weeks and come back then?"

Notations for problems encountered or variations used: _____

_____

_____ ■

□ SUGGESTED READINGS

Benson, H. (1974 July–August). Your innate asset for combating stress. *Harvard Business Review, 52,* 49–60.

Benson, H. (1976). *The relaxation response.* New York: Avon Books.

Bernstein, D. A., & Borkovec, T. D. (1973). *Progressive relaxation training: A manual for the helping professions.* Champaign, IL: Research Press.

Carrington, P. (1978a). *Clinically standardized meditation (CSM). Instructor's manual.* Kendall Park, NJ: Pace Educational Systems.

Carrington, P. (1978b). *Learning to meditate: Clinically standardized meditation (CSM). Course workbook.* Kendall Park, NJ: Pace Educational Systems.

Carrington, P., Collings, G. H., Benson, H., Robinson, H., Wood, L. W., Lehrer, P. M., Woolfolk, R. L., & Cole, J. W. (1980). The use of meditation-relaxation techniques for the management of stress in a working population. *Journal of Occupational Medicine, 22,* 221–231.

Cautela, J. R., & Groden, J. (1978). *Relaxation: A comprehensive manual for adults, children, and children with special needs.* Champaign, IL: Research Press.

Credidio, S. G. (1982). Comparative effectiveness of patterned biofeedback vs. meditation training on EMG and skin temperature changes. *Behaviour Research and Therapy, 20,* 233–241.

Ferguson, J. M., Marquis, J. N., & Taylor, C. B. (1977). A script for deep muscle relaxation. *Diseases of the Nervous System, 38,* 703–708.

Hillenberg, J. B., & Collins, F. L., Jr. (1982). A procedural analysis and review of relaxation training research. *Behaviour Research and Therapy, 20,* 251–260.

Lehrer, P. M. (1982). How to relax and how not to relax: A reevaluation of the work of Edmund Jacobson—I. *Behaviour Research and Therapy, 20,* 417–428.

Lehrer, P. M., Woolfolk, R. L., Rooney, A. J., McCann, B., & Carrington, P. (1983). Progressive relaxation and meditation: A study of psychophysiological and therapeutic differences between two techniques. *Behaviour Research and Therapy, 21,* 651–662.

Redfering, D. L., & Bowman, M. J. (1981). Effects of a meditative relaxation exercise on non-attending behaviors of behaviorally disturbed children. *Journal of Clinical Child Psychology, 10,* 126–127.

Shapiro, D. H. (1980). *Meditation: Self-regulation strategy and altered state of consciousness.* New York: Aldine.

Shapiro, D. H. (1982). Overview: Clinical and physiological comparison of meditation with other self-control strategies. *American Journal of Psychiatry, 139,* 267–274.

Southam, M. A., Agras, W. S., Taylor, C. B., & Kraemer, H. C. (1982). Relaxation training: Blood pressure lowering during the working day. *Archives of General Psychiatry, 39,* 715–717.

Throll, D. A. (1982). Transcendental meditation and progressive relaxation: Their physiological effects. *Journal of Clinical Psychology, 38,* 522–530.

Woolfolk, R. L., & Lehrer, P. M. (Eds.). (1984). *Principles and practice of stress management.* New York: Guilford Press.

Woolfolk, R. L., Lehrer, P. M., McCann, B. S., & Rooney, A. J. (1982). Effects of progressive relaxation and meditation on cognitive and somatic manifestations of daily stress. *Behaviour Research and Therapy, 20,* 461–467.

FEEDBACK: POSTEVALUATION

PART ONE

1. *Homework* (practice).
2. *Instruction* about body comfort.
3. *Rationale* — telling the client how the procedure is used.
4. *Instruction* about breathing.
5. *Homework* — giving the client instructions about how to carry out the practice.
6. *Instructing* the client to meditate for 10 to 20 minutes.
7. *Rationale* — providing a brief overview of the procedure.
8. *Probing* about the meditative experience — assessing the client's reactions.
9. *Instruction* about a passive attitude.
10. *Selection* of a mental device such as a syllable or a number.

PART TWO

1. *Rationale* — reason.
2. *Homework* — when to practice.
3. *Instructions* about distracting thoughts.
4. *Preparation* about drinks and drugs.
5. *Selection* of a mantra, or sound.
6. *Instructions* about coming out of meditation.

7. *Instructions* about the use of mantra.
8. *Preparation* about chewing gum and about lighting in the room.

PART THREE

Use the Interview Checklist for Relaxation Response and Zen Meditation or the Interview Checklist for Clinically Standardized Meditation as a guide to assess your teaching.

PART FOUR

1. Rationale for client:
   a. Purpose: "This procedure, if you practice it regularly, can help you become relaxed. The relaxation benefits you derive can help you sleep better."
   b. Overview: "This procedure involves learning to tense and relax different muscle groups in your body. By doing this, you can contrast the difference between tenseness and relaxation. This will help you to recognize tension so you can instruct yourself to relax."
2. Instructions about dress: "You don't want anything to distract you, so wear comfortable, loose clothes for training. You may want to remove your glasses or contact lenses."
3. Environmental factors:
   a. Quiet room with reclining chair
   b. No obvious distractions or interruptions
4. Modeling of exercises: "Let me show you exactly what you'll be doing. Watch my right arm closely. I'm going to clench my fist and tighten my forearm, studying the tension as I do this. Now I'm going to relax it like this [hand goes limp], letting all the tension just drain out of the arm and hand and fingertips."
5. Muscle groups used in the procedure include:
   a. fist of each arm
   b. wrist of each arm
   c. biceps of each arm
   d. shoulders
   e. facial muscles — forehead, eyes, nose, jaws, lips
   f. head, chin, and neck muscles
   g. back
   h. chest
   i. stomach
   j. legs and feet
6. Some possible probes are:
   a. "On a scale from 0 to 100, 0 being very relaxed and 100 very tense, how do you feel now?"

    b. "What is your overall reaction to what you just did?"

    c. "How did the contrast between the tensed and relaxed muscles feel?"

    d. "How easy or hard was it for you to do this?"

7. Homework instructions should include:

    a. practice twice daily

    b. practice in a quiet place; avoid interruptions

    c. use a reclining chair, the floor, or a bed with pillow support for your head

PART FIVE

Use the Interview Checklist for Muscle Relaxation to assess your performance.

SYSTEMATIC DESENSITIZATION

EIGHTEEN

Consider the following cases:

A man has been a successful high school teacher. He is teaching while plagued with a personal problem: he is married yet is in love with another person. One day at school he is overcome with anxiety. He leaves school to go home; the next day, the thought of school elicits so much anxiety he feels sick. For the last few months, he has not returned to school. Because of this, he is convinced he is "going crazy."

A high school student gets good grades on homework and self-study assignments. Whenever he takes a test, he "freezes." Some days, if he can, he avoids or leaves the class because he feels so anxious about the test even the day before. When he takes a test, he feels overcome with anxiety, he cannot remember very much, and his resulting test grades are quite low.

These two case descriptions reflect instances in which a person learned an anxiety response to a situation. According to Bandura (1969), anxiety is a persistent, learned maladaptive response resulting from stimuli that have acquired the capacity to elicit very intense emotional reactions. In addition, both persons described in these cases felt fear in situations where there was no obvious external danger (sometimes called a *phobia;* Morris, 1980, p. 248). Further, to some degree, each person managed to avoid the nondangerous feared situation (sometimes called a *phobic reaction;* Morris, p. 248). These persons will probably require counseling or therapy.

In contrast, in the next two cases, a person is prevented from learning an anxiety response to a certain situation.

A child is afraid to learn to swim because of a prior bad experience with water. The child's parent or teacher gradually introduces the child to swimming, first by visiting the pool, dabbling hands and feet in the water, getting in up to the knees, and so on. Each approach to swimming is accompanied by a pleasure — being with a parent, having a toy or an inner tube, or playing water games.

A person has been in a very bad car accident. The person recovers and learns to get back in a car by sitting in it, going for short distances first, often accompanied by a friend or the music on the radio.

In the two descriptions you just read, the situation never got out of hand; that is, it never acquired the capacity to elicit a persistent anxiety response, nor did the persons learn to avoid the situation continually. Why? See whether you can identify common elements in these situations that prevented these two persons from becoming therapy candidates. Go over these last two cases again. Do you notice that, in each case, some type of stimulus or emotion was present that counteracted the fear or anxiety? The parent used pleasurable activities to create enjoyment for the child while swimming; the person in the car took a friend or listened to music. In addition, these persons learned to become more comfortable with a potentially fearful situation gradually. Each step of the way represented a larger or more intense dose of the feared situation.

In a simplified manner, these elements reflect some of the processes that seem to occur in the procedure of *systematic desensitization,* a widely used anxiety-reduction strategy. According to Wolpe (1982, p. 133),

Systematic desensitization is one of a variety of methods for breaking down neurotic anxiety-response habits in piecemeal fashion . . . a physiological state inhibitory of anxiety is induced in the patient by means of muscle relaxation, and he is then exposed to a weak anxiety-evoking stimulus for a few seconds. If the exposure is repeated several times, the stimulus progressively loses its ability to evoke anxiety. Successively "stronger" stimuli are then introduced and similarly treated.

□ OBJECTIVES

1. Using written examples of four sample hierarchies, identify at least three hierarchies by type (spatiotemporal, thematic, personal).
2. Given a written client case description, identify and describe at least 9 of the following 11 procedural steps of desensitization:
   a. A rationale.
   b. An overview.
   c. A method for identifying client emotion-provoking situations.
   d. A type of hierarchy appropriate for this client.
   e. A method of ranking hierarchy items the client could use.
   f. An appropriate counterconditioning or coping response.
   g. A method of imagery assessment.
   h. A method of scene presentation.
   i. A method of client signaling during scene presentation.
   j. A written notation method to record scene-presentation progress.
   k. An example of a desensitization homework task.
3. Demonstrate at least 22 out of 28 steps of systematic desensitization in several role-play interviews.

□ REPORTED USES OF DESENSITIZATION

Systematic desensitization was used widely as early as 1958 by Wolpe. In 1961 Wolpe reported its effectiveness in numerous case reports, which were substantiated by successful case reports cited by Lazarus (1967). Since 1963, when Lang and Lazovik conducted the first controlled study of systematic desensitization, its use as a therapy procedure has been the subject of numerous empirical investigations and case reports.

Desensitization has been used to treat speech anxiety (Kirsch & Henry, 1979; Lent, Russell, & Zamostny, 1981), cases of multiple phobias in children (Van Hasselt, Hersen, Bellack, Rosenblum, & Lamparski, 1979), chronic vomiting (Redd, 1980), blood phobia (Elmore, Wildman, & Westefeld, 1980), nightmares (Schindler, 1980), driving phobia (Levine & Wolpe, 1980), and fear of water (Ultee, Griffioen, & Schellekens, 1982), to name just a few. It has also been used extensively with common phobias, including acrophobia (fear of heights), agoraphobia (fear of open places), and claustrophobia (fear of enclosed places). It has been used to treat fear of flying, fear of death, fear of criticism or rejection — and, after the stimulus movie *Jaws III,* fear of sharks. Of course, one should not apply desensitization automatically whenever a client reports "anxiety." In some cases, the anxiety may be the logical result of another problem. For example, a person who continually procrastinates on work deadlines may feel anxious. Using this procedure would only help the person become desensitized or numb to the possible consequences of continued procrastination. A more logical approach might be to help the client reduce the procrastination behavior that is clearly the antecedent for the experienced anxiety. This illustration reiterates the importance of thorough problem assessment (Chapters 7 and 8) as a prerequisite for selecting and implementing counseling strategies.

Generally, desensitization is appropriate when a client has the capability or the skills to handle a situation or perform an activity but avoids the situation or performs less than adequately because of anxiety. For example, in the two cases described at the beginning of this chapter, the teacher had a history of successful teaching yet persistently avoided school (or related thoughts) because of the associated anxiety. The high school student had the ability to do well and adequate study skills, yet his performance on tests was not up to par because of his response. In contrast, if a person avoids a situation because of skill deficits, then desensitization is inadequate and probably inappropriate (Rimm & Masters, 1979). As you may recall from Chapter 13, modeling procedures work very well with many kinds of skill-deficit problems. People with many fears or with general, pervasive anxiety may benefit more from cognitive change strategies (Chapters 15 and 16) or from combinations of strategies in which desensitization may play some role. In addition, some anxiety may be maintained by the client's maladaptive self-verbalizations. In such instances, cognitive restructuring or stress inoculation (Chapter 16) may be a first treatment choice or may be used in conjunction with desensitization. Densensitization should not be used when the client's anxiety is nonspecific, or freefloating (Foa, Stekette, & Ascher, 1980). As you may recall from Chapter 11, generalized anxiety is often treated initially with client-centered therapy. Biofeedback, meditation, and muscle relaxation may also be useful supplemental strategies (Meyer, 1983).

At the same time, desensitization should not be overlooked as a possible treatment strategy for client problems that do not involve anxiety. Marquis, Morgan, and Piaget (1973) suggest that desensitization can be used with any conditioned emotion. It has been used to reduce anger (Hearn & Evans, 1972) and to increase tolerance of White students toward Black peers (Cotharin & Mikulas, 1975). Dengrove (1966) reports the use of desensitization to treat situations of loss and grief, such as separation from a loved one or loss of a valued job or object.

□ COMPARISON WITH OTHER TREATMENT APPROACHES

A great many studies have compared desensitization with other therapy methods on certain dependent measures. In the treatment of test anxiety, desensitization has been compared with covert positive reinforcement (Kostka & Galassi, 1974), hypnosis (Melnick & Russell, 1976), cognitive therapy (Holroyd, 1976; Leal, Baxter, Martin, & Marx, 1981), cue-controlled relaxation (Russell, Wise & Stratoudakis, 1976), and modeling, flooding, and study skills training (Horne & Matson, 1977). In treating speech anxiety, desensitization has been compared with an insight treatment focusing on maladaptive self-verbalizations (Meichenbaum, Gilmore, & Fedoravicius, 1971), with cue-controlled relaxation (Lent et al., 1981; Russell & Wise, 1976), and with meditation (Kirsch & Henry, 1979). Shaw and Thoresen (1974) compared desensitization with modeling in treating dental phobia; Curran (1975) compared it with skills training consisting of modeling and behavior rehearsal on social-anxiety measures. Rudestam and Bedrosian (1977) compared flooding and desensitization in anxiety reduction of animal phobias and social phobias of college students. *In vitro* and *in vivo* systematic desensitization were compared in reducing the fear of water for children aged 5–10 years (Ultee et al., 1982).

Although desensitization has enjoyed substantial empirical support, a great deal of controversy surrounds its current status. There is general agreement that desensitization is effective in reducing fears and neurotic behavior. The controversy centers on how and why the procedure works, or what processes surrounding densensitization are responsible for its results (Kazdin & Wilcoxon, 1976). After a critical review of the literature, Kazdin and Wilcoxon (1976) concluded that nonspecific factors such as the rationale presented to the client and client expectancy may account for some of the therapeutic effects of desensitization. For example, Kirsch, Tennen, Wickless, Saccone, and Cody (1983) found that a credible expectancy modification procedure was just as effective as desensitization in reducing experienced fear.

☐ EXPLANATIONS OF DESENSITIZATION

We will briefly summarize some of the possible theoretical explanations of the desensitization procedure. This will help you understand both the counterconditioning and the self-control models for implementing desensitization.

Desensitization by Reciprocal Inhibition

In 1958 Wolpe explained the way in which desensitization ostensibly works with the principle of *reciprocal inhibition.* When reciprocal inhibition occurs, a response such as fear is inhibited by another response or activity that is stronger than and incompatible with the fear response (or any other response to be inhibited). In other words, if an incompatible response occurs in the presence of fear of a stimulus situation, and if the incompatible response is stronger than the fear, desensitization occurs, and the stimulus situation loses its capacity to evoke fear. The reciprocal inhibition theory is based on principles of classical conditioning. In order for desensitization to occur, according to the reciprocal inhibition principle, three processes are required:

1. A strong anxiety-competing or counterconditioning, response must be present. Usually this competing or inhibiting response is deep muscle relaxation. Although other responses (such as eating, assertion, and sexual ones) can be used, Wolpe (1982) believes relaxation is most helpful.

2. A graded series of anxiety-provoking stimuli is presented to the client. These stimulus situations are typically arranged in a hierarchy with low-intensity situations at the bottom and high-intensity situations at the top.

3. Contiguous pairing of one of these aversive stimulus situations and the competing, or counterconditioning, response (relaxation) must occur. This is usually accomplished by having the client achieve a state of deep relaxation and then imagine an aversive stimulus (presented as a hierarchy item) while relaxing. The client stops imagining the situation whenever anxiety (or any other emotion to be inhibited) occurs. After additional relaxation, the situation is represented several times.

In recent years, some parts of the reciprocal inhibition principle have been challenged, both by personal opinion and by empirical explorations. There is some doubt that relaxation functions in the manner suggested by Wolpe — as a response that is inherently antagonistic to anxiety (Lang, 1969). As Kazdin and Wilcoxon (1976) observe, some research indicates that desensitization is not dependent on muscle relaxation or a hierarchical arrangement of anxiety-provoking stimuli or the pairing of these stimuli with relaxation as an incompatible response (p. 731). These research results have led some people to abandon a reciprocal inhibition explanation for desensitization.

Desensitization by Extinction

Lomont (1965) proposed that extinction processes account for the results of desensitization. In other words, anxiety responses diminish as a result of presenting conditioned stimuli without reinforcement. This theory is based on principles of operant conditioning. Wolpe (1976) agrees that desensitization falls within this operational definition of extinction and that extinction may play a role in desensitization. Similarly, Wilson and Davison (1971) have argued that desensitization reduces a client's anxiety level sufficiently that the client gradually approaches the feared stimuli and the fear is then extinguished.

Some studies indicate that other factors, including habituation (Mathews, 1971; van Egeren, 1971), gender of the counselor and the client (Geer & Hurst, 1976), and reinforcement and instructions (Leitenberg, Agras, Barlow, & Oliveau, 1969) may be at least partly responsible for the results of desensitization.

Desensitization as Self-Control Training

In 1971 Goldfried challenged the idea that desensitization was a relatively passive process of deconditioning. Goldfried proposed that desensitization involved learning a general anxiety-reducing skill, rather than mere desensitization to some specific aversive stimulus (p. 228). According to this self-control explanation, the client learns to use relaxation as a way to cope with anxiety or to bring anxiety under control, not simply to replace anxiety. Eventually the client learns to identify the cues for muscular tension, to respond by relaxing away the tension, and to relabel the resulting emotion (p. 229). As learning occurs, Goldfried hypothesized, the relaxation responses may become "anticipatory," having the effect of partly or completely "short-circuiting" the anxiety or fear (p. 229).

Goldfried (1971) suggested certain modifications in the desensitization procedure that are more consistent with his view of the process. The client is told that desensitization involves learning the skill of relaxation as a way to cope with anxiety. During relaxation training, emphasis is placed on having the client become aware of sensations associated with tension and learning to use these sensations as a cue to relax. Since emphasis is placed on training the client to cope with anxiety cues and responses, the situations that elicit the anxiety are less important. Therefore, a single hierarchy can be used that reflects a variety of stimulus situations, not just those involving one theme (the latter is the procedure advocated by Wolpe, 1982). According to the reciprocal inhibition theory, the relaxation response must be stronger than the anxiety response. Therefore, the client is taught to stop visualizing the anxiety-provoking situation when anxious and to relax. In Goldfried's model, the client is instructed to maintain the image even though anxious and to relax away the tension. Finally, the client is taught to apply the skill to *in vivo* situations (pp. 231–232).

These procedural aspects of the self-control desensitization model were compared with the traditional (reciprocal inhibition) procedure of desensitization for the treatment of speech and test anxiety in college students (Zemore, 1975). Both methods produced improvements in treated *and* untreated fears of clients. Another study comparing these two methods of desensitization as a test-anxiety treatment found that they were comparable on the dependent measures; the self-control model showed significantly greater anxiety reduction on one test-anxiety self-report measure (Spiegler et al., 1976). These authors noted that, in the self-control model, only 4 of the 21 hierarchy items used dealt specifically with test-anxiety situations, supporting Goldfried's (1971) assumption that not all situations in the problem area need be included in the hierarchy for desensitization to occur (Spiegler et al., 1976). Further support for this position was reported by Goldfried and Goldfried (1977), who found no difference between speech-anxious subjects desensitized with a hierarchy relevant to speech anxiety and other speech-anxious people desensitized with a totally unrelated hierarchy. In another study, test-anxious students treated by self-control desensitization did better on both self-report and performance measures than students receiving standardized desensitization from a reciprocal inhibition framework (Denney & Rupert, 1977). More recent evidence of the efficacy of self-control desensitization was

provided in the treatment of a multiphobic child (Bornstein & Knapp, 1981) and in the treatment of fear of flying (Rebman, 1983).

Given the controversy surrounding the process of desensitization, what conclusions can be drawn about the possible ways to implement the procedure? First of all, perhaps there is no single right way to proceed with desensitization. A variety of procedural steps may be effective. Second, the specific ways in which desensitization is used will reflect the counselor's biases and preferences. To the extent that you believe a particular way of using desensitization works, this belief will only enhance the outcomes. Third, the details of the desensitization procedure should be adapted to each client. Very few studies have explored possible interactions between procedural variations in desensitization and client characteristics. Individual clients may respond differently to the particular rationale they receive or to the particular way a hierarchy is used. The counselor should always try to implement desensitization in a way that is likely to produce the best results for each client. Finally, perhaps the overall procedure of desensitization should integrate a variety of components from several theoretical explanations to ensure that no important contributing variable is overlooked. We have tried to do this in our presentation of the procedural aspects of desensitization in the following section. Figure 18-1 shows the seven major components of systematic desensitization. A summary of the procedural steps associated with each component is found in the Interview Checklist for Systematic Desensitization at the end of the chapter.

☐ COMPONENTS OF DESENSITIZATION

Treatment Rationale

The purpose and overview given to the client about desensitization are very important for several reasons. First, the rationale and overview establish the particular model or way in which the counselor plans to implement the procedure. The client is therefore informed of the principles of desensitization. Second, the outcomes of desensitization may be enhanced when the client is given very clear instructions and a positive expectancy set (Leitenberg et al., 1969). The *particular* rationale and overview you present to the client depend on the actual way you plan to implement desensitization.

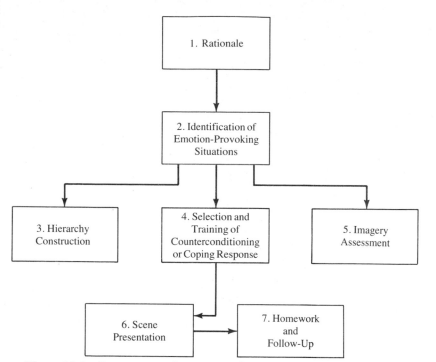

Figure 18-1. *Components of systematic desensitization procedure*

Rationale and overview of counterconditioning model. If you plan to use a counterconditioning model, you would present a rationale that explains how the client's fear or other conditioned emotion can be counterconditioned using desensitization. Your overview of the procedure would emphasize the use of an anxiety-free response to replace the conditioned emotion, the construction of a hierarchy consisting of a graduated series of items representing the emotion-provoking situations, and the pairing of these hierarchy items with the anxiety-free response (such as relaxation).

One rationale and overview based on a counterconditioning model has been used by Osterhouse (1976) in group-administered desensitization for test anxiety. Portions of this rationale are reprinted below:

The procedure we will use to help you overcome any unusually strong fears of examinations is called desensitization. . . . This approach is based upon the fact that it is impossible to be afraid and relaxed at the same time. For example, a student might want to ask a professor a question, or perhaps criticize something the professor has said. He may find, however, when he starts to speak that he experiences shortness of breath, his heart pounds, or his hands perspire. He is unable to make his point.

These are anxiety reactions and don't occur when the student is relaxed. Therefore, an important part of the method involves teaching you to relax as completely as possible. You may think that you don't have to be taught how to relax, but the fact is that most people are frequently unaware of their tensions.

Once you have learned how to relax, then this group will develop a list of situations in which the anxiety occurs. This list will be made up so that it contains items representing many different degrees of anxiety. . . . This list is called a hierarchy. . . .

One of the most interesting aspects of this procedure is that it tends to generalize to real life situations. Even though the procedure only requires you to imagine yourself in situations related to fear of examinations, there is a strong tendency for fear to decrease in the actual situation [p. 270].*

Rationale and overview of self-control model. If you plan to implement desensitization by emphasizing coping and self-control skills for tension management, your rationale and overview should

* From "Group Systematic Desensitization of Test Anxiety," by R. A. Osterhouse. In J. D. Krumboltz and C. E. Thoresen (Eds.), *Counseling methods.* Copyright 1976 by Holt, Rinehart and Winston. Reprinted by permission of CBS College Publishing.

reflect this emphasis. Goldfried (1971) suggests the following rationale and overview for explaining desensitization as training in self-control:

> There are various situations where, on the basis of your past experience, you have learned to react by becoming tense (anxious, nervous, fearful). What I plan to do is help you to learn how to cope with these situations more successfully, so that they do not make you as upset. This will be done by taking note of a number of those situations which upset you to varying degrees, and then having you learn to cope with the less stressful situations before moving on to the more difficult ones. Part of the treatment involves learning how to relax so that in situations where you feel yourself getting nervous you will be better able to eliminate this tenseness. Learning to relax is much like learning any other skill. When a person learns to drive, he initially has difficulty in coordinating everything, and often finds himself very much aware of what he is doing. With more and more practice, however, the procedures involved in driving become easier and more automatic. You may find the same thing occurring to you when you try to relax in those situations where you feel yourself starting to become tense. You will find that as you persist, however, it will become easier and easier [p. 231].*

In one study, test-anxious students who received this sort of active coping rationale for desensitization achieved significantly better grade-point averages than students who received a rationale explaining desensitization according to the principle of classical conditioning (Denney & Rupert, 1977).

☐ MODEL DIALOGUE: RATIONALE

Here is an example of a rationale the counselor could use to explain to Joan how desensitization can help her with her fear and avoidance of math class:

> "Joan, we've talked about how you get very nervous before and during your math class. Sometimes you try to skip it. But you realize you haven't always felt this way about math. You've *learned* to feel this way. There is a procedure called desensitization that can help you replace your tension with

relaxation. Eventually, the things about math class you now fear will not be tense situations for you. This procedure has been used very successfully to help other people reduce their fear of a certain situation.

> "In desensitization, you will learn how to relax. After you're relaxed, I'll ask you to imagine some things about your math class—starting with not too stressful things and gradually working with more stressful things. As we go along, the relaxation will start to replace the anxiety. These stressful situations then will no longer seem so stressful to you.

> "What questions do you have about this?"

Identification of Emotion-Provoking Situations

If the counselor and client have defined the problem thoroughly, there will already be some indications about the dimensions or situations that provoke anxiety (or any other emotional arousal) in the client. However, the counselor and client must be sure to isolate the most crucial situations in which the client should become less anxious or upset (Goldfried & Davison, 1976, p. 114). This is not always an easy task, as first appearances can be deceiving. Wolpe (1973) cites cases in which the initial problem seemed to indicate fear of open places (agoraphobia), yet the complaint was related to difficult unresolved situations in the client's marriage. Goldfried and Davison recommend that counselors ask themselves and their clients what the consequences may be of desensitization to one thing or another (p. 115).

The emotion-provoking situations must be defined idiosyncratically for each client. Marquis, Ferguson, and Taylor (1973) observe that, even among clients who have the same type of fear or phobia, the specific anxiety-provoking situations associated with the fear can vary greatly.

There are at least three ways in which the counselor can try to identify past and present situations that are anxiety-provoking to the client. These three methods are the interview assessment, client self-monitoring, and client completion of related self-report questionnaires.

Interview assessment. The interview assessment will be similar to the interview assessment we proposed in Chapters 7 and 8 on problem assessment. The counselor should use leads that will establish the particular circumstances and situations that elicit the conditioned emotion. For instance, does the client feel anxious in all social situations or only those with strangers present? Does the client's

---

* From "Systematic Desensitization as Training in Self-Control" by M. R. Goldfried. *Journal of Consulting and Clinical Psychology, 37,* 228–234. Copyright © 1971 by the American Psychological Association. Reprinted by permission.

anxiety vary with the number of people present? with whether the client is accompanied or alone? Does the client experience more anxiety with people of the same or the other sex? These are examples of the kinds of information the interview assessment could provide about a client's anxiety in certain social situations.

Client self-monitoring. In addition to the information obtained during the session, the counselor may obtain even more data by having the client observe and record on a log the emotion-provoking situations as they occur during the week. The client would observe and note what was going on, where, with whom, and when the emotion, such as anxiety, was detected. The client also might rate the level of anxiety felt during the situation on a scale of 1 (low) to 10 (high) or on a scale of 0 (no anxiety) to 100 (panic).*

Self-report questionnaires. Some counselors find that additional data about particular emotion-provoking situations can be gained by having the client complete one or more self-report questionnaires. A commonly used questionnaire is the Wolpe-Lang (1964) Fear Survey Schedule (FSS). Lick and Katkin (1976) present descriptions of other self-report measures of fear and anxiety.

The counselor should persist in this identification process until specific emotion-provoking situations are identified. Marquis et al. (1973, p. 2) indicate that information gathering is not complete until the counselor knows the factors related to the onset and maintenance of the client's problem and until the client believes that all pertinent information has been shared with the counselor. At this point, the counselor and client are ready to construct a hierarchy.

□ MODEL DIALOGUE: IDENTIFYING EMOTION-PROVOKING SITUATIONS

Counselor: Joan, we've already discussed some of the situations about your math class that make you feel anxious. What are some of these?

Client: Well, before class, just thinking about having to go bothers me. Sometimes at night I get anxious

---

* Although 1–5 and 1–7 rating scales are recommended in Chapter 10, the 0–100 rating scale is typically used in desensitization because it corresponds to the suds scaling method described later in this chapter.

—not so much doing math homework but studying for tests.

Counselor: OK. Can you list some of the things that happen during your math class that you feel anxious about?

Client: Well, always when I take a test. Sometimes when I am doing problems and don't know the answers—having to ask Mr. _____ for help. And, of course, when he calls on me or asks me to go to the board.

Counselor: OK, good. And I believe you said before that you feel nervous about volunteering answers, too.

Client: Right—that, too.

Counselor: And yet these sorts of situations don't seem to upset you in your other classes?

Client: No. And really math class has never been as bad as it is this year. I guess part of it is the pressure of getting closer to graduating and, well, my teacher makes me feel dumb. I felt scared of him the first day of class. Yet I've always felt somewhat nervous about working with numbers.

Counselor: So some of your fear centers on your teacher, too—and then perhaps there's some worry about doing well enough to graduate.

Client: Right. Although I know I won't do *that* badly.

Counselor: OK, good. You realize that, even with not liking math and worrying about it, you won't get a bad grade.

Client: Not worse than a C.

Counselor: There's one thing I'd like you to do this week. Could you make a list of anything about the subject of math—and your math class—that has happened and has made you nervous? Also, write down anything about math or your class that *could* happen that you would feel anxious about. Then, if you think it's a situation that makes you a little anxious, mark *L* by it. If it's average, mark *A*. If it does or could make you very nervous, mark *V*.

Client: OK.

Counselor: Earlier, too, you had mentioned that sometimes these same feelings occur in situations with your parents, so after we work with math class, we'll come back and work on the situations with you and your parents.

Hierarchy Construction

A hierarchy is a list of stimulus situations to which the client reacts with graded amounts of anxiety or some other emotional response (Wolpe, 1958). Hierarchy construction can consume a good deal of interview time because of the various factors involved in constructing an adequate hierarchy. These factors include selection of a type of hierarchy, the number of hierarchies (single or multiple), identification of hierarchy items, identification of control items, and ranking and spacing of items.

Types of hierarchies.   On the basis of the stimulus situations that evoke anxiety (or any emotion to be counterconditioned), the counselor should select an appropriate type of hierarchy in which to cast individual items or descriptions of the aversive situations. Marquis et al. (1973, pp. 3–4) describe three kinds of hierarchies: spatiotemporal, thematic, and personal. Spatiotemporal and thematic hierarchies are used more commonly than personal ones, and an occasional hierarchy may be a combination of any of these three types. The particular type used will depend on the client's problem, the counselor's preferences, and the client's preferences.

A spatiotemporal hierarchy is developed by using items that represent physical or time dimensions, such as distance from one's house or time before taking an exam. In either case, anxiety, for example, seems to vary with proximity to the feared object or situation. Someone who is afraid to leave the house will get more anxious as the distance from home increases. A client who has "exam panic" will get more anxious as the exam draws closer. Therefore, in developing a spatiotemporal hierarchy, usually more items are put at the high end of the scale than at the low end, so the space or time differences at the high end of the scale are smaller.

Here is an example of a *spatiotemporal hierarchy* used with a client who was very fearful of taking tests. The items are arranged in terms of time:

1. Your instructor announces on the first day of class that the first exam will be held in one month. You know that the month will go quickly.
2. A week before the exam, you are sitting in class and the instructor reminds the class of the exam date. You realize you have a lot of studying to do during the week.
3. You are sitting in the class and the instructor mentions the exam, scheduled for the next class session, two days away. You realize you still have a lot of pages to read.
4. Now it is one day before the exam. You are studying in the library. You wonder whether you have studied as much as everyone else in the class.
5. It is the night before the test. You are in your room studying. You think about the fact that this exam grade is one-third of your final grade.
6. It is the night before the exam—late evening. You have just finished studying and have gone to bed. You're lying awake going over your reading in your mind.
7. You wake up the next morning and your mind flashes to this being exam day. You wonder how much you will remember of what you read the night and day before.
8. It is later in the day, one hour before the exam. You do some last-minute scanning of your lecture notes. You start to feel a little hassled—even a little sick. You wish you had more time to prepare.
9. It is 15 minutes before the class—time to walk over to the classroom. As you're walking over, you realize how important this grade will be. You hope you don't "blank out."
10. You go into the building, stop to get a drink of water, and then enter the classroom. You look around and see people laughing. You think that they are more confident and better prepared than you.
11. The instructor is a little late. You are sitting in class waiting for the teacher to come and pass out the tests. You wonder what will be on the test.
12. The instructor has just passed out tests. You receive your copy. Your first thought is that the test is so long—will you finish in time?
13. You start to work on the first portion of the test. There are some questions you aren't sure of. You spend time thinking and then see that people around you are writing. You skip these questions and go on.
14. You look at your watch. The class is half over—only 25 minutes left. You feel you have dawdled on the first part of the test. You wonder how much your grade will be pulled down if you don't finish.
15. You continue to work as fast as you can; occasionally you worry about the time. You glance at your watch—five minutes left. You still have a lot of unanswered questions.
16. Time is just about up. There are some questions you had to leave blank. You worry again about this test being one-third of your grade.

A *thematic hierarchy* consists of items exposing the client to various components or parameters of feared objects, activities, or situations. For example, a client who is afraid of criticism or disapproval may find that the fear varies depending on who criticizes, what is criticized, and how the criticism is delivered. Here is an example of a thematic hierarchy used with a person who found criticism very stressful:

1. A classmate whom you don't especially respect tells you you're too quiet and asks "What's the matter with you?"
2. A casual friend tells you that you looked tired today.
3. A good friend points out that the color of your attire isn't really "your best color."
4. Your tennis date, a person you consider to be just "OK," tells you that you need to improve your tennis game.
5. You're in class and the teacher assigns a group project. Your group is meeting and you offer an idea for the project — no one responds to it.
6. You run into a person you used to date regularly; he or she avoids speaking to you.
7. Your sister comes in and complains you've been too busy to pay much attention to her.
8. Your best friend comments that you seem moody today and aren't too much fun to be around.
9. Your mother suggests you're putting on a little weight and need to exercise more.
10. You meet someone you like and ask him or her to go to a game with you. The person turns down your invitation.
11. You get a paper back that you worked hard on. You only get a C. The teacher writes across the top "Some good ideas, but you didn't develop them at all."
12. You are in front of the class making an individual presentation. Several people in the class are talking and laughing as you speak.
13. Your father complains that your grades aren't as good as they should be and implies that you're lazy.
14. You're in your honors class. The class is engaged in a big discussion. You offer one idea. Someone responds with "That's dumb."

A *personal hierarchy* is not used as often as the other two types, but it is very useful with clients who are persistently bothered by thoughts or memories of a certain individual. Dengrove (1966) recommends the use of a personal hierarchy to desensitize anxiety related to the separation or termination of a relationship. Items at the bottom of the hierarchy may consist of blissful or pleasant scenes or memories, progressing toward items at the top of the hierarchy representing painful or anxiety-provoking memories or thoughts (Marquis et al., 1973).

Here is an example of a personal hierarchy used with a male client who was bothered by painful memories of the termination of a close relationship:

1. You have been with Susie every day for the last month. You're sitting holding her in your arms and feeling like she's the only woman you'll ever love like this.
2. You and Susie are sitting on the floor in your apartment, drinking wine and listening to records.
3. You've just returned from taking Susie to her first race. She's ecstatic about the experience.
4. You and Susie are studying together in the library.
5. You and Susie are drinking beer at the local pub.
6. You and Susie aren't spending every day together. Sometimes she wants to study alone now. You're in the library by yourself studying.
7. You call Susie up late at night. The phone rings continuously without any answer. You wonder where she is.
8. You call Susie to ask her out for dinner and she turns you down — says she doesn't feel well.
9. You're walking down the street by the tennis court. You see Susie playing there with another person. You wonder why she hasn't told you about him.
10. You go over to Susie's. She isn't there. You wait until she comes. She sees you, goes back to her car, and drives away.
11. You call Susie on the phone. She says she doesn't want to see you anymore, that she never has really loved you, and hangs up on you.

Number of hierarchies. Whether you use one or several hierarchies also depends on the client's problem and preferences and on your preferences. Some therapists believe separate hierarchies should be constructed for different themes or different parameters of one theme (Marquis et al., 1973; Wolpe & Lazarus, 1966). Using multiple hierarchies may be less confusing but can require more time for hierarchy construction and presentation. Goldfried (1971) asserts that establishing separate hierarchies for carefully determined themes is not essential. He recommends constructing a single hierarchy composed of situations eliciting increasing amounts of tension, regardless of whether the hierarchy items represent any particular theme (p. 232). According to Goldfried, construction of a single hierarchy with items reflecting a variety of anxiety-provoking situations may facilitate generalization of the desensitization process from the session to the client's environment. Whether to use one or several hierarchies is a choice you will need to make during the process of hierarchy construction.

Identification of hierarchy items. The counselor must initiate a method of generating the items for the hierarchy. The client's role in this process is extremely important. Generally, the counselor can ask the client to aid in identifying hierarchy items by interview questions or by a homework assignment. The counselor can question the client about particular emotion-provoking scenes during the interview. Goldfried and Davison (1976) instruct clients to think of a large balloon and to draw items from different parts of the balloon that represent all the elements in the balloon. However, questioning the client about the scenes should not occur simultaneously with relaxation training. If the client is queried about hierarchy items after engaging in a period of deep relaxation, her or his responses may be altered.

If the client has difficulty responding concretely to interview questions, the counselor can assign homework for item identification. The counselor can give the client a stack of blank 3 × 5 index cards. The client is asked to generate items during the week and to write down each item on a separate note card. Often this homework assignment is useful even with clients who respond very thoroughly to the interview questions. During the week, the client has time to add items that were not apparent during the session.

The counselor should continue to explore and generate hierarchy items until a number have been identified that represent a range of aversive situations and varying degress of emotional arousal. A hierarchy typically contains 10 to 20 items but occasionally may have more or fewer. Goldfried and Davison (1976) and Marquis et al. (1973) suggest some criteria to use to construct adequate hierarchy items:

1. Some of the items should represent situations that, if carried out by the client *in vivo,* are under the client's control (do not require instigation from others).
2. An item must be concrete and specific. Embellishing the item description with sufficient details may help the client obtain a clear and vivid visualization of the item during scene presentation. As an example, an item that reads "Your best friend disapproves of you" is too general. A more concrete item would be "Your best friend disapproves of your boyfriend and tells you that you are stupid for going out with him."
3. Items should be similar to or represent actual situations the client has faced or may have to face in the future. If dialogue is written into an item, the language used should be adapted to the client.
4. Items selected should reflect a broad range of situations in which the client's fear (or other emotion) does or could occur.
5. Items should be included that reflect all different levels of the emotion, ranging from low to high intensity.

After the hierarchy items are identified, the client and counselor can identify several control items.

Identification of control items. A control item consists of a relaxing or neutral scene to which the client is not expected to have any strong emotional reaction. Control scenes are placed at the bottom of the hierarchy and represent a zero or "no anxiety" ranking. Some examples of control items are to "imagine a colored object," "imagine you're sitting in the sun on a day with a completely blue sky," or "imagine you're looking at a field of vivid yellow daffodils." A control item is often used to test the client's ability to visualize anxiety-free material and to give the client a relaxing or pleasant scene to imagine during scene presentation in order to enhance the level of relaxation. After all the hierarchy and control items have been identified, the client can arrange the items in order of increasing emotional arousal through a ranking method.

Ranking and spacing of hierarchy items. The counselor and client work together to identify an appropriate order for the items in the hierarchy. Generally, the client plays the major role in ranking, but the counselor must ensure that the spacing between items is satisfactory. The hierarchy items are ranked in order of increasing difficulty, stress, or emotional arousal. The control items are placed at the bottom of the hierarchy, and each item that represents more difficulty or greater anxiety is placed in a successively higher position in the hierarchy. Items at the top of the hierarchy represent the situations that are most stressful or anxiety-producing for the client.

The counselor should explain how the hierarchy items are arranged before asking the client to rank them. The counselor should also explain the purpose of this type of hierarchy arrangement so that the client fully understands the necessity of spending time to rank the items. The counselor can point out that desensitization occurs gradually and that the function of a hierarchy is to identify low-stress items to which the client will be desensitized before higher-stress items. The client's learning to face or cope with a feared situation will begin with more manageable situations first and gradually extend to more difficult situations. The counselor may emphasize that at no point will the client be asked to imagine or cope with a scene or situation that is very stressful before learning to deal successfully with less stressful scenes. This point is often reassuring to an occasional client whose anxiety is so great that the desensitization procedure itself is viewed with great trepidation.

There are several methods the client can use to order the hierarchy items. Three commonly used methods are rank-ordering; "suds" scaling; and low, medium, and high ordering. Rank-ordering is the simplest method. Each hierarchy item is written on a 3×5 note card (this note card is also useful later for the counselor to make notations about the item presentation). The client takes the stack of note cards and rank-orders the cards, with the least stressful situations at the bottom and successively more stressful items in an ascending order. The bottom item, a control item, can be assigned a 1; each successive item can be assigned one higher number. These numbers can be written at the top of each card in pencil, since the order of the items may change. After the client has rank-ordered the cards, the counselor can go over the order to determine whether there are too many or too few gaps between items. Items should be graduated evenly, with a fairly equal amount of difference between them. If items are bunched together, a few can be deleted. If there are large spaces between items, new ones can be added.

In the "suds" scaling method, items are arranged according to a point system in which the various points represent levels of the emotion referred to as "suds," or "subjective units of disturbance" (Wolpe & Lazarus, 1966). The most common scale is 100 points, where 0 suds represents complete relaxation and 100 suds indicates panic or an extremely stressful reaction. However, occasionally a 10-point suds scale is used, with 0 representing relaxation and 10 indicating panic. We think the 100-point scale is simpler to use, because the greater range of points makes adequate spacing between items easier. If a client uses the suds scale to arrange items, each item is assigned a number representing the amount of stress it generates for the client. If the item doesn't generate much stress, the client may assign it 10, 15, or 20 suds. Average amounts of stress might be assigned 35, 40, 45, or 50; whereas 85, 90, 95, and 100 suds represent situations that produce much anxiety or stress.

After the items are arranged according to the assigned suds, the counselor should make sure that no item is separated from the previous item by more than 10 suds; at the high end of the scale, spacing of no more than 5 suds between items is often necessary (Marquis et al., 1973). If there are large gaps (greater than 10 or 5 suds), the counselor and client should write additional, intermediate items to fill in. If there are too many items around the same level, particularly at the lower end of the hierarchy, some may be deleted. The suds system may require more explanation to the client and more time for item arrangement. However, it has advantages. First, the point system makes it easy to determine whether there is too much or too little space between items. Second, the use of the suds scale at this point in desensitization introduces the client to a way to discriminate and label varying degrees of relaxation and tension. Often this kind of labeling system is useful during relaxation training and scene presentation.

If the client has difficulty assigning exact suds ratings, a "low, medium, high" ranking method can be used instead. In this method, suggested by Goldfried and Davison (1976), the client rates items that produce little anxiety, which represent the bottom one-third of the hierarchy, or 0 to 33 suds; then rates average anxiety-producing items, which make up the middle of the hierarchy, or 34 to 66 suds; and finally the items that produce much anxiety, which compose the top end of the hierarchy, or 67 to 100 suds. After the items are sorted into these three groups, the client can rank-order items within each group. Then the counselor can go over the items to make sure the spacing is reasonable.

Whichever ranking method is used, the counselor should emphasize that it is flexible and subject to change. Any type of hierarchy or order of items is useful only to the degree that it helps desensitize the emotion or helps the client to cope. Many times, a carefully constructed hierarchy will require some change during scene presentations.

Although we have described how to construct a hierarchy for an individual client, hierarchy construction can also be adapted for groups of clients. For some clients standardized hierarchies may work as well as individualized ones (Emery & Krumboltz, 1967; Howard, Murphy, & Clarke, 1983; McGlynn, Wilson, & Linder, 1970; Nawas, Fishman, & Pucel, 1970). For a description of hierarchy construction with a group of clients, see Osterhouse (1976).

☐ MODEL DIALOGUE: HIERARCHY CONSTRUCTION

Counselor: Hi, Joan. I see you brought your list with you. That's great, because today we're going to work on a list that's called a hierarchy, which is like a staircase or a ladder. In your case, it will center on the theme or the idea of math anxiety. It's a list of all the situations about math that are anxiety-producing for you. We'll list these situations and then I'll ask you to rank them, starting with the less stressful ones. Does this seem clear?

Client: Yes. Actually I did something like that this week in making my list, didn't I?

Counselor: Right, you did. Now what we want to do is take your list, add any other situations that are stressful that aren't on here, and make sure each item on this list is specific. We may need to add some details to some of the items. The idea is to get a close description of the way the situation actually is or actually does or could happen. Let's take a look at your list now.

1. Sitting in English think about math class (L)
2. On way to math class (L)
3. At home, doing math homework (L)
4. At home, studying for a math test (A)
5. In math class, teacher giving out test (V)
6. In math class, taking test (V)
7. In math class, teacher asks me question (V)
8. In math class, at board, having trouble (V)
9. In math class, working problems at desk, don't know some answers (A)
10. Asking teacher for help (A)
11. Volunteering an answer (V)
12. Getting test or assignment back with low grade (V)
13. Teacher telling me I'll flunk or barely pass (V)
14. Doing anything with numbers, even outside math class, like adding up a list of numbers (A)
15. Talking about math with someone (A)

Counselor: Well, it looks like you've really worked hard at putting down some math situations that are stressful for you and indicating just how stressful they are. OK, let's go over this list and fill in some details. For each item here, can you write in one or two more details about the situation? What exactly happens that you feel nervous about? For instance, when you're sitting in English, what is it you're thinking that makes you nervous?

Client: OK, I see what you mean.

Counselor: Let's go over each item here, and as you tell me the details, I'll jot these down. [This step proceeds until a concrete description is obtained for each item. Counselor checks them to see whether items meet necessary criteria, which, with added details, these do. The criteria are: some items are under client's control; items are concrete; items represent past, present, or future anxiety-provoking scenes; items sample a broad range of situations; items represent varying levels of anxiety.]

Counselor: What else can you think of about math that is or could be stressful?

Client: Nothing right now. Not everything on my list has happened, but like if my teacher did tell me I was going to flunk, that would be very tense.

Counselor: You've got the idea. Now can you think of something not related to math that would be pleasant or relaxing for you to think about—like skiing down a slope or lying on the beach?

Client: Well, what about sitting in front of a campfire roasting marshmallows?

Counselor: Good. Now later on, as we proceed, I might ask you to relax by imagining a pleasant scene. Then you could imagine something like that.

Client: OK.

Counselor: I'd like you now to take these items we've listed on these cards and rank-order each item. We're going to put this pleasant item having to do with the campfire at the bottom of the list. Then go through the cards and put each card in an order from the least stressful to the most stressful situation. Is that clear?

Client: You mean the thing that bothers me least to the thing that makes me most nervous?

Counselor: Exactly. Each item as you go up the stack of cards should be a little more stressful than the previous item.

Client: OK. [Takes about ten minutes to rank-order the 16 cards.]

Counselor: OK. I'm going to lay each card out to see what you've got here, starting at the bottom.

Card 1: Sitting in front of a campfire on a cool night with friends, singing songs and roasting marshmallows [control item].

Card 2: Sitting in my room at my desk doing routine math homework over fairly easy material.

Card 3: Sitting in English about ten minutes before the bell. Thinking about going to math class next and wondering if I can hide or if I'll get called on.

Card 4: Walking down the hall with a couple of classmates to math class. Walking in the door and seeing the teacher looking over our homework. Wondering how I did.

Card 5: A girlfriend calls up and talks about our upcoming test in math—wonder if I'll pass it.

Card 6: Seeing a big list of numbers, like on a store receipt, and having to check the total to make sure it's OK.

Card 7: In math class, sitting at my desk; having to work on problems and coming across some that are confusing. Don't have much time to finish.

Card 8: Working on problems at my desk. I'm stumped on a couple. Nothing I try works. Having to go up and ask Mr. _____ for help. He tries to do it for me; I feel dumb.

Card 9: Sitting in my room at home the night before a big math test; studying for the test and wondering if I'll blank out on it.

Card 10: In math class taking a test and coming across some problems I don't know how to do.

Card 11: Waiting to get a test or an assignment back and worrying about a low grade.

Card 12: Sitting in math class and the teacher asks for the answer; raising my hand to volunteer it; wonder if it's right.

Card 13: Sitting in math class waiting for a big test to be passed out. Wondering what's on it and if I'll be able to remember things.

Card 14: Sitting in math class and suddenly the teacher calls on me and asks me for an answer. I feel unprepared.

Card 15: Sitting in math class and the teacher sends me to the board. I'm at the board trying to work a problem in front of the class. I'm getting stuck.

Card 16: The teacher calls me in for a conference after school. Mr. _____ is telling me I'm in big trouble and barely passing. There's a good chance I could flunk math.

Counselor: OK, now it seems like each of these items represents a somewhat more stressful situation. Do you feel that there are any large jumps between items—like going from a very low-stress situation to a higher-stress one suddenly?

Client (looks over list): No, I don't think so.

Counselor: OK, we'll stick with this list and this order for now. Of course, this is tentative. Later on, if we feel something needs to be moved around or added, we will do so.

LEARNING ACTIVITY #47: HIERARCHY CONSTRUCTION

This learning activity is designed to give you some practice in constructing different kinds of hierarchies. You can do this activity by yourself or with another person.

Part One: Spatiotemporal Hierarchy

Think of for yourself, or have your partner identify, a situation you fear and avoid. This situation should be something where the fear increases as the distance or time proximity toward the feared object or situation gets closer. For example, you might fear and avoid approaching certain kinds of animals or high places (distance). Or you might get increasingly anxious as the time before an exam, a speech, or an interview diminishes (time). For this situation, identify the specific situations that are anxiety-provoking. Try to identify all the relevant parameters of the situation.

For example, does your anxiety vary if you're alone or with another person, if you're taking a midterm or a quiz, if you're speaking before a large or a small group? List each anxiety-provoking situation that could be a hierarchy item on a separate index card. Also list one control (pleasant) item on a card. After you or your partner believes all the relevant items are listed, take the cards and rank-order them. The control item will be at the bottom, followed by items that evoke successively greater anxiety. Check the rank order to make sure items are equally spaced. Add or delete items as necessary.

Part Two: Thematic Hierarchy

This time, you or your partner should identify a situation you fear and avoid that is related to a certain

(continued)

LEARNING ACTIVITY #47: HIERARCHY CONSTRUCTION (continued)

theme: fear of being rejected or criticized, fear of engaging in risk-taking situations, fear of failure, fear of losing control, fear of getting ill or of death, and so on. Identify the particular anxiety-provoking situations associated with this theme, ones that have made or could make you anxious. Identify all the relevant parameters: does your fear vary with what you do? who is with you? List each anxiety-provoking situation that could represent a hierarchy item on a card or a piece of paper. After all the relevant items are listed, rank-order them, using the suds scale. Assign each item a number from 0 (no anxiety) to 100 (panic), depending on the intensity and amount of anxiety it provokes. Then arrange the items in order of increasing suds. Check to make sure there are no more than 10 suds between adjacent items and 5 suds between high-intensity items. Add or delete items as necessary.

Part Three: Personal Hierarchy

See whether you or your partner can identify a situation about which you have painful or unpleasant memories. Such situations might include loss of a prized object, loss of a job or friend, or termination of a close relationship. Generate emotion-provoking situations associated with pleasant memories and unpleasant memories. List each situation on a separate card. When all items are identified and listed, rank-order the cards into low, medium, and high groupings. Pleasant memories would constitute the low grouping, less pleasant the middle grouping, and very unpleasant the high grouping. Then, within each group, you can arrange the cards in another order from most pleasant at the bottom of the hierarchy to most painful at the top.

Selection and Training of Counterconditioning or Coping Response

According to the principles of reciprocal inhibition and counterconditioning, for desensitization to take place, the client must respond in a way that inhibits (or counterconditions) the anxiety or other conditioned emotion. A self-control model of desensitization emphasizes the client's learning of a skill to use to cope with the anxiety. In either model, the counselor selects, and trains the client to use, a response that can be considered either an alternative to anxiety or incompatible with anxiety.

Selection of a response. The counselor's first task is to select an appropriate counterconditioning or coping response for the client to use. Typically, the anxiety-inhibiting or counterconditioning response used in desensitization is deep muscle relaxation (Marquis et al., 1973; Wolpe, 1982). Goldfried (1971) also recommends muscle relaxation for use as the coping response. Muscle relaxation has some advantages. As you may remember from Chapter 17, its use in anxiety reduction and management is well documented. Wolpe (1982) prefers muscle relaxation because it doesn't require any sort of motor activity to be directed from the client toward the sources of anxiety (p. 135). Muscle relaxation is easily learned by most clients and easily taught in the interview. It is also adapt-

able for daily client practice. However, an occasional client may have difficulty engaging in relaxation. Further, relaxation is not always applicable to *in vivo* desensitization, in which the client carries out rather than imagines the hierarchy items (Marquis et al., 1973).

When deep muscle relaxation cannot be used as the counterconditioning or coping response, the counselor may decide to proceed without this sort of response or to substitute an alternative response. In some cases, clients have been desensitized without relaxation (Daniels, 1974; Rachman, 1968). However, with a client who is very anxious, it may be risky to proceed without any response to counteract the anxiety. Many other examples of counterconditioning and coping responses have been used in desensitization, including emotive imagery and meditation (Boudreau, 1972), assertion responses, feeding responses, ginger ale (Mogan & O'Brien, 1972), music (Lowe, 1973), laughter (Ventis, 1973), sexual responses (Bass, 1974), anger (Goldstein, Serber, & Piaget, 1970), kung fu (Gershman & Stedman, 1976), and coping thoughts (Weissberg, 1975). Some of these responses quite obviously are less easily applied in an office setting but may be suitable for certain cases of *in vivo* or self-administered desensitization.

If muscle relaxation is not suitable for a client, emotive imagery (Chapter 14), meditation (Chapter 17), and coping thoughts (Chapter 16) may be reasonable substitutes that are practical to use in the interview and easy to teach. For example, if the counselor selects emotive imagery, the client can focus on pleasant scenes during desensitization. If meditation is selected, the client can focus on breathing and counting. In the case of coping thoughts, the client can whisper or subvocalize coping statements.

Explanation of response to the client. Whatever counterconditioning or coping response is selected, its use and purpose in desensitization should be explained to the client. The client will be required to spend a great deal of time in the session and at home learning the response. Usually a large amount of client time will result in more payoffs if the client understands how and why this sort of response should be learned.

In emphasizing that the response is for counterconditioning, the counselor can explain that one of the ways desensitization can help the client is by providing a substitute for anxiety (or other emotions). The counselor should emphasize that this substitute response is incompatible with anxiety and will minimize the felt anxiety so that the client does not continue to avoid the anxiety-provoking situations.

Goldfried (1971) recommends that explanations of relaxation as a coping response should inform clients that they will be made aware of sensations associated with tension and will learn to use these sensations as a signal to cope and to relax away the tension. After the client indicates understanding of the need for learning another response, the counselor can begin to teach the client how to use the selected response.

Training in the response. The counselor will need to provide training for the client in the particular response to be used. The training in muscle relaxation or any other response may require at least portions of several sessions to complete. The training in a counterconditioning or coping response can occur simultaneously with hierarchy construction. Half of the interview can be used for training; the rest can be used for hierarchy construction. Remember, though, that identifying hierarchy items should not occur simultaneously with relaxation. The counselor can follow portions of the interview protocol for cognitive restructuring (Chapter 16) for training in coping statements; the interview checklists for emotive imagery

(Chapter 14), muscle relaxation, and meditation (Chapter 17) can be used to provide training in these responses.

Before and after each training session, the counselor should ask the client to rate the felt level of stress or anxiety. This is another time when the suds scale is very useful. The client can use the 0-to-100 scale and assign a numerical rating to the level of anxiety. Generally, training in the counterconditioning or coping response should be continued until the client can discriminate different levels of anxiety and can achieve a state of relaxation after a training session equivalent to 10 or less on the 100-point suds scale (Marquis et al., 1973). If, after successive training sessions, the client has difficulty using the response in a nonanxious manner, another response may need to be selected.

After the client has practiced the response with the counselor's direction, daily homework practice should be assigned. An adequate client demonstration of the counterconditioning or coping response is one prerequisite for actual scene presentation. A second prerequisite involves a determination of the client's capacity to use imagery.

☐ MODEL DIALOGUE: SELECTION OF AND TRAINING IN COUNTERCONDITIONING OR COPING RESPONSE

Counselor: Joan, perhaps you remember that when I explained desensitization to you, I talked about replacing anxiety with something else, like relaxation. What I'd like to do today is show you a relaxation method you can learn. How does that sound?

Client: OK, is it like yoga?

Counselor: Well, it's carried out differently than yoga, but it is a skill you can learn with practice and it has effects similar to yoga. This is a process of body relaxation. It involves learning to tense and relax different muscle groups in your body. Eventually you will learn to recognize when a part of you starts to get tense, and you can signal to yourself to relax.

Client: Then how do we use it in desensitization?

Counselor: After you learn this, I will ask you to imagine the items on your hierarchy—but only when you're relaxed, like after we have a relaxation session. What happens is that you're imagining something stressful, only you're relaxed. After you keep working with this, the stressful situations become less and less anxiety-provoking for you.

Client: That makes sense to me, I think. The relaxation can help the situation to be less tense.

Counselor: Yes, it plays a big role — which is why I consider the time we'll spend on learning the relaxation skill so important. Now, one more thing, Joan. Before and after each relaxation session, I'll ask you to tell me how tense or how relaxed you feel at that moment. You can do this by using a number from 0 to 100 — 0 would be total relaxation and 100 would be total anxiety or tenseness. How do you feel right now, on that scale?

Client: Well, not totally relaxed, but not real tense. Maybe around a 30.

Counselor: OK. Would you like to begin with a relaxation-training session now?

Client: Sure. [Training in muscle relaxation following the interview checklist presented in Chapter 17 is given to Joan. An abbreviated version of this is also presented in the model dialogue on scene presentation, later in this chapter.]

Imagery Assessment

The typical administration of desensitization relies heavily on client imagery. The relearning (counterconditioning) achieved in desensitization occurs during the client's visualization of the hierarchy items. This, of course, assumes that imagination of a situation is equivalent to a real situation and that the learning that occurs in the imagined situation generalizes to the real situation (Goldfried & Davison, 1976, p. 113). M. J. Mahoney (1974) points out that recent evidence indicates there may be considerable variability in the degree to which these assumptions about imagery really operate. Still, if desensitization is implemented, the client's capacity to generate images is vital to the way this procedure typically is used.

Explanation to the client. The counselor can explain that the client will be asked to imagine the hierarchy items as if the client were a participant in the situation. The counselor might say that imagining a feared situation can be very similar to actually being in the situation. If the client becomes desensitized while imagining the aversive situation, then the client will also experience less anxiety when actually in the situation. The counselor can suggest that because people respond differently to using their imagination, it is a good idea to practice visualizing several situations.

Assessment of client imagery. The client's capacity to generate clear and vivid images can be assessed by use of practice (control) scenes or by a questionnaire, as described in Chapter 14. Generally, it is a good idea to assess the client's imagery for desensitization at two times — when the client is deliberately relaxed and when the client is not deliberately relaxed. According to Wolpe (1982), imagery assessment of a scene under relaxation conditions serves two purposes. First, it gives the therapist information about the client's ability to generate anxiety-free images. Second, it suggests whether any factors are present that may inhibit the client's capacity to imagine anxiety-free material. For example, a client who is concerned about losing self-control may have trouble generating images of a control item (Wolpe, 1982, p. 158). After each visualization, the counselor can ask the client to describe the details of the imagined scene aloud. Clients who cannot visualize scenes may have to be treated with an alternative strategy for fear reduction that does not use imagery, such as participant modeling or *in vivo* desensitization (see also page 507).

Criteria for effective imagery. Remember that, in the typical administration of desensitization, the client's use of imagery plays a major role. A client who is unable to use imagery may not benefit from a hierarchy that is presented in imagination. From the results of the client's imagery assessment, the counselor should determine whether the client's images meet the criteria for effective therapeutic imagery. These four criteria have been proposed by Marquis et al. (1973, p. 10):

1. The client must be able to imagine a scene concretely, with sufficient detail and evidence of touch, sound, smell, and sight sensations.
2. The scene should be imagined in such a way that the client is a participant, not an observer.
3. The client should be able to switch a scene image on and off upon instruction.
4. The client should be able to hold a particular scene as instructed without drifting off or changing the scene.

If these or other difficulties are encountered during imagery assessment, the counselor may decide to continue to use imagery and provide imagery training or to add a dialogue or a script; to present the hierarchy in another manner (slides, role plays, or *in vivo*); or to terminate desensitization and use an alternative therapeutic strategy. Whenever the client is able to report clear, vivid images that meet most of the necessary criteria, the counselor can initiate the "nuts and bolts" of desensitization — presentation of the hierarchy items.

☐ MODEL DIALOGUE: IMAGERY ASSESSMENT

The following assessment should be completed two times: once after a relaxation session and once when Joan is not deliberately relaxed.

Counselor: Joan, I will be asking you in the procedure to imagine the items we've listed in your hierarchy. Sometimes people use their imagination differently, so it's a good idea to see how you react to imagining something. Could you just sit back and close your eyes and relax? Now get a picture of a winter snow scene in your mind. Put yourself in the picture, doing something. [Pauses.] Now, can you describe exactly what you imagined?

Client: Well, it was a cold day, but the sun was shining. There was about a foot of snow on the ground. I was on a toboggan with two friends going down a big hill very fast. At the bottom of the hill we rolled off and fell in the snow. That was cold!

Counselor: So you were able to imagine sensations of coldness. What colors do you remember?

Client: Well, the hill, of course, was real white and the sky was blue. The sun kind of blinded you. I had on a bright red snow parka.

Counselor: OK, good. Let's try another one. I'll describe a scene and ask you to imagine it for a certain amount of time. Try to get a clear image as soon as I've described the scene. Then, when I say "Stop the image," try to erase it from your mind. OK, here's the scene. It's a warm, sunny day with a good breeze. You're out on a boat on a crystal-clear lake. OK — now imagine this — put in your own details. [Pauses.] OK, Joan, stop the image. Can you tell me what you pictured? [Joan describes the images.] How soon did you get a clear image of the scene after I described it?

Client: Oh, not long. Maybe a couple of seconds.

Counselor: Were you able to erase it when you heard me say *stop?*

Client: Pretty much. It took me a couple of seconds to get completely out of it.

Counselor: Did you always visualize being on a boat, or did you find your imagination wandering or revising the scene?

Client: No, I was on the boat the entire time.

Counselor: How do you feel about imagining a scene now?

Client: These are fun. I don't think imagination is hard for me anyway.

Counselor: Well, you do seem pretty comfortable with it, so we can go ahead.

Joan's images meet the criteria for effective imagery: the scenes are imagined concretely; she sees herself in a scene as a participant; she is able to turn the image on and off fairly well on instruction; she holds a scene constant; there is no evidence of any other difficulties.

Hierarchy Scene Presentation

Scenes in the hierarchy are presented after the client has been given training in a counterconditioning or coping response and after the client's imagery capacity has been assessed. Each scene presentation is paired with the counterconditioning or coping response so that the client's anxiety (or other emotion) is counterconditioned, or decreased. There are different ways to present scenes to the client. Our discussion of this component of desensitization reflects some of the possible variations of scene presentation. The counselor must select a method for presenting scenes and a method for client signaling before progressing with actual scene presentation. Scene presentations follow a certain format and usually are concluded after 15 to 20 minutes.

Identify and explain a method of scene presentation. The counselor will first need to decide on the method of scene presentation to use and explain it in detail to the client before proceeding. There are three methods of scene presentation; the alphabetical labels for these methods (R, H, and A) were coined by Evans (1974).

Method R is used mainly when implementing desensitization according to a traditional model based on the principles of reciprocal inhibition, or counterconditioning. In method R, when the client visualizes an item and reports anxiety associated with the visualization, the client is instructed to *remove* or stop the image, then to relax. According to Wolpe (1982), the timing of scene presentation should maximize the amount of time the client imagines a situation without anxiety and minimize the amount of time the client imagines a scene eliciting anxiety.

There are several reasons for having the client remove the image when anxiety occurs. First, the principle of reciprocal inhibition assumes that, for a response such as anxiety to be successfully counterconditioned, the relaxation (or other counterconditioning) response must be stronger than the anxiety response. This principle is applied to scene presentation, so that the reaction any given item elicits from the client is never stronger than the nonanxiety response being used. In the presence of anxiety, the client is told to stop the image to prevent the anxiety from escalating to the point where it might be stronger than the client's state of relaxation. According to Wolpe (1982), continued exposure to a disturbing scene may even increase the client's sensitivity to it. This is an added reason to terminate the scene when it evokes a strong client reaction. However, some studies have found that sensitivity to a scene does not increase when' clients are asked to hold the image in spite of tension (Spiegler et al., 1976; Zemore, 1975). These findings have lent some credence to a method of scene presentation based on a self-control model of desensitization. This has been identified by Evans (1974) as method H.

In method H, when the client indicates anxiety associated with any given scene, the counselor asks the client to *hold* the image, to continue with the visualization, and to relax away the tension. Goldfried (1971) asserts that this is a more realistic method of scene presentation, since in real life the client can't "eliminate" a situation on becoming tense. This method of scene presentation was used successfully in three studies (Denney & Rupert, 1977; Spiegler et al., 1976; Zemore, 1975).

A third method of scene presentation is called method A (Evans, 1974). In method A, when the client indicates tension, he or she is instructed to switch the image to an "*adaptive alternative*" (p. 45). This might consist in an appropriate response in the feared situation or a coping response, similar to the coping thoughts taught to clients in cognitive restructuring and stress inoculation (Chapter 16). For example, a client who feared losing control of his temper with his children might be presented with the hierarchy item: "It is 5:00 at night. You are trying to fix dinner. Your three children are running underfoot and screaming. The telephone and doorbell both ring at the same time." If this item is tension-producing for the client (what parent wouldn't be tense!), he would be instructed to switch off this image and to visualize an adaptive coping response, something he can do that is under his control, such as "Think of staying calm and collected. Ask one child to get the door, the other to answer the phone. Make sure things in the oven are under control before going to the phone or to the door." These coping scenes should be worked out with the client before the hierarchy items are actually presented. This method also has some empirical support (Meichenbaum, 1972).

According to Meichenbaum, client use of coping imagery is based on the premise that when clients imagine hierarchy items, they provide themselves with "a model for their own behavior" (p. 372).

Identify and explain a signaling system. After explaining the scene-presentation method, the counselor will need to explain the use of a signaling process. During the presentation of hierarchy items, there are several times when the counselor and client need to communicate. In order not to interrupt the client's achievement of a relaxed state, it is useful to work out a signaling system the client can use in a relatively nondistracting manner. To prevent the signals from "getting crossed," it is a good idea to identify and explain a signaling system to the client before actually starting to present the hierarchy items.

There is no one right signaling method, and several can be used. You should select one that is clear to both you and the client to prevent any confusion. One signaling method advocated by Wolpe (1982) is to instruct the client to raise the left index finger one inch as soon as a clear image of the item is formed. Wolpe presents the item for a specified time (usually about seven seconds) and then asks the client to stop the image and to rate the level of anxiety felt during the visualization with a number on the 0-to-100 suds scale. This signaling method allows the counselor to determine whether and when the visualization begins. It also provides immediate feedback about the client's suds level of disturbance.

An alternative signaling method is to ask the client to imagine the scene and to indicate whether any anxiety is felt by raising an index finger. This signaling system has the advantage of letting the counselor know the time when the client started to notice the tension. However, with this method, the counselor cannot be sure when the visualization began, nor does the counselor obtain an exact rating of the client's anxiety.

Another signaling method used to indicate quantitative changes in anxiety is to instruct the client to raise a hand as the anxiety goes up (say, above 10 suds) and to lower it as the anxiety decreases (Marquis et al., 1973). This signaling method might be advantageous when the counselor asks the client to hold a scene image and to relax away the tension. The counselor can determine when the client does successfully lower the tension level.

A fourth method of signaling involves use of the words *tense* and *calm* in lieu of hand or finger signals. The client is instructed to say "tense" when anxiety is noticed and "calm" when relaxation is achieved. Marquis et al. (1973, p. 9) point out that this method may be slightly more disruptive of relaxation than hand or finger signals, but it may be clearer and prevent misunderstanding of signals.

None of these methods needs to be used arbitrarily. The counselor may wish to discuss possible signaling methods and encourage the client to choose one. Such choices strengthen the client's belief that she or he is an active, responsible participant in the treatment process. If one signaling method is used initially and seems distracting or confusing, it can be changed.

Format of a scene-presentation session. As soon as the scene-presentation and signaling methods are determined, the counselor can initiate scene presentation. Scene presentation follows a fairly standardized format. Each scene-presentation session should be preceded by a training session involving the designated counterconditioning or coping response. As you will recall, the idea is to present the hierarchy items concurrently with some counterconditioning or coping response. For example, the counselor can inform the client that they will go through a period of relaxation, after which the counselor will ask the client to imagine a scene from the hierarchy. Depending on the particular counterconditioning or coping response to be used, the client should engage in a brief period of muscle relaxation, meditation, or emotive imagery. The client's relaxation rating following this period should be 10 or less on the 100-point suds scale before the counselor presents a hierarchy item.

At this point, the counselor begins by describing a hierarchy item to the client and instructing the client to evoke the scene in imagination. The initial session begins with the first (least anxiety-provoking) item in the hierarchy. Successive scene presentations always begin with the last item successfully completed at the preceding session. This helps to make a smooth transition from one session to the next and checks on learning retention. Starting with the last successfully completed item may also prevent spontaneous recovery of the anxiety response (Marquis et al., 1973, p. 11). Sometimes relapse between two scene-presentation ses-

sions does occur (Agras, 1965; Rachman, 1966), and this procedure is a way to check for it.

In presenting the item, the counselor should describe it and ask the client to imagine it. Usually the counselor presents an item for a specified amount of time before asking the client to stop the image. There is no set duration for scene presentation. Marquis et al. (1973) point out that typically the client is asked to visualize the scene for 20 seconds. Even clients who signal anxiety before 20 seconds are up may be asked to continue to picture the scene for the full time. Clients are then asked to remove the image and relax (the R method), or to switch to an adaptive alternative (the A method).

There are several reasons that a visualization period of at least 20 (and perhaps up to 40) seconds may be important. First, if the client signals anxiety before this time and the counselor immediately instructs the client to stop the image, some avoidance responses may be inadvertently reinforced (Miller & Nawas, 1970). Second, some evidence indicates that both physiological and self-report indexes of anxiety show greater reduction with a longer scene duration, such as 30 seconds per scene (Eberle, Rehm, & McBurney, 1975; Ross & Proctor, 1973; Rudestam & Bedrosian, 1977). Longer scene presentation may result in even greater anxiety reduction for high-intensity items (Eberle et al., 1975) and faster desensitization of high-intensity items (Watts, 1971, 1974). Watts also found that a longer scene presentation of 30 to 45 seconds tended to prevent spontaneous recovery of previously desensitized items.

If the client holds the scene for the specified duration and does not report any tension, the counselor can instruct the client to stop the scene and to take a little time to relax. This relaxation time serves as a breather between item presentations. During this time, the counselor can cue the onset of relaxation with descriptive words such as "let all your muscles relax" or with the presentation of a control item. There is no set time for a pause between items. Generally a pause of 30 to 60 seconds is sufficient, although some clients may need as much as two or three minutes (Marquis et al., 1973).

If the client indicates that anxiety was experienced during the visualization, the counselor will instruct the client to remove the image and relax (method R), hold the image and relax away the tension (method H), or switch the image to an adaptive or coping alternative (method A). Generally, the counselor will pause for 30 to 60 seconds and then present the same item again. Successful coping or anxiety reduction with one item is required before presenting the next hierarchy item. Marquis et al. (1973, p. 11) indicate that an item can be considered successfully completed with two successive no-anxiety presentations. However, items that are very anxiety-arousing, such as those at the high end of the hierarchy, may require three or four successive no-anxiety repetitions or altering items in the hierarchy (Foa et al., 1980).

If an item continues to elicit anxiety after three presentations, this may indicate some trouble and a need for adjustment. Continued anxiety for one item may indicate a problem in the hierarchy or in the client's visualization. There are at least three things a counselor can try to alleviate continual anxiety resulting from the same item: a new, less anxiety-provoking item can be added to the hierarchy; the same item can be presented to the client more briefly; or the client's visualization can be

assessed to determine whether the client is drifting from or revising the scene.

The counselor should be careful to use standardized instructions at all times during scene-presentation sessions. Standardized instructions are important regardless of whether the client signals anxiety or reports a high or a low anxiety rating on the suds scale. Rimm and Masters (1979) observe that a counselor can inadvertently reinforce a client for not signaling anxiety by saying "Good." The client, often eager to please the counselor, may learn to avoid giving reports of anxiety because these are not similarly reinforced.

Each scene-presentation session should end with an item that evokes no anxiety or receives a low suds rating, since the last item of a series is well remembered (Lazarus & Rachman, 1957). At times, the counselor may need to return to a lower item on the hierarchy so that a non-anxiety-provoking scene can end the session. Generally, any scene-presentation session should be terminated

Subject's Name: Jane Doe

Theme of Hierarchy: Criticism

Time needed to relax at the beginning of the session: 15 minutes

Time needed to visualize the scene presented: 10 sec./8 sec./9 sec./5 sec.

Date and Total Time Spent in Session	Item Hierarchy Number	Anxiety + or − or Suds Rating		Time between Items	Comments, Observations, Changes in Procedure, or Other Special Treatment
7-14-84 45 minutes	4	+8 +20	−15 +30	60 sec./ 60 sec./ 30 sec./ 60 sec./	

Figure 18-2. Desensitization record sheet (from *A guidebook for systematic desensitization* (3rd ed.), by J. Marquis, W. Morgan, and G. Piaget. 1973, Veterans' Workshop, Palo Alto, California. Reprinted by permission.)

when three to five hierarchy items have been completed successfully or at the end of 15 to 30 minutes, whichever comes first. A session may be terminated sooner if the client seems restless. Desensitization requires a great deal of client concentration, and the counselor should not try to extend a session beyond the client's concentration limits.

Identify notation method. Desensitization also requires some concentration and attention on the counselor's part. Just think about the idea of conducting perhaps four or five scene-presentation sessions with one client and working with one or more hierarchies with 10 to 20 items per hierarchy! The counselor has a great deal of information to note and recall. Most counselors use some written recording method during the scene-presentation sessions. There are several ways to make notations of the client's progress in each scene-presentation session. We will describe three. These methods are only suggestions; you may discover a notation system that parallels more closely your own procedural style of desensitization.

Marquis et al. (1973) use a "Desensitization Record Sheet" to record the hierarchy item numbers and the anxiety or suds rating associated with each item presentation. Their record sheet is shown in Figure 18-2, with a sample notation provided at the top of the sheet.

Goldfried and Davison (1976) use a notation system written on the 3 × 5 index card that contains the description of the hierarchy item and the item number. Under the item description is space for the counselor to note the duration of the item presentations and whether item presentation elicited anxiety. An example is presented in Figure 18-3. In this example, the numbers refer to the time in seconds that the client visualized each presentation of the item. The plus sign indicates a no-anxiety or low-suds visualization, and the minus sign indicates an anxiety or high-suds visualization. Note that there were two successive no-anxiety visualizations (+ 30 and + 40) before the item was terminated.

One of the most comprehensive notation methods has been developed by Evans (1974), using the front and back of a preprinted 4 × 6 index card. Notations about the client's progress in scene presentation are made on categories listed on the back of the card.

The front of this record is shown in Figure 18-4. On this side of the card, the hierarchy scene itself is

---

Item No. 6
Date 7-14-84

ITEM DESCRIPTION

You are walking to class thinking about the
upcoming exam. Your head feels crammed full of details.
You are wondering whether you've studied the right
material.

+5 −9 +10 −15 +20 −25 +30 +40

Figure 18-3. Notation card (From *Clinical behavior therapy* by Marvin R. Goldfried and Gerald C. Davison. Copyright © 1976 by Holt, Rinehart and Winston, Inc. Reprinted by permission of CBS College Publishing.)

HIERARCHY SCENE
1. You are walking to class thinking about the upcoming exam. Your head feels crammed full of details. You are wondering whether you've studied the right material.

VARIATIONS
2.

3.

4.

Figure 18-4. *Front of record card* (from "A handy record-card for systematic desensitization hierarchy items," by I. M. Evans, *Journal of Behavior Therapy and Experimental Psychiatry,* 1974, *5,* 43–46. Copyright 1974 by Pergamon Press, Inc. Reprinted by permission.)

Item: 6   Theme: Test anxiety   Anxiety Rating: 70 Suds   Rank Order: 6
Adaptive Alternative: Concentrate on what you've studied, not
                     whether it is right or wrong.

PRESENTATION:	1	2	3	4	5	
Version	#1					Starting Suds: 5
Image Latency	8 sec.					Difficulties:
Duration Held	15 sec.					
Image Clarity	08					
Anxiety Latency	10 sec.					Physiological:
Strategy: R/H/A/	A					Some flushing of
Anxiety Decrease	25 sec.					neck.
Duration Held	5 sec.					Date Completed:
Anxiety Suds	45 suds					7-14-84

Success *In Vivo:*
7-28-84

Figure 18-5. *Back of record card* (from "A handy record-card for systematic desensitization hierarchy items," by I. M. Evans, *Journal of Behavior Therapy and Experimental Psychiatry,* 1974, *5,* 43–46. Copyright 1974 by Pergamon Press, Inc. Reprinted by permission.)

described. If, during scene presentation, any variations or revisions are made, these can be recorded below the scene description. A sample hierarchy item has been completed.

The back of the card, used to complete details about the scene-presentation session, is shown in Figure 18-5. Sample descriptions have been completed on this card. The back includes a place at the top of the card for the client's anxiety or suds rating of the item (Anxiety Rating) and the order of the item in the hierarchy (Rank Order). Each item can also be numbered (Item) and identified by the theme of the hierarchy (Theme). If the counselor plans to incorporate coping images into the scene presentation, these can be discussed and noted next to "Adaptive Alternative."

In the right-hand column of this card, there is a place to indicate the client's suds rating after relaxation at the beginning of the session (this should be 10 or less). Any problems encountered in the session can be recorded under "Difficulties." Signs of client anxiety can be noted under "Physiological." The date each hierarchy item is successfully completed is noted under "Date Completed," and the date the client reports an anxiety-free experience of the item in real life can be noted with "Success In Vivo."

The items in the left-hand column of the card under "Presentation" refer to methods of scene presentation and, as Evans (1974) points out, were designed to reflect the major variations in this part of the procedure. The counselor can record the version of the hierarchy item used (from the front of the card), the time required for the client to obtain a clear image (Image Latency), the duration of the scene held by the client (Duration Held), and, if necessary, a rating of the image clarity from 1 (not clear) to 10 (very clear). If the client reports anxiety during the scene visualization, the time at which this is reported after the image is obtained can be noted (Anxiety Latency). Once the client indicates anxiety, the counselor can instruct the client to remove the scene (method R), hold the scene (method H), or switch to the adaptive alternative (method A). The particular method used can be recorded next to "Strategy: R/H/A." If you ask the client to indicate when the anxiety diminishes, the length of time this takes is noted after "Anxiety Decrease." If you ask the client to continue to hold an image despite anxiety, this duration can be noted after "Duration Held." A report of the client's suds level of anxiety during the scene presentation can be noted after "Anxiety Suds."

Although this recording system does take more time to complete, its comprehensiveness can aid the progress of a given session and can pinpoint trouble spots as they occur.

☐ MODEL DIALOGUE: SCENE PRESENTATION

Counselor: Joan, after our relaxation session today, we're going to start working with your hierarchy. I'd like to explain how this goes. After you've relaxed, I'll ask you to imagine the first item on the low end of your hierarchy—that is, the pleasant one. It will help you relax even more. Then I'll describe the next item. I will show you a way to let me know if you feel any anxiety while you're imagining it. If you do, I'll ask you to stop or erase the image and to relax. You'll have some time to relax before I give you an item again. Does this seem clear?

Client: I believe so.

Counselor: One more thing. If at any point during the time you're imagining a scene you feel nervous or anxious about it, just raise your finger. This will signal that to me. OK?

Client: OK.

Counselor: Just to make sure we're on the same track, could you tell me what you believe will go on during this part of desensitization?

Client: Well, after relaxation you'll ask me to imagine an item at the bottom of the hierarchy. If I feel any anxiety, I'll raise my finger and you'll ask me to erase the scene and relax.

Counselor: Good. And even if you don't signal anxiety after a little time of imagining an item, I'll tell you to stop and relax. This gives you a sort of breather. Ready to begin?

Client: Yep.

Counselor: OK, first we'll begin with some relaxation. Just get in a comfortable position and close your eyes and relax. . . . Let the tension drain out of your body. . . . Now, to the word *relax,* just let your arms go limp. . . . Now relax your face. . . . Loosen up your face and neck muscles. . . . As I name each muscle group, just use the word *relax* as the signal to let go of all the tension. . . . Now, Joan, you'll feel even more relaxed by thinking about a pleasant situation. . . . Just imagine you're sitting around a campfire on a cool winter night. . . . You're with some good friends, singing songs and roasting marshmallows. [Presentation of item 1, or control item]. [Gives Joan about 40 seconds for this image.] Now I'd like you to imagine you're sitting in your room at your desk doing math homework that's pretty routine and is fairly easy. [Presentation of item 2 in hierarchy]. [Counselor notes duration of presentation on stopwatch. At 25 seconds Joan has not signaled. Counselor records "+25" for item 2.] OK, Joan, stop that image and erase it from your mind. Just concentrate on feeling very relaxed. [Pauses 30 to 60 seconds.] Now I'd like you to again imagine you're in your room sitting at your desk doing math homework that is routine and fairly simple. [Second presentation of item 2]. [Counselor notes 35 seconds and no signal. Records "+35" on card for item 2.] OK, Joan, now just erase the image from your mind and relax. Let go of all your muscles. [Pause of 40 seconds. Since two successive presentations of this item did not elicit any anxiety, the counselor will move on to item 3.]

Now I'd like you to imagine you're sitting in English class. It's about ten minutes before the bell. Your mind drifts to math class. You wonder if anything will happen like getting called on. [Presentation of item 3 in hierarchy]. [Counselor notes duration of presentation with stopwatch. At 12 seconds, Joan's finger goes up. Counselor records "−12" on card for item 3. Waits 3 more seconds.] OK, Joan, just erase that image from your mind. . . . Now relax. Let relaxation flood your body. . . . Think again about being in front of a campfire. [Pauses for about 40 seconds for relaxation.]

Now I'd like you to again imagine you're sitting in English class. It's almost time for the bell. You think about math class and wonder if you'll be called on. [Second presentation of item 3 in the hierarchy]. [Counselor notes duration with stopwatch. At 30 seconds, Joan has not signaled. Counselor notes "+30" on card.] OK, Joan, now just erase that image and concentrate on relaxing. [Pauses about 40 seconds.] OK, again imagine yourself sitting in English class. It's just a few minutes before the bell. You think about math class and wonder if you'll be called on. [Third presentation of item 3]. [At 30 seconds, no signal. Notation of "+30" recorded on card. Since the last two presentations of this item did not evoke anxiety, the counselor can move on to item 4 or can terminate this scene-presentation session on this successfully completed item if time is up or if Joan is restless.]

Ok, Joan, stop imagining that scene. Think about a campfire. . . . Just relax. [Another control item can be used for variation. After about 30 to 40 seconds, item 4 is presented or session is terminated.]

If this session had been terminated after the successful completion of item 3, the next scene-presentation session would begin with item 3. Other hierarchy items would be presented in the same manner as in this session. If Joan reported anxiety for three successive presentations of one item, the session would be interrupted, and an adjustment in the hierarchy would be made.

LEARNING ACTIVITY #48: SCENE PRESENTATION

This learning activity is designed to familiarize you with some of the procedural aspects of scene presentation. You can complete this activity by yourself or with a partner who can serve as your client.

PART ONE

1. Select one of the hierarchies you or your partner developed in Learning Activity #47, on hierarchy construction.
2. Select a counterconditioning or coping response to use, such as muscle relaxation or imagery.
3. Administer relaxation or imagery to yourself or to your partner.
4. If you have a partner, explain the use of method R of scene presentation and the signaling system in which the person raises a finger when anxiety is noticed or reports a suds rating after the scene is terminated.

5. By yourself or with your partner, start by presenting the lowest item in the hierarchy. If no anxiety is signaled after a specified duration, instruct your partner to remove the image and relax; then re-present the same scene. Remember, two successive no-anxiety presentations are required before presenting the next item. If anxiety is signaled, instruct yourself or your partner to remove the image and relax. After about 30 to 60 seconds, re-present the same item.
6. Select a notation system to use. Record at least the number of times each item was presented, the duration of each presentation, and whether each presentation did or did not evoke anxiety (or the anxiety rating if suds is used).

(continued)

PART TWO

1. Complete the activity again. This time, for step 4, substitute the following: Explain the use of method H of scene presentation and the signaling method in which the client raises a finger when anxiety is increased and lowers it when anxiety is decreased.

2. For step 5: Present the next item in the hierarchy. If no anxiety is indicated by a raised finger after about a 30-second presentation, instruct the person to relax; then present the same item again before moving on.

3. If anxiety is indicated, instruct yourself or the person to hold the scene and try to relax away the tension, indicating decreased tension by a lowered finger.

PART THREE

1. Again, with yourself or a partner, complete Part One. This time, for step 4, do the following. Instruct the person in method A of scene presentation. Identify one or two coping images you or the person could use. Instruct the person in the signaling method in which the word *tense* is used to indicate anxiety and *calm* is used to indicate relaxation.

2. For step 5: Present an item. When you or the person says "tense," instruct yourself or the person to switch to the adaptive alternative (the coping image) and to report relaxation by saying "calm."

PART FOUR

Reflect on or discuss with your partner the different methods of scene presentation and signaling used in this activity. Which ones did you or your partner feel comfortable or uncomfortable using? Did any method seem less confusing or easier than another? If so, why?

Homework and Follow-Up

Homework is essential to the successful completion of desensitization! Homework may include daily practice of the selected relaxation procedure, visualization of the items completed in the previous session, and exposure to *in vivo* situations.

Assignment of homework tasks. Most counselors instruct clients to practice the relaxation method being used once or twice daily. This is especially critical in the early sessions, in which training in the counterconditioning or coping response occurs. In addition, a counselor can assign the client to practice visualizing the items covered in the last session after the relaxation session. Goldfried and Davison (1976) record three to five items on a cassette tape so that clients can administer this assignment themselves. Gradually, *in vivo* homework tasks can be added. As desensitization progresses, the client should be encouraged to participate in real-life situations that correspond to the situations covered in hierarchy-item visualization during the sessions. This is very important in order to facilitate generalization from imagined to real anxiety-producing situations. However, there may be some risk in the client's engaging in a real situation corresponding to a hierarchy item that has not yet been covered in the scene-presentation sessions (Rimm & Masters, 1979).

Homework log sheets and follow-up. The client should record completion of all homework assignments on daily log sheets. After all desensitization sessions are completed, a follow-up session or contact should be arranged.

☐ MODEL DIALOGUE: HOMEWORK AND FOLLOW-UP

Counselor: Joan, you've been progressing through the items on your list very well in our session. I'd like you to try some practice on your own similar to what we've been doing.

Client: OK, what is it?

Counselor: Well, I'm thinking of an item that's near the middle of your list. It's something you've been able to imagine last week and this week without reporting any nervousness. It's the one on your volunteering an answer in class.

Client: You think I should do that?

Counselor: Yes, although there is something I'd like to do first. I will put this item and the two before it on tape. Each day after you practice your relaxation, I'd like you to use the tape and go over these three items just as we do here. If this goes well for you, then next week we can talk about your actually starting to volunteer a bit more in class.

Client: OK with me.

Counselor: One more thing. Each time you use the tape this week, write it down on a blank log sheet.

Also note your tension level before and after the practice with the tape on the 0-to-100 scale. Then I'll see you next week.

Figure 18-6 summarizes all the components of systematic desensitization. You may find this to be a useful review of procedural aspects of this strategy.

☐ PROBLEMS ENCOUNTERED DURING DESENSITIZATION

Although desensitization can be a very effective therapeutic procedure, occasionally problems are encountered that make it difficult or impossible to administer. Sometimes these problems can be minimized or alleviated. At other times, a problem may require the counselor to adopt an alternative strategy.

Wolpe (1982) and Marquis et al. (1973) discuss some of the barriers to effective implementation of desensitization. Some of the more common difficulties include problems in relaxation, imagery, and hierarchy arrangement and presentation. An occasional client may not be able to relax. Sometimes relaxation can be enhanced with additional training or with a gradual shaping process (Morris, 1980). An alternative method of relaxation can be used, or a different type of counterconditioning response can be selected. Another source of difficulty may be the client's inability to generate vivid, clear images. Marquis et al. report that a counselor may be able to strengthen a client's imagery by adding dialogue or a script to the item descriptions. Phillips (1971) has proposed a method of imagery training used to heighten a person's ability to imagine scenes. If imagery continues to be a problem, then *in vivo* desensitization that does not require imagery may be used. Or the hierarchy may be presented by other means, such as slides (O'Neil & Howell, 1969), videocassette tapes

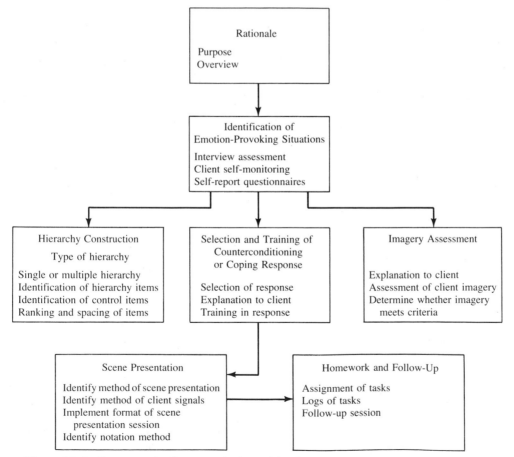

Figure 18-6. Components of systematic desensitization

(Caird & Wincze, 1974), or role play (Hosford, 1969).

An inaccurate hierarchy arrangement, selection of the wrong theme, and inadequacies in the method of hierarchy presentation can also be trouble spots. Sometimes these problems can be alleviated by reordering the hierarchy, reanalyzing the client's fear, or varying the method of scene presentation. Occasionally clients will benefit from a different form of desensitization. Some of the possible variations of desensitization are discussed in the next section.

□ VARIATIONS OF SYSTEMATIC DESENSITIZATION

The desensitization procedure described in this chapter reflects the traditional procedure applied over a series of sessions to an individual client by a counselor, using an individualized hierarchy imagined by the client. This section briefly describes the many possible variations of this method of desensitization. For more detailed information, we encourage you to consult the references mentioned in this section and those listed in the suggested readings at the end of the chapter.

Group-Administered Desensitization
Administration of desensitization to a group of clients who share similar concerns or fears is effective and is more efficient than individual administration. For example, Osterhouse (1976) and Altmaier and Woodward (1981) administered desensitization to a group of test-anxious college students. Other examples of group-administered desensitization have been reported by Paul and Shannon (1966) and Denholtz and Mann (1974). Group-administered desensitization often follows a specific treatment protocol. Standardized relaxation instructions are given to the entire group, and a standardized hierarchy is administered to the group en masse.

Self-Administered Desensitization
Some studies of desensitization have indicated that the presence of a therapist is not critical to the effectiveness of the strategy (Cornish & Dilley, 1973; Nawas et al., 1970; Rebman, 1983). Rosen, Glasgow, and Barrera (1976) found that clients who administered desensitization to themselves continued to improve after posttesting more than clients who were administered desensitization by a

counselor. In self-administered desensitization, the client administers the procedure with the assistance of written instructions, audiotapes (Cornish & Dilley, 1973), or a treatment manual such as the one developed by Dawley and Wenrich (1973). Recent evidence has suggested that self-administered desensitization may incur more dropouts than therapist-administered desensitization (Marshall, Presse, & Andrews, (1976). However, this problem seems to be eliminated by even minimal counselor contact, such as a weekly telephone call to the client.

In Vivo Desensitization
In vivo desensitization involves actual client exposure to the situations in the hierarchy. The client engages in the graded series of situations instead of imagining each item. This variation is used when a client has difficulty using imagery or does not experience anxiety during imagery or when a client's actual exposure to the situations will have more therapeutic effects. If the client can actually be exposed to the feared stimuli, then *in vivo* desensitization is preferable to imagined exposure because it will produce more rapid results and will foster greater generalization. At times the counselor may accompany the client to the feared situation (Sherman, 1972). *In vivo* desensitization resembles participant modeling (Chapter 13), in which the client performs a graduated series of difficult tasks with the help of induction aids. MacDonald and Bernstein (1974) and Turnage and Logan (1974) have reported clinical cases involving *in vivo* desensitization. O'Neil and Howell (1969) found that snake-phobic clients who were exposed to *in vivo* desensitization achieved greater anxiety reduction at follow-up than clients who imagined hierarchy items or clients who saw the items portrayed on color slides. *In vivo* desensitization was effective in reducing children's fear of water (Ultee et al., 1982). Finally, Rovetto (1983) used *in vivo* desensitization to treat driving phobia with the aid of radio contact and telemonitoring of neurophysiological reactions.

The main procedural problem associated with *in vivo* desensitization involves adequate use and control of a counterconditioning response (Marquis et al., 1973). Sometimes it is difficult for a client to achieve a state of deep relaxation while simultaneously performing an activity. However, it is not always necessary to use a counterconditioning response to decrease the client's anxiety in threatening situations. Often exposure alone will result in sufficient anxiety reduction, particularly if the exposure occurs in graduated amounts and with induction aids.

□ SUMMARY

Historically, desensitization probably has the longest track record of any of the therapeutic strategies presented in this book. Its results are well and frequently documented. Yet there is far more controversy surrounding its use than existed 15 years ago, mainly because of alternative explanations to account for its results. We do not believe that de-

sensitization has outlived its usefulness as a method for reducing extreme anxiety or conditioned emotional reactions. But today, desensitization does not occupy a singular place in many practitioners' repertoires of possible anxiety-reduction methods. As an anxiety-management strategy, it currently may be supplemented with or replaced by a variety of other methods for reducing and coping with fears and tension. And, as Krumboltz and Thoresen (1976) assert, the aim of *any* anxiety-reduction strategy should be to teach a client self-control skills so that future stress does not push the client's anxiety beyond "tolerable limits" (p. 247).

POSTEVALUATION

PART ONE

Objective One states that you should be able to identify accurately at least three out of four hierarchies by type. Read each hierarchy carefully and then identify on a piece of paper whether the hierarchy is spatiotemporal, thematic, or personal. Feedback is provided at the end of the postevaluation.

Hierarchy 1 (fear of heights)
1. You are walking along the sidewalk. It is on a completely level street.
2. You are walking along the sidewalk, ascending. At the top of the street, you look down and realize you've climbed a hill.
3. You are climbing a ladder up to a second-story window.
4. You are riding in a car, and the road curves higher and higher.
5. You are riding in a car and you look outside. You notice you are driving on the edge of a good-sized hill.
6. You are starting to climb to the top of a fire tower. You are halfway up. You look down and see how far you've climbed.
7. You are climbing a ladder to the roof of a three-story house.
8. You have climbed to the top of a fire tower and look down.
9. You are riding in a car and are at the edge of a cliff on a mountain.
10. You are at the very top of a mountain, looking down into the surrounding valley.

Hierarchy 2 (fear of being rejected)
1. You speak to a stranger on the street. He doesn't hear you.

2. You go into a department store and request some information from one of the clerks. The clerk snaps at you in response.
3. You ask a stranger to give you change. She gives you a sarcastic reply.
4. You ask a casual acquaintance to lend you a book. He refuses.
5. You ask a friend over to dinner. The friend is too busy to come.
6. You apply for a membership in a social club, and your application is denied.
7. You are competing for a job. You and another person are interviewed. The other person is hired; you are not chosen.
8. You have an argument with your best friend. She leaves suddenly. You don't hear from her for a while.
9. You have an argument with your husband. Your husband says he would rather do things alone than with you.
10. Your husband asks you for a divorce and says he doesn't love you any more.

Hierarchy 3 (loss of a close relationship)
1. You remember a warm, starry night. You ask this woman you love to marry you. She accepts. You are very happy.
2. The two of you are traveling together soon after your marriage, camping out and traveling around in a van.
3. The two of you are running in the water together at the beach and having a good time being together.
4. You and this person are eating dinner together at home.

(continued)

5. The two of you are disagreeing over how to spend money. She wants to save it; you are arguing to use some of it for camping supplies.
6. The two of you are arguing over your child. She wants the child to go with you on all trips; you want a babysitter occasionally.
7. The two of you are starting to eat some meals apart. You are working late to avoid coming home for dinner.
8. She is wrapped up in her social activities; you, in your work. On the weekends you go your separate ways.
9. You have a discussion about your relationship and separate activities. You start sleeping on the couch.
10. The two of you go to see a lawyer to initiate discussion about a separation.

Hierarchy 4 (fear of giving speeches)
1. Your instructor casually mentions a required speech to be given by the end of the course.
2. Your instructor passes around a sign-up sheet for the speeches. You sign up.
3. You talk about the speech with some of your classmates. You aren't sure what to say.
4. You go to the library to look up some resource material for your speech. You don't find too much.
5. Some of your classmates start to give speeches. You think about how good their speeches are and wonder how yours will be.
6. It is a week before the speech. You're spending a lot of time working on it.
7. It is the day before the speech. You're going over your notes religiously.
8. It is the night before the speech. You lie awake thinking about it.
9. It is the next morning. You wake up and remember it is speech day. You don't feel hungry at breakfast.
10. Later that morning you're walking to speech class. A classmate comes up and says "Well, I guess you're on today."
11. You're sitting in speech class. The instructor will call on you any moment. You keep going over your major points.

PART TWO

Objective Two asks you to identify and describe at least 9 out of 11 procedural steps of desensitization, using a written client case description. Read this case description carefully; then respond by identifying and describing the 11 items listed after the description.

Your client is a fifth-grade boy at a local elementary school. This year, the client's younger sister has entered first grade at the same school. After a few weeks at school, your client, Ricky, began to complain about school to his teacher and parents. He would come to school and get sick. His parents would come and take him home. After a medical check-up, the doctor can find nothing physically wrong with Ricky. Yet Ricky continues either to get sick at school or to wake up sick in the morning. He appears to be better on weekends. He says he hates school and it makes him sick to his stomach to have to go. On occasion, he has vomited in the morning. The parents report that it is getting harder and harder to get Ricky to attend school. Suppose you were to use desensitization as one strategy in this case to help Ricky overcome his tension and avoidance of school. Identify and describe how you would implement the following 11 steps of desensitization with Ricky. Adapt your language to words that a 10-year-old could understand.

1. Your rationale of desensitization.
2. Your description of an overview of desensitization.
3. A method for helping Ricky identify the anxiety-provoking situations about school.
4. The type of hierarchy that would be used with Ricky.
5. A ranking method Ricky could use to arrange the hierarchy items.
6. An appropriate counterconditioning or coping response you could train Ricky to use.
7. A method of assessing Ricky's imagery capacity.
8. A method of scene presentation you would use with Ricky.
9. A method Ricky could use for signaling during scene presentation.
10. A notation method you might use to keep track of hierarchy presentation.
11. An example of one homework task associated with desensitization that you might assign to Ricky to complete.

Feedback follows the Postevaluation.

PART THREE

Objective Three asks you to demonstrate at least 22 out of 28 steps of systematic desensitization with a role-play client. Several role-play interviews may be required in order for you to include all the major procedural components of desensitization. Use the Interview Checklist for Systematic Desensitization on pages 512–518 as an assessment tool.

510

☐ SUGGESTED READINGS

Altmaier, E. M., & Woodward, M. (1981). Group vicarious desensitization of test anxiety. *Journal of Counseling Psychology, 28,* 467–469.

Bornstein, P. H., & Knapp, M. (1981). Self-control desensitization with a multi-phobic boy: A multiple baseline design. *Journal of Behavior Therapy and Experimental Psychiatry, 12,* 281–285.

Elmore, R. T., Wildman, R. W., & Westefeld, J. S. (1980). The use of systematic desensitization in the treatment of blood phobia. *Journal of Behavior Therapy and Experimental Psychiatry, 11,* 277–279.

Foa, E. B., Stekette, G. S., & Ascher, L. M. (1980). Systematic desensitization. In A. Goldstein & E. B. Foa (Eds.), *Handbook of behavioral interventions: A clinical guide.* New York: Wiley.

Howard, W. A., Murphy, S. M., & Clarke, J. C. (1983). The nature and treatment of fear of flying: A controlled investigation. *Behavior Therapy, 14,* 557–567.

Kirsch, I., & Henry, D. (1979). Self-desensitization and meditation in the reduction of public speaking anxiety. *Journal of Consulting and Clinical Psychology, 47,* 536–541.

Kirsch, I., Tennen, H., Wickless, C., Saccone, A. J., & Cody, S. (1983). The role of expectancy in fear reduction. *Behavior Therapy, 14,* 520–533.

Leal, L., Baxter, E. G., Martin, J., & Marx, R. W. (1981). Cognitive modification and systematic desensitization with test anxious high school students. *Journal of Counseling Psychology, 28,* 525–528.

Lent, R. W., Russell, R. K., & Zamostny, K. P. (1981). Comparison of cue-controlled desensitization, rational structuring and credible placebo in the treatment of speech anxiety. *Journal of Consulting and Clinical Psychology, 49,* 608–610.

Levine, B. A., & Wolpe, J. (1980). *In vivo* desensitization of a severe driving phobia through radio contact. *Journal of Behavior Therapy and Experimental Psychiatry, 11,* 281–282.

Marquis, J., Morgan, W., & Piaget, G. (1973). *A guidebook for systematic desensitization* (3rd ed.). Palo Alto, CA: Veterans' Workshop.

Miller, W. R., & DiPilato, M. (1983). Treatment of nightmares via relaxation and desensitization: A controlled evaluation. *Journal of Consulting and Clinical Psychology, 51,* 870–877.

Morris, R. J. (1980). Fear reduction methods. In F. H. Kanfer & A. P. Goldstein (Eds.), *Helping people change.* New York: Pergamon Press.

Rebman, V. L. (1983). Self-control desensitization with cue controlled relaxation for treatment of a conditioned vomiting response to air travel. *Journal of Behavior Therapy and Experimental Psychiatry, 14,* 161–164.

Redd, W. H. (1980). *In vivo* desensitization in the treatment of chronic emesis following gastrointestinal surgery. *Behavior Therapy, 11,* 421–427.

Rimm, D. C., & Masters, J. C. (1979). *Behavior therapy: Techniques and empirical findings* (2nd ed.). New York: Academic Press.

Rovetto, F. M. (1983). *In vivo* desensitization of a severe driving phobia through radio contact with telemonitoring of neurophysiological reactions. *Journal of Behavior Therapy and Experimental Psychiatry, 14,* 49–54.

Schindler, F. E. (1980). Treatment by systematic desensitization of a recurring nightmare of a real life trauma. *Journal of Behavior Therapy and Experimental Psychiatry, 11,* 53–54.

Ultee, C. A., Griffioen, D., & Schellekens, J. (1982). The reduction of anxiety in children: A comparison of the effects of "systematic desensitization *in vitro*" and "systematic desensitization *in vivo*." *Behaviour Research and Therapy, 20,* 61–67.

Van Hasselt, V. B., Hersen, M., Bellack, A. S., Rosenblum, N. D., & Lamparski, D. (1979). Tripartite assessment of the effects of systematic desensitization in a multi-phobic child: An experimental analysis. *Journal of Behavior Therapy and Experimental Psychiatry, 10,* 51–55.

Wolpe, J. (1958). *Psychotherapy by reciprocal inhibition.* Stanford, CA: Stanford University Press.

Wolpe, J. (1976). *Theme and variations: A behavior therapy casebook.* New York: Pergamon Press. Chapter 2, "The Reciprocal Inhibition Theme and the Emergence of Its Role in Psychotherapy."

Wolpe, J. (1982). *The practice of behavior therapy* (3rd ed.). New York: Pergamon Press.

FEEDBACK: POSTEVALUATION

PART ONE

1. Spatiotemporal. Items are arranged by increasing height off the ground.
2. Thematic. Items are arranged around the theme of rejection.
3. Personal. Items are arranged from pleasant to unpleasant memories of an ex-spouse.
4. Spatiotemporal. Items are arranged by time; as the time approaching the situation diminishes, the fear intensifies.

PART TWO

Here are some possible descriptions of the 11 procedural steps of desensitization you were asked to identify and describe. See whether your responses are in some way similar to these.

1. Rationale: "Ricky, it seems that it's very hard for you to go to school now or even think about school without feeling sick. There are some things about school that upset you this much. We can work together to find out what bothers

(continued)

you, and I can help you learn to be able to go to school without feeling so upset or sick to your stomach, so you can go to school again and feel OK about it. How does that sound?"

2. Overview: "There are several things you and I will do together. First we'll talk about the things about school that upset you. I'll ask you to think about these situations, only instead of feeling upset when you do, I'll show you a way to stay calm and keep the butterflies out of your stomach. It will take a lot of practice in this room, but after a while you will be able to go back to your class and feel calm and OK about it!"

3. Method for identifying the anxiety-provoking situations:

   a. Use of interview leads such as "Ricky, what do you do in school that makes you feel sick? What about school makes you want to stay at home? What happens at school that bothers you? When do you feel most upset about school?"

   b. Use of client self-monitoring: "Ricky, could you keep a chart for me this week? Each time you feel upset about school, mark down what has happened or what you're thinking about that makes you feel upset or sick."

4. Type of hierarchy: A thematic hierarchy would be used. One hierarchy might consist of school-related anxiety-provoking situations. Depending on the anxiety-provoking situations identified, another thematic hierarchy may emerge, dealing with jealousy. It is possible that the avoidance of school is a signal that Ricky really fears being upstaged by his younger sister.

5. Ranking method: Because of Ricky's age, an easy ranking method should be used. Probably it would be easiest to start with the low, medium, high method. You would ask Ricky to sort the cards of the hierarchy items into three piles: a low pile (things that upset him only a little), a medium pile (things that upset him somewhat), and a high pile (things that really upset him). You might give him a pictorial or visual "anchor point" to describe the three piles: "The low pile is like going to the dentist to have your teeth examined. The middle pile is like going to the dentist to have your teeth cleaned. The high pile is going to the dentist to have a cavity in your tooth filled."

6. Counterconditioning or coping response: Muscle relaxation can be used easily with a child Ricky's age as long as you just show him (by modeling) the different muscle groups and the way to tighten and let go of a muscle.

7. Method of imagery assessment: Ask Ricky to tell you some daydreams he has or some things he loves to do. Before and after a relaxation-training session, ask him to imagine or pretend he is doing one of these things. Then have him describe the details of his imagined scene. Children often have a capacity for more vivid and descriptive imagery than adults.

8. Method of scene presentation: We would probably try method R or method A. Method R is simple to use and easily understood (stop imagining _____; now relax). Method A could be useful, since Ricky is legally required to attend school and does need to learn to cope with it. Method H may be less easily understood by a child, who might find it difficult to know what is meant by "hold the image and relax away the tension."

9. Signaling method: Again, you want to suggest something that is easily understood and used by Ricky. Perhaps the use of *word* signals might minimize any confusion. You would instruct him to say "tense" when he's upset or anxious and "calm" when he's less bothered or more relaxed.

10. Notation method: The easiest notation method might be to use each hierarchy card and note the number of times each item is presented, the duration of each presentation, and an indication of whether Ricky did or did not report being "tense" during or after the item. This notation system looks like this:

    Item No. _____ Date _____
    Item description
    $+10 - 15 + 15 + 20$

    The item was presented four times; the numbers 10, 15, 15, and 20 refer to the duration of each presentation; the + indicates no anxiety report; the — indicates a "tense" signal.

11. Examples of possible homework tasks:

    a. A list of anxiety-related situations.

    b. Practice of muscle relaxation.

    c. Practice of items covered in the interview, possibly with the use of coping imagery.

    d. Exposure to certain school-related *in vivo* situations.

PART THREE

You or an observer can rate your desensitization interviews using the Interview Checklist for Systematic Desensitization that follows.

(continued)

FEEDBACK: POSTEVALUATION (continued)

INTERVIEW CHECKLIST FOR SYSTEMATIC DESENSITIZATION

Instructions to observer: Listed below are some procedural steps of systematic desensitization. Check which of these steps were used by the counselor in implementing this procedure. Some possible examples of these leads are described in the right column of the checklist.

Item	Examples of counselor leads
I. Rationale	
_____ 1. Counselor gives client rationale for desensitization, clearly explaining how it works.	"This procedure is based on the idea that you can learn to replace your fear (or other conditioned emotion) in certain situations with a better or more desirable response, such as relaxation or general feelings of comfort." "You have described some situations in which you have learned to react with fear (or some other emotion). This procedure will give you skills to help you cope with these situations so they don't continue to be so stressful."
_____ 2. Counselor describes brief overview of desensitization procedure.	"There are three basic things that will happen—first, training you to relax, next, constructing a list of situations in which you feel anxious, and finally, having you imagine scenes from this list, starting with low-anxiety scenes, while you are deeply relaxed." "First you will learn how to relax and how to notice tension so you can use it as a signal to relax. Then we'll identify situations that, to varying degrees, upset you or make you anxious. Starting with the least discomforting situations, you will practice the skill of relaxation as a way to cope with the stress."
_____ 3. Counselor checks to see whether client is willing to use strategy.	"Are you ready to try this now?"
II. Identification of Emotion-Provoking Situations	
_____ 4. Counselor initiates at least one of the following means of identifying anxiety-provoking stimulus situations:	
_____a. Interview assessment through problem leads.	"When do you notice that you feel most _____?" "Where are you when this happens?" "What are you usually doing when you feel _____?" "What types of situations seem to bring on this feeling?"
_____b. Client self-monitoring.	"This week I'd like you to keep track of any situation that seems to bring on these feelings. On your log, write down where you are, what you're doing, whom you're with, and the intensity of these feelings."
_____c. Self-report questionnaires.	"One way that we might learn more about some of the specific situations that you find stressful is for you to complete this short questionnaire. There are no right or wrong answers—just describe how you usually feel or react in the situations presented."
_____ 5. Counselor continues to assess anxiety-provoking situations until client identifies some specific situations.	"Let's continue with this exploration until we get a handle on some things. Right now you've said that you get nervous and upset around certain kinds of people. Can you tell me some types or characteristics of people that bother you or make you anxious almost always?"

(continued)

Item	Examples of counselor leads
	"OK, good, so you notice you're always very anxious around people who can evaluate or criticize you, like a boss or teacher."

III. Hierarchy Construction

_____ 6. Counselor identifies a type of hierarchy to be constructed with client:

    _____ a. Spatiotemporal.

    _____ b. Thematic.

    _____ c. Personal.

    _____ d. Combination.

"Now we're going to make a list of these anxiety-provoking situations and fill in some details and arrange these in an order, starting with the least anxiety-provoking situation all the way to the most anxiety-provoking one."

"Since you get more and more anxious as the time for the speech gets closer and closer, we'll construct these items by closer and closer times to the speech."

"We'll arrange these items according to the different kinds of situations in which people criticize you — depending on who does it, what it's about, and so on."

"We'll construct a hierarchy of items that represent your memories about her, starting with pleasant memories and proceeding to unpleasant or painful memories."

_____ 7. Counselor identifies the number of hierarchies to be developed:

    _____ a. Single hierarchy.

    _____ b. Multiple hierarchies.

"We will take all these items that reflect different situations that are anxiety-producing for you and arrange them in one list."

"Since there are a number of types of situations you find stressful, we'll construct one list for situations involving criticism and another list for situations involving social events."

_____ 8. Counselor initiates identification of hierarchy items through one or more methods:

    _____ a. Interview questions (_not_ when client is engaged in relaxation).

    _____ b. Client completion of note cards (homework).

"I'd like us to write down some items that describe each of these anxiety-provoking scenes with quite a bit of detail."

"Describe for me what your mother could say that would bother you most. How would she say it? Now who, other than your mother, could criticize you and make you feel worse? What things are you most sensitive to being criticized about?"

"This week I'd like you to add to this list of items. I'm going to give you some blank index cards. Each time you think of another item that makes you get anxious or upset about criticism, write it down on one card."

_____ 9. Counselor continues to explore hierarchy items until items are identified that meet the following criteria:

    _____ a. Some items, if carried out _in vivo_, are under client's control (do not require instigation from others).

    _____ b. Items are concrete and specific.

    _____ c. Items are similar to or represent past, present, or future situations that _have_ provoked or _could_ provoke the emotional response from client.

"Can you think of some items that, if you actually were to carry them out, would be things you could initiate without having to depend on someone else to make the situation happen?"

"OK, now just to say that you get nervous at social functions is a little vague. Give me some details about a social function in which you might feel pretty comfortable and one that could make you feel extremely nervous."

"Think of items that represent things that have made you anxious before or currently — and things that could make you anxious if you encountered them in the future."

(continued)

FEEDBACK: POSTEVALUATION (continued)

Item	Examples of counselor leads
———d. Items have sampled broad range of situations in which emotional response occurs.	"Can you identify items representing different types of situations that seem to bring on these feelings?"
———e. Items represent different levels of emotion aroused by representative stimulus situations.	"Let's see if we have items here that reflect different amounts of the anxiety you feel. Here are some items that don't make you too anxious. What about ones that are a little more anxiety-provoking, up to ones where you feel panicky?"
———10. Counselor asks client to identify several control items (neutral, non-emotion-arousing).	"Sometimes it's helpful to imagine some scenes that aren't related to things that make you feel anxious. Could you describe something you could imagine that would be pleasant and relaxing?"
———11. Counselor explains purpose of ranking and spacing items according to increasing levels of arousal.	"It may take a little time, but you will rank these hierarchy items from least anxiety-producing to most anxiety-producing. This gives us an order to the hierarchy that is gradual, so we can work just with more manageable situations before moving on to more stressful ones."
———12. Counselor asks client to arrange hierarchy items in order of increasing arousal, using one of the following ranking methods, and explains method to client:	"Now I would like you to take the items and arrange them in order of increasing anxiety, using the following method."
———a. Rank-ordering.	"We have each hierarchy item written on a separate note card. Go through the cards and rank-order them according to increasing levels of anxiety. Items that don't provoke much anxiety go on the bottom, followed by items that are successively more anxiety-producing."
———b. "Suds."	"I'd like you to arrange these items using a 0-to-100 scale. 0 represents total relaxation and 100 is comparable to complete panic. If an item doesn't give you any anxiety, give it a 0. If it is just a little stressful, may be a 15 or 20. Very stressful items would get a higher number, depending on how stressful."
———c. Low/medium/high ordering.	"Take the items written on these cards and sort them into one of three groups. One group, small amounts of anxiety. The second group would consist of items provoking an average amount of anxiety. The third group would consist of items that are very anxiety-producing for you."
———13. Counselor adds or deletes items if necessary in order to achieve reasonable spacing of items in hierarchy.	"Let's see, at the lower end of the hierarchy you have many items. We might drop out a few of these. But you have only three items at the upper end, so we have some big gaps here. Can you think of a situation provoking a little bit more anxiety than this item but not quite as much as this next one? We can add that in here."

IV. Selection and Training of Counterconditioning or Coping Response

———14. Counselor selects appropriate counterconditioning or coping response to use to countercondition or cope with anxiety (or other conditioned emotion):	
———a. Deep muscle relaxation.	(contrasting tensed and relaxed muscles)
———b. Emotive imagery.	(evoking pleasurable scenes in imagination)
———c. Meditation.	(focusing on breathing and counting)

(continued)

Item	Examples of counselor leads
——d. Coping thoughts or statements.	(concentrating on coping or productive thoughts incompatible with self-defeating ones)
——15. Counselor explains purpose of particular response selected and describes its role in desensitization.	"This response is like a substitute for anxiety. It will take time to learn it, but it will help to decrease your anxiety so that you can face rather than avoid these feared situations." "This training will help you recognize the onset of tension. You can use these cues you learn as a signal to relax away the tension."
——16. Counselor trains client in use of counterconditioning or coping response and suggests daily practice of this response.	"We will spend several sessions learning this so you can use it as a way to relax. This relaxation on your part is a very important part of this procedure. After you practice this here, I'd like you to do this at home two times each day over the next few weeks. Each practice will make it easier for you to relax."
——17. Counselor asks client before and after each training session to rate felt level of anxiety or arousal.	"Using a scale from 0 to 100, with 0 being complete relaxation and 100 being intense anxiety, where would you rate yourself now?"
——18. Counselor continues with training until client can discriminate different levels of anxiety and can use nonanxiety response to achieve 10 or less rating on 0-to-100 scale.	"Let's continue with this until you feel this training really has an effect on your relaxation state after you use it."

V. Imagery Assessment

——19. Counselor explains use of imagery in desensitization.	"In this procedure, I'll ask you to imagine each hierarchy item as if you were actually there. We have found that imagining a situation can be very similar to actually being in the situation. Becoming desensitized to anxiety you feel while imagining an unpleasant situation will transfer to real situations, too."
——20. Counselor assesses client's capacity to generate vivid images by:	"It might be helpful to see how you react to using your imagination."
——a. Presenting control items when client is using a relaxation response.	"Now that you're relaxed, get a picture in your mind of sitting in the sun on a warm day. The sky is very blue, not a cloud in it. The grass and trees are green. You can feel the warmth of the sun on your body."
——b. Presenting hierarchy items when client is not using a relaxation response.	"OK, just imagine that you're at this party. You don't know anyone. Get a picture of yourself and the other people there. It's a very large room."
——c. Asking client to describe imagery evoked in *a* and *b*.	"Can you describe what you imagined? What were the colors you saw? What did you hear or smell?"
——21. Counselor, with client's assistance, determines whether client's imagery meets the following criteria and, if so, decides to continue with desensitization:	
——a. Client is able to imagine scene concretely with details.	"Were you able to imagine the scene clearly? How many details can you remember?"
——b. Client is able to imagine scene as participant, not onlooker.	"When you imagined the scene, did you feel as if you were actually there and involved—or did it seem as if you were just an observer, perhaps watching it happen to someone else?"
——c. Client is able to switch scene on and off when instructed to.	"How soon were you able to get an image after I gave it to you? When did you stop the image after I said *Stop?*"
——d. Client is able to hold scene without drifting off or revising it.	"Did you ever feel as if you couldn't concentrate on the scene and started to drift off?"

(continued)

FEEDBACK: POSTEVALUATION (continued)

Item	*Examples of counselor leads*
——e. Client shows no evidence of other difficulties.	"Did you ever change anything about the scene during the time you imagined it?" "What else did you notice that interfered with getting a good picture of this in your mind?"

VI. Hierarchy Scene Presentation

Item	*Examples of counselor leads*
——22. Counselor identifies and explains method of scene presentation to be used:	"I'd like to explain exactly how we will proceed. I'm going to present an item in the hierarchy to you after we go through relaxation. Here is what I'll instruct you to do."
——a. Method R — client will be instructed to stop image when anxiety is felt and to relax.	"When you tell me that you feel some anxiety while imagining the scene, I'll ask you to stop or remove the scene from your mind. Then I'll instruct you to relax. You'll have some time to relax before I ask you to imagine the scene another time."
——b. Method H — client will be instructed to hold image when anxiety is felt and to relax away tension.	"When you indicate you're imagining a scene, I'll ask you to continue to visualize the scene but to relax away the tension as you do so."
——c. Method A — client will be instructed to switch image to coping image when anxiety is felt.	"When you indicate that you feel some anxiety while you're imagining the scene, I'll ask you to switch the scene to a type of coping scene and to concentrate for a few minutes on the coping image."
——23. Counselor identifies and explains method of signaling to be used:	"It's very important that we work out a signaling system for you to use when I present the hierarchy items to you. I'll explain how you can signal. Make sure to tell me if it doesn't seem clear."
——a. Client is instructed to raise index finger when clear image is visualized.	"When I present an item, I'd like you to raise your index finger slightly at the point when you obtain a clear picture of the scene in your mind."
——b. Client is instructed to raise index finger when anxiety is noticed while visualizing.	"I'll ask you to imagine an item. If at any point during this imagination, you feel tension, signal this by raising your index finger."
——c. Client is instructed to raise finger to signal increased anxiety and to lower finger to indicate decreased anxiety.	"When you feel anxiety building up as you imagine the item, signal this by raising your finger. As the anxiety decreases and calmness takes over, signal this by lowering your finger."
——d. Client is instructed to indicate anxiety with the word *tense* and to signal relaxation with the word *calm*.	"When, during the visualization of an item, you notice anxiety, say 'tense.' When you feel calmer and more relaxed, say 'calm.'"
——24. For each session of scene presentation:	
——a. Counselor precedes scene presentation with muscle relaxation or other procedures to help client achieve relaxation before scenes are presented.	"Let your whole body become heavier and heavier as all your muscles relax. . . . Feel the tension draining out of your body. . . . Relax the muscles of your hands and arms. . . ."
——b. Counselor begins initial session with lowest (least anxiety-provoking) item in hierarchy and for successive sessions begins with last item successfully completed at previous session.	"I'm going to start this first session with the item that is at the bottom of the hierarchy." "Today we'll begin with the item we ended on last week for a review."
——c. Counselor describes item and asks	"Just imagine you are sitting in the classroom waiting for the

(continued)

Item	Examples of counselor leads
client to imagine it for 20 to 40 seconds.	test to be passed to you, wondering how much you can remember." [Counts 20 to 40 seconds, then instructs client in either R, H, or A method.]
____(1) If client held image and did not signal anxiety, counselor instructs client to stop image and relax for 30 to 60 seconds.	"Now, stop visualizing this scene and just take a little time to relax. Think of sitting in the sun on a warm day, with blue sky all around you."
____(2) If client indicated anxiety during or after visualizing scene, counselor uses method R, H, or A, selected in no. 22.	(R) "Now remove the image and just relax." (H) "Now hold the image but relax away the tension." (A) "Switch the image to the coping one we discussed earlier."
____d. After pause of 30 to 60 seconds between items, counselor presents each item to client a second time.	"Now I want you to imagine the same thing. Concentrate on being very relaxed, then imagine that you are sitting in the classroom waiting for the test to be passed to you, wondering how much you can remember."
____e. Each item is successfully completed (with no anxiety) at least two successive times (more for items at top of hierarchy) before new item is presented.	"I'm going to present this scene to you once more now. Just relax, then imagine that. . . ."
____f. If an item elicits anxiety after three presentations, counselor makes some adjustments in hierarchy or in client's visualization process.	"Let's see what might be bogging us down here. Do you notice that you are drifting away from the scene while you're imagining it—or revising it in any way? Can you think of a situation we might add here that is just a little bit less stressful for you than this one?"
____g. Standardized instructions are used for each phase of scene presentation; reinforcement of *just* the no-anxiety items is avoided.	"OK, I see that was not stressful for you. Just concentrate on relaxing a minute." "What was your feeling of anxiety on the 0-to-100 scale? 20. OK, I want you to just relax for a minute, then I'll give you the same scene."
____h. Each scene-presentation session ends with a successfully completed item (no anxiety for at least two successive presentations).	"OK, let's end today with this item we've just been working on, since you reported 5 suds during the last two presentations."
____ i. Each session is terminated:	"We've done quite a bit of work today. Just spend a few minutes relaxing, and then we will stop."
____(1) When three to five items are completed.	
____(2) After 15 to 20 minutes of scene presentation.	
____(3) After indications of client restlessness or distractibility.	
____25. Counselor uses written recording method during scene presentation to note client's progress through hierarchy.	"As we go through this session, I'm going to make some notes about the number of times we work with each item and your anxiety rating of each presentation."

VII. Homework and Follow-Up

____26. Counselor assigns homework tasks that correspond to treatment progress of desensitization procedure:	"There is something I'd like you to do this week on a daily basis at home."

(continued)

FEEDBACK: POSTEVALUATION (continued)

Item	Examples of counselor leads
____a. Daily practice of selected relaxation procedure.	"Practice this relaxation procedure two times each day in a quiet place."
____b. Visualization of items successfully completed at previous session.	"On this tape there are three items we covered this week. Next week at home, after your relaxation sessions, practice imagining each of these three items."
____c. Exposure to *in vivo* situations corresponding to successfully completed hierarchy items.	"You are ready now to actually go to a party by yourself. We have gotten to a point where you can imagine doing this without any stress."
____27. Counselor instructs client to record completion of homework on daily log sheets.	"Each time you complete a homework practice, record it on your log sheets."
____28. Counselor arranges for follow-up session or check-in.	"Check in with me in two weeks to give me a progress report."

Observer comments: _____

SELF-MANAGEMENT STRATEGIES: SELF-MONITORING, STIMULUS CONTROL, AND SELF-REWARD

NINETEEN

Self-management is a process in which clients direct their own behavior change with any one therapeutic strategy or a combination of strategies. For self-management to occur, the client must take charge of manipulating either internal or external variables to effect a desired change. Although a counselor may instigate self-management procedures and train the client in them, the client assumes the control for carrying out the process. Kanfer (1975, p. 310) distinguishes between therapist-managed procedures, in which a majority of the "therapeutic work" occurs *during* the interviews, and self-managed (or client-managed) procedures, in which most of the work takes place *between* sessions.

Self-management is a relatively recent phenomenon in counseling, and reports of clinical applications and theoretical descriptions have mushroomed since 1970. During this time, definitions of self-management have remained unclear, partly because of terminological confusion. Self-change methods have been referred to as self-control (Cautela, 1969; Thoresen & Mahoney, 1974), self-regulation (Kanfer, 1970, 1975), and self-management (M. J. Mahoney, 1971, 1972). We prefer the label *self-management* because it suggests conducting and handling one's life in a somewhat skilled manner. The term *self-management* also avoids the concepts of inhibition and restraint often associated with the words *control* and *regulation* (Thoresen & Mahoney).

In using self-management procedures, a client directs change efforts by modifying aspects of the environment or by manipulating and administering consequences (Jones, Nelson & Kazdin, 1977, p. 151). This chapter describes three self-management strategies:

Self-monitoring—self-observing and self-recording particular behaviors (thoughts, feelings, and actions) about oneself and the interactions with environmental events.

Stimulus control—the prearrangement of antecedents or cues to increase or decrease a target behavior.

Self-reward — self-presentation of a self-determined positive stimulus following a desired response.

These three strategies are typically classified as self-management because in each procedure the client, in a self-directed fashion, prompts, alters, or controls antecedents and consequences to produce the desired behavioral changes. However, none of these strategies is entirely independent of environmental variables and external sources of influence (Jones et al., 1977).

In addition to these three self-management procedures, it should be noted that a client can use virtually any helping strategy in a self-directed manner. For example, a client could apply relaxation training to manage anxiety by using a relaxation-training audiotape without the assistance of a counselor. In fact, some degree of client self-management may be a necessary component of every successful therapy case. For example, in all the other helping strategies described in this book, some elements of self-management are suggested in the procedural guidelines for strategy implementation. These self-managed aspects of any therapy procedure typically include —

1. Client self-directed practice in the interview.
2. Client self-directed practice in the *in vivo* setting (often through homework tasks).
3. Client self-observation and recording of target behaviors or of homework.
4. Client self-reward (verbal or material) for successful completion of action steps and homework assignments.

☐ OBJECTIVES

1. Given a written client case description, describe the use of the six components of self-monitoring for this client.
2. Teach another person how to engage in self-monitoring as a self-change strategy.
3. Given a client case description, describe how the client could use stimulus-control methods to reduce or increase the rate of a behavior.
4. Given a written client case description, be able to describe the use of the four components of self-reward for this client.
5. Teach another person how to use self-reward.

☐ CHARACTERISTICS OF AN EFFECTIVE SELF-MANAGEMENT PROGRAM

Well-constructed and well-executed self-management programs have some advantages that are not so apparent in counselor-administered procedures. For instance, use of a self-management procedure may increase a person's perceived control over the environment and decrease dependence on the counselor or others. Perceived control over the environment often motivates a person to take some action (Rotter, Chance, & Phares, 1972). Second, self-management approaches are practical — inexpensive and portable (Thoresen & Mahoney, 1974, p. 7). Third, such strategies are usable. By this we mean that occasionally a person will refuse to go "into therapy" to stop drinking or to lose weight (for example) but will agree to use the self-administered instructions that a self-management program provides. In fact, one study found that people who had never received counseling were more agreeable than clients to the idea of using self-management (Williams, Canale, & Edgerly, 1976). Finally, self-management strategies may enhance generalization of learning — both from the interview to the environment and from problematic to nonproblematic situations (Thoresen & Mahoney, 1974, p. 7). These are some of the possible advantages of self-management that have spurred both researchers and practitioners to apply and explore some of the components and effects of successful self-management programs. Although many questions remain unanswered, we can say tentatively that the following factors may be important in an effective self-management program:

1. A combination of strategies, some focusing on antecedents of behavior and others on consequences.
2. Consistent use of strategies over a period of time.
3. Evidence of client self-evaluation, goal setting with fairly high standards.
4. Use of covert, verbal, or material self-reinforcement.
5. Some degree of external, or environmental, support.

Combination of Strategies

A combination of self-management strategies is usually more useful than a single strategy. In a weight-control study, Mahoney, Moura, and

Wade (1973) found that the addition of self-reward significantly enhanced the procedures of self-monitoring and stimulus control. Further, people who combined self-reward and self-punishment lost more weight than those who used just one of the procedures. Greiner and Karoly (1976) found that students who used self-monitoring, self-reward, and planning strategies improved their study behavior and academic performance more than students who used only one strategy. Mitchell and White (1977) found that the frequency of clients' reported migraine headaches was reduced in direct proportion to the number of self-management skills they used. Similarly, Perri and Richards (1977) and Heffernan and Richards (1981) discovered that successful self-controllers reported using a greater number of techniques for a longer time than unsuccessful self-controllers. (In these studies, successful self-controllers were defined as persons who had increased or decreased the target behavior at least 50% and had maintained this level for several months.) Problem areas for which comprehensive self-management programs have been developed include weight control (Fremouw & Heyneman, 1983; Mahoney & Mahoney, 1976), interpersonal skills training (McFall & Dodge, 1982), developmental disabilities (Litrownik, 1982), anxiety (Deffenbacher & Suinn, 1982), addictive disorders (Marlatt & Parks, 1982), depression (Rehm, 1982), insomnia (Bootzin, 1977), and academic performance (Neilans & Israel, 1981).

Consistent Use of Strategies

Consistent, regular use of the strategies is a very important component of effective self-management. Seeming ineffectiveness may be due not to the impotence of the strategy but to its inconsistent or sporadic application (Thoresen & Mahoney, 1974, p. 107). Perri and Richards (1977) and Heffernan and Richards (1981) found that successful self-controllers reported using methods more frequently and more consistently than unsuccessful self-controllers. Similarly, another investigation noted that the "failures" in a self-management smoking-reduction program cheated in using the procedures and their contracts, whereas the "successes" did not (Hackett et al., 1976). In a case study of self-management, Greenberg and Altman (1976) found that smoking decrements occurred quite slowly (two to four months). If self-management efforts are not used over a certain period of time, their effectiveness may be too limited to produce any change.

Self-Evaluation and Standard Setting

Self-evaluation in the form of standard setting (or goal setting) and intention statements seems to be an important component of a self-management program. Spates and Kanfer (1977) found that children's performance on a learning task was enhanced only after the children had been trained to set standards or performance criteria. Greiner and Karoly (1976) also reported the importance of standard setting in a self-management program designed to improve the study behavior of college students. Some evidence also suggests that self-selected stringent standards affect performance more positively than lenient standards (Bandura, 1971b; Brownell, Colletti, Ersner-Hershfield, Hershfield, & Wilson, 1977). Perri and Richards (1977) described successful self-controllers as setting higher goals and criteria for change than unsuccessful self-controllers. However, the standards set should be realistic and within reach, or it is unlikely that self-reinforcement will ever occur.

Use of Self-Reinforcement

Self-reinforcement, either covert, verbal, or material, appears to be an important ingredient of an effective self-management program. Being able to praise oneself covertly or to note positive improvement seems to be correlated with self-change (Perri & Richards, 1977; Heffernan & Richards, 1981). In contrast, self-criticism (covert and verbal) seems to militate against change (Hackett et al., 1976; Mahoney & Mahoney, 1976). Mahoney, Moura, and Wade (1973) found that a material self-reward (such as money) was more effective than either self-monitoring or self-punishment in a weight reduction program. And across four problem areas of college students (eating, smoking, studying, and dating), successful self-controllers reported using self-reward far more frequently (67%) than unsuccessful self-controllers (19%) (Perri & Richards, 1977).

Environmental Support

Some degree of external support is necessary to effect and maintain the changes resulting from a self-management program. For example, public display of self-monitoring data and the help of another person provide opportunities for social reinforcement that often augment behavior change (Rutner & Bugle, 1969; Van Houten, Hill, & Parsons, 1975). Successful participants in a smoking-reduction program reported effective use of environmental contracts, whereas "failures" reported sabotage of the contracts by significant others (Hackett et al., 1976). Similarly, Perri and Richards (1977) observed that successful self-controllers reported receiving more positive feedback from others about their change efforts than unsuccessful self-controllers. To maintain any self-managed change, there must be some support from the social and physical environment (Kanfer, 1980; Thoresen & Mahoney, 1974).

☐ STEPS IN DEVELOPING A CLIENT SELF-MANAGEMENT PROGRAM

We have incorporated these five characteristics of effective self-management into a description of the steps associated with a self-management program. These steps are applicable to any program in which the client uses stimulus control, self-monitoring, or self-reward. Figure 19-1 summarizes the steps associated with developing a self-management program; the characteristics of effective self-management reflected in the steps are noted in the left column of the figure.

In developing a self-management program, steps 1 and 2 both involve aspects of standard setting and self-evaluation. In step 1, the client identifies and records the target behavior and its antecedents and consequences. This step involves self-monitoring in which the client collects baseline data about the behavior to be changed. If baseline data have not been collected as part of problem assessment (Chapter 8), it is imperative that such data be collected now, before using any self-management strategies. In step 2, the client explicitly identifies the desired behavior, conditions, and level of change. As you may remember from Chapter 9, the behavior, conditions, and level of change are the three parts of a counseling outcome goal. Defining the goal is an important part of self-management because of the possible motivating effects of standard setting. Establishing goals may interact with some of the self-management procedures and contribute to the desired effects (Jones et al., 1977).

Steps 3 and 4 are directed toward helping the client select a combination of self-management strategies to use. The counselor will need to explain all the possible self-management strategies to the client (step 3). The counselor should emphasize that the client should select some strategies that involve prearrangement of the antecedents and some that involve manipulation and self-administration of consequences. Ultimately, the client is responsible for selecting which self-management strategies should be used (step 4). Client selection of the strategies is an important part of the overall *self-directed* nature of self-management.

Steps 5 through 9 all involve procedural considerations that may strengthen client commitment and may encourage consistent use of the strategies over time. First, the client commits himself or herself verbally by specifying what and how much change is desired and the action steps (strategies) the client will take to produce the change (step 5). Next, the counselor will instruct the client in how to carry out the selected strategies (step 6). (The counselor can follow the guidelines listed in Table 19-1 for self-monitoring, those listed in Table 19-2 for stimulus control, and the ones presented for self-reward on p. 540.) Explicit instructions and modeling by the counselor may encourage the client to use a procedure more accurately and effectively. The instructional set given by a counselor may contribute to some degree to the overall treatment outcomes (Jones et al., 1977). The client also may use the strategies more effectively if there is an opportunity to rehearse the procedures in the interview under the counselor's direction (step 7). Finally, the client applies the strategies *in vivo* (step 8) and records (monitors) the frequency of use of each strategy and the level of the target behavior (step 9). Some of the treatment effects of self-management may also be a function of the client's self-recording (Jones et al.).

Steps 10 and 11 involve aspects of self-evaluation, self-reinforcement, and environmental support. The client has an opportunity to evaluate progress toward the goal by reviewing the self-recorded data collected during strategy implementation (step 10). Review of the data may indicate that the program is progressing smoothly or that some adjustments are needed. When the data suggest that some progress toward the goal is being made, the client's self-evaluation may set the occasion for self-reinforcement. Charting or posting the data (step 11) can enhance self-reinforcement and can elicit important environmental support for long-term maintenance of client change.

The following section describes how self-monitoring can be used to record the target behavior. Such recording can occur initially for problem assessment and goal setting, or it can be introduced later as a self-change strategy. We will discuss specifically how self-monitoring can be used to promote behavior change.

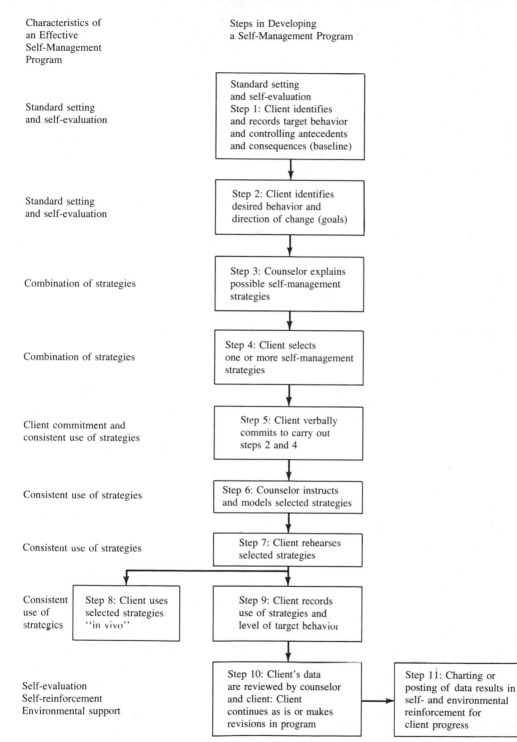

Figure 19-1. *Developing an effective self-management program*

☐ SELF-MONITORING

Purposes of Self-Monitoring

In Chapter 8 we defined self-monitoring as a process in which clients observe and record things about themselves and their interactions with environmental situations. Self-monitoring is a useful adjunct to problem assessment because the observational data can verify or change the client's verbal report about the problem behavior. We recommend that clients record their daily self-observations over a designated time period on a behavior log. Usually the client observes and records the problem behavior, controlling antecedents, and resulting consequences. Thoresen and Mahoney (1974) assert that self-monitoring is a major *first* step in any self-change program (as in any change program!). The client must be able to discover what is happening *before* implementing a self-change strategy, just as the counselor must know what is going on before using any other therapeutic procedure. In other words, any self-management strategy, like any other strategy, should be preceded by a baseline period of self-observation and recording. During this period, the client collects and records data about the behavior to be changed (B), the antecedents (A) of the behavior, and the consequences (C) of the behavior. In addition, the client may wish to note how much or how often the behavior occurs. For example, a client might record the daily amount of study time or the number of times he or she left the study time and place to do something else. The behavior log presented in Chapter 8 for problem-assessment data can also be used by a client to collect baseline data before implementing a self-management program. If the counselor introduces self-management strategies *after* problem assessment, these self-observation data should be already available.

As we discussed in Chapter 10, self-monitoring is also very useful for evaluation. When a client self-monitors the target behavior either before or during a treatment program, "the primary utility of self-monitoring lies in its assessment or data collection function" (Ciminero et al., 1977, p. 196). In recent years, however, practitioners and researchers have realized that the mere act of self-observation can produce change. As one collects data about oneself, the data collection may influence the behavior being observed. We now know that self-monitoring is useful not only to collect data but also to promote client change. If properly structured and executed, self-monitoring can be used as one type of self-management strategy.

Clinical Uses of Self-Monitoring

A number of research reports and clinical studies have explored self-monitoring as the major treatment strategy. In many cases, a self-monitoring procedure alone has been sufficient to produce at least short-term changes in the behavior being observed. McFall (1970), one of the first to investigate self-monitoring, found that college students who monitored their urge to smoke decreased the number of cigarettes smoked and the time spent smoking per cigarette. More recently, Abrams and Wilson (1979) found that self-monitoring of nicotine content resulted in significantly greater reductions in smoking than self-monitoring of the number of cigarettes smoked. Gormally and Rardin (1981) had overweight women monitor their daily caloric intake, activity levels, and minutes of calisthenics. Coates and Thoresen (1981) had three overweight female adolescents keep a "daily energy diary" that included duration in minutes and number of meals eaten, number of places at home where food was eaten, number of times food was eaten, number of activities while eating, and minutes of exercise (p. 388). Self-monitoring plus self-reward was effective in increasing academic behaviors and grades and in decreasing procrastination behaviors (Green, 1982). Fremouw and Heyneman (1983) used self-monitoring of behaviors and cognitions (mood and self-statements) to assess and treat obesity.

Self-monitoring has been used to record the degree of headache pain a person experiences four times a day (breakfast, lunch, dinner, and bedtime), using a 6-point scale (Blanchard, Andrasik, Neff, Jurish, & O'Keefe, 1981). Hiebert and Fox (1981) found that self-monitoring decreased the perceived level of anxiety. Hollon and Kendall (1981) have reported the use of self-monitoring client moods throughout the day. Frederiksen (1975) found that self-monitoring of antecedents, consequences, and frequency of episodes of ruminative thinking of a 25-year-old woman decreased these episodes significantly. Finally, Coates and Thoresen (1984) had two clients keep a daily sleep diary that included ratings of tension and mood, mental activity, and energy level on a 9-point scale before retiring and on arising in the morning.

Factors Influencing the Reactivity of Self-Monitoring

As you may recall from Chapter 10, two issues involved in self-monitoring are the reliability of the self-recording and its reactivity. Reliability, the accuracy of the self-recorded data, is important when self-monitoring is used to evaluate the goal behaviors. However, when self-monitoring is used as a change strategy, the accuracy of the data is less crucial. From a counseling perspective, the reactivity of self-monitoring makes it suitable for a change strategy. McFall (1970, p. 140) explains the potential reactivity of self-monitoring this way: "When an individual begins paying unusually close attention to one aspect of his behavior, that behavior is likely to change, even though no change may be intended or desired." As an example of reactivity, Kanfer (1980) noted that a married couple using self-monitoring to observe their frequent arguments reported that whenever the monitoring device (a taperecorder) was turned on, the argument was avoided.

Although the reactivity of self-monitoring can be a problem in data collection, it can be an asset when self-monitoring is used intentionally as a helping strategy. In using self-monitoring as a change strategy, it is important to try to maximize the reactive effects of self-monitoring — at least to the point of producing desired behavioral changes. Self-monitoring for *long* periods of time maintains reactivity. Nelson, Boykin, and Hayes (1982) found self-monitoring to be accurate over a long period of time. Reactivity persisted over a long period but discontinued when self-monitoring ceased.

A number of factors seem to influence the reactivity of self-monitoring. A summary of these factors suggests that self-monitoring "is most likely to produce positive behavioral changes when change-motivated subjects continuously monitor a limited number of discrete, positively-valued target behaviors; when performance feedback and goals or standards are made available and are unambiguous; and when the monitoring act is both salient and closely related in time to the target behaviors" (McFall, 1977b, p. 208).

Nelson (1977) has identified eight variables that seem to be related to the occurrence, intensity, and direction of the reactive effects of self-monitoring:

1. Motivation. Clients who are interested in changing the self-monitored behavior are more likely to show reactive effects when they self-monitor.

2. Valence of target behaviors. Behaviors a person values positively are likely to increase with self-monitoring; negative behaviors are likely to decrease; neutral behaviors may not change.

3. Type of target behaviors. The nature of the behavior that is being monitored may affect the degree to which self-monitoring procedures effect change.

4. Standard setting (goals), reinforcement, and feedback. Reactivity is enhanced for people who self-monitor in conjunction with goals and the availability of performance reinforcement or feedback.

5. Timing of self-monitoring. The time when the person self-records can influence the reactivity of self-monitoring. Results may differ depending on whether self-monitoring occurs before or after the target response.

6. Devices used for self-monitoring. More obtrusive or visible recording devices seem to be more reactive than unobtrusive devices.

7. Number of target responses monitored. Self-monitoring of only one response increases reactivity. As more responses are concurrently monitored, reactivity decreases.

8. Schedule for self-monitoring. The frequency with which a person self-monitors can affect reactivity. Continuous self-monitoring may result in more behavior change than intermittent self-recording.

Fremouw and Brown (1980) suggest three factors that can contribute to the reactive effects of self-monitoring:

1. Client characteristics. Client intellectual and physical abilities may be associated with greater reactivity when self-monitoring.

2. Expectations. Clients seeking help may have some expectations for desirable behavior changes. However, it is probably impossible to separate client expectations from implicit or explicit therapeutic "demands" to change the target behavior.

3. Behavior change skills. Reactivity may be influenced by the client's knowledge and skills associated with behavior change. For example, the reactivity of addictive behaviors may be affected by the client's knowledge of "simple, short-term strategies such as fasting or abstinence" (Fremouw & Brown, 1980, p. 213).

□ STEPS OF SELF-MONITORING

The effectiveness of self-monitoring seems to vary with several parameters, including the characteristics of the client and of the target behavior (Lipinski, Black, Nelson, & Ciminero, 1975; Nelson, Lipinski, & Black, 1976a), the demand characteristics of the situation (Kazdin, 1974e), and the various components of the monitoring procedure (Bellack, Rozensky, & Schwartz, 1974; Kanfer, 1980; Mahoney & Thoresen, 1974). Some of the important steps of self-monitoring will be explored in this section.

Self-monitoring involves at least six important steps: *rationale* for the strategy, *discrimination* of a response, *recording* of a response, *charting* of a response, *display* of data, and *analysis* of data (Thoresen & Mahoney, 1974, pp. 43–44). Each of these six steps and guidelines for their use will be discussed, and they are summarized in Table 19-1. However, remember that the steps are all interactive, and the presence of all of them may be required for a person to use self-monitoring effectively.

Treatment Rationale

First, the therapist explains the rationale for self-monitoring. Before using the strategy, the client should be aware of what the self-monitoring procedure will involve and how the procedure will help with the client's problem. Fremouw and Heyneman (1983) offer this rationale (overview) to treat obese clients:

"A critical part of this program is keeping the self-monitoring diaries. On these two diaries (one for meals and one for between meal eating), you will keep track of everything you eat, the situation you eat in, and your thoughts and feelings associated with eating. This will require a good deal of effort. However, it has been our experience that although people find this recording difficult at first, it soon becomes more automatic—and it certainly is well worth the effort" [p. 182].

TABLE 19-1. Steps of self-monitoring

1. *Rationale* for self-monitoring	A. Purpose
	B. Overview of procedure
2. *Discrimination* of a response	A. Selection of target response to monitor
	1. Type of response
	2. Valence of response
	3. Number of responses
3. *Recording* of a response	A. Timing of recording
	1. Prebehavior recording to decrease a response; postbehavior recording to increase a response
	2. Immediate recording
	3. Recording when no competing responses distract recorder
	B. Method of recording
	1. Frequency counts
	2. Duration measures
	a. Continuous recording
	b. Time sampling
	C. Devices for recording
	1. Portable
	2. Accessible
	3. Economical
	4. Somewhat obtrusive
4. *Charting* of a response	A. Charting and graphing of daily totals of recorded behavior
5. *Displaying* of data	A. Public display of chart for environmental support
6. *Analysis* of data	A. Accuracy of data interpretation
	B. Knowledge of results for self-evaluation and self-reinforcement

You could conclude the above rationale for self-monitoring with a statement about the purpose of self-monitoring, such as "The self-monitoring diaries will increase your awareness of your eating episodes, help to assess specific behaviors associated with your eating episodes, and help to formulate treatment strategies and plans for desired target behaviors. Are you willing to keep the diaries?"

Discrimination of a Response

When a client engages in self-monitoring, first an observation, or discrimination, of a response is required. For example, a client who is monitoring fingernail biting must be able to discriminate instances of nail biting from instances of other behavior. Discrimination of a response occurs whenever the client is able to identify the presence or absence of the behavior, whether overt, like nail biting, or covert, like a positive self-thought. Thoresen and Mahoney (1974, p. 43) point out that making behavioral discriminations can be thought of as the "awareness" facet of self-monitoring.

Discrimination of a response involves helping the client identify *what* to monitor. Often this decision will require counselor assistance. There is some evidence that the type of the monitored response affects the results of self-monitoring. For example, Romanczyk (1974) found that self-monitoring produced greater weight loss for people who recorded their daily weight and daily caloric intake than for those who recorded only daily weight. As McFall (1977b) has observed, it is not very clear why some target responses seem to be better ones to self-monitor than others; at this point, the selection of target responses remains a pragmatic choice. Mahoney (1977b, pp. 244–245) points out that there may be times when self-monitoring of certain responses could detract from therapeutic effectiveness, as in asking a suicidal client to monitor depressive thoughts.

The effects of self-monitoring also vary with the valence of the target response. There are always "two sides" of a behavior that could be monitored—the positive and the negative (Mahoney & Thoresen, 1974, p. 37). There seem to be times when one side is more important for self-monitoring than the other (Kanfer, 1970; Mahoney & Thoresen, p. 37).

Most of the evidence indicates that self-monitoring of positive responses increases these responses. In contrast, self-monitoring decreases the frequency of negative behaviors (Broden, Hall, & Mitts, 1971; Cavior & Marabotto, 1976; Kirschenbaum, Ordman, Tomarken, & Holtzbauer, 1982; Nelson, Lipinski, & Black, 1976a). Unfortunately, there are very few data to guide a decision about the exact type and valence of responses to monitor. Because the reactivity of self-monitoring is affected by the value assigned to a behavior (Watson & Tharp, 1981), one guideline might be to have the client monitor the behavior that she or he cares *most* about changing. Generally, it is a good idea to encourage the client to limit monitoring to one response, at least initially. If the client engages in self-monitoring of one behavior with no problems, then more items can be added.

Recording of a Response

After the client has learned to make discriminations about a response, the counselor can provide instructions and examples about the method for recording the observed response. Most clients have probably never recorded their behavior *systematically*. Systematic recording is crucial to the success of self-monitoring, so it is imperative that the client understand the importance and methods of recording. The client needs instructions in when and how to record and devices for recording. The timing, method, and recording devices all can influence the effectiveness of self-monitoring.

Timing of self-monitoring: When to record. One of the least understood processes of self-monitoring involves timing, or the point when the client actually records the target behavior. Instances have been reported of both prebehavior and postbehavior monitoring. In prebehavior monitoring, the client records the intention or urge to engage in the behavior *before* doing so. In postbehavior monitoring, the client records each completed instance of the target behavior—*after* the behavior has occurred. Kazdin (1974f, p. 239) points out that the precise effects of self-monitoring may depend on the point at which monitoring occurs in the chain of responses relative to the response being recorded. Kanfer (1980) concludes that existing data are insufficient to judge whether pre- or postbehavior monitoring will have maximal effects. Nelson (1977) indicates that the effects of the timing of self-monitoring may depend partly on whether other responses are competing for the person's attention at the time the response is recorded. Another factor influencing the timing of self-monitoring is the amount of time between the response and the actual recording. Most people agree that delayed recording of the behavior weakens the efficacy of the monitoring process (Kanfer, 1980; Kazdin, 1974f).

We suggest four guidelines that may help the counselor and client decide when to record. First, if the client is using monitoring as a way to *decrease* an undesired behavior, prebehavior monitoring may be more effective, as this seems to interrupt the response chain early in the process. An example of the rule of thumb for self-monitoring an undesired response would be "Record whenever you have the urge to smoke or to eat." McFall (1970) found that prebehavior monitoring did reduce smoking behavior. Similarly, Bellack et al. (1974) found that prebehavior monitoring resulted in more weight loss than postbehavior monitoring. If the client is using self-monitoring to *increase* a desired response, then postbehavior monitoring may be more helpful. As Bellack et al. observe, postbehavior monitoring can make a person more aware of a "low frequency, desirable behavior" (p. 529). Third, recording instances of a desired behavior as it occurs or immediately after it occurs may be most helpful. The rule of thumb is to "record *immediately* after you have the urge to smoke — or *immediately* after you have covertly praised yourself; do not wait even for 15 or 20 minutes, as the impact of recording may be lost." Fourth, the client should be encouraged to self-record the response when not distracted by the situation or by other competing responses. However, as mentioned in Chapter 10, the client should be instructed to record the behavior *in vivo* as it occurs, if possible, rather than at the end of the day, when he or she is dependent on retrospective recall. *In vivo* recording may not always be feasible, and in some cases the client's self-recording may have to be performed later.

Method of self-monitoring: How to record. The counselor also needs to instruct the client in a *method* for recording the target responses. McFall (1977b) points out that the method of recording can vary in a number of ways:

> It can range from a very informal and unstructured operation, as when subjects are asked to make mental notes of any event that seems related to mood changes, to something fairly formal and structured, as when subjects are asked to fill out a mood-rating sheet according to a time-sampling schedule. It can be fairly simple, as when subjects

are asked to keep track of how many cigarettes they smoke in a given time period; or it can be complex and time-consuming, as when they are asked to record not only how many cigarettes they smoke, but also the time, place, circumstances, and affective response associated with lighting each cigarette. It can be a relatively objective matter, as when counting the calories consumed each day; or it can be a very subjective matter, as when recording the number of instances each day when they successfully resist the temptation to eat sweets [p. 197].

Ciminero et al. (1977, p. 198) suggest that the recording method should be "easy to implement, must produce a representative sample of the target behavior, and must be sensitive to changes in the occurrence of the target behavior."

As you may remember from our description of outcome evaluation in Chapter 10, frequency, latency, duration, and intensity can be recorded with either a continuous recording or a time-sampling method. Selection of one of these methods will depend mainly on the type of target response and the frequency of its occurrence. To record the *number* of target responses, the client can use a frequency count. Frequency counts are most useful for monitoring responses that are discrete, do not occur all the time, and are of short duration (Ciminero et al., 1977, p. 190). For instance, clients might record the number of times they have an urge to smoke or the number of times they praise or compliment themselves covertly.

Other kinds of target responses are recorded more easily and accurately by latency or duration. Any time a client wants to record the amount or length of a response, a duration count can be used. Ciminero et al. (1977, p. 198) recommend the use of a duration measure whenever the target response is not discrete and varies in length. For example, a client might use a duration count to note the amount of time spent reading textbooks or practicing a competitive sport. Or a client might want to keep track of the length of time spent in a "happy mood." Latency would be used to self-record the amount of time that elapses before the onset of a response, such as the number of minutes elapsed between feeling angry and subsequently losing one's temper.

Sometimes a client may want to record two different responses and use both the frequency and duration methods. For example, a client might use a frequency count to record each urge to smoke and a duration count to monitor the time spent smoking a cigarette. Watson and Tharp (1981) suggest that the counselor can recommend frequency counts whenever it is easy to record clearly separate occurrences of the behavior and duration counts whenever the behavior continues for long periods.

Clients can also self-record intensity of responses whenever data are desired about the relative severity of a response. For example, a client might record the intensity of happy, anxious, or depressed feelings or moods.

Format of self-monitoring instruments. There are many formats of self-monitoring instruments a client can use to record frequency, duration, or severity of the target response as well as information about contributing variables. The particular format of the instrument can affect reactivity and can increase client compliance with self-monitoring. The format of the instrument should be tailored to the client problem. Figure 19-2 shows examples of four formats for self-monitoring instruments. Example 1 in the figure illustrates a variety of response dimensions that Fremouw and Heyneman (1983) used in the cognitive-behavioral diary for their weight reduction program: duration of snacks or binges, types of situations, recordings and self-ratings of self-statements, number of calories, and self-ratings of stress, control over eating or binging, and mood states. Example 2 illustrates a self-monitoring format used for assertive situations. The client is to record the situation, time and date, thoughts, behavior, self-rated satisfaction about the situation, and what behaviors should have been performed (Barlow et al., 1983, p. 103). Example 3 shows a format we use with couples in marital therapy for self-monitoring of content and quality of marital interactions. In this format, adapted from Williams (1979), each person records the content of the interaction with the spouse (for example, having dinner together, talking about finances, discussing work, going to movies) and self-rates the quality of that interaction. Example 4 shows a format we use with clients to self-record aspects of anxiety responses. This format can be adapted to other covert (internal) responses. Each of these formats can use a variety of self-recording devices.

Devices for self-monitoring. Often clients report that one of the most intriguing aspects of self-monitoring involves the device or mechanism used for recording. In order for recording to occur systematically and accurately, the client must have access to some recording device. A variety of devices have been used to help clients keep accurate records. Note cards, daily log sheets, and diaries can be used to make written notations. A popular self-recording device is a wrist counter, such as a golf counter. Lindsley (1968) adapted the golf counter for self-recording in different settings. If several behaviors are being counted simultaneously, the client can wear several wrist counters or use knitting tallies. K. Mahoney (1974) describes a wrist counter with rows of beads that permits the recording of several behaviors. Audio- and videotapes, toothpicks, or small plastic tokens can also be used as recording devices. Watson and Tharp (1981) report the use of pennies to count: a client can carry pennies in one pocket and transfer one penny to another pocket each time a behavior occurs. Children can record frequencies by pasting stars on a chart or by using a "countoon" (Kunzelmann, 1970), which has pictures and numbers for three recording columns: "What do I do," "My count," and "What happens." Clocks, watches, and kitchen timers can be used for duration counts.

The counselor and client select a recording device. Here is an opportunity to be inventive! There are several practical criteria to consider in helping a client select a recording device. The device should be portable and accessible so that it is present whenever the behavior occurs (Watson & Tharp, 1981). It should be easy and convenient to use and economical. The obtrusiveness of the device should also be considered. The recording device can function as a cue (discriminative stimulus) for the client to self-monitor, so it should be noticeable enough to remind the client to engage in self-monitoring. However, a device that is too obtrusive may draw attention from others who could reward or punish the client for self-monitoring (Ciminero et al., 1977, p. 202). Finally, the device should be capable of giving cumulative frequency data so that the client can chart daily totals of the behavior (Thoresen & Mahoney, 1974).

After the client has been instructed in the timing and method of recording, and after a recording device has been selected, the client should practice using the recording system. Breakdowns in self-monitoring often occur because a client did not understand the recording process clearly. Rehearsal of the recording procedures may ensure that the client will record accurately. Generally, a client should engage in self-recording for three to four weeks. Usually the effects of self-monitoring are not apparent in only one or two weeks' time.

Date_____

1. Cognitive-behavioral diary (Fremouw & Heyneman, 1983, p. 176)*

Prior to eating

Day & time start/stop (duration)	Snacks/ binges	Situation	Stress	Mood	Self-statements	Rate −5 + 5

Following eating

Food + quantity +calories	Mood	Self-statement	Rate −5 + 5	Control

Stress: 0 = none, 7 = extreme
Mood: *B*ored, *D*epressed, *F*rustrated, *G*uilty, *H*appy, *N*eutral
Rate self-statements: −5 = extremely negative, 0 = neutral, +5 = extremely positive
Control over eating or binge: 0 = none, 7 = extreme

* From "Obesity" by W. J. Fremouw and N. Heyneman. In M. Herson (Ed.), *Outpatient behavior therapy.* Copyright © 1983 by Grune & Stratton. Reprinted by permission of Grune & Stratton, Inc. and the author.

2. Assertiveness situations (Barlow, Hayes, & Nelson, 1984, p. 103)**

Date and time	Situation	What did you do?	What were you thinking?

How did situation end?	How did you feel about the outcome? (0 = very dissatisfied, 10 = very satisfied)	What could you have done differently?

** From *The scientist practitioner* by D. H. Barlow, S. C. Hayes, & R. O. Nelson. Copyright © 1984 by Pergamon Press. Reprinted by permission.

3. Content and quality of marital interactions
   Record the type of interaction under "Contents." For *each* interaction circle one category that best represents the quality of that interaction.

Time	Content of interaction	Quality of interaction				
		Very pleasant	Pleasant	Neutral	Unpleasant	Very unpleasant
6:30 A.M.		++	+	0	−	− −
7:00		++	+	0	−	− −
7:30		++	+	0	−	− −
8:00		++	+	0	−	− −

4. Self-monitoring log for recording anxiety responses

	Date and time	Frequency of anxiety response	External events	Internal dialogue (self-statements)	Behavioral factors	Degree of arousal	Skill in handling situation
Instructions for recording:	Record day and time of incident	Describe each situation in which anxiety occurred	Note what triggered the anxiety	Note your thoughts or things you said to yourself when this occurred	Note how you responded —what you did	Rate the intensity of the anxiety: (1) a little intense, (2) somewhat intense, (3) very intense, (4) extremely intense	Rate the degree to which you handled the situation effectively: (1) a little, (2) somewhat, (3) very, (4) extremely

Figure 19-2. *Four examples of formats for self-monitoring instruments*

Charting of a Response

The data recorded by the client should be translated onto a more permanent storage record such as a chart or graph that enables the client to inspect the self-monitored data visually. This type of visual guide may provide the occasion for client self-reinforcement (Kanfer, 1980), which, in turn, can influence the reactivity of self-monitoring. The data can be charted by days, using a simple line graph. For example, a client counting the number of urges to smoke a cigarette could chart these by days, as in Figure 19-3. A client recording the amount of time spent studying daily could use the same sort of line graph to chart duration of study time. The vertical axis would be divided into time intervals such as 15 minutes, 30 minutes, 45 minutes, or 1 hour.

The client should receive either oral or written instructions on a way to chart and graph the daily totals of the recorded response. The counselor can assist the client in interpreting the chart in the sessions on data review and analysis. If a client is using self-monitoring to increase a behavior, the line on the graph should go up gradually if the self-monitoring is having the desired effect; if self-monitoring is influencing an undesired response to decrease, the line on the graph should go down gradually.

Display of Data

After the graph has been made, the counselor should encourage the client to display the completed chart. If the chart is displayed in a "public" area, this display may prompt environmental reinforcement, a necessary part of an effective self-management program. Several studies have found that the effects of self-monitoring are augmented when the data chart is displayed as a public record (McKenzie & Rushall, 1974; Rutner & Bugle, 1969; Van Houten et al., 1975).

Analysis of Data

If the client's recording data are not reviewed and analyzed, the client may soon feel as if he or she was told to make a graph just for practice in drawing straight lines! A very important facet of self-monitoring is the information it can provide to the client. There is some evidence that people who receive feedback about their self-recording change more than those who do not (Kazdin, 1974e). The recording and charting of data should be used *explicitly* to provide the client with knowledge of results about behavior or performance. Specifically, the client should bring the data to weekly counseling sessions for review and analysis. In these sessions, the counselor can encourage the client to compare the data with the desired goals and stan-

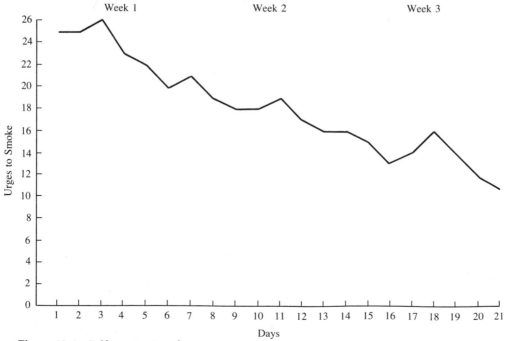

Figure 19-3. Self-monitoring chart

dards. The client can use the recorded data for self-evaluation and determine whether the data indicate that the behavior is within or outside the desired limits. The counselor can also aid in data analysis by helping the client interpret the data correctly. As Thoresen and Mahoney observe, "Errors about what the charted data represent can seriously hinder success in self-control" (1974, p. 44).

☐ MODEL EXAMPLE: SELF-MONITORING

As you may recall from Joan's goal chart in Chapter 9, one of Joan's goals was to increase her positive thoughts (and simultaneously decrease her negative thoughts) about her ability to do well with math. This goal lends itself well to application of self-management strategies for several reasons. First, the goal represents a covert behavior (positive thoughts), which is observable only by Joan. Second, the "flip side" of the goal (the negative thoughts) represents a very well-learned habit. Probably most of these negative thoughts occur *outside* the counseling sessions. To change this thought pattern, Joan will need to use strategies she can apply frequently (as needed) *in vivo*, and she will need to use strategies she can administer to herself.

Here is a description of the way self-monitoring could be used to help Joan achieve this goal.

1. *Treatment rationale.* The counselor would provide an explanation of what Joan will self-monitor and why, emphasizing that this is a strategy she can apply herself, can use with a "private" behavior, and can use as frequently as possible in the actual setting.

2. *Discrimination of a response.* The counselor would need to help Joan define the target response explicitly. One definition could be "Any time I think about myself doing math or working with numbers successfully." The counselor should provide some possible examples of this response, such as "Gee, I did well on my math homework today" or "I was able to balance the checkbook today." Joan should also be encouraged to identify some examples of the target response. Since Joan wants to increase this behavior, the target response would be stated in the "positive."

3. *Recording of a response.* The counselor should instruct Joan in timing, a method, and a device for recording. In this case, because Joan is

using self-monitoring to increase a desired behavior, she would use postbehavior monitoring. Joan should be instructed to record *immediately* after a target thought has occurred. She is interested in recording the *number* of such thoughts, so she could use a frequency count. A tally on a note card or a wrist counter could be selected as the device for recording. After these instructions, Joan should practice recording before actually doing it. She should be instructed to engage in self-monitoring for about four consecutive weeks.

4. *Charting of a response.* After each week of self-monitoring, Joan can add her daily frequency totals and chart them by days on a simple line graph.

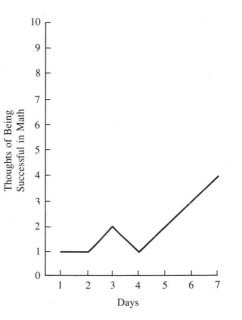

Joan is using self-monitoring to increase a behavior; as a result, if the monitoring has the desired effect, the line on her graph should gradually rise. It is just starting to do so here; additional data for the next few weeks should show a greater increase if the self-monitoring is influencing the target behavior in the desired direction.

5. *Display of data.* After Joan has made a data chart, she may wish to post it in a place such as her room, where her friends could see it and encourage her for progress. Public posting may also cue Joan to reinforce herself for progress.

6. *Analysis of data.* During the period of self-monitoring, Joan should bring in her data for

weekly review sessions with the counselor. The counselor can provide reinforcement and help Joan interpret the data accurately. Joan can use the data for self-evaluation by comparing the "story" of the data with her stated desired behavior and level of change.

LEARNING ACTIVITY #49: SELF-MONITORING

This learning activity is designed to help you use self-monitoring yourself. The instructions describe a self-monitoring plan for you to try out.

1. Discrimination of a target response:
   a. Specify one target behavior you would like to change. Pick either the positive or the negative side of the behavior to monitor—depending on which you value more and whether you want to increase or decrease this response.
   b. Write down a definition of this behavior. How clear is your definition?
   c. Can you write some examples of this behavior? If you had trouble with these, try to "tighten up" your definition—or else contrast positive and negative instances of the behavior.
2. Recording of the response:
   a. Specify the *timing* of your self-recording. Remember the "rules of thumb":
      1. Prebehavior monitoring to decrease an undesired response.
      2. Postbehavior monitoring to increase a desired response.
      3. Record immediately—don't wait.
      4. Record when there are no competing responses.

Write down the timing you choose.
   b. Select a *method* of recording (frequency, duration, and so on). Remember:
      1. Frequency counts for clearly separate occurrences of the response.
      2. Duration or latency measures for responses that occur for a period of time.
      3. Intensity measures to determine the severity of a response.
   c. Select a *device* to assist you in recording. Remember that the device should be—
      1. Portable.
      2. Accessible.
      3. Economical.
      4. Obtrusive enough to serve as a reminder to self-record.
   d. After you have made these determinations, engage in self-monitoring for at least a week (preferably two). Then complete steps 3, 4, and 5.
3. Charting of response: Take your daily self-recording data and chart them on a simple line graph for each day that you self-monitored.
4. Displaying of data: Arrange a place to display your chart where it may elicit strokes from others.
5. Analysis of data: Compare your chart with your stated desired behavior change. What has happened to the behavior?

☐ STIMULUS CONTROL: PREARRANGEMENT OF ANTECEDENTS

Kanfer (1980, p. 361) defines stimulus control as the predetermined arrangement of environmental conditions that makes it impossible or unfavorable for an undesired behavior to occur. Stimulus-control methods emphasize rearranging or modifying environmental conditions that serve as cues or antecedents of a particular response. As you may recall from the discussion of the ABC model of behavior in Chapter 7, a behavior often is guided by certain things that precede it (antecedents) and is maintained by positive or negative events that follow it (consequences). You may also remember that both antecedents and consequences can be external (overt) or internal (co-

vert). For example, an antecedent could be a situation, an emotion, a cognition, or an overt or covert verbal instruction.

Clinical Uses of Stimulus Control

Stimulus-control procedures have been used for behavior change and weight loss (Carroll & Yates, 1981; Fremouw, Callahan, Zitter, & Katell, 1981), to decrease nocturnal awakenings (Norton & DeLuca, 1979), to decrease insomnia (Lacks, Bertelson, Sugerman, & Kunkel, 1983; Turner & Ascher, 1982; Zwart & Lisman, 1979), with thought stopping to decrease persistent disturbing thoughts (Martin, 1982), to increase exercise (Keefe & Blumenthal, 1980), to decrease worry (Borkovec, Wilkinson, Folensbee, & Lerman, 1983), and to enhance social interaction and activity among elderly nursing-home residents (Quattrochi-Turbin & Jason, 1980). According to Gambrill (1977), stimulus-control procedures are most useful when the client's behavior exists but occurs in the wrong context or does not occur frequently enough in the same context.

How Antecedents Acquire Stimulus Control

When antecedents are consistently associated with a behavior that is reinforced in the *presence* (not the absence) of these antecedent stimuli, they gain control over the behavior. You might think of this as "stimulus control," since an antecedent is a stimulus for a certain response. When an antecedent gains stimulus control over the response, there is a high probability that the response will be emitted in the presence of these particular antecedent events. For example, most of us "automatically" slow down, put our foot on the brake, and stop the car when we see a red traffic light. The red light is a stimulus that has gained control over our stopping-the-car behavior. Generally, the fact that antecedents exert stimulus control is helpful, as it is in driving when we go ahead with a green light and stop at the sight of a red light.

Inappropriate Stimulus Control in Problem Behavior

Client problem behaviors may occur because of *inappropriate* stimulus control. For example, Ferster, Nurnberger, and Levitt (1962) were perhaps the first to note that inappropriate stimulus control was related to obesity. They found that eating responses of overweight people tended to be associated with many environmental cues. If a person eats something not only at the dining table but also when working in the kitchen, watching television, walking by the refrigerator, and stopping at a Dairy Queen, the sheer number of eating responses could soon result in obesity. Too many environmental cues often are related to other client problems, particularly "excesses" such as smoking and drinking. In these cases, the primary aim of a self-management stimulus-control method is to reduce the number of cues associated with the undesired response, such as eating or smoking.

Other problem behaviors have been observed that seem to involve excessively narrow stimulus control. At the opposite pole from obesity are people who eat so little that their physical and psychological health suffers (a condition called "anorexia nervosa"). For these people, there are too few eating cues. Lack of exercise can be a function of too

narrow stimulus control. For some people, the paucity of environmental cues associated with exercise results in very little physical activity. In these cases, the primary aim of a stimulus-control strategy is to establish or increase the number of cues that will elicit the desired behavior.

To summarize, stimulus-control self-management involves reducing the number of antecedent stimuli associated with an undesirable behavior and simultaneously increasing the antecedent cues associated with a desirable response (Mahoney & Thoresen, 1974; Thoresen & Mahoney, 1974). Table 19-2 shows the principal methods of stimulus control and some examples.

Using Stimulus Control to Decrease Behavior

To decrease the rate of a behavior, the antecedent cues associated with the behavior should be reduced in frequency or prearranged or altered in terms of time and place of occurrence. When cues are separated from the habitual behavior by alteration or elimination, the old, undesired habit can be terminated (Mahoney & Thoresen, 1974, p. 42). Many behavioral "excesses," such as eating, smoking, drinking, or self-criticism, are tied to a great number of antecedent situations. Reducing these cues can restrict the occurrence of the undesired behavior. For instance, Nolan (1968) and Roberts (1969) reported case studies in which smoking was restricted to one special "smoking chair." Existing cues can be prearranged to make the target behavior so hard to execute that the person is unlikely to do it. An example would be altering the place of smoking by moving one's smoking chair to an inconvenient place like the basement. The smoker would have to go downstairs each time she or he wanted a cigarette. Cues can also be prearranged by placing their control in the hands of another person. Giving your pack of cigarettes to a friend is an example of this method. The friend should agree to help you reduce smoking and should agree not to reinforce or punish any instances of your smoking behavior (the undesired response).

A behavior can also be reduced through stimulus control by interrupting the learned pattern or sequence that begins with one or more antecedent cues and results in the undesired response. This sequence may be called a *chain*. A problem behavior is often the result of a long chain of events. For example, a variety of behaviors make up the sequence of smoking. Before puffing on a cigarette, a person has to go to a cigarette machine, put money

TABLE 19-2. Principles and examples of stimulus-control strategies

Principle of change	Example
To decrease a behavior: Reduce or narrow the frequency of cues associated with the behavior.	
1. Prearrange or alter cues associated with the place of the behavior:	
a. Prearrange cues that make it hard to execute the behavior.	Place fattening foods in high, hard-to-reach places.
b. Prearrange cues so that they are controlled by others.	Ask friends or family to serve you only one helping of food and to avoid serving fattening foods to you.
2. Alter the time or sequence (chain) between the antecedents cues and the resulting behaviors:	
a. Break up the sequence.	Buy and prepare food only on a full stomach.
b. Change the sequence.	Substitute and engage in nonfood activities when you start to move toward snacking (toward refrigerator, cupboard, or candy machine).
c. Build pauses into the sequence.	Delay second helpings of food or snacks for a predetermined amount of time.
To increase a behavior: Increase or prearrange the cues associated with the response.	
1. Seek out these cues deliberately to perform the desired behavior.	Initially arrange only one room with a desk to study. When you need to study, go to this place.
2. Concentrate on the behavior when in the situation.	Concentrate only on studying in the room. If you get distracted, get up and leave. Don't mix study with other activities, such as listening to records or talking.
3. Gradually extend the behavior to other situations.	When you have control over studying in one room, extend the behavior to another conducive room or place.
4. Promote the occurrence of helpful cues by other people or by self-generated reminders.	Ask your roommate to remind you to leave the desk when talking or when distracted; remind yourself of good study procedures by posting a list over your study desk or by using verbal or covert self-instructions.

in the machine, take out a pack of cigarettes, take out one cigarette from the pack, and light the cigarette.

This chain might be interrupted in one of three ways: breaking up the chain of events, changing the chain, or building pauses into the chain (Watson & Tharp, 1981, pp. 113–115). All these methods involve prearranging or altering the time of occurrence of the behavior. A chain of events can be broken up by discovering and interrupting an event early in the sequence or by scrambling the typical order of events. For example, the smoker could break up the chain by not carrying the change required for a cigarette machine. Or, if the smoker typically smokes at certain times, the usual order of events leading up to smoking could be mixed up. The smoker could also change the typi-

cal chain of events. A person who starts to light up a cigarette whenever bored, tense, or lacking something to do with his or her hands could perform a different activity at this point, such as calling a friend when bored, relaxing when tense, or knitting or playing cards to provide hand activity. Finally, the smoker could interrupt the chain by deliberately building pauses into it. As you may recall, when antecedents exert control over a behavior, the behavior occurs almost automatically. As Watson and Tharp point out, one way to deal with this automatic quality is to pause before responding to a cue (p. 114). For instance, whenever the smoker has an urge to light up in response to a stress cue, a deliberate pause of ten minutes can be built in before the person actually does light up. Gradually this time interval can be increased.

Sometimes you can even strengthen the pause procedure by covertly instructing yourself on what you want to do or by thinking about the benefits of not smoking. The pause itself can then become a new antecedent "for a more desirable link in the chain of events" (Watson & Tharp, p. 114).*

Two studies illustrate the use of stimulus-control procedures to decrease worry (Borkovec et al., 1983) and to change eating patterns to decrease weight (Fremouw et al., 1981). In the first study, worriers were instructed "(1) to learn to identify and to distinguish worrisome thoughts that were unnecessary or unpleasant and thoughts that were necessary or pleasant, (2) to establish a half-hour worry period to take place at the same time and in the same location each day, (3) when worrying, to postpone worrying to a worry period and replace it with attending to present-moment experience, and (4) to make use of the half-hour worry period to worry about concerns and to engage in problem solving to eliminate those concerns" (Borkovec et al., p. 248).

Fremouw et al. (1981) used instructions in stimulus control to promote behavior change and weight loss. Clients were instructed to use the following procedures to change the antecedents for eating:

> (a) Designate one place to eat all meals and snacks; (b) avoid all other activities, such as reading, when eating; (c) buy nonfattening foods; (d) rearrange the cupboards and refrigerator to make snack foods less accessible and visible; (e) store foods in opaque containers; (f) shop from a prepared list when not hungry; (g) serve food on plates in the kitchen, do not leave serving bowls on the table; (h) use smaller plates, bowls, and glasses to make food appear larger; and (i) buy and prepare a variety of low calorie snacks such as vegetables or fruits [p. 292].

Using Stimulus Control to Increase Behavior

Stimulus-control methods can also be used to increase a desired response. As noted in Table 19-2, to increase the rate of a response, a person increases or prearranges the antecedent cues associated with the desired behavior. The person deliberately seeks out these cues to perform the

* This and all other quotations from this source are from *Self-directed behavior: Self-modification for personal adjustment* (3rd ed.), by D. L. Watson and R. G. Tharp. Copyright © 1981, 1977, 1974 by Wadsworth Publishing Company, Inc. Reprinted by permission of the publisher, Brooks/Cole Publishing Company, Monterey, California.

behavior and concentrates only on this behavior when in the situation. Competing or distracting responses must be avoided. Gradually, as stimulus control over the behavior in one situation is achieved, the person can extend the behavior by performing it in another, similar situation. This process of stimulus generalization means that a behavior learned in one situation can be performed in different but similar situations (Watson & Tharp, 1981, p. 126). The person can promote the occurrence of new antecedent cues by using reminders from others, self-reminders, or overt or covert self-instructions (Watson & Tharp). The rate of a desired response is increased by increasing the times and places in which the person performs the response.

As an example, suppose you are working with a client who wants to increase his or her amount of daily exercise. First, more cues would be established to which the person would respond with isometric or physical activity. For example, the person might perform isometric activities whenever sitting in a chair or waiting for a traffic light. Or the person might perform physical exercises each morning and evening on a special exercise mat. The client would seek out these prearranged cues and concentrate on performing the activity while in the situation. Other behaviors should not be performed while in these situations, since a competing response could interfere with the exercise activity (Watson & Tharp, 1981, p. 125). Gradually, the client could extend the exercise activities to new but similar situations—for example, doing isometrics while sitting on the floor or waiting for a meeting to start. The person could also promote exercise behavior in these situations by reminders—posting an exercise chart on the wall or carrying it around in a pocket or wallet, displaying an exercise list, and so forth.

As an illustration of the use of stimulus-control procedures to increase behavior, Keefe and Blumenthal (1980) used stimulus control and self-reinforcement to enhance maintenance of an exercise program. Clients were asked to use the following stimulus-control procedures: (1) exercise at the same time and in a similar place each day, (2) engage in a warm-up consisting of stretching exercises for a minimum of ten minutes before beginning exercise, (3) set an exercise goal not greater than 10% of the distance previously covered in walking during the preceding week (p. 32). Stimulus-control instructions also have been used to increase sleep. For example, clients were instructed: (1) Go to bed or lie down to sleep only when sleepy. (2) Do not read, watch TV, or eat in bed — use the bed only for sleeping and/or sexual activities. (3) If unable to fall asleep after 10 to 20 minutes, get out of bed and engage in some activity. Return to bed only when sleepy — and continue this procedure throughout the night as necessary. (4) Set the alarm clock and get up at the same time every morning regardless of the amount of sleep obtained during the night. (5) Do not take naps during the day (Turner & Ascher, 1982, pp. 35–36; Zwart & Lisman, 1979, p. 114).

According to Kanfer (1980, p. 361), one advantage of stimulus control is that only minimal self-initiated steps are required to trigger environmental changes that effect desired or undesired responses. Blechman, Olson, and Hellman (1976) found that one exposure to a family contract game was sufficient to achieve stimulus control over the family's discussion behavior. The participation in the game accelerated family problem-solving behavior and decreased their antagonistic, off-task discussion. However, stimulus-control methods often are insufficient to modify behavior without the support of other strategies. As Mahoney and Thoresen (1974) observe, stimulus-control methods are not usually sufficient for long-term self-change unless accompanied by other self-management methods that exert control over the *consequences* of the target behavior. One self-management method that involves self-presented consequences is discussed in the following section.

☐ MODEL EXAMPLE: STIMULUS CONTROL

This model example will illustrate how stimulus control can be used as *one way* to help Joan achieve her goal of increasing positive thoughts about her math ability. Recall that the principle of change in using stimulus control to increase a behavior is to increase the cues associated with the behavior. Here's how we would implement this principle with Joan.

1. Establish at least one cue that Joan could use as an antecedent for positive thoughts. We might suggest something like putting a piece of tape over her watch.
2. Develop a list of several positive thoughts about math. Each thought could be written on a blank card that Joan could carry with her.
3. Instruct Joan to read or think about a thought on one card *each* time she looks at her watch. Instruct her to seek out the opportunity deliberately by looking at her watch frequently and then concentrating on one of these positive thoughts.
4. When Joan gets to the point where she automatically thinks of a positive thought after looking at her watch, other cues can be established that she can use in the same way. For instance, she can put a ☺ on her math book. Each time she gets out her math book and sees the "smily face," she can use this cue to concentrate on another positive thought.
5. She can promote more stimulus control over these thoughts by using reminders. For instance, Joan could put a list of positive thoughts on the mirror or the closet door in her room. Each time she sees the list, it serves as a reminder. Or she can ask a friend or classmate to remind her to "think positively" whenever the subject of math or math class is being discussed.

LEARNING ACTIVITY #50: STIMULUS CONTROL

Since the emphasis in this chapter is on self-management, the learning activities in this chapter are designed to help you use these strategies yourself! The purpose of this learning activity is to help you reduce an unwanted behavior, using stimulus-control methods.

1. Specify a behavior that you find undesirable and you wish to decrease. It can be an overt one, such as smoking, eating, biting your nails, or making sarcastic comments, or it can be a covert behavior, such as thinking about yourself in negative ways or thinking how great food or smoking tastes.

2. Select one or more stimulus-control methods to use for behavior reduction from the list and examples given in Table 19-2. Remember, you will be reducing the number of cues or antecedent events associated with this behavior by altering the times and places the undesired response occurs.
3. Implement these stimulus-control methods daily for two weeks.
4. During the two weeks, engage in self-monitoring of your target response. Record the type and use of your method and amount of your target behav-

(continued)

ior, using frequency or duration methods of recording.

5. *At the end of two weeks, review your recording data. Did you use your selected method consistently? If not, what contributed to your infrequent use? If you used it consistently, did you notice any* gradual *reduction in the target behavior by the end of two weeks? What problems did you encounter in applying a stimulus-control method with yourself? What did you learn about stimulus control that might help you when using it with clients?*

☐ SELF-REWARD

Self-reward procedures are used to help clients regulate and strengthen their behavior with the aid of self-produced consequences. Many actions of an individual are controlled by self-produced consequences as much as by external consequences (Bandura, 1974, 1976b). As Bandura (1974) explains, "People typically set themselves certain standards of behavior and self-administer rewarding or punishing consequences depending on whether their performances fall short of, match, or exceed their self-prescribed demands" (p. 87). There is evidence that most patterns of self-reinforcement and self-punishment are acquired and modified by learning (Bandura, 1971b).

According to Bandura (1971b), there are several necessary conditions of self-reinforcement, or self-reward:

1. The individual (rather than someone else) determines the criteria for adequacy of her or his performance and for resulting reinforcement.
2. The individual (rather than someone else) controls access to the reward.
3. The individual (rather than someone else) is his or her own reinforcing agent and administers the rewards.

Note that self-reward involves *both* the self-determination and the self-administration of a reward. This distinction has, at times, been overlooked in self-reinforcement research and application. The characteristics of self-reward proposed by Bandura (1971b, 1981) suggest that the person has free access to the rewards; this is considered an essential feature of self-reward procedures. Nelson, Hayes, Spong, Jarrett, and McKnight (1983, p. 565) propose that "self-reinforcement is effective primarily because of its stimulus properties in cuing natural environmental consequences."

As a self-management procedure, self-reward is used to strengthen or increase a desired response. It is assumed that the operations involved in self-reward parallel those that occur in external reinforcement. In other words, a self-presented reward, like an externally administered reward, is defined by the function it exerts on the target behavior. A reinforcer (self- or external) is something that, when administered following a target response, tends to maintain or increase the probability of that response in the future. A major advantage of self-reward over external reward is that a person can use and apply this strategy independently.

Self-rewards can be classified into two categories: positive and negative. In positive self-reward, one presents onself with a positive stimulus (to which one has free access) *after* engaging in a specified behavior. Examples of positive reward include praising yourself after you have completed a long and difficult term paper, buying yourself a new record after you have engaged in a specified amount of piano practice, or imagining that you are resting on your favorite beach after you have completed your daily exercises. Negative self-reward involves the removal of a negative stimulus after execution of a target response. For example, obese clients removed portions of suet from their refrigerators after certain amounts of weight loss (Penick, Filion, Fox, & Stunkard, 1971). Taking down an uncomplimentary picture or chart from your wall after performing the target response is another example of negative self-reward.

Our discussion of self-reward as a therapeutic strategy is limited to the use of positive self-reward for several reasons. First, there has been very little research to validate the negative self-reward procedure. Second, by definition, negative self-reward involves an aversive activity. It is usually unpleasant for a person to keep suet in the refrigerator or to put an ugly picture on the wall. Many people will not use a strategy that is aversive. Second, we do not recommend that counselors suggest strategies that seem aversive, because the client may feel that terminating the counseling is preferable to engaging in an unpleasant change process.

Clinical Uses of Self-Reward

Self-reward has been explored as a convenient and

effective classroom-management procedure (Bolstad & Johnson, 1972; McLaughlin, 1976; Neilans & Israel, 1981). It has been used as a major component in comprehensive self-change programs involving weight control (Mahoney & Mahoney, 1976; Polly, Turner, & Sherman, 1976) and exercise programming (Turner, Polly, & Sherman, 1976). Jackson (1972) used self-reward to treat a woman who was depressed and very critical of herself. Self-reinforcement decreased the client's depressive moods, as indicated by daily self-ratings.

Self-reward has been investigated in several controlled studies that have presented evidence for the utility of self-reinforcement as a clinical treatment strategy. For example, Mahoney et al. (1973) found that self-reward was a more effective weight reduction strategy than self-monitoring, self-punishment, or stimulus control. In this study, self-reward consisted in having the people give themselves money to buy desired items after certain amounts of weight loss. M. J. Mahoney (1974) also found that self-reward strategies resulted in more weight loss than self-monitoring, especially when the clients made the rewards contingent on improved eating habits rather than weekly weight losses. Bellack (1976) reported that self-reward was more effective than self-monitoring in producing weight reduction, even without therapist contacts. He concluded that self-reward may substantially augment the role of self-monitoring in effecting behavior change.

Both the case studies and controlled investigations of self-reward indicate that this strategy has a promising place in clinical treatment programs. In a review of self-reinforcement, Jones et al. (1977, p. 160) note that "overall, self-reinforcement has been shown to be a viable technique in treating a plethora of both clinical and educational problems." However, these authors point out that some of the clinical effects typically attributed to the self-reinforcement procedure may also be due to certain external factors, including a client's previous reinforcement history, client goal setting, the role of client self-monitoring, surveillance by another person, external contingencies in the client's environment, and the instructional set given to the client about the self-reward procedure. The exact role these external variables may play in self-reward is still relatively little known. However, a counselor should acknowledge and perhaps try to capitalize on some of these factors to heighten the clinical effects of a self-reward strategy.

Components of Self-Reward

Self-reward involves planning by the client of appropriate rewards and of the conditions in which they will be used. Self-reward can be described by four major components: (1) selection of appropriate self-rewards, (2) delivery of self-rewards, (3) timing of self-rewards, and (4) planning for self-change maintenance. These components are described in this portion of the chapter and are summarized in the following list. Although these components are discussed separately, remember that all of them are integral parts of an effective self-reward procedure.

1. Selection of appropriate rewards
   a. Individualize the reward.
   b. Use accessible rewards.
   c. Use several rewards.
   d. Use different types of rewards (verbal/symbolic, material, imaginal, current, potential).
   e. Use potent rewards.
   f. Use rewards that are not punishing to others.
   g. Match rewards to target response.
2. Delivery of self-rewards
   a. Self-monitor for data of target response.
   b. Specify what and how much is to be done for a reward.
   c. Specify frequent reinforcement in small amounts for different levels of target response.
3. Timing of self-reward
   a. Reward should come after, not before, behavior.
   b. Rewards should be immediate.
   c. Rewards should follow performance, not promises.
4. Planning for self-change maintenance.
   a. Enlist help of others in sharing or dispensing rewards.
   b. Review data with counselor.

Selection of Appropriate Rewards

In helping a client to use self-reward effectively, some time and planning must be devoted to selecting rewards that are appropriate for the client and the desired target behavior. Selecting rewards can be time-consuming. However, effective use of self-reward is somewhat dependent on the availability of events that are truly reinforcing to the client. The counselor can assist the client in selecting appropriate self-rewards; however, the client should have the major role in determining the specific contingencies.

Rewards can take many different forms. A self-reward may be verbal/symbolic, material, or imaginal. One verbal/symbolic reward is self-praise, such as thinking or telling oneself "I did a good job." A material reward is something tangible—an event (such as a movie), a purchase (such as a banana split), or a token or point that can be exchanged for a reinforcing event or purchase. An imaginal reinforcer is the covert visualization of a scene or situation that is pleasurable and produces good feelings. Imaginal reinforcers might include picturing yourself as a thin person after losing weight or imagining that you are water-skiing on a lake you have all to yourself.

Self-rewards can also be classified as current or potential. A current reward is something pleasurable that happens routinely or occurs daily, such as eating, talking to a friend, or reading a newspaper. A potential reward is something that would be new and different if it happened, something a person does infrequently or anticipates doing in the future. Examples of potential rewards include going on a vacation or buying a "luxury" item (something you love but rarely buy for yourself, not necessarily something expensive). Engaging in a "luxury" activity—something you rarely do—can be a potential reinforcer. For a person who is very busy and constantly working, "doing nothing" might be a luxury activity that is a potential reinforcer.

In selecting appropriate self-rewards, a client should consider the availability of these various kinds of rewards. We believe that a well-balanced self-reward program involves a *variety* of types of self-rewards. A counselor might encourage a client to select *both* verbal/symbolic and material rewards. Relying only on material rewards may ignore the important role of positive self-evaluations in a self-change program. Further, material rewards have been criticized for overuse and misuse (O'Leary, Poulos, & Devine, 1972). Imaginal reinforcers may not be so powerful as verbal/symbolic and material ones. However, they are completely portable and can be used to supplement verbal/symbolic and material rewards when it is impossible for an individual to use these other types (Watson & Tharp, 1981).

In selecting self-rewards, a client should also consider the use of both current and potential rewards. One of the easiest ways for a client to use current rewards is to observe what daily thoughts or activities are reinforcing and then to rearrange these so that they are used in contingent rather than noncontingent ways (Kanfer, 1975; Watson & Tharp, 1981). However, whenever a client uses a current reward, some deprivation or self-denial is involved. For example, agreeing to read the newspaper only after cleaning the kitchen involves initially denying oneself some pleasant, everyday event in order to use it to reward a desired behavior. As Thoresen and Mahoney (1974) point out, this initial self-denial introduces an aversive element into the self-reward strategy. Some people do not respond well to any aversiveness associated with self-change or self-directed behavior. One of the authors, in fact, consistently "abuses" the self-reward principle by doing the reward before the response (reading the paper before cleaning the kitchen)—precisely as a reaction against the aversiveness of this "programmed" self-denial. One way to prevent self-reward from becoming too much like programmed abstinence is to have the client select novel or potential reinforcers to use in addition to current ones.

There are several ways a counselor can help a client identify and select various kinds of self-rewards. One way is simply with verbal report. The counselor and client can discuss current self-reward practices and desired luxury items and activities (Kanfer, 1980). The client can also identify rewards by using *in vivo* observation. The client should be instructed to observe and list current consequences that seem to maintain some behaviors. Finally, the client can identify and select rewards by completing preference and reinforcement surveys. A preference survey is designed to help the client identify preferred and valued activities. Here is an example of one that Watson and Tharp (1981, p. 170) recommend:

1. What will be the rewards of achieving your goal?
2. What kind of praise do you like to receive, from yourself or from others?
3. What kinds of things do you like to have?
4. What are your major interests?
5. What are your hobbies?
6. What people do you like to be with?
7. What do you like to do with those people?
8. What do you do for fun?
9. What do you do to relax?
10. What do you do to get away from it all?

11. What makes you feel good?
12. What would be a nice present to receive?
13. What kinds of things are important to you?
14. What would you buy if you had an extra $20? $50? $100?
15. On what do you spend your money each week?
16. What behaviors do you perform every day? (Don't overlook the obvious or the commonplace.)
17. Are there any behaviors that you usually perform instead of the target behavior?
18. What would you hate to lose?
19. Of the things you do every day, which would you hate to give up?
20. What are your favorite daydreams and fantasies?
21. What are the most relaxing scenes you can imagine?

The client can complete this sort of preference survey in writing or in a discussion. Clients who find it difficult to identify rewarding events might also benefit from completing a more formalized reinforcement survey, such as the Reinforcement Survey Schedule or the Children's Reinforcement Survey Schedule, written by Cautela (1977). The client can be given homework assignments to identify possible verbal/symbolic and imaginal reinforcers. For instance, the client might be asked to make a daily list for a week of positive self-thoughts or of the positive consequences of desired change. Or the client could make a list of all the things about which she or he likes to daydream or of some imagined scenes that would be pleasurable (Watson & Tharp, 1981).

Sometimes a client may seem thwarted in initial attempts to use self-reward because of difficulties in identifying rewards. Watson and Tharp (1981) note that people whose behavior consumes the reinforcer (such as smoking or eating), whose behavior is reinforced intermittently, or whose avoidance behavior is maintained by negative reinforcement may not be able to identify reinforcing consequences readily. Individuals who are "locked into" demanding schedules cannot find daily examples of reinforcers. Sometimes depressed people have trouble identifying reinforcing events. In these cases, the counselor and client have several options that can be used to overcome difficulties in selecting effective self-rewards.

A client who does not have the time or money for material rewards might use imaginal rewards.

Imagining pleasant scenes following a target response has been described by Cautela (1970) as *covert positive reinforcement* (CPR). In the CPR procedure, the client usually imagines performing a desired behavior, followed by imagination of a reinforcing scene. In one example, dieters imagined more positive body images as their reinforcing scene (Horan, Baker, Hoffman, & Shute, 1975). Watson and Tharp (1981) recommend that a client use imaginal reinforcers only when other kinds are not available, since some of the research on the CPR procedure has produced very mixed results. As an example, in at least one study (Bajtelsmit & Gershman, 1976), having the person imagine the reinforcer *before* the desired behavior was just as effective in reducing test anxiety as having the person imagine the reinforcer *after* the desired behavior. For these reasons, some people have questioned the exact method by which CPR really operates (Ladouceur, 1974).

A second available option for problem cases is to use a client's everyday activity as a self-reward. Some clinical cases have used a mundane activity such as answering the phone (Lawson & May, 1970) or opening the daily mail (Spinelli & Packard, 1975) as the self-reward. (Actually, such an activity may work more as a cuing device than a reinforcer; see Thoresen and Mahoney, 1974). If a frequently occurring behavior is used as a self-reward, it should be a desirable or at least a neutral activity. As Watson and Tharp (1981) note, clients should not use as a self-reward any high-frequency behavior that they would stop immediately if they could. Using a negative high-frequency activity as a reward may seem more like punishment than reinforcement.

With depressed clients, selecting self-rewards is often difficult, because many events lose their reinforcing value for someone who is depressed. Before using self-reward with a depressed client, it might be necessary to increase the reinforcing value of certain events. Anton, Dunbar, and Friedman (1976) describe the procedure of "anticipation training" designed to increase depressed clients' positive anticipations of events. In anticipation training, a client identifies and schedules several pleasant events to perform and then constructs three positive anticipation statements for each activity. The client imagines engaging in an activity and imagines the anticipation statements associated with the activity. An example adapted from Anton et al. of some anticipation statements for one activity might be:

Activity planned: *Spending an afternoon at the lake*

Date to be carried out: *Tuesday; Wednesday if it rains Tuesday*

I will enjoy: *sitting on the beach reading a book*

I will enjoy: *getting in the water on a hot day*

I will enjoy: *getting a suntan*

No thought, event, or imagined scene is reinforcing for everyone. Often what one person finds rewarding is very different from the rewards selected by someone else. In using self-reward, it is important to help clients choose rewards that will work well for *them*—not for the counselor, a friend, or a spouse. Kanfer notes that "it is crucial that the selected reinforcers relate to the client's personal history. They must be acceptable to him as something he wants, could easily acquire or do, and that would make him feel good" (1980, p. 369).

The counselor should use the following guidelines to help the client determine some self-rewards that might be used effectively.

1. *Individualize* the reward to the client (Homme, Csanyi, Gonzales, & Rechs, 1969).
2. The reward should be *accessible* and *convenient* to use after the behavior is performed.
3. *Several* rewards should be used interchangeably to prevent satiation (a reward can lose its reinforcing value because of repeated presentations).
4. Different *types* of rewards should be selected (verbal/symbolic, material, imaginal, current, potential).
5. The rewards should be *potent* but not so valuable that an individual will not use them contingently.
6. The rewards should not be *punishing* to others. Watson and Tharp (1981) suggest that if a reward involves someone else, the other person's agreement should be obtained.
7. The reward should be *compatible* with the desired response (Kanfer, 1980). For instance, a person losing weight might use new clothing as a reward or thoughts of a new body image after weight loss. Using eating as a reward is not a good match for a weight-loss target response.

Delivery of Self-Reward

The second part of working out a self-reward strategy with a client involves specifying the conditions and method of delivering the self-rewards. First of all, a client cannot deliver or administer a self-reward without some data base. Self-reward delivery is dependent on systematic data gathering; self-monitoring is an essential first step.

Second, the client should determine the precise conditions under which a reward will be delivered. The client should, in other words, state the rules of the game. The client should know *what* and *how much* has to be done before administering a self-reward. Usually self-reward is more effective when clients reward themselves for small steps of progress (Homme et al., 1969). In other words, performance of a subgoal should be rewarded. Waiting to reward oneself for demonstration of the overall goal usually introduces too much of a delay between responses and rewards.

Finally, the client should indicate how much and what kind of reward will be given for performing various responses or different levels of the goals. The client should specify that doing so much of the response results in one type of reward and how much of it. Usually reinforcement is more effective when broken down into smaller units that are self-administered more frequently (Homme et al., 1969). The use of tokens or points provides for frequent, small units of reinforcement; these can be exchanged for a "larger" reinforcer after a certain number of points or tokens are accumulated.

Timing of Self-Reward

The counselor also needs to instruct the client about the timing of self-reward—when a self-reward should be administered. There are three ground rules for the timing of a self-reward suggested by Homme et al. (1969):

1. A self-reward should be administered *after* performing the specified response, not before.
2. A self-reward should be administered *immediately* after the response. Long delays may render the procedure ineffective.
3. A self-reward should follow *actual performance,* not promises to perform.

Planning for Self-Change Maintenance

Self-reward, like any self-change strategy, needs environmental support for long-term maintenance of change (Kanfer, 1980; M. J. Mahoney, 1974). The last part of using self-reward involves helping the client find ways to plan for self-change maintenance. First, the counselor can encourage the client to enlist the help of others in a self-reward program. Other people can share in or dispense some of the reinforcement (Watson & Tharp, 1981). Some evidence indicates that people who receive rewards from others at least initially may benefit more from self-reward (Mahoney & Thoresen, 1974). Second, the client should plan to review the data collected during self-reward with the counselor. The review sessions give the counselor a chance to reinforce the client and to help the client make any necessary revisions in the use of the strategy. Therapist expectations and approval for client progress may add to the overall effects of the self-reward strategy (Jones et al., 1977).

Some Cautions in Using Rewards

The use of rewards as a motivational and informational device is a controversial issue. Using rewards, especially material ones, as incentives has been criticized on the grounds that tangible rewards are overused, are misused, and often discourage rather than encourage the "rewardee" (Levine & Fasnacht, 1974; O'Leary et al., 1972). Furthermore, McKeachie (1974, 1976) observes high levels of reward (or punishment) are not necessarily optimal for performance (1976, p. 823).

As a therapy technique, self-reward should not be used indiscriminately. Before suggesting self-reward, the counselor should carefully consider the individual client, the client's previous reinforcement history, and the client's desired change. When a counselor and client do decide to use self-reward, two cautionary guidelines should be followed. First, material rewards should not be used solely or promiscuously. Levine and Fasnacht (1974) recommend that the therapist seek ways to increase a person's intrinsic satisfaction in performance before automatically resorting to extrinsic rewards as a motivational technique. Second, the counselor's role in self-reward should be limited to providing instructions about the procedure and encouragement for progress. The client should be the one who selects the rewards and determines the criteria for delivery and timing of reinforcement. As Jones et al. (1977) observe, when the target behaviors and the contingencies are specified by someone other than the person using self-reward, the procedure can hardly be described accurately as a self-change operation (p. 174).

□ MODEL EXAMPLE: SELF-REWARD

This example will illustrate how self-reward could be used to help Joan increase her positive thoughts about her ability to do well in math.

1. *Selection of rewards:* First the counselor would help Joan select some appropriate rewards to use for reaching her predetermined goal. The counselor would encourage Joan to identify some self-praise she could use to reward herself symbolically or verbally ("I did it"; "I can gradually see my attitude about math changing"). Joan could give herself points for daily positive thoughts. She could accumulate and exchange the points for material rewards, including current rewards (such as engaging in a favorite daily event) and potential rewards (such as a purchase of a desired item). These are suggestions; Joan should be responsible for the actual selection. The counselor could suggest that Joan identify possible rewards through observation or completion of a preference survey. The counselor should make sure that the rewards Joan selects are accessible and easy to use. Several rewards should be selected to prevent satiation. The counselor should also make sure that the rewards selected are potent, compatible with Joan's goal, and not punishing to anyone else.

2. *Delivery of rewards:* The counselor would help Joan determine guidelines for delivery of the rewards selected. Joan might decide to give herself a point for each positive thought. This allows for reinforcement of small steps toward the overall goal. A predetermined number of daily points, such as 5, might result in delivery of a current reward, such as watching TV or going over to her friend's house. A predetermined number of weekly points could mean delivery of a potential self-reward, such as going to a movie or purchasing a new item. Joan's demonstration of her goal beyond the specified level could result in delivery of a bonus self-reward.

3. *Timing of rewards:* The counselor would instruct Joan to administer the reward *after* the positive thoughts or after the specified number of points is accumulated. The counselor can emphasize that the rewards follow performance, not promises. The counselor should encourage Joan to engage in the rewards as soon as possible after the daily and weekly target goals have been met.

4. *Planning for self-change maintenance:* The counselor can help Joan find ways to plan for self-change maintenance. One way is to schedule periodic "check-ins" with the counselor. In addition, Joan might select a friend who could help her share in the reward by watching TV or going shopping with her or by praising Joan for her goal achievement.

LEARNING ACTIVITY #51: SELF-REWARD

This learning activity is designed to have you engage in self-reward.

1. Select a target behavior you want to increase. Write down your goal (the behavior to increase, desired level of increase, and conditions in which behavior will be demonstrated).
2. Select several types of self-rewards to use and write them down. The types to use are verbal/symbolic, material (both current and potential), and imaginal. See whether your selected self-rewards meet the following criteria:
   a. Individually tailored to you?
   b. Accessible and convenient to use?
   c. Several self-rewards?
   d. Different types of self-rewards?
   e. Are rewards potent?
   f. Are rewards not punishing to others?
   g. Are rewards compatible with your desired goal?
3. Set up a plan for delivery of your self-reward: What type of reinforcement and how much will be administered? How much and what demonstration of the target behavior are required?
4. When do you plan to administer a self-reward?
5. How could you enlist the aid of another person?
6. Apply self-reward for a specified time period. Did your target response increase? To what extent?
7. What did you learn about self-reward that might help you in suggesting this to a client?

☐ PROMOTING CLIENT COMMITMENT TO USE SELF-MANAGEMENT STRATEGIES

A critical issue in any self-management strategy that is still unresolved has been termed "the contract problem" (Mahoney, 1970). Finding ways to strengthen a client's stated commitment to using a self-management strategy consistently is a major challenge to any helper (Kanfer, 1980; Thoresen & Mahoney, 1974). There are several things a counselor might do to increase the probability that a client will use self-management strategies consistently. First, some clients seem to be more hesitant about self-management methods on first entering therapy (Williams et al., 1976). Perhaps clients who decide to seek the assistance of a helper are discouraged with their own self-change efforts. For this reason, therapists may want to avoid introducing self-management strategies in early counseling sessions (Williams et al., p. 234).

Second, clients' regular use of self-management may depend partly on their motivation to change. People who are very motivated to change a behavior seem to benefit more from self-management than those who aren't interested in modifying the target response (Ciminero et al., 1977). In view of the importance of the client's desire to change the goal behavior, the counselor might precede initiating a self-management strategy with some assessment of the client's motivation level. Brown (1978) recommends that the following questions be answered orally or in writing by the client:

1. How much money would you be willing to spend to do _____? (Put any maximum dollar amount between 0 and 10,000.)
2. If unpleasant activity—real, unpaid, work—were required instead of money, how many *minutes* each day would you be willing to spend to reach your goal? (Put in any maximum number of *minutes* between 0 and 480.)
3. On the following scale, please circle the number that best indicates how motivated you are to make this change.

   4—Extremely motivated. . . . Nothing is more important to me.
   3—Very motivated. . . .
   2—Moderately motivated. . . .
   1—Not motivated [p. 127].*

Third, in using self-management programs, the help and support of other people should not be ignored. The use of significant others to aid the client in the use of a strategy may greatly enhance the behavior change. Self-help groups are one example: clients' self-directed change programs are supported by friends or by other clients working toward similar goals (Stuart, 1977).

The helper, too, should maintain at least minimal contact with the client while the self-management strategies are being used. These strategies are an excellent way to bridge the gap from regular weekly counseling sessions to termination of

---

* From *An analysis of self-monitoring-provided feedback in a behavioral weight reduction program,* by J. Brown. Unpublished doctoral dissertation, West Virginia University, 1978. Reprinted by permission.

counseling. Use of self-management procedures at this point may promote generalization of client changes from the interview setting to the client's environment. However, the counselor should maintain some contact with the client during this period, even if it involves only informal telephone calls. Using self-management strategies in the concluding sessions can also help the counselor and client achieve a gradual and successful termination.

☐ SUMMARY

Self-management is a process in which clients direct their own behavior change with any one therapeutic strategy or a combination of strategies. The self-monitoring strategy provides a method by which a client can become more aware of his or her overt behavior or internal responses such as thoughts or feelings. Self-monitoring may also provide information about the social and environmental context that influences these behaviors. Stimulus-control procedures require predetermined arrangement of environmental conditions that are antecedents of a target behavior, or cues to increase or decrease that behavior. As a self-management strategy, self-reward involves presenting oneself with a positive stimulus *after* engaging in a specified behavior. These three strategies typically are classified as self-management because in each procedure the client prompts, alters, or controls antecedents and consequences to produce desired changes in behavior in a self-directed fashion. Promoting client commitment to use self-management strategies can be achieved by introducing these strategies later in therapy, assessing the client's motivation for change, creating a social support system to aid the client in the use of the strategy, and maintaining contact with the client while self-management strategies are being used.

POSTEVALUATION

PART ONE

Objective One asks you to describe the application of the six components of self-monitoring to a written client case. Read the following case carefully. Then respond in writing to the questions listed.

Client Case Description

The client is a 30-year-old woman who has been married for ten years. Over the last two years she has been troubled by constant thoughts that her husband will die young and she will be left alone. She realizes there is no basis for these thoughts. Her baseline data indicate that these episodes of ruminative thinking occur anywhere from five to ten times daily. Suppose you were to use self-monitoring to help this client *decrease* these thoughts.

1. Provide an example *rationale* that you could give this client about this strategy.
2. Explain the process of *response discrimination* as it would be used with this client.
3. Give brief examples of the instructions you would give to this client about *response recording*. Include instructions about (a) *timing* of the recording, (b) *method* of recording, and (c) a *device* for recording.
4. Provide an example of a *chart* the client could use to plot the daily totals of the monitored behavior.
5. What are some examples of places where you would instruct this client to *display* the charted data?
6. Describe at least one way the client could engage in *data analysis*.

Feedback follows the Postevaluation on page 548.

PART TWO

Objective Two asks you to teach someone else how to engage in self-monitoring. Your teaching should follow the six guidelines listed in Table 19-1: rationale, response discrimination, self-recording, data charting, data display, and data analysis. Feedback follows.

PART THREE

Objective Three asks you to describe how stimulus-control methods could be used to increase or reduce a behavior for a given client. Using the following case description, describe in writing how you would use stimulus control to reduce the client's eating behavior and to increase her control over her study behavior. Feedback follows.

Case Description

The client is a freshman in college, living at home. She is concerned because she is under more pressure and has gained 25 pounds recently. She is having trouble

(continued)

keeping up with her course work because she lacks discipline to study. She wants help in reducing her weight and increasing her studying.

1. Describe how the client could use stimulus control to reduce her eating behavior:
   a. How could she reduce or narrow the cues associated with eating?
   b. How could she prearrange cues that make overeating or eating snacks or fattening foods difficult?
   c. How could she prearrange some cues to be controlled by other people?
   d. How could she break up the sequence, or chain, of eating behavior?
   e. How could she change the typical chain resulting in eating?
   f. How could she build pauses into the eating chain?
2. Describe how she could increase control of her study behavior, using stimulus control, by—
   a. Prearranging the cues associated with studying.
   b. Concentrating on the behavior while in the prearranged situations.
   c. Promoting the occurrence of helpful cues by reminders.

PART FOUR

Objective Four asks you to describe the application of the four components of self-reward for a written client case. Read the following case; then respond in writing to the questions that follow it. Feedback follows.

Case Description

The client is a young man who wants to increase the number of women he asks out for dates; he has set a goal of asking at least three different women out per week. You have instructed the client about how to self-monitor this target behavior. In addition, you plan to instruct the client to use self-reward. He will count and chart the number of women he actually invites, then administer a self-reward if he meets his weekly goal.

Selection of Rewards

1. What would be two examples of a verbal/symbolic reward the client could use? Two examples of a material reward? Two examples of an imaginal reward?

2. List at least three characteristics of an effective self-reward.

3. If the client had trouble identifying material reinforcers, what is one alternative that could be used?

Delivery of Rewards

4. Given an example of how you would instruct the client to administer and deliver a self-reward (for example, what type and how much reinforcement for levels of goal achievement).

Timing of Self-Rewards

5. List at least two instructions you would give the client about *when* to administer the reward.

Planning for Self-Change Maintenance

6. Write at least one thing the client could do to plan for self-change maintenance.

PART FIVE

Objective Five asks you to teach someone else how to use a self-reward procedure to increase or strengthen a behavior. You can use the list on page 540 as a guide. You should teach the person how to select appropriate self-rewards, how to deliver self-reinforcement, when to administer self-rewards, and how to plan for self-change maintenance.

□ SUGGESTED READINGS

Bandura, A. (1981). In search of pure unidirectional determinants. *Behavior Therapy, 12,* 30–40.

Barlow, D. H., Hayes, S. C., & Nelson, R. O. (1984). *The scientist practitioner.* New York: Pergamon Press.

Blanchard, E. B., Andrasik, F., Neff, D. F., Jurish, S. E., & O'Keefe, C. M. (1981). Social validation of the headache diary. *Behavior Therapy, 12,* 711–715.

Borkovec, T. D., Wilkinson, L., Folensbee, R., & Lerman, C. (1983). Stimulus control applications to the treatment of worry. *Behavior Research and Therapy, 21,* 247–251.

Carroll, L. J., & Yates, B. T. (1981). Further evidence for the role of stimulus control training in facilitating weight reduction after behavioral therapy. *Behavior Therapy, 12,* 287–291.

Coates, T. J., & Thoresen, C. E. (1984). Assessing daytime thoughts and behavior associated with good and poor sleep: Two exploratory case studies. *Behavioral Assessment, 6,* 153–167.

Fremouw, W. J., & Brown, J. P., Jr. (1980). The reactivity of addictive behaviors to self-monitoring: A functional analysis. *Addictive Behaviors, 5,* 209–217.

Fremouw, W. J., Callahan, E. J., Zitter, R. E., & Katell, A. (1981). Stimulus control and contingency contracting for behavior change and weight loss. *Addictive Behaviors, 6,* 289–300.

Fremouw, W. J., & Heyneman, N. (1983). Obesity. In M. Hersen (Ed.), *Outpatient behavior therapy.* New York: Grune & Stratton.

Heffernan, T., & Richards, C. S. (1981). Self-control of study behavior: Identification and evaluation of natural methods. *Journal of Counseling Psychology, 28,* 361–364.

Hollon, S. D., & Kendall, P. C. (1981). *In vivo* assessment techniques for cognitive-behavioral processes. In P. C. Kendall & S. D. Hollon (Eds.). *Assessment strategies for cognitive-behavioral interventions.* New York: Academic Press.

Jones, J. E. (1981). Self-monitoring of stuttering: Reactivity and accuracy. *Behaviour Research and Therapy, 19,* 291–296.

Karoly, P., & Kanfer, F. A. (Eds.). (1982). *Self-management and behavior change.* New York: Pergamon Press.

Keefe, F. J., & Blumenthal, J. A. (1980). The life fitness program: A behavioral approach to making exercise a habit. *Journal of Behavior Therapy and Experimental Psychiatry, 11,* 31–34.

Litrownik, A. J. (1982). Special considerations in the self-management training of the developmentally disabled. In P. Karoly & F. H. Kanfer (Eds.), *Self-management and behavior change.* New York: Pergamon Press.

Marlatt, G. A., & Parks, G. A. (1982). Self-management of addictive behaviors. In P. Karoly & F. H. Kanfer (Eds.). *Self-management and behavior change.* New York: Pergamon Press.

McFall, R. M., & Dodge, K. A. (1982). Self-management and interpersonal skills learning. In P. Karoly & F. H. Kanfer (Eds.), *Self-management and behavior change.* New York: Pergamon Press.

Nelson, R. O., Boykin, R. A., & Hayes, S. C. (1982). Long-term effects of self-monitoring on reactivity and on accuracy. *Behaviour Research and Therapy, 20,* 357–363.

Nelson, R. O., Hayes, S. C., Spong, R. T., Jarrett, R. B., & McKnight, D. L. (1983). Self-reinforcement: Appealing misnomer or effective mechanism. *Behaviour Research and Therapy, 21,* 557–566.

Quattrochi-Turbin, S., & Jason, L. A. (1980). Enhancing social interaction and activity among the elderly through stimulus control. *Journal of Applied Behavior Analysis, 13,* 159, 163.

Rehm, L. P. (1982). Self-management in depression. In P. Karoly & F. H. Kanfer (Eds.), *Self-management and behavior change.* New York: Pergamon Press.

Watson, D. L., & Tharp, R. G. (1981). *Self-directed behavior: Self-modification for personal adjustment* (3rd ed.). Monterey, CA: Brooks/Cole.

Zwart, C. A., & Lisman, S. A. (1979). Analysis of stimulus control treatment of sleep-onset insomnia. *Journal of Consulting and Clinical Psychology, 47,* 113–118.

FEEDBACK: POSTEVALUATION

PART ONE

1. In the rationale you would emphasize how this strategy could help obtain information about the client's thoughts as well as modify them in the desired direction. You would also explain that she would be recording defined thoughts *in vivo* on a daily basis for several weeks.

2. Response-discrimination training would involve selecting, defining, and giving examples of the response to be monitored. The counselor should model some examples of the defined behavior and elicit some others from the client. Specifically, you would help the client define the nature and content of the thoughts she would be recording, such as "being alone."

3. *Timing of the recording:* Since this client is using self-monitoring to decrease an undesired behavior, she would engage in prebehavior monitoring; each time she had the urge or started to think about being left alone, she would record.

Method of recording: The client would be instructed to use a frequency count and record the number of times she started to think about being left alone. If she was unable to discern when these thoughts started and ended, she could record with time sampling. For example, she could divide a day into equal time intervals and use the "all or none" method. If such thoughts occurred during an interval, she would record *yes;* if they did not, she would record *no.* Or, during each interval, she could rate the approximate frequency of these thoughts on a numerical scale, such as 0 for "never occurring," 1 for "occasionally," 2 for "often," and 3 for "very frequently."

Device for recording: There is no one right device to assist this client in recording. She could count the frequency using a tally on a note card or a golf wrist counter. Or she could use a daily log sheet to keep track of interval occurrences.

4. A simple chart might have days along the horizontal axis and frequency of thought urges along the vertical axis.

5. This client may or may not wish to display the data in a public place at home. If not, she could carry the data in her purse or knapsack.

6. The client could engage in data analysis by reviewing the data with the counselor or by comparing the data with the baseline or with her goal (desired

(continued)

level of behavior change). The latter involves self-evaluation and may set the stage for self-reinforcement.

PART TWO

Use Table 19-1 as a guide to assist your teaching. You might also determine whether the person you taught implemented self-monitoring accurately.

PART THREE

Refer to Table 19-2 for examples of stimulus control to reduce eating behavior and to increase study behavior.

PART FOUR

1. The *verbal symbolic rewards* used by this client could consist in self-praise for inviting a woman or covert verbalizations about the positive consequences of his behavior. Here are some examples:

   "I did it! I asked her out."
   "I did just what I wanted to do."
   "Now that I called her, I've got a great date."
   "Wow! What a good time I'll have with _____."

   Material rewards would be things or events the client indicates he prefers or enjoys. These might include buying a record, eating a snack, smoking, listening to music, or playing ball. Both current and potential rewards should be used. Of course, these activities are only possibilities; the client has to decide whether they are reinforcing.

   Examples of an *imaginal* reward may include either pleasant scenes or scenes related to going out:
   a. Imagining oneself on a raft on a lake.
   b. Imagining oneself on a football field.
   c. Imagining oneself with one's date at a movie.
   d. Imagining oneself with one's date lying on a warm beach.

2. See whether you identified at least three of the following seven characteristics of an effective self-reward:
   a. The rewards should be individualized for the client.
   b. The rewards should be accessible and easy to use.
   c. There should be several rewards.
   d. Different types of rewards should be selected.
   e. The rewards should be potent.
   f. The rewards should not be punishing to others.
   g. The rewards should be compatible with the client's desired goal.

3. If the client had trouble identifying some material reinforcers, here are some possible options:
   a. The client could use high-frequency behaviors as rewards as long as these behaviors were desirable, not aversive.
   b. The client could use imagery to reinforce himself covertly in lieu of material rewards.
   c. Perhaps the client could increase the potency of certain material events or activities with the use of "anticipation training." In anticipation training, a client preselects several activities in which to engage and rehearses anticipation statements about each activity.

4. Each woman this client asks out is a step in the desired direction. After the client asks out one woman, he might administer a verbal/symbolic or imaginal reward. When he reaches his desired weekly level of asking out three, he could administer a larger material reward.

5. See whether your instructions about the timing of self-reward included at least two of the following:
   a. The reward should be administered after, not before, the target behavior is carried out.
   b. The reward should be administered immediately and without delay.
   c. The reward should be administered for actual behavior, not promises.

6. The client could plan for self-change maintenance by holding review sessions with the counselor and by enlisting the aid of another person to share in or dispense the rewards.

PART FIVE

Use the list on page 540 as a guide to evaluate your teaching of the self-reward strategy. You also may wish to have your "student" keep data on the use of the procedure and the change in the target behavior.

STRATEGIES FOR MANAGING RESISTANCE

TWENTY

Resistance. The word itself is enough to make many therapists shudder. Yet many practitioners acknowledge that most clients, even self-referred ones, behave in resistive ways during the therapeutic process. For example, a client may be overtly resistant by refusing or sabotaging homework assignments or covertly resistant by using overcompliance or excessive cooperation to avoid dealing with an important issue. This chapter defines resistance, describes the most common sources of resistance, and identifies therapeutic techniques to manage resistance.

☐ OBJECTIVES

After completing this chapter, you will be able to—

1. Respond to client pessimism with listening responses that match, or pace, the client's feelings, given a role-play situation.
2. Identify dysfunctional behaviors and their reinforcers, or "payoffs," and ways in which the client can achieve the same reinforcement with more adaptive behaviors, given two written descriptions of client cases.
3. Identify four aspects of "patient position," given two written descriptions of clients and their presenting problems, and describe the implications of these positions for the management of therapy.
4. Select the most appropriate type of paradoxical intervention and write a description of a corresponding task and rationale, given two written descriptions of clients.
5. Deliver a compliance-based paradoxical intervention and a defiance-based paradoxical intervention, given a role-play interview.

☐ DEFINITION OF RESISTANCE

The concept of resistance originated with psychoanalysis. Freud (1900;1952) viewed resistance as a defensive reaction that served to protect the client against awareness of anxiety due to unresolved psychic conflicts or unacceptable thoughts and impulses. Freud speculated that, in spite of an expressed request for help, clients were resistant to giving up their symptoms because the symptoms were used to maintain internal equilibrium and avoid intrapsychic conflict. Bringing these sources of conflict into the client's awareness and working through the resistance are important goals of psychoanalytically oriented therapists.

Family systems literature views resistance as resulting from a need to keep a system homeostatic, or stable (Jackson, 1968). Efforts to change are resisted because such change implies too much deviation from "the way things are." According to Anderson and Stewart (1983, p. 29), "the need for stability in family systems is so strong that it is usually not the desire for change that leads families to seek therapy, but rather it is the *failure* to accommodate to change. Most families come to therapy *in response to changes* which they do not like or have not adjusted to." * From this perspective, clients tend to cling to the way things are and respond ambivalently to the threat of loss of control that seems to accompany change. In other words, clients often behave as if they wanted only more of what they already have (Gottman & Leiblum, 1974).

Although psychoanalysis and family therapy have contributed a great deal of literature about resistance, very little has been written about it from a cognitive-behavioral perspective. Some of the behavioral literature has minimized the concept of resistance by arguing that people will continue to behave in certain ways only as long as these behaviors are maintained by controlling consequences. Change will occur given the proper set of contingencies. Lack of change is attributed to failure to identify correctly the controlling contingencies or consequences rather than to "resistant behavior." An absence of available reinforcers and inability of the therapist to identify reinforcers are common reasons used to "explain away" client resistance.

In one of the first articles on the subject, Hersen (1971) acknowledged the presence of resistance in behavior therapy and asserted that it cannot always be explained away on the basis of operant

conditioning (a learning paradigm in which learning occurs because of positive, negative, or neutral consequences that follow a response). In a more recent article, Jahn and Lichstein (1980) noted that a resistive client directly defies the contingencies set by the therapist. They observed that it is impossible to blame incorrect contingency identification for all forms of client resistance or failure to change.

Other behavioral therapists tend to equate client resistance with noncompliance, or failure to achieve the desired behavior change because the client did not complete a prescribed task or assignment. Shelton and Levy (1981, p. 37) define compliance as "the client's carrying out an assignment in the way originally planned, discussed, and agreed upon by both him or herself and the therapist." As Anderson and Stewart (1983, p. 8) observe, "Most of the techniques described by behavioral therapists to increase compliance are ones which would serve to avoid the emergence of resistance." These techniques include such things as using relevant and appropriate tasks, giving the client choices, presenting tasks in a form acceptable to the client, keeping tasks small, concrete, and simple, and actively involving the client in devising the tasks.

We believe that resistance can be defined simply as any client *or* therapist behavior that interferes with or reduces the likelihood of a successful therapeutic process and outcome. Although the focus of this chapter is on client resistance, therapists also engage in resistive behavior. (This concept will be addressed in a later section of this chapter.) We also believe that most if not all clients engage in resistive behavior at some time during therapy. Perhaps most resistive are those clients who might be called "reluctant" or "involuntary"—that is, persons who would not be in the presence of a counselor and would prefer not to talk about themselves, given a choice (Patterson & Eisenberg, 1983). Often, involuntary clients are "required" to be counseled by a referring source such as the courts, a teacher, or a parent. However, even many voluntary and self-referred clients engage in some resistive behaviors during therapy, often in initial counseling contacts or when the need for change becomes apparent.

Resistance in therapy can stem from a variety of sources, including client variables, environmental variables, and therapist variables (Gottman & Leiblum, 1974; Munjack & Oziel, 1978). The particular sources of resistance can be identified by a

* This and all other quotations from this source are from *Mastering resistance* by C. M. Anderson and S. Stewart. Copyright © 1983 by The Guilford Press. Reprinted by permission.

careful assessment of the problem. For instance, questions asked during the problem assessment process can be directed to discovery of reinforcing and punishing contingencies, secondary gains, environmental competing stimuli, past attempts to resolve the problem, and so on. (See also Chapters 7 and 8.)

In the following three sections of the chapter, we elaborate on these three sources of resistance and suggest strategies for managing resistance effectively.

□ RESISTANCE DUE TO CLIENT VARIABLES

When Clients Lack Necessary Skills or Knowledge

Some clients may seem resistant but simply don't understand what to do or how to go about doing a task or activity. In some instances, the client is too preoccupied to understand the therapist's instructions or feels inept at carrying out the instructions. Other clients may not understand the counselor's instructions or the rationale for a particular strategy or task. Resistance that occurs when the client lacks necessary skills or knowledge can be managed with the following strategies.

Provide detailed instructions. Instructions are defined as one or more verbal statements in which the therapist instructs or directs a client to do something, either in the counseling session or as take-home instructions. Instructions have both influencing and informative effects. Instructions encourage a client to respond in a certain way and also provide information to help a client complete a particular task or activity. Effective instructions increase the likelihood of client compliance. Instructions are most effective if they are (1) specific rather than general (inform the client *what* to do and *how* to do it), (2) brief and concise rather than lengthy, and (3) delivered in a friendly rather than dogmatic manner.

To ensure that clients understand instructions, ask them to repeat the instructions to you. Written or typed summaries that clients can take home and display in a prominent place are useful adjuncts. Instructions may need to be supplemented with modeled demonstrations of the task or activity to be performed. Finally, it is important to follow up the instructions by asking about the client's experience at a later session.

Give direct skill training. Clients who are accustomed to refusing unreasonable requests are unlikely to "become more assertive" or comply with assertion homework tasks simply because the therapist exhorts them to do so. These clients need assurance that they can exercise the skill without humiliating themselves or important others. Compliance is enhanced when the counselor provides opportunities for skill acquisition that include breaking the behaviors into small steps or actions of increasing difficulty, modeling, role playing and imaginary rehearsal, feedback, and reinforcement (see also Chapter 12).

When Clients Have Pessimistic Expectations

Often therapists view some clients as "unmotivated." Usually this means these clients have minimal or even negative expectations about therapy and successful problem resolution. Resistance that occurs when clients present pessimistic expectations can be managed with the following strategies.

Acknowledge the client's pessimism. If the client expresses pessimistic ideas or expectations, a natural tendency is to counter these with expressions of optimism. Rather than encouraging the client to become less pessimistic, such comments may engender more resistance because they sound inflammatory and "preachy" or moralistic to the client. According to Fisch et al. (1982, p. 100), such comments "run counter to the client's position of pessimism, and one might predict that they will impede the client's cooperation and a successful outcome in treatment, especially if the client has already been discouraged by previous therapists who began treatment on a positive, optimistic note, only to terminate with no improvement."

What is likely to be more useful with these clients *initially* is to match your comments to those of the clients. This can be accomplished by the use of listening responses (Chapter 5) such as paraphrase and reflection that pace, or are in synchrony with, the client. Thus, instead of saying "You don't sound very hopeful about what we might accomplish, but I can assure you we can work this out successfully" the therapist might say "I can understand your wish to have this thing resolved, but after what has happened before, perhaps it would be better to start off being a little uncertain or doubtful about how this might turn out." According to Fisch et al. (1982, p. 100), "By stating this position, the therapist can, paradoxically, lessen the patient's pessimism, since he will be implying that he recognizes the patient's discouragement and its validity and that he will not patronize him through false hope." An alternative way of dealing with initial pessimism is to ask clients to recall any changes they may have experienced in the past that were preceded by an initial period of pessimism (Goldfried, 1982, p. 107). This is also more likely to bring about attitude change than trying to convince clients that their pessimistic attitudes are useless and unwarranted.

When Clients Have Negative or Anxious Thoughts

Other clients engage in resistive behaviors because of negative self-statements or cognitions about change. These clients often imagine the consequences of change as worse than the consequences of the problem. Resistance that occurs when the client's self-statements and cognitions are negative or anxiety-arousing can be managed with the following strategies.

Explore client fantasies, expectations, and fears in detail. Encourage clients to share their fears and anticipated reactions to change with you. Detailed and explicit expressions of anxious thoughts and feelings may actually help the client gain control of these feelings. Sometimes clients are reluctant to express such fears, believing that "talking about them will make them come true." On the contrary, clients are usually pleasantly surprised to find that expressing anxious feelings in the presence of a warm, nonjudgmental person actually reduces the intensity of such feelings. Having clients share aloud or role play their fantasies and fears about change also enables the counselor to correct any misperceptions. Some clients, for example, may resist change because of inaccurate or illogical beliefs such as "If I choose to get a divorce, I'll lose my job or everyone will think I'm a terrible person." The counselor can help the client sort out realistic and irrational anticipated results of change. Catastrophic expectations can be diffused in this process.

Provide support. Clients' avoidance of change may be reduced if you are highly supportive of their change efforts. Clients also benefit from hearing that their concerns are natural and that change often occurs slowly over a long period. At the same time, the counselor can challenge the client to change by suggesting that one way to discover whether fears of change are valid is to experiment with change and see what happens.

Set up what seems to be a small alteration in handling the problem. Clients who are pessimistic or fearful about change are more likely to engage in a small task than an overwhelming one. To clients, a small change in the way they handle a problem is more acceptable and is resisted less because it seems minor and inconsequential and does not require a great change in routine (Fisch et al., 1982). Therapeutic change is often like a kaleidoscope: change one small piece and the whole pattern changes.

Use a force-field analysis. The force-field analysis technique was developed by Lewin (1951) as a strategy for managing resistance to change. In this technique, the counselor assists the client in listing all possible avoidance behaviors (called "resisting forces") and all possible approach behaviors ("driving forces"). Next, the counselor and client plan ways to reduce the number and impact of the avoidance behaviors and increase the number and impact of the approach behaviors. An alternative strategy is to have the client "play out the polarity," or identify the self-talk associated with both sides of the conflict (approach and avoidance). Notice which side feels stronger. If it is the avoidance side, work on strengthening the approach side.

Give the suggestions when the client is most relaxed. A basic principle of hypnosis is to offer suggestions during the time a client is in a trance and therefore is most relaxed. The therapist can note when the client is most relaxed—or use imagery, relaxation, or focused breathing to reduce the client's tension—and offer a suggestion at this time.

Use rehearsal to practice new behaviors and to anticipate reactions from others. Very often clients are reluctant to implement a counselor's suggestion because they feel unable to do it or are unsure how it will turn out. Compliance can be increased if the counselor arranges for client practice of desired behaviors *before* having the client try these out in the real environment. Sometimes, too, clients are afraid to "handle" a situation because of anticipated responses from others. For example, a female client states "I'd really like to tell my mother I'm going to move, but I just can't, because of her reaction. She'll just go to pieces." Once you have determined that the client's perception of her mother's reaction is realistic (often it is just "mind reading"), then have the client rehearse how she will handle such a reaction. Anticipating and preparing for negative reactions helps clients comply with the task and carry it out more effectively.

Interpret the client's resistance.   At some point it may be useful to provide an interpretation of the client's resistance. Tentative hypotheses, or guesses, about the source and functions of the resistance can be offered. An effective interpretation (Chapter 6) can provide the client with greater self-understanding and can decrease some expressions of resistance. Interpretations may also show the client that the counselor does not skirt behavior or issues just because they make people feel uncomfortable (Dyer & Vriend, 1975).

The overall objective of interpreting resistance is for the client to identify and discuss unspoken feelings or issues. The interpretation focuses on what the client is doing to resist and provides an alternative explanation of the underlying issue, or "hidden agenda." For example, a counselor may interpret a very hostile client's resistance as follows:

> "I'm aware that every time I mention anything that has to do with "cutting the strings" from your parents, you become very upset and change the subject or deny it. You keep insisting that your parents are very dependent on you; could it be that you are the one who is more emotionally and financially dependent on them?"

As we mentioned in Chapter 6, it is important to be tentative rather than dogmatic when interpreting. It is also helpful to be accepting of clients and their resistance even while interpreting about it. Since interpretation is an action-oriented technique, it may work best with clients who are somewhat aware of their resistance. With other clients, a listening response such as reflection may be more helpful.

LEARNING ACTIVITY #52: CLIENT SOURCES OF RESISTANCE

In this activity, we present five statements that clients may make to a therapist at the beginning of or during therapy. Your task is to discriminate whether the statement suggests client *optimism* or *pessimism* about therapy and then construct a listening response (see also Chapter 5) that *matches,* or *paces,* the client's optimistic or pessimistic feelings. The first one is completed as an example. Feedback follows on page 556.

Example

Client, a middle-aged man: "I'm here only because my wife insisted I come in or else she would leave me and take my kids with her. I don't really think this will do much good."
    ____Optimism   ✔ Pessimism
Matching response(s):
"Given the pressure you feel to be here, I can understand your skepticism."
or
"You may be right. It's awfully difficult to make changes when someone insists that you do so."

Client Practice Messages

1. *Client,* a teenager: "I just have to talk to someone. I'm in trouble. I thought I could handle it, but I've gotten in over my head."
    ✔ Optimism   ____Pessimism
Matching response:

2. *Client,* an older retired man: "Yes, I've been having some trouble sleeping, but all I really need is some sleeping pills. My doctor doesn't seem to agree. He thinks it's my nerves and I need to see you instead."
    ____Optimism   ____Pessimism
Matching response:

3. *Client,* a graduate student: "I just can't stand this feeling of pressure. I'm desperate. I've got to have some immediate relief."
    ✔ Optimism   ____Pessimism
Matching response:

4. *Client,* a young woman: "I just don't feel very comfortable talking to other people about myself. How can talking like this help me with my problems anyway?"
    ____Optimism   ____Pessimism
Matching response:

5. *Client,* a teenager: "Of course I don't want to be here. But my parents gave me an ultimatum—shape up or ship out. They see this as a way to get me to behave. Ha!"
    ____Optimism   ✔ Pessimism
Matching response:

☐ RESISTANCE DUE TO ENVIRONMENTAL VARIABLES

Some clients resist treatment or fail to comply because of environmental variables that interfere with compliance. The client's environment may be arranged in a way that makes it difficult to engage in desired responding or in performing a desired activity. For example, the behavior may not be performed because of low visibility, competing stimuli, interactional variables, or differing norms of client's system. As Goldfried (1982, p.111) notes, "In cases where environmental determinants undermine therapeutic progress, it is clear that such variables must be the target of change."

When Environmental Variables Are Incompatible with Change

Resistance that occurs when environmental variables are incompatible with change can be managed with the following strategies.

Arrange cues that make the target response more visible. Environmental variables can contribute to client resistance when the environment is arranged in such a way that the cues or stimuli to set off and follow a particular response are not visible. For example, a student may find it difficult to study if her room is so crowded that it is hard to find space to work or if her books and school papers get lost easily. Rearranging the room to make it a less dense environment and posting reminders to study in highly visible places are ways to make the target response more visible and therefore more likely to occur. (See also "Stimulus Control" in Chapter 19.)

Reduce competing stimuli. Environmental variables can also produce resistance if the environment is arranged so that competing or distracting stimuli interfere with completion of the desired behavior or task. For example, students may find it difficult to study if the norms of their peer group are "to party." These norms compete with or distract the person from completing the desired response of studying. Students may also be less likely to study if there is so much conflict in their families that it is distracting and interfering with their ability to sustain a concentrated focus over a period of time. Finally, students may find it difficult to study if they are involved in a great many other time-consuming activities, such as sports, band, and work, that interfere with study behavior. Finding an alternative peer group, reducing family conflicts, and reducing participation in extracurricular activities would be ways to diminish competing stimuli that prevent the occurrence of desired study behavior. For other kinds of problems, an actual shift in environmental setting (for example, change of job) or involvement in a different support system that will reinforce desired change may be warranted (Goldfried, 1982).

Change the client's pattern and routine; avoid doing what has already been attempted. Some clients find it difficult to study because good study habits have never been incorporated into their daily routine. Simply having the client continue the same routine and pattern with the addition of inserting a time and a place for studying is not likely to work, because the new behavior doesn't fit with or is not supported by the old pattern. It would be more effective to scramble the client's typical pattern and routine and incorporate studying into an entirely different and new way of doing things each day.

Another reason to avoid simply inserting some study time into the client's old pattern is that that is probably the way the client tried to resolve the problem — and did so unsuccessfully. Although it seems obvious, people are often not sensitive to whether a particular solution is successful or not. When a solution is not working, instead of simply discarding it, most people do more of it or do it more frequently, thus increasing the problem. In this way, ordinary life difficulties are turned into more severe problems because the typical difficulty has been mishandled and remains unresolved (Fisch et al., 1982).

Remember that often the very ways clients try to alter problems — the "attempted solutions" — can maintain the problem or make it even worse (Fisch et al., 1982). It is much more helpful to get the client to abandon any previous unsuccessful solutions and to implement different solutions. Scrambling one's daily pattern to increase studying is likely to be a solution that the client has not yet attempted. Of course, this needs to be checked out during the assessment interviews (see also Chapters 7 and 8).

When Problem Behavior Is Maintained by Environmental Events

Some clients are resistant because environmental variables called "consequences" are primary factors maintaining the problem. In Chapter 7 we discussed the concept of consequences in detail. Simply stated, consequences include environmen-

FEEDBACK #52: CLIENT SOURCES OF RESISTANCE

Client 1
a. Optimism
b. Examples of matching responses: "You're feeling pretty overwhelmed right now and want someone to help pull you out of the deep."

or

"You've tried for a while to do it alone—now it's time to reach out and have someone there with you."

Client 2
a. Pessimism
b. Examples of matching responses: "It's irritating and upsetting that you are not to be able to just solve this problem immediately in a real, concrete way."

or

"It's pretty difficult to make sense of having to talk to me when taking a pill seems so easy and workable."

Client 3
a. Optimism
b. Examples of matching responses: "You've been feeling desperate long enough—like a cork on a bottle ready to pop. Now you need something to make an instant difference."

or

"This tremendous pressure has gone on long enough—too long. Now it's time for a change."

Client 4
a. Pessimism
b. Examples of matching responses: "It may or may not help. There's certainly no guarantee that talking like this will be the right avenue for you. Maybe it isn't."

or

"Yes. How can talk—just talk—really do anything concrete for anyone anyway?"

Client 5
a. Pessimism
b. Examples of matching responses: "I can certainly understand your skepticism, especially considering the fact that you're here mainly to avoid getting put out of your home."

or

"I can see where those feelings of disillusionment are coming from. How could someone think about making honest changes when feeling forced to do so?"

tal variables that maintain or exacerbate a problem—things that keep a problem going or make it worse. Although consequences may also include internal, covert events such as irrational or self-defeating thoughts, in this section we are concerned with overt variables such as situations or people in the client's environment.

Resistance that occurs when the problem behavior is maintained by environmental events and persons can be managed with the following strategies.

Find effective reinforcement for new or replacement behaviors. Behavior is followed by negative, neutral, or positive consequences (see also Chapter 7). Recall that new behaviors are more likely to be maintained when they are linked to positive, or rewarding, consequences. Melamed and Siegel (1980, p. 115) explain as follows the use of positive consequences to promote compliance:

> Consequences that immediately follow the desired behavior also affect the probable occurrence of that behavior. If the consequences are pleasant or reinforcing, the [desired] behavior is more likely to occur, whereas compliance with the therapist regimen is less likely to occur if the compliance behavior results in either no reinforcing consequences or aversive events.

To use this principle most effectively, begin with changes that are likely to make the client feel better in a short time or are likely to result in dramatic or at least visible improvement. When clients notice the benefits achieved from these initial steps, they will be more likely to engage in behaviors that make greater demands on them and take longer to effect the desired results.

Change can also be augmented by arranging for positive consequences to follow the desired behavior, in the form of either positively reinforcing activities or social reinforcement. For example, a client might engage in a daily desirable activity, such as watching television or reading, only after engaging in desired behavior or after completing some portion of assigned homework (see also "Self-Reward," in Chapter 19). Make sure the consequences selected are relevant and rewarding to the client.

Clients who receive strong doses of social reinforcement—"strokes," or encouragement and support, from counselors and significant others—are more motivated to change. The use of "social allies," persons who have frequent contact with the client and can assist the client in carrying out desired strategies and behaviors, is often very helpful (Stuart & Davis, 1972). Having a phobic client paired with a former phobic and using exercise partners to engage in daily aerobics are examples of this principle. Social allies also form the keystone of successful programs such as Alcoholics Anonymous and Weight Watchers International.

Find alternative or additional sources of rewards. In some instances, significant others in the client's environment may react negatively to client change, causing the client to experience punitive or aversive rather than positive consequences. For example, consider the case of a woman who is very dependent on her husband and behaves very nonassertively in his presence. Simply persuading the client to be less dependent and more assertive because that is better for her own mental health is unlikely to be helpful. Even providing her with overt skill training in assertive behavior may not work if, when she is assertive, her husband yells at her. As another example, consider the case of a college-aged female with the eating disorder of "anorexia." In spite of her parents' expressed concern for her, she becomes the object of strong criticism from her parents when she begins to eat again. In all probability, the client's defined problem (anorexia), though tragic, was serving an important function in her family environment. (The exact function could be determined during the assessment interviews.) When her problem got better, the family got worse and had difficulty coping with the loss of this function. This client is a likely candidate for a relapse, which would be a way for her to avoid further punishment from the family.

In such cases, the client is unlikely to want to give up the problem unless alternative sources of positive consequences can be found. Although the counselor can provide strong doses of encouragement, the client should develop his or her own sources of rewards as well. For example, clients might learn how to arrange for positive events in their environment that do not depend strongly on the reactions of significant others such as family members. The client could engage in rewarding activities, imagine rewarding activities, or learn to use positive self-talk or self-praise ("I did a great job") following completion of the desired response. (See also "Self-Reward," Chapter 19.) Eventually, however, the new behavior itself will need to *feel* rewarding for the client in this kind of situation — for example, "It feels good to be less

dependent, and I want to continue expressing more of my opinions because I like to — even though I get yelled at or punished for it."

An alternative approach when significant others punish rather than reinforce behavior change is to try to include them in counseling and use a systems approach to intervention (Minuchin, 1974).

Teach adaptive means of attaining "payoffs." As we mentioned in Chapters 7 and 8, "payoffs" (secondary gains) for dysfunctional, maladaptive behavior can have a powerful influence in maintaining that behavior, no matter how painful or uncomfortable it is for the client. Such payoffs may include — but are not limited to — money, attention from significant others, immediate (rather than delayed) gratification of needs and wants, or avoidance of work and stress.

An important and often overlooked secondary gain is security. Clients gain security in their present behavior patterns, no matter how dysfunctional or painful they may be. Maintaining problematic behavior enhances security by retaining predictability and helps the client avoid undue anxiety elicited by changing one's behavior. As Gottman & Leiblum (1974) observe, "Symptoms may be subjectively distressful, but they may produce a certain degree of consistency . . . in an otherwise unpredictable world" (p. 108).

Another important payoff is the control value, or relationship gains, that the problem behavior represents for the client. Haley (1963, p. 15) explains relationship gain this way: "The crucial aspect of a symptom is the advantage it gives the patient in gaining control of what is to happen in a relationship with someone else." When the client's problem behavior is maintained by reinforcing or useful payoffs, the client is not likely to eliminate the undesired behavior unless such benefits can be found in other ways. The counselor needs to help the client determine how such benefits could be met in other, more adaptive ways that do not jeopardize the welfare of the client or of other people. For example, if a child is using "aggressive behaviors" at school to have other kids notice him, the child needs to learn more adaptive ways of getting his peers to include him and pay attention to him. Similarly, if a wife is constantly criticizing her husband, which makes her feel better about herself, she needs to learn more productive ways of improving her self-esteem that do not threaten to disrupt her marriage.

LEARNING ACTIVITY #53: ENVIRONMENTAL SOURCES OF RESISTANCE

In this learning activity, we present two examples of behaviors that are partially maintained by environmental variables and that you or a client may wish to modify. For each behavior, your task is to generate as many suggestions/alternatives you can think of to (1) make the target response more visible in the person's environment and (2) reduce competing environmental stimuli. We have provided several suggestions as examples, and additional suggestions are found in the feedback section following the learning activity on page 560.

Behavior One:

Decrease amount of overeating done each week (leading to weight loss)

1. Ways to make the target response (overeating) more visible in your (or someone else's) environment:
   a. Post reminders.
   b. Contract for weight loss with spouse or friend.
   c.
   d.
   e.
   (see feedback for other ideas)
2. Ways to reduce environmental stimuli that compete with eating control:
   a. Don't socialize with overeaters.

b. Put locks on cupboards or refrigerator.
c.
d.
e.
(see feedback for other ideas)

Behavior Two:

Increase number of positive thoughts about oneself (leading to a good mood)

1. Ways to make the target response more visible in your (or someone else's) environment:
   a. Post reminders to think positively or rationally.
   b. Make a list of strengths or attributes.
   c.
   d.
   e.
   (see feedback for other ideas)
2. Ways to reduce environmental stimuli that compete with thinking positively about oneself:
   a. Avoid engaging in depressing or failure-oriented activities.
   b. Avoid being around people who get down on you.
   c.
   d.
   e.
   (see feedback for other ideas)

☐ RESISTANCE DUE TO THERAPIST OR THERAPEUTIC VARIABLES

According to Lazarus and Fay (1982, p. 115), resistance "is probably the most elaborate rationalization that therapists employ to explain their treatment failures." They assert that what appears to be client resistance often has its source within the therapist. Therapist resistance can be defined as those thoughts, feelings, and actions that contribute to failure to engage with or treat a client successfully (Anderson & Stewart, 1983, p. 210). When resistance is engendered by therapist or relationship variables, the following strategies may be helpful.

Avoiding Personalizing Client Resistance

It is important for therapists to be accepting of themselves and of resistive client behavior when working with pessimistic or discouraged clients. Some therapists may personalize client resistance and feel as if they are the target of the client's resist-

ive behavior. In such instances, acceptance of the client and of *yourself* is important. Dyer and Vriend (1975, pp. 98–99) note that when a counselor is unable or unwilling to accept a reluctant client and contracounseling behaviors, either the client, the counselor, or both are often declared *persona non grata,* and the counselor will experience failure in efforts to be helpful. Because therapists often experience client resistance as irritating, they may either give up on the client or subtly retaliate. In this case, they give clients a ticket to leave counseling (J. H. Fast, personal communication, December 1983). Attempts to detach yourself from therapeutic and client outcomes may help you to be more accepting of yourself and of clients, especially when your own expectations are not met.

Encouraging Client Participation in Therapy

According to the theory of psychological reactance (J. W. Brehm, 1966; S. S. Brehm, 1976), individuals are likely to resist attempts by others to change them whenever their perception of freedom has been diminished or eliminated. Encouraging active client participation in the therapy process has a number of important benefits, all of which serve to counteract the effects of psychological reactance. First, active participation increases the client's sense of control, or perception of choice. Second, clients are in a better position to select strategies and tasks that work in *their* world (Shelton & Levy, 1981). Third, clients may be more likely to comply and be less resistant in a cooperative rather than controlling counseling environment. Oppositional behavior is less likely to occur if clients are *asked* to do something instead of *told* to (Lazarus & Fay, 1982).

There are a number of ways to encourage greater participation by clients. First, deemphasize your role in any changes made by the client. Focus on the client contributions instead. Avoid taking credit for success. Self-attributed change is more likely to be maintained than change attributed by the client to someone else, such as the therapist (Kopel & Arkowitz, 1975).

Second, actively attempt to reduce the visibility of your influence efforts. Take a low profile, speak softly, and carry a tiny stick. The distinction between constructive influence, such as genuine efforts to help, and destructive influence, such as exploitation and coercion, is often blurred (Lazarus & Fay, 1982). Although a few clients respond positively to the use of authority or active influence, the majority of clients are either intimidated by or resistant to a great deal of therapeutic influence. Since the therapeutic relationship implies a position of presumed therapist power, the therapist must take deliberate actions to engage in what Fisch et al. (1982) call "one-downsmanship." Kiesler (1971, pp. 164–165) suggests that "if you want someone not only to behave in a particular way, but also to believe accordingly, then induce the behavior under conditions of very little apparent external pressure. Give the person the feeling that he was free to do otherwise if he wished." For example, instead of always directing a client when to do something, give some options. Say something like "Wouldn't it be interesting if sometime in the next week, you . . . ?" Most persons resist if they feel any pressure to do something *now*.

Third, solicit client input. Clients often are the best source of information about their intentions, problems, and proposed solutions. Take advantage of this resource in front of you!

Use of Timing and Pacing

Timing and pacing have to do with the speed with which a counselor moves through an interview. If the counselor proceeds too fast or paces too far ahead of the client, resistance may be engendered. Ways to decrease the resistance produced by timing and pacing include changing the pace, leaving a sensitive topic temporarily and returning to it later, or lessening the emotional intensity of the session (Brammer & Shostrom, 1982).

Timing and pacing also have to do with the process of taking small steps throughout therapy and assessing the client's reactions to each step before proceeding further or starting on a new task (Fisch et al., 1982, p. 27). The therapist times and paces his or her comments and actions in accordance with client responses. If the client responds in any way other than a definite verbal or nonverbal acceptance of the therapist's lead, the therapist should change the pace or strategy. If the therapist persists in using an approach or a strategy that is not working, there is a risk of increased resistance or reduced credibility (Fisch et al., 1982).

Another aspect of appropriate use of timing and pacing is to avoid taking a stand prematurely. The therapist must first assess the client's views about problems, treatment, and outcome and then offer suggestions that are likely to fit the client.

Offering Strategies and Homework Tasks That Are Relevant to the Client

The therapist needs to present alternative strategies and homework tasks that are relevant to each client. For example, assertion training may be incompatible with a client whose strongly held religious beliefs emphasize compliant behavior toward other people. Similarly, a client from a culture with a relatively unstructured concept of time may be mortified at the idea of using a kitchen timer to monitor study time or depressed thoughts. Strategies and homework should be individually tailored for each client. Haley (1978, p. 56) writes:

> The therapist must fit the task to the people. As he interviews a family, he will observe what sort of people the members are and can fit the task to the family style. If the family members emphasize doing things in an orderly, logical manner, the task offered to them should be an orderly, logical task — they will be more likely to do it. If they form a casual, disorderly household, a casual framework for the task may be more appropriate. If they are concerned about money, the therapist emphasizes

FEEDBACK #53: ENVIRONMENTAL SOURCES OF RESISTANCE

Behavior One: Overeating

Here are some ideas. Are some of yours similar? What can you add to this list?

1. *Ways to make target response more visible:*
   a. Post reminders (preferably on refrigerator or in kitchen).
   b. Contract for weight loss with spouse or friend.
   c. Keep a daily record of everything you eat.
   d. Post a picture of yourself (or someone else) when you have been slim.
   e. Keep a chart of weight loss and post it.
   Others:
2. *Ways to reduce competing environmental stimuli:*
   a. Don't socialize with overeaters.
   b. Put locks on cupboards or refrigerators.
   c. Put snacks in hard-to-reach places.
   d. Shop for food on a full stomach.
   e. Confine eating to certain times and places.
   Others:

Behavior Two: Positive Thoughts about Self

1. Ways to make target response more visible:
   a. Post reminders to think positively or rationally.
   b. Make a list of strengths or attributes.
   c. Carry a stack of note cards around with one strength or attribute listed on each card — plus a blank card. At different times during the day, examine and reflect on one card. Use the next card the next time. Each time you come to the blank card, write down another strength or something about yourself you value.
   d. Use an alarm to cue you to think positively.
   e. Make positive or rational thoughts contingent on rewarding things you do each day.
   Others:
2. *Ways to reduce competing environmental stimuli:*
   a. Avoid engaging in depressing or failure-oriented activities.
   b. Avoid being around people who get down on you.
   c. Practice thought stopping for negative or irrational thoughts about yourself.
   d. Put a timer on negative thinking; "wallow" in it for 15 minutes; stop when the buzzer goes off.
   e. Confine negative thinking to a certain place such as one room or one chair.
   Others:

that the task costs nothing. . . . The way they go about doing [tasks in therapy] will give the therapist information on how to frame the outside task more acceptably for them.

One way to ensure that a strategy is appropriate for a given client is to ask the client to spend a few minutes imagining what it would be like to spend time on such a task (Anderson & Stewart, 1983). If the client is not enthusiastic about actually using the strategy or engaging in the task, it is not suitable for this particular client.

Assessing and Utilizing Patient Position

Fisch et al. (1982) have made a major contribution to the literature on change with the concept of patient position. *Patient position* refers to clients'

> strongly held beliefs, values, and priorities, which determine how they will act or not act. Thus, the importance of "position" is that it represents an inclination within patients which can be utilized to enhance the acceptance and carrying out of therapist directives. . . . Knowing what the client's position is allows one to formulate guidelines on how to couch—or frame—a suggestion in a way that the client is most likely to accept [p. 90].

The therapist must first listen carefully to what the client says in order to assess the client's important position statements. It is important to listen to the words clients select and use, since clients indicate their positions in specific wording. The most useful positions are those strongly held by the client and, hence, repeated over and over during the sessions. For example, Tom, a 30-year-old male client, sought help from a counselor about career choice. During the initial interview, the client said things about himself like "It is difficult for me to decide whether to go for a graduate degree or to get a good job and start earning some money. *I don't know how much you'll be able to help me* because I'm a very *complex* person. I've had an *unusual* background for someone my age. I've always been *on top* or *achieved* more than what was expected of me in school and in jobs I've held, and all at a young age. I now consider myself very *mature* and *experienced* about life. I've done a lot of things I wasn't supposed to have the ability to do. *I always rise to a challenge.* If someone says 'Tom, you can't do this,' *I set out to prove the person wrong. I guess I'm sort of a rebel.*"

In this brief example, Tom has revealed several "patient positions," such as the following:

1. He is somewhat pessimistic about whether the counselor can help him or whether counseling will benefit him ("I don't know how much you'll be able to help me").
2. He regards himself as someone special, unique, and complicated ("I'm a very complex person. I've had an unusual background. Mature and experienced, I've been on top and achieved.").
3. He functions best when told he can't do something; he may be likely to display oppositional behavior when told or asked to do something ("I rise to a challenge. I set out to prove the person wrong. I guess I'm sort of a rebel").

"Patient positions" that have most bearing on the course of therapy include the client's notions about the nature of the problem and its assumed cause, about who is responsible for the problem, about how the problem can be resolved, and about the therapy process itself and the client's role during therapy.

If the therapist cannot detect these types of positions from listening to the client's words, use of selective questions such as the following can be an additional assessment tool:

"What is your interpretation of the problem?"
"If someone described your problem this way: _____, would you agree, or would that description be all wrong?"
"What is your best guess about why this problem exists?"
"Whom do you see as creating the problem?"
"How do you explain the fact that this problem has been so persistent [or gotten better or worse]?"
"Who do you feel needs to solve the problem?"
"This may or may not work for your problem, but have you tried _____?"
"How do you feel therapy will help you?"
"What is your thinking about my role [or your role] during therapy?"
"How would you describe yourself?"

After assessment, the therapist can use client position advantageously in several ways. First, the therapist can avoid making any comments that might create resistance—that is, comments that might be inflammatory to the client or might reduce your credibility because they are too discrepant from the client's values and beliefs. For example, with Tom, the counselor would need to *avoid* inflammatory comments such as—

1. "You have a very *simple* decision to make." (The word *simple* is likely to be inflammatory because it contradicts Tom's perception of himself and his problem as difficult and complex.)
2. "*Lots of people* find it hard to make this kind of career choice." (The phrase *lots of people* may be inflammatory because it is discrepant from Tom's view that he and his problem are unique.)
3. "It would be a good idea to make this decision in the next few months so you don't end up without a job or without a degree." (This statement is likely to be too "preachy" and may elicit oppositional behavior from Tom.)

Similarly, statements that might reduce the counselor's credibility with Tom include—

4. "I'm sure I can help you."
5. "If you work at it, counseling can be of great help to you." (These two statements do not match Tom's pessimistic view of the counselor and of the value of counseling.)

or

6. "Let's discuss the pros and cons of graduate school or employment and you can find a solution *fairly easily.*" (This statement does not match Tom's view that his decision is a hard one that cannot easily be reached.)

It would be more helpful to make comments that match the views and positions of this client, such as the following ones:

1. "Since this is a *difficult* and *unique* problem, it will be important to *go slowly* and *take time* to work it through."
2. "Perhaps considering your *unusual background,* it would be best to start off by being a *little more skeptical* about counseling than the *average person* might be."
3. "This is an *important* and *weighty* dilemma. It is worthy of *careful analysis* and *attention.*"

The counselor also needs to present suggestions and tasks in such a way that the client is likely to cooperate. To accomplish this, present tasks or actions in a way consistent with the client's position (Fisch et al., 1982, p. 101). Talk the client's language and suggest ideas that match the client's values and beliefs. As Erickson (quoted in Haley, 1973, p. 206) has observed, "People come for help, but they also come to be substantiated in their attitudes and they come to have face saved. I pay attention to this and I'm likely to speak in a fashion that makes them think I'm on their side." Restating or reframing ideas in such a way that the client is likely to accept them. For example, with Tom, the way the purpose or objective of therapy is framed can enlist or discourage his cooperation in working toward the purpose. Saying something like "It would be important to work toward a choice that will be satisfactory to you now and in the future, considering your background, achievements, and maturity" is likely to have more appeal to Tom than stating "You need to choose between school and a job." The strategies and actions suggested to Tom should also consider his perception of the problem and of himself. He is more likely to comply with strategies and tasks seen as unusual, grandiose, challenging, and risk-taking, because they appeal more to his perception of himself as extraordinary and uncommon, than tasks that are relatively mundane, routine, and unobtrusive.

Acknowledging Anxiety/Discomfort about Your Competence

Therapist resistance is greater with inexperienced therapists who are concerned about their competence and effectiveness with clients. Competence anxiety has to do with commitment and is worsened, in fact, by the sense of overwhelming responsibility that beginning therapists take for their clients (Anderson & Stewart, 1983). An initial step useful for dealing with competence anxiety is to acknowledge it. Expressing your anxiety with a peer, colleague, or supervisor often diminishes it and reduces your preoccupation with yourself. Seeking consultation and supervision from supportive and knowledgeable persons is another strategy for dealing with concern about your effectiveness (Anderson & Stewart, 1983).

A third strategy is to establish your own limits in counseling. Distinguish between things that you are legitimately responsible for and things that the client must be responsible for. Avoid doing work for the client! Weeks and L'Abate (1982) observe that a common myth surrounding counseling and therapy is that a therapist is always responsible for producing change. They note:

The therapist is expected to be optimistic about the future. Therapists are expected to be supportive. When therapy is not proceeding smoothly, then the therapist works harder. The therapist may even work on one problem more as the client works on it less. This kind of approach may eventually lead to a dependency relationship, with the therapist assuming a rescuing role [pp. 125–126].

Taking Care of Yourself

The axiom "Charity begins at home" has important implications for therapists. Therapist resistance is worse with therapists who are fatigued and overworked, who are so busy trying to take care of the lives of other people that they neglect their own needs. Eventually, what we refer to as "burnout" occurs. Signs of burnout include feeling relieved when a client cancels or postpones a session, having little energy available for sessions, lacking interest in client outcomes, and having persistent, recurring thoughts about whether you are in the right profession or about changing jobs (Anderson & Stewart, 1983). In severe cases of burnout, health problems may develop and work may be missed. Tired and overworked therapists tend to show resistance by being slow to return a client's phone call or to reschedule a canceled session, by showing pessimism about outcomes, and by displaying less enthusiasm and intensity toward clients. Clients are very sensitive about whether the therapist wants to see them, and such resistive behaviors are easily transmitted to clients, even over the telephone. Thus clients who show up late or postpone or cancel appointments may be reacting to therapist resistance rather than their own (Anderson & Stewart, 1983).

The best way to avoid resistance due to fatigue, overwork, and burnout is to prevent it. Arrange working and environmental conditions so that fatigue and burnout are not likely to occur. For example, schedule short "breathing spaces" between clients, always take a lunch break, develop a support system with other colleagues, consult frequently with your supervisor, arrange your office in a pleasing manner. When you're not working, learn to engage in relaxing activities, and don't bring your work home with you or dwell on what happened at work during leisure time.

If you are beyond this point and fatigue and burnout have already set in, start taking better care of yourself. Let off steam about your feelings to an empathic listener. Change the size or type of caseload you carry. Use vacation days or sick leave to take time off from work. Arrange for time-out periods when you are at work. Develop an ongoing support system for yourself. Do something each day that in some way is pleasing to you and meets your needs. Otherwise you are likely to feel bad about yourself and increasingly resentful of clients. Above all, remember—don't jeopardize the needs of your clients because you haven't learned or cared enough to take care of your own.

LEARNING ACTIVITY #54: THERAPIST SOURCES OF RESISTANCE

PART ONE

This activity is to be done in triads; one person assumes the role of client, another the counselor, and the third is the observer. Roles can then be switched twice so each person has an opportunity to function once in each of the three roles. As the client, decide on an issue you want to work on from the following list and tell the counselor what it is:

Assertiveness behavior
Marital (or relationship) communication
Weight control
Study skills
Rational thinking

As the counselor, give several *direct* suggestions to the client about things he or she could do to resolve this issue. Direct suggestions are framed as "I want you to," "You need to," and so on. After delivering each suggestion, watch and listen to the client's verbal and nonverbal behavior for "yes" and "no" clues that suggest receptivity or lack of interest in your suggestion. On the basis of the client's reactions, either stick with your suggestion if you get "yes" cues or modify it if you get "no" cues. As the observer, observe and monitor the client's reactions to the counselor's suggestions and note whether the counselor accurately discriminated the client's reactions by continuing with or changing the original suggestion.

PART TWO

The first part of this activity is done in writing; the second occurs in role play. First, recall the direct suggestions you gave to your client in the previous activity. Jot them down. Now reframe each direct suggestion into an *indirect* suggestion that presents an illusion of choice. For example, instead of "I want you to study two hours each day this week," try "How much do you want to study—one hour, two hours, or three hours a day?" Write down your indirect suggestions. Second, assuming the same roles you did in the previous activity, this time deliver the *indirect* suggestion and do it in a *one-down manner.* Then observe the client's reactions. The observer can also give input about the client's "yes" and "no" cues. In which activity was the client more receptive to your ideas and suggestions?

PART THREE

In dyads or small groups, discuss the problem of therapist resistance due to fatigue and burnout. Identify your own cognitive and behavioral signs of burnout and fatigue. Describe how you may communicate being resistant to clients. Identify ways to manage burnout or prevent it from occurring for yourself.

□ WHEN ALL ELSE FAILS: LAST-RESORT STRATEGIES

Occasionally the strategies mentioned so far in this chapter to manage resistance seem to have no effect. The client becomes increasingly resistant, and the counselor becomes more frustrated. In this section we describe some strategies that can be tried when all else fails.

Contracting to Change for One Week

If the client seems extremely reluctant to try out new behavior, contract to change for only one week. (This is based on the principle of successive approximations, described in Chapter 9.) Point out that change is not irreversible. Try to have the client agree to change for just one week (or any other specified time period) with the stipulation that the client can resort to the old behavior at the end of the week. At the end of the week, most

clients are pleasantly surprised and desire to continue the new behavior or some variation of it. A few, however, continue to sabotage this brief plan, especially if they have a vested interest in defeating the therapist (Anderson & Stewart, 1983).

Antisabotage Procedures

"Antisabotage procedures are 'designed' to anticipate, identify and modify those interactional tendencies to resist progress" (Spinks & Birchler, 1982, p. 180). They are used with clients who tend to sabotage plans and tasks that they have agreed to carry out. There are four steps in creating antisabotage procedures (Spinks & Birchler, 1982):

1. Have the client brainstorm all the possible reasons for and ways of being noncompliant with the accepted plan or task.
2. Identify high-risk sabotage behaviors—that is, what the client is likely to do *instead* of carrying

out the task or plan (watching TV instead of talking to spouse after dinner).

3. Develop ways for the client to deal with the high-risk sabotage behaviors so that they do not interfere with completion of the plan (talk to my spouse first and then watch TV).

4. Reinforce the client for follow-through and completion of the plan.

Although the therapist could easily list possible sabotage procedures, it is more effective to encourage *clients* to think of ways they might avoid the plan (Haley, 1978).

Metaphors

A metaphor is a word or phrase that implies a comparison. In therapy, metaphors are used as cognitive cues to suggest a likeness between the client and the object or person referred to in the metaphor. A classic metaphor used by Erickson (in Haley, 1967) with a cancer patient in great pain is that of a tomato plant growing from a seed. In the metaphor, Erickson described how the seed is planted and carefully nurtured, with special emphasis on the good, comfortable, peaceful feelings the plant has as it grows. What Erickson was doing was embedding within the story a number of suggestions for the client about relaxation, comfort, and disassociation from pain.

A metaphor is a useful way to tell a story that relates to a particular problem the client will recognize as his or her own without raising the client's anxiety level to the point where the client cannot assimilate the idea. A metaphor can function as an indirect confrontation or interpretation and is especially useful with denial. Metaphors also "are handy for saving face in that they often provide a vehicle for people to change without having to admit that they've been mistaken or that their ways of coping haven't worked" (Anderson & Stewart, 1983, p. 194).

For example, a counselor was working with a young man who had recently married a medical intern. The client was having difficulty accepting his wife's frequent absences while she was on call at the hospital. The client believed that his wife did not care for him as much as she should because occasionally, while on call, the wife did not telephone and check in with him. The client disputed the counselor's suggestion that a more rational interpretation might be that the wife had too many admissions or very ill patients that night in order to call him. At this point, the counselor offered the following metaphor:

"By the way, I am reminded of this story about a man and his neighbor. Now, it might seem curious to you that we are going to talk about a man and his neighbor. But perhaps this story will be interesting.

A man was enjoying a relaxing time at home one evening. There was a sudden knock on his door. His neighbor's husband was standing there. His wife had stopped breathing. He wanted his neighbor to come help him revive her. The man felt a pang; he had not been able to keep in touch with his neighbors as frequently as he wanted, because after a period of unemployment, he had started to work as a telephone switchboard operator. After finding the woman lying on the floor, he began to administer CPR. She started to breathe again. In the middle of the process, the phone began to ring. He started to stop the massage as if he felt he would answer it. The woman stopped breathing. Then he continued the massage and worked feverishly to try to get his neighbor to breathe again, which she did as he ignored the phone and continued the CPR."

Six steps are involved in creating a suitable metaphor:

1. Examine the nature of the client's problem. Identify any metaphoric themes within the problem (for example, intimacy, role behavior, self-image) and construct a metaphor that parallels the theme.

2. Select a representative "character" for the metaphor (person, animal, object, and so on).

3. Use words in the metaphor that match the client's visual, auditory, or kinesthetic representational system.

4. Create a process in the metaphor for each process in the problem. However, the actual content of the metaphor should be different enough from the client's problem so that the client does not overtly recognize it as her or his own story.

5. In order to use metaphors to promote behavior change, specify and elaborate on the character's behaviors. The intent is to detail "particular behaviors at specific choice points with sufficient precision and elaboration that the prescribed acts can be approximated by the listener" (Lankton & Lankton, 1983, p. 82).

6. Design the story line to provide a solution or a desired response that includes some element of suspense or mystery for attention holding (Lankton, 1980; Lankton & Lankton, 1983). The solution usually portrays the consequences of the behaviors specified in the story.

In the CPR example, a person was selected to use in the metaphor, and kinesthetic words *(feel, touch, experience)* were selected to match the client's primary representational system. The story reflected processes found in the client's problem:

1. Recent marriage = sudden knock on door; recent job.
2. Wife's frequent absences = man's absence from contact with neighbors.
3. Wife's not calling him on phone because of patient demands = ringing phone — man does not answer phone because of life-threatening situation.

The story also contained several descriptions of the character's actions or behaviors — starting CPR, stopping CPR as if he were going to answer the phone, but ignoring it and continuing the CPR.

The end of the story provided the desired response and consequences of the character's behavior: the man chose to ignore the phone, even though answering phones was his job, in order to continue CPR and to avoid his friend's death. The story provides an alternative explanation of the failure of the client's wife to call that is less threatening than a direct interpretation.

To be most effective, deliver metaphors as "stories" and offer them casually at times when telling a story seems appropriate, such as at the beginning or end of a session or during a natural break or change in focus. Since metaphors are more effective if they are told with conviction and congruence, draw on your own personal experiences and convey true stories if possible.

An object can also be used to confront clients metaphorically or to illustrate a point. A pocket calculator can be used to calculate percentages of time with clients who tend to catastrophize and generalize about the amount of time a problem or symptom occurs (Harvill, Jacobs, & Masson, 1984). We have found the use of a collapsible camping cup to be useful with some clients whose self-esteem goes up (pull cup up) or down (push cup down) depending on the reactions of other people to them or to their environment.

For further information about and examples of clinical metaphors, we suggest you peruse *Advanced Techniques of Hypnosis and Therapy: Selected Papers of Milton H. Erickson, M.D.* (Haley, 1967), *Therapeutic Metaphors* (Gordon, 1978),

and *The Answer Within* (Lankton & Lankton, 1983).

Shortening Sessions or Terminating

As a final resort, the therapist always has the option of shortening the sessions, reducing their frequency, or terminating treatment until the client makes some attempt to fulfill the therapeutic agreement. According to Fisch et al. (1982, p. 23), "The therapist cannot deal effectively with patient resistance unless he is prepared to exercise this ultimate option should it become necessary."

There are many times in therapy when this option may need to be discussed explicitly with the client. Exercise of this option, however, occurs infrequently. Before exercising this option, the counselor must first understand the nature of the client's resistance. Furthermore, this option should be used only after *several* unfulfilled promises or uncompleted tasks. Finally, the therapist should not terminate as punishment but rather "to demonstrate to the client the therapist's concern and unwillingness" to have the client waste his or her time and money (Gottman & Leiblum, 1974, p. 113).

Some clients display resistance only near the termination phase of therapy. In other words, the clients become anxious and concerned about how they will do without the therapist and resist termination. With panicky clients, one option is to *insist* on one more appointment (Fisch et al., 1982). Another option is to treat termination paradoxically, by prescribing or predicting a relapse (see also "A Taxonomy of Paradoxical Interventions," later in this chapter).

Clients are less likely to resist termination if it is done gradually and slowly. One way to do this is to gradually increase the time between sessions. Sessions can occur less and less frequently over a period of several months. It is also important to focus explicitly on the client's resources, strengths, and coping skills. According to Anderson and Stewart (1983, p. 117), "Placing an emphasis on [client's] strengths and abilities while providing some sort of cognitive distance on the experience of therapy helps to provide the closure needed to leave therapy comfortably."

A final option that is often useful either for approaching termination or as a "last resort" strategy is paradoxical intervention. Because this strategy requires great skill to implement, we discuss it in some detail in the next section.

LEARNING ACTIVITIES #55: LAST-RESORT STRATEGIES

Part One: Antisabotage Procedures

This activity can be done by yourself or in a dyad. It is designed to assist you in creating an antisabotage plan for a behavior that you (or a partner) wish to change but are likely to sabotage instead. Some examples are procrastination and meeting deadlines, weight control, smoking cessation, and exercise. These are just examples — pick a behavior relevant to yourself. An example of what one of us did for such a behavior follows the instructions.

Instructions for yourself or your partner:

1. Identify the behavior you wish to change. State the desired change in positive terms — that is, what you want to be able to do, think, or feel differently.
2. Describe (or have the partner describe) an action plan/steps to meet this desired goal. Make sure the plan is reasonable for you (or your partner) and is consistent with your (or your partner's) values.
3. Identify (or have the partner identify) all the possible reasons you might not comply with the plan (for example, too much time, too much trouble or energy).
4. Identify (or have the partner identify) "high-risk sabotage behaviors" — that is, what you are likely to do, think, or feel *instead* of carrying out the agreed-on plan (for example, watching TV, eating, talking on phone, partying, and so on, and so on!).
5. Develop ways for yourself (or have the partner develop ways) to deal with these high-risk sabotage behaviors so that they are less likely to interfere with completion of the action plan (comply with plan first, then watch TV or party).
6. Identify (or have the partner identify) ways to get different kinds of reinforcement such as those described under "Self-Reward," in Chapter 19, for compliance with the action plan and progress toward the goal.

Example

1. Desired behavior: Wish to exercise three times a week for 40 minutes each time.
2. Action plan:
   a. Set aside three times each week, every other day, for exercise.
   b. Build exercise into my daily routine — exercise at same time each week.
   c. Use music to make it more pleasant.
3. Possible reasons I might not comply:
   a. Not enough time to exercise — should be doing housework, job work, writing, or being with family.
   b. Don't feel as if I have the energy to exercise.
4. High-risk sabotage behaviors: Sleep late instead of exercise; stay at work longer to avoid exercise time.
5. Ways to deal with sabotage behaviors: Schedule exercise sessions in late afternoon or evening instead of morning on arising: exercise with a friend (exercise partner) so I won't "cop out."
6. Reinforcement:
   a. Social — obtain praise from spouse and friend.
   b. Self — feel better after exercising, also keep weight at desired level, body looks better.

End result: Went from 0 exercise a week to 2–3 exercise sessions a week over a nine-month period.

Part Two: Metaphors, Stories

Listed below are four descriptions of various client situations. Try to pick at least one or two situations that seem personally relevant to you. For each situation, construct a metaphor you could use with this client. Try to use a real story if possible or at least one that arises out of your personal experiences. The metaphor you construct will be more effective if it parallels themes or issues reflected in the client problem. Design the story line to provide a solution or indication of a desired response. Also include an element of mystery or suspense to hold the client's attention. The first situation is used as an example. After you construct your metaphors, discuss them with a colleague or instructor.

Example
Situation One

The client is a child who gets down on herself very easily. After making one mistake in school or at home, she tends to become very frustrated and wants to give up rather than completing the task or following through in the situation. The metaphor below, a true story, was offered to her by one of the authors who is a "closet pianist."

"Jane, would you be interested in hearing about something that happened to me when I was about your age? If so, I'd like to share this story with you. Listen and watch and see what you get out of it.

When I was 6 years old, I started taking piano lessons every week. My teacher was very good, and every year she rented a huge auditorium for all her students to have their yearly piano recital in. It was a big deal! There was a story written up about
(continued)

it in the newspaper and programs printed up with the students' names on them and the titles of the songs you would play. Then there was a big stage with lights and two big pianos and a beautiful bouquet of red roses. For a couple of years, I went to these recitals and did my thing and played my song and never thought twice about it. Really enjoyed myself. Then when I was about 9 or 10, something happened. Want to know what it was? I was supposed to play a duet with my sister, who also took lessons. We had practiced and practiced together. We had learned how to start playing at the same time—which was important—by my lifting my chin up and then, as my head came down, our fingers would start touching the keys simultaneously. Well, guess what? That day I started playing. I played for about a half a minute—although it seemed like an eternity—and then I stopped. Something was wrong! I was playing, but my sister was not. I realized I had forgotten to give her the "chins up" signal and she wasn't at all ready to start. I had just jumped in. So I stopped playing and felt horrified. I was ready to quit and walk off the stage and end my piano career right there, even though I loved music very much. But I didn't. Because I looked and saw my piano teacher in the wings. She had a smile on her face and whispered to me—"The show goes on. Forget about it and just start over." That's exactly what we did. And after we finished, the applause was just as loud as it would have been if I hadn't made that one mistake. After that, I never got through a recital in which I didn't make at least one mistake or play one wrong note. But it never really mattered, because for that one wrong note there were always ten thousand other notes that were just right."

Situation Two

A female client feels very dependent on her husband. When she is alone at work or attends a social function alone, she functions well and feels comfortable and confident. When she is with her husband, she feels insecure and anxious and doesn't trust herself or her decisions.

Situation Three

A male client wants his wife to depend on him to make him feel important. When she gets too close, however, he gets upset and angry and finds something about her to criticize.

Situation Four

A male client behaves very appropriately and assertively with other men but feels unable to refuse almost any request made to him by a woman, even if the request is inappropriate or costly to him in terms of time or money.

□ PARADOXICAL INTERVENTIONS

Paradoxical interventions have been used in various ways for many years. Dunlap's (1928) negative, or massed, practice is a form of paradoxical intervention. In this strategy, the behavior decreases or stops because of *satiation;* as a result of cumulative, or massed, repetition, the behavior loses its reinforcing properties and stops.

Another form of therapy, logotherapy (developed by Frankl, 1960), also uses paradoxical intervention. In this technique clients reach a certain goal by exaggerating an undesirable response. Implied in this directive is the assumption that by engaging in the problem behavior, the client will eventually be able to eliminate it.

An important hallmark of paradoxical intervention is the therapist's *acceptance* of the client's noncompliant behavior (Haley, 1973). Therapists must avoid becoming frustrated, defensive, or counteroppositional. Perhaps the most important principle to remember in dealing with highly resistant clients is *never* to fight with them. Haley (1973) likens resistance to a river. If a therapist opposes the river by blocking it, the river simply goes over and around her or him. If, however, the therapist accepts the force of the river and diverts it in a new direction, the force of the river will create a new channel. As Shelton and Levy (1981) observe, "When the therapist accepts the resistance, the client is caught in a position where resistance becomes cooperation" (p. 72). Acceptance of clients' resistant behavior is synonymous with respecting their polarity and pacing (matching) it (Lankton, 1980). Accepting, or pacing, turns a resistant client into a potentially very cooperative client.

Regardless of the origins of paradoxical interventions, all forms have one similar feature. The client is encouraged either to produce symptomatic behavior at will or to avoid trying to get better (Omer, 1981). The paradox in these messages is that the client can change by remaining unchanged. Further, in all paradoxical treatments, the context surrounding the symptomatic behavior is changed. In paradoxical interventions, the affective, cognitive, and/or interpersonal context of the symptom may be changed. The client may be instructed to exaggerate the symptom, do it more often or with more intensity, or carry it out at different times or places. Omer (1981) asserts that, in paradoxical treatments, change may result more from the change in context than from the type of directive. Because the context is changed, the "symptom loses its function and meaning" (p. 322). Similarly, Raskin and Klein (1976) note that instructions to engage in a problem behavior *voluntarily* change the stimuli that elicit the behavior so that the client is then less likely to engage in the problem behavior in the original setting.

Uses of Paradoxical Interventions

Ascher has reported the effective use of paradoxical interventions with insomnia (Ascher & Efran, 1978; Ascher & Turner, 1979), urinary retention (Ascher, 1979), and agoraphobia (Ascher, 1981; Mavissakalian, Michelson, Greenwald, Kornblith, & Greenwald, 1983). Paradoxical interventions have also been used effectively in reducing procrastination of college students (Lopez & Wambach, 1982; Wright & Strong, 1982). Birchler (1981) cites the effectiveness of this strategy in promoting change in behavioral marital therapy.

Paradoxical interventions are useful for clients who are disturbed by the frequency of a response. Clients may be concerned that an undesirable behavior occurs too often or that a desired response occurs rarely (Ascher, 1979). Lopez (1983) notes that paradoxical interventions are highly useful for facilitating voluntary control over specific, habitual, or reportedly 'involuntary' behaviors. Ascher (1980) asserts that paradoxical interventions may be used as the primary treatment whenever the designated change program fails to produce desired results: "When progress is impeded in the context of an appropriate behavioral analysis and a currently administered behavioral program, then enhancing the client's ability to cooperate may become the focus of attention" (p. 268).

Paradoxical interventions should be avoided with clients who have strong self-doubts, homicidal or suicidal tendencies, or are very dependent and in situations of crisis or extreme instability (Shelton & Levy, 1981; Rohrbaugh, Tennen, Press, & White, 1981). Weeks and L'Abate (1982) observe that paradoxical interventions will not work well with sociopathic personalities, who will change the task to fit their own needs, or paranoid personalities, who may become more suspicious.

Cautions in Using Paradoxical Interventions

One caution in using paradoxical interventions has to do with the timing of the directive. Use of paradoxical interventions in *initial* therapy sessions is usually *not* advised, for several reasons. First, in order for paradoxical interventions to be effective, the therapist must formulate an accurate functional analysis that explains in a plausible way the functions of the major presenting symptoms. This formulation is not always readily achieved. Second, paradoxical interventions should be reserved only for situations of *major* noncompliance (Papp, 1980). Before using a paradoxical intervention, the therapist should first use more direct interventions. Even then, some resistance is to be expected. As Gurman (1981, p. 120) observes, "The crucial issue that the therapist must address is, thus, not whether noncompliance exists, but whether and how readily it can be overcome, especially by the use of more direct interventions, such as further development of the therapeutic alliance [and] confrontation or interpretation."

Birchler (1981, p. 125) cites three criteria to be met before paradoxical intervention should be used:

1. The client's resistant behaviors are repetitive and persistent.
2. The resistant behaviors significantly obstruct the progress of therapy.
3. The resistant behaviors are not modified by more usual direct interventions.

A second issue has to do with the ethics of using a strategy such as paradoxical intervention, which appears to violate the behavioral principle of explicitly informing clients of the treatment rationale and technique. Shelton and Levy (1981) assert that, on occasion, the therapist may use a change strategy that is not explicitly agreed on, as long as the therapist is pursuing the client's choice of treatment goals. According to Birchler (1981), if paradoxical intervention is based on an accurate functional analysis, it is possible to tell the client quite openly why an assignment is being given. Birchler asserts:

It is tempting and all too easy to make isolated paradoxical prescriptions without preparing the [client] by providing a plausible, airtight rationale for the particular assignment. The necessity for the assignment should also be explained in the context of past failure of the [client] to make the expected progress, using whatever previous techniques. . . . Obviously, the therapist does not indicate that the assignment is meant to be a paradox or have a paradoxical effect [pp. 124–126].

A final caution is to remember that paradoxical interventions are complex and require great skill and energy to implement effectively. A paradoxical intervention can be difficult to administer properly, particularly by persons who have had little training or experience in the use of this technique. We strongly recommend that no one attempt to use a paradoxical intervention with real clients from reading about it in this or any other book without first practicing it in role-play situations and obtaining feedback on your use of the strategy. Additionally, it would be important to seek supervision for your initial attempts in using paradoxical intervention with clients.

Counselors should be aware that directives of any type can have important ethical and legal implications. In a recent case in California, for example, a counselor was found negligent because she instructed the client to "sit on the client's unruly son." The client, who happened to be rather obese, took the counselor's instruction literally and went home and sat on her son for two hours. The son subsequently died by asphyxiation. In a similar vein, a jury might have a difficult time understanding why a therapist would tell an insomniac to "try to stay awake at night" or another client to deliberately engage in the problematic behavior.

A Taxonomy of Paradoxical Interventions

There are a variety of ways in which paradoxical interventions can be organized. In this section we present a taxonomy to assist you in conceptualizing the various forms of this technique.

Focus of paradoxical interventions: Individual, dyadic, systemic. The focus of paradoxical interventions can be on individuals, couples (dyadic), or groups and families (transactional or systemic). The focus of the intervention chosen depends on the therapist's theoretical orientation, the number of clients present, and the results of the problem assessment. Dyadic and systemic interventions are the most difficult because they require understanding of the relationship and/or system as well as experience in working with couples and families. Individually oriented interventions are the easiest to prescribe and the most prevalent in the literature. Some of these interventions can be carried out alone by the client; some require the involvement of other people (Weeks & L'Abate, 1982). Examples of tasks that focus on the individ-

ual client are instructing a client who can't sleep to get up and do obnoxious household chores such as cleaning the oven, instructing a client who puts off studying to schedule 30 minutes nightly to practice procrastination, or directing a client who is plagued with negative, self-defeating thoughts to dwell on and exaggerate the thoughts as they occur. Our discussion deals with individually oriented interventions. We believe that effective dyadic and systemic interventions require some additional training and supervision in marriage and family therapy, which is beyond the scope of this book.

Purpose of interventions: Compliance or defiance. Paradoxical interventions can be divided into two categories, depending on whether the purpose of the intervention is to have the client carry out (comply with) or reject (defy) the task (Rohrbaugh et al., 1981: Tennen, Rohrbaugh, Press, & White, 1981). In compliance-based prescriptions the client's attempt to comply with the therapist's request "interrupts or short-circuits the process that perpetuates the problem" (Rohrbaugh et al., 1981, p. 457).* Tennen et al. (1981) note that compliance-based interventions emphasize the *intrapersonal* domain. Compliance-based interventions are most likely

> to work with symptoms such as obsessions, anxiety attacks, and various somatic complaints that are maintained to some extent by the patient's attempts to stave them off. By attempting to bring on such a symptom deliberately, one cannot continue in the usual ways of trying to prevent it, and under these conditions, the symptom often dissolves or comes more under voluntary control [Rohrbaugh et al., 1981, p. 457].

For further descriptions of compliance-based paradoxes, see the work of Watzlawick, Weakland, and Fisch (1974).

Defiance-based interventions assume that the client will oppose carrying out the directive. This directive is meant to influence the client to change by resisting or rebelling. Defiance-based interventions emphasize the *interpersonal* domain by reflecting the client's need to oppose, defeat, or be

---

* This and all other quotations from this source are reprinted with permission, from "Compliance, Defiance, and Therapeutic Paradox" by M. Rohrbaugh, H. Tennen, S. Press, and L. White. *American Journal of Orthopsychiatry, 51,* 454–467. Copyright © 1981 by the American Orthopsychiatric Association Inc.

one-up on the therapist (Tennen et al., 1981). Defiance-based interventions include predicting that something will happen when you know the client will oppose it and asking for even more extreme behavior than the client has shown. In both cases, the client is likely to rebel and decrease or eliminate the problem behavior. Defiance-based interventions work well with many relationship issues. For futher descriptions of defiance-based paradoxes, consult Haley (1976).

The therapist must decide when to use compliance- or defiance-based interventions. As Rohrbaugh et al. (1981, p. 458) observe, "In order to enhance the power of a given intervention, it is important for the therapist to decide when paradox is being used with the expectation of compliance, and when it is being used with the expectation of defiance." Rohrbaugh et al. (1981) suggest two parameters for therapists to use in deciding whether the purpose of the paradox should be compliance or defiance. The first parameter is the *reactance potential* of the client (J. W. Brehm, 1966, 1972; S. S. Brehm, 1976). Psychological reactance is the need to preserve one's freedom. Clients who are high in reactance are typically oppositional and often find ways to say or do the opposite of what the therapist suggests. Clients who are low on reactance potential are typically cooperative and comply with what the therapist suggests. Therapists can assess this dimension by noticing early whether the client consistently takes positions opposite or complementary to the therapist's views and/or by assigning a straightforward task and noticing whether the client carries out or forgets the task (Rohrbaugh et al., 1981).

The second parameter to assess is the client's *perceived freedom* of his or her symptoms. An "unfree" symptom is one that the client believes is out of his or her control—one that occurs *spontaneously*. A "free" symptom is one that the patient defines as something that can be done *voluntarily* — either now or in the future. Therapists can assess this dimension by asking the client or by "reading" cues from the client's verbal and nonverbal behavior (Rohrbaugh et al., 1981).

In general, *compliance-based* interventions are used for clients with *low* reactance potential and with *unfree,* or spontaneous, symptoms. *Defiance-based* interventions work better when reactance is *high* and the symptom is perceived as *free,* or voluntary. Paradoxical interventions are usually not necessary in cases of *low* reactance potential and *free,* or voluntary, behavior. The most difficult combination to treat is high reactance potential coupled with an unfree symptom. In such instances, the therapist's first task is to shift the focus of intervention temporarily away from the symptom, until reactance potential lowers (Rohrbaugh et al., 1981).

Types of intervention: Prescribing and restraining. The most common forms of paradoxical interventions are labeled as prescribing or restraining. Rohrbaugh et al. (1981) define prescriptions as follows:

> When using a paradoxical *prescribing* strategy, the therapist encourages or instructs someone to engage in the specific piece of behavior to be eliminated. For example, a patient may be asked to practice an obsessional thought or bring on an anxiety attack, a rebellious adolescent may be encouraged to rebel, or an overinvolved mother to be more protective of her child [p. 456].

Prescribing tactics are used for *compliance*-based interventions and are based on the assumption that engaging in the problem behavior or exaggerating the symptom will eliminate it. When using restraining interventions, the therapist discourages change or may even deny it is possible. The therapist may instruct the client to go slow or may gently suggest that change may not be feasible (Rohrbaugh et al., 1981). Restraining tactics are reserved for *defiance*-based interventions and are based on the assumption that the client will change by rebelling against the therapist's directive. The decision to use compliance- or defiance-based interventions depends on the level of the client's resistance, the nature of the problem, and the therapist's assessment of what and who constitute the problem.

A *symptom prescription* is the most common compliance-based paradoxical intervention used. The underlying rationale of a prescriptive paradox is (1) in order to ease your symptom, keep it, and (2) will your uncontrollable symptom to occur voluntarily (Tennen et al., 1981). Symptom prescription is not meant to trick clients but instead to help clients change under their own power, with their own resources, and to their own credit (Zeig, 1980a). As Lankton and Lankton (1983, p. 74) observe, "If a client can purposefully alter a symptom previously considered involuntary, a new measure of hope is realized." In all forms of symptom prescription, the therapist is introducing a small modification of the target behavior. Sometimes one small change is sufficient to disrupt a self-defeating behavior pattern. In other cases, this small change can be built on and added to with other changes.

In using a prescriptive paradox, the therapist first selects one or more elements of the symptom to prescribe such as thoughts, feelings, or behaviors. Next, the therapist decides how to prescribe the symptom. One type of prescriptive paradox is simply to ask the client to engage in or perform some element of the symptom—for example, "This week I'd like you to be aware of and keep track of all these times when you feel nervous [act nervous, have nervous thoughts, and so on]" or "This week you might try to bring on an anxiety attack deliberately." A variation is to ask the client to increase, decrease, or exaggerate some element of the symptom, such as intensity (this is similar to what occurs in implosion, or flooding). For example: "This week I'd like you to act [think, feel] even more nervous than before. Now, you said your nervousness is about a 5 on a 1-to-10 scale. Shoot for doubling its intensity this week." Or "When you realize you are blushing, exaggerate it. Get even hotter and redder in your face."

It is also important to offer the client a rationale for the prescription in order to increase the likelihood of compliance. For these forms of symptom prescription, one believable rationale is to emphasize *control.* You might tell the client that learning to turn on the symptom or do it more will help the client later to turn it off or do it less. Another useful rationale is based on *understanding.* Depending on the client's views about the problem, you could note that carrying out the directive "would help you to gain awareness" (Gestalt therapy), "would help us to get concrete data" (behavioral therapy), or "would help to get at the underlying causes of the problem" (psychodynamic therapy).

A second type of symptom prescription involves adding a positive or negative connotation to some part of the symptom. The most common way of adding a *negative* aspect to the symptom is by making its performance an *ordeal.* For example, with a client who wants to stop smoking or eating high-calorie foods, the therapist could instruct the client to put cigarettes or snacks in a hard-to-reach, locked cupboard accessible only with a footstool and a certain key, or could recommend that the client smoke or snack only in a straight-backed chair in his damp basement or in his cold garage. A client who has difficulty going to sleep at night might be instructed to get up and clean the oven if still awake after lying in bed for 30 minutes. When the symptom is scheduled as an ordeal, it is made too cumbersome and unpleasant to continue in the same way or at the same rate as before.

Positive connotations in the form of reframing can also be added to aspects of symptoms. Recall from Chapter 16 that positive connotation involves reconceptualizing the problem by describing the problem behavior in a positive manner. For example, with a client who has few good relationships because of her "bossiness," the bossiness may be described as a need for control; a client who engages in frequent negative ruminations about himself can be shown that such ruminations can produce humorous as well as unpleasant consequences; a client who has trouble going to sleep at night might be instructed to list positive aspects of staying awake. In marital therapy, a spouse's unproductive behavior, such as criticism, may be described as something the person is doing for the welfare of someone else—such as trying to get close to the partner. A rationale for these forms of interventions is to emphasize the client's *attitude* about the symptom. The therapist might say that by locking up food or cigarettes or by using time at night to clean, the client has opportunities to examine her or his attitude about the symptom under *different* conditions.

A third type of symptom prescription has to do with time. The most common form of symptom prescription based on time is *symptom scheduling.* The problem can be experienced more or less frequently, in different durations, or at different times or locations. The client is directed to try to bring on the symptom at particular times and/or in particular places. For example, the therapist may say "This week try to bring on an anxiety attack every morning before you leave the house." Scheduling of the symptom should occur before the time of its spontaneous occurrence, provided there is a typical time of day that the symptom occurs. In lieu of scheduling the symptom at prescribed times, the enactment of the symptom can be prescribed *contingent* on certain feelings, thoughts, or activities of the client or others. For example, the therapist could instruct the client to "get into your anxious feelings whenever the thoughts about your speech crop up." Usually in such cases, the client is also instructed to stay with the feelings or thoughts for a specified time period or even to exaggerate them—for example, "Once you get these anxious feelings going, keep them there for 15 minutes and make them more intense." A variation of symptom scheduling described by Weeks and L'Abate (1982) is to instruct the client to extend the feeling state. For example, depressed clients can be told to notice when they start to feel better and then to make themselves stay depressed for another 15 minutes before allowing themselves to feel better. This type of prescription is designed to show clients how they control their moods and feelings. As Weeks and L'Abate (1982) observe,

> Usually, clients following this prescription realize what they do to place themselves in an undesirable mood because they use those ideas to keep themselves in the mood longer. At the same time they are learning to keep themselves in the mood longer, they are also learning what they can do to control the mood [p. 122].

A useful rationale for all forms of symptom scheduling involves *prediction*. The client is told that since the symptom is going to occur anyway, at least the client could be in a position to predict it and therefore deal with it better when it happens.

One caution on prescription-based paradoxes — never prescribe suicidal or homicidal *behavior*. If self- or other-destructive *fantasies* are prescribed, make sure the client understands that whereas having such ideas is acceptable, acting them out is not (Zeig, 1980b).

In contrast to prescribing interventions, *restraining* interventions are those in which the therapist discourages or inhibits change. The underlying message in a restraining paradox is: In order to change, stay the same or give up (Rohrbaugh et al., 1981). *Restraining* interventions are used mainly when prescriptions have failed or when the therapist expects the client to defy the directive.

The first type of restraining strategy is *delaying change*. In "delaying change," the therapist moves more slowly than the client expects. Messages that encourage *delayed* compliance reduce resistance by decreasing threat. Fisch et al. (1982, p. 159) refer to this intervention as the injunction to "go slow." They explain this strategy as follows:

> The client is not instructed to do anything, certainly nothing specific. Whatever instructions are given are general and vague: "This week, it would be very important not to do anything to bring about further improvement." More of the intervention consists in offering believable rationales for "going slow": that change, even for the better, requires adjusting to; or that one needs to determine, a step

at a time, how much change would be optimal as opposed to maximal: "You might be better off with a 75 percent improvement rather than a 100 percent improvement"; or "Change occurring slowly and step by step makes for a more solid change than change which occurs too suddenly" [p. 159].

The "go slow" or "slow down" injunction works either directly, by reassuring the client, or paradoxically, by enhancing the client's sense of control and confidence in his or her ability to move more quickly (Anderson & Stewart, 1983, p. 183). This strategy is particularly useful for clients who deny problems, for clients whose main attempted solution is trying too hard, and for clients who press the therapist for urgent solutions while remaining passive and uncooperative (Anderson & Stewart, 1983; Fisch et al., 1982). Delaying changes is sometimes also called "soft restraining."

The second type of restraining intervention is *forbidding change*. Forbidding change is a slightly more extreme restraining tactic than delaying change. There are two typical ways to restrain in this way. The first way is called "giving in" (Watzlawick et al., 1974). In this intervention, the client is told to give in to the symptom (or some element of it), and then the symptom is prescribed. For example: "In order to find out how often your symptom occurs this week, just give in to it and let it happen" or "In order to get some information about your problem, I want you to do something new this week. Give up trying to stop _____ [for example, arguing] and then pay attention to what is happening before and during this time."

The second way to forbid change is just to tell the client directly not to engage in the target behavior. For instance, often in sex therapy clients are told not to engage in intercourse or not to have an erection or an orgasm. Similarly, an insomniac might be instructed "not to go to sleep this week."

The most extreme type of restraining (often called "hard restraining" for this reason) is to *declare hopelessness* and to predict that change or improvement will not be possible. Through the therapist's attitude of resignation, a challenge is issued and the stage is set for the client to prove the therapist wrong. This strategy is analogous to therapeutic impotence. In using it, it is important to accept responsibility for one's impotence without blaming the client (Selvini-Palazzoli, Cecchin, Prata, & Boscolo, 1978). In other words, the therapist owns the feelings of hopelessness and does not project them onto the client. This strategy is not needed very frequently, since with most "yes, but" clients, delaying and forbidding change are tried first and usually work. Declaring hopelessness is a last resort and is usually reserved for clients who are highly reactant and repeatedly seek help but fail to benefit (Rohrbaugh et al., 1981). In such instances, the therapist can say something like "I know I made an error in judgment in initially assessing your situation and assuming we could work together to make some changes. It is my belief that I can't really offer you anything at this point that will improve your situation. It would be a disservice to you to continue. Probably stopping and reassessing the situation and learning to live with the situation as it is would be the best possible course."

The fourth type of restraining strategy is *predicting a relapse*. This type of intervention is used frequently and is essential to most paradoxical tasks (Weeks & L'Abate, 1982). Predicting a relapse is used mainly to nurture incipient changes that result from symptom prescription. When the prescription works, the symptom disappears—often rather suddenly. Then the therapist predicts a relapse by telling the client the symptom will suddenly reappear. Again, the therapist has issued a therapeutic double bind. If the symptom does return, the therapist has predicted it, so it is under the therapist's control. If it doesn't return, it is under the client's control. In either case, it is impossible for the client to continue to view the symptom as unfree, or spontaneous. When a symptom is defined in such a way as to be under someone's control, it is less disturbing to the client and gives the client more energy to deal with the situation or person producing the problem (Weeks & L'Abate, 1982). Predicting a relapse can also be used when it is time to terminate treatment. Inform the client that, after termination, reappearance of the problem is normal and expected and will occur in the near future. A defiant client will probably prove the therapist wrong by not relapsing, and a compliant, overly anxious client will be less anxious about getting along without therapy.

Prescribing a relapse is an extension of predicting a relapse. Erickson (quoted in Haley, 1973) recommended this approach with clients who improve too quickly. Clients are requested to experience themselves as they were before treatment "to see if there is anything from that time that they wish to recover or salvage" (p. 4). Another option is to prescribe reenactment of the symptom—for example, "This week it would be a good idea to

conjure up all those old angry feelings [or thoughts]" or "At this time I'd like to see whether you can still fight by screaming at each other. Have that kind of fight each day." The relapse prescription helps clients see how they can fall back into the same patterns and find ways of preventing this from happening, particularly after therapy is over (Weeks & L'Abate, 1982).

All the restraining strategies described in this chapter require careful timing and delivery and need to be offered with warmth and empathy. Sarcasm and anger must be avoided in order for these interventions to be most helpful.

Steps in Working Paradoxically

There are seven steps in formulating and delivering paradoxical interventions with clients.

Therapeutic relationship. Before a paradoxical intervention is attempted, a therapeutic relationship in which the client is an active participant must exist. Both Weeks and L'Abate (1982) and Ascher (1980) observe that paradoxical interventions do not work well unless the client is actively involved in therapy and a supportive and therapeutic relationship exists. This is why paradoxical intervention may not work well for clients who are ordered to have counseling by experts or otherwise required to seek help. A good relationship creates the rapport necessary when instructing clients to do something that seems illogical from their current frame of reference.

Assessment. Paradoxical interventions are much more effective when they are accurate; that is, the therapist's functional analysis of the symptom or interactional system must be conceivable, if not highly probable (Birchler, 1981). Accurate paradoxical interventions are based on careful assessments that lead to a concrete understanding of the client's problem. Such an assessment includes analysis of repetitive behavior patterns, sequence of events leading up to the problem, chain of events in the problem, and interactional patterns (see also Chapters 7 and 8). Failure to base a paradoxical intervention on careful functional analysis may create difficulties because other controlling contingencies have been overlooked (Ascher, 1980).

Goals. Paradoxical interventions should be based on the direction and degree of change desired by the client. It is important that the client's reasons and hopes for treatment be carefully delineated so that the therapist is not pursuing the wrong ends.

Formulation. After the therapist has completed a functional analysis and is aware of the client's goals, the therapist may formulate a paradoxical intervention *if* he or she feels it is the treatment of choice for this particular client at this time. Paradoxical interventions are formulated as homework tasks. In formulating the directive, the therapist must first (1) be able to see the symptom in functionally positive terms (closeness, care, protection, stability, and so forth), (2) understand how the problem is perpetuated and maintained, and finally (3) hypothesize the function or purpose that the symptom serves for the client. It is extremely important to keep the prescribed task simple and to formulate an intervention that incorporates the client's language (Todd, 1980). The therapist may also formulate other (nonparadoxical) interventions to be used to complement the paradoxical task.

Assignment. Questions about the task are usually postponed until the next session. Delivery or assignment of the paradox can be the most crucial and difficult part. Often it is useful to write out the task before the session. Paradoxical interventions are usually assigned to the client as homework to be completed between sessions. To avoid assigning prematurely or for the wrong issue, reserve assigning a paradoxical intervention until the end of the session. Another important reason not to give a paradoxical instruction too early is that its effectiveness may be reduced if the client comments on it. When assigning a paradoxical intervention, it is also important to suggest a rationale that is likely to motivate the client to follow through or to resist —depending on whether you expect the client to comply with or defy the directive.

Evaluation. Once you assign a paradoxical intervention, it is important to monitor the results. Record the type of task given to the client and track its effects. In later sessions, ask about the client's response to the assigned task in detail. The effects usually occur one week to one month after assignment of the task (Weeks & L'Abate, 1982). Note whether the effects are similar to or different from the changes you predicted would occur. If the desired results did not occur, be sure to obtain information about why the task failed, because such information is critical for formulating a different task (Weeks & L'Abate, 1982).

Follow-up. If the task does succeed, the therapist must nurture and solidify the resulting changes. In addition to the use of nonparadoxical techniques, the therapist can strengthen change by tactics and comments likely to encourage continued change efforts. For example, with compliance-based paradoxical interventions, it is important to follow through with more of the same. For example, if a therapist tells a client to "dwell on the negative thoughts when they occur" and the client returns saying that there were too few that occurred on which to dwell, the therapist should urge the client to continue to concentrate on dwelling on them, until the client believes the problem has truly disappeared (Rohrbaugh et al., 1981). Other approaches to maintaining change described earlier include predicting and prescribing a relapse.

LEARNING ACTIVITIES #56: PARADOXICAL INTERVENTIONS

PART ONE
Below we list six examples of various paradoxical interventions. Read each one carefully and then identify whether the intervention is an example of a prescribing (compliance-based) or restraining (defiance-based) intervention. The first one is completed as an example. Feedback follows on page 576.

Example
1. "This week it is important not to try to change anything about your relationship."
    ____Prescribing   ✓Restraining
Restraining because it prohibits change this week.

2. "Whatever you decide to do about it, it would be important to do it at a very slow pace."
    ____Prescribing   ____Restraining
3. "Since you've noticed these anxiety attacks at work, you might consider trying to predict when they will occur by seeing whether you could have one at home each day before you go to work."
    ____Prescribing   ____Restraining
4. "I'm absolutely sure that you will begin to yell at each other again sometime soon."
    ____Prescribing   ____Restraining

(continued)

5. "If after 30 minutes you find you're still awake, you may find it helpful to get up and clean the toilets before going back to sleep. This may help to change your attitude about sleeping."

_____Prescribing   _____Restraining

6. "This week you may find you can gain more control of your depressed feelings by extending them when they occur another 15 or 20 minutes."

_____Prescribing   _____Restraining

PART TWO

In this activity we list five types of symptoms along with a description of the client's reactance potential. Using this information, match the five descriptions with the three types of interventions listed below. The first one is completed as an example. Feedback follows.

Type of Intervention

A. Compliance-based paradoxical interventions

B. Defiance-based paradoxical interventions

C. Nonparadoxical interventions

Description

Example

__B__ 1. Symptom: Marital couple has frequent fights. Reactance potential: High (Defiance-based paradoxical intervention is likely to match best because symptom is free and reactance potential is high.)

_____ 2. Symptom: Mother and son argue constantly. Reactance potential: Low

_____ 3. Symptom: Panic attacks. Reactance potential: Low

_____ 4. Symptom: Mother is very protective of only child, even though child is 17 years old. Reactance potential: High

_____ 5. Symptom: Frequent headaches for which no organic basis has been found. Reactance potential: Low

□ STRATEGIES FOR INVOLUNTARY CLIENTS

As we noted earlier, involuntary clients who are under some pressure to seek counseling are likely to present more resistant behaviors than voluntary clients, at least initially. Although all of the preceding strategies suggested to manage resistance also apply to involuntary clients, this section describes some special tactics that may be particularly useful for these clients.

Working with clients who are there under duress requires flexibility, creativity, and resourcefulness. Since an absent client can hardly be counseled, the counselor needs to engage the client somehow, at least until counseling makes a difference (Dyer & Vriend, 1975).

A useful beginning point is to start where the client is. Show interest in what the client wants to talk about. As Dyer and Vriend note, "A productive assumption in converting involuntariness into a commitment to be counseled is that any client's chief interest is himself" (p. 102). Since many involuntary clients are oriented toward self-protection, avoid demanding or even expecting that the client self-disclose or engage in other behaviors that rob him or her of any masks. Adapt your methods and style to the client's needs and style. If the client talks in a stilted and pedantic manner, a more formal approach is in order than if the client presents a casual interactional style.

Another initial strategy is to do something—anything—that is likely to be perceived as helpful by the client (Anderson & Stewart, 1983). Even a small intervention such as summarizing the situation or reflecting the client's resentment may enhance the client's expectations about therapy and may increase the helper's credibility. Sometimes a more involved intervention such as teaching the client relaxation, meditation, or a way to analyze irrational thinking may be immediately useful to this type of client.

Another strategy to use is to do anything that gives the client more control over what happens. When clients have little or no control over the process and outcome of therapy, they are more likely to view the counselor as a representative of the referring agency or person, and resistance will increase (Anderson & Stewart, 1983). Discuss openly the pressures that have resulted in the client's being referred for counseling. If the court has ordered the client to have treatment, the therapist can restore the client's control by pointing out that the client can refuse therapy and accept the consequences. As Anderson and Stewart (1983, p. 241) observe, "While the consequences are usually serious enough to mean that this is not a desirable choice, it should be made clear that refusal is an option or [the client] will continue to resist the therapist at every turn."

Another strategy useful for some involuntary clients is called "metered counseling" (M. A. Kirk, personal communication, December 1983). In this strategy, the counselor indicates that the client can choose to talk about whatever she or he wishes for about one-third of the session. During the other two-thirds of each session, the client must talk about something "interesting"; the therapist decides what issues are interesting. Or if the client is required to meet with a counselor for ten 50-minute sessions, the client can choose what to do or say for about 1500 minutes; for the remaining 3500 minutes, the client talks about something "interesting."

Another way to increase the client's control and responsibility is to renegotiate the "contract" if possible. Ask clients whether they are bothered by anything in addition to what they were sent or referred for. The object of this approach is to come up with a complaint that the *client* is interested in changing (Fisch et al., 1982). If it is impossible to do this, an alternative is to jointly negotiate an explicit treatment contract that meets the needs of the referring agency or person but also gives the client some control. It is also important not to exacerbate a client's loss of control by being vague about what you as the therapist will or won't do, what you will and won't report to the referring agency, and so on (Anderson & Stewart, 1983). If you are required to write a report to the referring agency, part of the treatment contract you develop with the client might be that the report will be shared just with the client (Anderson & Stewart, 1983).

If all else fails, and the client is not interested in renegotiating a contract that reflects his or her other interests, a final strategy is to try to get the client interested in treatment. Fisch et al. (1982) describe this strategy as follows:

> If this can be accomplished, it will *not* be done by exhorting him to take his problem seriously, to buckle down to treatment, and the like. This is the one pitfall to avoid. The therapist has some chance of success, however, if he applies a different pressure by going the other way—by taking the position with the "client" that treatment probably is inadvisable. The identified patient now has the opportunity to convince the therapist why it could be in his own best interest to do something about *his* problem [pp. 43–44].

If the identified client is still not interested in therapy, the counselor has the option of terminating treatment and working with the complainant, who is usually the person pressuring the client to seek help. Often the complainant is more interested in solving the problem and more willing to make changes than the involuntary client.

☐ A FINAL NOTE

There are three thoughts we would like to leave you with as we terminate this journey with you. First, set careful and realistic personal and professional limits for yourself as a therapist. Learn what you can and cannot do for and with clients. A critical part of effective helpgiving is to know when to back off and stop and hand some responsibility over to the person in front of you. The more you do for your clients, the less they will do for themselves.

Second, examine your expectations for yourself and your clients. Therapists often find that their expectations for change differ markedly from clients', particularly with reluctant or pessimistic clients. In such instances, therapists often are meeting more of their own needs for change and success than pursuing the needs and issues of clients. Therapy is endangered when the counselor wants more for clients than they want for themselves. In such cases, the therapist fights with the client (on the client's behalf), but the client loses an important ally.

Finally, above all, be flexible. The skills and strategies offered in this book are simply methodology that is more or less effective depending on the creativity and intuition of the user. Some of what gets labeled "client resistance" is nothing more than inflexibility of the therapist. Therapists who are flexible regard each client as unique and each helping strategy as a tool to be used or set aside depending on its effectiveness in producing client-generated outcomes.

POSTEVALUATION

PART ONE

In this part of the postevaluation, we give three descriptions of client roles. Use triads in which one person assumes the role of the client, another the role of the counselor, and the third person an observer. As the client, present one of the roles described below to the therapist (change the sex of the client, if necessary). As the counselor, respond to the client with listening responses that match, or pace, the client's pessimism (Chapter Objective One). As the observer, note whether the counselor successfully matches the client's pessimism and provide feedback following the role play.

Client 1: The client is a teenager who is very courteous and polite and also very stubborn. She says that she is willing to try anything you suggest to improve her school performance but that she doubts whether there is any successful solution.

Client 2: The client is an older male who has been missing work recently because of alcohol problems. The client says that he is willing to talk to you but that his alcohol problems are largely the result of job stress, for which he blames his immediate supervisor.

Client 3: Background: The clients are a mother, father and his 8-year-old son, whom the school personnel have described as "incorrigible." The father is very protective and overinvolved with the son to the point of nagging, which the son resents. The father and son have constant arguments.

Client role for purposes of role play: As the client, assume the role of the "underinvolved" mother. Inform the counselor that you are willing to come in and sit in on the sessions but you don't have much to contribute or much to learn, since the problem is basically between your husband and your son.

PART TWO

Listed below are two descriptions of clients. For each situation, identify the client's dysfunctional behaviors and the identified "payoffs," or reinforcers. Also identify and describe ways the client could achieve the same kind of reinforcement with other, more adaptive and less self-defeating behaviors (Chapter Objective Two). Feedback follows the Postevaluation (on page 580).

Client 1: The client is a 40-year-old married man who reports feelings of depression largely due to dissatisfaction with his job, in which he feels he works "like a horse," yet receives no credit or notice for his accomplishments. He also states that he feels his life is "going nowhere." During the past year, to compensate for his bad feelings, he has become very argumentative with and critical toward his wife and three children. He is seeking counseling because his wife, who has a good job with an adequate salary, is threatening to leave him and take the children with her unless he stops "verbally abusing" them. He would like to "save his marriage" but admits that he doesn't really know how or what to do.

a. Identify the client's dysfunctional or self-defeating behavior(s).

b. For each behavior identified in #1, list the presumed reinforcer, or payoff.

c. Describe some ways in which this client might achieve the same reinforcement through more adaptive behaviors.

Client 2: The client, a 16-year-old, has had repeated behavior problems in school over the last few years, resulting in poor grades and numerous phone calls to his parents. He has skipped school, gone to school late, and missed tests and assignments. Last month, he was caught shoplifting, and on the third incident the store pressed charges. For his sentence, he was required to do four hours of community service each week for 16 weeks and also see a counselor weekly. On talking with him, you discover that he is the younger of two boys. His brother just graduated with honors from college and has been accepted into a prestigious law school. The client states that he has always resented his parents' constant comparisons between himself and his brother and he never felt he could

(continued)

POSTEVALUATION (continued)

live up to their expectations for him, no matter what he did or how hard he tried. He describes his parents' relationship as quiet — says both are reserved and don't communicate very much with each other except for yelling and nagging at him.

   a. Identify the client's dysfunctional or self-defeating behavior(s).
   b. For each behavior identified in #1, list the prescribed reinforcers, or payoffs.
   c. Describe some ways in which this client might achieve the same reinforcement through more adaptive behaviors.

PART THREE

In this part of the Postevaluation, you are given two written descriptions of clients and their presenting complaints and problems. From these descriptions, Chapter Objective Three asks you to identify in writing four aspects of "patient position" and describe the implications of these positions for the management of therapy. Tune in carefully to the language and words used by the client in making your identifications. Feedback follows the Postevaluation.

Client 1, a teenage boy: "Actually, I'm doing OK in school. Yeah, I get stuck in detention center once in a while, mostly for lateness — showing up for class late or turning in my work late — but that's pretty normal. I'm not the only one in there. My mom thinks it's a major crime, though. She says she's at her wit's end, so maybe a counselor would help. Now, don't get me wrong, but I think I could work this out without much help from you if I just took the time to sit down and write out a schedule."

Identify:

   a. Client's notions about nature/cause of problem.
   b. Client's notions about who is responsible for the problem.
   c. Client's notions about how the problem can be resolved.
   d. Client's notions about therapy.
   e. Implications for managing therapy.

Client 2, a middle-aged woman: "My son is talking about doing himself in, and I just don't know where we went wrong. We tried to be good, loving, and understanding parents. We worked so hard at giving him a supportive environment so that he could feel good about himself and develop his own interests and abilities. Now it doesn't

seem like it's done any good — so maybe you can figure out what we should do next."

Identify:

   a. Client's notions about nature/cause of problem.
   b. Client's notions about who is responsible for the problem.
   c. Client's notions about how the problem can be resolved.
   d. Client's notions about therapy.
   e. Implications for managing therapy.

PART FOUR

In this part of the postevaluation, we give two descriptions of clients. For each client, select the most appropriate type of paradoxical intervention and write a description of a corresponding task, including a rationale (Chapter Objective Four). Then, using triads or small groups, practice delivering the paradoxical intervention in a role-play situation (Chapter Objective Five).

Client 1: The client is a college student who wants to go to med school but is having trouble making decent grades because of putting things off until the last moment. Often this results in careless or missed work or poor preparation. The client says it is very important for him to get into med school, and regardless of how hard he tries to get his work done on time, it doesn't seem to help. He just can't seem to get it done.

1. Select the most appropriate type of paradoxical intervention, based on the type of symptom and on the client's reactance level. (You may wish to check the feedback for question #1 before going on.)
2. For the type of intervention you select, write a description of a task to give this client, including a rationale for the task.
3. Deliver the task to a role-play client. In triads or small groups, one person assumes the role of the client, another the counselor, and the other(s) the observer(s). The client should take the role described above (that is, college student, procrastination, low reactance). The counselor's job is to deliver the task and the rationale for it in a way that is likely to promote client *compliance* with the task, since this situation calls for a compliance-based intervention. The observer(s) can give feedback after the role play, using the Checklist for

(continued)

Paradoxical Interventions at the bottom of this page as a guide. Roles can be switched several times to give each person an opportunity to assume the three roles.

Client 2: The client is a 25-year-old woman who refers herself to you to discuss her long-standing difficulties in relationships with men. She has never had a satisfactory or lengthy relationship with a man. She seems to get easily involved, becomes suspicious of the man's motives, and backs off from the relationship. After a short period of initial cooperation with you, the client becomes rather quiet, reserved, and noncommittal. Slowly this leads into a more active "yes, but" stance in which she refutes almost every idea or suggestion you have (high reactance). (By the way, note the relationship parallels between the way the client behaves with the therapist and her presenting problem.)

1. Select the most appropriate type of paradoxical intervention, given the type of symptom and the reactance level of the client. (You may wish to check the feedback for question #1 before going on.)
2. For the type of intervention you select, write a description of a task to give this client, including a rationale for the task.
3. Deliver the task to a role-play client, using triads or small groups. The client should take the role described above (young woman or man, relationship problem with opposite sex, high reactance). The counselor's job is to deliver the task and its rationale in a way that is likely to promote client *defiance* of the task, since this situation calls for a defiance-based intervention. The observer(s) can give feedback, using the Checklist for Paradoxical Interventions as a guide.

CHECKLIST FOR PARADOXICAL INTERVENTIONS

Name of Counselor_____   Date_____

I. Type of symptom client presents (circle one):   Free   Unfree

II. Reactance level of client (circle one):   High   Low

III. Type of paradoxical intervention used by counselor (check ✔ appropriate category):

Compliance	*Defiance*
_____symptom prescription	_____delay change
_____negative connotation (ordeal)	_____prohibit change
_____positive connotation (reframing)	_____predict relapse
_____symptom scheduling	_____declare hopelessness

IV. Note rationale used by counselor to accompany intervention (check ✔ appropriate category):

Compliance	*Defiance*
_____control	_____change others slowly
_____understanding	_____give in to symptom; let it happen
_____gain information	_____important not to engage in symptom
_____examine attitude	_____symptom needs to reappear for control
_____prediction	_____other:_____
_____other:_____	

Observer comments: _____

☐ SUGGESTED READINGS

Anderson, C. M., & Stewart, S. (1983). *Mastering resistance: A practical guide to family therapy.* New York: Guilford Press.

Ascher, L. M. (1980). Paradoxical intention. In A. Goldstein & E. B. Foa (Eds.), *Handbook of behavioral interventions: A clinical guide.* New York: Wiley.

Cavanaugh, M. E. (1982). *The counseling experience.* Monterey, CA: Brooks/Cole. Chapter 10, "Resistance in Counseling."

Chamberlain, P., Patterson, G., Reid, J., Kavanagh, K., & Forgatch, M. (1984). Observation of client resistance. *Behavior Therapy, 15,* 144–155.

Fisch, R., Weakland, J., & Segal, L. (1982). *The tactics of change.* San Francisco: Jossey-Bass.

Haley, J. (1984). *Ordeal therapy: Unusual ways to change behavior.* San Francisco: Jossey-Bass.

Jahn, D., & Lichstein, K. (1980). The resistive client. *Behavior Modification, 4,* 303–320.

King, M., Novik, L., & Citrenbaum, C. (1983). *Irresistible communication.* Philadelphia: Saunders.

Kolko, D., & Milan, M. (1983). Reframing and paradoxical instruction to overcome "resistance" in the treatment of delinquent youths: A multiple baseline analysis. *Journal of Consulting and Clinical Psychology, 51,* 655–660.

Lopez, F. G. (1983). A paradoxical approach to vocational indecision. *Personnel and Guidance Journal, 61,* 410–412.

Martin, G., & Worthington, E. (1982). Behavioral homework. In M. Hersen, R. Eisler, & P. Miller (Eds.), *Progress in behavior modification* (Vol. 13). New York: Academic Press.

Munjack, D. J., & Oziel, R. J. (1978). Resistance in behavioral treatment of sexual dysfunctions. *Journal of Sex and Marital Therapy, 4,* 122–138.

Papp, P. (1984). *The process of change.* New York: Guilford Press.

Rohrbaugh, M., Tennen, H., Press, S., & White, L. (1981). Compliance, defiance, and therapeutic paradox: Guidelines for strategic use of paradoxical interventions. *American Journal of Orthopsychiatry, 51,* 454–467.

Shelton, J., & Levy, R. (1981). *Behavioral assignments and treatment compliance.* Champaign, IL: Research Press.

Spinks, S., & Birchler, G. (1982). Behavioral-systems marital therapy: Dealing with resistance. *Family Process, 21,* 169–185.

Wachtel, P. (Ed.). (1982). Resistance: Psychodynamic and behavioral approaches. New York: Plenum.

Weeks, G. R., & L'Abate, L. (1982). *Paradoxical psychotherapy: Theory and practice with individuals, couples, and families.* New York: Brunner/Mazel.

Zeig, J. (1980). Symptom prescription techniques: Clinical applications using elements of communication. *American Journal of Clinical Hypnosis, 23,* 23–33.

FEEDBACK: POSTEVALUATION

PART TWO

Client 1:   a. Dysfunctional, self-defeating behavior: arguing with and being critical toward wife and children

b. Presumed reinforcers: increases his self-esteem, gives him power and control he feels are missing in his life and job

c. Other possible ways to increase his self-esteem and power and control:
Change jobs
Talk to his boss or supervisor
Get involved in a personally fulfilling leisure time activity
Others: (list yours)

Client 2:   a. Dysfunctional, self-defeating behaviors:

school-related problems such as skipping class and missing tests; shoplifting

b. Presumed reinforcers: (1) probable attention from parents and others (for both school-related problems and shoplifting); (2) possibly is helping parents avoid marital issues by creating an issue about himself they can invest their energy in (that is, negative reinforcement)

c. Other ways of getting reinforcers:
Change to a new school where he can start off differently
Get involved in sports or other activities of interest to client
Social skills training
Family counseling
Others: (list yours)

PART THREE

Client 1:

a. Notions about nature and cause of his problem: In his view, "problem" is nothing more than a typical developmental issue for someone his age.

b. Notions about who is responsible for the problem: Since he does not consider it a problem, the problem is created by his mom, according to his view.

c. Notions about how the problem can be resolved: Something very simple, concrete, and nontherapeutic, such as time management.

d. Notions about therapy: Therapy is not necessary, from this client's point of view, to resolve the "problem."

e. Implications for management of therapy:

1. Avoid communicating the idea that the client has a "big problem," since he doesn't see it this way.

2. Consider consulting with or seeing the mother (or parents), since she has a stake in the issue.

3. Avoid being overly pushy or optimistic about therapy, since the client doesn't believe it is necessary.

4. Any initial strategy/option you suggest should be one that fits with the client's values and seems concrete, specific, and not overly therapeutic to him.

Client 2:

a. Notions about nature and cause of the problem: A result of something missing from home environment.

b. Notions about who is responsible for the problem: Client feels responsible for problem (as the parent).

c. Notions about how the problem can be resolved: Therapeutically oriented strategies that focus and build on self-exploration, self-understanding, and self-esteem.

d. Notions about therapy: Therapy is necessary and important—client is looking to therapist as the "expert."

e. Implications for management of therapy:
   1. Avoid implying that the son has a problem, since the parents don't see it this way; at the same time, avoid reinforcing their assumption that they are the ones who are responsible—can do this initially by ignoring this assumption so you don't make opposing statements that are inflammatory.
   2. Build on their hopes and optimism about therapy, including use of "expertness" of your role without being one-up.
   3. Offer strategies that fit with their value system and focus on self-exploration and understanding.

PART FOUR

Client 1:
1. The most appropriate type of paradoxical intervention would be some form of a prescription or compliance-based intervention, since the symptom is unfree and the reactance potential is low.
2. Examples of various prescribing tasks and corresponding rationales—see whether your task is similar to any of these:
   a. Element of symptom is prescribed—rationale is understanding: "This week you might practice putting your studies off or trying to procrastinate deliberately. This will give us a greater understanding of what we're working with."
   b. Frequency of symptom is prescribed—rationale is control. "This week you may want to consider procrastinating an extra 30 minutes each evening before you tackle your homework. This will give you more control over the problem eventually."
   c. Connotation is prescribed; symptom is made an ordeal. Rationale is contrast. "This week, if you find you're still having trouble getting your work done on time, after about an hour or so of putting if off, it could be useful to get up and do something more physical, like jogging, exercising, doing laundry, or cleaning your room. This may help give a contrast you need between

physical work and mental work, thus making the mental work easier."
   d. Connotation is prescribed; symptom is reframed. Rationale is understanding of symptom. "Something you might think about this week is the idea that you may put off your studies so that your life is not overly controlled. Thinking about this may help you to understand this problem better."
   e. Symptom is scheduled; rationale is prediction. "This week it may be useful to try to procrastinate, but instead of waiting until evening, do it earlier in the day—as early as possible. This will help you learn to predict better when it seems to happen most."

Client 2:
1. The most appropriate type of paradoxical intervention would be some form of delaying or prohibiting change or defiance-based intervention, since the symptom is free and the client's reactance potential is high.
2. Examples of defiance-based tasks and their corresponding rationales:
   a. Delay change or go slow. Rationale: change occurs slowly. "You know it's important not to push too hard on an issue like this because the best change usually occurs very slowly, like a snail's pace. So this week it is very important that, above all else, you don't work on this problem too much or do too much about it."
   b. Prohibit change. Rationale: stop change, gain perspective. "After you've been working on a problem hard as you have, it's usually a good idea to back off from it for a while to give you some perspective. So this week, it is very important not to do anything about this problem—just go on as you have been and don't change your relationship with these guys [gals] in any way."
(Predicting a relapse is not useful yet for this client, since change has not yet occurred. Declaring hopelessness should not be tried unless the above two interventions are unsuccessful.)

ETHICAL STANDARDS, AMERICAN PERSONNEL AND GUIDANCE ASSOCIATION*

APPENDIX A

(Approved by Executive Committee upon referral of the Board of Directors, January 17, 1981.)

☐ PREAMBLE

The American Personnel and Guidance Association is an educational, scientific, and professional organization whose members are dedicated to the enhancement of the worth, dignity, potential, and uniqueness of each individual and thus to the service of society.

The Association recognizes that the role definitions and work settings of its members include a wide variety of academic disciplines, levels of academic preparation and agency services. This diversity reflects the breadth of the Association's interest and influence. It also poses challenging complexities in efforts to set standards for the performance of members, desired requisite preparation or practice, and supporting social, legal, and ethical controls.

The specification of ethical standards enables the Association to clarify to present and future members and to those served by members, the nature of ethical responsibilities held in common by its members.

The existence of such standards serves to stimulate greater concern by members for their own professional functioning and for the conduct of fellow professionals such as counselors, guidance and student personnel workers, and others in the helping professions. As the ethical code of the Association, this document establishes principles that define the ethical behavior of Association members.

Section A: General

1. The member influences the development of the profession by continuous efforts to improve professional practices, teaching, services, and research. Professional growth is continuous

throughout the member's career and is exemplified by the development of a philosophy that explains why and how a member functions in the helping relationship. Members must gather data on their effectiveness and be guided by the findings.

2. The member has a responsibility both to the individual who is served and to the institution within which the service is performed to maintain high standards of professional conduct. The member strives to maintain the highest levels of professional services offered to the individuals to be served. The member also strives to assist the agency, organization, or institution in providing the highest caliber of professional services. The acceptance of employment in an institution implies that the member is in agreement with the general policies and principles of the institution. Therefore the professional activities of the member are also in accord with the objectives of the institution. If, despite concerted efforts, the member cannot reach agreement with the employer as to acceptable standards of conduct that allow for changes in institutional policy conducive to the positive growth and development of clients, then terminating the affiliation should be seriously considered.

3. Ethical behavior among professional associates, both members and nonmembers, must be expected at all times. When information is possessed that raises doubt as to the ethical behavior of professional colleagues, whether Association members or not, the member must take action to attempt to rectify such a condition. Such action shall use the institution's channels first and then use procedures established by the state Branch, Division, or Association.

4. The member neither claims nor implies professional qualifications exceeding those possessed and is responsible for correcting any misrepresentations of these qualifications by others.

5. In establishing fees for professional counseling services, members must consider the financial status of clients and locality. In the event that the established fee structure is inappropriate for a client, assistance must be provided in finding comparable services of acceptable cost.

6. When members provide information to the public or to subordinates, peers or supervisors, they have a responsibility to ensure that the content is general, unidentified client information that is accurate, unbiased, and consists of objective, factual data.

7. With regard to the delivery of professional services, members should accept only those positions for which they are professionally qualified.

8. In the counseling relationship the counselor is aware of the intimacy of the relationship and maintains respect for the client and avoids engaging in activities that seek to meet the counselor's personal needs at the expense of that client. Through awareness of the negative impact of both racial and sexual stereotyping and discrimination, the counselor guards the individual rights and personal dignity of the client in the counseling relationship.

Section B: Counseling Relationship

This section refers to practices and procedures of individual and/or group counseling relationships.

The member must recognize the need for client freedom of choice. Under those circumstances where this is not possible, the member must apprise clients of restrictions that may limit their freedom of choice.

1. The member's *primary* obligation is to respect the integrity and promote the welfare of the client(s), whether the client(s) is (are) assisted individually or in a group relationship. In a group setting, the member is also responsible for taking reasonable precautions to protect individuals from physical and/or psychological trauma resulting from interaction within the group.

2. The counseling relationship and information resulting therefrom [must] be kept confidential, consistent with the obligations of the member as a professional person. In a group counseling setting, the counselor must set a norm of confidentiality regarding all group participants' disclosures.

3. If an individual is already in a counseling relationship with another professional person, the member [must] not enter into a counseling relationship without first contacting and receiving the approval of that other professional. If the member discovers that the client is in another counseling relationship after the counseling relationship begins, the member must gain the consent of the other professional or terminate the relationship, unless the client elects to terminate the other relationship.

4. When the client's condition indicates that there is clear and imminent danger to the client or others, the member must take reasonable personal action or inform responsible authorities. Consul-

tation with other professionals must be used where possible. The assumption of responsibility for the client's behavior must be taken only after careful deliberation. The client must be involved in the resumption of responsibility as quickly as possible.

5. Records of the counseling relationship, including interview notes, test data, correspondence, tape recordings, and other documents, are to be considered professional information for use in counseling and they should not be considered a part of the records of the institution or agency in which the counselor is employed unless specified by state statute or regulation. Revelation to others of counseling material must occur only upon the expressed consent of the client.

6. Use of data derived from a counseling relationship for purposes of counselor training or research shall be confined to content that can be disguised to ensure full protection of the identity of the subject client.

7. The member must inform the client of the purposes, goals, techniques, rules of procedure and limitations that may affect the relationship at or before the time that the counseling relationship is entered.

8. The member must screen prospective group participants, especially when the emphasis is on self-understanding and growth through self-disclosure. The member must maintain an awareness of the group participants' compatibility throughout the life of the group.

9. The member may choose to consult with any other professionally competent person about a client. In choosing a consultant, the member must avoid placing the consultant in a conflict of interest situation that would preclude the consultant's being a proper party to the member's efforts to help the client.

10. If the member determines an inability to be of professional assistance to the client, the member must either avoid initiating the counseling relationship or immediately terminate that relationship. In either event, the member must suggest appropriate alternatives. (The member must be knowledgeable about referral resources so that a satisfactory referral can be initiated.) In the event the client declines the suggested referral, the member is not obligated to continue the relationship.

11. When the member has other relationships, particularly of an administrative, supervisory and/or evaluative nature with an individual seeking counseling services, the member must not serve as the counselor but should refer the individual to another professional. Only in instances where such an alternative is unavailable and where the individual's situation warrants counseling intervention should the member enter into and/or maintain a counseling relationship. Dual relationships with clients that might impair the member's objectivity and professional judgment (e.g., as with close friends or relatives, sexual intimacies with any client) must be avoided and/or the counseling relationship terminated through referral to another competent professional.

12. All experimental methods of treatment must be clearly indicated to prospective recipients and safety precautions are to be adhered to by the member.

13. When the member is engaged in short-term group treatment/training programs (e.g., marathons and other encounter-type or growth groups), the member ensures that there is professional assistance available during and following the group experience.

14. Should the member be engaged in a work setting that calls for any variation from the above statements, the member is obligated to consult with other professionals whenever possible to consider justifiable alternatives.

Section C: Measurement and Evaluation

The primary purpose of educational and psychological testing is to provide descriptive measures that are objective and interpretable in either comparative or absolute terms. The member must recognize the need to interpret the statements that follow as applying to the whole range of appraisal techniques including test and nontest data. Test results constitute only one of a variety of pertinent sources of information for personnel, guidance, and counseling decisions.

1. The member must provide specific orientation or information to the examinee(s) prior to and following the test administration so that the results of testing may be placed in proper perspective with other relevant factors. In so doing, the member must recognize the effects of socioeconomic, ethnic and cultural factors on test scores. It is the member's professional responsibility to use additional unvalidated information carefully in modifying interpretation of the test results.

2. In selecting tests for use in a given situation or with a particular client, the member must consider carefully the specific validity, reliability, and appropriateness of the test(s). *General* validity, reliability and the like may be questioned legally as well as ethically when tests are used for vocational and educational selection, placement, or counseling.

3. When making any statements to the public about tests and testing, the member must give accurate information and avoid false claims or misconceptions. Special efforts are often required to avoid unwarranted connotations of such terms as *IQ* and *grade equivalent scores.*

4. Different tests demand different levels of competence for administration, scoring, and interpretation. Members must recognize the limits of their competence and perform only those functions for which they are prepared.

5. Tests must be administered under the same conditions that were established in their standardization. When tests are not administered under standard conditions or when unusual behavior or irregularities occur during the testing session, those conditions must be noted and the results designated as invalid or of questionable validity. Unsupervised or inadequately supervised test-taking, such as the use of tests through the mails, is considered unethical. On the other hand, the use of instruments that are so designed or standardized to be self-administered and self-scored, such as interest inventories, is to be encouraged.

6. The meaningfulness of test results used in personnel, guidance, and counseling functions generally depends on the examinee's unfamiliarity with the specific items on the test. Any prior coaching or dissemination of the test materials can invalidate test results. Therefore, test security is one of the professional obligations of the member. Conditions that produce most favorable test results must be made known to the examinee.

7. The purpose of testing and the explicit use of the results must be made known to the examinee prior to testing. The counselor must ensure that instrument limitations are not exceeded and that periodic review and/or retesting are made to prevent client stereotyping.

8. The examinee's welfare and explicit prior understanding must be the criteria for determining the recipients of the test results. The member must see that specific interpretation accompanies any release of individual or group test data. The

interpretation of test data must be related to the examinee's particular concerns.

9. The member must be cautious when interpreting the results of research instruments possessing insufficient technical data. The specific purposes for the use of such instruments must be stated explicitly to examinees.

10. The member must proceed with caution when attempting to evaluate and interpret the performance of minority group members or other persons who are not represented in the norm group on which the instrument was standardized.

11. The member must guard against the appropriation, reproduction, or modifications of published tests or parts thereof without acknowledgment and permission from the previous publisher.

12. Regarding the preparation, publication and distribution of tests, reference should be made to:

a. *Standards for Educational and Psychological Tests and Manuals,* revised edition, 1974, published by the American Psychological Association on behalf of itself, the American Educational Research Association and the National Council on Measurement in Education.

b. The responsible use of tests: A position paper of AMEG, APGA, and NCME. *Measurement and Evaluation in Guidance,* 1972, 5, 385–388.

c. "Responsibilities of Users of Standardized Tests," APGA, *Guidepost,* October 5, 1978, pp. 5–8.

Section D: Research and Publication

1. Guidelines on research with human subjects shall be adhered to, such as:

a. *Ethical Principles in the Conduct of Research with Human Participants,* Washington, D.C.: American Psychological Association, Inc., 1973.

b. Code of Federal Regulations, Title 45, Subtitle A, Part 46, as currently issued.

2. In planning any research activity dealing with human subjects, the member must be aware of and responsive to all pertinent ethical principles and ensure that the research problem, design, and execution are in full compliance with them.

3. Responsibility for ethical research practice lies with the principal researcher, while others involved in the research activities share ethical obligation and full responsibility for their own actions.

4. In research with human subjects, researchers are responsible for the subjects' welfare through-

out the experiment and they must take all reasonable precautions to avoid causing injurious psychological, physical, or social effects on their subjects.

5. All research subjects must be informed of the purpose of the study except when withholding information or providing misinformation to them is essential to the investigation. In such research the member must be responsible for corrective action as soon as possible following completion of the research.

6. Participation in research must be voluntary. Involuntary participation is appropriate only when it can be demonstrated that participation will have no harmful effects on subjects and is essential to the investigation.

7. When reporting research results, explicit mention must be made of all variables and conditions known to the investigator that might affect the outcome of the investigation or the interpretation of the data.

8. The member must be responsible for conducting and reporting investigations in a manner that minimizes the possibility that results will be misleading.

9. The member has an obligation to make available sufficient original research data to qualified others who may wish to replicate the study.

10. When supplying data, aiding in the research of another person, reporting research results, or in making original data available, due care must be taken to disguise the identity of the subjects in the absence of specific authorization from such subjects to do otherwise.

11. When conducting and reporting research, the member must be familiar with, and give recognition to, previous work on the topic, as well as . . . observe all copyright laws and follow the principles of giving full credit to all to whom credit is due.

12. The member must give due credit through joint authorship, acknowledgment, footnote statements, or other appropriate means to those who have contributed significantly to the research and/or publication, in accordance with such contributions.

13. The member must communicate to other members the results of any research judged to be of professional or scientific value. Results reflecting unfavorably on institutions, programs, services, or vested interests must not be withheld for such reasons.

14. If members agree to cooperate with another individual in research and/or publication, they incur an obligation to cooperate as promised in terms of punctuality of performance and with full regard to the completeness and accuracy of the information required.

15. Ethical practice requires that authors not submit the same manuscript, or one essentially similar in content, for simultaneous publication consideration by two or more journals. In addition, manuscripts published in whole or in substantial part in another journal or published work should not be submitted for publication without acknowledgment and permission from the previous publication.

Section E: Consulting

Consultation refers to a voluntary relationship between a professional helper and help-needing individual, group or social unit in which the consultant is providing help to the client(s) in defining and solving a work-related problem or potential problem with a client or client system. (This definition is adapted from Kurpius, DeWayne. Consultation theory and process: An integrated model. *Personnel and Guidance Journal,* 1978, 56.)

1. The member acting as consultant must have a high degree of self-awareness of his/her own values, knowledge, skills, limitations, and needs in entering a helping relationship that involves human and/or organizational change and . . . the focus of the relationship [must] be on the issues to be resolved and not on the person(s) presenting the problem.

2. There must be understanding and agreement between member and client for the problem definition, change goals, and predicted consequences of interventions selected.

3. The member must be reasonably certain that she/he or the organization represented has the necessary competencies and resources for giving the kind of help that is needed now or may develop later and that appropriate referral resources are available to the consultant.

4. The consulting relationship must be one in which client adaptability and growth toward self-direction are encouraged and cultivated. The member must maintain this role consistently and not become a decision maker for the client or create a future dependency on the consultant.

5. When announcing consultant availability

for services, the member conscientiously adheres to the Association's *Ethical Standards.*

6. The member must refuse a private fee or other remuneration for consultation with persons who are entitled to these services through the member's employing institution or agency. The policies of a particular agency may make explicit provisions for private practice with agency clients by members of its staff. In such instances, the clients must be apprised of other options open to them should they seek private counseling services.

Section F: Private Practice

1. The member should assist the profession by facilitating the availability of counseling services in private as well as public settings.

2. In advertising services as a private practitioner, the member must advertise the services in such a manner so as to accurately inform the public as to services, expertise, profession, and techniques of counseling in a professional manner. A member who assumes an executive leadership role in the organization shall not permit his/her name to be used in professional notices during periods when not actively engaged in the private practice of counseling.

The member may list the following: highest relevant degree, type and level of certification or license, type and/or description of services, and other relevant information. Such information must not contain false, inaccurate, misleading, partial, out-of-context, or deceptive material or statements.

3. Members may join in partnership/corporation with other members and/or other professionals provided that each member of the partnership or corporation makes clear the separate specialties by name in compliance with the regulations of the locality.

4. A member has an obligation to withdraw from a counseling relationship if it is believed that employment will result in violation of the *Ethical Standards.* If the mental or physical condition of the member renders it difficult to carry out an effective professional relationship or if the member is discharged by the client because the counseling relationship is no longer productive for the client, then the member is obligated to terminate the counseling relationship.

5. A member must adhere to the regulations for private practice of the locality where the services are offered.

6. It is unethical to use one's institutional affiliation to recruit clients for one's private practice.

Section G: Personnel Administration

It is recognized that most members are employed in public or quasi-public institutions. The functioning of a member within an institution must contribute to the goals of the institution and vice versa if either is to accomplish their respective goals or objectives. It is therefore essential that the member and the institution function in ways to (a) make the institution's goals explicit and public; (b) make the member's contribution to institutional goals specific; and (c) foster mutual accountability for goal achievement.

To accomplish these objectives, it is recognized that the member and the employer must share responsibilities in the formulation and implementation of personnel policies.

1. Members must define and describe the parameters and levels of their professional competency.

2. Members must establish interpersonal relations and working agreements with supervisors and subordinates regarding counseling or clinical relationships, confidentiality, distinction between public and private material, maintenance, and dissemination of recorded information, work load and accountability. Working agreements in each instance must be specified and made known to those concerned.

3. Members must alert their employers to conditions that may be potentially disruptive or damaging.

4. Members must inform employers of conditions that may limit their effectiveness.

5. Members must submit regularly to professional review and evaluation.

6. Members must be responsible for inservice development of self and/or staff.

7. Members must inform their staff of goals and programs.

8. Members must provide personnel practices that guarantee and enhance the rights and welfare of each recipient of their service.

9. Members must select competent persons and assign responsibilities compatible with their skills and experiences.

Section H: Preparation Standards

Members who are responsible for training others must be guided by the preparation standards of the

Association and relevant Division(s). The member who functions in the capacity of trainer assumes unique ethical responsibilities that frequently go beyond that of the member who does not function in a training capacity. These ethical responsibilities are outlined as follows:

1. Members must orient students to program expectations, basic skills development, and employment prospects prior to admission to the program.

2. Members in charge of learning experiences must establish programs that integrate academic study and supervised practice.

3. Members must establish a program directed toward developing students' skills, knowledge, and self-understanding, stated whenever possible in competency or performance terms.

4. Members must identify the levels of competencies of their students in compliance with relevant Division standards. These competencies must accommodate the para-professional as well as the professional.

5. Members, through continual student evaluation and appraisal, must be aware of the personal limitations of the learner that might impede future performance. The instructor must not only assist the learner in securing remedial assistance but also screen from the program those individuals who are unable to provide competent services.

6. Members must provide a program that includes training in research commensurate with levels of role functioning. Para-professional and technician-level personnel must be trained as consumers of research. In addition, these personnel must learn how to evaluate their own and their program's effectiveness. Graduate training, espe-cially at the doctoral level, would include preparation for original research by the member.

7. Members must make students aware of the ethical responsibilities and standards of the profession.

8. Preparatory programs must encourage students to value the ideals of service to individuals and to society. In this regard, direct financial remuneration or lack thereof must not influence the quality of service rendered. Monetary considerations must not be allowed to overshadow professional and humanitarian needs.

9. Members responsible for educational programs must be skilled as teachers and practitioners.

10. Members must present thoroughly varied theoretical positions so that students may make comparisons and have the opportunity to select a position.

11. Members must develop clear policies within their educational institutions regarding field placement and the roles of the student and the instructor in such placements.

12. Members must ensure that forms of learning focusing on self-understanding or growth are voluntary, or if required as part of the education program, are made known to prospective students prior to entering the program. When the education program offers a growth experience with an emphasis on self-disclosure or other relatively intimate or personal involvement, the member must have no administrative, supervisory, or evaluating authority regarding the participant.

13. Members must conduct an educational program in keeping with the current relevant guidelines of the American Personnel and Guidance Association and its Divisions.

ETHICAL PRINCIPLES OF PSYCHOLOGISTS, AMERICAN PSYCHOLOGICAL ASSOCIATION*

APPENDIX B □ PREAMBLE

Psychologists respect the dignity and worth of the individual and strive for the preservation and protection of fundamental human rights. They are committed to increasing knowledge of human behavior and of people's understanding of themselves and others and to the utilization of such knowledge for the promotion of human welfare. While pursuing these objectives, they make every effort to protect the welfare of those who seek their services and of the research participants that may be the object of study. They use their skills only for purposes consistent with these values and do not knowingly permit their misuse by others. While demanding for themselves freedom of inquiry and communication, psychologists accept the responsibility this freedom requires: competence, objectivity in the application of skills, and concern for the best interests of clients, colleagues, students, research participants, and society. In the pursuit of these ideals, psychologists subscribe to principles in the following areas: 1. Responsibility, 2. Competence, 3. Moral and Legal Standards, 4. Public Statements, 5. Confidentiality, 6. Welfare of the Consumer, 7. Professional Relationships, 8. Assessment Techniques, 9. Research with Human Participants, and 10. Care and Use of Animals.

* *Ethical Principles of Psychologists* (revised edition), by the American Psychological Association. Copyright 1981 by the American Psychological Association. Reprinted by permission of the publisher.

This version of the *Ethical Principles of Psychologists* (formerly entitled *Ethical Standards of Psychologists*) was adopted by the American Psychological Association's Council of Representatives on January 24, 1981. The revised *Ethical Principles* contain both substantive and grammatical changes in each of the nine ethical principles constituting the *Ethical Standards of Psychologists* previously adopted by the Council of Representatives in 1979, plus a new tenth principle entitled "Care and Use of Animals." Inquiries concerning the *Ethical Principles of Psychologists* should be addressed to the Administrative Officer for Ethics, American Psychological Association, 1200 Seventeenth Street, N.W., Washington, D.C. 20036.

Acceptance of membership in the American Psychological Association commits the member to adherence to these principles.

Psychologists cooperate with duly constituted committees of the American Psychological Association, in particular, the Committee on Scientific and Professional Ethics and Conduct, by responding to inquiries promptly and completely. Members also respond promptly and completely to inquiries from duly constituted state association ethics committees and professional standards review committees.

Principle 1: Responsibility

In providing services, psychologists maintain the highest standards of their profession. They accept responsibility for the consequences of their acts and make every effort to ensure that their services are used appropriately.

a. As scientists, psychologists accept responsibility for the selection of their research topics and the methods used in investigation, analysis, and reporting. They plan their research in ways to minimize the possibility that their findings will be misleading. They provide thorough discussion of the limitations of their data, especially where their work touches on social policy or might be construed to the detriment of persons in specific age, sex, ethnic, socioeconomic, or other social groups. In publishing reports of their work, they never suppress disconfirming data, and they acknowledge the existence of alternative hypotheses and explanations of their findings. Psychologists take credit only for work they have actually done.

b. Psychologists clarify in advance with all appropriate persons and agencies the expectations for sharing and utilizing research data. They avoid relationships that may limit their objectivity or create a conflict of interest. Interference with the milieu in which data are collected is kept to a minimum.

c. Psychologists have the responsibility to attempt to prevent distortion, misuse, or suppression of psychological findings by the institution or agency of which they are employees.

d. As members of governmental or other organizational bodies, psychologists remain accountable as individuals to the highest standards of their profession.

e. As teachers, psychologists recognize their primary obligation to help others acquire knowledge and skill. They maintain high standards of scholarship by presenting psychological information objectively, fully, and accurately.

f. As practitioners, psychologists know that they bear a heavy social responsibility because their recommendations and professional actions may alter the lives of others. They are alert to personal, social, organizational, financial, or political situations and pressures that might lead to misuse of their influence.

Principle 2: Competence

The maintenance of high standards of competence is a responsibility shared by all psychologists in the interest of the public and the profession as a whole. Psychologists recognize the boundaries of their competence and the limitations of their techniques. They only provide services and only use techniques for which they are qualified by training and experience. In those areas in which recognized standards do not yet exist, psychologists take whatever precautions are necessary to protect the welfare of their clients. They maintain knowledge of current scientific and professional information related to the services they render.

a. Psychologists accurately represent their competence, education, training, and experience. They claim as evidence of educational qualifications only those degrees obtained from institutions acceptable under the Bylaws and Rules of the Council of the American Psychological Association.

b. As teachers, psychologists perform their duties on the basis of careful preparation so that their instruction is accurate, current, and scholarly.

c. Psychologists recognize the need for continuing education and are open to new procedures and changes in expectations and values over time.

d. Psychologists recognize differences among people, such as those that may be associated with age, sex, socioeconomic, and ethnic backgrounds. When necessary, they obtain training, experience, or counsel to assure competent service or research relating to such persons.

e. Psychologists responsible for decisions involving individuals or policies based on test results have an understanding of psychological or educational measurement, validation problems, and test research.

f. Psychologists recognize that personal problems and conflicts may interfere with professional effectiveness. Accordingly, they refrain from undertaking any activity in which their personal problems are likely to lead to inadequate performance or harm to a client, colleague, student, or research participant. If engaged in such activity when they become aware of their personal problems, they seek competent professional assistance to determine whether they should suspend, terminate, or limit the scope of their professional and/or scientific activities.

Principle 3: Moral and Legal Standards

Psychologists' moral and ethical standards of behavior are a personal matter to the same degree as they are for any other citizen, except as these may compromise the fulfillment of their professional responsibilities or reduce the public trust in psychology and psychologists. Regarding their own behavior, psychologists are sensitive to prevailing community standards and to the possible impact that conformity to or deviation from these standards may have upon the quality of their performance as psychologists. Psychologists are also aware of the possible impact of their public behavior upon the ability of colleagues to perform their professional duties.

a. As teachers, psychologists are aware of the fact that their personal values may affect the selection and presentation of instructional materials. When dealing with topics that may give offense, they recognize and respect the diverse attitudes that students may have toward such materials.

b. As employees or employers, psychologists do not engage in or condone practices that are inhumane or that result in illegal or unjustifiable actions. Such practices include, but are not limited to, those based on considerations of race, handicap, age, gender, sexual preference, religion, or national origin in hiring, promotion, or training.

c. In their professional roles, psychologists avoid any action that will violate or diminish the legal and civil rights of clients or of others who may be affected by their actions.

d. As practitioners and researchers, psychologists act in accord with Association standards and guidelines related to practice and to the conduct of research with human beings and animals. In the ordinary course of events, psychologists adhere to relevant governmental laws and institutional regulations. When federal, state, provincial, organiza-

tional, or institutional laws, regulations, or practices are in conflict with Association standards and guidelines, psychologists make known their commitment to Association standards and guidelines and, wherever possible, work toward a resolution of the conflict. Both practitioners and researchers are concerned with the development of such legal and quasi-legal regulations as best serve the public interest, and they work toward changing existing regulations that are not beneficial to the public interest.

Principle 4: Public Statements

Public statements, announcements of services, advertising, and promotional activities of psychologists serve the purpose of helping the public make informed judgments and choices. Psychologists represent accurately and objectively their professional qualifications, affiliations, and functions, as well as those of the institutions or organizations with which they or the statements may be associated. In public statements providing psychological information or professional opinions or providing information about the availability of psychological products, publications, and services, psychologists base their statements on scientifically acceptable psychological findings and techniques with full recognition of the limits and uncertainties of such evidence.

a. When announcing or advertising professional services, psychologists may list the following information to describe the provider and services provided: name, highest relevant academic degree earned from a regionally accredited institution, date, type, and level of certification or licensure, diplomate status, APA membership status, address, telephone number, office hours, a brief listing of the type of psychological services offered, an appropriate presentation of fee information, foreign languages spoken, and policy with regard to third-party payments. Additional relevant or important consumer information may be included if not prohibited by other sections of these Ethical Principles.

b. In announcing or advertising the availability of psychological products, publications, or services, psychologists do not present their affiliation with any organization in a manner that falsely implies sponsorship or certification by that organization. In particular and for example, psychologists do not state APA membership or fellow status in a way to suggest that such status implies specialized professional competence or qualifications. Public statements include, but are not limited to, communication by means of periodical, book, list, directory, television, radio, or motion picture. They do not contain (i) a false, fraudulent, misleading, deceptive, or unfair statement; (ii) a misinterpretation of fact or a statement likely to mislead or deceive because in context it makes only a partial disclosure of relevant facts; (iii) a testimonial from a patient regarding the quality of a psychologist's services or products; (iv) a statement intended or likely to create false or unjustified expectations of favorable results; (v) a statement implying unusual, unique, or one-of-a-kind abilities; (vi) a statement intended or likely to appeal to a client's fears, anxieties, or emotions concerning the possible results of failure to obtain the offered services; (vii) a statement concerning the comparative desirability of offered services; (viii) a statement of direct solicitation of individual clients.

c. Psychologists do not compensate or give anything of value to a representative of the press, radio, television, or other communication medium in anticipation of or in return for professional publicity in a news item. A paid advertisement must be identified as such, unless it is apparent from the context that it is a paid advertisement. If communicated to the public by use of radio or television, an advertisement is prerecorded and approved for broadcast by the psychologist, and a recording of the actual transmission is retained by the psychologist.

d. Announcements or advertisements of "personal growth groups," clinics, and agencies give a clear statement of purpose and a clear description of the experiences to be provided. The education, training, and experience of the staff members are appropriately specified.

e. Psychologists associated with the development or promotion of psychological devices, books, or other products offered for commercial sale make reasonable efforts to ensure that announcements and advertisements are presented in a professional, scientifically acceptable, and factually informative manner.

f. Psychologists do not participate for personal gain in commercial announcements or advertisements recommending to the public the purchase or use of proprietary or single-source products or services when that participation is based solely upon their identification as psychologists.

g. Psychologists present the science of psychology and offer their services, products, and publications fairly and accurately, avoiding misrepresentation through sensationalism, exaggeration, or superficiality. Psychologists are guided by the primary obligation to aid the public in developing informed judgments, opinions, and choices.

h. As teachers, psychologists ensure that statements in catalogs and course outlines are accurate and not misleading, particularly in terms of subject matter to be covered, bases for evaluating progress, and the nature of course experiences. Announcements, brochures, or advertisements describing workshops, seminars, or other educational programs accurately describe the audience for which the program is intended as well as eligibility requirements, educational objectives, and nature of the materials to be covered. These announcements also accurately represent the education, training, and experience of the psychologists presenting the programs and any fees involved.

i. Public announcements or advertisements soliciting research participants in which clinical services or other professional services are offered as an inducement make clear the nature of the services as well as the costs and other obligations to be accepted by participants in the research.

j. A psychologist accepts the obligation to correct others who represent the psychologist's professional qualifications, or associations with products or services, in a manner incompatible with these guidelines.

k. Individual diagnostic and therapeutic services are provided only in the context of a professional psychological relationship. When personal advice is given by means of public lectures or demonstrations, newspaper or magazine articles, radio or television programs, mail, or similar media, the psychologist utilizes the most current relevant data and exercises the highest level of professional judgment.

l. Products that are described or presented by means of public lectures or demonstrations, newspaper or magazine articles, radio or television programs, or similar media meet the same recognized standards as exist for products used in the context of a professional relationship.

Principle 5: Confidentiality

Psychologists have a primary obligation to respect the confidentiality of information obtained from persons in the course of their work as psychologists.

They reveal such information to others only with the consent of the person or the person's legal representative, except in those unusual circumstances in which not to do so would result in clear danger to the person or to others. Where appropriate, psychologists inform their clients of the legal limits of confidentiality.

a. Information obtained in clinical or consulting relationships, or evaluative data concerning children, students, employees, and others, is discussed only for professional purposes and only with persons clearly concerned with the case. Written and oral reports present only data germane to the purposes of the evaluation, and every effort is made to avoid undue invasion of privacy.

b. Psychologists who present personal information obtained during the course of professional work in writings, lectures, or other public forums either obtain adequate prior consent to do so or adequately disguise all identifying information.

c. Psychologists make provisions for maintaining confidentiality in the storage and disposal of records.

d. When working with minors or other persons who are unable to give voluntary, informed consent, psychologists take special care to protect these persons' best interests.

Principle 6: Welfare of the Consumer

Psychologists respect the integrity and protect the welfare of the people and groups with whom they work. When conflicts of interest arise between clients and psychologists' employing institutions, psychologists clarify the nature and direction of their loyalties and responsibilities and keep all parties informed of their commitments. Psychologists fully inform consumers as to the purpose and nature of an evaluative, treatment, educational, or training procedure, and they freely acknowledge that clients, students, or participants in research have freedom of choice with regard to participation.

a. Psychologists are continually cognizant of their own needs and of their potentially influential position vis-à-vis persons such as clients, students, and subordinates. They avoid exploiting the trust and dependency of such persons. Psychologists make every effort to avoid dual relationships that could impair their professional judgment or increase the risk of exploitation. Examples of such dual relationships include, but are not limited to,

research with and treatment of employees, students, supervisees, close friends, or relatives. Sexual intimacies with clients are unethical.

b. When a psychologist agrees to provide services to a client at the request of a third party, the psychologist assumes the responsibility of clarifying the nature of the relationships to all parties concerned.

c. Where the demands of an organization require psychologists to violate these Ethical Principles, psychologists clarify the nature of the conflict between the demands and these principles. They inform all parties of psychologists' ethical responsibilities and take appropriate action.

d. Psychologists make advance financial arrangements that safeguard the best interests of and are clearly understood by their clients. They neither give nor receive any remuneration for referring clients for professional services. They contribute a portion of their services to work for which they receive little or no financial return.

e. Psychologists terminate a clinical or consulting relationship when it is reasonably clear that the consumer is not benefiting from it. They offer to help the consumer locate alternative sources of assistance.

Principle 7: Professional Relationships

Psychologists act with due regard for the needs, special competencies, and obligations of their colleagues in psychology and other professions. They respect the prerogatives and obligations of the institutions or organizations with which these other colleagues are associated.

a. Psychologists understand the areas of competence of related professions. They make full use of all the professional, technical, and administrative resources that serve the best interests of consumers. The absence of formal relationships with other professional workers does not relieve psychologists of the responsibility of securing for their clients the best possible professional service, nor does it relieve them of the obligation to exercise foresight, diligence, and tact in obtaining the complementary or alternative assistance needed by clients.

b. Psychologists know and take into account the traditions and practices of other professional groups with whom they work and cooperate fully with such groups. If a person is receiving similar services from another professional, psychologists do not offer their own services directly to such a person. If a psychologist is contacted by a person who is already receiving similar services from another professional, the psychologist carefully considers that professional relationship and proceeds with caution and sensitivity to the therapeutic issues as well as the client's welfare. The psychologist discusses these issues with the client so as to minimize the risk of confusion and conflict.

c. Psychologists who employ or supervise other professionals or professionals in training accept the obligation to facilitate the further professional development of these individuals. They provide appropriate working conditions, timely evaluations, constructive consultation, and experience opportunities.

d. Psychologists do not exploit their professional relationships with clients, supervisees, students, employees, or research participants sexually or otherwise. Psychologists do not condone or engage in sexual harassment. Sexual harassment is defined as deliberate or repeated comments, gestures, or physical contacts of a sexual nature that are unwanted by the recipient.

e. In conducting research in institutions or organizations, psychologists secure appropriate authorization to conduct such research. They are aware of their obligations to future research workers and ensure that host institutions receive adequate information about the research and proper acknowledgment of their contributions.

f. Publication credit is assigned to those who have contributed to a publication in proportion to their professional contributions. Major contributions of a professional character made by several persons to a common project are recognized by joint authorship, with the individual who made the principal contribution listed first. Minor contributions of a professional character and extensive clerical or similar nonprofessional assistance may be acknowledged in footnotes or in an introductory statement. Acknowledgment through specific citations is made for unpublished as well as published material that has directly influenced the research or writing. Psychologists who compile and edit material of others for publication publish the material in the name of the originating group, if appropriate, with their own name appearing as chairperson or editor. All contributors are to be acknowledged and named.

g. When psychologists know of an ethical violation by another psychologist, and it seems appropriate, they informally attempt to resolve the issue by bringing the behavior to the attention of the psychologist. If the misconduct is of a minor nature and/or appears to be due to lack of sensitivity, knowledge, or experience, such an informal solution is usually appropriate. Such informal corrective efforts are made with sensitivity to any rights to confidentiality involved. If the violation does not seem amenable to an informal solution, or is of a more serious nature, psychologists bring it to the attention of the appropriate local, state, and/or national committee on professional ethics and conduct.

Principle 8: Assessment Techniques

In the development, publication, and utilization of psychological assessment techniques, psychologists make every effort to promote the welfare and best interests of the client. They guard against the misuse of assessment results. They respect the client's right to know the results, the interpretations made, and the bases for their conclusions and recommendations. Psychologists make every effort to maintain the security of tests and other assessment techniques within limits of legal mandates. They strive to ensure the appropriate use of assessment techniques by others.

a. In using assessment techniques, psychologists respect the right of clients to have full explanations of the nature and purpose of the techniques in language the clients can understand, unless an explicit exception to this right has been agreed upon in advance. When the explanations are to be provided by others, psychologists establish procedures for ensuring the adequacy of these explanations.

b. Psychologists responsible for the development and standardization of psychological tests and other assessment techniques utilize established scientific procedures and observe the relevant APA standards.

c. In reporting assessment results, psychologists indicate any reservations that exist regarding validity or reliability because of the circumstances of the assessment or the inappropriateness of the norms for the person tested. Psychologists strive to ensure that the results of assessments and their interpretations are not misused by others.

d. Psychologists recognize that assessment results may become obsolete. They make every effort to avoid and prevent the misuse of obsolete measures.

e. Psychologists offering scoring and interpretation services are able to produce appropriate evidence for the validity of the programs and procedures used in arriving at interpretations. The public offering of an automated interpretation service is considered a professional-to-professional consultation. Psychologists make every effort to avoid misuse of assessment reports.

f. Psychologists do not encourage or promote the use of psychological assessment techniques by inappropriately trained or otherwise unqualified persons through teaching, sponsorship, or supervision.

Principle 9: Research with Human Participants

The decision to undertake research rests upon a considered judgment by the individual psychologist about how best to contribute to psychological science and human welfare. Having made the decision to conduct research, the psychologist considers alternative directions in which research energies and resources might be invested. On the basis of this consideration, the psychologist carries out the investigation with respect and concern for the dignity and welfare of the people who participate and with cognizance of federal and state regulations and professional standards governing the conduct of research with human participants.

a. In planning a study, the investigator has the responsibility to make a careful evaluation of its ethical acceptability. To the extent that the weighing of scientific and human values suggests a compromise of any principle, the investigator incurs a correspondingly serious obligation to seek ethical advice and to observe stringent safeguards to protect the rights of human participants.

b. Considering whether a participant in a planned study will be a "subject at risk" or a "subject at minimal risk," according to recognized standards, is of primary ethical concern to the investigator.

c. The investigator always retains the responsibility for ensuring ethical practice in research. The investigator is also responsible for the ethical treatment of research participants by collaborators, assistants, students, and employees, all of whom, however, incur similar obligations.

d. Except in minimal-risk research, the investigator establishes a clear and fair agreement with research participants, prior to their participation, that clarifies the obligations and responsibilities of each. The investigator has the obligation to honor all promises and commitments included in that agreement. The investigator informs the participants of all aspects of the research that might reasonably be expected to influence willingness to participate and explains all other aspects of the research about which the participants inquire. Failure to make full disclosure prior to obtaining informed consent requires additional safeguards to protect the welfare and dignity of the research participants. Research with children or with participants who have impairments that would limit understanding and/or communication requires special safeguarding procedures.

e. Methodological requirements of a study may make the use of concealment or deception necessary. Before conducting such a study, the investigator has a special responsibility to (i) determine whether the use of such techniques is justified by the study's prospective scientific, educational, or applied value; (ii) determine whether alternative procedures are available that do not use concealment or deception; and (iii) ensure that the participants are provided with sufficient explanation as soon as possible.

f. The investigator respects the individual's freedom to decline to participate in or to withdraw from the research at any time. The obligation to protect this freedom requires careful thought and consideration when the investigator is in a position of authority or influence over the participant. Such positions of authority include, but are not limited to, situations in which research participation is required as part of employment or in which the participant is a student, client, or employee of the investigator.

g. The investigator protects the participant from physical and mental discomfort, harm, and danger that may arise from research procedures. If risks of such consequences exist, the investigator informs the participant of that fact. Research procedures likely to cause serious or lasting harm to a participant are not used unless the failure to use these procedures might expose the participant to risk of greater harm, or unless the research has great potential benefit and fully informed and voluntary consent is obtained from each participant. The participant should be informed of procedures for contacting the investigator within a reasonable time period following participation should stress, potential harm, or related questions or concerns arise.

h. After the data are collected, the investigator provides the participant with information about the nature of the study and attempts to remove any misconceptions that may have arisen. Where scientific or humane values justify delaying or withholding this information, the investigator incurs a special responsibility to monitor the research and to ensure that there are no damaging consequences for the participant.

i. Where research procedures result in undesirable consequences for the individual participant, the investigator has the responsibility to detect and remove or correct these consequences, including long-term effects.

j. Information obtained about a research participant during the course of an investigation is confidential unless otherwise agreed upon in advance. When the possibility exists that others may obtain access to such information, this possibility, together with the plans for protecting confidentiality, is explained to the participant as part of the procedure for obtaining informed consent.

Principle 10: Care and Use of Animals

An investigator of animal behavior strives to advance understanding of basic behavioral principles and/or to contribute to the improvement of human health and welfare. In seeking these ends, the investigator ensures the welfare of animals and treats them humanely. Laws and regulations notwithstanding, an animal's immediate protection depends upon the scientist's own conscience.

a. The acquisition, care, use, and disposal of all animals are in compliance with current federal, state or provincial, and local laws and regulations.

b. A psychologist trained in research methods and experienced in the care of laboratory animals closely supervises all procedures involving animals and is responsible for ensuring appropriate consideration of their comfort, health, and humane treatment.

c. Psychologists ensure that all individuals using animals under their supervision have received explicit instruction in experimental methods and in the care, maintenance, and handling of the species being used. Responsibilities and activities of individuals participating in a research project are consistent with their respective competencies.

d. Psychologists make every effort to minimize discomfort, illness, and pain of animals. A procedure subjecting animals to pain, stress, or deprivation is used only when an alternative procedure is unavailable and the goal is justified by its prospective scientific, educational, or applied value. Surgical procedures are performed under appropriate anesthesia; techniques to avoid infection and minimize pain are followed during and after surgery.

e. When it is appropriate that the animal's life be terminated, it is done rapidly and painlessly.

CODE OF ETHICS, NATIONAL ASSOCIATION OF SOCIAL WORKERS*

APPENDIX C □ I. THE SOCIAL WORKER'S CONDUCT AND COMPORTMENT AS A SOCIAL WORKER

A. *Propriety.* The social worker should maintain high standards of personal conduct in the capacity or identity as social worker.
   1. The private conduct of the social worker is a personal matter to the same degree as is any other person's, except when such conduct compromises the fulfillment of professional responsibilities.
   2. The social worker should not participate in, condone, or be associated with dishonesty, fraud, deceit, or misrepresentation.
   3. The social worker should distinguish clearly between statements and actions made as a private individual and as a representative of the social work profession or an organization or group.

B. *Competence and professional development.* The social worker should strive to become and remain proficient in professional practice and the performance of professional functions.
   1. The social worker should accept responsibility or employment only on the basis of existing competence or the intention to acquire the necessary competence.
   2. The social worker should not misrepresent professional qualifications, education, experience, or affiliations.

C. *Service.* The social worker should regard as primary the service obligation of the social work profession.
   1. The social worker should retain ultimate responsibility for the quality and extent of the service that individual assumes, assigns, or performs.
   2. The social worker should act to prevent practices that are inhumane or discriminatory against any person or group of persons.

* Code of Ethics of the National Association of Social Workers, as adopted by the 1979 NASW Delegate Assembly, effective July 1, 1980. Reprinted by permission.

D. *Integrity.* The social worker should act in accordance with the highest standards of professional integrity and impartiality.
   1. The social worker should be alert to and resist the influences and pressures that interfere with the exercise of professional discretion and impartial judgment required for the performance of professional functions.
   2. The social worker should not exploit professional relationships for personal gain.
E. *Scholarship and research.* The social worker engaged in study and research should be guided by the conventions of scholarly inquiry.
   1. The social worker engaged in research should consider carefully its possible consequences for human beings.
   2. The social worker engaged in research should ascertain that the consent of participants in the research is voluntary and informed, without any implied deprivation or penalty for refusal to participate, and with due regard for participants' privacy and dignity.
   3. The social worker engaged in research should protect participants from unwarranted physical or mental discomfort, distress, harm, danger, or deprivation.
   4. The social worker who engages in the evaluation of services or cases should discuss them only for the professional purposes and only with persons directly and professionally concerned with them.
   5. Information obtained about participants in research should be treated as confidential.
   6. The social worker should take credit only for work actually done in connection with scholarly and research endeavors and credit contributions made by others.

☐ II. THE SOCIAL WORKER'S ETHICAL RESPONSIBILITY TO CLIENTS

F. *Primacy of clients' interests.* The social worker's primary responsibility is to clients.
   1. The social worker should serve clients with devotion, loyalty, determination, and the maximum application of professional skill and competence.
   2. The social worker should not exploit relationships with clients for personal advantage, or solicit the clients of one's agency for private practice.
   3. The social worker should not practice, condone, facilitate, or collaborate with any form of discrimination on the basis of race, color, sex, sexual orientation, age, religion, national origin, marital status, political belief, mental or physical handicap, or any other preference or personal characteristic, condition, or status.
   4. The social worker should avoid relationships or commitments that conflict with the interests of clients.
   5. The social worker should under no circumstances engage in sexual activities with clients.
   6. The social worker should provide clients with accurate and complete information regarding the extent and nature of the services available to them.
   7. The social worker should apprise clients of their risks, rights, opportunities, and obligations associated with social service to them.
   8. The social worker should seek advice and counsel of colleagues and supervisors whenever such consultation is in the best interest of clients.
   9. The social worker should terminate service to clients, and professional relationships with them, when such service and relationships are no longer required or no longer serve the clients' needs or interests.
   10. The social worker should withdraw services precipitously only under unusual circumstances, giving careful consideration to all factors in the situation and taking care to minimize possible adverse effects.
   11. The social worker who anticipates the termination or interruption of service to clients should notify clients promptly and seek the transfer, referral, or continuation of services in relation to the clients' needs and preferences.
G. *Rights and prerogatives of clients.* The social worker should make every effort to foster maximum self-determination on the part of clients.
   1. When the social worker must act on behalf of a client who has been adjudged legally

incompetent, the social worker should safeguard the interests and rights of that client.

2. When another individual has been legally authorized to act in behalf of a client, the social worker should deal with that person always with the client's best interest in mind.

3. The social worker should not engage in any action that violates or diminishes the civil or legal rights of clients.

H. *Confidentiality and privacy.* The social worker should respect the privacy of clients and hold in confidence all information obtained in the course of professional service.

1. The social worker should share with others confidences revealed by clients, without their consent, only for compelling professional reasons.

2. The social worker should inform clients fully about the limits of confidentiality in a given situation, the purposes for which information is obtained, and how it may be used.

3. The social worker should afford clients reasonable access to any official social work records concerning them.

4. When providing clients with access to records, the social worker should take due care to protect the confidences of others contained in those records.

5. The social worker should obtain informed consent of clients before taping, recording, or permitting third party observation of their activities.

I. *Fees.* When setting fees, the social worker should ensure that they are fair, reasonable, considerate, and commensurate with the service performed and with due regard for the clients' ability to pay.

1. The social worker should not divide a fee or accept or give anything of value for receiving or making a referral.

☐ III. THE SOCIAL WORKER'S ETHICAL RESPONSIBILITY TO COLLEAGUES

J. *Respect, fairness, and courtesy.* The social worker should treat colleagues with respect, courtesy, fairness, and good faith.

1. The social worker should cooperate with colleagues to promote professional interests and concerns.

2. The social worker should respect confidences shared by colleagues in the course of their professional relationships and transactions.

3. The social worker should create and maintain conditions of practice that facilitate ethical and competent professional performance by colleagues.

4. The social worker should treat with respect, and represent accurately and fairly, the qualifications, views, and findings of colleagues and use appropriate channels to express judgments on these matters.

5. The social worker who replaces or is replaced by a colleague in professional practice should act with consideration for the interest, character, and reputation of that colleague.

6. The social worker should not exploit a dispute, between a colleague and employers to obtain a position or otherwise advance the social worker's interest.

7. The social worker should seek arbitration or mediation resolution for compelling professional reasons.

8. The social worker should extend to colleagues of other professions the same respect and cooperation that is extended to social work colleagues.

9. The social worker who serves as an employer, supervisor, or mentor to colleagues should make orderly and explicit arrangements regarding the conditions of their continuing professional relationship.

10. The social worker who has the responsibility for employing and evaluating the performance of other staff members should fulfill such responsibility in a fair, considerate, and equitable manner, on the basis of clearly enunciated criteria.

11. The social worker who has the responsibility for evaluating the performance of employees, supervisees, or students should share evaluations with them.

K. *Dealing with colleagues' clients.* The social worker has the responsibility to relate to the clients of colleagues with full professional consideration.

1. The social worker should not solicit the clients of colleagues.

2. The social worker should not assume pro-

fessional responsibility for the clients of another agency or a colleague without appropriate communication with that agency or colleague.

3. The social worker who serves the clients of colleagues, during a temporary absence or emergency, should serve those clients with the same consideration as that afforded any client.

☐ IV. THE SOCIAL WORKER'S ETHICAL RESPONSIBILITY TO EMPLOYERS AND EMPLOYING ORGANIZATIONS

L. *Commitments to employing organization.* The social worker should adhere to commitments made to the employing organization.

1. The social worker should work to improve the employing agency's policies and procedures, and the efficiency and effectiveness of its services.

2. The social worker should not accept employment or arrange student field placements in an organization which is currently under public sanction by NASW for violating personnel standards, or imposing limitations on or penalties for professional actions on behalf of clients.

3. The social worker should act to prevent and eliminate discrimination in the employing organization's work assignments and in its employment policies and practices.

4. The social worker should use with scrupulous regard, and only for the purpose for which they are intended, the resources of the employing organization.

☐ V. THE SOCIAL WORKER'S ETHICAL RESPONSIBILITY TO THE SOCIAL WORK PROFESSION

M. *Maintaining the integrity of the profession.* The social worker should uphold and advance the values, ethics, knowledge, and mission of the profession.

1. The social worker should protect and enhance the dignity and integrity of the profession and should be responsible and vigorous in discussion and criticism of the profession.

2. The social worker should take action through appropriate channels against unethical conduct by any other member of the profession.

3. The social worker should act to prevent the unauthorized and unqualified practice of social work.

4. The social worker should make no misrepresentation in advertising as to qualifications, competence, service, or results to be achieved.

N. *Community service.* The social worker should assist the profession in making social services available to the general public.

1. The social worker should contribute time and professional expertise to activities that promote respect for the utility, the integrity, and the competence of the social work profession.

2. The social worker should support the formulation, development, enactment, and implementation of social policies of concern to the profession.

O. *Development of knowledge.* The social worker should take responsibility for identifying, developing, and fully utilizing knowledge for professional practice.

1. The social worker should base practice upon recognized knowledge relevant to social work.

2. The social worker should critically examine and keep current with emerging knowledge relevant to social work.

3. The social worker should contribute to the knowledge base of social work and share research knowledge and practice wisdom with colleagues.

☐ VI. THE SOCIAL WORKER'S ETHICAL RESPONSIBILITY TO SOCIETY

P. *Promoting the general welfare.* The social worker should promote the general welfare of society.

1. The social worker should act to prevent and eliminate discrimination against any person or group on the basis of race, color, sex, sexual orientation, age, religion, national origin, marital status, political belief, mental or physical handicap, or any other

preference or personal characteristic, condition, or status.

2. The social worker should act to ensure that all persons have access to the resources, services, and opportunities which they require.

3. The social worker should act to expand choice and opportunity for all persons, with special regard for disadvantaged or oppressed groups and persons.

4. The social worker should promote conditions that encourage respect for the diversity of cultures which constitute American society.

5. The social worker should provide appropriate professional services in public emergencies.

6. The social worker should advocate changes in policy and legislation to improve social conditions and to promote social justice.

7. The social worker should encourage informed participation by the public in shaping social policies and institutions.

STANDARDS FOR THE PRIVATE PRACTICE OF CLINICAL SOCIAL WORK, NATIONAL ASSOCIATION OF SOCIAL WORKERS*

APPENDIX D □ QUALIFICATIONS FOR THE CLINICAL SOCIAL WORKER IN PRIVATE PRACTICE

I. The clinical social worker in private practice shall meet the educational and practice requirements of the National Association of Social Workers, shall maintain current knowledge of scientific and professional developments, and shall obtain additional training when required for effective practice.

A. The practitioner shall have a Master's or Doctoral degree from an accredited school of social work plus two years or 3,000 hours of postdegree direct practice experience, supervised by a Master's level clinical social worker, in a hospital, clinic, agency, or other institutional setting.

B. The practitioner shall abide by NASW's continuing education requirements and other standards relating to competence in clinical practice which shall be established by the Association.

C. The clinical social worker practicing privately for the first time should obtain consultation from an experienced clinical social worker.

D. The practitioner shall limit the practice to demonstrated areas of professional competence.

E. When using specialized methods of practice which range beyond those normally learned in a school of social work or social work practice setting, the practitioner shall obtain training or professional supervision in the modalities employed.

* *Standards for the Private Practice of Clinical Social Work,* by the National Association of Social Workers (draft of April 22, 1981). Reprinted with permission from the NASW Policy Statement Series.

☐ LEGAL ASPECTS OF PRIVATE CLINICAL PRACTICE

II. The clinical social worker in private practice shall comply with the laws of the jurisdiction within which s/he practices. The practitioner shall adhere to the educational, experiential, and other practice requirements of law in those jurisdictions which regulate clinical social work.

☐ PROFESSIONAL IDENTIFICATION AND COMMITMENT

III. The privately practicing clinician whose training is in social work: (a) identifies himself/herself as a member of the social work profession, regardless of clinical orientation; and (b) is committed to the profession.
  A. Commitment to the profession is demonstrated through organizational participation, teaching, writing, and other activities.
  B. The practitioner should belong to the NASW, ACSW, the NASW Register of Clinical Social Workers and shall adhere to the NASW Code of Ethics.
  C. The privately practicing clinical social worker, like all social workers, should seek modification within the client and within those societal systems and institutions which affect the client.
  D. The practitioner shall be subject to NASW standards and grievance procedures and to peer and utilization review depending upon state and local law and customary professional practice.

☐ THE MAINTENANCE OF CONFIDENTIALITY

IV. The clinical social worker in private practice shall abide by the provisions of confidentiality in the NASW Code of Ethics. (See Appendix C.)
  A. The social worker should share with others confidences revealed by clients, without their consent, only for compelling professional reasons.
    1. The clinical social worker in private practice may find it necessary to reveal confidential information disclosed by the patient to protect the patient or the community from imminent danger.
    2. When the clinical social worker in private practice is ordered by the court to reveal the confidences entrusted by patients, the practitioner may comply or may ethically hold the right to dissent within the framework of the law.

☐ THE MANAGEMENT ASPECTS OF A PRIVATE CLINICAL PRACTICE

V. To render the best possible service to the client, the clinical social worker shall be capable of managing the business aspects of a private practice.
  A. The clinical practitioner shall be familiar with relevant state and local laws on the conduct of a business.
  B. The practitioner should carry malpractice and premises liability insurance.
  C. The practitioner shall deal expediently and efficiently with insurance companies covering clinical social work services. This includes maintenance of records and the use of diagnostic categories in billing private and governmental carriers.
  D. The private practitioner and client shall agree to a contract during the initial visit(s). Conditions of the contract shall be clear and explicit. These shall include:
    1. Agreement about fees; insurance; length, frequency, and location of sessions; appointments missed or cancelled without adequate notice; vacation coverage during an absence; collateral contacts. (The foregoing information may be provided on a standardized form.)
    2. Agreement regarding goals of treatment.
    3. Informing the client of his/her rights.
  E. Private clinical practitioners shall keep up-to-date, accurate records on the treatment of the client. (Records should protect confidentiality while recording subjects discussed in sufficient detail to justify therapeutic action.)
  F. Offices in which services are rendered

shall be located for client safety, accessibility, and privacy.

G. A social worker in private practice may advertise. The advertisement should clearly inform a prospective client of the nature of the services to be received. Advertisements shall not misrepresent qualifications, competence, service, or results to be achieved. (See Code of Ethics V.M.4.)

H. When a clinical social worker terminates a private practice, there is a responsibility to refer clients elsewhere. If the clinical social worker chooses, s/he may carefully select a successor to whom the practice may be sold. Clients should be given the choice of transferring to the successor or to another clinician. The responsible practitioner collaborates with the successor for the maximum benefit of their mutual clients.

I. The privately practicing clinical social worker's rates shall be commensurate with services performed and with fees charged by mental health professionals practicing in the community. Clients who cannot pay the practitioner's fee should be referred to a mental health or family agency or to a private practitioner with lower rates.

J. The practitioner's bill shall reflect services actually rendered.

K. The clinical social worker shall not divide a fee or accept or give anything of value for receiving or making a referral. (See Code of Ethics II.I.1.)

L. Unpaid accounts may be collected through a collection agency [or] small claims court or through other legal action when efforts to collect directly from the client have failed.

☐ MODALITIES AND METHODS OF TREATMENT

VI. A variety of professionally acceptable and ethically sanctioned modalities and methods of treatment may be used in the private practice of clinical social work.

A. The practitioner shall be familiar with the client's physical condition, collaborating with a physician when the client is chronically ill or disabled and/or using medication. The practitioner shall refer the client to a physician for treatment or medication when necessary.

B. The privately practicing clinical social worker may certify or admit clients to institutional facilities depending upon state or local practice.

C. An appointment with a relative or collateral shall be made only when the client's permission has been obtained.

D. The privately practicing clinical social worker shall not discriminate against or refuse to treat a client because of race, sex, color, sexual orientation, religion, lifestyle, mental or physical handicap. (See Code of Ethics II.F.3.)

E. The private practice may be limited to certain specialties but clients outside the practitioner's area of expertise should be referred to appropriate resources.

F. The private practitioner shall not engage in sexual activities with clients. (See Code of Ethics II.F.5.)

G. Clients should be treated as expeditiously as possible. Consultation should be sought when there is a lack of progress in treatment.

☐ RELATIONSHIPS WITH OTHER PROFESSIONALS AND COMMUNITY AGENCIES

VII. The privately practicing clinical social worker shall maintain the highest professional and business ethics in dealing with other professionals and community agencies.

A. The practitioner shall be familiar with the network of professional and self-help systems in the community and shall link clients with relevant services and resources.

B. When the client is referred to another resource, the role of the primary provider of care and the specific responsibility of each party concerned with the client should be delineated clearly.

C. When the clinical social worker is unable to continue service to an individual(s), there is a responsibility to offer suitable referral(s).

D. The practitioner shall cooperate with

professionals who subsequently treat former clients.

E. The clinical social worker leaving an agency for private practice shall abide by that agency's explicit policy regarding transfer of clients. If the agency permits transfer of the client to a private practice, there shall be advance agreement between the agency and the practitioner before discussing options with the client.

F. The clinical social worker employing others in the private practice shall assume professional responsibility and accountability for all services provided.

☐ APPENDIX I: CONFIDENTIALITY AND PRIVACY

The social worker should respect the privacy of clients and hold in confidence all information obtained in the course of professional service.

The social worker should share with others confidences revealed by clients, without consent, only for compelling professional reasons.

The social worker should inform clients fully about the limits of confidentiality in a given situation, the purposes for which information is obtained, and how it may be used.

The social worker should afford clients reasonable access to any official social work records concerning them.

When providing clients with access to records, the social worker should take due care to protect the confidences of others contained in those records.

The social worker should obtain informed consent of clients before taping, recording, or permitting third party observation of their activities.

MULTIMODAL LIFE HISTORY QUESTIONNAIRE*

APPENDIX E ☐ PURPOSE OF THIS QUESTIONNAIRE:

The purpose of this questionnaire is to obtain a comprehensive picture of your background. In psychotherapy, records are necessary, since they permit a more thorough dealing with one's problems. By completing these questions as fully and as accurately as you can, you will facilitate your therapeutic program. You are requested to answer these routine questions in your own time instead of using up your actual consulting time. It is understandable that you might be concerned about what happens to the information about you because much or all of this information is highly personal. Case records are strictly confidential. NO OUTSIDER IS PERMITTED TO SEE YOUR CASE RECORD WITHOUT YOUR PERMISSION.

If you do not desire to answer any questions, merely write "Do Not Care to Answer."

Date: _____

1. General Information:

Name: _____

Address: _____

Telephone Numbers: (days) _____ (evenings) _____

Age: _____ Occupation _____ Sex _____

By whom were you referred? _____

Marital Status (circle one): Single Engaged Married Separated Divorced Widowed

Remarried (how many times? _____) Living with someone _____

Do you live in: house, hotel, room, apartment _____

2. Description of Presenting Problems:

State in your own words the nature of your main problems _____

_____

_____

_____

_____

_____

On the scale below please estimate the severity of your problem(s):

Mildly Upsetting	Moderately Upsetting	Very Severe	Extremely Severe	Totally Incapacitating

When did your problems begin (give dates): _____

_____

_____

_____

* *The Multimodal Life History Questionnaire* by Arnold Lazarus. Copyright © 1980 by the Multimodal Therapy Institute. Reprinted by permission.

Please describe significant events occurring at that time, or since then, which may relate to the development or maintenance of your problems: _____
_____

What solutions to your problems have been most helpful? _____
_____

Have you been in therapy before or received any prior professional assistance for your problems? If so, please give name(s), professional title(s), dates of treatments and results: _____
_____

3. Personal and Social History

(a) Date of Birth _____ Place of Birth _____
(b) Siblings: Number of Brothers _____ Brothers' Ages: _____
Number of Sisters _____ Sisters' Ages: _____
(c) Father: Living? _____ If alive, give father's present age _____
Deceased? _____ If deceased, give his age at time of death _____
How old were you at the time? _____
Cause of Death _____
Occupation _____ Health _____
(d) Mother: Living? _____ If alive, give mother's present age _____
Deceased? _____ If deceased, give her age at time of her death _____
How old werc you at the time? _____
Cause of Death _____
Occupation _____ Health _____
(e) Religion: As a Child: _____ As an Adult: _____
(f) Education: What is the last grade completed (degree)? _____
(g) Scholastic Strengths and Weaknesses: _____
_____

(h) Underline any of the following that applied during your childhood/adolescence:

Happy Childhood	School Problems	Medical Problems
Unhappy Childhood	Family Problems	Alcohol Abuse
Emotional/Behavior Problems	Strong Religious Convictions	Others:
Legal Trouble	Drug Abuse	

(i) What sort of work are you doing now? _____
(j) What kinds of jobs have you held in the past? _____
_____

(k) Does your present work satisfy you? If not, please explain _____
_____

(l) What is your annual family income? _____ How much
does it cost you to live? _____
(m) What were your past ambitions? _____
_____

(n) What are your current ambitions? _____
_____

(o) What is your height? _____ ft. _____ inches What is your weight? _____ lbs.
(p) Have you ever been hospitalized for psychological problems? Yes _____ No _____
If yes, when and where? _____
(q) Do you have a family physician? Yes _____ No _____ If so, please
give his/her name(s) and telephone number(s) _____
(r) Have you ever attempted suicide? Yes _____ No _____
(s) Does any member of your family suffer from alcoholism, epilepsy, depression or anything else that might be considered a "mental disorder"? _____

(t) Has any relative attempted or committed suicide? _____

(u) Has any relative had serious problems with the "law"? _____

Modality Analysis of Current Problems

The following section is designed to help you describe your current problems in greater detail and to identify problems which might otherwise go unnoticed. This will enable us to design a comprehensive treatment program and tailor it to your specific needs. The following section is organized according to the seven (7) modalities of *Behavior, Feelings, Physical Sensations, Images, Thoughts, Interpersonal Relationships and Biological Factors.*

4. Behavior:

Underline any of the following behaviors that apply to you:

Overeat	Suicidal attempts	Can't keep a job
Take drugs	Compulsions	Insomnia
Vomiting	Smoke	Take too many risks
Odd behavior	Withdrawal	Lazy
Drink too much	Nervous tics	Eating problems
Work too hard	Concentration difficulties	Aggressive behavior
Procrastination	Sleep disturbance	Crying
Impulsive reactions	Phobic avoidance	Outbursts of temper
Loss of control		

Are there any specific behaviors, actions or habits that you would like to change? _____

What are some special talents or skills that you feel proud of? _____

What would you like to do more of? _____

What would you like to do less of? _____

What would you like to start doing? _____

What would you like to stop doing? _____

How is your free time spent? _____

Do you keep yourself compulsively busy doing an endless list of chores or meaningless activities? _____

Do you practice relaxation or meditation regularly? _____

5. Feelings

Underline any of the following feelings that often apply to you:

Angry	Guilty	Unhappy
Annoyed	Happy	Bored
Sad	Conflicted	Restless
Depressed	Regretful	Lonely
Anxious	Hopeless	Contented
Fearful	Hopeful	Excited
Panicky	Helpless	Optimistic
Energetic	Relaxed	Tense
Envious	Jealous	Others:

List your five main fears:

1.
2.
3.

4.

5.

What feelings would you most like to experience more often? _____

_____

What feelings would you like to experience less often? _____

_____

What are some positive feelings you have experienced recently? _____

_____

When are you most likely to lose control of your feelings? _____

_____

Describe any situations that make you feel calm or relaxed _____

_____

_____

Please complete the following:

If I told you what I'm feeling now _____

One of the things I feel proud of is _____

One of the things I feel guilty about is _____

I am happiest when _____

One of the things that saddens me the most is _____

If I weren't afraid to be myself, I might _____

I get so angry when _____

If I get angry with you _____

What kinds of hobbies or leisure activities do you enjoy or find relaxing?

_____

Do you have trouble relaxing and enjoying weekends and vacations? (If "yes," please explain) _____

_____

6. Physical Sensations:

Underline any of the following that often apply to you:

Headaches	Stomach trouble	Skin problems
Dizziness	Tics	Dry mouth
Palpitations	Fatigue	Burning or itchy skin
Muscle spasms	Twitches	Chest pains
Tension	Back pain	Rapid heart beat
Sexual disturbances	Tremors	Don't like being touched
Unable to relax	Fainting spells	Blackouts
Bowel disturbances	Hear things	Excessive sweating
Tingling	Watery eyes	Visual disturbances
Numbness	Flushes	Hearing problems

MENSTRUAL HISTORY:

Age of first period _____ Were you informed or did it come

as a shock? _____

Are you regular? _____ Date of last period _____

Duration _____ Do you have pain? _____

Do your periods affect your mood? _____

What sensations are especially:

Pleasant for you? _____

_____

Unpleasant for you? _____

_____

7. Images
Underline any of the following that apply to you:

Pleasant sexual images
Unpleasant childhood images
Helpless images
Aggressive images

Unpleasant sexual images
Lonely images
Seduction images
Images of being loved

Check which of the following applies to you:

I PICTURE MYSELF:

being hurt
not coping
succeeding
losing control
being followed
being talked about
Others:

hurting others
being in charge
failing
being trapped
being laughed at
being promiscuous

What picture comes into your mind most often?

Describe a very pleasant image, mental picture, or fantasy.

Describe a very unpleasant image, mental picture, or fantasy.

Describe your image of a completely "safe place."

How often do you have nightmares?

8. Thoughts:
Underline each of the following thoughts that apply to you:

I am worthless, a nobody, useless and/or unlovable.
I am unattractive, incompetent, stupid and/or undesirable.
I am evil, crazy, degenerate and/or deviant.
Life is empty, a waste; there is nothing to look forward to.
I make too many mistakes, can't do anything right.

Underline each of the following words that you might use to describe yourself:

intelligent, confident, worthwhile, ambitious, sensitive, loyal, trustworthy, full of regrets, worthless, a nobody, useless, evil, crazy, morally degenerate, considerate, a deviant, unattractive, unlovable, inadequate, confused, ugly, stupid, naive, honest, incompetent, horrible thoughts, conflicted, concentration difficulties, memory problems, attractive, can't make decisions, suicidal ideas, persevering, good sense of humor, hard-working.

What do you consider to be your most irrational thought or idea?

Are you bothered by thoughts that occur over and over again?

On each of the following items, please circle the number that most accurately reflects your opinions:

	STRONGLY DISAGREE	DISAGREE	NEUTRAL	AGREE	STRONGLY AGREE
I should not make mistakes.	1	2	3	4	5
I should be good at everything I do.	1	2	3	4	5
When I do not know, I should pretend that I do.	1	2	3	4	5

I should not disclose personal information.	1	2	3	4	5
I am a victim of circumstances.	1	2	3	4	5
My life is controlled by outside forces.	1	2	3	4	5
Other people are happier than I am.	1	2	3	4	5
It is very important to please other people.	1	2	3	4	5
Play it safe; don't take any risks.	1	2	3	4	5
I don't deserve to be happy.	1	2	3	4	5
If I ignore my problems, they will disappear.	1	2	3	4	5
It is my responsibility to make other people happy.	1	2	3	4	5
I should strive for perfection.	1	2	3	4	5
Basically, there are two ways of doing things — the right way and the wrong way.	1	2	3	4	5

Expectations regarding therapy:

In a few words, what do you think therapy is all about?

How long do you think your therapy should last?

How do you think a therapist should interact with his or her clients? What personal qualities do you think the ideal therapist should possess?

(Please complete the following:)
I am a person who _____
All my life _____
Ever since I was a child _____
It's hard for me to admit _____
One of the things I can't forgive is _____
A good thing about having problems is _____
The bad thing about growing up is _____
One of the ways I could help myself but don't is _____

9. Interpersonal Relationships

A. Family of Origin

(1) If you were not brought up by your parents, who raised you and between what years?

(2) Give a description of your father's (or father substitute's) personality and his attitude toward you (past and present):

(3) Give a description of your mother's (or mother substitute's) personality and her attitude toward you (past and present):

(4) In what ways were you disciplined (punished) by your parents as a child?

(5) Give an impression of your home atmosphere (i.e., the home in which you grew up). Mention state of compatibility between parents and between children.

(6) Were you able to confide in your parents?
(7) Did your parents understand you?
(8) Basically, did you feel loved and respected by your parents?
(9) If you have a step-parent, give your age when parent remarried.
(10) Has anyone (parents, relatives, friends) ever interfered in your marriage, occupation, etc.?
(11) Who are the most important people in your life?

B. Friendships
(1) Do you make friends easily?

(2)   Do you keep them?

(3)   Were you ever bullied or severely teased?

(4)   Describe any relationship that gives you:
(a) Joy

(b) Grief

(5)   Rate the degree to which you generally feel comfortable and relaxed in social situations:
Very relaxed ____   Relatively comfortable ____   Relatively uncomfortable ____   Very anxious ____

(6)   Generally, do you express your feelings, opinions, and wishes to others in an open, appropriate manner? Describe those individuals with whom (or those situations in which) you have trouble asserting yourself.

(7)   Did you date much during High School? College?

(8)   Do you have one or more friends with whom you feel comfortable sharing your most private thoughts and feelings?

C. Marriage:

(1)   How long did you know your spouse before your engagement?

(2)   How long have you been married?

(3)   What is your spouse's age?

(4)   What is your spouse's occupation?

(5)   Describe your spouse's personality.

(6)   In what areas are you compatible?

(7)   In what areas are you incompatible?

(8)   How do you get along with your in-laws (this includes brothers and sisters-in-law)?

(9)   How many children do you have? _____ Please give their names, ages and sexes:

(10)   Do any of your children present special problems?

(11)   Any relevant information regarding abortions or miscarriages?

D. Sexual Relationships:

(1)   Describe your parents' attitude toward sex. Was sex discussed in your home?

(2)   When and how did you derive your first knowledge of sex?

(3)   When did you first become aware of your own sexual impulses?

(4)   Have you ever experienced any anxiety or guilt feelings arising out of sex or masturbation? If yes, please explain.

(5)   Any relevant details regarding your first or subsequent sexual experiences?

(6)   Is your present sex life satisfactory? If not, please explain.

(7)   Provide information about any significant homosexual reactions or relationships.

(8)   Please note any sexual concerns not discussed above.

E. Other Relationships

(1)   Are there any problems in your relationships with people at work? If so, please describe.

(2)   Please complete the following:
(a)   One of the ways people hurt me is _____
_____

(b) I could shock you by _____

_____

(c) A mother should _____

_____

(d) A father should _____

_____

(e) A true friend should _____

_____

(3) Give a brief description of yourself as you would be described by:
  (a) Your spouse (if married):

  (b) Your best friend:

  (c) Someone who dislikes you:

(4) Are you currently troubled by any past rejections or loss of a love relationship? If so, please explain.

10. Biological factors:

Do you have any current concerns about your physical health? Please specify:

_____

Please list any medicines you are currently taking, or have taken during the past 6 months (including aspirin, birth control pills, or any medicines that were prescribed or taken over the counter) _____

_____

Do you eat three well-balanced meals each day? If not, please explain

_____

Do you get regular physical exercise? If so, what type and how often?

_____

Check any of the following that apply to you:

	NEVER	RARELY	FREQUENTLY	VERY OFTEN
Marijuana				
Tranquilizers				
Sedatives				
Aspirin				
Cocaine				
Painkillers				
Alcohol				
Coffee				
Cigarettes				
Narcotics				
Stimulants				
Hallucinogens (LSD, etc.)				
Diarrhea				
Constipation				
Allergies				
High blood pressure				
Heart problems				
Nausea				
Vomiting				
Insomnia				
Headaches				
Backache				
Early morning awakening				

Fitful sleep _____

Overeat _____

Poor appetite _____

Eat "junk foods" _____

Underline any of the following that apply to you or members of your family: thyroid disease, kidney disease, asthma, neurological disease, infectious diseases, diabetes, cancer, gastrointestinal disease, prostate problems, glaucoma, epilepsy, other:

Have you ever had any head injuries or loss of consciousness? Please give details. _____

_____

Please describe any surgery you have had (give dates) _____

_____

Please describe any accidents or injuries you have suffered (give dates)

_____

Sequential History

Please outline your most significant memories and experiences within the following ages:

0–5 _____

6–10 _____

11–15 _____

16–20 _____

21–25 _____

26–30 _____

31–35 _____

36–40 _____

41–45 _____

46–50 _____

51–55 _____

56–60 _____

61–65 _____

Over 65 _____

BEHAVIORAL ANALYSIS
HISTORY QUESTIONNAIRE (BAHQ)*

APPENDIX F

This questionnaire is used to supply us with information from your past history and present situation that will help us to change your undesirable behavior. Your answers will be strictly confidential and will not be revealed to anyone without your full consent.

Name: _____ Date _____

Address: _____

_____

Age: _____ Date of Birth: _____

Telephone Number: (Home) _____ (Work) _____

Sex: Male _____ Female _____

Height: _____ ft. _____ in.   Weight: _____ lbs.

Race: White _____ Black _____ Oriental _____ Other _____

Color of Eyes: Blue _____ Brown _____ Green _____ Black _____

Glasses: Yes _____ No _____

Complexion: Dark _____ Medium-dark _____ Medium _____ Fair _____ Very Fair _____

Distinguishing features: _____

_____

Referral

Who referred you? _____

What present complaints (maladaptive behaviors) do you have that make you feel you need help? _____

_____

_____

How often do these occur? times per week _____ times per month _____

What do you think is presently causing these behaviors? _____

_____

Have you sought treatment before? Yes _____ No _____

If yes, please list in chronological order the therapists and dates seen.

* From "The behavioral inventory battery: The use of self-report measures" by J. R. Cautela and D. Upper. In *Behavioral assessment: A practical handbook.* Copyright 1976 by Pergamon Press. Reprinted by permission.

Name of therapist: _____   Dates seen: _____

_____   _____

_____   _____

_____   _____

_____   _____

Have you ever been hospitalized for mental illness?   Yes _____   No _____

If so, list hospital(s) and dates

Hospital(s):   Dates:

_____   _____

_____   _____

_____   _____

Fears and Negative Thoughts

List below some of the fears that you have:

_____

_____

_____

If you have any thoughts as listed below, check the frequency of the occurrence:

	Hardly ever	*Occasionally*	*Frequently*
Life is hopeless.	_____	_____	_____
I am lonely.	_____	_____	_____
The future is hopeless.	_____	_____	_____
Nobody cares about me.	_____	_____	_____
I feel like killing myself.	_____	_____	_____
I am a failure.	_____	_____	_____
I am intellectually inferior to other people.	_____	_____	_____
People usually don't like me.	_____	_____	_____
I am going to faint.	_____	_____	_____
I am going to have a panic attack.	_____	_____	_____
Other negative thoughts you may have:	_____	_____	_____

Marital Status

Married _____   Single _____   Divorced _____   Separated _____   Widowed _____

If married, wife's/husband's age and occupation.

Age: _____   Occupation: _____

If any children, list their names and ages:

Name   *Age*

_____   _____

_____   _____

_____   _____

_____   _____

_____   _____

If divorced or separated, for what reason: _____

_____

_____

_____

List the people who currently live in your household, and their relationship to you.

Name   *Relationship to you* (e.g., Mother-in-law,
                                                daughter, roommate, etc.)

_____   _____

_____   _____

_____   _____

_____   _____

_____   _____

_____   _____

_____   _____

Family History

Mother: Name _____   Age: _____

Height: ____ ft. ____ in.   Weight: ____ lbs.   Religion _____

Occupation: _____

How did she punish you? _____

How did she reward you? _____

What did she punish? _____

What did she reward? _____

How would others describe your mother? _____

_____

How would you describe your mother? _____

_____

What activities did you do with your mother when you were a child? _____

_____

How did you get along with your mother? _____

_____

Father: Name: _____   Age: _____

Height: _____ ft. _____ in.   Weight: _____ lbs.   Religion _____

Occupation: _____

How did he punish you? _____

How did he reward you? _____

What did he punish? _____

What did he reward? _____

How would others describe your father? _____

_____

How would you describe your father? _____

_____

What activities did you do with your father when you were a child? _____

_____

How did you get along with your father? _____

Names of Brothers and Sisters	*Age*	*How did you get along with him/her?*
_____	_____	_____
_____	_____	_____
_____	_____	_____
_____	_____	_____
_____	_____	_____

Does (did) your mother favor any one?   Yes _____   No _____

If so, who and why? _____

_____

How do (did) your mother and father get along? _____

_____

Educational History

	Name of School	*Location*	*Dates*	*How were your grades?*
Grammar:				
Secondary:				
College:				
Post-Graduate school(s):				

_____

How well did you adjust to school situations?   poorly _____   fairly _____   well _____   excellently _____

List any significant events relating to school that you think had a bearing on your present problem:

_____

_____

_____

Childhood interests and hobbies: _____

_____

Present interests and hobbies: _____

_____

Job History

List the jobs you have held and their dates. Then note which aspects of each job were the most pleasurable for you (e.g., working with people, type of work, etc.) and which aspects gave you the most anxiety or trouble.

Dates	Job Titles	Salaries	Liked	Disliked

How often did you miss work?

  a. As a general estimate for all your jobs: _____

  b. For the jobs you enjoyed: _____

  c. For the jobs you disliked: _____

How did you get along with your fellow employees?   not at all _____   fairly well _____   very well _____

What bothered you most about your fellow employees? _____

_____

How did you get along with your supervisors? _____

_____

What bothered you about your supervisors? _____

_____

What training or education have you had relevant to occupational skills? (List on-the-job training as well as course work.)

_____

_____

_____

What job, if any, are you presently holding? _____

_____

Does it satisfy you: intellectually ——   emotionally ——   physically ——

What ambitions do you have at the present time? _____

_____

Sexual History

When and how did you first learn about sex? _____

_____

Was sex ever discussed at home:

    not at all ——   occasionally ——   a fair amount of time ——   frequently ——

What was the attitude of your parents concerning sex?

    It was considered shameful to discuss ——   Not exactly shameful, but not discussed much ——

    A natural function to be discussed without embarrassment ——

Describe your first sexual experience _____

_____

If you masturbate, when did you first start? _____

When did you have your first sexual intercourse? _____

Have you ever had any homosexual experience? _____

_____

What is your sexual activity at the present time?

	Times per week	Times per month
a. Masturbation	————	————

    What do you imagine when you masturbate? _____

_____

	Times per week	Times per month
b. Light petting (kissing & hugging)	————	————
c. Heavy petting (touching sexual organs)	————	————
d. Homosexual contacts	————	————
e. Intercourse	————	————

(For female clients)

When did you have your first period? _____

Are your periods regular at the present time?   Yes ——   No ——

How comfortable are your periods?

    very uncomfortable ——   uncomfortable ——   fairly comfortable ——   comfortable ——

Do you often feel depressed just before your period? _____

Do you use birth control devices or pills?   Yes ——   No ——   If so, what type? ——

Marital History

How well do you and your wife/husband get along? Rate your relationship on a scale from 1 to 5:

    1 very poor   2 poor   3 fair   4 good   5 excellent

How often do you and your wife/husband go out socially?   per week _____   per month _____

Who is the dominant member of your relationship?   you _____   your husband/wife _____

List some of the behaviors of your husband/wife that you find disagreeable:

_____

_____

_____

List some of the behaviors of your husband/wife that you find agreeable:

_____

_____

_____

Health History

List any childhood diseases you've had: _____

_____

List any operations you've had: _____

_____

Have you had any significant illnesses in the past? _____

List present physical ailments (for example, high blood pressure, diabetes, etc.) _____

_____

When was the last time you had a complete physical exam? _____

   Results? _____

_____

Name and address of your physician:

   Name: _____   Address: _____

Do you have trouble falling asleep?   Yes _____   No _____

Do you wake up during the night? _____

If you do wake up, can you get back to sleep easily? _____

_____

How is your appetite?   poor _____   average _____   good _____   very good _____

Which drugs are you presently taking and why? _____

_____

_____

Religious History

In which religion were you raised?   Protestant _____   Catholic _____   Jewish _____   other _____

Do you presently engage in any religious activity?   Yes _____   No _____

If so, please describe: _____

_____

Personality Assessment

List any faults you think you have: _____

_____

_____

_____

List your good points: _____

_____

_____

_____

Please add anything you feel might help us understand your problem: _____

_____

_____

_____

_____

REFERENCES

Abrams, D. B., & Wilson, G. T. (1979). Self-monitoring and reactivity in the modification of cigarette smoking. *Journal of Consulting and Clinical Psychology, 47,* 243–251.

Adler, A. (1964). *Social interest: A challenge to mankind.* New York: Capricorn Books.

Agras, W. S. (1965). An investigation in the decrements of anxiety responses during systematic desensitization therapy. *Behaviour Research and Therapy, 2,* 267–270.

Agras, W. S., Schneider, J. A., & Taylor, C. B. (1984). Relaxation training in essential hypertension: A failure of retraining in relaxation procedures. *Behavior Therapy, 15,* 191–196.

Alagna, F. J., Whitcher, S. J., Fisher, J. D., & Wicas, E. A. (1979). Evaluative reaction to interpersonal touch in a counseling interview. *Journal of Counseling Psychology, 26,* 265–472.

Alexander, J., & Parsons, B. (1982). *Functional family therapy.* Monterey, Calif.: Brooks/Cole.

Altmaier, E. M., Ross, S. L., Leary, M. R., & Thornbrough, M. (1982). Matching stress inoculation's treatment components to clients' anxiety mode. *Journal of Counseling Psychology, 29,* 331–334.

Altmaier, E. M., & Woodward, M. (1981). Group vicarious desensitization of test anxiety. *Journal of Counseling Psychology, 28,* 467–469.

American Association for Counseling and Development. (1981). *Ethical standards* (Rev. ed.). Alexandria, VA: Author.

American Psychiatric Association. (1980). *Diagnostic and statistical manual of mental disorders* (3rd ed.). Washington, DC: Author.

American Psychological Association. (1981). *Ethical principles of psychologists* (Rev. ed.). Washington, DC: Author.

Anderson, C. M., & Stewart, S. (1983). *Mastering resistance: A practical guide to family therapy.* New York: Guilford Press.

Andolfi, M. (1979). *Family therapy: An interactional approach.* New York: Plenum.

Anthony, J., & Edelstein, B. (1975). Thought-stopping treatment of anxiety attacks due to seizure-related obsessive ruminations. *Journal of Behavior Therapy and Experimental Psychiatry, 6,* 343–344.

Anton, J. L., Dunbar, J., & Friedman, L. (1976). Anticipation training in the treatment of depression. In J. D. Krumboltz & C. E. Thoresen (Eds.), *Counseling methods* (pp. 67–74). New York: Holt, Rinehart and Winston.

Arrick, M., Voss, J. R., & Rimm, D. C. (1981). The relative efficacy of thought-stopping and covert assertion. *Behaviour Research and Therapy, 19,* 17–24.

Ascher, L. M. (1979). Paradoxical intention in the treatment of urinary retention. *Behaviour Research and Therapy, 17,* 267–270.

Ascher, L. M. (1980). Paradoxical intention. In A. Goldstein

& E. B. Foa (Eds.), *Behavioral interventions: A clinical guide.* New York: Wiley.

Ascher, L. M. (1981). Employing paradoxical intention in the treatment of agoraphobia. *Behaviour Research and Therapy, 19,* 533–547.

Ascher, L. M., & Efran, J. (1978). Use of paradoxical intention in a behavioral program for sleep onset insomnia. *Journal of Consulting and Clinical Psychology, 46,* 547–550.

Ascher, L. M., & Phillips, D. (1975). Guided behavior rehearsal. *Journal of Behavior Therapy and Experimental Psychiatry, 6,* 215–218.

Ascher, L. M., & Turner, R. (1979). Paradoxical intention and insomnia: An experimental investigation. *Behaviour Research and Therapy, 17,* 408–411.

Auerswald, M. C. (1974). Differential reinforcing power of restatement and interpretation on client production of affect. *Journal of Counseling Psychology, 21,* 9–14.

Azrin, N. H., & Besale, V. A. (1980). *Job club counselor's manual: A behavioral approach to vocational counseling.* Baltimore, MD: University Park Press.

Bain, J. A. (1928). *Thought control in everyday life.* New York: Funk & Wagnalls.

Bajtelsmit, J., & Gershman, L. (1976). Covert positive reinforcement: Efficacy and conceptualization. *Journal of Behavior Therapy and Experimental Psychiatry, 7,* 207–212.

Baker, S. B. (1981). *Cleaning up our thinking: A unit in self-improvement.* Unpublished manuscript, Division of Counseling and Educational Psychology, Pennsylvania State University, University Park.

Baker, S. B., & Butler, J. N. (1984). Effects of preventive cognitive self-instruction training on adolescent attitudes, experiences and state anxiety. *Journal of Primary Prevention, 5,* 10–14.

Baker, S. B., Thomas, R. N., & Munson, W. W. (1983). Effects of cognitive restructuring and structured group discussion as primary prevention strategies. *School Counselor, 31,* 26–33.

Bandler, R., & Grinder, J. (1975). *The structure of magic I: A book about language and therapy.* Palo Alto, CA: Science and Behavior Books.

Bandler, R., & Grinder, J. (1982). *Reframing.* Moab, Utah: Real People Press.

Bandura, A. (1969). *Principles of behavior modification.* New York: Holt, Rinehart and Winston.

Bandura, A. (1971a). Psychotherapy based upon modeling principles. In A. E. Bergin & S. L. Garfield (Eds.), *Handbook of psychotherapy and behavior change: An empirical analysis* (pp. 653–708). New York: Wiley.

Bandura, A. (1971b). Vicarious and self-reinforcement processes. In R. Glaser (Ed.), *The nature of reinforcement.* New York: Academic Press.

Bandura, A. (1974). Self-reinforcement processes. In M. J. Mahoney & C. E. Thoresen (Eds.), *Self-control: Power to the person* (pp. 86–110). Monterey, CA: Brooks/Cole.

Bandura, A. (1976a). Effecting change through participant modeling. In J. D. Krumboltz & C. E. Thoresen (Eds.), *Counseling methods* (pp. 248–265). New York: Holt, Rinehart and Winston.

Bandura, A. (1976b). Self-reinforcement: Theoretical and methodological considerations. *Behaviorism, 4,* 135–155.

Bandura, A. (1981). In search of pure unidirectional determinants. *Behavior Therapy, 12,* 30–40.

Bandura, A., & Adams, N. E. (1977). Analysis of self-efficacy theory of behavioral change. *Cognitive Therapy and Research, 1,* 287–310.

Bandura, A., Adams, N. E., & Beyer, J. (1977). Cognitive processes mediating behavioral change. *Journal of Personality and Social Psychology, 35,* 125–139.

Bandura, A., Blanchard, E. B., & Ritter, B. (1969). Relative efficacy of desensitization and modeling approaches for inducing behavioral, affective, and attitudinal changes. *Journal of Personality and Social Psychology, 13,* 173–199.

Bandura, A., & Jeffery, R. W. (1973). Role of symbolic coding and rehearsal processes in observational learning. *Journal of Personality and Social Psychology, 26,* 122–130.

Bandura, A., Jeffery, R. W., & Gajdos, E. (1975). Generalizing change through participant modeling with self-directed mastery. *Behaviour Research and Therapy, 13,* 141–152.

Bandura, A., Jeffery, R. W., & Wright, C. (1974). Efficacy of participant modeling as a function of response induction aids. *Journal of Abnormal Psychology, 83,* 56–64.

Bandura, A., & Simon, K. (1977). The role of proximal intentions in self-regulation of refractory behavior. *Cognitive Therapy and Research, 1,* 177–193.

Banikiotes, P. G., Kubinski, J. A., & Pursell, S. A. (1981). Sex role orientation, self-disclosure, and gender-related perceptions. *Journal of Counseling Psychology, 28,* 140–146.

Barak, A., Patkin, J., & Dell, D. M. (1982). Effects of certain counselor behaviors in perceived expertness and attractiveness. *Journal of Counseling Psychology, 29,* 261–267.

Barber, T. (1980). Personal communication. Cited in D. H. Shapiro, Jr., *Meditation: Self-regulation strategy and altered state of consciousness.* New York: Aldine.

Barlow, D. H. (Ed.). (1981a). *Behavioral assessment of adult disorders.* New York: Guilford Press.

Barlow, D. H. (1981b). On the relation of clinical research to clinical practice: Current issues, new directions. *Journal of Consulting and Clinical Psychology, 49,* 147–155.

Barlow, D. H., Hayes, S. C., & Nelson, R. O. (1984). *The scientist practitioner.* New York: Pergamon Press.

Barrett-Lennard, G. T. (1981). The empathy cycle: Refinement of a nuclear concept. *Journal of Counseling Psychology, 28,* 91–100.

Bass, B. A. (1974). Sexual arousal as an anxiety inhibitor. *Journal of Behavior Therapy and Experimental Psychiatry, 5,* 151–152.

Bateson, G., & Jackson, D. (1964). Some varieties of pathogenic organization. In D. McK. Rioch (Ed.), *Disorders of communication* (Vol. 42) (pp. 270–283). Research Publications, Association for Research in Nervous and Mental Disease.

Battle, C. C., Imber, S. D., Hoehn-Saric, R., Stone, A. R., Nash, E. R., & Frank, J. D. (1966). Target complaints as criteria of improvement. *American Journal of Psychotherapy, 20,* 184–192.

Beck, A. T. (1970). Cognitive therapy: Nature and relation to behavior therapy. *Behavior Therapy, 1,* 184–200.

Beck, A. T. (1972). *Depression: Causes and treatment.* Philadelphia: University of Pennsylvania Press.

Beck, A. T. (1976). *Cognitive therapy and the emotional disorders.* New York: International Universities Press.

Beck, A. T., & Emery, G. (1979). *Cognitive therapy of anxiety.* Philadelphia: Center for Cognitive Therapy.

Beck, A. T., Ward, C. H., Mendelson, M., Mock, J., & Erbaugh, J. (1961). An inventory for measuring depression. *Archives of General Psychiatry, 4,* 561–571.

Beck, J. T., & Strong, S. R. (1982). Stimulating therapeutic change with interpretations: A comparison of positive and negative connotation. *Journal of Counseling Psychology, 29,* 551–559.

Bellack, A. S. (1976). A comparison of self-reinforcement and self-monitoring in a weight reduction program. *Behavior Therapy, 7,* 68–75.

Bellack, A. S., & Hersen, M. (1977). Self-report inventories in behavioral assessment. In J. D. Cone & R. P. Hawkins (Eds.), *Behavioral assessment: New directions in clinical psychology* (pp. 52–76). New York: Brunner/Mazel.

Bellack, A. S., Rozensky, R., & Schwartz, J. (1974). A comparison of two forms of self-monitoring in a behavioral weight reduction program. *Behavior Therapy, 5,* 523–530.

Bemis, K. (1980). Personal communication. Cited in P. C. Kendall & S. D. Hollon (Eds.), *Assessment strategies for cognitive-behavioral interventions.* New York: Academic Press.

Benjamin, A. (1974). *The helping interview* (2nd ed.). Boston: Houghton Mifflin.

Benson, H. (1974). Your innate asset for combating stress. *Harvard Business Review, 52,* 49–60.

Benson, H. (1976). *The relaxation response.* New York: Avon Books.

Berenson, B. C., & Mitchell, K. M. (1974). *Confrontation: For better or worse.* Amherst, MA: Human Resource Development Press.

Berne, E. (1964). *Games people play.* New York: Grove Press.

Bernstein, D. A., & Borkovec, T. D. (1973). *Progressive relaxation training: A manual for the helping professions.* Champaign, IL: Research Press.

Bijou, S. W., & Baer, D. M. (1961). *Child development I: A systematic and empirical theory.* Englewood Cliffs, NJ: Prentice-Hall.

Birchler, G. (1981). Paradox and behavioral marital therapy. In A. S. Gurman (Ed.), *Questions and answers in the practice of family therapy* (Vol. 1) (pp. 123–127). New York: Brunner/Mazel.

Birdwhistell, R. L. (1970). *Kinesics and context.* Philadelphia: University of Pennsylvania Press.

Birholtz, L. (1981). Neurolinguistic programming: Testing some basic assumptions. *Dissertation Abstracts International, 42,* 356 SB. (University Microfilms No. 8118324)

Bixler, R. H. (1949). Limits are therapy. *Journal of Consulting Psychology, 13,* 1–11.

Blanchard, E. B. (1982). Biofeedback and relaxation training with three kinds of headache: Treatment effects and their prediction. *Journal of Consulting and Clinical Psychology, 50,* 562–575.

Blanchard, E. B., Andrasik, F., Neff, D. F., Jurish, S. E., & O'Keefe, D. M. (1981). Social validation of the headache diary. *Behavior Therapy, 12,* 711–715.

Blanchard, E. B., Theobald, D. E., Williamson, D. A., Silver, B. V., & Brown, D. A. (1978). Temperature biofeedback in the treatment of migraine headaches. *Archives of General Psychiatry, 35,* 581–588.

Blechman, E., Olson, D., & Hellman, I. (1976). Stimulus control over family problem-solving behavior: The family contract game. *Behavior Therapy, 7,* 686–692.

Bloomfield, H. H., Cain, M. P., Jaffe, D. T., & Kory, R. B. (1975). *TM: Discovering inner energy and overcoming stress.* New York: Dell.

Bolstad, O. D., & Johnson, S. M. (1972). Self-regulation in the modification of disruptive classroom behavior. *Journal of Applied Behavior Analysis, 5,* 443–454.

Bootzin, R. R. (1972). Stimulus control treatment for insomnia. *American Psychological Association Proceedings,* 395–396.

Bootzin, R. R. (1977). Effects of self-control procedures for insomnia. In R. B. Stuart (Ed.), *Behavioral self-management: Strategies, techniques, and outcomes* (pp. 176–195). New York: Brunner/Mazel.

Borck, L. E., & Fawcett, S. B. (1982). *Learning counseling and problem-solving skills.* New York: Haworth Press.

Borkovec, T., Grayson, J. B., & Cooper, K. (1978). Treatment of general tension: Subjective and physiological effects of progressive relaxation. *Journal of Consulting and Clinical Psychology, 46,* 518–528.

Borkovec, T. D., Grayson, J. B., O'Brien, G. T., & Weerts, T. C. (1979). Relaxation treatment of pseudoinsomnia and idiopathic insomnia: An electroencephalographic evaluation. *Journal of Applied Behavior Analysis, 12,* 37–54.

Borkovec, T. D., Wilkinson, L., Folensbee, R., & Lerman, C. (1983). Stimulus control applications to the treatment of worry. *Behaviour Research and Therapy, 21,* 247–251.

Bornstein, P. H., & Devine, D. A. (1980). Covert modeling-hypnosis in the treatment of obesity. *Psychotherapy: Theory, Research and Practice, 17,* 272–275.

Bornstein, P. H., Hamilton, S. B., Carmody, T. B., Rychtarik, R. G., & Veraldi, D. M. (1977). Reliability enhancement: Increasing the accuracy of self-report through meditation-based procedures. *Cognitive Therapy and Research, 1,* 85–98.

Bornstein, P. H., & Knapp, M. (1981). Self-control desensitization with a multi-phobic boy: A multiple baseline design. *Journal of Behavior Therapy and Experimental Psychiatry, 12,* 281–285.

Boudreau, L. (1972). Transcendental meditation and yoga as reciprocal inhibitors. *Journal of Behavior Therapy and Experimental Psychiatry, 3,* 97–98.

Bourque, P., & Ladouceur, R. (1980). An investigation of various performance-based treatments with acrophobics. *Behaviour Research and Therapy, 18,* 161–170.

Brammer, L. M., & Shostrom, E. L. (1982). *Therapeutic psychology: Fundamentals of counseling and psychotherapy* (4th ed.). Englewood Cliffs, NJ: Prentice-Hall.

Brauer, A. P., Horlick, L., Nelson, E., Farquhar, J. W., & Agras, W. S. (1979). Relaxation therapy for essential hypertension: A Veterans Administration outpatient study. *Journal of Behavioral Medicine, 2,* 21–29.

Brehm, J. W. (1966). *A theory of psychological reactance.* New York: Academic Press.

Brehm, J. W. (1972). *Response to loss of freedom: A theory of psychological resistance.* Morristown, NJ: General Learning Press.

Brehm, S. S. (1976). *The application of social psychology to clinical practice.* Washington, DC: Hemisphere.

Brockman, W. P. (1980). *Empathy revisited: The effect of representational system matching on certain counseling process and outcome variables.* Unpublished doctoral dissertation, College of William and Mary, Williamsburg, VA.

Broden, M., Hall, R., & Mitts, B. (1971). The effect of self-recording on the classroom behavior of two eighth-grade students. *Journal of Applied Behavior Analysis, 4,* 191–199.

Broverman, I., Broverman, D., Clarkson, F., Rosenkrantz, P., & Vogel, S. (1970). Sex-role stereotypes and clinical judgments of mental health. *Journal of Consulting and Clinical Psychology, 34,* 1–7.

Brown, J. H., & Brown, S. (1977). *Systematic counseling: A guide for the practitioner.* Champaign, IL: Research Press.

Brown, J. P. (1978). *An analysis of self-monitoring-provided feedback in a behavioral weight reduction program.* Unpublished doctoral dissertation, West Virginia University, Morgantown.

Brownell, K., Colletti, G., Ersner-Hershfield, R., Hershfield, S., & Wilson, G. (1977). Self-control in school children: Stringency and leniency in self-determined and externally imposed performance standards. *Behavior Therapy, 8,* 442–455.

Bruch, M. A., Juster, H. R., & Heisler, B. D. (1982). Conceptual complexity as a mediator of thought content and negative affect: Implications for cognitive restructuring interventions. *Journal of Counseling Psychology, 29,* 343–353.

Bry, A., & Bair, M. (1979). *Visualization: Directing the movies of your mind.* New York: Barnes and Noble.

Bucher, B., & Fabricatore, J. (1970). Use of patient-administered shock to suppress hallucinations. *Behavior Therapy, 1,* 382–385.

Buggs, D. C. (1975). *Your child's self-esteem.* New York: Doubleday.

Burish, T. G., & Lyles, J. N. (1979). Effectiveness of relaxation training in reducing the aversiveness of chemotherapy in the treatment of cancer. *Journal of Behavior Therapy and Experimental Psychiatry, 10,* 357–361.

Caird, W. K., & Wincze, J. P. (1974). Videotaped desensitization of frigidity. *Journal of Behavior Therapy and Experimental Psychiatry, 5,* 175–178.

Carkhuff, R. R. (1969a). *Helping and human relations.* Vol. 1: *Selection and training.* New York: Holt, Rinehart and Winston.

Carkhuff, R. R. (1969b). *Helping and human relations.* Vol. 2: *Practice and research.* New York: Holt, Rinehart and Winston.

Carkhuff, R. R. (1972). *The art of helping.* Amherst, MA: Human Resource Development Press.

Carkhuff, R. R., & Anthony, W. A. (1979). *The skills of helping.* Amherst, MA: Human Resource Development Press.

Carkhuff, R. R., & Pierce, R. M. (1975). *Trainer's guide: The art of helping.* Amherst, MA: Human Resource Development Press.

Carkhuff, R. R., Pierce, R. M., & Cannon, J. R. (1977). *The art of helping III.* Amherst, MA: Human Resource Development Press.

Carrington, P. (1978a). *Clinically standardized meditation (CSM): Instructor's manual.* Kendall Park, NJ: Pace Educational Systems.

Carrington, P. (1978b). *Learning to meditate: Clinically standardized meditation (CSM) course workbook.* Kendall Park, NJ: Pace Educational Systems.

Carrington, P., Collings, G. H., Benson, H., Robinson, H., Wood, L. W., Lehrer, P. M., Woolfolk, R. L., & Cole, J. W. (1980). The use of meditation-relaxation techniques for the management of stress in a working population. *Journal of Occupational Medicine, 22,* 221–231.

Carroll, L. J., & Yates, B. T. (1981). Further evidence for the role of stimulus control training in facilitating weight reduction after behavioral therapy. *Behavior Therapy, 12,* 287–291.

Cash, T. F., & Salzbach, R. F. (1978). The reality of counseling: Effects of counselor physical attractiveness and self-disclosure on perceptions of counselor behavior. *Journal of Counseling Psychology, 25,* 283–291.

Cautela, J. R. (1969). Behavior therapy and self-control: Techniques and implications. In C. Franks (Ed.), *Behavior therapy: Appraisal and status* (pp. 323–340). New York: McGraw-Hill.

Cautela, J. R. (1970). Covert reinforcement. *Behavior Therapy, 1,* 33–50.

Cautela, J. R. (1971). *Covert modeling.* Paper presented at the fifth annual meeting of the Association for Advancement of Behavior Therapy, Washington, DC.

Cautela, J. R. (1976). The present status of covert modeling. *Journal of Behavior Therapy and Experimental Psychiatry, 6,* 323–326.

Cautela, J. R. (1977). *Behavior analysis forms for clinical intervention.* Champaign, IL: Research Press.

Cautela, J. R. (1981). *Behavior analysis forms for clinical intervention* (Vol. 2). Champaign, IL: Research Press.

Cautela, J. R., Flannery, R., & Hanley, S. (1974). Covert modeling: An experimental test. *Behavior Therapy, 5,* 494–502.

Cautela, J. R., & Groden, J. (1978). *Relaxation: A comprehensive manual for adults, children, and children with special needs.* Champaign, IL: Research Press.

Cautela, J. R., & Upper, D. (1975). The process of individual behavior therapy. In M. Hersen, R. Eisler, & P. Miller (Eds.), *Progress in behavior modification I* (pp. 275–305). New York: Academic Press.

Cautela, J. R., & Upper, D. (1976). The behavioral inventory battery: The use of self-report measures in behavioral analysis and therapy. In M. Hersen & A. S. Bellack (Eds.), *Behavioral assessment: A practical handbook* (pp. 77–109). New York: Pergamon Press.

Cavanaugh, M. E. (1982). *The counseling experience.* Monterey, CA: Brooks/Cole.

Cavior, N., & Marabotto, C. M. (1976). Monitoring verbal behaviors in a dyadic interaction. *Journal of Consulting and Clinical Psychology, 44,* 68–76.

Celotta, B., & Telasi-Golubscow, H. (1982). A problem taxonomy for classifying clients' problems. *Personnel and Guidance Journal, 61,* 73–76.

Chamberlain, P., Patterson, G., Reid, J., Kavanagh, K., & Forgatch, M. (1984). Observation of client resistance. *Behavior Therapy, 15,* 144–155.

Chassan, J. B. (1962). Probability processes in psychoanalytic psychiatry. In J. Scher (Ed.), *Theories of the mind.* New York: Free Press.

Chaves, J., & Barber, T. (1974). Cognitive strategies, experimenter modeling, and expectation in the attenuation of pain. *Journal of Abnormal Psychology, 83,* 356–363.

Ciminero, A. R. (1977). Behavioral assessment: An overview. In A. R. Ciminero, K. S. Calhoun, & H. E. Adams (Eds.), *Handbook of behavioral assessment* (pp. 3–13). New York: Wiley.

Ciminero, A. R., Nelson, R. O., & Lipinski, D. P. (1977). Self-monitoring procedures. In A. R. Çiminero, K. S. Calhoun, & H. E. Adams (Eds.), *Handbook of behavioral assessment* (pp. 195–232). New York: Wiley.

Claiborn, C. D. (1979). Counselor verbal intervention, nonverbal behavior, and social power. *Journal of Counseling Psychology, 26,* 378–383.

Claiborn, C. D. (1982). Interpretation and change in counseling. *Journal of Counseling Psychology, 29,* 439–453.

Claiborn, C. D., Ward, S. R., & Strong, S. R. (1981). Effects of congruence between counselor interpretations and client beliefs. *Journal of Counseling Psychology, 28,* 101–109.

Clarke, J. C., & Jackson, J. A. (1983). *Hypnosis and behavior therapy.* New York: Springer.

Coates, T. J., & Thoresen, C. E. (1981). Behavior and weight changes in three obese adolescents. *Behavior Therapy, 12,* 383–399.

Coates, T. J., & Thoresen, C. E. (1984). Assessing daytime thoughts and behavior associated with good and poor sleep: Two exploratory case studies. *Behavioral Assessment, 6,* 153–167.

Coe, W. C. (1980). Expectation, hypnosis, and suggestion methods. In F. H. Kanfer & A. P. Goldstein (Eds.), *Helping people change* (2nd ed.) (pp. 423–469). New York: Pergamon Press.

Collins, F. L., Jr., Martin, J. E., & Hillenberg, J. B. (1982). Assessment of relaxation compliance: A pilot validation study. *Behavioral Assessment, 4,* 221–225.

Condon, W. S., & Ogston, W. D. (1966). Soundfilm analysis of normal and pathological behavior patterns. *Journal of Nervous and Mental Disease, 143,* 338–347.

Connolly, P. R. (1975). The perception of personal space among black and white Americans. *Central States Speech Journal, 26,* 21–28.

Cooley, E. J., & Spiegler, M. D. (1980). Cognitive versus emotional coping responses as alternatives to test anxiety. *Cognitive Therapy and Research, 4,* 159–166.

Copeland, A. P. (1981). The relevance of subject variables in cognitive self-instructional programs for impulsive children. *Behavior Therapy, 12,* 520–529.

Corey, G., Corey, M., & Callanan, P. (1984). *Professional and ethical issues in counseling and psychotherapy* (2nd ed.). Monterey, CA: Brooks/Cole.

Cormier, L. S., & Cormier, W. H. (1975). *Behavioral counseling: Operant procedures, self-management strategies, and recent innovations.* Boston: Houghton Mifflin.

Cormier, L. S., Cormier, W. H., & Weisser, R. J., Jr. (1984). *Interviewing and helping skills for health professionals.* Monterey, CA.: Wadsworth Health Sciences.

Cormier, W. H., & Cormier, L. S. (1975). *Behavioral counseling: Initial procedures, individual and group strategies.* Boston: Houghton Mifflin.

Cornish, R. D., & Dilley, J. S. (1973). Comparison of three methods of reducing test anxiety: Systematic desensitization, implosive therapy, and study counseling. *Journal of Counseling Psychology, 20,* 499–503.

Corrigan, J. D., Dell, D. M., Lewis, K. N., & Schmidt, L. D. (1980). Counseling as a social influence process: A review. *Journal of Counseling Psychology, 27,* 395–441.

Cotharin, R., & Mikulas, W. (1975). Systematic desensitization of racial emotional responses. *Journal of Behavior Therapy and Experimental Psychiatry, 6,* 347–348.

Cozby, P. C. (1973). Self-disclosure: A literature review. *Psychological Bulletin, 79,* 73–91.

Craigie, F. C., Jr., & Ross, S. M. (1980). The case of a videotape pretherapy training program to encourage treatment-seeking among alcohol detoxification patients. *Behavior Therapy, 11,* 141–147.

Credidio, S. G. (1982). Comparative effectiveness of patterned biofeedback vs. meditation training on EMG and skin temperature changes. *Behaviour Research and Therapy, 20,* 233–241.

Cronbach, L. J. (1970). *Essentials of psychological testing* (3rd ed.). New York: Harper & Row.

Cronbach, L. J. (1975). Beyond the two disciplines of scientific psychology. *American Psychologist, 30,* 116–127.

Cronbach, L. J. (1984). *Essentials of psychological testing* (4th ed.). New York: Harper & Row.

Cullen, C. (1983). Implications of functional analysis. *British Journal of Clinical Psychology, 22,* 137–138.

Cureton, E. E. (1951). Validity. In E. F. Lindquist (Ed.), *Educational measurement* (pp. 621–694). Washington, DC: American Council on Education.

Curran, J. P. (1975). Social skills training and systematic desensitization in reducing dating anxiety. *Behaviour Research and Therapy, 13,* 65–68.

Daniels, L. K. (1974). A single session desensitization without relaxation training. *Journal of Behavior Therapy and Experimental Psychiatry, 5,* 207–208.

D'Augelli, A., D'Augelli, J., & Danish, S. (1981). *Helping others.* Monterey, CA: Brooks/ Cole.

Davis, A., Rosenthal, T. L., & Kelley, J. E. (1981). Actual fear cues, prompt therapy, and rationale enhance participant modeling with adolescents. *Behavior Therapy, 12,* 536–542.

Davis, R. (1979). The impact of self-modeling on problem behaviors in school-age children. *School Psychology Digest, 8,* 128–132.

Davison, G. C., & Wilson, G. T. (1973). Processes of fear-reduction in systematic desensitization: Cognitive and social reinforcement factors in humans. *Behavior Therapy, 4,* 1–21.

Dawidoff, D. J. (1973). *The malpractice of psychiatrists.* Springfield, IL: Charles C Thomas.

Dawley, H. H., & Wenrich, W. W. (1973). *Patient's manual for systematic desensitization.* Palo Alto, CA: Veterans' Workshop.

Day, R. W., & Sparacio, R. T. (1980). Structuring the counseling process. *Personnel and Guidance Journal, 59,* 246–250.

Deffenbacher, J. L., & Hahnloser, R. M. (1981). Cognitive and relaxation coping skills in stress inoculation. *Cognitive Therapy and Research, 5,* 211–215.

Deffenbacher, J. L., & Suinn, R. M. (1982). The self-control of anxiety. In P. Karoly & F. H. Kanfer (Eds.), *Self-management and behavior change* (pp. 393–442). New York: Pergamon Press.

Dengrove, E. (1966). *Treatment of non-phobic disorders by the behavioral therapies.* Paper presented at the meeting of the Association for Advancement of Behavior Therapy, New York.

Denholtz, M., & Mann, E. (1974). An audiovisual program for group desensitization. *Journal of Behavior Therapy and Experimental Psychiatry, 5,* 27–29.

Denney, D. R., & Rupert, P. (1977). Desensitization and self-control in the treatment of test anxiety. *Journal of Counseling Psychology, 24,* 272–280.

Denniston, D., & McWilliams, P. (1975). *The TM book.* New York: Warner Books.

Dentch, G. E., O'Farrell, T. J., & Cutter, H. S. G. (1980). Readability of marital assessment measures used by behavioral marriage therapists. *Journal of Consulting and Clinical Psychology, 48,* 790–792.

Derogatis, L. R., Rickels, K., & Rock, A. F. (1976). The SCL-90 and the MMPI: A step in the validation of a new self-report scale. *British Journal of Psychiatry, 128,* 280–289.

Devine, D. A., & Fernald, P. S. (1973). Outcome effects of receiving a preferred, randomly assigned, or non-preferred therapy. *Journal of Consulting and Clinical Psychology, 41,* 104–107.

Dittmann, A. T. (1962). The relationship between body movements and moods in interviews. *Journal of Consulting Psychology, 26,* 480.

Dixon, D. N., & Glover, J. A. (1984). *Counseling: A problem-solving approach.* New York: Wiley.

Dorn, F. J. (1984a). *Counseling as applied social psychology: An introduction to the social influence model.* Springfield, IL: Charles C Thomas.

Dorn, F. J. (1984b). The social influence model: A social psychological approach to counseling. *Personnel and Guidance Journal, 62,* 342–345.

Doster, J. A., & Nesbitt, J. G. (1979). Psychotherapy and self-disclosure. In G. J. Chelune (Ed.), *Self-disclosure: Origins, patterns, and implications of openness in interpersonal relationships.* San Francisco: Jossey-Bass.

Dowrick, P. W., & Dove, C. (1980). The use of self-modeling to improve the swimming performance of spina bifida children. *Journal of Applied Behavior Analysis, 13,* 51–56.

Duhl, F. J., Kantor, D., & Duhl, B. S. (1973). Learning, space and action in family therapy: A primer of sculpture. In D. A. Bloch (Ed.), *Techniques of family psychotherapy.* New York: Grune & Stratton.

Duley, S. M., Cancelli, A. A., Kratochwill, T. R., Bergan, J. R., & Meredith, K. E. (1983). Training and generalization of motivational analysis interview assessment skills. *Behavioral Assessment, 5,* 281–293.

Duncan, S. P., Jr. (1972). Some signals and rules for taking speaking turns in conversations. *Journal of Personality and Social Psychology, 23,* 283–292.

Duncan, S. P., Jr. (1974). On the structure of speaker-audi-

tor interaction during speaking turns. *Language in Society, 2,* 161–180.

Dunlap, K. (1928). A revision of the fundamental law of habit formation. *Science, 57,* 360–362.

Dush, D. M., Hirt, M. L., & Schroeder, H. (1983). Self-statement modification with adults: A meta-analysis. *Psychological Bulletin, 94,* 408–422.

Dyer, W. W. (1976). *Your erroneous zones.* New York: Funk & Wagnalls.

Dyer, W. W., & Vriend, J. (1975). *Counseling techniques that work.* Washington, DC: American Personnel and Guidance Association.

Eberle, T., Rehm, L., & McBurney, D. (1975). Fear decrement to anxiety hierarchy items: Effects of stimulus intensity. *Behaviour Research and Therapy, 13,* 225–261.

Edelstein, B., & Eisler, R. (1976). Effects of modeling and modeling with instructions and feedback on the behavioral components of social skills. *Behavior Therapy, 7,* 382–389.

Egan, G. (1975). *The skilled helper: A model for systematic helping and interpersonal relating.* Monterey, CA: Brooks/Cole.

Egan, G. (1976). *Interpersonal living: A skills contract approach to human-relations training in groups.* Monterey, CA: Brooks/Cole.

Egan, G. (1982). *The skilled helper: Model, skills, and methods for effective helping* (2nd ed.). Monterey, CA.: Brooks/Cole.

Eisenberg, S., & Delaney, D. J. (1977). *The counseling process* (2nd ed.). Chicago: Rand McNally.

Eisler, R. M., & Frederiksen, L. W. (1980). *Perfecting social skills: A guide to interpersonal behavior development.* New York: Plenum.

Ekman, P. (1964). Body position, facial expression and verbal behavior during interviews. *Journal of Abnormal and Social Psychology, 68,* 295–301.

Ekman, P., & Friesen, W. V. (1967). Head and body cues in the judgment of emotion: A reformulation. *Perceptual and Motor Skills, 24,* 711–724.

Ekman, P., & Friesen, W. V. (1969a). Nonverbal leakage and clues to deception. *Psychiatry, 32,* 88–106.

Ekman, P., & Friesen, W. V. (1969b). The repertoire of nonverbal behavior: Categories, origins, usage, and coding. *Semiotica, 1,* 49–98.

Ekman, P., & Friesen, W. V. (1972). Hand movements. *Journal of Communication, 22,* 353–374.

Ekman, P., & Friesen, W. V. (1975). *Unmasking the face.* Englewood Cliffs, NJ: Prentice-Hall.

Ekman, P., Friesen, W. V., & Ellsworth, P. (1972). *Emotion and the human face: Guidelines for research and an integration of findings.* New York: Pergamon Press.

Ekman, P., Friesen, W. V., & Tomkins, S. S. (1971). Facial affect scoring technique: A first validity study. *Semiotica, 3,* 37–58.

Elder, J. P. (1978). *Comparison of cognitive restructuring and response acquisition in the enhancement of social competence in college freshmen.* Unpublished doctoral dissertation, West Virginia University, Morgantown.

Elder, J. P., Edelstein, B. A., & Fremouw, W. J. (1981). Client by treatment interactions in response acquisition and cognitive restructuring approaches. *Cognitive Therapy and Research, 5,* 203–210.

Elliott, R. (1980). *Therapy session report: Short-forms for client and therapist.* Unpublished instrument, University of Toledo, Toledo, Ohio.

Elliott, R., Barker, C. B., Caskey, N., & Pistrang, N. (1982). Differential helpfulness of counselor verbal response modes. *Journal of Counseling Psychology, 29,* 354–361.

Elliott, R., Filipovich, H., Harrigan, L., Gaynor, J., Reimschuessel, C., & Zapadka, J. (1982). Measuring response empathy: The development of a multicomponent rating scale. *Journal of Counseling Psychology, 29,* 379–389.

Ellis, A. (1974). *Humanistic psychotherapy.* New York: McGraw-Hill.

Ellis, A. (1975). *Growth through reason.* North Hollywood, CA: Wilshire Book Company.

Ellis, A. (1984). *Rational-emotive therapy and cognitive behavior therapy.* New York: Springer.

Ellis, A., & Grieger, R. (1977). *Handbook of rational-emotive therapy.* New York: Springer.

Elmore, R. T., Wildman, R. W., & Westefeld, J. S. (1980). The use of systematic desensitization in the treatment of blood phobia. *Journal of Behavior Therapy and Experimental Psychiatry, 11,* 277–279.

Emery, J. R., & Krumboltz, J. D. (1967). Standard versus individualized hierarchies in desensitization to reduce test anxiety. *Journal of Counseling Psychology, 14,* 204–209.

Epstein, N. B., & Bishop, D. S. (1981). Problem-centered systems therapy of the family. *Journal of Marital and Family Therapy, 7,* 23–31.

Erickson, F. (1975). One function of proxemic shifts in face-to-face interaction. In A. Kendon, R. M. Harris, & M. R. Keys (Eds.), *Organization of behavior in face to face interactions* (pp. 175–187). Chicago: Aldine.

Erickson, M. H., Rossi, E., & Rossi, S. (1976). *Hypnotic realities.* New York: Irvington.

Etringer, B. D., Cash, T. F., & Rimm, D. C. (1982). Behavioral, affective, and cognitive effects of participant modeling and an equally credible placebo. *Behavior Therapy, 13,* 476–485.

Evans, I. M. (1974). A handy record-card for systematic desensitization hierarchy items. *Journal of Behavior Therapy and Experimental Psychiatry, 5,* 43–46.

Evans, R. (1970). Exhibitionism. In G. C. Costello (Ed.), *Symptoms of psychopathology: A handbook.* New York: Wiley.

Exline, R. V., & Winters, L. C. (1965). Affective relations and mutual glances in dyads. In S. S. Tompkins & C. E. Izard (Eds.), *Affect, cognition, and personality.* New York: Springer.

Falzett, W. C. (1981). Matched versus unmatched primary representational systems and their relationship to perceived trustworthiness in a counseling analogue. *Journal of Counseling Psychology, 28,* 305–308.

Fay, A. (1980). *The invisible diet.* New York: Manor Books.

Feindler, E. L., & Fremouw, W. J. (1983). Stress inoculation training for adolescent problems. In D. Meichenbaum & M. E. Jaremko (Eds.), *Stress reduction and prevention* (pp. 451–485). New York: Plenum.

Fensterheim, H. (1983). Basic paradigms, behavioral formulation and basic procedures. In H. Fensterheim & H. Glazer (Eds.), *Behavioral psychotherapy. Basic principles and case studies in an integrative clinical model* (pp. 40–87). New York: Brunner/Mazel.

Ferguson, J. M., Marquis, J. N., & Taylor, C. B. (1977). A script for deep muscle relaxation. *Diseases of the Nervous System, 38,* 703–708.

Ferster, C. B., Nurnberger, J. I., & Levitt, E. B. (1962). The control of eating. *Journal of Mathetics, 1,* 87–109.

Fisch, R., Weakland, J., & Segal, L. (1982). *The tactics of change: Doing therapy briefly.* San Francisco: Jossey-Bass.

Fishman, S. T., & Lubetkin, B. S. (1983). Office practice of behavior therapy. In M. Hersen (Ed.), *Outpatient behavior therapy: A clinical guide.* New York: Grune & Stratton.

Fling, S., Thomas, A., & Gallaher, M. (1981). Participant characteristics and the effects of two types of meditation vs. quiet sitting. *Journal of Clinical Psychology, 37,* 784–790.

Flowers, J. V., & Booraem, C. D. (1980). Simulation and role playing methods. In F. A. Kanfer & A. P. Goldstein (Eds.), *Helping people change* (pp. 172–209). New York: Pergamon Press.

Foa, E. B., Steketee, G. S., & Ascher, L. M. (1980). Systematic desensitization. In A. Goldstein & E. B. Foa (Eds.), *Handbook of behavioral interventions: A clinical guide* (pp. 38–91). New York: Wiley.

Fong, M. L., & Cox, B. G. (1983). Trust as an underlying dynamic in the counseling process: How clients test trust. *Personnel and Guidance Journal, 62,* 163–166.

Forman, S. G. (1980). A comparison of cognitive training and response cost procedures in modifying aggressive behavior of elementary school children. *Behavior Therapy, 11,* 594–600.

Forsyth, N. L., & Forsyth, D. R. (1982). Internality, controllability, and the effectiveness of attributional interpretations in counseling. *Journal of Counseling Psychology, 29,* 140–150.

Framer, E. M., & Sanders, S. H. (1980). The effects of family contingency contracting on disturbed sleeping behaviors of a male adolescent. *Journal of Behavior Therapy and Experimental Psychiatry, 11,* 235–237.

Frank, J. D. (1961). *Persuasion and healing.* Baltimore: Johns Hopkins Press.

Frankl, V. (1960). Paradoxical intention: A logotherapeutic technique. *American Journal of Psychotherapy, 14,* 520–535.

Frederiksen, L. W. (1975). Treatment of ruminative thinking by self-monitoring. *Journal of Behavior Therapy and Experimental Psychiatry, 6,* 258–259.

Frederiksen, L. W., Epstein, L. H., & Kosevsky, B. P. (1975). Reliability and controlling effects of three procedures for self-monitoring smoking. *Psychological Record, 25,* 255–264.

Freedman, N. (1972). The analysis of movement behavior during the clinical interview. In A. W. Siegman & B. Pope (Eds.), *Studies in dyadic communication.* New York: Pergamon Press.

Freeman, A. (1981). Dreams and images in cognitive therapy. In G. Emery, S. D. Hollon, & R. C. Bedrosian (Eds.), *New directions in cognitive therapy* (pp. 224–238). New York: Guilford Press.

Fremouw, W. J. (1977). A client manual for integrated behavior treatment of speech anxiety. *JSAS Catalogue of Selected Documents in Psychology, 1,* 14.MS.1426.

Fremouw, W. J., & Brown, J. P., Jr. (1980). The reactivity of addictive behaviors to self-monitoring: A functional analysis. *Addictive Behaviors, 5,* 209–217.

Fremouw, W. J., Callahan, E. J., Zitter, R. E., & Katell, A. (1981). Stimulus control and contingency contracting for behavior change and weight loss. *Addictive Behaviors, 6,* 289–300.

Fremouw, W. J., & Harmatz, M. G. (1975). A helper model for behavioral treatment of speech anxiety. *Journal of Consulting and Clinical Psychology, 43,* 652–660.

Fremouw, W. J., & Heyneman, N. (1983). Obesity. In M. Hersen (Ed.), *Outpatient behavior therapy* (pp. 173–202). New York: Grune & Stratton.

Fremouw, W. J., & Zitter, R. E. (1978). A comparison of skills training and cognitive restructuring-relaxation for the treatment of speech anxiety. *Behavior Therapy, 9,* 248–259.

Fretz, B. R., Corn, R., Tuemmler, J. M., & Bellet, W. (1979). Counselor nonverbal behaviors and client evaluations. *Journal of Counseling Psychology, 26,* 304–311.

Freud, S. (1952). *A general introduction to psychoanalysis.* New York: Washington Square Press. (Original work published 1900)

Frey, D. H. (1975). The anatomy of an idea: Creativity in counseling. *Personnel and Guidance Journal, 54,* 22–27.

Frey, D. H., & Raming, H. E. (1979). A taxonomy of counseling goals and methods. *Personnel and Guidance Journal, 58,* 26–33.

Galassi, J. P., Delo, J. S., Galassi, M. D., & Bastien, S. (1974). The college self-expression scale: A measure of assertiveness. *Behavior Therapy, 5,* 165–171.

Galassi, M. D., & Galassi, J. P. (1976). The effects of role playing variations on the assessment of assertive behavior. *Behavior Therapy, 7,* 343–347.

Galassi, M. D., & Galassi, J. P. (1977). *Assert yourself! How to be your own person.* New York: Human Sciences.

Gallagher, J. W., & Arkowitz, H. (1978). Weak effects of covert modeling treatment of test anxiety. *Journal of Behavior Therapy and Experimental Psychiatry, 9,* 23–26.

Gambrill, E. D. (1977). *Behavior modification: Handbook of assessment, intervention, and evaluation.* San Francisco: Jossey-Bass.

Gambrill, E. D., & Richey, C. (1975). An assertion inventory for use in assessment and research. *Behavior Therapy, 6,* 550–561.

Gazda, G. M., Asbury, F. S., Balzer, F. J., Childers, W. C., & Walters, R. P. (1977). *Human relations development.* (2nd ed.). Boston: Allyn & Bacon.

Gazda, G. M., Asbury, F. S., Balzer, F. J., Childers, W. C., & Walters, R. P. (1984). *Human relations development: A manual for educators* (3rd ed.). Boston: Allyn & Bacon.

Geer, C. A., & Hurst, J. C. (1976). Counselor-subject sex variables in systematic desensitization. *Journal of Counseling Psychology, 23,* 296–301.

Geis, G. L., & Chapman, R. (1971). Knowledge of results and other possible reinforcers in self-instructional systems. *Educational Technology, 11,* 38–50.

Gelatt, H., Varenhorst, B., Carey, R., & Miller, G. (1973). *Decisions and outcomes: A leader's guide.* Princeton, NJ: College Entrance Examination Board.

Gelder, M. G., Bancroft, J. H. J., Gath, D. H., Johnson, D. W., Matthews, A. M., & Shaw, P. M. (1973). Specific and non-specific factors in behavior therapy. *British Journal of Psychiatry, 123,* 445–462.

George, R., & Cristiani, T. (1981). *Theory, methods, and processes of counseling and psychotherapy.* Englewood Cliffs, NJ: Prentice-Hall.

Gershman, L. (1970). Case conference: A transvestite fantasy treated by thought-stopping, covert sensitization and aversive shock. *Journal of Behavior Therapy and Experimental Psychiatry, 1,* 153–161.

Gershman, L., & Clouser, R. A. (1974). Treating insomnia with relaxation and desentitization in a group setting by an automated approach. *Journal of Behavior Therapy and Experimental Psychiatry, 5,* 31–35.

Gershman, L., & Stedman, J. M. (1976). Using Kung Fu to reduce anxiety in a claustrophobic male. In J. D. Krumboltz & C. E. Thoresen (Eds.), *Counseling methods* (pp. 312–316). New York: Holt, Rinehart and Winston.

Gilbert, B. O., Johnson, S. B., Spillar, R., McCallum, M., Silverstein, J. H., & Rosenbloom, A. (1982). The effects of a peer-modeling film on children learning to self-inject insulin. *Behavior Therapy, 13,* 186–193.

Gillen, R. W., & Heimberg, R. G. (1980). Social skills training for the job interview: Review and prospectus. In M. Hersen, R. M. Eisler, & P. M. Miller, *Progress in behavior modification* (Vol. 10) (pp. 183–206). New York: Academic Press.

Gilliland, B., James, R., Roberts, G., & Bowman, J. (1984). *Theories and strategies in counseling and psychotherapy.* Englewood Cliffs, NJ: Prentice-Hall.

Girodo, M. (1974). Yoga meditation and flooding in the treatment of anxiety neurosis. *Journal of Behavior Therapy and Experimental Psychiatry, 5,* 157–160.

Gladstein, G. (1983). Understanding empathy: Integrating counseling, developmental, and social psychology perspectives. *Journal of Counseling Psychology, 30,* 467–482.

Glaister, B. (1982). Muscle relaxation training for fear reduction of patients with psychological problems: A review of controlled studies. *Behaviour Research and Therapy, 20,* 493–504.

Glasgow, R. E. & Rosen, G. M. (1978). Behavioral bibliotherapy: A review of self-help behavior therapy manuals. *Psychological Bulletin, 85,* 1–23.

Glasgow, R. E., & Rosen, G. M. (1979). Self-help behavior therapy manuals: Recent developments and clinical usage. *Clinical Behavior Therapy Review, 1,* 1–20.

Glogower, F. D., Fremouw, W. J., & McCroskey, J. C. (1978). A component analysis of cognitive restructuring. *Cognitive Therapy and Research, 2,* 209–223.

Goldfried, M. R. (1971). Systematic desensitization as training in self-control. *Journal of Consulting and Clinical Psychology, 37,* 228–234.

Goldfried, M. R. (1976a). Behavioral assessment. In I. B. Weiner (Ed.), *Clinical methods in psychology.* New York: Wiley.

Goldfried, M. R. (1976b). *Exercise manual and log for self-modification of anxiety: To accompany audio cassette #T44B.* New York: Biomonitoring Applications.

Goldfried, M. R. (1977). The use of relaxation and cognitive relabeling as coping skills. In R. B. Stuart (Ed.), *Behavioral self-management: Strategies, techniques and outcomes* (pp. 82–116). New York: Brunner/Mazel.

Goldfried, M. R. (1982). Behavioral assessment: An overview. In A. S. Bellack, M. Hersen, & A. E. Kazdin (Eds.), *International handbook of behavior modification and therapy.* New York: Plenum.

Goldfried, M. R. (1983). The behavior therapist in clinical practice. *Behavior Therapist, 6,* 45–46.

Goldfried, M. R., & Davison, G. C. (1976). *Clinical behavior therapy.* New York: Holt, Rinehart and Winston.

Goldfried, M. R., Decenteceo, E. T., & Weinberg, L. (1974). Systematic rational restructuring as a self-control technique. *Behavior Therapy, 5,* 247–254.

Goldfried, M. R., & Goldfried, A. P. (1977). Importance of hierarchy content in the self-control of anxiety. *Journal of Consulting and Clinical Psychology, 45,* 124–134.

Goldfried, M. R., & Goldfried, A. P. (1980). Cognitive change methods. In F. H. Kanfer & A. P. Goldstein (Eds.), *Helping people change* (pp. 97–130). New York: Pergamon Press.

Goldfried, M. R., Linehan, M. M., & Smith, J. L. (1978). The reduction of test anxiety through cognitive restructuring. *Journal of Consulting and Clinical Psychology, 46,* 32–39.

Goldfried, M. R., & Padawer, W. (1982). Current status and future directions in psychotherapy. In M. R. Goldfried (Ed.), *Converging themes in the practice of psychotherapy* (pp. 3–49). New York: Springer.

Goldiamond, I. (1965). Self-control procedures in personal behavior problems. *Psychological Reports, 17,* 851–868.

Goldiamond, I., & Dyrud, J. E. (1967). Some applications and implications of behavioral analysis in psychotherapy. In J. Schlein (Ed.), *Research in psychotherapy* (Vol. 3). Washington, DC: American Psychological Association.

Goldstein, A. J., Serber, M., & Piaget, G. (1970). Induced anger as a reciprocal inhibitor of fear. *Journal of Behavior Therapy and Experimental Psychiatry, 1,* 67–70.

Goldstein, A. P. (1971). *Psychotherapeutic attraction.* New York: Pergamon Press.

Goldstein, A. P. (1980). Relationship-enhancement methods. In F. H. Kanfer & A. P. Goldstein (Eds.), *Helping people change* (pp. 18–57). New York: Pergamon Press.

Goldstein, A. P., & Stein, N. (1976). *Prescriptive psychotherapies.* New York: Pergamon Press.

Goodwin, D. L. (1969). Consulting with the classroom teacher. In J. D. Krumboltz & C. E. Thoresen (Eds.), *Behavioral counseling: Cases and techniques* (pp. 260–264). New York: Holt, Rinehart and Winston.

Goodyear, R. K., & Bradley, F. O. (1980). The helping process as contractual. *Personnel and Guidance Journal, 58,* 512–515.

Goodyear, R. K., & Robyak, J. (1981). Counseling as an interpersonal influence process: A perspective for counseling practice. *Personnel and Guidance Journal, 60,* 654–657.

Gordon, D. (1978). *Therapeutic metaphors.* Cupertino, CA: Meta Publications.

Gormally, J., & Rardin, D. (1981). Weight loss and maintenance and changes in diet and exercise for behavioral counseling and nutrition education. *Journal of Counseling Psychology, 28,* 295–304.

Gormally, J., Varvil-Weld, D., Raphael R., & Sipps, G. (1981). Treatment of socially anxious college men using cognitive counseling and skills training. *Journal of Counseling Psychology, 28,* 147–157.

Gottman, J. M., & Leiblum, S. R. (1974). *How to do psychotherapy and how to evaluate it.* New York: Holt, Rinehart and Winston.

Graves, J. R., & Robinson, J. D. (1976). Proxemic behavior as a function of inconsistent verbal and nonverbal messages. *Journal of Counseling Psychology, 23,* 333–338.

Green, K. D., Webster, J., Beeman, I., Rosmarin, D., & Holliway, P. (1981). Progressive and self-induced relaxation training: Their relative effects on subjective and autonomic arousal to fearful stimuli. *Journal of Clinical Psychology, 37,* 309–315.

Green, L. (1982). Minority students' self-control of procrastination. *Journal of Counseling Psychology, 29,* 636–644.

Greenberg, I., & Altman, J. (1976). Modifying smoking behavior through stimulus control: A case report. *Journal of Behavior Therapy and Experimental Psychiatry, 7,* 97–99.

Greenberg, L. S., & Safran, J. D. (1981). Encoding and cognitive therapy: Changing what clients attend to. *Psychotherapy: Theory, Research & Practice, 18,* 163–169.

Greiner, J., & Karoly, P. (1976). Effects of self-control training on study activity and academic performance: An analysis of self-monitoring, self-reward and systematic-planning components. *Journal of Counseling Psychology, 23,* 495–502.

Gresham, F. M., & Nagle, R. J. (1980). Social skills training with children: Responsiveness of modeling and coaching as a function of peer orientation. *Journal of Consulting and Clinical Psychology, 48,* 718–729.

Grinder, J., & Bandler, R. (1976). *The structure of magic II.* Palo Alto, CA: Science and Behavior Books.

Gurman, A. S. (1981). Using "paradox" in psychodynamic marital therapy. In A. S. Gurman (Ed.), *Questions and answers in the practice of family therapy,* Vol. 1 (pp. 119–122). New York: Brunner/Mazel.

Gurman, A. S. (Ed.) (1982). *Questions and answers in the practice of family therapy* (Vol. 2). New York: Brunner/Mazel.

Haase, R. F., & Tepper, D. (1972). Nonverbal components of empathic communication. *Journal of Counseling Psychology, 19,* 417–424.

Hackett, G., & Horan, J. J. (1980). Stress inoculation for pain: What's really going on? *Journal of Counseling Psychology, 27,* 107–116.

Hackett, G., Horan, J. J., Stone, C., Linberg, S., Nicholas, W., & Lukaski, H. (1976). *Further outcomes and tentative predictor variables from an evolving comprehensive program for the behavioral control of smoking.* Paper presented at the annual meeting of the American Educational Research Association, San Francisco.

Hackmann, A., & McLean, C. A. (1975). A comparison of flooding and thought stopping in the treatment of obsessional neurosis. *Behaviour Research and Therapy, 13,* 263–269.

Hackney, H., & Cormier, L. S. (1979). *Counseling strategies and objectives* (2nd ed.). Englewood Cliffs, NJ: Prentice-Hall.

Haley, J. (1963). *Strategies of psychotherapy.* New York: Grune & Stratton.

Haley, J. (1967). *Advanced techniques of hypnosis and therapy: Selected papers of Milton H. Erickson, M.D.* New York: Grune & Stratton.

Haley, J. (1973). *Uncommon therapy: The psychiatric techniques of Milton Erickson, M.D.* New York: Norton.

Haley, J. (1976). *Problem-solving therapy.* San Francisco: Jossey-Bass.

Haley, J. (1978). Ideas which handicap therapists. In M. M. Berger (Ed.), *Beyond the double bind: Communication and family systems, theories, and techniques with schizophrenics.* New York: Brunner/Mazel.

Haley, J. (1984). *Ordeal therapy.* San Francisco: Jossey-Bass.

Hall, E. T. (1963). A system for the notation of proxemic behavior. *American Anthropologist, 65,* 1003–1026.

Hall, E. T. (1966). *The hidden dimension.* Garden City, NY: Doubleday.

Hamilton, S. A., & Fremouw, W. J. (in press). Cognitive-behavioral training for college basketball foul-shooting performance. *Cognitive Therapy and Research.*

Hammer, A. (1983). Matching perceptual predicates: Effect on perceived empathy in a counseling analogue. *Journal of Counseling Psychology, 30,* 172–179.

Hansen, J. C., Stevic, R. R., & Warner, R. W., Jr. (1977). *Counseling theory and process* (2nd ed.). Boston: Allyn & Bacon.

Hare-Mustin, R. T., Maracek, J., Kaplan, A. G., & Liss-Levinson, N. (1979). Rights of clients, responsibilities of therapists. *American Psychologist, 34,* 3–16.

Harper, R. G., Wiens, A. N., & Matarazzo, J. D. (1978). *Nonverbal communication: The state of the art.* New York: Wiley.

Harris, G. M., & Johnson, S. B. (1983). Coping imagery and relaxation instructions in a covert modeling treatment for text anxiety. *Behavior Therapy, 14,* 144–157.

Harvill, R., Jacobs, E., & Masson, R. (1984). Using "props" to enhance your counseling. *Personnel and Guidance Journal, 62,* 273–275.

Hathaway, S. R., & McKinley, J. C. (1951). *MMPI manual.* New York: Psychological Corporation.

Hawkins, R. P., & Dobes, R. W. (1977). Behavioral definitions in applied behavior analysis: Explicit or implicit. In B. C. Etzel, J. M. LeBlanc, & D. M. Baer (Eds.), *New developments in behavioral research: Theory, method, and application* (pp. 167–188). Hillsdale, NJ: Erlbaum.

Hay, W. M., Hay, L. R., Angle, H. V., & Nelson, R. O. (1979). The reliability of problem identification in the behavioral interview. *Behavioral Assessment, 1,* 107–118.

Hay, W. M., Hay, L. R., & Nelson, R. O. (1977). The adaptation of covert modeling procedures to the treatment of chronic alcoholism and obsessive-compulsive behavior: Two case reports. *Behavior Therapy, 8,* 70–76.

Hayes, S. C. (1981). Single case experimental design and empirical clinical practice. *Journal of Consulting and Clinical Psychology, 49,* 193–211.

Haynes, S. N. (1978). *Principles of behavioral assessment.* New York: Gardner Press.

Haynes, S. N., & Jensen, B. J. (1979). The interview as a behavioral assessment instrument. *Behavioral Assessment, 1,* 97–106.

Haynes, S. N., Jensen, B. J., Wise, E., & Sherman, D. (1981). The marital intake interview: A multimethod criterion validity assessment. *Journal of Consulting and Clinical Psychology, 49,* 379–387.

Haynes, S. N., & Wilson, C. C. (1979). *Behavioral assessment.* San Francisco: Jossey-Bass.

Hays, V., & Waddell, K. J. (1976). A self-reinforcing procedure for thought stopping. *Behavior Therapy, 7,* 559.

Hearn, M., & Evans, D. (1972). Anger and reciprocal inhibition therapy. *Psychological Reports, 30,* 943–948.

Heffernan, T., & Richards, C. S. (1981). Self-control of study behavior: Identification and evaluation of natural methods. *Journal of Counseling Psychology, 28,* 361–364.

Hein, E. C. (1980). *Communication in nursing practice* (2nd ed.) Boston: Little, Brown.

Heppner, P. P., & Dixon, D. N. (1981). Effects of client perceived need and counselor role in clients' behaviors. *Journal of Counseling Psychology, 59,* 542–550.

Heppner, P. P., & Heesacker, M. (1982). Interpersonal influence process in real-life counseling: Investigating client perceptions, counselor experience level, and counselor power over time. *Journal of Counseling Psychology, 29,* 215–223.

Heppner, P. P., & Heesacker, M. (1983). Perceived counselor characteristics, client expectations, and client satisfaction with counseling. *Journal of Counseling Psychology, 30,* 31–39.

Hersen, M. (1971). Resistance to direction in behavior therapy: Some comments. *Journal of Genetic Psychology, 118,* 121–127.

Hersen, M., & Barlow, D. H. (1976). *Single-case experimental designs: Strategies for studying behavior change.* New York: Pergamon Press.

Hersen, M., & Bellack, A. S. (Eds.). (1976). *Behavioral assessment: A practical handbook.* New York: Pergamon Press.

Hersen, M., & Bellack, A. S. (Eds.). (1981). *Behavioral assessment: A practical handbook* (2nd ed.). New York: Pergamon Press.

Hess, E. H. (1975). *The tell-tale eye.* New York: Van Nostrand Reinhold.

Hiebert, B., & Fox, E. E. (1981). Reactive effects of self-monitoring anxiety. *Journal of Counseling Psychology, 28,* 187–193.

Higgins, R. L., Frisch, M. B., & Smith, D. (1983). A comparison of role-played and natural responses to identical circumstances. *Behavior Therapy, 14,* 148–169.

Highlen, P. S., & Baccus, G. K. (1977). Effect of reflection of feeling and probe on client self-referenced affect. *Journal of Counseling Psychology, 24,* 440–443.

Hill, C. E. (1975). A process approach for establishing counseling goals and outcomes. *Personnel and Guidance Journal, 53,* 571–576.

Hill, C. E., Carter, J. A., & O'Farrell, M. K. (1983). A case study of the process and outcome of time-limited counseling. *Journal of Counseling Psychology, 30,* 3–18.

Hill, C. E., & Gormally, J. (1977). Effects of reflection, restatement, probe, and nonverbal behaviors on client affect. *Journal of Counseling Psychology, 24,* 92–97.

Hill, C. E., Siegelman, L., Gronsky, B. R., Sturniolo, F., & Fretz, B. R. (1981). Nonverbal communication and counseling outcome. *Journal of Counseling Psychology, 28,* 203–212.

Hillenberg, J. B., & Collins, F. L., Jr. (1982). A procedural analysis and review of relaxation training research. *Behaviour Research and Therapy, 20,* 251–260.

Hoffman-Graff, M. A. (1977). Interviewer use of positive

and negative self-disclosure and interviewer-subject sex pairing. *Journal of Counseling Psychology, 24,* 184–190.

Hollon, S. D., & Kendall, P. C. (1981). *In vivo* assessment techniques for cognitive-behavioral processes. In P. C. Kendall & S. D. Hollon (Eds.), *Assessment strategies for cognitive-behavioral interventions* (pp. 319–362). New York: Academic Press.

Holroyd, K. A. (1976). Cognition and desensitization in the group treatment of test anxiety. *Journal of Consulting and Clinical Psychology, 44,* 991–1001.

Holroyd, K. A., Appel, M. A., & Andrasik, F. (1983). A cognitive-behavioral approach to psychophysiological disorders. In D. Meichenbaum & M. E. Jaremko (Eds.), *Stress reduction and prevention* (pp. 219–259). New York: Plenum.

Homme, L., Csanyi, A., Gonzales, M., & Rechs, J. (1969). *How to use contingency contracting in the classroom.* Champaign, IL: Research Press.

Hopkins, J., Krawitz, G., & Bellack, A. S. (1981). The effects of situational variations in role-play scenes on assertive behavior. *Journal of Behavioral Assessment, 3,* 271–280.

Horan, J. J. (1973). "In vivo" emotive imagery: A technique for reducing childbirth anxiety and discomfort. *Psychological Reports, 32,* 1328.

Horan, J. J. (1976). Coping with inescapable discomfort through in vivo emotive imagery. In J. D. Krumboltz & C. E. Thoresen (Eds.), *Counseling methods* (pp. 316–320). New York: Holt, Rinehart and Winston.

Horan, J. J., Baker, S. B., Hoffman, A. M., & Shute, R. E. (1975). Weight loss through variations in the coverant control paradigm. *Journal of Counseling and Clinical Psychology, 43,* 68–72.

Horan, J. J., & Dellinger, J. K. (1974). "In vivo" emotive imagery: A preliminary test. *Perceptual and Motor Skills, 39,* 359–362.

Horan, J. J., Hackett, G., Buchanan, J. D., Stone, C. I., & Demchik-Stone, D. (1977). Coping with pain: A component analysis of stress inoculation. *Cognitive Therapy and Research, 1,* 211–221.

Horan, J. J., Layng, F. C., & Pursell, C. H. (1976). Preliminary study of the effects of "in vivo" emotive imagery on dental discomfort. *Perceptual and Motor Skills, 42,* 105–106.

Horne, A. M., & Matson, J. L. (1977). A comparison of modeling, desensitization, flooding, study skills, and control groups for reducing test anxiety. *Behavior Therapy, 8,* 1–8

Horney, K. (1950). *Neurosis and human growth: The struggle toward self-realization.* New York: Norton.

Hosford, R. E. (1969). Overcoming fear of speaking in a group. In J. D. Krumboltz & C. E. Thoresen (Eds.), *Behavioral counseling: Cases and techniques* (pp. 80–83). New York: Holt, Rinehart and Winston.

Hosford, R. E. (1974). *Counseling techniques: Self-as-a-model film.* Washington, DC: American Personnel and Guidance Press.

Hosford, R. E. (1980). Self-as-a-model: A cognitive social learning technique. *Counseling Psychologist, 9,* 45–62.

Hosford, R. E., & de Visser, L. (1974). *Behavioral approaches to counseling: An introduction.* Washington, DC: American Personnel and Guidance Press.

Hosford, R. E., Moss, C., & Morrell, G. (1976). The self-as-

a-model technique: Helping prison inmates change. In J. D. Krumboltz & C. E. Thoresen (Eds.), *Counseling methods* (pp. 487–495). New York: Holt, Rinehart and Winston.

Howard, W. A., Murphy, S. M., & Clarke, J. C. (1983). The nature and treatment of fear of flying: A controlled investigation. *Behavior Therapy, 14,* 557–567.

Hubble, M. A., Noble, F. C., & Robinson, S. E. (1981). The effect of counselor touch in an initial counseling session. *Journal of Counseling Psychology, 28,* 533–535.

Huck, S. W., Cormier, W. H., & Bounds, W. G. (1974). *Reading statistics and research.* New York: Harper & Row.

Hudson, J., & Danish, S. (1980). The acquisition of information: An important life skill. *Personnel and Guidance Journal, 59,* 164–167.

Hughes, H., & Haynes, S. (1978). Structured laboratory observation in the behavioral assessment of parent-child interactions: A methodological critique. *Behavior Therapy, 9,* 428–447.

Hull, C. L. (1952). *A behavior system.* New Haven, Conn.: Yale University Press.

Hutchins, D. E. (1979). Systematic counseling: The T-F-A model for counselor intervention. *Personnel and Guidance Journal, 57,* 529–531.

Ivey, A. E. (1983). *Intentional interviewing and counseling.* Monterey, CA: Brooks/Cole.

Ivey, A. E., & Gluckstern, N. (1974). *Basic attending skills: Participant manual.* Amherst, MA: Microtraining Associates.

Ivey A. E., & Gluckstern, N. (1976). *Basic influencing skills: Participant manual.* Amherst, MA: Microtraining Associates.

Ivey, A. E., & Simek-Downing, L. (1980). *Counseling and psychotherapy: Skills, theories, and practice.* Englewood Cliffs, NJ: Prentice-Hall.

Jackson, B. (1972). Treatment of depression by self-reinforcement. *Behavior Therapy, 3,* 298–307.

Jackson, D. (1968). *Therapy, communication and change.* Palo Alto, CA: Science and Behavior Books.

Jacobs, M. K., & Cochran, S. D. (1982). The effects of cognitive restructuring on assertive behavior. *Cognitive Therapy and Research, 6,* 63–76.

Jacobsen, R., & Edinger, J. D. (1982). Side effects of relaxation treatment. *American Journal of Psychiatry, 139,* 952–953.

Jacobson, E. (1929). *Progressive relaxation.* Chicago: University of Chicago Press.

Jacobson, E. (1964). *Anxiety and tension control.* Philadelphia: Lippincott.

Jacobson, N. S. (1981). Marital problems. In J. L. Shelton & R. L. Levy (Eds.), *Behavioral assignments and treatment compliance* (pp. 147–166). Champaign, IL: Research Press.

Jacobson, N. S. & Margolin, G. (1979). *Marital therapy: Strategies based on social learning and behavior exchange principles.* New York: Brunner/Mazel.

Jahn, D. L., & Lichstein, K. L. (1980). The resistive client. *Behavior Modification, 4,* 303–320.

James, J. E. (1981). Self-monitoring of stuttering: Reactivity and accuracy. *Behaviour Research and Therapy, 19,* 291–296.

Janis, I. L. (1983). Stress inoculation in health care: Theory and research. In D. Meichenbaum & M. E. Jaremko (Eds.), *Stress reduction and prevention* (pp. 67–100). New York: Plenum.

Jaremko, M. E. (1983). Stress inoculation training for social anxiety, with emphasis on dating anxiety. In D. Meichenbaum & M. E. Jaremko (Eds.), *Stress reduction and prevention* (pp. 419–450). New York: Plenum.

Jaremko, M. E. (1984). Stress inoculation training: A generic approach for the prevention of stress-related disorders. *Personnel and Guidance Journal, 62,* 544–550.

Jarvinen, P. J., & Gold, S. R. (1981). Imagery as an aid in reducing depression. *Journal of Clinical Psychology, 37,* 523–529.

Jayaratne, S., & Levy, R. L. (1979). *Empirical clinical practice.* New York: Columbia University Press.

Jeffery, K. M. (1977). *The effects of goal-setting on self-motivated persistence.* Unpublished doctoral dissertation, Stanford University, Stanford, CA.

Jeffery, R. W. (1976). Reducing fears through participant modeling and self-directed practice. In J. D. Krumboltz & C. E. Thoresen (Eds.), *Counseling methods* (pp. 301–312). New York: Holt, Rinehart and Winston.

Johnson, D. W. (1981). *Reaching out: Interpersonal effectiveness and self-actualization.* Englewood Cliffs, NJ: Prentice-Hall.

Johnston, J. M., & O'Neill, G. (1973). The analysis of performance criteria defining course grades as a determinant of college student academic performance. *Journal of Applied Behavior Analysis, 6,* 261–268.

Jones, R. T., Nelson, R. E., & Kazdin, A. E. (1977). The role of external variables in self-reinforcement: A review. *Behavior Modification, 1,* 147–178.

Kanfer, F. H. (1970). Self-monitoring: Methodological limitations and clinical applications. *Journal of Consulting and Clinical Psychology, 35,* 148–152.

Kanfer, F. H. (1975). Self-management methods. In F. H. Kanfer & A. P. Goldstein (Eds.), *Helping people change* (pp. 309–355). New York: Pergamon Press.

Kanfer, F. H. (1980). Self-management methods. In F. H. Kanfer & A. P. Goldstein (Eds.), *Helping people change* (2nd ed.) (pp. 334–389). New York: Pergamon Press.

Kanfer, F. H., and Goldstein, A. P. (1975). Introduction. In F. H. Kanfer & A. P. Goldstein (Eds.), *Helping people change* (pp. 1–14). New York: Pergamon Press.

Kanfer, F. H., & Grimm, L. G. (1977). Behavioral analysis: Selecting target behaviors in the interview. *Behavior Modification, 1,* 7–28.

Kanfer, F. H., & Phillips, J. S. (1970). *Learning foundations of behavior therapy.* New York: Wiley.

Kanfer, F. H., & Saslow, G. (1969). Behavioral diagnosis. In C. M. Franks (Ed.), *Behavior therapy: Appraisal and status* (pp. 417–444). New York: McGraw-Hill.

Kantor, J. R. (1970). An analysis of the experimental analysis of behavior (TEAB). *Journal of the Experimental Analysis of Behavior, 13,* 101–108.

Kaplan, D. A. (1982). Behavioral, cognitive, and behavioral-cognitive approaches to group assertion training therapy. *Cognitive Therapy and Research, 6,* 301–314.

Kaplan, H. I., & Sadock, B. J. (1981). *Modern synopsis of comprehensive textbook of psychiatry III* (3rd ed.). Baltimore: Williams & Wilkins.

Karoly, P. (1975). Operant methods. In F. H. Kanfer & A. P. Goldstein (Eds.), *Helping people change* (pp. 195–228). New York: Pergamon Press.

Karoly, P., & Kanfer, F. A. (Eds.). (1982). *Self-management and behavior change.* New York: Pergamon Press.

Kazdin, A. E. (1973a). Covert modeling and the reduction of avoidance behavior. *Journal of Abnormal Psychology, 81,* 89–95.

Kazdin, A. E. (1973b). Methodological and assessment considerations in evaluating reinforcement programs in applied settings. *Journal of Applied Behavior Analysis, 6,* 517–531.

Kazdin, A. E. (1974a). Comparative effects of some variations of covert modeling. *Journal of Behavior Therapy and Experimental Psychiatry, 5,* 225–231.

Kazdin, A. E. (1974b). Covert modeling, model similarity, and reduction of avoidance behavior. *Behavior Therapy, 5,* 325–340.

Kazdin, A. E. (1974c). Effects of covert modeling and model reinforcement on assertive behavior. *Journal of Abnormal Psychology, 83,* 240–252.

Kazdin, A. E. (1974d). The effect of model identity and fear-relevant similarity on covert modeling. *Behavior Therapy, 5,* 624–635.

Kazdin, A. E. (1974e). Reactive self-monitoring: The effects of response desirability, goal setting, and feedback. *Journal of Consulting and Clinical Psychology, 42,* 704–716.

Kazdin, A. E. (1974f). Self-monitoring and behavior change. In M. J. Mahoney & C. E. Thoresen (Eds.), *Self-control: Power to the person* (pp. 218–246). Monterey, CA: Brooks/Cole.

Kazdin, A. E. (1975). Covert modeling, imagery assessment, and assertive behavior. *Journal of Consulting and Clinical Psychology, 43,* 716–724.

Kazdin, A. E. (1976a). Assessment of imagery during covert modeling of assertive behavior. *Journal of Behavior Therapy and Experimental Psychiatry, 7,* 213–219.

Kazdin, A. E. (1976b). Developing assertive behavior through covert modeling. In J. D. Krumboltz & C. E. Thoresen (Eds.), *Counseling methods* (pp. 475–486). New York: Holt, Rinehart and Winston.

Kazdin, A. E. (1976c). Effects of covert modeling, multiple models, and model reinforcement on assertive behavior. *Behavior Therapy, 7,* 211–222.

Kazdin, A. E. (1976d). Statistical analyses for single-case experimental designs. In M. Hersen & D. H. Barlow, *Single-case experimental designs: Strategies for studying behavior change* (pp. 265–316). New York: Pergamon Press.

Kazdin, A. E. (1977). Assessing the clinical or applied importance of behavior change through social validation. *Behavior Modification, 1,* 427–452.

Kazdin, A. E. (1979a). Effects of covert modeling and coding of modeled stimuli on assertive behavior. *Behaviour Research and Therapy, 17,* 53–61.

Kazdin, A. E. (1979b). Imagery elaboration and self-efficacy in covert modeling treatment of unassertive behavior. *Journal of Consulting and Clinical Psychology, 47,* 725–733.

Kazdin, A. E. (1980a). Covert and overt rehearsal and elaboration during treatment in development of assertive behavior. *Behaviour Research and Therapy, 18,* 191–201.

Kazdin, A. E. (1980b). *Research design in clinical psychology.* New York: Harper & Row.

Kazdin, A. E. (1981). Drawing valid inferences from case studies. *Journal of Consulting and Clinical Psychology, 49,* 183–192.

Kazdin, A. E. (1982). The separate and combined effects of covert and overt rehearsal in developing assertive behavior. *Behaviour Research and Therapy, 20,* 17–25.

Kazdin, A. E., & Krouse, R. (1983). The impact of variations in treatment rationales on expectancies for therapeutic change. *Behavior Therapy, 14,* 657–671.

Kazdin, A. E., & Mascitelli, S. (1982a). Behavioral rehearsal, self-instructions, and homework practice in developing assertiveness. *Behavior Therapy, 13,* 346–360.

Kazdin, A. E., & Mascitelli, S. (1982b). Covert and overt rehearsal and homework practice in developing assertiveness. *Journal of Consulting and Clinical Psychology, 50,* 250–258.

Kazdin, A. E., Matson, J. L., & Esveldt-Dawson, K. (1984). The relationship of role-play assessment of children's social skills to multiple measures of social competence. *Behaviour Research and Therapy, 22,* 129–139.

Kazdin, A. E., & Wilcoxon, L. A. (1976). Systematic desensitization and nonspecific treatment effects: A methodological evaluation. *Psychological Bulletin, 83,* 729–758.

Keane, T. M., Black, J. L., Collins, F. L., Jr., & Venson, M. C. (1982). A skills training program for teaching the behavioral interview. *Behavioral Assessment, 4,* 53–62.

Keefe, F. J., & Blumenthal, J. A. (1980). The life fitness program: A behavioral approach to making exercise a habit. *Journal of Behavior Therapy and Experimental Psychiatry, 11,* 31–34.

Keefe, F. J., Surwit, R. S., & Pilon, R. N. (1980). Biofeedback, autogenic training and progressive relaxation in the treatment of Raynaud's disease: A comparative study. *Journal of Applied Behavior Analysis, 13,* 3–11.

Kendall, P. C. (1983). Stressful medical procedures: Cognitive-behavioral strategies for stress management and prevention. In D. Meichenbaum & M. E. Jaremko (Eds.), *Stress reduction and prevention* (pp. 159–180). New York: Plenum.

Kendall, P. C., & Braswell, L. (1982). Cognitive-behavioral self-control therapy for children: A component analysis. *Journal of Consulting and Clinical Psychology, 50,* 672–689.

Kendall, P. C., & Hollon, S. D. (Eds.). (1981). *Assessment strategies for cognitive-behavioral interventions.* New York: Academic Press.

Kern, J. M. (1982). The comparative external and concurrent validity of three role-plays for assessing heterosocial performance. *Behavior Therapy, 13,* 666–680.

Kern, J. M., Miller, C., & Eggers, J. (1983). Enhancing the validity of role-play tests: A comparison of three role-play methodologies. *Behavior Therapy, 14,* 482–492.

Kiesler, C. A. (1971). *The psychology of commitment.* New York: Academic Press.

Kiesler, D. J. (1966). Some myths of psychotherapy research and the search for a paradigm. *Psychological Bulletin, 65,* 110–136.

King, M., Novik, L., & Citrenbaum, C. (1983). *Irresistible communication: Creative skills for the health professional.* Philadelphia: Saunders.

Kiresuk, T. J. & Sherman, R. E. (1968). Goal attainment scaling: A general method for evaluating comprehensive mental health programs. *Community Mental Health Journal, 4,* 443–453.

Kirsch, I., & Henry, D. (1979). Self-desensitization and meditation in the reduction of public speaking anxiety. *Journal of Consulting and Clinical Psychology, 47,* 536–541.

Kirsch, I., Tennen, H., Wickless, C., Saccone, A. J., & Cody, S. (1983). The role of expectancy in fear reduction. *Behavior Therapy, 14,* 520–533.

Kirschenbaum, D. S., Ordman, A. M., Tomarken, A. J., & Holtzbauer, R. (1982). Effects of differential self-monitoring and level of mastery of sports performance: Brain power bowling. *Cognitive Therapy and Research, 6,* 335–342.

Klepac, R. K., Hauge, G., Dowling, J., & McDonald, M. (1981). Direct and generalized effects of three components of stress inoculation for increased pain tolerance. *Behavior Therapy, 12,* 417–424.

Klorman, R., Hilpert, P. L., Michael, R., LaGana, C., & Sveen, O. B. (1980). Effects of coping and mastery modeling on experienced and inexperienced pedodontic patients' disruptiveness. *Behavior Therapy, 11,* 156–168.

Knapp, M. L. (1972). *Nonverbal communication in human interaction.* New York: Holt, Rinehart and Winston.

Knapp, M. L. (1978). *Nonverbal communication in human interaction* (2nd ed.). New York: Holt, Rinehart and Winston.

Knox, J. (1972). *Cognitive strategies for coping with pain: Ignoring vs. acknowledging.* Unpublished doctoral dissertation, University of Waterloo, Waterloo, Ontario, Canada.

Kolko, D., & Milan, M. (1983). Reframing and paradoxical instruction to overcome "resistance" in the treatment of delinquent youths: A multiple baseline analysis. *Journal of Consulting and Clinical Psychology, 51,* 655–660.

Kopel, S., & Arkowitz, H. (1975). The role of attribution and self-perception in behavior change: Implications for behavior therapy. *Genetic Psychology Monographs, 92,* 175–212.

Kostka, M. P., & Galassi, J. P. (1974). Group systematic desensitization versus covert positive reinforcement in the reduction of test anxiety. *Journal of Counseling Psychology, 21,* 464–468.

Kothandapani, V. (1971). Validation of feeling, belief, and intention to act as three components of attitude and their contribution to prediction of contraceptive behavior. *Journal of Personality and Social Psychology, 19,* 321–333.

Krivonos, P. D., & Knapp, M. L. (1975). Initiating communication: What do you say when you say hello? *Central States Speech Journal, 26,* 115–125.

Krumboltz, J. D. (1966). Behavioral goals for counseling. *Journal of Counseling Psychology, 13,* 153–159.

Krumboltz, J. D., & Thoresen, C. E. (Eds.) (1969). *Behavioral counseling: Cases and techniques.* New York: Holt, Rinehart and Winston.

Krumboltz, J. D., & Thoresen, C. E. (Eds.) (1976). *Counseling methods.* New York: Holt, Rinehart and Winston.

Kunzelmann, H. D. (Ed.). (1970). *Precision teaching.* Seattle: Special Child Publications.

L'Abate, L. (1981). Toward a systematic classification of counseling and therapy theorists, methods, processes, and goals: The E-R-A model. *Personnel and Guidance Journal, 59,* 263–266.

Laborde, G. (1984). *Influencing with integrity.* Palo Alto, CA: Science and Behavior Books.

Lacks, P., Bertelson, A. D., Sugerman, J., & Kunkel, J. (1983). The treatment of sleep maintenance insomnia with stimulus-control techniques. *Behaviour Research and Therapy, 21,* 291–295.

LaCrosse, M. B. (1980). Perceived counselor social influence and counseling outcomes: Validity of the counselor rating form. *Journal of Counseling Psychology, 27,* 320–327.

Ladouceur, R. (1974). An experimental test of the learning paradigm of covert positive reinforcement in deconditioning anxiety. *Journal of Behavior Therapy and Experimental Psychiatry, 5,* 3–6.

Ladouceur, R. (1983). Participant modeling with or without cognitive treatment for phobias. *Journal of Consulting and Clinical Psychology, 51,* 930–932.

LaFromboise, T. D., & Dixon, D. N. (1981). American Indian perception of trustworthiness in a counseling interview. *Journal of Counseling Psychology, 28,* 135–139.

Lamaze, F. (1958). *Painless childbirth: Psychoprophylactic method.* London: Burke.

Lang, P. J. (1969). The mechanics of desensitization and the laboratory study of human fear. In C. M. Franks (Ed.), *Behavior therapy: Appraisal and status* (pp. 160–191). New York: McGraw-Hill.

Lang, P. J., & Lazovik, A. (1963). Experimental desensitization of a phobia. *Journal of Abnormal and Social Psychology, 66,* 519–525.

Lankton, S. R. (1980). *Practical magic: A translation of basic neurolinguistic programming into clinical psychotherapy.* Cupertino, CA: Meta Publications.

Lankton, S. R., & Lankton, C. H. (1983). *The answer within: A clinical framework of Ericksonian hypnotherapy.* New York: Brunner/Mazel.

Lawson, D. M., & May, R. B. (1970). Three procedures for the extinction of smoking behavior. *Psychological Record, 20,* 151–157.

Lazarus, A. A. (1966). Behavioral rehearsal vs. non-directive therapy vs. advice in effecting behaviour change. *Behaviour Research and Therapy, 4,* 209–212.

Lazarus, A. A. (1967). In support of technical eclecticism. *Psychological Reports, 21,* 415–416.

Lazarus, A. A. (1968). Variations in desensitization therapy. *Psychotherapy: Theory, Research and Practice, 5,* 50–52.

Lazarus, A. A. (1970). *Daily living: Coping with tension and anxieties* [Tape of relaxation exercises]. Chicago: Instructional Dynamics.

Lazarus, A. A. (1971). *Behavior therapy and beyond.* New York: McGraw-Hill.

Lazarus, A. A. (1973). Multimodal behavior therapy: Treating the "basic id." *Journal of Nervous and Mental Disease, 156,* 404–411.

Lazarus, A. A. (1976). *Multimodal behavior therapy.* New York: Springer.

Lazarus, A. A. (1978). Multimodal behavior therapy. Part 3. In E. Shostrom (Ed.), *Three approaches to psychotherapy II* [16-mm film or ¾″ videocassette]. Orange, CA: Psychological Films.

Lazarus, A. A. (1981). *The practice of multimodal therapy.* New York: McGraw-Hill.

Lazarus, A. A. (1982). *Personal enrichment through imagery,* Workbook [Audiotape]. New York: BMA Audio Cassettes.

Lazarus, A. A., & Abramovitz, A. (1962). The use of "emotive imagery" in the treatment of children's phobias. *Journal of Mental Science, 108,* 191–195.

Lazarus, A. A., & Fay, A. (1982). Resistance or rationalization? A cognitive-behavioral perspective. In P. L. Wachtel (Ed.), *Resistance: Psychodynamic and behavioral approaches* (pp. 115–132). New York: Plenum.

Lazarus, A. A., & Rachman, S. (1957). The use of systematic desensitization in psychotherapy. *South African Medical Journal, 32,* 934–937.

Leal, L., Baxter, E. G., Martin, J., & Marx, R. W. (1981). Cognitive modification and systematic desensitization with test anxious high school students. *Journal of Counseling Psychology, 28,* 525–528.

Leaman, D. R. (1978). Confrontation in counseling. *Personnel and Guidance Journal, 56,* 630–633.

Lecomte, C., Bernstein, B. L., & Dumont, F. (1981). Counseling interactions as a function of spatial-environmental conditions. *Journal of Counseling Psychology, 28,* 536–539.

Lee, D. Y., Hallberg, E. T., Kocsis, M., & Haase, R. F. (1980). Decoding skills in nonverbal communication and perceived interviewer effectiveness. *Journal of Counseling Psychology, 27,* 89–92.

Lehrer, P. M. (1982). How to relax and how not to relax: A reevaluation of the work of Edmund Jacobson — I. *Behaviour Research and Therapy, 20,* 417–428.

Lehrer, P. M., & Woolfolk, R. L. (1982). Self-report assessment of anxiety: Somatic, cognitive, and behavioral modalities. *Behavioral Assessment, 4,* 167–177.

Lehrer, P. M., & Woolfolk, R. L. (1984). Are stress-reduction techniques interchangeable, or do they have specific effects? A review of the comparative empirical literature. In R. L. Woolfolk & P. M. Lehrer (Eds.), *Principles and practice of stress management* (pp. 404–477). New York: Guilford Press.

Lehrer, P. M., Woolfolk, R. L., Rooney, A. J., McCann, B., & Carrington, P. (1983). Progressive relaxation and meditation: A study of psychophysiological and therapeutic differences between two techniques. *Behaviour Research and Therapy, 21,* 651–662.

Leitenberg, H., Agras, W. S., Barlow, D. H., & Oliveau, D. (1969). Contribution of selective positive reinforcement and therapeutic instructions to systematic desensitization therapy. *Journal of Abnormal Psychology, 74,* 113–118.

Lent, R. W., Russell, R. K., & Zamostny, K. P. (1981). Comparison of cue-controlled desensitization, rational restructuring and a credible placebo in the treatment of speech anxiety. *Journal of Consulting and Clinical Psychology, 49,* 608–610.

Levendusky, P., & Pankratz, L. (1975). Self-control techniques as an alternative to pain medication. *Journal of Abnormal Psychology, 84,* 165–168.

Leventhal, H., & Nerenz, D. R. (1983). A model for stress research with some implications for the control of stress disorders. In D. Meichenbaum & M. G. Jaremko (Eds.), *Stress reduction and prevention* (pp. 67–100). New York: Plenum.

Levin, F. M., & Gergen, K. J. (1969). Revealingness, ingratiation, and the disclosure of self. *Proceedings of the 77th Annual Convention of the American Psychological Association, 4* (Pt. 1), 447–448.

Levine, B. A., & Wolpe, J. (1980). *In vivo* desensitization of a severe driving phobia through radio contact. *Journal of Behavior Therapy and Experimental Psychiatry, 11,* 281–282.

Levine, F., & Fasnacht, G. (1974). Token rewards may lead to token learning. *American Psychologist, 29,* 816–820.

Levy, L. H. (1963). *Psychological interpretation.* New York: Holt, Rinehart and Winston.

Levy, R. I. (1977). Relationship of an overt commitment to task compliance in behavior therapy. *Journal of Behavior Therapy and Experimental Psychiatry, 8,* 25–29.

Lewin, K. (1951). *Field theory in social science.* New York: Harper & Row.

Lewis, E. C. (1970). *The psychology of counseling.* New York: Holt, Rinehart and Winston.

Lewis, G. K. (1978). *Nurse-patient communication* (3rd ed.). Dubuque, IA: William C. Brown.

Ley, P. (1976). Toward better doctor-patient communications. In A. E. Bennett (Ed.), *Communication between doctors and patients.* London: Oxford University Press.

Lick, J. R., & Katkin, E. S. (1976). Assessment of anxiety and fear. In M. Hersen & A. S. Bellack (Eds.), *Behavioral assessment: A practical handbook* (pp. 175–206). New York: Pergamon Press.

Lick, J. R., & Unger, T. (1977). The external validity of behavioral fear assessment: The problem of generalizing from the laboratory to the natural environment. *Behavior Modification, 1,* 283–306.

Lidz, C. W., Meisel, A., Zerbavel, G. E., Carter, M., Sestak, R., & Roth, L. (1984). *Informed consent: A study of decision-making in psychiatry.* New York: Guilford Press.

Lindsley, O. R. (1968). A reliable wrist counter for recording behavior rates. *Journal of Applied Behavior Analysis, 1,* 77–78.

Linehan, M. (1977). Issues in behavioral interviewing. In J. D. Cone & R. P. Hawkins (Eds.), *Behavioral assessment: New directions in clinical psychology* (pp. 30–51). New York: Brunner/Mazel.

Lipinski, D. P., Black, J. L., Nelson, R. O., & Ciminero, A. (1975). Influence of motivational variables on the reactivity and reliability of self-recording. *Journal of Consulting and Clinical Psychology, 43,* 637–646.

Lipinski, D. P., & Nelson, R. (1974). The reactivity and unreliability of self-recording. *Journal of Consulting and Clinical Psychology, 42,* 118–123.

Litrownik, A. J. (1982). Special considerations in the self-management training of the developmentally disabled. In P. Karoly & F. H. Kanfer (Eds.), *Self management and behavior change* (pp. 315–352). New York: Pergamon Press.

Livingston, S. A. (1977). Psychometric techniques for criterion-referenced testing and behavioral assessment. In J.

D. Cone & R. P. Hawkins (Eds.), *Behavioral assessment: New directions in clinical psychology* (pp. 308–383). New York: Brunner/Mazel.

Lloyd, M. E. (1983). Selecting systems to measure client outcome in human service agencies. *Behavioral Assessment, 5,* 55–70.

Locke, E. A., Shaw, K. N., Saari, L. M., & Latham, G. P. (1981). Goal-setting and task performance, 1969–1980. *Psychological Bulletin, 90,* 125–152.

Locke, H. J., & Wallace, K. N. (1957). Short marital adjustment and prediction tests: Their reliability and validity. *Marriage and Family Living, 21,* 251–255.

Lomont, J. F. (1965). Reciprocal inhibition or extinction? *Behaviour Research and Therapy, 3,* 209–219.

Long, L., Paradise, L., & Long, T. (1981). *Questioning: Skills for the helping process.* Monterey, CA: Brooks/Cole.

Long, L., & Prophit, P. (1981). *Understanding/responding: A communication manual for nurses.* Monterey, CA: Wadsworth Health Sciences.

Lopez, F. G. (1983). A paradoxical approach to vocational indecision. *Personnel and Guidance Journal, 61,* 410–412.

Lopez, F. G., & Wambach, C. A. (1982). Effects of paradoxical and self-control directives in counseling. *Journal of Counseling Psychology, 29,* 115–124.

LoPiccolo, J., & Steger, J. C. (1974). The sexual interaction inventory: A new instrument for assessment of sexual dysfunction. *Archives of Sexual Behavior, 6,* 585–595.

Lowe, J. C. (1973). Excitatory response to music as a reciprocal inhibitor. *Journal of Behavior Therapy and Experimental Psychiatry, 4,* 297–299.

Lum, L. C. (1976). The syndrome of habitual chronic hyperventilation. In O. Hill (Ed.), *Modern trends in psychosomatic medicine* (Vol. 3). Boston: Butterworths.

Lyles, J. N., Burish, T. G., Krozely, M. G., & Oldham, R. K. (1982). Efficacy of relaxation training and guided imagery in reducing the aversiveness of cancer chemotherapy. *Journal of Consulting and Clinical Psychology, 50,* 509–524.

MacDonald, M. L., & Bernstein, D. A. (1974). Treatment of a spider phobia by *in vivo* and imaginal desensitization. *Journal of Behavior Therapy and Experimental Psychiatry, 5,* 47–52.

Mahaney, M. M., & Kern, J. M. (1983). Variations in role-play tests of heterosocial performance. *Journal of Consulting and Clinical Psychology, 51,* 151–152.

Mahoney, K. (1974). Count on it: A simple self-monitoring device. *Behavior Therapy, 5,* 701–703.

Mahoney, K., & Mahoney, M. J. (1976). Cognitive factors in weight reduction. In J. D. Krumboltz & C. E. Thoresen (Eds.), *Counseling methods* (pp. 99–105). New York: Holt, Rinehart and Winston.

Mahoney, M. J. (1970). Toward an experimental analysis of covariant control. *Behavior Therapy, 1,* 510–521.

Mahoney, M. J. (1971). The self-management of covert behavior: A case study. *Behavior Therapy, 2,* 575–578.

Mahoney, M. J. (1972). Research issues in self-management. *Behavior Therapy, 3,* 45–63.

Mahoney, M. J. (1974). *Cognition and behavior modification.* Cambridge, MA: Ballinger.

Mahoney, M. J. (1977a). Cognitive therapy and research: A

question of questions. *Cognitive Therapy and Research, 1,* 5–16.

Mahoney, M. J. (1977b). Some applied issues in self-monitoring. In J. Cone & R. Hawkins (Eds.), *Behavioral assessment: New directions in clinical psychology* (pp. 241–254). New York: Brunner/Mazel.

Mahoney, M. J., Moura, N. G., & Wade, T. C. (1973). Relative efficacy of self-reward, self-punishment, and self-monitoring techniques for weight loss. *Journal of Consulting and Clinical Psychology, 40,* 404–407.

Mahoney, M. J., & Thoresen, C. E. (Eds.). (1974). *Self-control: Power to the person.* Monterey, CA: Brooks/Cole.

Manthei, R. J. (1983). Client choice of therapist or therapy. *Personnel and Guidance Journal, 61,* 334–340.

Margolin, G. (1981). Behavior exchange in happy and unhappy marriages: A family cycle perspective. *Behavior Therapy, 12,* 329–343.

Marlatt, G. A., & Marques, J. K. (1977). Meditation, self-control and alcohol use. In R. B. Stuart (Ed.), *Behavioral self-management: Strategies, techniques and outcomes* (pp. 117–153). New York: Brunner/Mazel.

Marlatt, G. A., & Parks, G. A. (1982). Self-management of addictive behaviors. In P. Karoly & F. H. Kanfer (Eds.), *Self-management and behavior change* (pp. 443–448). New York: Pergamon Press.

Marlatt, G. A., & Perry, M. A. (1975). Modeling methods. In F. H. Kanfer & A. P. Goldstein (Eds.), *Helping people change* (pp. 117–158). New York: Pergamon Press.

Marquis, J. N., Ferguson, J. M., & Taylor, C. B. (1980). Generalization of relaxation skills. *Journal of Behavior Therapy and Experimental Psychiatry, 11,* 95–99.

Marquis, J. N., Morgan, W., & Piaget, G. (1973). *A guidebook for systematic desensitization* (3rd ed.). Palo Alto, CA: Veterans' Workshop.

Marshall, W., Presse, L., & Andrews, W. A. (1976). A self-administered program for public speaking anxiety. *Behaviour Research and Therapy, 14,* 33–39.

Martin, G. A., & Worthington, E. L. (1982). Behavioral homework. In M. N. Hersen, R. M. Eisler, & P. M. Miller (Eds.), *Progress in behavior modification* Vol. 13 (pp. 197–226). New York: Academic Press.

Martin, G. L. (1982). Thought-stopping and stimulus control to decrease persistent disturbing thoughts. *Journal of Behavior Therapy and Experimental Psychiatry, 13,* 215–220.

Martin, J. E., Collins, F. L., Jr., Hillenberg, J. B., Zabin, M. A., & Katell, A. D. (1981). Assessing compliance to home relaxation: A simple technology for a critical problem. *Behavioral Assessment, 3,* 193–198.

Martinez, J. A., & Edelstein, B. (1977, December). *The effects of demand characteristics on the assessment of heterosocial competence.* Paper presented at the annual meeting of the Association for the Advancement of Behavior Therapy, Atlanta.

Maslin, A., & Davis, J. L. (1975). Sex-role stereotyping as a factor in mental health standards among counselors-in-training. *Journal of Counseling Psychology, 22,* 87–91.

Maslow, A. H. (1966). *The psychology of science: A reconnaisance.* New York: Harper & Row.

Matarazzo, J. D., & Wiens, A. N. (1972). *The interview: Research on its anatomy and structure:* Chicago: Aldine-Atherton.

Mathews, A. M. (1971). Psychophysiological approaches to the investigation of desensitization and related procedures. *Psychological Bulletin, 76,* 73–91.

Maultsby, R. C. (1984). *Rational behavior therapy.* Englewood Cliffs, NJ: Prentice-Hall.

Maurer, R. E., & Tindall, J. H. (1983). Effect of postural congruence on client's perception of counselor empathy. *Journal of Counseling Psychology, 30,* 158–163.

Mavissakalian, M., Michelson, L., Greenwald, D., Kornblith, S., & Greenwald, M. (1983). Cognitive-behavioral treatment of agoraphobia: Paradoxical intention vs. self-statement training. *Behaviour Research and Therapy, 21,* 75–86.

McCarthy, P. (1982). Differential effects of counselor self-referent responses and counselor status. *Journal of Counseling Psychology, 29,* 125–131.

McCarthy, P., & Betz, N. (1978). Differential effects of self-disclosing versus self-involving counselor statements. *Journal of Counseling Psychology, 25,* 251–256.

McCordick, S. M., Kaplan, R. M., Smith, S., & Finn, M. E. (1981). Variations in cognitive behavior modification for test anxiety. *Psychotherapy: Theory, Research & Practice, 18,* 170–178.

McDonald, F. J. (1973). Behavior modification in teacher education. In *Behavior modification in education: 72nd yearbook of the National Society for the Study of Education* (Pt. 1). Chicago: University of Chicago Press.

McFall, R. M. (1970). Effects of self-monitoring on normal smoking behavior. *Journal of Consulting and Clinical Psychology, 35,* 135–142.

McFall, R. M. (1977a). Analogue methods in behavioral assessment: Issues and prospects. In J. D. Cone & R. P. Hawkins (Eds.), *Behavioral assessment: New directions in clinical psychology* (pp. 152–177). New York: Brunner/Mazel.

McFall, R. M. (1977b). Parameters of self-monitoring. In R. B. Stuart (Ed.), *Behavioral self-management: Strategies, techniques and outcomes* (pp. 196–214). New York: Brunner/Mazel.

McFall, R. M., & Dodge, K. A. (1982). Self-management and interpersonal skills learning. In P. Karoly & F. H. Kanfer (Eds.), *Self-management and behavior change* (pp. 353–392). New York: Pergamon Press.

McFall, R. M., & Twentyman, C. (1973). Four experiments on the relative contributions of rehearsal, modeling, and coaching to assertion training. *Journal of Abnormal Psychology, 81,* 199–218.

McGlynn, F. D. (1980). Successful treatment of anorexia nervosa with self-monitoring and long distance praise. *Journal of Behavior Therapy and Experimental Psychiatry, 11,* 283–286.

McGlynn, F. D., Bichajian, C., Giesen, J. M., & Rose, R. L. (1981). Effects of cue-controlled relaxation, a credible placebo treatment and no treatment on shyness among college males. *Journal of Behavior Therapy and Experimental Psychiatry, 12,* 299–306.

McGlynn, F. D., Wilson, A., & Linder, L. (1970). Systematic desensitization of snake-avoidance with individualized and non-individualized hierarchies. *Journal of Behavior Therapy and Experimental Psychiatry, 1,* 201–204.

McGuigan, F. J. (1984). Progressive relaxation: Origins, principles, and clinical applications. In R. L. Woolfolk & P. M. Lehrer (Eds.), *Principles and practice of stress management* (pp. 12–42). New York: Guilford Press.

McGuire, D., & Thelen, M. H. (1983). Modeling, assertion training, and the breadth of the target assertive behavior. *Behavior Therapy, 14,* 275–285.

McGuire, D., Thelen, M. H., & Amolsch, T. (1975). Interview self-disclosure as a function of length of modeling and descriptive instructions. *Journal of Consulting and Clinical Psychology, 43,* 356–362.

McKeachie, W. J. (1974). The decline and fall of the laws of learning. *Educational Researcher, 3,* 7–11.

McKeachie, W. J. (1976). Psychology in America's bicentennial year. *American Psychologist, 31,* 819–833.

McKenzie, T. L., & Rushall, B. S. (1974). Effects of self-recording on attendance and performance in a competitive swimming training environment. *Journal of Applied Behavior Analysis, 7,* 199–206.

McLaughlin, T. F. (1976). Self-control in the classroom. *Review of Educational Research, 46,* 631–663.

Meador, B., & Rogers, C. (1984). Person-centered therapy. In R. J. Corsini (Ed.), *Current psychotherapies* (pp. 142–195). Itasca, IL: Peacock.

Mehrabian, A. (1976). *Public places and private spaces.* New York: Basic Books.

Meichenbaum, D. H. (1971). Examination of model characteristics in reducing avoidance behavior. *Journal of Personality and Social Psychology, 17,* 298–307.

Meichenbaum, D. H. (1972). Cognitive modification of test anxious college students. *Journal of Consulting and Clinical Psychology, 39,* 370–380.

Meichenbaum, D. H. (1974). *Therapist manual for cognitive behavior modification.* Unpublished manuscript, University of Waterloo, Waterloo, Ontario, Canada.

Meichenbaum, D. H. (1976). A cognitive-behavior modification approach to assessment. In M. Hersen & A. S. Bellack (Eds.), *Behavioral assessment: A practical handbook* (pp. 143–171). New York: Pergamon Press.

Meichenbaum, D. H. (1977). *Cognitive-behavior modification: An integrative approach.* New York: Plenum.

Meichenbaum, D. H. (1985). *Stress-inoculation training.* New York: Pergamon Press.

Meichenbaum, D. H., & Cameron, R. (1973a). *Stress inoculation: A skills training approach to anxiety management.* Unpublished manuscript, University of Waterloo, Waterloo, Ontario, Canada.

Meichenbaum, D. H., & Cameron, R. (1973b). Training schizophrenics to talk to themselves. A means of developing attentional control. *Behavior Therapy, 4,* 515–534.

Meichenbaum, D. H., & Cameron, R. (1983). Stress inoculation training: Toward a general paradigm on training coping skills. In D. H. Meichenbaum & M. E. Jaremko (Eds.), *Stress reduction and prevention* (pp. 115–157). New York: Plenum.

Meichenbaum, D. H., Gilmore, J., & Fedoravicius, A. (1971). Group insight versus group desensitization in treating speech anxiety. *Journal of Counseling and Clinical Psychology, 36,* 410–421.

Meichenbaum, D. H., & Goodman, J. (1971). Training impulsive children to talk to themselves: A means of developing self-control. *Journal of Abnormal Psychology, 77,* 115–126.

Meichenbaum, D. H., & Turk, D. (1976). The cognitive-behavioral management of anxiety, anger, and pain. In P. O. Davidson (Ed.), *The behavioral management of anxiety, depression and pain.* New York: Brunner/Mazel.

Melamed, B. G., & Siegel, L. J. (1975). Reduction of anxiety in children facing hospitalization and surgery by use of filmed modeling. *Journal of Consulting and Clinical Psychology, 43,* 511–521.

Melamed, B. G., & Siegel, L. J. (1980). *Behavioral medicine: Practical applications in health care.* New York: Springer.

Melnick, J. (1973). A comparison of replication techniques in the modification of minimal dating behavior. *Journal of Abnormal Psychology, 81,* 51–59.

Melnick, J., & Russell, R. W. (1976). Hypnosis versus systematic desensitization in the treatment of test anxiety. *Journal of Counseling Psychology, 23,* 291–295.

Melnick, J., & Stocker, R. (1977). An experimental analysis of the behavioral rehearsal with feedback technique in assertiveness training. *Behavior Therapy, 8,* 222–228.

Meyer, R. G. (1983). *The clinician's handbook: The psychopathology of adulthood and late adolescence.* Boston: Allyn & Bacon.

Meyer, V., & Turkat, I. (1979). Behavioral analysis of clinical cases. *Journal of Behavioral Assessment, 1,* 259–270.

Miklich, D., Chida, T., & Danker-Brown, P. (1977). Behavior modification by self-modeling without subject awareness. *Journal of Behavior Therapy and Experimental Psychiatry, 8,* 125–130.

Miller, H. R., & Nawas, M. M. (1970). Control of aversive stimulus termination in systematic desensitization. *Behaviour Research and Therapy, 8,* 57–61.

Miller, R. C., & Berman, J. S. (1983). The efficacy of cognitive behavior therapies: A quantitative review of the research evidence. *Psychological Bulletin, 94,* 39–53.

Miller, W. R., & DiPilato, M. (1983). Treatment of nightmares via relaxation and desensitization: A controlled evaluation. *Journal of Consulting and Clinical Psychology, 51,* 870–877.

Milne, C. R., & Dowd, E. T. (1983). Effect of interpretation style on counselor social influence. *Journal of Counseling Psychology, 30,* 603–606.

Minuchin, S. (1974). *Families and family therapy.* Cambridge, MA: Harvard University Press.

Mischel, W. (1968). *Personality and assessment.* New York: Wiley.

Mischel, W. (1971). *Introduction to personality.* New York: Holt, Rinehart and Winston.

Mitchell, K. M., Bozarth, J. D., & Krauft, C. C. (1977). A reappraisal of the therapeutic effect of accurate empathy, nonpossessive warmth, and genuineness. In A. S. Gurman & A. M. Razin (Eds.), *Effective psychotherapy: A handbook of research* (pp. 482–502). New York: Pergamon Press.

Mitchell, K. R., & White, R. G. (1977). Behavioral self-management: An application to the problem of migraine headaches. *Behavior Therapy, 8,* 213–221.

Mogan, J., & O'Brien, J. S. (1972). The counterconditioning of a vomiting habit by sips of ginger ale. *Journal of Behavior Therapy and Experimental Psychiatry, 3,* 135–137.

Moos, R. H. (1972). Assessment of the psychosocial environments of community-oriented psychiatric treatment programs. *Journal of Abnormal Psychology, 79,* 9–18.

Morganstern, K. P., & Tevlin, H. E. (1981). Behavioral interviewing. In M. Hersen & A. S. Bellack (Eds.), *Behavioral assessment: A practical handbook* (pp. 71–100). New York: Pergamon Press.

Morris, K. T., & Kanitz, H. M. (1975). *Rational emotive therapy.* Boston: Houghton Mifflin.

Morris, R. J. (1980). Fear reduction methods. In F. H. Kanfer & A. P. Goldstein (Eds.), *Helping people change* (pp. 248–293). New York: Pergamon Press.

Munjack, D. J., & Oziel, R. J. (1978). Resistance in the behavioral treatment of sexual dysfunctions. *Journal of Sex and Marital Therapy, 4,* 122–138.

National Association of Social Workers (1979). *Code of ethics.* Washington, DC: Author.

Nawas, M., Fishman, S., & Pucel, J. (1970). A standardized desensitization program applicable to group and individual treatments. *Behaviour Research and Therapy, 8,* 49–56.

Nay, W. R. (1979). *Multimethod clinical assessment.* New York: Gardner Press.

Neilans, T. H., & Israel, A. C. (1981). Towards maintenance and generalization of behavior change: Teaching children self-regulation and self-instructional skills. *Cognitive Therapy and Research, 5,* 189–195.

Nelson, R. O. (1977). Methodological issues in assessment via self-monitoring. In J. D. Cone & R. P. Hawkins (Eds.), *Behavioral assessment: New directions in clinical psychology* (pp. 217–254). New York: Brunner/Mazel.

Nelson, R. O. (1981). Realistic dependent measures for clinical use. *Journal of Consulting and Clinical Psychology, 49,* 168–182.

Nelson, R. O. (1983). Behavioral assessment: Past, present, and future. *Behavioral Assessment, 5,* 195–206.

Nelson, R. O., & Barlow, D. H. (1981). Behavioral assessment: Basic strategies and initial procedures. In D. H. Barlow (Ed.), *Behavioral assessment of adult disorders* (pp. 13–43). New York: Guilford Press.

Nelson, R. O., Boykin, R. A., & Hayes, S. C. (1982). Long-term effects of self-monitoring on reactivity and on accuracy. *Behaviour Research and Therapy, 20,* 357–363.

Nelson, R. O., & Hayes, S. C. (1979). Some current dimensions of behavioral assessment. *Behavioral Assessment, 1,* 1–16.

Nelson, R. O., Hayes, S. C., Spong, R. T., Jarrett, R. B., & McKnight, D. L. (1983). Self-reinforcement: Appealing misnomer or effective mechanism. *Behaviour Research and Therapy, 21,* 557–566.

Nelson, R. O., Lipinski, D. P., & Black, J. L. (1976a). The reactivity of adult retardates' self-monitoring: A comparison among behaviors of different valences, and a comparison with token reinforcement. *Psychological Record, 26,* 189–201.

Nelson, R. O., Lipinski, D., & Black, J. L. (1976b). The relative reactivity of external observations and self-monitoring. *Behavior Therapy, 7,* 314–321.

Nelson, R. O., Lipinski, D. P., & Boykin, R. A. (1978). The effects of self-recorders' training and the obtrusiveness of the self-recording device on the accuracy and reactivity of self-monitoring. *Behavior Therapy, 9,* 200–208.

Nelson, W. M., III. (1981). A cognitive-behavioral treatment for disproportionate dental anxiety and pain: A case study. *Journal of Clinical Child Psychology, 10,* 79–82.

Nesse, M., & Nelson, R. O. (1977). Variations of covert modeling on cigarette smoking. *Cognitive Therapy and Research, 1,* 343–354.

Nicassio, P., & Bootzin, R. (1974). A comparison of progressive relaxation and autogenic training as treatment for insomnia. *Journal of Abnormal Psychology, 83,* 253–260.

Nietzel, M. T., & Bernstein, D. A. (1981). Assessment of anxiety and fear. In M. Hersen & A. S. Bellack (Eds.), *Behavioral assessment* (2nd ed.) (pp. 215–245). New York: Pergamon Press.

Nietzel, M. T., Martorano, R., & Melnick, J. (1977). The effects of covert modeling with and without reply training on the development and generalization of assertive responses. *Behavior Therapy, 8,* 183–192.

Nilsson, D., Strassberg, D., & Bannon, J. (1979). Perceptions of counselor self-disclosure: An analogue study. *Journal of Counseling Psychology, 26,* 399–404.

Nolan, J. D. (1968). Self-control procedures in the modification of smoking behavior. *Journal of Consulting and Clinical Psychology, 32,* 92–93.

Norton, G. R., & DeLuca, R. V. (1979). The use of stimulus control procedures to eliminate persistent nocturnal awakenings. *Journal of Behavior Therapy and Experimental Psychiatry, 10,* 65–67.

Novaco, R. W. (1975). *Anger control: The development and evaluation of an experimental treatment.* Lexington, MA: Heath.

Novaco, R. W. (1977). A stress inoculation approach to anger management in the training of law enforcement officers. *American Journal of Community Psychology, 5,* 327–346.

Nye, L. S. (1973). Obtaining results through modeling. *Personnel and Guidance Journal, 51,* 380–384.

Okun, B. F. (1976). *Effective helping: Interviewing and counseling techniques.* North Scituate, MA: Duxbury Press.

Okun, B. F. (1982). *Effective helping: Interviewing and counseling techniques* (2nd ed.). Monterey, CA: Brooks/Cole.

O'Leary, K., Poulos, R., & Devine, V. (1972). Tangible reinforcers: Bonuses or bribes. *Journal of Consulting and Clinical Psychology, 38,* 1–8.

Olin, R. J. (1976). Thought stopping: Some cautionary observations. *Behavior Therapy, 7,* 706–707.

Omer, H. (1981). Paradoxical treatments: A unified concept. *Psychotherapy: Theory, Research and Practice, 18,* 320–324.

O'Neil, D., & Howell, R. (1969). Three modes of hierarchy presentation in systematic desensitization therapy. *Behaviour Research and Therapy, 7,* 289–294.

Orne, M. T. (1969). Demand characteristics and the concept of quasi-controls. In R. Rosenthal & R. Rosnow (Eds.), *Artifact in behavioral research* (pp. 147–179). New York: Academic Press.

Ornstein, R. E. (1972). *The psychology of consciousness.* New York: Viking.

Osberg, J. W., III. (1981). The effectiveness of applied relaxation in the treatment of speech anxiety. *Behavior Therapy, 12,* 723–729.

Öst, L.-G., Jerremalm, A., & Johannson, J. (1981). Individual response patterns and the effects of different behavioral methods in the treatment of social phobia. *Behaviour Research and Therapy, 19,* 1–16.

Öst, L.-G., Johannson, J., & Jerremalm, A. (1982). Individual response patterns and the effects of different behavioral methods in the treatment of claustrophobia. *Behaviour Research and Therapy, 20,* 445–460.

Osterhouse, R. A. (1976). Group systematic desensitization of test anxiety. In J. D. Krumboltz & C. E. Thoresen (Eds.), *Counseling methods* (pp. 269–279). New York: Holt, Rinehart and Winston.

Otter, S. B., & Guerra, J. J. (1976). *Assertion training.* Champaign, IL: Research Press.

Owens, R. G., & Ashcroft, J. B. (1982). Functional analysis in applied psychology. *British Journal of Clinical Psychology, 21,* 181–189.

Papp, P. (1976). Family choreography. In P. J. Guerin, Jr. (Ed.), *Family therapy: Theory and practice* (pp. 465–479). New York: Gardner Press.

Papp, P. (1980). The Greek chorus and other techniques of paradoxical therapy. *Family Process, 19,* 45–57.

Papp, P. (1984). *The process of change.* New York: Guilford Press.

Pascal, G. R. (1959). *Behavioral change in the clinic.* New York: Grune & Stratton.

Passons, W. R. (1975). *Gestalt approaches in counseling.* New York: Holt, Rinehart and Winston.

Patterson, L. E., & Eisenberg, S. (1983). *The counseling process* (3rd ed.). Boston: Houghton Mifflin.

Paul, G. L. (1966). *Insight versus desensitization in psychotherapy: An experiment in anxiety reduction.* Stanford, CA: Stanford University Press.

Paul, G. L. (1967). Strategy of outcome research in psychotherapy. *Journal of Consulting Psychology, 31,* 109–118.

Paul, G. L., & Shannon, D. T. (1966). Treatment of anxiety through systematic desensitization in therapy groups. *Journal of Abnormal Psychology, 71,* 124–135.

Penick, S. B., Filion, R., Fox, S., & Stunkard, A. J. (1971). Behavior modification in the treatment of obesity. *Psychosomatic Medicine, 33,* 49–55.

Perls, F. S. (1973). *The Gestalt approach and eyewitness to therapy.* Palo Alto, CA: Science and Behavior Books.

Perri, M. G., & Richards, C. S. (1977). An investigation of naturally occurring episodes of self-controlled behaviors. *Journal of Counseling Psychology, 24,* 178–183.

Perry, M. A., & Furukawa, M. J. (1980). Modeling methods. In F. H. Kanfer & A. P. Goldstein (Eds.), *Helping people change* (pp. 131–171). New York: Pergamon Press.

Peterson, L., & Shigetomi, C. (1981). The use of coping techniques to minimize anxiety in hospitalized children. *Behavior Therapy, 12,* 1–14.

Philips, C., & Hunter, M. (1981). The treatment of tension headache: II. EMG "normality" and relaxation. *Behaviour Research and Therapy, 19,* 499–507.

Phillips, L. W. (1971). Training of sensory and imaginal responses in behavior therapy. In R. D. Rubin, H. Fensterheim, A. A. Lazarus, & C. M. Franks (Eds.), *Advances in behavior therapy* (pp. 111–122). New York: Academic Press.

Pickett, C., & Cloum, G. A. (1982). Comparative treatment strategies and their interaction with locus of control in the reduction of postsurgical pain and anxiety. *Journal of Consulting and Clinical Psychology, 50,* 439–441.

Pietrofesa, J. J., Hoffman, A., Splete, H. H., & Pinto, D. V. (1978). *Counseling: Theory, research, and practice.* Chicago: Rand McNally.

Polly, S., Turner, R. D., & Sherman, A. R. (1976). A self-control program for the treatment of obesity. In J. D. Krumboltz & C. E. Thoresen (Eds.), *Counseling methods* (pp. 106–117). New York: Holt, Rinehart and Winston.

Pope, B. (1979). *The mental health interview.* New York: Pergamon Press.

Potter, S. (1965). Language and society. In P. Hazard & M. Hazard (Eds.), *Language and literacy today.* Chicago: Science Research Associates.

Prinz, R. J., Foster, S., Kent, R. N., & O'Leary, K. D. (1979). Multivariate assessment of conflict in distressed and nondistressed mother-adolescent dyads. *Journal of Applied Behavior Analysis, 12,* 691–700.

Quattrochi-Turbin, S., & Jason, L. A. (1980). Enhancing social interaction and activity among the elderly through stimulus control. *Journal of Applied Behavior Analysis, 13,* 159–163.

Rachman, A. W. (1981). Clinical meditation in groups. *Psychotherapy: Theory, Research and Practice, 18,* 250–252.

Rachman, S. (1966). Studies in desensitization—III: Speed of generalization. *Behaviour Research and Therapy, 4,* 7–15.

Rachman, S. (1968). The role of muscular relaxation in desensitization therapy. *Behaviour Research and Therapy, 6,* 159–166.

Rachman, S. (1972). Clinical applications of observational learning, imitation and modeling. *Behavior Therapy, 3,* 379–397.

Rappaport, A. F., & Cammer, L. (1977). Breath meditation in the treatment of essential hypertension. *Behavior Therapy, 8,* 269–270.

Raskin, D., & Klein, Z. (1976). Losing a symptom through keeping it: A review of paradoxical treatment techniques and rationale. *Archives of General Psychiatry, 33,* 548–555.

Raths, L., Harmin, M., & Simon, S. (1966). *Values and teaching.* Columbus, OH: Charles E. Merrill.

Rathus, S. A. (1973). A 30-item schedule for assessing assertive behavior. *Behavior Therapy, 4,* 398–406.

Raush, H. L., & Bordin, E. S. (1957). Warmth in personality development and in psychotherapy. *Psychiatry, 20,* 351–363.

Ray, W. J., & Raczynski, J. M. (1981). Psychophysiological assessment. In M. Hersen & A. S. Bellack (Eds.), *Behavioral assessment* (pp. 175–211). New York: Pergamon Press.

Reade, M. N., & Smouse, A. D. (1980). Effect of inconsistent verbal-nonverbal communication and counselor response mode on client estimate of counselor regard and effectiveness. *Journal of Counseling Psychology, 27,* 546–553.

Rebman, V. L. (1983). Self-control desensitization with cue controlled relaxation for treatment of a conditioned vomiting response to air travel. *Journal of Behavior Therapy and Experimental Psychiatry, 14,* 161–164.

Redd, W. H. (1980). *In vivo* desensitization in the treatment of chronic emesis following gastrointestinal surgery. *Behavior Therapy, 11,* 421–427.

Redfering, D. L., & Bowman, M. J. (1981). Effects of a meditative relaxation exercise on non-attending behaviors of behaviorally disturbed children. *Journal of Clinical Child Psychology, 10,* 126–127.

Reeder, C., & Kunce, J. (1976). Modeling techniques, drug-abstinence behavior, and heroin addicts: A pilot study. *Journal of Counseling Psychology, 23,* 560–562.

Rehm, L. P. (1982). Self-management in depression. In P. Karoly & F. H. Kanfer (Eds.), *Self-management and behavior change* (pp. 522–567). New York: Pergamon Press.

Reid, W. H. (1983). *Treatment of the DSM-III psychiatric disorders.* New York: Brunner/Mazel.

Reiser, D. E., & Schroder, A. K. (1980). *Patient interviewing.* Baltimore: Williams & Wilkins.

Richardson, B., & Stone, G. L. (1981). Effects of a cognitive adjunct procedure within a microtraining situation. *Journal of Counseling Psychology, 28,* 168–175.

Rimm, D. C. (1973). Thought stopping and covert assertion in the treatment of phobias. *Journal of Consulting and Clinical Psychology, 41,* 466–467.

Rimm, D. C., & Masters, J. C. (1979). *Behavior therapy: Techniques and empirical findings* (2nd ed.). New York: Academic Press.

Rinn, R. C., & Vernon, J. C. (1975). Process evaluation of outpatient treatment in a community mental health center. *Journal of Behavior and Experimental Psychiatry, 6,* 5–11.

Risley, T., & Hart, B. (1968). Developing correspondence between the nonverbal and verbal behavior of preschool children. *Journal of Applied Behavior Analysis, 1,* 267–281.

Roberts, A. H. (1969). Self-control procedures in modification of smoking behavior: Replication. *Psychological Reports, 24,* 675–676.

Rogers, C. (1942). *Counseling and psychotherapy.* Boston: Houghton Mifflin.

Rogers, C. (1951). *Client-centered therapy.* Boston: Houghton Mifflin.

Rogers, C. (1957). The necessary and sufficient conditions of therapeutic personality change. *Journal of Consulting Psychology, 21,* 95–103.

Rogers, C. (1977). *Carl Rogers on personal power: Inner strength and its revolutionary impact.* New York: Delacorte Press.

Rogers, C., Gendlin, E., Kiesler, D., & Truax, C. (1967). The therapeutic relationship and its impact: A study of psychotherapy with schizophrenics. Madison: University of Wisconsin Press.

Rohrbaugh, M., Tennen, H., Press, S., & White, L. (1981). Compliance, defiance and therapeutic paradox: Guidelines for strategic use of paradoxical interventions. *American Journal of Orthopsychiatry, 51,* 454–467.

Romanczyk, R. G. (1974). Self-monitoring in the treatment of obesity: Parameters of reactivity. *Behavior Therapy, 5,* 531–540.

Rose, S. D. (1973). *Treating children in groups: A behavioral approach.* San Francisco: Jossey-Bass.

Rosen, A., & Proctor, E. (1981). Distinctions between treatment outcomes and their implications for treatment

evaluation. *Journal of Consulting and Clinical Psychology, 49,* 418–425.

Rosen, G. M., Glasgow, R. E., & Barrera, M. (1976). A controlled study to assess the clinical efficacy of totally self-administered systematic desensitization. *Journal of Consulting and Clinical Psychology, 44,* 208–217.

Rosen, R. C., & Schnapp, B. J. (1974). The use of a specific behavioral technique (thought-stopping) in the context of conjoint couples therapy: A case report. *Behavior Therapy, 5,* 261–264.

Rosenthal, T. L. (1976). Modeling therapies. In M. Hersen, R. Eisler, & P. Miller (Eds.), *Progress in behavior modification* (Vol. 2) (pp. 53–97). New York: Academic Press.

Rosenthal, T. L., & Bandura, A. (1978). Psychological modeling: Theory and Practice. In S. L. Garfield & A. E. Bergin (Eds.), *Handbook of Psychotherapy and Behavior Change* (2nd ed.) (pp. 621–658). New York: Wiley.

Rosenthal, T. L., Hung, J. H., & Kelley, J. E. (1977). Therapist social influence: Sternly strike while the iron is hot. *Behaviour Research and Therapy, 15,* 253–259.

Rosenthal, T. L., & Reese, S. L. (1976). The effects of covert and overt modeling on assertive behavior. *Behaviour Research and Therapy, 14,* 463–469.

Roskies, E. (1983). Stress management for Type A individuals. In D. Meichenbaum & M. E. Jaremko (Eds.), *Stress reduction and prevention* (pp. 261–288). New York: Plenum.

Ross, S. M., & Proctor, S. (1973). Frequency and duration of hierarchy item exposure in a systematic desensitization technique. *Behaviour Research and Therapy, 11,* 303–312.

Rothmeier, R. C., & Dixon, D. N. (1980). Trustworthiness and influence: A reexamination in an extended counseling analogue. *Journal of Counseling Psychology, 27,* 315–319.

Rotter, J. B., Chance, J. E., & Phares, E. J. (Eds.). (1972). *Applications of a social learning theory of personality.* New York: Holt, Rinehart and Winston.

Rovetto, F. M. (1983). *In vivo* desensitization of a severe driving phobia through radio contact with telemonitoring of neurophysiological reactions. *Journal of Behavior Therapy and Experimental Psychiatry, 14,* 49–54.

Rudestam, K., & Bedrosian, R. (1977). An investigation of the effectiveness of desensitization and flooding with two types of phobias. *Behaviour Research and Therapy, 15,* 23–30.

Russell, M. L. (1974). *The decision-making book for children.* Unpublished manuscript, Stanford University, Stanford, CA.

Russell, M. L., & Thoresen, C. E. (1976). Teaching decision-making skills to children. In J. D. Krumboltz & C. E. Thoresen (Eds.), *Counseling methods* (pp. 377–383). New York: Holt, Rinehart and Winston.

Russell, R. K., & Lent, R. W. (1982). Cue-controlled relaxation and systematic desensitization versus nonspecific factors in treating test anxiety. *Journal of Counseling Psychology, 29,* 100–103.

Russell, R. K., & Wise, F. (1976). Treatment of speech anxiety by cue-controlled relaxation and desensitization with professional and paraprofessional counselors. *Journal of Counseling Psychology, 23,* 583–586.

Russell, R. K., Wise, F., & Stratoudakis, J. P. (1976). Treatment of test anxiety by cue-controlled relaxation and systematic desensitization. *Journal of Counseling Psychology, 23,* 563–566.

Rutner, I. T., & Bugle, C. (1969). An experimental procedure for the modification of psychotic behavior. *Journal of Consulting and Clinical Psychology, 33,* 651–653.

Safran, J. D., Alden, L. E., & Davidson, P. O. (1980). Client anxiety level as a moderator variable in assertion training. *Cognitive Therapy and Research, 4,* 189–200.

Safran, J. D., & Greenberg, L. S. (1982). Cognitive appraisal and reappraisal: Implications for clinical practice. *Cognitive Therapy and Research, 6,* 251–258.

Saha, G. B., Palchoudhury, S., & Mardal, M. K. (1982). A study on facial expression of emotion. *Psychologia, 25,* 255–259.

Samaan, M. (1975). Thought-stopping and flooding in a case of hallucinations, obsessions, and homicidal-suicidal behavior. *Journal of Behavior Therapy and Experimental Psychiatry, 6,* 65–67.

Sarason, I. G. (1973). Test anxiety and cognitive modeling. *Journal of Personality and Social Psychology, 28,* 58–61.

Sarason, I. G., & Sarason, B. R. (1981). Teaching cognitive and social skills to high school students. *Journal of Consulting and Clinical Psychology, 49,* 908–918.

Schindler, F. E. (1980). Treatment by systematic desensitization of a recurring nightmare of a real life trauma. *Journal of Behavior Therapy and Experimental Psychiatry, 11,* 53–54.

Schlichter, K. J., & Horan, J. J. (1981). Effects of stress inoculation on the anger and aggression management skills of institutionalized juvenile delinquents. *Cognitive Therapy and Research, 5,* 359–365.

Schulz, R., & Barefoot, J. (1974). Nonverbal responses and affiliative conflict theory. *British Journal of Social and Clinical Psychology, 13,* 237–243.

Schutz, B. (1982). *Legal liability in psychotherapy.* San Francisco: Jossey-Bass.

Schutz, W. (1967). *Joy: Expanding human awareness.* New York: Grove Press.

Schwartz, A., & Goldiamond, I. (1975). *Social casework: A behavioral approach.* New York: Columbia University Press.

Schwartz, G. E., Davidson, R. J., & Goleman, D. J. (1978). Patterning of cognitive and somatic processes in the self-regulation of anxiety: Effects of meditation versus exercise. *Psychosomatic Medicine, 40,* 321–328.

Seay, T. A. (1978). *Systematic eclectic therapy.* Jonesboro, TN: Pilgrimage Press.

Seay, T. A., & Altekruse, M. K. (1979). Verbal and nonverbal behavior in judgments of facilitative conditions. *Journal of Counseling Psychology, 26,* 108–119.

Seer, P., & Raeburn, J. M. (1980). Meditation training and essential hypertension: A methodological study. *Journal of Behavioral Medicine, 3,* 59–71.

Seidner, M. L., & Kirschenbaum, D. S. (1980). Behavioral contracts: Effects of pretreatment information and intention statements. *Behavior Therapy, 11,* 689–698.

Selby, J. W., & Calhoun, L. G. (1980). Psychodidactics: An undervalued and underdeveloped treatment tool of psychological intervention. *Professional Psychology, 11,* 236–241.

Selvini-Palazzoli, M., Cecchin, G., Prata, G., & Boscolo, L. (1978). *Paradox and counterparadox.* New York: Jason Aronson.

Semb, G., Hopkins, B. L., & Hursh, D. E. (1973). The effects of study questions and grades on student test performance in a college course. *Journal of Applied Behavior Analysis, 6,* 631–642.

Senour, M. (1982). How counselors influence clients. *Personnel and Guidance Journal, 60,* 345–350.

Shaffer, W. F. (1976). *Heuristics for the initial diagnostic interview.* Paper presented at the annual meeting of the American Psychological Association, Washington, DC.

Shaffer, W. F. (1984). Personal communication, June 1, 1984.

Shapiro, D. H. (1978a). Behavioral and attitudinal changes resulting from a "Zen experience" workshop and Zen meditation. *Journal of Humanistic Psychology, 18,* 21–29.

Shapiro, D. H. (1978b). Instructions for a training package combining formal and informal Zen meditation with behavioral self-control strategies. *Psychologia, 31,* 70–76.

Shapiro, D. H. (1980). *Meditation: Self-regulation strategy and altered state of consciousness.* New York: Aldine.

Shapiro, D. H., (1982). Overview: Clinical and physiological comparison of meditation with other self-control strategies. *American Journal of Psychiatry, 139,* 267–274.

Shapiro, D. H., & Zifferblatt, S. M. (1976). Zen meditation and behavioral self-control: Similarities, differences, and clinical applications. *American Psychologist, 31,* 519–532.

Shapiro, M. B. (1966). The single case in clinical psychology research. *Journal of General Psychology, 74,* 3–23.

Sharpley, C. F. (1984). Predicate matching in NLP: A review of research on the preferred representational system. *Journal of Counseling Psychology, 31,* 238–248.

Shaw, D. W., & Thoresen, C. E. (1974). Effects of modeling and desensitization in reducing dentist phobia. *Journal of Counseling Psychology, 21,* 415–420.

Sheehan, P. W. (1967). A shortened form of Betts' questionnaire upon mental imagery. *Journal of Clinical Psychology, 23,* 386–389.

Sheikh, A. A. (Ed.). (1983). *Imagery: Current theory, research and application.* New York: Wiley.

Shelton, J. L., & Ackerman, J. M. (1974). *Homework in counseling and psychotherapy.* Springfield, IL: Charles C Thomas.

Shelton, J. L., & Levy, R. L. (1981). *Behavioral assignments and treatment compliance.* Champaign, IL: Research Press.

Sherer, M., & Rogers, R. (1980). Effects of therapist's nonverbal communication on rated skill and effectiveness. *Journal of Clinical Psychology, 26,* 696–700.

Sherman, A. R. (1972). Real-life exposure as a primary therapeutic factor in the desensitization treatment of fear. *Journal of Abnormal Psychology, 79,* 19–28.

Sherman, T. M., & Cormier, W. H. (1972). The use of subjective scales for measuring interpersonal reactions. *Journal of Behavior Therapy and Experimental Psychiatry, 3,* 279–280.

Shoemaker, J. E., & Tasto, D. L. (1975). The effects of muscle relaxation on blood pressure of essential hypertensives. *Behaviour Research and Therapy, 13,* 29–43.

Shorr, J. E., Sobel-Whittington, G., Robin, P., & Connella, J. A. (Eds.). (1984). *Imagery.* Vol. 3: *Theoretical and clinical applications.* New York: Plenum.

Siegel, J. C. (1980). Effects of objective evidence of expertness, nonverbal behavior, and subject sex in client-perceived expertness. *Journal of Counseling Psychology, 27,* 117–121.

Sierra-Franco, M. (1978). *Therapeutic communication in nursing.* New York: McGraw-Hill.

Simkins, L. (1971). The reliability of self-recorded behaviors. *Behavior Therapy, 2,* 83–87.

Simonson, N. (1976). The impact of therapist disclosure on patient disclosure. *Journal of Counseling Psychology, 23,* 3–6.

Simonton, O. C., Matthews-Simonton, S., & Creighton, J. (1980). *Getting well again.* New York: Bantam Books.

Simonton, O. C., & Simonton, S. S. (1975). Belief systems and management of the emotional aspects of malignancy. *Journal of Transpersonal Psychology, 7,* 29–47.

Singer, J. L. (1975). Navigating the stream of consciousness: Research in daydreaming and related inner experience. *American Psychologist, 30,* 727–738.

Singer, J. L. & Antrobus, J. S. (1972). Daydreaming, imaginal processes, and personality: A normative study. In P. W. Sheehan (Ed.), *The function and nature of imagery* (pp. 175–202). New York: Academic Press.

Sitton, S. C., & Griffin, S. T. (1981). Detection of deception from clients' eye contact patterns. *Journal of Counseling Psychology, 28,* 269–271.

Slade, P. (1982). Towards a functional analysis of anorexia nervosa and bulimia nervosa. *British Journal of Clinical Psychology, 21,* 167–179.

Smith, D. L. (1976). Goal attainment scaling as an adjunct to counseling. *Journal of Counseling Psychology, 23,* 22–27.

Smith, E. J. (1977). Counseling Black individuals: Some stereotypes. *Personnel and Guidance Journal, 55,* 390–396.

Smith, G. P., & Coleman, R. E. (1977). Processes underlying generalization through participant modeling with self-directed practice. *Behaviour Research and Therapy, 15,* 204–206.

Smith, J. C. (1975). Meditation as psychotherapy: A review of the literature. *Psychological Bulletin, 82,* 558–564.

Smith-Hanen, S. S. (1977). Effects of nonverbal behaviors on judged levels of counselor warmth and empathy. *Journal of Counseling Psychology, 24,* 87–91.

Snow, R. E. (1974). Representative and quasi-representative designs for research on teaching. *Review of Educational Research, 44,* 265–291.

Southam, M. A., Agras, W. S., Taylor, C. B., & Kraemer, H. C. (1982). Relaxation training: Blood pressure lowering during the working day. *Archives of General Psychiatry, 39,* 715–717.

Spates, C. R., & Kanfer, F. H. (1977). Self-monitoring, self-evaluation, and self-reinforcement in children's learning: A test of a multistage self-regulation model. *Behavior Therapy, 8,* 9–16.

Spiegler, M., Cooley, E., Marshall, G., Prince, H., Puckett, S., & Skenazy, J. (1976). A self-control versus a counterconditioning paradigm for systematic desensitization: An experimental comparison. *Journal of Counseling Psychology, 23,* 83–86.

Spinelli, P. R., & Packard, T. (1975, February). *Behavioral self-control delivery systems.* Paper presented at the National Conference on Behavioral Self-Control, Salt Lake City.

Spinks, S., & Birchler, G. (1982). Behavioral-systems marital therapy: Dealing with resistance. *Family Process, 21,* 169–185.

Spirito, A., Finch, A. J., Smith, T. L., & Cooley, W. H. (1981). Stress inoculation for anger and anxiety control: A case study with one emotionally disturbed boy. *Journal of Clinical Child Psychology, 10,* 67–70.

Spitzer, R. L., Skodol, A. E., Gibbon, M., & Williams, J. (1981). *DSM-III Case-book.* Washington, DC: American Psychiatric Association.

Spooner, S. E., & Stone, S. C. (1977). Maintenance of specific counseling skills over time. *Journal of Counseling Psychology, 24,* 66–71.

Srebalus, D. J. (1975). Rethinking change in counseling. *Personnel and Guidance Journal, 53,* 415–421.

Stiles, W. B. (1980). Measurement of the impact of psychotherapy sessions. *Journal of Consulting and Clinical Psychology, 48,* 176–185.

Stone, C. I., Demchik-Stone, D. A., & Horan, J. J. (1977). Coping with pain: A component analysis of Lamaze and cognitive-behavioral procedures. *Journal of Psychosomatic Research, 21,* 451–456.

Strong, S. R. (1968). Counseling: An interpersonal influence process. *Journal of Counseling Psychology, 15,* 215–224.

Strong, S. R., & Claiborn, C. (1982). *Change through interaction: Social psychological processes of counseling and psychotherapy.* New York: Wiley-Interscience.

Strong, S. R., & Schmidt, L. (1970). Expertness and influence in counseling. *Journal of Counseling Psychology, 17,* 81–87.

Strong, S. R., Wambach, C. A., Lopez, F. G., & Cooper, R. K. (1979). Motivational and equipping functions of interpretation in counseling. *Journal of Counseling Psychology, 26,* 98–107.

Strupp, H. H. (1980). Success and failure in time-limited psychotherapy: A systematic comparison of two cases: Comparison 1. *Archives of General Psychiatry, 37,* 595–603.

Stuart, R. B. (1971). Behavioral contracting within the families of delinquents. *Journal of Behavior Therapy and Experimental Psychiatry, 2,* 1–11.

Stuart, R. B. (1977). Self-help group approach to self-management. In R. B. Stuart (Ed.), *Behavioral self-management: Strategies, techniques and outcomes* (pp. 275–305). New York: Brunner/Mazel.

Stuart, R. B., & Davis, B. (1972). *Slim chance in a fat world.* Champaign, IL: Research Press.

Sue, D. W. (1977). Consumerism in counseling. *Personnel and Guidance Journal, 56,* 197.

Sue, D. W., & Sue, D. (1977). Barriers to effective cross-cultural counseling. *Journal of Counseling Psychology, 24,* 420–429.

Sweeney, G. A., & Horan, J. J. (1982). Separate and combined effects of cue-controlled relaxation and cognitive restructuring in the treatment of medical performance anxiety. *Journal of Counseling Psychology, 29,* 486–497.

Sweeney, M. A., Cottle, W. C., & Kobayashi, M. J. (1980). Nonverbal communication: A cross-cultural comparison of American and Japanese counseling students. *Journal of Counseling Psychology, 27,* 150–156.

Swensen, C. H. (1968). *An approach to case conceptualization.* Boston: Houghton Mifflin.

Tasto, D. L. (1977). Self-report schedules and inventories. In A. R. Ciminero, K. S. Calhoun, & H. E. Adams (Eds.), *Handbook of behavioral assessment* (pp. 153–193). New York: Wiley.

Taylor, C. B. (1983). DSM-III and behavioral assessment. *Behavioral Assessment, 5,* 5–14.

Taylor, C. B., Pfenninger, J. L., & Candelaria, T. (1980). The use of treatment contracts to reduce Medicaid costs of a difficult patient. *Journal of Behavior Therapy and Experimental Psychiatry, 11,* 77–82.

Taylor, J. G. (1963). A behavioral interpretation of obsessive-compulsive neurosis. *Behaviour Research and Therapy, 1,* 237–244.

Tearnan, B. H., Lahey, B. B., Thompson, J. R., & Hammer, D. (1982). The role of coping self-instructions combined with covert modeling in specific fear reduction. *Cognitive Therapy and Research, 6,* 185–190.

Teders, S. J., Blanchard, E. B., Andrasik, F., Jurish, S. E., Neff, D. F., & Arena, J. G. (1984). Relaxation training for tension headache: Comparative efficacy and cost-effectiveness of a minimal therapist contact versus a therapist-delivered procedure. *Behavior Therapy, 15,* 59–70.

Tennen, H., Rohrbaugh, M., Press, S., & White, L. (1981). Reactance theory and therapeutic paradox: A compliance-defiance model. *Journal of Counseling Psychology, 18,* 14–22.

Thomas, E. J. (1977). *Marital communication and decision making.* New York: Free Press.

Thompson, A., & Wise, W. (1976). Steps toward outcome criteria. *Journal of Counseling Psychology, 23,* 202–208.

Thoresen, C. E., & Mahoney, M. J. (1974). *Behavioral self-control.* New York: Holt, Rinehart and Winston.

Thorpe, G. L. (1973). *Short-term effectiveness of systematic desensitization, modeling and behavior rehearsal, and self-instructional training in facilitating assertive-refusal behavior.* Unpublished doctoral dissertation, Rutgers University, New Brunswick, NJ.

Throll, D. A. (1982). Transcendental meditation and progressive relaxation: Their physiological effects. *Journal of Clinical Psychology, 38,* 522–530.

Todd, T. C. (1980). *Paradoxical prescriptions: Application of consistent paradox using a strategic team.* Paper presented at the annual meeting of the American Psychological Association, Montreal, Canada.

Trager, G. L. (1958). Paralanguage: A first approximation. *Studies in Linguistics, 1,* 1–12.

Truax, C. B., & Carkhuff, R. R. (1967). *Toward effective counseling and psychotherapy: Training and practice.* Chicago: Aldine.

Truax, C. B., & Mitchell, K. M. (1971). Research on certain therapist interpersonal skills in relation to process and outcome. In A. Bergin & S. Garfield (Eds.), *Handbook of psychotherapy and behavior change: An empirical analysis* (pp. 299–344). New York: Wiley.

Tryon, G. S. (1979). A review and critique of thought stopping research. *Journal of Behavior Therapy and Experimental Psychiatry, 10,* 189–192.

Tryon, G. S., & Pallandino, J. J. (1979). Thought stopping:

A case study and observation. *Journal of Behavior Therapy and Experimental Psychiatry, 10,* 151–154.

Turk, D. (1975). *Cognitive control of pain: A skills training approach for the treatment of pain.* Unpublished master's thesis, University of Waterloo, Waterloo, Ontario, Canada.

Turk, D., & Genest, M. (1979). Regulation of pain: The application of cognitive and behavioral techniques for prevention and remediation. In P. Kendall & S. Hollon (Eds.), *Cognitive-behavioral interventions: Theory, research, and procedures* (pp. 287–314). New York: Academic Press.

Turnage, J. R., & Logan, D. L. (1974). Treatment of a hypodermic needle phobia by *in vivo* systematic desensitization. *Journal of Behavior Therapy and Experimental Psychiatry, 5,* 67–69.

Turner, J. A. (1982). Comparison of group progressive-relaxation training and cognitive-behavioral group therapy for chronic low back pain. *Journal of Consulting and Clinical Psychology, 50,* 757–765.

Turner, R. D., Polly, S., & Sherman, A. R. (1976). A behavioral approach to individualized exercise programming. In J. D. Krumboltz & C. E. Thoresen (Eds.), *Counseling methods.* New York: Holt, Rinehart and Winston.

Turner, R. M., & Ascher, L. M. (1982). Therapist factor in the treatment of insomnia. *Behaviour Research and Therapy, 20,* 33–40.

Turock, A. (1980). Immediacy in counseling: Recognizing clients' unspoken•messages. *Personnel and Guidance Journal, 59,* 168–172.

Uhlemann, M. R., Lea, G. W., & Stone, G. L. (1976). Effect of instructions and modeling on trainees low in interpersonal-communication skills. *Journal of Counseling Psychology, 23,* 509–513.

Ullmann, L. P., & Krasner, L. (1969). *A psychological approach to abnormal behavior.* Englewood Cliffs, NJ: Prentice-Hall.

Ultee, C. A., Griffioen, D., & Schellekens, J. (1982). The reduction of anxiety in children: A comparison of the effects of "systematic desensitization *in vitro*" and "systematic desensitization *in vivo.*" *Behaviour Research and Therapy, 20,* 61–67.

Valerio, H. P., & Stone, G. L. (1982). Effects of behavioral, cognitive, and combined treatments for assertion as a function of differential deficits. *Journal of Counseling Psychology, 29,* 158–168.

van Egeren, L. F. (1971). Psychophysiological aspects of systematic desensitization: Some outstanding issues. *Behaviour Research and Therapy, 9,* 65–77.

Van Hasselt, V. B., Hersen, M., Bellack, A. S., Rosenblum, N. D., & Lamparski, D. (1979). Tripartite assessment of the effects of systematic desensitization in a multi-phobic child: An experimental analysis. *Journal of Behavior Therapy and Experimental Psychiatry, 10,* 51–55.

Van Hoose, W. H., & Kottler, J. A. (1977). *Ethical and legal issues in counseling and psychotherapy.* San Francisco: Jossey-Bass.

Van Houten, R., Hill, S., & Parsons, M. (1975). An analysis of a performance feedback system: The effects of timing and feedback, public posting, and praise upon academic performance and peer interaction. *Journal of Applied Behavior Analysis, 8,* 449–457.

Vargas, A. M., & Borkowski, J. G. (1982). Physical attractiveness and counseling skills. *Journal of Counseling Psychology, 29,* 246–255.

Varni, J. W. (1980). Behavioral treatment of disease-related chronic insomnia in a hemophiliac. *Journal of Behavior Therapy and Experimental Psychiatry, 11,* 143–145.

Varni, J. W. (1981). Self-regulation techniques in the management of chronic arthritic pain in hemophilia. *Behavior Therapy, 12,* 185–194.

Ventis, W. (1973). Case history: The use of laughter as an alternative response in systematic desensitization. *Behavior Therapy, 4,* 120–122.

Veronen, L. J., & Kilpatrick, D. G. (1983). Stress management for rape victims. In D. Meichenbaum & M. E. Jaremko (Eds.), *Stress reduction and prevention* (pp. 341–374). New York: Plenum.

Wachtel, P. L. (Ed.). (1982). *Resistance: Psychodynamic and behavioral approaches.* New York: Plenum.

Wahler, R. G., & Fox, J. J. (1981). Setting events in applied behavior analysis: Toward a conceptual and methodological expansion. *Journal of Applied Behavior Analysis, 14,* 327–338.

Walls, R. T., Werner, T. J., Bacon, A., & Zane, T. (1977). Behavior checklists. In J. D. Cone & R. P. Hawkins (Eds.), *Behavioral assessment: New directions in clinical psychology* (pp. 77–145). New York: Brunner/Mazel.

Watkins, C. E., Jr. (1983). Transference phenomena in the counseling situation. *Personnel and Guidance Journal, 62,* 206–210.

Watson, D. L., & Friend, R. (1969). Measurement of social-evaluative anxiety. *Journal of Consulting and Clinical Psychology, 33,* 448–457.

Watson, D. L., & Tharp, R. G. (1981). *Self-directed behavior: Self-modification for personal adjustment* (3rd ed.). Monterey, CA: Brooks/Cole.

Watson, L. (1976). *The effects of covert modeling and covert reinforcement on job-interview skills of youth offenders.* Unpublished doctoral dissertation, West Virginia University, Morgantown.

Watson, O. M. (1970). *Proxemic behavior: A cross-cultural study.* The Hague: Mouton.

Watts, F. N. (1971). Desensitization as an habituation phenomenon: I. Stimulus intensity as determinant of the effects of stimulus lengths. *Behavior and Therapy, 12,* 209–217.

Watts, F. N. (1974). The control of spontaneous recovery of anxiety in imaginal desensitization. *Behaviour Research and Therapy, 12,* 57–59.

Watzlawick, P. (1978). *The language of change: Elements of therapeutic communication.* New York: Basic Books.

Watzlawick, P. (1982). In Ard, B. Reality, reframing and resistance in therapy: Interview with P. Watzlawick. *AAMFT Family Therapy News, 13,* 1.

Watzlawick, P., Beavin, J. H., & Jackson, D. D. (1967). *Pragmatics of human communication—A study of interactional patterns, pathologies, and paradoxes.* New York: Norton.

Watzlawick, P., Weakland, J., & Fisch, R. (1974). *Change:*

Principles of problem formation and problem resolution. New York: Norton.

Webb, L. J., DiClemente, C. C., Johnstone, E. E., Sanders, J. L., & Perley, R. A. (1981). *DSM-III training guide.* New York: Brunner/Mazel.

Webster-Stratton, C. (1981a). Modification of mothers' behaviors and attitudes through a videotape modeling group discussion program. *Behavior Therapy, 12,* 634–642.

Webster-Stratton, C. (1981b). Videotape modeling: A method of parent education. *Journal of Clinical Child Psychology, 10,* 93–98.

Webster-Stratton, C. (1982). The long-term effects of a videotape parent-training program: Comparison of immediate and 1-year follow-up results. *Behavior Therapy, 13,* 702–714.

Weeks, G. R., & L'Abate, L. (1982). *Paradoxical psychotherapy: Theory and practice with individuals, couples, and families.* New York: Brunner/Mazel.

Weissberg, M. (1975). Anxiety-inhibiting statements and relaxation combined in two cases of speech anxiety. *Journal of Behavior Therapy and Experimental Psychiatry, 6,* 163–164.

Wernick, R. L. (1983). Stress inoculation in the management of clinical pain: Application to burn pain. In D. Meichenbaum & M. E. Jaremko (Eds.), *Stress reduction and prevention* (pp. 191–217). New York: Plenum.

West, D. J., Jr., Horan, J. J., & Games, P. A. (1984). Component analysis of occupational stress inoculation applied to registered nurses in an acute care hospital setting. *Journal of Counseling Psychology, 31,* 209–218.

White, K., Sheehan, P. W., & Ashton, R. (1977). Imagery assessment: A survey of self-report measures. *Journal of Mental Imagery, 1,* 145–170.

Widiger, T. A., & Rorer, L. G. (1984). The responsible psychotherapist. *American Psychologist, 39,* 503–515.

Williams, A. M. (1979). The quantity and quality of marital interaction related to marital satisfaction: A behavioral analysis. *Journal of Applied Behavior Analysis, 12,* 665–678.

Williams, R. L., Canale, J., & Edgerly, J. (1976). Affinity for self-management: A comparison between counseling clients and controls. *Journal of Behavior Therapy and Experimental Psychiatry, 7,* 231–234.

Wilson, G. T., & Davison, G. C. (1971). Processes of fear reduction in systematic desensitization: Animal studies. *Psychological Bulletin, 76,* 1–14.

Wilson, G. T., & Evans, I. M. (1977). The therapist-client relationship in behavior therapy. In A. S. Gurman & A. M. Razin (Eds), *Effective psychotherapy: A handbook of research.* New York: Pergamon Press.

Wing, J. K., Cooper, J. E., & Sartorius, N. (1974). *The measurement and classification of psychiatric symptoms.* Cambridge, England: Cambridge University Press.

Wisocki, P. A., & Rooney, E. J. (1974). A comparison of thought stopping and covert sensitization techniques in the treatment of smoking: A brief report. *Psychological Record, 24,* 191–192.

Wolf, M. M. (1978). Social validity: The case for subjective measurement; or, how applied behavior analysis is finding its heart. *Journal of Applied Behaviour Analysis, 11,* 203–214.

Wollersheim, J. P., Bordewick, M., Knapp, M., McLellarn, R., & Paul, W. (1982). The influence of therapy rationales upon perceptions of clinical problems. *Cognitive Therapy and Research, 6,* 167–172.

Wolpe, J. (1958). *Psychotherapy by reciprocal inhibition.* Stanford, CA: Stanford University Press.

Wolpe, J. (1961). The systematic desensitization treatment of neuroses. *Journal of Nervous and Mental Disease, 132,* 189–203.

Wolpe, J. (1969). *The practice of behavior therapy.* New York: Pergamon Press.

Wolpe, J. (1971). Dealing with resistance to thought-stopping: A transcript. *Journal of Behavior Therapy and Experimental Psychiatry, 2,* 121–125.

Wolpe, J. (1973). *The practice of behavior therapy* (2nd ed.). New York: Pergamon Press.

Wolpe, J. (1976). *Theme and variations: A behavior/therapy casebook.* New York: Pergamon Press.

Wolpe, J. (1982). *The practice of behavior therapy* (3rd ed.). New York: Pergamon Press.

Wolpe, J., & Lang, P. J. (1964). A fear survey schedule for use in behavior therapy. *Behaviour Research and Therapy, 2,* 27–30.

Wolpe, J., & Lazarus, A. A. (1966). *Behavior therapy techniques.* New York: Pergamon Press.

Woodward, R., & Jones, R. B. (1980). Cognitive restructuring treatment: A controlled trial with anxious patients. *Behaviour Research and Therapy, 18,* 401–407.

Woolfolk, R. L. (1976). The multimodal model as a framework for decision-making in psychotherapy. In A. A. Lazarus (Ed.), *Multimodal behavior therapy* (pp. 20–24). New York: Springer.

Woolfolk, R. L., Carr-Kaffashan, L., McNulty, T. F., & Lehrer, P. M. (1976). Meditation training as a treatment for insomnia. *Behavior Therapy, 7,* 359–365.

Woolfolk, R. L., & Lehrer, P. M. (Eds.). (1984). *Principles and practice of stress management.* New York: Guilford Press.

Woolfolk, R. L., Lehrer, P. M., McCann, B. S., & Rooney, A. J. (1982). Effects of progressive relaxation and meditation on cognitive and somatic manifestations of daily stress. *Behaviour Research and Therapy, 20,* 461–467.

Woolfolk, R. L., & McNulty, T. F. (1983). Relaxation treatment for insomnia: A component analysis. *Journal of Consulting and Clinical Psychology, 51,* 495–503.

Woollams, S., & Brown, M. (1979). *TA: The total handbook of transactional analysis.* Englewood Cliffs, NJ: Prentice-Hall.

Worthington, E. L., & Shumate, M. (1981). Imagery and verbal counseling methods in stress inoculation training for pain control. *Journal of Counseling Psychology, 28,* 1–6.

Woy, J. R., & Efran, J. S. (1972). Systematic desensitization and expectancy in the treatment of speaking anxiety. *Behaviour Research and Therapy, 10,* 43–49.

Wright, R. M., & Strong, S. R. (1982). Stimulating therapeutic change with directives: An exploratory study. *Journal of Counseling Psychology, 29,* 199–202.

Wysocki, T., Hall, G., Iwata, B., & Riordan, M. (1979). Behavioral management of exercise: Contracting for aerobic points. *Journal of Applied Behavior Analysis, 12,* 55–64.

Yamagami, T. (1971). The treatment of an obsession by thought-stopping. *Journal of Behavior Therapy and Experimental Psychiatry, 2,* 133–135.

Yeaton, W. H., & Sechrest, L. (1981). Critical dimensions in the choice and maintenance of successful treatments: Strength, integrity, and effectiveness. *Journal of Consulting and Clinical Psychology, 49,* 156–167.

Youell, K. J., & McCullough, J. P. (1975). Behavioral treatment of mucous colitis. *Journal of Consulting and Clinical Psychology, 43,* 740–745.

Young, D. W. (1980). Meanings of counselor nonverbal gestures: Fixed or interpretive? *Journal of Counseling Psychology, 27,* 447–452.

Zamostny, K. P., Corrigan, J. D., & Eggert, M. A. (1981). Replication and extension of social influence processes in counseling: A field study. *Journal of Counseling Psychology, 28,* 481–489.

Zeig, J. (1980a). Symptom prescription and Ericksonian principles of hypnosis and psychotherapy. *American Journal of Clinical Hypnosis, 23,* 16–22.

Zeig, J. (1980b). Symptom prescription techniques: Clinical applications using elements of communication. *American Journal of Clinical Hypnosis, 23,* 22–33.

Zemore, R. (1975). Systematic desensitization as a method of teaching a general anxiety-reducing skill. *Journal of Counseling and Clinical Psychology, 43,* 157–161.

Zlotlow, S. F., & Allen, G. J. (1981). Comparison of analogue strategies for investigating the influence of counselors' physical attractiveness. *Journal of Counseling Psychology, 28,* 194–202.

Zwart, C. A., & Lisman, S. A. (1979). Analysis of stimulus control treatment of sleep-onset insomnia. *Journal of Consulting and Clinical Psychology, 47,* 113–118.

AUTHOR INDEX

Abramovitz, A., 352, 355
Abrams, D. B., 524, 525
Ackerman, J. M., 203
Adams, H. E., 291
Adams, N. E., 303
Agras, W. S., 464, 478, 483, 499
Alagna, F. J., 77
Alden, L. E., 405, 445
Alexander, J., 418
Allen, G. J., 52
Altekruse, M. K., 27, 41, 81
Altmaier, E. M., 423, 507, 510
Amolsch, T., 330
Anderson, C. M., 551, 558, 560, 562, 563, 564, 565, 572, 575, 576, 579
Andolfi, M., 419
Andrasik, F., 423, 524, 547
Andrews, W. A., 507
Angle, H. V., 291
Anthony, J., 386, 389
Anthony, W. A., 99, 111, 233, 238, 239, 243, 254
Anton, J. L., 542
Antrobus, J. S., 352
Appel, M. A., 423
Arkowitz, H., 356, 559
Arrick, M., 387, 388, 401
Asbury, F. S., 21, 41, 86, 144
Ascher, L. M., 317, 482, 510, 534, 538, 568, 573, 579
Ashcroft, J. B., 170
Ashton, R., 352
Auerswald, M. C., 126
Azrin, N. J., 309

Baccus, G. K., 92
Bacon, A., 261, 292
Baer, D. M., 158
Bain, J. A., 385
Bair, M., 375
Bajtelsmit, J., 542
Baker, S. B., 185, 405, 445, 542
Balzer, F. J., 21, 41, 86, 144
Bandler, R., 24, 50, 63, 417, 420, 445
Bandura, A., 184, 187, 219, 220, 226, 228, 233, 234, 238, 239, 248, 281, 294,

Bandura, A. (continued)
303, 310, 311, 313, 318, 325, 331, 335, 336, 337, 338, 340, 348, 357, 358, 360, 480, 521, 539, 547
Banikiotes, P. G., 29, 53
Bannon, J., 29, 41
Barak, A., 48, 52, 63
Barber, T., 425, 450
Barefoot, J., 77
Barker, C. B., 126, 144
Barlow, D. H., 162, 170, 216, 256, 258, 264, 268, 269, 270, 272, 291, 483, 529, 530, 547
Barrera, M., 507
Barrett-Lennard, G. T., 22, 41
Bass, B. A., 494
Bastien, S., 266
Baxter, E. G., 482, 510
Beavin, J. H., 181
Beck, A. T., 155, 204, 266, 268, 291, 378, 401
Beck, J. T., 125, 126, 144
Bedrosian, R. C., 78, 482, 499
Bellack, A. S., 216, 266, 267, 268, 269, 291, 292, 481, 510, 526, 528, 540
Bellet, W., 81
Bemis, K., 204
Benjamin, A., 54
Benson, H., 448, 449, 450, 452, 453, 477
Berenson, B. C., 21
Bergan, J. R., 174, 216
Berman, J. S., 405, 445
Berne, E., 33
Bernstein, B. L., 77, 86
Bernstein, D. A., 292, 458, 460, 461, 463, 464, 465, 477, 507
Bertelson, A. D., 534
Besalel, V. A., 309
Betts, G. H., 352
Betz, N., 28, 30, 34
Beyer, J., 303
Bijou, S. W., 158
Birchler, G., 563, 568, 573, 580
Birdwhistell, R. L., 65, 66
Birholtz, L., 24
Bishop, D. S., 207, 216
Bixler, R. H., 54

Black, J. L., 174, 216, 258, 526, 527
Blanchard, E. B., 266, 291, 336, 357, 524, 547
Blechman, E., 538
Bloch, D. A., 86
Bloomfield, H. H., 448
Blumenthal, J. A., 534, 537, 548
Bolstad, O. D., 540
Booraem, C. D., 325
Bootzin, R. R., 258, 265, 448, 521
Borck, L. E., 144
Bordin, E. S., 31
Borkovec, T. D., 458, 460, 461, 463, 464, 465, 477, 534, 537, 547
Borkowski, J. G., 52, 64
Bornstein, P. H., 266, 356, 358, 361, 375, 484, 510
Boscolo, L., 572
Boudreau, L., 449, 494
Bounds, W. S., 256
Bourque, P., 325, 339, 348
Bowman, J., 3, 21
Bowman, M. J., 449, 478
Boykin, R. A., 265, 525, 548
Bozarth, J. D., 298
Bradley, F. O., 322, 326
Brammer, L. M., 11, 12, 18, 20, 21, 53, 54, 111, 124, 127, 144, 559
Braswell, L., 379, 401
Brehm, J. W., 558, 570
Brehm, S. S., 407, 558, 570
Brockman, W. P., 24, 25
Broden, M., 527
Broverman, D., 17
Broverman, I., 17
Brown, D. A., 266, 291
Brown, J. H., 182, 227, 235
Brown, J. P., Jr., 525, 545, 547
Brown, M., 79
Brown, S., 182, 227, 235
Brownell, K., 521
Bruch, M. A., 405, 445
Bry, A., 375
Buchanan, J. D., 423
Bucher, B., 386
Buggs, D. C., 98
Bugle, C., 521, 532
Burish, T. G., 353, 376
Butler, J. N., 405, 445

Cain, M. P., 448
Caird, W. K., 507
Calhoun, K. S., 291
Calhoun, L. G., 130, 144
Callahan, E. G., 534, 548
Callanan, P., 16, 20, 41

Cameron, R., 190, 379, 401, 423, 424, 425, 426, 427, 428, 429, 430, 445
Cammer, L., 449
Canale, J., 520
Cancelli, A. A., 174, 216
Candelaria, T., 322
Cannon, J. R., 102
Carey, L., 130, 318
Carkhuff, R. R., 21, 22, 23, 32, 99, 102, 106, 111, 121, 233, 238, 239, 243, 254
Carmody, T. B., 266
Carrington, P., 448, 449, 454, 455, 456, 477
Carr-Kaffasham, L., 449
Carroll, L. J., 534, 547
Carter, M., 307
Cash, T. F., 52, 336, 349
Caskey, N., 126, 144
Cautela, J. R., 178, 216, 223, 266, 291, 352, 356, 357, 361, 362, 363, 375, 385, 458, 477, 519, 542
Cavanaugh, M. E., 41, 547
Cavior, N., 527
Cecchin, G., 572
Celotta, B., 170
Chamberlain, D., 579
Chance, J. E., 520
Chapman, R., 314
Chassan, J. B., 272
Chaves, J., 425
Chelune, G. J., 41
Chida, T., 332, 349
Childers, W. C., 21, 41, 86, 144
Ciminero, A. R., 260, 264, 291, 524, 526, 528, 529, 545
Citrenbaum, C., 86, 580
Claiborn, C. D., 4, 64, 81, 124, 125, 126, 144
Clarke, J. C., 352, 375, 450, 492, 510
Clarkson, F., 17
Cloum, G. A., 353, 376
Clouser, R. A., 459
Coates, T. J., 524, 547
Cochran, S. D., 405
Cody, S., 482, 510
Coe, W. C., 325
Cole, J. W., 477
Coleman, R. E., 336, 340
Colletti, G., 521
Collings, G. H., 477
Collins, F. L., Jr., 174, 216, 458, 464, 477
Condon, W. S., 75
Cone, J. D., 292
Connella, J. A., 376
Cooley, E. J., 484
Cooper, J. E., 178

Cooper, R. K., 125, 144
Copeland, A. P., 379, 401
Corey, G., 16, 20, 41
Corey, M., 16, 20, 41
Cormier, L. S., 4, 77, 94, 111, 115, 294, 295, 311, 454
Cormier, W. H., 256, 266, 311, 454
Corn, R., 81
Cornish, R. D., 507
Corrigan, J. D., 44, 46, 47, 48, 53, 63
Cotharin, R., 482
Cottle, W. C., 82, 86
Cox, B. G., 55, 56, 57, 58, 64
Cozby, D. C., 28, 29, 30
Craigie, F. C., Jr., 330, 348
Credidio, S. G., 477
Cristiani, T., 32
Cronbach, L. J., 261, 267, 268, 277
Csanyi, A., 543
Cullen, C., 161
Cureton, E. E., 259, 291
Curran, J. P., 482
Cutter, H. S. G., 268, 291

Daniels, L. K., 494
Danish, S., 41, 116, 144
Danker-Brown, P., 332, 349
D'Augelli, A., 41, 116, 131
D'Augelli, J., 41, 116
Davidson, P. O., 405, 445
Davis, A., 349
Davis, B., 557
Davis, J. L., 17
Davis, R., 332, 349
Davison, G. C., 296, 298, 300, 317, 326, 412, 458, 459, 465, 483, 486, 490, 496, 501, 505
Dawidoff, D. J., 228
Dawley, H. H., 507
Day, R. W., 53, 54, 63
Decenteceo, E. T., 405
Deffenbacher, J. L., 521
Delaney, D. J., 34, 226, 295
Dell, D. M., 44, 48, 52, 63
Delo, J. S., 266
DeLuca, R. V., 534
Demchik-Stone, D., 352, 423
Dengrove, E., 482, 489
Denholtz, M., 507
Denney, D. R., 484, 486, 498
Denniston, D., 448
Dentch, G. E., 268, 291
Derogatis, L. R., 266, 291
Devine, D. A., 299, 356, 358, 361, 375
Devine, V., 541
de Visser, L., 235, 257, 294, 331, 332

DiClemente, C. C., 171
Dilley, J. S., 507
DiPilato, M., 510
Dittmann, A. T., 76
Dixon, D. N., 55, 64, 219, 222, 224, 225, 233, 234, 238, 239, 241, 254, 286, 299, 300, 307
Dobes, R. W., 265
Dodge, K. A., 521, 548
Dorn, F. J., 43, 64
Doster, J. A., 41
Dove, C., 332, 349
Dowd, E. T., 125, 127, 144
Dowling, J., 423, 445
Dowrick, P. W., 332, 349
Duhl, B. S., 79, 86
Duhl, F. J., 79, 86
Duley, S. M., 174, 216
Dumont, F., 77, 86
Dunbar, J., 542
Duncan, S. P., Jr., 75
Dunlap, K., 567
Dush, D. M., 405
Dyer, W. W., 434, 554, 558, 575
Dyrud, J. E., 159

Eberle, T., 499
Edelstein, B., 258, 269, 349, 386, 389, 405, 445
Edgerly, J., 520
Efran, J. S., 258, 568
Egan, G., 21, 22, 23, 27, 28, 29, 31, 33, 34, 41, 46, 47, 55, 90, 113, 118, 120, 121, 124, 130, 133, 256, 271, 296, 297, 298
Eggers, J., 269, 292
Eggert, M. A., 46
Eisenberg, S., 34, 118, 120, 226, 295, 551
Eisler, R. M., 79, 86, 309, 326, 349
Ekman, P., 66, 67, 74, 76, 86
Elder, J. P., 405, 445
Elliott, R., 126, 144, 286
Ellis, A., 184, 403, 404, 405, 406
Ellsworth, P., 74
Elmore, R. T., 481, 510
Emery, G., 204
Emery, J. R., 492
Epstein, L. H., 265
Epstein, N. B., 207, 216
Erbaugh, J., 266, 291
Erickson, F., 77
Erickson, M. H., 66, 418, 561, 565, 573
Ersner-Hershfield, R., 521
Esveldt-Dawson, K., 268, 292
Etringer, B. D., 336, 349
Evans, D., 482

Evans, I. M., 310, 497, 498, 501, 502, 503
Evans, R., 162
Exline, R. V., 73

Fabricatore, J., 386
Falzett, W. C., 24, 25
Fashnacht, G., 544
Fast, J. H., 558
Fawcett, S. B., 144
Fay, A., 181, 558, 559
Fedoravicius, A., 482
Feindler, E. L., 423, 445
Fensterheim, H., 181, 207
Ferguson, J. M., 477, 486
Fernald, P. S., 299
Ferster, C. B., 535
Filion, R., 539
Finn, M. E., 405, 445
Fisch, R., 190, 191, 417, 552, 553, 555, 559, 560, 561, 565, 569, 572, 576, 579
Fisher, J. D., 77
Fishman, S., 492
Fishman, S. T., 160, 170, 189
Flannery, R. B., 356
Flowers, J. V., 325
Foa, E. B., 482, 500, 510
Folensbee, R., 534, 547
Fong, M. L., 55, 56, 57, 58, 64
Forgatch, M., 579
Forsyth, D. R., 125
Forsyth, N. L., 125
Foster, S., 271, 292
Fox, E. E., 524
Fox, J. J., 159, 171
Fox, S., 539
Framer, E. M., 322
Frank, J. D., 258
Frankl, V., 567
Frederiksen, L. W., 79, 86, 265, 309, 524
Freedman, N., 76
Fremouw, W. J., 266, 405, 406, 408, 409, 423, 431, 445, 521, 524, 525, 526, 529, 530, 534, 537, 547, 548
Fretz, B. R., 81, 86
Freud, S., 550
Frey, D. H., 8, 219, 254, 299
Friedman, L., 542
Friend, R., 266, 277, 290
Friesen, W., 66, 67, 74, 76, 86
Frisch, M. B., 269, 291
Furukawa, M. J., 311, 326, 328, 349

Gajdos, E., 318, 325, 336, 348
Galassi, J. P., 266, 269, 309, 482
Galassi, M. D., 266, 269, 309

Gallagher, J. W., 356
Gambrill, E., 184, 186, 187, 223, 224, 225, 226, 227, 236, 239, 242, 243, 266, 273, 296, 297, 298, 300, 535
Games, P. A., 423, 445
Gazda, G. M., 21, 33, 35, 41, 83, 86, 106, 116, 133, 144
Geer, C. A., 483
Geis, G. L., 314
Gelatt, H., 130, 134, 318
Gendlin, E., 21
Genest, M., 423, 445
George, R., 32
Gergen, K. J., 29
Gershman, L., 386, 389, 459, 494, 542
Gibbon, M., 162, 170
Gilbert, B. O., 329, 349
Gilliland, B., 3, 21
Gilmore, J., 482
Girodo, M., 449
Gladstein, G., 22, 41
Glasgow, R. E., 309, 330, 349, 507
Glogower, F. D., 405, 408, 410
Glover, J. A., 219, 222, 224, 225, 233, 234, 238, 239, 241, 254, 286, 299, 300, 307
Gluckstern, N., 30, 92, 103, 124, 127
Gold, S. R., 353, 375
Goldfried, A. P., 8, 225
Goldfried, M. R., 2, 8, 182, 216, 225, 266, 295, 296, 298, 300, 317, 326, 405, 406, 407, 410, 412, 458, 459, 465, 483, 484, 486, 489, 490, 494, 495, 496, 498, 501, 505, 553, 555
Goldiamond, I., 157, 159, 203, 204, 240
Goldstein, A. J., 494
Goldstein, A. P., 11, 32, 44, 53, 63, 294, 325, 326, 349, 510
Gonzales, M., 543
Goodman, J., 379, 380, 401
Goodwin, D. L., 157
Goodyear, R., 64, 322, 326
Gordon, D., 127, 565
Gormally, J., 92, 405, 524
Gottman, J. M., 222, 226, 227, 228, 551, 557, 565
Graves, J. R., 83
Green, L., 524
Greenberg, I., 521
Greenberg, L. S., 405, 417, 419, 420, 445

Greenwald, D., 568
Greiner, J., 521
Gresham, F. M., 330, 349
Griffin, S. T., 73
Griffioen, D., 481, 510
Grimm, L. G., 181
Grinder, J., 24, 50, 63, 417, 420, 445
Groden, J., 458, 477
Gronsky, B. R., 81, 86
Guerra, J. J., 79, 86
Gurman, A. S., 568

Haase, R. F., 23, 86
Hackett, G., 423, 521, 522
Hackmann, A., 386, 387
Hackney, H., 4, 77, 94, 111, 115, 294, 295
Haley, J., 557, 559, 561, 564, 565, 567, 570, 573, 579
Hall, E. T., 66, 77
Hall, G., 322
Hall, R., 527
Hallberg, E. T., 86
Hamilton, S. A., 405, 445
Hamilton, S. B., 266
Hammer, A., 22, 24, 25, 41
Hammer, D., 358, 376
Hanley, S., 356
Hansen, J. C., 54
Hare-Mustin, R. T., 19
Harmatz, M. G., 405, 431
Harmin, M., 16
Harper, R. G., 74, 77, 86
Hart, B., 403
Harvill, R., 565
Hathaway, S. R., 266
Hauge, G., 423, 445
Hawkins, R. P., 265, 292
Hay, L. R., 291, 356
Hay, W. M., 291, 356, 360, 363
Hayes, S. C., 170, 256, 268, 291, 292, 525, 530, 539, 547, 548
Haynes, S. N., 174, 216, 258, 263, 266, 291
Hays, V., 389
Hearn, M., 482
Heesacker, M., 43, 48, 52, 64
Heffernan, T., 521, 548
Hein, E. C., 92
Heisler, B. D., 405, 445
Hellman, I., 538
Henry, D., 481, 482, 510
Heppner, P. P., 43, 48, 52, 64
Hersen, M., 216, 256, 266, 267, 268, 272, 291, 292, 326, 481, 510, 548, 551
Hershfield, S., 521
Hess, E. H., 73, 86

Heyneman, N., 266, 521, 524, 526, 529, 530, 548
Hiebert, B., 524
Higgins, R. L., 269, 291
Highlen, P. S., 92
Hill, C. E., 81, 83, 86, 92, 219, 234
Hill, S., 521
Hillenberg, J. B., 458, 464, 477
Hilpert, P. L., 329
Hirt, M. L., 405, 445
Hoffman, A., 54
Hoffman, A. M., 542
Hoffman-Graff, M. S., 28, 29
Hollon, S. D., 170, 203, 204, 207, 263, 266, 413, 445, 524, 548
Holroyd, K. A., 423, 482
Holtzbauer, R., 527
Homme, L., 315, 543
Hopkins, B. L., 6
Hopkins, J., 269, 291
Horan, J. J., 352, 353, 354, 375, 405, 423, 424, 425, 445, 542
Horne, A. M., 482
Hosford, R. E., 235, 257, 294, 331, 332, 333, 349, 507
Howard, K. I., 266, 267
Howard, W. A., 492, 510
Howell, R., 507
Hubble, M. A., 77, 86
Huck, S. W., 256
Hudson, J., 144
Hughes, H., 258
Hull, C., 161
Hursh, D. E., 6
Hurst, J. C., 483
Hutchins, D. E., 151, 170

Israel, A. C., 521, 540
Ivey, A. E., 30, 33, 92, 95, 98, 99, 103, 111, 113, 114, 115, 118, 120, 124, 127, 144
Iwata, B., 322

Jackson, B., 540
Jackson, D., 551
Jackson, D. D., 181
Jackson, J. A., 352, 375, 450
Jacobs, E., 565
Jacobs, M. K., 405
Jacobson, E., 448, 458
Jacobson, N. S., 258, 316
Jaffe, D. T., 448
Jahn, D. L., 551, 580
James, R., 3, 21
Janis, I. L., 445
Jaremko, M. E., 423, 445
Jarrett, R. B., 539, 548

Jarvinen, P. J., 353, 375
Jason, L. A., 535, 548
Jayaratne, S., 263, 268, 270, 272, 291
Jeffery, K. M., 238
Jeffery, R. W., 310, 313, 318, 325, 336, 348, 349
Jensen, B. J., 174, 216, 263, 291
Jerremalm, A., 298, 307
Johannson, J., 298, 307
Johnson, D. W., 32, 41, 55, 56, 64, 120, 121, 124, 144
Johnson, S. B., 349
Johnson, S. M., 540
Johnston, J. M., 6
Johnstone, E. E., 171
Jones, J. E., 548
Jones, R. B., 405
Jones, R. T., 519, 520, 522, 540, 544
Jurish, S. E., 524, 547
Juster, H. R., 405, 445

Kanfer, F. H., 64, 147, 157, 181, 325, 326, 349, 510, 519, 521, 522, 525, 526, 527, 528, 532, 534, 538, 541, 543, 545, 548
Kanitz, H. M., 403, 404
Kantor, D., 79, 86
Kantor, J. R., 158
Kaplan, A. G., 19
Kaplan, D. A., 405
Kaplan, H. I., 178
Kaplan, R. M., 405, 445
Karoly, P., 181, 521, 548
Katell, A. D., 464, 534, 548
Katkin, E. S., 264, 267, 269, 272, 487
Kavanagh, K., 579
Kazdin, A. E., 256, 258, 263, 264, 268, 271, 272, 292, 310, 311, 313, 316, 326, 351, 352, 356, 357, 358, 359, 360, 361, 362, 363, 375, 376, 379, 401, 482, 483, 519, 526, 527, 528, 532
Keane, T. M., 174, 216
Keefe, F. J., 534, 537, 548
Kelley, J. E., 349
Kendall, P. C., 170, 203, 204, 207, 263, 266, 379, 401, 413, 423, 445, 524, 548
Kent, R. N., 271, 292
Kern, J. M., 269, 292
Kiesler, C. A., 559
Kiesler, D. J., 12, 21, 22, 294
Kilpatrick, D. G., 423, 445
King, M., 86, 580
Kiresuk, T. J., 235

Kirk, M. A., 575
Kirsch, I., 481, 482, 510
Kirschenbaum, D. S., 238, 254, 322, 527
Klein, Z., 568
Klepac, R. K., 423, 445
Klorman, R., 329
Knapp, M., 510
Knapp, M. L., 65, 66, 67, 73, 75, 76, 77, 86
Knox, J., 427
Kobayashi, M. J., 82, 86
Kocsis, M., 86
Kolko, D., 580
Kopel, S., 559
Kornblith, S., 568
Kory, R. B., 448
Kosevsky, B. P., 265
Kostka, M. P., 482
Kottler, J. A., 228, 297
Kraemer, H. C., 478
Krasner, L., 404
Kratochwill, T. R., 174, 216
Krauft, C. C., 298
Krawitz, G., 269, 291
Krivonos, P. D., 75
Krouse, R., 258, 310, 326
Krozely, M. G., 352, 376
Krumboltz, J. D., 2, 22, 155, 180, 219, 220, 226, 235, 315, 348, 353, 354, 358, 375, 378, 485, 492, 508
Kubinski, J. A., 29, 53
Kunce, J., 329, 330
Kunkel, J., 534
Kunzelmann, H. D., 529

L'Abate, L., 151, 170, 562, 568, 569, 572, 573, 574, 580
Laborde, G., 41
Lacks, P., 534
LaCrosse, M. B., 46, 64
Ladouceur, R., 325, 336, 339, 348, 349, 542
LaFromboise, T. D., 55, 64
LaGana, C., 329
Lahey, B. B., 358, 376
Lamaze, F., 352, 355, 426, 458
Lamparski, D., 481, 510
Lang, P. J., 266, 481, 483, 487
Lankton, C. H., 564, 565, 570
Lankton, S. R., 22, 24, 25, 48, 95, 564, 565, 567, 570
Latham, G. P., 224, 254
Lawson, D. M., 542
Layng, F. C., 352
Lazarus, A. A., 147, 151, 152, 153, 155, 156, 167, 170, 178, 180, 181, 183, 184, 185, 190, 191, 192, 216, 294, 298, 299, 300,

Lazarus, A. A. *(continued)* 307, 314, 323, 352, 353, 355, 376, 385, 386, 404, 481, 489, 500, 558, 559
Lazovik, A., 481
Lea, G. W., 23
Leal, L., 482, 510
Leaman, D. R., 144
Leary, M. R., 423
Lecomte, C., 77, 86
Lee, D. Y., 86
Lehrer, P. M., 287, 292, 298, 302, 307, 448, 449, 458, 477, 478
Leiblum, S. R., 222, 226, 227, 228, 551, 557, 565
Leitenberg, H., 483, 484
Lent, R. W., 481, 482, 510
Lerman, C., 534, 547
Leventhal, H., 424, 445
Levin, F. M., 29
Levine, B. A., 481, 510
Levine, F., 544
Levitt, E. B., 535
Levy, L. H., 124
Levy, R. L., 263, 265, 268, 270, 272, 291, 292, 316, 317, 326, 551, 559, 567, 568, 580
Lewin, K., 147, 553
Lewis, E. C., 131, 133
Lewis, K. N., 44, 63
Ley, D., 134
Lichstein, K. L., 551, 580
Lick, J. R., 258, 264, 265, 267, 268, 269, 272, 487
Lidz, C. W., 307
Linder, L., 492
Lindquist, E. F., 291
Lindsley, O. R., 529
Linehan, M. M., 179, 203
Lipinski, D. P., 258, 260, 264, 265, 291, 526, 527
Lisman, S. A., 534, 538, 548
Liss-Levenson, N., 19
Litrownik, A. J., 521, 548
Livingston, S. A., 259, 292
Lloyd, M. E., 220, 235, 254, 257
Locke, E. A., 224, 254
Locke, H. J., 266, 292
Logan, D. L., 507
Lomont, J. F., 483
Long, L., 98, 99, 114, 115, 116, 144
Long, T., 114, 144
Lopez, F. G., 125, 144, 568, 580
Lo Piccolo, J., 266, 292
Lowe, J. C., 494
Lubetkin, B. S., 160, 170, 189
Lum, L. C., 155
Lyles, J. N., 353, 376

MacDonald, M. L., 507
Mahaney, M. M., 269
Mahoney, K., 10, 411, 434, 521, 529, 540
Mahoney, M. J., 10, 157, 256, 258, 261, 264, 265, 303, 351, 378, 386, 388, 401, 411, 434, 496, 519, 520, 521, 522, 524, 526, 527, 529, 533, 535, 538, 540, 541, 542, 543, 544, 545
Mann, E., 507
Manthei, R. J., 299, 307
Marabotto, C. M., 527
Maracek, J., 19
Margolin, G., 271, 292, 316
Marlatt, G. A., 311, 449, 524, 548
Marques, J. K., 449
Marquis, J. N., 477, 482, 486, 487, 488, 489, 490, 491, 494, 495, 496, 498, 499, 500, 501, 506, 507, 510
Marshall, G., 484
Marshall, W., 507
Martin, G. A., 316, 326, 580
Martin, G. L., 386, 401, 534
Martin, J., 482, 510
Martin, J. E., 464
Martinez, J. A., 258, 269
Martorano, R., 360
Marx, R. W., 482, 510
Mascitelli, S., 313, 316, 326, 360, 361, 363, 376, 379, 401
Maslin, A., 17
Maslow, A. H., 297
Masson, R., 565
Masters, J. C., 155, 385, 387, 388, 389, 401, 482, 500, 505, 510
Matarazzo, J. D., 74, 86
Mathews, A. M., 483
Matson, J. L., 268, 292, 482
Maultsby, M. C., 223
Maurer, R. E., 22, 23, 41, 83, 86
Mavissakalian, M., 568
May, R. B., 542
McBurney, D., 499
McCallum, M., 349
McCann, B. S., 448, 449, 477, 478
McCarthy, P., 28, 29, 30, 34, 41, 53
McCordick, S. M., 405, 445
McCroskey, J. C., 405
McCullough, J. P., 235
McDonald, F. J., 331
McDonald, M., 423, 445

McFall, R. M., 264, 265, 266, 268, 313, 521, 524, 525, 527, 528, 548
McGlynn, F. D., 492
McGuigan, F. J., 458
McGuire, D., 330
McKeachie, W. J., 9, 315, 544
McKenzie, T. L., 532
McKinley, J. C., 266
McKnight, D. L., 539, 548
McLaughlin, T. F., 540
McLean, C. A., 386, 387
McNulty, T. F., 449
McWilliams, P., 448
Meador, B., 21
Mehrabian, A., 78, 86
Meichenbaum, D. H., 155, 180, 190, 311, 358, 379, 380, 401, 405, 406, 407, 408, 409, 410, 423, 424, 425, 426, 427, 428, 429, 430, 445, 498
Meisel, A., 307
Melamed, B. G., 329, 556
Melnick, J., 314, 315, 360, 482
Mendelson, M., 266, 291
Meredith, K. E., 174, 216
Meyer, R. G., 178, 298, 302, 307, 482
Meyer, V., 170
Michael, R., 329
Michelson, L., 568
Miklich, D., 332, 349
Mikulas, W., 482
Milan, M., 580
Miller, C., 269, 292
Miller, G., 130
Miller, H. R., 499
Miller, P. M., 326
Miller, R. C., 405, 445
Miller, W. R., 510
Milne, C. R., 125, 127, 144
Minuchin, S., 557
Mischel, W., 156, 158, 264, 312
Mitchell, K. M., 21, 298
Mitchell, K. R., 521
Mitts, B., 527
Mock, J., 266, 291
Mogan, J., 494
Moos, R. H., 266
Morgan, W., 482, 500, 510
Morganstern, K. P., 106, 174, 179, 226, 227
Morrell, G., 331
Morris, K. T., 403, 404
Morris, R. J., 480, 506, 510
Moss, C., 331
Moura, N. G., 520
Munjack, D. J., 551, 580
Munson, W. W., 405
Murphy, S. M., 492, 510

Nagle, R. J., 330, 349
Nawas, M. M., 492, 499, 507
Nay, W. R., 216
Neff, D. F., 524, 547
Neilans, T. H., 521, 548
Nelson, R. E., 519
Nelson, R. O., 162, 170, 174, 207, 216, 256, 258, 259, 260, 264, 265, 266, 267, 268, 269, 270, 291, 292, 356, 361, 363, 525, 526, 527, 530, 539, 547, 548
Nelson, W. M., III., 423
Nerenz, D. R., 424, 445
Nesbitt, J. G., 41
Nesse, M., 356, 361, 363
Nicassio, P., 258, 265, 448
Nietzel, M. T., 292, 360
Nilsson, D., 29, 41
Noble, F. C., 77, 86
Nolan, J. D., 535
Norton, G. R., 534
Novaco, R. W., 423, 424, 425, 426, 427, 428, 429, 430, 445
Novik, L., 86, 580
Nurnberger, J. I., 534
Nye, L. S., 330

O'Brien, J. S., 494
O'Farrell, T. J., 268, 291
Ogston, W. D., 75
O'Keefe, D. M., 524, 547
Okun, B. F., 17, 41, 263, 281, 294, 295, 296, 297
Oldham, R. K., 353, 376
O'Leary, K. D., 271, 292, 541, 544
Olin, R. J., 386
Oliveau, D., 483
Olson, D., 538
Omer, H., 567, 568
O'Neil, D., 507
O'Neill, G., 6
Ordman, A. M., 527
Orlinsky, D. E., 266, 267
Orne, M. T., 258, 269, 292
Ornstein, R. E., 452, 453
Öst, L. G., 298, 307
Osterhouse, R. A., 485, 492, 507
Otter, S. B., 79, 86
Owens, R. G., 170
Oziel, R. J., 551, 580

Packard, T., 542
Palchoudhury, S., 86
Pallandino, J. J., 386, 388, 402
Papp, P., 79, 568, 580
Paradise, L., 114, 144
Parks, G. A., 521, 548

Parsons, B., 418
Parsons, M., 521
Pascal, G. R., 147
Passons, W. R., 66, 67, 79, 80, 86
Patkin, J., 48, 52, 63
Patterson, G., 579
Patterson, L. E., 118, 120, 551
Paul, G. L., 147, 258, 294, 507
Penick, S. B., 539
Perley, R. A., 171
Perls, F. S., 66
Perri, M. G., 521, 522
Perry, M. A., 311, 326, 328, 349
Peterson, L., 329, 349
Pfenninger, J. L., 322
Phares, E. J., 520
Phillips, D., 217
Phillips, L. W., 352, 506
Piaget, G., 482, 494, 500, 510
Pickett, C., 376
Pierce, R. M., 22, 23, 102
Pietrofesa, J. J., 54
Pinto, D. V., 54
Pistrang, N., 126, 144
Polly, S., 540
Pope, B., 126
Potter, S., 89
Poulos, R., 541
Prata, G., 572
Press, S., 568, 569, 580
Presse, L., 507
Prince, H., 484
Prinz, R. J., 271, 292
Proctor, F., 254
Proctor, S., 499
Prophit, P., 98, 99
Pucel, J., 492
Puckett, S., 484
Pursell, C. H., 352
Pursell, S. A., 29, 53

Quattrochi-Tubin, S., 535, 548

Rachman, S., 328, 494, 499, 500
Raczynski, J. M., 270, 292
Raming, H. E., 219, 254
Rappaport, A. F., 449
Rapshall, R., 405
Rardin, D., 524
Raskin, D., 568
Raths, L., 16
Rathus, S. A., 266
Raush, H. L., 31
Ray, W. J., 270, 292
Reade, M. N., 83, 86
Rebman, V. L., 484, 507, 510
Rechs, J., 543
Redd, W. H., 481, 510

Redfering, D. L., 449, 478
Reeder, C., 329, 330
Reese, S. L., 361
Rehm, L., 499, 521, 548
Reid, J., 579
Reid, W. H., 302, 307
Reiser, D. E., 20
Richards, C. S., 521, 522, 548
Richardson, B., 6, 89, 100, 111
Richey, C., 266
Rickels, K., 266, 291
Rimm, D. C., 155, 336, 349, 385, 387, 388, 389, 401, 482, 500, 505, 510
Rinn, R. C., 286
Riordan, M., 322
Risley, T., 403
Rittenhouse, R., 50
Ritter, B., 336, 357
Roberts, A. H., 535
Roberts, G., 3, 21
Robin, P., 376
Robinson, H., 477
Robinson, J. D., 83
Robinson, S. E., 77, 86
Robyak, J. K., 64
Rock, A. F., 266, 291
Rogers, C., 4, 12, 21, 23, 28, 31
Rogers, R., 86
Rohrbaugh, M., 568, 569, 570, 572, 573, 574, 580
Romanczyk, R. G., 537
Rooney, A. J., 448, 449, 477, 478
Rooney, F. J., 386, 387
Rorer, L. G., 308
Rose, S. D., 315, 317
Rosen, A., 254
Rosen, G. M., 309, 330, 349, 507
Rosen, R. C., 386
Rosenbloom, A., 349
Rosenblum, N. D., 481, 510
Rosenkrantz, P., 17
Rosenthal, R., 292
Rosenthal, T. L., 311, 349, 361
Roskies, E., 423, 445
Rosnow, R., 292
Ross, S. L., 423
Ross, S. M., 330, 348, 499
Rossi, E., 66
Rossi, S., 66
Roth, L., 307
Rothmeier, R. C., 64
Rotter, J. B., 520
Rovetto, F. M., 507, 510
Rozensky, R., 526
Rudestam, K., 482, 499
Rupert, P., 484, 486, 498
Rushall, B. S., 532

Russell, M. L., 329, 331
Russell, R. K., 481, 482, 510
Russell, R. W., 482
Rutner, I. T., 521, 532
Rychtarik, R. G., 266

Saari, L. M., 224, 254
Saccone, A. J., 482, 510
Sadock, B. J., 178
Safran, J. D., 405, 417, 419, 420, 445
Saha, G. B., 86
Salzbach, R. F., 52
Samaan, M., 386, 389
Sanders, J. L., 171
Sanders, S. H., 322
Sarason, B. R., 326, 329, 330, 331, 349
Sarason, I. G., 326, 329, 330, 331, 349, 379, 401
Sartorious, N., 178
Saslow, G., 147, 157
Schellekens, J., 481, 510
Schindler, F. E., 481, 510
Schlichter, K. J., 423
Schmidt, L. D., 44, 63
Schnapp, B. J., 386
Schneider, J. A., 464
Schroeder, H., 20, 405, 445
Schulz, R., 77
Schutz, B., 41
Schutz, W., 65
Schwartz, A., 203, 204, 240
Schwartz, J., 526
Seay, T. A., 27, 41, 81, 147, 150, 167, 170
Sechrest, L., 308
Segal, L., 190
Seidner, M. L., 238, 254, 322
Selby, J. W., 130, 144
Selvini-Palazzoli, M., 572
Semb, G., 6
Senour, M., 43, 64
Serber, M., 494
Sestak, R., 307
Shaffer, W. F., 296, 298, 300, 301, 308
Shannon, D. T., 507
Shapiro, D. H., 449, 450, 451, 452, 453, 454, 455, 456, 478
Shapiro, M. B., 256
Sharpley, C. F., 24, 25, 41
Shaw, D. W., 482
Shaw, K. N., 224, 254
Sheehan, P. W., 352
Sheikh, A. A., 376
Shelton, J. L., 203, 316, 317, 326, 551, 559, 567, 568, 580
Sherer, M., 86
Sherman, A. R., 507, 540
Sherman, D., 216

Sherman, R. E., 235
Sherman, T. M., 266
Shigetomi, C., 329, 349
Shoemaker, J. E., 448
Shostrom, E. L., 11, 12, 18, 20, 21, 53, 54, 111, 124, 127, 144, 559
Shumate, M., 352
Shute, R. E., 542
Siegel, J. C., 64
Siegel, L. J., 329, 556
Siegelman, L., 81, 86
Silver, B. V., 266, 291
Silverstein, J. H., 349
Simek-Downing, L., 33, 95, 98, 114, 115
Simkins, L., 265
Simon, K., 233, 234, 238, 239
Simonson, N., 28
Simonton, O. C., 353
Simonton, S. S., 353
Singer, J. L., 73, 352
Sipps, G., 405
Sitton, S. C., 73
Skenazy, J., 484
Skinner, B. F., 155
Skodol, A. E., 162, 170
Slade, P., 170
Smith, D., 269, 291
Smith, D. L., 219, 220
Smith, E. J., 17
Smith, G. P., 336, 340
Smith, J. C., 448, 449
Smith, S., 405, 445
Smith-Hanen, S. S., 23, 83
Smouse, A. D., 83, 86
Snow, R. E., 9
Sobel-Whittington, G., 376
Southam, M. A., 478
Sparacio, R. T., 53, 54, 63
Spates, C. R., 521
Spiegler, M., 484, 498
Spillar, R., 349
Spinelli, P. R., 542
Spinks, S., 563, 580
Spitzer, R. L., 162, 170
Splete, H. H., 54
Spong, R. T., 539, 548
Spooner, S. E., 114
Srebalus, D. J., 222
Stedman, J. M., 494
Steger, J. C., 266, 292
Stein, N., 294
Stekette, G. S., 482, 510
Stevic, R. R., 54
Stewart, S., 551, 558, 560, 562, 563, 564, 565, 572, 575, 576, 579
Stiles, W. B., 292
Stocker, R., 315
Stone, C. I., 352, 423
Stone, G. L., 6, 23, 89, 100, 111, 405

Stone, S. C., 114
Strassberg, D., 29, 41
Stratoudakis, J. P., 482
Strong, S. R., 4, 44, 55, 64, 125, 126, 144, 568
Stuart, R. B., 264, 322, 326, 545, 557
Stunkard, A. J., 539
Sturniolo, F., 81, 86
Sue, D., 76, 80
Sue, D. W., 76, 80, 299
Sugerman, J., 534
Suinn, R. M., 521
Sveen, O. B., 329
Sweeney, G. A., 405, 445
Sweeney, M. A., 82, 86
Swensen, C. H., Jr., 147, 148, 149, 150, 167, 171

Tasto, D. L., 266, 448
Taylor, C. B., 162, 171, 322, 464, 477, 478, 486
Taylor, J. G., 385
Tearnan, B. H., 358, 376
Teders, S. J., 463
Telasi-Golubscow, H., 170
Tennen, H., 482, 510, 568, 569, 570, 580
Tepper, D., 23
Tevlin, H. E., 106, 174, 179, 226, 227
Tharp, R. G., 527, 528, 529, 536, 537, 541, 542, 543, 548
Thelen, M., 330
Theobald, D. E., 266, 291
Thomas, E. J., 315
Thomas, R. N., 405
Thompson, A., 248
Thompson, J. R., 358, 376
Thoresen, C. E., 2, 22, 157, 180, 235, 261, 315, 331, 348, 353, 354, 358, 375, 378, 482, 485, 508, 519, 520, 521, 522, 524, 526, 527, 529, 533, 535, 538, 541, 542, 544, 545, 547
Thornbrough, M., 423
Thorpe, G. L., 406, 407
Throll, D. A., 478
Tindall, J. H., 22, 23, 41, 83, 86
Todd, T. C., 574
Tomarken, A. J., 527
Tomkins, S. S., 74
Trager, G. L., 66
Truax, C., 21, 32
Tryon, G. S., 386, 388, 401, 402
Tuemmler, J. M., 81
Turk, D., 423, 424, 425, 427, 428, 429, 431, 445
Turkat, I., 170
Turnage, J. R., 507

Turner, R., 534, 568
Turner, R. D., 540
Turner, R. M., 538
Turock, A., 34, 35, 42
Twentyman, C., 313

Uhlemann, M. R., 23
Ullmann, L. P., 404
Ultee, C. A., 481, 482, 507, 510
Unger, T., 258, 264, 265, 268, 269
Upper, D., 223, 266

Valerio, H. P., 405
van Egeren, L. F., 483
Van Hasselt, V. B., 481, 510
Van Hoose, W. H., 228, 297
Van Houten, R., 521, 532
Varenhorst, B., 130, 318
Vargas, A. M., 52, 64
Varni, J. W., 352, 376
Varvil-Weld, D., 405
Vensen, M. C., 174, 216
Ventis, W., 494
Veraldi, D. M., 266
Vernon, J. C., 286
Veronen, L. J., 423, 445
Voss, J. R., 387, 401
Vriend, J., 554, 558, 575

Wachtel, P. L., 580
Waddell, K. J., 389
Wade, T. C., 521
Wahler, R. G., 159, 171
Wallace, K. N., 266, 292
Walls, R. T., 261, 262, 292
Walters, R. P., 21, 41, 86, 144
Wambach, C. A., 125, 144, 568
Ward, C. H., 266, 291
Ward, S. R., 125, 144
Warner, R. W., 54
Watkins, C. E., Jr., 42
Watson, D. L., 266, 277, 290, 527, 528, 529, 536, 537, 541, 542, 543, 548
Watson, L., 356, 358, 359, 360
Watson, O. M., 67, 77
Watts, F. N., 499
Watzlawick, P., 181, 300, 417, 418, 569, 572
Weakland, J., 190, 417, 569, 579
Webb, L. J., 171
Webster-Stratton, C., 330, 349
Weeks, G. R., 562, 568, 569, 572, 573, 574, 580
Weinberg, L., 405
Weissberg, M., 494
Weisser, R. J., Jr., 454

Wenrich, W. W., 507
Werner, T. J., 261, 292
Wernick, R. L., 423, 445
West, D. J., Jr., 423, 445
Westefeld, J. S., 481, 510
Whitcher, S. J., 77
White, K., 352
White, L., 568, 569, 580
White, R. G., 521
Wicas, E. A., 77
Wickless, C., 482, 510
Widiger, T. A., 308
Wiens, A. N., 74, 86
Wilcoxon, L. A., 482, 483
Wildman, R. W., 481, 510
Wilkinson, L., 534
Williams, A. M., 529
Williams, J., 162, 170

Williams, R. L., 520, 545
Williamson, D. A., 266, 291
Wilson, A., 492
Wilson, C. C., 216, 266, 291
Wilson, G., 521
Wilson, G. T., 310, 483, 524, 525
Wincze, J. P., 507
Wing, J. K., 178
Winters, L. C., 73
Wise, E., 216
Wise, F., 482
Wise, W., 248
Wisocki, P. A., 386, 387
Wolf, M. M., 292
Wolpe, J., 155, 266, 385, 386, 387, 389, 458, 481, 483, 484, 486, 487, 489,

Wolpe, J. (continued)
494, 496, 497, 498, 506, 510
Wood, L. W., 477
Woodward, M., 507, 510
Woodward, R., 405
Woolfolk, R. L., 182, 287, 292, 298, 302, 307, 448, 449, 477, 478
Woollams, S., 79
Worthington, E. L., 316, 326, 352, 580
Woy, J. R., 258
Wright, C., 313, 336, 348
Wright, R. M., 568
Wysocki, T., 322

Yamagami, T., 386, 387, 389

Yates, B. T., 534, 547
Yeaton, W. H., 308
Youell, K. J., 235
Young, D. W., 86

Zabin, M. A., 464
Zamostny, K. P., 46, 481, 510
Zane, T., 261, 292
Zeig, J., 570, 572, 580
Zemore, R., 484, 498
Zerbavel, G. E., 307
Zifferblatt, S. M., 449, 450, 453
Zitter, R. E., 405, 534, 548
Zlotlow, S. F., 52
Zwart, C. A., 534, 538, 548

SUBJECT INDEX

ABC model, 157–161, 187, 192, 208
ABCDE model, 404
Abnormal behavior, *see* Maladaptive behavior
Abusive behavior, 426
Action responses, 113, 114–136, 137
   purposes of, 113, 114, 136–137
Action steps, *see* Subgoals
Adaptive behavior, 148, 155, 190, 553
Adaptors (nonverbal), 76
Addictive disorders, 169–170, 279, 525
   alcohol abuse, 169–170, 302
Adjustment disorders, 163, 169
Adlerian counseling, 3, 79, 124, 125, 128, 149, 186, 302
Advice, 130–131
Affect, 91, 94–95, 97, 104, 150, 151, 153, 158, 159, 161,
    182–183, 187, 188
   affect words, 99, 100
   expression of, 426
Affective disorders, 163, 170
Ageism, 17
Alcoholics Anonymous, 557
Ambiguity (of client messages), 92
American Association for Counseling and Development,
    ethical standards of, 18, 53, 78, 582–588
American Psychological Association, ethical principles of,
    18, 78, 589–596
Anger, 183, 184, 207, 302
   control of, 423, 424, 425, 426, 427, 428–429, 430, 431,
    441–444, 482
Anorexia nervosa, 204, 557
Antecedents, 157, 158–159, 208, 520, 522, 524, 534
   definition of, 157, 158, 187
   identifying antecedents, 187–188, 524
   relationship to history-taking, 174–175
   setting events, 158–159
   sources of, 159, 187–188
   and stimulus control, 534, 535, 536, 546
   stimulus events, 158–159
Anticipation training, 542–543
Antisabotage procedures, 242, 563–564, 566
Anxiety (*see also* Stress):
   antecedents for, 159, 481–482
   anxiety disorders, 163, 302
   cognitive factors in, 184, 388, 405, 406, 428–429
   components of, 158, 298
   consequences of, 161
   definition of, 480
   generalized, 4, 298, 301, 302, 482
   measurement of, 270
   monitoring of, 204, 207
   panic attacks, 156, 302, 491, 569, 571–572
   phobias, 163, 302, 336, 337, 338, 339, 352, 423, 425,
    480, 481, 482
   ranking intensity of, 491, 495, 498, 499

Anxiety *(continued)*
  somatic symptoms of, 155, 156, 183
  specific (focal), 301, 303
Arbitrary inference, 184
Arousal, 424, 429, 430, 431, 486, 490, 491
Assertion Inventory, 266
Assertion training, 79, 150, 302, 309, 323, 332, 333, 337, 338, 339, 340, 357, 358–359, 379, 405, 494, 557, 559
  covert assertion, 307, 388–389
Assessment, 4, 47, 49, 52, 55, 146–172, 173–217, 458, 482, 522, 524, 552, 555, 557, 573, 594–595
  and ABC model of behavior, 157–161
  assumptions of, 155–157
  in crisis counseling, 207
  definition of, 146
  and diagnostic classifications, 161–164
  hypothesis-testing, 199–200
  interview assessment, 174–217
  methods of, 173
  models of, 147–155
  multitrait, 259
  purposes of, 146–147, 173, 207
  reliability of, 259
  termination of, 207
  and treatment (strategy) selection, 277–281, 298
  validity of, 259
Attention, 310
  diversion, 427
  focusing, 449, 450
Attractiveness, 43, 44, 45, 47, 52–54, 60
  interpersonal, 52, 60, 81
  physical, 52, 60
Attributions, 152, 224, 318, 405, 418, 419, 559
Audiotaping, 263, 268, 269, 271, 315, 329, 330, 332–333, 363, 458, 463, 464, 505, 507, 520
Auditory processing, 24, 25, 90, 95, 100, 185
Avoidance behavior, 160, 296, 298, 419, 449, 542, 553

Baseline data, 147, 192, 203–204, 207, 208, 236, 270, 272–277, 522, 524
  retrospective baseline and history-taking, 174
  and strategy selection, 296
Basic ID, 151–153
Beck Depression Inventory, 266
Beck Depression Scale, 268
Behavior, 150–151, 157, 158, 183–184, 188, 189, 524, 525
  acquisition of, 236, 238, 312
  adaptive, 148, 155, 190, 553
  avoidance, 160, 296, 298, 419, 499, 542, 553
  components of, 158
  as components of outcome goals, 233–234
  deficits, 151, 184, 236, 302, 336, 482
  deviant, 147–148
  escape, 160
  excesses, 151, 184, 236, 302, 535
  maladaptive, 148, 155, 185, 557
  overt, 158, 183–184, 185
Behavioral approaches, 2, 3, 149, 153, 155, 186, 571
  and nonverbal behavior, 79
  and interpretation, 124, 125, 128
Behavioral assessment, *see* Assessment
Behavioral diary, 529, 530, 531
Behavioral Self-Rating Checklist (BSRC), 223

Belief systems, *see* Cognitions
Bibliotherapy, 330
Biofeedback, 302, 482
Body sensations, *see* Somatic variables
Body therapies, 79, 298
Breathing techniques, 412, 427, 432, 450, 451, 452, 453, 454, 459, 553
Burnout, 562

Card-sort, 269
Case conceptualization, 147–155
  definition of, 147
  models of, 147–153
Chain, 535, 536
Change:
  direction of, in outcome goals, 234–237
  evaluation of, 257
  issues, 222, 223, 236–238, 299, 301
  resistance to, 225, 551, 553, 557, 570, 572
Charting, 522, 523, 526, 532, 533
Checklists, 261–262, 268, 269, 276–277
Childhood, adolescent disorders, 163
Children's Reinforcement Survey Schedule, 542
Choice issues, 222, 236–238, 299
Clarification, 91, 92–94
  definition of, 92
  purpose of, 92
  steps in, 92–93
Classical conditioning, 483
Client-centered therapy, 3, 4, 21, 79, 124, 149, 298, 300, 301, 302, 482
Client rights, 19, 224, 299, 598–599, 603
Clinically standardized meditation, 448, 449, 454–457, 468
  checklist for, 471–473
Coaching, 313 (*see also* Induction aids)
Cognitions, 150–151, 152, 155, 158, 159, 161, 184–185, 188, 189, 219, 301, 403, 404, 425, 427–430, 434
Cognitive-behavioral therapy, 150, 298, 301–302, 403, 404–417, 482
  assumptions of, 155–157, 403, 404
  definition of, 155
  notions of resistance, 551, 552
Cognitive modeling, 302, 379–385, 392, 434
  checklist for, 395–398
Cognitive restructuring, 153, 298, 299, 302, 392, 403, 404–417, 423, 427, 434, 482, 495, 498
  checklist for, 436–439
Cognitive self-instruction, 6, 379–385
Cognitive therapy, 124, 125, 128, 149, 153, 185, 301, 302, 378, 482
College Self-Expression Scale, 266
Commitment:
  in self-management, 522, 523, 545–546
  and strategy selection, 296
Competence (*see also* Expertness):
  anxiety about, 562
  and goal-setting, 227
  intellectual, 12
  and self-image, 14
  standards of, 590–591, 597, 598, 602
Compliance:
  with assertive behavior, 360

Compliance *(continued)*
  compliance-based paradox, 569–570, 574
  definition of, 551
  with homework, 553, 556
  with instructions, 552
  with relaxation training, 464
  with self-monitoring, 265, 529
Concreteness, 48–50
Concurrent validity, 259, 268
Confidentiality, 19, 56, 271, 583, 592–593, 596, 598, 599, 603, 605
Conflict, 551, 555
Confrontation, 114, 118–124, 564, 568
  client reactions to, 121–122
  definition of, 118
  ground rules for, 120
  of mixed messages, 118–119
  purposes of, 118
  steps in, 122–123
  timing of, 120–121
Congruence, 21, 27–31, 79–80, 82–83
  of clients, 79–80
  of counselors, 82–83
  and genuineness, 27–28
  in therapeutic relationship, 27–31
  and trustworthiness, 55
Consequences, 157, 159–161, 208, 520, 522, 524, 534, 538, 546, 551
  definition of, 157, 159, 187, 188, 555–556
  identification of, 188–189, 524
  negative, 159–160
  positive, 159–160
  secondary gains, 160, 189–190, 208, 243, 552, 557
  in self-reward, 539–557
  sources of, 161, 188–189
  and stimulus control, 538
Construct validity, 259
Consultation, 586–587
Consumerism (in counseling), 299–300
Content messages, 91, 94–95, 104
Content validity, 259, 267
Context, 158, 159, 161, 185–186, 188, 189
  of goals, 234
  in paradoxical interventions, 567–568
  reframes of, 420
Contingencies, *see* Antecedents; Consequences; Controlling variables
Contingency contracts, 322
Continuous recording, 261, 526, 528
Contracts (treatment), 300, 322–323, 576, 603
  elements of, 322
  purposes of, 322
  sample of, 323
  types of, 322
  use of in self-management, 521–522
Control, 557, 559, 571, 575
  of symptoms, 570, 573
Controlling variables, 147, 150, 157, 159, 162, 187, 203–204, 521, 551, 552, 573 *(see also* Antecedents; Consequences)
Coping model, 311, 329, 358, 380
Coping skills, 190, 318, 423, 458, 565
  cognitive, 427–430, 431, 432

Coping skills *(continued)*
  direct-action, 425–427, 430–431, 432, 465
    use of in systematic desensitization, 494–495, 497, 498, 499, 505
Coping statements (or thoughts), 380, 388–389, 405, 408, 409, 410, 411, 412, 427, 428–429, 430, 463, 494, 495, 498
Cost/benefit effects, 225–226
Counseling Outcome Inventory (COI), 234
Counterconditioning approaches, 30, 412, 468, 483, 485, 494, 495, 496, 497, 499, 505, 506, 507–508
Countertransference, 20
Covert modeling, 300, 302, 344, 351, 352, 356–368
  checklist for, 371–374
Covert positive reinforcement, 482, 542
Credibility, 47
Crisis counseling, 12
Cross-cultural issues, 17–18, 55, 559
  effects on client behavior, 185–186
  and ethical issues, 584, 601
  and nonverbal behavior, 67, 74–77, 80
  and the use of questions, 116
Cue-controlled relaxation, 482
Cues, 555 *(see also* Antecedents)

Decision-making, 130, 222, 299, 301, 318–321, 329, 331
Deep structure, 48
Defiance-based paradox, 569, 570
Deletions, 48–50
Demand characteristics, 258, 266, 267, 269, 270, 317, 363, 525, 526
Depression, 162, 183, 184, 203, 204, 207, 302, 353, 572
  affective disorders, 163, 170
Deviant behavior, 147–148
Diagnosis, 161–164, 167, 168, 191–192
  cues and strategy selection, 300–303
  limitations of, 163–164
  major classes of, 162–163
  mental-status exam, 178, 208
  multiaxial evaluation, 162, 191–192
  purposes of, 162–163
Diagnostic and Statistical Manual of Mental Disorders, III, 161–164, 167–168
Dialogue work, 153, 299, 301, 553
Dichotomous reasoning, 184
Directives, 569
Disassociative disorders, 163
Discrepancies, *see* Mixed messages
Discrimination (of behavioral responses), 526, 527, 533
Discrimination Inventory, 23
Dissonance, 44
Distance (between counselor & client), 77 *(see also* Proxemics)
Distortions, 48–50
  in cognitions, 184–185
  of feelings, 183
Drugs, 152, 156 *(see also* Medication)
Dual relationships, 19, 584, 590, 593
Due care, 19, 228
Duration (of problem behavior), 191, 192, 203
  of imagery scenes, 361
  measures of, 260–261, 269, 272, 526, 528, 529

Eclectic counseling, 3, 128, 151
Educational counseling, 299, 301
Electrocardiogram (EKG), 270
Electromyogram (EMG), 270
Emotions, *see* Affect
Emotive imagery, 344, 351, 352–356, 368, 494, 495, 499
    (*see also* Imagery)
    checklist for, 369–371
Empathy, 21–27, 31, 298, 573
    additive or advanced, 23, 124
    definition of, 22
    interchangeable or primary, 23
    nonverbal empathy behaviors, 23–24, 81
    purposes of, 22
    verbal empathy messages, 22–23
Encoding, 412, 417, 418, 419, 420
Energy, 12
Enhancing statements, 33
Environments:
    effects in strategy selection, 297–298
    effects of on clients, 66, 78
    in meditation, 450, 451, 452, 455, 456
    in muscle relaxation, 458
    in self-management, 521–522, 523, 526, 532, 543
ERA model, 151
Escape behavior, 160
Ethical issues, 18–20, 53, 78, 202–203, 568, 569
    ethical standards, 582–605
    in evaluation, 271
    in goal-setting, 226–228
    in strategy selection, 297, 299
Evaluation (of helping), 4, 46, 55, 147, 157, 219–220,
    256–293, 584–585
    methods of evaluation, 262–272, 289
    nontreatment factors in evaluation, 257–259
    outcome, 257, 259–286
    of paradoxical interventions, 574
    process, 257, 286–287
    purposes of, 257, 288
    what to evaluate, 260–262, 289
    when to evaluate, 272–286, 289
Existential approaches, 302
Expectancy set, 258, 266, 270, 299, 463, 482, 484, 525,
    552, 575, 576
Experiencing, 21
Expertness, 44, 45, 46–51, 60, 77
External validity, 268, 271
Extinction, 483

Facilitative conditions, 21 (*see also* Empathy;
    Genuineness; Positive regard)
Factitious disorders, 163
Family choreography, 79
Family sculpture, 79
Family therapy, 149, 181, 186, 223–224, 236–237, 301,
    302, 417–418, 557
    problem-solving, 538
    resistance to, 551
    seating and spatial arrangements in, 77, 79
Fear of failure, 224
Fear of Negative Evaluation (FNE) Scale, 266, 277
Fear Survey Schedule, 266, 487
Feedback, 7, 314–316, 331, 333, 338–339, 522, 525, 532

Feelings, *see* Affect
Fight or flight response, 450
Flexibility, 12, 575, 576
Flooding, 482
Focus, 91, 95, 102, 103, 115, 118, 125
Follow-up, 281–286, 505, 574
    methods of, 282
    reasons for, 281
    use of, with homework assignments, 317–318, 505
Force-field analysis, 553
Frequency (of problem behavior), 191, 192, 203
    counts of, 260, 269, 272, 526, 528, 529, 533
Functional relationship, 157, 159, 161, 199, 568, 573

Generalization (of change), 312, 316, 318, 340, 363, 431,
    505, 520, 537, 546
Generalizations (in language), 48, –50, 420
Genuineness, 27–31
    components of, 27–28
    definition of, 27
    purposes of, 27
Gestalt therapy, 3, 79, 124, 149, 150, 153, 299, 301, 302, 571
Goal-attainment scaling (GAS), 235–236
Goal pyramid, 239, 240, 242–243
Goals (outcome), 4, 47, 49, 52, 55, 147, 157, 207,
    218–255, 260, 568, 573
    definition of, 220–221, 233–247
    evaluation of, 257, 260, 271, 280
    in self-management, 521, 522, 525, 533
    purposes of, 219–220, 247–248
    relationship to strategy selection, 296, 299
    selection of, 220, 221–233
    subgoals, 238–242, 246–247
    and treatment contracts, 322, 323
Good will, 12, 52
Gradient of reinforcement, 161
Graphs:
    of interview data, 276
    of role-play data, 277
    of self-monitoring, 273, 280, 281, 282, 532, 533
    of self-ratings, 275
    of self-report data, 277–278
Group counseling/therapy, 301, 302, 583, 584
Growth, personal, 2, 584, 588
Guided participation, 338–340

Health history, 176, 183, 609, 613–614, 621
Helping:
    characteristics of effective helpers, 11–15
    core skills in, 2, 21
    definition of, 4
    evaluation of, 257
    stages of, 4, 45–49, 52, 55
Hidden agendas, 180, 183, 554
Hierarchy:
    in covert modeling, 361
    in goal-setting, 239–240
    of imagery scenes, 269–270
    in participant modeling, 337, 340
    in systematic desensitization, 483, 484, 485, 487–494,
        495, 496, 497–505, 507
History-taking, 174–178, 207–208
    Behavioral Analysis History Questionnaire, 615–622
    Multimodal Life History Questionnaire, 606–614

Homework, 223, 258, 309, 316–318, 323, 382, 389, 408, 490, 505, 542
  benefits of, 316
  checklist for, 325
  components of, 316–317
  in vivo, 317, 318, 333, 355, 363, 390, 412, 420, 431, 454
  paradoxical tasks, 574
  selection of, 559–560, 561–562
  self-monitoring of, 317–318
Hyperventilation, 155
Hypnosis, 352, 450, 465, 482, 553
Hypochondriasis, 183
Hypothesis formulation, 199–200, 203, 207, 256, 574

Identified patient, 223–224, 418
"I" language, 35
Imagery, 152, 173, 180, 185, 208, 223, 351, 419, 420, 431, 432, 553 (*see also* Emotive imagery)
  ability of client to use, 300, 496
  assessment of client's, 351–352, 353, 496, 497
  during baseline, 277
  as an evaluation tool, 269–270, 271
    advantages of, 270
    guidelines for use, 270
    limitations of, 270
  as a helping strategy, 299, 302, 351–356, 426–427
  imagery elaboration, 362
  imaginal rewards, 541, 542
  in systematic desensitization, 490, 491, 494, 495, 496–497, 499, 500, 505, 506
Imagery Survey Schedule, 352
Imaginal Processes Inventory, 352
Immediacy, 33–35, 80–81
  definition of, 33
  ground rules for, 35
  and nonverbal behavior, 80–81
  purposes of, 34
  steps in, 34
  of subgoals, 239
Impulse control disorders, 163, 379, 380
Individualized client treatment plan, 202–203
Induction aids, 313, 339, 465, 507 (*see also* Coaching; Props)
Informal meditation, 453–454
Information, 425, 426
Information-giving, 114, 130–136
  definition of, 130
  differences between, and advice, 130–131
  emotional impact of, 134
  ground rules for, 131–132
  purposes of, 130
  role of, in decision-making, 130
  steps in, 134–135
Informed consent, 19, 299–300, 595, 596, 599
  checklist for, 306
  components of, 299–300
  consent from a minor and institutionalized clients, 299–300, 593
  documentation of consent, 300
  and treatment contracts, 322, 323
Initial interviews, 45, 46, 47, 52, 53, 55, 180, 568 (*see also* Intake interviews)
Inner circle strategy, 180

Instructions, 258, 269, 483, 484, 522, 523, 536, 544
  for covert modeling, 359, 361
  to manage resistance, 552
  for participant modeling, 338
  for rehearsal, 313
  self-instructions, 536, 537
  for self-monitoring, 265, 532
  for symbolic models, 330
  in systematic desensitization, 500, 507
Intake interviews, 174–178, 207–208
  written report of, 202
Intensity (of problems), 191, 192, 203
  measures of, 261, 528, 529
  ratings of, 269–270, 275–276
Intention statements, 322, 323
Interpretation, 114, 124–129, 564, 568
  client reactions to, 126–127
  of client resistance, 554
  definition of, 124
  depth of, 125
  ground rules for, 127
  purposes of, 124
  relationship to counseling theories, 124–125
  steps in, 127–128
  timing of, 127
  wording of, 125–126
Interviewing, 173, 174, 207–208
  as assessment method, 174, 179–193, 486–487
  during baseline, 276
  as evaluation method, 262–263, 271
    advantages of, 263
    guidelines for, 263
    limitations of, 263
  intake interviews, 174–178, 207
  limitations of, 192–193
Intimacy, 5
Intrapsychic conflict, 155, 550–551
Involuntary clients, 181, 551, 575–576
Irrational beliefs, 152, 161, 183, 184, 385, 386, 387, 403–404, 405, 406, 417, 553, 556, 575
  effects of, on goal-setting, 224–225
  types of, 403–404

Job interview skills, 309, 359, 395–398

Kinesics, 65, 67–76
  adaptors, 76
  turn signals, 75–76
Kinesthetic processing, 24–25, 90, 95, 100, 183, 185

Latency, 261, 332, 337, 528
Learning, 155, 156, 159, 160, 486
  classical conditioning, 483
  observational learning, *see* Modeling
  operant conditioning, 483, 551
  shaping, 239, 506
  successive approximations, 239, 243, 337, 464, 563
Liability (legal), 228, 603
Life themes, 150–151
Listening:
  listening responses, 91–106, 552
  process of, 89–90
  purposes of, 90, 106–107, 114

Listening *(continued)*
  relationship to action, 113, 114, 136–137
  and sensory modalities, 90
  use of, with confrontation, 122
  use of, with questions, 116
Logotherapy, 567
Logs, 192, 203–207, 317–318, 487, 529–531
  behavior, 203, 204, 524
  descriptive, 203–204, 205
  homework, 317–318, 333, 355, 363, 390, 408, 409,
    412–413, 431–432, 450, 453, 454, 457, 463–464,
    505–506
  uses of, 204–207, 317

Magnification, 184, 185
Maladaptive behavior, 148, 155, 185, 557
Mantra, 449, 450, 451, 452, 454–455, 456
Marital Adjustment Test, 266
Marital counseling, 316, 568, 571 *(see also* Family therapy)
Mastery model, 311, 329, 358
Mastery thoughts, 409–410
Media, 330, 332–333, 344 *(see also* Audiotaping)
Mediation, 155, 163
Medication, 156, 302, 604 *(see also* Drugs)
Meditation, 298, 299, 302, 448, 449–457, 468, 482, 494,
  495, 499, 575
  checklists for, 469–471, 471–473
Mental-status examination, 178, 208
Metaphors:
  to manage client resistance, 564–565, 566–567
  use of, in interpreting, 127
Metered counseling, 575–576
Minnesota Multiphasic Personality Inventory (MMPI), 266
Misrepresentation, 297, 592, 597, 600, 604
Mixed messages, 118–120
Modeling, 299, 302, 309, 310–312, 323, 328–350, 430,
  459, 482, 522, 523
  characteristics of the model, 311–312, 331, 358
  checklist for, 324–325
  cognitive modeling, 379–385, 434
  covert, 351, 352, 356–368
  definition of, 310, 324–325
  live, 310, 311–312
  participant, 335–344
  processes in, 310–311
  role models, 187, 324
  self-as-a-model, 331–335
  symbolic, 310, 311, 329–331
  uses of, 310, 328
Mood states, *see* Affect
Motivation, 219, 238, 311, 525, 545
Motor responses, *see* Behavior, overt
Muscle relaxation, 299, 302, 352, 427, 448, 451, 452,
  457–468, 481, 482, 483, 485, 494, 495, 496, 499,
  503–504
  checklist for, 473–477

National Association of Social Workers, ethical standards
  of, 18, 597–601, 602–605
Negative practice, 567
Negative reinforcement, 160

Neurolinguistics programming (NLP), 24, 153, 301, 302
  (see also Representational systems)
Noncompliance, 551, 567, 568
Nonjudgmental behavior (of counselors), 31–32
Nonspecific factors, 257–259, 289
  demand characteristics, 258, 266, 267, 269, 270, 317,
    363, 525, 526
  expectancy set, 258, 266, 270
  instructions, 258, 269
  reactivity of measurement, 258–259, 267, 270, 279
  social influence factors, 44–45, 257–258
Nonverbal behavior:
  and attractiveness, 52
  of the client, 66–79
  of the counselor, 81–84, 420
  cultural differences in, 67, 74–77, 80
  definition of, 65
  effects of environment on, 66, 78
  effects of time on, 66, 78
  and empathy, 23
  and expertness, 48
  and genuineness, 27
  kinesics, 65, 67–76
  paralinguistics, 66, 76–77
  proxemics, 66, 77–78
  relationship to verbal messages, 66–67
  and trustworthiness, 55
  and warmth, 32–33
  ways to work with, 79–81
Norms, 266, 267, 268, 555

Obesity, 159, 160, 526–527, 535 *(see also* Weight loss)
Objectives, 5 *(see also* Goals)
Observation, 173, 271
Observational skills, 6
  and nonverbal behavior, 79–82, 99–100
  client observation checklist, 138–139
Obsessive-compulsive behavior, 204, 302, 386, 392
Obstacles (of goals), 242, 248
Occurrence (of response), 261–262
Operant:
  approaches, 301
  conditioning, 483, 551
  extinction, 160
Operational definitions, 156–157
Ordeal therapy, 571
Organic dysfunction, 155–156, 178, 301, 458
  organic mental disorders, 163
Outcomes, *see* Goals

Pacing, 23, 24, 25, 83, 122, 552, 559, 561, 567
Pain, 352, 353, 355, 426, 427, 428–429
Paper and pencil techniques, 134, 225–226, 239, 552
Paradoxical intention, 299, 302, 565, 567–575
Paralanguage, 66, 76–77
  pauses and silence, 76
  voice and vocal cues, 76
Paranoid disorders, 163, 568
Paraphrase, 91, 95–97, 552
  definition of, 95
  purpose of, 95
  steps in, 95–96

Participant modeling, 151, 297, 298, 302, 335–344, 496, 507
  checklist for, 347–348
Patient position, 190, 300, 560–562
Percentage scores, 260
Perceptions, 417, 418, 419, 420
Performance discrepancy, 222
Personal hierarchy, 489, 494, 508–509
Personality disorders, 163, 302
Person-centered therapy, *see* Client-centered therapy
Pessimism, 552–553, 562
Phobias, 163, 302, 336, 337, 338, 339, 352, 423, 425, 480, 481, 482
Phone-mate system, 363
Positive connotation, 125–126, 418, 420, 571
Positive regard, 31–35, 298
  components of, 31–35
  definition of, 31
  purposes of, 31
Power:
  expert, 44
  legitimate, 44, 46
  referent, 44, 52
  and self-image, 14–15
Practice, *see* Rehearsal
Predictive validity, 259, 264
Prescribing directives, 570, 571, 572, 573
Presenting problems, 181, 417–418
  change problems, 222
  choice problems, 222
Prioritization (of client problems), 181–182
Probes, 114–117
  closed questions, 115–116
  definition of, 114
  guidelines for, 116
  open-ended questions, 114–115
  purposes of, 115
  steps in, 116–117
Problem solving, 155
  skills for, 190
  relationship to client goals, 219, 222, 223
Process evaluation, 286–287, 289
Progressive relaxation, 448, 449, 458 (*see also* Muscle relaxation; Relaxation training)
Projection, 223
Prompts, 317
Props, 159, 312, 565 (*see also* Induction aids)
Proxemics, 66, 77–78
  distance 77
  in family therapy, 77
  furniture arrangements, 77
  shifts in, 77
  touch, 77
Psychoanalytic therapy, 3, 124, 128, 186, 550, 571
Psychophysiological measures, 173
  during baseline, 277
  as evaluation tool, 270
    advantages of, 270
    guidelines for use, 270
    limitations of, 270
Psychosexual disorders, 163, 170, 183, 270, 302
Psychotic disorders, 163

Punishment, 159, 160, 542, 543, 544, 557 (*see also* Consequences)

Questions, 114–117 (*see also* Probes)
  and concreteness, 48–49
Quid pro quo contract, 322

Rathus Assertiveness Scale, 266
Rating scales, 261, 269
Rational beliefs, 185, 190, 404, 406
  effects of, on goal-setting, 224–225
Rationale (treatment), 299, 309, 310, 311
  checklist for, 324
  for clinically standardized meditation, 451, 454, 456
  for cognitive modeling, 380
  for cognitive restructuring, 405–407
  for covert modeling, 357
  for emotive imagery, 353
  for homework, 316–317
  for muscle relaxation, 322, 458–459
  for paradoxical interventions, 568, 571, 572, 573, 574
  for participant modeling, 337
  for relaxation response and Zen meditation, 450, 451, 452
  for self-as-a-model, 332
  for self-monitoring, 526, 527, 533
  for stress inoculation, 322–323, 424, 427
  for systematic desensitization, 482, 484–486
  for thought stopping, 387
  and treatment contracts, 322, 323
Rational-emotive therapy, 3, 125, 149, 150, 298, 302, 403–404, 405, 408 (*see also* Cognitive therapy)
Reactance, 558–559, 570, 573
Reactivity, 147, 407, 450
  in goal-setting, 220
  of measurement, 258–259, 267, 270, 279
  of self-monitoring, 207, 258, 264–265, 525, 529, 532
Reality therapy, 3, 149
Reciprocal inhibition, 483, 484, 494, 497
Recording (of behavior), 526, 527–528, 533
Record-keeping, 202–203, 576, 584, 599, 603, 605
Redecision work, 153, 299, 301
Referral, 17, 19–20, 181, 226–228, 247, 301, 576, 584, 598, 599, 604
Reflection (of feelings), 23, 91, 97–102, 552, 575
  definition of, 97
  purposes of, 98–99
  steps in, 99–102
Reframing, 153, 299, 301, 302, 403, 404, 417–423, 434, 562, 571
  checklist for, 439–441
  of interpretations, 125–126
Rehearsal, 6, 309, 312–316, 323, 325, 331, 338, 354–355, 363, 410, 430, 522, 523, 553–554, 552
  coaching and, 313
  cognitive, 380–381
  covert, 312–313
  criteria for effective, 314
  feedback and, 314–316, 323, 338–339
  overt, 312–313
  self-directed, 313–314, 318, 339–340

Reinforcers, 155, 157, 159, 160, 483, 539, 541, 542, 543, 544, 551 (*see also* Consequences)
  experiences with, in participant modeling, 340
  in managing resistance, 555–558
  self-statements, 409, 411–412, 425, 427, 429
  social, 186–187
  surveys of, 541–542
  use of, in covert modeling scenes, 360
  use of, in rehearsal, 315–316
Reinforcement Survey Schedule, 542
Relapse, 573, 574
Relationship, therapeutic or helping, 4, 11, 573
  and emotional objectivity, 20
  ethics of, 583–584, 593–594
  and immediacy, 33–34
  and strategy selection, 295
  with use of confrontation, 120–121
Relationship enhancers, 46 (see also Attractiveness; Expertness; Trustworthiness)
Relationships (interpersonal), 152, 153, 158, 159, 161, 186–187, 188, 189
Relaxation response, 448, 449, 450–454, 468
  checklist for, 469–471
Relaxation training, 302, 303–305, 358, 412, 423, 430, 458, 520, 553, 575 (*see also* Muscle relaxation)
  in covert modeling, 357
  mental, 426–427
  physical, 427
  in systematic desensitization, 490, 491, 494–495, 503–504, 505, 506
Reliability, 259, 525, 585, 594
  of imagery measures, 270
  of interview data, 263
  of physiological measures, 270
  of self-monitoring, 264–265
  of self-ratings, 266
  of self-report measures, 267, 271
Representational systems, 24–25, 82–83, 90, 95, 100, 103, 122, 127–129, 183, 185, 564, 565
Research, 585–586, 595–596, 598 (*see also* Evaluation)
Resistance, 189, 190, 248, 300, 418, 550–581
  and client variables, 552–554
  definition of, 550–552, 558
  and environmental variables, 555–558
  and involuntary clients, 575–576
  last resort strategies for, 563–575
  and therapist variables, 558–563
Resources (of clients), 242–243
Respect, *see* Positive regard
Response:
  cost, 160
  deficits, 236, 238, 336
  excesses, 236, 238
  inhibition, 236, 238
  restructuring, 236–237, 238
Restraining directives, 570, 572, 573
Rewards, *see* Reinforcers
Role-play, 6, 7, 121, 137, 173, 180, 184, 208, 299, 310, 312–313, 410, 419, 420, 431, 507, 552, 553
  during baseline, 276–277
  as evaluation method, 268–269, 271
    advantages of, 268

Role-play (*continued*)
    guidelines for use, 269
    limitations of, 268–269
Role reversal, 311, 315

Sandwiching technique, 315
Satiation, 543, 544, 567
Schizophrenic disorders, 163, 167, 379
Secondary gains (payoffs), 160, 189–190, 208, 243, 552, 557
Self-as-a-model, 311, 331–335, 344, 358
  checklist for, 345–346
Self-awareness, 12
Self-control, 190, 300, 379, 508, 519, 521
Self-defeating thoughts, 406–407, 408, 409, 410, 411, 412, 427, 556 (*see also* Irrational beliefs)
Self-disclosure, 28–30, 52–53
  and attractiveness, 52–53
  definition of, 28
  depth of, 30
  effects of, on clients, 30, 575
  ground rules for, 29–30
  purposes of, 29
  types of, 28–29
Self-efficacy, 303
Self-enhancing thoughts, 406–407, 408 (*see also* Coping statements; Rational beliefs)
Self-evaluation, 521, 522, 526, 533, 534, 541
Self-help, 309, 545
Self-hypnosis, 450
Self-image, 14–15
Self-instructional models, 329–331
Self-instructional training, 379, 380
Self-labeling, 184
Self-management, 153, 190, 302, 519–549
  characteristics of, 520–522
  commitment to use, 545–546
  steps in, 522–523
Self-modeling, 430 (*see also* Self-as-a-model)
Self-monitoring, 192, 207, 208, 234, 237, 315, 521, 522, 540, 543, 546
  as assessment tool, 203–207, 487
  during baseline, 272–275
  definition of, 203, 263, 519, 524
  as evaluation tool, 263–266, 271, 524
    advantages of, 264
    guidelines for use, 265–266
    limitations of, 264–265
  during follow-up, 282
  as helping strategy, 299, 302, 524–534
  with homework assignments, 317–318
  during posttreatment, 281
  purposes of, 203, 263
  reactivity of, 207, 258, 264–265, 525, 529, 532
  during treatment, 277–280
Self-observation, 173, 520, 527 (*see also* Self-monitoring)
Self-punishment, 521, 539, 540
Self-ratings, 266, 267, 271
  during baseline, 275–276
  of headaches, 267
  of therapy progress, 267
  with role-play, 268

Self-ratings (continued)
  as evaluation tool, 266
    advantages of, 266
    guidelines for use, 266
    limitations of, 266
Self-reinforcement, 360, 380, 389, 431, 520, 521, 522,
  523, 525, 526, 532, 537, 539, 540 (see also Self-reward)
Self-report measures, 173, 208, 223, 266–268, 271, 487
  during baseline, 277–278
  as evaluation tool, 267–268
    advantages of, 267
    guidelines for use, 268
    limitations of, 267–268
Self-reward, 161, 299, 315, 429, 520, 521, 522, 539–545,
  546, 556, 557
Self-statements, 157, 161, 184, 190, 380, 381, 405, 406,
  411–412, 424, 428, 429, 553–554
Self-verbalizations, 362, 379, 482
Sensation, 151
Sensitivity:
  and nonverbal behavior, 82
Sensory channels, see Representational systems
Setting events, 158–159
Severity (of problems), 162 (see also Intensity)
Sexist counseling, 17
Sexual dysfunction, 183 (see also Psychosexual disorders)
Sexual Interaction Inventory, 266
Shaping, 239, 506
Silence, 76–77, 80
Similarity:
  between helper and helpee, 52–53
  between model and client, 311–312, 358
Situation-specificity (of behavior), 186
Skill integration, 137, 139–142
Skill training, 153, 298, 299, 302, 309, 310, 318, 412,
  482, 552 (see also Assertion training)
  deficits, 302
  study skills, 298
Social:
  allies, 556–557
  desirability, 266, 267
  interest, 152
  modeling, see Modeling
  reinforcement, 186–187, 298, 411, 521, 556
  skills, 79, 276, 300, 329, 330, 331
Social Avoidance and Distress Scale (SADS), 266, 277
Social influence theory, 4, 43, 44–45
  and attractiveness, 43, 44, 47, 52–54, 60
  client characteristics in, 44–45, 60
  counselor characteristics of, 46, 60
  effects on counseling outcomes, 257–258
  and expertness, 44, 46–51, 60
  models of, 43, 44–45
  and resistance, 559
  and trustworthiness, 44, 47, 55–59, 60
Sociopathic personality, 568
Somatic variables, 156, 158, 159, 161, 183, 187–188,
  188–189, 569
Somatoform disorders, 163
Spatiotemporal hierarchies, 488, 493, 508, 509
Speech errors, 66, 76
Sphygmomanometer, 270

Spontaneity, 28
Stability (of behavior), 272, 273, 278, 279
Standard-setting, 521, 522, 523, 525
Stereotyping, 17, 199, 583, 584, 585
Stimulus:
  control, 237, 238, 299, 302, 426, 455, 519–520, 521,
    522, 534–539, 540, 546, 555
  events, 158–159
  screening, 77
Strategies, helping:
  characteristics of effective strategies, 297
  decision rules for, 300–303
  definition of, 294
  evaluation of, 277–280
  intervention strategies, 47, 49, 55
  selection of, 4, 49, 147, 159, 161, 163, 219, 294–308,
    559–560
  timing of, in counseling, 295–296
Strengths, 148 (see also Coping skills)
Stress, 148, 424, 425, 426, 428–429, 431, 448, 450, 468,
  490, 495 (see also Anxiety)
  checklist for, 441–444
  inoculation, 298, 299, 302, 304, 392, 403, 404,
    423–434, 465, 482, 498
  management, 448
Structuring, 53–54, 310
Subgoals, 238–242, 246–247, 248
  intermediate, 239
  review of, 242–243
  sequencing of, 239–240
Subjective Units of Disturbance (SUDS) Scale, 487, 491,
  495, 498, 499, 500, 501, 502, 503
Subjective Units of Irritation (SUI) scale, 266
Substance use disorders, 163, 170, 360
Successive approximations, 239, 243, 337, 464, 563
Suicide, 203, 527, 568, 572
Summarization, 91, 102–106, 312, 579
  definition of, 102
  of modeled performances, 312, 331
  purposes of, 102–103
  steps in, 103–105
Support, 12
  environmental, 520, 521
  systems of, 242–243, 295, 426, 555, 563
  techniques, 302, 553, 556
Surface structure, 48
Symbolic modeling, 310, 311, 329–331, 344
  checklist for, 345
Symbolic processes, 183–184
Symptom Checklist (SCL-90), 266
Symptom prescription, see Prescribing directives
Symptom scheduling, 571–572
Synchrony:
  between body movements and speech, 75
  between counselor and client, 83, 552
  of counselor verbal and nonverbal behavior, 83
Systematic desensitization, 298, 299, 300, 301, 302,
  304–305, 412, 423, 458, 468, 480–518
  contact desensitization, 298
  coping skills desensitization, 298, 299, 483–484,
    485–486, 494, 498
  group-administered desensitization, 507

Systematic densensitization *(continued)*
  in vitro desensitization, 482
  in vivo desensitization, 482, 494, 496, 506, 507–508
  record cards for, 500–503
  self-administered desensitization, 507
Systematic rational restructuring, 405 (*see also* Cognitive
    restructuring)
Systems interventions, 301, 551, 557, 569

Termination (of helping), 53–54, 55, 103, 545–546, 565,
    573, 576, 593, 597, 604
Tests (standardized), 173, 584, 594–595
TFA model, 151
Thematic hierarchies, 488–489, 493–494, 508
Themes (of client messages), 102–103, 150–151, 564
Therapy session report, 267, 286
Thermistor, 270
Thought stopping, 278, 279, 298, 299, 302, 385–392,
    411, 434
  checklist for, 398–400
Time:
  effects of, on clients, 66, 78
  sampling, 261, 526, 528
  time-limited counseling, 298
  unit of, in data collection, 274–275, 279
Tokens, 543
Touch, 33, 77
Trait and factor counseling, 3
Trance, 553
Transactional analysis, 3, 79, 124, 125, 128, 149, 150,
    153, 199–200, 299, 301

Transcendental meditation, 449 (*see also* Meditation)
Transference, 20
Transfer-of-training, 340 (*see also* Generalization;
    Homework)
Trend (of behavior), 272, 273, 278, 279
Trustworthiness, 44, 45, 47, 55–59, 60, 271
Turn signals, 75–76 (*see also* Kinesics)

Uniformity myth, 294

Valence (of a response), 525, 527
Validity, 259, 264, 266, 267, 268, 270, 585, 594, 595
Values, 16, 247, 560–562, 591, 600
  conflict of, 181, 226–228
  stereotypical, 17–18
V codes, 163, 165, 166
Verbal summary codes, 362, 363
Visualization, 351, 352, 490, 496, 498, 499, 500, 505, 541
    (*see also* Imagery)
Visual processing, 24–25, 90, 95, 100, 185, 386
Vocational counseling, 299, 301

Warmth, 32, 298, 573 (*see also* Positive regard)
Weight loss, 240–241, 242, 521, 536, 537, 540
Weight Watchers International, 557

Zen meditation, 449, 450–454, 457, 468
  checklist for, 469–471